COBOL

for the 80's

COBOL

for the 80's

J. Wayne Spence
North Texas State University

WEST PUBLISHING COMPANY
St. Paul / New York / Los Angeles / San Francisco

COPY EDITOR: Rick DiBello
DESIGN AND COMPOSITION: Carlisle Graphics

COPYRIGHT © 1982 By WEST PUBLISHING CO.
                        50 West Kellogg Boulevard
                        P.O. Box 3526
                        St. Paul, Minnesota 55165

Printed in the United States of America

Library of Congress Cataloging in Publication Data

Spence, J. Wayne.
    COBOL for the 80's.
    Includes index.
    1. COBOL (Computer program language)
I. Title.
QA76.73.C25S65   001.64′24   81-19852
ISBN 0-314-63290-5   AACR2

2nd Reprint—1982

TO
JAN, PAT, AND CARI
(I'll be *home* for dinner)

Contents

Preface to the Instructor   xiii
Preface to the Student   xiv
Acknowledgments   xv

Part 1   Introductory Concepts   **1**

1   Introduction   **3**

COBOL: The Past   **3**
COBOL: The Present   **4**
COBOL: The Future   **5**
COBOL: The Environment   **6**
Creation of a Keyed File   **10**
Summary   **11**
Questions   **11**

2   COBOL: A Matter of Structure   **13**

Overall Organization of COBOL   **13**
The COBOL Coding Form   **16**
Some Definitions, Rules, and Guidelines   **18**
Summary   **26**
Notes on Programming Style   **26**
Questions   **27**
Exercises   **29**
Problems   **30**

3   The IDENTIFICATION DIVISION   **31**

Purpose of the Division   **31**
Overall View of the IDENTIFICATION DIVISION   **31**
Summary   **33**
Notes on Programming Style   **33**
Questions   **33**
Exercises   **34**

4 The ENVIRONMENT DIVISION 35

Purpose of the Division **35**
Overall View of the ENVIRONMENT DIVISION **35**
SPECIAL-NAMES **36**
INPUT-OUTPUT SECTION **37**
SELECT and ASSIGN Clauses **37**
Other FILE-CONTROL Paragraph Clauses **38**
Summary **42**
Notes on Programming Style **42**
Questions **43**
Exercises **44**

5 The DATA DIVISION 45

Purpose of the Division **45**
Overall Description of the DATA DIVISION **45**
FILE SECTION **46**
Record Descriptions **47**
PICTURE Clauses **49**
Examples of FILE SECTION Entries **52**
The WORKING-STORAGE SECTION **56**
Summary **59**
Notes on Programming Style **60**
Questions **62**
Exercises **64**

6 The PROCEDURE DIVISION 67

Purpose of the DIVISION **67**
Overall Structure of the PROCEDURE DIVISION **67**
OPEN and CLOSE Statements **68**
READ Statement **70**
WRITE Statement **72**
The MOVE Statement **76**
The Simple GO TO Statement **77**
The STOP Statement **78**
A Comprehensive Example **79**
A Second Example—Producing Mailing Labels **83**
Summary **86**
Notes on Programming Style **86**
Questions **87**
Exercises **89**
Problems **92**

Part 2 More Advanced COBOL Concepts 97

7 Programming: The Traditional versus a Structured Approach 99

Flowcharting **100**
Structured Programming **104**
The Case Structure **121**
Summary **123**
Notes on Programming Style **123**
Questions **124**

8 Coding the Basic Structures (The Relational IF and Simple PERFORM Statements)   127

IF Statements in General   **127**
The Relational Test   **128**
Compound IF Statements   **131**
Nested IF Statements   **134**
PERFORM Statements in General   **135**
The Simple PERFORM Statement   **136**
The PERFORM/UNTIL Statement   **139**
The EXIT Statement   **142**
An Example: Two-Up Mailing Labels   **142**
The Control Break   **146**
Paragraphs versus Sections   **149**
Summary   **153**
Notes on Programming Style   **153**
Questions   **156**
Exercises   **158**
Problems   **162**

9 Editing Data for Printed Output   167

Fixed Insertion   **167**
Floating-Insertion   **169**
Replacement   **171**
Edited Data and the MOVE Statement   **171**
The Student Listing Program (with Edited Output)   **173**
Inventory Listing Program   **176**
Summary   **180**
Notes on Programming Style   **181**
Questions   **181**
Exercises   **183**
Problems   **184**

10 Arithmetic Statements   189

The ADD Statement   **189**
The SUBTRACT Statement   **191**
The MULTIPLY Statement   **192**
The DIVIDE Statement   **193**
The COMPUTE Statement   **195**
The Sales Tax Program   **196**
The Letter-Grade Assignment Problem   **202**
The Electric Utility Company Program   **207**
The Page Break   **217**
Summary   **217**
Notes on Programming Style   **218**
Questions   **219**
Exercises   **221**
Problems   **223**

11 More on the IF Statements 229

The Sign Test **229**
The Class Test **230**
The Condition-Name Test **230**
An Inventory-Control Example **233**
Inventory Data Editing **240**
Summary **252**
Notes on Programming Style **252**
Questions **253**
Exercises **253**
Problems **255**

12 More on the PERFORM Statements 261

The PERFORM/TIMES Statement **261**
The PERFORM/VARYING Statement **263**
PERFORM/VARYING: An Example **270**
Summary **280**
Notes on Programming Style **280**
Questions **281**
Exercises **283**
Problems **284**

13 Table Handling with Subscripts 289

Single-Dimension Tables **289**
Multi-Dimension Tables **292**
Sales Summary Report **297**
Character Processing with Tables **302**
Variable-Length Tables **309**
Summary **309**
Notes on Programming Style **310**
Questions **311**
Exercises **313**
Problems **315**

14 Table Handling with Indexes 321

The PERFORM Statement **322**
The SET Statement **323**
The SEARCH Statement **326**
Sales Summary Report with Indexed Tables **332**
The Sales Analysis Program with SEARCH Statements **337**
The Sales Analysis Program with a Variable-Length Table **346**
Summary **349**
Notes on Programming Style **350**
Questions **350**
Exercises **352**
Problems **354**

Part 3 Fundamental File Processing Concepts 359

15 The SORT Statement 361

The Sorting Process **361**
The SORT File **362**
The Specification of Sort Keys **363**
The Input Process **366**
The Output Process **370**
The Inventory Sort Problem **371**
General Limitations **376**
Summary **377**
Notes on Programming Style **377**
Questions **377**
Exercises **379**
Problems **380**

16 Sequential File Processing 385

ENVIRONMENT DIVISION Considerations **388**
DATA DIVISION Considerations **390**
Processing Sequential Files—New Statement Options **392**
Building a Sequential File **393**
Updating a Sequential File **398**
Adding to a Sequential File **406**
Deleting from a Sequential File **412**
Sequential File Processing with Magnetic Disk **413**
Summary **414**
Notes on Programming Style **414**
Questions **415**
Problems **417**

17 Indexed File Processing 425

ENVIRONMENT DIVISION Considerations **425**
DATA DIVISION Considerations **428**
PROCEDURE DIVISION Considerations **428**
Building an Indexed Sequential File **431**
Updating an Indexed Sequential File **436**
Adding to an Indexed Sequential File **442**
Summary **447**
Notes on Programming Style **447**
Questions **448**
Problems **449**

Part 4 Special Usage COBOL Concepts 451

18 More GO TO Statements 453

The GO TO/DEPENDING ON Statement **453**
Summary **460**
Notes on Programming Style **460**
Questions **460**

19   Multiple Record Descriptions, Redefinitions, and Renaming of Data Items   461

Multiple Record Descriptions   **461**
The REDEFINES Clause   **464**
Redefinition of Tables   **466**
The RENAMES Clause   **467**
Summary   **472**
Notes on Programming Style   **474**
Questions   **474**

20   Non-Character-Oriented Data Storage   477

DISPLAY Data Items   **478**
Binary Data Items   **479**
Packed-Decimal Data Items   **480**
Floating-Point Data Items   **481**
Other Clauses Related to the Description of Data   **482**
Non-Character-Oriented Data, Tables, and the SYNCHRONIZED
  Clause   **485**
Summary   **488**
Notes on Programming Style   **488**
Questions   **490**

21   Character-Oriented Data Processing   493

The STRING Statement   **493**
The UNSTRING Statement   **495**
Key Word in Context   **503**
The INSPECT Statement   **510**
The EXAMINE and TRANSFORM Statements   **515**
Summary   **519**
Notes on Programming Style   **519**
Questions   **520**

Appendixes   523

A   List of Reserved Words   525
B   General Forms of COBOL Statements   529
C   Table of Allowable Data Movements   541
D   Answers to Selected Questions and Exercises   543
E   Debugging COBOL Programs   561
F   COBOL '81—Suggestions for the New Standard   581

Index   587

Preface to the Instructor

This text is specifically designed for those institutions where the COBOL programming language is taught in two or more courses or a single accelerated course. The text addresses introductory COBOL topics and does not stress advanced concepts, such as those related to tape and disk file manipulations. Introductory topics have been separated from advanced topics because the author's experience over the past 10 years at four universities has shown that students learn better this way.

Prior to publication, over 500 students have *learned* introductory COBOL concepts using the framework provided in this text. Evaluations of each student and feedback from the ultimate employers of the students have demonstrated that a true learning process has taken place.

Those selecting this text should be forewarned. The text is *not* designed to fit well into a course that provides just a basic familiarity with COBOL. It *is* designed for those seeking employment in the commercial computing field. The text includes several (in some cases rather detailed) example programs. Besides providing illustrations of the function and syntax of a particular statement or clause in the context of a program, these example programs give the student insight into coding conventions and techniques they should find useful in coding assignments.

The instructor should also find useful teaching tools in the instructor's manual. The manual includes references to transparency masters, problem assignments, sample data sets (on magnetic tape), and answers to all text questions and exercises in the text.

J. Wayne Spence

Preface to the Student

You are about to embark upon an area of study in computing which is the life blood of the commercial applications programmer. The COBOL programming language is a vital part of most business data processing environments. Nationwide, as much as 80 percent of all new applications are written in COBOL. Knowledge of COBOL and skill in writing programs are the single most important talents to those seeking entry-level jobs in commercial data processing.

COBOL is not the easiest language to learn. In fact, if COBOL is not your first programming language, you might find yourself longing for the days when you were using that *other* language. However, if the past is any predictor of the future, COBOL is here to stay—if for no other reason but that billions of dollars have been spent on COBOL programs.

I encourage you not only to learn COBOL but to learn it well. Your future in the data processing field could depend on it.

J. Wayne Spence

Acknowledgments

The following acknowledgment has been reproduced from COBOL Edition, U.S. Department of Defense, at the request of the Conference on Data Systems Languages.

Any organization interested in reproducing the COBOL report and specifications in whole or in part, using ideas taken from this report as the basis for an instruction manual or for any other purpose is free to do so. However, all such organizations are requested to reproduce this section as part of the introduction to the document. Those using a short passage, as in a book review, are requested to mention "COBOL" in acknowledgment of the source, but need not quote this entire section.

COBOL is an industry language and is not the property of any company or group of companies, or of any organization or group of organizations.

No warranty, expressed or implied, is made by any contributor or by the COBOL Committee as to the accuracy and functioning of the programming system and language. Moreover, no responsibility is assumed by any contributor, or by the committee, in connection therewith.

Procedures have been established for the maintenance of COBOL. Inquiries concerning the procedures for proposing changes should be directed to the Executive Committee of the Conference on Data Systems Languages.

The authors and copyright holders of the copyrighted material used herein

FLOW-MATIC (Trademark of Sperry Rand Corporation), Programming for the Univac (R) I and II, Data Automation Systems copyrighted 1958, 1959, by Sperry Rand Corporation: IBM Commercial Translator Form No. F 28-8013, copyrighted 1959 by IBM; FACT, DSI 27A5260-2760, copyrighted 1960 by Minneapolis-Honeywell

have specifically authorized the use of this material in whole or in part, in the COBOL specifications. Such authorization extends to the reproduction and use of COBOL specifications in programming manuals or similar publications.

Finally, I would like to express my deepest appreciation to the following individuals, whose considerable efforts, helpful suggestions and professional expertise aided the author in the development of this text:

Gary Block, Onondaga Community College—New York
Marilyn Bohl, Scientific Research Associates (SRA)—California
John B. Crawford, California Polytech Institute—Pomona
Tom Dart, Valdosa State University—Georgia
Robert W. Duvall, Virginia Commonwealth University—Richmond

Robert J. Fedrick, El Camino State University—California
David Greenblatt, Queens College—New York
Robert B. Kirklin, L.A. Harbor Community College—California
James L. Landre, California State University—Sacramento
J. David Naulmann, University of Minnesota
Ruth Schwartz, Arizona State University

and a special note of thanks to my wife Jan for her constant encouragement and assistance in the preparation of the manuscript.

While acknowledging the assistance of others, the author takes full responsibility for any errors or omissions in this text.

part 1 Introductory Concepts

1 Introduction

COBOL (COmmon Business-Oriented Language) is a high-level programming language. COBOL began to be developed in 1959 as a standard programming language that could be used on several different computers. Thus, the word *common* should be taken literally. COBOL is common to commercially oriented large- and medium-sized computers, many minicomputers, and some microcomputers.

Because COBOL is business-oriented, it is particularly well suited to commercial data processing applications. Compared to scientific applications, business applications require limited mathematic manipulations and many input and output operations. Thus, COBOL handles input and output operations efficiently, but its mathematical capabilities are limited.

COBOL: The Past

During the late 1950s, the Department of Defense was awarding many defense contracts to companies throughout the United States. To document contract progress, costs, and many other control factors each company had its own computer programs. Before long, the Department of Defense found it impossible to verify these figures because of the wide variety of programming languages used (some high-level and some low-level). Thus, the Defense Department either had to train its investigators (auditors) to work with a variety of programming languages or force all companies under Defense Department contract to use a common language.

Consequently, the idea of one language for all government contracts was adopted. But, no existing language could be adopted by all of these companies, primarily because of the differences in their equipment. In addition, most available languages were ill-suited to the task. To address the problem, the CODASYL (Committee On DAta SYstems Language) was created in 1959 to study the problems of business computer applications. The committee included representatives of U.S. government agencies (primarily the Department of Defense), computer manufacturers, universities, and computer users. CODASYL decided to create a new language with common elements for all computers. The language was to be understandable by people with very little computer training.

The results of the CODASYL Conference were produced in April 1960. Included were the initial specifications for COBOL. (The language came to be known as COBOL-60, after the year of its birth.) Later revisions were produced in 1963 and 1965. As COBOL began to be changed, computer manufacturers recognized the importance of new capabilities, with each manufacturer taking a different approach to implementation. It soon became apparent that if computer manufacturers were left to their own devices, COBOL would no longer be the common language intended by the CODASYL. Consequently, in 1968, the American National Standards Institute (ANSI) published suggestions for making COBOL a standard programming language, making one standard available for the construction of COBOL compilers. COBOL compilers that *generally* conform to the ANSI recommendations are often referred to as Standard COBOL or ANSI COBOL compilers. (Recently, ANSI COBOL has been shortened to ANS COBOL.) In 1974, ANSI revised the standard COBOL specifications (USA Standard COBOL, X3-1974, American National Standards Institute, New York, 1974). This publication is the current COBOL standard.

COBOL: The Present

Currently, COBOL is the most widely used language for business data processing applications. Some estimate that COBOL is used for as much as 80 percent of new business applications. One widely known study supporting this claim was performed by Andreas Phillippakis (*Datamation*, December, 1977), and has historically been supported by other surveys.

Why is COBOL so widely used? There are five reasons. First, many government contractors adopted the language because of the urging of the Defense Department. This resulted in a ripple effect—from contractor to subcontractor, down the long chain of companies involved in large government contracts. Thus, because COBOL was widely used during its infancy, it was somewhat easier for other companies to adopt. Some companies adopted COBOL as they changed computer systems, and others adopted it as their primary language when they went from manual to computer procedures.

Second, COBOL was designed to be a common language, i.e., machine independent. Because of the standardization of COBOL by ANSI, it *should* be a very simple matter to convert a program written for one manufacturer's computer to run on another manfacturer's computer.

Third, in keeping with the initial requirements for the language, COBOL is said to be "self-documenting." That is, very little of COBOL is symbolic or cryptic. Many of the statements in COBOL are English-like sentences. For the programming novice, it is not as difficult to read as many other programming languages.

Fourth, COBOL is one of the most efficient high-level languages for data handling. It possesses extensive data-editing features and more importantly, excellent file management capabilities.

Finally, COBOL is not a "dead" language. It is being continually updated, modified, and improved to meet the demands of a business-oriented programming language. Both CODASYL and ANSI continue to monitor changing demands on COBOL. For example, in the early 1970s, CODASYL suggested a new series of capabilities for COBOL so that it might be more easily used as a *host* programming language in a data base management environment. Some computer manufacturers have extended COBOL to handle these new demands; however, these extensions are not yet standard.

A recent major development, which has promoted the continued use of COBOL, was the birth and adoption of *structured programming*. This concept (discussed in Chapter 7) does not require any changes to COBOL, (although some have been suggested), but, rather, a new look at the capabilities of the language. Structured programming is a disciplined approach to the programming of medium to large projects (although it may be applied to projects of any size).

With all of these advantages, why is COBOL not *the* universal language? First, the most critical shortcoming of COBOL is its lack of mathematical capabilities. Thus, for mathematical or scientific applications, COBOL is ill-suited. More scientifically oriented languages, such as FORTRAN, have extensive mathematical capabilities. Second, COBOL is "wordy." That is, due to its "self-documenting" nature, COBOL requires more coding and keying (e.g., key-punching) time than most other languages. BASIC and APL are much more concise languages that require little program preparation time. Third, COBOL is both comprehensive and coherent. It is comprehensive in that a programmer must know a great deal about COBOL before attempting to construct a COBOL program. It is coherent in that simply knowing the parts of COBOL is not sufficient; the programmer must know the relationships of the parts. COBOL is not for the individual interested in occasional use or in a language that can be quickly mastered. Finally, COBOL in its present form is not considered the best language for a structured approach. Both PL/I and ALGOL contain all of the "structures" used in structured programming, and both are modular in design.

In this text COBOL has been broken into major topical areas. The next five chapters (Chapters 2 through 6) present the basic framework (nucleus) of COBOL. That is, only the essential details are presented in these chapters so that the programmer can begin writing programs. The topics in Part 2 present other details that may be inserted into the basic framework to extend the programmer's ability to solve certain types of program-related problems.

COBOL: The Future

The basic framework of COBOL, as presented in this text, should be basically the same for several years, partly because many currently used commercial programs are written in COBOL. To redesign or rewrite these programs would be a monumental (if not insurmountable) task.

The future of COBOL's file-handling capabilities, however, is not as certain, for two reasons. (Note that only elementary concepts in file handling are discussed in this text.) First, file handling (management) is the least consistent aspect of COBOL. Each firm producing a COBOL compiler has a different viewpoint on the physical manipulations of each file-oriented statement, even though the statements themselves may look the same from one system to another. Thus, for COBOL to become a truly standard language, a consensus must be reached with regard to file handling.

The second reason is the concept of *data base management systems*, which became a reality in the early 1970s. This approach abandons the "file" in favor of a "pooled data source." Though many data base management systems are now in use, continuing research will probably result in new and more efficient methods of handling data. Thus, files (and data base management systems) as we know them today may become obsolete in the future.

COBOL: The Environment

Although this text is devoted to the COBOL programming language, there are other elements in any data processing installation of which the programmer must be aware. Among these other elements are *hardware*, *system software*, *application software*, a *job control language*, and *data*. Of these, hardware is probably the most easily identifiable. *Hardware* is generally any and all equipment in a data processing installation, i.e., central processing units (computers), internal storage (primary memory or "core"), and peripheral devices (card readers, line printers, tape drives, and disk drives—the latter two are often referred to as *secondary* or *mass storage* units.) These devices can be referred to as hardware, either collectively or individually. These devices collectively can be referred to as the *computer system*. Of course, there are other hardware elements in computer systems, such as input-output channels, which connect the peripheral devices to the central processing unit, or telecommunication devices, which permit the transmission of data over telephone lines, but knowledge of these is not necessary to understand how a programmer uses a programming language.

Software, in general, encompasses all programs regardless of their nature or purpose. System software and application software are separated above because of their different functions. A *program* is simply a list of commands to which the computer system reacts. Specifically, a program (or algorithm) is a set of nonambiguous, step-by-step instructions that direct the computer to fulfill a specified objective. System software is the set of programs that directs the overall activity of the computer—it controls the computer. Computer operating systems fall into this category.

Operating systems vary in both name and capability from one manufacturer to another. For example, IBM produces three basic types of operating systems, which are referred to as DOS (disk operating system), OS (operating system), and OS/VS (operating system for virtual storage machines). This is not an exhaustive list of the operating systems produced by IBM, but it gives you an idea of the variability of operating systems within just one manufacturer.

System software also includes *assemblers*, *compilers*, and *interpreters*. These programs translate programming languages (such as COBOL) into machine-understandable (computer) instructions. COBOL is a compiler-oriented language. That is, before the computer can react to a program written in COBOL, the program must be compiled (translated) from a *source program* (a program written in a high-level programming language such as COBOL) into an *object program* (a set of instructions in machine language). Only after the compilation process is completed can the program be executed by the computer.

Application software are programs written to perform a specific function needed by a user, such as payroll, accounts receivable, and inventory control programs. Programs written in COBOL fall into this category. Utility programs and processors are also considered to be application software. Utility programs generally sort data, copy data from one medium to another (e.g., from cards to magnetic tape), or format reports. It is the development of the various types of application software that occupies most of the programmer's time.

The distinction between hardware, system software, and application software becomes blurred in a relatively new area called *firmware.* Firmware is a component (integrated-circuit chips) of a piece of hardware (generally the central processor). However, these chips may contain operating systems, utility programs, and under some circumstances may be programmed by a programmer.

Job Control Language (JCL) is used by the programmer to communicate with the operating system to interface his program with the operating system. Generally, it is not used to write application programs. JCL instructions act as flags to the operating system. JCL instructions may be used to communicate accounting information to the operating system, indicate the types of resources needed to execute an application program, invoke a compiler, specify the location of data, and terminate a procedure. All of these functions may be called to execute a single program. However, since JCL instructions are a direct function of the operating system, further explanation is beyond the scope of this text. Consult your installation for information regarding job control language. Many installations will provide "canned" JCL streams for the novice user.

The last element, data, is the entity to be manipulated. That is, data may be composed of names, addresses, quantities, dollar amounts, etc. These numeric or character "values" are accepted by application software and manipulated to a useful end—perhaps a report. The data may represent information about a customer, an employee, or an inventory item.

Here is a scenario of the interaction of some of these elements using the framework of this text. The programmer begins creating a COBOL application program, which is supposed to perform a definable task. To this application program, the programmer adds JCL and data to create a group of elements (a *job*) arranged in the sequence illustrated in Figure 1.1. Notice that the COBOL program and the data are concentrated into units, and JCL (in this case identified by "/ /" in the first two columns) is spread throughout the job stream.

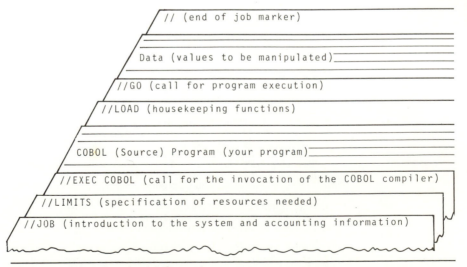

Figure 1.1 Illustration of a Job Stream*

*This illustration does not represent any known directly usable Job Control Language, but rather is intended to illustrate the relationship between a Job Control Language, a COBOL source program, and data. / / indicates a message to be communicated to the operating system. Depending on the operating system, other characters may be substituted for / /.

After the job stream has been prepared, the programmer submits it to the computer by having the job stream read into the computer system by a card reader. Within the computer system, each element of the procedure is identified, examined, and acted upon by the computer. The job card (the first JCL command) is accessed, and information on the card is examined for accuracy (e.g., a valid account number, correct format, etc.). If the job card is acceptable, the operating system begins collecting job statistics (e.g., elapsed job time, compile time, execution time, number of cards read, etc.) and in many cases assigns a job number to the procedure. The second JCL command may call for specific computer resources—amount of internal memory, expected compilation and execution time, specific print forms, etc.—and if the resources are available, the procedure takes the next step. See Figure 1.2a. The third JCL command calls for the COBOL compiler. The compiler (or at least elements of the compiler) are copied into the computer's memory to begin the translation process. Once the compiler is available, the COBOL (source) program is placed in memory, and the translation process begins. The COBOL instructions are examined one at a time by the compiler, under the supervision of the operating system. As each instruction is examined, the compiler produces the

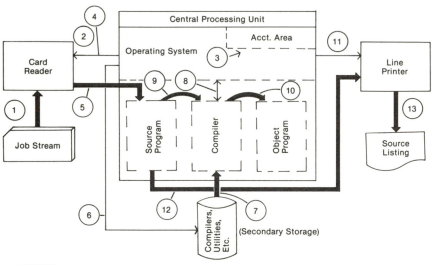

LEGEND
1. Job stream loaded into card reader.
2. Operating system initiates card reader and reads job card.
3. If job card valid, user accounting and statistical information initiated.
4. Operating system causes remainder of job stream to be read.
5. Source program placed in internal memory.
6. Operating system calls for appropriate compiler (indicated in job stream).
7. Compiler placed in internal memory.
8. Operating system interacts with compiler to initiate compiling process.
9. Instructions from source program examined by compiler.
10. Translated version of source-program instruction placed in object program.
11. After compilation complete, operating system invokes line printer.
12. Source program (perhaps with errors) copied to line printer.
13. Source program listing produced on printout.

Control Operations: ⟶

Data Transfer Operations: ➡

Figure 1.2a Illustration of Source Program Compilation

machine-language equivalent in the object-program area. When compilation has been completed, the *object* program will be the essence of the source program but in machine language. (*Machine language* is an extremely elementary language peculiar to particular computers and is understood by the computer without additional interpretation.)

After the object program has been produced, "loading" takes place. (See Figure 1.2b.) Loading is basically a housekeeping process, wherein loose ends, such as external references, internal address locations, and so forth are resolved. Finally, the program is linked to the devices called for and the program is executed. It is only during execution that data will be accepted and manipulated by the program. Eventually, the program terminates. The program termination causes the last of the JCL commands to be encountered—generally a marker declaring the end of the job stream.

To review, the general procedure required to complete a job stream containing an application program is: (1) compile the source program into an object program, (2) load the object program, and (3) execute the object program and accept data. These steps are often termed "compile-load-and-go."

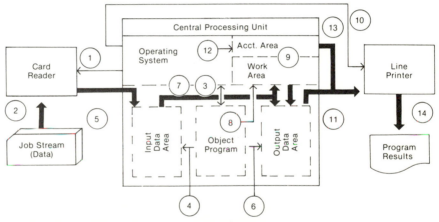

LEGEND
1. After object program is created, operating system checks job stream for "load" and "execute" JCL commands and data availability.
2. Records from job stream made available.
3. Operating system initiates object-program execution.
4. Object program requests input of data (READ operation).
5. Data is transferred from input device to input data area (internal memory) under control of operating system.
6. Object program requests output of data (WRITE operation).
7. Data transferred from input data area to output data area.
8. Object program requests movement of data to work area.
   (Step 7 repeated, but data transferred to work area.)
9. Data transferred from work area to output data area.
   (Step 8 precedes this operation when object program requests movement of data from work area to output data area.)
10. Operating system checks printer availability and initiates output sequence.
11. Data transferred from output data area to the line printer.
12. End-of-job-stream data collected under operating-system control.
13. Job statistics transmitted to line printer.
14. Line printer produces program results (printout).

Control Operations: ⟶

Data Transfer Operations: ⟹

Figure 1.2b Illustration of Program Execution

**Creation of
a Keyed File**

In the preceding illustration, a batch job stream was developed on punched cards and submitted to the computer system via a card reader, with all of the elements necessary to process a program (JCL, source language statements, and data references) being submitted as a single unit.

Today, many computer systems, indeed most larger commercial installations, do not develop programs in the "batch" mode because it is not the most productive use of programmer time. In these installations, *on-line* facilities permit the programmer to develop, modify, and often execute a program via a remote terminal. This means the programmer is in direct communication with the computer system through a *CRT* (Cathode Ray Tube—a video display unit with an integral keyboard) or a *hard-copy* (printing) terminal. Like the batch mode of operation, the programmer must have a means of modifying or correcting his program. In the batch mode this means correcting and moving card records within a program deck. In the on-line mode, however, the programmer develops a program (or procedure) file—a system reference point which contains the "images" of records which might otherwise exist in a card form.

The program file created through on-line operations may be called a *source* file, a *keyed* file, or a *text editor* file depending on the computer system in use. However, all program files have characteristics in common; they all contain images of program statements. Each record (line of the program) is accessible, and individual records can be inserted, deleted, modified, or moved. Beyond these characteristics, however, commonality between computer systems often ends. For example, some systems attach an addressable record number to each line (record) in the procedure; others do not. The significance of line numbers is that individual lines may be addressed by number without having to address those lines which precede the specified line. Without the line numbers, one must sequentially search the procedure file until the desired record is located. In addition, some systems automatically "save" or retain for future reference the records as they are entered; others must be instructed to save the records. Some systems automatically incorporate any changes made to the file in the file itself; others provide for a primary (original) file and a secondary (working) file for the purpose of making changes. In a system that does not automatically save a procedure file when it is addressed, the programmer normally is provided with a command like "SAVE file-name," permitting the existing program to be copied and retained for future reference.

Finally, some systems permit the programmer to compile and execute a program only by submitting it to the batch system; others provide the capability for compiling and executing the program in both the batch mode and an *interactive* mode. (*Interactive* means that the program is compiled and executed on-line so that the programmer can "converse" with his program as it is executing.) All computer systems permit programs to be executed in the batch mode. However, in many computer systems it is possible to develop a procedure file, which looks as if it were punched on cards, through the use of a terminal. In this situation, program compilation and execution is accomplished by a command such as "BATCH file-name," thus causing the procedure file to be placed in the batch job queue (or waiting line) of the system. The procedure file in this case would likely include JCL, COBOL statements, and perhaps even data.

As an additional capability, many computer systems permit compilation and execution of programs on-line. Although on-line operations in systems vary, the procedure file might contain just the statements of a COBOL program. The programmer may call for on-line compilation of this program by entering a command such as "COBOL file-name." During the compiling process, diagnostic messages and other operator prompts may be displayed on the terminal that initiated the compilation. Then, after the program has been successfully compiled, the program could be executed immediately, or the object program could be saved in a separate file and executed later by using commands such as "RUN file-name" or "EXECUTE file-name."

The variability of on-line program development in today's environment makes it virtually impossible to describe the process in detail without addressing individual computers, support equipment, and operating systems. You will have to rely on your instructor and computer center support personnel for assistance in this area. You will find that learning this newer mode of program development will be well worth the effort, especially in modifying or changing a program.

Summary

COBOL, which was conceived by the CODASYL committee in 1959, is the most widely used language for programming commercial applications. COBOL is common to a wide variety of computers and, to a large extent, it has been standardized by the American National Standards Institute.

Since COBOL's inception, it has been frequently updated and expanded. COBOL has also been enhanced so that it may be used as a host programming language in a data base management system environment.

COBOL is not *the* universal language, yet it has been widely adopted. COBOL is more English-oriented than other languages, it handles input-output operations efficiently, and it is capable of supporting the structured approach to programming. However, COBOL's mathematical capabilities are limited. It is not one of the easiest languages to learn, and it is not the *best* language for structured programming.

COBOL (as well as other programming languages) is used in a data processing environment composed of hardware, system software, application software, a job control language, and data. Each of these elements of a data processing installation interact to become a useful tool for solving business data processing problems.

Questions

Below, fill in the blank(s) with the appropriate word, words, or phrases.

1. COBOL is an acronym for _____ .

2. COBOL is referred to as a common language because _____ .

3. COBOL is intended for use in _____ applications (programs).

4. Unlike scientific data processing, commercial data processing requires _____ calculations and _____ input-output operations.

5. CODASYL is an acronym for _____ .

6. CODASYL's purpose was _____ .

7. The CODASYL committee had representatives from _____ , _____ , and _____ .

8. The latest version of COBOL is referred to as _____ .

9. ANSI is an acronym for _____ .

10. Standard COBOL is also referred to as _____ COBOL.

11. The programming language currently most widely used for commercial applications is _____ .

12. A host programming language is one which is used in a(n) _____ environment.

13. Structured programming is a(n) _____ approach to programming.

14. Another term for equipment or devices is _____ .

15. Internal storage or primary memory resides within the _____ and secondary storage resides on _____ .

16. The total of all combined devices within a data processing installation may be called a _____ .

17. A collection of all programs in a data processing installation is known as _____ .

18. A list of commands to which the computer reacts or a set of nonambiguous, step-by-step instructions aimed at a specific objective is the definition of a(n) _____ or a(n) _____ .

19. One of the primary entities in the system software group is a(n) _____ .

20. A program written in a language such as COBOL may also be referred to in general terms as a(n) _____ program.

21. A program written in machine language is known as a(n) _____ program.

22. A(n) _____ translates a source program into an object program.

23. _____ software are programs written to satisfy a specific user-oriented function and when written in COBOL usually satisfies business need.

24. Firmware is _____ , _____ , and _____ .

25 _____ is used by the programmer to communicate with the operating system and to interface his program to the operating system.

26. A compiler is generally invoked by a(n) _____ command.

27. _____ are generally manipulated by application programs in data processing installations.

28. What are the advantages of using COBOL?

29. What are the disadvantages of using COBOL?

30. List the components (elements) of a computer system. Of a data processing installation.

2 COBOL: A Matter of Structure

The COBOL programming language is one of the most structured programming languages in general use today. Initially, the programmer may think some of the structure of COBOL is unnecessary especially if he or she had been exposed to other programming languages. However, as the programmer becomes familiar with the structure of COBOL, he or she will begin to understand the principles behind this structure.

Overall Organization of COBOL

COBOL is organized much like a book. A book, such as a novel, is broken into major segments called chapters. In COBOL, these major segments are called *divisions.* In some books chapters have subparts which might be called sections. Most of the COBOL divisions have subparts called *sections.* Within major sections of a book, one might expect to find paragraphs. Each section of a COBOL program may have a *paragraph* or some similar method of division. Paragraphs in books generally comprise one or more sentences. Paragraphs in a COBOL program also comprise *sentences* (or *entries*). Finally, a sentence in a novel might be made up of one or more statements. In a COBOL program, a sentence is also one or more *statements* (and an entry is represented by one or more *clauses*).

A COBOL program is always composed of four divisions—IDENTIFICATION, ENVIRONMENT, DATA, and PROCEDURE. The divisions always appear in this order. The IDENTIFICATION, ENVIRONMENT, and DATA DIVISIONS are made up of sections, paragraphs, entries and clauses (except for the IDENTIFICATION DIVISION which has no sections). This is the hierarchy (from highest to lowest) of these three divisions. The PROCEDURE DIVISION hierarchy is sections, paragraphs, sentences, and statements. Each one of the four divisions is responsible for a specific function within a COBOL program.

The IDENTIFICATION DIVISION (shown as lines 10 through 70 in Figure 2.1) identifies the program to anyone unfamiliar with it. It gives the program a name and other basic information. The ENVIRONMENT DIVISION (lines 80 through 160 in Figure 2.1) is responsible for identifying the type of computers being used to compile and execute the program (the CONFIGURATION SECTION) and the types of equipment being used to provide data to and accept output from the program (the INPUT-OUTPUT SECTION). The DATA DIVISION, the third major part, is responsible for describing data items to be used in the program. It is generally one of the larger segments of a COBOL program (see lines 170 through 490 in Figure 2.1). The DATA DIVISION is generally composed of at least two sections. The FILE SECTION is used to describe the form in which data will be either input to the program or output from the program. The last major part of a COBOL program, the PRO-

Line	Code	DIVISION	SECTION	Paragraph	Entry or Sentence
000010	IDENTIFICATION DIVISION.	X			
000020	PROGRAM-ID. SAMPLE-PROGRAM.			X	X
000030	AUTHOR. J. WAYNE SPENCE.			X	X
000040	DATE-WRITTEN. JANUARY 1, 1981.			X	X
000050	DATE-COMPILED. JANUARY 1, 1981.			X	X
000060*	THIS PROGRAM IS FOR THE PURPOSE OF DEMONSTRATING				X
000070*	THE PARTS OF A COBOL PROGRAM.				X
000080	ENVIRONMENT DIVISION.	X			
000090	CONFIGURATION SECTION.		X		
000100	SOURCE-COMPUTER. IBM-370-158.			X	X
000110	OBJECT-COMPUTER. IBM-370-158.			X	X
000120	SPECIAL-NAMES. C01 IS TOP-OF-NEXT-PAGE.			X	X
000130	INPUT-OUTPUT SECTION.		X		
000140	FILE-CONTROL.			X	
000150	SELECT STUDENT-FILE ASSIGN TO UR-S-SYSIN.				X
000160	SELECT PRINTOUT ASSIGN TO UR-S-SYSPRINT.				X
000170	DATA DIVISION.	X			
000180	FILE SECTION.		X		
000190	FD STUDENT-FILE LABEL RECORDS ARE OMITTED.			X	X
000200	01 STUDENT-REC.				X
000210	05 STUDENT-IDENTIFICATION.				X
000220	10 LAST-NAME PIC X(10).				X
000230	10 FIRST-NAME PIC X(10).				X
000240	10 MIDDLE-INITIAL PIC X(01).				X
000250	10 STUDENT-ID PIC 9(09).				X
000260	05 FILLER PIC X(05).				X
000270	05 ENROLLMENT-INFO.				X
000280	10 CLASSIFICATION PIC X(02).				X
000290	10 TOTAL-HOURS PIC 9(03).				X
000300	10 HOURS-THIS-SEM PIC 9(02).				X
000310	10 MAJOR PIC X(03).				X
000320	05 FILLER PIC X(35).				X
000330	FD PRINTOUT LABEL RECORDS ARE OMITTED.			X	X
000340	01 OUTPUT-REC.				X
000350	05 FILLER PIC X(03).				X
000360	05 1ST-NAME PIC X(11).				X
000370	05 M-I PIC X(02).				X
000380	05 SUR-NAME PIC X(10).				X
000390	05 FILLER PIC X(04).				X
000400	05 ID-NUM PIC 9(09).				X
000410	05 FILLER PIC X(05).				X
000420	05 CLASS PIC X(02).				X
000430	05 FILLER PIC X(06).				X
000440	05 MAJ PIC X(03).				X
000450	05 FILLER PIC X(05).				X
000460	05 CURRENT-HOURS PIC 9(02).				X
000470	05 FILLER PIC X(06).				X
000480	05 TOT-HOURS PIC 9(03).				X
000490	05 FILLER PIC X(03).				X
000500	PROCEDURE DIVISION.	X			
000510	START-UP.			X	
000520	OPEN INPUT STUDENT-FILE, OUTPUT PRINTOUT.				X
000530	MOVE SPACES TO OUTPUT-REC.				X
000540	READ-DATA.			X	
000550	READ STUDENT-FILE AT END GO TO END-JOB.				X
000560	MOVE STUDENT-ID TO ID-NUM.				X
000570	MOVE LAST-NAME TO SUR-NAME.				X
000580	MOVE FIRST-NAME TO 1ST-NAME.				X
000590	MOVE MIDDLE-INITIAL TO M-I.				X
000600	MOVE CLASSIFICATION TO CLASS.				X
000610	MOVE TOTAL-HOURS TO TOT-HOURS.				X
000620	MOVE HOURS-THIS-SEM TO CURRENT-HOURS.				X
000630	MOVE MAJOR TO MAJ.				X
000640	WRITE OUTPUT-REC AFTER 2 LINES.				X
000650	GO TO READ-DATA.				X
000660	END-JOB.			X	
000670	CLOSE STUDENT-FILE, PRINTOUT.				X
000680	STOP RUN.				X

(All code lines are marked FIG 2.1)

Figure 2.1 A Sample COBOL Program

CEDURE DIVISION (lines 500 through 680 in Figure 2.1) provides the process to be performed (e.g., the records to be read, the data to be manipulated, the output to be written, etc.).

Figure 2.1 demonstrates a more "traditional" approach to programming style; Figure 2.2 illustrates a structured program. The two programs produce exactly the same results; however, experts generally concede that the program in Figure 2.2 is easier to develop and change. Examine these two illustrations. Notice that the lines are exactly the same down to line 500. At line 500, a new section has been added to the program in Figure 2.2. The WORKING-STORAGE SECTION generally comprises all data items not directly related to input-output activity. In this illustration, a data item called INDICATOR has been introduced. INDICATOR is often called a *control variable*, because its primary function is to control the activity in the PROCEDURE DIVISION.

In the PROCEDURE DIVISION (lines 530 through 750 in Figure 2.2), a new procedure (CONTROL-LOGIC) has been added. In a structured program, the first procedure generally controls the overall function of the program. Thus, in this example, the CONTROL-LOGIC procedure initiates the operation of the program by performing the START-UP procedure (line 550), repetitively ex-

```
|          1   1   2   2   2   3   3   4   4   4   5   5   6   6   6   7   7   8|
|      4   8   2   6   0   4   8   2   6   0   4   8   2   6   0   4   8   2   6   0|
----------------------------------------------------------------------------------
|000010 IDENTIFICATION DIVISION.                                        FIG  2.2|
|000020 PROGRAM-ID. SAMPLE-PROGRAM.                                     FIG  2.2|
|000030 AUTHOR. J. WAYNE SPENCE.                                        FIG  2.2|
|000040 DATE-WRITTEN. JANUARY 1, 1981.                                  FIG  2.2|
|000050 DATE-COMPILED. JANUARY 1, 1981.                                 FIG  2.2|
|000060*    THIS PROGRAM IS FOR THE PURPOSE OF DEMONSTRATING            FIG  2.2|
|000070*    THE PARTS OF A COBOL PROGRAM.                               FIG  2.2|
|000080 ENVIRONMENT DIVISION.                                           FIG  2.2|
|000090 CONFIGURATION SECTION.                                          FIG  2.2|
|000100 SOURCE-COMPUTER. IBM-370-158.                                   FIG  2.2|
|000110 OBJECT-COMPUTER. IBM-370-158.                                   FIG  2.2|
|000120 SPECIAL-NAMES. C01 IS TOP-NEXT-PAGE.                            FIG  2.2|
|000130 INPUT-OUTPUT SECTION.                                           FIG  2.2|
|000140 FILE-CONTROL.                                                   FIG  2.2|
|000150     SELECT STUDENT-FILE ASSIGN TO UR-S-SYSIN.                   FIG  2.2|
|000160     SELECT PRINTOUT ASSIGN TO UR-S-SYSPRINT.                    FIG  2.2|
|000170 DATA DIVISION.                                                  FIG  2.2|
|000180 FILE SECTION.                                                   FIG  2.2|
|000190 FD  STUDENT-FILE LABEL RECORDS ARE OMITTED.                     FIG  2.2|
|000200 01  STUDENT-REC.                                                FIG  2.2|
|000210     05 STUDENT-IDENTIFICATION.                                  FIG  2.2|
|000220        10 LAST-NAME          PIC X(10).                         FIG  2.2|
|000230        10 FIRST-NAME         PIC X(10).                         FIG  2.2|
|000240        10 MIDDLE-INITIAL     PIC X(01).                         FIG  2.2|
|000250        10 STUDENT-ID         PIC 9(09).                         FIG  2.2|
|000260     05 FILLER                PIC X(05).                         FIG  2.2|
|000270     05 ENROLLMENT-INFO.                                         FIG  2.2|
|000280        10 CLASSIFICATION     PIC X(02).                         FIG  2.2|
|000290        10 TOTAL-HOURS        PIC 9(03).                         FIG  2.2|
|000300        10 HOURS-THIS-SEM     PIC 9(02).                         FIG  2.2|
|000310        10 MAJOR              PIC X(03).                         FIG  2.2|
|000320     05 FILLER                PIC X(35).                         FIG  2.2|
|000330 FD  PRINTOUT LABEL RECORDS ARE OMITTED.                         FIG  2.2|
|000340 01  OUTPUT-REC.                                                 FIG  2.2|
|000350     05 FILLER                PIC X(03).                         FIG  2.2|
|000360     05 1ST-NAME              PIC X(11).                         FIG  2.2|
|000370     05 M-I                   PIC X(02).                         FIG  2.2|
|000380     05 SUR-NAME              PIC X(10).                         FIG  2.2|
|000390     05 FILLER                PIC X(04).                         FIG  2.2|
|000400     05 ID-NUM                PIC 9(09).                         FIG  2.2|
|000410     05 FILLER                PIC X(05).                         FIG  2.2|
|000420     05 CLASS                 PIC X(02).                         FIG  2.2|
|000430     05 FILLER                PIC X(06).                         FIG  2.2|
|000440     05 MAJ                   PIC X(03).                         FIG  2.2|
|000450     05 FILLER                PIC X(08).                         FIG  2.2|
```

Figure 2.2 A Sample (Structured) COBOL Program

```
--------------------------------------------------------------------------------
|        1   1   2   2   2   3   3   4   4   4   5   5   6   6   6   7   7   8|
|    4   8   2   6   0   4   8   2   6   0   4   8   2   6   0   4   8   2   6   0|
--------------------------------------------------------------------------------
|000460      05 CURRENT-HOURS           PIC 9(02).                    FIG  2.2|
|000470      05 FILLER                  PIC X(08).                    FIG  2.2|
|000480      05 TOT-HOURS               PIC 9(03).                    FIG  2.2|
|000490      05 FILLER                  PIC X(03).                    FIG  2.2|
|000500  WORKING-STORAGE SECTION.                                     FIG  2.2|
|000510  01  WORKING-VARIABLES.                                       FIG  2.2|
|000520      05 INDICATOR               PIC X(05) VALUE 'START'.      FIG  2.2|
|000530  PROCEDURE DIVISION.                                          FIG  2.2|
|000540  CONTROL-LOGIC.                                               FIG  2.2|
|000550      PERFORM START-UP.                                        FIG  2.2|
|000560      PERFORM READ-DATA UNTIL INDICATOR = 'DONE'.              FIG  2.2|
|000570      PERFORM END-JOB.                                         FIG  2.2|
|000580      STOP RUN.                                                FIG  2.2|
|000590  START-UP.                                                    FIG  2.2|
|000600      OPEN INPUT STUDENT-FILE, OUTPUT PRINTOUT.                FIG  2.2|
|000610      MOVE SPACES TO OUTPUT-REC.                               FIG  2.2|
|000620      READ STUDENT-FILE AT END MOVE 'DONE' TO INDICATOR.       FIG  2.2|
|000630  READ-DATA.                                                   FIG  2.2|
|000640      MOVE STUDENT-ID TO ID-NUM.                               FIG  2.2|
|000650      MOVE LAST-NAME TO SUR-NAME.                              FIG  2.2|
|000660      MOVE FIRST-NAME TO 1ST-NAME.                             FIG  2.2|
|000670      MOVE MIDDLE-INITIAL TO M-I.                              FIG  2.2|
|000680      MOVE CLASSIFICATION TO CLASS.                            FIG  2.2|
|000690      MOVE TOTAL-HOURS TO TOT-HOURS.                           FIG  2.2|
|000700      MOVE HOURS-THIS-SEM TO CURRENT-HOURS.                    FIG  2.2|
|000710      MOVE MAJOR TO MAJ.                                       FIG  2.2|
|000720      WRITE OUTPUT-REC AFTER 2 LINES.                          FIG  2.2|
|000730      READ STUDENT-FILE AT END MOVE 'DONE' TO INDICATOR.       FIG  2.2|
|000740  END-JOB.                                                     FIG  2.2|
|000750      CLOSE STUDENT-FILE, PRINTOUT.                            FIG  2.2|
```

Figure 2.2 A Sample (Structured) COBOL Program *Continued*

ecuting the READ-DATA procedure (line 560), and terminating the procedure by invoking END-JOB (line 570). After these operations have been performed, the procedure is halted. The CONTROL-LOGIC paragraph summarizes the procedure for the programmer, making it unnecessary to read the entire program, something that is often required to understand a program designed along "traditional" lines.

The remaining chapters in this part are designed to acquaint the programmer with the four divisions, how they are coded, what they mean, and various alternatives available within them. Chapter 3 deals with the IDENTIFICATION DIVISION, Chapter 4 discusses the ENVIRONMENT DIVISION, Chapter 5 is an initial investigation of the DATA DIVISION, and Chapter 6 explores a few of the most important statements in the PROCEDURE DIVISION.

The COBOL Coding Form

As with most programming languages, there are specific rules for each line of a COBOL program. The layout of the COBOL coding form is presented in Figure 2.3. The body of the form (eliminating the top portion, which includes nonprogramming entries), provides specific column designations for the COBOL entries. These designations represent five parts of COBOL lines (statements)—sequence numbers, continuation and comment, Area A, Area B, and identification (shown in the upper right-hand corner of the form).

The sequence numbers occupy columns 1 through 6. The numbers act only as a means of recording the sequence of lines from coding forms. Most COBOL compilers, unless directed otherwise, will ignore the numbers placed in these columns, and they may be omitted without any detrimental effects. They can be an effective means of insuring that the statements (or cards) are in

COBOL Coding Form

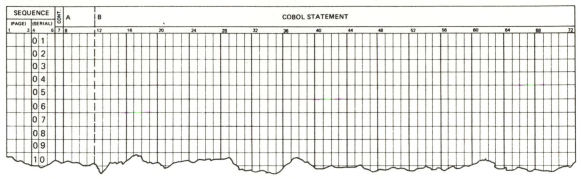

Figure 2.3 The COBOL Coding Form

the prescribed sequence, however. COBOL compilers, if directed, will check the sequence of these numbers during the compiling process and will mark (with a warning message) any lines that are out of sequence. To be in the proper order, the sequence numbers must be in an ascending order, but not necessarily in fixed increments.

Many coding forms subdivide these six columns so that columns 1 through 3 represent page numbers and columns 4 through 6 represent serial numbers. This procedure provides slightly better control. The page number represents the page number of the coding form from which the line was taken. The serial number represents the specific line on that page. Thus, a programmer could return to the original coding form for a program if necessary. Serial or line numbers are generally printed on the coding form in increments of 10 to allow for inserting new lines later, while still maintaining the ascending order.

The second part of the coding form serves a dual function. Column 7 may be used for indicating the continuation of a COBOL statement (entry) from one line to the next, or it may be used for entering a comment entry. If a continuation is necessary, the programmer enters a hyphen (-) in column 7 of each line following the start of the statement and for every additional line needed to complete the statement. This is necessary because the COBOL compiler assumes a space between column 72 of one line and column 12 of the line immediately following it. The significance of this will become more apparent after reading the discussion on Area B.

A continuation is usually required only if (1) a reserved word is being continued from one line to another, (2) a programmer-supplied name cannot be completed on one line, or (3) a literal does not begin and end on the same line. Therefore, just because a statement, entry, or clause is not completed on one line does not necessarily mean a continuation is needed. In some cases, a statement may take two or more lines with no continuations. Conversely, two or more statements may be recorded on the same line. This will be discussed more fully later in this chapter under COBOL punctuation.

Column 7 is also used for comment entries. Any line in a COBOL program with an asterisk (*) in column 7 will be ignored by the compiler. Thus, comments or a verbal commentary on the purpose of specific segments of code require an asterisk in column 7 of each of the affected lines.

Area A of the coding form, columns 8 through 11, is used to record the major segments of a COBOL program. That is, all division headings, section headings, paragraph-names, FD entries, and level numbers Ø1, 66, and 77 should begin in columns 8 through 11. (Some of these terms are new, but they will be discussed in later chapters.) Only these items should appear in Area A. It is *desirable* to record these entries in a special way to make them easy to locate. Examine Figure 2.1. Notice that some of the lines extend more to the left than others. All of these entries are major segments.

Area B, columns 12 through 72, is the portion of the coding form in which statements and clauses are recorded. Notice that the bulk of the coding in Figure 2.1 begins four positions to the right of the beginning of the division headings in column 12.

The final part of the coding form lies in columns 73 through 80, which is not scanned by the COBOL compiler. The programmer can put any information in these columns he or she desires or leave it blank. Generally, this area is used to identify the program by placing some code or series of symbols in these columns on all lines. Because this area is not checked by the compiler, the programmer should be careful not to use it for any portion of a COBOL command.

One final note about the COBOL coding form. Each line of the coding form represents one card (line) in a COBOL program. Consequently, when a character appears in column 1 of the coding form, it should be placed in column 1 of the medium used to record the program.

Some Definitions, Rules, and Guidelines

The valid *character set* for COBOL statements is represented in Table 2.1. Only the characters presented in this table may be used in the formation of COBOL statements. There are three basic groups of characters represented in the table—*numeric, alphabetic* (including the space) and *special characters.* Each of these symbols has a specific use.

Table 2.1 The COBOL Character Set

Character(s)	Meaning			
	space or blank			
+	plus sign			
−	minus sign or hyphen	used as		
*	asterisk	arithmetic		
/	slash (stroke or virgule)	operators	used in	
=	equal sign		condition	
>	"greater than" symbol		tests	characters
<	"less than" symbol			composing
$	currency (dollar) sign			the COBOL
.	period			character
,	comma			set
" or '	quote characters	punctuation		
;	semicolon			
(	left (open) parenthesis			
)	right (close) parenthesis			
0,1,...9	numeric characters (digits)			
A,B,...Z	alphabetic characters (letters)			

The first use of the characters in the COBOL character set is *punctuation*. As previously noted, a COBOL program is structured to parallel a written text. Since there are punctuation rules for textual material, there are also punctuation rules for COBOL programs. The punctuation characters are as follows:

Character	Meaning
	space
,	comma
;	semicolon
.	period
" or '	quote characters
(	left (open) parenthesis
)	right (close) parenthesis

Remember that the hierarchy of COBOL is division, section, paragraph, sentence (or entry), and statement (or clause). Each of these parts is shown in Figure 2.1. The required punctuation for both division and section headings (within the scope of this text) is that each must be coded on a line by itself and followed immediately by a period. Each paragraph, though it *may* be coded on a line by itself, is terminated by a period and at least one space. Sentences and entries follow the same rules as paragraphs. (However, they must be recorded in Area B— columns 12 through 72—and there may be one or more sentences (or entries) on one line.) Other rules related to punctuation are listed below.

1. Any punctuation shown in the format of clauses or statements in subsequent chapters is required of that clause or statement.
2. As with a period, a space must appear after any use of a comma or semicolon. However, there should not be a space immediately before these characters.
3. Two successive words in COBOL are required to have at least one space separating them. This rule applies equally to reserved words, programmer-supplied-names, literals, and figurative constants (each of which is discussed shortly).
4. Any arithmetic operator (a symbol indicating the operation of adding, subtracting, multiplying, or dividing) or an equal sign is required to have at least one space before and after the symbol. (See the COMPUTE statement and the IF statements.)
5. A left parenthesis should be preceded by a space and must not be followed by a space. The right parenthesis should not be preceded by a space but must be followed by either a space or some other form of punctuation such as a period. (See the COMPUTE and IF statements and table handling.)
6. A comma may be used to separate multiple operands in a statement. (See, for example, the MOVE statement.)
7. A comma or semicolon may be used to separate several clauses which form an entry or several statements which form a sentence.

The first nonpunctuation use of the COBOL character set is in the formation of *words* in COBOL. A word is a combination of numeric and alphabetic characters and the special character hyphen (-) to form a reference symbol that has meaning to the COBOL compiler and the programmer. There are two types of words—*reserved words* and *programmer-supplied-names*. A reserved word is a symbol with which the COBOL compiler associates special meaning. The first two words found in any COBOL program are the symbols IDENTIFICATION and DIVISION. Both are reserved words and should be used only in the context permitted (or established) by the COBOL compiler. For example, all division names, and the word DIVISION itself, are reserved words. A reserved word has special connotation to the COBOL compiler, and its use should be avoided except as directed by the language. To aid in identifying the reserved words, Table 2.2 is provided. This is a list of all ANS COBOL reserved words. (A word of caution—all compilers have additional reserved words. Thus, to avoid the use of a reserved word, review the reserved-word list for the COBOL compiler available at your installation.)

Table 2.2 ANS COBOL Reserved Words**

ACCEPT*	COLUMN*	DETAIL*	GO
ACCESS	COMMA	DISABLE*	GREATER
ADD	COMMUNICATION*	DISPLAY	GROUP*
ADVANCING	COMP	DIVIDE	
AFTER	COMPUTATIONAL	DIVISION	HEADING*
ALL	COMPUTE	DOWN	HIGH-VALUE
ALPHABETIC	CONFIGURATION	DUPLICATES*	HIGH-VALUES
ALSO*	CONTAINS	DYNAMIC*	
ALTER*	CONTROL*		I-O*
ALTERNATE	CONTROLS*	EGI*	I-O-CONTROL*
AND	COPY*	ELSE	IDENTIFICATION
ARE	CORR*	EMI*	IF
AREA	CORRESPONDING*	ENABLE*	IN
AREAS	COUNT*	END	INDEX
ASCENDING	CURRENCY	END-OF-PAGE	INDEXED
ASSIGN		ENTER*	INDICATE*
AT	DATA	ENVIRONMENT	INITIAL*
AUTHOR	DATE*	EOP	INITIATE*
	DATE-COMPILED	EQUAL	INPUT
BEFORE	DATE-WRITTEN	ERROR	INPUT-OUTPUT
BLANK	DAY*	ESI*	INSPECT
BLOCK*	DE*	EVERY	INSTALLATION
BOTTOM*	DEBUG-CONTENTS	EXCEPTION*	INTO
BY	DEBUG-LINE	EXIT	INVALID
	DEBUG-ITEM	EXTEND*	IS
CALL*	DEBUG-NAME		
CANCEL*	DEBUG-SUB-1	FD	JUST
CD*	DEBUG-SUB-2	FILE	JUSTIFIED
CF*	DEBUG-SUB-3	FILE-CONTROL	
CH*	DEBUGGING	FILLER	KEY
CHARACTER	DECIMAL-POINT	FINAL*	
CHARACTERS	DECLARATIVES	FIRST	LABEL
CLOCK-UNITS*	DELETE*	FOOTING*	LAST
CLOSE	DELIMITED	FOR*	LEADING
COBOL*	DELIMITER	FROM	LEFT
CODE*	DEPENDING		LENGTH
CODE-SET*	DESCENDING	GENERATE*	LESS
COLLATING*	DESTINATION*	GIVING	LIMIT*

Table 2.2 ANS COBOL Reserved Words** *Continued*

LIMITS*	PERFORM	REWIND	SYMBOLIC*
LINAGE*	PF*	REWRITE	SYNC
LINAGE-COUNTER*	PH*	RF*	SYNCHRONIZED
LINE*	PIC	RH*	
LINE-COUNTER*	PICTURE	RIGHT	TABLE*
LINES	PLUS*	ROUNDED	TALLY
LINKAGE*	POINTER	RUN	TALLYING
LOCK*	POSITION*		TAPE*
LOW-VALUE	POSITIVE	SAME*	TERMINAL*
LOW-VALUES	PRINTING*	SD	TERMINATE*
	PROCEDURE	SEARCH	TEXT*
MEMORY*	PROCEDURES	SECTION	THAN
MERGE*	PROCEEDING*	SECURITY	THROUGH
MESSAGE*	PROGRAM*	SEGMENT*	THRU
MODE	PROGRAM-ID	SEGMENT-LIMIT*	TIME*
MODULES*		SELECT	TIMES
MOVE	QUEUE*	SEND*	TO
MULTIPLE*	QUOTE	SENTENCE	TOP*
MULTIPLY	QUOTES	SEPARATE*	TRAILING*
		SEQUENCE*	TYPE*
NATIVE*	RANDOM	SEQUENTIAL	
NEGATIVE	RD*	SET	UNIT
NEXT	READ	SIGN	UNSTRING
NO	RECEIVE*	SIZE	UNTIL
NOT	RECORD	SORT	UP
NUMBER*	RECORDS	SORT-MERGE*	UPON
NUMERIC	REDEFINES	SOURCE*	USAGE
	REEL*	SOURCE-COMPUTER	USE
OBJECT-COMPUTER	REFERENCES*	SPACE	USING
OCCURS	RELATIVE*	SPACES	
OF	RELEASE	SPECIAL-NAMES	VALUE
OFF*	REMAINDER	STANDARD	VALUES
OMITTED	REMOVAL*	STANDARD-1*	VARYING
ON	RENAMES	START	
OPEN	REPLACING	STATUS*	WHEN
OPTIONAL*	REPORT*	STOP	WITH
OR	REPORTING*	STRING	WORDS*
ORGANIZATION*	REPORTS*	SUB-QUEUE-1*	WORKING-STORAGE
OUTPUT	RERUN	SUB-QUEUE-2*	WRITE
OVERFLOW	RESERVE	SUB-QUEUE-3*	
	RESET	SUBTRACT	ZERO
PAGE*	RETURN	SUM*	ZEROES
PAGE-COUNTER*	REVERSED	SUPPRESS*	ZEROS

*Reserved words not mentioned or discussed in this text.
**Additional non-ANS COBOL reserved words are listed in Appendix A.

The second class of words in COBOL is programmer-supplied-names. This includes all names in a program that are *not* reserved words. The rules for the creation of a programmer-supplied-name are listed below.

1. It may not exceed a total of thirty (30) consecutive nonblank characters.
2. The characters in the name must be alphabetic or numeric or a hyphen.
3. The hyphen may not be the first or last character in a name.
4. The name is terminated by the first occurrence of a space, period, comma, semicolon, or right parenthesis.

There are three basic types of programmer-supplied-names—*data-names*, *condition-names*, and *procedure-names*. Data-names have one additional requirement over standard programmer-supplied-names. All data-names must include at least one alphabetic character. Data-names as the term implies are used to represent some form of data. The following types of names are all data-names.

file-names	index-data-items
record-names	report-names
group-names	sort-file-names
elementary-item-names	sort-record-names
independent-elementary-item-names	mnemonic-names
index-names	

All of these names, if needed, must be described (or defined) in the DATA DIVISION of a COBOL program, except for mnemonic-names, which are described in the ENVIRONMENT DIVISION (SPECIAL-NAMES paragraph). These names can also be referenced in the PROCEDURE DIVISION.

The second type of programmer-supplied-name is a condition-name. It is assigned a particular value or set of values provided through a data-name. It is used solely in testing operations, and it cannot be used to reference data in the same fashion as data-names. A condition-name must also contain at least one alphabetic character; it is described in the DATA DIVISION and may be referenced in the PROCEDURE DIVISION.

A procedure-name is the last type of programmer-supplied-name. A procedure-name, as the name implies, is used to reference segments of the

Programmer-supplied-name	Valid data-name* or condition-name	Valid procedure-name*
EMPLOYEE-NAME	YES	YES
NUMBER	NO[1]	NO[1]
GO-TO	YES[2]	YES[2]
DATE-COMPILED	NO[3]	NO[3]
1ST-NAME	YES	YES
RATE-PER-HOUR	YES	YES
475	NO[4]	YES
HOURS-WORKED-	NO[5]	NO[5]
ANNUAL-INTEREST-RATE	YES[6]	YES[6]

1. Although NUMBER is not generally considered an ANS COBOL reserved word, it is a reserved word in a sufficient number of compilers to warrant its avoidance. Instead of NUMBER, an abbreviation such as NUM or NUMB could be used. (NO is another reserved word.)
2. Even though the words GO and TO are reserved words, when a hyphen is placed between them, they no longer fall into the reserved word category. There are relatively few reserved words containing a hyphen. Thus, hyphenated words are often used as programmer-supplied-names.
3. DATE-COMPILED is an ANS COBOL reserved word. Note that it also contains a hyphen.
4. A data-name or condition-name must contain at least one alphabetic character.
5. Programmer-supplied-names must not begin or end with a hyphen.
6. Even though the name is rather long, it falls within the 30-character limit. (Hyphens are included in the character count.)

*It is assumed that the same name is not being used as both a data-name (or condition-name) and a procedure-name in the same program.

Figure 2.4 Sample Programmer-Supplied-Names

PROCEDURE DIVISION. Procedure-names do not reference data but rather reference the location of one or more statements in the PROCEDURE DIVISION. Procedure-names, which are commonly referred to as paragraph or SECTION names in the PROCEDURE DIVISION, need *not* contain an alphabetic character.

Figure 2.4 lists some possible programmer-supplied-names. Note that in some cases, the name does not conform to the rules for name formation.

The next category of items used in COBOL are *constants*. Unlike data-names, constants retain the same "value" from the beginning of the program to the end of the program. There are three classes of constants used in COBOL—*numeric literals, non-numeric literals,* and *figurative constants.* Numeric and non-numeric literals as a group are sometimes referred to as literals.

A numeric literal is what one generally thinks of as a constant. It is a numeric value. That is, the digits in the numeric literal represent its numeric "value." A numeric literal must conform to the following rules.

1. It must contain one or more of the characters 0 through 9.
2. It may have a leading plus or minus sign.
3. If a portion of the number represents a decimal fraction, it may contain a decimal point in any position except following the last character of the value.
4. It may generally be from 1 to 18 digits in length.

A non-numeric literal is a textual string of characters, generally messages (e.g., column headings). A non-numeric literal must conform to the following rules.

1. It may contain any character acceptable to the computer being utilized (i.e., generally all characters in either the EBCDIC or ASCII coding systems). This is generally a larger set of characters than the COBOL character set in Table 2.1.
2. It must be contained within quotes (i.e., it begins and ends with a quote character). The quote characters themselves are not part of the non-numeric literal. The quote character may be either a quote mark (") or the apostrophe ('). Check at your installation to determine which character is assumed by default by your compiler. In most cases it is the apostrophe.
3. It may contain reserved words.
4. Each space (or blank) represents a character.
5. The length of the non-numeric literal may generally be from 1 through 120 characters (excluding the quote character). (Some compilers permit slightly longer non-numeric literals.)

The final category in the constant group is the figurative constant. The figurative constant is a COBOL reserved word which represents the value(s) signified by the word. Since they are reserved words, no other special designation is necessary. The figurative constants, their alternate spellings, and meanings are presented below. Whether the singular or plural form of the word is used, the meaning is the same.

ZERO ZEROS ZEROES	One or more occurrences of the number zero. (This is the only figurative constant that can be used in conjunction with a numeric data item.)

SPACE SPACES	One or more occurrences of a space (or blank).
HIGH-VALUE HIGH-VALUES	One or more occurrences of the character considered to be the highest in a particular computer's collating (character-value) sequence.
LOW-VALUE LOW-VALUES	One or more occurrences of the character considered to be the lowest in a particular computer's collating (character-value) sequence.
QUOTE QUOTES	One or more occurrences of the quote character, i.e., either the quote mark (") or the apostrophe ('). The figurative constant QUOTE(S) is not intended to replace the quote character in non-numeric literals.
ALL literal	One or more occurrences of the character string that composes the literal. The literal must be either a non-numeric literal or a figurative constant. In the case of figurative constants, the word ALL is redundant.

In the case of HIGH-VALUE(S) and LOW-VALUE(S), the particular internal representation used depends on the coding system used by the computer (EBCDIC or ASCII). Several examples of numeric and non-numeric literals are presented in Figure 2.5.

It is possible to code literals as portions of entries or statements that do not lie totally within Area B of one line. For example, when coding a non-numeric literal, it is possible for one literal, which could reach 120 characters, to exceed the space provided in Area B, which is only 61 characters. If it is necessary to continue a non-numeric literal from one line to another, the continuation character (hyphen) should be placed in column 7 of all additional lines used. It

Text of literal*	Type of literal (comments)
12345	numeric
123.45	numeric
.12345	numeric
12345.	illegal numeric—a decimal point cannot appear as the last character in a numeric literal
– 12345	numeric—all previous numeric literals are treated as positive, although no sign is physically recorded
'END OF JOB'	non-numeric—10 characters in length
'12345'	non-numeric—even though the literal is composed entirely of digits, the literal is treated as non-numeric.
'ED'S PLACE'	illegal non-numeric—one of the characters in the literal is the quote character
'12,345.67—BALANCE'	non-numeric—18 characters in length

*In these examples, it is assumed that the apostrophe (') is the character used by the compiler to represent the quote character.

Figure 2.5 Sample Numeric and Non-numeric Literals

is also necessary to repeat the quote character in Area B (column 12) of each line for which the literal continues. Thus, a continued non-numeric literal might appear as shown in Figure 2.6. No continuation character is necessary on the first line containing the literal. However, on the second line a hyphen is placed in column 7, and the quote character is repeated in column 12. The literal includes any remaining spaces (up to and including column 72) from the first line. Therefore, to continue a non-numeric literal, as much of the literal as possible should be written on the first line before it is continued on subsequent lines. This insures that no unanticipated spaces are "added" to the literal. Continuation of lines containing numeric literals, figurative constants and other reserved words, and programmer-supplied-names is a simpler task, as demonstrated in Figure 2.6. Only the hyphen in column 7 is necessary for a continuation.

The final set of rules and guidelines are not rules for the COBOL language itself but rather an aid to understanding the form of the language. The rules below have been widely adopted to describe COBOL clauses and statements. They have been applied in programming manuals of every computer manufacturer and textbook on COBOL with which this author is familiar. The rules are provided here to make the transition from this text to other manuals or texts simpler.

1. Any reserved word in a statement or clause will appear in capital letters.
2. Any reserved word that is underlined is a required reserved word. If an underscored reserved word appears in an optional portion of a statement or clause, the word is required only if the option is used. Any reserved word which is not underscored may be employed at the programmer's discretion.
3. Any word in lower-case letters is a programmer-supplied-name (e.g., data-name, condition-name, etc.). It is the programmer's responsibility to supply these words in an appropriate context.

COBOL Coding Form

SYSTEM An Introduction to ANS COBOL | PUNCHING INSTRUCTIONS | PAGE 1 OF 1
PROGRAM Illustrations of Statement Continuation | GRAPHIC | CARD FORM # FIG 2.6
PROGRAMMER J. Wayne Spence | DATE 01/01/81 | PUNCH

```
SEQUENCE  CONT A    B   COBOL STATEMENT                                    IDENTIFICATION
01        *         CONTINUATION OF A NON-NUMERIC LITERAL
02                                                          ... 'GENERALLY S
03        -         'PEAKING, SOMETHING WOULD PRECEED THIS LITERAL'.
04
05
06        *         CONTINUATION OF A NUMERIC LITERAL
07                                                                   ... 12
08
09        -         3456.
10
11        *         CONTINUATION OF RESERVED WORDS (SUCH AS FIGURATIVE CONSTANTS)
12        *               AND PROGRAMMER-SUPPLIED-NAMES
13
14                                                                    ... Z
15        -         EROES.
16
17
```

Figure 2.6 Examples of Continuations

4. Words in brackets ([ ]) indicate that this portion of the statement or clause is optional. It may be included in the statement or clause at the programmer's discretion.

5. Any option followed by an ellipsis (. . .) indicates that the option may be repeated at the programmer's discretion.

6. Any portion of a statement or clause within braces ({ }) indicates that the programmer must make a selection between (or among) the items listed. This is a forced choice unless the braces are shown within a set of brackets.

Summary COBOL is based upon a hierarchical structure. This structure, from the highest level to the lowest level, includes DIVISION headings, SECTION headings, paragraphs, entries or sentences, and clauses or statements. There are four divisions in every COBOL program—IDENTIFICATION, ENVIRONMENT, DATA, and PROCEDURE—and they must be recorded in that order. Each division satisfies a particular purpose within the program:

IDENTIFICATION—general documentation and definition;
ENVIRONMENT—definition of equipment (hardware) used by the program;
DATA—definition and description of all data items used in the program and interrelationships of data items; and
PROCEDURE—definition of the process to be executed.

As with most programming languages, the COBOL language conforms to a series of coding rules. These rules specify that columns 1 through 6 of each line are reserved for sequence numbers; column 7 may be used for continuations or comments; columns 8 through 11, Area A, is used for recording major headings; columns 12 through 72, Area B, is used to record entries and sentences; and columns 73 through 80 may be used for additional program identification.

Entries and sentences are composed of reserved words, programmer-supplied-names, punctuation, and perhaps constants. Reserved words have special meaning to the COBOL compiler and should only be used in the prescribed context. Programmer-supplied-names are those names selected by the programmer and include data-names, condition-names, and procedure-names. Programmer-supplied-names must conform to specific formation rules, and each name type has a specific use. Punctuation—periods, commas, and semicolons—is necessary for the completion of entries and sentences. Commas, for example, may be used to separate clauses within an entry, while the entry itself is terminated by a period. Finally, some clauses and statements require the use of constants. Three categories of constants are available in COBOL—numeric literals, non-numeric literals, and figurative constants. Thus, through hierarchical design and sublevel components of clauses and statements, COBOL is one of the most highly structured programming languages.

Notes on Programming Style Although COBOL compilers allow entries and statements to appear on the same line as paragraph names, most commercial programmers record paragraph names on a line by themselves as an additional visual cue.

COBOL compilers also permit multiple statements (and clauses) *per line*. However, recording multiple statements per line is *not* advisable for three reasons. First, program modifications become more difficult, especially when other statements need to be inserted between existing statements. Secondly, debugging (logical error correcting) is often more difficult because of each statement's lack of isolation. Finally, statements are more readable when recorded one per line. In addition. since all compilers ignore blanks in Area B (except in non-numeric literals), the programmer may choose to indent certain segments of the program to improve readability.

Comments are frequently helpful in explaining a certain approach or the significance of a particular procedure. However, work cautiously! Too many comments distract from otherwise readable code. Furthermore, comments that are too specific should be avoided. Historically when programs are modified after extended use, the comments are rarely modified to reflect the changes. Thus, specific comments may no longer be accurate. Finally, *never* use comments to try to "improve" or make up for poorly written procedures! The procedure should speak for itself if at all possible.

Questions

Below, fill in the blank(s) with the appropriate word, words, or phrases.

1. The largest (most encompassing) segment of a COBOL program is at the _____ level.

2. Within a COBOL program there are _____ (number) divisions.

3. Divisions are subdivided into segments called _____ , which are in turn broken into _____ .

4. Sentences are composed of one or more _____ , while entries are composed of one or more _____ .

5. The first division of a COBOL program is always the _____ DIVISION, and the last division is always the _____ DIVISION.

6. The _____ DIVISION contains no sections.

7. Sentences appear only in the _____ DIVISION.

8. The function of the IDENTIFICATION DIVISION is to _____ .

9. The function of the ENVIRONMENT DIVISION is to _____ .

10. All data items are described in the _____ DIVISION.

11. The FILE SECTION may be found in the _____ DIVISION.

12. The INPUT-OUTPUT SECTION may be found in the _____ DIVISION.

13. The process to be performed by a COBOL program is provided in the _____ DIVISION.

14. Columns 1 through 6 of a COBOL coding form are reserved for _____ .

15. If a COBOL statement is to be continued, a(n) _____ should appear in column(s) _____ .

16. When an asterisk appears in column 7, the line is treated as a(n) _____ .

17. Paragraph names should begin in Area _____ .

18. Clauses should begin in Area _____ .

19. The COBOL character set is composed of _____ , _____ , and _____ characters.

20. Both _____ and _____ must be recorded on a line by themselves and be followed by a period.

21. An entry is terminated by a(n) _____ .

22. Clauses in an entry may be separated by _____ or _____ .

23. There are two types of words in COBOL, _____ which have special meaning to the COBOL compiler and _____ which have special meaning to the programmer.

24. A data-name differs from a procedure-name in that it must include at least one _____ character.

25. All data-names must appear in the _____ DIVISION.

26. A programmer-supplied-name is a generic term that includes _____ , _____ , and _____ .

27. Numeric literals, non-numeric literals, and figurative constants are all generically known as _____ .

28. The maximum length of a numeric literal is _____ digits.

29. The maximum length of a non-numeric literal is _____ characters.

30. The figurative constant associated with the maximum quantity of a computer is _____ .

31. All figurative constants are _____ words.

Respond to the following questions by circling either "T" for true or "F" for false.

T F 32. The proper order of divisions within a COBOL program is ENVIRONMENT, IDENTIFICATION, DATA, AND PROCEDURE.
T F 33. All divisions may contain sections.
T F 34. Paragraphs are always composed of sentences.
T F 35. The lowest-level item in the PROCEDURE DIVISION is the clause.
T F 36. The WORKING-STORAGE SECTION may be a part of the DATA DIVISION.
T F 37. Sequence numbers (in columns 1 through 6) are necessary on each line of a COBOL program.
T F 38. A hyphen is the only character permitted in column 7 of a COBOL statement.

T F 39. Each time a COBOL statement requires two or more lines to record, continuation (a hyphen in column 7) is required.

T F 40. Division headings must begin in column 8.

T F 41. Section headings should begin in Area A.

T F 42. Entries and sentences should begin in Area A.

T F 43. In COBOL, there is a distinction between alphabetic and special characters.

T F 44. In COBOL, only one statement may be recorded per line.

T F 45. Paragraph names must be recorded on a line by themselves.

T F 46. A period must be followed by a space.

T F 47. A sentence may be terminated by a semicolon.

T F 48. A data-name may be selected for use by the programmer from the list of reserved words.

T F 49. All programmer-supplied-names are used to reference data values.

T F 50. All programmer-supplied-names must contain at least one alphabetic character.

T F 51. Numeric literals may contain digits.

T F 52. Non-numeric literals may contain digits.

T F 53. Figurative constants may contain digits.

T F 54. The value − 12.5 could be used as a numeric literal.

T F 55. The value 147. could be used as a numeric literal.

Exercises

1. Below is a list of programmer-supplied-names. Identify those names which are legal names. If the name is illegal, indicate the reason it is illegal.

   a. ANNUAL-SALES
   b. DOLLAR-INVESTMENT
   c. W2-FORM
   d. 1040
   e. MONTH-OF-THE-WEEK
   f. DAY OF THE WEEK
   g. FEDERAL-WITHHOLDING-TAX-DEDUCTION
   h. F.I.C.A.
   i. DATE-COMPILED
   j. TAX

2. In the program that follows, identify at least one of each of the following:

   division heading
   paragraph name
   clause
   statement
   data-name
   numeric literal
   figurative constant
   section heading
   entry
   sentence
   programmer-supplied-name
   procedure-name
   non-numeric literal

```
000010 IDENTIFICATION DIVISION.
000020 PROGRAM-ID. PROB-EXAMPLE.
000030 ENVIRONMENT DIVISION.
000040 CONFIGURATION SECTION.
000050 SOURCE-COMPUTER. IBM.
000060 OBJECT-COMPUTER. IBM.
000070 INPUT-OUTPUT SECTION.
000080 FILE-CONTROL.
000090     SELECT PRINT-FILE ASSIGN TO UR-1403-S-PROUT.
000100 DATA DIVISION.
000110 FILE SECTION.
000120 FD  PRINT-FILE LABEL RECORDS ARE OMITTED.
000130 01  PRINT-LINE.
000140     02 FILLER                  PIC X.
000150     02 POSITION-1              PIC X(10).
000160     02 FILLER                  PIC X(5).
000170     02 POSITION-2              PIC X(10).
000180     02 FILLER                  PIC X(107).
000190 WORKING-STORAGE SECTION.
000200 01  VALUE-RECORD.
000210     02 VALUE-1                 PIC X(10) VALUE 'FIELD NO 1'.
000220     02 VALUE-2                 PIC 9(5) VALUE 145.
000230 PROCEDURE DIVISION.
000240 PROCEDURAL-COMMANDS.
000250     OPEN OUTPUT PRINT-FILE.
000260     MOVE SPACES TO PRINT-LINE.
000270     MOVE VALUE-1 TO POSITION-1.
000280     MOVE VALUE-2 TO POSITION-2.
000290     WRITE PRINT-LINE AFTER ADVANCING 2 LINES.
000300     MOVE ALL '-' TO PRINT-LINE.
000301     WRITE PRINT-LINE AFTER ADVANCING 2 LINES.
000320     MOVE 'END REPORT' TO POSITION-1.
000330     MOVE ALL '*' TO POSITION-2.
000340     WRITE PRINT-LINE AFTER ADVANCING 2 LINES.
000350 CONCLUDING-COMMANDS.
000360     CLOSE PRINT-FILE.
000370     STOP RUN.
```

Problems

With the help of your instructor, run the program shown in question #2 above. You will need the necessary job control language instructions for compiling and executing a COBOL program which requires no external data. Also, you may need to modify the ASSIGN clause provided in line 90 of the program so that it conforms to the type of compiler and equipment available at your installation. Good Luck!

3 The IDENTIFICATION DIVISION

Purpose of the Division

The IDENTIFICATION DIVISION is always present in a COBOL program or routine and is always the first division. The IDENTIFICATION DIVISION, as its name implies, identifies the program by providing documentation. The IDENTIFICATION DIVISION provides information about the program, such as the title of the program, who wrote it, when it was written, the date it was *compiled* (translated) from the *source program* (a high-level language program such as COBOL) into an *object program* (a program in the computer's language), who it was written for, whether it is to be protected from unauthorized use or access, and the purpose of the program. Thus, to familiarize oneself quickly with a program in COBOL, one need only refer to the IDENTIFICATION DIVISION.

Overall View of the IDENTIFICATION DIVISION

The permitted entries in the IDENTIFICATION DIVISION are shown in Figure 3.1. The IDENTIFICATION DIVISION heading is always the first entry of the division. The one major difference between the structure of this division and that of the other divisions is that no section names are permitted. The IDENTIFICATION DIVISION is composed totally of paragraph names.

```
IDENTIFICATION DIVISION.

PROGRAM-ID.  program-name.

[AUTHOR.  [comment entry.]. . .]

[INSTALLATION. [comment entry.]. . .]

[DATE-WRITTEN. [comment entry.]. . .]

[DATE-COMPILED.[comment entry.]. . .]

[SECURITY. [comment entry.]. . .]
```

Figure 3.1 Format of the IDENTIFICATION DIVISION

The paragraph names (which are reserved words) should be coded in the order shown in Figure 3.1. The paragraph names should begin in Area A of the COBOL coding form, be spelled exactly as shown, and be terminated with a period and at least one blank space. The entries following the paragraph names may follow on the same line or start on a new line beginning in Area B. Each entry is terminated by the next paragraph name (or division heading) but should be ended with a period.

Of the paragraph names, only the PROGRAM-ID paragraph is required. The program-name provides an external name by which the program is recognized by the computer's *operating system* (a program that controls the overall operation of the computer). The program-name is a programmer-supplied-name and must, at a minimum, conform to the rules (see Chapter 2) for the creation of programmer-supplied-names. Following these rules will provide a satisfactory program-name for any COBOL compiler (although some compilers will truncate and/or translate the program-name into a form acceptable to the operating system).

All other paragraph names in the IDENTIFICATION DIVISION are optional; however, programmers are encouraged to use them to improve their documentation. All "comment entries" give the programmer complete freedom of content. The entries may be English sentences or paragraphs and may contain numbers, special characters and symbols, and reserved words. All comment entries must appear totally within Area B.

The only benefit of including optional paragraph names in the IDENTIFICATION DIVISION is that any comment entries that appear after the DATE-COMPILED paragraph will be replaced by the current date, i.e. the month, day, and year the program was last compiled (see Figure 3.2).

A note about Figure 3.2—the area of the coding form labeled "Punching Instructions" is used to avoid misinterpretation of characters printed on the coding form. The area marked "Graphic" identifies specific characters that

COBOL Coding Form

SEQUENCE		COBOL STATEMENT
SYSTEM	INTRODUCTION TO COBOL	PUNCHING INSTRUCTIONS
PROGRAM	IDENTIFICATION DIVISION	GRAPHIC
PROGRAMMER	R. D. WILLIAMS DATE 1/1/81	PUNCH

```
01   IDENTIFICATION DIVISION.
02   PROGRAM-ID. PAYROLL-CHECKS
03   AUTHOR. ORIGINAL CODE -- J. WAYNE SPENCE -- 5/31/68.
04          REVISED CODE -- ROBERT D. WILLIAMS -- 4/2/81.
05   INSTALLATION.
06          KLINGON ENTERPRISES, INC.
07   DATE-WRITTEN.
08          JANUARY 1, 1968.
09   DATE-COMPILED.  7/25/81.
10   SECURITY.
11          THIS PROGRAM UTILIZES CONTROLLED DOCUMENTS (PAYCHECK FORMS)
12          AND SENSITIVE DATA INVOLVING POSSIBLE VIOLATIONS OF
13          PERSONAL PRIVACY OF EMPLOYEES.  EXECUTE APPROPRIATE
14          SAFEGUARDS AS DIRECTED BY THE COMPTROLLERS OFFICE IN
15          POLICY STATEMENT SGP-1793, DATED SEPTEMBER 1, 1980.
16
17
18
```

Figure 3.2 An Illustration of the IDENTIFICATION DIVISION

may be similar in physical appearance (e.g., S and 5). The area marked "Punch" demonstrates the hole locations in a punched card that correspond to the characters. This information is especially useful if the person coding the information is not the individual keying the information into a machine-media form.

Summary
The IDENTIFICATION DIVISION is the first division of each COBOL program. Its purpose is to provide information to someone unfamiliar with the program. The division has one required paragraph—PROGRAM-ID—as well as other paragraphs, which are designed to provide information about the author of the program, the date the program was written, the date the program was last compiled, and so forth. Thus, there are very few functional components in the IDENTIFICATION DIVISION.

Notes on Programming Style
Documentation is the primary purpose of the IDENTIFICATION DIVISION. Little effort is required to program this division, yet the effort is well worth the rewards. Assume for the moment that you are required to change a program that is unfamiliar to you and that was written by someone else over two years ago. Wouldn't you like to have most, if not all, of the information allowed in this division before beginning your work?

Questions

Below, fill in the blank(s) with the appropriate word, words, or phrases.

1. The first division of a COBOL program is the _____ DIVISION .

2. The purpose of the IDENTIFICATION DIVISION is to provide _____ .

3. Although there are paragraphs in the IDENTIFICATION DIVISION, the division permits no _____ headings.

4. The only paragraph the COBOL compiler requires to be present in the IDENTIFICATION DIVISION is the _____ paragraph.

5. All paragraph names in the IDENTIFICATION DIVISION should appear in Area _____ of the COBOL coding form.

6. All entries following the paragraph names in the IDENTIFICATION DIVISION should appear in Area _____ .

7. The only paragraph that will have its comment entry modified when executed is the comment entry following the _____ paragraph.

8. The entry following the PROGRAM-ID paragraph at a minimum must conform to the rules for a(n) _____ .

9. Comment entries in the IDENTIFICATION DIVISION should be terminated by a(n) _____ .

10. Comment entries may include _____ .

Answer the following questions by circling either "T" for true or "F" for false.

T F 11. The paragraph names in the IDENTIFICATION DIVISION may be written (listed in the program) in any order desired by the programmer.

T F 12. If the DATE-WRITTEN paragraph is present in the IDENTIFICATION DIVISION, the DATE-COMPILED paragraph must also be present.

T F 13. It is possible for the DATE-WRITTEN paragraph to be the first paragraph in a COBOL program.

T F 14. It is possible for the DATE-WRITTEN paragraph to be the second paragraph in a COBOL program.

T F 15. Division names must be coded on a line by themselves.

T F 16. Entries following paragraph names in the IDENTIFICATION DIVISION may be coded on a separate line from the paragraph name itself.

T F 17. A paragraph name must be followed by a period.

T F 18. In the comment entry following the AUTHOR paragraph, more than one period may be present.

T F 19. Comment entries that follow paragraph names may be several lines long and may appear anywhere between columns 8 and 72.

T F 20. PROGRAM-ID is a section name.

Exercises

1. Below is the IDENTIFICATION DIVISION of a COBOL program. Locate the errors, and correct them.

```
IDENTIFICATION DIVISION
AUTHOR. JOHN DOE
DATE COMPILED. JANUARY 1, 1980.
DATE-WRITEN.
    01/-1/80.
SECURITY .  PART-I:  EXAMINE THIS PROBLEM CLOSELY.
PART-II:  CORRECT ALL ERRORS.
```

2. Write the code for an IDENTIFICATION DIVISION that gives the following details:

Comments:	This procedure provides the basic computational requirements for demand forecasting based on historical data collected over the past twelve months.
Programmer:	(insert your name)
Original coding:	(insert the current date)
Procedure name:	DFCM214
Precautionary measures:	Procedure requires history tapes, which should be returned to the tape vault after use.

3. Rewrite the code provided in Question 2 so that the code conforms to the minimum requirements of the COBOL compiler.

4 The ENVIRONMENT DIVISION

Purpose of the Division

The ENVIRONMENT DIVISION is the second COBOL division. It documents the types of hardware used and the types and number of input and output files, such as card readers and line printers. The division also includes several functional entries.

Because of the differences in COBOL compilers, even between those labeled "standard" ANS COBOL, the programmer must know exactly what hardware is to be used to compile and execute the program. The differences between types of computers (e.g., between IBM and CDC) are definite and very distinct, but the differences between ANS COBOL compilers are minimal and more subtle. At times a program may even have to be changed before it will run on two different computer models made by the same manufacturer. Therefore, although COBOL is called a machine-independent language, it is not completely so. Where it is practical throughout the rest of this text, differences among COBOL compilers will be mentioned.

Overall View of the ENVIRON- MENT DIVISION

The ENVIRONMENT DIVISION heading is the first entry of the division. It is followed immediately by the CONFIGURATION SECTION heading, the first section heading of a COBOL program. The CONFIGURATION SECTION heading is then followed, in order, by two required paragraphs, SOURCE-COMPUTER and OBJECT-COMPUTER and one optional paragraph, SPECIAL-NAMES. The SOURCE-COMPUTER and OBJECT-COMPUTER paragraphs are followed by "comment-entries," which show both the type of computer used to compile the source program and the type used to execute the object program. In most cases these "comment-entries" are nonfunctional and are treated as comments. They differ slightly from the comment entries of the IDENTIFICATION DIVISION, however, in that they are required. The format of the ENVIRONMENT DIVISION is shown in Figure 4.1. (The ENVIRONMENT DIVISION in this part of the text will be discussed only to the extent it is needed for punched-card input and line-printer output.)

SPECIAL-NAMES The SPECIAL-NAMES paragraph is an optional paragraph, but it is the first paragraph that contains information related to specific COBOL compilers. The clause(s) that follows the paragraph heading is of the form

```
system-name IS mnemonic-name
```

The system-name, an *external name* known to the COBOL compiler, must conform to the requirements of the computer being used. The mnemonic-name, an *"internal name,"* is known to the COBOL program, is a programmer-supplied name, and it must conform to the rules for data-name formation in Chapter 2. Thus the clause allows a COBOL program to "communicate" with a COBOL compiler.

```
      ENVIRONMENT DIVISION.*
      CONFIGURATION SECTION.
      SOURCE-COMPUTER.   comment-entry.
      OBJECT-COMPUTER.   comment-entry.
     [SPECIAL-NAMES.   system-name-1 IS mnemonic-name-1.**
          [system-name-2 IS mnemonic-name-2.] . . .]
     [INPUT-OUTPUT SECTION.
      FILE-CONTROL.
          SELECT file-name ASSIGN TO system-name
          [RESERVE {NO       } ALTERNATE [AREA ] ]
                   {integers}            [AREAS]
          [ACCESS MODE IS SEQUENTIAL**]
          [PROCESSING MODE IS SEQUENTIAL] . . . .]

      *The division, as shown, is incomplete.
     **The paragraph, as shown, is incomplete.
```

Figure 4.1 The Format of the ENVIRONMENT DIVISION

The SPECIAL-NAMES clause has a variety of uses; all are generally related to input or output commands. The clause can be used with the DISPLAY statement (discussed in Appendix E) and with the WRITE statement (discussed in Chapter 6). The clause is most often used with the WRITE statement (as one means of indicating vertical spacing or carriage control on the line printer).

WRITE statements used for a line printer are generally limited (without the use of the SPECIAL-NAMES clause) to advancing a specified number of lines from the last line written. Often, it is desirable to advance to either the top of the page or a fixed number of lines from the top of a page (e.g., to produce page headings). Then, the SPECIAL-NAMES clause is used.

Two of the more popular system-names that indicate top-of-page are CØ1 (used by IBM machines) and '1' (used by CDC, Honeywell, Xerox, and others). The SPECIAL-NAMES clause for an IBM machine might be

```
CØ1 IS TOP-OF-PAGE.
```

The same clause for a CDC machine might be

```
'1' IS TOP-OF-PAGE
```

where "TOP-OF-PAGE" represents the mnemonic-name that appears in the PROCEDURE DIVISION with WRITE statements. These are not the only system-names applicable to most computers. Check with your computer installation for the system-names it permits.

INPUT-OUTPUT SECTION

The INPUT-OUTPUT SECTION heading appears next in the ENVIRON-MENT DIVISION. It appears in all programs, except where the routine is a subprogram without input-output capability. For the purposes of this text, the INPUT-OUTPUT SECTION appears in all programs.

The FILE-CONTROL paragraph follows the INPUT-OUTPUT SECTION heading. Within the FILE-CONTROL paragraph, each file used is described by the clauses shown in Figure 4.1. If a program requires punched-card input and line-printer output, two sets of descriptions are presented. Like the SPECIAL-NAMES clause, part of the description of each file uses external-system-names, and some of the entries use internal-names.

SELECT and ASSIGN Clauses

The only entries required to indicate the presence of a file are the SELECT and ASSIGN clauses. The SELECT clause is used to provide an internal-name for a file. This internal-name must conform to the rules for formation of data-names presented in Chapter 2. A SELECT clause might appear as

```
SELECT CARD-INPUT-FILE
```

or

```
SELECT PRINTED-OUTPUT-FILE
```

The file-names, CARD-INPUT-FILE and PRINTED-OUTPUT-FILE, become internal file names and would appear later in other entries and statements of the program. (CARD-INPUT-FILE would likely appear in a file description entry of the DATA DIVISION and OPEN, READ, and CLOSE statements in the PROCEDURE DIVISION. The file-name PRINTED-OUTPUT-FILE would likely appear in a file description entry of the DATA DIVISION and OPEN and CLOSE statements of the PROCEDURE DIVISION.)

The ASSIGN clause is used to provide an external-system-name for the type of external peripheral device (e.g., a card reader or a line printer) to be associated with a file. Since these are external-names, they must conform to the names used by the computer manufacturer. These differences are shown in Table 4.1 for card readers and line printers of the many popular computer manufacturers. For example, the ASSIGN statements for a card reader and a line printer in a system using an IBM-370-145 operating under OS might be

```
...ASSIGN UR-S-CARDIN.
```

and

```
...ASSIGN UR-S-PRTOUT.
```

where CARDIN and PRTOUT are further described in the program job control language. The same ASSIGN clauses for an IBM-360-H50 operating under DOS might be

```
...ASSIGN SYS005-UR-2501-S.
```

and

```
...ASSIGN SYS007-UR-1403-S.
```

where the card-input file is to be read from an IBM model-2501 card reader at system address 005 and output is to be printed on an IBM model-1403 line

Table 4.1 Device Designations for Popular Computer Manufacturers

Manufacturer	Card Reader Designation	Line Printer Designation
IBM 360 or 370 (OS or VS)	$\left\{\begin{array}{c}UR\\UT\end{array}\right\} - \left[\begin{array}{c}1442R\\2501\\2520R\\2540R\end{array}\right]$ -S[-name].	$\left\{\begin{array}{c}UR\\UT\end{array}\right\} - \left[\begin{array}{c}1132\\1403\\1404\\1443\end{array}\right]$ -S[-name].
IBM 360 or 370 (DOS)	SYSnnn- $\left\{\begin{array}{c}UR\\UT\end{array}\right\} - \left\{\begin{array}{c}1442R\\2501\\2520R\\2540R\end{array}\right\}$ -S.	SYSnnn- $\left\{\begin{array}{c}UR\\UT\end{array}\right\} - \left\{\begin{array}{c}1132\\1403\\1404\\1443\end{array}\right\}$ -S.
Honeywell	CARD-READER	PRINTER
CDC	INPUT or SYSTEM-INPUT	OUTPUT or SYSTEM-OUTPUT
UNIVAC	CARD-READER	PRINTER
DEC/PDP	Literal	Literal
Burroughs	READER	PRINTER
General Electric*	file-code CARDS	file-code LISTING
RCA*	SYSIN	SYSOUT
Xerox*	CARD-READER	PRINTER

*Computers manufactured under this name are currently supported by one of the computer manufacturers listed above.

printer at system address 007. The ASSIGN clause for a CDC model 6600 operating under KRONOS might be

```
...ASSIGN INPUT.
```

and

```
...ASSIGN OUTPUT.
```

where INPUT represents the system card reader and OUTPUT represents the system line printer.

Note that with IBM external device names under the OS and VS operating systems, the optional name at the end of the ASSIGN clause entry may or may not be required. With IBM systems under DOS, the system addresses may be other than those shown in the example. Regardless of the type of system to be used, it is wise to consult with your computer installation for any special requirements.

Other FILE-CONTROL Paragraph Clauses

Although only the SELECT and ASSIGN clauses are required to indicate the presence of card-reader and line-printer files, other clauses may be used to improve input or output speed or to improve documentation. These clauses must have a period only after the *last* clause for the file (although other types of punctuation are permitted).

The only other clause that has a functional effect on card readers and line printers is the RESERVE clause. The RESERVE clause, which is optional, is used to manipulate the number of input and output buffers. A *buffer* is simply an area of internal computer memory set aside to store input and output

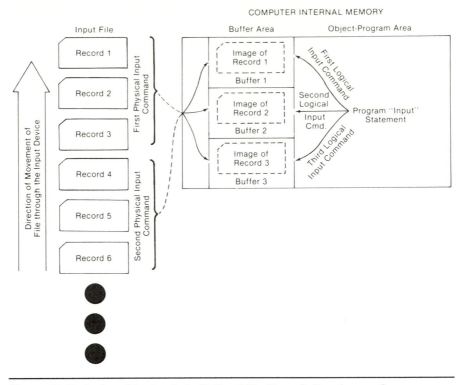

Figure 4.2 Illustration of the Input of a Buffered File (Three Buffers Assumed)

records. It has no logical impact on the programming of a problem, but it is simply used to reduce the numbers of physical input and output operations that the computer must perform. Thus, although every input statement *appears* to cause a single record to be introduced from an external medium, not every such statement causes the computer to interact with the input device. Some input statements physically cause several records to be input; others cause no physical input operation.

An illustration of a buffered input operation is given in Figure 4.2. When the computer executes the first input statement (a READ statement in COBOL) for the first time, the computer reacts by reading the first *three* records from the input file; in one physical read operation all assigned buffers will be filled. Each time the buffers are filled, the operation system automatically sets a *pointer* that *addresses* the first buffer, which is the area addressed by the execution of the first logical input statement. Data is now available for processing. Upon encountering the second logical input statement, the pointer is simply repositioned to address the second input buffer, and, consequently, the image of the second data record, so no physical input takes place. When the third logical input statement is executed the pointer is repositioned again to the buffer assigned.

With the attempted access to the fourth buffer by execution of the fourth logical input statement, no more buffers are found. As a result, the operating system responds by refilling the three assigned buffers with the next three input records. Thus, record 4 is placed in the first buffer, record 5 is placed in the second buffer, record 6 is recorded in the third buffer, and the addressing pointer is repositioned to the first buffer. This cyclic execution of three logical input statements to one physical input operation continues throughout the execution of the program. The same process is used for all files. For example, if a printed output file were assigned three buffers, three logical output commands would have to be executed before the program "dumps" output to the line printer. That is, output physically occurs only when the output buffers are full or upon termination of the program.

This process seems unnecessary, but since no currently available input or output device operates as fast as the computer, it is possible to improve the total input and output speed (efficiency) of a program by increasing the number of input and output buffers. Of course, there must be enough internal memory space available for the buffers since records will be placed in internal memory. This is important for most business applications since they generally use many input-output operations. Again, the use of additional input or output buffers has *no* logical impact on a program; buffers simply improve speed by the use of more internal memory.

The format of the RESERVE clause from Figure 4.1 is:

$$\text{RESERVE} \left\{ \frac{\text{NO}}{\text{integer}} \right\} \quad \text{ALTERNATE} \left[\begin{array}{c} \text{AREA} \\ \text{AREAS} \end{array} \right]$$

The programmer may choose to specify NO if no *additional* input or output areas are required. This allows *one-physical-record-at-a-time* either to enter or exit the computer. The programmer may also choose to indicate an integer (generally between a minimum of 1 and maximum of 254), which allocates enough internal memory for the necessary single buffer plus the additional "integer" number of buffers. And, of course, since the clause is optional, the programmer may choose to leave it out.

One note of caution: All COBOL compilers do not treat buffers in the same way. For example, IBM DOS allows a maximum of only two buffers, which is generally the default when the RESERVE clause is omitted. In addition, many operating systems do not print the contents of output buffers until all buffers are full or until the program is complete. The difficulty here is that if a program terminates abnormally, one or more lines of output may not appear (on the printout). This sometimes makes it a problem to locate the source of the error. You should consult with your installation to determine the maximum number of buffers available to a file and the disposition of the contents of output buffers in cases of abnormal termination.

The remaining clauses, ACCESS MODE and PROCESSING MODE, are documentation clauses. When using punched-card input and line-printer output, only sequential access and processing are possible. If the clauses are omitted, sequential access and processing will be assumed.

Now look at the examples in Figure 4.3. The examples illustrate the different forms of the ENVIRONMENT DIVISION, but they are not the only approaches to the formation of the division, although the coding and indention procedure used in the second illustration is generally the preferred approach in commercial computer installations. The first example shows only the required

COBOL Coding Form

SYSTEM	INTRODUCTION TO ANSI COBOL		PUNCHING INSTRUCTIONS		PAGE 1	OF 1
PROGRAM	ILLUSTRATIVE EXAMPLE FORMAT DIVISION	GRAPHIC				
PROGRAMMER	PATRICK THOMAS SPENCE	DATE 2/18/81	PUNCH		CARD FORM #	

```
01  ENVIRONMENT DIVISION.
02  CONFIGURATION SECTION.
03  SOURCE-COMPUTER.  HONEYWELL-200.
04  OBJECT-COMPUTER.  HONEYWELL-200.
05  INPUT-OUTPUT SECTION.
06  FILE-CONTROL.  SELECT PAY-RECORDS ASSIGN CARD-READER.  SELECT
07      PAY-CHECKS ASSIGN PRINTER.
08
09
10  ENVIRONMENT DIVISION.
11  CONFIGURATION SECTION.
12  SOURCE-COMPUTER.
13      IBM-370-145-OS.
14  OBJECT-COMPUTER.
15      IBM-370-145-OS.
16  SPECIAL-NAMES.
17      C01 IS HEAD-OF-NEXT-PAGE.
18  INPUT-OUTPUT SECTION.
19  FILE-CONTROL.
20      SELECT MASTER FILE ASSIGN TO UR-2540R-S-INCARD;
            RESERVE 15 ALTERNATE AREAS;
            ACCESS MODE IS SEQUENTIAL.
        SELECT EXCEPTION-REPORT ASSIGN TO UR-1403-S-OUTLINE
            RESERVE NO ALTERNATE AREA.
```

Figure 4.3 Examples of the ENVIRONMENT DIVISION

entries of the ENVIRONMENT DIVISION. The entries include the division heading, the section headings, and the three required paragraph names (SOURCE-COMPUTER, OBJECT-COMPUTER, and FILE-CONTROL). The FILE-CONTROL paragraph indicates that a punched-card input file and a line printer will be used. The computer name suggests that a Honeywell computer will be used to compile and execute the program, so the ASSIGN clauses conform to the external device names used by Honeywell equipment. In this case, the ENVIRONMENT DIVISION could be used without changes on a UNIVAC computer because many system names used by UNIVAC are the same as those used by Honeywell.

The second example uses more optional clauses of the ENVIRONMENT DIVISION. The first optional clause is the SPECIAL-NAMES paragraph, which provides a new-page carriage control. In the FILE-CONTROL paragraph, the ASSIGN clauses conform to the format for IBM systems using an OS operating system. The input-card file uses a model 2540 multifunction card unit, has sixteen buffers allocated (the necessary one plus fifteen alternates), and is explicitly a sequentially accessed file. The output is ASSIGNed to a 1403 line printer, has only the necessary single output buffer (which makes it extremely slow), and is implicitly a sequentially accessed file. Both the input and output files are further described by the additional labels of INCARD and OUTLINE.

The first example could be used for several different computers, but the second example could be used only for an IBM 360 or 370 system utilizing OS.

Even on these systems, warning messages could be generated if the model numbers of the specific devices (254OR and 1403) are not the devices used at the installation. Thus, in the second example, several changes (including the SPECIAL-NAMES clause) might be necessary if a different type of computer system were used.

After looking at the ENVIRONMENT DIVISION, you might think it will be difficult to learn COBOL. This is true for the ENVIRONMENT DIVISION because you specify the types of equipment, but there are few differences in the other three divisions from one ANS COBOL compiler to another. Most of any COBOL program is in the DATA and PROCEDURE DIVISIONs, making COBOL a "standardized" language, aside from the ENVIRONMENT DIVISION. The "programming" of COBOL is in the DATA DIVISION and the PROCEDURE DIVISION, to which the remainder of this text is devoted.

Summary

The ENVIRONMENT DIVISION, the second division of a COBOL program, defines the computer resources needed by a program. Although COBOL is known as a "standard" language, the ENVIRONMENT DIVISION provides the means for tailoring a program to specific hardware. The ENVIRONMENT DIVISION comprises two sections, the CONFIGURATION SECTION (in which the computer to be used to compile and execute a program is specified) and the INPUT-OUTPUT SECTION (in which the files and peripheral devices to be used by a program are enumerated). Establishing files and devices in a program is done with SELECT and ASSIGN clauses.

Although there are several special clauses possible in the ENVIRON-MENT DIVISION, the clauses associated with the SPECIAL-NAMES paragraph and the RESERVE clause are probably the most often used. In the SPECIAL-NAMES paragraph, an entry may establish a top-of-form carriage control for output statements in the PROCEDURE DIVISION. The RESERVE clause may be used to establish the number of input-output buffers for a file.

Notes on Programming Style

Two points should be emphasized about the ENVIRONMENT DIVISION. First, you should not feel that mastering COBOL is going to be impossible because of the variability you see in the ENVIRONMENT DIVISION. On the contrary, after you have completed your first few programs, you will find that coding the first *two* divisions is automatic compared to the DATA and PRO-CEDURE DIVISIONs.

Second, understanding the concept of buffer utilization is vital to understanding why COBOL is so frequently used for commercial application programs. However, this is often forgotten, even by experienced program-mers, because COBOL tends to "take care of you." That is, COBOL is more ef-ficient in handling input and output operations than most high-level languages. We, as programmers, should never forget that input and output ef-ficiency is more critical in commercial applications than internal processing ef-ficiency. Therefore, we should avoid coding situations that hamper I/O han-dling. For example, beginning programmers will frequently move spaces to an output line and write it—hardly an efficient means of creating a report. This mistake is the result of their failure to understand the buffering process, and the result is "garbage" (undefined or uninitialized memory area) on a printout. How this happens will become evident in the next two chapters.

Questions

Below, fill in the blank(s) with the appropriate word, words, or phrases.

1. The purpose of the ENVIRONMENT DIVISION is to describe _____ .

2. The ENVIRONMENT DIVISION is composed of the _____ SECTION and the _____ SECTION.

3. The two required paragraphs of the CONFIGURATION SECTION are _____ and _____.

4. In the SPECIAL-NAMES paragraph an external _____ name is assigned to a program-oriented _____ name.

5. The system names CØ1 or '1' are used to represent _____ .

6. A mnemonic-name can appear in the SPECIAL-NAMES paragraph of the ENVIRONMENT DIVISION and in the _____ DIVISION.

7. All files and devices used in a program appear in the _____ SECTION.

8. The clause which is used to assign a file-name to a program is the _____ clause.

9. The clause which is used to assign a device to a file is the _____ clause.

10. One _____ clause and one _____ clause will appear in the FILE-CONTROL paragraph for each file used in a COBOL program.

11. A(n) _____ is an area of internal memory which is set aside for the purpose of conducting input or output operations.

12. The number of buffers assigned to a file is controlled by the _____ clause.

13. The minimum number of buffers necessary for a file to be used in input or output operations is _____ (number).

14. If a file is assigned five buffers, one physical input-output operation takes place for every _____ (number) logical input-output operation(s).

Respond to the following questions by circling either "T" for true or "F" for false.

T F 15. The ENVIRONMENT DIVISION of a COBOL program is the same regardless of the type of computer used to compile and execute the program.

T F 16. COBOL is independent of the computer upon which it is executed.

T F 17. The ENVIRONMENT DIVISION provides information concerning the types of peripheral devices needed by a program.

T F 18. The CONFIGURATION SECTION is an optional section and may be omitted from the ENVIRONMENT DIVISION of a COBOL program.

T F 19. The entries which appear in the SPECIAL-NAMES paragraph are comment entries and have no functional purpose.

T F 20. It is possible to conduct input-output operations in a COBOL program without an INPUT-OUTPUT SECTION.

T F 21. The same file may be assigned to two different devices in the same program.
T F 22. The external device names are the same regardless of the computer being used.
T F 23. Physical input-output operations are the same as logical input-output operations.
T F 24. Buffers are used to improve the efficiency of physical input-output operations.
T F 25. If the clause RESERVE 7 ALTERNATE AREAS is used for a file, the file is assigned 8 buffers.
T F 26. If the clause RESERVE NO ALTERNATE AREAS is used for a file, the file has no buffers.

Exercises

1. Below is the ENVIRONMENT DIVISION of a program. The coding of the division contains errors. Locate the error and demonstrate what correction is necessary.

```
ENVIROMENT DIVISION.
CONFIGURATION-SECTION.
SOURCE-COMPUTER.  UNKNOWN.
OBJECT COMPUTER   IBM.
    SPECIAL-TERMS.  C Ø 1  IS NEXT-PAGE
INPUT-OUTPUT.
    SELECT MY-INPUT-FILE.  ASSIGN TO UR-254ØR-S-CARDIN.
SELECT MY-PRINT-FILE ASSIGN UR-14Ø3-S-PROUT.
    RESERVE 4 ALTERNATIVE AREAS.
```

2. Write the ENVIRONMENT DIVISION of a program on the basis of the following information:

FILE INFORMATION—

File Name	Device Designation	Number of Buffers
BANK BALANCE	UR-254ØR-S-INPTCDS	10
ACCOUNT BALANCE REPORT	UR-14Ø3-S-RPTOUT	—

COMPUTER INFORMATION—
Program will be compiled and executed on an IBM 370 model 145 utilizing the OS operating system. The term to be used in the program to represent the top of form for the printer will be NEXT-ACCOUNT-HEADING.

5 The DATA DIVISION

Purpose of the Division

The DATA DIVISION provides a description of the characteristics of *all* data items that will be used in a program as well as the groupings of those items and other data interrelationships. This chapter is just an initial examination of the DATA DIVISION. Many of the chapters in Parts 2, 3, and 4 deal with additional specific details of the DATA DIVISION not covered in this chapter.

Overall Description of the DATA DIVISION

The DATA DIVISION generally comprises two parts—the FILE SECTION and the WORKING-STORAGE SECTION. The FILE SECTION is used to present a detailed description of the input and output files and records. The WORKING-STORAGE SECTION provides the description of data items or records to be used within the program, but which are not directly connected to either an input or an output file. A very basic description of the DATA DIVISION is provided in Figure 5.1.

```
DATA DIVISION.*
FILE SECTION.
FD   file description entries.
Ø1   record description entries.
       .
       .
       .

WORKING-STORAGE SECTION.
77   independent elementary item description entries.
       .
       .
       .

Ø1   record description entries.
       .
       .
       .

*DATA DIVISION is incomplete as shown; only the basic framework of the division is shown.
```

Figure 5.1 Basic Format of the DATA DIVISION

The coding of the DATA DIVISION requires patience and planning. These are sometimes neglected by beginning COBOL programmers with the result being later correction and longer debugging time. Many of the entries in the DATA DIVISION are also used in the PROCEDURE DIVISION. So the DATA DIVISION should be coded such that the programmer can remember the structure and characteristics of the DATA DIVISION entries without continued reference. The programmer can then code the PROCEDURE DIVISION more easily. Thus, the choices for data references, groupings, etc., should have meaning (both to the programmer and to the problem).

FILE SECTION

The FILE SECTION of the DATA DIVISION provides a description of all files to be used in the program. There is a direct association between the FILE-CONTROL paragraph of the ENVIRONMENT DIVISION and the FILE SECTION of the DATA DIVISION. In the FILE-CONTROL paragraph (in Chapter 4) all files to be used in a program were ASSIGNed to their external devices. The SELECT clause coupled with *each* ASSIGN clause provided a file-name. In the FILE SECTION of the DATA DIVISION there are a series of entries associated with each file-name in the SELECT clauses. Thus, if two SELECT clauses appear in the ENVIRONMENT DIVISION, two sets of file-describing entries appear in the FILE SECTION.

The first part of the description of each file is a series of entries and clauses showing the characteristics of the file. A list of these clauses, in their appropriate format, is presented in Figure 5.2. The first entry following the FILE SECTION heading is an FD (File Description) entry, which is coded in AREA A. All other entries and clauses should be coded in AREA B. Following the FD entry, one of the file-names from a SELECT clause is coded. After the file-name, on the same line or on another line, the other clauses may be entered in any order. The only "required" clause is the LABEL RECORDS clause, which may use either of the combinations of words shown in Figure 5.2. While the LABEL RECORDS clause is "required," some compilers will assume it to be present if it is omitted. The LABEL RECORDS clause is not particularly useful when files are using only punched-card input and line-printer output. (When

```
FILE SECTION.*

FD   file-name

     LABEL  {RECORD IS / RECORDS ARE}  OMITTED**

     [RECORD CONTAINS integer CHARACTERS]

     [DATA {RECORD IS / RECORDS ARE}  data-name-1  [data-name-2 . . .] .

Ø1  record description entries.
```

*FILE SECTION is incomplete as shown; only references to card readers and line printers are shown.
**Clause is incomplete as shown.

Figure 5.2 Format of the File Description Entries and Clauses

magnetic tape or disk is used, however, it is possible for the programmer to have to record labeling information within the file itself. For example, additional security may be provided to make sure the correct tape or disk file is used with a program.)

The RECORD CONTAINS clause is also generally more useful when used with tape or disk files. It is used to specify the number of characters in a record description, generally 80 characters for punched cards and 133 characters for a line printer. Thus, the integer numbers are 80 for punched cards and 133 for most line printers. This is true even if an input-card record does not use all 80 columns or if the output print line does not use 133 columns. If the clause does not reflect the sum of all PICTURE string lengths, the compiler will respond with at least a warning message.

The DATA RECORDS clause is used to provide the record-name(s) of all records used with a file. It is not a functional clause and therefore is only used for documentation.

One final note before leaving the file description clauses. All of the major portions of the descriptions are clauses. As such, *only one period is permitted from the beginning of the file description entries (the FD) to the beginning of the (first) record description (the Ø1 level)*; however, other types of punctuation (commas and semicolons) are permitted.

Record Descriptions

Record descriptions follow a specific order. Figure 5.3 illustrates their form. The description begins with the name of the record itself. Records are composed of *groups* (possibly at several levels) and *elementary-items.* The elementary-items describe data (fields), as indicated by PICTURE clauses. Collections of elementary-items are called *groups* (which may be collected into other groups).

Record descriptions are presented in an outline or hierarchical form similar to that used in division organization. However, since record-names, group-names, and elementary-item-names are data-names, a data-name itself does not distinguish among different levels of inclusiveness. (Data-names must follow the rules in Chapter 2 on data-name formation.) Therefore, *level numbers* are coupled with data-names to indicate different levels of in-

```
Ø1  record-name.*
   [[Ø2 - 48] group-name.]

   [[Ø2 - 49] elementary-item-name { PICTURE }  field-description-entry.
                                    { PIC     }

   [[Ø2 - 49] FILLER { PICTURE }  field-description-entry.
                     { PIC     }
         .
         .
         .


   *Record description is incomplete as shown. Only essential elements are included.
```

Figure 5.3 Format of a Record Description

clusiveness. The lower the level number, the higher the level of inclusiveness. The permitted level numbers are Ø1 through 49.

Since the Ø1 level is the most inclusive level of a record description, it is always associated with the record-name. It should be coded in AREA A, with the record-name itself in AREA B. The record-name can be used as a data reference in other portions of a program, and if used, it will refer to all groups and elementary-items subordinate to it (all data-names at a lower level). Thus, by using the record-name as a data reference, it is possible to address jointly all data-items associated within the record.

The level numbers Ø2 through 48 may be used for either group or elementary-item designations. The lowest-level number, 49, cannot represent a group; it must be an elementary-item. A group represents a series of entries in a record begun by an entry without a PICTURE clause and ended by the next entry that has an equal or higher level number. By definition, a record-name is also a group-name. In addition, however, records may contain groups, and groups may contain groups.

For example, look at the illustration in Figure 5.4. By definition, any entry *with* a PICTURE clause cannot be a group-name and must be an elementary-item. ITEM-3, ITEM-4, ITEM-5, ITEM-8, ITEM-9, ITEM-1Ø, and ITEM-11 are elementary-items. Those data-names without PICTURE clauses are, by definition, group-names at various levels. MASTER-RECORD is a group-name (and a record-name), and it may be used to reference all data items from ITEM-1 through ITEM-11. ITEM-1 is a group-name. It has a level number of Ø3. Thus, all data items listed under it until the next occurrence of an Ø1, Ø2, or Ø3 level are part of this group (and subordinate to) ITEM-1. ITEM-2 through ITEM-1Ø are part of ITEM-1. ITEM-2 is also a group-name. It includes all entries until the next occurrence of a level number less than or equal to Ø5 (down to, but not including, ITEM-5). Thus, ITEM-3 and ITEM-4 are part of group ITEM-2.

```
Ø1   MASTER-RECORD.

    Ø3  ITEM-1.

        Ø5  ITEM-2.

            Ø7  ITEM-3          PICTURE . . .

            Ø7  ITEM-4          PICTURE . . .

        Ø5  ITEM-5             PICTURE . . .

        Ø5  ITEM-6

            1Ø  ITEM-7.

                15  ITEM-8      PICTURE . . .

            1Ø  ITEM-9          PICTURE . . .

        Ø5  ITEM-1Ø            PICTURE . . .

    Ø3  ITEM-11                PICTURE . . .
```

Figure 5.4 An Illustration of a Record Description

Recall that ITEM-3 and ITEM-4 are elementary-items. This might generally mean that the next level number which is lower than Ø7 would be another group-name. Such is not the case, however, ITEM-5 is the next higher level number, but it is an elementary-item. Thus, level numbers by themselves *do not* necessarily indicate the grouping of data items. ITEM-6 is at the same level as ITEM-5, but it is a group-name. It contains ITEM-7 through ITEM-9. ITEM-7 is a group-name containing ITEM-8. ITEM-8 through ITEM-11 all contain PICTURE clauses and are therefore elementary-items.

Two more conclusions can be drawn from Figure 5.4. First, it is not necessary to use consecutive level numbers. Notice that level numbers Ø2, Ø4, Ø6, etc., do not appear in the example. The only requirement is that the higher the number used in a record description, the less data it describes in that record. (However, the reverse is not also true, as is illustrated by ITEM-11.) Second, level numbers do not have to occur at any specific interval. For example, ITEM-2 is an Ø5 level, and its subordinate items are Ø7 levels. On the other hand, ITEM-6 is an Ø5 level, but its subordinate items are 1Ø and 15 levels.

Four additional points need to be made. First, every entry (line) should end with a period because compilers react differently to their omission. Second, the indention shown in the example is not required. It simply reflects a popular convention used by most COBOL programmers so that different levels can be easily seen. (This is one of the tenets of structured programming, discussed in Chapter 7.) Third, it is a good idea to use nonconsecutive level numbers. Though the record description is carefully planned, unforeseen circumstances are not unusual (at least in the beginning) and may necessitate adding groups to a record description. If consecutive level numbers are used (i.e., Ø1, Ø2, Ø3, etc.) it is impossible to add new group-names without renumbering some items. However, if a nonconsecutive numbering system is used (e.g., Ø1, Ø5, 1Ø, 15, etc.), several new groupings could be inserted without renumbering.

Finally, the reserved word, FILLER, as indicated in Figure 5.3, may be placed in a record description at any level number except Ø1 and is always used with a PICTURE clause. Thus, it follows the same basic characteristics of an elementary-item-entry, except that FILLER is used in place of a data-name. FILLER is used to represent one or more spaces or data that is not to be accessed. Thus, when data fields are noncontiguous in an input record or spacing is desired in an output line, FILLER is generally used. In addition, FILLER is generally characterized as being an alphanumeric data-type and cannot be referenced in the PROCEDURE DIVISION (even if it should happen to contain data).

PICTURE Clauses

PICTURE clauses are used to describe the characteristics of a field whether the field internally describes a data item or describes a field connected with an input or output medium (e.g., punched cards or lines of print). An accompanying PICTURE clause distinguishes an elementary-item from a group-name. Every elementary-item will have a PICTURE clause.

The PICTURE-clause field-description entries discussed here are limited to nonedited (DISPLAY) PICTURE character strings. Other types of PICTURE characters are presented in Chapter 9, and other forms of data representation are presented in Chapter 20.

The nonedited PICTURE characters and their meanings are presented in Table 5.1. The table shows the three different types of data representation allowed in COBOL. The first is alphabetic data. A programmer may input, output, or internally store alphabetic data using the PICTURE character "A" for every alphabetic character in the field. Alphabetic characters are the characters A through Z and blanks. The allowable character set for alphabetic fields is not universal, however. A few compilers permit any allowable character for an alphanumeric field to be placed in an alphabetic field. Check at your installation to determine the restrictions on "A" fields.

Table 5.1 Nonedited (DISPLAY) PICTURE Characters

Character	Meaning	Use	Maximum Size for Data
A	Alphabetic	Elementary-items used to represent or store alphabetic data (not for computational purposes)	30 characters
X	Alphanumeric	Elementary-items used to represent or store alphabetic, numeric, and special characters. All group-names are treated as alphanumeric even though they do not have a PICTURE clause. Not for computational purposes.	30 characters*
9	Numeric	Elementary-items used to represent or store numbers. May be used for computation purposes.	18 digits
S	Operational Sign	Numeric elementary-items for which the capability to store a sign (+ or −) is desired.	no space used
V	Implied Decimal	Numeric elementary-item for which decimal positions are desired.	no space used
P	Scaling Factor	Numeric elementary-item to which zeros are to be added when transferred from an external medium to the computer's memory.	no space used

*The maximum length of an alphanumeric data item, when used to represent non-numeric literals, is 120 characters. FILLER items are permitted to be as long as is required to describe a given data area (within practical limitations of approximately 32,000 on most computers).

Alphanumeric PICTURE clauses are created with the character "X." Thus, a number of consecutive Xs (a string) is a representation of alphanumeric data. Any character that means something to the computer may be recorded in an X field. Modern computers use one of two popular character codes, either EBC-DIC (Extended Binary Coded Decimal Interchange Code) or ASCII (American Standard Code II). These character sets are shown in Table 5.2. Since this set of characters includes alphabetic characters, X PICTURE fields are sometimes substituted for A fields.

The PICTURE character "9" is used to represent numeric data, whether or not computation is planned for the data item. For every "9" in the character string describing a numeric item, one digit position is reserved. The allowable characters in a numeric field are the digits 0 through 9. Spaces are not allowed. Consequently, in a numeric field, any column not containing a digit must contain a zero.

Another problem with numeric input data is recording negative numbers. If negative numeric data is to be entered, a negative sign should be overpunched in the last column of the field on the card. Then, the digit in the last column

Table 5.2 The COBOL Character Sets (in Collating-Sequence Order from Lowest Value to Highest Value)

EBCDIC		ASCII	
	space		space
.	period or decimal point	"	quote symbol
<	less than symbol	$	currency symbol
(	left parenthesis	'	apostrophe
+	plus symbol	(	left parenthesis
$	currency symbol	)	right parenthesis
*	asterisk	*	asterisk
)	right parenthesis	+	plus symbol
;	semicolon	,	comma
−	hyphen or minus symbol	−	hyphen or minus symbol
/	slash	.	period or decimal point
,	comma	/	slash
>	greater than symbol	0 – 9	numeric characters (digits)
'	apostrophe	;	semicolon
=	equal symbol	<	less than symbol
"	quote symbol	=	equal symbol
A – Z	alphabetic characters (letters)	>	greater than symbol
Ø – 9	numeric characters (digits)	A – Z	alphabetic characters (letters)

will appear with a minus sign. If the number −123 were to be punched on a card in a four-column field, it would have to be punched as Ø12$\overline{3}$. The last position requires both the digit "3" and a minus sign. Do this by punching the digit "3", backspacing, and punching the minus sign. Or, use the multipunch key available on most keypunch machines and punch both characters in one position. Or, the easiest way to perform this operation is to use a substitute character. In Hollerith code the digit "3" produces a punch in row 3. The minus sign produces a punch in row 11. The combination of these is the Hollerith code representation for the character "L." Thus, −123 could be punched as Ø12L, where the character L in a numeric field is treated as a minus sign *and* the digit 3. A list of all the Hollerith code combinations of numerals with a punch in row 11 is presented in Table 5.3.

In addition, unless the PICTURE string contains the operational sign (the character S), the sign of the number will not be stored within the computer.

Table 5.3 Hollerith code representations in which a punch in row 11 (minus sign) is combined with a numeral.

Hollerith Code	Character Representation
11 - 1	J
11 - 2	K
11 - 3	L
11 - 4	M
11 - 5	N
11 - 6	O
11 - 7	P
11 - 8	Q
11 - 9	R
11 - 0	Nonprintable character*

*Even though this character is nonprintable, it can be created on a punched card with the "multipunch" key on most keypunch machines.

Any numeric field that does not contain the operational sign treats the numeric data it contains as unsigned regardless of the sign actually in the data. The character S, if used, can appear only once per PICTURE clause as the leftmost character. It does not occupy space either internally or externally.

The character V is used to indicate an implied decimal point. Without this character in a numeric PICTURE clause, all numbers are treated as integers (whole numbers). Thus, to record data with decimal-fraction storage capability, the character V must appear in the PICTURE string. The character V can appear only once in a PICTURE string and cannot be the rightmost character. It does not occupy internal or external space.

The last of the nonediting PICTURE characters is the "P." The least used of the nonediting characters, P is used to insert additional zeros either before or after a string of 9s. That is, a number may be either scaled up (by adding zeros after the last digit taken from an external medium) or scaled down (by adding zeros before the first digit, assuming an implied decimal point is the leftmost character).

Table 5.4 illustrates the use of each of these nonedited PICTURE characters. The complete PICTURE clause requires coding the reserved word *PICTURE* (or its abbreviation *PIC*), followed by at least one space and the character string representing the data field, without any intervening spaces. Provided no additional clauses are attached to the elementary-item, the entry is terminated with a period.

Two additional comments should be made about PICTURE clauses. First, though A, X, and 9 are generally used exclusively of one another, combinations of these characters in one PICTURE clause are permitted. When this is done, however, the entire field is treated as being alphanumeric. Second, if several consecutive positions include the same PICTURE character, the character may be shown either by repeating it (for example, a five-character alphabetic field could be recorded as AAAAA), or a *replication factor* could be used. A replication factor is an integer number, placed in parentheses following the character to be repeated. Thus, to show a five-character alphabetic field, code A(5)—meaning five consecutive A characters. PICTURE clauses may also contain multiple replication factors if warranted, i.e., S9(4)P(5).

Examples of FILE SECTION Entries

The following examples will help you fully understand how the FILE SECTION entries are used in context. First, look at Figure 5.5. It shows the type of input data record one might expect to see in a banking application. The

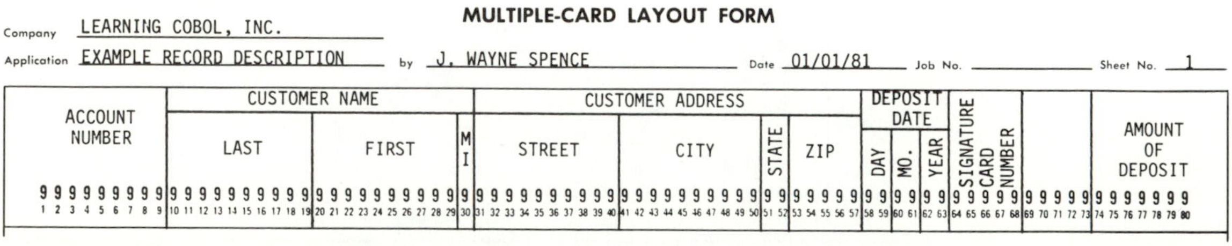
MULTIPLE-CARD LAYOUT FORM

Company LEARNING COBOL, INC.

Application EXAMPLE RECORD DESCRIPTION by J. WAYNE SPENCE Date 01/01/81 Job No. Sheet No. 1

ACCOUNT NUMBER	CUSTOMER NAME			CUSTOMER ADDRESS				DEPOSIT DATE			SIGNATURE CARD NUMBER		AMOUNT OF DEPOSIT
	LAST	FIRST	MI	STREET	CITY	STATE	ZIP	DAY	MO.	YEAR			
9 9 9 9 9 9 9 9 9	9 9 9 9 9 9 9 9 9 9	9 9 9 9 9 9 9 9 9 9	9	9 9 9 9 9 9 9 9 9 9	9 9 9 9 9 9 9 9 9 9	9 9	9 9 9 9 9	9 9	9 9	9 9	9 9 9 9 9	9 9 9 9 9	9 9 9 9 9 9 9
1 2 3 4 5 6 7 8 9	10 11 12 13 14 15 16 17 18 19	20 21 22 23 24 25 26 27 28 29	30	31 32 33 34 35 36 37 38 39 40	41 42 43 44 45 46 47 48 49 50	51 52	53 54 55 56 57	58 59	60 61	62 63	64 65 66 67 68	69 70 71 72 73	74 75 76 77 78 79 80

Figure 5.5 Graphic Sample of an Input (Punched Card) Record

Table 5.4 Illustrations of Nonedited (DISPLAY) PICTURE Clause Characters

Data Class	PICTURE String	Meaning	Number of Columns Represented on a Punched Card or a Line of Print
Alphabetic	A	a single alphabetic character of storage	1
	AAAA or A(4)	4 characters of alphabetic storage	4
	A(20)	20 characters of alphabetic storage	20
Alphanumeric	X	a single alphanumeric character of storage	1
	XXXX or X(4)	4 characters of alphanumeric storage	4
	X(20)	20 characters of alphanumeric storage	20
Numeric	9	an unsigned single digit of numeric storage	1
	9999 or 9(4)	a 4-digit integer of numeric storage	4
	9(18)	an 18-digit integer (the maximum) storage position	18
	99V99	a 4-digit numeric field with 2 digits preceding the implied decimal point and 2 digits after	4
	9(5)V99	an unsigned, 7-digit storage position with 5 digits preceding the implied decimal point and 2 digits after	7
	9(4)V9(5)	an unsigned, 9-digit storage position with 4 digits preceding the implied decimal point and 5 digits after	9
	V99	an unsigned, 2-digit numeric storage position with both digits following the implied decimal point	2
	999V	Illegal use of an implied decimal point (V should be omitted)	-
	S9(6)	a 6-digit integer storage position capable of recording a sign	6
	S9V9(8)	a 9-digit numeric storage position capable of storing 1 digit preceding the implied decimal point, 8 digits after, and a sign	9
	VPPP99	an unsigned 5-digit numeric storage position with all 5 digits following the implied decimal point. The 9s represent digit storage positions which in general come from an external medium (e.g., punched cards), with the Ps replaced by zeros. The internal data storage would appear as .000nn where n is replaced by a digit from an external source.	2
	S9(4)P(5)	a signed, 9-digit storage position where Ps are replaced by zeros. This yields an internally stored value of nnnn00000 where ns are replaced by digits.	4

punched card is a representation of an initial deposit slip for opening of a checking account. The relevant information from this card includes:

1. the account number—a nine-digit numeric field appearing in card columns 1 through 9;
2. customer's last name—a ten-character alphabetic field appearing in card columns 10 through 19;
3. customer's first name—a ten-character alphabetic field appearing in card columns 20 through 29;
4. customer's middle initial—a one-character alphabetic field appearing in card column 30;
5. customer's street address—a ten-character alphanumeric field appearing in card columns 31 through 40;
6. customer's city address—a ten-character alphabetic field appearing in card columns 41 through 50;
7. customer's state name abbreviation—a two-character alphabetic field appearing in card columns 51 and 52;
8. customer's zip code—a five-digit numeric field appearing in card columns 53 through 57;
9. the day of the date of deposit—a two-digit numeric field appearing in card columns 58 and 59;
10. the month of the date of deposit—a two-digit numeric field appearing in card columns 60 and 61;
11. the year of the date of deposit—a two-digit numeric field appearing in card columns 62 and 63;
12. customer's signature-card number—a five-digit numeric field appearing in card columns 64 through 68;
13. a blank field consisting of five card columns and appearing in card columns 69 through 73; and
14. the amount of deposit (in dollars and cents)—a seven-digit numeric field appearing in card columns 74 through 80.

Compare Figure 5.5 with Figure 5.6. The FILE SECTION begins with an FD entry; subsequent clauses describe the characteristics of the file. The file-name is DEPOSITS (and would also appear in a SELECT clause in the FILE-CONTROL paragraph of the ENVIRONMENT DIVISION). The one required clause after the file-name is the LABEL RECORDS clause (which could have been coded on the same line as the file-name). The RECORD CONTAINS clause and the DATA RECORDS clause are optional. The RECORD CONTAINS clause shows that the record description which follows is 80 characters long. (With standard cards, 80 characters would be assumed if the clause was omitted. However, for documentation purposes, it is a good habit to describe as much as possible, including standard (80-character) punched-card descriptions, even if the trailing part of the record is blank.) The DATA RECORDS clause is only for documentation; it shows the record-names which follow. Note that only one period appears in the entire file description entry—after the last clause.

The record description (which begins with Ø1) should match, column by column, the record description given in Figure 5.5. The results of this record description in Figure 5.6 are given in Table 5.5. Any data-name listed in this table references data and may be used in the PROCEDURE DIVISION.

COBOL Coding Form

SYSTEM FILE SECTION ENTRIES	PUNCHING INSTRUCTIONS	PAGE 1 OF 1
PROGRAM BANK DEPOSITS (INITIAL)	GRAPHIC	CARD FORM #FIG 5.6
PROGRAMMER J. WAYNE SPENCE DATE 01/01/81	PUNCH	

SEQUENCE		COBOL STATEMENT	IDENTIFICATION
01		FILE SECTION.	
02	FD	DEPOSITS	
03		LABEL RECORDS ARE OMITTED	
04		RECORD CONTAINS 80 CHARACTERS	
05		DATA RECORD IS DEPOSIT-CARDS.	
06	01	DEPOSIT CARDS.	
07		03 ACCOUNT-NUMBER PIC 9(9).	
08		03 CUSTOMER-NAME.	
09		05 LAST-NAME PIC X(10).	
10		05 FIRST-NAME PIC X(10).	
11		05 MIDDLE-INITIAL PIC X.	
12		03 CUSTOMER-ADDRESS.	
13		05 STREET PIC X(10).	
14		05 CITY PIC X(10).	
15		05 STATE-ABBR PIC XX.	
16		05 ZIP-CODE PIC 9(5).	
17		03 DATE-OF-DEPOSIT.	
18		05 DEP-DAY PIC 99.	
19		05 DEP-MONTH PIC 99.	
20		05 DEP-YEAR PIC 99.	
		03 SIGNATURE-CARD-NUMBER PIC 9(5).	
		03 FILLER PIC X(5).	
		03 AMOUNT-OF-DEPOSIT PIC 9(5)V99.	

Figure 5.6 A Sample of FILE SECTION Entries for a Punched Card File

Table 5.5 Data Description Results

Data Name	Type of Data-Name Record (R); Group (G); Elementary-Item (E)	Number of Characters Represented	Type of Data Represented
DEPOSIT-CARDS	R/G	80	Alphanumeric
ACCOUNT-NUMBER	E	9	Numeric
CUSTOMER-NAME	G	21	Alphanumeric
LAST-NAME	E	10	Alphanumeric
FIRST-NAME	E	10	Alphanumeric
MIDDLE-INITIAL	E	1	Alphanumeric
CUSTOMER-ADDRESS	G	27	Alphanumeric
STREET	E	10	Alphanumeric
CITY	E	10	Alphanumeric
STATE-ABBR	E	2	Alphanumeric
ZIP-CODE	E	5	Numeric
DATE-OF-DEPOSIT	G	6	Alphanumeric
DEP-DAY	E	2	Numeric
DEP-MONTH	E	2	Numeric
DEP-YEAR	E	2	Numeric
SIGNATURE-CARD-NUMBER	E	5	Numeric
(FILLER)	-	5	Alphanumeric
AMOUNT-OF-DEPOSIT	E	7	Numeric (with 2 decimal positions)

Suppose one wants to describe an output file that might be used to print some of the data from the input record of the previous example. Examine Figure 5.7 and Figure 5.8. In Figure 5.8 note the multiple uses of the reserved word FILLER which provides spaces between data fields. Obviously, FILLER is not limited to a single occurrence within a record description, and it is likely to appear in the DATA DIVISION several times.

The FD entry for this file is the minimum requirement. As Figure 5.8 indicates, only the file-name (NEW-CUSTOMER-LIST) and the LABEL RECORDS clause are used. In a program, the FD might immediately follow the last entry shown in Figure 5.5, i.e., the input-file description may precede the output-file description. However, this is not required, and FDs do not have to appear in the same order as the SELECT clauses in the ENVIRONMENT DIVISION—they are independent of each other.

As with the input-record description, the output-record descriptions in Figure 5.7 and Figure 5.8 should correspond, column by column. The major differences between the input-record description and the output-record description are that different data-names are used so that unique storage positions are addressed (this is not a requirement), the number of data-names is different and the output is longer (the output line shown is for 133 characters—a standard print-line length). Another difference not shown in the diagram is that output-record descriptions may contain edited data fields (see Chapter 9).

Other entries related to the FILE SECTION will be discussed in later chapters.

The WORKING-STORAGE SECTION

The WORKING-STORAGE SECTION is used to provide storage space for those data items not directly related to an input or an output file. There are two forms of storage in the WORKING-STORAGE SECTION—records and independent-elementary-items. As Figure 5.9 indicates, the WORKING-STORAGE SECTION is an optional section, but when used it must follow the FILE SECTION. The entries in the WORKING-STORAGE SECTION may either take the form of independent-elementary-items or record descriptions. Record descriptions in the WORKING-STORAGE SECTION are structurally no different than those in the FILE SECTION, except that they are not connected with a file.

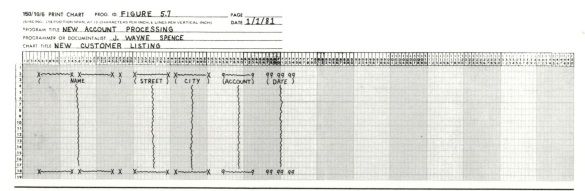

Figure 5.7 A Graphic Description of a Desired Report

COBOL Coding Form

SYSTEM FILE SECTION ENTRIES (OUTPUT)	PUNCHING INSTRUCTIONS	PAGE 1 OF 1
PROGRAM BANK DEPOSITS (INITIAL)	GRAPHIC	CARD FORM # FIG 5.8
PROGRAMMER J. Wayne Spence	DATE 01/01/81 PUNCH	

SEQUENCE	CONT	A	B	COBOL STATEMENT	IDENTIFICATION
01		FD	NEW-CUSTOMER-LIST LABEL RECORDS ARE OMITTED.		
02		01	REPORT-LINE.		
03			02 FILLER	PIC X(4).	
04			02 NAME.		
05			03 LAST-N	PIC X(10).	
06		/	03 FILLER	PIC X.	
07			03 FIRST-N	PIC X(10).	
08			03 FILLER	PIC X.	
09			03 MIDDLE-I	PIC X.	
10			02 FILLER	PIC XXX.	
11			02 ACCOUNT	PIC 9(9).	
12			02 FILLER	PIC XXX.	
13			02 DATE-OF-ENTRY.		
14			03 DA	PIC 99.	
15			03 FILLER	PIC X.	
16			03 MO	PIC 99.	
17			03 FILLER	PIC X.	
18			03 YR	PIC 99.	
19			02 FILLER	PIC X(59).	
20					

Figure 5.8 A Sample of FILE SECTION Entries for a Printed Output Line

```
 WORKING-STORAGE SECTION.*

 [77  independent-elementary-item  {PICTURE / PIC}  field-description-entry

           [VALUE IS {figurative-constant
                      numeric-literal
                      non-numeric-literal   }]]
                      ALL literal


 [01  record-description.

    [[02 - 48] group-name.]

      [02 - 49]{elementary-item-name / FILLER}  {PICTURE / PIC}  field-description-entry

           [VALUE IS {figurative-constant
                      numeric-literal
                      non-numeric-literal  }]]]
                      ALL literal
```

*Section, as shown, is incomplete. Only basic elements are included.

Figure 5.9 Format of the WORKING-STORAGE SECTION

Independent-elementary-items, on the other hand, have no equivalent in the FILE SECTION. They should be listed first in the WORKING-STORAGE SECTION (prior to record descriptions). They are always assigned level-number 77 and should appear in Area A. These items are referred to as independent-elementary-items since they are independent of any record description.

One other difference between data items described in the FILE SECTION and those described in the WORKING-STORAGE SECTION is that in the WORKING-STORAGE SECTION, each independent-elementary-item requires additional internal space. Each record also requires additional internal space, unless explicitly REDEFINED. This is covered in greater depth in Chapter 19.

Another major difference between data items in the FILE SECTION and those in the WORKING-STORAGE SECTION is that VALUE clauses are permitted in the latter. As indicated in Figure 5.9, a VALUE clause may be used in conjunction with independent-elementary-items or elementary-items of record descriptions in the WORKING-STORAGE SECTION. VALUE clauses are used for initial (or constant) values for elementary-items, i.e., level-77 items, elementary-items in records, and FILLERs. As indicated in Figure 5.9, the VALUE of an elementary-item could be a figurative constant (e.g., SPACE or ZERO), a numeric literal (a constant composed of digits and a possible decimal point and sign), a non-numeric literal (a character string), or the figurative constant ALL followed by a non-numeric literal.

Figure 5.10 includes some examples of how the VALUE clause might be used in the WORKING-STORAGE SECTION. Obviously, the examples do not list all of its uses. Also, the VALUEs created in this WORKING-STORAGE SEC-TION may be assigned in the PROCEDURE DIVISION. Finally, although every item shown in the example uses a VALUE clause, it is not required.

In Figure 5.10, the figurative constant ZERO used as a VALUE for COUNT-OF-CUSTOMERS (and ZEROS used with AVERAGE-DEPOSIT-PER-CUST) places the number Ø in each position of the field. The same result is achieved by using the numeric literal Ø with TOTAL-DEPOSITS. In the case of PAGE-COUNT, the VALUE 1 is a numeric constant, which is placed in the *last* digit position with the other digit position(s) filled with zero(s). TOTAL-SERVICE-CHARGE has a value of 4.5 which is aligned on the (implied) decimal point to result in Ø4∧5Ø. (The same alignment as with PAGE-COUNT since the decimal point is assumed to be located after the last digit.)

The record descriptions, which follow level-77 entries in the WORKING-STORAGE SECTION, are provided as headings to the output shown in Figure 5.7. The record YEAR-BEGINNING is used to illustrate one very important point: The type of VALUE used should be consistent with the field description, i.e., a numeric field should only be VALUEd with a numeric-oriented figurative constant or numeric literals; alphabetic fields, with alphabetic-oriented figurative constants and non-numeric literals; and alphanumeric fields, with figurative constants and non-numeric literals. The VALUE Ø1/Ø1/78 is a non-numeric literal because it is enclosed in the "quote" character (apostrophe). It would be a non-numeric literal even if the slash characters were eliminated.

The record descriptions YEAR-BEGINNING, PAGE-HEADING, COL-UMN-HEADING, and UNDER-LINE all have FILLER as the elementary-item

COBOL Coding Form

SYSTEM WORKING-STORAGE ENTRIES			PUNCHING INSTRUCTIONS						PAGE 1	OF 1
PROGRAM BANK-DEPOSITS (WORKING STORAGE)		GRAPHIC								
PROGRAMMER J. WAYNE SPENCE	DATE 01/01/81	PUNCH						CARD FORM # FIG 5.10		

SEQUENCE		A	B	COBOL STATEMENT	IDENTIFICATION
01	77		COUNT-OF-CUSTOMERS	PIC 999 VALUE ZERO.	
02	77		TOTAL-DEPOSITS	PIC 9(5)V99 VALUE IS 0.	
03	77		AVERAGE-DEPOSIT-PER-CUST	PIC 9(5)V999 VALUE ZEROES.	
04	77		PAGE-COUNT	PIC 99 VALUE 1.	
05	77		TOTAL-SERVICE-CHARGE	PIC 99V99 VALUE 4.5.	
06	01		YEAR-BEGINNING.		
07		02	FILLER	PIC X(8) VALUE '01/01/78'.	
08	01		PAGE-HEADING.		
09		02	FILLER	PIC X(27) VALUE SPACE.	
10		02	FILLER	PIC X(20) VALUE	
11			'NEW CUSTOMER LISTING'.		
12	01		COLUMN-HEADING.		
13		02	FILLER	PIC X(9) VALUE SPACES.	
14		02	FILLER	PIC X(13) VALUE	
15			'CUSTOMER NAME'.		
16		02	FILLER	PIC X(12) VALUE SPACES.	
17		02	FILLER	PIC X(13) VALUE	
18			'LOCAL ADDRESS'.		
19		02	FILLER	PIC X(8) VALUE SPACE.	
20		02	FILLER	PIC X(7) VALUE 'ACCOUNT'.	
		02	FILLER	PIC X(6) VALUE SPACES.	
		02	FILLER	PIC X(4) VALUE 'DATE'.	
	01		UNDER-LINE.		
		02	FILLER	PIC X((77) VALUE ALL '*'.	

Figure 5.10 An Illustration of the WORKING-STORAGE SECTION

description. The only data-name reference that may be used to access these descriptions are the record-names. Note that in the last three record descriptions FILLER may contain SPACE (or SPACES) and non-numeric literals. Those FILLER items that contain SPACES have a blank character in every position of the field and are used to provide horizontal spacing. The other FILLER items are used to provide "message-oriented" output.

Field descriptions may be either longer or shorter than the VALUE to be placed in the field. If the VALUE is shorter than the field length, the compiler will place the data in the leftmost positions of alphanumeric or alphabetic fields (left-justify). Enough blanks will be added in the trailing positions to fill the field with data. If the VALUE is too long for the field, it will be truncated (characters dropped off) from the right until it is exactly the same size as the field. (Most compilers will generate a WARNING message when truncation occurs.) SPACE or SPACES will always fill the field, as will the use of "ALL literal." A literal character(s) will be generated to fill the field exactly. In the example, the FILLER of UNDER-LINE contains exactly 77 asterisks (because the PICTURE size is 77 characters).

Summary

The DATA DIVISION, the third division of a COBOL program, provides for the descriptions of all data-names. Because each data-name is described, the DATA DIVISION is generally one of the more time-consuming to construct. The DATA DIVISION may be divided into several sections; the most common are the FILE SECTION and the WORKING-STORAGE SECTION.

In the FILE SECTION, each file-name defined in the ENVIRONMENT DIVISION with a SELECT clause is further described. The file description (FD) entries include record descriptions. Each record is defined with level number Ø1. Subparts of records (groups and elementary-items) may be described using a hierarchy of level numbers (Ø2 through 49). Only elementary-items describe fields. PICTURE clauses are used to describe the characteristics of fields and may be classified as alphabetic (A), alphanumeric (X), or numeric (9). Only numeric fields may be used for computation. Numeric fields may be further defined with the PICTURE characters S (operational sign) and V (implied decimal point).

The second section—the WORKING-STORAGE SECTION—provides for the description of those data-items *not* directly related to input-output activities, i.e., internal or working variables. In addition to record descriptions, the WORKING-STORAGE SECTION permits the use of independent-elementary-items (items not associated with any record) by the use of level-77 entries. Finally, the WORKING-STORAGE SECTION also permits the use of VALUE clauses at the elementary-item level to assign initial values to data-names.

Notes on Programming Style

Several programming conventions are commonly used to record DATA DIVISION entries. The most widely used convention is appropriate indention. For example, level numbers dictate the hierarchy of the record description. However, the grouping of data items may be easier to see if subordinate items are indented to the right of "superior" items. For example, the syntax of the two record descriptions below is equivalent, but the record description to the right is easier to understand at a glance because it is more visually appealing.

```
Ø1   INVOICE.                    Ø1   INVOICE.
     Ø2   INV-NUM . . .               Ø2   INV-NUM . . .
     Ø2   CUST-ID.                    Ø2   CUST-ID.
     Ø3   CUST-NO . . .                    Ø3   CUST-NO . . .
     Ø3   CUST-NAME . . .                  Ø3   CUST-NAME . . .
     Ø2   DATE-OF-SALE.               Ø2   DATE-OF-SALE.
     Ø3   SALE-MONTH . . .                 Ø3   SALE-MONTH . . .
     Ø3   SALE-DAY . . .                   Ø3   SALE-DAY . . .
     Ø3   SALE-YEAR . . .                  Ø3   SALE-YEAR . . .
```

PICTURE clauses of elementary-items also are indented, usually to column 40, to make it easy to locate the characteristic of each item.

The second most frequent convention used in the DATA DIVISION is the elimination of level-77 independent-elementary-items from the WORKING-STORAGE SECTION. To replace level-77 items, each item is recorded as an ordinary elementary-item within a record description. Thus, the description:

```
WORKING-STORAGE SECTION.
77 FIELD-1                   PIC 9(5).
77 FIELD-2                   PIC X(1Ø).
77 FIELD-3                   PIC 99V99 VALUE Ø.
```

could be recorded as

```
WORKING-STORAGE SECTION.
Ø1 WORKING-VARIABLES.
   Ø2 FIELD-1                PIC 9(5).
   Ø2 FIELD-2                PIC X(1Ø).
   Ø2 FIELD-3                PIC 99V99 VALUE Ø.
```

Consequently, adjusting level-77 items to the indicated structure removes these "special cases," thus permitting these data items to be used in much the same way as other data items (e.g., group operations, qualifications, redefinition, etc.).

The third convention is sometimes used in the FILE SECTION. Although the programmer is permitted to record extremely detailed record descriptions with each FD, only minimal definition of records is really necessary in the FILE SECTION. More detailed descriptions can be coded in the WORKING-STORAGE SECTION. Thus,

```
FD   INPUT-FILE LABEL RECORDS ARE OMITTED.
Ø1   INPUT-REC.
     Ø2 IN-FIELD-1              PIC 99.
     Ø2 IN-FIELD-2              PIC X(1Ø).
     Ø2 IN-FIELD-3              PIC 99V99.
     Ø2 FILLER                  PIC X(64).
```

would become

```
FD   INPUT-FILE LABEL RECORDS ARE OMITTED.
Ø1   INPUT-REC                 PIC X(8Ø).
     .
     .
     .
WORKING-STORAGE SECTION.
Ø1   WORKING-INPUT-REC.
     Ø2 WS-FIELD-1              PIC 99.
     Ø2 WS-FIELD-2              PIC X(1Ø).
     Ø2 WS-FIELD-3              PIC 99V99.
```

Again, the purpose of such a move is to remove "special cases" in favor of more uniform definitions (even though the latter requires additional internal memory). Thus, *all* useful definitions of data appear in the WORKING-STORAGE SECTION. Data placed in the input-record (FD) description would simply be copied INTO its WORKING-STORAGE definition and output-record (FD) descriptions would be filled by copying its contents FROM a WORKING-STORAGE record description.

In conjunction with more extensive uses of the WORKING-STORAGE SECTION (and more comprehensive applications) the creation of meaningful and unique data-names for two or more fields that represent the same data sometimes becomes a problem. The convention used to overcome this problem is to tag each data name with a prefix denoting the function it is to serve. For example, if we used the letter "I" to denote input and "O" to denote output we might develop the following data-names:

```
I-CUSTOMER-NUMBER
O-CUSTOMER-NUMBER
I-QUANTITY
O-QUANTITY
```

It is immediately obvious that data-names preceded by "I" are from the input record and those preceded by "O" are from the output record. Furthermore, if a third or fourth name is necessary, it may be developed without modifying the "root" data-names. For example, data-names that appear in the WORKING-STORAGE SECTION could begin with the prefix W or WS.

The most recently developed coding convention is to make PICTURE clauses as uniform as possible. This convention goes beyond the simple alignment previously mentioned. Consider for a moment the following PICTURE descriptions:

```
. . . PIC XXX.
. . . PIC X(3).
. . . PIC X(Ø3).
```

The data described in all three PICTURE descriptions is the same. Now consider the following sequence of PICTURE clauses taken from Figure 5.6:

```
Original            Modified
PIC 9(9).           PIC 9(Ø9).
PIC X(1Ø).          PIC X(1Ø).
PIC X(1Ø).          PIC X(1Ø).
PIC X.              PIC X(Ø1).
PIC X(1Ø).          PIC X(1Ø).
PIC X(1Ø).          PIC X(1Ø).
PIC XX.             PIC X(Ø2).
PIC 9(5).           PIC 9(Ø5).
PIC 99.             PIC 9(Ø2).
PIC 99.             PIC 9(Ø2).
PIC 99.             PIC 9(Ø2).
PIC 9(5).           PIC 9(Ø5).
PIC X(5).           PIC X(Ø5).
PIC 9(5)V99.        PIC 9(Ø5)V9(Ø2).
```

Again, the data described in both records is exactly the same; however, it is much easier to verify the record length (by summing the length specifications) since they are all in the same columns (except for implied decimal fields). In addition, this format is somewhat easier to use when it is necessary to identify the data types (X or 9) of each field.

Questions

Below, fill in the blank(s) with the appropriate word, words, or phrases.

1. The DATA DIVISION may contain both a(n) _____ SECTION and a(n) _____ SECTION.

2. All files defined in the INPUT-OUTPUT SECTION of the ENVIRONMENT DIVISION are described in detail in the _____ SECTION of the DATA DIVISION.

3. Data items not directly related to input-output operations are described in the _____ SECTION.

4. For each FD entry, the file-name and the _____ clause must be specified before the first level Ø1.

5. A punched-card record is assumed to be _____ (number) columns long.

6. The _____ clause serves only as documentation in the FD entry.

7. Records may contain _____ , which are always treated as alphanumeric fields, and _____ , which may be represented by PICTURE clauses.

8. _____ determines the inclusiveness of a data-name.

9. The level number _____ is always associated with a record-name.

10. The level number(s) _____ always appear in Area A, and the level number(s) _____ always appear in Area B.

11. All elementary-item-descriptions include a level number, a data-name, and a(n) _____ clause.

12. The three different types of data items that can be described with a PICTURE clause are _____ , _____ , and _____ .

13. _____ data may be described with the PICTURE character A, _____ , with the PICTURE character X, and _____ , with the PICTURE character 9.

14. When an area of an input record contains no data, that area may be referred to as the reserved word _____ in the record description.

15. When negative numeric data is required, the PICTURE should contain a(n) _____ character in the _____ position of the PICTURE string, and the data itself should contain a(n) _____ in the _____ position (column).

16. Anytime a decimal fraction is anticipated in a numeric field, the PICTURE string should contain the character _____ .

17. When a series of the same PICTURE character appear adjacent to each other, the character could be repeated in the PICTURE string, or a single PICTURE character could be written followed by a(n) _____ .

18. In the WORKING-STORAGE SECTION, data may be described within the context of a record or as a(n) _____ .

19. Two 80-byte record descriptions associated with a single file in the FILE SECTION require _____ (number) bytes of internal memory, while two 80-byte records in the WORKING-STORAGE SECTION require _____ (number) bytes of internal memory.

20. VALUE clauses are permitted only in the _____ SECTION and only at the _____ level.

Answer the following questions by circling either "T" for true or "F" for false.

T F 21. A description of all data items used in a program may be found in the DATA DIVISION.
T F 22. All COBOL programs require a WORKING-STORAGE SECTION.
T F 23. For every SELECT clause in the FILE-CONTROL paragraph, there should be an FD entry in the FILE SECTION.
T F 24. The FDs in the FILE SECTION must be in the same order as the SELECT clauses in the INPUT-OUTPUT SECTION.
T F 25. In a record description, one group may appear within another group.
T F 26. Elementary-items are composed of groups.
T F 27. Within a record description the level numbers Ø1 through 1ØØ may be used.
T F 28. The level number Ø2 is always used to indicate a group.
T F 29. The level number Ø2 may be used in the representation of an elementary-item.
T F 30. When used in a record description, level numbers must appear in a consecutive sequence (Ø1, Ø2, Ø3, etc.).
T F 31. Each item within a record (whether a record, a group, or an elementary-item) should appear on a line by itself and should be followed by a period.
T F 32. Both alphanumeric and numeric fields may be used for computation.

T	F	33.	All group items are treated as though they were defined as alphanumeric data items.
T	F	34.	The operational sign character (S) should be used in a PICTURE clause anytime negative numeric data is anticipated.
T	F	35.	The character V can appear anywhere in a numeric PICTURE string.
T	F	36.	Multiple replication factors could be used in one PICTURE string.
T	F	37.	The reserved word FILLER may appear in a record description more than once.
T	F	38.	A level-77 item is permitted in the FILE SECTION.
T	F	39.	The level numbers 01 through 49 may appear in the WORKING-STORAGE SECTION.
T	F	40.	The WORKING-STORAGE SECTION is required in every COBOL program.
T	F	41.	Independent elementary items may follow record descriptions in the WORKING-STORAGE SECTION.
T	F	42.	In the WORKING-STORAGE SECTION, a VALUE clause may be used in conjunction with a FILLER.
T	F	43.	A numeric elementary-item may have a value of SPACES assigned through a VALUE clause.
T	F	44.	The values assigned to an alphanumeric field may be shorter than the field length.
T	F	45.	An alphanumeric field of 20 characters with a VALUE ALL '-' will produce 20 hyphens (or dashes) in the field.

Exercises

1. Below is a record description associated with a file in the FILE SECTION. Complete a table with the indicated headings using the information presented within the record description.

```
Ø1 INVOICE=RECORD.
   Ø5 DESCRIPTIVE-INFORMATION.
      1Ø INVOICE-NUMBER                 PIC 9(Ø5).
      1Ø CUSTOMER-NUMBER.
         15 CUSTOMER-GROUP              PIC 9(Ø2).
         15 CUSTOMER-SUFFIX             PIC 9(Ø7).
      1Ø ITEM-INFORMATION.
         15 ITEM-NUMBER                 PIC 9(1Ø).
         15 ITEM-DESCRIPTION            PIC X(3Ø).
         15 QUANTITY-PURCHASED          PIC 9(Ø5).
         15 PRICE-PER-UNIT              PIC 9(Ø3)V9(Ø2).
         15 COST-PER-UNIT               PIC 9(Ø3)V9(Ø2).
         15 UNIT-MEASUREMENT            PIC X(Ø1).
   Ø5 FILLER                            PIC X(Ø5).
```

RECORD DESCRIPTION

DATA NAME	GROUP OR ELEMENTARY ITEM	LENGTH	COLUMNS OR POSITIONS

2. Below is a record that might be associated with a record description in the FILE SECTION. Complete a table with the indicated headings using the information presented within the record description.

```
Ø1 PAYROLL-SUMMARY-RECORD.
   Ø3 INDIVIDUAL-IDENTIFICATION.
      Ø5 EMPLOYEE-NUMBER              PIC X(Ø4).
      Ø5 DEPARTMENT                   PIC 9(Ø3).
      Ø5 EMPLOYEE-NAME.
         1Ø LAST-NAME                 PIC X(1Ø).
         1Ø FIRST-NAME                PIC X(1Ø).
         1Ø MIDDLE-NAME               PIC X(1Ø).
      Ø5 MONETARY-BASE-DATA.
         1Ø RATE-PER-HOUR             PIC 9(Ø4)V9(Ø2).
         1Ø SALARIED-HOURLY           PIC X(Ø1).
         1Ø FEDERAL-TAX-INFORMATION.
            15 MARRIED-SINGLE         PIC X(Ø1).
            15 NO-DEPENDENTS          PIC 9(Ø2).
            15 EXTRA-DEDUCTION        PIC 9(Ø3)V9(Ø2).
```

	RECORD DESCRIPTION		
DATA NAME	GROUP OR ELEMENTARY ITEM	LENGTH	COLUMNS OR POSITIONS

3. The graphic record layout shown in this exercise contains three records. Write the DATA DIVISION entries necessary to describe these records. (Assume each record is independent of the others.)

Company __LEARNING COBOL, INC.__

Application __DATA DIVISION EXAMPLES__ by __M. JANET SPENCE__ Date __06/01/81__ Job No. _____ Sheet No. __1__

MULTIPLE-CARD LAYOUT FORM

a) NAME/ADDRESS LABELS

CONTACT NAME	BUSINESS NAME	STREET ADDRESS/P.O. BOX	CITY	ST. (A/N)	ZIP CODE
(Alphanumeric--A/N)	(A/N)	(A/N)	(Alphabetic--A)		(A/N)

b) INVENTORY RECORD

IDENTIFICATION INFORMATION		CURRENT INFORMATION				STATISTICAL INFO.		
ITEM NUMBER (Numeric--N)	ITEM DESCRIPTION (A/N)	PRICE GROUP (N)	UNIT PRICE (N)	UNIT COST (N)	ON HAND (N)	MONTH TO DATE SALES (N)	YEAR TO DATE SALES (N)	

c) STUDENT GRADE RECORD

STUDENT NAME	STUDENT ID NUMBER	EXAM GRADES						COURSE DATA	
(A/N)	(N)	EXAM 1 (N)	EXAM 2 (N)	EXAM 3 (N)	EXAM 4 (N)	PRE-FIX (A/N)	NUM-BER (N)	COURSE TITLE (A/N)	

4. Given the following information about a record, write the record description. The record-name is to be PAYMENT-RECORD. Use your discretion in the coding of groups and subgroups.

Column	Description	Type*
1–8	Customer number	N
10–19	Amount of payment (dollars and cents)	N
20–21	Month of payment	N
22–23	Day of payment	N
24–25	Year of payment	N
30–31	Month of receipt	N
32–33	Day of receipt	N
34–35	Year of receipt	N
40–45	Check number	N
50–52	Receipt clerk	A/N
60–80	Special notes	A/N

*N—numeric field; A/N—alphanumeric field

5. The layout below represents a report and column headings for output to be created by a program. Write the record description(s) necessary to create this form. Assume the record description(s) appear in the WORKING-STORAGE SECTION, and use VALUE clauses (where appropriate) to load the text of the heading. The numbers that appear in the layout represent column numbers. The "99" designations indicate the location of data fields—use your own data names as appropriate.

6. Assume the report layout below represents the form of an output report. Write the record description(s) necessary to form both the column headings and data record(s). The numbers which appear on the layout represent column locations and the names in parentheses should be used to represent data names in the output record description.

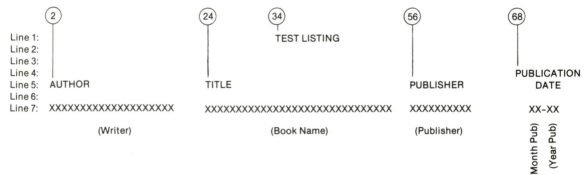

6 The PROCEDURE DIVISION

Purpose of the DIVISION

The PROCEDURE DIVISION is the portion of a COBOL program that provides the procedure, process, or algorithm to be executed. Thus, it is the "doing" part of the program. All input and output operations, data manipulation and movement, and decisions (testing of data values) occur during the execution of this division. The PROCEDURE DIVISION is logically the most complex portion of a COBOL program. Though the IDENTIFICATION, ENVIRONMENT, and DATA DIVISIONs may be very similar between programs, there may be little similarity between the PROCEDURE DIVISION of one program and another. Therefore, the PROCEDURE DIVISION, unlike the first three divisions, has no general format, i.e., required section and paragraph names, entries, and clauses. (This chapter is limited to those commands necessary to input and output records. Additional capabilities of the PROCEDURE DIVISION are discussed in Parts 2, 3, and 4.)

Overall Structure of the PROCEDURE DIVISION

The lack of a required structure in the PROCEDURE DIVISION may be a bit disconcerting at first; however, it gives the programmer the benefit of a rather wide latitude in structure choice. The programmer structures the PROCEDURE DIVISION with his selection, organization, and use of the section names, paragraph names, sentences, and statements that may be included in the division. To form a section or paragraph name, refer to the rules for the creation of data-names in Chapter 2. Recall that the principal difference between data-names and procedure-names is that section and paragraph names do not require an alphabetic character. There is little difference in the rules for creating these names, but there is a vast difference in how they are employed. Data-names, presented in both the DATA and PROCEDURE DIVISIONs, are used to refer internally to data-storage positions. Section and paragraph names in the PROCEDURE DIVISION are used to reference or mark the location of one or more statements. For instance, to perform a branching operation (go from one location in the PROCEDURE DIVISION to somewhere other than the next sequential statement), section or paragraph names may be used to indicate the destination of the branching instruction.

As data-names should indicate the type of data the name represents, so should section and paragraph names in the PROCEDURE DIVISION indicate their functions. If a part of the PROCEDURE DIVISION is responsible for accepting data from an external data source (e.g., reading data cards into the computer's memory), the paragraph name DATA-INPUT might be used. DATA-INPUT should include only those statements necessary for the acquisition of data. (This isolation of functions may require paragraph names which are seemingly useless; however, in Chapter 7 you will see that this approach makes a program easier to *debug* (to correct errors in logic) and adds to the "structure" of the program.)

So far, section names have not been discussed. In the PROCEDURE DIVISION, the programmer may have section names, paragraph names, or both; sections are not required if paragraphs are used and vice versa. The differences between section names and paragraph names are: (1) a section name must be followed by the word SECTION; and (2) sections, as in the other divisions, may include one or more paragraphs.

One final note about the structure of the PROCEDURE DIVISION. Some COBOL compilers require a procedure name immediately following the division heading (on another line). Other compilers do not. All compilers, however, *permit* a procedure name to follow the division heading. Because the additional name also improves program clarity, a procedure name should follow the PROCEDURE DIVISION heading.

OPEN and CLOSE Statements

In COBOL, a program's access to a file may be localized. If a file is not needed from the beginning of the procedure to the end, the programmer, by using OPEN and CLOSE statements, may make a file available only during certain segments of the procedure (e.g., when reading data or producing printed output). This has the effect of releasing resources (e.g., card readers, line printers, etc.) to other programs that might also be requesting their use.

The OPEN statement (see Figure 6.1) is responsible for "preparing" a file for use by a program. Following the required reserved word OPEN, either INPUT (reading operations) or OUTPUT (writing operations) must be declared. The word INPUT or OUTPUT can appear only once in an OPEN STATEMENT; however, a program could have many OPEN statements. After the reserved word INPUT (or OUPUT) one or more file-names are listed—the same file-names used in SELECT clauses in the ENVIRONMENT DIVISION and in FD entries in the DATA DIVISION. Once a file has been opened it cannot be reopened, unless it has previously been closed.

```
OPEN   INPUT    file-name-1 [file-name-2]...
       OUTPUT

       ⎰OUTPUT⎱  *  file-name-m  [file-name-n]...⎤
       ⎱INPUT ⎰                                  ⎦

*The reserved word used in the first set of braces cannot be repeated in the second set of
braces.
```

Figure 6.1 Format of the OPEN Statement. (Only clauses used in conjunction with a card reader or a line printer are shown.)

The CLOSE statement, shown in Figure 6.2, is the natural complement of the OPEN statement. The CLOSE statement "disconnects" the file-names listed in the statement from the program. It is not necessary to indicate whether the file was being used for input or output operations, only that the files are no longer needed. A CLOSE statement should not be executed for a file until it has been opened, and it should not be closed again until it has been reopened.

```
CLOSE file-name-1 [file-name-2] ...
```

Figure 6.2 Format of the CLOSE Statement. (Only clauses used in conjunction with a card reader or a line printer are shown.)

Figure 6.3 illustrates the use of OPEN and CLOSE statements to "localize" input or output resources. Notice that the file-names are "tied together" through the ENVIRONMENT, DATA, and PROCEDURE DIVISIONs. FILE-1 appears in the first SELECT clause and is ASSIGNed to a card reader (in the ENVIRONMENT DIVISION). For the remainder of the program, the description of FILE-1 should be consistent with the device being employed. For example, the file description (FD in the DATA DIVISION) should not exceed 80 characters and should not reflect edited data. Also, the data should be described in "character" form as demonstrated in Chapter 5. In the PRO-

Figure 6.3 Nonoverlapping INPUT and OUTPUT Operations

CEDURE DIVISION, FILE-1 should be opened as an input file—CARD-READER signifies an input device. In the PROCEDURE DIVISION, FILE-1 is opened, all input is presumed to occur, and the file is closed before FILE-2 is referenced. Presumably the requirements for this program never call for the card reader to be available at the same time as the line printer. (Your initial programs will generally require some overlap of input and output operations.) The characteristics of FILE-2 must be consistent with a "hard-copy" printing device. The data should be described in "character" form, could be edited (as explained in Chapter 9), and should generally not be over 133 characters in length. In addition, a line printer is always used for OUTPUT.

Figure 6.4 illustrates how the OPEN and CLOSE operations may be performed when input and output operations are needed in the same segment of a program. Using the same SELECT clauses and FD entries as presented in Figure 6.3, FILE-1 and FILE-2 are both available during the same phase of the program. Since FILE-1 and FILE-2 are opened and closed together, at any point between the OPEN and CLOSE statements data could be input from the card reader, or output could be created on the line printer. In both examples, files were opened and closed in the same manner. This does not mean that you are forced to OPEN and CLOSE files using a consistent form of OPEN and CLOSE statements. For example, several files could be opened in the same statement and each closed separately, or *vice versa*. Also, the order of the SELECT clauses in the ENVIRONMENT DIVISION is not necessarily related to the order in which files are opened or closed in the PROCEDURE DIVISION. However, for purposes of clarity, ordering of SELECTs often establishes the logical order for file use in the PROCEDURE DIVISION.

READ Statement

Once a file has been OPENed as an INPUT file, the file is available for the input of records via the READ statement. When a READ statement is executed, data in one record (punched-card) will be transferred into the computer's memory. The data in the punched-card record will then be available for use by the program by referencing the data-names of the FD record.

COBOL Coding Form

SYSTEM	LEARNING COBOL, INC.			PUNCHING INSTRUCTIONS		PAGE 1	OF 1
PROGRAM	OVERLAPPED INPUT/OUTPUT OPERATIONS		GRAPHIC			CARD FORM # FIG 6.4	
PROGRAMMER	J. Wayne Spence	DATE 01/01/81	PUNCH				

```
PROCEDURE DIVISION.
1ST-PARAGRAPH.
    OPEN INPUT FILE-1, OUTPUT FILE-2.
* INPUT AND OUTPUT OPERATIONS PERFORMED.

* INPUT AND OUTPUT COMPLETED.
    CLOSE FILE-1, FILE-2.
```

Figure 6.4 Overlapped INPUT and OUTPUT Operations

```
READ file-name RECORD [INTO identifier] AT END* imperative-statement
```
*One other clause is generally available at this position, which makes the AT END clause an optional clause.

Figure 6.5 Format of the READ Statement

The format of the READ statement is presented in Figure 6.5. The key-word READ is required, followed by the *file-name* from which a record is to be read. The file-name must appear in an OPEN statement prior to the execution of the first READ statement for that file. The keyword RECORD is not required. The INTO identifier phase is also optional. INTO makes it possible to read a record into an "alternate" record description. During the execution of the READ statement, data are automatically placed in the record descriptions that appear in the FD for that file. However, if INTO is specified, data from the input record will also be placed in a second description provided by the programmer. The "alternate" description is generally in the WORKING-STORAGE SECTION. The READ statement with an INTO option is therefore equivalent to a READ statement followed by a "MOVE" statement (discussed shortly).

The AT END phrase is required when reading from a card reader. The phrase indicates (in the imperative statement) the procedure to be followed when an end-of-file (EOF) condition is found. When repetitive READ operations are executed, eventually the list of records or deck of data cards will be exhausted. At that time the imperative statement is executed.

Remember that, in COBOL, a statement is one executable instruction. However, the imperative *statement* shown with the AT END phrase is really an imperative *sentence*. That is, one or more statements could be used. The imperative statement directs what happens when the end-of-file is reached. If the imperative statement includes a GO TO statement (discussed shortly), the GO TO should be the *last* statement in the imperative statement. Any statement following an unconditional branch in a sentence will not be executed.

Figure 6.6 illustrates the use of a READ statement in a program. In this example, when the first READ statement is executed, data from the first record of CARD-FILE is placed in the IN-REC record description. From that point, the data in columns 1 through 5 of the input record would be placed in ITEM-1; columns 16 through 21, in ITEM-2; columns 22 through 41, in ITEM-3; and columns 45 through 48 in ITEM-4. If no data were available when an attempt was made to read from card file, an unconditional branch to the FINISH-UP paragraph would be executed.

When the second READ statement is executed, the same data alignment would be made for ITEM-1 through ITEM-4 as described above. In addition the contents of ITEM-1 would also be placed in EMPLOYEE-NUMBER; RATE-PER-HOUR would be the same as ITEM-2; EMPLOYEE-NAME (which is made up of LAST-NAME and FIRST-NAME) would be the same as ITEM-3; and ITEM-4 and HOURS-WORKED would share the same digits. Note the minor differences in the PICTURE clauses on IN-REC and IN-REC-ALT. It is not necessary that the PICTURE clauses be the same, or even that the fields align on the same columns of the input records.

COBOL Coding Form

SYSTEM LEARNING COBOL, Inc.	PUNCHING INSTRUCTIONS / PAGE 1 OF 2
PROGRAM Sample Input Operations	GRAPHIC
PROGRAMMER J. Wayne Spence DATE 01/01/81	PUNCH CARD FORM # FIG 6.6

```
01      SELECT CARD-FILE ASSIGN TO SYS007-UR-2501-S.
02
03    DATA DIVISION.
04    FILE SECTION.
05    FD  CARD FILE LABEL RECORDS ARE OMITTED.
06    01  IN REC.
07        03  ITEM-1              PIC  9(05).
08        03  FILLER              PIC  X(10).
09        03  ITEM-2              PIC  S9(04)V9(02).
10        03  ITEM-3              PIC  X(20).
11        03  FILLER              PIC  X(03).
12        03  ITEM-4              PIC  9(03).
13        03  FILLER              PIC  X(33).
14    WORKING-STORAGE SECTION.
15
16    01  IN-REC-ALT.
17        03  EMPLOYEE-NUMBER     PIC  9(05).
18        03  FILLER              PIC  X(10).
19        03  RATE-PER-HOUR       PIC  9(04)V9(02).
20        03  EMPLOYEE-NAME.
              05  LAST-NAME        PIC  X(10).
              05  FIRST-NAME       PIC  X(10).
          03  FILLER              PIC  X(03).
          03  HOURS-WORKED        PIC  9(02)V9(01).
```

Figure 6.6 Illustration of the READ Statement

The presence of an alternate description has three important advantages. First, the alternate may be used to describe the data fields differently. Second, any change made to the data fields in IN-REC, which is independent of IN-REC-ALT, will not affect the contents of the data in IN-REC-ALT; the reverse of this is also true. Third, the FD description is a "buffer" description which should not be changed other than by reading data from an external source. The IN-REC-ALT description is a WORKING-STORAGE record and is not directly associated with any file (although in the example the INTO option is an indirect reference). Thus, the WORKING-STORAGE record description may be used for purposes other than holding input data. The contents of the elementary-items could be manipulated and changed without causing processing problems.

In the example (Figure 6.6), the AT END phrase includes a sentence, not a simple statement. The execution of the imperative statement will cause the non-numeric literal INPUT PHASE COMPLETE to be moved to an output line, the output line to be written, and an unconditional branch to the FINISH-UP paragraph. The full significance of this should become clear while reading the rest of this chapter.

WRITE Statement

A WRITE statement takes data which have been stored internally and causes it to be placed on an external medium. Within the scope of this part of the text, the WRITE statement causes lines of printed output to be created. Each time a WRITE statement is executed, one record (line of output) is printed. Prior to

COBOL Coding Form

SYSTEM	LEARNING COBOL, INC.			PUNCHING INSTRUCTIONS					PAGE 2	OF 2

PROGRAM Sample Input Operations — GRAPHIC

PROGRAMMER J. Wayne Spence DATE 1/1/81 PUNCH — CARD FORM # FIG 6.6

```
01   PROCEDURE DIVISION.
02   START-UP.
03       OPEN INPUT CARD-FILE.
04
05
06   READ CARD-FILE AT END GO TO FINISH-UP.
07
08
09   READ CARD-FILE INTO IN-REC-ALT AT END
10       MOVE ' INPUT PHASE COMPLETE ' TO PRINT-LINE;
11       WRITE PRINT-LINE AFTER ADVANCING 1 LINES;
12       GO TO FINISH-UP.
13
14
15   FINISH-UP.
```

Figure 6.6 Illustration of the READ Statement *Continued*

the first execution of a WRITE, the file used in conjunction with the WRITE statement must be OPENed in an OUTPUT mode.

The format of the WRITE statement appears in Figure 6.7. Within this statement the reserved word WRITE is followed by the name of the *record* to be written. *A record-name, not the file-name, is used in WRITE statements.* The record-name to be written must appear in the FD for the output file. There may be one or more record descriptions (depending upon the requirements of the output) within a single FD.

The FROM option of the WRITE statement can be used to move an alternate record description—referenced by identifier-1—to the output record before the WRITE statement takes place. The record description, referenced by identifier-1, is generally located in the WORKING-STORAGE SECTION.

The next optional clause (BEFORE/AFTER ADVANCING) specifies the carriage control or vertical spacing for printed output. The programmer chooses whether the vertical positioning should take place BEFORE or AFTER the line is printed. If BEFORE is specified, the line is written before any vertical movement takes place. With AFTER, the carriage control is invoked, and then the line of output is produced. Once BEFORE or AFTER has been specified, all other WRITE statements to the same file must contain the same reserved word. The word ADVANCING is not required but is provided for clarity. The programmer then has a choice of entries for specifying the line to which the printer is to be positioned. If identifier-2 is specified, identifier-2 must be described as a nonedited-numeric field. The field should not contain an integer value less than zero or greater than 100. The value associated with identifier-2 will cause that number of lines to be advanced on the line printer. If the value is zero, there will be no advance. When either identifier-2 or integer is specified, the optional word LINES may follow.

Most compilers support the use of a mnemonic-name as one of the options indicating the number of lines to be advanced. Remember the SPECIAL-NAMES paragraph in the ENVIRONMENT DIVISION. One of the entries in the SPECIAL-NAMES paragraph is "system-name IS mnemonic-name." Most

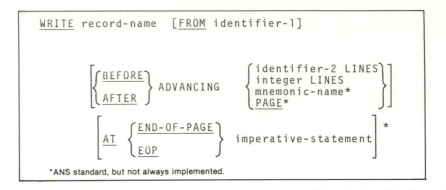

Figure 6.7 Format of the WRITE Statement. (Statement, as shown, is designed for printed output only.)

compilers provide a series of system-names which indicate a particular location or channel on a printer carriage-control tape. If it is desirable to use system-names to indicate paper advancement, SPECIAL-NAMES is used with the WRITE statement. The most used system-names for indicating top-of-the page are CØ1 (IBM) and '1' (e.g., CDC). Of course, other system-names could be used for other methods of line advancement, but this is the only practical means for advancing to the top of a new page without regard to the present location on the previous page.

The final option that indicates paper advancement on a line printer is PAGE. In Figure 6.7 note that PAGE is an American National Standard (ANS) option but is not always implemented. Furthermore, not all implementations are uniform. In some cases PAGE is used to indicate a top-of-page advancement (e.g., UNIVAC), and in other cases it is replaced with TO *TOP* OF PAGE (e.g., Honeywell).

The last clause associated with the WRITE statement is the END-OF-PAGE clause. As noted in Figure 6.7, it is among the ANS options but is not always implemented. It is implemented in a large number of COBOL compilers; however, they diverge widely in how the END-OF-PAGE condition is detected. For further information on how the END-OF-PAGE imperative-statement is invoked, consult with your installation.

Figure 6.8 illustrates the use of WRITE statements in a COBOL program. The first WRITE statement of the illustration produces a "page heading." In this statement, the record-name to be printed is PRINT-LINE. PRINT-LINE has already been described in general terms in the FILE SECTION. The FROM option is used to provide more detailed information from a record (identifier-1) labeled HEADING-LINE. The description of HEADING-LINE in the WORKING-STORAGE SECTION indicates that a series of non-numeric literals are to be written with interspersed blank columns (indicated by FILLER). This output record is to be placed at the top of the next page of print. NEXT-PAGE is the mnemonic-name identified in the SPECIAL-NAMES paragraph.

The next line of output created by the program would be located four lines below the top of the page. This WRITE statement is designed to produce

```
ENVIRONMENT DIVISION.
CONFIGURATION SECTION.
SOURCE-COMPUTER.  IBM-37Ø-145.
OBJECT-COMPUTER.  IBM-37Ø-145.
SPECIAL-NAMES.    CØ1 IS NEXT-PAGE.
INPUT-OUTPUT SECTION.
FILE-CONTROL.
     SELECT PRINT-FILE ASSIGN TO UR-S-PROUT.
      .
      .
      .

DATA DIVISION.
FILE SECTION.
FD   PRINT-FILE LABEL RECORDS ARE OMITTED.
Ø1   PRINT-LINE                    PIC X(133).
      .
      .
      .

WORKING-STORAGE SECTION.
Ø1   WORKING-VARIABLES.
     Ø2 NUMBER-OF                  PIC 9(Ø2) VALUE 4.
Ø1   HEADING-LINE.
     Ø2 FILLER                     PIC X(57) VALUE SPACES.
     Ø2 FILLER                     PIC X(18) VALUE 'STUDENT GRADE ROLL'.
Ø1   COLUMN-HEADINGS.
     Ø2 FILLER                     PIC X(2Ø) VALUE SPACES.
     Ø2 FILLER                     PIC X(4Ø) VALUE 'STUDENT NAME'.
     Ø2 FILLER                     PIC X(23) VALUE 'STUDENT ID. NUMBER'.
     Ø2 FILLER                     PIC X(11) VALUE 'CLASS'.
     Ø2 FILLER                     PIC X(1Ø) VALUE 'MAJOR'.
     Ø2 FILLER                     PIC X(1Ø) VALUE 'MINOR'.
Ø1   DETAIL-LINE.
     Ø2 FILLER                     PIC X(15) VALUE SPACES.
     Ø2 STUDENT-NAME               PIC X(3Ø).
     Ø2 FILLER                     PIC X(19) VALUE SPACES.
     Ø2 ID-NUMBER                  PIC 9(Ø9).
     Ø2 FILLER                     PIC X(11) VALUE SPACES.
     Ø2 CLASS                      PIC X(Ø3).
     Ø2 FILLER                     PIC X(Ø8) VALUE SPACES.
     Ø2 MAJOR                      PIC X(Ø2).
     Ø2 FILLER                     PIC X(Ø7) VALUE SPACES.
     Ø2 MINOR                      PIC X(Ø2).
      .
      .
      .

PROCEDURE DIVISION.
OPENING-PARA.
     OPEN OUTPUT PRINT-FILE,
     WRITE PRINT-LINE FROM HEADING-LINE
          AFTER ADVANCING NEXT-PAGE.
     WRITE PRINT-LINE FROM COLUMN-HEADINGS
          AFTER ADVANCING NUMBER-OF LINES.
       .
       .
       .

     MOVE DETAIL-LINE TO PRINT-LINE,
     WRITE PRINT-LINE AFTER ADVANCING 2 LINES.
       .
       .
       .
```

Figure 6.8 An Illustration of the WRITE Statement

"column headings." Again the record-name PRINT-LINE signifies the output line, and again, the FROM option is used to provide the text for the output line. In this instance, however, a data-name (identifier-2) is used to indicate the number of lines to be advanced. In the WORKING-STORAGE SECTION, the data item NUMBER-OF contains a value of 4, signifying that four lines are to be advanced. Since a data item is used, the value of the variable could be changed later to provide variably spaced output.

The last line of output is produced from DETAIL-LINE. DETAIL-LINE is moved to PRINT-LINE prior to the execution of the WRITE statement so that individual data items will be printed. A procedure for placing data into each of the elementary-items of DETAIL-LINE prior to the execution of this WRITE statement is assumed. In this final example the integer 2 is specified, indicating that two lines are to be advanced. Thus, if the third WRITE statement were executed repeatedly the output would be double-spaced.

In the example the AFTER ADVANCING option is also employed. Thus, all of the WRITE statements in the program using PRINT-LINE must use the AFTER keyword to indicate when vertical position is to take place.

The MOVE Statement

The MOVE statement provides the means for moving data from one location to another within internal memory. Though the MOVE statement appears to be "simple," it is one of the most powerful commands in COBOL. The format of the MOVE statement is provided in Figure 6.9. It is composed of two parts, the sending field and the receiving field(s). The "sending" field in the statement is either identifier-1, a literal, or a figurative constant. The sending field acts as the source of the data to be transmitted to the receiving field(s), which are those identifiers listed after the reserved word TO.

```
MOVE  {identifier-1    }  TO  identifier-2 [identifier-3]...
      {literal         }
      {figurative constant}
```

Figure 6.9 Format of the MOVE Statement

Valid movements of data from a sending field to a receiving field are listed in Table 6.1. In the table, sending fields are classified by the types of data represented. The same approach is used for the receiving fields. The contents of the sending field are not affected by this movement. The (new) contents of the receiving field are determined by the sending field.

There is a fundamental difference between alphanumeric data (including record- and group-names), alphabetic data, and numeric data. Alphanumeric and alphabetic data either in a sending or a receiving field are generally *left-justified* (occupy the leftmost positions of the field); unused positions (to the right) are filled with spaces. If the sending field is longer than the receiving field, data are truncated from right to left as much as necessary.

For numeric data, the rules are different. Normally, data from the sending field are aligned on the (implied) decimal point of the receiving field. In the absence of a decimal point, it is presumed to follow the rightmost digit. If the

Table 6.1 Permissible Moves of Nonedited Data

Sending Fields	Receiving Fields			
	Records or Groups	Elementary Items		
		Alphanumeric (X)	Alphabetic (A)	Numeric (9)
Record or Group	YES	YES	YES[1]	YES[3]
Alphanumeric (X)	YES	YES	YES[1]	YES[3]
Alphabetic (A)	YES	YES	YES	NO
Numeric (9)	YES[3]	YES[4]	NO	YES
Figurative Constants				
ZEROS	YES	YES	NO	YES
SPACES	YES	YES	YES	NO
HIGH-VALUE, LOW-VALUE, and QUOTES	YES	YES	NO	NO
ALL Literal	YES	YES	YES[1]	YES[2]
Numeric Literal	YES[3]	YES[4]	NO	YES
Non-numeric Literal	YES	YES	YES[1]	YES[2]

1. When the field contains only alphabetic characters and spaces.
2. When the field contains only numeric characters. The field is treated as a numeric integer.
3. The movement of data is treated the same as an alphanumeric to alphanumeric move.
4. When the numeric data item represents an integer number.

sending field is too long, the data may be truncated to the size of the receiving field from either the right or the left. If there are not enough digit positions to the left of the decimal point in the receiving field to accommodate the data from the sending field, high-order (leading) digits will be truncated. If there are not sufficient positions following the decimal location in the receiving field, data will be truncated from the low-order (trailing) digit positions. If the sending field is larger than the receiving field (either to the left or right or both), zeros will replace unused digit positions.

The examples in Figure 6.10 show some results of the MOVE statement.

The Simple GO TO Statement

The simple GO TO statement is often referred to as an *unconditional branch* instruction. The execution of a GO TO causes the execution sequence to begin again with the statement immediately below or adjacent to the paragraph- or SECTION-name provided in the GO TO statement. The instruction to be executed may be either above or below the GO TO statement itself. Be careful not to go immediately to the GO TO statement being executed or to another series of statements that would cause a *closed* or *continuous loop* (a series of statements with no mechanism for terminating itself, so the program "spins its wheels"). In many installations, a closed loop will cause an execution time limit error.

As noted in Figure 6.11, the GO TO statement provides a branch to either a paragraph- or SECTION-name. For this reason, paragraph-names must be unique within the PROCEDURE DIVISION—at least within SECTIONs of the PROCEDURE DIVISION. The differences between paragraph-and SECTION-names are that (1) paragraphs are less inclusive than SECTIONs, (2) a SECTION-name is always followed with the reserved word SECTION, and (3) paragraph-names can be qualified by SECTION names.

The results of "MOVE ITEM-1 TO ITEM-2," when ITEM-1 and ITEM-2 are described as follows (each example should be considered separately):

ITEM-1 Picture Clause	ITEM-1 Contains*	ITEM-2 PICTURE Clause	ITEM-2 After MOVE* Contains
X(5)	ABCDE	X(5)	ABCDE
X(5)	ABCDE	X(3)	ABC
X(5)	ABCDE	X(7)	ABCDEƀƀ
X(5)	ABCDE	A(4)	ABCD
X(5)	ƀ1234	9(5)	ƀ1234
A(4)	ABƀƀ	A(3)	ABƀ
A(4)	ABCD	A(6)	ABCDƀƀ
A(4)	ABCD	X(5)	ABCDƀ
9(5)	12345	9(5)	12345
9(5)	12345	9(4)	2345
9(5)	12345	9(6)	Ø12345
999V99	123∧45	99	23
999V99	123∧45	9(4)	Ø123
999V99	123∧45	V99	∧45
999V99	123∧45	9V9	3∧4
9(4)	1234	X(4)	1234
9(4)	1234	X(5)	ƀ1234

The results of "MOVE ---- TO ITEM-2." when the sending field is described as follows:

Sending Field Type	Sending Field Form	ITEM-2* PICTURE Clause	ITEM-2* After MOVE Contains
Figurative constant	ZERO	9(4)	ØØØØ
Figurative constant	SPACES	X(5)	ƀƀƀƀƀ
Figurative constant	ALL '*'	X(7)	*******
Numeric literal	1234	9(4)	1234
Numeric literal	1234	999V99	234∧ØØ
Numeric literal	123.4	999V99	123∧4Ø
Non-numeric literal	'ENDƀOFƀJOB'	X(10)	ENDƀOFƀJOB
Non-numeric literal	'1234'	9(4)	1234
Non-numeric literal	'A'	A(3)	Aƀƀ

* The symbol ƀ represents a blank; the symbol Ø represents a zero.

Figure 6.10 Illustrations of the MOVE Statement

```
GO TO procedure-name.
```

Figure 6.11 Format of the GO TO Statement

```
STOP  {RUN
       literal}
```

Figure 6.12 Format of the STOP Statement

The STOP Statement

The STOP statement is used to terminate the execution of a program. The format of the statement is shown in Figure 6.12. The STOP statement is placed at the *logical* termination point of a program, not necessarily the last statement in a program. If a program has several logical termination points, several STOP statements could be used.

When the statement is coded as STOP RUN, the program is permanently terminated. If STOP RUN appears in a sentence (such as the imperative statement in the READ command), it should be the last statement. The programmer is responsible for closing all active files prior to the execution of the STOP RUN statement. All programs in this text assume a permanent termination of program execution, so only the STOP RUN form of the statement is used.

The second form of the STOP statement temporarily halts a program; direct intervention by the computer operator is required before the program will continue. Then, execution continues with the statement immediately following the STOP. The literal used in this form of the STOP may be numeric or non-numeric or any figurative constant except ALL. During the learning/experimenting process, this form of the STOP statement should be avoided.

A Comprehensive Example

The program presented in Figure 6.13 (same program as Figure 2.1 with a few embellishments) incorporates many of the features of COBOL presented in Part 1. The function of the program is to accept data records (punched cards) and produce a listing of the records on a printed output form. The design of the input records is shown in Figure 6.13 (Record Layout). The desired output from the program is shown in Figure 6.13 (Report Layout). Note that the output data items are determined by the input data items. The difference between the input-record description and the output record is that the order of the STUDENT-IDENTIFICATION data items and of the ENROLLMENT-INFO are slightly different. The only added information on the output is the report and column headings.

The Record Layout of Figure 6.13 is described in lines 290 through 410 of the COBOL program. Each field is described in the input-record description of STUDENT-REC. In addition, group data items (STUDENT-IDENTIFICA-TION and ENROLLMENT-INFO) have been added. Finally, the blank fields on the input record are described by FILLER entries. The STUDENT-REC description is associated with STUDENT-FILE (line 240), which has been assigned to a card reader in line 200. The second file described in the program is PRINTOUT. This file will be used to produce the printed output. PRINT-OUT is assigned to a line printer (line 210) and the output PRINT-LINE is provided with a utility (general) description (lines 260 and 270).

The WORKING-STORAGE SECTION provides additional details of the description of the printed output. REPORT-HEADING (lines 420 through 450) provides the record description necessary to produce SEMESTER STUDENT LIST. SEPARATOR-LINE (lines 460 through 480) is used to produce rows of asterisks above and below the column headings. COLUMN-HEADING-1 (lines 490 through 530) provides the first line of the column headings. Note the use of continuation of the non-numeric literal message producing this part of the column headings. It was necessary to use three cards (lines) to produce a "message" 79 characters in length. Thus, lines 520 and 530 have a hyphen in column 7 (the continuation column and character), and the non-numeric literal is restarted with each new line. (The apostrophe in column 12 of lines 520 and 530 is necessary to continue non-numeric literals.) The second line of the column headings is presented in COLUMN-HEADING-2 (lines 540 through 600). A continuation was also needed on line 600. The final record description in the WORKING-STORAGE SECTION is OUTPUT-REC. This record description provides data-names that closely resemble those in the input-record description (with asterisks inserted at the proper points to provide the illusion of column boundaries on the output).

The PROCEDURE DIVISION begins at line 780. The START-UP paragraph is responsible for opening the files needed by the program (the OPEN statement in line 800) and producing the report and column headings indicated on the Report Layout. The WRITE statement appearing in lines 810 and 820 pro-

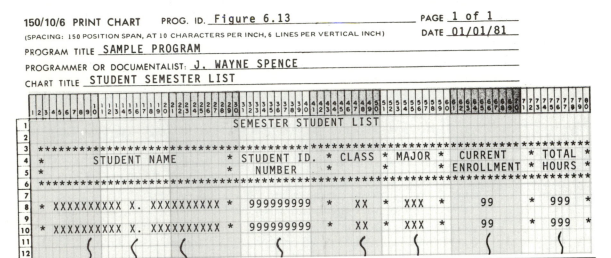

MULTIPLE-CARD LAYOUT FORM

Company ABC MANUFACTURING COMPANY

Application SAMPLE PROGRAM   by J. WAYNE SPENCE   Date 01/01/81   Job No. _____   Sheet No. ___1

Figure 6.13 A Sample Program (Card Layout)

150/10/6 PRINT CHART   PROG. ID. **Figure 6.13**   PAGE **1 of 1**

(SPACING: 150 POSITION SPAN, AT 10 CHARACTERS PER INCH, 6 LINES PER VERTICAL INCH)   DATE **01/01/81**

PROGRAM TITLE **SAMPLE PROGRAM**

PROGRAMMER OR DOCUMENTALIST: **J. WAYNE SPENCE**

CHART TITLE **STUDENT SEMESTER LIST**

Figure 6.13 A Sample Program (Report Layout) *Continued*

```
|000010 IDENTIFICATION DIVISION.                                     FIG 6.13|
|000020 PROGRAM-ID.  SAMPLE-PROGRAM.                                 FIG 6.13|
|000030 AUTHOR. J. WAYNE SPENCE.                                     FIG 6.13|
|000040 DATE-WRITTEN. JANUARY 1, 1981.                               FIG 6.13|
|000050 DATE-COMPILED. JANUARY 1, 198|                               FIG 6.13|
|000060*    THIS PROGRAM ILLUSTRATES A COMPLETE COBOL                FIG 6.13|
|000070*    PROGRAM.  IT DEMONSTRATES (PRIMARILY) RECORD DESCRIPTIONS FIG 6.13|
|000080*    IN THE FILE SECTION AND WORKING-STORAGE SECTION OF       FIG 6.13|
|000090*    THE DATA DIVISION AND THE USE OF OPEN, READ, MOVE,       FIG 6.13|
|000100*    WRITE, GO TO, CLOSE AND STOP RUN STATEMENTS IN THE       FIG 6.13|
|000110*    PROCEDURE DIVISION.  RECORD DESCRIPTIONS IN THE WORKING- FIG 6.13|
|000120*    STORAGE SECTIONS EMPLOY VALUE CLAUSES.                   FIG 6.13|
|000130 ENVIRONMENT DIVISION.                                        FIG 6.13|
|000140 CONFIGURATION SECTION.                                       FIG 6.13|
|000150 SOURCE-COMPUTER. IBM-370-145.                                FIG 6.13|
|000160 OBJECT-COMPUTER. IBM-370-145.                                FIG 6.13|
|000170 SPECIAL-NAMES.  C01 IS TOP-OF-NEXT-PAGE.                     FIG 6.13|
|000180 INPUT-OUTPUT SECTION.                                        FIG 6.13|
|000190 FILE-CONTROL.                                                FIG 6.13|
|000200     SELECT STUDENT-FILE ASSIGN TO UR-S-SYSIN.               FIG 6.13|
|000210     SELECT PRINTOUT ASSIGN TO UR-S-SYSPRINT.                FIG 6.13|
|000220 DATA DIVISION.                                               FIG 6.13|
|000230 FILE SECTION.                                                FIG 6.13|
|000240 FD  STUDENT-FILE LABEL RECORDS ARE OMITTED.                  FIG 6.13|
|000250 01  DUMMY-RECORD              PIC X(80).                     FIG 6.13|
|000260 FD  PRINTOUT LABEL RECORDS ARE OMITTED.                      FIG 6.13|
```

Figure 6.13 The Student List Program *Continued*

```
|          1 . 1   2   2   2   3   3   4   4   4   5   5   6   6   6   7   7   8|
|   4    8 2   6   0   4   8   2   6   0   4   8   2   6   0   4   8   2   6   0|
|-----------------------------------------------------------------------------|
|000270 01  PRINT-LINE                 PIC X(133).                 FIG 6.13|
|000280 WORKING-STORAGE SECTION.                                  FIG 6.13|
|000290 01  STUDENT-REC.                                          FIG 6.13|
|000300     05 STUDENT-IDENTIFICATION.                            FIG 6.13|
|000310        10 LAST-NAME            PIC X(10).                 FIG 6.13|
|000320        10 FIRST-NAME           PIC X(10).                 FIG 6.13|
|000330        10 MIDDLE-INITIAL       PIC X(01).                 FIG 6.13|
|000340        10 STUDENT-ID           PIC 9(09).                 FIG 6.13|
|000350     05 FILLER                  PIC X(05).                 FIG 6.13|
|000360     05 ENROLLMENT-INFO.                                   FIG 6.13|
|000370        10 CLASSIFICATION       PIC X(03).                 FIG 6.13|
|000380        10 TOTAL-HOURS          PIC 9(03).                 FIG 6.13|
|000390        10 HOURS-THIS-SEM       PIC 9(02).                 FIG 6.13|
|000400        10 MAJOR                PIC X(03).                 FIG 6.13|
|000410     05 FILLER                  PIC X(35).                 FIG 6.13|
|000420 01  REPORT-HEADING.                                       FIG 6.13|
|000430     03 FILLER                  PIC X(29) VALUE SPACES.    FIG 6.13|
|000440     03 FILLER                  PIC X(21) VALUE            FIG 6.13|
|000450     *SEMESTER STUDENT LIST*.                              FIG 6.13|
|000460 01  SEPARATOR-LINE.                                       FIG 6.13|
|000470     03 FILLER                  PIC X(01)  VALUE SPACE.    FIG 6.13|
|000480     03 FILLER                  PIC X(79)  VALUE ALL '*'.  FIG 6.13|
|000490 01  COLUMN-HEADING-1.                                     FIG 6.13|
|000500     02 FILLER                  PIC X(01)  VALUE SPACE.    FIG 6.13|
|000510     02 FILLER                  PIC X(79) VALUE '*        STUDENT FIG 6.13|
|000520-    *NAME      * STUDENT ID. * CLASS * MAJOR *  CURRENT   * TOTAFIG 6.13|
|000530-    *L *'.                                                FIG 6.13|
|000540 01  COLUMN-HEADING-2.                                     FIG 6.13|
|000550     02 FILLER                  PIC X(28) VALUE '  *'.     FIG 6.13|
|000560     02 FILLER                  PIC X(14) VALUE '*  NUMBER'. FIG 6.13|
|000570     02 FILLER                  PIC X(08) VALUE '*'.       FIG 6.13|
|000580     02 FILLER                  PIC X(08) VALUE '*'.       FIG 6.13|
|000590     02 FILLER                  PIC X(22) VALUE '* ENROLLMENT * HFIG 6.13|
|000600-    *OURS *'.                                             FIG 6.13|
|000610 01  OUTPUT-REC.                                           FIG 6.13|
|000620        08 FILLER               PIC X(03) VALUE '  *'.     FIG 6.13|
|000630        08 1ST-NAME             PIC X(11).                 FIG 6.13|
|000640        08 M-I                  PIC X(01).                 FIG 6.13|
|000650        08 FILLER               PIC X(02) VALUE '.'.       FIG 6.13|
|000660        08 SUR-NAME             PIC X(10).                 FIG 6.13|
|000670        08 FILLER               PIC X(04) VALUE ' *'.      FIG 6.13|
|000680        08 ID-NUM               PIC 9(09).                 FIG 6.13|
|000690        08 FILLER               PIC X(05) VALUE '  *'.     FIG 6.13|
|000700        08 CLASS                PIC X(02).                 FIG 6.13|
|000710        06 FILLER               PIC X(06) VALUE '   *'.    FIG 6.13|
|000720        08 MAJ                  PIC X(03).                 FIG 6.13|
|000730        08 FILLER               PIC X(08) VALUE '   *'.    FIG 6.13|
|000740        08 CURRENT-HOURS        PIC 9(02).                 FIG 6.13|
|000750        08 FILLER               PIC X(08) VALUE '      *'. FIG 6.13|
|000760        08 TOT-HOURS            PIC 9(03).                 FIG 6.13|
|000770        08 FILLER               PIC X(03) VALUE '  *'.     FIG 6.13|
|000780 PROCEDURE DIVISION.                                       FIG 6.13|
|000790 START-UP.                                                 FIG 6.13|
|000800     OPEN INPUT STUDENT-FILE, OUTPUT PRINTOUT.             FIG 6.13|
|000810     WRITE PRINT-LINE FROM REPORT-HEADING AFTER            FIG 6.13|
|000820        TOP-OF-NEXT-PAGE.                                  FIG 6.13|
|000830     WRITE PRINT-LINE FROM SEPARATOR-LINE AFTER 2 LINES.   FIG 6.13|
|000840     WRITE PRINT-LINE FROM COLUMN-HEADING-1 AFTER 1.       FIG 6.13|
|000850     WRITE PRINT-LINE FROM COLUMN-HEADING-2 AFTER 1.       FIG 6.13|
|000860     WRITE PRINT-LINE FROM SEPARATOR-LINE AFTER 1.         FIG 6.13|
|000870 READ-DATA.                                                FIG 6.13|
|000880     READ STUDENT-FILE INTO STUDENT-REC                    FIG 6.13|
|000890        AT END GO TO END-JOB.                              FIG 6.13|
|000900     MOVE STUDENT-ID TO ID-NUM.                            FIG 6.13|
|000910     MOVE LAST-NAME TO SUR-NAME.                           FIG 6.13|
|000920     MOVE FIRST-NAME TO 1ST-NAME.                          FIG 6.13|
|000930     MOVE MIDDLE-INITIAL TO M-I.                           FIG 6.13|
|000940     MOVE CLASSIFICATION TO CLASS.                         FIG 6.13|
|000950     MOVE TOTAL-HOURS TO TOT-HOURS.                        FIG 6.13|
|000960     MOVE HOURS-THIS-SEM TO CURRENT-HOURS.                 FIG 6.13|
|000970     MOVE MAJOR TO MAJ.                                    FIG 6.13|
|000980     WRITE PRINT-LINE FROM OUTPUT-REC AFTER 2 LINES.       FIG 6.13|
|000990     GO TO READ-DATA.                                      FIG 6.13|
|001000 END-JOB.                                                  FIG 6.13|
|001010     CLOSE STUDENT-FILE, PRINTOUT.                         FIG 6.13|
|001020     STOP RUN.                                             FIG 6.13|
```

Figure 6.13 The Student List Program *Continued*

```
-------------------------------------------------------------------------------------------------------
|       |           1         2         3         4         5         6         7         8| FIGURE  |
|RECORD|1234567890123456789012345678901234567890123456789012345678901234567890123456789 0| NUMBER  |
-------------------------------------------------------------------------------------------------------
|    1|ADAMS      JOHN      Q343564321      GR21900CSC                                    |FIG 6.13|
|    2|BROWN      JOHN      A555667777      FR03515MKT                                    |FIG 6.13|
|    3|CULVER     MATT      N456789012      JR09408MGT                                    |FIG 6.13|
|    4|DORSETT    ANTHONY   R353492761      SR13816ECO                                    |FIG 6.13|
|    5|ELDRIDGE   DAVID     G376495268      S004712FIN                                    |FIG 6.13|
|    6|FRANKLIN   BEN       V000000002      GR18912GBU                                    |FIG 6.13|
|    7|GERBER     KENNETH   A537903251      S002816MGT                                    |FIG 6.13|
|    8|HAMILTON   MARK      C486762389      JR09618CSC                                    |FIG 6.13|
|    9|ISSACS     MATT      H474653790      SR12018ECO                                    |FIG 6.13|
|   10|JENNINGS   HAROLD    Q502326955      FR01818MGT                                    |FIG 6.13|
|   11|KENNIMER   FLOYD     R476329092      JR06012MKT                                    |FIG 6.13|
|   12|LINCOLN    STEVEN    0442648942      S004515MKT                                    |FIG 6.13|
|   13|MARCUS     JEFF      V546677219      SR09918CSC                                    |FIG 6.13|
-------------------------------------------------------------------------------------------------------
```

Figure 6.13 The Student List Program (Data) *Continued*

```
                                  SEMESTER STUDENT LIST

************************************************************************************
*             STUDENT NAME          * STUDENT ID. * CLASS * MAJOR *  CURRENT    * TOTAL *
*                                    *  NUMBER     *       *       * ENROLLMENT  * HOURS *
************************************************************************************

  *JOHN        Q. ADAMS      *  343564321  *  GR   *  CSC  *    00    *  219  *

  *JOHN        A. BROWN      *  555667777  *  FR   *  MKT  *    15    *  035  *

  *MATT        N. CULVER     *  456789012  *  JR   *  MGT  *    08    *  094  *

  *ANTHONY     R. DORSETT    *  353492761  *  SR   *  ECO  *    16    *  138  *

  *DAVID       G. ELDRIDGE   *  376495268  *  SO   *  FIN  *    12    *  047  *

  *BEN         V. FRANKLIN   *  000000002  *  GR   *  GBU  *    12    *  189  *

  *KENNETH     A. GERBER     *  537903251  *  SO   *  MGT  *    16    *  028  *

  *MARK        C. HAMILTON   *  486762389  *  JR   *  CSC  *    18    *  096  *

  *MATT        H. ISSACS     *  474653790  *  SR   *  ECO  *    18    *  120  *

  *HAROLD      Q. JENNINGS   *  502326955  *  FR   *  MGT  *    18    *  018  *

  *FLOYD       R. KENNIMER   *  476329092  *  JR   *  MKT  *    12    *  060  *

  *STEVEN      0. LINCOLN    *  442648942  *  SO   *  MKT  *    15    *  045  *

  *JEFF        V. MARCUS     *  546677219  *  SR   *  CSC  *    18    *  099  *
```

Figure 6.13 The Student List Program (Output) *Continued*

duces the report heading SEMESTER STUDENT LIST. The WRITE statement using the FROM option causes the REPORT-HEADING record description to be moved to the PRINT-LINE. (All output produced by the program must be directed through PRINT-LINE, since this is the record description that is directly associated with the line printer.) Further, notice that the mnemonic-name TOP-OF-NEXT-PAGE is used to indicate the appropriate carriage control. TOP-OF-NEXT-PAGE is described in the SPECIAL-NAMES paragraph (line 170). The remainder of the WRITE statements in the START-UP paragraph are responsible for producing the column headings. The primary difference between these WRITE statements and the previous WRITE statement is that each indicates a specific (integer) number of lines to be advanced before the output is printed.

The READ-DATA paragraph (lines 870 through 990) represents the body of the program. That is, the majority of the "work" done by the program occurs within the READ-DATA paragraph. The first statement (the READ statement in line 880) causes data to be accepted from the card reader. Thus, the data on a punched card in STUDENT-FILE is transferred into the input-record description (STUDENT-REC). From this point forward, the program has access to the data of the first data card, until the READ statement is again executed. The program then transfers the data from the input record to the output record with a series of MOVE statements (lines 900 through 970). Notice that each field name in STUDENT-REC is moved to a similar representation of that data item in the OUTPUT-REC description. The WRITE statement in line 980 causes the data represented by the OUTPUT-REC description to be placed in the PRINT-LINE. The PRINT-LINE is written after two lines have been advanced. Finally, the statement GO TO READ-DATA causes an unconditional branch to the READ-DATA paragraph. The process just described is repeated until all data cards have been read. When the end of the STUDENT-FILE is reached, the AT END phrase of the READ statement is executed, causing a branch to the END-JOB paragraph.

When the END-JOB paragraph is encountered, the requirements of the program have been fulfilled. The card reader (STUDENT-FILE) and the line printer (PRINTOUT) files are released from the program (line 1010), and the program is terminated with the STOP RUN statement (line 1020). The results of this program are shown in Figure 6.13 (Output).

A Second Example— Producing Mailing Labels

To illustrate the differences that might exist between programs written in COBOL, consider the program presented in Figure 6.13 (the student listing program) and Figure 6.14 (the mailing-label program). In Figure 6.13, once the report and column headings have been produced, the program falls into a basic read/write mode whereby student records are read, i.e., the data in those records are moved to the output area, and the output area is written to the line printer as a single line of output. In Figure 6.14, a single record read by the program causes three printed lines and two blank lines to be produced on the line printer.

Examine the IDENTIFICATION DIVISION of both programs. In the student listing program the IDENTIFICATION DIVISION (lines 10–120) is more detailed than in the mailing-label program (lines 10–20). The primary dif-

```
|           1    1    2    2    2    3    3    4    4    4    5    5    6    6    6    7    7    8|
|      4    8    2    6    0    4    8    2    6    0    4    8    2    6    0    4    8    2    6    0|
-----------------------------------------------------------------------------------------------
|000010  IDENTIFICATION DIVISION.                                              FIG 6.14|
|000020  PROGRAM-ID. ONE-UP-LABELS.                                            FIG 6.14|
|000030  ENVIRONMENT DIVISION.                                                 FIG 6.14|
|000040  CONFIGURATION SECTION.                                                FIG 6.14|
|000050  SOURCE-COMPUTER. IBM-370-145-DOS.                                     FIG 6.14|
|000060  OBJECT-COMPUTER. IBM-370-145-DOS.                                     FIG 6.14|
|000070  SPECIAL-NAMES. C01 IS ALIGNING-LABELS.                                FIG 6.14|
|000080  INPUT-OUTPUT SECTION.                                                 FIG 6.14|
|000090  FILE-CONTROL.                                                         FIG 6.14|
|000100      SELECT CLIENT-FILE ASSIGN TO SYS003-UR-2501-S.                    FIG 6.14|
|000110      SELECT ONE-UP-LABELS ASSIGN TO SYS005-UR-1403-S.                  FIG 6.14|
|000120  DATA DIVISION.                                                        FIG 6.14|
|000130  FILE SECTION.                                                         FIG 6.14|
|000140  FD  CLIENT-FILE LABEL RECORDS ARE OMITTED.                            FIG 6.14|
|000150  01  CLIENT-RECORD.                                                    FIG 6.14|
|000160      02 CLIENT-NAME            PIC X(20).                              FIG 6.14|
|000170      02 CLIENT-ADDRESS         PIC X(30).                              FIG 6.14|
```

Figure 6.14 One-up Labels

```
|          1   1   2   2   2   3   3   4   4   4   5   5   6   6   6   7   7   8|
|   4   8   2   6   0   4   8   2   6   0   4   8   2   6   0   4   8   2   6   0|
--------------------------------------------------------------------------------
|000180        02 CLIENT-CITY              PIC X(20).                 FIG 6.14|
|000190        02 CLIENT-STATE             PIC X(02).                 FIG 6.14|
|000200        02 CLIENT-ZIP               PIC X(05).                 FIG 6.14|
|000210        02 FILLER                   PIC X(03).                 FIG 6.14|
|000220 FD  ONE-UP-LABELS LABEL RECORDS ARE OMITTED.                  FIG 6.14|
|000230 01  LABEL-LINE.                                               FIG 6.14|
|000240        02 FILLER                   PIC X(05).                 FIG 6.14|
|000250        02 INFORMATION-LINE         PIC X(30).                 FIG 6.14|
|000260 WORKING-STORAGE SECTION.                                      FIG 6.14|
|000270 01  ORGANIZE-CITY-STATE-ZIP.                                  FIG 6.14|
|000280        02 CITY-PART                PIC X(20).                 FIG 6.14|
|000290        02 FILLER                   PIC X(02) VALUE ', '.      FIG 6.14|
|000300        02 STATE-PART               PIC X(02).                 FIG 6.14|
|000310        02 FILLER                   PIC X(01) VALUE SPACES.    FIG 6.14|
|000320        02 ZIP-PART                 PIC X(05).                 FIG 6.14|
|000330 PROCEDURE DIVISION.                                           FIG 6.14|
|000340 INITIALIZATION.                                               FIG 6.14|
|000350     OPEN INPUT CLIENT-FILE, OUTPUT ONE-UP-LABELS.             FIG 6.14|
|000360     MOVE SPACES TO LABEL-LINE.                                FIG 6.14|
|000370     WRITE LABEL-LINE AFTER ALIGNING-LABELS.                   FIG 6.14|
|000380 READ-AND-PRINT-LABEL.                                         FIG 6.14|
|000390     READ CLIENT-FILE AT END GO TO TERMINATION.               FIG 6.14|
|000400     MOVE CLIENT-NAME TO INFORMATION-LINE.                     FIG 6.14|
|000410     WRITE LABEL-LINE AFTER ADVANCING 3 LINES.                 FIG 6.14|
|000420     MOVE CLIENT-ADDRESS TO INFORMATION-LINE.                  FIG 6.14|
|000430     WRITE LABEL-LINE AFTER ADVANCING 1 LINES.                 FIG 6.14|
|000440     MOVE CLIENT-CITY TO CITY-PART.                            FIG 6.14|
|000450     MOVE CLIENT-STATE TO STATE-PART.                          FIG 6.14|
|000460     MOVE CLIENT-ZIP TO ZIP-PART.                              FIG 6.14|
|000470     MOVE ORGANIZE-CITY-STATE-ZIP TO INFORMATION-LINE.         FIG 6.14|
|000480     WRITE LABEL-LINE AFTER ADVANCING 1 LINES.                 FIG 6.14|
|000490     GO TO READ-AND-PRINT-LABEL.                               FIG 6.14|
|000500 TERMINATION.                                                  FIG 6.14|
|000510     CLOSE CLIENT-FILE, ONE-UP-LABELS.                         FIG 6.14|
|000520     STOP RUN.                                                 FIG 6.14|
```

Figure 6.14 One-up Labels *Continued*

```
|       |        1         2         3         4         5         6         7         8| FIGURE  |
|RECORD|12345678901234567890123456789012345678901234567890123456789012345678901234567890| NUMBER  |
--------------------------------------------------------------------------------------------------
|    1|GARY BRYAN           CANYON EXPRESSWAY           AMARILLO            TX79220 |FIG 6.14|
|    2|PHILLIP P. HARRISON 2219 W. 7TH STREET           PERRYTON            TX79070 |FIG 6.14|
|    3|LARRY K. SPENCE      509 44TH STREET APT. 21     GRUVER              TX79021 |FIG 6.14|
|    4|PATRICK THOMAS       335 TEASLEY LANE             DENTON              TX79201 |FIG 6.14|
|    5|MARTHA WORKMAN       1444 COLGATE AVE.            TULIA               TX79321 |FIG 6.14|
```

Figure 6.14 One-up Labels (Data) *Continued*

```
GARY BRYAN
CANYON EXPRESSWAY
AMARILLO          , TX 79220


PHILLIP P. HARRISON
2219 W. 7TH STREET
PERRYTON          , TX 79070


LARRY K. SPENCE
509 44TH STREET APT. 21
GRUVER            , TX 79021


PATRICK THOMAS
335 TEASLEY LANE
DENTON            , TX 79201


MARTHA WORKMAN
1444 COLGATE AVE.
TULIA             , TX 79321
```

Figure 6.14 One-Up Labels (Output) *Continued*

ference between the two programs is that the student listing program provides better documentation than the mailing-label program. The ENVIRONMENT DIVISIONs of the two programs are similar. In the student listing program (lines 130–210) a computer manufactured by IBM is used, and in the mailing-label program (lines 30–110) an IBM computer is used. Notice, however, that even though the same company manufactured both computers, the ASSIGN clauses are slightly different. The student listing program uses IBM's operating system (OS), and the mailing-label program uses IBM's disk operating system (DOS). The ASSIGN clauses are modified accordingly.

The major differences between the two programs lie in the DATA and PRO-CEDURE DIVISIONs. In the student listing program, the DATA DIVISION is rather extensive (lines 220–770); however, the bulk of the division lies in the WORKING-STORAGE SECTION (lines 280–770). In the student listing pro-gram a rather complicated set of headings was to be produced; in the mailing-label program, the DATA DIVISION (lines 120–320) is shorter because no headings are produced. The input file (CLIENT-FILE) is described by CLIENT-RECORD (lines 150–210). CLIENT-RECORD describes the type of data nor-mally associated with a mailing label—name, address, city, state, and zip code. The output files of both programs are similar since both programs pro-duce generalized lines of output. However, the file description entries for LABELS (lines 220–250) are more detailed than the output-file description for the student listing program. The output-record description of the mailing-label program is in two parts—FILLER (line 240) and INFORMATION-LINE (line 250). The FILLER is used to provide five spaces at the beginning of each line; INFORMATION-LINE contains the name and address data. In the WORK-ING-STORAGE SECTION of the mailing-label program (lines 260–320), a special record-description (ORGANIZE-CITY-STATE-ZIP) is provided. This record is used to position the data values of client city, state, and zip code within a record, with a comma between the city and state.

In the PROCEDURE DIVISION of the student listing program (lines 780–1020), the files are opened and a heading is produced (lines 800–860), stu-dent records are read, data are moved to the output area, and lines of output are written until no more data are available for reading (lines 880–990), and the files are closed and the program is stopped (lines 1010–1020). In the mailing-label program's PROCEDURE DIVISION (lines 330–520), the files are opened and a WRITE statement aligns the label forms. The MOVE statement (line 360) is important for two reasons. First, the output line (LABEL-LINE) is initialized to contain blanks so that the following WRITE statement will not produce garbage on the printed output. Second, the MOVE statement initial-ized the FILLER part of LABEL-LINE to blanks. Since no other reference is made to LABEL-LINE (except to write it), the value placed in the FILLER at the beginning of the process will be maintained throughout the process. Thus, the first five positions of each printed line will contain blanks.

The procedure followed in the READ-AND-PRINT-LABEL paragraph (lines 380–490) is somewhat different from the main procedure of the student listing program. In the mailing-label program, each record read (line 390) causes the execution of three WRITE statements (lines 410, 430, and 480), producing a three-line mailing label. The first WRITE statement (line 410) prints the client-name (the first line of each label) after advancing three lines. The line advance leaves two blank lines before the location of the client-name on the label. (This program assumes the label form can hold a maximum of five lines.) The client-name is placed in LABEL-LINE by a MOVE statement (line 400). Note that INFORMATION-LINE is the receiving field of this move, not LABEL-LINE. The second line of the label is produced by moving CLIENT-ADDRESS to INFORMATION-LINE and writing LABEL-LINE (lines 420–430). The last line of the label requires a bit more organization before printing is possible. The city, state, and zip code of the input record are first moved to corresponding fields in ORGANIZE-CITY-STATE-ZIP (lines 440–460) before the data is moved to INFORMATION-LINE and label line is printed (lines 470–480). The GO TO statement (line 490) completes the loop, which continues until all client records have been read.

When the end of the client file is reached, the read statement causes a transfer to the TERMINATION paragraph (lines 500–520). Both files are closed in this paragraph, and the program is terminated.

Summary

The PROCEDURE DIVISION is the last division in a COBOL program. The PROCEDURE DIVISION establishes the process or algorithm to be executed. The procedure is supported by entries, especially by the data definitions in the DATA DIVISION. No structure is prescribed in the PROCEDURE DIVISION, and the programmer has complete latitude with SECTION and paragraph names.

Several types of statements are permitted in the PROCEDURE DIVISION. The statements described in this chapter include:

the OPEN statement, which "enables" files to the procedure,

the CLOSE statement, which "disconnects" files from the procedure,

the READ statement, which causes records from an input file to be placed in internal memory,

the WRITE statement, which causes internally stored data to be placed on an output medium,

the MOVE statement, which copies data from one field to another,

the GO TO statement, which causes an interruption of the sequential execution of statements, and

the STOP RUN statement, which permanently terminates the execution of the program.

Other statements will be discussed later in this text.

Notes on Programming Style

As mentioned in the notes at the end of Chapter 5, record descriptions that could appear in the FILE SECTION are frequently transferred to the WORKING-STORAGE SECTION. Printed output in the form of headings is frequently developed in the WORKING-STORAGE SECTION and moved to the output-record description by using a "WRITE record-name FROM identifier" form of the statement. In fact, all WRITE statements may be written in this form. Likewise, the READ-INTO form of the input statement may be used to conform to the same style by reading the data into the input-record description and moving the input data into a WORKING-STORAGE record description.

From a program design standpoint, your first objective should be to obtain an overall grasp of the program requirements. The next step should be to identify the general functions to be performed, such as a start-up or initialization function, a repetitive-processing function, and a termination function. After the general functions have been isolated, you should examine each to determine its suitability for further subdivision. Try to isolate each separate, identifiable, functional element of the problem. Only when you have broken the problem into its most basic elements should you begin coding statements and clauses. The next chapter is largely dedicated to this process.

Questions

Below, fill in the blank(s) with the appropriate word, words, or phrases.

1. The structure of the PROCEDURE DIVISION includes a division heading, sections, paragraphs, _____ , and _____ .

2. In the PROCEDURE DIVISION, section and paragraph names are also referred to as _____ names.

3. Data-names appear in both the _____ and the _____ division, but procedure-names appear only in the _____ division.

4. A procedure-name which is also a SECTION name may be composed of one or more _____ names.

5. A file-name that appears in an OPEN statement in the PROCEDURE DIVISION must also appear in a(n) _____ clause in the ENVIRONMENT DIVISION and in a(n) _____ entry in the DATA DIVISION.

6. In the OPEN statement, a file processing of _____ must be declared for read-oriented files, while the file must be opened _____ for write-oriented files.

7. Each file-name that appears in an OPEN statement should also appear in a(n) _____ statement before the program is terminated.

8. Data from an external medium is available for use within the program (in internal memory) once a(n) _____ statement has been executed.

9. A READ statement causes one _____ (logical/physical) input operation to be executed.

10. When an end-of-file condition is detected for an input file, the _____ phrase of the READ statement is executed.

11. In a READ statement, an imperative statement is really an imperative _____ .

12. When a file has been assigned to a line printer it should be opened as a(n) _____ file.

13. A single WRITE statement will cause _____ (number) lines to be printed.

14. For an output file, the WRITE statement should reference the output file _____ name.

15. The READ statement may use an INTO option to place data from an input record into an alternate area, whereas the WRITE statement may use a(n) _____ option to move data from an alternate area to an output record.

16. The BEFORE/AFTER clause of the WRITE statement is used for _____ .

17. Carriage control may be specified in a WRITE statement through _____ LINES, _____ LINES, or a(n) _____ .

18. If a WRITE statement is always to advance to the top of the next page a(n) _____ should be used in the WRITE statement.

19. When a mnemonic-name appears in a WRITE statement, the mnemonic-name should also appear in the _____ paragraph of the _____ DIVISION.

20. The COBOL statement that causes data from one field to be copied to another field is the _____ statement.

21. In a MOVE statement, the field that contains the data to be moved to another location is often called the _____ field.

22. The field that has its value altered as a result of a MOVE statement is the _____ field.

23. Numeric data is generally _____ -justified in an integer field, whereas alphanumeric data is generally _____ -justified.

24. A GO TO statement is often referred to as a(n) _____ instruction.

25. A closed loop is _____ .

26. A GO TO statement causes a branch to a(n) _____ name or a(n) _____ name.

27. The _____ statement causes the termination of a program and should be placed at the _____ termination point of a program.

Answer the following questions by circling either "T" for true or "F" for false.

T F 28. A READ operation may be referred to as destructive, i.e., the data accessible by the first READ operation is replaced (destroyed) by the data accessed by the second READ operation.

T F 29. READ statements read a record, and WRITE statements write a file.

T F 30. When the AFTER option is used in a WRITE statement, the output line is printed and then carriage control takes place.

T F 31. When an identifier is used to indicate vertical spacing of printed output, the identifier is permitted to contain zero as its value.

T F 32. There is no condition under which a group-item may be moved to an elementary-item.

T F 33. An elementary-item can always be moved to a group.

T F 34. To be able to move data from one field to another, the lengths of the two fields must be the same.

T F 35. The PROCEDURE DIVISION may be omitted from some COBOL programs.

T F   36. The PROCEDURE DIVISION may appear prior to the DATA DIVISION in a COBOL program.

T F   37. The algorithm or process to be performed by a program is presented in the PROCEDURE DIVISION.

T F   38. The PROCEDURE DIVISION has a number of required SECTIONS and paragraphs.

T F   39. The PROCEDURE DIVISION does not require the use of section names.

T F   40. The word "SECTION" must follow each section name in the PROCEDURE DIVISION.

T F   41. In COBOL, data files are available for input/output operations at any location within the PROCEDURE DIVISION without any kind of preparatory operation.

T F   42. The word "INPUT" may appear more than once in a single OPEN statement.

T F   43. Only a single file may be opened in a single OPEN statement.

T F   44. Multiple OPEN statements are permitted in a single COBOL program.

T F   45. The same file-name may be opened as both INPUT and OUTPUT at the same time.

T F   46. A particular file may be opened several times without ever being closed.

T F   47. A file may be read from or written to after it has been closed.

T F   48. A file that was opened in an output mode must be closed in an output mode, i.e., the word "OUTPUT" must appear in the CLOSE statement preceding the file-name.

T F   49. Files must be opened in the same order as the SELECT clauses in the ENVIRONMENT DIVISION.

T F   50. Once a file has been opened in an input mode, records may be read from that file.

T F   51. More than one logical record can be accessed by the program with a single execution of one READ statement.

T F   52. An input file-name always appears in a READ statement.

T F   53. With a READ statement, it is possible to have input data stored in two separately addressable areas of internal memory.

T F   54. Any statements following an unconditional branch in a sentence will not be executed.

T F   55. To be able to move data from one field to another, the field types of the two fields must be the same type (e.g., both must be numeric).

T F   56. A GO TO statement may be used to alter the sequential execution of statements.

Exercises

---

1. Below is an input-record description, PROCEDURE DIVISION statements, and two data records. After each input operation, record the values associated with each data-name of the input record.

```
ENVIRONMENT DIVISION.
      .
      .
      .
INPUT-OUTPUT SECTION.
FILE-CONTROL.
     SELECT INSURANCE-POLICIES ASSIGN UR-2540R-S-CARDIN.
      .
      .
      .
DATA DIVISION.
FILE SECTION.
FD  INSURANCE-POLICIES LABEL RECORDS ARE OMITTED.
Ø1  INSURANCE-RECORD.
     Ø3 POLICY-NUMBER              PIC X(1Ø).
     Ø3 CLIENT-NUMBER              PIC 9(Ø8).
     Ø3 POLICY-ANNIVERSARY-DATE.
        Ø5 ANNIVERSARY-MONTH       PIC 9(Ø2).
        Ø5 ANNIVERSARY-DAY         PIC 9(Ø2).
```

```
                    Ø3 POLICY-EXPIRATION-DATE.
                       Ø5 EXPIRATION-MONTH        PIC 9(Ø2).
                       Ø5 EXPIRATION-DAY          PIC 9(Ø2).
                       Ø5 EXPIRATION-YEAR         PIC 9(Ø2).
                    Ø3 PREMIUM-AMOUNT             PIC 9(Ø5)V9(Ø2).
                    Ø3 COMMISSION-AMOUNT          PIC 9(Ø3)V9(Ø2).
                    Ø3 SALESMAN-CODE              PIC X(Ø3).
                    Ø3 STATE-CODE                 PIC X(Ø2).
                    Ø3 FILLER                     PIC X(35).
                 .
                 .
                 .
            PROCEDURE DIVISION.
                 .
                 .
                 .
                 OPEN INPUT INSURANCE-POLICIES.
                 .
                 .
                 .
            READ-INSURANCE-POLICY.
                 READ INSURANCE-POLICIES AT END GO TO EXERCISE-COMPLETE.
                 .
                 .
                 .
            EXERCISE-COMPLETE.
                 CLOSE INSURANCE-POLICIES.
                 STOP RUN.
```

```
Record 1: AX-14293-4ØØ5Ø214 8Ø415Ø226 82ØØ7238 8Ø869ØJWSTX ----- blank -----
Record 2: R42219-C  1Ø8521Ø2Ø 83 11Ø288 1Ø19117611612DEWIL ----- blank -----
```

DATA-NAME	VALUE FROM FIRST READ	VALUE FROM SECOND READ

2. The following procedure produces a printed output form. Describe (using a printer layout form, if available), the output created by the program.

```
            IDENTIFICATION DIVISION.
            PROGRAM-ID. EXERCISE-2.
            ENVIRONMENT DIVISION.
            CONFIGURATION SECTION.
            SOURCE-COMPUTER. IBM-37Ø-OS.
            OBJECT-COMPUTER. IBM-37Ø-OS.
            SPECIAL-NAMES. CØ1 IS NEXT-PAGE.
            INPUT-OUTPUT SECTION.
                 SELECT PATIENTS ASSIGN UR-S-CARDIN.
                 SELECT CASE-REPORT ASSIGN UR-S-PROUT.
            DATA DIVISION.
            FILE-SECTION.
            FD  PATIENTS LABEL RECORDS ARE OMITTED.
            Ø1  PATIENT-RECORD.
                 Ø5 PATIENT-NUMBER            PIC 9(Ø5).
                 Ø5 PATIENT-NAME              PIC X(2Ø).
                 Ø5 DATE-OF-SERVICE           PIC X(Ø6).
                 Ø5 DIAGNOSIS-CODE            PIC X(Ø4).
                 Ø5 PROCEDURE-TIME.
                    1Ø HOURS                  PIC 9(Ø2).
                    1Ø MINUTES                PIC 9(Ø2).
                 Ø5 DIAGNOSIS-COMMENTS        PIC X(4Ø).
                 Ø5 VERIFICATION-CODE         PIC X(Ø1).
            FD  CASE-REPORT LABEL RECORDS ARE OMITTED.
            Ø1  REPORT-LINE.
                 Ø2 FILLER                    PIC X(Ø1).
                 Ø2 PAT-NUMBER-OUT            PIC 9(Ø5).
```

```
        02 FILLER                       PIC X(05).
        02 PAT-NAME-OUT                 PIC X(20).
        02 FILLER                       PIC X(05).
        02 DIAG-CODE-OUT                PIC X(04).
        02 FILLER                       PIC X(05).
        02 DIAG-COMMENT-OUT             PIC X(40).
        02 FILLER                       PIC X(05).
        02 HOURS-OUT                    PIC 9(02).
        02 TIME-SEPARATOR               PIC X(01).
        02 MINUTES-OUT                  PIC 9(02).
        02 FILLER                       PIC X(05).
        02 SERVICE-DATE-DAY             PIC 9(02).
        02 DASH-1                       PIC X(01).
        02 SERVICE-DATE-MONTH           PIC 9(02).
        02 DASH-2                       PIC X(01).
        02 SERVICE-DATE-YEAR            PIC 9(02).
        02 FILLER                       PIC X(25).
WORKING-STORAGE SECTION.
01   DATE-RECORD.
        02 REPORT-DAY                   PIC 9(02).
        02 REPORT-MONTH                 PIC 9(02).
        02 REPORT-YEAR                  PIC 9(02).

01   REPORT-HEADING.
        02 FILLER                       PIC X(46) VALUE SPACES.
        02 FILLER                       PIC X(33) VALUE
        'DAILY CASE FOR THE DATE OF '.
        02 REPORT-DAY-OUT               PIC 9(02).
        02 FILLER                       PIC X(01) VALUE '/'.
        02 REPORT-MONTH-OUT             PIC 9(02).
        02 FILLER                       PIC X(01) VALUE '/'.
        02 REPORT-YEAR-OUT              PIC 9(02).
01   COLUMN-HEADING-2.
        05 FILLER                       PIC X(11) VALUE 'NUMBER'.
        05 FILLER                       PIC X(25) VALUE 'PATIENT NAME'.
        05 FILLER                       PIC X(09) VALUE 'CODE'.
        05 FILLER                       PIC X(45) VALUE 'COMMENTS:'.
        05 FILLER                       PIC X(12) VALUE 'TIME'.
        05 FILLER                       PIC X(04) VALUE 'DATE'.
01   COLUMN-HEADING-1.
        05 FILLER                       PIC X(01) VALUE SPACES.
        05 FILLER                       PIC X(07) VALUE 'PATIENT'.
        05 FILLER                       PIC X(28) VALUE SPACES.
        05 FILLER                       PIC X(04) VALUE 'DIAG'.
        05 FILLER                       PIC X(50) VALUE SPACES.
        05 FILLER                       PIC X(16) VALUE '***** SERVICE *****'.
PROCEDURE DIVISION.
INITIAL-OPERATIONS.
        OPEN INPUT PATIENTS, OUTPUT CASE-REPORT.
        READ PATIENTS INTO DATE-RECORD
            AT END GO TO PROCEDURE-TERMINATION.
HEADING-PRODUCTION.
        MOVE REPORT-DAY TO REPORT-DAY-OUT.
        MOVE REPORT-MONTH TO REPORT-MONTH-OUT.
        MOVE REPORT-YEAR TO REPORT-YEAR-OUT.
        WRITE REPORT-LINE FROM REPORT-HEADING AFTER NEXT-PAGE.
        WRITE REPORT-LINE FROM COLUMN-HEADING-1 AFTER 2 LINES.
        WRITE REPORT-LINE FROM COLUMN-HEADING-2 AFTER 1 LINES.
        MOVE ALL '-' TO REPORT-LINE.
        WRITE REPORT-LINE AFTER 1 LINES.
        MOVE SPACES TO REPORT-LINE.
        MOVE '-' TO DASH-1, DASH-2.
        MOVE ':' TO TIME-SEPARATOR.
BODY-OF-REPORT.
        READ PATIENTS
            AT END GO TO PROCEDURE-TERMINATION.
        MOVE PATIENT-NUMBER TO PAT-NUMBER-OUT.
        MOVE PATIENT-NAME TO PAT-NAME-OUT.
```

```
            MOVE DATE-OF-SERVICE TO DATE-RECORD.
            MOVE REPORT-DAY TO SERVICE-DATE-DAY.
            MOVE REPORT-MONTH TO SERVICE-DATE-MONTH.
            MOVE REPORT-YEAR TO SERVICE-DATE-YEAR.
            MOVE DIAGNOSIS-CODE TO DIAG-CODE-OUT.
            MOVE HOURS TO HOURS-OUT.
            MOVE MINUTES TO MINUTES-OUT.
            MOVE DIAGNOSIS-COMMENTS TO DIAG-COMMENTS-OUT.
            WRITE REPORT-LINE AFTER ADVANCING 2 LINES.
            GO TO BODY-OF-REPORT.

        PROCEDURE-TERMINATION.
            MOVE SPACES TO REPORT-LINE.
            MOVE ' END OF REPORT' TO DIAG-COMMENT-OUT.
            WRITE REPORT-LINE AFTER ADVANCING 3 LINES.
            CLOSE PATIENTS, CASE-REPORT.
            STOP RUN.
(DATA)

19Ø58Ø ----- blank -----
14827PHILLIPøHARRISTONøøø14Ø58ØA471Ø245REMOVALøOFøFOREIGNøBODYøøøøøøøøøøøøøøøøøR
29884ELIZABETHøFREDERICKS15Ø58ØNØ46Ø115TREATMENTøOFøSEVEREøINSULT--LEFTøHANDøøJ

(END OF FILE)
```

3. Assume the following items are situations in which the statement "MOVE FIRST-FIELD TO SECOND-FIELD." is to be executed. Indicate what the result of each movement of data would be. Be sure to indicate the location of blanks and zeros, where applicable.

FIRST-FIELD		SECOND-FIELD	
DATA VALUE	PICTURE STRING	PICTURE STRING	RESULT
482	999	999	_____
3976	9(4)	999	_____
1872	9(4)	9(5)	_____
Ø672∧88	9(4)V99	9(3)	_____
2118∧69	9(4)V99	9(3)V99	_____
Ø	9	9(4)	_____
112∧Ø4	9(3)V99	9(5)V99	_____
SAVE	X(4)	X(4)	_____
MONIES	X(6)	XXX	_____
UNITS	X(5)	X(7)	_____
ONE	XXX	X	_____
1234	X(4)	9(4)	_____
2417	9(4)	X(4)	_____
Ø8271	9(5)	XXX	_____
4Ø5	XXX	9(4)	_____
5Ø4	XXX	99	_____
JOHN	AAAA	A(5)	_____
ø	A	XXXX	_____
OUT	XXX	AAA	_____
FOUR	X(4)	AA	_____

Problems

1. Periodically, your company performs a manual count of all items in inventory. Although there are records for the sale and purchase of each item, sometimes mistakes are made, items are returned and are not accounted for, and items may be

damaged, lost, or stolen. Thus, the actual count is necessary. What is needed is a report (as shown) on which the inventory clerks can record items present in the specified locations. The record format (as shown) contains the following fields:

1. Item number—8-digit number to be split into two parts (group and item) when printed.
2. Item description—30 characters
3. Item location—5 characters composed of (a) Asile—2 characters and (b) Bin number—3 digits
4. Lot size (e.g., per foot, pound, etc.)—3 characters
5. Estimated contents (what we think should be in the bin)—5 digits

The report format should be followed as closely as possible. Each data record should be reflected on the report. A blank area (flanked by less-than and greater-than symbols) should appear under the actual-location column so the clerks can record an item's actual location in the event it has been moved. Likewise, a blank area should appear under the actual-contents column to record the corrected count. Finally, a hyphen is to appear between the group and item numbers. All detail lines should be double spaced (as shown) and the report is to begin at the top of a page.

MULTIPLE-CARD LAYOUT FORM

Company: LEARNING COBOL, INC.

Application: INVENTORY by J. Wayne Spence Date 01/01/81 Job No. PROB 6.1 Sheet No. 1

150/10/8 PRINT CHART PROG. ID INVENTORY P6.1 PAGE 1 DATE 01/01/80
(SPACING: 150 POSITIONS AT 10 CHARACTERS PER INCH, 8 LINES PER VERTICAL INCH)
PROGRAM TITLE INVENTORY CONTROL
PROGRAMMER OR DOCUMENTALIST J. WAYNE SPENCE
CHART TITLE INVENTORY CONTROL REPORT

2. During the course of business, passengers make reservations for flights on our airline. We keep a permanent record of all reservation information for each passenger in a printer-report form for future reference. Therefore, even though the computer records may be replaced, modified, or destroyed, we will have some record of the reservation. Each reservation request contains the following information (also see the graphic record layout):

1. Ticket number—5 digits (appears on our records, but is not printed on the report)

2. Passengers name:
   (a) First name—10 characters (to be printed second on the report)
   (b) Middle initial—1 character (to be printed last)
   (c) Last name—10 characters (to be printed first)
3. Date of the flight—6 digits in the format MMDDYY (two digits each for the month, day, and year)
4. Flight number—3 digits
5. Passenger class—1 character (e.g., first class, tourist, economy, etc.)
6. Estimated time of departure—4 digits in the format HHMM (two digits each for hours and minutes)
7. Departure gate number—3 characters
8. Flight status—2 characters (e.g., delayed, cancelled, on time, etc.)
9. Estimated time of arrival—4 digits in the format HHMM
10. Comments—10 characters (status spelled out plus other entries)

On the report, column headings are to be printed flanked (above and below) by a row of asterisks. The passenger's name is to be printed in the format of last, first, middle. The date of the flight should have a slash (/) between the month-day and the day-year. The departure and arrival times should have a colon (:) between the hours and minutes. All detail lines are to be single spaced (as shown), and the report should begin at the top of a page.

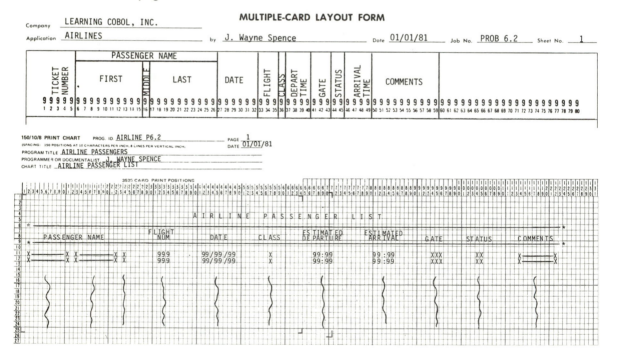

3. The personnel department has requested a status report on all company employees. Records in an applicable format have been constructed in the format shown, and each record contains the following fields:

   1. Employee number—3 digits (not used on the report)
   2. Employee name—20 characters
   3. Job classification—4 digits
   4. Job title—20 characters
   5. Department—10 characters

6. Date of employment—6 digits in the format MMDDYY
7. Date of last promotion—6 digits in the format MMDDYY
8. Employee status—10 characters (e.g., vacation, on leave, laid off, etc.)

On the printed Status Report, the employee number is not to be printed. However, a field called "Hourly/Salaried" has been added. The data to be placed in this field is the first digit of the job classification. (The job classification report field should include all four digits.) In addition, the two dates are to be edited as shown and should be printed in the format of DD/MM/YY. The report should begin at the top of a page, and the detail lines should be double spaced.

Company LEARNING COBOL, INC.

MULTIPLE-CARD LAYOUT FORM

Application PERSONNEL   by J. Wayne Spence   Date 01/01/81   Job No. PROB 6.3   Sheet No. 1

EMPLOYEE NUMBER	EMPLOYEE NAME	JOB CLASS	JOB TITLE	DEPARTMENT	DATE EMPLOYED	DATE PROMOTED	STATUS

150/10/8 PRINT CHART   PROG. ID. PERSONNEL P6.3   PAGE 1
(SPACING: 150 POSITIONS AT 10 CHARACTERS PER INCH, 8 LINES PER VERTICAL INCH)   DATE 01/01/81
PROGRAM TITLE PERSONNEL STATUS
PROGRAMMER OR DOCUMENTALIST J. WAYNE SPENCE
CHART TITLE PERSONNEL STATUS REPORT

3525 CARD PRINT POSITIONS

```
                            PERSONNEL STATUS REPORT

EMPLOYEE NAME        DEPARTMENT    CLASS  JOB    * DATE OF *      HOURLY/   PRESENT
                                         TITLE  EMPLOYMENT  LAST PROMOTION  SALARIED  STATUS
X-----------X   X------X   9999  X------X   XX/XX/XX   XX/XX/XX    X    X------X
X-----------X   X------X   9999  X------X   XX/XX/XX   XX/XX/XX    X    X------X
```

part **2 More Advanced COBOL Concepts**

7 Programming: The Traditional versus a Structured Approach

Two primary considerations related to running a computer installation are the cost of computer *hardware* (equipment) and the cost of *software* (programs) or program development within an organization. The cost of hardware is declining, while the cost of software development is increasing, and this trend is likely to continue for the foreseeable future. To combat the rising cost of program development, two techniques have been developed to reduce the amount of time required from program initiation to program completion. These techniques are called *flowcharting* and *structured programming*. Before discussing these, we will look briefly at the program development process.

The development of programs follows a pattern with at least three distinct phases. The first phase is generally called program *analysis* (often referred to as analysis, design, and planning). In the analysis phase, the requirements of the program are determined (e.g., types of input and output, decisions, calculations, etc.). Once these requirements have been identified, the programmer (or analyst) may begin the design and planning of the program. The programmer must begin to develop the logical flow of the program, which is often done with the aid of a *program flowchart*.

Beginning programmers often overlook the importance of *flowcharting*—of planning a program solution before attempting to write the program. Perhaps this is because beginning programmers start with simple programs so the programmer can remember all the details. With larger programs, however, even the best programmers need a way to keep track of where they have been and where they are going. Program planning is similar to coding a program—the more you practice, the better you get. Do not wait until an extremely complex program comes along to start thinking about program planning; practice program planning so you will have the necessary skills when they are needed.

The second phase of program development is *implementation*. During this phase, the program is organized and coded in a programming language. After coding is complete, *testing* and *debugging* begin, which involve attempting to execute the program. Most programs will not run the first time. Usually they contain keypunching or program-planning errors. Thus, testing and debugging are the repetitive processes of correcting errors or "bugs" (debugging) and verifying the results of the program (testing). Once these are satisfactorily concluded, implementation is complete, and the program is executed under "real life" conditions.

The third phase is called *modification and maintenance*, which involves altering or enhancing an existing program to keep it up to date, to correct a previously undiscovered error, or to expand its ability to handle more operations. Often, the person responsible for creating a program is *not* the individual who performs the modification and maintenance work. Thus, one step in this phase is to understand at least the portion of the program that will be changed. After this step is complete, modification and maintenance activities continue with a repeat of the analysis and implementation phases.

Flowcharting

Flowcharting is a technique for diagramming a procedure. More specifically, *program flowcharting* is the technique of planning a program by expressing it in terms of symbols or blocks prior to coding. The flowchart consists of symbols or blocks, which represent types of operations; (presented in Figure 7.1), notations, which identify the operations to be performed; and flowlines, which represent the logical relationship of one operation to another.

Symbol	Description
	Any processing function; operation(s) causing change in value, form, or location of data.
	General input/output function; data available for processing (input), or recording of processed data (output).
	A decision or switching-type operation that determines which of a number of alternative paths is followed.
	A terminal point in a flowchart—start, stop, halt, delay, or interrupt; may show entry to or exit from a closed subroutine.
	Connector used to demonstrate the exit to or entry from another part of the flowchart on the same page. Often used to eliminate flowlines.
	Predefined process, used to indicate one or more named operations or program steps specified in a subroutine or another set of flowcharts.
	Annotation or comment, used to provide additional descriptive clarification. Attached to another symbol by a dotted line.

Figure 7.1 Program Flowcharting Symbols

There are several advantages to flowcharting programs before coding. First, by logically arranging the program's sequence of events, the program designer can trace through the flowchart to determine if the procedure performs as anticipated. If not, the flowchart can be modified and retested. Second, drawing flowcharts is usually less time-consuming than coding. In case of error, it is easier to redraw the flowchart than it is to modify the program code. Third, the flowchart acts as documentation. Someone unfamiliar with programming should be able to comprehend the program's sequence of events through the flowchart. In large corporations, the individual responsible for program implementation may not be the individual who performs the analysis. Then, the flowchart can be used to communicate program requirements from the analyst to the program coder.

The flowchart should be written independent of the programming language, primarily to avoid "coding" of the flowchart. Each MOVE statement should *not* be represented by a block in the flowchart. Rather, each block should capture the essence of the operation to take place at that point in the process. The details are added during coding.

Figure 7.2 presents a program flowchart for the program presented in Chapter 6 (Figure 6.13). In this problem, a report and column heading were to be produced, records were to be used from a card file, the data contained in the records were to be reorganized, and the data were to be printed on a line printer. The reading and writing cycle was to continue until all records had been processed. (When flowlines go from left to right or from top to bottom, arrowheads are normally omitted; this is a standard convention in flowcharting. Further, notice the connector symbol used to eliminate the flowline that could have been drawn from the "Print Detail Line" block to the area just above the "Read a Record" block.) As an aid to understanding the relationship between the flowchart and the program, the corresponding COBOL statements are shown where they relate to the flowchart.

Now compare Figure 7.3 with the problem statement below. The process in the flowchart might be used to calculate employee payroll information and produce an earnings report, by department. (It is assumed that the data for this problem has been ordered, at a minimum, by department.)

The payroll-computation procedure contains these requirements:

1. computation of employee's gross pay,
2. computation of federal and state taxes,
3. computation of FICA taxes, and
4. determination of the employee's net pay.

The problem is complicated by the following:

1. gross pay may include an overtime factor,
2. federal and state taxes normally vary with the employee's marital status,
3. employee records may be coded to reflect savings and hospitalization deductions,
4. departmental pay totals are to be produced, and
5. companywide totals are to be produced.

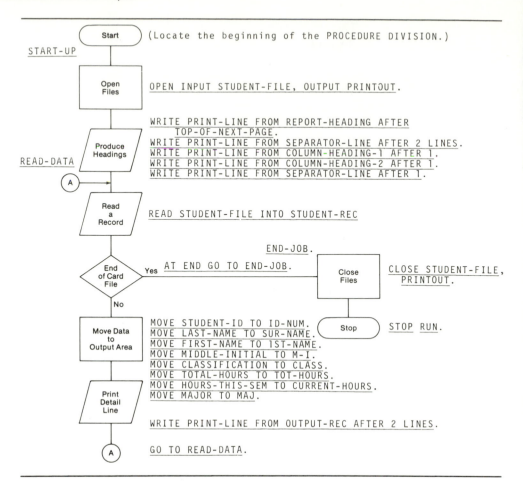

Figure 7.2 A Simple Program Flowchart

Though it is slightly more complex than the basic "read-move-write" sequence of the student listing problem, the development procedure for the payroll-computation-procedure flowchart incorporates the same philosophy as that used in the simpler problem.

Notice that some latitude is possible in the more complex problem. Although the flowchart demonstrates that the computation sequence for deductions should be (a) federal and state taxes, (b) FICA tax, (c) savings deduction, and (d) hospitalization deduction; this sequence may be reordered and still achieve the same result. The location of some of the steps in the procedure is critical, however. For example, gross pay must be determimed before taxes may be computed, and as a precondition to any computation, data must have been provided (through the reading of a payroll record). Therefore, to design a flowchart properly (and test its accuracy), concentrate on those key steps that *must* precede other steps.

The flowchart may have to be refined as other considerations are discovered (e.g., other deductions or a modification of the FICA computation); however, it should be a great deal easier to code the solution to the problem with a flowchart in hand than to remember all details of the problem while developing the code.

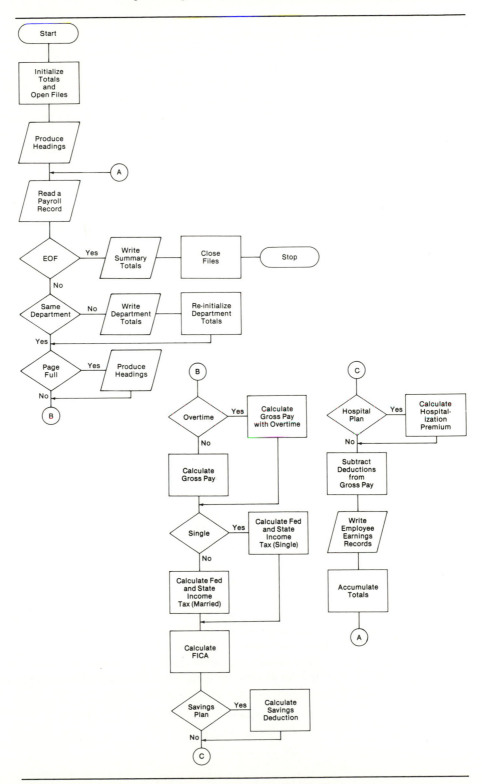

Figure 7.3 Payroll Computation Procedure (Program Flowchart)

Structured Programming

Although the program flowcharts in Figures 7.2 and 7.3 are concise and solve the problems for which they are intended, they violate almost every rule of structured programming. Imagine increasing the complexity of the second problem by a factor of 10. The flowchart for such a problem would be extremely difficult to construct and next to impossible to understand. This is due to flowcharting's attempt to solve the entire problem in one giant step.

The most significant advantage of structured programming is that the programmer no longer has to consider all the details of a problem with the idea of solving it in one step. The program is viewed as a series of *modules* (a collection of program statements) connected through "driving" or control routines. Each module should be clearly defined and functionally oriented, if possible. In a payroll-computation procedure, for example, one module could be dedicated to handle the payroll computations, and other modules could perform the functions necessary to get the process started and stopped. The payroll computation module might be further subdivided into modules to calculate taxes and other deductions. An additional module might be used to interface all other modules in the same way a table of contents shows the interrelationship between chapters of a book.

Many proponents of structured programming argue that if a module cannot be adequately described in a one-page narrative, the function should be further subdivided. In addition, each module should permit only one entry and one exit point. Single-entry, single-exit modules greatly facilitate program understanding and the location of logic errors in programming because the programmer does not have to worry that the code may be executed from some other point later in the block, thereby jumping the code which would "normally" be executed first. Furthermore, the programmer knows exactly where the module ends and, therefore, does not have to worry that one or more statements within the module might cause a jump to some other part of the program before the end of the module is reached.

What advantages can be gained through the structured approach to developing a program? Most important, large and complex problems can be attacked as smaller, simplified subproblems, which reduces the time required to develop a program. If the project is extremely large, the programming effort can be easily divided among several individuals. Because program functions can be isolated into specific modules, execution errors and logical bugs can be located and eliminated more quickly. Portions of the program code may be tested independently of other modules or functions. This may call for the insertion of *stubs* during the development process. Stubs are nothing more than dummy statements which indicate the presence of modules which are to be more fully coded at a later time.

Structured programming also encourages and supports a standardized style, which facilitates maintenance and modification. This standardized style uses three basic approaches to module design:

1. the *sequence*,
2. the *if-then-else*, and
3. the *do-while*.

Each of the three structures, shown in flowcharts in Figure 7.4, is supported by COBOL. The sequence structure is a series of process (or input/output) operations that are executed sequentially from the first statement to the last. In COBOL, this type of structure could be written as a series of READ, WRITE, MOVE, and arithmetic statements.

The function of the if-then-else is provided through the COBOL IF statement (see Chapter 8). Often, structured programs incorporate nested IF statements. That is, on the basis of one decision, another decision is made. An illustration of this operation is shown in Figure 7.5. For example, suppose that a programmer wants to determine a customer discount from purchases on the following schedule:

Purchase	Discount
Up to $500	0%
$501 to $1,000	5%
$1,001 to $2,000	10%
Over $2,000	20%

One approach to the problem would be to examine the conditions in a "tree" form. Condition-1 might determine if the amount of purchase is $1,000 or less. If the first answer is "true", condition-2 might determine if the purchase is $500 or less. If this is true, the discount would be zero percent. However, if condition-2 is false, the discount would be 5 percent. If the first test (condition-1) was false, condition-3 might determine if the purchase was $2,000 or less. If this is true, the discount would be 10 percent; but if false, the discount would be 20 percent.

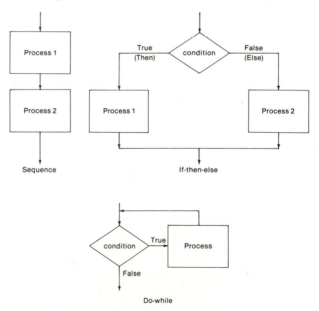

Figure 7.4 Three Forms Used in Structured Programming

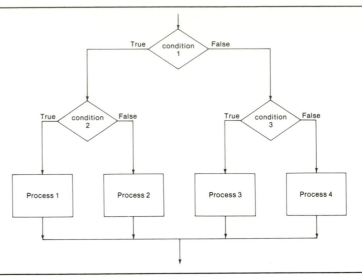

Figure 7.5 Nested IF Statement in a "Tree" Form

Another way to view this series of decisions is to check each category in stages or "stair-step" form. Figure 7.6 provides this type of decision process. For example, condition-1 might determine if the amount of purchase is $500 or less. If this condition is true, the discount would be zero; if false, the second condition would determine if the amount of purchase was $1,000 or less. If condition-2 is true, the discount would be 5 percent; if false, the third condition would determine if the amount of purchase was $2,000 or less. If condition-3 is true, the discount would be 10 percent; if false, the discount would be 20 percent.

These two approaches to decision logic are frequently used; however, both examples suffer from the same problem—they require the programmer to remember a sequence of events in a testing cycle. Although the example is easy to understand, as testing complexity increases, so does the programmer's difficulty in understanding and programming the decision logic. Furthermore, complex decision logic requires more indepth study when it becomes necessary to modify the program. For this reason, simple independent testing procedures are generally preferred.

For example, the same series of decisions presented above could be redesigned into individual tests executed in serial fashion. (See Figure 7.7.) Condition-1 determines if the purchase amount is $500 or less, and if true, assigns a discount of zero. Condition-2 determines if the purchase amount is greater than $500 and less than $1,001, and if true, sets the discount to 5 percent. Condition-3 determines if the purchase amount is greater than $1,000 and less than $2,001, and if true sets the discount at 10 percent. Finally, condition-4 determines if the purchase amount is greater than $2,000, and if true, sets the discount to 20 percent. In this form, one of the tests could be altered without altering other tests. For example, suppose another category is added, say, if the amount of purchase was $3,001 or more, the discount would be 25 percent. It would only be necessary to add a fifth condition and a fifth process to the tests to incorporate the new category into the program.

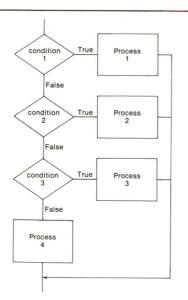

Figure 7.6 Nested IF Statements in a "Staged" Form

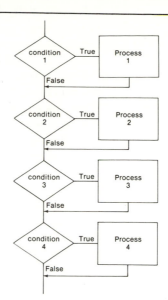

Figure 7.7 Independent IF Statements

To alter the decision "tree" form of nested IFs would require an "unbalanced tree," and exact placement of the new test would require careful study and the alteration of existing statements. In the "stair-step" form of nested IFs the "default" value would probably no longer be valid, and the existing structure would have to be altered to incorporate the new test. Independent IF statements, however, are simpler, easier to modify, and less prone to new logic errors as a program is modified.

The last of the fundamental structures of structured programming is the do-while. Though COBOL does not totally embrace the do-while structure, the structure can be approximated in the PERFORM statement. (See Chapter 8) The PERFORM statement incorporates a *do-until* structure, illustrated in Figure 7.8. The do-while structure specifies that a process is to be repeated so long as the indicated condition is *true*. The do-until structure indicates that a process is to be repeated so long as the specified condition is *false*. Thus, the control of *looping* operations (the repetitive execution of a series of statements) is geared to a positive response to a condition with a do-while and to a negative response to a condition with do-until. Though there is a fundamental difference between the two structures, most programmers can easily translate the do-while structure to the do-until structure.

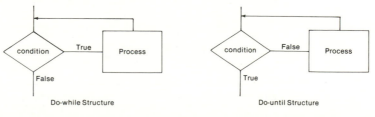

Figure 7.8 Do-while Versus Do-until (PERFORM)

Figure 7.9 illustrates structured programming in the context of a program. The flowchart and program illustrated demonstrate the redesign of the student listing program from Chapter 6. The flowchart decomposes (divides) the procedure into small single-function modules.

The *control procedure* module is added to control the execution of individual functional modules. This module is a simple sequence structure. Each block (statement) will be executed in sequence until the module has been completed. However, note that the symbols used in the body of this module are *predefined-process* symbols. This means that the actual details of these blocks are more clearly spelled out in another part of the flowchart with a corresponding label. Thus, although the *Initialize* module is present in the control sequence, the actual procedure may be found in more detail elsewhere. The *Initialize* procedure of this program is responsible only for opening files. Although this is an artificially small module (one statement), it does represent a singular function. In more complex programs, the initialization procedure might also include such procedures as setting variables to their initial values, placing zeros in individual cells of a table, and so forth.

The second block in the control module indicates the generation of a report heading. In the *Report Heading* module, one block is used to indicate that a report heading and column headings are to be printed. Though only one block is present in this module, several statements are present in the program to fulfill the requirements of this block. This block of the flowchart should clearly represent the essence of the activity to be performed in the program.

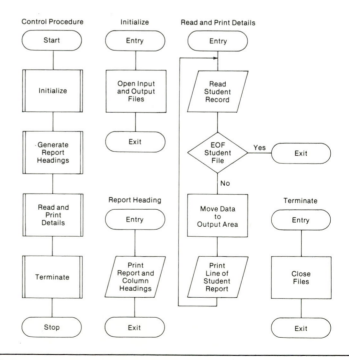

Figure 7.9 Student List Program (Structured Flowchart)

```
|          1  1   2   2   2   3   3   4   4   4   5   5   6   6   6   7   7   8|
|    4   8  2  6   0   4   8   2   6   0   4   8   2   6   0   4   8   2   6   0|
-------------------------------------------------------------------------------
|000010 IDENTIFICATION DIVISION.                                       FIG  7.9|
|000020 PROGRAM-ID.  STUDENT-LIST.                                     FIG  7.9|
|000030 AUTHOR. J. WAYNE SPENCE.                                       FIG  7.9|
|000040 DATE-WRITTEN. JANUARY 1, 1981.                                 FIG  7.9|
|000050 DATE-COMPILED. JANUARY 1, 1981.                                FIG  7.9|
|000060*    THIS PROGRAM ILLUSTRATES A COMPLETE COBOL                  FIG  7.9|
|000070*    PROGRAM.  IT DEMONSTRATES (PRIMARILY) RECORD DESCRIPTIONS  FIG  7.9|
|000080*    IN THE FILE SECTION AND WORKING-STORAGE SECTION OF         FIG  7.9|
|000090*    THE DATA DIVISION AND THE USE OF OPEN, READ, MOVE,         FIG  7.9|
|000100*    WRITE, GO TO, PERFORM, CLOSE AND STOP RUN STATEMENTS IN THE FIG 7.9|
|000110*    PROCEDURE DIVISION.  RECORD DESCRIPTIONS IN THE WORKING-   FIG  7.9|
|000120*    STORAGE SECTIONS EMPLOY VALUE CLAUSES.                     FIG  7.9|
|000130 ENVIRONMENT DIVISION.                                          FIG  7.9|
|000140 CONFIGURATION SECTION.                                         FIG  7.9|
|000150 SOURCE-COMPUTER. HONEYWELL.                                    FIG  7.9|
|000160 OBJECT-COMPUTER. HONEYWELL.                                    FIG  7.9|
|000170 SPECIAL-NAMES. '1' IS TOP-OF-NEXT-PAGE.                        FIG  7.9|
|000180 INPUT-OUTPUT SECTION.                                          FIG  7.9|
|000190 FILE-CONTROL.                                                  FIG  7.9|
|000200     SELECT STUDENT-FILE ASSIGN TO CARD-READER.                 FIG  7.9|
|000210     SELECT PRINTOUT ASSIGN TO PRINTER.                         FIG  7.9|
|000220 DATA DIVISION.                                                 FIG  7.9|
|000230 FILE SECTION.                                                  FIG  7.9|
|000240 FD  STUDENT-FILE LABEL RECORDS ARE OMITTED.                    FIG  7.9|
|000250 01  DUMMY-RECORD              PIC X(80).                       FIG  7.9|
|000260 FD  PRINTOUT LABEL RECORDS ARE OMITTED.                        FIG  7.9|
|000270 01  PRINT-LINE                PIC X(133).                      FIG  7.9|
|000280 WORKING-STORAGE SECTION.                                       FIG  7.9|
|000290 01  STUDENT-REC.                                               FIG  7.9|
|000300     05 STUDENT-IDENTIFICATION.                                 FIG  7.9|
|000310        10 LAST-NAME           PIC X(10).                       FIG  7.9|
|000320        10 FIRST-NAME          PIC X(10).                       FIG  7.9|
|000330        10 MIDDLE-INITIAL      PIC X(01).                       FIG  7.9|
|000340        10 STUDENT-ID          PIC 9(09).                       FIG  7.9|
|000350     05 FILLER                 PIC X(05).                       FIG  7.9|
|000360     05 ENROLLMENT-INFO.                                        FIG  7.9|
|000370        10 CLASSIFICATION      PIC X(02).                       FIG  7.9|
|000380        10 TOTAL-HOURS         PIC 9(03).                       FIG  7.9|
|000390        10 HOURS-THIS-SEM      PIC 9(02).                       FIG  7.9|
|000400        10 MAJOR               PIC X(03).                       FIG  7.9|
|000410     05 FILLER                 PIC X(35).                       FIG  7.9|
|000420 01  REPORT-HEADING.                                            FIG  7.9|
|000430     03 FILLER                 PIC X(29) VALUE SPACES.          FIG  7.9|
|000440     03 FILLER                 PIC X(21) VALUE                  FIG  7.9|
|000450     'SEMESTER STUDENT LIST'.                                   FIG  7.9|
|000460 01  SEPARATOR-LINE.                                            FIG  7.9|
|000470     03 FILLER                 PIC X(01)  VALUE SPACE.          FIG  7.9|
|000480     03 FILLER                 PIC X(79)  VALUE ALL '*'.        FIG  7.9|
|000490 01  COLUMN-HEADING-1.                                          FIG  7.9|
|000500     02 FILLER                 PIC X(01) VALUE SPACE.           FIG  7.9|
|000510     02 FILLER                 PIC X(79) VALUE '*      STUDENT  FIG  7.9|
|000520-    'NAME     * STUDENT ID. * CLASS * MAJOR *  CURRENT  * TOTA FIG  7.9|
|000530-    'L *'.                                                     FIG  7.9|
|000540 01  COLUMN-HEADING-2.                                          FIG  7.9|
|000550     02 FILLER                 PIC X(28) VALUE ' *'.            FIG  7.9|
|000560     02 FILLER                 PIC X(14) VALUE '*  NUMBER'.     FIG  7.9|
|000570     02 FILLER                 PIC X(08) VALUE '*'.             FIG  7.9|
|000580     02 FILLER                 PIC X(08) VALUE '*'.             FIG  7.9|
|000590     02 FILLER                 PIC X(22) VALUE '* ENROLLMENT * H FIG 7.9|
|000600-    'OURS *'.                                                  FIG  7.9|
|000610 01  OUTPUT-REC.                                                FIG  7.9|
|000620        08 FILLER              PIC X(03) VALUE ' *'.            FIG  7.9|
|000630        08 1ST-NAME            PIC X(11).                       FIG  7.9|
|000640        08 M-I                 PIC X(01).                       FIG  7.9|
|000650        08 FILLER              PIC X(02) VALUE '.'.             FIG  7.9|
|000660        08 SUR-NAME            PIC X(10).                       FIG  7.9|
|000670        08 FILLER              PIC X(04) VALUE ' *'.            FIG  7.9|
|000680        08 ID-NUM              PIC 9(09).                       FIG  7.9|
|000690        08 FILLER              PIC X(05) VALUE '  *'.           FIG  7.9|
|000700        08 CLASS               PIC X(02).                       FIG  7.9|
|000710        08 FILLER              PIC X(06) VALUE '   *'.          FIG  7.9|
|000720        08 MAJ                 PIC X(03).                       FIG  7.9|
|000730        08 FILLER              PIC X(08) VALUE '   *'.          FIG  7.9|
|000740        08 CURRENT-HOURS       PIC 9(02).                       FIG  7.9|
|000750        08 FILLER              PIC X(08) VALUE '     *'.        FIG  7.9|
```

Figure 7.9 Student List Program (Structured) *Continued*

```
|                 1   1   2   2   2   3   3   4   4   4   5   5   6   6   6   7   7   8|
|   4       8     2   6   0   4   8   2   6   0   4   8   2   6   0   4   8   2   6   0|
-------------------------------------------------------------------------------------------
|000760          08  TOT-HOURS           PIC 9(03).                              FIG  7.9|
|000770          08  FILLER              PIC X(03) VALUE '  **'.                  FIG  7.9|
|000780 PROCEDURE DIVISION.                                                      FIG  7.9|
|000790 CONTROL-PROCEDURE.                                                       FIG  7.9|
|000800     PERFORM INITIALIZATION.                                              FIG  7.9|
|000810     PERFORM WRITE-REPORT-HEADING.                                        FIG  7.9|
|000820     PERFORM READ-AND-PRINT-DETAILS THRU READ-AND-PRINT-EXIT.             FIG  7.9|
|000830     PERFORM TERMINATION.                                                 FIG  7.9|
|000840     STOP RUN.                                                            FIG  7.9|
|000850 INITIALIZATION.                                                          FIG  7.9|
|000860     OPEN INPUT STUDENT-FILE, OUTPUT PRINTOUT.                            FIG  7.9|
|000870 WRITE-REPORT-HEADING.                                                    FIG  7.9|
|000880     WRITE PRINT-LINE FROM REPORT-HEADING AFTER                           FIG  7.9|
|000890         TOP-OF-NEXT-PAGE.                                                FIG  7.9|
|000900     WRITE PRINT-LINE FROM SEPARATOR-LINE AFTER 2 LINES.                  FIG  7.9|
|000910     WRITE PRINT-LINE FROM COLUMN-HEADING-1 AFTER 1.                      FIG  7.9|
|000920     WRITE PRINT-LINE FROM COLUMN-HEADING-2 AFTER 1.                      FIG  7.9|
|000930     WRITE PRINT-LINE FROM SEPARATOR-LINE AFTER 1.                        FIG  7.9|
|000940 READ-AND-PRINT-DETAILS.                                                  FIG  7.9|
|000950     READ STUDENT-FILE INTO STUDENT-REC                                   FIG  7.9|
|000960         AT END GO TO READ-AND-PRINT-EXIT.                                FIG  7.9|
|000970     MOVE STUDENT-ID TO ID-NUM.                                           FIG  7.9|
|000980     MOVE LAST-NAME TO SUR-NAME.                                          FIG  7.9|
|000990     MOVE FIRST-NAME TO 1ST-NAME.                                         FIG  7.9|
|001000     MOVE MIDDLE-INITIAL TO M-I.                                          FIG  7.9|
|001010     MOVE CLASSIFICATION TO CLASS.                                        FIG  7.9|
|001020     MOVE TOTAL-HOURS TO TOT-HOURS.                                       FIG  7.9|
|001030     MOVE HOURS-THIS-SEM TO CURRENT-HOURS.                                FIG  7.9|
|001040     MOVE MAJOR TO MAJ.                                                   FIG  7.9|
|001050     WRITE PRINT-LINE FROM OUTPUT-REC AFTER 2 LINES.                      FIG  7.9|
|001060     GO TO READ-AND-PRINT-DETAILS.                                        FIG  7.9|
|001070 READ-AND-PRINT-EXIT.                                                     FIG  7.9|
|001080     EXIT.                                                                FIG  7.9|
|001090 TERMINATION.                                                             FIG  7.9|
|001100     CLOSE STUDENT-FILE, PRINTOUT.                                        FIG  7.9|
```

Figure 7.9 Student List Program (Structured) *Continued*

```
-------------------------------------------------------------------------------------------------------
|        |          1         2         3         4         5         6         7        8| FIGURE  |
|RECORD |1234567890123456789012345678901234567890123456789012345678901234567890| NUMBER  |
-------------------------------------------------------------------------------------------------------
|    1 |ADAMS     JOHN      Q343564321     GR21900CSC                          |FIG  7.9|
|    2 |BROWN     JOHN      A555667777     FR03515MKT                          |FIG  7.9|
|    3 |CULVER    MATT      N456789012     JR09408MGT                          |FIG  7.9|
|    4 |DORSETT   ANTHONY   R353492761     SR13816ECO                          |FIG  7.9|
|    5 |ELDRIDGE  DAVID     Q376495268     S004712FIN                          |FIG  7.9|
|    6 |FRANKLIN  BEN       V000000002     GR18912GBU                          |FIG  7.9|
|    7 |GERBER    KENNETH   A537903251     S002816MGT                          |FIG  7.9|
|    8 |HAMILTON  MARK      C486762389     JR09618CSC                          |FIG  7.9|
|    9 |ISSACS    MATT      H474653790     SR12018ECO                          |FIG  7.9|
|   10 |JENNINGS  HAROLD    G502326955     FR01818MGT                          |FIG  7.9|
|   11 |KENNIMER  FLOYD     R476329092     JR06012MKT                          |FIG  7.9|
|   12 |LINCOLN   STEVEN    0442648942     S004515MKT                          |FIG  7.9|
|   13 |MARCUS    JEFF      V546677219     SR09918CSC                          |FIG  7.9|
```

Figure 7.9 Student List Program (Structured—Data) *Continued*

The third module, *Read and Print*, represents a looping activity. During each cycle of this loop, a record containing student data is to be read, the data contained in this record is to be moved to the output area of the program, and the output area is to be written to the printer. This looping activity is to continue until there are no more records in the student file.

The *Terminate* module is similar in design to the *Initialize* block. The *Terminate* module is responsible for closing files, but in more complex programs, it might be used to perform such activities as print footings on the last page of a report or producing a summary report. Finally, control of the program is

SEMESTER STUDENT LIST

STUDENT NAME		STUDENT ID. NUMBER	CLASS	MAJOR	CURRENT ENROLLMENT	TOTAL HOURS
JOHN	G. ADAMS	343564321	GR	CSC	00	219
JOHN	A. BROWN	555667777	FR	MKT	15	035
MATT	N. CULVER	456789012	JR	MGT	08	094
ANTHONY	R. DORSETT	353492761	SR	ECO	16	138
DAVID	Q. ELDRIDGE	376495268	SO	FIN	12	047
BEN	V. FRANKLIN	000000002	GR	GBU	12	189
KENNETH	A. GERBER	537903251	SO	MGT	16	028
MARK	C. HAMILTON	486762389	JR	CSC	18	096
MATT	H. ISSACS	474653790	SR	ECO	18	120
HAROLD	Q. JENNINGS	502326955	FR	MGT	18	018
FLOYD	R. KENNIMER	476329092	JR	MKT	12	060
STEVEN	O. LINCOLN	442648942	SO	MKT	15	045
JEFF	V. MARCUS	546677219	SR	CSC	18	099

Figure 7.9 Student List Program (Structured—Output) *Continued*

returned to the *Control Procedure* module, where the STOP RUN statement is encountered.

Although the *Read and Print* activity is probably understandable from a logical standpoint (it has a single entry and exit point), it does not clearly represent one of the three fundamental structures of a structured program. If the decision block were eliminated, the structure would be a simple sequence. Yet the decision is necessary to exit from this loop. But, the inclusion of the decision does not yield an if-then-else structure since the module has an initial input operation.

The *Read and Print* module is an example of the type of module that separates the structured programming "purist" from those who use structured programming only so long as clarity is maintained. The purists believe that the tenets of structured programming should be followed to the letter—only the three programming structures should be employed. *GO TO* statements should never be used since they may be overused and could result in multiple exit points, mulitple entry points, or large blocks of code tied together by a series of unconditional branches (GO TOs).

The second group, which strives for clarity in program code, argues that structured programming is only a means to an end, not an end in itself. Under most circumstances the tenets of structured programming are followed; however, when use of a particular structure would result in less clarity, this group opts for the clearest, most understandable code possible.

The programmer should be aware of both approaches to structured programming. Both approaches are used in industry, and new programmers should be able to conform to either. Figure 7.10 illustrates a structured program that would satisfy the structured programming purist.

Figure 7.9 and Figure 7.10 are, of course, highly similar. In fact, the *Report Heading* and *Terminate* modules are exactly the same. And except for the type of PERFORM statement used to control the *Read and Print* module, the *Control Procedure* is the same. This change in PERFORM statements is significant, however, the PERFORM statement in Figure 7.10 provides the do-until structure, whereas all previous PERFORMS were simply interpreted as "do" (or "do it once"). The use of this form also requires the introduction of a control variable or INDICATOR to the program. INDICATOR (a level-∅1 entry in the WORKING-STORAGE SECTION) is used by the program to determine the status of the last READ statement executed, i.e., either the READ statement accepted a new record (the value of INDICATOR remains as assigned in the *Initialize* module) or an end-of-file condition was encountered upon attempting to read a record from the student file (the value of INDICATOR is changed to PROCESS COMPLETE in either the *Initialize* or *Read and Print* module).

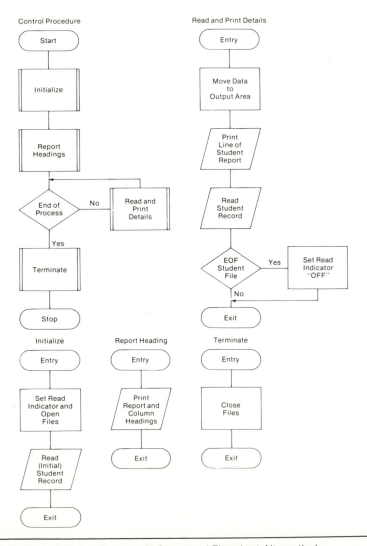

Figure 7.10 Student Listing Program (A Structured Flowchart Alternative)

```
|                1 1 2 2 2 3 3 4 4 4 5 5 6 6 6 7 7 8|
|   4    8       2 6 0 4 8 2 6 0 4 8 2 6 0 4 8 2 6 0|
---------------------------------------------------------
|000010 IDENTIFICATION DIVISION.                              FIG 7.10|
|000020 PROGRAM-ID. STUDENT-LIST.                             FIG 7.10|
|000030 AUTHOR. J. WAYNE SPENCE.                              FIG 7.10|
|000040 DATE-WRITTEN. JANUARY 1, 1981.                        FIG 7.10|
|000050 DATE-COMPILED. JANUARY 1, 1981.                       FIG 7.10|
|000060*    THIS PROGRAM ILLUSTRATES A COMPLETE COBOL         FIG 7.10|
|000070*    PROGRAM.  IT DEMONSTRATES (PRIMARILY) RECORD DESCRIPTIONS  FIG 7.10|
|000080*    IN THE FILE SECTION AND WORKING-STORAGE SECTION OF FIG 7.10|
|000090*    THE DATA DIVISION AND THE USE OF OPEN, READ, MOVE, FIG 7.10|
|000100*    THE DATA DIVISION AND THE USE OF OPEN, READ, MOVE, FIG 7.10|
|000110*    WRITE, PERFORM, CLOSE AND STOP RUN STATEMENTS IN THE FIG 7.10|
|000120*    PROCEDURE DIVISION.  RECORD DESCRIPTIONS IN THE WORKING- FIG 7.10|
|000130*    STORAGE SECTIONS EMPLOY VALUE CLAUSES.            FIG 7.10|
|000140 ENVIRONMENT DIVISION.                                 FIG 7.10|
|000150 CONFIGURATION SECTION.                                FIG 7.10|
|000160 SOURCE-COMPUTER. HONEYWELL.                           FIG 7.10|
|000170 OBJECT-COMPUTER. HONEYWELL.                           FIG 7.10|
|000180 SPECIAL-NAMES. '1' IS TOP-OF-NEXT-PAGE.               FIG 7.10|
|000190 INPUT-OUTPUT SECTION.                                 FIG 7.10|
|000200 FILE-CONTROL.                                         FIG 7.10|
|000210     SELECT STUDENT-FILE ASSIGN TO CARD-READER.        FIG 7.10|
|000220     SELECT PRINTOUT ASSIGN TO PRINTER.                FIG 7.10|
|000230 DATA DIVISION.                                        FIG 7.10|
|000240 FILE SECTION.                                         FIG 7.10|
|000250 FD  STUDENT-FILE LABEL RECORDS ARE OMITTED.           FIG 7.10|
|000260 01  DUMMY-RECORD            PIC X(80).                FIG 7.10|
|000270 FD  PRINTOUT LABEL RECORDS ARE OMITTED.               FIG 7.10|
|000280 01  PRINT-LINE              PIC X(133).               FIG 7.10|
|000290 WORKING-STORAGE SECTION.                              FIG 7.10|
|000300 01  INDICATOR               PIC X(16).                FIG 7.10|
|000310 01  STUDENT-REC.                                      FIG 7.10|
|000320     05 STUDENT-IDENTIFICATION.                        FIG 7.10|
|000330        10 LAST-NAME         PIC X(10).                FIG 7.10|
|000340        10 FIRST-NAME        PIC X(10).                FIG 7.10|
|000350        10 MIDDLE-INITIAL    PIC X(01).                FIG 7.10|
|000360        10 STUDENT-ID        PIC 9(09).                FIG 7.10|
|000370     05 FILLER               PIC X(05).                FIG 7.10|
|000380     05 ENROLLMENT-INFO.                               FIG 7.10|
|000390        10 CLASSIFICATION    PIC X(02).                FIG 7.10|
|000400        10 TOTAL-HOURS       PIC 9(03).                FIG 7.10|
|000410        10 HOURS-THIS-SEM    PIC 9(02).                FIG 7.10|
|000420        10 MAJOR             PIC X(03).                FIG 7.10|
|000430     05 FILLER               PIC X(35).                FIG 7.10|
|000440 01  REPORT-HEADING.                                   FIG 7.10|
|000450     03 FILLER               PIC X(29) VALUE SPACES.   FIG 7.10|
|000460     03 FILLER               PIC X(21) VALUE           FIG 7.10|
|000470     'SEMESTER STUDENT LIST'.                          FIG 7.10|
|000480 01  SEPARATOR-LINE.                                   FIG 7.10|
|000490     03 FILLER               PIC X(01)  VALUE SPACE.   FIG 7.10|
|000500     03 FILLER               PIC X(79)  VALUE ALL '*'. FIG 7.10|
|000510 01  COLUMN-HEADING-1.                                 FIG 7.10|
|000520     02 FILLER               PIC X(01) VALUE SPACE.    FIG 7.10|
|000530     02 FILLER               PIC X(79) VALUE '*      STUDENT FIG 7.10|
|000540-  'NAME     * STUDENT ID. * CLASS * MAJOR *  CURRENT  * TOTAFIG 7.10|
|000550-  'L *'.                                              FIG 7.10|
|000560 01  COLUMN-HEADING-2.                                 FIG 7.10|
|000570     02 FILLER               PIC X(28) VALUE ' *'.     FIG 7.10|
|000580     02 FILLER               PIC X(14) VALUE '*  NUMBER'. FIG 7.10|
|000590     02 FILLER               PIC X(08) VALUE '*'.      FIG 7.10|
|000600     02 FILLER               PIC X(08) VALUE '*'.      FIG 7.10|
|000610     02 FILLER               PIC X(22) VALUE '* ENROLLMENT * HFIG 7.10|
|000620-  'OURS *'.                                           FIG 7.10|
|000630 01  OUTPUT-REC.                                       FIG 7.10|
|000640        08 FILLER            PIC X(03) VALUE ' *'.     FIG 7.10|
|000650        08 1ST-NAME          PIC X(11).                FIG 7.10|
|000660        08 M-I               PIC X(01).                FIG 7.10|
|000670        08 FILLER            PIC X(02) VALUE '.'.      FIG 7.10|
|000680        08 SUR-NAME          PIC X(10).                FIG 7.10|
|000690        08 FILLER            PIC X(04) VALUE ' *'.     FIG 7.10|
|000700        08 ID-NUM            PIC 9(09).                FIG 7.10|
|000710        08 FILLER            PIC X(05) VALUE '  *'.    FIG 7.10|
|000720        08 CLASS             PIC X(02).                FIG 7.10|
|000730        08 FILLER            PIC X(06) VALUE '   *'.   FIG 7.10|
|000740        08 MAJ               PIC X(03).                FIG 7.10|
|000750        08 FILLER            PIC X(08) VALUE '   *'.   FIG 7.10|
|000760        08 CURRENT-HOURS     PIC 9(02).                FIG 7.10|
|000770        08 FILLER            PIC X(08) VALUE '    *'.  FIG 7.10|
|000780        08 TOT-HOURS         PIC 9(03).                FIG 7.10|
|000790        08 FILLER            PIC X(03) VALUE '  *'.    FIG 7.10|
```

Figure 7.10 Student Listing Program (Structured Alternative) *Continued*

```
|--------------------------------------------------------------------------------|
|        1   1   2   2   2   3   3   4   4   4   5   5   6   6   6   7   7   8|
|   4    8   2   6   0   4   8   2   6   0   4   8   2   6   0   4   8   2   6   0|
|--------------------------------------------------------------------------------|
|000800 PROCEDURE DIVISION.                                             FIG 7.10|
|000810 CONTROL-PROCEDURE.                                              FIG 7.10|
|000820     PERFORM INITIALIZATION.                                     FIG 7.10|
|000830     PERFORM WRITE-REPORT-HEADING.                               FIG 7.10|
|000840     PERFORM READ-AND-PRINT-DETAILS                              FIG 7.10|
|000850         UNTIL INDICATOR = 'PROCESS COMPLETE'.                   FIG 7.10|
|000860     PERFORM TERMINATION.                                        FIG 7.10|
|000870     STOP RUN.                                                   FIG 7.10|
|000880 INITIALIZATION.                                                 FIG 7.10|
|000890     MOVE 'PROCESS START' TO INDICATOR.                          FIG 7.10|
|000900     OPEN INPUT STUDENT-FILE, OUTPUT PRINTOUT.                   FIG 7.10|
|000910     READ STUDENT-FILE INTO STUDENT-REC                          FIG 7.10|
|000920         AT END MOVE 'PROCESS COMPLETE' TO INDICATOR.            FIG 7.10|
|000930 WRITE-REPORT-HEADING.                                           FIG 7.10|
|000940     WRITE PRINT-LINE FROM REPORT-HEADING AFTER                  FIG 7.10|
|000950         TOP-OF-NEXT-PAGE.                                       FIG 7.10|
|000960     WRITE PRINT-LINE FROM SEPARATOR-LINE AFTER 2 LINES.         FIG 7.10|
|000970     WRITE PRINT-LINE FROM COLUMN-HEADING-1 AFTER 1.             FIG 7.10|
|000980     WRITE PRINT-LINE FROM COLUMN-HEADING-2 AFTER 1.             FIG 7.10|
|000990     WRITE PRINT-LINE FROM SEPARATOR-LINE AFTER 1.               FIG 7.10|
|001000 READ-AND-PRINT-DETAILS.                                         FIG 7.10|
|001010     MOVE STUDENT-ID TO ID-NUM.                                  FIG 7.10|
|001020     MOVE LAST-NAME TO SUR-NAME.                                 FIG 7.10|
|001030     MOVE FIRST-NAME TO 1ST-NAME.                                FIG 7.10|
|001040     MOVE MIDDLE-INITIAL TO M-I.                                 FIG 7.10|
|001050     MOVE CLASSIFICATION TO CLASS.                               FIG 7.10|
|001060     MOVE TOTAL-HOURS TO TOT-HOURS.                              FIG 7.10|
|001070     MOVE HOURS-THIS-SEM TO CURRENT-HOURS.                       FIG 7.10|
|001080     MOVE MAJOR TO MAJ.                                          FIG 7.10|
|001090     WRITE PRINT-LINE FROM OUTPUT-REC AFTER 2 LINES.             FIG 7.10|
|001100     READ STUDENT-FILE INTO STUDENT-REC                          FIG 7.10|
|001110         AT END MOVE 'PROCESS COMPLETE' TO INDICATOR.            FIG 7.10|
|001120 TERMINATION.                                                    FIG 7.10|
|001130     CLOSE STUDENT-FILE, PRINTOUT.                               FIG 7.10|
```

Figure 7.10 Student Listing Program (Structured Alternative) *Continued*

```
|--------------------------------------------------------------------------------|
|              1         2         3         4         5         6         7     8| FIGURE |
|RECORD|12345678901234567890123456789012345678901234567890123456789012345678901234567890| NUMBER |
|--------------------------------------------------------------------------------|
|    1|ADAMS     JOHN       Q343564321      GR21900CSC                    |FIG 7.10|
|    2|BROWN     JOHN       A555667777      FR03515MKT                    |FIG 7.10|
|    3|CULVER    MATT       N456789012      JR09408MGT                    |FIG 7.10|
|    4|DORSETT   ANTHONY    R353492761      SR13816ECO                    |FIG 7.10|
|    5|ELDRIDGE  DAVID      Q376495268      S004712FIN                    |FIG 7.10|
|    6|FRANKLIN  BEN        V000000002      GR18912GBU                    |FIG 7.10|
|    7|GERBER    KENNETH    A537903251      S002816MGT                    |FIG 7.10|
|    8|HAMILTON  MARK       C486762389      JR09618CSC                    |FIG 7.10|
|    9|ISSACS    MATT       H474653790      SR12018ECO                    |FIG 7.10|
|   10|JENNINGS  HAROLD     Q502326955      FR01818MGT                    |FIG 7.10|
|   11|KENNIMER  FLOYD      R476329092      JR06012MKT                    |FIG 7.10|
|   12|LINCOLN   STEVEN     0442648942      S004515MKT                    |FIG 7.10|
|   13|MARCUS    JEFF       V546677219      SR09918CSC                    |FIG 7.10|
```

Figure 7.10 Student Listing Program (Structured Alternative—Data) *Continued*

The condition specified in the PERFORM statement using the UNTIL option (UNTIL INDICATOR = 'PROCESS COMPLETE') is tested upon encountering the PERFORM statement and again each time the *bottom* of the module is encountered. This testing procedure forms the adjustment of the *Initialize* and *Read and Print* modules. In the *Initialize* module the INDICATOR is initialized to some meaningful value, which would not cause the do-until structure to terminate on the first execution of the PERFORM statement. (The initialization of INDICATOR could have been accomplished in the DATA DIVISION through a VALUE clause.)

SEMESTER STUDENT LIST

```
******************************************************************************
*          STUDENT NAME          * STUDENT ID. * CLASS * MAJOR *  CURRENT   * TOTAL *
*                                *   NUMBER    *       *       * ENROLLMENT * HOURS *
******************************************************************************
*  JOHN      G. ADAMS            *  343564321  *  GR   *  CSC  *     00     *  219  *
*  JOHN      A. BROWN            *  555667777  *  FR   *  MKT  *     15     *  035  *
*  MATT      N. CULVER           *  456789012  *  JR   *  MGT  *     08     *  094  *
*  ANTHONY   R. DORSETT          *  353492761  *  SR   *  ECO  *     16     *  138  *
*  DAVID     Q. ELDRIDGE         *  376495268  *  SO   *  FIN  *     12     *  047  *
*  BEN       V. FRANKLIN         *  000000002  *  GR   *  GRU  *     12     *  189  *
*  KENNETH   A. GERBER           *  537903251  *  SO   *  MGT  *     16     *  028  *
*  MARK      C. HAMILTON         *  486762389  *  JR   *  CSC  *     18     *  096  *
*  MATT      H. ISSACS           *  474653790  *  SR   *  ECO  *     18     *  120  *
*  HAROLD    G. JENNINGS         *  502326955  *  FR   *  MGT  *     18     *  018  *
*  FLOYD     R. KENNIMER         *  476329092  *  JR   *  MKT  *     12     *  060  *
*  STEVEN    O. LINCOLN          *  442648942  *  SO   *  MKT  *     15     *  045  *
*  JEFF      V. MARCUS           *  546677219  *  SR   *  CSC  *     18     *  099  *
```

Figure 7.10 Student Listing Program (Structured Alternative—Output) *Continued*

The next step in the *Initialize* module is to open all files. All input variables are initialized with a READ statement. A READ operation is necessary in the *Initialize* module because of the structure of the *Read and Print* module. However, if the student file is read and there is no record in the file, the IN-DICATOR is set up to PROCESS COMPLETE, which will cause the *Read and Print* module to be skipped in the execution sequence.

When the *Read and Print* module is executed, the first step is to move existing input data (either from the READ process performed during the initialization step or from the READ operation at the bottom of the module) to the output area. The data are then written to the printer. Finally, the next record is read. The READ statement *must* be the last statement in the module so that if the end-of-file is reached, the INDICATOR is set to PROCESS COMPLETE just before reaching the bottom of the module. After the READ statement has been executed, the PERFORM condition is tested. If the condition is true, the looping activity is stopped, and the *Terminate* module is invoked. If INDICATOR is not equal to PROCESS COMPLETE, however, the *Read and Print* module is repeated until the end of the student file is encountered. Now, examine Figure 7.11; it illustrates a structured version of the payroll-computation procedure in Figure 7.3. Since this problem is fairly complex, a *hierarchy chart* (sometimes called a *Visual Table of Contents*—VTOC) is used to get a grasp of the overall logic of the problem while identifying the major modules of the program. The hierarchy chart shows a *logic tree* of a process. That is, the blocks of the chart indicate the logical relationships between operations and the sequence in which the operations are to be executed. Normally, the tree is "executed" from top to bottom, traversing each branch of the

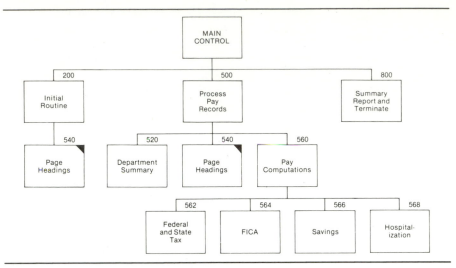

Figure 7.11 Payroll Computation Procedure (Hierarchy Chart)

tree from left to right. Tracing the hierarchy chart of the payroll-computation procedure produces the sequence in Table 7.1.

Note that when a module is being "continued," rather than "started," the completion of the routine will cause control to be returned to the module that originally "called" it. Thus, when the MAIN CONTROL module invokes the INITIAL ROUTINE module (Step 2), the sequence will ultimately return to the MAIN CONTROL module when the INITIAL ROUTINE module has been completed (Step 5).

Again look at Figure 7.11, and notice the series of numbers recorded at the upper right-hand corner of each block. This numbering system is used to provide an understanding of the superior-subordinate relationship between modules. Each identifying number is composed of three digits (although four- and five-digit numbers could be used on more complex problems). The first module (MAIN CONTROL) should be unnumbered or numbered "000." One level below the MAIN CONTROL module, all "hundred" series modules are recorded. The numbers are not necessarily consecutive to permit later addition of other modules. All remaining numbers in the hierarchy chart should be from the same series as those at the first level. For example, all blocks subordinate to PROCESS PAY RECORDS (500) should be from the 500 series—520, 540, and 560, and so on. Thus, not only is each block uniquely identified by name and number, but the numbering system helps to determine the relationships between modules and the order in which the modules should appear in the PROCEDURE DIVISION. Although other numbering systems may be used in the hierarchy chart, the numbering system presented is both meaningful and concise. Its biggest limitation is that it permits only nine (1–9) different modules to be subordinate to a single superior module.

As with all procedures, there are exceptions to the rules. In the hierarchy chart in Figure 7.11, module 540 (PAGE HEADING) is duplicated under

Table 7.1 Sequence of Events in the Payroll-Computation
Procedure Hierarchy Chart

Step	Module Number	Start/Continue*	Called From/Returned To
1	–	MAIN CONTROL (S)	–
2	200	INITIAL ROUTINE (S)	MAIN CONTROL
3	540	PAGE HEADING (S)	INITIAL ROUTINE
4	200	INITIAL ROUTINE (C)	–
5	–	MAIN ROUTINE (C)	–
6	500	PROCESS PAY RECORDS (S)	MAIN ROUTINE
7	520	DEPARTMENT SUMMARY (S)	PROCESS PAY RECORDS
8	500	PROCESS PAY RECORDS (C)	–
9	540	PAGE HEADING (S)	PROCESS PAY RECORDS
10	500	PROCESS PAY RECORDS (C)	–
11	560	PAY COMPUTATIONS (S)	PROCESS PAY RECORDS
12	562	FEDERAL AND STATE TAX (S)	PAY COMPUTATIONS
13	560	PAY COMPUTATIONS (C)	–
14	564	FICA (S)	PAY COMPUTATIONS
15	560	PAY COMPUTATIONS (C)	–
16	566	SAVINGS (S)	PAY COMPUTATIONS
17	560	PAY COMPUTATIONS (C)	–
18	568	HOSPITALIZATION (S)	PAY COMPUTATIONS
19	560	PAY COMPUTATIONS (C)	–
20	500	PROCESS PAY RECORDS (C)	–
21	–	MAIN CONTROL (C)	–
22	800	SUMMARY REPORT AND TERMINATE (S)	MAIN ROUTINE
23	–	MAIN CONTROL (C)—Stop	

*S = start processing module
 C = continue processing module

540

PAGE
HEADINGS

modules 200 and 500. Because module 540 is not unique to a single branch of the logic tree, it is a *utility* or *service* module. For purposes of visual clarity, utility modules are often drawn with a shaded upper right-hand corner. Thus, the module might appear as shown here.

Now, examine the payroll computation procedure in Figure 7.12. Processing begins with the MAIN CONTROL module, which calls the INITIAL ROUTINE (200). Since a summary report is to be produced, data-names used to accumulate values are set to zero, and the files used in the process are opened. Next, the initial page heading is printed by calling PAGE HEADINGS (540). After control is returned to the INITIAL ROUTINE, the initial pay record is read, initializing all data-names for that file, so data for the first employee are now available for processing. But what if the Pay File is not available for processing, thus yielding an end-of-file condition? If EOF on the Pay File is encountered, an indicator used to control the PROCESS PAY RECORDS module is set to "off" (no more data are available in the Pay File). This is done so that when processing of the MAIN CONTROL module resumes, the PROCESS PAY RECORDS module will be omitted from the sequence. This "fall through" condition then causes a summary report containing zeros to be printed and closes all files. Finally, MAIN CONTROL again resumes and the program halts. This process is obviously a response to an unusual circumstance—no Pay File—but programs should be able to respond to unusual circumstances without terminating because of a fatal error.

If data were sucessfully read from the Pay File during execution of the IN-ITIAL ROUTINE, control is still passed back to the MAIN CONTROL module. However, rather than falling through to the termination sequence, the PROCESS PAY RECORDS module (500) is initiated with a series of tests. The first test determines whether the last record contains a department value other than that on the previous record. Though this would *not* be the case for the first record, this condition could exist at any time after that. If the department values are different, the DEPARTMENT SUMMARY module (540) is invoked. During the execution of the 540 module, subtotals are printed, the ac-cumulating fields for the department are reset to zero, and the new department value is recorded. Whether or not the department value was changed, the next step is to determine whether a new page heading is necessary. Again, one

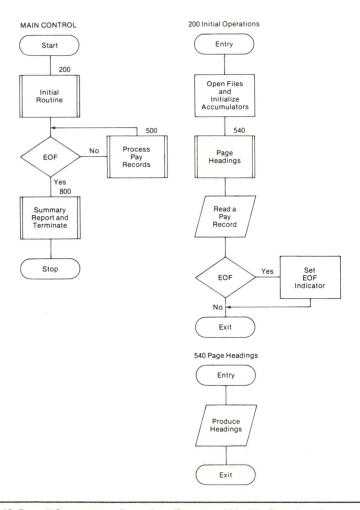

Figure 7.12 Payroll Computation Procedure (Structured Module Flowcharts)

would *not* expect a new page heading to be necessary on the first record, but periodically a new heading will be necessary, and the PAGE HEADINGS module (540) will be executed.

After the initial tests have been performed, the PAY COMPUTATIONS module (560) is invoked. Although it is not absolutely necessary to invoke a separate routine to perform this function, the PROCESS PAY RECORDS module becomes simpler as a result. When the PAY COMPUTATIONS module is executed, the first operation is represented by an if-then-else structure to determine the necessity of computing gross pay with or without an overtime component. Once the gross-pay value has been determined, the remainder of the module is constructed along the lines of a simple sequence. That is, the FEDERAL AND STATE TAX module (562), the FICA module

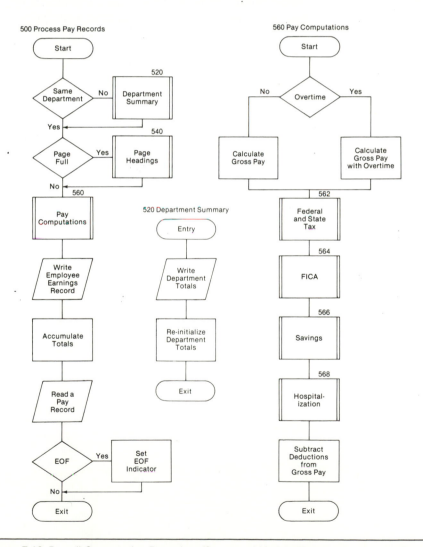

Figure 7.12 Payroll Computation Procedure (Structured Module Flowcharts) *Continued*

(564), the SAVINGS module (566), the HOSPITALIZATION module (568), and a determination of net pay (gross pay less deductions) are executed in a simple sequence.

The FEDERAL AND STATE TAX module (562) is represented by an if-then-else structure. One branch of the structure is reserved for the computation of taxes for married taxpayers, and the other branch is used to compute taxes for single taxpayers. The FICA module (564), a simple sequence (not necessarily a single step), computes the FICA tax based on gross pay. The SAVINGS module (566), another if-then-else structure, is without an operation if the employee record is not coded for the savings plan. Otherwise, the savings deducation is calculated. The final computational module, HOSPITALIZA-TION (568), is similar in structure to the SAVINGS module. The difference lies in the employee-code field tested (hospital plan) and the details of how the hospitalization premium (a deduction) is computed.

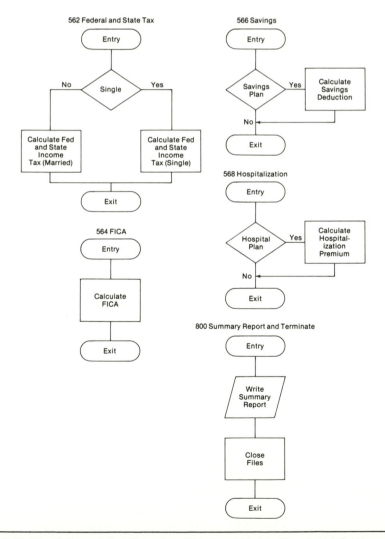

Figure 7.12 Payroll Computation Procedure (Structured Module Flowcharts) *Continued*

After each of the previous modules have been invoked and executed, all possible deductions have been calculated. All that remains is to subtract these deductions from gross pay to produce the net pay value—the final operation in the PAY COMPUTATIONS module.

When the exit from the PAY COMPUTATIONS module is executed, control returns to the PROCESS PAY RECORDS module, and another simple sequence is initiated. All the calculated fields related to the employee record are printed in a report format, these fields are accumulated in the department and companywide totals, and the next employee record is read. Provided the end-of-file condition does not exist upon reading the next record, the PROCESS PAY RECORDS module is repeated. Upon encountering the end-of-file condition, the end-of-file indicator is set, causing the termination of the PROCESS PAY RECORDS module. When control is returned to the MAIN CONTROL module, the next step is to invoke the SUMMARY REPORT AND TER-MINATE module (800). In this module, a companywide summary report is produced from those data values accumulated during the course of execution, and all files are closed. The exit returns control to the MAIN CONTROL routine, where the stop block is encountered and the procedure terminates.

The Case Structure

Besides the three fundamental structures already discussed, one additional structure—the *case*—is often added to make it easier to represent and code a certain class of problems. In some situations a decision is to be made on the basis of a known set of alternatives. This set is referred to as a *mutually exclusive, collectively exhaustive set*. That is, by choosing one alternative, all other alternatives are excluded. Furthermore, a list of all the alternatives in the set would contain all possibilities.

With the case structure, after the appropriate alternative has been selected, one and only one process is executed. Figure 7.13 illustrates the case structure.

The first mechanism in the case structure performs switching operations. One such mechanism is provided in COBOL through the GO TO/DEPENDING ON statement (See Chapter 18). Thus, depending upon the data provided

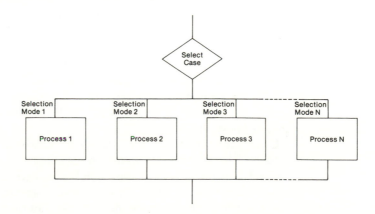

Figure 7.13 The Case Structure

to the selection mechanism, one (and only one) of the processes is performed. After the process is performed, the structure is complete.

Figure 7.14 illustrates how the case structure might be used in a structured flowchart. Again using the payroll-computation procedure, suppose an employee had a choice of three hospitalization plans according to the following schedule:

Plan	Description	Premium
1.	Self only	$65.00
2.	Self and spouse	100.00
3.	Family	125.00

The case structure would permit the selection of one of the plans followed by the appropriate process (in this case, a premium-value assignment).

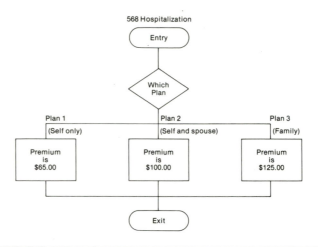

Figure 7.14 An Illustration of the Case Structure (Hospitalization Plan Selection)

Now that you have seen examples of structured flowcharting, you are probably wondering how to begin the design of the diagrams. There are several recommended approaches to structured-program design. The most popular of these is the *top-down* approach. A flowchart designed from the top down begins with the major aspects of the problem and progresses to the level of least importance. In Figure 7.12 for example, this would mean that the CONTROL routine is designed first. The INITIAL ROUTINE, the SELECT PROCESS, and SUMMARY REPORT AND TERMINATE modules would be designed next, and so on.

Other alternatives are the *bottom-up* approach and the *critical-event* approach. The bottom-up approach is simply a reversal of the top-down method. The critical-event approach begins with the most important module, regardless of its level. Work then begins on superior and subordinate routines, which either drive or service the critical-event routine. For example, in Figure 7.12, the SELECT PROCESS routine may be viewed as being the most important. The subordinate modules which service this routine are identified when the SELECT PROCESS module is complete. The final module to be designed might be the routine that determines when the SELECT PROCESS module is to be executed.

Regardless of which alternative is selected to begin the design of procedures, the guidelines of structured program development should be followed. The result will be easily implemented, maintainable, and clear programs.

Summary

As program development has become more costly, tools and techniques have been developed that aid the programmer in the program development. The program-development cycle generally includes at least three distinct (but perhaps overlapping) phases—analysis, implementation, and modification and maintenance. During the analysis phase both program flowcharting and structured programming have been used as planning and cost-reduction tools.

Program flowcharting is a means of representing the logic of a problem in a block diagram form which includes blocks or symbols, notations, and flowlines. The intent of the flowchart is to demonstrate the operation to be performed and the interrelationships between operations. Flowcharts have many advantages including the capability for the programmer to trace his logic through the diagram, the conservation of programmer time, and enhanced documentation.

The discipline of structured programming is enforced through three fundamental program structures: (a) simple sequence, (b) if-then-else, and (c) do-while. The do-while structure is translated into a do-until in COBOL. These three structures may be augmented by the case structure when the program involves a "select one from a set" situation.

The structured approach also provides several advantages including the division of the procedure into small concise subproblems; functional orientation of modules; and the ability to easily divide programming among several programmers. Also, execution and logic errors may be isolated more quickly, and the procedure may be coded and tested in stages. For ease of implementation, hierarchy charts are available to provide the overall interrelationships of modules, and program flowcharts are redesigned into module flowcharts with single entry and exit points.

Notes on Programming Style

Beyond raw intelligence, three factors seem to play a role in learning how to write programs. The first factor is experience—on-the-job training. Learning from mistakes is admittedly painful at times and time consuming, but one rarely makes the same mistake twice, and a certain amount of knowledge gained in the solution to one problem can be directly transported to the next problem, and so on.

The second factor is planning. "Playing computer" (tracing the process step by step as the computer will do when it executes your solution) to determine strengths and weaknesses, even before committing to code, is a good method of planning a solution. Do not measure your progress toward solving a problem in lines of COBOL code, but rather in solutions to elements of the overall problem. Determine the shortcomings and pitfalls of each element of your solution, and plan contingencies for each.

It is often said that "he who codes last, codes best." So planning has an additional advantage—it helps you avoid a vested interest in work performed. Unfortunately, it is human nature to avoid scrapping a product in which a great deal of time (or money) is invested. When we spend a lot of time writing a computer program and later realize that our solution is not viable, we often attempt to "patch" it. Unfortunately, the more we patch a program, the less manageable it becomes. And, as we continue, it becomes increasingly harder to give up and try a new angle. Appropriate planning should help you avoid ever approaching this stage.

The third factor is closely related to planning. It is in essence a planning methodology called *recursive decomposition* or *stepwise refinement*. Recursive decomposition consists of breaking larger (perhaps more poorly defined) problems into smaller, clearly defined subproblems. One decomposing pass is made on each subproblem until each subproblem is clearly understood.

When viewed from the programming angle, the process is referred to as stepwise refinement. That is, a partial solution to the problem is devised, providing the basic structured for the ultimate solution. After the first partial solution has been implemented and tested, a new element is added to solve an additional aspect of the problem. The process continues one step at a time until all aspects of the problem have been incorporated into the solution.

Questions

Below, fill in the blank(s) with the appropriate word, words, or phrases.

1. The program development phase in which the procedure requirements are determined is called the _____ phase.

2. The process of transforming a planned approach to a problem into program code is called _____ .

3. Program errors are called _____ .

4. The implementation step in which the programmer determines whether or not his program will work is called _____ .

5. A(n) _____ is a technique for expressing the logic of a program in a block diagram form.

6. Flowcharting a problem has many advantages including (a) _____ , (b) _____, and (c) _____ .

7. When flowlines on a flowchart go from top to bottom or from left to right, _____ are generally omitted.

8. One of the advantages of _____ is that the programmer does not have to "solve" a problem in one step.

9. In a structured flowchart, a module should be _____ oriented.

10. Each module should have _____ entry and exit point(s).

11. The three basic structures used to design modules are (a) _____ , (b) _____ , and (c) _____ .

12. A(n) _____ is simply a representation in a procedure which will exist, but has not yet been coded.

13. Among the advantages of structured progamming are (a) _____ , (b) _____ , and (c) _____ .

14. A sequence structure describes processes which are in _____ form to be executed one after the other.

15. Decisions made in either a(n) _____ or a(n) _____ form suffer some type of limitation when compared to simple decision logic using independent tests.

16. A do-while structure repeats a process so long as a specified condition is _____ , while the do-until structure repeats the process so long as the condition is _____ .

17. A program variable used to control looping operations is often called a(n) _____ .

18. An overview of a procedure in logic-tree form is called a(n) _____ .

19. When a control module invokes (calls) an initialization module, execution resumes with the _____ module when the initialization module has been completed.

20. A subordinate module invoked by two or more superior modules is often referred to as a(n) _____ module.

21. The structure which indicates that one of a series of choices is to be selected is called the _____ structure.

Answer the following questions by circling either "T" for true or "F" for false.

T F 22. In most computer installations the cost of hardware exceeds the expenditure on software.
T F 23. Programs generally "work" the first time they are executed.
T F 24. A program flowchart is a tool used by a programmer to plan his program.
T F 25. Each block of a flowchart should contain a single program statement such as a MOVE statement.
T F 26. In a flowchart, a MOVE operation is normally represented by a parallelogram symbol.
T F 27. Structured flowcharts are oriented toward modules.
T F 28. A module should encompass as many functions as possible.
T F 29. Each module should have a specific beginning point, although multiple ending points are desirable.
T F 30. The intent of the do-while structure is to test conditions.
T F 31. The overall logic of a structured program may be gained from a control module.
T F 32. A hierarchy chart is not used to show relationships between modules, but rather the functional elements of each module.
T F 33. Flowlines of a flowchart indicate the interrelationships between blocks.
T F 34. Development of a program in a structured form from the highest-level to the lowest-level modules is called the _____ approach.

8 Coding the Basic Structures (The Relational IF and Simple PERFORM Statements)

This chapter will discuss the if-then-else structure through the use of the relational IF statement. Use of the do-until structure will also be described through the use of the simple PERFORM and the PERFORM/UNTIL statements. After completing this chapter, you will be acquainted with how the three structures typically used in a structured program are implemented in COBOL. Combinations of statements, including OPEN, CLOSE, READ, WRITE, and MOVE statements, form the simple sequence structure. The IF statement forms the if-then-else structure, and the PERFORM statements form the do-until structure.

IF Statements in General

Many programming applications require portions of a program to be executed under one set of circumstances, and other statements, under other circumstances. This "selective" execution of statements is made possible through IF statements. IF statements are capable of determining the relationships between data values and selecting "paths" of execution on the basis of those relationships. For example, if the programmer wants to perform one set of operations when data-value-1 is greater than data-value-2, an IF statement can be employed to "test" for this relationship.

Although there are four categories of conditions used to describe the test to be performed, only the relational form of the IF statement will be discussed in this chapter. The *relational test* examines the relationship between two or more data values (in less-than, equal-to, or greater-than form) to determine the appropriate action. The other forms of the IF statement (presented in Chapter 11) are referred to as the *sign test*, the *class test*, and the *condition-name test*. The sign test is used to determine whether a data value (represented by an identifier or an expression) is algebraically positive, negative, or zero. The class test is used to determine the type of data (numeric or alphabetic) contained in an identifier. The condition-name test is used to determine whether a pre-set condition is true or false, i.e., the presence or absence of a particular value associated with a condition-name.

The Relational Test

The format of the relational test, presented in Figure 8.1, includes a number of parts. The identifiers in the relational IF statement may be any type of data item (e.g., an elementary-item, group-name, or record-name), and elementary-items can be numeric, alphabetic, and alphanumeric. The literals may be numeric, non-numeric, or figurative constants. The arithmetic expressions must conform to the format for arithmetic expressions (see Chapter 10, the COMPUTE statement). Thus, the relationships that can be tested are numerous.

```
IF  {identifier-1          }                     {identifier-2          }
    {literal-1             }  relational-operator {literal-2             }
    {arithmetic-expression-1}                     {arithmetic-expression-2}

    {imperative-statement-1}  [     {imperative-statement-2}]
    {                      }  [ELSE {                      }]
    {NEXT SENTENCE         }  [     {NEXT SENTENCE         }]
```

Figure 8.1 Format of the Relational IF Statement

A relational operator must be specified between the items being compared. The relational operator indicates the relationship to be evaluated. The allowable relational operators are:

```
IS [NOT] GREATER THAN    or IS [NOT] >
IS [NOT] EQUAL TO        or IS [NOT] =
IS [NOT] LESS THAN       or IS [NOT] <
```

The reserved word IS is not required. The reserved word NOT is optional. NOT represents the logical negation of the statement. For example, if the relational operator NOT GREATER is indicated, the test could be considered to be equivalent to "less than or equal to." After the reserved word NOT, the relation to be tested is specified i.e., GREATER, EQUAL TO, LESS, or their symbols.

The portion of the IF statement that follows the second set of items is used to indicate the process(es) to be executed. Imperative-statement-1 (or NEXT SENTENCE) will be executed if the result of the comparison is *true*. Imperative-statement-2 (or NEXT SENTENCE) will be executed when the result is *false*. Each of the imperative statements may be either simple (single) statements or compound (multiple) statements. However, note that only one period should appear in the IF statement—at the end. When NEXT SENTENCE is provided in the place of an imperative statement, the statement that immediately follows the IF statement is executed. The NEXT SENTENCE phrase may be used for either the true or the false "branch"; however, there is no practical reason for the ELSE NEXT SENTENCE phrase as a false branch. (The next statement in the program will be executed by default in the event that the result of the comparison is false. Thus, the ELSE phrase can be omitted.) Furthermore, if either the true or the false branch is not an unconditional branching statement, (i.e., a GO TO statement) after the true or false branch is executed, the next sequential statement will be executed.

An example will help to clarify these points. Assume one wishes to execute the statement MOVE ZERO TO A if the value of A exceeds the value of B. If the value of A is not greater than B, the programmer wishes to execute the statement MOVE 1∅ TO A. Figure 8.2 illustrates the program steps necessary to perform this operation. In Case 1, an unconditional branch is executed on either the true condition or the false condition, thereby executing the appropriate statement. However, after the unconditional branch takes place (GO TO ZERO-A or GO TO MOVE-TO-A is executed), the flow of the program proceeds from two separate points. This could be desirable in some circumstances, but generally, it is better to maintain a singular flow through the program as in Case 2. In this IF statement, the operations to be executed on a true or a false condition are entered as imperative statements in the IF statement rather than as separate statements. After either the true or false branch is executed, the next operation is indicated by the statement immediately following the IF statement. Consequently, the major difference between Cases 1 and 2 is that Case 1 concludes with two possible directions while Case 2 yields only one, which, for the sake of program simplicity and control, is the type recommended.

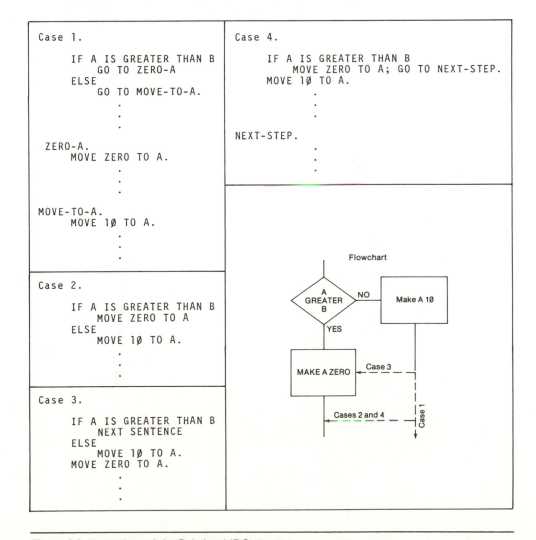

Figure 8.2 Illustrations of the Relational IF Statement

Case 3 of Figure 8.2 demonstates the use of NEXT SENTENCE. The result of this sequence is different from those in the two previous cases. In Case 3, if A is greater than B, A will be modified to zero. Otherwise, the value 1Ø is placed in A. The difference is that after the false branch is executed, the next operation is MOVE ZERO TO A—destroying the result produced by the false branch, obviously *not* the intent of the program. This form of the IF statement should be used only if the true and false branches do not modify the same data item.

The last case presented in Figure 8.2 provides only a true branch within the IF statement. However, the IF statement provides both true and false capabilities. In the event that A is greater than B, A is set to zero, and a branch to NEXT-STEP takes place. (Note that two COBOL statements have been coded in the true branch and are separated by a semicolon.) If A is not greater than B (the comparison is false) and there is no false branch, the next executable statement is encountered (MOVE 1Ø TO A). This produces a temporary two-direction path through the program with the paths merging at paragraph NEXT-STEP. Consequently, the *result* of Case 4 is the same as the result of Case 2; however, the form in Case 2 is still better from a structured programming standpoint.

Figure 8.3 illustrates the use of relational IF statements in a program. Assume the problem is to determine the letter grade of the course from a numeric average. For the purposes of this problem, any student averaging over 89.4 should receive an A. A student scoring between 89.4 and 79.5 (inclusive) should receive a B; between 79.4 and 69.5, a C; and so forth. (See Chapter 10 for a complete program.)

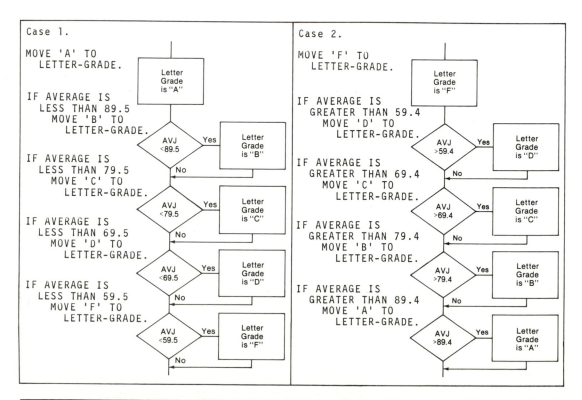

Figure 8.3 Illustrations of Relational IF Statements

In Figure 8.3, IF statements capable of making the proper letter-grade assignments based on the above information are shown. Both Case 1 and Case 2 are based on *default logic*. That is, when *all* possible outcomes for a set of decisions can be stated, it is necessary to test for all but one possible situation. In the case of letter-grade assignments, five grades are possible (A, B, C, D, and F). If a student is not assigned one of the first four grades, he must have received the fifth grade.

In Case 1 of Figure 8.3, the student is assigned a letter grade of A until subsequent decisions determine that the grade assignment should have been lower. The first IF statement may override the original letter-grade assignment if the average is less than 89.5. The letter-grade B then becomes the default grade until subsequent IF statements prove the assignment is incorrect. Consequently, the student is assigned successively lower letter grades until the appropriate grade is reached. After the correct assignment, all remaining IF statements will be false. For example, if the student's average was 75, the following sequence would be executed.

TEST	TEST RESULT	LETTER-GRADE
----	---	A
Average < 89.5	True	B
Average < 79.5	True	C
Average < 69.5	False	-
Average < 59.5	False	-

Thus, the last assigned letter grade would be a C.

Case 2 performs the same function as Case 1; however, the sequence begins with the assumption the student has earned the letter-grade F. The letter grade is altered upward if the average is higher than the numeric values associated with that letter grade. Thus , if the student's average was 75, the assignment of letter grades would be as follows:

TEST	TEST RESULTS	LETTER-GRADE
----	---	F
Average > 59.4	True	D
Average > 69.4	True	C
Average > 79.4	False	-
Average > 89.4	False	-

Compound IF Statements

Under some circumstances it is desirable to make a comparison between (or among) several data items. Perhaps a program requires two separate operations depending on the outcomes of several comparisons. To allow several sets to be compared within one IF statement, COBOL includes two logical operators—the reserved words AND and OR.

When two or more sets of relational conditions are combined using AND, and all conditions are true, the true branch of the IF statement is executed. (This type of operation is sometimes referred to as a logical or Boolean AND or the *union* of two or more sets.) When two or more sets of relational conditions are connected by the reserved word OR, and any condition is true, the true branch will be executed. (This is referred to as a logical, inclusive, or Boolean OR or the *intersection* of two or more sets.)

Suppose the requirements of a program called for a certain set of instructions to be executed when both A is greater than B and C is not equal to D. The COBOL IF statement could be written as

IF A IS GREATER THAN B AND C NOT = D true-instructions
ELSE false-instructions.

By the same token, suppose that a certain set of instructions was to be executed if *either* of the two relations stated above was true. Then this series of conditions could be written as two separate IF statements or a single statement, such as

IF A IS GREATER THAN B OR C NOT = D true-instructions
ELSE false-instructions.

In some cases, the coding of an IF statement becomes so complex a programmer becomes confused about how the compiler will interpret the instruction. For that reason, there is a six-step operation sequence for IF statements that indicates the order in which the statement will be evaluated. First, the programmer may specify the sequence of relationships to be evaluated by enclosing within parentheses those relationships to be examined first. The second component of the IF statement to be examined is arithmetic expressions, if present. Third, relational operators are examined. Fourth, NOT conditions are evaluated. Fifth, the portions of IF statements connected with the logical operator AND are analyzed. And finally any relationship connected by the logical operator OR is checked. If more than one AND or OR is present in a logical expression, the expression is evaluated from left to right.

The meaning of these relationships (using OR, AND, NOT, and parentheses) is presented in Table 8.1. In this table, two logical expressions are presented in conjunction with OR, AND, NOT, and parentheses. Suppose that the first logical expression is of the form ITEM1 LESS THAN ITEM2 (expression A), and the second logical expression is of the form ITEM3 EQUAL TO ITEM4 (expression B). Given these logical expressions, there are four possible outcomes. These combinations are:

Expression A	Expression B
True	True
True	False
False	True
False	False

Table 8.1 Results of the Evaluation of Logical Operators

A	B	A AND B	A OR B	NOT A	NOT (A AND B)	NOT A AND B	NOT (A OR B)	NOT A OR B
True	True	True	True	False	False	False	False	True
True	False	False	True	False	True	False	False	False
False	True	False	True	True	True	True	False	True
False	False	False	False	True	True	False	True	True

Often it is unnecessary to repeat the *subject* of an IF statement. In those circumstances where the same identifier, literal, or arithmetic expression (subject) is being compared to two or more objects in the test; it is unnecessary to repeat the subject; this is called an *implied* subject. For example, the statement

```
IF A LESS THAN B AND A GREATER THAN C . . .
```

has the same subject for two comparisons—A is the subject of two relationships. In this case, the statement could also be coded as:

```
IF A LESS THAN B AND GREATER THAN C . . .
```

Thus, the subject (A) was not repeated for the second relationship—it is assumed to be the same as for the previous relationship.

If the subject and relational operator are the same for several conditions, both the subject and the relational operator may be implied. For example, the statement

```
IF A IS EQUAL TO B AND A IS EQUAL TO C . . .
```

could be written such that both the subject and relational operator are assumed for the second relationship, i.e.,

```
IF A IS EQUAL TO B AND C . . .
```

Obviously, if the same subject and relational operator are used for three or more relationships, they may also be implied. However, the logical operator is not implied. This is true whether the logical connective is AND or OR.

Figure 8.4 illustrates the use of compound IF statements with a repeat of the letter-grade determination process. In this series of statements, each numeric average is placed in a bracket much the same as in the original statement of the problem. That is, the first IF statement examines the average to determine whether or not it is greater than 89.4. This statement could have been written:

```
IF AVERAGE IS GREATER THAN 89.5 OR AVERAGE IS EQUAL
    TO 89.5 MOVE 'A' TO LETTER-GRADE.
```

However, the same result is achieved by the noncompound IF statement in the example (assuming the PICTURE description of AVERAGE can contain no more than one digit following the decimal point—e.g., 999V9). Other IF statements in the example utilize the logical operator AND. For example, for a letter grade of B to be assigned, the average must be between (but should not include) 89.5 and 79.4. And, since each letter grade is placed in its own specific bracket, a fifth IF statement must be added to the sequence of tests. Thus, a letter grade of F is assigned in the last IF statement if the average is below 59.5.

Comparing Figure 8.3 with Figure 8.4, notice the different number of IF statements—four and five, respectively. However, use of compound IF statements, even with the extra IF statement, is more efficient because no erroneous letter grades are assigned in the progression from one IF statement to the next. Only one grade is assigned—the correct one!

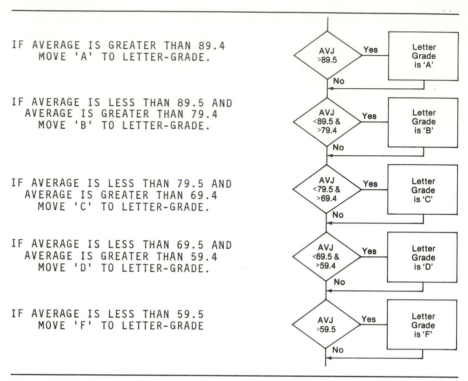

```
IF AVERAGE IS GREATER THAN 89.4
    MOVE 'A' TO LETTER-GRADE.


IF AVERAGE IS LESS THAN 89.5 AND
    AVERAGE IS GREATER THAN 79.4
    MOVE 'B' TO LETTER-GRADE.



IF AVERAGE IS LESS THAN 79.5 AND
    AVERAGE IS GREATER THAN 69.4
    MOVE 'C' TO LETTER-GRADE.



IF AVERAGE IS LESS THAN 69.5 AND
    AVERAGE IS GREATER THAN 59.4
    MOVE 'D' TO LETTER-GRADE.



IF AVERAGE IS LESS THAN 59.5
    MOVE 'F' TO LETTER-GRADE
```

Figure 8.4 Compound IF Statements

Nested IF Statements

The imperative statements used as the true and false branches of an IF statement may contain any type of statement in the COBOL language. True and false imperative statements may even contain other IF statements. A combination of IF statements leads to the *nested IF statement*. A nested IF statement is an IF statement that appears as the imperative statement of another IF statement.

This combination of IF statements is illustrated in Figure 8.5. In the letter-grade problem the relational IF statements (of Figure 8.3) can be replaced with one nested IF statement. Case 1 of Figure 8.5 presents the nesting of IF statements on false branches. In this case, as long as the responses to the conditions remain false, the next level of the statement (the next false branch) is examined. If, at any point in the chain of IF statements, a true branch is taken, the entire statement is terminated with the appropriate MOVE statement, and other false branches are not examined. This is the *affirmative* approach to the nesting of IF statements—that is, the positive action (or true branch) is closely coupled with the IF statement, which causes the completion of the "decision-making" process. This type of nested IF statement is very easy to understand and code. If an indention convention is used to begin the reserved words IF and ELSE in the same column, this grouping of IF statements should create a stair-step appearance in the program code. This approach makes understanding the nested IF statements and their relationship to each other a more manageable task.

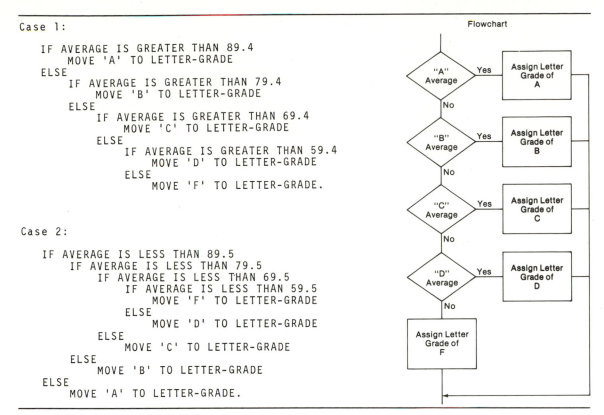

```
Case 1:

    IF AVERAGE IS GREATER THAN 89.4
        MOVE 'A' TO LETTER-GRADE
    ELSE
        IF AVERAGE IS GREATER THAN 79.4
            MOVE 'B' TO LETTER-GRADE
        ELSE
            IF AVERAGE IS GREATER THAN 69.4
                MOVE 'C' TO LETTER-GRADE
            ELSE
                IF AVERAGE IS GREATER THAN 59.4
                    MOVE 'D' TO LETTER-GRADE
                ELSE
                    MOVE 'F' TO LETTER-GRADE.


Case 2:

    IF AVERAGE IS LESS THAN 89.5
        IF AVERAGE IS LESS THAN 79.5
            IF AVERAGE IS LESS THAN 69.5
                IF AVERAGE IS LESS THAN 59.5
                    MOVE 'F' TO LETTER-GRADE
                ELSE
                    MOVE 'D' TO LETTER-GRADE
            ELSE
                MOVE 'C' TO LETTER-GRADE
        ELSE
            MOVE 'B' TO LETTER-GRADE
    ELSE
        MOVE 'A' TO LETTER-GRADE.
```

Figure 8.5 Nested Relational IF Statements

The second method of nesting IF statements is to use the true branch for coding imbedded IF's (Case 2 of Figure 8.5). In this form, one IF statement is immediately followed by another. This is the *negative* approach to coding nested IF statements, since the false branch of each statement is separated from the true branch by one or more intervening IF statements. This nested IF statement appears much like brackets, where one IF statement falls totally within the code of another. If the code indention procedure illustrated in Case 2 of Figure 8.5 is used, the connection between true and false branches of the parent IF statement is somewhat more easily determined; however, this type of nesting of IF statement is still much more difficult to code properly and understand than the form presented in Case 1. If coded correctly and all true and false branches are present, the code should appear as a V-shape.

PERFORM Statements in General

The PERFORM statement allows a programmer to execute one or more contiguous procedures (paragraphs or sections), which are not necessarily physically close to the location of the PERFORM statement itself. The capabilities of the PERFORM statement far exceed those of the simple GO TO statement. The GO TO statement permits the execution of a procedure, that is not the next sequential procedure, but it does not provide any further control of the execution of a program, once the GO TO itself has been executed. The

```
Format 1:   The Simple PERFORM Statement

    PERFORM procedure-name-1     ⎡⎧THROUGH⎫  procedure-name-2⎤
                                 ⎣⎩THRU   ⎭                  ⎦
──────────────────────────────────────────────────────────────

Format 2:   The PERFORM/UNTIL Statement

    PERFORM procedure-name-1     ⎡⎧THROUGH⎫  procedure-name-2⎤ UNTIL condition-1
                                 ⎣⎩THRU   ⎭                  ⎦
```

Figure 8.6 Formats of the PERFORM Statement

PERFORM statement, on the other hand, regains control of execution after the procedure or procedures have been completed. When all operations within the procedure are completed, execution continues from a point immediately after the PERFORM statement. Thus, the PERFORM statement permits a programmer to "go to" a particular procedure or set of procedures and "return" to the location of the PERFORM statement after the procedure has been completed.

Although there are four formats of the PERFORM statement, only the two most frequently used in structured programs are described in this chapter (see Figure 8.6). The remaining two are discussed in Chapter 12. All PERFORM formats have one phrase in common—the name(s) of the procedure(s) to be executed. In Figure 8.6, Format 1 of the PERFORM statement (and the other formats, as well) shows that, at a minimum, procedure-name-1 must be specified. A procedure-name is a paragraph or SECTION name located in the PROCEDURE DIVISION. The procedure may be located either above or below the PERFORM statement itself. The PERFORM statement may never specify the procedure-name containing itself unless precautions are taken to avoid an endless loop.

If the optional phrase THROUGH (THRU) procedure-name-2 is specified, procedure-name-2 is a paragraph or SECTION name that is physically below (but not necessarily immediately below) procedure-name-1. The THROUGH option should be avoided where possible to improve program clarity and maintenance. The statements in either procedure-name-1 or procedure-name-2 may be any COBOL statements, including GO TO statements and other PERFORM statements.

The Simple PERFORM Statement

The Format-1 PERFORM statement is terminated (control passes to the statement following the PERFORM statement) when the last statement in the specified set of procedures is executed, resulting in the logical effect of the insertion of the statements in the set of procedures at the location of the PERFORM statement. The same PERFORM statement could appear at several locations in a program (e.g., a utility or service module) without repetition of the procedure. The PERFORM statement may be placed anywhere in the PROCEDURE DIVISION, even imbedded in sentences or imperative statements.

Figure 8.7 illustrates how the simple PERFORM statement might be used in a program. This figure presents a series of example PERFORM statements. For a more complete understanding of the sequence of operation of these statements, review the list of procedures executed. Also, remember that when a PERFORM has completed execution, *control* of the program *returns* to the statement immediately following the PERFORM statement. Thus, unless some provision is placed in a program to avoid re-execution of procedures following the PERFORM statement, they will be executed again.

In Figure 8.7a, the TERMINATION paragraph is invoked by a PERFORM statement. When the next paragraph-name is encountered (or the physical end of the program is reached), procedural control is passed to the statement following the PERFORM statement. The STOP RUN statement is executed, and the program is halted. In this particular example, the TERMINATION paragraph may include operations such as report footings, a summary report, or file closings.

Figure 8.7b illustrates what happens when a PERFORM operation is not protected from "fall through." The sequence indicates that GET-A-RECORD is executed twice—once as a result of the PERFORM and once because GET-A-RECORD follows the PERFORM statement.

In Figure 8.7c the sequence of paragraphs executed begins with a series of paragraphs. Only after the PROCEDURE-BODY paragraph is encountered is a PERFORM statement executed. However, in this case, the paragraph being performed is located above the PERFORM statement itself. Thus, when the PAGE-HEADING paragraph is invoked by the PERFORM statement, execution will remain in the paragraph until the next paragraph (PROCEDURE-BODY) is reached. Then execution continues in the PROCEDURE-BODY paragraph at a point immediately following the PERFORM statement. From there, execution proceeds sequentially to the EOJ paragraph.

Figure 8.7d illustrates the THROUGH (THRU) option. Although similar to Figure 8.7a this example causes the execution of a series of paragraphs under the control of the PERFORM statement. Execution begins with the PERFORM statement, which causes SUMMARY-REPORT to be invoked. Control, under these circumstances, does not return to the point after the PERFORM statement until the last statement of FILE-CLOSINGS has been executed.

Figure 8.7e is similar to Figure 8.7d in that the PERFORM statement causes a series of paragraphs to be executed; however, the first paragraph (FED-WITHHOLDING) is physically separated from the last paragraph to be executed (DEDUCTS) by an intervening paragraph (FICA-CALCULATIONS).

Figure 8.7f illustrates multiple PERFORM statements in one procedure. The first PERFORM statement caused the execution of three paragraphs (READ-A-RECORD, WRITE-A-RECORD, and MOVE-DATA). After the first PERFORM has been completed, the second PERFORM invokes the READ-A-RECORD paragraph. Despite the reference to the paragraph in a previous PERFORM statement, the use of the paragraph name is not restricted in other PERFORM statements even though the context of its use may be different. Thus, when READ-A-RECORD has been completed, the third PERFORM

PROCEDURE DIVISION STRUCTURE	SEQUENCE OF PARAGRAPHS EXECUTED

a)
```
        PERFORM TERMINATION.─────────────────────TERMINATION
        STOP RUN
            ⋛
     TERMINATION.
            ⋛
```

b)
```
        PERFORM GET-A-RECORD.────────────────────GET-A-RECORD
     GET-A-RECORD.                 (fall through) GET-A-RECORD
            ⋛
```

c)
```
     PAGE-HEADING.                 (fall through)⎰PAGE-HEADING
            ⋛                                      ⎱PROCEDURE-BODY
     PROCEDURE-BODY.                               PAGE-HEADING
            ⋛                      (fall through)  EOJ
         PERFORM PAGE-HEADING.
            ⋛
     EOJ.
            ⋛
```

d)
```
        PERFORM SUMMARY-REPORT THRU FILE-CLOSINGS.─⎰SUMMARY-REPORT
        STOP RUN.                                   ⎱FILE-CLOSINGS
     SUMMARY-REPORT.
            ⋛

     FILE-CLOSINGS.
            ⋛
```

e)
```
        PERFORM FED-WITHHOLDING THROUGH DEDUCTS.──⎰FED-WITHHOLDING
        STOP RUN.                                  ⎨FICA-CALCULATION
     FED-WITHHOLDING.                              ⎩DEDUCTS
            ⋛
     FICA-CALCULATION.
            ⋛
     DEDUCTS.
            ⋛
```

f)
```
        PERFORM READ-A-RECORD THRU MOVE-DATA.──⎰READ-A-RECORD
        PERFORM READ-A-RECORD.                  ⎨WRITE-A-RECORD
        PERFORM WRITE-A-RECORD.                 ⎩MOVE-DATA
     READ-A-RECORD.                             READ-A-RECORD
            ⋛                                   WRITE-A-RECORD
     WRITE-A-RECORD.                            ⎰READ-A-RECORD
            ⋛                                   ⎪WRITE-A-RECORD
     MOVE-DATA.                  (fall through)⎨MOVE-DATA
            ⋛                                   ⎩EOJ
     EOJ.
            ⋛
```

g)
```
        PERFORM UNIT-1.                          ⎰UNIT-1
        PERFORM UNIT-4.                          ⎰UNIT-2
        STOP RUN.                                 UNIT-4
     UNIT-1.                                      ⎱UNIT-3
            ⋛                                     ⎰UNIT-3
         PERFORM UNIT-2 THRU UNIT-3.             ⎰UNIT-4
            ⋛                                     ⎱UNIT-3
     UNIT-2.
            ⋛
         PERFORM UNIT-4.
            ⋛
     UNIT-3.
            ⋛
     UNIT-4.
            ⋛
         PERFORM UNIT-3.
```

Figure 8.7 Illustrations of the Simple PERFORM Statement

statement is executed, and WRITE-A-RECORD is invoked. Finally, once WRITE-A-RECORD has been completed, a "fall through" causes the repeated execution of all four remaining paragraphs.

The final illustration, Figure 8.7g, demonstrates PERFORM statements being performed within paragraphs. When UNIT-1 is executed as a result of the first PERFORM statement, another PERFORM statement is encountered. The second PERFORM statement (PERFORM UNIT-2 THRU UNIT-3) invokes UNIT-2. While UNIT-2 is being executed, a third PERFORM statement is encountered, which causes UNIT-4 to be invoked. Finally, during the execution of UNIT-4, a fourth PERFORM is discovered, causing the execution of UNIT-3 to begin. At this point, all four PERFORM statements are "active" and an "unfolding" operation begins. When UNIT-3 is completed, execution of UNIT-4 resumes. When UNIT-4 is completed, execution of UNIT-2 resumes. When UNIT-2 is completed, execution of UNIT-3 begins (for the second time) because the PERFORM which originally invoked this operation was PERFORM UNIT-2 THRU UNIT-3. When UNIT-3 is completed for the second time, execution of UNIT-1 resumes. When UNIT-1 is completed, execution proceeds with the statement that originally caused UNIT-1 to be invoked. Thus, the statement PERFORM UNIT-4 is executed, causing UNIT-4 to be invoked. Again, during the execution of UNIT-4, a PERFORM statement invoking UNIT-3 is encountered. UNIT-3 is completed, UNIT-4 is resumed and completed, the original PERFORM statement is thus completed, and finally STOP RUN is encountered.

The PERFORM/ UNIT Statement

The second format of the PERFORM statement, the PERFORM/UNTIL, allows the programmer to control, from within the procedure itself, the number of times a procedure is executed. As indicated in Format 2 of Figure 8.6, the PERFORM/UNTIL statement provides for the testing of a specified condition. The condition itself may be any condition or combination of conditions permitted within the context of an IF statement. Thus, the condition in a PERFORM/UNTIL statement might be a relational condition, a sign condition, a class condition, or a condition-name condition. The condition is tested by the PERFORM statement *when the PERFORM statement is encountered and prior to each execution of the procedure* specified in the PERFORM statement.

Figure 8.8 illustrates the PERFORM/UNTIL statement. Note that where the PERFORM/UNTIL statement is used, a statement (or combination of statements) in some way affects the condition specified in the PERFORM/UNTIL statement.

In Figure 8.8a, the data-name DAYS is used to control the performed activity. DAYS is initialized in a MOVE statement (DAYS=1) and the PERFORM statement is encountered. If, at this point, DAYS is greater than five, WEEKDAYS is not performed at all. However, since DAYS is equal to one, the PERFORM statement invokes WEEKDAYS, which is repeatedly executed until DAYS is greater than five. While executing WEEKDAYS, an ADD statement is encountered (The ADD statement is discussed in detail in Chapter 10) and DAYS is incremented by one. At this point, DAYS is equal to two, thus WEEKDAYS is repeated. When DAYS=6 and the end of the WEEKDAYS paragraph is encountered, the condition is true, the PERFORM statement is terminated, and the STOP RUN statement is encountered.

The second illustration, Figure 8.8b, demonstrates the use of multiple PERFORM/UNTIL statements. The sequence begins when NUM is initialized to

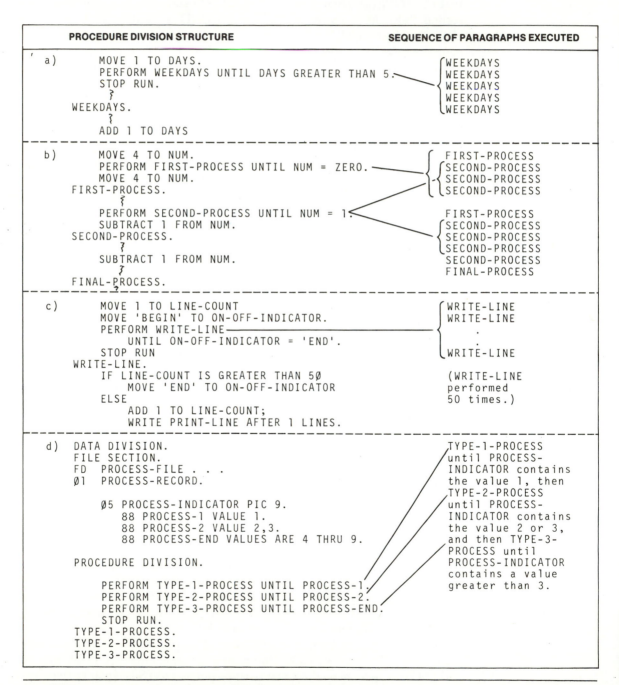

Figure 8.8 Illustrations of the PERFORM/UNTIL Statement

four. The first PERFORM statement is then encountered. In this instance the condition uses a sign test based on the value of NUM. Thus, FIRST-PROCESS continues to be executed until NUM has been decremented to zero. However, while FIRST-PROCESS is being executed for the first time, PERFORM SECOND-PROCESS is encountered. The condition necessary for the termination of SECOND-PROCESS is for NUM to be equal to one. While SECOND-PROCESS is being executed, a SUBTRACT statement is encountered, which decrements the value of NUM each time SECOND-PROCESS is executed. (The SUBTRACT statement is described in detail in Chapter 10.) As a consequence, SECOND-PROCESS will be executed three times before NUM is equal to one at the end of the paragraph. After SECOND-PROCESS has been completed, execution of FIRST-PROCESS resumes, where NUM is again decremented (and NUM should contain a value of zero). Thus, the first time the end of FIRST-PROCESS is encountered, the condition specified for no longer executing the paragraph is true. Again, the value of four is moved to NUM and execution "falls through" to the FIRST-PROCESS paragraph. Within FIRST-PROCESS, SECOND-PROCESS is again repeated three times. However, when the PERFORM SECOND-PROCESS has been completed, the procedure falls through SECOND-PROCESS to the FINAL-PROCESS paragraph.

A few comments about Figure 8.8b: first, it is not often desirable to have several perform statements controlled in a "nested" arrangement, especially when all the procedures have the opportunity to modify the same "control" data-name. The nested control structure is generally difficult to construct properly, it rarely works the first time executed, and it is a nightmare to maintain. Second, the conditions "NUM = ZERO" and "NUM = 1" are dangerous because if the SUBTRACT statement were eliminated accidentally from the illustration, the procedure would be executed until it was canceled by the computer operator or the program time limit was exceeded. To make the procedure self-checking, the first condition could be stated in terms of "LESS THAN OR EQUAL TO 1" and the second condition could test for "LESS THAN OR EQUAL TO 1." Finally, procedure "fall through," used extensively in this illustration, should be reduced (if not totally eliminated) in favor of more explicit control structures. For example, the execution sequence achieved in this illustration could be created by totally separating the execution of FIRST-PROCESS from SECOND-PROCESS (e.g., PERFORM FIRST-PROCESS and then PERFORM SECOND-PROCESS).

The third illustration, Figure 8.8c, is controlled by an interrelationship between the values of two data-names—LINE-COUNT and ON-OFF-INDICATOR. LINE-COUNT is initialized to one, and ON-OFF-INDICATOR is set to "BEGIN" to start the procedure. The next statement initiates the execution of the WRITE-LINE paragraph. Within the WRITE-LINE paragraph, LINE-COUNT is tested to determine if it exceeds 50. When LINE-COUNT is 50 or less, one is added to LINE-COUNT, and a line is written to a line printer. When LINE-COUNT is greater than 50, "END" is moved to ON-OFF-INDICATOR, the UNTIL condition is true when the end of the WRITE-LINE paragraph is reached, and the procedure is terminated. Also note that since LINE-COUNT is initialized to 1 and incremented by 1 *before* the first line is written, only 50 lines of output will be printed.

In Figure 8.8d, the final example, condition-name conditions (and names) are used to control the procedure. (Condition-name tests are discussed in Chapter 11.) Because the content of input records is not shown, the precise number of iterations of each process cannot be determined. However, this much can be determined: (1) until the data-name PROCESS-INDICATOR is equal to 1, TYPE-1-PROCESS is executed; (2) until PROCESS-INDICATOR contains a value of 2 or 3, TYPE-2-PROCESS is executed; and (3) TYPE-3-PROCESS is executed until PROCESS-INDICATOR contains a value greater than 3.

The EXIT Statement

Some problems may require many possible paths through a set of procedures, while some systems (e.g., IBM) often require a PERFORM procedure to be terminated in a special manner. To satisfy both requirements for the use of the PERFORM statement, a common ending point is required. That is, regardless of the logical processes in several paragraphs or sections being performed, the procedure must have a single point at which it begins (procedure-name-1) and a single point at which it ends (procedure-name-2). COBOL provides a common ending point through the EXIT statement. The EXIT statement is composed of a single reserved word—EXIT. To qualify as a common reference point, the EXIT statement *must be a single-statement sentence* and *must appear in a paragraph by itself* (see Figure 8.9). The EXIT statement serves no function other than as a common ending point for a series of procedures. Thus, it is possible to use the paragraph name containing the EXIT statement in a PERFORM statement as procedure-name-2. To complete a single execution of the procedure, it would be necessary to encounter procedure-name-2 (by branching to it or by encountering it serially) and execute the statement in procedure-name-2.

```
EXIT.
```

Figure 8.9 The EXIT Statement

An Example: Two-Up Mailing Labels

Figure 8.10 illustrates the use of the simple PERFORM and the PERFORM/ UNTIL statements. The procedure shown in this example is an embellishment on the one-up mailing-label program in Chapter 6. In Figure 8.10, two-up (side-by-side) labels are produced. Although the mailing-label programs are

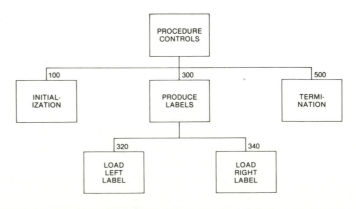

Figure 8.10 Two-Up Labels (Hierarchy Chart)

similar the procedure for multiple labels is logically more complex. Because it must read more than one record before a single label can be produced the procedure must be designed very carefully. For example, even though the reading of data is initialized in the same manner as in previous programs (line 620 of the PROCEDURE DIVISION), note that the procedure continues thereafter by reading two records in sequence (320-LOAD-LEFT-LABEL, lines 730–810, and 340-LOAD-RIGHT-LABEL, lines 820–900). In addition, it is possible that an odd number of labels may be produced, i.e., data may be available for the left label, but not the right label. Thus, the procedure must not attempt to read past the end-of-file, and it must insure that all labels are printed—even if data is available for only one label of a two-label set.

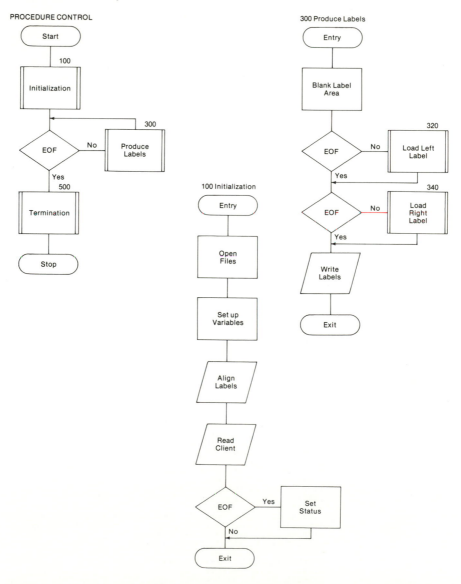

Figure 8.10 Two-Up Labels (Module Flowcharts) *Continued*

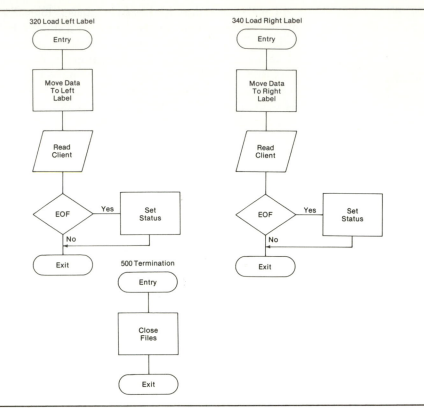

Figure 8.10 Two-Up Labels (Module Flowcharts) *Continued*

```
----------------------------------------------------------------------------
|         1  1   2   2   2   3   3   4   4   4   5   5   6   6   6   7   7   8|
|  4   8  2  6   0   4   8   2   6   0   4   8   2   6   0   4   8   2   6   0|
----------------------------------------------------------------------------
|000010 IDENTIFICATION DIVISION.                                   FIG 8.10|
|000020 PROGRAM-ID. TWO-UP-LABELS.                                 FIG 8.10|
|000030 DATE-WRITTEN. JANUARY 1, 1981.                             FIG 8.10|
|000040 DATE-COMPILED JANUARY 1, 1981.                             FIG 8.10|
|000050 ENVIRONMENT DIVISION.                                      FIG 8.10|
|000060 CONFIGURATION SECTION.                                     FIG 8.10|
|000070 SOURCE-COMPUTER. HONEYWELL.                                FIG 8.10|
|000080 OBJECT-COMPUTER. HONEYWELL.                                FIG 8.10|
|000090 SPECIAL-NAMES. *1* IS ALIGNING-LABELS.                     FIG 8.10|
|000100 INPUT-OUTPUT SECTION.                                      FIG 8.10|
|000110 FILE-CONTROL.                                              FIG 8.10|
|000120     SELECT CLIENT-FILE ASSIGN TO CARD-READER.             FIG 8.10|
|000130     SELECT TWO-UP-LABELS ASSIGN TO PRINTER.               FIG 8.10|
|000140 DATA DIVISION.                                             FIG 8.10|
|000150 FILE SECTION.                                              FIG 8.10|
|000160 FD  CLIENT-FILE LABEL RECORDS ARE OMITTED.                FIG 8.10|
|000170 01  CLIENT-RECORD.                                         FIG 8.10|
|000180     02 CLIENT-NAME          PIC X(20).                    FIG 8.10|
|000190     02 CLIENT-ADDRESS       PIC X(30).                    FIG 8.10|
|000200     02 CLIENT-CITY          PIC X(20).                    FIG 8.10|
|000210     02 CLIENT-STATE         PIC X(02).                    FIG 8.10|
|000220     02 CLIENT-ZIP           PIC X(05).                    FIG 8.10|
|000230     02 FILLER               PIC X(03).                    FIG 8.10|
|000240 FD  TWO-UP-LABELS LABEL RECORDS ARE OMITTED.              FIG 8.10|
|000250 01  LABEL-LINE              PIC X(133).                   FIG 8.10|
|000260 WORKING-STORAGE SECTION.                                   FIG 8.10|
|000270 01  RECORD-STATUS-INDICATOR.                              FIG 8.10|
|000280     02 FILE-STATUS          PIC X(20).                    FIG 8.10|
|000290 01  LINES-OF-THE-LABEL.                                   FIG 8.10|
|000300     02 LINE-1.                                            FIG 8.10|
|000310        04 FILLER            PIC X(05).                    FIG 8.10|
|000320        04 LEFT-LINE-1       PIC X(30).                    FIG 8.10|
```

Figure 8.10 Two-Up Labels *Continued*

```
|        1 1 2 2 2 3 3 4 4 4 5 5 6 6 6 7 7 8|
|  4   8 2 6 0 4 8 2 6 0 4 8 2 6 0 4 8 2 6 0|
|000330          04 FILLER              PIC X(05).                  FIG 8.10|
|000340          04 RIGHT-LINE-1        PIC X(30).                  FIG 8.10|
|000350       02 LINE-2.                                            FIG 8.10|
|000360          04 FILLER              PIC X(05).                  FIG 8.10|
|000370          04 LEFT-LINE-2         PIC X(30).                  FIG 8.10|
|000380          04 FILLER              PIC X(05).                  FIG 8.10|
|000390          04 RIGHT-LINE-2        PIC X(30).                  FIG 8.10|
|000400       02 LINE-3.                                            FIG 8.10|
|000410          04 FILLER              PIC X(05).                  FIG 8.10|
|000420          04 LEFT-LINE-3         PIC X(30).                  FIG 8.10|
|000430          04 FILLER              PIC X(05).                  FIG 8.10|
|000440          04 RIGHT-LINE-3        PIC X(30).                  FIG 8.10|
|000450 01  ORGANIZE-CITY-STATE-ZIP.                                FIG 8.10|
|000460       02 CITY-PART              PIC X(20).                  FIG 8.10|
|000470       02 FILLER                 PIC X(02) VALUE ', '.       FIG 8.10|
|000480       02 STATE-PART             PIC X(02).                  FIG 8.10|
|000490       02 FILLER                 PIC X(01) VALUE SPACE.      FIG 8.10|
|000500       02 ZIP-PART               PIC X(05).                  FIG 8.10|
|000510 PROCEDURE DIVISION.                                         FIG 8.10|
|000520 PROCEDURE-CONTROL.                                          FIG 8.10|
|000530       PERFORM 100-INITIALIZATION.                           FIG 8.10|
|000540       PERFORM 300-PRODUCE-LABELS                            FIG 8.10|
|000550          UNTIL FILE-STATUS = 'PROCESS COMPLETE'.            FIG 8.10|
|000560       PERFORM 500-TERMINATION.                              FIG 8.10|
|000570       STOP RUN.                                             FIG 8.10|
|000580 100-INITIALIZATION.                                         FIG 8.10|
|000590       OPEN INPUT CLIENT-FILE, OUTPUT TWO-UP-LABELS.         FIG 8.10|
|000600       MOVE SPACES TO LABEL-LINE.                            FIG 8.10|
|000610       WRITE LABEL-LINE AFTER ALIGNING-LABELS.               FIG 8.10|
|000620       MOVE 'PROCESSING' TO FILE-STATUS.                     FIG 8.10|
|000630       READ CLIENT-FILE AT END                               FIG 8.10|
|000640          MOVE 'PROCESS COMPLETE' TO FILE-STATUS.            FIG 8.10|
|000650 300-PRODUCE-LABELS.                                         FIG 8.10|
|000660       MOVE SPACES TO LINE-1, LINE-2, LINE-3.                FIG 8.10|
|000670       IF FILE-STATUS = 'PROCESSING'                         FIG 8.10|
|000680          PERFORM 320-LOAD-LEFT-LABEL.                       FIG 8.10|
|000690       IF FILE-STATUS = 'PROCESSING'                         FIG 8.10|
|000700          PERFORM 340-LOAD-RIGHT-LABEL.                      FIG 8.10|
|000710       WRITE LABEL-LINE FROM LINE-1 AFTER ADVANCING 2 LINES. FIG 8.10|
|000720       WRITE LABEL-LINE FROM LINE-2 AFTER ADVANCING 1 LINES. FIG 8.10|
|000730       WRITE LABEL-LINE FROM LINE-3 AFTER ADVANCING 1 LINES. FIG 8.10|
|000740 320-LOAD-LEFT-LABEL.                                        FIG 8.10|
|000750       MOVE CLIENT-NAME TO LEFT-LINE-1.                      FIG 8.10|
|000760       MOVE CLIENT-ADDRESS TO LEFT-LINE-2.                   FIG 8.10|
|000770       MOVE CLIENT-CITY TO CITY-PART.                        FIG 8.10|
|000780       MOVE CLIENT-STATE TO STATE-PART.                      FIG 8.10|
|000790       MOVE CLIENT-ZIP TO ZIP-PART.                          FIG 8.10|
|000800       MOVE ORGANIZE-CITY-STATE-ZIP TO LEFT-LINE-3.          FIG 8.10|
|000810       READ CLIENT-FILE AT END                               FIG 8.10|
|000820          MOVE 'PROCESS COMPLETE' TO FILE-STATUS.            FIG 8.10|
|000830 340-LOAD-RIGHT-LABEL.                                       FIG 8.10|
|000840       MOVE CLIENT-NAME TO RIGHT-LINE-1.                     FIG 8.10|
|000850       MOVE CLIENT-ADDRESS TO RIGHT-LINE-2.                  FIG 8.10|
|000860       MOVE CLIENT-CITY TO CITY-PART.                        FIG 8.10|
|000870       MOVE CLIENT-STATE TO STATE-PART.                      FIG 8.10|
|000880       MOVE CLIENT-ZIP TO ZIP-PART.                          FIG 8.10|
|000890       MOVE ORGANIZE-CITY-STATE-ZIP TO RIGHT-LINE-3.         FIG 8.10|
|000900       READ CLIENT-FILE AT END                               FIG 8.10|
|000910          MOVE 'PROCESS COMPLETE' TO FILE-STATUS.            FIG 8.10|
|000920 500-TERMINATION.                                            FIG 8.10|
|000930       CLOSE CLIENT-FILE, TWO-UP-LABELS.                     FIG 8.10|
```

Figure 8.10 Two-Up Labels *Continued*

```
|       |        1         2         3         4         5         6         7         8| FIGURE  |
|RECORD |12345678901234567890123456789012345678901234567890123456789012345678901234567890| NUMBER  |
|    1|CINDY ALLAN       520 TRAILDUST ROAD       DALLAS            TX75222    |FIG 8.10|
|    2|DANA ARMSTRONG    9396 MOCKINGBIRD LN.      DALLAS            TX75234    |FIG 8.10|
|    3|GARY BRYAN        CANYON EXPRESSWAY         AMARILLO          TX79220    |FIG 8.10|
|    4|RALPH P. COMSTOCK 852 E. 14TH STREET        STUART            TX72059    |FIG 8.10|
|    5|DAVID DAVIDSON    552 DOVER DRIVE           PARIS             TX78563    |FIG 8.10|
|    6|PHILLIP P. HARRISON 2219 W. 7TH STREET      PERRYTON          TX79070    |FIG 8.10|
|    7|CHARLOTTE HELM    579 LAKE ROAD             BROWNSVILLE       TX74329    |FIG 8.10|
|    8|MICHAEL POOLE     2549 MUNSON STREET        WACO              TX79568    |FIG 8.10|
|    9|LARRY K. SPENCE   509 44TH STREET APT. 21   GRUVER            TX79021    |FIG 8.10|
|   10|PATRICK THOMAS    335 TEASLEY LANE          DENTON            TX79201    |FIG 8.10|
|   11|MARTHA WORKMAN    1444 COLGATE AVE.         TULIA             TX79321    |FIG 8.10|
```

Figure 8.10 Two-Up Labels (Data) *Continued*

```
CINDY ALLAN                          DANA ARMSTRONG
520 TRAILDUST ROAD                   9396 MOCKINGBIRD LN.
DALLAS                , TX 75222     DALLAS              , TX 75234

GARY BRYAN                           RALPH P. COMSTOCK
CANYON EXPRESSWAY                    852 E. 14TH STREET
AMARILLO              , TX 79220     STUART              , TX 72059

DAVID DAVIDSON                       PHILLIP P. HARRISON
552 DOVER DRIVE                      2219 W. 7TH STREET
PARIS                 , TX 78563     PERRYTON            , TX 79070

CHARLOTTE HELM                       MICHAEL POOLE
579 LAKE ROAD                        2549 MUNSON STREET
BROWNSVILLE           , TX 74329     WACO                , TX 79568

LARRY K. SPENCE                      PATRICK THOMAS
509 44TH STREET APT. 21              335 TEASLEY LANE
GRUVER                , TX 79021     DENTON              , TX 79201

MARTHA WORKMAN
1444 COLGATE AVE.
TULIA                 , TX 79321
```

Figure 8.10 Two-Up Labels (Output) *Continued*

The Control Break

A process common to many programs is the control break. The control break is a process through which an out-of-the-ordinary programming situation is executed. For example, examine Figure 8.11. This program produces a simple listing of employees. However, the employees are to be listed by department. So, the data must be arranged by department. The control break is executed when the value in the department field *changes*. Thus, so long as the department value stays the same, the program does nothing out of the ordinary. Examine the COBOL program for a moment. The control-break process is accomplished by the statement on lines 670 and 680. Upon encountering this statement the first time, note that DEPT-NO-IN (defined at line 180) contains a value by virtue of the READ statement at line 640. However, PREVIOUS-DEPT (defined at line 280) contains no previously defined value. As a result, the first page heading is produced. Thus, this control break produces output *ahead* of the actual printing of information regarding the department. To perform the control break *after* the department changes (e.g., subtotals by department), all that is necessary is to move the DEPT-NO-IN value to the PREVIOUS-DEPT field immediately after the READ statement at line 640.

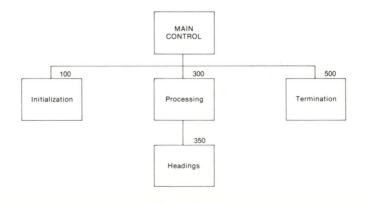

Figure 8.11 Employee Report by Department (Hierarchy Chart)

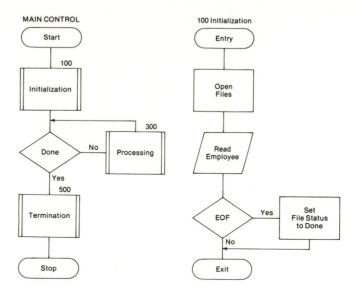

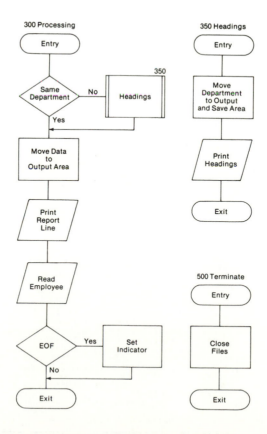

Figure 8.11 Employee Report by Department (Module Flowcharts) *Continued*

```
-----------------------------------------------------------------------
|        1   1   2   2   2   3   3   4   4   4   5   5   6   6   6   7   7   8|
|  4   8   2   6   0   4   8   2   6   0   4   8   2   6   0   4   8   2   6   0|
|000010 IDENTIFICATION DIVISION.                                    FIG 8.11|
|000020 PROGRAM-ID. BREAKER.                                        FIG 8.11|
|000030 ENVIRONMENT DIVISION.                                       FIG 8.11|
|000040 CONFIGURATION SECTION.                                      FIG 8.11|
|000050 SOURCE-COMPUTER. IBM-3033.                                  FIG 8.11|
|000060 OBJECT-COMPUTER. IBM-3033.                                  FIG 8.11|
|000070 SPECIAL-NAMES.                                              FIG 8.11|
|000080     C01 IS PAGE-TOP.                                        FIG 8.11|
|000090 INPUT-OUTPUT SECTION.                                       FIG 8.11|
|000100 FILE-CONTROL.                                               FIG 8.11|
|000110     SELECT EMPLOYEE ASSIGN TO UT-S-DATA1.                   FIG 8.11|
|000120     SELECT DEPT-REPORT ASSIGN TO UT-S-PROUT.                FIG 8.11|
|000130 DATA DIVISION.                                              FIG 8.11|
|000140 FILE SECTION.                                               FIG 8.11|
|000150 FD  EMPLOYEE                                                FIG 8.11|
|000160     LABEL RECORDS ARE OMITTED.                              FIG 8.11|
|000170 01  INPUT-REC.                                              FIG 8.11|
|000180     05  DEPT-NO-IN            PIC X(05).                    FIG 8.11|
|000190     05  EMP-NO-IN             PIC X(05).                    FIG 8.11|
|000200     05  EMP-NAME-IN           PIC X(20).                    FIG 8.11|
|000210     05  FILLER                PIC X(50).                    FIG 8.11|
|000220 FD  DEPT-REPORT                                             FIG 8.11|
|000230     LABEL RECORDS ARE OMITTED.                              FIG 8.11|
|000240 01  PRINT-LINE.                                             FIG 8.11|
|000250     05  FILLER                PIC X(133).                   FIG 8.11|
|000260 WORKING-STORAGE SECTION.                                    FIG 8.11|
|000270 01  WORKING-VARIABLES.                                      FIG 8.11|
|000280     05  PREVIOUS-DEPT         PIC X(05).                    FIG 8.11|
|000290     05  FILE-STATUS           PIC X(04) VALUE SPACES.       FIG 8.11|
|000300 01  HEADING1-REC.                                           FIG 8.11|
|000310     05  FILLER                PIC X(49) VALUE SPACES.       FIG 8.11|
|000320     05  FILLER                PIC X(20) VALUE               FIG 8.11|
|000330     'LEARNING COBOL, INC.'.                                 FIG 8.11|
|000340 01  HEADING2-REC.                                           FIG 8.11|
|000350     05  FILLER                PIC X(51) VALUE SPACES.       FIG 8.11|
|000360     05  FILLER                PIC X(10) VALUE 'DEPARTMENT'. FIG 8.11|
|000370     05  FILLER                PIC X(01) VALUE SPACES.       FIG 8.11|
|000380     05  DEPT-HEADING-OUT      PIC X(05).                    FIG 8.11|
|000390 01  HEADING3-REC.                                           FIG 8.11|
|000400     05  FILLER                PIC X(30) VALUE SPACES.       FIG 8.11|
|000410     05  FILLER                PIC X(10) VALUE 'DEPARTMENT'. FIG 8.11|
|000420     05  FILLER                PIC X(10) VALUE SPACES.       FIG 8.11|
|000430     05  FILLER                PIC X(15) VALUE               FIG 8.11|
|000440     'EMPLOYEE NUMBER'.                                      FIG 8.11|
|000450     05  FILLER                PIC X(10) VALUE SPACES.       FIG 8.11|
|000460     05  FILLER                PIC X(13) VALUE 'EMPLOYEE NAME'. FIG 8.11|
|000470 01  REPORT-LINE.                                            FIG 8.11|
|000480     05  FILLER                PIC X(32) VALUE SPACES.       FIG 8.11|
|000490     05  DEPT-NO-OUT           PIC X(05).                    FIG 8.11|
|000500     05  FILLER                PIC X(17) VALUE SPACES.       FIG 8.11|
|000510     05  EMP-NO-OUT            PIC X(05).                    FIG 8.11|
|000520     05  FILLER                PIC X(15) VALUE SPACES.       FIG 8.11|
|000530     05  EMP-NAME-OUT          PIC X(20).                    FIG 8.11|
|000540 PROCEDURE DIVISION.                                         FIG 8.11|
|000550 MAIN-CONTROL.                                               FIG 8.11|
|000560     PERFORM 100-INITIALIZATION.                             FIG 8.11|
|000570     PERFORM 300-PROCESSING                                  FIG 8.11|
|000580         UNTIL FILE-STATUS = 'DONE'.                         FIG 8.11|
|000590     PERFORM 500-TERMINATION.                                FIG 8.11|
|000600     STOP RUN.                                               FIG 8.11|
|000610 100-INITIALIZATION.                                         FIG 8.11|
|000620     OPEN INPUT EMPLOYEE                                     FIG 8.11|
|000630          OUTPUT DEPT-REPORT.                                FIG 8.11|
|000640     READ EMPLOYEE                                           FIG 8.11|
|000650         AT END MOVE 'DONE' TO FILE-STATUS.                  FIG 8.11|
|000660 300-PROCESSING.                                             FIG 8.11|
|000670     IF DEPT-NO-IN NOT EQUAL TO PREVIOUS-DEPT                FIG 8.11|
|000680         PERFORM 350-HEADINGS.                               FIG 8.11|
|000690     MOVE DEPT-NO-IN TO DEPT-NO-OUT.                         FIG 8.11|
|000700     MOVE EMP-NO-IN TO EMP-NO-OUT.                           FIG 8.11|
|000710     MOVE EMP-NAME-IN TO EMP-NAME-OUT.                       FIG 8.11|
|000720     WRITE PRINT-LINE FROM REPORT-LINE                       FIG 8.11|
|000730         AFTER ADVANCING 2 LINES.                            FIG 8.11|
|000740     READ EMPLOYEE                                           FIG 8.11|
|000750         AT END MOVE 'DONE' TO FILE-STATUS.                  FIG 8.11|
|000760 350-HEADINGS.                                               FIG 8.11|
|000770     MOVE DEPT-NO-IN TO DEPT-HEADING-OUT,                    FIG 8.11|
|000780                       PREVIOUS-DEPT.                        FIG 8.11|
|000790     WRITE PRINT-LINE FROM HEADING1-REC                      FIG 8.11|
```

Figure 8.11 Employee Report by Department *Continued*

```
|           1  1  2  2  2  3  3  4  4  4  5  5  6  6  6  7  7  8|
|    4    8 2  6  0  4  8  2  6  0  4  8  2  6  0  4  8  2  6  0|
----------------------------------------------------------------
|000800            AFTER ADVANCING PAGE-TOP.              FIG 8.11|
|000810    WRITE PRINT-LINE FROM HEADING2-REC             FIG 8.11|
|000820            AFTER ADVANCING 1 LINES.               FIG 8.11|
|000830    WRITE PRINT-LINE FROM HEADING3-REC             FIG 8.11|
|000840            AFTER ADVANCING 3 LINES.               FIG 8.11|
|000850 500-TERMINATION.                                  FIG 8.11|
|000860    CLOSE EMPLOYEE,                                FIG 8.11|
|000870          DEPT-REPORT.                             FIG 8.11|
```

Figure 8.11 Employee Report by Department *Continued*

```
|         1         2         3         4         5         6         7        8| FIGURE |
|RECORD|1234567890123456789012345678901234567890123456789012345678901234567890| NUMBER |
----------------------------------------------------------------------------------------
|     1|1111110001MARY KAY GRIFFIN                                            |FIG 8.11|
|     2|1111111200JOHN BAKER                                                  |FIG 8.11|
|     3|1111120050GEORGE MONTGOMERY                                           |FIG 8.11|
|     4|1111140095LINDA JOHNSON                                               |FIG 8.11|
|     5|1111175500LONNIE ANDERSON                                             |FIG 8.11|
|     6|1111195220HAROLD WILLIAMS                                             |FIG 8.11|
|     7|2222210500HOWARD PHELPS                                               |FIG 8.11|
|     8|2222225000MICHAEL REED                                                |FIG 8.11|
|     9|2222229850DONNA EDWARDS                                               |FIG 8.11|
|    10|2222230045WILLIAM HARGROVE                                            |FIG 8.11|
|    11|2222235025KARLA SAUNDERS                                              |FIG 8.11|
|    12|2222265300RONALD MCVAY                                                |FIG 8.11|
|    13|2222295225DEWAYNE RICHARDSON                                          |FIG 8.11|
|    14|3333312399ANDREA KRUMWELL                                             |FIG 8.11|
|    15|3333330005JANICE TRIMBLE                                              |FIG 8.11|
|    16|3333335422LAURA WELLINGTON                                            |FIG 8.11|
|    17|3333340030JERRY DOBSON                                                |FIG 8.11|
|    18|3333355550ANDREW KNIGHT                                               |FIG 8.11|
|    19|3333364900HERMAN YARBOROUGH                                           |FIG 8.11|
|    20|3333375400BRENDA SMITH                                                |FIG 8.11|
|    21|3333388505GARY JAMISON                                                |FIG 8.11|
|    22|3333399950THOMAS WHITTINGTON                                          |FIG 8.11|
```

Figure 8.11 Employee Report by Department (Data) *Continued*

To avoid reproducing the heading each time line 670 is encountered, notice that while the new heading is being produced, the value in DEPT-NO-IN is moved to PREVIOUS-DEPT. Thus, these two fields contain the same value so long as the value of DEPT-NO-IN does not change; however, when this value does change (as is the case when record number 7 is read), a new heading is produced and the PREVIOUS-DEPT field is updated.

Paragraphs versus SECTIONs

Thus far, all the programs illustrated have used only paragraphs in the PROCEDURE DIVISION. Such is also the case in Figure 8.11. The procedure from Figure 8.11 is illustrated again in Figure 8.12. The hierarchy chart for these two procedures is the same, the data is the same, and the output is the same. Yet there is only one paragraph in the PROCEDURE DIVISION of Figure 8.12—the 300-EXIT paragraph on line 730. The differences between these two programs are worth noting. The first notable modification appears in line 560 of Figure 8.12. Instead of using the PERFORM/UNTIL statement to control execution of 300-PROCESSING, a simple PERFORM is used. As a result, the FILE-STATUS data item is not needed in this procedure. The next difference is that a READ statement *does not* appear in the 100-INITIALIZATION procedure. Next, 300-PROCESSING begins (rather than ends) with a READ state-

```
                         LEARNING COBOL, INC.
                         DEPARTMENT 11111


     DEPARTMENT           EMPLOYEE NUMBER           EMPLOYEE NAME
       11111                  10001              MARY KAY GRIFFIN
       11111                  11200              JOHN  BAKER
       11111                  20050              GEORGE  MONTGOMERY
       11111                  40095              LINDA  JOHNSON
       11111                  75500              LONNIE  ANDERSON
       11111                  95220              HAROLD  WILLIAMS


                         LEARNING COBOL, INC.
                         DEPARTMENT 22222


     DEPARTMENT           EMPLOYEE NUMBER           EMPLOYEE NAME
       22222                  10500              HOWARD  PHELPS
       22222                  25000              MICHAEL  REED
       22222                  29850              DONNA  EDWARDS
       22222                  30045              WILLIAM  HARGROVE
       22222                  35025              KARLA  SAUNDERS
       22222                  65300              RONALD  MCVAY
       22222                  95225              DEWAYNE  RICHARDSON


                         LEARNING COBOL, INC.
                         DEPARTMENT 33333


     DEPARTMENT           EMPLOYEE NUMBER           EMPLOYEE NAME
       33333                  12399              ANDREA  KRUMWELL
       33333                  30005              JANICE  TRIMBLE
       33333                  35422              LAURA  WELLINGTON
       33333                  40030              JERRY  DOBSON
       33333                  55550              ANDREW  KNIGHT
       33333                  64900              HERMAN  YARBOROUGH
       33333                  75400              BRENDA  SMITH
       33333                  88505              GARY  JAMISON
       33333                  99950              THOMAS  WHITTINGTON
```

Figure 8.11 Employee Report by Department (Output) *Continued*

ment, and the AT END phrase transfers control to 300-EXIT upon encountering the end-of-file condition. Finally, a GO TO statement is placed at the bottom of 300-PROCESSING to transfer control back to the top of this procedure. (Of course, all of the paragraphs, except for 300-EXIT, are SECTIONs.) This style has been widely adopted in industry for two reasons. First, the MAIN-CONTROL procedure becomes a true simple sequence, thereby simplifying the overall picture of the program. Second, statements need not be duplicated (as has been the case with the READ statements). Therefore, if input-related changes are necessary (e.g., the file type changes), only one READ statement has to be located and modified.

Both coding styles demonstrated thus far are used in industry. Therefore, the remaining program illustrations will vary between these two styles. Since you have no way of knowing which style your employer may use, it is suggested that you familiarize yourself with both styles (and even, heaven forbid, unstructured programs).

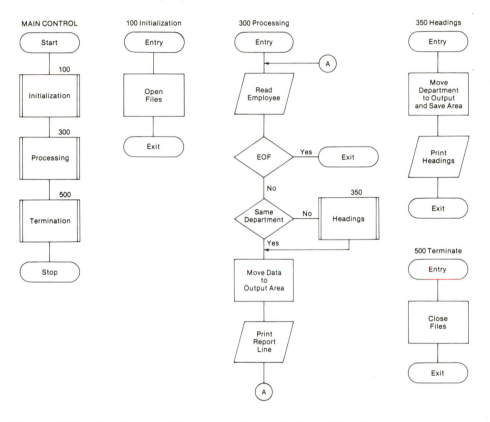

Figure 8.12 Employee Report by Department (with SECTIONs) (Module Flowcharts)

```
|           1   1   2   2   2   3   3   4   4   4   5   5   6   6   6   7   7   8|
|   4   8   2   6   0   4   8   2   6   0   4   8   2   6   0   4   8   2   6   0|
|-----------------------------------------------------------------------------|
|000010 IDENTIFICATION DIVISION.                                       FIG 8.12|
|000020 PROGRAM-ID. BREAKER.                                           FIG 8.12|
|000030 ENVIRONMENT DIVISION.                                          FIG 8.12|
|000040 CONFIGURATION SECTION.                                         FIG 8.12|
|000050 SOURCE-COMPUTER. IBM-3033.                                     FIG 8.12|
|000060 OBJECT-COMPUTER. IBM-3033.                                     FIG 8.12|
|000070 SPECIAL-NAMES.                                                 FIG 8.12|
|000080     C01 IS PAGE-TOP.                                           FIG 8.12|
|000090 INPUT-OUTPUT SECTION.                                          FIG 8.12|
|000100 FILE-CONTROL.                                                  FIG 8.12|
```

Figure 8.12 Employee Report by Department (with SECTIONs) *Continued*

```
|              1   1   2   2   2   3   3   4   4   4   5   5   6   6   6   7   7   8|
|   4   8      2   6   0   4   8   2   6   0   4   8   2   6   0   4   8   2   6   0|
|000110     SELECT EMPLOYEE ASSIGN TO UT-S-DATA1.                          FIG 8.12|
|000120     SELECT DEPT-REPORT ASSIGN TO UT-S-SYSPRINT.                    FIG 8.12|
|000130 DATA DIVISION.                                                     FIG 8.12|
|000140 FILE SECTION.                                                      FIG 8.12|
|000150 FD  EMPLOYEE                                                       FIG 8.12|
|000160     LABEL RECORDS ARE OMITTED.                                     FIG 8.12|
|000170 01  INPUT-REC.                                                     FIG 8.12|
|000180     05  DEPT-NO-IN          PIC X(05).                             FIG 8.12|
|000190     05  EMP-NO-IN           PIC X(05).                             FIG 8.12|
|000200     05  EMP-NAME-IN         PIC X(20).                             FIG 8.12|
|000210     05  FILLER              PIC X(50).                             FIG 8.12|
|000220 FD  DEPT-REPORT                                                    FIG 8.12|
|000230     LABEL RECORDS ARE OMITTED.                                     FIG 8.12|
|000240 01  PRINT-LINE.                                                    FIG 8.12|
|000250     05  FILLER              PIC X(133).                            FIG 8.12|
|000260 WORKING-STORAGE SECTION.                                           FIG 8.12|
|000270 01  WORKING-VARIABLES.                                             FIG 8.12|
|000280     05 PREVIOUS-DEPT        PIC X(05).                             FIG 8.12|
|000290 01  HEADING1-REC.                                                  FIG 8.12|
|000300     05  FILLER              PIC X(49) VALUE SPACES.                FIG 8.12|
|000310     05  FILLER              PIC X(20) VALUE                        FIG 8.12|
|000320     'LEARNING COBOL, INC.'.                                        FIG 8.12|
|000330 01  HEADING2-REC.                                                  FIG 8.12|
|000340     05  FILLER              PIC X(51) VALUE SPACES.                FIG 8.12|
|000350     05  FILLER              PIC X(10) VALUE 'DEPARTMENT'.          FIG 8.12|
|000360     05  FILLER              PIC X(01) VALUE SPACES.                FIG 8.12|
|000370     05  DEPT-HEADING-OUT    PIC X(05).                             FIG 8.12|
|000380 01  HEADING3-REC.                                                  FIG 8.12|
|000390     05  FILLER              PIC X(30) VALUE SPACES.                FIG 8.12|
|000400     05  FILLER              PIC X(10) VALUE 'DEPARTMENT'.          FIG 8.12|
|000410     05  FILLER              PIC X(10) VALUE SPACES.                FIG 8.12|
|000420     05  FILLER              PIC X(15) VALUE                        FIG 8.12|
|000430     'EMPLOYEE NUMBER'.                                             FIG 8.12|
|000440     05  FILLER              PIC X(10) VALUE SPACES.                FIG 8.12|
|000450     05  FILLER              PIC X(13) VALUE 'EMPLOYEE NAME'.       FIG 8.12|
|000460 01  REPORT-LINE.                                                   FIG 8.12|
|000470     05  FILLER              PIC X(32) VALUE SPACES.                FIG 8.12|
|000480     05  DEPT-NO-OUT         PIC X(05).                             FIG 8.12|
|000490     05  FILLER              PIC X(17) VALUE SPACES.                FIG 8.12|
|000500     05  EMP-NO-OUT          PIC X(05).                             FIG 8.12|
|000510     05  FILLER              PIC X(15) VALUE SPACES.                FIG 8.12|
|000520     05  EMP-NAME-OUT        PIC X(20).                             FIG 8.12|
|000530 PROCEDURE DIVISION.                                                FIG 8.12|
|000540 MAIN-CONTROL SECTION.                                              FIG 8.12|
|000550     PERFORM 100-INITIALIZATION.                                    FIG 8.12|
|000560     PERFORM 300-PROCESSING.                                        FIG 8.12|
|000570     PERFORM 500-TERMINATION.                                       FIG 8.12|
|000580     STOP RUN.                                                      FIG 8.12|
|000590 100-INITIALIZATION SECTION.                                        FIG 8.12|
|000600     OPEN INPUT EMPLOYEE                                            FIG 8.12|
|000610          OUTPUT DEPT-REPORT.                                       FIG 8.12|
|000620 300-PROCESSING SECTION.                                            FIG 8.12|
|000630     READ EMPLOYEE                                                  FIG 8.12|
|000640          AT END GO TO 300-EXIT.                                    FIG 8.12|
|000650     IF DEPT-NO-IN NOT EQUAL TO PREVIOUS-DEPT                       FIG 8.12|
|000660          PERFORM 350-HEADINGS.                                     FIG 8.12|
|000670     MOVE DEPT-NO-IN TO DEPT-NO-OUT.                                FIG 8.12|
|000680     MOVE EMP-NO-IN TO EMP-NO-OUT.                                  FIG 8.12|
|000690     MOVE EMP-NAME-IN TO EMP-NAME-OUT.                              FIG 8.12|
|000700     WRITE PRINT-LINE FROM REPORT-LINE                              FIG 8.12|
|000710          AFTER ADVANCING 2 LINES.                                  FIG 8.12|
|000720     GO TO 300-PROCESSING.                                          FIG 8.12|
|000730 300-EXIT.                                                          FIG 8.12|
|000740     EXIT.                                                          FIG 8.12|
|000750 350-HEADINGS SECTION.                                              FIG 8.12|
|000760     MOVE DEPT-NO-IN TO DEPT-HEADING-OUT,                           FIG 8.12|
|000770                        PREVIOUS-DEPT.                              FIG 8.12|
|000780     WRITE PRINT-LINE FROM HEADING1-REC                             FIG 8.12|
|000790          AFTER ADVANCING PAGE-TOP.                                 FIG 8.12|
|000800     WRITE PRINT-LINE FROM HEADING2-REC                             FIG 8.12|
|000810          AFTER ADVANCING 1 LINES.                                  FIG 8.12|
|000820     WRITE PRINT-LINE FROM HEADING3-REC                             FIG 8.12|
|000830          AFTER ADVANCING 3 LINES.                                  FIG 8.12|
|000840 500-TERMINATION SECTION.                                           FIG 8.12|
|000850     CLOSE EMPLOYEE,                                                FIG 8.12|
|000860          DEPT-REPORT.                                              FIG 8.12|
```

Figure 8.12 Employee Report by Department (with SECTIONs) *Continued*

Summary

In COBOL, most decision-oriented instructions take the form of IF statements. The relational conditions, discussed in this chapter, permit the comparison of two values based on greater than, equal to, or less than relationships. All IF statements provide for an imperative statement whether the specified condition is true or false; however, the false imperative statement may be omitted if no action is required. Furthermore, multiple actions may be executed in an imperative "statement."

IF statements use the logical operators AND and OR to create compound conditions. Where the subject of a compound condition is the source for several tests in a sequence, the subject may be implied after the first condition. If both the subject and the relational operator are the same for a series of conditions in a compound test, they may be implied.

The PERFORM statement is *the* COBOL statement that permits the modular design of programs required of structured programming. In general, the PERFORM statement causes procedures which are physically separated from the location of the PERFORM statement to be invoked (executed). Unlike the GO TO statement, after the PERFORM statement has been executed, the procedure continues with the statement immediately following the PERFORM statement.

Two forms of the PERFORM statement were discussed in this chapter—the simple PERFORM and the PERFORM/UNTIL statements. The simple PERFORM causes a single execution of the procedure(s) specified in the statement. The PERFORM/UNTIL statement is the COBOL equivalent of the "do-while" program structure. The PERFORM/UNTIL specifies the condition for the termination of the indicated procedure; however testing the specified condition will occur *only* upon encountering the end (the last statement) of the procedure.

Notes on Programming Style

Since the IF statement is very flexible, one should exercise caution and good judgement when constructing the code in which a series of decisions are to be made. You may be tempted to use nested IF statements under conditions that do not warrant their use. You might (eventually) get the structure to work properly, but have a little sympathy for those who have to "follow in your tracks." Remember that modification and maintenance of most programs used commercially is inevitable, so use the K-I-S-S principle (Keep It Simple Stupid) whenever possible. Who knows, you may have to modify *your own* program some day.

Because simplicity is the goal, the following design constraints should be followed whenever possible:

1. Do not use the logical relation NOT.
2. Use proper indention procedure, i.e.,

```
IF conditional expression
    true statement(s)
ELSE
    false statement(s).
```

3. Do not use nested IFs.
4. Do not use compound conditions.

The only one of these constraints that should always be used is the indention rule. Occasionally, the other rules will have to be broken because of the nature of the application. But, under all conditions, strive for the simplest possible expression of the decision.

SPECIAL NOTE. Even though it is theoretically possible to reference any COBOL statement in either the true or false imperative statements—even other IF statements—many compilers have difficulty properly translating an IF statement when an imperative statement includes a READ statement. Both the IF statement and the READ statement permit imperative statements, which could feasibly contain several instructions. The difficulty arises when the compiler tries to "decide" where one imperative statement ends and the other begins (or continues). For example, suppose a READ statement is to be executed when a specified condition is true. Assume a MOVE operation is also to be executed after the READ operation and only when the previously indicated condition is true. Where does the imperative statement for the READ operation end so that the MOVE statement is also a part of the IF statement's imperative statement? This seems like a problem with no solution, but these operations can be executed in the proper sequence by using two IF statements or by using the PERFORM statement in the IF's imperative statement to invoke the proper procedure.

Now, a few observations about the use of the PERFORM statement.

Although the PERFORM statement permits the use of the THRU option (procedure-name-1 THRU procedure-name-2), most programmers avoid its use. If a functional procedure is to be executed, the programmer should be able to structure the program so that only one procedure-name is necessary. When several procedures are to be executed, a lower level module (below the primary control procedure of the hierarchy chart) may constitute a sublevel control procedure. Suppose, for example, you found the following situation:

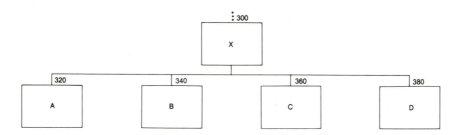

The module 300-X becomes a control module, but it does not control the entire program, only those elements subordinate to it. Thus, though we might be tempted to say "PERFORM 320-A THRU 380-D" in the 300-X module, an alternative to this would be :

```
300-X.
    PERFORM 320-A.
    PERFORM 340-B.
    PERFORM 360-C.
    PERFORM 380-D.
```

```
300-X SECTION.                    300-X SECTION.
300-Y. .                          300-Y.
        .                             PERFORM 320-A.
        .                             PERFORM 340-B.
320-A.  .                             PERFORM 360-C.
        .                             PERFORM 380-D.
        .                             GO TO 399-EXIT.
        .                         320-A.
340-B.  .                                 .
        .                                 .
        .                         340-B.  .
360-C.  .                                 .
        .                                 .
        .                         360-C.  .
380-D.  .                                 .
        .                                 .
        .                         380-D.  .
400-X SECTION.                            .
                                          .
                                  399-EXIT.
                                      EXIT.
                                  400-X SECTION.
```

There are two advantages to this approach. First, only the specified procedures will be executed. If other procedures had been placed between two of these modules (by accident or otherwise), they would not be executed. This way, code may be placed in a program and not executed until other modules have been executed and fully tested. Second, if one of the executed procedures turns out to be executed only on a conditional basis, only a minor modification is necessary. Another way to avoid use of the THRU option is to design your program around SECTIONs, such as the first example above. Here, the paragraph labeled "300-Y" becomes a control procedure, as paragraph 300-X was previously. We still have one small problem, however. To terminate the PERFORM of a SECTION, the end of the SECTION must be encountered serially (not under the control of a PERFORM from within the SECTION). We can do this with the sequence at the right above. Without the GO TO statement in this structure, the procedure would encounter the end of the section by "fall through," i.e., the procedure 320-A through 380-D would be executed first by the PERFORM operation in paragraph 300-Y and then repeated by serial execution. Thus, the GO TO statement is used to "jump" to the bottom of the SECTION to avoid the unintentional re-execution of the procedures that follow.

We have now studied all of the structure types that are fundamental to structured programming—the simple sequence (MOVE, READ, WRITE, and other statement types executed in a serial fashion), the if-then-else (IF statement), and the do-until (PERFORM/UNTIL statement).

Questions

Below, fill in the blank(s) with the appropriate word, words, or phrases.

1. IF statements appear in the _____ DIVISION.

2. COBOL permits _____ (number) different types of IF statements.

3. The _____ test is used to test the relationship between two values.

4. The _____ test is used to determine whether a numeric identifier is positive, zero, or negative.

5. The _____ test may be used to determine whether a value is numeric or alphabetic.

6. The relational equivalent to NOT LESS THAN is _____ .

7. Compound tests may be constructed in COBOL by using the logical operators _____ and _____ .

8. The logical operator _____ should join two relational tests when both tests must be true for the true branch to be executed.

9. The logical operator _____ should join two relational tests when the true branch is to be executed when either test is true.

10. In a complex logical expression _____ may be used to force the sequences of examination by the compiler.

11. The PERFORM statement permits the execution of a(n) _____ name or a(n) _____ name.

12. After the procedure(s) indicated in the PERFORM statements have been executed, execution continues with/at _____ .

13. A simple PERFORM statement is completed only when _____ .

14. With a simple PERFORM statement, the indicated procedure is executed _____ (number) time(s).

15. A PERFORM/UNTIL statement is completed only when _____ and _____ .

16. With a PERFORM/UNTIL, when the condition is true upon encountering the PERFORM statement, the procedure is executed _____ (number) time(s).

Answer the following questions by circling either "T" for True or "F" for False.

T F 17. An IF statement may be used to determine the relationship between two numeric values.

T F 18. An IF statement may be used to determine the relationship between two alphanumeric values.

T F 19. A relational IF statement permits the comparison of a numeric literal to an arithmetic expression.

T F   20. A relational IF statement permits the comparison of an alphanumeric elementary-item to the figurative constant SPACES.

T F   21. When a testing operation requires no false branch, ELSE NEXT SENTENCE may be omitted from the IF statement.

T F   22. When a testing operation requires no true branch, ELSE NEXT SENTENCE may be omitted from the IF statement.

T F   23. The imperative statement of either a true or a false branch may contain multiple COBOL statements.

T F   24. The true branch is terminated in the IF statement by the occurrence of either a period or the reserved word ELSE.

T F   25. There is only one way to code true and false branches once the condition to be tested has been specified.

T F   26. Within complex logical expressions, the logical operator OR takes precedence over (is examined prior to) AND.

T F   27. When the same subject is used in two or more relational expressions of a compound test, only the subject for the first relationship need be stated.

T F   28. If the relational operator used in two adjacent relational tests is the same, the relational operator may be implied even though the subjects of the two tests may be different.

T F   29. Logical operators, when they are the same for several relational tests in a sequence, may be implied.

T F   30. When nesting IF statements, the nested IF may appear in only the true branch of the parent IF statement.

T F   31. Types of conditions (e.g., relational and sign tests) may be combined in one logical expression by using AND or OR.

T F   32. Any COBOL statement may be used in the false branch of an IF statement.

T F   33. The PERFORM statement may be used to invoke a paragraph, so long as that paragraph appears physically below the PERFORM statement itself in the PROCEDURE DIVISION.

T F   34. With the PERFORM statement, the programmer is permitted to invoke a procedure and return to the location of the PERFORM when the procedure has been completed.

T F   35. The PERFORM statement only permits the execution of one paragraph or section.

T F   36. When a THROUGH option is used in a PERFORM statement, the second procedure-name does not necessarily have to follow the first procedure-name.

T F   37. If the THROUGH option is used in a PERFORM, the procedure-names listed must be paragraphs.

T F   38. A PERFORM statement may invoke a procedure containing another PERFORM statement.

T F   39. Once a paragraph has been executed by one PERFORM statement, it may not be re-executed by another PERFORM statement in another part of the program.

T F   40. A program that contains PERFORM statements is permitted to also include GO TO statements.

T F   41. A PERFORM statement could appear in the imperative statement portion of an IF statement.

T F   42. A PERFORM statement could appear in the imperative statement portion of a READ statement.

T F   43. In a PERFORM/UNTIL, the only condition permitted is a relational condition.

T F   44. In a PERFORM/UNTIL, compound conditions are permitted.

Exercises

1. Below is a series of IF statements. Indicate whether or not the statement has been coded in an acceptable form. If the form is correct, indicate which statement(s) constitute the "true" and "false" imperative statements. If the statement is in error, indicate the probable cause of the error.

a) ```
IF HOURS > 4Ø

    MOVE 'OVERTIME WORKED' TO MESSAGE

ELSE

    MOVE 'NO OVERTIME' TO MESSAGE.
```

b) ```
IF PAY-AMOUNT IS NOT LESS THAN DEDUCTION-LIMIT

    NEXT SENTENCE

ELSE

    MOVE Ø TO DEDUCTION-AMOUNT.
```

c) ```
IF LAST-EMPLOYEE NOT EQUAL THIS-EMPLOYEE

    WRITE EMPLOYEE-RECORD AFTER ADVANCING 4 LINES.
```

d) ```
IF SPECIAL-PROVISION = 'EARNED INCOME CREDIT'

    PERFORM EIC-LOOKUP.
```

e) ```
IF HOSPITALIZATION = ZERO

    GO TO NO-HOSPITALIZATION;

    GO TO NEXT-OPERATION

ELSE

    GO TO DEDUCT-HOSPITALIZATION.
```

f) ```
IF FICA-YTD > FICA-LIMIT

ELSE

    PERFORM FICA-CALCULATION.
```

2. Write the COBOL IF statement(s) necessary to fulfill the following set of conditions. (If any DATA DIVISION support is required, show that code also.)

a) When the cumulative salary for an employee exceeds $22,900 for the year, no (additional) FICA deduction is to be taken; otherwise a procedure is to be executed that calculates and deducts the FICA tax for the pay period.

b) When a W-5 form has been filed (a code value of 1 or 2), an Earned Income Credit (EIC) is to be calculated. When the form is filed by only one member of a family unit (a code value of 1), calculations are to be based on a single-filing party basis. When the code is 2, both husband and wife have (jointly) filed a W-5 form and calculations should be based on a two-party filing basis.

c) When (and if) the amount of net pay is less than or equal to zero or when it is greater than $5,000.00 move the word "void" to an output message and write the output message; otherwise, move the amount of net-pay to the output field and write the record.

3. Below is a series of simple PERFORM statement combinations. For each set, record the paragraphs executed. If a paragraph is executed an indeterminate number of times, indicate under what circumstances the perform is terminated. When a paragraph is encountered by "fall through" indicate that condition adjacent to the paragraph name.

a)   PERFORM A-PART.

        PERFORM B-PART.

        STOP RUN.

        A-PART.

        B-PART.

b)   PERFORM 1ST-PARA.

        STOP RUN.

        1ST-PARA.

            PERFORM 2ND-PARA.

        2ND-PARA.

            PERFORM 1ST-PARA.

c)   PERFORM PARA-A.

        STOP RUN.

        PARA-A.

            PERFORM PARA-B.

            PERFORM PARA-C.

        PARA-B.

        PARA-C.

            PERFORM PARA-B.

d)   PERFORM PART-1.

        PART-1.

            PERFORM PART-2.

        PART-2.

        PART-3.

        STOP RUN.

e)   PERFORM DO-1ST THRU DO-LAST.

        STOP RUN.

        DO-1ST.

            PERFORM DO-2ND THRU DO-3RD.

        DO-2ND.

        DO-3RD.

            PERFORM DO-2ND.

            PERFORM DO-LAST.

        DO-LAST.

            PERFORM DO-2ND.

4. Below is a series of PERFORM statement combinations. For each set, record the paragraph(s) executed. If a paragraph is executed an indeterminate number of times, indicate under what circumstances the perform is terminated. When a paragraph is encountered by "fall through" indicate that condition adjacent to the paragraph name.

a)
```
      MOVE 'COMPLETE' TO STATUS-INDICATOR.

      PERFORM 1ST-PARA

          UNTIL STATUS-INDICATOR = 'COMPLETE'.

      STOP RUN.

   1ST-PARA.
```

b)
```
      MOVE SPACES TO DONE.

      PERFORM PART-1

          UNTIL DONE = 'YES'.

      STOP RUN.

   PART-1.

      PERFORM PART-2.


   PART-2.

      MOVE 'YES' TO DONE.
```

c)
```
      MOVE SPACES TO COMPLETION-STATUS.

      PERFORM 1ST-PART

          UNTIL COMPLETION-STATUS = 'DONE'.

   1ST-PART.

      MOVE SPACES TO COMPLETION-STATUS.

      IF COMPLETION-STATUS NOT = 'DONE'

          PERFORM 2ND-PART

      MOVE 'DONE' TO COMPLETION-STATUS.



   2ND-PART.



      IF COMPLETION-STATUS NOT = 'DONE'

          PERFORM 3RD-PART.


   3RD-PART.
```

```
d)    MOVE 'PROCESS' TO REPETITION-STATUS.

      PERFORM A-PART THRU C-PART
          UNTIL REPETITION-STATUS = 'COMPLETE'.

      STOP RUN.

   A-PART.
```

```
   B-PART.

      PERFORM A-PART.

      PERFORM D-PART.
```

```
   C-PART.
```

```
   D-PART.

      MOVE 'COMPLETE' TO REPETITION-STATUS.


e)    PERFORM PROCEDURE-SETUP

      PERFORM INITIAL-PROCEDURE
          UNTIL FILE-STATUS = 'FINISHED'.

      PERFORM PROCEDURE-SETUP.

      PERFORM FOLLOW-UP-PROCEDURE
          UNTIL FILE-STATUS = 'FINISHED'.

      STOP RUN.

   PROCEDURE-SETUP.

      IF FILE-STATUS = 'FINISHED'

          OPEN INPUT SECOND-FILE;

          READ SECOND-FILE

             AT END CLOSE SECOND-FILE

                 STOP RUN

      ELSE

          OPEN INPUT FIRST-FILE;

          READ FIRST-FILE

             AT END CLOSE FIRST-FILE

                 STOP RUN.

      MOVE SPACES TO FILE-STATUS.
```

```
INITIAL-PROCEDURE.
        ⌇
    READ FIRST-FILE
        AT END CLOSE FIRST-FILE
            MOVE 'FINISHED' TO FILE-STATUS.
FOLLOW-UP-PROCEDURE.
        ⌇
    READ SECOND-FILE
        AT END CLOSE SECOND-FILE
            MOVE 'FINISHED' TO FILE-STATUS.
```

Problems

1. You are to write a generalized mailing-label program capable of producing 1-to 4-up labels and 3- or 4-line addresses. Two record types are to be used to accomplish this task. The first record is a control record (see the mulitple-card layout form) and is composed of three fields:
   1. Form used—1 digit and may contain the digits 1 through 4 to indicate the number of labels across the form (1-up to 4-up labels)
   2. Number of lines per label—1 digit and may contain either 3 or 4—to reflect 3- or 4-line labels, (On 4-line labels all data fields from the type-2 record are used).
   3. First-line print indicator—1 digit and may contain either 1 or 2.

   The first-line print indicator is used only when 3-line labels are to be printed and is used to indicate whether the individual's name (indicator = 1) or the company's name (indicator = 2) is to be printed as the first line of the address. On 4-line labels, the individual's name should appear first, followed by the company name (line 2), street or P.O. Box (line 3) and the city-state-zip code (line 4).

   The second record type contains the data to be printed and is represented by the following fields (see multiple-card layout form):

   1. Individual name—20 characters
   2. Company name—20 characters
   3. Street or P.O. Box—20 characters
   4. City—10 characters
   5. State—2 characters (2-character state abbreviation
   6. Zip code—5 characters

   The print chart demonstrates the possible variation in label printing. The elliptical shapes on the printer layout indicate the actual location and size of the mailing labels. Note: Multiple executions of the program will be required to demonstrate your program's capability to print 3- and 4-line labels and 1-, 2-, 3-, and 4-up labels.

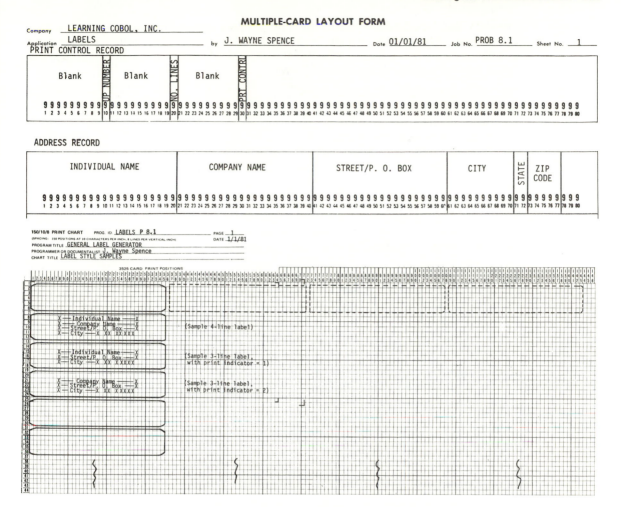

2. Our corporate library contains a series of publication types, including books, government documents, magazines and other periodicals, pamphlets, manuals, and internal working papers. Each time one of these holdings is checked out of the library, the patron's name and the date are recorded. Periodically, we need to account for all publications. Obviously, a physical inventory of the library would indicate what materials are outstanding (have not been returned to the library). However, an examination of the "checkout" records would be faster. Unfortunately, the date of return has not been recorded on some of the records, thus, we cannot simply examine the records to see which do not have a return date. We must examine the checkout date (which *is* available for each record) to find the last user (most current checkout date). Once the last user is located, we examine the return date—if it is blank, the publication has not been returned, and the details of the record should be printed (as indicated on the print chart).

The data, described below and on the multiple-card layout form, has been organized by publication type (all books are first, followed by government documents, etc.) and by publication number, i.e., all records for a given publication will be in one group. The fields of the checkout record are as follows:

1. Publication number—7 characters
2. Publication title—30 characters
3. Publication type—1 character
4. Patron name—30 characters
5. Checkout date—6 digits in the format MMDDYY
6. Return date—6 digits in the format MMDDYY

As previously noted, only the record of the most recent checkout is to be printed, and only if the return date for that record is blank. There are typically several checkout records for a single publication. The publication types are to be grouped—every time the publication type changes, a new heading is to be printed. The heading is to contain the name of the publication type according to the following list:

B—BOOK
G—GOVERNMENT DOCUMENT
M—MAGAZINE/PERIODICAL
P—PAMPHLET
N—MANUAL
W—WORKING PAPER

See the print chart for further details.

3. Inventory-status records have been created for the purchasing department to determine whether or not particular items should be ordered. Each of the inventory records consist of the following fields:

1. Item number—6 digits
2. Item description—30 characters
3. Vendor/supplier code—3 characters
4. Product group—3 digits
5. Quantity on hand—5 digits
6. Minimum stocking quantity—5 digits
7. Date of last order—6 digits in the format MMDDYY
8. Order flag—1 character
9. Quantity ordered—5 digits
10. Purchase-lot size—5 digits

You are to produce an inventory-reorder report based on this data. You may assume the data has been ordered by vendor code, product group, and item number. The report (see the print chart) is to include only those items for which the quantity on hand is less than the minimum stocking quantity. (All others should not appear on the report.)

Once you have decided whether or not an item is to be placed on the report, other considerations come into play. The order flag set to "Y" means an order has been previously placed and has not yet arrived. In this case, the date of the last order and the ordered quantity should appear under the COMMENTS heading (99999 UNITS ORDERED ON XX/XX/XX). The order flag set to "S" means all further purchases have been suspended, and the message "PURCHASES SUSPENDED" should appear under the COMMENTS heading. If the order flag is blank or set to "N," a current order is not pending and a new order should be placed. In this case, the message "BELOW MINIMUM STOCK LEVEL OF 99999—ORDER UNITS" should appear below the COMMENTS heading.

Other considerations are:

1. The reorder list should begin on a new page for each vendor code encountered.
2. A blank line should appear between each new product group, i.e., product groups of different values.

MULTIPLE-CARD LAYOUT FORM

Company __LEARNING COBOL, INC.__

Application __REORDER REPORT__ by __J. Wayne Spence__ Date __01/01/81__ Job No. __PROB 8.3__ Sheet No. __1__

IDENTIFICATION INFORMATION				ORDERING INFORMATION						
ITEM NUMBER	ITEM DESCRIPTION	VENDOR CODE	PRODUCT GROUP	QTY ON HAND	MIN. STOCK QTY	DATE OF LAST ORDER	ORD FLG	QTY ORDERED	PUR. LOT SIZE	
9 9 9 9 9 9	9 9 9 9 9 9 9 9 9 9 9 9 9 9 9 9 9 9 9 9 9 9 9 9 9 9 9 9 9 9	9 9 9	9 9 9	9 9 9 9 9	9 9 9 9 9	9 9 9 9 9 9	9	9 9 9 9 9	9 9 9 9 9	9 9 9 9 9 9 9 9 9 9
1 2 3 4 5 6	7 8 9 10 11 12 13 14 15 16 17 18 19 20 21 22 23 24 25 26 27 28 29 30 31 32 33 34 35 36	37 38 39	40 41 42	43 44 45 46 47	48 49 50 51 52	53 54 55 56 57 58	59 60	61 62 63 64	65 66 67 68 69	70 71 72 73 74 75 76 77 78 79 80

150/10/8 PRINT CHART   PROG. ID. INVENTORY P 8.3   PAGE 1
(SPACING: 150 POSITIONS AT 10 CHARACTERS PER INCH, 8 LINES PER VERTICAL INCH)   DATE 1/1/81
PROGRAM TITLE REORDER REPORT
PROGRAMMER OR DOCUMENTALIST: J. WAYNE SPENCE
CHART TITLE INVENTORY REORDER REPORT

Print chart layout showing:

INVENTORY REORDER REPORT
FOR VENDOR XXX

ITEM NUMBER | DESCRIPTION | PRODUCT GROUP | QTY ON HAND | --------- COMMENTS ---------

999 999 | X ... X | 999 | 9 9999
999 999 | X ... X | 999 | 9 9999 | 99999 UNITS ORDERED ON XX/XX/XX
BELOW MINIMUM STOCK LEVEL OF 99999--ORDER 999.99 UNITS
PURCHASES SUSPENDED
(Printed, as needed on the basis of the ORDER FLAG)

999 999 | X ... X | 999 | 9 9999

999 999 | X ... X | 999 | 9 9999 ← (Change of Product Group value)
999 999 | X ... X | 999 | 9 9999

999 999 | X ... X | 999 | 9 9999

9 Editing Data for Printed Output

In Chapter 5 (The DATA DIVISION), the basic PICTURE characters—A, X, 9, V, S, and P—were presented. These characters are sufficient for the internal description of input data or data items needed for internal purposes only; however, printed output should be easy for users to read. To improve its readability, we can edit printed output, using PICTURE characters specifically designed for that purpose.

The PICTURE characters used for editing are presented with their meanings in Table 9.1. Editing PICTURE characters fall into three categories—*fixed- insertion, floating-insertion,* and *replacement* characters. Some of these fall into two of these categories. Each one of these categories has a precise set of rules for its use.

Fixed Insertion

A fixed-insertion character is printed on the output in the position it occupies in the PICTURE string. The fixed-insertion characters are shown at the left.

1. +
2. −
3. $
4. .
5. ,
6. Ø
7. B
8. CR
9. DB

However, +, −, and $ also fall into the floating-insertion category. These three characters are considered to be fixed-insertion characters if they appear only once in a PICTURE string.

The rules for the fixed-insertion category are as follows:

1. The +, −, CR, and DB symbols are mutually exclusive. If one of the characters appears in a PICTURE string, the other three symbols must not appear in that PICTURE string.
2. The + or − symbol may appear only once per PICTURE string. It must appear as either the leftmost or the rightmost character in the PICTURE string.
3. The CR or DB symbol may appear only once in a PICTURE string. It must appear to the right of the least-significant-digit position in the PIC-TURE string.
4. The $ symbol may appear only once in a PICTURE string. It must appear to the left of the most-significant-digit position in the PICTURE string.

5. The . symbol may appear only once in a PICTURE string. It must not appear as the rightmost character of the PICTURE string.

6. The , symbol may appear several times in a PICTURE string. It must never be the leftmost or rightmost character in a PICTURE string, and two commas should not be adjacent to each other.

7. The Ø symbol may be used in numeric-, alphabetic-, or alphanumeric-edited fields. Zeros may be adjacent and may appear as either the leftmost or the rightmost characters in a PICTURE string.

8. The B symbol may be used in numeric-, alphabetic-, or alphanumeric-edited fields. Blanks may be inserted in adjacent positions, as the leftmost characters or the rightmost characters in a PICTURE string.

Table 9.2 shows how fixed-insertion characters can be used.

Table 9.1 Editing PICTURE Characters

Character	Meaning	Editing Category	Data Type Used With
+	The plus sign causes either a plus or minus sign to be printed, depending on the algebraic value of the data item.	Fixed Insertion Floating Insertion	Numeric
—	The minus sign causes only the minus sign to be printed if the algebraic value of the data item is negative.	Fixed Insertion Floating Insertion	Numeric
*	The "check protection" character causes leading zeros to be replaced with asterisks (*).	Replacement	Numeric
$	The currency symbol causes the "dollar sign" to be printed. It may be printed at the beginning of a PICTURE string or it may be used as a floating character (the symbol appears adjacent to the most significant digit in a numeric field).	Fixed Insertion Floating Insertion	Numeric
.	The decimal point causes a decimal point to be printed at the point where it is located in a PICTURE string, it may appear only once in a PICTURE string.	Fixed Insertion	Numeric
,	The comma causes a comma to be printed at the point(s) where it is located in a PICTURE string. Although a fixed-insertion character, it may be replaced by floating or replacement characters.	Fixed Insertion	Numeric
Ø	The zero causes a zero to appear on the output in every position it occupies in a PICTURE string.	Fixed Insertion	Numeric Alphanumeric Alphabetic
B	The blank symbol causes a blank to be printed on the output at the point(s) where it is located in PICTURE string.	Fixed Insertion	Numeric Alphanumeric Alphabetic
Z	The zero-suppression symbol causes leading zeros to be replaced with blanks (spaces) on the printed output.	Replacement	Numeric
CR	The "credit" symbol appears on the printed output if the field it is in contains a negative value.	Fixed Insertion	Numeric
DB	The "debit" symbol appears on the printed output if the field it is in contains a negative value.	Fixed Insertion	Numeric

Floating-Insertion   The second category of editing characters is floating-insertion characters. Floating insertion gives the appearance that the field is exactly large enough to accommodate the number. As the name implies, these characters "float" from left to right and appear adjacent to the most significant digit (assuming the floating character is coded to the most significant digit position of the PIC-

Table 9.2 Examples of the Use of Fixed-Insertion Characters

Data Value	PICTURE String Used for Output	Resulting Output*	Comments
123456	+ 9(6)	+ 123456	Length of the output field is 7 columns; unsigned source field is interpreted as containing a positive value.
− 123456	9(6) +	123456 −	Note that the + symbol may be recorded on the right and that it produces a minus sign when the data is negative.
+ 1234∧56	− 9(5).99	∅∅1234.56	The length of the output field is 9 characters, the minus sign does not cause the sign to be printed (consequently leaving a blank), and data is aligned on the decimal point in the PICTURE string such that a zero is added to the output.
− 1234∧56	9(4) −	1234 −	The minus sign is recorded at the rightmost position of this 5-character output field, and since the assumed decimal position follows the last digit, the fractional portion of the source field is truncated.
+ 123∧45	$99.99B	$23.45∅	A high-order digit is truncated, but the dollar sign and the blank of the PICTURE string are printed—a digit cannot replace a fixed-insertion character.
− 123456	99B99B99B∅∅	12∅34∅56∅∅∅	The length of the output field is 11 characters, multiple nonadjacent Bs are used, and adjacent 0s are inserted at the rightmost character positions of the PICTURE string. Note that the minus sign is ignored.
12345∧67	$999,999.99CR	$∅12,345.67∅∅	The output field is 13 characters long, and several fixed-insertion characters appear—note that since the data is not negative, the CR symbol is not produced, but it does require 2 spaces.
− 1234	$9999.∅∅BDB	$1234.∅∅∅DB	Again, several fixed-insertion characters are used—since the data is negative, the DB symbol is produced.
− 1234∧56	− $9(4).99	− $1234.56	Both the dollar sign and the minus sign appear in the PICTURE string.
∧1234	.999∅∅B(4)	.123∅∅∅∅∅∅	The decimal point may appear as the leftmost character; the field is not sufficiently large to accommodate the "4," and editing characters may use replication factors (such as B in the example).
ABCDEF	AAABBAAA	ABC∅∅DEF	Example shows the use of blank insertion in an alphabetic field.
123∅ABC	XXBB∅X(5)	12∅∅∅3∅ABC	Example shows the use of blank and zero insertion in an alphanumeric field. Note that the first 2 blanks are caused by the blank insertion, and the single blank is part of the data field.

* The symbol ∅ is used to represent the location of a blank; the symbol ∅ indicates the presence of the numeric zero.

TURE string). The floating-insertion characters are $+$, $-$, and $. To be interpreted as a floating character, two or more of the same floating-insertion characters must be recorded adjacent to each other. In other words, a single $+$ recorded adjacent to a single $ in a PICTURE string is not floating insertion, but rather two fixed-insertion characters recorded together. Two floating-insertion characters are not allowed in the same PICTURE string; however, a floating character could be preceded by, followed by, or interspersed with other PICTURE characters. (Remember that when one "sign-oriented" character is used in a PICTURE string, no other "sign-oriented" character can be used. Thus, if $+$ is used as a floating-insertion character, $-$, CR, and DB cannot also be used as a fixed-insertion character).

All of the floating-insertion characters are used with numeric data fields. Since floating-insertion characters are placed adjacent to the most-significant-digit position of a numeric field, a floating-insertion character may not appear to the right of a 9 in a PICTURE string. If fixed-insertion character, (e.g., comma) are used in conjunction with a floating-insertion character, the floating-insertion character is capable of either replacing the fixed insertion character or causing the fixed-insertion character to be replaced with a blank. Examples of floating-insertion characters are presented in Table 9.3.

Table 9.3 Examples of the Use of Floating-Insertion Characters

Data Value	PICTURE String Used for Output	Resulting Output*	Comments
$+12345$	$+ + + + +9$	$+12345$	No "floating" is apparent because the number exactly fills the field.
$+123$	$+(6)$	ƀƀ$+123$	The $+$ symbol is floated 2 positions to the right to appear adjacent to the most-significant-digit position, and the field may be composed totally of an insertion character.
-12345	$+(5)$	-2345	The field is not sufficiently large to accommodate the data value. Consequently the data is decimal-point aligned (assumed to be after the rightmost digit) and placed in the field. Note: the floating-insertion character must be written in the output field, even to the exclusion of a significant digit.
$-123456\wedge78$	$- - - , - - - . - -$	$-123,456.78$	The floating-insertion character may be interspersed with fixed-insertion characters.
$+123\wedge45$	$- - - , - - - . - -$	ƀƀƀƀƀ123.45	Note the disappearance of the comma as the $-$ sign is floated from left to right (except the sign of the number is positive so the $-$ symbol is not printed).
$+12345\wedge67$	$$$,$$$,$$$.$$B +$	ƀƀƀƀ$12,345.67ƀ +$	The length of the output field is 16 characters, the $ symbol floats from left to right to become adjacent to the most significant digit—it is replaced by blanks as it moves.
Ø	$(5).$$	ƀƀƀƀƀƀƀƀ	If the field contains zero, the field on the output will be blank.
$\wedge$Ø1	$(5).$$	ƀƀƀƀ$.Ø1	If there is a significant digit to the right of the decimal point, the floating character will be printed adjacent to the decimal point.

* The symbol ƀ is used to represent the location of a blank; the symbol Ø indicates the presence of the numeric zero.

Replacement   The final category of editing characters is replacement characters. These characters (*and Z) are used to replace insignificant zeros (from left to right) in an output field. The * replaces zeros with asterisks, and the Z replaces zeros with blanks. Since replacement characters and floating-insertion characters are for somewhat the same purpose, both replacement and floating-insertion characters cannot appear in the same PICTURE string. And, the two replacement characters cannot appear in the same PICTURE string; however, replacement characters can be interspersed with fixed-insertion characters.

The replacement characters, like floating-insertion characters, are used only with numeric fields. A replacement character cannot appear after a 9 in a PICTURE string. The replacement character will cause a fixed-insertion character (e.g., comma or period) to be replaced by an asterisk or a blank if there is not a significant digit to the left of the fixed-insertion character. Table 9.4 gives examples of the use of replacement characters.

Edited Data and the MOVE Statement   The use of edited data (numeric-edited, alphabetic-edited, and alphanumeric-edited fields) affects the use of the COBOL statements previously discussed, primarily the MOVE statement. There are specific rules for the movement of data into and from edited data fields. Table 9.5 shows the permitted movements of edited data.

One note of caution: Beginning programmers sometimes forget that numeric data are not the same as numeric-*edited* data. In terms of data manipulation (e.g., adding, subtracting, etc.) numeric-edited data fields are more limited than simple numeric fields. Often, the beginning programmer temporarily forgets that, in a numeric PICTURE string, the decimal point is an editing character. Thus, *use the decimal point* (as well as other editing characters) *only in a data field that will be directly written to the line printer*. Otherwise,

Table 9.4 Examples of the Use of Replacement Characters

Data Value	PICTURE String Used for Output	Resulting Output*	Comments
1234	ZZZZ9	ϐ1234	The first character of the output, which would normally be a zero, is replaced with a blank.
123	Z(5)	ϐϐ123	The first 2 positions are replaced with blanks.
12345	Z(5)	12345	Unlike a floating-insertion character, the replacement character does not always have to be used.
− 1234∧56	+ ZZZ,ZZZ.ZZ	− ϐϐ1,234.56	Fixed-insertion characters may be used in conjunction with replacement characters.
12∧34	$***,***.99	$*****12.34	The fixed-insertion comma is replaced by an asterisk, and 9s are used in conjunction with the replacement character.
∅	$***,***.**	**********	All characters are replaced with the replacement character.
∧∅1	$***,***.**	$*******.∅1	The zero in the output field occupies a significant position.
− 1234	$*****.∅∅CR	$*1234.∅∅CR	The zero insertion character may be used with a zero suppression (replacement) character, as can other fixed-insertion characters.
∅	Z,ZZZ	ϐϐϐϐϐ	All zeros are replaced by blanks (insertion characters are replaced with blanks, if passed).

* The symbol ϐ is used to represent the location of a blank; the symbol ∅ is used to indicate the presence of the numeric zero.

you may spend a great deal of time trying to trace insignificant data errors. Chapter 10 (Arithmetic Statements) discusses, in detail, the numeric-edited versus numeric-nonedited fields. If you should have difficulty with edited data causing errors in your program, refer to Appendix E for an explanation of how the error may be located.

Table 9.5 PERMISSIBLE MOVES OF DATA**

| Sending Fields | Receiving Fields | | | | | | |
| | | Elementary-Items | | | | | |
	Record or group	Alphanumeric (X)	Alphanumeric-edited	Alphabetic (A)	Alphabetic-edited*	Numeric (9)	Numeric-edited
Record or group	YES	YES	YES	YES[1]	YES[1]	YES[3]	YES[3]
Alphanumeric (X)	YES	YES	YES	YES[1]	YES[1]	YES[3]	YES[3]
Alphanumeric-edited	YES	YES	YES	YES[1]	YES[1]	NO	NO
Alphabetic (A)	YES	YES	YES	YES	YES	NO	NO
Alphabetic-edited	YES	YES	YES	YES	YES	NO	NO
Numeric (9)	YES[3]	YES[4]	YES[4]	NO	YES[4]	YES	YES
Numeric-edited	YES	YES[3]	YES[3]	NO	YES[3]	NO	NO
Figurative Constants ZEROS	YES	YES	YES	NO	YES	YES	YES
SPACES	YES	YES	YES	YES	YES	NO	NO
HIGH-VALUES, LOW-VALUES, and QUOTES	YES	YES	YES	NO	YES	NO	NO
ALL literal	YES	YES	YES	YES[1]	YES	YES[2]	YES[2]
Numeric literal	YES[3]	YES[4]	YES[4]	NO	YES	YES	YES
Non-numeric literal	YES	YES	YES	YES[1]	YES	YES[2]	YES[2]

1. So long as the field contains only alphabetic characters and spaces.
2. So long as the field contains only numeric characters. The field is treated as a numeric integer.
3. The movement of data is treated the same as an alphanumeric to alphanumeric move.
4. So long as the numeric data item represents an integer number.

 * Alphabetic-edited data is treated the same as alphanumeric-edited data.
** The permissible moves of COMPUTATIONAL data items and INDEX data items are not presented in this table.

The Student Listing Program (with Edited Output)

Figure 9.1 illustrates the use of edited output in a program. This is the student listing program that was demonstrated in Chapter 2 (Figure 2.1) and again in Chapter 6 (Figure 6.13). In Figure 9.1 the OUTPUT-REC description has been modified. ID-NUM is now shown with a blank insertion character (B). Zero suppression (Z) is used in the description of the elementary-items CURRENT-HOURS and TOT-HOURS. Notice that on the output, two extra spaces appear in the ID-NUM field, and no leading zeros are produced in the output fields for CURRENT-HOURS and TOT-HOURS.

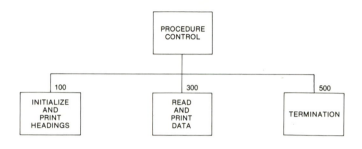

Figure 9.1 Student Listing Program (Hierarchy Chart)

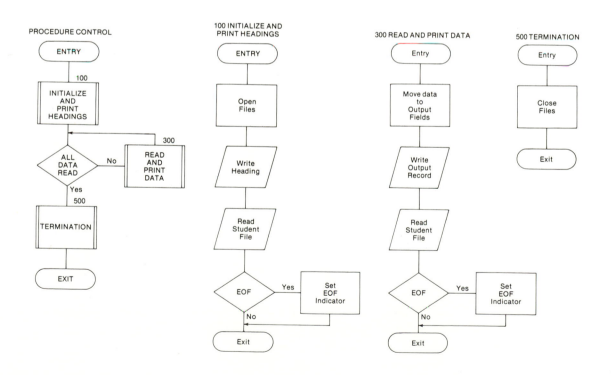

Figure 9.1 Student Listing Program (Module Flowcharts) *Continued*

```
|            1  1    2   2   2   3   3   4   4   4   5   5   6   6   6   7   7   8|
|    4   8   2  6    0   4   8   2   6   0   4   8   2   6   0   4   8   2   6   0|
--------------------------------------------------------------------------------
|000010 IDENTIFICATION DIVISION.                                         FIG  9.1|
|000020 PROGRAM-ID. EDITED-OUTPUT-EXAMPLE.                               FIG  9.1|
|000030 AUTHOR. J. WAYNE SPENCE.                                         FIG  9.1|
|000040 DATE-WRITTEN. JANUARY 1, 1981.                                   FIG  9.1|
|000050 DATE-COMPILED. JANUARY 1, 1981.                                  FIG  9.1|
|000060*       THIS PROGRAM ILLUSTRATES THE USE OF EDITING               FIG  9.1|
|000070*    CHARACTERS WITH OUTPUT.  IT FURTHER DEMONSTRATES             FIG  9.1|
|000080*    THE USE OF RECORDS IN THE WORKING-STORAGE                    FIG  9.1|
|000090*    SECTION AND VALUE CLAUSES -- ESPECIALLY THE                  FIG  9.1|
|000100*    VALUE ALL LITERAL.                                           FIG  9.1|
|000110 ENVIRONMENT DIVISION.                                            FIG  9.1|
|000120 CONFIGURATION SECTION.                                           FIG  9.1|
|000130 SOURCE-COMPUTER. CDC-6600.                                       FIG  9.1|
|000140 OBJECT-COMPUTER. CDC-6600.                                       FIG  9.1|
|000150 SPECIAL-NAMES.  C01 IS TOP-OF-NEXT-PAGE.                         FIG  9.1|
|000160 INPUT-OUTPUT SECTION.                                            FIG  9.1|
|000170 FILE-CONTROL.                                                    FIG  9.1|
|000180     SELECT STUDENT-FILE ASSIGN TO UT-S-SYSIN.                    FIG  9.1|
|000190     SELECT PRINTOUT ASSIGN TO UT-S-SYSPRINT.                     FIG  9.1|
|000200 DATA DIVISION.                                                   FIG  9.1|
|000210 FILE SECTION.                                                    FIG  9.1|
|000220 FD  STUDENT-FILE LABEL RECORDS ARE OMITTED.                      FIG  9.1|
|000230 01  STUDENT-REC.                                                 FIG  9.1|
|000240     05 STUDENT-IDENTIFICATION.                                   FIG  9.1|
|000250        10 LAST-NAME          PIC X(10).                          FIG  9.1|
|000260        10 FIRST-NAME         PIC X(10).                          FIG  9.1|
|000270        10 MIDDLE-INITIAL     PIC X(01).                          FIG  9.1|
|000280        10 STUDENT-ID         PIC 9(09).                          FIG  9.1|
|000290     05 FILLER                PIC X(05).                          FIG  9.1|
|000300     05 ENROLLMENT-INFO.                                          FIG  9.1|
|000310        10 CLASSIFICATION     PIC X(02).                          FIG  9.1|
|000320        10 TOTAL-HOURS        PIC 9(03).                          FIG  9.1|
|000330        10 HOURS-THIS-SEM     PIC 9(02).                          FIG  9.1|
|000340        10 MAJOR              PIC X(03).                          FIG  9.1|
|000350     05  FILLER               PIC X(35).                          FIG  9.1|
|000360 FD  PRINTOUT LABEL RECORDS ARE OMITTED.                          FIG  9.1|
|000370 01  PRINT-LINE               PIC X(133).                         FIG  9.1|
|000380 WORKING-STORAGE SECTION.                                         FIG  9.1|
|000390 01  WORKING-VARIABLES.                                           FIG  9.1|
|000400     05 INPUT-INDICATOR       PIC X(13) VALUE SPACES.             FIG  9.1|
|000410 01  REPORT-HEADING.                                              FIG  9.1|
|000420     03 FILLER                PIC X(29) VALUE SPACES.             FIG  9.1|
|000430     03 FILLER                PIC X(21) VALUE                     FIG  9.1|
|000440     'SEMESTER STUDENT LIST'.                                     FIG  9.1|
|000450 01  SEPARATOR-LINE.                                              FIG  9.1|
|000460     03 FILLER                PIC X(01) VALUE SPACES.             FIG  9.1|
|000470     03 FILLER                PIC X(79)  VALUE ALL '*'.           FIG  9.1|
|000480 01  COLUMN-HEADING-1.                                            FIG  9.1|
|000490     02 FILLER                PIC X(01) VALUE SPACES.             FIG  9.1|
|000500     02 FILLER                PIC X(79) VALUE '*       STUDENT FIG 9.1|
|000510-    'NAME      * STUDENT ID. * CLASS * MAJOR *  CURRENT   * TOTAFIG 9.1|
|000520-    'L *'.                                                       FIG  9.1|
|000530 01  COLUMN-HEADING-2.                                            FIG  9.1|
|000540     02 FILLER                PIC X(28) VALUE ' *'.               FIG  9.1|
|000550     02 FILLER                PIC X(14) VALUE '*    NUMBER'.      FIG  9.1|
|000560     02 FILLER                PIC X(08) VALUE '*'.                FIG  9.1|
|000570     02 FILLER                PIC X(08) VALUE '*'.                FIG  9.1|
|000580     02 FILLER                PIC X(22) VALUE '* ENROLLMENT * HFIG 9.1|
|000590-    'OURS *'.                                                    FIG  9.1|
|000600 01  OUTPUT-REC.                                                  FIG  9.1|
|000610        08 FILLER             PIC X(03) VALUE ' *'.               FIG  9.1|
|000620        08 1ST-NAME           PIC X(11).                          FIG  9.1|
|000630        08 M-I                PIC X(01).                          FIG  9.1|
|000640        08 FILLER             PIC X(02) VALUE '.'.                FIG  9.1|
|000650        08 SUR-NAME           PIC X(10).                          FIG  9.1|
|000660        08 FILLER             PIC X(03) VALUE ' *'.               FIG  9.1|
|000670        08 ID-NUM             PIC 99989989999.                    FIG  9.1|
|000680        08 FILLER             PIC X(04) VALUE ' *'.               FIG  9.1|
--------------------------------------------------------------------------------
```

Figure 9.1 Student Listing Program (With Edited Output) *Continued*

```
|          1   1   2   2   2   3   3   4   4   4   5   5   6   6   6   7   7   H|
|  4   8   2   6   0   4   8   2   6   0   4   8   2   6   0   4   8   2   6   0 |
-----------------------------------------------------------------------------
|000690          08 CLASS              PIC X(02).                        FIG  9.1|
|000700          08 FILLER             PIC X(06)   VALUE '  *'.          FIG  9.1|
|000710          08 MAJ                PIC X(03).                        FIG  9.1|
|000720          08 FILLER             PIC X(08)   VALUE '  *'.          FIG  9.1|
|000730          08 CURRENT-HOURS      PIC Z9.                           FIG  9.1|
|000740          08 FILLER             PIC X(08)   VALUE '     *'.       FIG  9.1|
|000750          08 TOT-HOURS          PIC ZZ9.                          FIG  9.1|
|000760          08 FILLER             PIC X(03)   VALUE '  *'.          FIG  9.1|
|000770 PROCEDURE DIVISION.                                              FIG  9.1|
|000780 PROCEDURE-CONTROL.                                               FIG  9.1|
|000790     PERFORM 100-INIT-AND-PRINT-HEADINGS.                         FIG  9.1|
|000800     PERFORM 300-READ-AND-PRINT-DATA                              FIG  9.1|
|000810         UNTIL INPUT-INDICATOR = 'ALL DATA READ'.                 FIG  9.1|
|000820     PERFORM 500-TERMINATION.                                     FIG  9.1|
|000830     STOP RUN.                                                    FIG  9.1|
|000840 100-INIT-AND-PRINT-HEADINGS.                                     FIG  9.1|
|000850     OPEN INPUT STUDENT-FILE, OUTPUT PRINTOUT.                    FIG  9.1|
|000860     WRITE PRINT-LINE FROM REPORT-HEADING AFTER                   FIG  9.1|
|000870         TOP-OF-NEXT-PAGE.                                        FIG  9.1|
|000880     WRITE PRINT-LINE FROM SEPARATOR-LINE AFTER 2 LINES.          FIG  9.1|
|000890     WRITE PRINT-LINE FROM COLUMN-HEADING-1 AFTER 1.              FIG  9.1|
|000900     WRITE PRINT-LINE FROM COLUMN-HEADING-2 AFTER 1.              FIG  9.1|
|000910     WRITE PRINT-LINE FROM SEPARATOR-LINE AFTER 1.                FIG  9.1|
|000920     MOVE 'READING DATA' TO INPUT-INDICATOR.                      FIG  9.1|
|000930     READ STUDENT-FILE                                            FIG  9.1|
|000940         AT END MOVE 'ALL DATA READ' TO INPUT-INDICATOR.          FIG  9.1|
|000950 300-READ-AND-PRINT-DATA.                                         FIG  9.1|
|000960     MOVE STUDENT-ID TO ID-NUM.                                   FIG  9.1|
|000970     MOVE LAST-NAME TO SUR-NAME.                                  FIG  9.1|
|000980     MOVE FIRST-NAME TO 1ST-NAME.                                 FIG  9.1|
|000990     MOVE MIDDLE-INITIAL TO M-I.                                  FIG  9.1|
|001000     MOVE CLASSIFICATION TO CLASS.                                FIG  9.1|
|001010     MOVE TOTAL-HOURS TO TOT-HOURS.                               FIG  9.1|
|001020     MOVE HOURS-THIS-SEM TO CURRENT-HOURS.                        FIG  9.1|
|001030     MOVE MAJOR TO MAJ.                                           FIG  9.1|
|001040     WRITE PRINT-LINE FROM OUTPUT-REC AFTER 2 LINES.              FIG  9.1|
|001050     READ STUDENT-FILE                                           FIG  9.1|
|001060         AT END MOVE 'ALL DATA READ' TO INPUT-INDICATOR.          FIG  9.1|
|001070 500-TERMINATION.                                                 FIG  9.1|
|001080     CLOSE STUDENT-FILE, PRINTOUT.                                FIG  9.1|
```

Figure 9.1 Student Listing Program (with Edited Output) *Continued*

```
|        |       1         2         3         4         5         6         7        8| FIGURE |
|RECORD|12345678901234567890123456789012345678901234567890123456789012345678901234567890| NUMBER |
----------------------------------------------------------------------------------------
|   1|ADAMS     JOHN      G343564321    GR21900CSC                                |FIG  9.1|
|   2|BROWN     JOHN      A555667777    FR03515MKT                                |FIG  9.1|
|   3|CULVER    MATT      N456789012    JR09408MGT                                |FIG  9.1|
|   4|DORSETT   ANTHONY   R353492761    SR13816ECO                                |FIG  9.1|
|   5|ELDRIDGE  DAVID     G376495268    S004712FIN                                |FIG  9.1|
|   6|FRANKLIN  BEN       V000000002    GR18912GBU                                |FIG  9.1|
|   7|GERBER    KENNETH   A537903251    S002816MGT                                |FIG  9.1|
|   8|HAMILTON  MARK      C486762389    JR09618CSC                                |FIG  9.1|
|   9|ISSACS    MATT      H474653790    SR12018ECO                                |FIG  9.1|
|  10|JENNINGS  HAROLD    Q502326955    FR01818MGT                                |FIG  9.1|
|  11|KENNIMER  FLOYD     R476329092    JR06012MKT                                |FIG  9.1|
|  12|LINCOLN   STEVEN    0442648942    S004515MKT                                |FIG  9.1|
|  13|MARCUS    JEFF      V546677219    SR09918CSC                                |FIG  9.1|
```

Figure 9.1 Student Listing Program (with Edited Output—Data) *Continued*

```
                              SEMESTER STUDENT LIST

  **************************************************************************
  *            STUDENT NAME      *  STUDENT ID. * CLASS * MAJOR *  CURRENT   * TOTAL *
  *                              *   NUMBER      *       *       * ENROLLMENT * HOURS *
  **************************************************************************

  *  JOHN       Q. ADAMS        *  343 56 4321 *  GR   *  CSC  *     0      *  219  *

  *  JOHN       A. BROWN        *  555 66 7777 *  FR   *  MKT  *    15      *   35  *

  *  MATT       N. CULVER       *  456 78 9012 *  JR   *  MGT  *     8      *   94  *

  *  ANTHONY    R. DORSETT      *  353 49 2761 *  SR   *  ECO  *    16      *  138  *

  *  DAVID      Q. ELDRIDGE     *  376 49 5268 *  SO   *  FIN  *    12      *   47  *

  *  BEN        V. FRANKLIN     *  000 00 0002 *  GR   *  GBU  *    12      *  189  *

  *  KENNETH    A. GERBER       *  537 90 3251 *  SO   *  MGT  *    16      *   28  *

  *  MARK       C. HAMILTON     *  486 76 2389 *  JR   *  CSC  *    18      *   96  *

  *  MATT       H. ISSACS       *  474 65 3790 *  SR   *  ECO  *    18      *  120  *

  *  HAROLD     G. JENNINGS     *  502 32 6955 *  FR   *  MGT  *    18      *   18  *

  *  FLOYD      R. KENNIMER     *  476 32 9092 *  JR   *  MKT  *    12      *   60  *

  *  STEVEN     O. LINCOLN      *  442 64 8942 *  SO   *  MKT  *    15      *   45  *

  *  JEFF       V. MARCUS       *  546 67 7219 *  SR   *  CSC  *    18      *   99  *
```

Figure 9.1 Student Listing Program (with Edited Output) *Continued*

Inventory Listing Program

Figure 9.2 provides an additional program example of the use of editing characters. The program is designed to input a series of data cards and produce from these cards a master list of inventory items. Because the first digit of the item number is used to indicate the product category, on the output, the first digit of the item number is separated from the other digits by a blank insertion. The output also shows the price per unit for each item. This is produced on the output with a floating dollar sign and a decimal-point insertion. The last column of the report represents the number of units available. Zero suppression is used to eliminate leading zeros in the field; however, if no units are available, zero is printed as a single digit.

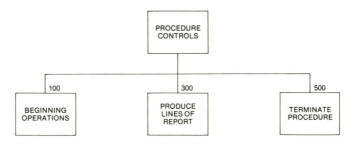

Figure 9.2 Inventory Listing Program (Hierarchy Chart)

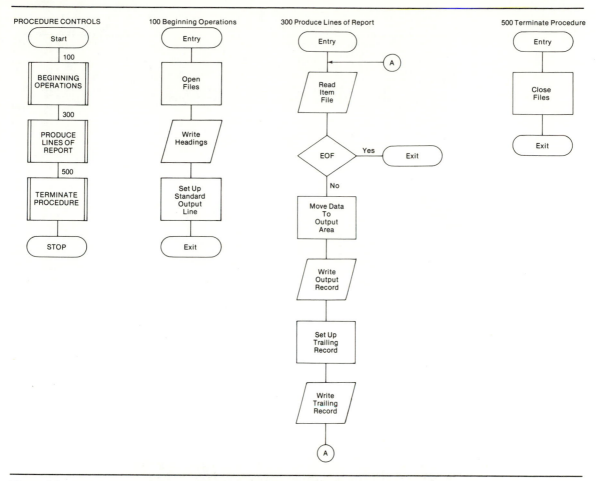

Figure 9.2 Inventory Listing Program (Module Flowcharts) *Continued*

```
|            1   1   2   2   2   3   3   4   4   4   5   5   6   6   6   7   7   8|
|   4    8   2   6   0   4   8   2   6   0   4   8   2   6   0   4   8   2   6   0|
------------------------------------------------------------------------------
|000010 IDENTIFICATION DIVISION.                                       FIG  9.2|
|000020 PROGRAM-ID.  MASTER-LIST.                                      FIG  9.2|
|000030 AUTHOR.  J. WAYNE SPENCE.                                      FIG  9.2|
|000040 DATE-WRITTEN.  JANUARY 1, 1981.                                FIG  9.2|
|000050 DATE-COMPILED.  JANUARY 1, 1981.                               FIG  9.2|
|000060*   PROGRAM PRODUCES MASTER INVENTORY LIST FOR ABC              FIG  9.2|
|000070*   BUILDING SUPPLY COMPANY.  PROGRAM ILLUSTRATES THE USE       FIG  9.2|
|000080*   OF EDITED OUTPUT AND THE USE OF VALUE CLAUSES WITH          FIG  9.2|
|000090*   NON-NUMERIC LITERALS IN THE WORKING-STORAGE SECTION.        FIG  9.2|
|000100 ENVIRONMENT DIVISION.                                          FIG  9.2|
|000110 CONFIGURATION SECTION.                                         FIG  9.2|
|000120 SOURCE-COMPUTER.  IBM-360.                                     FIG  9.2|
```

Figure 9.2 Inventory Listing Program *Continued*

```
|         1   1   2   2   2   3   3   4   4   4   5   5   6   6   6   7   7   8|
|   4   8  2   6   0   4   8   2   6   0   4   8   2   6   0   4   8   2   6   0|
------------------------------------------------------------------------------
|000130 OBJECT-COMPUTER.  IBM-360.                                  FIG  9.2|
|000140 SPECIAL-NAMES.                                              FIG  9.2|
|000150      C01 IS TOP-OF-PAGE.                                    FIG  9.2|
|000160 INPUT-OUTPUT SECTION.                                       FIG  9.2|
|000170 FILE-CONTROL.                                               FIG  9.2|
|000180      SELECT ITEM-FILE ASSIGN TO UT-S-SYSIN.                 FIG  9.2|
|000190      SELECT MASTER-LIST ASSIGN TO UT-S-SYSPRINT.            FIG  9.2|
|000200 DATA DIVISION.                                              FIG  9.2|
|000210 FILE SECTION.                                               FIG  9.2|
|000220 FD  ITEM-FILE                                               FIG  9.2|
|000230      LABEL RECORDS ARE OMITTED.                             FIG  9.2|
|000240 01  INPUT-RECORD                 PIC X(80).                 FIG  9.2|
|000250 FD  MASTER-LIST                                             FIG  9.2|
|000260      LABEL RECORDS ARE OMITTED                              FIG  9.2|
|000270      RECORD CONTAINS 133 CHARACTERS.                        FIG  9.2|
|000280 01  LINE-OF-TABLE                PIC X(133).                FIG  9.2|
|000290 WORKING-STORAGE SECTION.                                    FIG  9.2|
|000300 01  ITEM-RECORD.                                            FIG  9.2|
|000310     05  ITEM-DESCRIPTION         PIC X(24).                 FIG  9.2|
|000320     05  FILLER                   PIC X(12).                 FIG  9.2|
|000330     05  ITEM-NUMBER              PIC 9(06).                 FIG  9.2|
|000340     05  FILLER                   PIC X(04).                 FIG  9.2|
|000350     05  NUMBER-OF-UNITS          PIC 9(03).                 FIG  9.2|
|000360     05  FILLER                   PIC X(02).                 FIG  9.2|
|000370     05  PACKING-UNIT             PIC A(03).                 FIG  9.2|
|000380     05  FILLER                   PIC X(02).                 FIG  9.2|
|000390     05  PRICE-PER-UNIT           PIC 9(02)V9(02).           FIG  9.2|
|000400 01  TITLE-LINE-1.                                           FIG  9.2|
|000410     06 FILLER                    PIC X(22) VALUE SPACES.    FIG  9.2|
|000420     06 FILLER                    PIC X(27) VALUE            FIG  9.2|
|000430     *ABC BUILDING SUPPLY COMPANY*.                          FIG  9.2|
|000440 01  TITLE-LINE-2.                                           FIG  9.2|
|000450     06 FILLER                    PIC X(25) VALUE SPACES.    FIG  9.2|
|000460     06 FILLER                    PIC X(21) VALUE            FIG  9.2|
|000470     *MASTER INVENTORY LIST*.                                FIG  9.2|
|000480 01  ASTK-LINE.                                              FIG  9.2|
|000490     06 FILLER                    PIC X(01) VALUE SPACES.    FIG  9.2|
|000500     06 FILLER                    PIC X(72) VALUE ALL '*'.   FIG  9.2|
|000510 01  STANDARD-LINE.                                          FIG  9.2|
|000520     08 FILLER                    PIC X(01) VALUE SPACES.    FIG  9.2|
|000530     08 FILLER                    PIC X(01) VALUE '*'.       FIG  9.2|
|000540     08 FILLER                    PIC X(09) VALUE SPACES.    FIG  9.2|
|000550     08 FILLER                    PIC X(01) VALUE '*'.       FIG  9.2|
|000560     08 FILLER                    PIC X(26) VALUE SPACES.    FIG  9.2|
|000570     08 FILLER                    PIC X(01) VALUE '*'.       FIG  9.2|
|000580     08 FILLER                    PIC X(09) VALUE SPACES.    FIG  9.2|
|000590     08 FILLER                    PIC X(01) VALUE '*'.       FIG  9.2|
|000600     08 FILLER                    PIC X(12) VALUE SPACES.    FIG  9.2|
|000610     08 FILLER                    PIC X(01) VALUE '*'.       FIG  9.2|
|000620     08 FILLER                    PIC X(10) VALUE SPACES.    FIG  9.2|
|000630     08 FILLER                    PIC X(01) VALUE '*'.       FIG  9.2|
|000640 01  HEAD-LINE-1.                                            FIG  9.2|
|000650     06 FILLER                    PIC X(01) VALUE SPACES.    FIG  9.2|
|000660     06 FILLER                    PIC X(01) VALUE '*'.       FIG  9.2|
|000670     06 FILLER                    PIC X(02) VALUE SPACES.    FIG  9.2|
|000680     06 FILLER                    PIC X(04) VALUE 'ITEM'.    FIG  9.2|
|000690     06 FILLER                    PIC X(03) VALUE SPACES.    FIG  9.2|
|000700     06 FILLER                    PIC X(01) VALUE '*'.       FIG  9.2|
|000710     06 FILLER                    PIC X(07) VALUE SPACES.    FIG  9.2|
|000720     06 FILLER                    PIC X(11) VALUE 'DESCRIPTION'.  FIG  9.2|
|000730     06 FILLER                    PIC X(08) VALUE SPACES.    FIG  9.2|
|000740     06 FILLER                    PIC X(01) VALUE '*'.       FIG  9.2|
|000750     06 FILLER                    PIC X(01) VALUE SPACES.    FIG  9.2|
|000760     06 FILLER                    PIC X(07) VALUE 'PACKING'. FIG  9.2|
|000770     06 FILLER                    PIC X(04) VALUE ' * '.     FIG  9.2|
|000780     06 FILLER                    PIC X(09) VALUE 'PRICE PER'. FIG  9.2|
|000790     06 FILLER                    PIC X(04) VALUE ' * '.     FIG  9.2|
|000800     06 FILLER                    PIC X(06) VALUE 'NUMBER'.  FIG  9.2|
|000810     06 FILLER                    PIC X(03) VALUE '  *'.     FIG  9.2|
|000820 01  HEAD-LINE-2.                                            FIG  9.2|
|000830     06 FILLER                    PIC X(01) VALUE SPACES.    FIG  9.2|
|000840     06 FILLER                    PIC X(02) VALUE '* '.      FIG  9.2|
|000850     06 FILLER                    PIC X(06) VALUE 'NUMBER'.  FIG  9.2|
|000860     06 FILLER                    PIC X(02) VALUE SPACES.    FIG  9.2|
|000870     06 FILLER                    PIC X(01) VALUE '*'.       FIG  9.2|
|000880     06 FILLER                    PIC X(26) VALUE SPACES.    FIG  9.2|
|000890     06 FILLER                    PIC X(01) VALUE '*'.       FIG  9.2|
|000900     06 FILLER                    PIC X(09) VALUE ' UNIT  '. FIG  9.2|
```

Figure 9.2 Inventory Listing Program *Continued*

```
I            1 1   2   2   2   3   3   4   4   4   5   5   6   6   6   7   7   8|
I    4    8  2 6   0   4   8   2   6   0   4   8   2   6   0   4   8   2   6   0|
-------------------------------------------------------------------------------
|000910        06 FILLER              PIC X(01) VALUE '*'.              FIG  9.2|
|000920        06 FILLER              PIC X(12) VALUE '    UNIT     '.  FIG  9.2|
|000930        06 FILLER              PIC X(01) VALUE '*'.              FIG  9.2|
|000940        06 FILLER              PIC X(11) VALUE ' OF UNITS *'.    FIG  9.2|
|000950  01    ITEM-RECORD-2.                                          FIG  9.2|
|000960        06 FILLER              PIC X(03).                        FIG  9.2|
|000970        06 ITEM-NO             PIC 9B9(5).                       FIG  9.2|
|000980        06 FILLER              PIC X(03).                        FIG  9.2|
|000990        06 DESCRIPTION         PIC X(24).                        FIG  9.2|
|001000        06 FILLER              PIC X(05).                        FIG  9.2|
|001010        06 PK-UNIT             PIC A(03).                        FIG  9.2|
|001020        06 FILLER              PIC X(07).                        FIG  9.2|
|001030        06 PRICE               PIC $$$.99.                       FIG  9.2|
|001040        06 FILLER              PIC X(07).                        FIG  9.2|
|001050        06 UNITS               PIC ZZ9.                          FIG  9.2|
|001060        06 FILLER              PIC X(05).                        FIG  9.2|
|001070 PROCEDURE DIVISION.                                            FIG  9.2|
|001080 PROCEDURE-CONTROLS.                                            FIG  9.2|
|001090        PERFORM 100-BEGINNING-OPERATIONS.                       FIG  9.2|
|001100        PERFORM 300-PRODUCE-LINES-OF-REPORT.                    FIG  9.2|
|001110        PERFORM 500-TERMINATE-PROCEDURE.                        FIG  9.2|
|001120        STOP RUN.                                               FIG  9.2|
|001130 100-BEGINNING-OPERATIONS SECTION.                              FIG  9.2|
|001140        OPEN INPUT ITEM-FILE OUTPUT MASTER-LIST.                FIG  9.2|
|001150        MOVE SPACES TO LINE-OF-TABLE.                           FIG  9.2|
|001160        WRITE LINE-OF-TABLE AFTER TOP-OF-PAGE.                   FIG  9.2|
|001170        WRITE LINE-OF-TABLE FROM TITLE-LINE-1 AFTER 1 LINES.     FIG  9.2|
|001180        WRITE LINE-OF-TABLE FROM TITLE-LINE-2 AFTER 1 LINES.     FIG  9.2|
|001190        WRITE LINE-OF-TABLE FROM ASTK-LINE AFTER 4 LINES.        FIG  9.2|
|001200        WRITE LINE-OF-TABLE FROM STANDARD-LINE AFTER 1 LINES.    FIG  9.2|
|001210        WRITE LINE-OF-TABLE FROM HEAD-LINE-1 AFTER 1 LINES.      FIG  9.2|
|001220        WRITE LINE-OF-TABLE FROM HEAD-LINE-2 AFTER 1 LINES.      FIG  9.2|
|001230        WRITE LINE-OF-TABLE FROM STANDARD-LINE AFTER 1 LINES.    FIG  9.2|
|001240        WRITE LINE-OF-TABLE FROM ASTK-LINE AFTER 1 LINES.        FIG  9.2|
|001250        WRITE LINE-OF-TABLE FROM STANDARD-LINE AFTER 1 LINES.    FIG  9.2|
|001260        MOVE STANDARD-LINE TO ITEM-RECORD-2.                     FIG  9.2|
|001270 199-EXIT.                                                      FIG  9.2|
|001280        EXIT.                                                   FIG  9.2|
|001290 300-PRODUCE-LINES-OF-REPORT SECTION.                           FIG  9.2|
|001300        READ ITEM-FILE INTO ITEM-RECORD                         FIG  9.2|
|001310            AT END GO TO 399-EXIT.                              FIG  9.2|
|001320        MOVE ITEM-NUMBER TO ITEM-NO.                            FIG  9.2|
|001330        MOVE ITEM-DESCRIPTION TO DESCRIPTION.                   FIG  9.2|
|001340        MOVE PACKING-UNIT TO PK-UNIT.                           FIG  9.2|
|001350        MOVE PRICE-PER-UNIT TO PRICE.                           FIG  9.2|
|001360        MOVE NUMBER-OF-UNITS TO UNITS.                          FIG  9.2|
|001370        MOVE SPACES TO LINE-OF-TABLE.                           FIG  9.2|
|001380        WRITE LINE-OF-TABLE FROM ITEM-RECORD-2 AFTER 1.         FIG  9.2|
|001390        MOVE SPACES TO LINE-OF-TABLE.                           FIG  9.2|
|001400        WRITE LINE-OF-TABLE FROM STANDARD-LINE AFTER 1.         FIG  9.2|
|001410        GO TO 300-PRODUCE-LINES-OF-REPORT.                      FIG  9.2|
|001420 399-EXIT.                                                      FIG  9.2|
|001430        EXIT.                                                   FIG  9.2|
|001440 500-TERMINATE-PROCEDURE SECTION.                               FIG  9.2|
|001450        CLOSE ITEM-FILE, MASTER-LIST.                           FIG  9.2|
|001460 599-EXIT.                                                      FIG  9.2|
|001470        EXIT.                                                   FIG  9.2|
```

Figure 9.2 Inventory Listing Program *Continued*

```
|          1          2          3          4          5          6          7          8| FIGURE |
|RECORD|12345678901234567890123456789012345678901234567890123456789012345678901234567890| NUMBER |
-------------------------------------------------------------------------------------------------
|    1|1/2 IN. FINISHING NAILS        131139    120  BOX  0075                   |FIG  9.2|
|    2|STOVE BOLTS--2 IN.             176414    065  BOX  0160                   |FIG  9.2|
|    3|1/2 IN. ROOFING NAILS          188217    030  BOX  0060                   |FIG  9.2|
|    4|DIE CAST ALUM. BOLTS--2"       191192    275  BOX  0195                   |FIG  9.2|
|    5|8 FT. 2 X 4 -- REDWOOD         221570    040  EA   0375                   |FIG  9.2|
|    6|8 FT. 2 X 4 --PINE             615523    500  EA   0220                   |FIG  9.2|
|    7|8 FT. 1 X 6 -- PINE            665227    115  EA   0205                   |FIG  9.2|
|    8|8 FT. 4 X 4 -- PINE            681874    015  EA   0595                   |FIG  9.2|
|    9|SPLIT CEDAR SHINGLES           721250    080  BUN  4250                   |FIG  9.2|
|   10|COMPOSITION SHINGLES           794825    120  BUN  3195                   |FIG  9.2|
```

Figure 9.2 Inventory Listing Program (Data) *Continued*

```
                    ABC BUILDING SUPPLY COMPANY
                       MASTER INVENTORY LIST

*****************************************************************************
*          *                          *          *            *           *
*   ITEM   *      DESCRIPTION         * PACKING  * PRICE PER  *  NUMBER   *
*  NUMBER  *                          *  UNIT    *    UNIT    * OF UNITS  *
*          *                          *          *            *           *
*****************************************************************************
*          *                          *          *            *           *
*  1 31139 * 1/2 IN. FINISHING NAILS  *   BOX    *    $.75    *    120    *
*          *                          *          *            *           *
*  1 76414 * STOVE BOLTS--2 IN.       *   BOX    *   $1.60    *     65    *
*          *                          *          *            *           *
*  1 88217 * 1/2 IN. ROOFING NAILS    *   BOX    *    $.60    *     30    *
*          *                          *          *            *           *
*  1 91192 * DIE CAST ALUM. BOLTS--2" *   BOX    *   $1.95    *    275    *
*          *                          *          *            *           *
*  2 21570 * 8 FT. 2 X 4 -- REDWOOD   *    EA    *   $3.75    *     40    *
*          *                          *          *            *           *
*  6 15523 * 8 FT. 2 X 4 --PINE       *    EA    *   $2.20    *    500    *
*          *                          *          *            *           *
*  6 65227 * 8 FT. 1 X 6 -- PINE      *    EA    *   $2.05    *    115    *
*          *                          *          *            *           *
*  6 81874 * 8 FT. 4 X 4 -- PINE      *    EA    *   $5.95    *     15    *
*          *                          *          *            *           *
*  7 21250 * SPLIT CEDAR SHINGLES     *   BUN    *  $42.50    *     80    *
*          *                          *          *            *           *
*  7 94825 * COMPOSITION SHINGLES     *   BUN    *  $31.95    *    120    *
*          *                          *          *            *           *
```

Figure 9.2 Inventory Listing Program (Output) *Continued*

Summary   In this chapter, you have been introduced to the means for improving the readability of printed reports—edited data fields. Although any elementary-item may be described by using editing characters, only those fields which are to be printed should include them.

Editing characters fall into three catagories, as indicated below:

Fixed-Insertion	Floating-Insertion	Replacement
+	+	*
−	−	Z
$	$	
.	.	
,		
Ø		
B		
CR		
DB		

Fixed-insertion characters are printed on output where they appear in the edited PICTURE string. Floating-insertion characters are used to suppress leading zeros in numeric fields. Replacement characters are similar to floating characters in that they react to nonsignificant (leading) zeros in numeric fields. Unlike floating characters, however, replacement characters replace leading zeros with another character.

Although all editing characters are permitted in numeric fields, the zero insertion (Ø) and blank insertion (B) characters may also be used in the description of alphabetic- and alphanumeric-edited fields. COBOL permits the mixing of fixed- and floating-insertion characters *or* fixed-insertion and replacement characters in the numeric-edited field.

Notes on Programming Style

Typically, the beginning programmer overuses editing characters, and this improper use of editing characters tends to detract from readability. A case in point is the overuse of the currency symbol ($). Examine the columns of figures below:

$123.45	$123.45	123.45
$ 6.78	$6.78	6.78
$ 90.12	$90.12	90.12
$ .34	$.34	.34

The left column uses a fixed-insertion dollar symbol and zero suppression. The center column uses a floating-insertion dollar symbol. The right column uses zero suppression only. Ask yourself which column you would rather look at if you were spending your day reading printed reports containing one of the three. You probably chose the right column, because *without* the dollar symbol the values are easier to read. When designing reports, especially when edited output is to be included, always ask yourself if the part the *user* reads is in its most usable form.

Remember also that editing characters may not appear in a numeric field if that field is to be used in mathematical processing. The most frequent violation of this requirement is the use of the decimal-point insertion character (.) in place of the implied decimal character (V).

Remember also, that when program requirements call for the use of negative data, it is the programmer's responsibility to incorporate that into his program and report design. Signed internal fields should be used, and a reflection of the sign should be incorporated into printed report formats. It is also the programmer's responsibility to be aware of the possibility of field truncation, especially in numeric fields.

The printed report is frequently the only visible product of a program. The printed report, more than any other single factor, may mean the success or failure of a given system. It is the programmer's responsibility to insure that the reports are meaningful, in the most useful format, and *accurate!* The printed report is your "window to the world" outside the commercial programming environment. *Treat it accordingly.*

Questions

Below fill in the blank(s) with the appropriate word, words, or phrases.

1. An editing character that will occupy a specific position in a field (regardless of the magnitude of the numeric value placed in the field) is referred to as a(n) _____ character.

2. The fixed-insertion character (symbol) that causes a sign (+ or −) to be printed regardless of the sign of a numeric field is the _____ character (symbol).

3. The fixed-insertion character (symbol) that causes a sign to be printed only if a numeric value is negative is the _____ character (symbol).

4. The only editing characters considered to be both fixed- and floating-insertion characters are _____ , _____ and _____ .

5. The asterisk (check protection) character is considered to be a(n) _____ insertion character and is used to replace leading zeros in numeric fields.

6. The editing picture characters _____ must never appear as the rightmost character.

7. The editing picture characters _____ and _____ may be used in numeric-, alphabetic-, and alphanumeric-edited fields.

8. The three floating-insertion characters are _____ , _____ , and _____ .

9. The replacement characters are _____ and _____ .

Answer the following questions by circling either "T" for True or "F" for False.

T	F	10.	It is possible to edit only numeric fields.
T	F	11.	Each picture character falls into a single-use category.
T	F	12.	The fixed-insertion character + may be used only with numeric-edited fields and may produce either the plus or minus sign in the output field depending upon the sign of the numeric value.
T	F	13.	The fixed-insertion character + may appear in a picture string only as the leftmost character.
T	F	14.	The editing character + is a fixed-insertion character only.
T	F	15.	All fixed-insertion characters are also floating-insertion characters.
T	F	16.	Only one sign-oriented picture character is permitted per picture string.
T	F	17.	The currency symbol ($) must appear to the left of the most-significant-digit position as a fixed-insertion character.
T	F	18.	The comma (,) editing character may appear more than once per picture string, but the decimal-point character may appear only once.
T	F	19.	Only one fixed-insertion character may appear in a picture string.
T	F	20.	To be considered a floating-insertion character, a currency symbol ($) must appear more than once in a picture string.
T	F	21.	Two floating characters may appear in the same picture string.
T	F	22.	A picture string may contain both a floating-insertion character and a fixed-insertion character.
T	F	23.	Floating-insertion characters may be used in conjunction with numeric fields only.
T	F	24.	A floating-insertion character may appear only to the left of a 9 in the same picture string.
T	F	25.	It is possible for a floating-insertion character to replace a comma in a numeric-edited picture string.
T	F	26.	It is possible for a floating-insertion character to replace a decimal point in a numeric-edited picture string.
T	F	27.	It is permitted to have a fixed-insertion character flanked by floating-insertion characters.
T	F	28.	Replacement characters may suppress zeros to the right of a significant digit position.
T	F	29.	Both replacement and floating-insertion characters may appear in the same picture string.
T	F	30.	Replacement characters should be used only in numeric edited-fields.
T	F	31.	If the first significant digit in a numeric field appears to the right of a fixed-insertion character, the fixed-insertion character may be replaced with a blank if replacement characters are in use.

Exercises

1. Below is a series of source data fields, with PICTURE clauses, blank receiving fields with PICTURE clauses. For each, indicate the result of the movement of data, and show the length (number of columns) the field would occupy if it appeared in a printed report.

		SOURCE FIELD		RECEIVING FIELD		
	DATA*	PICTURE	PICTURE	RESULT		LENGTH
a)	69274	9(5)	99,999	_____		_____
b)	3192∧88	9(4)V99	99,999.99	_____		_____
c)	− 24∧76	S99V99	+ 9(4).99	_____		_____
d)	− 627	S999	− 9(3).ØØ	_____		_____
e)	+ 821∧62	S9(3)V99	+ 99	_____		_____
f)	+ 677∧44	S999V99	9(3).99CR	_____		_____
g)	− 7621∧88	S9(4)V99	$9,999.99B −	_____		_____
h)	4562∧894	9999V999	$$$,$$$.$$	_____		_____
i)	ØØØ∧Ø1	9(3)V99	$(4).$$	_____		_____
j)	4855∧97	9(4)V99	$(4).99	_____		_____
k)	− 9884∧6Ø	S9(4)V99	− $$$,$$$.$$	_____		_____
l)	ØØØ	9(3)	$(4).$$	_____		_____
m)	462∧88	S9(4)V99	+ $*,***.**	_____		_____
n)	1286	9(4)	99B99BØØ	_____		_____
o)	HELPME	X(6)	X(4)BBXX	_____		_____

*∧ denotes the location of the implied decimal point. Signs are shown in leading characters for visual identificaiton.

2. Create an edited output-record description that accommodates the following situation:

An output line is to consist of an employee number, hourly rate, hours worked, total deductions, gross pay, and net pay. The employee number is six digits long, the first two of which indicate the employee's department. The field is to be printed with one space separating the department number from the remainder of the employee number. The hourly rate is recorded as dollars and cents. The total field width is five digits. Print the field to suppress all insignificant zeros. The field should be blank for salaried employees (rate per hour is equal to zero). In the hours-worked field only whole hours are recorded; suppress unnecessary zeros in this three-digit field, and insert a decimal point followed by two zeros at the end of the field. It is conceivable that total deductions (a dollars-and-cents field) could be a negative value or could exceed $1,000. Thus, this field should be printed such that the sign (if negative) should appear adjacent to the most-significant-digit position. Commas and decimal points should also appear in the field, as appropriate. However, the field (at a minimum) should be printed as ".00." Gross pay is a seven-digit, dollars-and-cents field. Use commas and decimal points as appropriate, and print a dollar sign adjacent to the most-significant-digit position. Finally, the seven-digit (dollars-and-cents) net-pay field should contain a dollar sign, a decimal point, and commas, as appropriate. Leading zeros should appear as a check protection character.

Supply your own data-names for this record, and reserve at least five columns (containing spaces) between fields.

Problems

1. The personnel department has asked you to create a data-verification sheet containing employee data. Because these reports are to be distributed to individual departments, when the department name changes, a new page is to begin (indicating the department name). You may assume the data has been ordered by department name and employee name. The records contain these fields as well as the fields indicated below (see multiple-card layout form):

   1. Employee number—4 digits
   2. Employee name—30 characters
   3. Social security number—9 digits
   4. Employment date—6 digits in the format MMDDYY
   5. Department name—10 characters
   6. Hourly/Salaried code—1 character
   7. Rate for regular time—8 digits, 2 of which are decimal positions (contains either the rate per hour or salary amount)
   8. Overtime rate—6 digits, 2 of which are decimal positions (contains either overtime rate per hour or zeros for salaried employees)
   9. Number of dependents—2 digits
   10. Medical plan code—1 character
   11. Retirement plan code—1 character
   12. Savings plan code—1 character

   From this data you are to produce the report indicated on the print chart that meets following requirements:

   1. The employee number should have leading digits suppressed.
   2. The social security number should have blanks inserted at the appropriate positions of the number (should be treated as *one* field).
   3. The regular rate per hour should have the dollar symbol printed adjacent to the most-significant-digit position.
   4. The overtime rate per hour should be zero suppressed.
   5. The number of dependents should be zero suppressed.

   Both the regular and overtime rate per hour should have a decimal point (except the overtime rate should be blank when the field contains zero). The regular rate per hour should have a comma inserted between hundreds and thousands (since a monthly salary could appear in this field).

MULTIPLE-CARD LAYOUT FORM

Company LEARNING COBOL, INC.

Application PERSONNEL   by J. WAYNE SPENCE   Date 01/01/81   Job No. PROB 9.1   Sheet No. 1

EMPLOYEE ID			STATUS ID			PAYMENT ID		CODES		
EMP. NUMBER	EMPLOYEE NAME	SOCIAL SECURITY NUMBER	EMPLOY. DATE	DEPARTMENT	HR/SAL	REGULAR RATE	OVER-TIME RATE	NO DEP	MEDICAL	RETIRE	SAVINGS

150/10/8 PRINT CHART PROG. ID. PERSONNEL P 9.1   PAGE 1
(SPACING: 150 POSITIONS AT 10 CHARACTERS PER INCH, 8 LINES PER VERTICAL INCH)   DATE 1/1/81
PROGRAM TITLE PERSONNEL DATA VERIFICATION
PROGRAMMER OR DOCUMENTALIST J. WAYNE SPENCE
CHART TITLE PERSONNEL DATA VERIFICATION SHEET

3525 CARD PRINT POSITIONS

```
(RECORD CORRECTIONS BELOW                    PERSONNEL DATA
THE AFFECTED ITEM)                         VERIFICATION SHEET
                                           DEPARTMENT X ——————— X

 EMP.                              SOCIAL     HOUR/  |------ RATE ------|          |--- DEDUCTION CODES ---|
 NBR.   EMPLOYEE NAME             SECURITY   SALARY  REGULAR    OVER      NO.
                                  NUMBER     CODE     TIME      TIME      DEP.   MED    RET    SAV

ZZ Z9   X————————————————X    XXX XX XXXX    X    $$$,$$$.99  Z,ZZZ.ZZ   Z9     X      X      X

ZZ Z9   X————————————————X    XXX XX XXXX    X    $$$,$$$.99  Z,ZZZ.ZZ   Z9     X      X      X
```

2. Your company has decided to implement a computer-generated payroll-check procedure. The procedure that develops the actual monetary amounts to be printed by the check-writing program is the responsibility of another programmer; however, he has indicated to you that the data will be provided in two formats—a single-data record, which will precede the remainder of the file, and a payment record for each employee to receive a paycheck. The date record is composed of the following fields (see multiple-card layout form):

1. Payment-period beginning date—6 digits in the format MMDDYY
2. Payment-period ending date—6 digits in the format MMDDYY
3. Check date (date on which the check is to be printed)—6 digits in the format MMDDYY

The payment record consists of the following fields (see multiple-card layout form):

1. Employee name—20 characters
2. Number of regular hours worked—5 digits with 2 decimal positions
3. Number of overtime hours worked—5 digits with 2 decimal positions
4. Gross pay amount—7 digits with 2 decimal positions
5. Net pay amount—7 digits with 2 decimal positions
6. Federal withholding tax—6 digits with 2 decimal positions
7. FICA amount—6 digits with 2 decimal positions
8. Medical deduction amount—6 digits with 2 decimal positions
9. Retirement deduction amount—6 digits with 2 decimal positions
10. Savings deduction amount—6 digits with 2 decimal positions
11. Other deduction amount—6 digits with 2 decimal positions

The information contained in the DATA and PAYMENT records are to be printed in the format indicated on the print chart. Note that this is a preprinted form—spacing should be followed *exactly*. Furthermore, as is the case with most preprinted forms, only the name, hours, monetary-amount, and date fields are to be printed by your procedure. That is, "NAME," "PERIOD BEGINNING," and so forth are already printed on the paper to be used by your program. (Obviously you will not have these preprinted forms, but assume you do.) As shown on the print chart, all hours and monetary-amount fields are to be zero suppressed and are to include a decimal point. In addition, comma insertion is to be used in the gross-pay and net-pay fields. The net-pay field will appear in this form on the check stub, on the actual paycheck the net-pay amount should use the check protection character, a fixed-insertion dollar symbol, a comma, and a decimal point. Also notice that the employee name is to be printed twice ("NAME" and "PAYEE" fields). Finally, the check number is preprinted on each individual check—you are not responsible for printing this information. Spacing is indicated on the preprinted form. *DO NOT ADVANCE TO THE TOP OF FORM FOR EACH PAYCHECK!*

MULTIPLE-CARD LAYOUT FORM

Company __LEARNING COBOL, INC.__

Application __CHECK__   by __J. WAYNE SPENCE__   Date __01/01/81__   Job No. __PROB 9.2__   Sheet No. __1__

PAYMENT RECORD

150/10/8 PRINT CHART   PROG. ID. __CHECK .P 9.2__   PAGE __1__

(SPACING: 150 POSITIONS AT 10 CHARACTERS PER INCH, 8 LINES PER VERTICAL INCH)   DATE __1/1/81__

PROGRAM TITLE __CHECK WRITER__

PROGRAMMER OR DOCUMENTALIST __J. WAYNE SPENCE__

CHART TITLE __PAYROLL CHECKS__

3. A series of purchase-order records have been prepared from a series of purchase requests which have been filled by one or more of our vendors. Each record is composed of a series of fields as indicated below (see the multiple-card layout form):

     1. Purchase-order number—5 characters

     2. Purchase-order date—6 characters in the format MMDDYY

     3. Vendor ID code—3 characters (initials)

     4. Vendor name—20 characters

     5. Inventory item number—6 digits

     6. Inventory item description—20 characters

     7. Quantity purchased—4 digits

8. Cost-per-item-purchased—6 digits (dollars and cents)
9. Tax-on-item-purchased—5 digits (dollars and cents)
10. Discount-on-item-purchased—5 digits (dollars and cents)

From these records, you are to produce the report presented on the print chart. The Purchase-Order Listing is to begin at the top of a new page. Since each purchase order contains several line items (multiple items purchased), several records in sequence will contain the same purchase-order number. However, when the purchase-order number changes, two blank lines are to appear on the report. The print editing to be performed should be as follows:

1. Purchase-order number should be printed such that the first digit is separated from the other four digits by a single space.
2. Purchase-order date should be printed such that a single space appears between the month and day and a single space appears between the day and year.
3. Vendor ID code should be printed with a single space between each of the individual characters in the field.
4. Inventory item number should be printed as three digits, a single space and the remaining three digits.
5. Quantity purchased should be printed such that leading zeros are suppressed; however, zero should be printed if the quantity is zero.
6. Cost-per-item purchased should contain a dollar sign, a comma between the thousands and hundreds positions, a decimal point, and nonsignificant zeros (excluding cents) should be suppressed.
7. Tax-on-items-purchased should be zero suppressed, with a decimal point (such that the field is blank if no tax is charged on the purchase).
8. Discount-on-items-purchased should have the same field characteristics as 7 above.

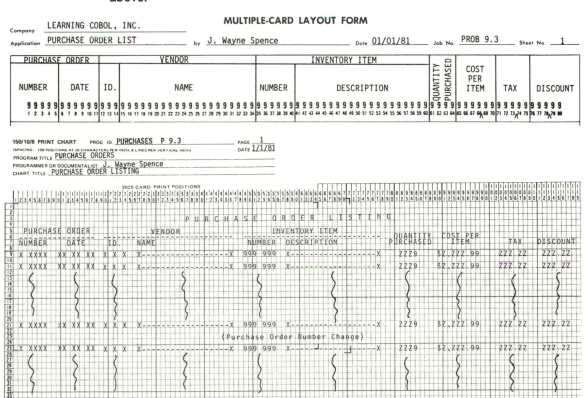

10 Arithmetic Statements

COBOL is limited arithmetically to addition, subtraction, multiplication, division, and exponentiation (raising a number to a power). Other programming languages (e.g., FORTRAN) provide more arithmetical versatility, but COBOL's arithmetic capability is generally adequate for business data processing applications.

There are five arithmetic statements in COBOL—ADD, SUBTRACT, MULTIPLY, DIVIDE, and COMPUTE. The first four of these statements (ADD, SUBTRACT, MULTIPLY, and DIVIDE) each perform a single arithmetic function. The COMPUTE statement can perform a variety of functions, including addition, subtraction, multiplication, division, and exponentiation.

The ADD Statement

The function of the ADD statement is to provide the sum of numeric items. There are two formats of the ADD statement, as presented in Figure 10.1. The first format of the ADD statement causes all identifiers and literals appearing

```
Format 1:

    ADD  {identifier-1}  [identifier-2]
         {literal-1   }  [literal-2  ]  . . . TO identifier-m [ROUNDED]

         [identifier-n [ROUNDED]] . . . .[ON SIZE ERROR imperative-statement]


Format 2:

    ADD  {identifier-1}  {identifier-2}  [identifier-3]
         {literal-1   }  {literal-2   }  [literal-3  ]  . . .

         GIVING identifiers-m [ROUNDED] [ON SIZE ERROR imperative-statement]
```

Figure 10.1 Formats of the ADD Statement

before the required word TO to be added to the identifier(s) following the word TO. As an example, if the statement

```
ADD ITEM-1, ITEM-2, 1Ø TO ITEM-3.
```

were to be executed, the values contained in ITEM-1 and ITEM-2 and the value 1Ø would be added to ITEM-3. Thus, if ITEM-1 contains 5, ITEM-2 contains 15, and ITEM-3 contains 30 before the execution of this statement, after the statement is executed, ITEM-1 and ITEM-2 are unchanged, and ITEM-3 contains the results of the operation—the value 60. Thus, ITEM-3 both takes part in the addition operation *and* acts as the receiving field of the operation. If additional identifiers are listed after TO, they likewise take part in the addition operation and act as receiving fields for the results of the addition.

All identifiers in this form of the ADD statement must be nonedited, numeric data items. (Remember that a decimal point is an editing character.) All literals in the statement must be numeric literals. The maximum size of each of the items in the ADD statement is set by the particular computer (but generally may be no more than 18 digits). The data items are decimal-point aligned before the addition takes place. Thus, overflow of the field to the left (high-order digits) or truncation to the right (after the decimal point) is possible.

Two optional clauses may be attached to the ADD statement. The ROUND-ED option rounds the result in the receiving field to the field's PICTURE size. Thus, if the result of the addition operation has more positions following the decimal point than does the receiving field, the result is rounded to the size of the receiving field.

The SIZE ERROR option allows the programmer to specify the action to be taken in response to an addition-operation result that is too large for the receiving field, i.e., the number of high-order digits in the result exceeds the available space in the receiving field. If the ROUNDED option is also specified, rounding occurs before the SIZE ERROR is checked. The SIZE ERROR applies only to the final result of the computation and not to any intermediate results. If a SIZE ERROR occurs, the imperative-statement is executed, and the receiving field is not altered. If several identifiers are listed after TO, a SIZE ERROR applies to all identifiers. Identifiers listed *after* (and including) the identifier causing the SIZE ERROR are not changed by the execution of the ADD statement. All identifiers listed *before* the identifier causing the error will be altered by the ADD statement. New values are assigned to receiving fields from left to right.

The remaining arithmetic statements also permit ROUNDED and SIZE ER-ROR options. The actions of these options are the same as discussed above. However, when division is possible and there is an attempted division by zero, the SIZE ERROR option is invoked. Thus, the SIZE ERROR option has an additional function for the DIVIDE and COMPUTE statements.

The second format of the ADD statement is the "ADD-GIVING" statement. It differs slightly from the first ADD statement. *Two* identifiers or literals are required before the word GIVING. *Only one* receiving field may be listed after the word GIVING. *TO does not appear in this format of the ADD.*

This ADD statement causes all of the identifiers and literals before the word GIVING to be summed, and their sum is placed in the identifier following the word GIVING. The difference between the first ADD and this ADD is that the identifier following the word GIVING is a receiving field *only*—it does not take part in the addition operation.

As with the first ADD statement, all identifiers, listed before the word GIVING must be numeric-nonedited elementary-items. Literals must be numeric literals. The identifier listed after the word GIVING (the receiving field) may be an *edited*-numeric field. And, since it acts as a receiving field only, it need not contain a value prior to the execution of the ADD statement. *Initialization is a requirement for all other identifiers in both formats of the ADD.* The programmer should exercise caution in describing edited-numeric field. If identifier-m is an edited-numeric field, it cannot be used as an operand in any other arithmetic operation, although it may appear again after the word GIVING. Thus, the value of the identifier is, for all intents and purposes, an end product. (Remember that the decimal point is an editing character.)

As an example of the ADD-GIVING statement, assume that ITEM-1 contains 123ᴧ45 and ITEM-2 contains 945ᴧØ2. If the statement

```
ADD ITEM-1, ITEM-2 GIVING ITEM-3.
```

is executed, and the PICTURE string of ITEM-3 is 999.9, the result stored in ITEM-3 will be Ø68.4 (regardless of the previous contents of ITEM-3). The result placed in ITEM-3 has been truncated from both ends to fit the PICTURE string. (Most compilers provide a warning message indicating that lower-order digits may be truncated, but no compiler warns that high-order digits will be truncated when the PICTURE string of the receiving field has as many digit positions before the decimal point as the items used to compute it.) IF the ROUNDED option is specified, i.e.,

```
ADD ITEM-1, ITEM-2 GIVING ITEM-3 ROUNDED.
```

then the result placed in ITEM-3 would be Ø68.5— the digit(s) to be truncated from the rightmost position(s) is 5 or greater. However, there is still no indication that ITEM-3 has been truncated from the left. If the SIZE ERROR option is added to the statement, i.e.,

```
ADD ITEM-1, ITEM-2 GIVING ITEM-3 ROUNDED ON SIZE ERROR
     DISPLAY 'ERROR OCCURRED DURING ADDITION OF ITEM-3'...
```

the value of ITEM-3 would be the value it contained before the ADD operation took place, and the message "ERROR OCCURRED DURING ADDITION OF ITEM-3" would appear on the output from the program. To complete the addition operation, the PICTURE string of ITEM-3 should be enlarged to at least 9999.9, if not larger. Remember that this PICTURE string is an edited-numeric field, so ITEM-3 can only be used as a receiving field in other arithmetic statements.

The SUBTRACT Statement

The SUBTRACT statement causes the subtraction (reduction or decrement) of an item (or items) from the value of one or more items. The two formats of the SUBTRACT statement appear in Figure 10.2.

Format 1 of the SUBTRACT statement causes the *algebraic* sum of the identifiers and literals preceding the word FROM to be subtracted from the identifier(s) listed after the word FROM. It is important to note that the algebraic sum is subtracted, because if the sum of the identifiers and literals is negative, the effect is to *add* the identifiers and literals before FROM to the identifier(s)

```
Format 1:

    SUBTRACT  {identifier-1}  [identifier-2]  . . . FROM identifier-m [ROUNDED]
              {literal-1   }  [literal-2   ]

              [identifier-n [ROUNDED]] . . .[ON SIZE ERROR imperative-statement]

- - - - - - - - - - - - - - - - - - - - - - - - - - - - - - - - - - - - - - - - - - -

Format 2:

    SUBTRACT  {identifier-1}  [identifier-2]  . . . FROM  {identifier-m}
              {literal-1   }  [literal-2   ]              {literal-m   }

        GIVING identifier-n [ROUNDED] [ON SIZE ERROR imperative-statement]
```

Figure 10.2 Formats of the SUBTRACT Statement

after FROM. If a negative result is anticipated (or is possible), the receiving field's PICTURE string should contain an operational sign (S).

All identifiers in this format of the SUBTRACT statement must be non-edited-numeric fields and must contain values. Literals must be numeric literals.

Suppose that the statement

SUBTRACT ITEM-1, 2∅.5 FROM ITEM-2.

was included in a program where ITEM-1 contains 5∅$_\wedge$3 and ITEM-2 contains 3∅ and has a PICTURE of S999. The result stored in ITEM-2 would be -∅4∅. Again, the fraction (.2) is truncated. If the PICTURE string of ITEM-3 did not contain the operational sign (S), the result of the subtraction would be ∅4∅ (an unsigned number).

Format 2 of the SUBTRACT statement allows the algebraic sum of the identifiers and literals appearing before the word FROM to be subtracted from the identifier listed after the word FROM—the result being stored in the identifier shown after the word GIVING. As before, all identifiers listed before the word GIVING must be nonedited-numeric fields. The identifier after GIVING may be an edited-numeric field and does not have to contain a value before the execution of the statement.

Suppose the statement

SUBTRACT ITEM-1 FROM ITEM-2 GIVING ITEM-3

was contained in a program, where ITEM-1 contained 22$_\wedge$4 and ITEM-2 contained 46$_\wedge$8. The result of the execution of this statement would place 24$_\wedge$4 in ITEM-3, regardless of its previous value. (The indicated value assumes the PICTURE clause of ITEM-3 is at least as large as 99.9.) The values of ITEM-1 and ITEM-2 are unchanged after this operation.

The MULTIPLY Statement

The MULTIPLY statement performs the multiplication of *two* data items only.

The first format of the MULTIPLY statement creates the product of the first identifier or numeric literal and the second identifier and stores the result in the second identifier. The identifiers in this format of the MULTIPLY statement must be nonedited-numeric fields containing values.

For example, in the following statement,

```
MULTIPLY 1Ø.1 BY ITEM-1
```

if ITEM-1 contained the value 4 before the execution of the statement, it would contain 4Ø.4 after the statement is executed. The numeric literal 1Ø.1 can be used *only* in the location shown. An identifier *must* follow the word BY to serve as the receiving field for the calculation.

Format 1:

    MULTIPLY {identifier-1 / literal-1} BY identifier-2 [ROUNDED]

        [ON SIZE ERROR imperative-statement]

- -

Format 2:

    MULTIPLY {identifier-1 / literal-1} BY {identifier-2 / literal-2} GIVING identifier-3 [ROUNDED]

        [ON SIZE ERROR imperative-statement]

Figure 10.3 Formats of the MULTIPLY Statement

Format 2 of the MULTIPLY statement allows identifiers and literals to appear before and after the word BY. The identifiers must be nonedited numeric fields; however, the field following the word GIVING may be an edited field that may or may not contain a value prior to the execution of the MULTIPLY statement. The result of the multiplication is stored in the identifier following the word GIVING.

If the statement

```
MULTIPLY ITEM-1 BY 1Ø GIVING ITEM-2.
```

is executed (with ITEM-1 containing $4_\wedge 5$ and ITEM-2 having a PICTURE string of 999V99), the result stored in ITEM-2 will be $\emptyset 45_\wedge \emptyset\emptyset$.

The DIVIDE Statement

The DIVIDE statement produces a quotient when one data is divided into another. As seen in Figure 10.4, the DIVIDE statement is similar to the MULTIPLY statement. In Format 1, identifier-1 (or literal-1) represents the divisor (or denominator), and identifier-2 represents the dividend (or numerator), i.e.,

$$\text{identifier-1 (or literal-1)} \sqrt{\text{identifier-2}}$$

or

$$\frac{\text{identifier-2}}{\text{identifier-1 (or literal-1)}} .$$

```
Format 1:

    DIVIDE  ⎧identifier-1⎫  INTO identifier-2 [ROUNDED]
            ⎨          ⎬
            ⎩literal-1  ⎭

            [ON SIZE ERROR imperative-statement]

--------------------------------------------------------------------------

Format 2:

    DIVIDE  ⎧identifier-1⎫ ⎧INTO⎫ ⎧identifier-2⎫  GIVING identifier-3 [ROUNDED]
            ⎨          ⎬ ⎨    ⎬ ⎨          ⎬
            ⎩literal-1  ⎭ ⎩BY  ⎭ ⎩literal-2  ⎭

            [REMAINDER identifier-4] [ON SIZE ERROR imperative-statement]
```

Figure 10.4 Formats of the DIVIDE Statement

The result of the division operation (the quotient) is placed in identifier-2 after the DIVIDE statement has been executed. In this form of the DIVIDE statement, the identifiers must be nonedited-numeric fields, and the literal must be a numeric literal. When an attempt is made to divide by zero, i.e., when identifier-1 is zero, a SIZE ERROR occurs. If the SIZE ERROR option is not specified, an attempted division by zero will result in an "ILLEGAL DECIMAL" or "DECIMAL DIVIDE EXCEPTION" error.

Suppose the statement

```
DIVIDE ITEM-1 INTO ITEM-2.
```

was included in a program, where ITEM-1 contained the value 1Ø and ITEM-2 contained the value 45 before the execution of the statement. After the statement was executed, ITEM-1 would be unchanged and ITEM-2 would contain $4_\wedge 5$ (provided the description of ITEM-2 permitted for decimal positions).

In the second format of the DIVIDE statement, the result of the division operation is placed in the identifier following the word GIVING. With Format 2, the programmer has a choice of the reserved words BY or INTO. When the reserved word INTO is provided, the designation of divisor and dividend is the same as for Format 1. However, when the keyword BY is present, divisor and dividend are reversed (identifier-2 becomes the divisor, and identifier-1 becomes the dividend).

The Format 2 DIVIDE statement provides one option that does not appear in any other COBOL arithmetic statement—the reserved word REMAINDER. REMAINDER makes it possible to perform a division and retain the remainder *modulo* division. Thus, the remainder is defined as being the dividend less the product of the quotient and the divisor.

Assume the statement

```
DIVIDE ITEM-1 INTO ITEM-2 GIVING ITEM-3.
```

is executed, where ITEM-1 contains the value 1Ø, ITEM-2 contains the value 45, and ITEM-3 has a PICTURE string of 99. The result of the division operation placed in ITEM-3 would be Ø4, with a remainder of 5, which is not retained. If the statement is modified to:

```
DIVIDE ITEM-1 INTO ITEM-2 GIVING ITEM-3 REMAINDER ITEM-4.
```

and ITEM-4 has a PICTURE string of 99, the division operation would result in ITEM-3 containing Ø4 and ITEM-4 containing Ø5. Finally, if the statement is further modified to:

```
DIVIDE ITEM-1 BY ITEM-2 GIVING ITEM-3 REMAINDER ITEM-4.
```

ITEM-3 would contain ØØ and ITEM-4 would contain 45.

The COMPUTE Statement

The most versatile arithmetic statement is the COMPUTE statement. The COMPUTE statement permits the coding of a series of operations in algebraic form. The general format of the COMPUTE statement is presented in Figure 10.5. Identifier-1 is the receiving field, and like the other arithmetic statements providing the GIVING phrase, the identifier may be an edited-numeric field not containing a value prior to the execution of the COMPUTE statement. This identifier is followed by an optional ROUNDED clause (allowing the result of the computation to be rounded to the PICTURE size of identifier-1). The identifier is then followed by an equal symbol, the only required punctuation for the COMPUTE statement other than the normal period at the end of the statement.

All identifiers listed after the equal symbol must be nonedited-numeric fields, and all identifiers must contain a value. All literals must be numeric literals. In the format of the COMPUTE statement, the programmer has a choice of an identifier, a literal, or an arithmetic expression. If an identifier or a literal is chosen, the identifier or literal is assigned to the storage position identifier-1. This in no way affects the contents of identifier-2. The COMPUTE statement is used much like the MOVE statement, and if the programmer chooses to use them, the arithmetic capabilities of the COMPUTE statement are extensive.

```
COMPUTE identifier-1 [ROUNDED] =  { identifier-2      }
                                  { literal-1         }
                                  { arithmetic-expression }

        [ON SIZE ERROR imperative-statement]
```

Figure 10.5 Format of the COMPUTE Statement

An arithmetic expression in COBOL may be composed of arithmetic operators, identifiers, literals, and parentheses. The symbols used to represent arithmetic operators are

+ — addition   / — division
− — subtraction   ** — exponentiation.
* — multiplication

Thus, the COMPUTE statement allows the same types of operations performed by the ADD, SUBTRACT, MULTIPLY, and DIVIDE statements plus exponentiation (raising a number to a power)— which is not easily done with the other arithmetic statements. The arithmetic operators should never appear adjacent to each other in an expression. When used, an operator should be preceded and followed by a space. And, in the absence of parentheses, exponentiation will be executed first; multiplication and division, second; and addition and subtraction, last. If multiple operations appear in an expression, and the operations are on the same "level" (as just described), the operations will be executed from left to right.

In some instances, the programmer may wish certain operations to be performed before others (e.g., an addition before a multiplication). To accomplish this the programmer may specify the sequence of operations by placing parentheses around the operation to be executed first. That is, if parentheses are present in an arithmetic expression, the COBOL compiler proceeds by first eliminating (or resolving) sets of parentheses. If there are multiple sets of parentheses, the compiler resolves the parentheses from left to right. If the parentheses are "nested" (one set of parentheses within another set of parentheses), the compiler will begin the execution of the statement with the innermost set of parentheses. When parentheses are coded in an expression, a left (open) parenthesis should be preceded, but not followed by a space. The right (close) parenthesis should not be preceded by a space, but should be followed by a space or a period.

Figure 10.6 illustrates the COMPUTE statement as it relates to various types of formulae. Carefully read the comments associated with each of the examples.

The Sales Tax Program

Figure 10.7 demonstrates how arithmetic statements might be used in a program. The program presented in Figure 10.7 determines the amount of sales tax (assumed to be 4 percent) when the amount of purchase is provided. In addition, the program "counts" the number of sales made and accumulates (calculates a grand total) the amount of sale, sales tax, and total amount due. The program flowchart of Figure 10.7 shows the sequence of events in the PROCEDURE DIVISION of the sales tax program. The hierarchy chart shows three functional modules (START-UP, READ-DATA, and FINISH-UP), the execution of which are controlled by the PROCEDURE CONTROL module (lines 58 through 62 of the program). The PROCEDURE CONTROL module follows a pattern similar to previous control modules. The procedure is initialized (START-UP), a repetitive function is executed until all data are read (READ-DATA), and the procedure is terminated (FINISH-UP).

In the START-UP module (100) and the START-UP paragraph (lines 63 through 67), after the input and output files are opened, the heading is produced by the WRITE and MOVE statements. The lines of output are produced by REPORT-HEADING (from lines 44 through 47 of the DATA DIVISION) through PRINT-LINE. Notice that PRINT-LINE (lines 26 through 37) provides a detailed description of the output record. It is a possible to produce headings through such a description, but to avoid having "garbage" in the output of detail information, any line printed through PRINT-LINE should be "erased" before a detailed record is written. This is one reason for the MOVE SPACES TO PRINT-LINE statement (line 66). The WRITE statement in line 67 causes one blank line to be produced after the heading (another reason for moving spaces to PRINT-LINE).

Formula*	COMPUTE Statement	Comments
$X = \dfrac{A}{B}$	COMPUTE X = A / B.	The same type of operation can be performed by the DIVIDE statement (e.g., DIVIDE A BY B GIVING X.)
$X = A + B - C$	COMPUTE X = A + B - C.	There is a direct translation between the formula and the COMPUTE statement. Addition is performed first, followed by subtraction, and then the assignment of the result to X.
$X = A + B^2$	COMPUTE X = A + B ** 2.	The representation B² in the formula is B ** 2 in the COMPUTE statement. This is called exponentiation. Note that the exponent (in this case 2) is placed after the double asterisk. Exponentiation occurs first, followed by addition.
$X = \dfrac{A + B}{C - D}$	COMPUTE X = (A + B) / (C - D).	Note that parentheses are required in both the numerator and demoninator. This forces the operations to be done in the order (1) add A and B, (2) subtract D from C, and (3) divide the numerator by the denominator.
$X = \sqrt{\dfrac{AB}{C^2}}$	COMPUTE X = (A * B / C ** 2) ** .5.	Inside the square-root symbol (radical), the formula suggests that A and B should be multiplied (A * B), C squared (C**2), the numerator divided by the denominator (/), and the square root of the expression determined (** .5). Since the expression is enclosed in a set of parentheses, exponentiation, multiplication, and division take place in that order. Once the parentheses are resolved, the expression is ''raised'' to the .5 power—the square root.
$X = -B + \sqrt{\dfrac{B^2 - 4AC}{2A}}$	COMPUTE X = -B + ((B ** 2 - 4 * A * C) / (2 * A)) ** .5.	Notice that in this expression, there are ''nested'' parentheses. The entire expression under the radical is enclosed in the outermost set of parentheses, while the numerator and denominator are each enclosed in a separate set of parentheses.

* All identifiers are assumed to be a single character in length.

Figure 10.6 Examples of the COMPUTE Statement

When the READ-DATA module (300) is invoked, the processing of data begins. The process is initiated through the READ statement (line 69). If an input operation is attempted and no data is found, the READ statement will cause an unconditional branch to take place (through the AT END phrase) to the exit for the section (lines 81 and 82). Provided data has been read, the statement MULTIPLY .Ø4 BY SALES-AMT GIVING TAX ROUNDED (line 70) creates an amount of tax based on the amount of sales. Note that the value .Ø4 is a numeric literal and SALES-AMT is a nonedited-numeric field (described in line 23 of the CUST-REC and provided a value through the READ statement in line 69). TAX—the result of the MULTIPLY statement—is described in the WORKING-STORAGE SECTION (line 40). TAX does not contain a value until the MULTIPLY statement is executed. Furthermore, TAX is a nonedited-numeric field permitting it to be used in later computations (the ADD statements in lines 75 and 78). The next four statements (lines 71 through 74) MOVE data items from CUST-REC (CUST-NO, CUST-NAME, and CUST-AMT) and the WORKING-STORAGE SECTION (TAX) to the output-record description (PRINT-LINE containing CUST-NAME-OUT, CUST-NO-OUT, SALES-AMT-OUT, and SALES-TAX). These operations prepare the output record for printing.

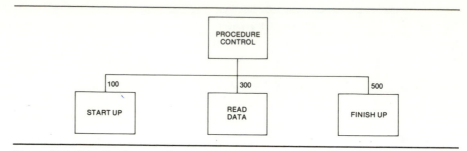

Figure 10.7 Sales Tax Program (Hierarchy Chart)

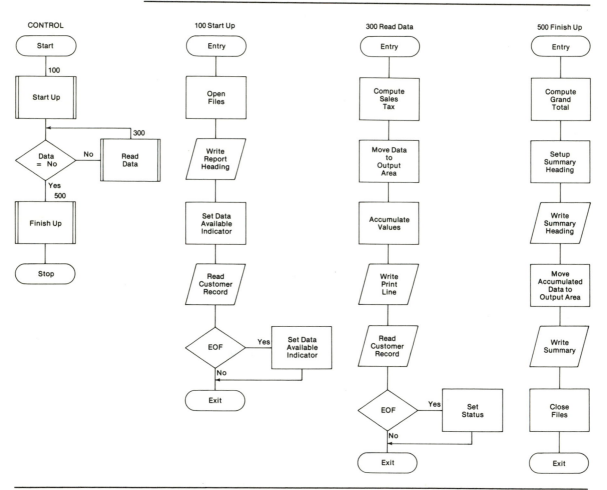

Figure 10.7 Sales Tax Program (Module Flowcharts) *Continued*

```
|           1   1   2   2   3   3   4   4   4   5   5   6   6   6   7   7   8|
|   4   8   2   6   0   4   8   2   5   0   4   8   2   6   0   4   8   2   6   0|
-------------------------------------------------------------------------------
|000010 IDENTIFICATION  DIVISION.                                    FIG 10.7|
|000020 PROGRAM-ID. SALES-TAX-PROG.                                  FIG 10.7|
|000030 AUTHOR. J. WAYNE SPENCE.                                     FIG 10.7|
|000040 DATE-WRITTEN. JAN 1, 1981.                                   FIG 10.7|
|000050 DATE-COMPILED JAN 1, 1981.                                   FIG 10.7|
|000060* THIS PROGRAM ILLUSTRATES THE USE OF ARITHMETIC             FIG 10.7|
|000070* STATEMENTS, COUNTERS AND ACCUMULATORS.                      FIG 10.7|
|000080 ENVIRONMENT DIVISION.                                        FIG 10.7|
|000090 CONFIGURATION SECTION.                                       FIG 10.7|
|000100 SOURCE-COMPUTER.  IBM.                                       FIG 10.7|
|000110 OBJECT-COMPUTER.  IBM.                                       FIG 10.7|
|000120 SPECIAL-NAMES.   C01 IS TOP-OF-PAGE.                         FIG 10.7|
|000130 INPUT-OUTPUT SECTION.                                        FIG 10.7|
|000140 FILE-CONTROL.                                                FIG 10.7|
|000150     SELECT CUSTOMER-FILE ASSIGN TO UT-S-SYSIN.               FIG 10.7|
|000160     SELECT REPORT-FILE ASSIGN TO UT-S-SYSPRINT.              FIG 10.7|
|000170 DATA DIVISION.                                               FIG 10.7|
|000180 FILE SECTION.                                                FIG 10.7|
|000190 FD  CUSTOMER-FILE LABEL RECORDS ARE OMITTED.                 FIG 10.7|
|000200 01  CUST-REC.                                                FIG 10.7|
|000210     05 CUST-NO              PIC 9(05).                       FIG 10.7|
|000220     05 CUST-NAME            PIC X(20).                       FIG 10.7|
|000230     05 SALES-AMT            PIC 9(04)V9(02).                 FIG 10.7|
|000240     05 FILLER               PIC X(49).                       FIG 10.7|
|000250 FD  REPORT-FILE LABEL RECORDS ARE OMITTED.                   FIG 10.7|
|000260 01  PRINT-LINE.                                              FIG 10.7|
|000270     02 FILLER               PIC X(35).                       FIG 10.7|
|000280     02 CUST-NAME-OUT        PIC X(20).                       FIG 10.7|
|000290     02 FILLER               PIC X(05).                       FIG 10.7|
|000300     02 CUST-NO-OUT          PIC Z(4)9.                       FIG 10.7|
|000310     02 FILLER               PIC X(05).                       FIG 10.7|
|000320     02 SALES-AMT-OUT        PIC $(5).99.                     FIG 10.7|
|000330     02 FILLER               PIC X(05).                       FIG 10.7|
|000340     02 SALES-TAX            PIC $$$$.99.                     FIG 10.7|
|000350     02 FILLER               PIC X(05).                       FIG 10.7|
|000360     02 TOTAL-AMT            PIC $$$,$$$.99.                   FIG 10.7|
|000370     02 FILLER               PIC X(58).                       FIG 10.7|
|000380 WORKING-STORAGE SECTION.                                     FIG 10.7|
|000390 01  WORKING-VARIABLES.                                       FIG 10.7|
|000400     05  TAX                 PIC 9(03)V9(02).                 FIG 10.7|
|000410     05  TRANS-COUNT         PIC 9(04)       VALUE ZERO.      FIG 10.7|
|000420     05  CUM-SALES-AMT       PIC 9(10)V9(02) VALUE ZERO.      FIG 10.7|
|000430     05  CUM-TAX             PIC 9(10)V9(02) VALUE ZERO.      FIG 10.7|
|000440 01  REPORT-HEADING.                                          FIG 10.7|
|000450     03 FILLER               PIC X(60) VALUE SPACES.          FIG 10.7|
|000460     03 FILLER               PIC X(06) VALUE 'SALES'.         FIG 10.7|
|000470     03 TYPE-OF-HEADING      PIC X(07) VALUE 'DETAIL'.        FIG 10.7|
|000480 01  SUMMARY-RECORD.                                          FIG 10.7|
|000490     02 FILLER               PIC X(31) VALUE SPACES.          FIG 10.7|
|000500     02 T-COUNT              PIC ZZZ9.                        FIG 10.7|
|000510     02 FILLER               PIC X(05) VALUE SPACES.          FIG 10.7|
|000520     02 C-SALES-AMT          PIC $$,$$$,$$$,$$$.99.           FIG 10.7|
|000530     02 FILLER               PIC X(05) VALUE SPACES.          FIG 10.7|
|000540     02 C-TAX                PIC $$,$$$,$$$,$$$.99.           FIG 10.7|
|000550     02 FILLER               PIC X(05) VALUE SPACES.          FIG 10.7|
|000560     02 C-TOTAL-AMT          PIC $$,$$$,$$$,$$$.99.           FIG 10.7|
|000570 PROCEDURE DIVISION.                                          FIG 10.7|
|000580 PROCEDURE-CONTROL SECTION.                                   FIG 10.7|
|000590     PERFORM 100-START-UP.                                    FIG 10.7|
|000600     PERFORM 300-READ-DATA.                                   FIG 10.7|
|000610     PERFORM 500-FINISH-UP.                                   FIG 10.7|
|000620     STOP RUN.                                                FIG 10.7|
|000630 100-START-UP SECTION.                                        FIG 10.7|
|000640     OPEN INPUT CUSTOMER-FILE, OUTPUT REPORT-FILE.            FIG 10.7|
|000650     WRITE PRINT-LINE FROM REPORT-HEADING AFTER TOP-OF-PAGE.  FIG 10.7|
|000660     MOVE SPACES TO PRINT-LINE.                               FIG 10.7|
|000670     WRITE PRINT-LINE AFTER ADVANCING 1 LINES.                FIG 10.7|
|000680 300-READ-DATA SECTION.                                       FIG 10.7|
|000690     READ CUSTOMER-FILE AT END GO TO 399-EXIT.                FIG 10.7|
|000700     MULTIPLY .04 BY SALES-AMT GIVING TAX ROUNDED.            FIG 10.7|
|000710     MOVE CUST-NO TO CUST-NO-OUT.                             FIG 10.7|
|000720     MOVE CUST-NAME TO CUST-NAME-OUT.                         FIG 10.7|
|000730     MOVE SALES-AMT TO SALES-AMT-OUT.                         FIG 10.7|
|000740     MOVE TAX TO SALES-TAX.                                   FIG 10.7|
|000750     ADD SALES-AMT, TAX GIVING TOTAL-AMT.                     FIG 10.7|
|000760     ADD SALES-AMT TO CUM-SALES-AMT.                          FIG 10.7|
|000770     ADD TAX TO CUM-TAX.                                      FIG 10.7|
```

Figure 10.7 Sales Tax Program *Continued*

```
|           1   1   2   2   2   3   3   4   4   4   5   5   6   6   6   7   7   8|
|   4   8   2   6   0   4   8   2   6   0   4   8   2   6   0   4   8   2   6   0|
-------------------------------------------------------------------------------
|000780      ADD 1 TO TRANS-COUNT.                                      FIG 10.7|
|000790      WRITE PRINT-LINE AFTER ADVANCING 1 LINES.                  FIG 10.7|
|000800      GO TO 300-READ-DATA.                                       FIG 10.7|
|000810 399-EXIT.                                                       FIG 10.7|
|000820      EXIT.                                                      FIG 10.7|
|000830 500-FINISH-UP.                                                  FIG 10.7|
|000840      ADD CUM-TAX, CUM-SALES-AMT GIVING C-TOTAL-AMT.             FIG 10.7|
|000850      MOVE 'SUMMARY' TO TYPE-OF-HEADING.                         FIG 10.7|
|000860      WRITE PRINT-LINE FROM REPORT-HEADING AFTER TOP-OF-PAGE.    FIG 10.7|
|000870      MOVE CUM-TAX TO C-TAX.                                     FIG 10.7|
|000880      MOVE TRANS-COUNT TO T-COUNT.                               FIG 10.7|
|000890      MOVE CUM-SALES-AMT TO C-SALES-AMT.                         FIG 10.7|
|000900      WRITE PRINT-LINE FROM SUMMARY-RECORD AFTER 2 LINES.        FIG 10.7|
|000910      CLOSE CUSTOMER-FILE, REPORT-FILE.                          FIG 10.7|
```

Figure 10.7 Sales Tax Program *Continued*

```
|      |        1         2         3         4         5         6         7        8| FIGURE |
|RECORD|12345678901234567890123456789012345678901234567890123456789012345678901234567890| NUMBER |
---------------------------------------------------------------------------------------------------
|    1|02643ADAMS, RICHARD       003515                                                 |FIG 10.7|
|    2|03647ANDERSON, FOREST     326520                                                 |FIG 10.7|
|    3|04753BALLES, FRANK        357025                                                 |FIG 10.7|
|    4|12893BEATTIE, WILLIAM     292720                                                 |FIG 10.7|
|    5|14438BOND, RONALD         006690                                                 |FIG 10.7|
|    6|14762BREW, GEORGE         441900                                                 |FIG 10.7|
|    7|17216BROADUS, JEFF        374765                                                 |FIG 10.7|
|    8|19506BUCKLEY, CATHY       152680                                                 |FIG 10.7|
|    9|24168CESARIO, MARK        114515                                                 |FIG 10.7|
|   10|24917CHOW, WINNIE         516815                                                 |FIG 10.7|
|   11|31588CLEMENT, GREGORY     000515                                                 |FIG 10.7|
|   12|31656DECK, DEBORA         003845                                                 |FIG 10.7|
|   13|32877DECKER, MIKE         734700                                                 |FIG 10.7|
|   14|33683DIMOND, LAWRENCE     444500                                                 |FIG 10.7|
|   15|33759EDMISTON, DAVID      342375                                                 |FIG 10.7|
|   16|34724ELLIOTT, GARY        412790                                                 |FIG 10.7|
|   17|35168ELLIOTT, ROGER       192260                                                 |FIG 10.7|
|   18|35295FLORES, JOSE         418100                                                 |FIG 10.7|
|   19|37081FORD, PATRICIA       612015                                                 |FIG 10.7|
|   20|41511FRYSTAK, JAMES       486160                                                 |FIG 10.7|
|   21|41682GAPINSKI, ALAN       419075                                                 |FIG 10.7|
|   22|42359GOVERN, MAUREEN      541740                                                 |FIG 10.7|
|   23|42487HAFFEY, JOHANNA      140765                                                 |FIG 10.7|
|   24|42620HARDEKOFF, ERNEST    000345                                                 |FIG 10.7|
|   25|43679HEALTON, BRUCE       552940                                                 |FIG 10.7|
|   26|44877HEMMERLING, TIM      532465                                                 |FIG 10.7|
|   27|45710HILL, CARY           457735                                                 |FIG 10.7|
|   28|45719HOMMOWUN, ROBERT     241770                                                 |FIG 10.7|
|   29|47631HOOSON, BEVERLY      001305                                                 |FIG 10.7|
|   30|49236HOUCK, KIM           376560                                                 |FIG 10.7|
|   31|51365KASKADDEN, KEN       957735                                                 |FIG 10.7|
|   32|51395KEYES, NANCY         211860                                                 |FIG 10.7|
|   33|51690KEYES, ROBERT        350005                                                 |FIG 10.7|
|   34|52188KILHOFFER, ANDY      635480                                                 |FIG 10.7|
|   35|52200KLAVON, MIKE         926325                                                 |FIG 10.7|
|   36|52809KLINE, KEVIN         526345                                                 |FIG 10.7|
|   37|52894KOS, JANE            448885                                                 |FIG 10.7|
|   38|53772LENSE, JAMIE         257010                                                 |FIG 10.7|
|   39|54104LORENZ, GARY         972810                                                 |FIG 10.7|
|   40|54440MACAS, LINDA         525000                                                 |FIG 10.7|
|   41|55046MEYER, DENISE        009635                                                 |FIG 10.7|
|   42|55088MILLER, ROBERT       992955                                                 |FIG 10.7|
|   43|55291MISFELDT, MARK       001410                                                 |FIG 10.7|
|   44|55541MYERS, LANA          427180                                                 |FIG 10.7|
|   45|57106OLSON, AUDREY        720755                                                 |FIG 10.7|
|   46|59236ROEHL, GARY          125700                                                 |FIG 10.7|
|   47|59354ROTHENBERG, MARTY    819305                                                 |FIG 10.7|
|   48|61144SENGER, ROBERT       524130                                                 |FIG 10.7|
|   49|61902SHENEFELT, MARVIN    315235                                                 |FIG 10.7|
|   50|61958SHOGREN, THOMAS      349820                                                 |FIG 10.7|
|   51|62745SIPOLT, MARCUS       919435                                                 |FIG 10.7|
|   52|63394SMITH, WYMAN         250725                                                 |FIG 10.7|
|   53|64044SNYDER, DENNIS       147525                                                 |FIG 10.7|
|   54|64198SWANSON, JOHN        156235                                                 |FIG 10.7|
|   55|67361SWEETEN, JEFF        340100                                                 |FIG 10.7|
|   56|67391TIDWELL, ALLEN       003045                                                 |FIG 10.7|
|   57|75139WHALEN, JANE         910280                                                 |FIG 10.7|
```

Figure 10.7 Sales Tax Program (Data) *Continued*

SALES DETAIL

ADAMS, RICHARD	2643	$2335.15	$93.41	$2,428.56
ANDERSON, FOREST	3647	$3265.20	$130.61	$3,395.81
BALLES, FRANK	4753	$3570.25	$142.81	$3,713.06
BEATTIE, WILLIAM	12893	$2927.20	$117.09	$3,044.29
BOND, RONALD	14438	$1566.90	$62.68	$1,629.58
BREW, GEORGE	14762	$4419.00	$176.76	$4,595.76
BROADUS, JEFF	17216	$3747.65	$149.91	$3,897.56
BUCKLEY, CATHY	19506	$1526.80	$61.07	$1,587.87
CESARIO, MARK	24168	$1145.15	$45.81	$1,190.96
CHOW, WINNIE	24917	$5168.15	$206.73	$5,374.88
CLEMENT, GREGORY	31588	$5505.15	$220.21	$5,725.36
DECK, DEBORA	31656	$9438.45	$377.54	$9,815.99
DECKER, MIKE	32877	$7347.00	$293.88	$7,640.88
DIMOND, LAWRENCE	33683	$4445.00	$177.80	$4,622.80
EDMISTON, DAVID	33759	$3423.75	$136.95	$3,560.70
ELLIOTT, GARY	34724	$4127.90	$165.12	$4,293.02
ELLIOTT, ROGER	35168	$1922.60	$76.90	$1,999.50
FLORES, JOSE	35295	$4181.00	$167.24	$4,348.24
FORD, PATRICIA	37081	$6120.15	$244.81	$6,364.96
FRYSTAK, JAMES	41511	$4861.60	$194.46	$5,056.06
GAPINSKI, ALAN	41682	$4190.75	$167.63	$4,358.38
GOVERN, MAUREEN	42359	$5417.40	$216.70	$5,634.10
HAFFEY, JOHANNA	42487	$1407.65	$56.31	$1,463.96
HARDEKOFF, ENNEST	42620	$3403.45	$136.14	$3,539.59
HEALTON, BRUCE	43679	$5529.40	$221.18.	$5,750.58
HEMMERLING, TIM	44877	$5324.65	$212.99	$5,537.64
HILL, CARY	45710	$4577.35	$183.09	$4,760.44
HOMMOWUN, ROBERT	45719	$2417.70	$96.71	$2,514.41
HOOSON, BEVERLY	47631	$4213.05	$168.52	$4,381.57
HOUCK, KIM	49236	$3765.60	$150.62	$3,916.22
KASKADDEN, KEN	51365	$9577.35	$383.09	$9,960.44
KEYES, NANCY	51395	$2118.60	$84.74	$2,203.34
KEYES, ROBERT	51690	$3500.05	$140.00	$3,640.05
KILHOFFER, ANDY	52188	$6354.80	$254.19	$6,608.99
KLAVON, MIKE	52200	$9263.25	$370.53	$9,633.78
KLINE, KEVIN	52809	$5263.45	$210.54	$5,473.99
KOS, JANE	52894	$4488.85	$179.55	$4,668.40
LENSE, JAMIE	53772	$2570.10	$102.80	$2,672.90
LORENZ, GARY	54104	$9728.10	$389.12	$10,117.22
MACAS, LINDA	54440	$5250.00	$210.00	$5,460.00
MEYER, DENISE	55046	$4496.35	$179.85	$4,676.20
MILLER, ROBERT	55088	$9929.55	$397.18	$10,326.73
MISFELDT, MARK	55291	$3214.10	$128.56	$3,342.66
MYERS, LANA	55541	$4271.80	$170.87	$4,442.67
OLSON, AUDREY	57106	$7207.55	$288.30	$7,495.85
ROEHL, GARY	59236	$1257.00	$50.28	$1,307.28
ROTHENBERG, MARTY	59354	$8193.05	$327.72	$8,520.77
SENGER, ROBERT	61144	$5241.30	$209.65	$5,450.95
SHENEFELT, MARVIN	61902	$3152.35	$126.09	$3,278.44
SHOGREN, THOMAS	61958	$3498.20	$139.93	$3,638.13
SIPOLT, MARCUS	62745	$9194.35	$367.77	$9,562.12
SMITH, WYMAN	63394	$2507.25	$100.29	$2,607.54
SNYDER, DENNIS	64044	$1475.25	$59.01	$1,534.26
SWANSON, JOHN	64198	$1562.35	$62.49	$1,624.84
SWEETEN, JEFF	67361	$3401.00	$136.04	$3,537.04
TIDWELL, ALLEN	67391	$1230.45	$49.22	$1,279.67
WHALEN, JANE	75139	$9102.80	$364.11	$9,466.91

SALES SUMMARY

57	$258,340.30	$10,333.60	$268,673.90

Figure 10.7 Sales Tax Program (Output) *Continued*

The next statement—ADD SALES-AMT, TAX GIVING TOTAL-AMT—
(line 75) completes the output record (PRINT-LINE). Note that although
SALES-AMT and TAX are nonedited-numeric fields, TOTAL-AMT *is* an
edited numeric field (line 36 of PRINT-LINE). TOTAL-AMT can be an edited
field because it will not be used for further computations. Lines 76 through 78
complete the computation procedure specified in the flowchart. The ADD
statement in line 76 accumulates (calculates a grand total) the cumulative sales
amount. That is, CUM-SALES-AMT will contain the total of all SALES-AMT
values because each time SALES-AMT changes (by reading the next record)
the new value of SALES-AMT is added to CUM-SALES-AMT. CUM-SALES-

AMT is described as a nonedited-numeric field with an initial value of zero (line 42 of the WORKING-STORAGE SECTION). Line 77 of the PROCEDURE DIVISION contains an ADD statement responsible for calculating the grand total for TAX (CUM-TAX in line 43 of the WORKING-STORAGE SECTION) and a count of the number of transactions for which TAX is computed (TRANS-COUNT in line 41). Adding 1 to TRANS-COUNT (line 78) every time a record is read (or every time an output record is printed) will cause TRANS-COUNT to contain a count of the number of times the READ-DATA procedure has been repeated.

The READ-DATA module is concluded by printing the data placed in PRINT-LINE (line 79). Thereafter, the GO TO statement at the bottom of the procedure causes the process to repeat. Again, when the READ statement is encountered and no data is found, the section exit will be executed.

The FINISH-UP module (500) contains operations that: (1) calculate the cumulative total amount and place it in the summary record (line 84), (2) write the summary report heading (line 86), (3) move accumulated data to the summary record to complete the summary record (lines 87 through 89), (4) write the summary record (line 90), and (5) close all files. When the FINISH-UP module is complete, execution of the PROCEDURE CONTROL module continues, the STOP RUN statement is encountered, and the procedure is terminated. The result of this process is demonstrated in the output portion of Figure 10.7.

The Letter-Grade Assignment Problem

In Chapter 8, a logical decision process was developed for translating student numeric averages into letter grades. Here, the entire process involved in that problem is described. First, examine the input-record description of STUDENT-FILE in Figure 10.8. Each record contains the student's name and scores on three exams. The student's average is to be computed from these exams prior to the assignment of letter grades. Overall or summary statistics are also to be produced by the procedure. The overall statistics include class averages for each of the three exams plus an overall class average based on all exam averages—a course average.

Now investigate the logic of the procedure to determine how each of the requirements is met. The hierarchy chart and the flowchart for PROCEDURE CONTROL present each of the major functional modules (and their interrelationships). The first module executed from the PROCEDURE-CONTROL paragraph is INITIAL-OPERATIONS (100). The module opens all input and output files, writes a report heading, sets the file indicators, and reads the first record from the student file. Provided data is available, the DETERMINE GRADE module (300) is invoked. Within this module, the student average is computed, exam values are counted and added to exam accumulators and the grand total, the letter grade is assigned, the data are printed (module 350), and the student record is read.

When the student file has been exhausted, control passes back to the PROCEDURE CONTROL module which calls the OVERALL STATS module (500). In the OVERALL STATS module, course averages by exam are calculated along with the course average, and the summary statistics are printed.

Control returns to the PROCEDURE CONTROL module, which calls the CLOSE FILES module, where the input and output files are closed, the module is completed, control is again returned to the PROCEDURE CONTROL module, and the procedure is terminated.

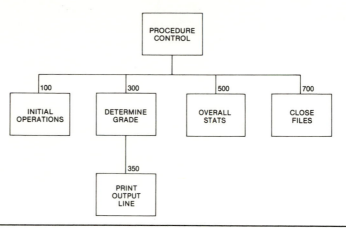

Figure 10.8 Letter-Grade Assignment (Hierarchy Chart)

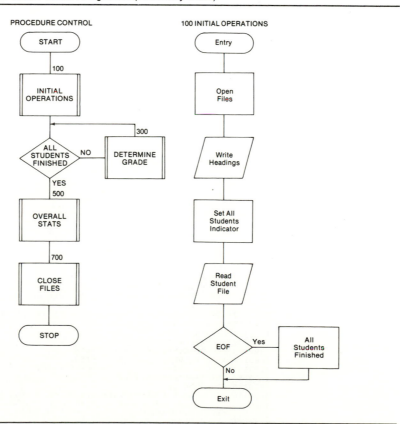

Figure 10.8 Letter-Grade Assignment (Module Flowcharts) *Continued*

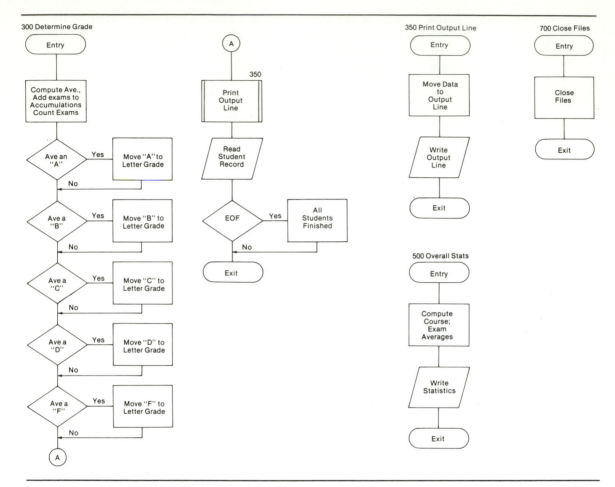

Figure 10.8 Letter-Grade Assignment (Module Flowcharts) *Continued*

```
            1   1   2   2   2   3   3   4   4   4   5   5   6   6   6   7   7   8|
    4   8   2   6   0   4   8   2   6   0   4   8   2   6   0   4   8   2   6   0|
|000010 IDENTIFICATION DIVISION.                                    FIG 10.8|
|000020 PROGRAM-ID. GRADES-ANALYSIS.                                FIG 10.8|
|000030 AUTHOR. J. WAYNE SPENCE.                                    FIG 10.8|
|000040 DATE-WRITTEN. JAN 1, 1981.                                  FIG 10.8|
|000050 DATE-COMPILED. JAN 1, 1981.                                 FIG 10.8|
|000060* THIS PROGRAM ILLUSTRATES THE USE OF                        FIG 10.8|
|000070* THE RELATIONAL IF STATEMENT.                               FIG 10.8|
|000080* IN ADDITION, ARITHMETIC STATEMENTS; ACCUMULATORS;          FIG 10.8|
|000090* EXAM-COUNTERS; EDITED OUTPUT AND VALUE CLAUSES ARE USED.   FIG 10.8|
|000100 ENVIRONMENT DIVISION.                                       FIG 10.8|
|000110 CONFIGURATION SECTION.                                      FIG 10.8|
|000120 SOURCE-COMPUTER. IBM-370-158.                               FIG 10.8|
|000130 OBJECT-COMPUTER. IBM-370-158.                               FIG 10.8|
|000140 SPECIAL-NAMES. C01 IS HEAD-OF-PAGE.                         FIG 10.8|
|000150 INPUT-OUTPUT SECTION.                                       FIG 10.8|
|000160 FILE-CONTROL.                                               FIG 10.8|
|000170    SELECT STUDENT-FILE ASSIGN TO UT-S-SYSIN.                FIG 10.8|
|000180    SELECT GRADE-REPORT ASSIGN TO UT-S-SYSPRINT.             FIG 10.8|
|000190 DATA DIVISION.                                              FIG 10.8|
|000200 FILE SECTION.                                               FIG 10.8|
|000210 FD  STUDENT-FILE LABEL RECORDS ARE OMITTED.                 FIG 10.8|
```

Figure 10.8 Letter-Grade Analysis *Continued*

```
|               1   1   2   2   2   3   3   4   4   4   5   5   6   6   6   7   7   8|
|   4   8       2   6   0   4   8   2   6   0   4   8   2   6   0   4   8   2   6   0|
-------------------------------------------------------------------------------------
|000220 01    CARD-REC.                                                    FIG 10.8|
|000230       03 NAME-STUDENT            PIC X(20).                        FIG 10.8|
|000240       03 FILLER                  PIC X(10).                        FIG 10.8|
|000250       03 GRADES.                                                   FIG 10.8|
|000260          05 EXAM-1               PIC 9(03).                        FIG 10.8|
|000270          05 EXAM-2               PIC 9(03).                        FIG 10.8|
|000280          05 EXAM-3               PIC 9(03).                        FIG 10.8|
|000290       03 FILLER                  PIC X(41).                        FIG 10.8|
|000300 FD  GRADE-REPORT LABEL RECORDS ARE OMITTED.                        FIG 10.8|
|000310 01  PRINT-LINE                   PIC X(133).                       FIG 10.8|
|000320 WORKING-STORAGE SECTION.                                           FIG 10.8|
|000330 01  WORKING-VARIABLES.                                             FIG 10.8|
|000340       05  EXAM-COUNTER           PIC 9(03)       VALUE ZERO.       FIG 10.8|
|000350       05  EXAM-1-TOTAL           PIC 9(05)       VALUE ZERO.       FIG 10.8|
|000360       05  EXAM-2-TOTAL           PIC 9(05)       VALUE ZERO.       FIG 10.8|
|000370       05  EXAM-3-TOTAL           PIC 9(05)       VALUE ZERO.       FIG 10.8|
|000380       05  GRAND-TOTAL            PIC 9(06)       VALUE ZERO.       FIG 10.8|
|000390       05  AVERAGE                PIC 9(03)V9(01).                  FIG 10.8|
|000400       05  ALL-STUDENTS           PIC X(08).                        FIG 10.8|
|000410 01  TITLE-LINE.                                                    FIG 10.8|
|000420       02 FILLER                  PIC X(55) VALUE SPACES.           FIG 10.8|
|000430       02 FILLER                  PIC X(22) VALUE                    FIG 10.8|
|000440       'STUDENT GRADE AVERAGES'.                                    FIG 10.8|
|000450       02 FILLER                  PIC X(56) VALUE SPACES.           FIG 10.8|
|000460 01  REPORT-COL-HEADINGS.                                           FIG 10.8|
|000470       02 FILLER                  PIC X(41) VALUE SPACES.           FIG 10.8|
|000480       02 FILLER                  PIC X(12) VALUE                    FIG 10.8|
|000490       'STUDENT NAME'.                                              FIG 10.8|
|000500       02 FILLER                  PIC X(10) VALUE SPACES.           FIG 10.8|
|000510       02 FILLER                  PIC X(07) VALUE 'AVERAGE'.        FIG 10.8|
|000520       02 FILLER                  PIC X(10) VALUE SPACES.           FIG 10.8|
|000530       02 FILLER                  PIC X(12) VALUE 'LETTER GRADE'.   FIG 10.8|
|000540 01  ASTER-ROW.                                                     FIG 10.8|
|000550       02 FILLER                  PIC X(41) VALUE SPACES.           FIG 10.8|
|000560       02 FILLER                  PIC X(51) VALUE ALL '*'.          FIG 10.8|
|000570 01  STUDENT-REC.                                                   FIG 10.8|
|000580       02 FILLER                  PIC X(41) VALUE SPACES.           FIG 10.8|
|000590       02 STUDENT-NAME            PIC X(20).                        FIG 10.8|
|000600       02 FILLER                  PIC X(03) VALUE SPACES.           FIG 10.8|
|000610       02 AVERAGE-GRADE           PIC ZZ9.9.                        FIG 10.8|
|000620       02 FILLER                  PIC X(16) VALUE SPACES.           FIG 10.8|
|000630       02 LETTER-GRADE            PIC X(01).                        FIG 10.8|
|000640 01  STATISTICS.                                                    FIG 10.8|
|000650       02 FILLER                  PIC X(27) VALUE SPACES.           FIG 10.8|
|000660       02 FILLER                  PIC X(24) VALUE                    FIG 10.8|
|000670       'SUMMARY CLASS STATISTICS'.                                  FIG 10.8|
|000680       02 FILLER                  PIC X(05) VALUE SPACES.           FIG 10.8|
|000690       02 EXAM-1-AVERAGE          PIC ZZ9.9.                        FIG 10.8|
|000700       02 FILLER                  PIC X(05) VALUE SPACES.           FIG 10.8|
|000710       02 EXAM-2-AVERAGE          PIC ZZ9.9.                        FIG 10.8|
|000720       02 FILLER                  PIC X(05) VALUE SPACES.           FIG 10.8|
|000730       02 EXAM-3-AVERAGE          PIC ZZ9.9.                        FIG 10.8|
|000740       02 FILLER                  PIC X(05) VALUE SPACES.           FIG 10.8|
|000750       02 OVERALL-AVERAGE         PIC ZZ9.9.                        FIG 10.8|
|000760 PROCEDURE DIVISION.                                                FIG 10.8|
|000770 PROCEDURE-CONTROL.                                                 FIG 10.8|
|000780       PERFORM 100-INITIAL-OPERATIONS.                             FIG 10.8|
|000790       PERFORM 300-DETERMINE-GRADES UNTIL ALL-STUDENTS = 'FINISHED'.FIG 10.8|
|000800       PERFORM 500-OVERALL-STATS.                                  FIG 10.8|
|000810       PERFORM 700-CLOSE-FILES.                                    FIG 10.8|
|000820       STOP RUN.                                                    FIG 10.8|
|000830 100-INITIAL-OPERATIONS.                                            FIG 10.8|
|000840       OPEN INPUT STUDENT-FILE, OUTPUT GRADE-REPORT.               FIG 10.8|
|000850       WRITE PRINT-LINE FROM TITLE-LINE AFTER HEAD-OF-PAGE.        FIG 10.8|
|000860       WRITE PRINT-LINE FROM REPORT-COL-HEADINGS AFTER 1 LINES.    FIG 10.8|
|000870       WRITE PRINT-LINE FROM ASTER-ROW AFTER 1 LINES.             FIG 10.8|
|000880       MOVE 'READING' TO ALL-STUDENTS.                             FIG 10.8|
|000890       READ STUDENT-FILE                                           FIG 10.8|
|000900          AT END MOVE 'FINISHED' TO ALL-STUDENTS.                  FIG 10.8|
|000910 300-DETERMINE-GRADES.                                             FIG 10.8|
|000920       COMPUTE AVERAGE ROUNDED = (EXAM-1 + EXAM-2 + EXAM-3) / 3.   FIG 10.8|
|000930       ADD EXAM-1 TO EXAM-1-TOTAL, GRAND-TOTAL.                    FIG 10.8|
|000940       ADD EXAM-2 TO EXAM-2-TOTAL, GRAND-TOTAL.                    FIG 10.8|
|000950       ADD EXAM-3 TO EXAM-3-TOTAL, GRAND-TOTAL.                    FIG 10.8|
|000960       ADD 1 TO EXAM-COUNTER.                                       FIG 10.8|
|000970       IF AVERAGE IS GREATER THAN 89.4                             FIG 10.8|
|000980          MOVE 'A' TO LETTER-GRADE.                                FIG 10.8|
|000990       IF AVERAGE IS GREATER THAN 79.4 AND LESS THAN 89.5          FIG 10.8|
|001000          MOVE 'B' TO LETTER-GRADE.                                FIG 10.8|
```

Figure 10.8 Letter-Grade Analysis *Continued*

```
                   1   1   2   2   2   3   3   4   4   4   5   5   6   6   6   7   7   8|
|    4       8      2   6   0   4   8   2   6   0   4   8   2   6   0   4   8   2   6   0|
|001010      IF AVERAGE IS GREATER THAN 69.4 AND LESS THAN 79.5                  FIG 10.8|
|001020         MOVE *C* TO LETTER-GRADE.                                        FIG 10.8|
|001030      IF AVERAGE IS GREATER THAN 59.4 AND LESS THAN 69.5                  FIG 10.8|
|001040         MOVE *D* TO LETTER-GRADE.                                        FIG 10.8|
|001050      IF AVERAGE IS LESS THAN 59.5                                        FIG 10.8|
|001060         MOVE *F* TO LETTER-GRADE.                                        FIG 10.8|
|001070      PERFORM 350-PRINT-OUTPUT-LINE.                                      FIG 10.8|
|001080      READ STUDENT-FILE                                                   FIG 10.8|
|001090         AT END MOVE *FINISHED* TO ALL-STUDENTS.                          FIG 10.8|
|001100  350-PRINT-OUTPUT-LINE.                                                  FIG 10.8|
|001110      MOVE NAME-STUDENT TO STUDENT-NAME.                                  FIG 10.8|
|001120      MOVE AVERAGE TO AVERAGE-GRADE.                                      FIG 10.8|
|001130      WRITE PRINT-LINE FROM STUDENT-REC AFTER 2 LINES.                    FIG 10.8|
|001140  500-OVERALL-STATS.                                                      FIG 10.8|
|001150      WRITE PRINT-LINE FROM ASTER-ROW AFTER 2 LINES.                      FIG 10.8|
|001160      DIVIDE EXAM-1-TOTAL BY EXAM-COUNTER GIVING EXAM-1-AVERAGE           FIG 10.8|
|001170         ROUNDED.                                                         FIG 10.8|
|001180      DIVIDE EXAM-2-TOTAL BY EXAM-COUNTER GIVING EXAM-2-AVERAGE           FIG 10.8|
|001190         ROUNDED.                                                         FIG 10.8|
|001200      DIVIDE EXAM-3-TOTAL BY EXAM-COUNTER GIVING EXAM-3-AVERAGE           FIG 10.8|
|001210         ROUNDED.                                                         FIG 10.8|
|001220      COMPUTE OVERALL-AVERAGE ROUNDED = GRAND-TOTAL /                     FIG 10.8|
|001230         (EXAM-COUNTER * 3).                                             FIG 10.8|
|001240      WRITE PRINT-LINE AFTER ADVANCING 2 LINES.                           FIG 10.8|
|001250      WRITE PRINT-LINE FROM STATISTICS AFTER 2 LINES.                     FIG 10.8|
|001260  700-CLOSE-FILES.                                                        FIG 10.8|
|001270      CLOSE STUDENT-FILE, GRADE-REPORT.                                   FIG 10.8|
```

Figure 10.8 Letter-Grade Analysis *Continued*

```
                1             2             3             4             5             6             7             8| FIGURE |
|RECORD|1234567890123456789012345678901234567890123456789012345678901234567890| NUMBER |
|     1|ADAMS, FOREST              053051051                                        |FIG 10.8|
|     2|BALLES, WILLIAM            070075072                                        |FIG 10.8|
|     3|BOND, GEORGE               090096090                                        |FIG 10.8|
|     4|BROADUS, CATHY             086080081                                        |FIG 10.8|
|     5|CESARIO, WINNIE            068051058                                        |FIG 10.8|
|     6|CLEMENT, DEBORA            094093085                                        |FIG 10.8|
|     7|DECKER, LAWRENCE           044045050                                        |FIG 10.8|
|     8|EDMISTON, GARY             079071074                                        |FIG 10.8|
|     9|ELLIOTT, JOSE              081080084                                        |FIG 10.8|
|    10|FORD, JAMES                086084061                                        |FIG 10.8|
|    11|GAPINSKI, MAUREEN          054057051                                        |FIG 10.8|
|    12|HAFFEY, ERNEST             093090094                                        |FIG 10.8|
|    13|HEALTON, TIM               084095098                                        |FIG 10.8|
|    14|HILL, ROBERT               077070071                                        |FIG 10.8|
|    15|HOOSON, KIM                076075076                                        |FIG 10.8|
|    16|KASKADDEN, NANCY           081086080                                        |FIG 10.8|
|    17|KEYES, ANDY                063054080                                        |FIG 10.8|
|    18|KLAVON, KEVIN              084088085                                        |FIG 10.8|
|    19|KCS, JANIE                 100099099                                        |FIG 10.8|
|    20|LORENZ, LINDA              082087081                                        |FIG 10.8|
|    21|MEYER, ROBERT              099092095                                        |FIG 10.8|
|    22|MILLER, MARK               071069068                                        |FIG 10.8|
|    23|MYERS, AUDREY              072075070                                        |FIG 10.8|
|    24|ROEHL, MARTY               081093095                                        |FIG 10.8|
|    25|SENGER, MARVIN             053053055                                        |FIG 10.8|
|    26|SHOGREN, MARCUS            091094089                                        |FIG 10.8|
|    27|SMITH, DENNIS              025072028                                        |FIG 10.8|
|    28|SWANSON, JEFF              100100100                                        |FIG 10.8|
|    29|TIDWELL, JANE              065066067                                        |FIG 10.8|
```

Figure 10.8 Letter-Grade Analysis (Data) *Continued*

```
                    STUDENT GRADE AVERAGES
      STUDENT NAME           AVERAGE              LETTER GRADE
      *************************************************************

      ADAMS, FOREST            51.7                    F

      BALLES, WILLIAM          72.3                    C

      BOND, GEORGE             92.0                    A

      BROADUS, CATHY           82.3                    B

      CESARIO, WINNIE          59.0                    F

      CLEMENT, DEBORA          90.7                    A

      DECKER, LAWRENCE         46.3                    F

      EDMISTON, GARY           74.7                    C

      ELLIOTT, JOSE            81.7                    B

      FORD, JAMES              77.0                    C

      GAPINSKI, MAUREEN        54.0                    F

      HAFFEY, ERNEST           92.3                    A

      HEALTON, TIM             92.3                    A

      HILL, ROBERT             72.7                    C

      HOOSON, KIM              75.7                    C

      KASKADDEN, NANCY         82.3                    B

      KEYES, ANDY              65.7                    D

      KLAVON, KEVIN            85.7                    B

      KOS, JANIE               99.3                    A

      LORENZ, LINDA            83.3                    B

      MEYER, ROBERT            95.3                    A

      MILLER, MARK             69.3                    D

      MYERS, AUDREY            72.3                    C

      ROEHL, MARTY             89.7                    A

      SENGER, MARVIN           53.7                    F

      SHOGREN, MARCUS          91.3                    A

      SMITH, DENNIS            41.7                    F

      SWANSON, JEFF           100.0                    A

      TIDWELL, JANE            66.0                    D

      *************************************************************

      *************************************************************

SUMMARY CLASS STATISTICS      75.9       77.3      75.4      76.2
```

Figure 10.8 Letter-Grade Analysis (Output) *Continued*

The Electric Utility Company Program

The program illustrated in Figure 10.9 might be used by an electric utility company to determine electricity usage and the amount due the utility based on that usage plus any unpaid balance in the customer's account. To provide all necessary data, three types of input records are required. The first record type for each customer contains the customer history—the meter reading from the last month and the customer balance from previous periods. The second record type contains the customer payments to prior account balances. There may be none, one, or several payments for each customer. (Assume that multiple payments are possible for multifamily dwellings. The total for all payments for a customer are not assumed to be exactly equal to the outstanding balance. The customer is issued a credit if he overpays his bill and he is charged a finance charge for underpayment. The final record type contains a meter reading for the current month's usage of electricity. Furthermore, the programmer has been cautioned to guard against meter "roll over"—i.e., where the meter exceeds its maximum reading and begins again from zero, like the odometer of an automobile. All of these records are assumed to be ordered (sorted) by customer number and type of record.

Other requirements of the program are to (1) produce a report with one line for each customer, (2) produce a summary report containing the totals of all pertinent details, and (3) properly compute current charges based on the amount of electricity used. The current charges are based on the following: (1) a customer who uses less than 10 kilowatt hours (KWH) is charged a flat fee of $2.50, (2) a customer who uses 10 KWH to 5,000 KWH is charged a rate of $0.0323 per KWH used, and (3) the customer who uses over 5,000 KWH is charged at the rate of $0.0255 per KWH. There is no charge for no usage.

The program CONTROL PROCEDURE provides the overall control for the program. That is, the execution of the procedure is controlled by the CONTROL-PROCEDURE of the PROCEDURE DIVISION. In the program listing itself, each statement of the control section is a PERFORM statement which causes other paragraphs to be executed.

The process performed by the program is the creation of a report to be used within the electric utility company. The program is responsible for accepting input records that represent the past month's results (history) for each customer. In addition, each account may be updated to include payments received from the customer and new meter readings recorded. After all data for a particular account had been read, the program is to determine the amount of electricity (in kilowatt hours) used by the customer, the rate charged per kilowatt hour used, the base bill based on the kilowatt hours used, the remaining balance for the account after payments have been recorded, the finance charges for outstanding balances (if any), and the new balance the customer owes the utility company. After the program has processed all the accounts in this manner, a summary of all accounts is to be produced. The flowchart, program listing, and printed output of the program are provided in Figure 10.9.

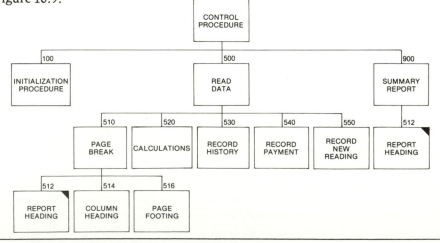

Figure 10.9 Electric Utility Program (Hierarchy Chart)

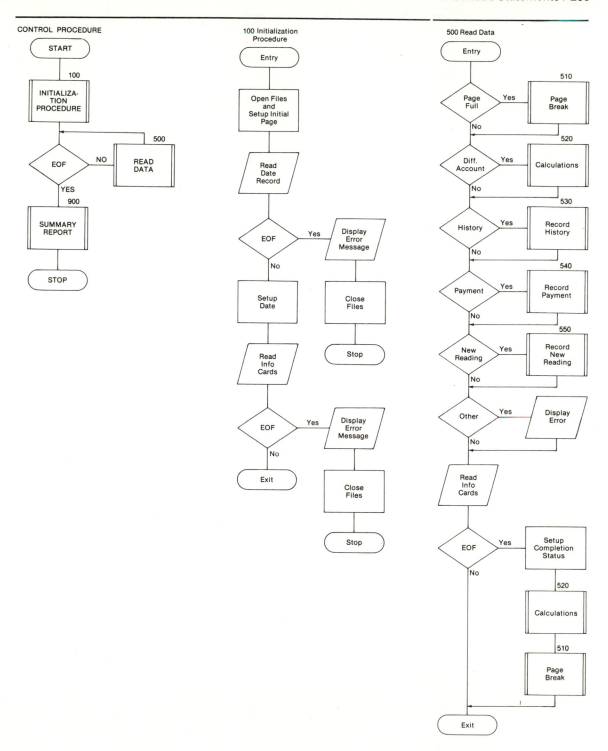

Figure 10.9 Electric Utility Program (Module Flowcharts) *Continued*

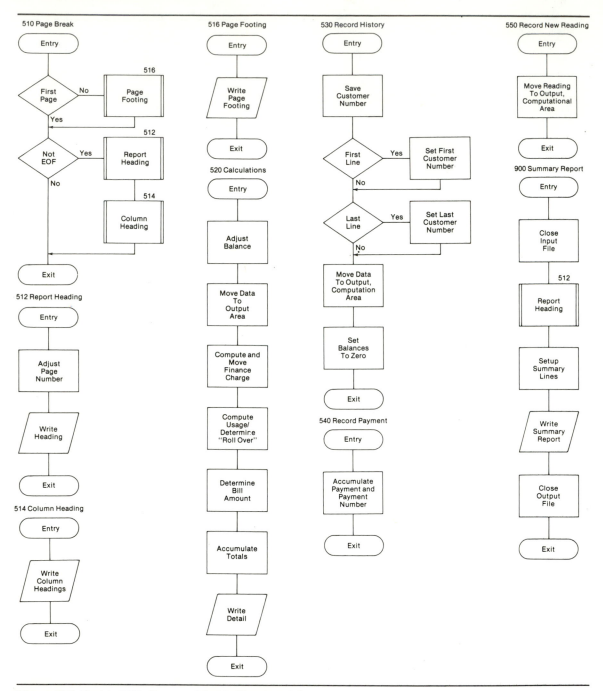

Figure 10.9 Electric Utility Program (Module Flowcharts) *Continued*

```
               1  1  2  2  2  3  3  4  4  4  5  5  6  6  6  7  7  8
         4  8  2  6  0  4  8  2  6  0  4  8  2  6  0  4  8  2  6  0
 000010 IDENTIFICATION DIVISION.                               FIG 10.9
 000020 PROGRAM-ID. ELECTRIC-COMPANY.                          FIG 10.9
 000030 AUTHOR. J. WAYNE SPENCE.                               FIG 10.9
 000040 DATE-WRITTEN. JANUARY 1, 1981.                         FIG 10.9
```

Figure 10.9 Electric Utility Program *Continued*

```
|--------------------------------------------------------------------------------
|          1   1   2   2   2   3   3   4   4   4   5   5   6   6   6   7   7   8|
|   4    8 2   6   0   4   8   2   6   0   4   8   2   6   0   4   8   2   6   0|
--------------------------------------------------------------------------------
|000050 DATE-COMPILED. JANUARY 1, 1981.                                FIG 10.9|
|000060*    THIS PROGRAM ILLUSTRATES THE USE OF A MULTIPLE RECORD      FIG 10.9|
|000070*    TYPE IN THE DATA FILE, CONDITION-NAMES AND CONDITION-NAME  FIG 10.9|
|000080*    TEST IN THE PROCEDURE DIVISION, 01-LEVELS IN THE           FIG 10.9|
|000090*    WORKING-STORAGE SECTION, AND A STRUCTURED PROCEDURE        FIG 10.9|
|000100*    DIVISION UTILIZING PERFORMS, SIMPLE IF'S AND NESTED IF'S.  FIG 10.9|
|000110 ENVIRONMENT DIVISION.                                          FIG 10.9|
|000120 CONFIGURATION SECTION.                                         FIG 10.9|
|000130 SOURCE-COMPUTER. HONEYWELL.                                    FIG 10.9|
|000140 OBJECT-COMPUTER. HONEYWELL.                                    FIG 10.9|
|000150 SPECIAL-NAMES. '1' IS TOP-OF-PAGE.                             FIG 10.9|
|000160 INPUT-OUTPUT SECTION.                                          FIG 10.9|
|000170 FILE-CONTROL.                                                  FIG 10.9|
|000180     SELECT ACTIVITY-REPORT ASSIGN TO PRINTER.                  FIG 10.9|
|000190     SELECT INFO-CARDS ASSIGN TO CARD-READER.                   FIG 10.9|
|000200 DATA DIVISION.                                                 FIG 10.9|
|000210 FILE SECTION.                                                  FIG 10.9|
|000220 FD  INFO-CARDS LABEL RECORDS ARE OMITTED.                      FIG 10.9|
|000230 01  HISTORY-CARD.                                              FIG 10.9|
|000240     03 CUSTOMER-NUMBER          PIC 9(06).                     FIG 10.9|
|000250     03 FILLER                   PIC X(08).                     FIG 10.9|
|000260     03 TYPE-INFORMATION         PIC X(21).                     FIG 10.9|
|000270     03 FILLER                   PIC X(44).                     FIG 10.9|
|000280     03 CARD-TYPE                PIC 9(01).                     FIG 10.9|
|000290 FD  ACTIVITY-REPORT LABEL RECORDS ARE OMITTED.                 FIG 10.9|
|000300 01  REPORT-LINE                 PIC X(133).                    FIG 10.9|
|000310 WORKING-STORAGE SECTION.                                       FIG 10.9|
|000320 01  WORKING-VARIABLES.                                         FIG 10.9|
|000330     03 FILE-STATUS              PIC X(15) VALUE SPACES.        FIG 10.9|
|000340     03  LINE-COUNT              PIC 9(02) VALUE 0.             FIG 10.9|
|000350     03  SAVE-ACCOUNT            PIC 9(06) VALUE 0.             FIG 10.9|
|000360     03  OLD-READING             PIC 9(05).                     FIG 10.9|
|000370     03  OLD-BALANCE             PIC S9(04)V9(02).              FIG 10.9|
|000380     03  T-PMTS                  PIC S9(04)V9(02).              FIG 10.9|
|000390     03  N-PMTS                  PIC 9(02).                     FIG 10.9|
|000400     03  THIS-READING            PIC 9(05).                     FIG 10.9|
|000410     03  KWATTS-USED             PIC S9(06).                    FIG 10.9|
|000420     03  FIN-CHRG                PIC 9(03)V9(02).               FIG 10.9|
|000430     03  AMT-BILL                PIC 9(04)V9(02).               FIG 10.9|
|000440     03  TOT-AMT                 PIC S9(06)V9(02).              FIG 10.9|
|000450     03  TOT-NUM-CUST            PIC 9(06) VALUE 0.             FIG 10.9|
|000460     03  TOT-KWH                 PIC 9(09) VALUE 0.             FIG 10.9|
|000470     03  TOT-BAL-BEFORE-PMT      PIC 9(09)V9(02) VALUE 0.       FIG 10.9|
|000480     03  TOT-BAL-AFTER-PMT       PIC 9(09)V9(02) VALUE 0.       FIG 10.9|
|000490     03  TOT-PMTS                PIC 9(09)V9(02) VALUE 0.       FIG 10.9|
|000500     03  TOT-N-PMTS              PIC 9(06) VALUE 0.             FIG 10.9|
|000510     03  TOT-AMT-BILL            PIC 9(09)V9(02) VALUE 0.       FIG 10.9|
|000520     03  TOT-FIN-CHRG            PIC 9(09)V9(02) VALUE 0.       FIG 10.9|
|000530     03  TOTAL-AMOUNT            PIC 9(09)V9(02) VALUE 0.       FIG 10.9|
|000540     03 HISTORY-INFORMATION.                                    FIG 10.9|
|000550        05 LAST-METER-READING    PIC 9(05).                     FIG 10.9|
|000560        05 FILLER                PIC X(10).                     FIG 10.9|
|000570        05 PREVIOUS-BALANCE      PIC 9(04)V9(02).               FIG 10.9|
|000580     03 PAYMENT-INFORMATION.                                    FIG 10.9|
|000590        05 FILLER                PIC X(15).                     FIG 10.9|
|000600        05 PAYMENT               PIC 9(04)V9(02).               FIG 10.9|
|000610     03 CURRENT-INFORMATION.                                    FIG 10.9|
|000620        05 CURRENT-METER-READING PIC 9(05).                     FIG 10.9|
|000630 01  DATE-CARD.                                                 FIG 10.9|
|000640     05 REPORT-DAY               PIC 9(02).                     FIG 10.9|
|000650     05 REPORT-MONTH             PIC 9(02).                     FIG 10.9|
|000660     05 REPORT-YEAR              PIC 9(02).                     FIG 10.9|
|000670 01  HEADING-1.                                                 FIG 10.9|
|000680     02 FILLER                   PIC X(38) VALUE SPACES.        FIG 10.9|
|000690     02 HEAD-1                   PIC X(30) VALUE                FIG 10.9|
|000700     'ELECTRIC POWER UTILITY COMPANY'.                          FIG 10.9|
|000710 01  HEADING-2.                                                 FIG 10.9|
|000720     02 FILLER                   PIC X(37) VALUE SPACES.        FIG 10.9|
|000730     02 FILLER                   PIC X(32) VALUE                FIG 10.9|
|000740     'CUSTOMER ACCOUNT ACTIVITY REPORT'.                        FIG 10.9|
|000750     02 FILLER                   PIC X(30) VALUE SPACES.        FIG 10.9|
|000760     02 FILLER                   PIC X(05) VALUE 'PAGE'.        FIG 10.9|
|000770     02 PAGE-NO-TOP              PIC 9(02).                     FIG 10.9|
|000780 01  HEADING-3.                                                 FIG 10.9|
|000790     02 FILLER                   PIC X(38) VALUE SPACES.        FIG 10.9|
|000800     02 FILLER                   PIC X(21) VALUE                FIG 10.9|
|000810     'FOR THE MONTH ENDING '.                                   FIG 10.9|
|000820     02 RPT-DAY                  PIC 9(02).                     FIG 10.9|
|000830     02 FILLER                   PIC X(01) VALUE '/'.           FIG 10.9|
|000840     02 RPT-MONTH                PIC 9(02).                     FIG 10.9|
|000850     02 FILLER                   PIC X(01) VALUE '/'.           FIG 10.9|
--------------------------------------------------------------------------------
```

Figure 10.9 Electric Utility Program *Continued*

```
----------------------------------------------------------------------------------
|         1   1   2   2   2   3   3   4   4   4   5   5   6   6   6   7   7   8|
|  4   8  2   6   0   4   8   2   6   0   4   8   2   6   0   4   8   2   6   0|
----------------------------------------------------------------------------------
|000860    02 RPT-YEAR                    PIC 9(02).                        FIG 10.9|
|000870 01 LINE-ACROSS.                                                     FIG 10.9|
|000880    02 FILLER                      PIC X(01) VALUE SPACES.           FIG 10.9|
|000890    02 FILLER                      PIC X(105) VALUE ALL '*'.         FIG 10.9|
|000900 01 HEADING-4.                                                       FIG 10.9|
|000910    02 FILLER                      PIC X(132) VALUE                  FIG 10.9|
|000920    '  *CUSTOMER*   METER READING   *KILOWATT*  PREVIOUS*    PAYMFIG 10.9|
|000930-   *ENTS   *BALANCE * BASE *FINANCE    TOTAL    *'.                 FIG 10.9|
|000940 01 HEADING-5.                                                       FIG 10.9|
|000950    02 FILLER                      PIC X(132) VALUE                  FIG 10.9|
|000960    '  *  ACCOUNT*--------------------*  HOURS   *  BALANCE *--------FIG 10.9|
|000970-   *--------*  AFTER *  BILL  *CHARGES*  AMOUNT    *'.              FIG 10.9|
|000980 01 HEADING-6.                                                       FIG 10.9|
|000990    02 FILLER                      PIC X(132) VALUE                  FIG 10.9|
|001000    '  *  NUMBER  *LAST MONTH*THIS MONTH*   USED   *        *  AMOUNTFIG 10.9|
|001010-   *  *NUMBER*PAYMENT *         *         *   DUE    *'.            FIG 10.9|
|001020 01 FOOTING-1.                                                       FIG 10.9|
|001030    02 FILLER                      PIC X(30) VALUE                   FIG 10.9|
|001040    '  CUSTOMER NUMBERS ON THIS PAGE'.                               FIG 10.9|
|001050 01 FOOTING-2.                                                       FIG 10.9|
|001060    02 FILLER                      PIC X(07) VALUE SPACES.           FIG 10.9|
|001070    02 1ST-NUMBER                  PIC 9(06).                        FIG 10.9|
|001080    02 FILLER                      PIC X(04) VALUE ' TO'.            FIG 10.9|
|001090    02 LAST-NUMBER                 PIC 9(06).                        FIG 10.9|
|001100    02 FILLER                      PIC X(76) VALUE SPACES.           FIG 10.9|
|001110    02 FILLER                      PIC X(05) VALUE 'PAGE'.           FIG 10.9|
|001120    02 PAGE-NO-BOTTOM              PIC 9(02).                        FIG 10.9|
|001130 01 DETAIL-RECORD.                                                   FIG 10.9|
|001140    02 FILLER                      PIC X(03) VALUE ' *'.             FIG 10.9|
|001150    02 ACCOUNT                     PIC 9(06).                        FIG 10.9|
|001160    02 FILLER                      PIC X(06) VALUE ' *'.             FIG 10.9|
|001170    02 LAST-READING                PIC ZZZZ9.                        FIG 10.9|
|001180    02 FILLER                      PIC X(06) VALUE ' *'.             FIG 10.9|
|001190    02 NEW-READING                 PIC ZZZZ9.                        FIG 10.9|
|001200    02 FILLER                      PIC X(03) VALUE ' *'.             FIG 10.9|
|001210    02 HOURS-USED                  PIC ZZZZZ9.                       FIG 10.9|
|001220    02 FILLER                      PIC X(02) VALUE ' *'.             FIG 10.9|
|001230    02 BALANCE                     PIC $$,$$$.99.                    FIG 10.9|
|001240    02 FILLER                      PIC X(01) VALUE '*'.              FIG 10.9|
|001250    02 PMT-AMT                     PIC $$,$$$.99.                    FIG 10.9|
|001260    02 FILLER                      PIC X(03) VALUE '*'.              FIG 10.9|
|001270    02 PMT-NO                      PIC Z9.                           FIG 10.9|
|001280    02 FILLER                      PIC X(03) VALUE '  *'.            FIG 10.9|
|001290    02 BAL-AFTER-PMT               PIC $$$$.99-.                     FIG 10.9|
|001300    02 FILLER                      PIC X(01) VALUE '*'.              FIG 10.9|
|001310    02 BASE-BILL                   PIC $$$$.99.                      FIG 10.9|
|001320    02 FILLER                      PIC X(02) VALUE '*'.              FIG 10.9|
|001330    02 FINANCE-CHRG                PIC $$$.99.                       FIG 10.9|
|001340    02 FILLER                      PIC X(01) VALUE '*'.              FIG 10.9|
|001350    02 AMOUNT-DUE                  PIC $$,$$$.99CR.                  FIG 10.9|
|001360    02 FILLER                      PIC X(01) VALUE '*'.              FIG 10.9|
|001370 01 SUMMARY-LINE.                                                    FIG 10.9|
|001380    02 FILLER                      PIC X(23) VALUE SPACES.           FIG 10.9|
|001390    02 FILLER                      PIC X(06) VALUE 'TOTAL'.          FIG 10.9|
|001400    02 DETAIL-SUMMARY              PIC X(53).                        FIG 10.9|
|001410 01 SUM-LINE-1.                                                      FIG 10.9|
|001420    02 FILLER                      PIC X(31) VALUE                   FIG 10.9|
|001430    'NUMBER OF CUSTOMERS PROCESSED'.                                 FIG 10.9|
|001440    02 GT-NUM-CUST                 PIC ZZZ,ZZ9.                      FIG 10.9|
|001450 01 SUM-LINE-2.                                                      FIG 10.9|
|001460    02 FILLER                      PIC X(21) VALUE                   FIG 10.9|
|001470    'KILOWATT HOURS USED'.                                          FIG 10.9|
|001480    02 GT-KWH                      PIC ZZZ,ZZZ,ZZ9.                  FIG 10.9|
|001490 01 SUM-LINE-3.                                                      FIG 10.9|
|001500    02 FILLER                      PIC X(38) VALUE                   FIG 10.9|
|001510    'OUTSTANDING BALANCES BEFORE PAYMENTS'.                          FIG 10.9|
|001520    02 GT-BAL-BEFORE-PMT           PIC $$$$,$$$,$$$.99.              FIG 10.9|
|001530 01 SUM-LINE-4.                                                      FIG 10.9|
|001540    02 FILLER                      PIC X(17) VALUE                   FIG 10.9|
|001550    'OF ALL PAYMENTS'.                                              FIG 10.9|
|001560    02 GT-PMTS                     PIC $$$$,$$$,$$$.99.              FIG 10.9|
|001570 01 SUM-LINE-5.                                                      FIG 10.9|
|001580    02 FILLER                      PIC X(29) VALUE                   FIG 10.9|
|001590    'NUMBER OF PAYMENTS RECEIVED'.                                   FIG 10.9|
|001600    02 GT-N-PMTS                   PIC ZZZ,ZZ9.                      FIG 10.9|
|001610 01 SUM-LINE-6.                                                      FIG 10.9|
|001620    02 FILLER                      PIC X(37) VALUE                   FIG 10.9|
|001630    'OUTSTANDING BALANCES AFTER PAYMENTS'.                           FIG 10.9|
|001640    02 GT-BAL-AFTER-PMT            PIC $$$$,$$$,$$$.99.              FIG 10.9|
|001650 01 SUM-LINE-7.                                                      FIG 10.9|
|001660    02 FILLER                      PIC X(19) VALUE                   FIG 10.9|
----------------------------------------------------------------------------------
```

Figure 10.9 Electric Utility Program *Continued*

```
|          1  1    2    2    2    3    3    4    4    4    5    5    6    6    6    7    7    8|
|  4    8  2  6    0    4    8    2    6    0    4    8    2    6    0    4    8    2    6    0|
--------------------------------------------------------------------------------------------
|001670       *OF ALL BASE BILLS*.                                           FIG 10.9|
|001680       02 GT-AMT-BILL              PIC $$$$,$$$,$$$.99.                FIG 10.9|
|001690 01  SUM-LINE-8.                                                      FIG 10.9|
|001700       02 FILLER                   PIC X(17) VALUE                     FIG 10.9|
|001710       *FINANCE CHARGES*.                                             FIG 10.9|
|001720       02 GT-FIN-CHRG              PIC $$$$,$$$,$$$.99.                FIG 10.9|
|001730 01  SUM-LINE-9.                                                      FIG 10.9|
|001740       02 FILLER                   PIC X(27) VALUE                     FIG 10.9|
|001750       *AMOUNT OF ALL RECEIVABLES*.                                   FIG 10.9|
|001760       02 GT-AMOUNT                PIC $$$$,$$$,$$$.99.                FIG 10.9|
|001770 PROCEDURE DIVISION.                                                  FIG 10.9|
|001780 CONTROL-PROCEDURE.                                                   FIG 10.9|
|001790       PERFORM 100-INITIALIZATION-PROCEDURE.                          FIG 10.9|
|001800       PERFORM 500-READ-DATA UNTIL FILE-STATUS = *FILE COMPLETED*.    FIG 10.9|
|001810       PERFORM 900-SUMMARY-REPORT.                                    FIG 10.9|
|001820       STOP RUN.                                                      FIG 10.9|
|001830 100-INITIALIZATION-PROCEDURE.                                        FIG 10.9|
|001840       OPEN INPUT INFO-CARDS, OUTPUT ACTIVITY-REPORT.                 FIG 10.9|
|001850       MOVE 0 TO PAGE-NO-TOP, PAGE-NO-BOTTOM.                         FIG 10.9|
|001860       MOVE 99 TO LINE-COUNT.                                         FIG 10.9|
|001870       READ INFO-CARDS INTO DATE-CARD                                 FIG 10.9|
|001880          AT END DISPLAY *NO DATA IN FILE*                            FIG 10.9|
|001890                 CLOSE INFO-CARDS, ACTIVITY-REPORT;                   FIG 10.9|
|001900                 STOP RUN.                                            FIG 10.9|
|001910       MOVE REPORT-DAY TO RPT-DAY.                                    FIG 10.9|
|001920       MOVE REPORT-MONTH TO RPT-MONTH.                                FIG 10.9|
|001930       MOVE REPORT-YEAR TO RPT-YEAR.                                  FIG 10.9|
|001940       READ INFO-CARDS                                                FIG 10.9|
|001950          AT END DISPLAY *NO DATA IN FILE*                            FIG 10.9|
|001960                 CLOSE INFO-CARDS, ACTIVITY-REPORT;                   FIG 10.9|
|001970                 STOP RUN.                                            FIG 10.9|
|001980       MOVE CUSTOMER-NUMBER TO SAVE-ACCOUNT.                          FIG 10.9|
|001990 500-READ-DATA.                                                       FIG 10.9|
|002000       IF LINE-COUNT GREATER THAN 19                                  FIG 10.9|
|002010          PERFORM 510-PAGE-BREAK.                                     FIG 10.9|
|002020       IF SAVE-ACCOUNT NOT EQUAL TO CUSTOMER-NUMBER                   FIG 10.9|
|002030          PERFORM 520-CALCULATIONS.                                   FIG 10.9|
|002040       IF CARD-TYPE = 1                                               FIG 10.9|
|002050          PERFORM 530-RECORD-HISTORY.                                 FIG 10.9|
|002060       IF CARD-TYPE = 2                                               FIG 10.9|
|002070          PERFORM 540-RECORD-PAYMENT.                                 FIG 10.9|
|002080       IF CARD-TYPE = 3                                               FIG 10.9|
|002090          PERFORM 550-RECORD-NEW-READING.                            FIG 10.9|
|002100       IF CARD-TYPE < 1 OR > 3                                        FIG 10.9|
|002110          DISPLAY *ERROR IN CODE*.                                    FIG 10.9|
|002120       READ INFO-CARDS AT END                                         FIG 10.9|
|002130          MOVE *FILE COMPLETED* TO FILE-STATUS                        FIG 10.9|
|002140          MOVE SAVE-ACCOUNT TO LAST-NUMBER                            FIG 10.9|
|002150          PERFORM 520-CALCULATIONS                                    FIG 10.9|
|002160          PERFORM 510-PAGE-BREAK.                                     FIG 10.9|
|002170 510-PAGE-BREAK.                                                      FIG 10.9|
|002180       IF LINE-COUNT NOT = 99                                         FIG 10.9|
|002190          PERFORM 516-PAGE-FOOTING.                                   FIG 10.9|
|002200       IF FILE-STATUS NOT = *FILE COMPLETED*                          FIG 10.9|
|002210          PERFORM 512-REPORT-HEADING                                  FIG 10.9|
|002220          PERFORM 514-COLUMN-HEADING.                                 FIG 10.9|
|002230       MOVE 0 TO LINE-COUNT.                                          FIG 10.9|
|002240 512-REPORT-HEADING.                                                  FIG 10.9|
|002250       ADD 1 TO PAGE-NO-TOP, PAGE-NO-BOTTOM.                          FIG 10.9|
|002260       WRITE REPORT-LINE FROM HEADING-1 AFTER TOP-OF-PAGE.            FIG 10.9|
|002270       MOVE SPACES TO HEAD-1.                                         FIG 10.9|
|002280       WRITE REPORT-LINE FROM HEADING-2 AFTER 2 LINES.                FIG 10.9|
|002290       WRITE REPORT-LINE FROM HEADING-3 AFTER 1 LINES.                FIG 10.9|
|002300       WRITE REPORT-LINE FROM LINE-ACROSS AFTER 3 LINES.              FIG 10.9|
|002310 514-COLUMN-HEADING.                                                  FIG 10.9|
|002320       WRITE REPORT-LINE FROM HEADING-4 AFTER 1 LINES.                FIG 10.9|
|002330       WRITE REPORT-LINE FROM HEADING-5 AFTER 1 LINES.                FIG 10.9|
|002340       WRITE REPORT-LINE FROM HEADING-6 AFTER 1 LINES.                FIG 10.9|
|002350       WRITE REPORT-LINE FROM LINE-ACROSS AFTER 1 LINES.              FIG 10.9|
|002360 516-PAGE-FOOTING.                                                    FIG 10.9|
|002370       WRITE REPORT-LINE FROM LINE-ACROSS AFTER 1 LINES.              FIG 10.9|
|002380       MOVE SPACES TO REPORT-LINE.                                    FIG 10.9|
|002390       WRITE REPORT-LINE AFTER 2 LINES.                               FIG 10.9|
|002400       WRITE REPORT-LINE FROM FOOTING-1 AFTER 2 LINES.                FIG 10.9|
|002410       WRITE REPORT-LINE FROM FOOTING-2 AFTER 1 LINES.                FIG 10.9|
|002420 520-CALCULATIONS.                                                    FIG 10.9|
|002430       SUBTRACT T-PMTS FROM OLD-BALANCE.                              FIG 10.9|
|002440       MOVE OLD-BALANCE TO BAL-AFTER-PMT.                             FIG 10.9|
|002450       MOVE T-PMTS TO PMT-AMT.                                        FIG 10.9|
|002460       MOVE N-PMTS TO PMT-NO.                                         FIG 10.9|
|002470       IF OLD-BALANCE GREATER THAN 0                                  FIG 10.9|
```

Figure 10.9 Electric Utility Program *Continued*

```
|-------------------------------------------------------------------------|
|        1   1   2   2   2   3   3   4   4   4   5   5   6   6   6   7   7   8|
|   4     8  2   6   0   4   8   2   6   0   4   8   2   6   0   4   8   2   6   0|
|-------------------------------------------------------------------------|
|002480          COMPUTE FIN-CHRG ROUNDED = OLD-BALANCE * .015.        FIG 10.9|
|002490      MOVE FIN-CHRG TO FINANCE-CHRG.                           FIG 10.9|
|002500      SUBTRACT OLD-READING FROM THIS-READING GIVING KWATTS-USED. FIG 10.9|
|002510      IF KWATTS-USED LESS THAN 0                               FIG 10.9|
|002520          COMPUTE KWATTS-USED =                               FIG 10.9|
|002530          THIS-READING + 100000 - OLD-READING.               FIG 10.9|
|002540      MOVE KWATTS-USED TO HOURS-USED.                          FIG 10.9|
|002550      IF KWATTS-USED EQUAL TO 0                               FIG 10.9|
|002560          MOVE 0 TO AMT-BILL.                                 FIG 10.9|
|002570      IF KWATTS-USED > 0 AND < 10                             FIG 10.9|
|002580          MOVE 2.50 TO AMT-BILL.                              FIG 10.9|
|002590      IF KWATTS-USED NOT < 10 AND < 5001                      FIG 10.9|
|002600          MULTIPLY KWATTS-USED BY .0255 GIVING AMT-BILL ROUNDED. FIG 10.9|
|002610      IF KWATTS-USED > 5000                                   FIG 10.9|
|002620          MULTIPLY KWATTS-USED BY .0323 GIVING AMT-BILL ROUNDED. FIG 10.9|
|002630      MOVE AMT-BILL TO BASE-BILL.                             FIG 10.9|
|002640      ADD AMT-BILL, OLD-BALANCE, FIN-CHRG GIVING TOT-AMT.     FIG 10.9|
|002650      MOVE TOT-AMT TO AMOUNT-DUE.                             FIG 10.9|
|002660      ADD 1 TO TOT-NUM-CUST.                                 FIG 10.9|
|002670      ADD KWATTS-USED TO TOT-KWH.                            FIG 10.9|
|002680      ADD OLD-BALANCE TO TOT-BAL-AFTER-PMT.                  FIG 10.9|
|002690      ADD T-PMTS TO TOT-PMTS.                               FIG 10.9|
|002700      ADD N-PMTS TO TOT-N-PMTS.                             FIG 10.9|
|002710      ADD AMT-BILL TO TOT-AMT-BILL.                         FIG 10.9|
|002720      ADD FIN-CHRG TO TOT-FIN-CHRG.                         FIG 10.9|
|002730      ADD TOT-AMT TO TOTAL-AMOUNT.                          FIG 10.9|
|002740      WRITE REPORT-LINE FROM DETAIL-RECORD AFTER 2 LINES.   FIG 10.9|
|002750      ADD 1 TO LINE-COUNT.                                  FIG 10.9|
|002760  530-RECORD-HISTORY.                                       FIG 10.9|
|002770      MOVE TYPE-INFORMATION TO HISTORY-INFORMATION.         FIG 10.9|
|002780      MOVE CUSTOMER-NUMBER TO ACCOUNT, SAVE-ACCOUNT.        FIG 10.9|
|002790      IF LINE-COUNT = 0                                     FIG 10.9|
|002800          MOVE CUSTOMER-NUMBER TO 1ST-NUMBER.              FIG 10.9|
|002810      IF LINE-COUNT = 19                                    FIG 10.9|
|002820          MOVE CUSTOMER-NUMBER TO LAST-NUMBER.            FIG 10.9|
|002830      MOVE LAST-METER-READING TO LAST-READING, OLD-READING, FIG 10.9|
|002840          NEW-READING, THIS-READING.                       FIG 10.9|
|002850      MOVE PREVIOUS-BALANCE TO BALANCE, OLD-BALANCE.        FIG 10.9|
|002860      MOVE 0 TO T-PMTS, N-PMTS, FIN-CHRG, KWATTS-USED.      FIG 10.9|
|002870      ADD PREVIOUS-BALANCE TO TOT-BAL-BEFORE-PMT.          FIG 10.9|
|002880  540-RECORD-PAYMENT.                                       FIG 10.9|
|002890      MOVE TYPE-INFORMATION TO PAYMENT-INFORMATION.         FIG 10.9|
|002900      ADD PAYMENT TO T-PMTS.                               FIG 10.9|
|002910      ADD 1 TO N-PMTS.                                     FIG 10.9|
|002920  550-RECORD-NEW-READING.                                   FIG 10.9|
|002930      MOVE TYPE-INFORMATION TO CURRENT-INFORMATION.         FIG 10.9|
|002940      MOVE CURRENT-METER-READING TO NEW-READING, THIS-READING. FIG 10.9|
|002950  900-SUMMARY-REPORT.                                       FIG 10.9|
|002960      CLOSE INFO-CARDS.                                     FIG 10.9|
|002970      MOVE '        S U M M A R Y' TO HEAD-1.              FIG 10.9|
|002980      PERFORM 512-REPORT-HEADING.                           FIG 10.9|
|002990      MOVE TOT-NUM-CUST TO GT-NUM-CUST.                     FIG 10.9|
|003000      MOVE SUM-LINE-1 TO DETAIL-SUMMARY.                    FIG 10.9|
|003010      WRITE REPORT-LINE FROM SUMMARY-LINE AFTER 2 LINES.    FIG 10.9|
|003020      MOVE TOT-KWH TO GT-KWH.                               FIG 10.9|
|003030      MOVE SUM-LINE-2 TO DETAIL-SUMMARY.                    FIG 10.9|
|003040      WRITE REPORT-LINE FROM SUMMARY-LINE AFTER 2 LINES.    FIG 10.9|
|003050      MOVE TOT-BAL-BEFORE-PMT TO GT-BAL-BEFORE-PMT.         FIG 10.9|
|003060      MOVE SUM-LINE-3 TO DETAIL-SUMMARY.                    FIG 10.9|
|003070      WRITE REPORT-LINE FROM SUMMARY-LINE AFTER 2 LINES.    FIG 10.9|
|003080      MOVE TOT-PMTS TO GT-PMTS.                             FIG 10.9|
|003090      MOVE SUM-LINE-4 TO DETAIL-SUMMARY.                    FIG 10.9|
|003100      WRITE REPORT-LINE FROM SUMMARY-LINE AFTER 2 LINES.    FIG 10.9|
|003110      MOVE TOT-N-PMTS TO GT-N-PMTS.                         FIG 10.9|
|003120      MOVE SUM-LINE-5 TO DETAIL-SUMMARY.                    FIG 10.9|
|003130      WRITE REPORT-LINE FROM SUMMARY-LINE AFTER 2 LINES.    FIG 10.9|
|003140      MOVE TOT-BAL-AFTER-PMT TO GT-BAL-AFTER-PMT.           FIG 10.9|
|003150      MOVE SUM-LINE-6 TO DETAIL-SUMMARY.                    FIG 10.9|
|003160      WRITE REPORT-LINE FROM SUMMARY-LINE AFTER 2 LINES.    FIG 10.9|
|003170      MOVE TOT-AMT-BILL TO GT-AMT-BILL.                     FIG 10.9|
|003180      MOVE SUM-LINE-7 TO DETAIL-SUMMARY.                    FIG 10.9|
|003190      WRITE REPORT-LINE FROM SUMMARY-LINE AFTER 2 LINES.    FIG 10.9|
|003200      MOVE TOT-FIN-CHRG TO GT-FIN-CHRG.                     FIG 10.9|
|003210      MOVE SUM-LINE-8 TO DETAIL-SUMMARY.                    FIG 10.9|
|003220      WRITE REPORT-LINE FROM SUMMARY-LINE AFTER 2 LINES.    FIG 10.9|
|003230      MOVE TOTAL-AMOUNT TO GT-AMOUNT.                       FIG 10.9|
|003240      MOVE SUM-LINE-9 TO DETAIL-SUMMARY.                    FIG 10.9|
|003250      WRITE REPORT-LINE FROM SUMMARY-LINE AFTER 2 LINES.    FIG 10.9|
|003260      WRITE REPORT-LINE FROM LINE-ACROSS AFTER 2 LINES.     FIG 10.9|
|003270      CLOSE ACTIVITY-REPORT.                               FIG 10.9|
|                                                                  FIG 10.9|
|-------------------------------------------------------------------------|
```

Figure 10.9 Electric Utility Program *Continued*

```
|        |         1         2         3         4         5         6         7        8| FIGURE |
|RECORD|12345678901234567890123456789012345678901234567890123456789012345678901234567890| NUMBER |
```

RECORD	data			FIGURE NUMBER
1	010181			|FIG 10.9|
2	110421	00598	043200	1|FIG 10.9|
3	110421		040000	2|FIG 10.9|
4	110421	04325		3|FIG 10.9|
5	111111	22222	123456	1|FIG 10.9|
6	111111		123456	2|FIG 10.9|
7	111111	33333		3|FIG 10.9|
8	114612	96182	003568	1|FIG 10.9|
9	114612		003568	2|FIG 10.9|
10	114612	00013		3|FIG 10.9|
11	118921	61984	005595	1|FIG 10.9|
12	118921	66418		3|FIG 10.9|
13	121212	11111	001500	1|FIG 10.9|
14	121212		001500	2|FIG 10.9|
15	121212	13425		3|FIG 10.9|
16	176257	23925	007655	1|FIG 10.9|
17	176257		076550	2|FIG 10.9|
18	176257	39876		3|FIG 10.9|
19	185792	34128	012367	1|FIG 10.9|
20	185792		012367	2|FIG 10.9|
21	185792	34134		3|FIG 10.9|
22	185794	06195	147620	1|FIG 10.9|
23	185794		147620	2|FIG 10.9|
24	185794		014762	2|FIG 10.9|
25	185794	09195		3|FIG 10.9|
26	195798	61622	014822	1|FIG 10.9|
27	195798		014820	2|FIG 10.9|
28	195798	65984		3|FIG 10.9|
29	199428	49462	004527	1|FIG 10.9|
30	234567	99827	012525	1|FIG 10.9|
31	234567		012000	2|FIG 10.9|
32	235698	33982	014570	1|FIG 10.9|
33	235698	63419		3|FIG 10.9|
34	237422	65922	205476	1|FIG 10.9|
35	237422		200000	2|FIG 10.9|
36	237422	73155		3|FIG 10.9|
37	241185	00002	026500	1|FIG 10.9|
38	241185		025400	2|FIG 10.9|
39	241185		001100	2|FIG 10.9|
40	241185	01496		3|FIG 10.9|
41	244488	75320	054378	1|FIG 10.9|
42	244488		030000	2|FIG 10.9|
43	244488		005000	2|FIG 10.9|
44	244488	78793		3|FIG 10.9|
45	245395	56218	052950	1|FIG 10.9|
46	245395		030000	2|FIG 10.9|
47	245395	57315		3|FIG 10.9|
48	251922	42417	000000	1|FIG 10.9|
49	252263	61538	057218	1|FIG 10.9|
50	252263		057218	2|FIG 10.9|
51	263477	04198	000650	1|FIG 10.9|
52	263477	07623		3|FIG 10.9|
53	293647	98690	019250	1|FIG 10.9|
54	293647		019250	2|FIG 10.9|
55	293647	00422		3|FIG 10.9|
56	321619	70041	052150	1|FIG 10.9|
57	321619		060000	2|FIG 10.9|
58	321619	76015		3|FIG 10.9|
59	377619	19576	000000	1|FIG 10.9|
60	377619	20461		3|FIG 10.9|
61	378906	98900	200000	1|FIG 10.9|
62	378906		140000	2|FIG 10.9|
63	378906		002000	2|FIG 10.9|
64	378906		003000	2|FIG 10.9|
65	378906		055000	2|FIG 10.9|
66	378906	01234		3|FIG 10.9|
67	422442	45370	008915	1|FIG 10.9|
68	422442		004000	2|FIG 10.9|
69	422442	47429		3|FIG 10.9|
70	588883	00039	016000	1|FIG 10.9|
71	588883		061000	2|FIG 10.9|
72	675782	07215	072575	1|FIG 10.9|

Figure 10.9 Electric Utility Program (Data) *Continued*

```
                    ELECTRIC POWER UTILITY COMPANY

                    CUSTOMER ACCOUNT ACTIVITY REPORT                        PAGE 01
                    FOR THE MONTH ENDING 01/01/81
```

CUSTOMER ACCOUNT NUMBER	METER READING LAST MONTH	THIS MONTH	*KILOWATT* HOURS USED	PREVIOUS* BALANCE	PAYMENTS AMOUNT	NUMBER	*BALANCE AFTER PAYMENT	BASE BILL	*FINANCE* CHARGES	TOTAL AMOUNT DUE
110421	598	4325	3727	$432.00	$400.00	1	$32.00	$95.04	$.48	$127.52
111111	22222	33333	11111	$1,234.56	$1,234.56	1	$.00	$358.89	$.00	$358.89
114612	96182	13	3831	$35.68	$35.68	1	$.00	$97.69	$.00	$97.69
118921	61984	66418	4434	$55.95	$.00	0	$55.95	$113.07	$.84	$169.86
121212	11111	13425	2314	$15.00	$15.00	1	$.00	$59.01	$.00	$59.01
176257	23925	39876	15951	$76.55	$765.50	1	$688.95-	$515.22-	$.00	$173.73CR
185792	34128	34134	6	$123.67	$123.67	1	$.00	$2.50	$.00	$2.50
185794	6195	9195	3000	$1,476.20	$1,623.82	2	$147.62-	$76.50	$.00	$71.12CR
195798	61622	65984	4362	$148.22	$148.20	1	$.02	$111.23	$.00	$111.25
199428	49462	49462	0	$45.27	$.00	0	$45.27	$.00	$.68	$45.95
234567	99827	99827	0	$125.25	$120.00	1	$5.25	$.00	$.08	$5.33
235698	33982	63419	29437	$145.70	$.00	0	$145.70	$950.82	$2.19	$1,098.71
237422	65922	73155	7233	$2,054.76	$2,000.00	1	$54.76	$233.63	$.82	$289.21
241185	2	1496	1494	$265.00	$265.00	2	$.00	$38.10	$.00	$38.10
244488	75320	78793	3473	$543.78	$350.00	2	$193.78	$88.56	$2.91	$285.25
245395	56218	57315	1097	$529.50	$300.00	1	$229.50	$27.97	$3.44	$260.91
251922	42417	42417	0	$.00	$.00	0	$.00	$.00	$.00	$.00
252263	61538	61538	0	$572.18	$572.18	1	$.00	$.00	$.00	$.00
263477	4198	7623	3425	$6.50	$.00	0	$6.50	$87.34	$.10	$93.94
293647	98690	422	1732	$192.50	$192.50	1	$.00	$44.17	$.00	$44.17

```
CUSTOMER NUMBERS ON THIS PAGE
    110421 TO 293647                                                        PAGE 01
```

```
                    CUSTOMER ACCOUNT ACTIVITY REPORT                        PAGE 02
                    FOR THE MONTH ENDING 01/01/81
```

CUSTOMER ACCOUNT NUMBER	METER READING LAST MONTH	THIS MONTH	*KILOWATT* HOURS USED	PREVIOUS* BALANCE	PAYMENTS AMOUNT	NUMBER	*BALANCE AFTER PAYMENT	BASE BILL	*FINANCE* CHARGES	TOTAL AMOUNT DUE
321619	70041	76015	5974	$521.50	$600.00	1	$78.50-	$192.96	$.00	$114.46
377619	19576	20461	885	$.00	$.00	0	$.00	$22.57	$.00	$22.57
378906	98900	1234	2334	$2,000.00	$2,000.00	4	$.00	$59.52	$.00	$59.52
422442	45370	47429	2059	$89.15	$40.00	1	$49.15	$52.50	$.74	$102.39
588883	39	39	0	$160.00	$610.00	1	$450.00-	$.00	$.00	$450.00CR
675782	7215	7215	0	$725.75	$.00	0	$725.75	$.00	$10.89	$736.64

```
CUSTOMER NUMBERS ON THIS PAGE
    110421 TO 675782                                                        PAGE 02
```

Figure 10.9 Electric Utility Company (Output—Pages 1 and 2) *Continued*

```
                        S U M M A R Y
              CUSTOMER ACCOUNT ACTIVITY REPORT                        PAGE 03
                FOR THE MONTH ENDING 01/01/81

**************************************************************************************

          TOTAL NUMBER OF CUSTOMERS PROCESSED        26

          TOTAL KILOWATT HOURS USED        107,879

          TOTAL OUTSTANDING BALANCES BEFORE PAYMENTS          $11,574.67

          TOTAL OF ALL PAYMENTS        $11,396.11

          TOTAL NUMBER OF PAYMENTS RECEIVED        25

          TOTAL OUTSTANDING BALANCES AFTER PAYMENTS          $1,380.56

          TOTAL OF ALL EASE BILLS        $3,227.29

          TOTAL FINANCE CHARGES        $23.17

          TOTAL AMOUNT OF ALL RECEIVABLES        $3,429.02

**************************************************************************************
```

Figure 10.9 Electric Utility Company (Output—Page 3) *Continued*

The Page Break   A relatively common programming concept is demonstrated in Figure 10.9—
the page break. The page break is actually a specialized control break. (The
control break was described in Chapter 8.) Unfortunately, few list-oriented
print reports will fit neatly on one page. It is often desirable (if not necessary)
to reproduce the heading at the top of *every* printed page. As a consequence,
we need to know when a page is full. Such a mechanism is shown in lines 2010
and 2020. In the example, if 20 or more lines have been printed on a page
(LINE-COUNT IS GREATER THAN 19), a new page heading is to be printed
(510-PAGE-BREAK is PERFORMed). The program keeps track of the lines
printed with line 2760, which increments LINE-COUNT by one each time the
WRITE statement at 2750 is executed. When a page break occurs, this ac-
cumulator is reset to zero (or some minimal value) at line 2240.

Control breaks and page breaks are similar in nature—both require initial
values to be set, and both check the content of at least one storage position.
The difference is that the control break seeks any change in value, but the page
break looks for a particular value. The control-break variable changes each
time a new value is available (in the example from an input operation) and the
page break variable (LINE-COUNT) is typically controlled internally (e.g., by
incrementing the variable each time a new line is printed).

Summary   This chapter has presented the arithmetic data-manipulation statements of
COBOL. Numeric data may be manipulated in COBOL through the use of the
ADD, SUBTRACT, MULTIPLY, DIVIDE, and COMPUTE statements. Generally, the ADD statement is capable of generating the algebraic sum of a series
of identifiers and literals. The SUBTRACT statement calculates the algebraic
sum of a series of data items that is deducted from another data value to
achieve the result. The MULTIPLY statement is capable of producing the product of two data values. The DIVIDE statement generates the result of dividing

one data value into (or by) another. Finally, the COMPUTE statement, through the creation of an arithmetic expression, may perform addition, subtraction, multiplication, division, and exponentiation (and combinations thereof).

Only numeric data, represented by identifier or numeric literals, may be manipulated by these statement types. Furthermore, unless an identifier serves only as a receiving field for the calculation, all data items must be described as nonedited-numeric elementary-items. In addition, each of these identifiers must contain a data value prior to being used in an arithmetic operation.

Two options are available with the arithmetic statement—ROUNDED and SIZE ERROR. The ROUNDED option allows the result of a calculation to be rounded to the size of the PICTURE clause of the receiving field, thus avoiding low-order digit truncation. The SIZE ERROR option gives the programmer the means to perform special processing in the event that overflow of a receiving field occurs.

Notes on Programming Style

It is obvious that all computational capabilities of the ADD, SUBTRACT, MULTIPLY, and DIVIDE statements are present in the COMPUTE statement. Simple forms of the statements can also be expressed in the GIVING form of the same statement. For example, the statement

ADD 1 TO C

can be rewritten as

ADD 1, C GIVING C.

or

COMPUTE C = C + 1.

However, let me urge you to use the statements as they were intended to be used. When other arithmetic statements are used to replace the simple ADD statement, the code typically becomes less clear. If a computation is complex, i.e., it cannot be performed with a single ADD, SUBTRACT, MULTIPLY, or DIVIDE statement or a limited number of these statements in combination, the COMPUTE statement is a superior choice for the calculation from the standpoint of computer execution time. However, compared to the other arithmetic statements, COMPUTE statements generally require more time during compilation—since the COMPUTE statement could contain a number of different operations. The reason the COMPUTE statement generally solves complex problems faster than the corresponding ADD, SUBTRACT, MULTIPLY, and DIVIDE statements is that intermediate results are stored in the computer's memory (registers) and not placed directly into a programmer-supplied-name until the final result is achieved. This could eliminate a number of movements from (and to) "working registers" to (and from) programmer-accessible storage areas.

Finally, extreme care should be exercised when dealing with numeric data. It is more likely than not that your first execution-type error will be caused by numeric data that does not correspond to its PICTURE description. Suppose, for example, a particular data item is represented by the PICTURE clause 99V9. If any of the following values were placed (moved or read) into the data item, it would result in an error:

$$X42$$
$$7.3$$
$$45$$

The first value contains the letter "X"—not a numeric value (or character). The second value contains a decimal point—not a numeric value. The third value contains a blank—not a numeric value. Internal numeric varibles (e.g., counters, accumulators, indicators, etc.) should always be initialized either directly in the DATA DIVISION with a VALUE clause or in the initializing processes in the PROCEDURE DIVISION. Use *edited* fields in output (printer) record descriptions only. Their use in other locations invariably tends to cause problems for programmers.

Questions

Below fill in the blank(s) with the appropriate word, words, or phrases.

1. The COBOL verbs associated with arithmetic operations are _____ , _____ , _____ , _____ and _____ .

2. Only the _____ statement permits multiple types of arithmetic operations in one statement.

3. The _____ statement may be used to generate the sum of two numeric items.

4. The PICTURE description of all identifiers in the simple ADD statement must be _____.

5. In the simple ADD statement, data values may be indicated before the reserved word TO by either _____ or _____ .

6. The optional phrases which may be associated with the simple ADD statement are _____ and _____ .

7. If the programmer wishes to identify situations in which receiving field overflow occurs, the _____ option should be used in arithmetic operations.

8. If the programmer wishes to identify situations in which division by zero has been attempted, the _____ option should be used.

9. In the simple ADD statement _____ (number) identifier(s) or literal(s) is/are required before the reserved word TO, while _____ (number) identifier(s) or literal(s),is/are required before the reserved word GIVING in the ADD-GIVING form of the statement.

10. The identifier following the reserved word GIVING in the ADD-GIVING statement may be a(n) _____ numeric field.

11. In the simple SUBTRACT statement, one or more _____ must follow the reserved word FROM.

12. The _____ statement causes the creation of the product of two data values.

13. A literal may appear after the reserved word BY only in the _____ form of the MULTIPLY statement.

14. The product of _____ (number) values is created by the MULTIPLY statement.

15. The SIZE ERROR option may be invoked in a DIVIDE statement when receiving field overflow occurs or when _____ is attempted.

16. When the REMAINDER option is provided in a DIVIDE statement, it is possible to perform _____ division.

17. When the reserved word BY appears in the DIVIDE-GIVING statement, identifier-1 is the _____ (divisor/dividend).

18. The only required punctuation in a COMPUTE statement (other than a period) is a(n) _____ .

19. An arithmetic expression in a COMPUTE statement may be composed of _____ , _____ , _____ , and _____ .

Answer the following questions by circling either "T" for True or "F" for False.

T F 20. COBOL is the most advanced programming language for performing computation.

T F 21. In the simple ADD statement, one or more identifiers may be added to another identifier.

T F 22. Only the identifier after the reserved word TO in the simple ADD statement is modified by the addition operation.

T F 23. It is possible to add to more than one identifier with the simple ADD statement.

T F 24. The identifier after the reserved word TO in a simple ADD statement does not necessarily have to contain a value prior to the addition operation.

T F 25. In the simple ADD statement it is permitted to record a literal after the reserved word TO.

T F 26. The ROUNDED option of the simple ADD statement causes rounding of the addition of the operation to an integer value.

T F 27. With the ADD statement it is possible to have receiving field overflow (high-order digit truncation) and underflow (low-order digit truncation).

T F 28. When a ROUNDED option is used in conjunction with an ADD statement, receiving field overflow will never occur.

T F 29. The reserved word TO appears in all forms of the ADD statement.

T F 30. Only one receiving field is permitted after the reserved word GIVING in the ADD-GIVING statement.

T F 31. All identifiers in the ADD-GIVING statement must contain a value.

T F 32. If an identifier in an ADD statement contained a negative value, the algebraic equivalent of subtraction could be achieved by the ADD statement.

T F 33. All identifiers in the simple SUBTRACT statement must be nonedited-numeric data items and contain a value.

T F 34. Both formats of the SUBTRACT statement require the reserved word FROM.

T F 35. In both formats of the SUBTRACT statement, the identifier following the reserved word FROM is modified by the subtraction operation.

T F 36. In both formats of the SUBTRACT statement, multiple identifiers could appear after the reserved word FROM.

T F 37. All identifiers used as receiving fields in both forms of the SUBTRACT statement must contain the operational-sign character(s) in their PICTURE string.

T F 38. Only two identifiers are permitted in the simple MULTIPLY, and both must be described as nonedited-numeric fields.

T F 39. The reserved word BY appears in both forms of the MULTIPLY statement.

T F 40. Multiple receiving fields are permitted in the simple form of the MULTIPLY statement.

T F 41. The reserved word BY is permitted in both forms of the DIVIDE statement.

T F 42. In the DIVIDE statement, the selection of the reserved words BY and INTO have no effect on the division operation of the DIVIDE-GIVING statement.

T F 43. The receiving field in the COMPUTE statement is the first identifier appearing in the statement.

T F 44. Multiple receiving fields are permitted in a COMPUTE statement.

T F 45. The receiving field of a COMPUTE statement may be an edited field.

T F 46. There is no arithmetic operation which can be performed by the ADD, SUBTRACT, MULTIPLY, and DIVIDE statements which cannot also be performed by a COMPUTE statement.

T F 47. In a COMPUTE statement, multiplication normally takes place before addition.

T F 48. It is possible to have "nested" parentheses in a COMPUTE statement.

Exercises

1. Below is a series of ADD statements. Given the data-names, PICTURE clauses, and VALUE clauses indicated, determine the result of the execution of each ADD statement. (Consider each statement independently.)

```
01  FIELD-RECORD.
    05 FIELD-1          PIC 99          VALUE 27.
    05 FIELD-2          PIC 99          VALUE 62.
    05 FIELD-3          PIC 999V99      VALUE 247.62.
    05 FIELD-4          PIC 9(4)V99.
    05 FIELD-5          PIC $$$$.$$.
```

a. ADD FIELD-1 TO FIELD-2.

b. ADD FIELD-1, FIELD-3 TO FIELD-2.

c. ADD FIELD-1, FIELD-3 GIVING FIELD-4.

d. ADD FIELD-1, FIELD-2, 4Ø.5 GIVING FIELD-3.

e. ADD FIELD-1, 1Ø7.698, GIVING FIELD-4 ROUNDED.

f. ADD 1Ø TO FIELD-2.

g. ADD -4Ø, FIELD-1 TO FIELD-2.

h. ADD -4Ø, FIELD-1 GIVING FIELD-2 ROUNDED.

i. ADD -2ØØ, FIELD-3 GIVING FIELD-1 ROUNDED.

j. ADD 7ØØ, FIELD-1, FIELD-2 TO FIELD-3
   ROUNDED ON SIZE ERROR
   MOVE Ø TO FIELD-3.

2. Below is a series of SUBTRACT statements. Given the data-names, PICTURE clauses, and VALUE clauses indicated, determine the result of the execution of each SUBTRACT statement. (Consider each statement independently.)

```
01   ITEM-RECORD.
     05  ITEM-1              PIC 99             VALUE 75.
     05  ITEM-2              PIC S999           VALUE -982.
     05  ITEM-3              PIC S999V99        VALUE 44.73.
     05  ITEM-4              PIC 9(4)           VALUE 64.
     05  ITEM-5              PIC Z(4).99.
```

  a. SUBTRACT 15 FROM ITEM-1.
  b. SUBTRACT 25 FROM ITEM-2, ITEM-3.
  c. SUBTRACT ITEM-2 FROM ITEM-4.
  d. SUBTRACT ITEM-1, ITEM-4 FROM ITEM-3.
  e. SUBTRACT ITEM-3, 4Ø FROM ITEM-1.
  f. SUBTRACT ITEM-1 FROM ITEM-2 GIVING ITEM-3.
  g. SUBTRACT ITEM-2 FROM ITEM-1 GIVING ITEM-4.
  h. SUBTRACT ITEM-3 FROM ITEM-4 ROUNDED.
  i. SUBTRACT ITEM-3 FROM ITEM-4 GIVING ITEM-5.
  j. SUBTRACT ITEM-3 FROM ITEM-1 GIVING ITEM-2.
    ON SIZE ERROR
      SUBTRACT ITEM-1 FROM ITEM-3 GIVING ITEM-2.

3. Below is a series of MULTIPLY statements. Given the data-names, PICTURE clauses, and VALUE clauses indicated, determine the result of the execution of each MULTIPLY statement. (Consider each statement independently.)

```
01   NUM-RECORD.
     05  NUM-1              PIC 99             VALUE 1Ø.
     05  NUM-2              PIC S999           VALUE -25.
     05  NUM-3              PIC 9(4)           VALUE 15Ø.
     05  NUM-4              PIC 99V99          VALUE 1.11.
     05  NUM-5              PIC $$,$$$.$$
```

  a. MULTIPLY 1Ø BY NUM-3.
  b. MULTIPLY -1 BY NUM-2.
  c. MULTIPLY NUM-1 BY NUM-4.
  d. MULTIPLY NUM-3 BY NUM-1.
  e. MULTIPLY -5 BY NUM-2.
  f. MULTIPLY NUM-3 BY 1Ø GIVING NUM-5.
  g. MULTIPLY NUM-2 BY NUM-4 GIVING NUM-3.
  h. MULTIPLY .9 BY NUM-4 GIVING NUM-2 ROUNDED.
  i. MULTIPLY NUM-2 BY NUM-4 GIVING NUM-5.
  j. MULTIPLY NUM-1 BY NUM-2 GIVING NUM-3
    ON SIZE ERROR
      MOVE Ø TO NUM-3.

4. Below is a series of DIVIDE statements. Given the data-names, PICTURE clauses, and VALUE clauses indicated, determine the result of the execution of each DIVIDE statement. (Consider each statement independently.)

```
01   DATA-RECORD.
     05  DATA-1             PIC 999            VALUE 2Ø.
     05  DATA-2             PIC S99V99         VALUE 9.25.
     05  DATA-3             PIC 9(3)V99        VALUE Ø.
     05  DATA-4             PIC V999           VALUE .Ø1.
     05  DATA-5             PIC +(4).++.
```

    a. DIVIDE 1Ø INTO DATA-1.
    b. DIVIDE .1 INTO DATA-1.
    c. DIVIDE DATA-2 INTO DATA-1.
    d. DIVIDE DATA-4 INTO DATA-4.
    e. DIVIDE DATA-1 INTO DATA-2 ROUNDED.
    f. DIVIDE DATA-4 BY DATA-2 GIVING DATA-3.
    g. DIVIDE DATA-3 INTO DATA-2 GIVING DATA-3.
       ON SIZE ERROR MOVE 1 TO DATA-3
           DIVIDE DATA-3 INTO DATA-2 GIVING DATA-3.
    h. DIVIDE DATA-2 BY .Ø1 GIVING DATA-4 ROUNDED.
    i. DIVIDE DATA-2 BY .1 GIVING DATA-1.
    j. DIVIDE DATA-2 BY DATA-1 GIVING DATA-3.

5. Below is a series of COMPUTE statements. Given the data-names, PICTURE clauses, and VALUE clauses indicated, determine the result of the execution of each COMPUTE statement. (Consider each statement independently.)

```
01  VAL-RECORD.
    05 VAL-1              PIC 9(3)          VALUE 125.
    05 VAL-2              PIC 99V99         VALUE 5.
    05 VAL-3              PIC S9(4)V99      VALUE 25.
    05 VAL-4              PIC S9V999        VALUE 1.1.
    05 VAL-5              PIC Z(4).ZZ.
```

    a. COMPUTE VAL-3 = VAL-1 / VAL-2 + 25.
    b. COMPUTE VAL-2 = VAL-1 + VAL-3 - 1ØØ.
    c. COMPUTE VAL-3 = VAL-2 − VAL-1 / 1Ø.
    d. COMPUTE VAL-2 = (VAL-1 + 5ØØ) **.5.
    e. COMPUTE VAL-4 = VAL-3 / VAL-2 / 1Ø.
    f. COMPUTE VAL-5 = VAL-3 ** 2.
    g. COMPUTE VAL-1 ROUNDED = VAL-4 + (VAL-3 / VAL-2) * 3.
    h. COMPUTE VAL-3 = (VAL-3 - VAL-1) * .6.

Problems

1. Customer records have been prepared for processing to create an accounts receivable schedule. The accounts receivable schedule is to list all customer records and their outstanding balances (see the multiple-card layout form). The current balance is the amount (dollars and cents) a customer owes us from the last (current) billing period. The 30-day balance is the amount of money owed to us, which has been due over 30 days (1 month). The 60-day balance is the amount owed, which has been due 60 days (2 months). The 90-day balance is the amount owed us, which has been due 90 days or more (3 months or more). The 30-day balance is not included in the 60-day balance field or vice versa—they are independent of each other. The same relationship is true between the 60-day and 90-day balances.

The report to be produced from this data is composed of two parts—a body which contains a listing of all customer records and a summary (see the print charts). The content of the body of the report is self-explanatory except that the pages are to be numbered, a heading is to appear on every page, and page totals are to be printed (the total of each monetary-amount column). Page totals reflect amounts appearing on that page only.

In the summary, several monetary values are presented. First, individual totals are to be printed for the current, 30-day, 60-day, and 90-day balances (along with the percentage each is of the grand total—total receivables). The second major group of data printed in the summary report is cumulative totals. In the order listed on the report, the cumulative current total is the same as the current total. The cumulative 30-day total is the 30-day total plus the current total, and so forth for the 60-day and 90-day cumulative totals. The cumulative percentages are again based on total receivables.

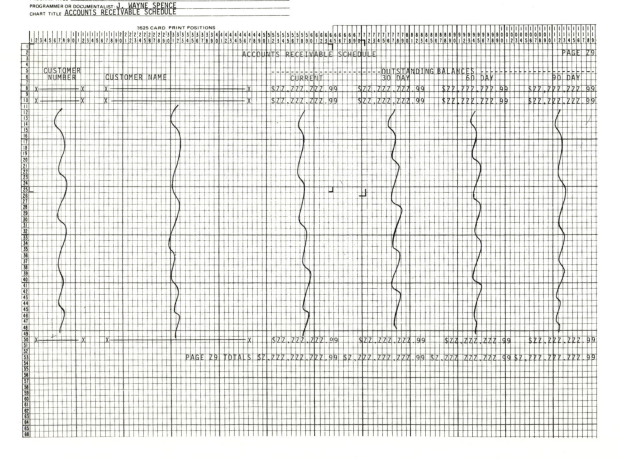

150/10/8 **PRINT CHART**   PROG. ID. RECEIVABLES P 10.1   PAGE 2 OF 2
(SPACING: 150 POSITIONS AT 10 CHARACTERS PER INCH, 8 LINES PER VERTICAL INCH)   DATE 1/1/81
PROGRAM TITLE ACCOUNTS RECEIVABLE
PROGRAMMER OR DOCUMENTALIST J. WAYNE SPENCE
CHART TITLE ACCOUNTS RECEIVABLE SCHEDULE

```
                        ACCOUNTS RECEIVABLE SCHEDULE                          PAGE Z9
                                S U M M A R Y

                          TOTALS                    CUMMULATIVE TOTALS
                   -------------------------    -------------------------
             BALANCES      $            %              $            %
             CURRENT   $ZZ,ZZZ,ZZZ,ZZZ.99    ZZZ.ZZZ   $ZZ,ZZZ,ZZZ,ZZZ.99   ZZZ.ZZZ
             30 DAY    $ZZ,ZZZ,ZZZ,ZZZ.99    ZZZ.ZZZ   $ZZ,ZZZ,ZZZ,ZZZ.99   ZZZ.ZZZ
             60 DAY    $ZZ,ZZZ,ZZZ,ZZZ.99    ZZZ.ZZZ   $ZZ,ZZZ,ZZZ,ZZZ.99   ZZZ.ZZZ
             90 DAY    $ZZ,ZZZ,ZZZ,ZZZ.99    ZZZ.ZZZ   $ZZ,ZZZ,ZZZ,ZZZ.99   ZZZ.ZZZ

                 TOTAL ACCOUNTS RECEIVABLE $ZZZ,ZZZ,ZZZ,ZZZ.99
```

2. In an effort to reduce the amount of money invested in on-hand inventory, the inventory control manager has asked us to develop a planning model to evaluate three possible alternatives:

   a. Do nothing—retain current inventory replenishment policies based on the reorder point (ROP).
   b. Establish a new reorder point based on annual historical usage.
   c. Establish a new reorder point based on annual historical usage, which does not include a safety stock margin.

   To forecast product demand for each inventory item, we will assume that annual usage (demand) is constant—i.e., demand does not fluctuate because of seasonal, cyclical, or trend influences.

   To establish the average inventory cost for each alternative, the following computations are necessary:

   The average number of units on-hand is equal to the reorder point (less safety stock, if any) divided by 2. (Again, a constant demand is assumed.) The safety stock, if any, is then added back, and the sum is multiplied by the cost per unit.

   The cost of alternative (a)—using the current policy—is based on the existing reorder point value.

   The reorder point value for alternative (b)—establish a new reorder point based on annual demand—is equal to the annual usage in units divided by the number-of-weeks-supply needed to cover the time lag between the placement of an order and the receipt of the order plus the safety stock. (Since there are 52 weeks in a year, the usage per week may be determined by dividing annual usage by 52. Then multiply the number of weeks between order and receipt to find the minimum quantity necessary to meet anticipated demand.) Now, with the new reorder point, proceed in the manner specified for alternative (a) to find the average cost of inventory.

   For alternative (c), the computation is the same as for alternative (b) except that the safety stock level is assumed to be zero units.

On the basis of the information specified above and after reviewing the graphic record layout, produce the report format specified on the print chart. Notice that the column INC/DEC ALT 1 has been added to the columns marked ALTERNATIVE 2 and ALTERNATIVE 3. This new column should reflect the increase or decrease in cost of the respective alternative with respect to ALTERNATIVE 1. Finally, totals are to be produced for each alternative.

MULTIPLE-CARD LAYOUT FORM

Company LEARNING COBOL, INC.
Application INVENTORY VALUATION   by J. Wayne Spence   Date 01/01/81   Job No. PROB 10.2   Sheet No. 1

Inventory Item		Vendor	Safety Stock	Reorder Point	Weeks Ord. to Receipt	Annual Usage in Units	Cost Per Unit	
Number	Description							

```
999999 9999999999999999999999 99 999 9999 99 9999999 99999 99999999999999999999999999999
1 2 3 4 5 6 7 8 9 10 11 12 13 14 15 16 17 18 19 20 21 22 23 24 25 26 27 28 29 30 31 32 33 34 35 36 37 38 39 40 41 42 43 44 45 46 47 48 49 50 51 52 53 54 55 56 57 58 59 60 61 62 63 64 65 66 67 68 69 70 71 72 73 74 75 76 77 78 79 80
```

150/10/8 PRINT CHART   PROG. ID. INVENTORY P 10.2   PAGE 1
(SPACING: 150 POSITIONS AT 10 CHARACTERS PER INCH, 8 LINES PER VERTICAL INCH)   DATE 01/01/81
PROGRAM TITLE INVENTORY EVALUATION
PROGRAMMER OR DOCUMENTALIST: J. Wayne Spence
CHART TITLE REORDER POINT ANALYSIS

```
                    REORDER   POINT   ANALYSIS                                      PAGE ZZ9

                    ALTERNATIVE #1        ALTERNATIVE #2                  ALTERNATIVE #3
ITEM                ----------------      ----------------  -----------   ----------------  -----------
NUMBER DESCRIPTION  ROP    COST           ROP    COST       INC/DEC ALT 1 ROP    COST        INC/DEC ALT 1
XXXXXX X----------X ZZZZZ9 $Z,ZZZ,ZZZ.99  ZZZZZ9 $Z,ZZZ,ZZZ.99 --,---,---.99  ZZZZZ9 $Z,ZZZ,ZZZ.99 --,---,---.99
XXXXXX X----------X ZZZZZ9 $Z,ZZZ,ZZZ.99  ZZZZZ9 $Z,ZZZ,ZZZ.99 --,---,---.99  ZZZZZ9 $Z,ZZZ,ZZZ.99 --,---,---.99

XXXXXX X----------X ZZZZZ9 $Z,ZZZ,ZZZ.99  ZZZZZ9 $Z,ZZZ,ZZZ.99 --,---,---.99  ZZZZZ9 $Z,ZZZ,ZZZ.99 --,---,---.99

                    REORDER   POINT   ANALYSIS                                      PAGE ZZ9

                    ALTERNATIVE #1        ALTERNATIVE #2                  ALTERNATIVE #3
ITEM                ----------------      ----------------  -----------   ----------------  -----------
NUMBER DESCRIPTION  ROP    COST           ROP    COST       INC/DEC ALT 1 ROP    COST        INC/DEC ALT 1
XXXXXX X----------X ZZZZZ9 $Z,ZZZ,ZZZ.99  ZZZZZ9 $Z,ZZZ,ZZZ.99 --,---,---.99  ZZZZZ9 $Z,ZZZ,ZZZ.99 --,---,---.99
XXXXXX X----------X ZZZZZ9 $Z,ZZZ,ZZZ.99  ZZZZZ9 $Z,ZZZ,ZZZ.99 --,---,---.99  ZZZZZ9 $Z,ZZZ,ZZZ.99 --,---,---.99

XXXXXX X----------X ZZZZZ9 $Z,ZZZ,ZZZ.99  ZZZZZ9 $Z,ZZZ,ZZZ.99 --,---,---.99  ZZZZZ9 $Z,ZZZ,ZZZ.99 --,---,---.99
             TOTALS        $Z,ZZZ,ZZZ.99         $Z,ZZZ,ZZZ.99 --,---,---.99         $Z,ZZZ,ZZZ.99 --,---,---.99
```

3. Your company has a fleet of automobiles used by both executives and sales personnel. The motor pool is responsible for maintaining the fleet and recording costs of vehicle operation. The fleet manager requests a report to assist in cost controls for the fleet as a whole and for individual vehicles. Each month the expense receipts are summarized, and a record is developed (as indicated in the multiple- card layout form). The key elements of the record are the odometer readings at the beginning and ending of each month, total receipts for gas and oil, receipts for repairs and other maintenance, average (historical) mileage per gallon for all past travel, and average (historical) cost per mile driven for all past travel.

The report the fleet manager requests contains the following features (see the print chart):

1. number of miles driven during the month for each vehicle
2. average miles per gallon for each vehicle during the month
3. average cost per mile (which includes the cost for gas and repairs) during the month for each vehicle
4. a new historical average miles per gallon (which includes the current month and all past performance)
5. a new historical average cost per mile (which includes the current month and all past performance)
6. if the average miles per gallon or the cost per mile shows any more than a 10 percent deviation over the historical average, it is to be indicated
7. any vehicle with a monthly mile per gallon of any value less than 10 mpg is to be indicated
8. any vehicle which exceeds 35 cents per mile for operating cost during the month is to be indicated

For this report, the fleet manager requests no more than 30 vehicles to be listed per page and that the pages be numbered.

MULTIPLE-CARD LAYOUT FORM

Company AMPEX CORPORATION

Application FLTSUM   by J. WAYNE SPENCE   Date 01/01/81   Job No. PROB 10.3   Sheet No. 1 OF 1

VEHICLE ID	VEHICLE DESCRIPTION	ODOMETER READING		GAS-OIL		REPAIR AND MAINT.	AVERAGE		
		BEGIN- ING	END- ING	EXPENSE	COST PER GAL		MPG	COST PER MILE	

150/10/8 PRINT CHART   PROG. ID. FLTSUM P 10.3   PAGE 1 of 1
(SPACING: 150 POSITIONS AT 10 CHARACTERS PER INCH, 8 LINES PER VERTICAL INCH)   DATE 01/01/81
PROGRAM TITLE FLEET UTILIZATION SUMMARY
PROGRAMMER OR DOCUMENTALIST J. WAYNE SPENCE
CHART TITLE FLEET UTILIZATION REPORT

```
                              AMPEX  CORPORATION

                          FLEET UTILIZATION REPORT                    PAGE XXX

                                                               AVERAGE
                                                      --------------------------------------
     VEHICLE     VEHICLE         ODOMETER READING   MILEAGE   EXPENDITURES    THIS MONTH       UPDATED HISTORY
                                                     THIS    -------------  -------------    ----------------
     ID NUM      DESCRIPTION      BEGIN     END      MONTH   GAS/OIL  REPAIR   MPG  COST/MILE   MPG  COST/MILE

     XXXXXXXXX   XXXXXXXXXXXXXXXXXXXXXX  XXXXXX   XXXXXX     XXXX   XXX.XX   XXX.XX   XX.X     XX,XXX  *   XX.X    XX,XXX
     XXXXXXXXX   XXXXXXXXXXXXXXXXXXXXXX  XXXXXX   XXXXXX     XXXX   XXX.XX   XXX.XX   XX.X  *  XX,XXX      XX.X    XX,XXX
     XXXXXXXXX   XXXXXXXXXXXXXXXXXXXXXX  XXXXXX   XXXXXX     XXXX   XXX.XX   XXX.XX   XX.X     XX,XXX  ** XX.X    XX,XXX



     XXXXXXXXX   XXXXXXXXXXXXXXXXXXXXXX  XXXXXX   XXXXXX     XXXX   XXX.XX   XXX.XX   XX.X     XX,XXX      XX.X    XX,XXX


     *  EXCEEDS 10% INCREASE
     ** EXCEEDS 35 CENTS
```

11 More on the IF Statements

In addition to the relational IF statement (discussed in Chapter 8) COBOL permits conditions to be stated in terms of a *sign test*, a *class test*, and a *condition-name test*. Many of the IF statement's properties described in Chapter 8 also apply to these new types of conditions.

The Sign Test

The sign test category of the IF statement (shown in Figure 11.1) provides the means for determining whether an item is positive, negative, or zero. One difference between the sign test and the relational test is that the subject of a sign test may be an identifier or an arithmetic expression only. The test compares the sign of an item, so the identifier (or arithmetic expression) must be a numeric data item. A literal cannot be the subject of a sign test. The subject of the sign test is followed by one of three reserved words—POSITIVE, NEGATIVE, or ZERO. (Here, the reserved word ZERO is not exactly the same as the figurative constant ZERO because the plural form of the word is not acceptable.) These reserved words are followed by true and false imperative statements (or NEXT SENTENCEs), as with the relational test.

The sign test does not possess a relational operator as does the relational IF statement. Thus, the operator (POSITIVE, NEGATIVE, or ZERO) cannot be implied; however, logical operators may be used with the sign test. For example, it is permissible to have the statement

```
IF ITEM-1 IS POSITIVE OR ITEM-1 ZERO. . .
```

which uses the logical connective OR. (The programmer is cautioned against using the logical operator AND, since one value cannot be both positive *and*

$$
\text{IF} \left\{ \begin{array}{l} \text{identifier} \\ \text{arithmetic-expression} \end{array} \right\} \text{IS [\underline{NOT}]} \left\{ \begin{array}{l} \underline{\text{POSITIVE}} \\ \underline{\text{NEGATIVE}} \\ \underline{\text{ZERO}} \end{array} \right\} \left\{ \begin{array}{l} \text{imperative-statement-1} \\ \underline{\text{NEXT}} \ \underline{\text{SENTENCE}} \end{array} \right\}
$$

$$
\left[\underline{\text{ELSE}} \left\{ \begin{array}{l} \text{imperative-statement-2} \\ \underline{\text{NEXT}} \ \underline{\text{SENTENCE}} \end{array} \right\} \right]
$$

Figure 11.1 Format of the Sign Text

zero at the same time.) Because the subject of both conditions is ITEM-1, the same statement could be written as

```
IF ITEM-1 IS POSITIVE OR ZERO . . .,
```

in which case the subject (ITEM-1) is implied. It is generally not necessary to use a compound sign test. In the statements above, the procedure is to be executed if ITEM-1 is either positive or zero. Another way of indicating the same condition is to say NOT NEGATIVE, i.e.,

```
IF ITEM-1 NOT NEGATIVE . . .
```

Like the relational test, the sign test also permits nesting, however, it is not generally necessary to nest sign tests which are using the same data item—such as in the grade assignment problem presented in Chapter 10. Nevertheless, the sign test could be used to determine which letter grade should be assigned to a student on the basis of a numeric average. Figure 11.2 provides this somewhat artificial use of the sign test. Note that in the case of this program, short arithmetic expressions are necessary to "bracket" the numeric averages into letter-grade categories. While the reserved word POSITIVE is used for each of these tests, it would be a simple matter to reverse the order of the tests; change the constants to 89.5, 79.5, etc., and use the reserved word NOT NEGATIVE for each of the tests.

```
IF AVERAGE - 89.4 IS POSITIVE
    MOVE 'A' TO LETTER-GRADE
ELSE
    IF AVERAGE - 79.4 IS POSITIVE
        MOVE 'B' TO LETTER-GRADE
    ELSE
        IF AVERAGE - 69.4 IS POSITIVE
            MOVE 'C' TO LETTER-GRADE
        ELSE
            IF AVERAGE - 59.4 IS POSITIVE
                MOVE 'D' TO LETTER-GRADE
            ELSE
                MOVE 'F' TO LETTER-GRADE
```

Figure 11.2 Examples of the Sign Test

The Class Test

The primary purpose of the class test is to determine whether an identifier is NUMERIC or ALPHABETIC. Note from Figure 11.3 that only an identifier is permitted to be the subject of the class test and the identifier must be described in a form consistent with the type of test being made. That is, in a numeric class test, the description of the identifier in the DATA DIVISION *must not* be described (either implicitly or explicitly) as an alphabetic data item. The identifier will be classified as NUMERIC only if the contents of the identifier are numeric—composed only of digits and perhaps an operational sign. The converse of this is also true. If the class test is to be made using the reserved word ALPHABETIC, the true branch of this IF statement will be executed only if the content of the identifier consists of alphabetic characters and spaces.

The Condition-Name Test

The condition-name test is somewhat different from the other IF tests in that support for the test is required in the DATA DIVISION. The basic format for this statement is provided in Figure 11.4. Note the appearance of the state-

```
IF identifier IS [NOT]  ⎧NUMERIC   ⎫ ⎧imperative-statement-1⎫
                        ⎩ALPHABETIC⎭ ⎩NEXT SENTENCE         ⎭

    ⎡       ⎧imperative-statement-2⎫⎤
    ⎢ELSE   ⎨                      ⎬⎥
    ⎣       ⎩NEXT SENTENCE         ⎭⎦
```

Figure 11.3 Format of the Class Test

```
IF condition-name  ⎧imperative-statement-1⎫ ⎡      ⎧imperative-statement-2⎫⎤
                   ⎨                      ⎬ ⎢ELSE  ⎨                      ⎬⎥
                   ⎩NEXT SENTENCE         ⎭ ⎣      ⎩NEXT SENTENCE         ⎭⎦
```

Figure 11.4 Format of the Condition-Name Test

ment. No relational operators or reserved words appear between the condition-name and the imperative statement (or NEXT SENTENCE) phrases of the statement. Thus, the test is made on the basis of the condition-name itself.

The condition-name is a special type of programmer-supplied-name in that it may be used only in conjunction with a condition-name test. While appearing to contain data values, condition-names cannot be used as data-names. Condition-names are specified in the DATA DIVISION of a COBOL program. Condition-names are *associated with preset values* which may be contained in an elementary data item to which the condition-names are subordinate. Furthermore, a condition-name is always accompanied by a level-88 number. The format for the coding of condition-names is presented in Figure 11.5. A condition-name and a particular value or set of values of the elementary data item are associated by the VALUE clause. As it is used here, the VALUE clause is slightly different from the VALUE clause presented in Chapter 5. The first major difference is that a condition-name may be associated with one literal, but it can also be associated with a series of literals. If more than one value is to be associated with a condition name, the values must be listed in ascending order (with literal-1 receiving the smallest value in the sequence). Also, the literals must be consistent with the PICTURE type of the elementary data item. That is, if the elementary-item is described as numeric, the literals should be numeric literals or figurative constants (e.g., ZERO). If the elementary-item is

```
level-number elementary-item-name  ⎧PICTURE⎫  picture-string . . .
                                    ⎩PIC    ⎭

    88 condition-name-1  ⎧VALUE IS  ⎫  literal-1 [THRU literal-2]
                         ⎩VALUES ARE⎭

        [literal-3 [THRU literal-4]] . . .
```

Figure 11.5 Format for the Creation of Condition-Names

described as alphabetic or alphanumeric, the literals should be non-numeric literals or figurative constants (e.g., SPACE). Finally, VALUE clauses connected with condition-names may appear in both the FILE SECTION and the WORKING-STORAGE SECTION.

Perhaps an example of the creation of condition-names is in order. In the illustration below, condition-names are employed to distinguish between courses taught by different departments or colleges within a university system. Assuming the university is organized by college (e.g., colleges of Arts and Sciences, Business, Education, etc.), with each college having one or more course-prefix designations, it would be possible to determine which college teaches a particular course by the following condition-names and codes.

```
04  COURSE-DESIGNATION.
    06  COURSE-PREFIX    PIC XXX.
        88 ARTS-AND-SCIENCES VALUES ARE 'ART', 'BIO', 'CHE', 'COM', 'ECO',
            'ENG', 'GEO', 'GOV', 'HIS', 'MAT', 'MUS', 'PE', 'PHY', 'PSY'.
        88 BUSINESS VALUES ARE 'ACC', 'CSC', 'FIN', 'MAN', 'MAR', 'OAD'.
        88 EDUCATION VALUES ARE 'EED', 'SED'.
```

If the following statements were placed in the PROCEDURE DIVISION, the first IF statement would be considered true if COURSE-PREFIX contained any of the values ART, BIO, CHE, COM, ECO, ENG, GEO, GOV, HIS, MAT, MUS, PE, PHY, or PSY. The second IF statement would be true for COURSE-PREFIX values of ACC, CSC, FIN, MAN, MAR, or OAD. The third IF statement would be true for values of EED and SED, and so forth.

```
IF ART-AND-SCIENCES . . .
IF BUSINESS . . .
IF EDUCATION . . .
```

To further demonstrate the use of the VALUE clause in the association of elementary-item values with condition-names, assume that college courses were numbered such that all 100s would represent freshman courses; 200s, sophomore courses; 300s, junior courses; and 400s, senior courses. The creation of condition-names under this situation might appear as:

```
06  COURSE-SUFFIX    PICTURE 999.
    88 FRESHMAN-LEVEL VALUES ARE 100 THRU 199.
    88 SOPHOMORE-LEVEL VALUES ARE 200 THRU 299.
    88 JUNIOR-LEVEL VALUES ARE 300 THRU 399.
    88 SENIOR-LEVEL VALUES ARE 400 THRU 499.
    88 GRADUATE-LEVEL VALUES ARE 500 THRU 999.
```

In the PROCEDURE DIVISION, the statements

```
IF FRESHMAN-LEVEL . . .
IF SOPHOMORE-LEVEL . . .
IF JUNIOR-LEVEL . . .
IF SENIOR-LEVEL . . .
IF GRADUATE-LEVEL . . .
```

could be used to distinguish between different course levels.

The grade-assignment problem can also be constructed to utilize condition-name tests. Figure 11.6 demonstrates the procedure for incorporating condition-name tests into the problem for the determination of letter grades. First, to use condition-name tests, the DATA DIVISION must be modified to create the condition-names. After the condition-names and their associated values have been provided, it is a very simple matter to modify the PRO-CEDURE DIVISION to use condition-name IF statements.

As you can see, programs may be written using a variety of IF statements. In some cases, types of IF statements can be interchanged, as in the grades problem. In other cases, only one of the IF statements will solve the problem.

```
DATA DIVISION entries.

01  AVERAGE-OF-GRADES.
    02 AVERAGE                          PIC 999V9.
        88 GRADE-A VALUES ARE 89.5 THRU 100.
        88 GRADE-B VALUES ARE 79.5 THRU 89.4.
        88 GRADE-C VALUES ARE 69.5 THRU 79.4.
        88 GRADE-D VALUES ARE 59.5 THRU 69.4.
        88 GRADE-F VALUES ARE 0 THRU 59.4.


PROCEDURE DIVISION statements.

    IF GRADE-A
        MOVE 'A' TO LETTER-GRADE.
    IF GRADE-B
        MOVE 'B' TO LETTER-GRADE.
    IF GRADE-C
        MOVE 'C' TO LETTER-GRADE.
    IF GRADE-D
        MOVE 'D' TO LETTER-GRADE.
    IF GRADE-F
        MOVE 'F' TO LETTER-GRADE.
```

Figure 11.6 An Illustration of the Use of Condition-Name IF Statements

An Inventory-Control Example

Figure 11.7 illustrates the use of condition-name tests in conjunction with the processing of records. In this illustration, data representing inventory records and transaction updates are read. The type of record is identified by the transaction-code value. Note that the data item TRANSACTION-CODE is defined in line 230 of the input-record description. The meaning of possible code values is explained by the condition-names (lines 240–310). Data records in the inventory file are assumed to have been ordered such that all records with a particular PART-NUMBER appear together. The procedure makes no assumption about the order of records within each group; however, it assumes that a beginning balance record (TRANSACTION-CODE=0) either has an initial amount-on-hand or is zero. The procedure is to be terminated on the basis of a specific value of TRANSACTION-CODE (a value of 9) *or* on encountering the end-of-file (line 420).

The predominant processing elements appear in the UPDATE-INVENTORY module (lines 910–1150). This procedure determines whether the transaction volume is to be added to existing stock (conditions of BEGINNING-BALANCE, UNITS-RETURNED-AFTER-SALE, or UNITS-RECEIVED), sub-

tracted from existing stock (conditions of UNITS-SOLD or UNITS-RE-
TURNED-AFTER-RECEIPT), ignored altogether (condition of TRANSAC-
TION-OMITTED), or identified as an error (ITEM-STATUS, line 430, does
not contain the literal "PROCESSED"). The first decision of UPDATE-IN-
VENTORY is to determine whether or not the current transaction record is for

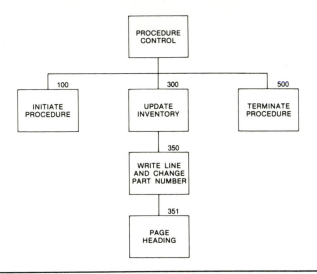

Figure 11.7 Inventory Control Program (Hierarchy Chart)

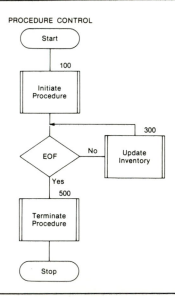

Figure 11.7 Inventory Control Program (Module Flowchart) *Continued*

the *same* PART-NUMBER as that which was previously processed. This decision is necessary because only one line of output is produced for each part number, regardless of the number of transactions processed (that is, unless a transaction is omitted or is in error).

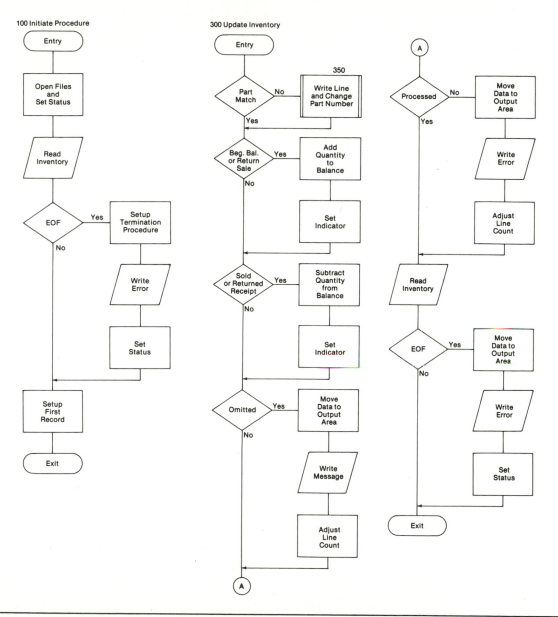

Figure 11.7 Inventory Control Program (Module Flowcharts) *Continued*

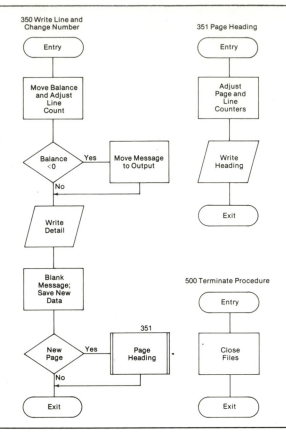

Figure 11.7 Inventory Control Program (Module Flowchart) *Continued*

```
|          .  1    1    2    2    2    3    3    4    4    4    5    5    6    6    6    7    7    8|
|     4       8    2    6    0    4    8    2    6    0    4    8    2    6    0    4    8    2    6    0|

|000010 IDENTIFICATION DIVISION.                                      FIG 11.7|
|000020 PROGRAM-ID. INVENTORY-CONTROL.                                FIG 11.7|
|000030 AUTHOR. EDWIN F. WILLIAMS.                                    FIG 11.7|
|000040 DATE-WRITTEN. JANUARY 1, 1981.                                FIG 11.7|
|000050 DATE-COMPILED. JANUARY 1, 1981.                               FIG 11.7|
|000060 ENVIRONMENT DIVISION.                                         FIG 11.7|
|000070 CONFIGURATION SECTION.                                        FIG 11.7|
|000080 SOURCE-COMPUTER. XEROX-560.                                   FIG 11.7|
|000090 OBJECT-COMPUTER. XEROX-560.                                   FIG 11.7|
|000100 SPECIAL-NAMES. *1* IS NEXT-PAGE.                              FIG 11.7|
|000110 INPUT-OUTPUT SECTION.                                         FIG 11.7|
|000120 FILE-CONTROL.                                                 FIG 11.7|
|000130     SELECT INVENTORY-FILE ASSIGN TO CARD-READER.              FIG 11.7|
|000140     SELECT PRINT-FILE ASSIGN TO PRINTER.                      FIG 11.7|
|000150 DATA DIVISION.                                                FIG 11.7|
|000160 FILE SECTION.                                                 FIG 11.7|
|000170 FD  INVENTORY-FILE LABEL RECORDS ARE OMITTED.                 FIG 11.7|
|000180 01  INVENTORY-TRANSACTION.                                    FIG 11.7|
|000190     02 PART-NUMBER           PIC 9(06).                       FIG 11.7|
|000200     02 ITEM-DESCRIPTION      PIC X(20).                       FIG 11.7|
|000210     02 TRANSACTION-UNIT-VOLUME  PIC 9(06).                    FIG 11.7|
|000220     02 FILLER                PIC X(47).                       FIG 11.7|
|000230     02 TRANSACTION-CODE      PIC 9(01).                       FIG 11.7|
|000240        88 BEGINNING-BALANCE       VALUE 0.                    FIG 11.7|
|000250        88 UNITS-SOLD              VALUE 1.                    FIG 11.7|
|000260        88 UNITS-RETURNED-AFTER-SALE VALUE 2.                  FIG 11.7|
|000270        88 UNITS-RECEIVED          VALUE 3.                    FIG 11.7|
|000280        88 UNITS-RETURNED-AFTER-RECEIPT VALUE 4.               FIG 11.7|
```

Figure 11.7 Inventory Control Program *Continued*

```
|          1  1  2  2  2  3  3  4  4  4  5  5  6  6  6  7  7  8|
|  4    8  2  6  0  4  8  2  6  0  4  8  2  6  0  4  8  2  6  0|
|000290          88 TRANSACTION-OMITTED   VALUE 5.              FIG 11.7|
|000300          88 UNKNOWN-CODE          VALUES 6 THRU 8.      FIG 11.7|
|000310          88 TERMINATE-PROCESSING VALUE 9.              FIG 11.7|
|000320 FD  PRINT-FILE LABEL RECORDS ARE OMITTED.              FIG 11.7|
|000330 01  PRINT-OUT               PIC X(133).                FIG 11.7|
|000340 WORKING-STORAGE SECTION.                                FIG 11.7|
|000350 01  WORKING-VARIABLES.                                  FIG 11.7|
|000360     05  LINE-COUNT             PIC 9(02).               FIG 11.7|
|000370     05  PAGE-COUNT             PIC 9(03) VALUE ZEROS.   FIG 11.7|
|000380     05  TRANSACTION-BALANCE    PIC S9(08).             FIG 11.7|
|000390     05  SAVE-PART-NUMBER       PIC 9(06) VALUE ZEROS.  FIG 11.7|
|000400 01  STATUS-INDICATOR.                                   FIG 11.7|
|000410     04  FILE-STATUS            PIC X(15).               FIG 11.7|
|000420         88 END-OF-FILE VALUE *TERMINATE*.              FIG 11.7|
|000430     04  ITEM-STATUS            PIC X(15).               FIG 11.7|
|000440         88 PROCESSED VALUE *PROCESSED*.                FIG 11.7|
|000450 01  REPORT-TITLE.                                       FIG 11.7|
|000460     02 FILLER                  PIC X(54) VALUE SPACES.  FIG 11.7|
|000470     02 FILLER                  PIC X(24) VALUE          FIG 11.7|
|000480     *INVENTORY CONTROL REPORT*.                         FIG 11.7|
|000490 01  PAGE-NUMBER.                                        FIG 11.7|
|000500     02 FILLER                  PIC X(115) VALUE SPACES. FIG 11.7|
|000510     02 FILLEP                  PIC X(05) VALUE *PAGE*.  FIG 11.7|
|000520     02 PAGE-NO                 PIC ZZ9.                 FIG 11.7|
|000530 01  HEADING-LINE.                                       FIG 11.7|
|000540     02 FILLER                  PIC X(33) VALUE SPACES.  FIG 11.7|
|000550     02 FILLER                  PIC X(16) VALUE *PART NUMBER*. FIG 11.7|
|000560     02 FILLER                  PIC X(26) VALUE          FIG 11.7|
|000570     *PART DESCRIPTION*.                                 FIG 11.7|
|000580     02 FILLER                  PIC X(20) VALUE          FIG 11.7|
|000590     *ENDING BALANCE*.                                   FIG 11.7|
|000600     02 FILLER                  PIC X(06) VALUE *NOTES:*. FIG 11.7|
|000610 01  DETAIL-LINE.                                        FIG 11.7|
|000620     02 FILLER                  PIC X(35) VALUE SPACES.  FIG 11.7|
|000630     02 PART-NUMBER-OUT         PIC 9(06).              FIG 11.7|
|000640     02 FILLER                  PIC X(07) VALUE SPACES.  FIG 11.7|
|000650     02 DESCRIPTION-OUT         PIC X(20).              FIG 11.7|
|000660     02 FILLER                  PIC X(08) VALUE SPACES.  FIG 11.7|
|000670     02 BALANCE-OUT             PIC -Z(08).             FIG 11.7|
|000680     02 FILLER                  PIC X(10) VALUE SPACES.  FIG 11.7|
|000690     02 MESSAGE                 PIC X(35) VALUE SPACES.  FIG 11.7|
|000700 PROCEDURE DIVISION.                                     FIG 11.7|
|000710 PROCEDURE-CONTROL.                                      FIG 11.7|
|000720     PERFORM 100-INITIATE-PROCEDURE.                    FIG 11.7|
|000730     PERFORM 300-UPDATE-INVENTORY                       FIG 11.7|
|000740         UNTIL TERMINATE-PROCESSING OR END-OF-FILE.     FIG 11.7|
|000750     PERFORM 500-TERMINATE-PROCEDURE.                   FIG 11.7|
|000760     STOP RUN.                                          FIG 11.7|
|000770 100-INITIATE-PROCEDURE.                                 FIG 11.7|
|000780     OPEN INPUT INVENTORY-FILE, OUTPUT PRINT-FILE.      FIG 11.7|
|000790     MOVE *PROCESSING* TO FILE-STATUS.                  FIG 11.7|
|000800     READ INVENTORY-FILE AT END                         FIG 11.7|
|000810         MOVE 0 TO PART-NUMBER-OUT, BALANCE-OUT         FIG 11.7|
|000820         MOVE SPACES TO DESCRIPTION-OUT                 FIG 11.7|
|000830         MOVE *ILLEGAL TERMINATION* TO MESSAGE          FIG 11.7|
|000840         WRITE PRINT-OUT FROM DETAIL-LINE AFTER 3 LINES FIG 11.7|
|000850         MOVE *TERMINATE* TO FILE-STATUS.               FIG 11.7|
|000860     MOVE PART-NUMBER TO SAVE-PART-NUMBER, PART-NUMBER-OUT. FIG 11.7|
|000870     MOVE ITEM-DESCRIPTION TO DESCRIPTION-OUT.          FIG 11.7|
|000880     MOVE ZERO TO TRANSACTION-BALANCE.                  FIG 11.7|
|000890     MOVE 99 TO LINE-COUNT.                             FIG 11.7|
|000900 300-UPDATE-INVENTORY.                                   FIG 11.7|
|000910     IF SAVE-PART-NUMBER NOT EQUAL TO PART-NUMBER       FIG 11.7|
|000920         PERFORM 350-WRITE-LINE-CHANGE-NUMBER.          FIG 11.7|
|000930     IF BEGINNING-BALANCE OR UNITS-RETURNED-AFTER-SALE OR FIG 11.7|
|000940         UNITS-RECEIVED                                 FIG 11.7|
|000950         MOVE *PROCESSED* TO ITEM-STATUS               FIG 11.7|
|000960         ADD TRANSACTION-UNIT-VOLUME TO TRANSACTION-BALANCE. FIG 11.7|
|000970     IF UNITS-SOLD OR UNITS-RETURNED-AFTER-RECEIPT      FIG 11.7|
|000980         MOVE *PROCESSED* TO ITEM-STATUS               FIG 11.7|
|000990         SUBTRACT TRANSACTION-UNIT-VOLUME FROM          FIG 11.7|
|001000         TRANSACTION-BALANCE.                           FIG 11.7|
|001010     IF TRANSACTION-OMITTED                             FIG 11.7|
|001020         MOVE *PROCESSED* TO ITEM-STATUS               FIG 11.7|
|001030         MOVE PART-NUMBER TO PART-NUMBER-OUT;          FIG 11.7|
|001040         MOVE TRANSACTION-UNIT-VOLUME TO BALANCE-OUT;  FIG 11.7|
|001050         MOVE *OMITTED* TO MESSAGE;                    FIG 11.7|
|001060         WRITE PRINT-OUT FROM DETAIL-LINE AFTER 1 LINES; FIG 11.7|
|001070         MOVE SPACES TO MESSAGE;                       FIG 11.7|
|001080         ADD 1 TO LINE-COUNT.                          FIG 11.7|
```

Figure 11.7 Inventory Control Program *Continued*

```
|        1  1  2  2  2  3  3  4  4  4  5  5  6  6  6  7  7  8|
|   4    8  2  6  0  4  8  2  6  0  4  8  2  6  0  4  8  2  6  0|
------------------------------------------------------------------
|001090      IF NOT PROCESSED                                    FIG 11.7|
|001100          MOVE PART-NUMBER TO PART-NUMBER-OUT             FIG 11.7|
|001110          MOVE ZEROS TO BALANCE-OUT                       FIG 11.7|
|001120          MOVE 'ILLEGAL TRANSACTION' TO MESSAGE           FIG 11.7|
|001130          WRITE PRINT-OUT FROM DETAIL-LINE AFTER 1 LINES  FIG 11.7|
|001140          MOVE SPACES TO MESSAGE                          FIG 11.7|
|001150          ADD 1 TO LINE-COUNT.                            FIG 11.7|
|001160      READ INVENTORY-FILE AT END                          FIG 11.7|
|001170          MOVE 0 TO PART-NUMBER-OUT, BALANCE-OUT          FIG 11.7|
|001180          MOVE SPACES TO DESCRIPTION-OUT                  FIG 11.7|
|001190          MOVE 'ILLEGAL TERMINATION' TO MESSAGE           FIG 11.7|
|001200          WRITE PRINT-OUT FROM DETAIL-LINE AFTER 3 LINES  FIG 11.7|
|001210          MOVE 'TERMINATE' TO FILE-STATUS.                FIG 11.7|
|001220 350-WRITE-LINE-CHANGE-NUMBER.                            FIG 11.7|
|001230      MOVE TRANSACTION-BALANCE TO BALANCE-OUT.            FIG 11.7|
|001240      ADD 2 TO LINE-COUNT.                                FIG 11.7|
|001250      IF TRANSACTION-BALANCE LESS THAN 0                  FIG 11.7|
|001260          MOVE 'ACCOUNT BALANCE LESS THAN ZERO' TO MESSAGE.  FIG 11.7|
|001270      WRITE PRINT-OUT FROM DETAIL-LINE AFTER 2 LINES.     FIG 11.7|
|001280      MOVE SPACES TO MESSAGE.                             FIG 11.7|
|001290      MOVE PART-NUMBER TO SAVE-PART-NUMBER, PART-NUMBER-OUT.  FIG 11.7|
|001300      MOVE ITEM-DESCRIPTION TO DESCRIPTION-OUT.           FIG 11.7|
|001310      MOVE ZERO TO TRANSACTION-BALANCE.                   FIG 11.7|
|001320      IF LINE-COUNT GREATER THAN 40                       FIG 11.7|
|001330          PERFORM 351-PAGE-HEADING.                       FIG 11.7|
|001340 351-PAGE-HEADING.                                        FIG 11.7|
|001350      ADD 1 TO PAGE-COUNT.                                FIG 11.7|
|001360      MOVE PAGE-COUNT TO PAGE-NO.                         FIG 11.7|
|001370      MOVE 0 TO LINE-COUNT.                               FIG 11.7|
|001380      WRITE PRINT-OUT FROM REPORT-TITLE AFTER NEXT-PAGE.  FIG 11.7|
|001390      WRITE PRINT-OUT FROM PAGE-NUMBER AFTER 2 LINES.     FIG 11.7|
|001400      WRITE PRINT-OUT FROM HEADING-LINE AFTER 2 LINES.    FIG 11.7|
|001410      MOVE SPACES TO PRINT-OUT. WRITE PRINT-OUT AFTER 1 LINES.  FIG 11.7|
|001420 500-TERMINATE-PROCEDURE.                                 FIG 11.7|
|001430      CLOSE INVENTORY-FILE, PRINT-FILE.                   FIG 11.7|
|001440      DISPLAY 'END OF JOB'.                               FIG 11.7|
------------------------------------------------------------------
```

Figure 11.7 Inventory Control Program *Continued*

```
------------------------------------------------------------------------------------
|       |         1         2         3         4         5         6         7         8| FIGURE  |
|RECORD |1234567890123456789012345678901234567890123456789012345678901234567890123456789 0| NUMBER  |
------------------------------------------------------------------------------------
|    1|101100LIGHT BROWN UMBRELLA000025                                               0|FIG 11.7|
|    2|101100                    000030                                               2|FIG 11.7|
|    3|101100                    000015                                               2|FIG 11.7|
|    4|101100                    000045                                               6|FIG 11.7|
|    5|101100                    000006                                               3|FIG 11.7|
|    6|101100                    000150                                               1|FIG 11.7|
|    7|101100                    000050                                               1|FIG 11.7|
|    8|454550100 WATT LIGHT BULBS088500                                               0|FIG 11.7|
|    9|454550                    000100                                               5|FIG 11.7|
|   10|454550                    000050                                               3|FIG 11.7|
|   11|454550                    007000                                               1|FIG 11.7|
|   12|454550                    000045                                               7|FIG 11.7|
|   13|454550                    000300                                               4|FIG 11.7|
|   14|1249006 OZ. CHOCOLATE BAR 150000                                               0|FIG 11.7|
|   15|124900                    000820                                               6|FIG 11.7|
|   16|124900                    000760                                               1|FIG 11.7|
|   17|124900                    005000                                               1|FIG 11.7|
|   18|124900                    000050                                               1|FIG 11.7|
|   19|124900                    000100                                               2|FIG 11.7|
|   20|132240YELLOW COMB         040000                                               0|FIG 11.7|
|   21|132240                    000460                                               5|FIG 11.7|
|   22|132240                    000790                                               4|FIG 11.7|
|   23|132240                    004000                                               1|FIG 11.7|
|   24|465465GREEN COMB          000431                                               0|FIG 11.7|
|   25|465465                    000200                                               3|FIG 11.7|
|   26|123450LAUNDRY SOAP        005900                                               0|FIG 11.7|
|   27|123450                    001000                                               1|FIG 11.7|
|   28|123450                    000030                                               2|FIG 11.7|
|   29|123450                    000020                                               3|FIG 11.7|
|   30|123450                    000040                                               4|FIG 11.7|
|   31|123450                    000010                                               5|FIG 11.7|
|   32|123450                    000100                                               1|FIG 11.7|
|   33|123450                    000040                                               1|FIG 11.7|
------------------------------------------------------------------------------------
```

Figure 11.7 Inventory Control Program (Data) *Continued*

```
|      |          1         2         3         4         5         6         7        8| FIGURE |
|RECORD|1234567890123456789012345678901234567890123456789012345678901234567890| NUMBER |
---------------------------------------------------------------------------------------
|    34|790000MICKEY MOUSE WATCH   000010                                      0|FIG 11.7|
|    35|790000                     000100                                      7|FIG 11.7|
|    36|790000                     000075                                      1|FIG 11.7|
|    37|790000                     000400                                      2|FIG 11.7|
|    38|222200HEADPHONES           033200                                      0|FIG 11.7|
|    39|222200                     000045                                      8|FIG 11.7|
|    40|222200                     000300                                      1|FIG 11.7|
|    41|222200                     000005                                      2|FIG 11.7|
|    42|222200                     000095                                      1|FIG 11.7|
|    43|222200                     000200                                      1|FIG 11.7|
|    44|222200                     000010                                      4|FIG 11.7|
|    45|152155TUB MARGARINE        000750                                      0|FIG 11.7|
|    46|152155                     000023                                      8|FIG 11.7|
|    47|152155                     000045                                      4|FIG 11.7|
|    48|152155                     000500                                      3|FIG 11.7|
|    49|457890HULA HOOP            002000                                      0|FIG 11.7|
|    50|457890                     000045                                      5|FIG 11.7|
|    51|457890                     000063                                      1|FIG 11.7|
|    52|457890                     000357                                      2|FIG 11.7|
|    53|123987RED FOOD COLORING    099910                                      0|FIG 11.7|
|    54|123987                     000246                                      6|FIG 11.7|
|    55|123987                     004631                                      1|FIG 11.7|
|    56|123987                     000005                                      1|FIG 11.7|
|    57|123987                     000462                                      4|FIG 11.7|
|    58|123987                     000050                                      3|FIG 11.7|
|    59|302100ASPIRIN              000100                                      0|FIG 11.7|
|    60|302100                     002045                                      1|FIG 11.7|
|    61|302100                     002065                                      1|FIG 11.7|
|    62|302100                     000050                                      3|FIG 11.7|
|    63|302100                     000009                                      2|FIG 11.7|
|    64|302100                     000030                                      5|FIG 11.7|
|    65|302100                     000200                                      4|FIG 11.7|
|    66|302100                     000200                                      6|FIG 11.7|
|    67|302100                     000500                                      1|FIG 11.7|
|    68|302100                     000010                                      8|FIG 11.7|
|    69|302100                     000020                                      7|FIG 11.7|
|    70|302100                     000046                                      2|FIG 11.7|
|    71|302100                     000403                                      9|FIG 11.7|
---------------------------------------------------------------------------------------
```

Figure 11.7 Inventory Control Program (Data) *Continued*

```
101100      LIGHT BROWN UMBRELLA         124    ACCOUNT BALANCE LESS THAN ZERO
454550      100 WATT LIGHT BULBS         100    OMITTED

454550      100 WATT LIGHT BULBS       81250

124900      6 OZ. CHOCOLATE BAR       144290
132240      YELLOW COMB                  460    OMITTED

132240      YELLOW COMB                35210

465465      GREEN COMB                   631
123450      LAUNDRY SOAP                  10    OMITTED

123450      LAUNDRY SOAP                4770

790000      MICKEY MOUSE WATCH          335

222200      HEADPHONES                32600

152155      TUB MARGARINE              1205
457890      HULA HOOP                    45    OMITTED

457890      HULA HOOP                  2294

123987      RED FOOD COLORING         94862
302100      ASPIRIN                      30    OMITTED
```

Figure 11.7 Inventory Control Program (Output) *Continued*

While creating output records, the procedure keeps track of the number of lines on a page and decides whether or not a new page heading is necessary. The output procedure also updates the saved part number so that the next sequence through the UPDATE-INVENTORY procedure reflects the new item number. Other elements of the procedure are similar to those presented in previous illustrations.

Inventory Data Editing

Data editing, the process of examining data for accuracy (or at least reasonableness) is often necessary in commercial applications to insure the proper execution of procedures. Most of the programs illustrated in this text assume the data are of the appropriate form (e.g., dates are legitimate, numeric fields contain numeric data, etc.). Unfortunately, data are frequently wrong, mostly because of keying errors. To maintain some level of data accuracy, data are often subjected to a number of tests before they are relied on for further processing. Figure 11.8 illustrates this process with an inventory data-editing problem.

The editing process often requires a series of tests for individual data fields. Editing of each field is performed in a separate module to permit easier procedure validation and to provide the opportunity to implement (and test) portions of the editing process while leaving other modules to be coded later. Furthermore, if editing requirements change, existing editing code for each field is easy to locate.

In Figure 11.8 a series of condition-names is provided in conjunction with the input-record description. The procedure assumes that a fixed number of vendor values are legitimate in the three categories of inventory items (general, lumber and paint, lines 270–300). It is assumed that the packaging unit and the vendor are related. That is, if we determine that an inventory item is purchased from a lumber vendor, we would expect the packaging unit to be in board-feet or linear-feet—condition-name values of "BF" and "LF." The condition-names specified in lines 360 through 390 establish the association between the vendor group and the packaging-unit value. Finally, condition-names are used to indicate the status of individual inventory records (e.g., in line 500, "A" represents an active record; "I," an inactive record; "H," a record to be held; and "D," a record to be deleted).

In the PROCEDURE DIVISION, the editing process begins in module 5000 (EDIT-INVENTORY-DATA). Beginning at line 2110, and for the next several lines, field-oriented edit modules are invoked, and the legitimacy of the field contents is established. In the several modules that follow, each type of IF statement is illustrated a number of times. The class test is demonstrated in line 2320 (CATALOG-NUMBER-TEST IS NOT NUMERIC). The condition-name test is illustrated in line 2370 (LUMBER-VENDOR AND NOT LUMBER-NUMBER). The sign test is illustrated in line 2570 (ON-HAND IS NEGA-

TIVE). And, the relational test is illustrated in line 3120 (CUST-PER-UNIT IS LESS THAN ZERO). In addition, the use of the logical operators AND and OR are illustrated in lines 2370 and 2440.

For each field to be edited, several field definitions are provided. Of course the input-record description for each field is necessary. Each of the numeric fields are also provided with an alphanumeric counterpart in TEST-INVENTORY-RECORD (lines 510–610). Thus, when it is necessary to examine these numeric fields (e.g., catalog number) we are permitted to address the field using the data-name CATALOG-NUMBER only if it contains numeric data. Otherwise, we must use CATALOG-NUMBER-TEST—an alphanumeric description of the same column positions of the input records. Thus, the initial test of the catalog number is "IF CATALOG-NUMBER- TEST IS NOT NUMERIC"—a test, which if passed, will insure us that we are dealing with numeric data. In addition, it is necessary to establish two fields for each numeric output field. For example, CATALOG-NUMBER-OUT is a numeric field to be used in the event that CATALOG-NUMBER is numeric. CATALOG-NUMBER-DISP (line 930) is used when CATALOG-NUMBER-TEST contains non-numeric characters. (Though we could have declared CATALOG-NUMBER-OUT alphanumeric without any detrimental effect, we might have problems with fields such as PRICE-PER-UNIT-OUT.)

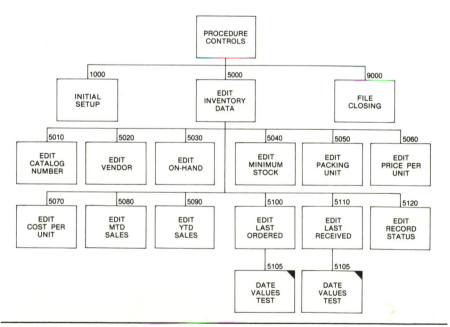

Figure 11.8 Inventory Data-Editing (Hierarchy Chart)

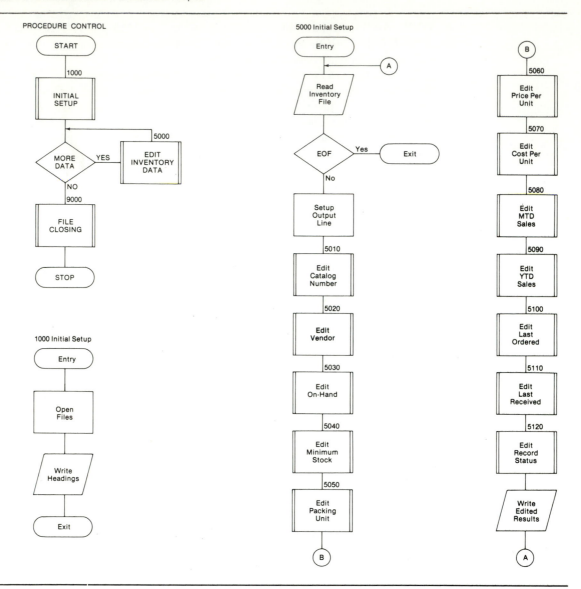

Figure 11.8 Inventory Data-Editing (Module Flowcharts) *Continued*

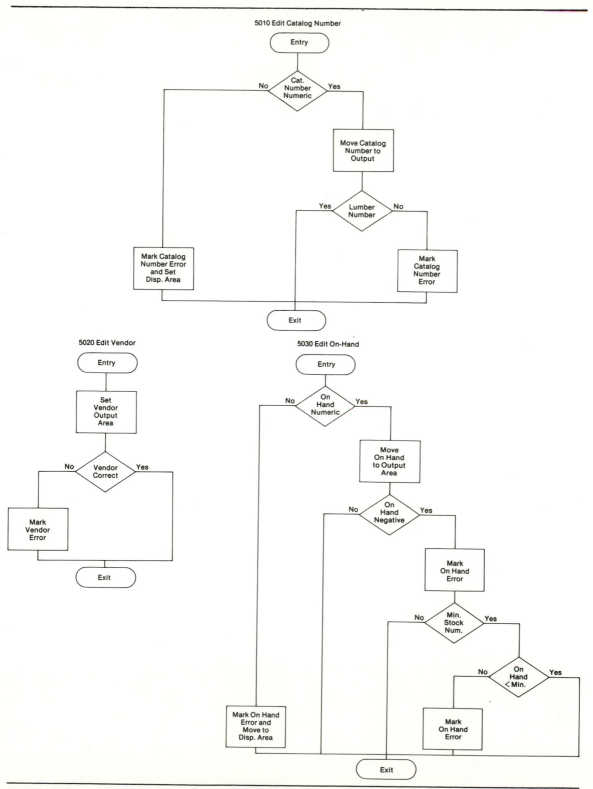

Figure 11.8 Inventory Data-Editing (Module Flowcharts) *Continued*

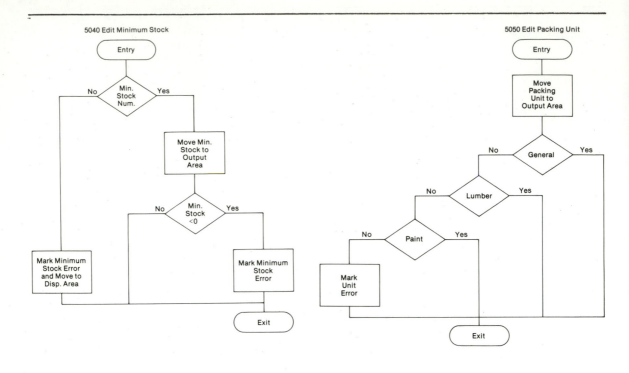

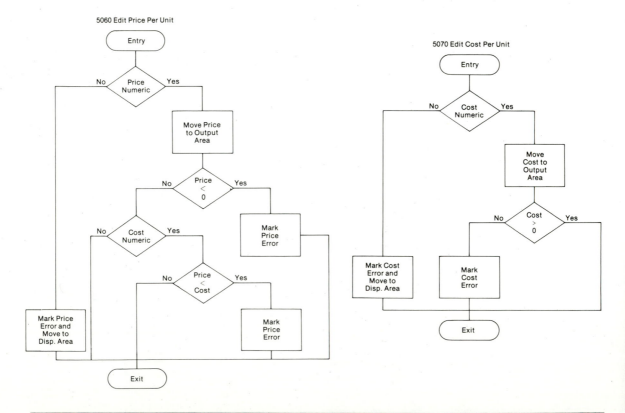

Figure 11.8 Inventory Data-Editing (Module Flowcharts) *Continued*

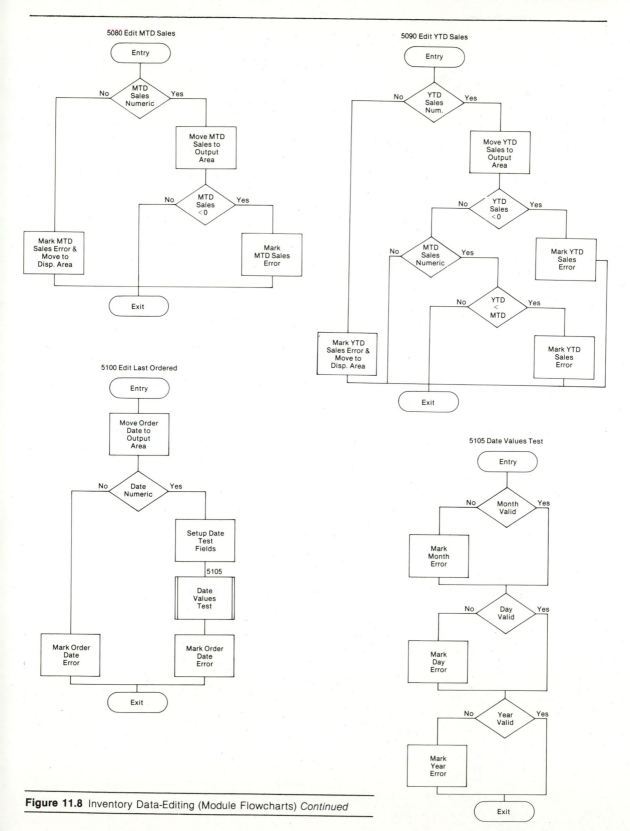

Figure 11.8 Inventory Data-Editing (Module Flowcharts) *Continued*

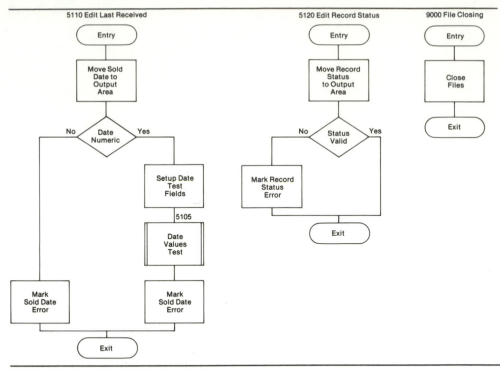

Figure 11.8 Inventory Data-Editing (Module Flowcharts) *Continued*

```
----------------------------------------------------------------------------
|              1    1    2    2    2    3    3    4    4    5    5    6    6    7    7    8|
|    4    8    2    6    0    4    8    2    6    0    4    8    2    6    0    4    8    2    6    0|
----------------------------------------------------------------------------
|000010 IDENTIFICATION DIVISION.                                          FIG 11.8|
|000020 PROGRAM-ID. INVENTORY-DATA-EDIT.                                  FIG 11.8|
|000030 AUTHOR. J. WAYNE SPENCE.                                          FIG 11.8|
|000040 DATE-WRITTEN. JANUARY 1, 1981.                                    FIG 11.8|
|000050 DATE-COMPILED. JANUARY 1, 1981.                                   FIG 11.8|
|000060*    THIS PROGRAM ILLUSTRATES THE USE OF A VARIETY                 FIG 11.8|
|000070*    OF IF STATEMENTS, WHICH IN COMBINATION SERVE TO               FIG 11.8|
|000080*    CHECK THE CONTENTS OF DATA RECORDS FOR ACCURACY (OR AT        FIG 11.8|
|000090*    LEAST REASONABLENESS).                                        FIG 11.8|
|000100 ENVIRONMENT DIVISION.                                             FIG 11.8|
|000110 CONFIGURATION SECTION.                                            FIG 11.8|
|000120 SOURCE-COMPUTER. IBM-370-158.                                     FIG 11.8|
|000130 OBJECT-COMPUTER. IBM-370-158.                                     FIG 11.8|
|000140 SPECIAL-NAMES. C01 IS TO-TOP-OF-FORM.                             FIG 11.8|
|000150 INPUT-OUTPUT SECTION.                                             FIG 11.8|
|000160 FILE-CONTROL.                                                     FIG 11.8|
|000170     SELECT INVENTORY-FILE ASSIGN TO UR-S-SYSIN.                   FIG 11.8|
|000180     SELECT EDIT-REPORT ASSIGN TO UR-S-SYSPRINT.                   FIG 11.8|
|000190 DATA DIVISION.                                                    FIG 11.8|
|000200 FILE SECTION.                                                     FIG 11.8|
|000210 FD  INVENTORY-FILE LABEL RECORDS ARE OMITTED.                     FIG 11.8|
|000220 01  INVENTORY-RECORD.                                             FIG 11.8|
|000230     05 DESCRIPTIVE-DATA.                                          FIG 11.8|
|000240        10 CATALOG-NUMBER              PIC 9(10).                  FIG 11.8|
|000250           88 LUMBER-NUMBER VALUES ARE 1000 THRU 1000000.          FIG 11.8|
|000260        10 VENDOR                      PIC X(03).                  FIG 11.8|
|000270           88 GENERAL-VENDOR VALUE IS 'GEN'.                       FIG 11.8|
|000280           88 LUMBER-VENDOR VALUES ARE 'WHR', 'UPA', 'IP ',        FIG 11.8|
|000290           88 PAINT-VENDOR VALUES ARE 'JMV', 'GLD', 'JB ',         FIG 11.8|
|000300              'PIT', 'BM '.                                        FIG 11.8|
|000310        10 DESCRIPTION                 PIC X(20).                  FIG 11.8|
|000320     05 UNIT-DATA.                                                 FIG 11.8|
|000330        10 ON-HAND                     PIC S9(05).                 FIG 11.8|
|000340        10 MINIMUM-STOCK-LEVEL         PIC S9(05).                 FIG 11.8|
|000350        10 PACKAGING-UNIT              PIC X(02).                  FIG 11.8|
|000360           88 GENERAL-UNIT VALUES ARE 'EA', 'X ', 'DZ', 'GR',      FIG 11.8|
|000370              'C ', 'M ', 'OZ'.                                    FIG 11.8|
```

Figure 11.8 Inventory Data-Editing *Continued*

```
|       1 1 2 2 2 3 3 4 4 4 5 5 6 6 6 7 7 8|
|  4  8  2 6 0 4 8 2 6 0 4 8 2 6 0 4 8 2 6 0|
----------------------------------------------------------------
|000380              88 LUMBER-UNIT VALUES ARE 'BF', 'LF'.            FIG 11.8|
|000390              88 PAINT-UNIT VALUES ARE 'PT', 'QT', 'GA'.       FIG 11.8|
|000400          05 PRICE-COST-DATA.                                  FIG 11.8|
|000410              10 PRICE-PER-UNIT              PIC S9(03)V9(02).  FIG 11.8|
|000420              10 COST-PER-UNIT               PIC S9(03)V9(02).  FIG 11.8|
|000430          05 SALES-DATA.                                       FIG 11.8|
|000440              10 MONTH-TO-DATE-SALES         PIC S9(04)V9(02).  FIG 11.8|
|000450              10 YEAR-TO-DATE-SALES          PIC S9(04)V9(02).  FIG 11.8|
|000460          05 DATE-DATA.                                        FIG 11.8|
|000470              10 DATE-LAST-ORDERED           PIC X(06).         FIG 11.8|
|000480              10 DATE-LAST-SOLD              PIC X(06).         FIG 11.8|
|000490          05 RECORD-STATUS                   PIC X(01).         FIG 11.8|
|000500              88 VALID-STATUS VALUES ARE 'A', 'I', 'H', 'D'.    FIG 11.8|
|000510 01    TEST-INVENTORY-RECORD.                                  FIG 11.8|
|000520          05 CATALOG-NUMBER-TEST             PIC X(10).         FIG 11.8|
|000530          05 FILLER                          PIC X(23).         FIG 11.8|
|000540          05 ON-HAND-TEST                    PIC X(05).         FIG 11.8|
|000550          05 MINIMUM-STOCK-LEVEL-TEST        PIC X(05).         FIG 11.8|
|000560          05 FILLER                          PIC X(02).         FIG 11.8|
|000570          05 PRICE-PER-UNIT-TEST             PIC X(05).         FIG 11.8|
|000580          05 COST-PER-UNIT-TEST              PIC X(05).         FIG 11.8|
|000590          05 MONTH-TO-DATE-SALES-TEST        PIC X(06).         FIG 11.8|
|000600          05 YEAR-TO-DATE-SALES-TEST         PIC X(06).         FIG 11.8|
|000610          05 FILLER                          PIC X(13).         FIG 11.8|
|000620 FD    EDIT-REPORT    LABEL RECORDS ARE OMITTED.               FIG 11.8|
|000630 01    OUTPUT-RECORD                          PIC X(133).       FIG 11.8|
|000640 01    EDIT-RECORD.                                            FIG 11.8|
|000650          02 FILLER                          PIC X(01).         FIG 11.8|
|000660          02 CATALOG-NUMBER-OUT              PIC 9(10).         FIG 11.8|
|000670          02 FILLER                          PIC X(02).         FIG 11.8|
|000680          02 VENDOR-OUT                      PIC X(03).         FIG 11.8|
|000690          02 FILLER                          PIC X(02).         FIG 11.8|
|000700          02 DESCRIPTION-OUT                 PIC X(20).         FIG 11.8|
|000710          02 FILLER                          PIC X(02).         FIG 11.8|
|000720          02 ON-HAND-OUT                     PIC 9(05).         FIG 11.8|
|000730          02 FILLER                          PIC X(02).         FIG 11.8|
|000740          02 MINIMUM-STOCK-LEVEL-OUT         PIC 9(05).         FIG 11.8|
|000750          02 FILLER                          PIC X(02).         FIG 11.8|
|000760          02 PACKAGING-UNIT-OUT              PIC X(02).         FIG 11.8|
|000770          02 FILLER                          PIC X(02).         FIG 11.8|
|000780          02 PRICE-PER-UNIT-OUT              PIC 9(03).9(02).   FIG 11.8|
|000790          02 FILLER                          PIC X(02).         FIG 11.8|
|000800          02 COST-PER-UNIT-OUT               PIC 9(03).9(02).   FIG 11.8|
|000810          02 FILLER                          PIC X(02).         FIG 11.8|
|000820          02 MONTH-TO-DATE-SALES-OUT         PIC 9(04).9(02).   FIG 11.8|
|000830          02 FILLER                          PIC X(02).         FIG 11.8|
|000840          02 YEAR-TO-DATE-SALES-OUT          PIC 9(04).9(02).   FIG 11.8|
|000850          02 FILLER                          PIC X(02).         FIG 11.8|
|000860          02 DATE-LAST-ORDERED-OUT           PIC XXBXXBXX.      FIG 11.8|
|000870          02 FILLER                          PIC X(02).         FIG 11.8|
|000880          02 DATE-LAST-SOLD-OUT              PIC XXBXXBXX.      FIG 11.8|
|000890          02 FILLER                          PIC X(02).         FIG 11.8|
|000900          02 RECORD-STATUS-OUT               PIC X(01).         FIG 11.8|
|000910 01    DISPLAY-RECORD.                                         FIG 11.8|
|000920          02 FILLER                          PIC X(01).         FIG 11.8|
|000930          02 CATALOG-NUMBER-DISP             PIC X(10).         FIG 11.8|
|000940          02 FILLER                          PIC X(29).         FIG 11.8|
|000950          02 ON-HAND-DISP                    PIC X(05).         FIG 11.8|
|000960          02 FILLER                          PIC X(02).         FIG 11.8|
|000970          02 MINIMUM-STOCK-LEVEL-DISP        PIC X(05).         FIG 11.8|
|000980          02 FILLER                          PIC X(02).         FIG 11.8|
|000990          02 PACKAGING-UNIT-DISP             PIC X(02).         FIG 11.8|
|001000          02 FILLER                          PIC X(02).         FIG 11.8|
|001010          02 PRICE-PER-UNIT-DISP             PIC X(06).         FIG 11.8|
|001020          02 FILLER                          PIC X(02).         FIG 11.8|
|001030          02 COST-PER-UNIT-DISP              PIC X(06).         FIG 11.8|
|001040          02 FILLER                          PIC X(02).         FIG 11.8|
|001050          02 MONTH-TO-DATE-SALES-DISP        PIC X(07).         FIG 11.8|
|001060          02 FILLER                          PIC X(02).         FIG 11.8|
|001070          02 YEAR-TO-DATE-SALES-DISP         PIC X(07).         FIG 11.8|
|001080 WORKING-STORAGE SECTION.                                      FIG 11.8|
|001090 01    HEADING-RECORD.                                         FIG 11.8|
|001100          02 FILLER                     PIC X(01) VALUE SPACE.  FIG 11.8|
|001110          02 CATALOG-NUMBER-HEAD        PIC X(10)               FIG 11.8|
|001120              VALUE 'CAT NUMBER'.                               FIG 11.8|
|001130          02 FILLER                     PIC X(02) VALUE SPACES. FIG 11.8|
|001140          02 VENDOR-HEAD                PIC X(03) VALUE 'VEN'.  FIG 11.8|
|001150          02 FILLER                     PIC X(02) VALUE SPACES. FIG 11.8|
|001160          02 DESCRIPTION-HEAD           PIC X(20) VALUE 'DESCRI FIG 11.8|
|001170-             'PTION'.                                          FIG 11.8|
```

Figure 11.8 Inventory Data-Editing *Continued*

```
|       1   1   2   2   2   3   3   4   4   4   5   5   6   6   6   7   7   8|
|  4   8   2   6   0   4   8   2   6   0   4   8   2   6   0   4   8   2   6   0|
-------------------------------------------------------------------------------
|001180        02 FILLER                          PIC X(02) VALUE SPACES.FIG 11.8|
|001190        02 ON-HAND-HEAD                    PIC X(05) VALUE 'QTY.'.FIG 11.8|
|001200        02 FILLER                          PIC X(02) VALUE SPACES.FIG 11.8|
|001210        02 MINIMUM-STOCK-LEVEL-HEAD        PIC X(05) VALUE 'MIN.'.FIG 11.8|
|001220        02 FILLER                          PIC X(02) VALUE SPACES.FIG 11.8|
|001230        02 PACKAGING-UNIT-HEAD             PIC X(02) VALUE 'PK'.  FIG 11.8|
|001240        02 FILLER                          PIC X(02) VALUE SPACES.FIG 11.8|
|001250        02 PRICE-PER-UNIT-HEAD             PIC X(06)             FIG 11.8|
|001260           VALUE 'PRICE'.                                        FIG 11.8|
|001270        02 FILLER                          PIC X(02) VALUE SPACES.FIG 11.8|
|001280        02 COST-PER-UNIT-HEAD              PIC X(06)             FIG 11.8|
|001290           VALUE ' COST'.                                        FIG 11.8|
|001300        02 FILLER                          PIC X(02) VALUE SPACES.FIG 11.8|
|001310        02 MONTH-TO-DATE-SALES-HEAD        PIC X(07)             FIG 11.8|
|001320           VALUE ' MTD $'.                                       FIG 11.8|
|001330        02 FILLER                          PIC X(02) VALUE SPACES.FIG 11.8|
|001340        02 YEAR-TO-DATE-SALES-HEAD         PIC X(07)             FIG 11.8|
|001350           VALUE '  YTD $'.                                      FIG 11.8|
|001360        02 FILLER                          PIC X(02) VALUE SPACES.FIG 11.8|
|001370        02 DATE-LAST-ORDERED-HEAD          PIC X(08)             FIG 11.8|
|001380           VALUE 'LAST ORD'.                                     FIG 11.8|
|001390        02 FILLER                          PIC X(02) VALUE SPACES.FIG 11.8|
|001400        02 DATE-LAST-SOLD-HEAD             PIC X(08)             FIG 11.8|
|001410           VALUE 'LAST SLD'.                                     FIG 11.8|
|001420        02 FILLER                          PIC X(02) VALUE SPACES.FIG 11.8|
|001430        02 RECORD-STATUS-HEAD              PIC X(02) VALUE 'ST'. FIG 11.8|
|001440 01 DATE-TEST-VALUES.                                            FIG 11.8|
|001450     05 TEST-MONTH                         PIC S9(02).           FIG 11.8|
|001460        88 VALID-MONTH VALUES ARE 1 THRU 12.                     FIG 11.8|
|001470     05 TEST-DAY                           PIC S9(02).           FIG 11.8|
|001480        88 VALID-DAY VALUES ARE 1 THRU 31.                       FIG 11.8|
|001490     05 TEST-YEAR                          PIC S9(02).           FIG 11.8|
|001500        88 VALID-YEAR VALUES ARE 77 THRU 81.                     FIG 11.8|
|001510     05 DATE-ERROR.                                              FIG 11.8|
|001520        10 MONTH-ERROR                     PIC X(02).            FIG 11.8|
|001530        10 DAY-ERROR                       PIC X(02).            FIG 11.8|
|001540        10 YEAR-ERROR                      PIC X(02).            FIG 11.8|
|001550 01 ERROR-RECORD.                                                FIG 11.8|
|001560     02 FILLER                             PIC X(01).            FIG 11.8|
|001570     02 CATALOG-NUMBER-ERROR               PIC X(10).            FIG 11.8|
|001580     02 FILLER                             PIC X(02).            FIG 11.8|
|001590     02 VENDOR-ERROR                       PIC X(03).            FIG 11.8|
|001600     02 FILLER                             PIC X(02).            FIG 11.8|
|001610     02 DESCRIPTION-ERROR                  PIC X(20).            FIG 11.8|
|001620     02 FILLER                             PIC X(02).            FIG 11.8|
|001630     02 ON-HAND-ERROR                      PIC X(05).            FIG 11.8|
|001640     02 FILLER                             PIC X(02).            FIG 11.8|
|001650     02 MINIMUM-STOCK-LEVEL-ERROR          PIC X(05).            FIG 11.8|
|001660     02 FILLER                             PIC X(02).            FIG 11.8|
|001670     02 PACKAGING-UNIT-ERROR               PIC X(02).            FIG 11.8|
|001680     02 FILLER                             PIC X(02).            FIG 11.8|
|001690     02 PRICE-PER-UNIT-ERROR               PIC X(06).            FIG 11.8|
|001700     02 FILLER                             PIC X(02).            FIG 11.8|
|001710     02 COST-PER-UNIT-ERROR                PIC X(06).            FIG 11.8|
|001720     02 FILLER                             PIC X(02).            FIG 11.8|
|001730     02 MONTH-TO-DATE-SALES-ERROR          PIC X(07).            FIG 11.8|
|001740     02 FILLER                             PIC X(02).            FIG 11.8|
|001750     02 YEAR-TO-DATE-SALES-ERROR           PIC X(07).            FIG 11.8|
|001760     02 FILLER                             PIC X(02).            FIG 11.8|
|001770     02 DATE-LAST-ORDERED-ERROR.                                 FIG 11.8|
|001780        04 DO-MONTH-ERROR                  PIC X(02).            FIG 11.8|
|001790        04 FILLER                          PIC X(01).            FIG 11.8|
|001800        04 DO-DAY-ERROR                    PIC X(02).            FIG 11.8|
|001810        04 FILLER                          PIC X(01).            FIG 11.8|
|001820        04 DO-YEAR-ERROR                   PIC X(02).            FIG 11.8|
|001830     02 FILLER                             PIC X(02).            FIG 11.8|
|001840     02 DATE-LAST-SOLD-ERROR.                                    FIG 11.8|
|001850        04 DS-MONTH-ERROR                  PIC X(02).            FIG 11.8|
|001860        04 FILLER                          PIC X(01).            FIG 11.8|
|001870        04 DS-DAY-ERROR                    PIC X(02).            FIG 11.8|
|001880        04 FILLER                          PIC X(01).            FIG 11.8|
|001890        04 DS-YEAR-ERROR                   PIC X(02).            FIG 11.8|
|001900     02 FILLER                             PIC X(02).            FIG 11.8|
|001910     02 RECORD-STATUS-ERROR                PIC X(01).            FIG 11.8|
|001920 PROCEDURE DIVISION.                                             FIG 11.8|
|001930 PROCEDURE-CONTROLS.                                             FIG 11.8|
|001940     PERFORM 1000-INITIAL-SETUP.                                 FIG 11.8|
|001950     PERFORM 5000-EDIT-INVENTORY-DATA.                           FIG 11.8|
|001960     PERFORM 9000-FILE-CLOSING.                                  FIG 11.8|
|001970     STOP RUN.                                                   FIG 11.8|
```

Figure 11.8 Inventory Data-Editing *Continued*

```
|       1   1   2   2   2   3   3   4   4   4   5   5   6   6   6   7   7   8|
|   4   8   2   6   0   4   8   2   6   0   4   8   2   6   0   4   8   2   6   0|
-----------------------------------------------------------------------------------
|001980 1000-INITIAL-SETUP SECTION.                                      FIG 11.8|
|001990 1001-INITIAL-SETUP.                                              FIG 11.8|
|002000     OPEN INPUT INVENTORY-FILE, OUTPUT EDIT-REPORT.               FIG 11.8|
|002010     WRITE OUTPUT-RECORD FROM HEADING-RECORD AFTER                FIG 11.8|
|002020         ADVANCING TO-TOP-OF-FORM.                                FIG 11.8|
|002030 1009-EXIT.                                                       FIG 11.8|
|002040     EXIT.                                                        FIG 11.8|
|002050 5000-EDIT-INVENTORY-DATA SECTION.                                FIG 11.8|
|002060 5001-EDIT-INVENTORY-DATA.                                        FIG 11.8|
|002070     READ INVENTORY-FILE AT END                                   FIG 11.8|
|002080         GO TO 5009-EXIT.                                         FIG 11.8|
|002090     MOVE SPACES TO OUTPUT-RECORD, ERROR-RECORD.                  FIG 11.8|
|002100     MOVE DESCRIPTION TO DESCRIPTION-OUT.                         FIG 11.8|
|002110     PERFORM 5010-CATALOG-NUMBER.                                 FIG 11.8|
|002120     PERFORM 5020-EDIT-VENDOR.                                    FIG 11.8|
|002130     PERFORM 5030-EDIT-ON-HAND.                                   FIG 11.8|
|002140     PERFORM 5040-EDIT-MINIMUM-STOCK.                             FIG 11.8|
|002150     PERFORM 5050-EDIT-PACKING-UNIT.                              FIG 11.8|
|002160     PERFORM 5060-EDIT-PRICE-PER-UNIT.                            FIG 11.8|
|002170     PERFORM 5070-EDIT-COST-PER-UNIT.                             FIG 11.8|
|002180     PERFORM 5080-EDIT-MTD-SALES.                                 FIG 11.8|
|002190     PERFORM 5090-EDIT-YTD-SALES.                                 FIG 11.8|
|002200     PERFORM 5100-EDIT-LAST-ORDERED.                              FIG 11.8|
|002210     PERFORM 5110-EDIT-LAST-SOLD.                                 FIG 11.8|
|002220     PERFORM 5120-EDIT-RECORD-STATUS.                             FIG 11.8|
|002230     WRITE OUTPUT-RECORD AFTER ADVANCING 2 LINES.                 FIG 11.8|
|002240     IF ERROR-RECORD NOT EQUAL TO SPACES                          FIG 11.8|
|002250         WRITE OUTPUT-RECORD FROM ERROR-RECORD AFTER              FIG 11.8|
|002260             ADVANCING 1 LINES.                                   FIG 11.8|
|002270     GO TO 5001-EDIT-INVENTORY-DATA.                              FIG 11.8|
|002280 5009-EXIT.                                                       FIG 11.8|
|002290     EXIT.                                                        FIG 11.8|
|002300 5010-CATALOG-NUMBER SECTION.                                     FIG 11.8|
|002310 5011-CATALOG-NUMBER.                                             FIG 11.8|
|002320     IF CATALOG-NUMBER-TEST IS NOT NUMERIC                        FIG 11.8|
|002330         MOVE ALL '*' TO CATALOG-NUMBER-ERROR                     FIG 11.8|
|002340         MOVE CATALOG-NUMBER-TEST TO CATALOG-NUMBER-DISP          FIG 11.8|
|002350         GO TO 5019-EXIT.                                         FIG 11.8|
|002360     MOVE CATALOG-NUMBER TO CATALOG-NUMBER-OUT.                   FIG 11.8|
|002370     IF LUMBER-VENDOR AND NOT LUMBER-NUMBER                       FIG 11.8|
|002380         MOVE ALL '*' TO CATALOG-NUMBER-ERROR.                    FIG 11.8|
|002390 5019-EXIT.                                                       FIG 11.8|
|002400     EXIT.                                                        FIG 11.8|
|002410 5020-EDIT-VENDOR SECTION.                                        FIG 11.8|
|002420 5021-EDIT-VENDOR.                                                FIG 11.8|
|002430     MOVE VENDOR TO VENDOR-OUT.                                   FIG 11.8|
|002440     IF GENERAL-VENDOR OR LUMBER-VENDOR OR PAINT-VENDOR           FIG 11.8|
|002450         NEXT SENTENCE                                            FIG 11.8|
|002460     ELSE                                                         FIG 11.8|
|002470         MOVE ALL '*' TO VENDOR-ERROR.                            FIG 11.8|
|002480 5029-EXIT.                                                       FIG 11.8|
|002490     EXIT.                                                        FIG 11.8|
|002500 5030-EDIT-ON-HAND SECTION.                                       FIG 11.8|
|002510 5031-EDIT-ON-HAND.                                               FIG 11.8|
|002520     IF ON-HAND-TEST IS NOT NUMERIC                               FIG 11.8|
|002530         MOVE ON-HAND-TEST TO ON-HAND-DISP                        FIG 11.8|
|002540         MOVE ALL '*' TO ON-HAND-ERROR                            FIG 11.8|
|002550         GO TO 5039-EXIT.                                         FIG 11.8|
|002560     MOVE ON-HAND TO ON-HAND-OUT.                                 FIG 11.8|
|002570     IF ON-HAND IS NEGATIVE                                       FIG 11.8|
|002580         MOVE ALL '*' TO ON-HAND-ERROR                            FIG 11.8|
|002590         GO TO 5039-EXIT.                                         FIG 11.8|
|002600     IF MINIMUM-STOCK-LEVEL-TEST IS NOT NUMERIC                   FIG 11.8|
|002610         GO TO 5039-EXIT.                                         FIG 11.8|
|002620     IF ON-HAND IS LESS THAN MINIMUM-STOCK-LEVEL                  FIG 11.8|
|002630         MOVE ALL '*' TO ON-HAND-ERROR.                           FIG 11.8|
|002640 5039-EXIT.                                                       FIG 11.8|
|002650     EXIT.                                                        FIG 11.8|
|002660 5040-EDIT-MINIMUM-STOCK SECTION.                                 FIG 11.8|
|002670 5041-EDIT-MINIMUM-STOCK.                                         FIG 11.8|
|002680     IF MINIMUM-STOCK-LEVEL-TEST IS NOT NUMERIC                   FIG 11.8|
|002690         MOVE MINIMUM-STOCK-LEVEL-TEST TO MINIMUM-STOCK-LEVEL-DISP FIG 11.8|
|002700         MOVE ALL '*' TO MINIMUM-STOCK-LEVEL-ERROR                FIG 11.8|
|002710         GO TO 5049-EXIT.                                         FIG 11.8|
|002720     MOVE MINIMUM-STOCK-LEVEL TO MINIMUM-STOCK-LEVEL-OUT.         FIG 11.8|
|002730     IF MINIMUM-STOCK-LEVEL IS LESS THAN ZERO                     FIG 11.8|
|002740         MOVE ALL '*' TO MINIMUM-STOCK-LEVEL-ERROR.               FIG 11.8|
|002750 5049-EXIT.                                                       FIG 11.8|
|002760     EXIT.                                                        FIG 11.8|
```

Figure 11.8 Inventory Data-Editing *Continued*

```
|             1   1   2   2   2   3   3   4   4   4   5   5   6   6   6   7   7   8|
|   4     8   2   6   0   4   8   2   6   0   4   8   2   6   0   4   8   2   6   0|
--------------------------------------------------------------------------------------
|002770 5050-EDIT-PACKING-UNIT SECTION.                                     FIG 11.8|
|002780 5051-EDIT-PACKING-UNIT.                                             FIG 11.8|
|002790     MOVE PACKAGING-UNIT TO PACKAGING-UNIT-OUT.                      FIG 11.8|
|002800     IF GENERAL-UNIT AND GENERAL-VENDOR                              FIG 11.8|
|002810         GO TO 5059-EXIT.                                            FIG 11.8|
|002820     IF LUMBER-UNIT AND LUMBER-VENDOR                                FIG 11.8|
|002830         GO TO 5059-EXIT.                                            FIG 11.8|
|002840     IF PAINT-UNIT AND PAINT-VENDOR                                  FIG 11.8|
|002850         GO TO 5059-EXIT.                                            FIG 11.8|
|002860     MOVE ALL '*' TO PACKAGING-UNIT-ERROR.                           FIG 11.8|
|002870 5059-EXIT.                                                          FIG 11.8|
|002880     EXIT.                                                           FIG 11.8|
|002890 5060-EDIT-PRICE-PER-UNIT SECTION.                                   FIG 11.8|
|002900 5061-EDIT-PRICE-PER-UNIT.                                           FIG 11.8|
|002910     IF PRICE-PER-UNIT-TEST IS NOT NUMERIC                           FIG 11.8|
|002920         MOVE PRICE-PER-UNIT-TEST TO PRICE-PER-UNIT-DISP             FIG 11.8|
|002930         MOVE ALL '*' TO PRICE-PER-UNIT-ERROR                        FIG 11.8|
|002940         GO TO 5069-EXIT.                                            FIG 11.8|
|002950     MOVE PRICE-PER-UNIT TO PRICE-PER-UNIT-OUT.                      FIG 11.8|
|002960     IF PRICE-PER-UNIT IS LESS THAN ZERO                             FIG 11.8|
|002970         MOVE ALL '*' TO PRICE-PER-UNIT-ERROR                        FIG 11.8|
|002980         GO TO 5069-EXIT.                                            FIG 11.8|
|002990     IF COST-PER-UNIT-TEST IS NOT NUMERIC                            FIG 11.8|
|003000         GO TO 5069-EXIT.                                            FIG 11.8|
|003010     IF PRICE-PER-UNIT < COST-PER-UNIT                               FIG 11.8|
|003020         MOVE ALL '*' TO PRICE-PER-UNIT-ERROR.                       FIG 11.8|
|003030 5069-EXIT.                                                          FIG 11.8|
|003040     EXIT.                                                           FIG 11.8|
|003050 5070-EDIT-COST-PER-UNIT SECTION.                                    FIG 11.8|
|003060 5071-EDIT-COST-PER-UNIT.                                            FIG 11.8|
|003070     IF COST-PER-UNIT-TEST IS NOT NUMERIC                            FIG 11.8|
|003080         MOVE COST-PER-UNIT-TEST TO COST-PER-UNIT-DISP               FIG 11.8|
|003090         MOVE ALL '*' TO COST-PER-UNIT-ERROR                         FIG 11.8|
|003100         GO TO 5079-EXIT.                                            FIG 11.8|
|003110     MOVE COST-PER-UNIT TO COST-PER-UNIT-OUT.                        FIG 11.8|
|003120     IF COST-PER-UNIT IS LESS THAN ZERO                              FIG 11.8|
|003130         MOVE ALL '*' TO COST-PER-UNIT-ERROR.                        FIG 11.8|
|003140 5079-EXIT.                                                          FIG 11.8|
|003150     EXIT.                                                           FIG 11.8|
|003160 5080-EDIT-MTD-SALES SECTION.                                        FIG 11.8|
|003170 5081-EDIT-MTD-SALES.                                                FIG 11.8|
|003180     IF MONTH-TO-DATE-SALES-TEST IS NOT NUMERIC                      FIG 11.8|
|003190         MOVE MONTH-TO-DATE-SALES-TEST TO MONTH-TO-DATE-SALES-DISPFIG 11.8|
|003200         MOVE ALL '*' TO MONTH-TO-DATE-SALES-ERROR                   FIG 11.8|
|003210         GO TO 5089-EXIT.                                            FIG 11.8|
|003220     MOVE MONTH-TO-DATE-SALES TO MONTH-TO-DATE-SALES-OUT.            FIG 11.8|
|003230     IF MONTH-TO-DATE-SALES IS < ZERO                                FIG 11.8|
|003240         MOVE ALL '*' TO MONTH-TO-DATE-SALES-ERROR.                  FIG 11.8|
|003250 5089-EXIT.                                                          FIG 11.8|
|003260     EXIT.                                                           FIG 11.8|
|003270 5090-EDIT-YTD-SALES SECTION.                                        FIG 11.8|
|003280 5091-EDIT-YTD-SALES.                                                FIG 11.8|
|003290     IF YEAR-TO-DATE-SALES-TEST IS NOT NUMERIC                       FIG 11.8|
|003300         MOVE YEAR-TO-DATE-SALES-TEST TO YEAR-TO-DATE-SALES-DISP     FIG 11.8|
|003310         MOVE ALL '*' TO YEAR-TO-DATE-SALES-ERROR                    FIG 11.8|
|003320         GO TO 5099-EXIT.                                            FIG 11.8|
|003330     MOVE YEAR-TO-DATE-SALES TO YEAR-TO-DATE-SALES-OUT.              FIG 11.8|
|003340     IF YEAR-TO-DATE-SALES IS NEGATIVE                               FIG 11.8|
|003350         MOVE ALL '*' TO YEAR-TO-DATE-SALES-ERROR                    FIG 11.8|
|003360         GO TO 5099-EXIT.                                            FIG 11.8|
|003370     IF MONTH-TO-DATE-SALES-TEST IS NOT NUMERIC                      FIG 11.8|
|003380         GO TO 5099-EXIT.                                            FIG 11.8|
|003390     IF YEAR-TO-DATE-SALES < MONTH-TO-DATE-SALES                     FIG 11.8|
|003400         MOVE ALL '*' TO YEAR-TO-DATE-SALES-ERROR.                   FIG 11.8|
|003410 5099-EXIT.                                                          FIG 11.8|
|003420     EXIT.                                                           FIG 11.8|
|003430 5100-EDIT-LAST-ORDERED SECTION.                                     FIG 11.8|
|003440 5101-EDIT-LAST-ORDERED.                                             FIG 11.8|
|003450     MOVE DATE-LAST-ORDERED TO DATE-LAST-ORDERED-OUT.                FIG 11.8|
|003460     MOVE SPACES TO DATE-ERROR.                                      FIG 11.8|
|003470     IF DATE-LAST-ORDERED IS NOT NUMERIC                             FIG 11.8|
|003480         MOVE ALL '*' TO DATE-LAST-ORDERED-ERROR                     FIG 11.8|
|003490         GO TO 5109-EXIT.                                            FIG 11.8|
|003500     MOVE DATE-LAST-ORDERED TO DATE-TEST-VALUES.                     FIG 11.8|
```

Figure 11.8 Inventory Data-Editing *Continued*

```
|                 1   1   2   2   3   3   4   4   4   5   5   6   6   6   7   7   8|
|   4     8       2   6   0   4   8   2   6   0   4   8   2   6   0   4   8   2   6   0|
------------------------------------------------------------------------------------
|003510          PERFORM 5105-DATE-VALUES-TEST.                           FIG 11.8|
|003520          MOVE MONTH-ERROR TO DO-MONTH-ERROR.                      FIG 11.8|
|003530          MOVE DAY-ERROR TO DO-DAY-ERROR.                          FIG 11.8|
|003540          MOVE YEAR-ERROR TO DO-YEAR-ERROR.                        FIG 11.8|
|003550          GO TO 5109-EXIT.                                         FIG 11.8|
|003560      5105-DATE-VALUES-TEST.                                       FIG 11.8|
|003570          IF NOT VALID-MONTH                                       FIG 11.8|
|003580              MOVE '**' TO MONTH-ERROR.                            FIG 11.8|
|003590          IF NOT VALID-DAY                                         FIG 11.8|
|003600              MOVE '**' TO DAY-ERROR.                              FIG 11.8|
|003610          IF NOT VALID-YEAR                                        FIG 11.8|
|003620              MOVE '**' TO YEAR-ERROR.                             FIG 11.8|
|003630      5109-EXIT.                                                   FIG 11.8|
|003640          EXIT.                                                    FIG 11.8|
|003650      5110-EDIT-LAST-SOLD SECTION.                                 FIG 11.8|
|003660      5111-EDIT-LAST-SOLD.                                         FIG 11.8|
|003670          MOVE DATE-LAST-SOLD TO DATE-LAST-SOLD-OUT.               FIG 11.8|
|003680          MOVE SPACES TO DATE-ERROR.                               FIG 11.8|
|003690          IF DATE-LAST-SOLD IS NOT NUMERIC                         FIG 11.8|
|003700              MOVE ALL '*' TO DATE-LAST-SOLD-ERROR                 FIG 11.8|
|003710              GO TO 5119-EXIT.                                     FIG 11.8|
|003720          MOVE DATE-LAST-SOLD TO DATE-TEST-VALUES.                 FIG 11.8|
|003730          PERFORM 5105-DATE-VALUES-TEST.                           FIG 11.8|
|003740          MOVE MONTH-ERROR TO DS-MONTH-ERROR.                      FIG 11.8|
|003750          MOVE DAY-ERROR TO DS-DAY-ERROR.                          FIG 11.8|
|003760          MOVE YEAR-ERROR TO DS-YEAR-ERROR.                        FIG 11.8|
|003770      5119-EXIT.                                                   FIG 11.8|
|003780          EXIT.                                                    FIG 11.8|
|003790      5120-EDIT-RECORD-STATUS SECTION.                            FIG 11.8|
|003800      5121-EDIT-RECORD-STATUS.                                     FIG 11.8|
|003810          MOVE RECORD-STATUS TO RECORD-STATUS-OUT.                 FIG 11.8|
|003820          IF NOT VALID-STATUS                                      FIG 11.8|
|003830              MOVE ALL '*' TO RECORD-STATUS-ERROR.                 FIG 11.8|
|003840      5129-EXIT.                                                   FIG 11.8|
|003850          EXIT.                                                    FIG 11.8|
|003860      9000-FILE-CLOSING SECTION.                                   FIG 11.8|
|003870      9001-FILE-CLOSING.                                           FIG 11.8|
|003880          CLOSE INVENTORY-FILE, EDIT-REPORT.                       FIG 11.8|
|003890      9009-EXIT.                                                   FIG 11.8|
|003900          EXIT.                                                    FIG 11.8|
```

Figure 11.8 Inventory Data-Editing *Continued*

```
|      |         1         2         3         4         5         6         7        8| FIGURE |
|RECORD|12345678901234567890123456789012345678901234567890123456789012345678901234567890| NUMBER |
--------------------------------------------------------------------------------------------------
|     1|0000001000GEN4 INCH NAILS          9000020000GR005000030000750002000012068002098 1H|FIG 11.8|
|     2|0000250500WHR4 X 4 PLYWOOD         0050000200BF0070000450FIFTY 075000MAY 80MAY 802|FIG 11.8|
|     3|0000385000PUAOAK PLANKS            0010000200LF0040000700045000029000070180070580A|FIG 11.8|
|     4|0004697000JMVSKY-BLUE FLAT PAINT   0006700020GA0110000925070000750001123800205 81A|FIG 11.8|
|     5|0000555550IP MAPLE LOGS            SIXTY00350LF030000220000500000075000329800116 80II|FIG 11.8|
|     6|0000709800GLDWHITE SEMI-GLOSS      0805006500QT005500065000950000850002018102138 1D|FIG 11.8|
|     7|0000100000GEN10FT LADDER           0010000050EA015000105000600000750013128011118 0D|FIG 11.8|
|     8|0000330030PITTURPENTINE            0105001500PT000950004500091000151005208002177 9H|FIG 11.8|
|     9|0000000101WHR2 X 4 REDWOOD         0005000040EA0220002500052500060500120580012581H|FIG 11.8|
|    10|0000600500IP WOOD PANELS           0025000300BF01100009000095000120001228780113 81U|FIG 11.8|
|    11|0000890200BM YELLOW EXTERIOR       0030600315DZTWELVE112500750000500000870790630 80A|FIG 11.8|
|    12|0000224200GENBOLTS AND NUTS        500005000002000500005000120001500020781020582II|FIG 11.8|
|    13|0000985040JB HOT PINK PAINT        00005 TWO PT00200001500002000020009157904218 0H|FIG 11.8|
|    14|0000765090UPA4 X 6 ASPEN           0054900500M 0220002100015000175000404810600797 9D|FIG 11.8|
|    15|0000382110PITRED INTERIOR          0015000200QT010000065000100000200001208012017 9D|FIG 11.8|
|    16|0001000000GENSMALL SCREWDRIVER     0080000500QT000950010000190000250010228010028 0E|FIG 11.8|
|    17|0000465470GLDAVOCADO-KITCHEN       0009500075GA01250NINE 00125000250004278004018 0R|FIG 11.8|
|    18|0000505020BM GOLDEN YELLOW FLAT    0009500100GA014900135000280 0SIXTY 03037903037 9E|FIG 11.8|
|    19|0000610010JMVBURNT ORANGE GLOSS    0005000075QT0092500720000925000925021481020781II|FIG 11.8|
|    20|0000765050UPASHEETROCK             0100001000BF0100000900009000050001128800205 81A|FIG 11.8|
```

Figure 11.8 Inventory Data-Editing (Data) *Continued*

CAT NUMBER	VEN	DESCRIPTION	QTY.	MIN.	PK	PRICE	COST	MTD $	YTD $	LAST ORD	LAST SLD	ST
0000001000	GEN	4 INCH NAILS	90000	20000	GR	005.00	003.00	0075.00	0200.00	12 06 80	02 09 81	H
0000250500	WHR	4 X 4 PLYWOOD	00500	00200	BF	007.00	004.50	FIFTY ******	0750.00	MA Y 80 ********	MA Y 80 ********	2 *
0000385000 ***	PUA	OAK PLANKS	00100	00200	LF **	004.00	007.00 ******	0450.00	0290.00 ******	07 01 80	07 05 80	A
0004697000	JMV	SKY-BLUE FLAT PAINT	00067	00020	GA	011.00	009.25	0700.00	0750.00	11 23 80	02 05 81	A
0000555550	IP	MAPLE LOGS	SIXTY *****	00350	LF	030.00	022.00	0050.00	0075.00	03 29 80	01 16 80	I
0000709800	GLD	WHITE SEMI-GLOSS	08050	06500	QT	005.50 ******	006.50	0095.00	0085.00 ******	02 01 81	02 13 81	D
0000100000	GEN	10FT LADDER	00100	00050	EA	015.00	010.50	0060.00	0075.00	13 12 80 **	11 11 80	D
0000330030	PIT	TURPENTINE	01050 *****	01500	PT	000.95	000.45	0009.10	0015.10	05 20 80	02 17 79	H
0000000101 *********	WHR	2 X 4 REDWOOD	00050	00040	EA **	022.00	025.00 ******	0525.00	0605.00	12 05 80	01 25 81	H
0000600500	IP	WOOD PANELS	00250 *****	00300	BF	011.00	009.00	0095.00	0120.00	12 28 78	01 13 81	U *
0000890200	BM	YELLOW EXTERIOR	00306 *****	00315	DZ **	TWELV ******	E1125 ******	0075.00	0050.00 ******	08 70 79 **	06 30 80	A
0000224200	GEN	BOLTS AND NUTS	50000	50000	OZ	000.50	000.50	0012.00	0015.00	02 07 81	02 05 82 **	I
0000985040	JB	HOT PINK PAINT	00005	TWO *****	PT	002.00	001.50	0002.00	0002.00	09 15 79	04 21 80	H
0000765090	UPA	4 X 6 ASPEN	00549	00500	M **	022.00	021.00	0150.00	0175.00	04 04 81	06 09 79	D
0000382110	PIT	RED INTERIOR	00150 *****	00200	QT	010.00	006.50	0010.00	0020.00	01 20 80	12 01 79	D
0001000000	GEN	SMALL SCREWDRIVER	00800	00500	QT **	000.95 ******	001.00	0019.00	0025.00	10 22 80	10 02 80	E *
0000465470	GLD	AVOCADO-KITCHEN	00095	00075	GA	012.50	NINE ******	0012.50	0025.00	04 27 80	04 01 80	R *
0000505020	BM	GOLDEN YELLOW FLAT	00095 *****	00100	GA	014.90	013.50	0028.00	SIXTY ******	03 03 79	03 03 79	E *
0000610010	JMV	BURNT ORANGE GLOSS	00050 *****	00075	QT	009.25	007.20	0009.25	0009.25	02 14 81	02 07 81	I
0000765050	UPA	SHEETROCK	01000	01000	BF	010.00	009.00	0090.00	0050.00 ******	11 28 80	02 05 81	A

Figure 11.8 Inventory Data-Editing (Output) *Continued*

Summary

With the IF statement conditions presented in this chapter, all possible condition types available in standard COBOL have been discussed. Thus, the programmer may choose among IF statement conditions stated in terms of:

1. a relational test,
2. a sign test,
3. a class test, or
4. a condition-name test.

Conditions stated in the PERFORM/UNTIL can also be altered to use these condition types. And, condition types may be joined in compound conditions (by using the logical operators AND and OR).

Notes on Programming Style

Although this chapter has introduced three new condition types, all the notes pertaining to IF statements presented in Chapter 8 still apply. You should select the condition type that makes your code the most readable and understandable. Some commercial installations have banned (or at least restricted) the use of the condition-name test. The rationale is that a person reading the code for the first time (e.g., a maintenance programmer) would be required to flip back and forth between the DATA DIVISION and the PRO-CEDURE DIVISION to determine the actual testing conditions each time a condition-name test is employed.

Questions

Below fill in the blank(s) with the appropriate word, words, or phrases.

1. If an identifier is used in a sign test, it must have a _____ PICTURE description.

2. The logical operator _____ may be used in a compound sign test, but the logical operator _____ results in an IF statement that will always be false.

3. The class test may be used to determine whether an identifier contains _____ or _____ data.

4. A condition-name is always associated with the level _____ number.

5. If a series of values are associated with a condition-name, they must be assigned in _____ order.

6. The values associated with a condition-name must be consistent with the _____ to which it is subordinate.

Answer the following questions by circling "T" for True or "F" for False.

T F   7. Literals may appear in a sign test.
T F   8. Both the subject and the sign test operator (e.g., ZERO) may be implied in a sign test.
T F   9. A class test in the NUMERIC test mode may be used to test the results of an arithmetic operation.
T F   10. A condition-name has the same characteristics as any other data-name (e.g., it could be used for computational purposes).
T F   11. A condition-name may be associated with a single value or a series of values.
T F   12. Any condition stated in terms of a sign test could be restated in terms of a relational test.
T F   13. Any condition stated in terms of a relational test could be restated in terms of a sign test.

Exercises

1. Below is a series of IF statements. Indicate whether or not each statement has been coded acceptably. If the form is correct, identify the type of condition in use and which statement(s) constitute the "true" and "false" imperative statements. If the statement is wrong, indicate the probable cause of the error.

   a. IF EXAM-TOTAL IS ZERO
   　　　　MOVE 'DIVISION ERROR—PROCEDURE ABORTED' TO OUTPUT-LINE
   　　　　WRITE OUTPUT-LINE AFTER ADVANCING 1 LINES
   　　　　STOP RUN.

   b. IF DEPENDENT-COUNT NUMERIC
   　　　　PERFORM DEPENDENT-DEDUCTIONS
   　　ELSE
   　　　　NEXT SENTENCE.

   c. IF 1000 IS POSITIVE
   　　　　GO TO DEDUCT-STANDARD
   　　ELSE
   　　　　GO TO DEDUCT-ITEMIZED.

   d. IF 'W2' IS ALPHABETIC
   　　　　MOVE 'W-2 FILED' TO EMPLOYEE-STATUS
   　　ELSE
   　　　　MOVE 'NO W-2' TO EMPLOYEE-STATUS.

2. Below is a series of IF statements. Determine whether or not each statement is correct, and if so, indicate the type of condition(s) which is (are) used. If the statement is incorrect, indicate the probable cause of the error.

   a. IF EMPLOYEE-TYPE IS HOURLY AND HOURS-WORKED GREATER THAN 40
         PERFORM OVERTIME-CALCULATIONS
    ELSE
         PERFORM STRAIGHT-TIME-CALCULATIONS.

   b. IF DAILY-HOURS IS GREATER THAN OR EQUAL TO 40
         PERFORM DAILY-OVERTIME.

   c. IF EXTRA-TAX-DEDUCTION IS POSITIVE AND NOT = 9999
         SUBTRACT EXTRA-TAX-DEDUCTION FROM NET-PAY.

   d.   05 MARITAL-STATUS   PIC X(01).
           88 SINGLE   VALUE 'S'.
           88 MARRIED   VALUE 'M'.
     IF MARITAL-STATUS = MARRIED
         PERFORM MARRIED-TAX-TABLE
     ELSE
         PERFORM SINGLE-TAX-TABLE.

   e.   05 SHIFT-WORKED   PIC 9(01).
           88 1ST-SHIFT   VALUE 1.
           88 2ND-SHIFT   VALUE 2.
           88 3RD-SHIFT   VALUE 3.

     IF 1ST-SHIFT
       MOVE 0 TO SHIFT-DIFFERENTIAL
     ELSE
       IF 2ND-SHIFT
         MOVE PREMIUM-SECOND TO SHIFT-DIFFERENTIAL
       ELSE
         IF 3RD-SHIFT
           MOVE PREMIUM-THIRD TO SHIFT-DIFFERENTIAL
         ELSE
           MOVE 'SHIFT VALUE ERROR' TO MESSAGE-OUT
           WRITE PRINT-LINE AFTER ADVANCING 2 LINES.

   f.   04 DEPARTMENT-NUMBER   PIC 9(03).
           88 EXECUTIVE-STAFF   VALUE 100 THRU 150.
           88 ACCOUNTING-STAFF   VALUE 200 THRU 299.
           88 MARKETING-RESEARCH   VALUE 300.
           88 PRODUCTION-DEPARTMENT   VALUE 400 THRU 599.
           88 SHIPPING-DEPARTMENT   VALUE 600 THRU 610.

     IF (EXECUTIVE-STAFF OR MARKETING-RESEARCH) AND
       (PAY-TYPE = 'H' OR 'X')
         MOVE 'PAY TYPE ERROR' TO MESSAGE
     ELSE
       PERFORM PAY-CALCULATIONS.

3. In a payroll application, employees are often divided into at least four categories:
   a. salaried-exempt (salaried with no overtime pay),
   b. salaried-non-exempt (salaried with overtime pay possible),
   c. hourly-exempt (pay is based on rate per hour with no provision for overtime), and
   d. hourly-non-exempt (pay is based on rate per hour with overtime pay when hours worked exceed the regular hourly limit).

Assume an input record contains a field called PAY-CODE. This field is a single character alphanumeric and should contain the following values:

VALUE	MEANING
S	salaried-exempt
O	salaried-non-exempt
X	hourly-exempt
H	hourly-non-exempt

Write the PROCEDURE DIVISION code necessary to distinguish between (among) the pay codes such that when PAY-CODE is S, the variable BASE contains "salary" and the variable OVERTIME contains "no." If an employee is non-exempt, OVERTIME should contain "yes." If an employee is paid on an hourly basis, BASE should contain "hours." Regardless of the values placed in BASE and OVERTIME, these values are to be written. Furthermore, do not assume that PAY-CODE contains only legitimate values. If PAY-CODE does not contain S, O, X, or H, both BASE and OVERTIME should contain "error."

Write this code using relational IF statements; then rewrite the code employing condition-name tests.

Problems

1. You are charged with checking all customer records for payment accuracy. Each customer has been sent a statement and has returned the statement along with a payment. Each record consists of the following (see multiple-card layout form):
   1. Customer number—5 characters
   2. Customer name—20 characters
   3. Street address—20 characters
   4. City—10 characters
   5. State—2 characters (State-name abbreviations)
   6. Zip code—5 digits
   7. Amount of statement—5 digits including 2 decimal positions (dollars and cents)
   8. Amount of payment—5 digits including 2 decimal positions (dollars and cents)
   9. Date payment due—4 digits in the format MMDD
   10. Date of payment—4 digits in the format MMDD

Check the amount of the statement against the amount of payment, and print one of the following messages in the PAYMENT STATUS field:

   1. "PAYMENT CORRECT"—amount of statement = payment
   2. "PAYMENT INSUFFICIENT"—amount of statement greater than payment
   3. "CREDIT DUE"—amount of statement less than payment

Then check the date the payment was due against the date the payment was received, and print one of the following messages in the DATE STATUS field:

   1. "PAYMENT EARLY"—payment received prior to due date
   2. "PAYMENT ON TIME"—payment received on due date
   3. "PAYMENT LATE"—payment received after due date

See the print chart for additional details.

MULTIPLE-CARD LAYOUT FORM

Company LEARNING COBOL, INC.

Application CUSTOMER PAYMENT STATUS   by J. Wayne Spence   Date 01/01/81   Job No. PROB 11.1   Sheet No. 1

| CUSTOMER NUMBER | CUSTOMER NAME | CUSTOMER ADDRESS | | | | | AMOUNT OF | DATE PAYMENT | |
| | | STREET | CITY | STATE | ZIP CODE | STMT | PAYMENT | DUE | REC'D |

```
150/10/8 PRINT CHART    PROG. ID. CUSTOMER  P 11.1              PAGE  1
(SPACING:  150 POSITIONS AT 10 CHARACTERS PER INCH, 8 LINES PER VERTICAL INCH)    DATE 1/1/81
PROGRAM TITLE CUSTOMER PAYMENT STATUS
PROGRAMMER OR DOCUMENTALIST J. WAYNE SPENCE
CHART TITLE CUSTOMER PAYMENT STATUS REPORT
```

CUSTOMER PAYMENT STATUS REPORT

NUMB   NAME/ADDRESS   AMOUNT STATUS   DATE STATUS

XXXXX   X   (Name)   X   X   X   X   X
X   (Street)   X
X (City) X XX 999 99

XXXXX   X   X   X   X   X   X
X   X XX 999 99

2. You are provided with a series of new employee records which are to be added to the Employee Data File. Before the records are added to the file, they should be edited for proper values. The new employee records have been ordered by department number, and the employee numbers should be in ascending order within each department.

The following editing is to be performed on the fields of each new employee record (see multiple-column layout form):

1. The employee number should be numeric and should be in ascending order within a department.
2. The social security number should be numeric.
3. The employee name should not be blank.
4. The department number should be 100, 200, 300, 400, or 500 (and should be grouped together—i.e., all 100s should be in a group, all 200s should be in a group, and so forth).
5. The pay type should be either H (hourly) or S (salaried).
6. The rate per hour or salary field should be numeric. If the pay type is H, the rate per hour should be in the range of $5.00 to $20.00. If the pay type is S, the salary should be between $200.00 and $800.00 if paid weekly, $400.00 to $1,600.00 if paid biweekly, $500.00 to $2,000.00 if paid semimontly, and $1,000.00 to $4,000.00 if paid monthly.
7. The pay frequency should be W (weekly), B (biweekly), S (semimonthly), or M (monthly).

8. The date of employment should be reasonable—the month value should be between 1 and 12, the day value should be between 1 and 31, and the year value should be the current year.
9. The health plan should be "NONE" (no health plan), "HIGH" (health plan—high option), or "LOW" (health plan—low option).
10. The retirement plan should be either "YES" (enrolled in a retirement plan) or "NO" (not enrolled in a retirement plan).
11. The savings plan should be either "YES" (employee desires a savings deduction) or "NO" (employee does not desire a savings deduction).
12. The savings amount should either be numeric, if the savings plan code is "YES," or blank, if the savings plan code is "NO."

The printed edit-results report should mark (with asterisk) any field that does not conform to these editing standards. In the event that no errors are encountered, the employee record is not to be printed on the report—only those records with errors are to be printed. The output line for each employee record in error should be an exact duplicate of the input record. Each field in error should have asterisks located immediately below it. (See the print chart). Furthermore, each department should begin on a new page; "ACCOUNTING" should be printed in the heading if the department number is 100; "SALES" if, 200; "MANUFACTURING" if, 300; "PURCHASING" if, 400; and "RECEIVING" if, 500.

MULTIPLE-CARD LAYOUT FORM

Company LEARNING COBOL, INC.

Application EMPLOYEE EDIT   by J. Wayne Spence   Date 01/01/81   Job No. PROB 11.2   Sheet No. 1

150/10/8 PRINT CHART   PROG. ID. EMPLOYEE P 11.2   PAGE 1 of 1
(SPACING: 150 POSITIONS AT 10 CHARACTERS PER INCH, 8 LINES PER VERTICAL INCH)   DATE 1/1/81
PROGRAM TITLE EMPLOYEE EDIT
PROGRAMMER OR DOCUMENTALIST: J. Wayne Spence
CHART TITLE DEPARTMENTAL EMPLOYEE ERRORS

3. Presume another procedure has been executed to produce records to govern the printing of a Balance Sheet. (A Balance Sheet is a formal financial statement generally produced by the accounting department for purposes of determining a company's financial status.) The contents of each of these records is as follows (see the graphic record layout):

1. account number—4 digits
2. account title—30 characters
3. monetary amount—8 digits (whole dollars)
4. print control indicator—1 character

The print control indicator is used to distinguish between the different types of accounts and to determine what is to be printed and where. (See the print chart.) The print control indicator should be used as described below.

If the print control indicator is "1," the record contains a regular (money) account, and the account number, title, and monetary amount should be printed in the specified locations in a single spaced format.

If the print control indicator is "2," the record contains a title account, and only the title is to be printed in the specified location, preceded by one blank line.

If the print control indicator is "3," the record contains a total account, and the account title and monetary amount should be printed in the specified locations preceded by one blank line. However, the preceding regular account-record monetary-amount field should be underscored (use a row of hyphens on the next line if your printer does not permit underscoring).

If the print control indicator is "4," the record contains a heading-account record, and only the account title is to be printed in the specified location, preceded by four blank lines.

If the print control indicator is "5," the record contains a grand total amount, and the account title and monetary amount are to be printed in the specified locations preceded by two blank lines. The monetary amount field should be double underscored (with a row of equal symbols) on the following line.

Special Options:

1. The *first* record in the data file contains the report date that is to appear in the heading. The date will appear in the account title field already formatted in the form needed for printing. (If this option is not used, the program due date should appear in the date field (as a literal).
2. The report heading is to be produced at the top of the page only when the first digit of the account number is 1 (assets) or 2 (liabilities) when a heading account record is processed. (If this option is not used, place the heading at the top of the first page only.)

MULTIPLE-CARD LAYOUT FORM

Company ___LEARNING COBOL, INC.___

Application ___BALANCE SHEET___ by ___J. Wayne Spence___ Date ___01/01/81___ Job No. ___PROB 11.3___ Sheet No. ___1___

ACCOUNT NUMBER	ACCOUNT TITLE	MONETARY AMOUNT	PRT CNTRL	
9999	9999999999999999999999999999999	999999	9	99999999999999999999999999999999999999
1 2 3 4	5 6 7 8 9 10 11 12 13 14 15 16 17 18 19 20 21 22 23 24 25 26 27 28 29 30 31 32 33 34	35 36 37 38 39 40 41 42	43	44 45 46 47 48 49 50 51 52 53 54 55 56 57 58 59 60 61 62 63 64 65 66 67 68 69 70 71 72 73 74 75 76 77 78 79 80

150/10/8 PRINT CHART PROG. ID. ___ACCOUNTING P 11.3___ PAGE ___1___

(SPACING: 150 POSITIONS AT 10 CHARACTERS PER INCH, 8 LINES PER VERTICAL INCH) DATE ___1/1/81___

PROGRAM TITLE ___BALANCE SHEET PRINT___

PROGRAMMER OR DOCUMENTALIST: ___J. WAYNE SPENCE___

CHART TITLE ___BALANCE SHEET___

```
          LEARNING  COBOL, INC.
                BALANCE SHEET
      X   FOR THE PERIOD ENDING        X          (Date)

             X                      X             (Heading Account)
          X                       X               (Title Account)
  9999 X                      X    99 99999 9
  9999 X                      X    99 99999 9
        {           {                  {
  9999 X                      X    99 99999 9     } (Regular Accounts)
          X                      X     999 99999   (Total Account)
          X                      X                 (Title Account)
  9999 X                      X    99 99999 9
  9999 X                      X    99 99999 9     } (Regular Accounts)
        {           {                  {
  9999 X                      X    99 99999 9
          X                      X     999 99999
          X                      X       999 99999  (Grand Total Account)
                                         === ======
```

12 More on the PERFORM Statements

In Chapter 8, two PERFORM statements were discussed—the simple PERFORM and the PERFORM/UNTIL. The remaining PERFORM statements—the PERFORM/TIMES and the PERFORM/VARYING—are generally controlled by counting operations.

The PERFORM/TIMES and PERFORM/VARYING statements, shown in Figures 12.1 and 12.3, are similar to the other PERFORM statements. The procedure-names specify the paragraphs or SECTIONs to be executed. If procedure-name-2 is specified with the THROUGH (THRU) option, it must be located below procedure-name-1 in the program. And, when the procedure has been completed, program control returns to the statement that follows the PERFORM statement.

The PERFORM/TIMES Statement

The PERFORM/TIMES statement permits the programmer to execute a procedure a fixed number of times with one execution of the statement. Prior to the reserved word TIMES, the programmer specifies identifier-1 or integer-1. Identifier-1 must be described in the DATA DIVISION as an elementary data item in a numeric-nonedited field. Identifier-1 should contain a positive integer value prior to the execution of the PERFORM statement. Later, that value may be changed to zero or a negative if the PERFORM statement is to be bypassed during execution. Integer-1 must be a positive integer value. Though the value of identifier-1 may be changed from one execution of the PERFORM statement to the next, each execution of the procedure will be repeated the number of times specified when the PERFORM begins, even if the value of the identifier is altered during execution of the procedure.

Figure 12.2 presents several illustrations of the PERFORM/TIMES statement. Each of the examples includes a list of the procedures executed.

In Figure 12.2a, a simple use of the PERFORM/TIMES statement is shown; HEADER-RECORD is executed two times. The paragraph is executed once when the procedure-name following HEADER-RECORD is encountered or when the end of the PROCEDURE DIVISION is reached. In Figure 12.2b, a set of procedures beginning with SETS-OF-LABELS and ending with LABEL-SUMMARY is executed three times. While processing SETS-OF-LABELS the

```
Format 3:  The PERFORM/TIMES Statement

    PERFORM procedure-name-1  [ {THROUGH}  procedure-name-2 ]
                                {THRU   }

    {identifier-1}  TIMES
    {integer-1   }
```

Figure 12.1 The PERFORM/TIMES Statement

first time, another PERFORM/TIMES statement is encountered causing DUPLICATE-LABELS to be executed twice. When the processing of DUPLICATE-LABELS has been completed, the execution sequence continues from the point where DUPLICATE-LABELS was originally invoked. LABEL-SUMMARY is then encountered in a "fall through" condition. When the end of LABEL-SUMMARY has been reached, the original PERFORM has completed one cycle. This cycle is completed two more times before the procedure is terminated.

In Figure 12.2c, a simple PERFORM statement is combined with a PERFORM/TIMES statement. In this example, the PERFORM/TIMES is based on the value of an identifier. Although the illustration shows the value of NUMBER-OF-DEPENDENTS being generated by a MOVE statement, the value could just as easily be derived from an input operation or through arithmetic manipulation. After the MOVE statement has been executed DEPENDENT-DEDUCTION is invoked. Within this paragraph, DE-DUCT-1000 is invoked—to be repeated five times (the current value of NUMBER-OF-DEPENDENTS). Within the DEDUCT-1000 paragraph, NUM-BER-OF-DEPENDENTS is set to zero, which has no effect on the number of times DEDUCT-1000 is executed in the illustrated procedure.

Figure 12.2d demonstrates a situation in which an identifier associated with a PERFORM/TIMES is modified, and the modification has an effect on the executed procedure. The illustration combines a PERFORM/UNTIL with a PERFORM/TIMES statement. The identifier COUNT-DOWN, used to control the activity of the procedure, is initialized to 3. Then a PERFORM/UNTIL is executed, to be terminated only when COUNT-DOWN is less than zero. While PYRAMID is being executed the first time, a PERFORM/TIMES statement is encountered causing LINE-OUT to be executed COUNT-DOWN times (3). When the execution of LINE-COUNT has been completed, COUNT-DOWN is decremented by one. The end of PYRAMID is encountered, but the current value of COUNT-DOWN (2) is not yet less than zero; thus, PYRAMID is repeated. With the re-execution of PYRAMID, the PERFORM/TIMES statement causes LINE-OUT to be executed twice. COUNT-DOWN is again decremented (to a value of one); COUNT-DOWN is still not less than zero. PYRAMID is re-executed, and LINE-OUT is performed one time. Finally, COUNT-DOWN is decremented to zero, PYRAMID is repeated, LINE-COUNT is *not* performed, COUNT-DOWN is decremented to minus one, the UNTIL condition is true, and the procedure is terminated.

PERFORM/TIMES Examples	Sequence of Paragraphs Executed

a)   `PERFORM HEADER-RECORD 2 TIMES.`
    `STOP RUN.`
`HEADER-RECORD.`
       ⌇
	`HEADER-RECORD`
	`HEADER-RECORD`

b)   `PERFORM SETS-OF-LABELS THRU LABEL-SUMMARY`
        `3 TIMES.`
    `STOP RUN.`
`SETS-OF-LABELS.`
    `PERFORM DUPLICATE-LABELS 2 TIMES.`
`LABEL-SUMMARY.`
 	
`DUPLICATE-LABELS.`
      ⌇
	`SETS-OF-LABELS`
	`DUPLICATE-LABLES`
	`DUPLICATE-LABELS`
	`LABEL-SUMMARY`
	`SETS-OF-LABELS`
	`DUPLICATE-LABELS`
	`DUPLICATE-LABELS`
	`LABEL-SUMMARY`
	`SETS-OF-LABELS`
	`DUPLICATE-LABELS`
	`DUPLICATE-LABELS`
	`LABEL-SUMMARY`

c)   `MOVE 5 TO NUMBER-OF-DEPENDENTS.`
    `PERFORM DEPENDENT-DEDUCTION.`
    `STOP RUN.`
`DEPENDENT-DEDUCTION.`
    `PERFORM DEDUCT-1000`
       `NUMBER-OF-DEPENDENT TIMES.`
`DEDUCT-1000.`
    `SUBTRACT 1000 FROM ANNUAL-TAXABLE-PAY.`
    `MOVE 0 TO NUMBER-OF-DEPENDENTS.`
      ⌇
	`DEPENDENT-DEDUCTION`
	`DEDUCT-1000`
	`DEDUCT-1000`
	`DEDUCT-1000`
	`DEDUCT-1000`
	`DEDUCT-1000`

d)   `MOVE 3 TO COUNT-DOWN.`
    `PERFORM PYRAMID`
       `UNTIL COUNT-DOWN < 0.`
    `STOP RUN.`
`PYRAMID.`
    `PERFORM LINE-OUT COUNT-DOWN TIMES.`
    `SUBTRACT 1 FROM COUNT-DOWN.`
`LINE-OUT.`
      ⌇
	`PYRAMID`
	`LINE-OUT`
	`LINE-OUT`
	`LINE-OUT`
	`PYRAMID`
	`LINE-OUT`
	`LINE-OUT`
	`PYRAMID`
	`LINE-OUT`
	`PYRAMID`

Figure 12.2 Illustrations of the PERFORM/TIMES Statement

The PERFORM/ VARYING Statement

The PERFORM/VARYING statement is most often (but not exclusively) used with the manipulation of tables in COBOL. (Table handling in COBOL is discussed in Chapters 13 and 14.) This type of PERFORM statement permits the modification of a data item (identifier-2) or data items (identifier-2, identifier-5, and identifier-8). (See Figure 12.3.) These data items may be either identifiers (numeric-nonedited elementary items) or index-names. Index-names are directly associated with table manipulations, and they will be discussed in detail in Chapter 14. This chapter will limit discussion to the use of identifiers and/or literals in the PERFORM/VARYING statement.

During the execution of the PERFORM/VARYING statement, the value of the identifier following the reserved word VARYING will be altered as a result of other portions of the statement. Identifier-3 (identifier-6 and identifier-9), which follows the reserved word FROM, should be an elementary item containing a positive-integer value. Literal-1 (literal-3, and literal-5) should be a positive-integer numeric literal. This data item or value represents the initial value to be placed in identifier-2 (identifier-5 and identifier-8, respectively). Thus, the value indicated after the reserved word FROM will be the value of the identifier when the PERFORM statement is executed initially.

The identifiers or literals after the reserved word BY represent an incremental value—that is, these identifiers or literals are added to the value contained in the identifier(s) following the reserved words VARYING or AFTER. The identifier(s) following VARYING or AFTER will continue to be incremented until their respective conditions are found to be true. The incremental identifiers (identifier-4, identifier-7, and identifier-10) and literals (literal-2, literal-4, and literal-6) should be integers (but not necessarily positive) with the same restrictions for the initial values as for the identifier(s) being modified. The identifiers continue to be modified until the conditions associated with them are true. When a condition is true, the next step depends on which condition the identifier was associated. If only the VARYING phrase is specified, the execution of the PERFORM statement is terminated when condition-1 is true. If the first optional AFTER phrase is provided, and condition-2 is true, only that part of the PERFORM statement is terminated, identifier-2 is incremented, and condition-1 is tested. The same operation takes place for the second AFTER phrase. When condition-3 is true, that portion of the PERFORM statement is terminated, identifier-5 is incremented, and condition-2 is tested.

Figure 12.4 shows the inner workings of the PERFORM/VARYING statement. Figure 12.4a flowcharts the process executed by the PERFORM/VARYING statement. If the statement is written with only the VARYING phrase, the process begins by initializing the data item following the reserved word VARYING and testing the condition associated with the phrase. If the condi-

```
Format 4:   The PERFORM/VARYING Statement

    PERFORM procedure-name-1  [{THROUGH}  procedure-name-2]
                               {THRU   }

       VARYING  {identifier-2}  FROM  {identifier-3}   BY  {identifier-4}
                {index-name-1}         {index-name-2}       {literal-2  }
                                       {literal-1   }

          UNTIL condition-1

    [AFTER  {identifier-5}  FROM  {identifier-6}   BY  {identifier-7}
            {index-name-3}         {index-name-4}       {literal-4  }
                                   {literal-3   }

          UNTIL condition-2

    [AFTER  {identifier-8}  FROM  {identifier-9}   BY  {identifier-10}
            {index-name-5}         {index-name-6}       {literal-6   }
                                   {literal-6   }

          UNTIL condition-3]]
```

Figure 12.3 The PERFORM/VARYING Statement

tion is false, the procedure or the set of procedures indicated immediately following the reserved word PERFORM is executed. After the procedure has been executed, the identifier is incremented, and the test of the condition is repeated. This process continues until the condition is true, at which time the PERFORM statement is terminated.

If the first optional AFTER phrase is added to the PERFORM/VARYING statement (Figure 12.4b), the function of the statement is the same as previously described up to the point when the procedure is executed. Prior to the execution of the procedure, the second indentifier is initialized. The second condi-

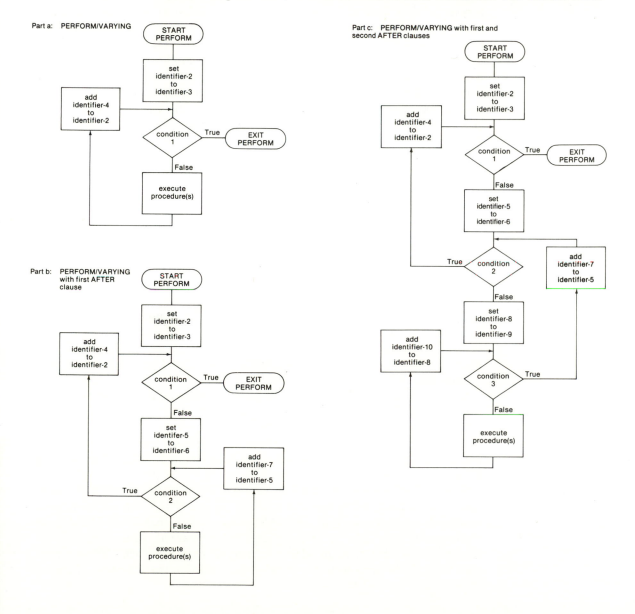

Figure 12.4 Flowcharts of the PERFORM/VARYING Statement

tion is then tested. If the condition is false, the procedure is executed. After the procedure has been executed, the second identifier is incremented, and the second condition is retested. This process continues until condition-2 is true. Then instead of the PERFORM statement being terminated, the first identifier is incremented, and condition-1 is retested. If condition-1 is false, the second identifier is re-initialized, and the process continues until condition-1 is true—terminating the PERFORM statement.

The final version of the PERFORM/VARYING statement calls for the addition of a second AFTER phrase (Figure 12.4c). As before, all of the boxes that appear prior to the initialization of the third identifier are executed. After the second condition is tested (and found to be false), however, the third data item is initialized, and condition-3 is tested. If the condition is false, the procedure is executed, and the third identifier is incremented. If condition-3 is true, the path from the decision on condition-3 to increment the second identifier is executed. Condition-2 is retested, and if false the third identifier is re-initialized, and the process is repeated. When condition-2 is true, the first identifier is incremented, condition-1 is retested, and if false the second identifier is re-initialized (which generally causes a re-initialization of the third identifier). When condition-1 is true, the PERFORM statement is terminated. Thus, regardless of the number of "levels" within the PERFORM statement, the only situation that terminates the statement is when condition-1 is true.

Figure 12.5 provides a series of examples. A list of the values of the identifier(s) modified by the statement and the names of the procedures executed are provided for each example.

Figure 12.5a illustrates the simplest use of the PERFORM/VARYING statement. The "indexing" identifier is initialized to 800, and the condition is tested. Since HOURS is *not* greater than 1800, the paragraph MILITARY-HOURS is invoked. Once the end of the paragraph is reached, HOURS is incremented by 100 (to 900), and the condition is rechecked. Since the condition is not yet true, the paragraph is repeated. MILITARY-HOURS will continue to be repeated until HOURS is greater than 1800, i.e., HOURS will be equal to 1900. At this point, the condition is true, the PERFORM is completed, and the procedure is terminated.

In Figure 12.5b, a PERFORM/VARYING statement is coupled with two simple PERFORM statements. In this example, however, the condition upon which the PERFORM/VARYING statement is terminated is *not* based on the data-name being changed by the statement. Rather, the statement is terminated upon encountering the end-of-file. The simple PERFORM statements are invoked on the conditions specified.

Figure 12.5c provides the first illustration of a PERFORM/VARYING statement with an AFTER option. Both MONTH and YEAR are initialized and modified (by increments of one). However, notice that MONTH will be incremented from 1 to 12 before YEAR is incremented. When YEAR is incremented, and provided its value is not greater than 1981, MONTH will proceed through the same sequence of values indicated for the first series of operations.

Figure 12.5d is different from Figure 12.5c in only two respects. First, the conditions used to terminate each phase of the PERFORM statement are based on a data-name rather than on a numeric literal. Second, the values of variables are different from the previous example to demonstrate that variables, rather than constants, may be used to control the activity of the PERFORM statement.

Figure 12.5e illustrates the maximum number of AFTER clauses that may be associated with a PERFORM/VARYING statement. In addition, a data-name is used to supply the incremental value of HOURS. As illustrated under the identifier values, HOURS is initialized to 0, along with DAYS-OF-WEEK and AM-PM (which are both set to 1). Further, notice that the full sequence of values to be associated with HOURS is generated before DAYS-OF-WEEK is incremented the first time. Eventually, enough sets of HOURS will be generated to cause DAYS-OF-WEEK to exceed 7. At that point, AM-PM is incremented the first time, and the entire process repeats itself. Thus, the last identifier associated with an AFTER option is the first identifier to be incremented and tested. When the condition associated with the clause is true, then and only then are previously listed AFTER/VARYING-clause variables modified.

PERFORM/VARYING Examples	Sequence of* Paragraphs Executed	Identifier(s) Values

a)   `PERFORM MILITARY-HOURS`
        `VARYING HOURS FROM 800 BY 100`
          `UNTIL HOURS GREATER THAN 1800.`
    `STOP RUN.`
  `MILITARY-HOURS.`
	`MILITARY-HOURS`
	`MILITARY-HOURS`
	`MILITARY-HOURS`
	`MILITARY-HOURS`
	`MILITARY-HOURS`
	`MILITARY-HOURS`
	`MILITARY-HOURS`
	`MILITARY-HOURS`
	`MILITARY-HOURS`
	`MILITARY-HOURS`
	`MILITARY-HOURS`
		<u>HOURS</u>
		800
		900
		1000
		1100
		1200
		1300
		1400
		1500
		1600
		1700
		1800
		1900

b)   `PERFORM INPUT-PROCEDURE`
        `VARYING RECORD-COUNT FROM 1 BY 1`
          `UNTIL FILE-STATUS = 'COMPLETE'.`
    `PERFORM AVERAGES.`
    `STOP RUN.`
  `INPUT-PROCEDURE.`
    `READ EMPLOYEE-RECORDS`
        `AT END MOVE 'COMPLETE'`
          `TO FILE-STATUS.`
    `IF FILE-STATUS NOT = 'COMPLETE'`
        `PERFORM COMPUTE-AND-WRITE.`
  `COMPUTE-AND-WRITE.`
 	
  `AVERAGES.`
    `SUBTRACT 1 FROM RECORD-COUNT.`
	`INPUT-PROCEDURE`
	`COMPUTE-AND-WRITE`
	`INPUT-PROCEDURE`
	`COMPUTE-AND-WRITE`
	.
	.
	.
	.
	`AVERAGES`
		<u>RECORD-COUNT</u>
		1
		1
		2
		2
		
		`End-of-file`
		`encountered on`
		`EMPLOYEE-RECORDS`

Figure 12.5 Illustrations of the PERFORM/VARYING Statement

The final illustration, Figure 12.5f, demonstrates the possibility for interaction between the VARYING and AFTER clauses. Note from the illustration that the data-name N is being varied. In addition, N is used as the initial value of the two AFTER options. Finally, note that the values associated with the data-name 0 decline with each iteration. Decrementing is achieved, in this case, by using the numeric literal-1 as the incremental value of 0.

PERFORM/VARYING Examples	Sequence of Paragraphs Executed	Identifier(s) Values	

c)
```
        PERFORM CALENDAR
            VARYING YEAR FROM 1980 BY 1
                UNTIL YEAR > 1981
            AFTER MONTH FROM 1 BY 1
                UNTIL MONTH > 12.
        STOP RUN.
    CALENDAR.
```

		MONTH	YEAR
	CALENDAR	1	1980
	CALENDAR	2	1980
	CALENDAR	3	1980
	CALENDAR	4	1980
	CALENDAR	5	1980
	CALENDAR	6	1980
	CALENDAR	7	1980
	CALENDAR	8	1980
	CALENDAR	9	1980
	CALENDAR	10	1980
	CALENDAR	11	1980
	CALENDAR	12	1980
	-	13	1980
	CALENDAR	1	1981
	CALENDAR	2	1981
	.	.	.
	.	.	.
	.	.	.
	CALENDAR	11	1981
	CALENDAR	12	1981
	-	13	1981
	-	13	1982

d)
```
    MOVE 5 TO WORKDAYS.
    MOVE 3 TO MONTH-DURATION.
    PERFORM PROJECT-CYCLE
        VARYING MONTH FROM 1 BY 1
            UNTIL MONTH > MONTH-DURATION
        AFTER DAYS FROM 1 BY 1
            UNTIL DAYS > WORKDAYS.
    STOP RUN.
PROJECT-CYCLE.
```

		DAYS	MONTH
	PROJECT-CYCLE	1	1
	PROJECT-CYCLE	2	1
	PROJECT-CYCLE	3	1
	PROJECT-CYCLE	4	1
	PROJECT-CYCLE	5	1
	-	6	1
	PROJECT-CYCLE	1	2
	PROJECT-CYCLE	2	2
	PROJECT-CYCLE	3	2
	PROJECT-CYCLE	4	2
	PROJECT-CYCLE	5	2
	-	6	2
	PROJECT-CYCLE	1	3
	PROJECT-CYCLE	2	3
	PROJECT-CYCLE	3	3
	PROJECT-CYCLE	4	3
	PROJECT-CYCLE	5	3
	-	6	3
	-	6	4

Figure 12.5 Illustrations of the PERFORM/VARYING Statement *Continued*

e)

```
        MOVE 15 TO HOURS-INCREMENT.
        PERFORM TIME-SLOTS
            VARYING AM-PM FROM 1 BY 1
                UNTIL AM-PM > 2
            AFTER DAYS-OF-WEEK FROM 1 BY 1
                UNTIL DAYS-OF-WEEK > 7
            AFTER HOURS FROM Ø BY
                HOURS-INCREMENT
                UNTIL HOURS > 6Ø.
        STOP RUN.
TIME-SLOTS.
```

Sequence of Paragraphs Executed	HOURS	DAYS-OF-WEEK	AM-PM
TIME-SLOT	0	1	1
TIME-SLOT	15	1	1
TIME-SLOT	30	1	1
TIME-SLOT	60	1	1
-	75	1	1
TIME-SLOT	0	2	1
TIME-SLOT	15	2	1
TIME-SLOT	30	2	1
TIME-SLOT	60	2	1
-	75	2	1
TIME-SLOT	0	3	1
TIME-SLOT	15	3	1
.	.	.	.
.	.	.	.
TIME-SLOT	60	7	1
-	75	7	1
-	75	8	1
TIME-SLOT	0	1	2
.	.	.	.
.	.	.	.
TIME-SLOT	60	7	2
-	75	8	2
-	75	8	3

f)

```
        PERFORM INVERSION-SEQUENCE
            VARYING N FROM 1 BY 1
                UNTIL N > 4
            AFTER M FROM N BY 1
                UNTIL M > 4
            AFTER O FROM N BY -1
                UNTIL O < 1.
        STOP RUN
INVERSION-SEQUENCE.
```

Sequence of Paragraphs Executed	O	M	N
INVERSION-SEQUENCE	1	1	1
-	Ø	1	1
INVERSION-SEQUENCE	1	2	1
-	Ø	2	1
INVERSION-SEQUENCE	1	3	1
-	Ø	3	1
INVERSION-SEQUENCE	1	4	1
-	Ø	4	1
-	Ø	5	1
INVERSION-SEQUENCE	2	2	2
INVERSION-SEQUENCE	1	2	2
-	Ø	2	2
INVERSION-SEQUENCE	2	3	2
INVERSION-SEQUENCE	1	3	2
-	Ø	3	2
INVERSION-SEQUENCE	2	4	2
INVERSION-SEQUENCE	1	4	2
-	Ø	4	2
-	Ø	5	2
INVERSION-SEQUENCE	3	3	3
INVERSION-SEQUENCE	2	3	3
INVERSION-SEQUENCE	1	3	3
-	Ø	3	3
INVERSION-SEQUENCE	3	4	3
INVERSION-SEQUENCE	2	4	3
INVERSION-SEQUENCE	1	4	3
-	Ø	4	3
-	Ø	5	3
INVERSION-SEQUENCE	4	4	4
INVERSION-SEQUENCE	3	4	4
INVERSION-SEQUENCE	2	4	4
INVERSION-SEQUENCE	1	4	4
-	Ø	4	4
-	Ø	5	4
-	Ø	5	5

*"-" indicates the procedure is not executed; "..." means the repetition of a previously established pattern.

Figure 12.5 Illustrations of the PERFORM/VARYING Statement *Continued*

**PERFORM/
VARYING:
An Example**

One of the most commonly accepted principles used in the recovery of the cost of any major business asset (such as equipment) is depreciation. The Internal Revenue Service permits a tax "write-off" on the basis of the expected useful life of the asset, thereby permitting the business to recoup (for possible later replacement) the cost of major investments. Although the intent of deducting depreciation from taxable income is a standard practice, the procedures for calculating the depreciation amount vary. The illustration in Figure 12.6 provides four different (but equally acceptable) ways of calculating depreciation.

In all cases, depreciation is based on the original value of the asset (less any salvage value after the expected useful life of the asset) spread over the useful life of the asset. In the straight-line depreciation method, the amount of depreciation is equal for all periods. Thus, if an asset were expected to last for six months, one-sixth of the original value of the asset would be depreciated each month. In other cases, depreciation based on the current book value (undepreciated value) is a more desirable alternative, more nearly representing the actual depletion of the business's asset, in which case the declining-values method may be used to calculate the depreciation amount each period. Declining values means that the percentage of depreciation is the same for each period, but the remaining balance (value) of the asset declines. This procedure generally leaves a balloon (larger amount) write-off during the last period.

The double-declining-balance depreciation method is procedurally the same as the declining-balance method; however, the percentage of depreciation per period is doubled. This procedure allows a business to accelerate depreciation during earlier periods of the life of the asset.

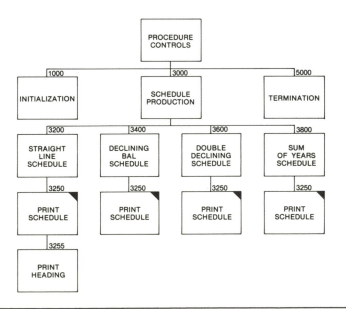

Figure 12.6 Depreciation Schedules (Hierarchy Chart)

Finally, depreciation can be calculated by the "sum-of-the-years-digits" method, which provides for the most rapid depreciation of an asset. For each period, depreciation is calculated on the original value of the asset; however, the percentage rate changes. For example, suppose an asset were estimated to last five periods. The sum-of-the-years-digits would be 15 (i.e., 1+2+3+4+5). The depreciation the first period would be 33.33 percent (5/15ths). The second period, the depreciation would be 26.67 percent (4/15ths). The remaining periods would be depreciated by 3/15ths, 2/15ths, and 1/15th of the value of the asset. Thus, the numerator for each fraction is a representation of the number of periods of *remaining* useful life, and the denominator is the sum of the different period values.

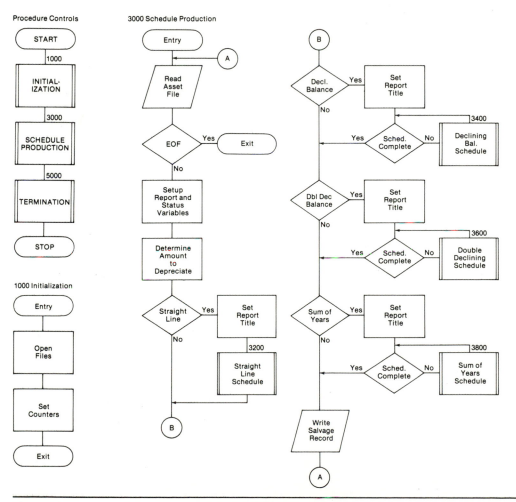

Figure 12.6 Depreciation Schedules (Module Flowcharts) *Continued*

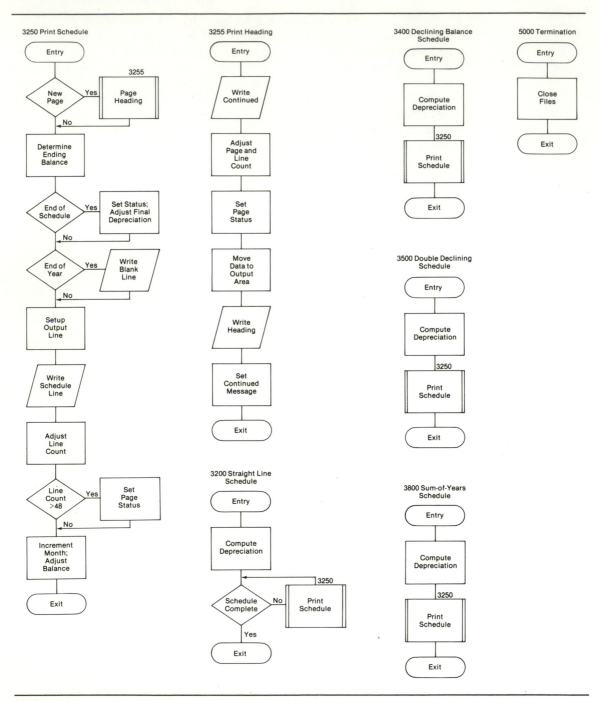

Figure 12.6 Depreciation Schedules (Module Flowcharts) *Continued*

```
|         1   1   2   2   2   3   3   4   4   4   5   5   6   6   6   7   7   8|
|  4   8  2   6   0   4   8   2   6   0   4   8   2   6   0   4   8   2   6   0|
-------------------------------------------------------------------------------
|000010 IDENTIFICATION DIVISION.                                    FIG 12.6|
|000020 PROGRAM-ID. DEPRECIATION-SCHEDULES.                         FIG 12.6|
|000030 AUTHOR. PATRICK THOMAS.                                     FIG 12.6|
|000040 DATE-WRITTEN. JANUARY 1, 1981.                              FIG 12.6|
|000050 DATE-COMPILED. JANUARY 1, 1981.                             FIG 12.6|
|000060 ENVIRONMENT DIVISION.                                       FIG 12.6|
|000070 CONFIGURATION SECTION.                                      FIG 12.6|
|000080 SOURCE-COMPUTER. IBM.                                       FIG 12.6|
|000090 OBJECT-COMPUTER. IBM.                                       FIG 12.6|
|000100 SPECIAL-NAMES. C01 IS START-SCHEDULE.                       FIG 12.6|
|000110 INPUT-OUTPUT SECTION.                                       FIG 12.6|
|000120 FILE-CONTROL.                                               FIG 12.6|
|000130     SELECT ASSET-FILE ASSIGN TO UT-S-SYSIN.                 FIG 12.6|
|000140     SELECT SCHEDULE-REPORT ASSIGN TO UT-S-SYSPRINT.         FIG 12.6|
|000150 DATA DIVISION.                                              FIG 12.6|
|000160 FILE SECTION.                                               FIG 12.6|
|000170 FD  ASSET-FILE LABEL RECORDS ARE OMITTED.                   FIG 12.6|
|000180 01  ASSET-RECORD.                                           FIG 12.6|
|000190     05 ITEM-NUMBER            PIC X(10).                    FIG 12.6|
|000200     05 ITEM-DESCRIPTION       PIC X(30).                    FIG 12.6|
|000210     05 PURCHASE-VALUE         PIC 9(07)V9(02).              FIG 12.6|
|000220     05 SALVAGE-VALUE          PIC 9(07)V9(02).              FIG 12.6|
|000230     05 PURCHASE-DATE.                                       FIG 12.6|
|000240        10 PURCHASE-MONTH       PIC 9(02).                   FIG 12.6|
|000250        10 PURCHASE-YEAR        PIC 9(02).                   FIG 12.6|
|000260     05 USEFUL-LIFE            PIC 9(03).                    FIG 12.6|
|000270     05 SCHEDULE-TYPE          PIC 9(01).                    FIG 12.6|
|000280        88 STRAIGHT-LINE VALUE IS 1.                         FIG 12.6|
|000290        88 DECLINING-BALANCE VALUE IS 2.                     FIG 12.6|
|000300        88 DOUBLE-DECLINING-BALANCE VALUE IS 3.              FIG 12.6|
|000310        88 SUM-OF-YEARS-DIGITS VALUE IS 4.                   FIG 12.6|
|000320        88 UNKNOWN-TYPE VALUE IS 0, 5 THRU 9.                FIG 12.6|
|000330     05 FILLER                 PIC X(14).                    FIG 12.6|
|000340 FD  SCHEDULE-REPORT LABEL RECORDS ARE OMITTED.              FIG 12.6|
|000350 01  SCHEDULE-LINE             PIC X(132).                   FIG 12.6|
|000360 WORKING-STORAGE SECTION.                                    FIG 12.6|
|000370 01  WORKING-STATUS-VARIABLES.                               FIG 12.6|
|000380     05 PAGE-STATUS            PIC X(10).                    FIG 12.6|
|000390        88 NEW-PAGE VALUE 'PAGE'.                            FIG 12.6|
|000400     05 SCHEDULE-STATUS        PIC X(10).                    FIG 12.6|
|000410        88 SCHEDULE-COMPLETE   VALUE 'COMPLETE'.             FIG 12.6|
|000420     05 PAGE-COUNT             PIC 9(03).                    FIG 12.6|
|000430     05 LINE-COUNT             PIC 9(02).                    FIG 12.6|
|000440     05 REMAINING-VALUE        PIC S9(07)V9(02).             FIG 12.6|
|000450     05 ENDING-VALUE           PIC S9(07)V9(02).             FIG 12.6|
|000460     05 DEPRECIATION           PIC S9(07)V9(02).             FIG 12.6|
|000470     05 DEPRECIATION-PERIOD     PIC 9(03).                   FIG 12.6|
|000480     05 ACCUMULATED-DEPR       PIC S9(07)V9(02).             FIG 12.6|
|000490 01  SCHEDULE-HEADER.                                        FIG 12.6|
|000500     05 FILLER                 PIC X(05) VALUE SPACES.       FIG 12.6|
|000510     05 ITEM-NO                PIC X(10).                    FIG 12.6|
|000520     05 FILLER                 PIC X(05) VALUE SPACES.       FIG 12.6|
|000530     05 ITEM-DESC              PIC X(30).                    FIG 12.6|
|000540     05 FILLER                 PIC X(05) VALUE SPACES.       FIG 12.6|
|000550     05 VALUE-OF-ASSET         PIC -$$,$$$,$$$.$$.           FIG 12.6|
|000560     05 FILLER                 PIC X(05) VALUE SPACES.       FIG 12.6|
|000570     05 LIFE                   PIC ZZ9.                      FIG 12.6|
|000580     05 FILLER                 PIC X(05) VALUE SPACES.       FIG 12.6|
|000590     05 SCHEDULE-TITLE         PIC X(30).                    FIG 12.6|
|000600 01  SCHEDULE-TEXT.                                          FIG 12.6|
|000610     05 FILLER                 PIC X(60) VALUE              FIG 12.6|
|000620 '     ITEM          ITEM DESCRIPTION'.                      FIG 12.6|
|000630     05 FILLER                 PIC X(25) VALUE              FIG 12.6|
|000640 '  BALANCE    LIFE'.                                        FIG 12.6|
|000650     05 FILLER                 PIC X(10) VALUE SPACES.       FIG 12.6|
|000660     05 FILLER                 PIC X(05) VALUE 'PAGE '.      FIG 12.6|
|000670     05 PAGE-NO                PIC ZZ9.                      FIG 12.6|
|000680 01  DEPR-RECORD.                                            FIG 12.6|
|000690     05 FILLER                 PIC X(05) VALUE SPACES.       FIG 12.6|
|000700     05 MONTH                  PIC 9(02).                    FIG 12.6|
```

Figure 12.6 Depreciation Schedules *Continued*

```
|          1   1   2   2   3   3   4   4   5   5   6   6   7   7   8|
|   4    8 2   6   0   4   8   2   6   0   4   8   2   6   0   4   2   6   0|
----------------------------------------------------------------------
|000710    05 FILLER                    PIC X(01) VALUE SPACES.      FIG 12.6|
|000720    05 YEAR                      PIC 9(02).                   FIG 12.6|
|000730    05 FILLER                    PIC X(05) VALUE SPACES.      FIG 12.6|
|000740    05 BEGINNING-BALANCE         PIC -$$,$$$,$$$.$$.          FIG 12.6|
|000750    05 FILLER                    PIC X(05) VALUE SPACES.      FIG 12.6|
|000760    05 DEPRECIATION-AMOUNT       PIC -$$,$$$,$$$.$$.          FIG 12.6|
|000770    05 FILLER                    PIC X(05) VALUE SPACES.      FIG 12.6|
|000780    05 ENDING-BALANCE            PIC -$$,$$$,$$$.$$.          FIG 12.6|
|000790    05 FILLER                    PIC X(05) VALUE SPACES.      FIG 12.6|
|000800    05 ACCUM-DEPRECIATION        PIC -$$,$$$,$$$.$$.          FIG 12.6|
|000810 01 COLUMN-HEADING.                                          FIG 12.6|
|000820    05 FILLER                    PIC X(55) VALUE             FIG 12.6|
|000830 *  MONTH YEAR     BEG. BALANCE                   DEPR*.      FIG 12.6|
|000840    05 FILLER                    PIC X(40) VALUE             FIG 12.6|
|000850 *END. BALANCE     ACCUM. DEPRECIATION*.                     FIG 12.6|
|000860 01 SALVAGE-RECORD.                                          FIG 12.6|
|000870    05 FILLER                    PIC X(52) VALUE             FIG 12.6|
|000880 *      ESTIMATED SALVAGE VALUE AFTER DEPRECIATION*.         FIG 12.6|
|000890    05 SALVAGE                   PIC -$$$,$$$,$$$.99.         FIG 12.6|
|000900 01 CONTINUED-LINE.                                          FIG 12.6|
|000910    05 FILLER                    PIC X(40).                  FIG 12.6|
|000920 PROCEDURE DIVISION.                                         FIG 12.6|
|000930 PROCEDURE-CONTROLS SECTION.                                 FIG 12.6|
|000940    PERFORM 1000-INITIALIZATION.                             FIG 12.6|
|000950    PERFORM 3000-SCHEDULE-PRODUCTION.                        FIG 12.6|
|000960    PERFORM 5000-TERMINATION.                                FIG 12.6|
|000970    STOP RUN.                                                FIG 12.6|
|000980 1000-INITIALIZATION SECTION.                                FIG 12.6|
|000990    OPEN INPUT ASSET-FILE, OUTPUT SCHEDULE-REPORT.           FIG 12.6|
|001000    MOVE 0 TO PAGE-COUNT, LINE-COUNT.                        FIG 12.6|

|001010 3000-SCHEDULE-PRODUCTION SECTION.                           FIG 12.6|
|001020    READ ASSET-FILE AT END                                  FIG 12.6|
|001030       GO TO 3999-EXIT.                                     FIG 12.6|
|001040    MOVE *PRODUCE* TO SCHEDULE-STATUS.                       FIG 12.6|
|001050    MOVE SPACES TO CONTINUED-LINE.                           FIG 12.6|
|001060    MOVE PURCHASE-MONTH TO MONTH.                            FIG 12.6|
|001070    MOVE PURCHASE-YEAR TO YEAR.                              FIG 12.6|
|001080    MOVE *PAGE* TO PAGE-STATUS.                              FIG 12.6|
|001090    MOVE 0 TO ACCUMULATED-DEPR.                              FIG 12.6|
|001100    SUBTRACT SALVAGE-VALUE FROM PURCHASE-VALUE               FIG 12.6|
|001110       GIVING REMAINING-VALUE.                              FIG 12.6|
|001120    IF STRAIGHT-LINE                                         FIG 12.6|
|001130       MOVE *STRAIGHT LINE* TO SCHEDULE-TITLE                FIG 12.6|
|001140       PERFORM 3200-STRAIGHT-LINE-SCHEDULE.                  FIG 12.6|
|001150    IF DECLINING-BALANCE                                     FIG 12.6|
|001160       MOVE *DECLINING BALANCE* TO SCHEDULE-TITLE            FIG 12.6|
|001170       PERFORM 3400-DECLINING-BAL-SCHEDULE                   FIG 12.6|
|001180          VARYING DEPRECIATION-PERIOD FROM 1 BY 1           FIG 12.6|
|001190          UNTIL SCHEDULE-COMPLETE.                          FIG 12.6|
|001200    IF DOUBLE-DECLINING-BALANCE                              FIG 12.6|
|001210       MOVE *DOUBLE DECLINING BALANCE* TO SCHEDULE-TITLE     FIG 12.6|
|001220       PERFORM 3600-DOUBLE-DECLINING-SCHEDULE                FIG 12.6|
|001230          VARYING DEPRECIATION-PERIOD FROM 1 BY 1           FIG 12.6|
|001240          UNTIL SCHEDULE-COMPLETE.                          FIG 12.6|
|001250    IF SUM-OF-YEARS-DIGITS                                   FIG 12.6|
|001260       MOVE *SUM OF THE YEARS* TO SCHEDULE-TITLE             FIG 12.6|
|001270       PERFORM 3800-SUM-OF-YEARS-SCHEDULE                    FIG 12.6|
|001280          VARYING DEPRECIATION-PERIOD FROM 1 BY 1           FIG 12.6|
|001290          UNTIL SCHEDULE-COMPLETE.                          FIG 12.6|
|001300    MOVE SALVAGE-VALUE TO SALVAGE.                           FIG 12.6|
|001310    WRITE SCHEDULE-LINE FROM SALVAGE-RECORD AFTER 2 LINES.   FIG 12.6|
|001320    GO TO 3000-SCHEDULE-PRODUCTION.                          FIG 12.6|
|001330 3999-EXIT.                                                  FIG 12.6|
|001340    EXIT.                                                    FIG 12.6|
|001350 3200-STRAIGHT-LINE-SCHEDULE SECTION.                        FIG 12.6|
|001360       COMPUTE DEPRECIATION ROUNDED =                        FIG 12.6|
|001370          REMAINING-VALUE * (1 / USEFUL-LIFE)               FIG 12.6|
|001380       PERFORM 3250-PRINT-SCHEDULE                           FIG 12.6|
|001390          VARYING DEPRECIATION-PERIOD FROM 1 BY 1           FIG 12.6|
|001400          UNTIL SCHEDULE-COMPLETE.                          FIG 12.6|
|001410 3250-PRINT-SCHEDULE SECTION.                                FIG 12.6|
|001420    IF NEW-PAGE                                              FIG 12.6|
```

Figure 12.6 Depreciation Schedules *Continued*

```
|              1   1   2   2   2   3   3   4   4   4   5   5   6   6   6   7   7   8|
|   4    8     2   6   0   4   8   2   6   0   4   8   2   6   0   4   8   2   6   0|
----------------------------------------------------------------------------------
|001430            PERFORM 3255-PRINT-HEADING.                               FIG 12.6|
|001440        SUBTRACT DEPRECIATION FROM REMAINING-VALUE                    FIG 12.6|
|001450            GIVING ENDING-VALUE.                                      FIG 12.6|
|001460        IF DEPRECIATION-PERIOD = USEFUL-LIFE                          FIG 12.6|
|001470            MOVE 'COMPLETE' TO SCHEDULE-STATUS                        FIG 12.6|
|001480            ADD ENDING-VALUE TO DEPRECIATION                         FIG 12.6|
|001490            MOVE 0 TO ENDING-VALUE.                                   FIG 12.6|
|001500        IF MONTH > 12                                                 FIG 12.6|
|001510            MOVE 1 TO MONTH                                           FIG 12.6|
|001520            ADD 1 TO YEAR                                             FIG 12.6|
|001530            MOVE SPACES TO SCHEDULE-LINE                              FIG 12.6|
|001540            WRITE SCHEDULE-LINE AFTER 1 LINES.                        FIG 12.6|
|001550        MOVE REMAINING-VALUE TO BEGINNING-BALANCE.                    FIG 12.6|
|001560        MOVE DEPRECIATION TO DEPRECIATION-AMOUNT.                     FIG 12.6|
|001570        MOVE ENDING-VALUE TO ENDING-BALANCE.                         FIG 12.6|
|001580        ADD DEPRECIATION TO ACCUMULATED-DEPR.                         FIG 12.6|
|001590        MOVE ACCUMULATED-DEPR TO ACCUM-DEPRECIATION.                  FIG 12.6|
|001600        WRITE SCHEDULE-LINE FROM DEPR-RECORD AFTER ADVANCING 1 LINES.FIG 12.6|
|001610        ADD 1 TO LINE-COUNT.                                          FIG 12.6|
|001620        IF LINE-COUNT > 48                                            FIG 12.6|
|001630            MOVE 'PAGE' TO PAGE-STATUS.                               FIG 12.6|
|001640        ADD 1 TO MONTH.                                               FIG 12.6|
|001650        MOVE ENDING-VALUE TO REMAINING-VALUE.                         FIG 12.6|
|001660 3400-DECLINING-BAL-SCHEDULE SECTION.                                 FIG 12.6|
|001670        COMPUTE DEPRECIATION ROUNDED =                                FIG 12.6|
|001680            REMAINING-VALUE * (1 / USEFUL-LIFE).                      FIG 12.6|
|001690        PERFORM 3250-PRINT-SCHEDULE.                                  FIG 12.6|
|001700 3600-DOUBLE-DECLINING-SCHEDULE SECTION.                              FIG 12.6|
|001710        COMPUTE DEPRECIATION ROUNDED =                                FIG 12.6|
|001720            REMAINING-VALUE * (2 / USEFUL-LIFE).                      FIG 12.6|
|001730        PERFORM 3250-PRINT-SCHEDULE.                                  FIG 12.6|
|001740 3800-SUM-OF-YEARS-SCHEDULE SECTION.                                  FIG 12.6|
|001750        COMPUTE DEPRECIATION ROUNDED =                                FIG 12.6|
|001760            (PURCHASE-VALUE - SALVAGE-VALUE) *                        FIG 12.6|
|001770            (USEFUL-LIFE - DEPRECIATION-PERIOD + 1) /                 FIG 12.6|
|001780            ((USEFUL-LIFE * (USEFUL-LIFE + 1)) / 2).                  FIG 12.6|
|001790        PERFORM 3250-PRINT-SCHEDULE.                                  FIG 12.6|
|001800 3255-PRINT-HEADING SECTION.                                          FIG 12.6|
|001810        WRITE SCHEDULE-LINE FROM CONTINUED-LINE AFTER 2 LINES.        FIG 12.6|
|001820        ADD 1 TO PAGE-COUNT.                                          FIG 12.6|
|001830        MOVE 0 TO LINE-COUNT.                                         FIG 12.6|
|001840        MOVE PAGE-COUNT TO PAGE-NO.                                   FIG 12.6|
|001850        MOVE 'NO PAGE' TO PAGE-STATUS.                                FIG 12.6|
|001860        WRITE SCHEDULE-LINE FROM SCHEDULE-TEXT                        FIG 12.6|
|001870            AFTER START-SCHEDULE.                                     FIG 12.6|
|001880        MOVE 0 TO LINE-COUNT.                                         FIG 12.6|
|001890        MOVE ITEM-NUMBER TO ITEM-NO.                                  FIG 12.6|
|001900        MOVE ITEM-DESCRIPTION TO ITEM-DESC.                           FIG 12.6|
|001910        MOVE PURCHASE-VALUE TO VALUE-OF-ASSET.                        FIG 12.6|
|001920        MOVE USEFUL-LIFE TO LIFE.                                     FIG 12.6|
|001930        WRITE SCHEDULE-LINE FROM SCHEDULE-HEADER AFTER 1 LINES.       FIG 12.6|
|001940        WRITE SCHEDULE-LINE FROM COLUMN-HEADING AFTER 2 LINES.        FIG 12.6|
|001950        MOVE SPACES TO SCHEDULE-LINE.                                 FIG 12.6|
|001960        WRITE SCHEDULE-LINE AFTER ADVANCING 1 LINES.                  FIG 12.6|
|001970        MOVE ' ***** CONTINUED ON NEXT PAGE *****' TO CONTINUED-LINE.FIG 12.6|
|001980 5000-TERMINATION SECTION.                                            FIG 12.6|
|001990        CLOSE ASSET-FILE, SCHEDULE-REPORT.                            FIG 12.6|
```

Figure 12.6 Depreciation Schedules *Continued*

```
|       |        1         2         3         4         5         6         7         8| FIGURE |
|RECORD |1234567890123456789012345678901234567890123456789012345678901234567890| NUMBER |
----------------------------------------------------------------------------------------------
|   1|      12345TEST ASSET DESC          001000000000000000001800121        |FIG 12.6|
|   2|ABCDE12345TEST ASSET DESCRIPTION    000253129000010000004800362        |FIG 12.6|
|   3|R2-X1147-3MILLING MACHINE           004786690000070000010790603        |FIG 12.6|
|   4|   T28-127CENTRAL WAREHOUSE BUILDING 006130000000000000006811204       |FIG 12.6|
```

Figure 12.6 Depreciation Schedules (Data) *Continued*

ITEM	ITEM DESCRIPTION		BALANCE	LIFE		PAGE	1
12345	TEST ASSET DESC		$10,000.00	12	STRAIGHT LINE		

MONTH YEAR	BEG. BALANCE	DEPR	END. BALANCE	ACCUM. DEPRECIATION
01 80	$10,000.00	$830.00	$9,170.00	$830.00
02 80	$9,170.00	$830.00	$8,340.00	$1,660.00
03 80	$8,340.00	$830.00	$7,510.00	$2,490.00
04 80	$7,510.00	$830.00	$6,680.00	$3,320.00
05 80	$6,680.00	$830.00	$5,850.00	$4,150.00
06 80	$5,850.00	$830.00	$5,020.00	$4,980.00
07 80	$5,020.00	$830.00	$4,190.00	$5,810.00
08 80	$4,190.00	$830.00	$3,360.00	$6,640.00
09 80	$3,360.00	$830.00	$2,530.00	$7,470.00
10 80	$2,530.00	$830.00	$1,700.00	$8,300.00
11 80	$1,700.00	$830.00	$870.00	$9,130.00
12 80	$870.00	$870.00		$10,000.00

ESTIMATED SALVAGE VALUE AFTER DEPRECIATION $.00

ITEM	ITEM DESCRIPTION		BALANCE	LIFE		PAGE	2
ABCDE12345	TEST ASSET DESCRIPTION		$2,531.29	36	DECLINING BALANCE		

MONTH YEAR	BEG. BALANCE	DEPR	END. BALANCE	ACCUM. DEPRECIATION
04 80	$1,531.29	$41.34	$1,489.95	$41.34
05 80	$1,489.95	$40.23	$1,449.72	$81.57
06 80	$1,449.72	$39.14	$1,410.58	$120.71
07 80	$1,410.58	$38.09	$1,372.49	$158.80
08 80	$1,372.49	$37.06	$1,335.43	$195.86
09 80	$1,335.43	$36.06	$1,299.37	$231.92
10 80	$1,299.37	$35.08	$1,264.29	$267.00
11 80	$1,264.29	$34.14	$1,230.15	$301.14
12 80	$1,230.15	$33.21	$1,196.94	$334.35
01 81	$1,196.94	$32.32	$1,164.62	$366.67
02 81	$1,164.62	$31.44	$1,133.18	$398.11
03 81	$1,133.18	$30.60	$1,102.58	$428.71
04 81	$1,102.58	$29.77	$1,072.81	$458.48
05 81	$1,072.81	$28.97	$1,043.84	$487.45
06 81	$1,043.84	$28.18	$1,015.66	$515.63
07 81	$1,015.66	$27.42	$988.24	$543.05
08 81	$988.24	$26.68	$961.56	$569.73
09 81	$961.56	$25.96	$935.60	$595.69
10 81	$935.60	$25.26	$910.34	$620.95
11 81	$910.34	$24.58	$885.76	$645.53
12 81	$885.76	$23.92	$861.84	$669.45
01 82	$861.84	$23.27	$838.57	$692.72
02 82	$838.57	$22.64	$815.93	$715.36
03 82	$815.93	$22.03	$793.90	$737.39
04 82	$793.90	$21.44	$772.46	$758.83
05 82	$772.46	$20.86	$751.60	$779.69
06 82	$751.60	$20.29	$731.31	$799.98
07 82	$731.31	$19.75	$711.56	$819.73
08 82	$711.56	$19.21	$692.35	$838.94
09 82	$692.35	$18.69	$673.66	$857.63
10 82	$673.66	$18.19	$655.47	$875.82
11 82	$655.47	$17.70	$637.77	$893.52
12 82	$637.77	$17.22	$620.55	$910.74
01 83	$620.55	$16.75	$603.80	$927.49
02 83	$603.80	$16.30	$587.50	$943.79
03 83	$587.50	$587.50		$1,531.29

ESTIMATED SALVAGE VALUE AFTER DEPRECIATION $1,000.00

Figure 12.6 Depreciation Schedules (Output) *Continued*

ITEM R2-X1147-3	ITEM DESCRIPTION MILLING MACHINE		BALANCE $47,866.90	LIFE 60	PAGE 3 DOUBLE DECLINING BALANCE
MONTH YEAR	BEG. BALANCE	DEPR	END. BALANCE	ACCUM. DEPRECIATION	
10 79	$40,866.90	$1,348.61	$39,518.29	$1,348.61	
11 79	$39,518.29	$1,304.10	$38,214.19	$2,652.71	
12 79	$38,214.19	$1,261.07	$36,953.12	$3,913.78	
01 80	$36,953.12	$1,219.45	$35,733.67	$5,133.23	
02 80	$35,733.67	$1,179.21	$34,554.46	$6,312.44	
03 80	$34,554.46	$1,140.30	$33,414.16	$7,452.74	
04 80	$33,414.16	$1,102.67	$32,311.49	$8,555.41	
05 80	$32,311.49	$1,066.28	$31,245.21	$9,621.69	
06 80	$31,245.21	$1,031.09	$30,214.12	$10,652.78	
07 80	$30,214.12	$997.07	$29,217.05	$11,649.85	
08 80	$29,217.05	$964.16	$28,252.89	$12,614.01	
09 80	$28,252.89	$932.35	$27,320.54	$13,546.36	
10 80	$27,320.54	$901.58	$26,418.96	$14,447.94	
11 80	$26,418.96	$871.83	$25,547.13	$15,319.77	
12 80	$25,547.13	$843.06	$24,704.07	$16,162.83	
01 81	$24,704.07	$815.23	$23,888.84	$16,978.06	
02 81	$23,888.84	$788.33	$23,100.51	$17,766.39	
03 81	$23,100.51	$762.32	$22,338.19	$18,528.71	
04 81	$22,338.19	$737.16	$21,601.03	$19,265.87	
05 81	$21,601.03	$712.83	$20,888.20	$19,978.70	
06 81	$20,888.20	$689.31	$20,198.89	$20,668.01	
07 81	$20,198.89	$666.56	$19,532.33	$21,334.57	
08 81	$19,532.33	$644.57	$18,887.76	$21,979.14	
09 81	$18,887.76	$623.30	$18,264.46	$22,602.44	
10 81	$18,264.46	$602.73	$17,661.73	$23,205.17	
11 81	$17,661.73	$582.84	$17,078.89	$23,788.01	
12 81	$17,078.89	$563.60	$16,515.29	$24,351.61	
01 82	$16,515.29	$545.00	$15,970.29	$24,896.61	
02 82	$15,970.29	$527.02	$15,443.27	$25,423.63	
03 82	$15,443.27	$509.63	$14,933.64	$25,933.26	
04 82	$14,933.64	$492.81	$14,440.83	$26,426.07	
05 82	$14,440.83	$476.55	$13,964.28	$26,902.62	
06 82	$13,964.28	$460.82	$13,503.46	$27,363.44	
07 82	$13,503.46	$445.61	$13,057.85	$27,809.05	
08 82	$13,057.85	$430.91	$12,626.94	$28,239.96	
09 82	$12,626.94	$416.69	$12,210.25	$28,656.65	
10 82	$12,210.25	$402.94	$11,807.31	$29,059.59	
11 82	$11,807.31	$389.64	$11,417.67	$29,449.23	
12 82	$11,417.67	$376.78	$11,040.89	$29,826.01	
01 83	$11,040.89	$364.35	$10,676.54	$30,190.36	
02 83	$10,676.54	$352.33	$10,324.21	$30,542.69	
03 83	$10,324.21	$340.70	$9,983.51	$30,883.39	
04 83	$9,983.51	$329.46	$9,654.05	$31,212.85	
05 83	$9,654.05	$318.58	$9,335.47	$31,531.43	
06 83	$9,335.47	$308.07	$9,027.40	$31,839.50	
07 83	$9,027.40	$297.90	$8,729.50	$32,137.40	
08 83	$8,729.50	$288.07	$8,441.43	$32,425.47	
09 83	$8,441.43	$278.57	$8,162.86	$32,704.04	
10 83	$8,162.86	$269.37	$7,893.49	$32,973.41	

***** CONTINUED ON NEXT PAGE *****

Figure 12.6 Depreciation Schedules (Output) *Continued*

ITEM	ITEM DESCRIPTION		BALANCE	LIFE	PAGE 4
R2-X1147-3	MILLING MACHINE		$47,866.90	60	DOUBLE DECLINING BALANCE

MONTH YEAR	BEG. BALANCE	DEPR	END. BALANCE	ACCUM. DEPRECIATION
11 83	$7,893.49	$260.49	$7,633.00	$33,233.90
12 83	$7,633.00	$251.89	$7,381.11	$33,485.79
01 84	$7,381.11	$243.58	$7,137.53	$33,729.37
02 84	$7,137.53	$235.54	$6,901.99	$33,964.91
03 84	$6,901.99	$227.77	$6,674.22	$34,192.68
04 84	$6,674.22	$220.25	$6,453.97	$34,412.93
05 84	$6,453.97	$212.98	$6,240.99	$34,625.91
06 84	$6,240.99	$205.95	$6,035.04	$34,831.86
07 84	$6,035.04	$199.16	$5,835.98	$35,031.02
08 84	$5,835.89	$192.58	$5,643.30	$35,223.60
09 84	$5,643.30	$5,643.30		$40,866.90

ESTIMATED SALVAGE VALUE AFTER DEPRECIATION $7,000.00

ITEM	ITEM DESCRIPTION		BALANCE	LIFE	PAGE 5
T28-127	CENTRAL WAREHOUSE BUILDING		$61,300.00	120	SUM OF THE YEARS

MONTH YEAR	BEG. BALANCE	DEPR	END. BALANCE	ACCUM. DEPRECIATION
06 81	$61,300.00	$1,013.22	$60,286.78	$1,013.22
07 81	$60,286.78	$1,004.78	$59,282.00	$2,018.00
08 81	$59,282.00	$996.34	$58,285.66	$3,014.34
09 81	$58,285.66	$987.89	$57,297.77	$4,002.23
10 81	$57,297.77	$979.45	$56,318.32	$4,981.68
11 81	$56,318.32	$971.01	$55,347.31	$5,952.69
12 81	$55,347.31	$962.56	$54,384.75	$6,915.25
01 82	$54,384.75	$954.12	$53,430.63	$7,869.37
02 82	$53,430.63	$945.67	$52,484.96	$8,815.04
03 82	$52,484.96	$937.23	$51,547.73	$9,752.27
04 82	$51,547.73	$928.79	$50,618.94	$10,681.06
05 82	$50,618.94	$920.34	$49,698.60	$11,601.40
06 82	$49,698.60	$911.90	$48,786.70	$12,513.30
07 82	$48,786.70	$903.46	$47,883.24	$13,416.76
08 82	$47,883.24	$895.01	$46,988.23	$14,311.77
09 82	$46,988.23	$886.57	$46,101.66	$15,198.34
10 82	$46,101.66	$878.13	$45,223.53	$16,076.47
11 82	$45,223.53	$869.68	$44,353.85	$16,946.15
12 82	$44,353.85	$861.24	$43,492.61	$17,807.39
01 83	$43,492.61	$852.80	$42,639.81	$18,660.19
02 83	$42,639.81	$844.35	$41,795.46	$19,504.54
03 83	$41,795.46	$835.91	$40,959.55	$20,340.45
04 83	$40,959.55	$827.47	$40,132.08	$21,167.92
05 83	$40,132.08	$819.02	$39,313.06	$21,986.94
06 83	$39,313.06	$810.58	$38,502.48	$22,797.52
07 83	$38,502.48	$802.13	$37,700.35	$23,599.65
08 83	$37,700.35	$793.69	$36,906.66	$24,393.34
09 83	$36,906.66	$785.25	$36,121.41	$25,178.59
10 83	$36,121.41	$776.80	$35,344.61	$25,955.39
11 83	$35,344.61	$768.36	$34,576.25	$26,723.75
12 83	$34,576.25	$759.92	$33,816.33	$27,483.67
01 84	$33,816.33	$751.47	$33,064.86	$28,235.14
02 84	$33,064.86	$743.03	$32,321.83	$28,978.17
03 84	$32,321.83	$734.59	$31,587.24	$29,712.76
04 84	$31,587.24	$726.14	$30,861.10	$30,438.90
05 84	$30,861.10	$717.70	$30,143.40	$31,156.60
06 84	$30,143.40	$709.26	$29,434.14	$31,865.86
07 84	$29,434.14	$700.81	$28,733.33	$32,566.67
08 84	$28,733.33	$692.37	$28,040.96	$33,259.04
09 84	$28,040.96	$683.93	$27,357.03	$33,942.97
10 84	$27,357.03	$675.48	$26,681.55	$34,618.45
11 84	$26,681.55	$667.04	$26,014.51	$35,285.49
12 84	$26,014.51	$658.60	$25,355.91	$35,944.09
01 85	$25,355.91	$650.15	$24,705.76	$36,594.24
02 85	$24,705.76	$641.71	$24,064.05	$37,235.95
03 85	$24,064.05	$633.26	$23,430.79	$37,869.21
04 85	$23,430.79	$624.82	$22,805.97	$38,494.03
05 85	$22,805.97	$616.38	$22,189.59	$39,110.41
06 85	$22,189.59	$607.93	$21,581.66	$39,718.34

***** CONTINUED ON NEXT PAGE *****

Figure 12.6 Depreciation Schedules (Output) *Continued*

ITEM T28-127	ITEM DESCRIPTION CENTRAL WAREHOUSE BUILDING		BALANCE $61,300.00	LIFE 120 SUM OF THE YEARS	PAGE 6
MONTH YEAR	BEG. BALANCE	DEPR	END. BALANCE	ACCUM. DEPRECIATION	
07 85	$21,581.66	$599.49	$20,982.17	$40,317.83	
08 85	$20,982.17	$591.05	$20,391.12	$40,908.88	
09 85	$20,391.12	$582.60	$19,808.52	$41,491.48	
10 85	$19,808.52	$574.16	$19,234.36	$42,065.64	
11 85	$19,234.36	$565.72	$18,668.64	$42,631.36	
12 85	$18,668.64	$557.27	$18,111.37	$43,188.63	
01 86	$18,111.37	$548.83	$17,562.54	$43,737.46	
02 86	$17,562.54	$540.39	$17,022.15	$44,277.85	
03 86	$17,022.15	$531.94	$16,490.21	$44,809.79	
04 86	$16,490.21	$523.50	$15,966.71	$45,333.29	
05 86	$15,966.71	$515.06	$15,451.65	$45,848.35	
06 86	$15,451.65	$506.61	$14,945.04	$46,354.96	
07 86	$14,945.04	$498.17	$14,446.87	$46,853.13	
08 86	$14,446.87	$489.72	$13,957.15	$47,342.85	
09 86	$13,957.15	$481.28	$13,475.87	$47,824.13	
10 86	$13,475.87	$472.84	$13,003.03	$48,296.97	
11 86	$13,003.03	$464.39	$12,538.64	$48,761.36	
12 86	$12,538.64	$455.95	$12,082.69	$49,217.31	
01 87	$12,082.69	$447.51	$11,635.18	$49,664.82	
02 87	$11,635.18	$439.06	$11,196.12	$50,103.88	
03 87	$11,196.12	$430.62	$10,765.50	$50,534.50	
04 87	$10,765.50	$422.18	$10,343.32	$50,956.68	
05 87	$10,343.32	$413.73	$9,929.59	$51,370.41	
06 87	$9,929.59	$405.29	$9,524.30	$51,775.70	
07 87	$9,524.30	$396.95	$9,127.45	$52,172.55	
08 87	$9,127.45	$388.40	$8,739.05	$52,560.95	
09 87	$8,739.05	$379.96	$8,359.09	$52,940.91	
10 87	$8,359.09	$371.52	$7,987.57	$53,312.43	
11 87	$7,987.57	$363.07	$7,624.50	$53,675.50	
12 87	$7,624.50	$354.63	$7,269.87	$54,030.13	
01 88	$7,269.87	$346.18	$6,923.69	$54,376.31	
02 88	$6,923.69	$337.74	$6,585.95	$54,714.05	
03 88	$6,585.95	$329.30	$6,256.65	$55,043.35	
04 88	$6,256.65	$320.85	$5,935.80	$55,364.20	
05 88	$5,935.80	$312.41	$5,623.39	$55,676.61	
06 88	$5,623.39	$303.97	$5,319.42	$55,980.58	
07 88	$5,319.42	$295.52	$5,023.90	$56,276.10	
08 88	$5,023.90	$287.08	$4,736.82	$56,563.18	
09 88	$4,736.82	$278.64	$4,458.18	$56,841.82	
10 88	$4,458.18	$270.19	$4,187.99	$57,112.01	
11 88	$4,187.99	$261.75	$3,926.24	$57,373.76	
12 88	$3,926.24	$253.31	$3,672.93	$57,627.07	
01 89	$3,672.93	$244.86	$3,428.07	$57,871.93	
02 89	$3,428.07	$236.42	$3,191.65	$58,108.35	
03 89	$3,191.65	$227.98	$2,963.67	$58,336.33	
04 89	$2,963.67	$219.53	$2,744.14	$58,555.86	
05 89	$2,744.14	$211.09	$2,533.05	$58,766.95	
06 89	$2,533.05	$202.64	$2,330.41	$58,969.59	
07 89	$2,330.41	$194.20	$2,136.21	$59,163.79	

***** CONTINUED ON NEXT PAGE *****

Figure 12.6 Depreciation Schedules (Output) *Continued*

ITEM T28-127	ITEM DESCRIPTION CENTRAL WAREHOUSE BUILDING		BALANCE $61,300.00	LIFE 120	SUM OF THE YEARS	PAGE 7

MONTH YEAR	BEG. BALANCE	DEPR	END. BALANCE	ACCUM. DEPRECIATION
08 89	$2,136.21	$135.76	$1,950.45	$59,349.55
09 89	$1,950.45	$177.31	$1,773.14	$59,526.86
10 89	$1,773.14	$168.87	$1,604.27	$59,695.73
11 89	$1,604.27	$160.43	$1,443.84	$59,856.16
12 89	$1,443.84	$151.98	$1,291.86	$60,008.14
01 90	$1,291.86	$143.54	$1,148.32	$60,151.68
02 90	$1,148.32	$135.10	$1,013.22	$60,286.78
03 90	$1,013.22	$126.65	$886.57	$60,413.43
04 90	$886.57	$118.21	$768.36	$60,531.64
05 90	$768.36	$109.77	$658.59	$60,641.41
06 90	$658.59	$101.32	$557.27	$60,742.73
07 90	$557.27	$92.88	$464.39	$60,835.61
08 90	$464.39	$84.44	$379.95	$60,920.05
09 90	$379.95	$75.99	$303.96	$60,996.04
10 90	$303.96	$67.55	$236.41	$61,063.59
11 90	$236.41	$59.10	$177.31	$61,122.69
12 90	$177.31	$50.66	$126.65	$61,173.35
01 91	$126.65	$42.22	$84.43	$61,215.57
02 91	$84.43	$33.77	$50.66	$61,249.34
03 91	$50.66	$25.33	$25.33	$61,274.67
04 91	$25.33	$16.89	$8.44	$61,291.56
05 91	$8.44	$8.44		$61,300.00

ESTIMATED SALVAGE VALUE AFTER DEPRECIATION $.00

Figure 12.6 Depreciation Schedules (Output) *Continued*

Summary

In this chapter the last two versions of the PERFORM statement have been discussed. Although the simple PERFORM and PERFORM/UNTIL statements are more often used in general structures in the PROCEDURE DIVISION, the PERFORM/TIMES and the PERFORM/VARYING are extremely useful when tackling certain problems (e.g., counting activities and table manipulation—to be discussed in Chapters 13 and 14).

The PERFORM/TIMES statement provides the programmer with the means to invoke a procedure (or set of procedures) a specified number of times. An identifier or a literal indicates the number of times the procedure is to be executed. If an identifier is modified during the execution of the procedure, the modification of the identifier in no way affects that execution of the procedure.

The PERFORM/VARYING statement also provides the programmer with the means to invoke a procedure repetitively. Unlike the PERFORM/TIMES statement, however, the PERFORM/VARYING has a built-in "counting" feature. That is, the statement is capable of initializing, incrementing, and testing the value of an identifier. In addition, the condition associated with this statement does not necessarily have to reference the "index" identifier being initiated and incremented. The PERFORM/VARYING statement can also initialize, increment, and test an associated condition for up to three semi-independent identifiers in a "nested" arrangement.

Notes on Programming Style

Although the processes involved in the PERFORM/VARYING and PERFORM/TIMES statements are similar to those of the simple PERFORM and PERFORM/UNTIL statements, you should be aware of several considerations in the use of these statements. First, the PERFORM/VARYING statement provides for the testing of conditions much like the PERFORM/UNTIL. One should be extremely careful in the construction of the condition to be tested in both of these statements. It is conceivable, even likely, that you will construct a condition that will never be true. For example, the statement

```
PERFORM PROCEDURE-1 VARYING I FROM 1 BY 2 UNTIL I = 10.
```

will never find a true condition, i.e., I will equal 1, 3, 5, 7, 9, 11, 13, and so forth, but never 10. Thus, avoid testing for the equality of the varied identifier in a PERFORM/VARYING statement whenever possible. Also, the condition in the PERFORM/VARYING statement does not necessarily have anything to do with the varied identifier (although this is frequently the case). For example, the statement

```
PERFORM READ-DATA
        VARYING ITEM-COUNT FROM 1 BY 1 UNTIL FILE-STATUS = 'DONE'.
```

could be used to perform two functions—execute a procedure until all data from a file have been processed *and* count the number of items read. (The count of the number of items read will be off by one since ITEM-COUNT is incremented *before* the condition is tested during the execution of READ-DATA.) Finally, do not code yourself into a corner. That is, when structuring a PERFORM/VARYING statement, carefully examine the problem requirements. Do not automatically assume the initial value, incremental value, or perhaps termination condition will be based on a static (numeric literal) value. Because program generalization is typically preferable, these values are not recorded as numeric literals, but rather as identifiers, which may be modified in value.

Questions

Below fill in the blank(s) with the appropriate word, words, or phrases.

1. In total there are _____ (number) different forms of the PERFORM statement.

2. The version of the PERFORM statement which permits a specified repetition of a procedure is referred to as the _____ statement.

3. The number of times a procedure is to be executed may be specified in the PERFORM/TIMES statement by either a(n) _____ or a(n) _____ .

4. The PERFORM statement that includes a "built-in" counter is referred to as the _____ statement.

5. The PERFORM/VARYING permits the individual modification of _____ (number) identifiers.

6. After the procedure has been invoked in a PERFORM/VARYING statement, the identifier is incremented _____ (before/after) the specified condition is tested.

7. The statement which may be used to represent a common end point for several procedures is called the _____ statement.

Answer the following questions by circling either "T" for True or "F" for False.

T F 8. COBOL does not permit the mixing of different forms of the PERFORM statement in a single procedure.

T F 9. COBOL permits a PERFORM statement to invoke a procedure containing another PERFORM statement.

T F 10. When an identifier is specified in the PERFORM/TIMES statement, it is possible to modify that identifier within the procedure being invoked.

T F 11. When an identifier is specified in the PERFORM/TIMES statement, it is possible to modify that identifier within the procedure being invoked and thereby alter the number of times the procedure is executed.

T F 12. When an identifier is specified in the PERFORM/TIMES statement and the value of the identifier is zero, the procedure is executed only once.

T F 13. An identifier specified in the PERFORM/TIMES statement may not contain a negative value.

T F 14. In the PERFORM/VARYING statement, an incremental value of one is always assumed.

T F 15. In the PERFORM/VARYING statement the incremental value must always be positive.

T F 16. In the PERFORM/VARYING statement, the condition used to terminate the perform activity must reference the identifier being incremented.

T F 17. The condition specified in a PERFORM/VARYING must be a relational condition.

T F 18. The same identifier may be incremented by both a VARYING phrase and an AFTER option in a PERFORM/VARYING statement.

T F 19. When a PERFORM/VARYING statement contains an AFTER option, only one condition may be specified.

T F 20. When a PERFORM/VARYING statement contains an AFTER option, the condition associated with the VARYING phrase is used to determine when the procedure has been completed.

T F 21. Compound conditions may be associated with a PERFORM/VARYING statement.

T F 22. If a relational condition is specified for the VARYING phrase of the PERFORM/VARYING statement, a relational condition must be specified for the first AFTER option, if used.

T F 23. A PERFORM/VARYING statement may invoke a procedure that contains another PERFORM/VARYING statement.

T F 24. A PERFORM/VARYING statement may invoke a procedure that contains another PERFORM/VARYING statement where both statements increment the same identifier.

T F 25. The PERFORM/VARYING statement may use the reserved word AFTER as a substitute for the reserved word VARYING.

T F 26. It is possible to encounter a PERFORM/VARYING statement and *not* execute the specified procedure.

T F 27. The EXIT statement must be coded in a single-statement paragraph, if used.

Exercises

1. Below are several situations in which the PERFORM/TIMES statement is used. Record the paragraph names encountered during the execution of each procedure. If a paragraph is encountered by "fall through," record this situation adjacent to the paragraph name.

a)
```
    PERFORM PARA-1
    STOP RUN.
PARA-1
    PERFORM PARA-2 5 TIMES.
PARA-2.
```

b)
```
    PERFORM PARA-1 THRU PARA-2 3 TIMES.
    STOP RUN.
PARA-1.

PARA-2.
    PERFORM PARA-3 2 TIMES.
PARA-3.
```

c)
```
    MOVE 4 TO NO-OF.
    PERFORM PARA-1 NO-OF TIMES.
    PERFORM PARA-2 NO-OF TIMES.
    STOP RUN.
PARA-1.
    MOVE 2 to NO-OF.

PARA-2.
```

d)
```
PARA-1.
    MOVE 0 TO MANY.
    PERFORM PARA-2 MANY TIMES.
    PERFORM PARA-3.
    STOP RUN.
PARA-2.

PARA-3.
    PERFORM PARA-2 4 TIMES.
```

e)
```
    MOVE 1 TO MAX-NUM.
    PERFORM PARA-1 THRU PARA-3
        MAX-NUM TIMES.
    STOP RUN.
PARA-1.
    ADD 1 TO MAX-NUM.

PARA-2.
    IF MAX-NUM IS LESS THAN 5
        PERFORM PARA-1.

PARA-3.
    PERFORM PARA-4 MAX-NUM TIMES.

PARA-4.
```

2. Below are several situations in which the PERFORM/VARYING statement is used. Record the paragraph names encountered during the execution of each procedure. If a paragraph is encountered by "fall through," record this situation adjacent to the paragraph name. Furthermore, record the values of the PERFORM/VARYING index.

a)
```
    PERFORM PARA-1 VARYING I FROM 1
        BY 1 UNTIL I IS GREATER THAN 5.
    STOP RUN.
PARA-1.
```

b)
```
    PERFORM PARA-1 VARYING I FROM 1 BY 1
        UNTIL I IS GREATER THAN 3.
    STOP RUN.
PARA-1.
    PERFORM PARA-2 VARYING J FROM 1 BY 1
        UNTIL J IS GREATER THAN 2.

PARA-2.
```

c)
```
    PERFORM PARA-1
        VARYING I FROM 1 BY 1
            UNTIL I IS GREATER THAN 4
        AFTER J FROM 10 BY -2
            UNTIL J < 0.
    STOP RUN.
PARA-1.
```

d)
```
    MOVE 2 TO M, O.
    MOVE 4 TO N, P.
    PERFORM PARA-1 THRU PARA-2
        VARYING I FROM M BY 1
            UNTIL I > N-1

        AFTER J FROM 1 BY O
            UNTIL J > P
        AFTER K FROM M BY N
            UNTIL K > 10.
    STOP RUN.
PARA-1.

PARA-2.
    PERFORM PARA-3 3 TIMES.

PARA-3.
```

Problems

1. Records have been developed to indicate both the number of employees in departments within the company and employee names of individuals within each department. The data is organized in such a way that multiple sets (departments) are possible. That is, each set will be organized such that the first record indicates the number of employees in the department and the second record type (multiple records) contains the employee name. (See the multiple-card layout form.)

You are to design a procedure to decide, based on the number of employees in each department, the number of columns in which the employee roster should be printed. That is, some departments have as many as 200 employees, while other departments have as few as 10 members. Your departmental employee roster should fit on one page. Thus, for example, if a department has as few as 50 members only one column should be printed. If the list is to contain up to 100 names, the list should be printed in two columns. Use three columns if the list contains up to 150 names and four columns for up to 200. The list, regardless of the number of employees, should appear centered on the page. Therefore, it will probably be desirable to have at least two output line formats—one when 1 or 3 columns are to be printed and one to be used if 2 or 4 columns are to be printed. (See the print chart.)

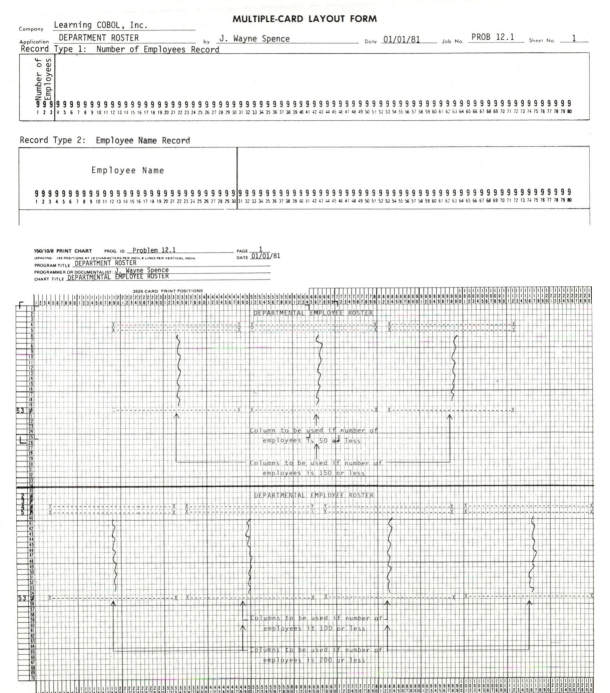

2. The Vice-President in Charge of Operations has received numerous complaints regarding the appointment and planning calendars purchased in bulk by the company. The current calendars are said to be difficult to use for at least two reasons. First, they do not provide an overview of the activities to be performed. Second, they do not provide sufficient space in which to record appointments and specifics of the subject of the appointment. The vice-president has decided to have a printer produce appointment and planning calendars in the future but has decided a number of alternate designs might be desirable. He has asked us to produce a series of possible calendar designs from a program.

One design which has been suggested is shown on the print chart. This design shows the time of the appointment across the top of the page and both day of the week and day of the month horizontally at the left margin of the page. Each appointment period is then marked off as a box. This calendar is to cover one month (regardless of the number of days in the month—assume 31). Finally, just to check the overall format, you are to produce two complete copies of the planning and appointment calendar in this format.

Note: This procedure does not require the use of input data.

3. When manufacturing a product, management often refers to a measurement known as the break-even point. The break-even point is that level of production (in units of a product) where the cost of manufacturing the item is exactly equal to the revenues received from selling the item. In its simplest form, the formula for determining the break-even point is:

a.   (Fixed Cost plus Variable Cost times Units Produced) less
                        (Selling Price times Units Produced) = 0

where

Fixed Cost is the cost incurred as a result of maintaining a production capacity (such as the building in which the manufacturing plant is housed),
Variable Cost is the cost directly associated with the production of units of an item (such as material and manpower costs), and Selling Price is the price at which we anticipate selling all units produced.

To find the break-even point (in units), this formula may be factored to yield:

b.
$$\text{Units Produced} = \frac{\text{Fixed Cost}}{\text{Sales Price less Variable Cost}}$$

Thus, if Fixed Cost were \$100.00, Variable Cost were \$1.00 per unit, and Selling Price were \$3.00 per unit; the company would have to produce 50 units to break-even. Stated another way, the cost of manufacturing the item is exactly equal to the revenues received from selling the item when 50 units are produced.

You have two problems. Your company is anticipating the manufacture of several new products. Information concerning each of these products has been placed in a record (see the multiple-card layout form). You are to determine the break-even point (in units) for each product and then produce a schedule which illustrates all levels of production (in incremental levels of units) ranging from 90 percent to 110 percent of the break-even point (see the print chart). Note that the production level increment for an item may not be in single units. For example, though it might be practical to build one automobile at a time, it is hardly practical to produce paint one gallon at a time. Further note that a single schedule may be several pages long.

Company LEARNING COBOL, INC.   **MULTIPLE-CARD LAYOUT FORM**

Application BREAK-EVEN   by J. Wayne Spence   Date 01/01/81   Job No. PROB 12.3   Sheet No. 1

Product Name	Production Cost		Selling Price Per Unit	Production Lot Size	
	Fixed	Variable Per Unit			
9 9 9 9 9 9 9 9 9 9 9 9 9 9 9 9 9 9 9 9 9 9 9 9 9 9 9 9 9 9	9 9 9 9 9 9 9 9 9 9	9 9 9 9 9 9 9 9 9 9	9 9 9 9 9 9 9 9	9 9 9 9	9 9 9 9 9 9 9 9 9 9 9 9 9 9 9 9 9 9 9 9
1 2 3 4 5 6 7 8 9 10 11 12 13 14 15 16 17 18 19 20 21 22 23 24 25 26 27 28 29 30	31 32 33 34 35 36 37 38 39 40	41 42 43 44 45 46 47 48	49 50 51 52 53 54 55 56	57 58 59 60 61	62 63 64 65 66 67 68 69 70 71 72 73 74 75 76 77 78 79 80

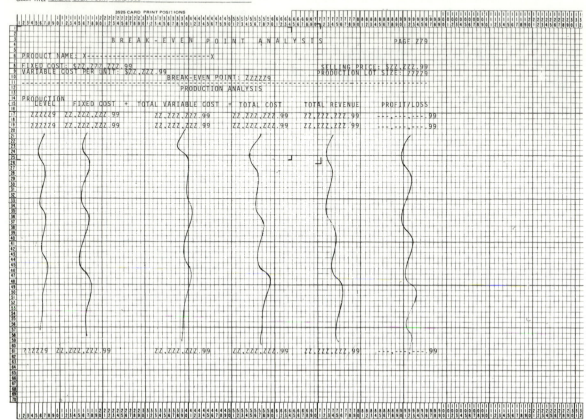

150/10/8 PRINT CHART   PROG. ID. **Problem 12.3**   PAGE **1**

(SPACING: 150 POSITIONS AT 10 CHARACTERS PER INCH, 8 LINES PER VERTICAL INCH)   DATE **01/01**/81

PROGRAM TITLE **BREAK-EVEN**

PROGRAMMER OR DOCUMENTALIST **J. Wayne Spence**

CHART TITLE **BREAK-EVEN POINT ANALYSIS**

```
              B R E A K - E V E N   P O I N T   A N A L Y S I S                    PAGE ZZ9

PRODUCT NAME: X---------------------------X
FIXED COST: $ZZ,ZZZ,ZZZ.99                                    SELLING PRICE: $ZZ,ZZZ.99
VARIABLE COST PER UNIT: $ZZ,ZZZ.99                           PRODUCTION LOT SIZE: ZZZZ9
                          BREAK-EVEN POINT: ZZZZZ9
---------------------------------------------------------------------------------------
                              PRODUCTION ANALYSIS

PRODUCTION
  LEVEL      FIXED COST  +  TOTAL VARIABLE COST  =  TOTAL COST    TOTAL REVENUE    PROFIT/LOSS
ZZZZZ9     ZZ,ZZZ,ZZZ.99      ZZ,ZZZ,ZZZ.99        ZZ,ZZZ,ZZZ.99  ZZ,ZZZ,ZZZ.99   ---,---,---.99
ZZZZZ9     ZZ,ZZZ,ZZZ.99      ZZ,ZZZ,ZZZ.99        ZZ,ZZZ,ZZZ.99  ZZ,ZZZ,ZZZ.99   ---,---,---.99



ZZZZZ9     ZZ,ZZZ,ZZZ.99      ZZ,ZZZ,ZZZ.99        ZZ,ZZZ,ZZZ.99  ZZ,ZZZ,ZZZ.99   ---,---,---.99
```

13 Table Handling with Subscripts

In many programming applications, massive amounts of data must be stored within the computer's memory. Without the capability to store interrelated or homogeneous data within one area or block of computer memory, programming some types of problems would be inconvenient, and other applications would be impractical or impossible. In COBOL, tables allow the programmer to store and reference bulk data easily without specifying an individual data-name for each location reserved for a data value.

A table is specified with the OCCURS clause in the DATA DIVISION. The OCCURS clause, pictured in Figure 13.1, specifies the number of storage positions to be associated with a single data-name. The OCCURS clause may be coded with data items at levels Ø2 through 49. The OCCURS clause cannot be used with data items at levels Ø1, 66, 77, or 88. Both groups and elementary-items may employ the OCCURS clause, making multi-dimensional tables possible. COBOL supports tables with a maximum of three dimensions by arranging OCCURS clauses in subordinate relationships to one another.

Single-Dimension Tables

As presented in Figure 13.1, the simple format of the OCCURS clause provides for the description of a table with static dimensions. That is, the size of the table described with this OCCURS clause does not change during the execution of a program. The programmer specifies the number of occurrences of a data-name within the table by providing a positive integer value for integer-2, which gives the integer-2 storage positions that can be referenced using the data-name associated with the clause. If the OCCURS clause is specified for a group item, each subordinate data item will occur integer-2 times. A data item so described in COBOL is a single-dimension table or vector.

When a data item associated with an OCCURS clause is addressed in the PROCEDURE DIVISION, it must be written with a *subscript*. The values of the subscript indicate the occurrence to be referenced during execution. The subscript must be enclosed in parentheses with one space preceding the left parenthesis and a space or a punctuation character following the right parenthesis. The subscript value may be provided by either a data-name that

```
Format 1 *


        OCCURS integer-2 TIMES


*Format, as written, is incomplete. Complete format
provided in Chapter 14.
```

Figure 13.1 Simple Format of the OCCURS Clause

```
Ø1  RATE-PER-HOUR-TABLE.
    Ø3 RATE-PER-HOUR OCCURS 1Ø TIME PICTURE 99V99.
```

```
┌─────────────────────┐  ╲
│ RATE-PER-HOUR (1)   │
├─────────────────────┤
│ RATE-PER-HOUR (2)   │
├─────────────────────┤
│ RATE-PER-HOUR (3)   │
├─────────────────────┤
│ RATE-PER-HOUR (4)   │
├─────────────────────┤
│ RATE-PER-HOUR (5)   │   RATE-PER-HOUR-TABLE
├─────────────────────┤
│ RATE-PER-HOUR (6)   │
├─────────────────────┤
│ RATE-PER-HOUR (7)   │
├─────────────────────┤
│ RATE-PER-HOUR (8)   │
├─────────────────────┤
│ RATE-PER-HOUR (9)   │
├─────────────────────┤
│ RATE-PER-HOUR (1Ø)  │
└─────────────────────┘  ╱
```

Figure 13.2 A Simple One-Dimensional Table

describes integer fields containing a positive value or by a positive integer value. In either case, the value of the subscript should be at least one but no greater than the number of occurrence positions in the table.

Figure 13.2 illustrates how a table is formed in COBOL. This illustration provides both the DATA DIVISION entries necessary to describe a table and the logical representation of the table in the computer's memory. In the figure, RATE-PER-HOUR-TABLE is a record-name that represents a subordinate table. When used in the PROCEDURE DIVISION, RATE-PER-HOUR-TABLE addresses all occurrences of the table subordinate to it (or 40 bytes of internal storage). RATE-PER-HOUR, since it is coded with a PICTURE clause, is an elementary data item. Since it is also coded with an OCCURS clause, RATE-PER-HOUR describes 10 positions in the computer's memory, each of which is described by the PICTURE clause. Each appearance of the data-name RATE-PER-HOUR in the PROCEDURE DIVISION must be accompanied by a subscript within the range of 1 through 10, inclusive. Each occurrence of RATE-PER-HOUR addresses a four-digit number. Remember that RATE-PER-HOUR-TABLE is not subordinate to (or directly associated with) an OCCURS clause. Thus, when RATE-PER-HOUR-TABLE is referenced in the PRO-CEDURE DIVISION, it should *not* be written with a subscript.

In Figure 13.3, a table that contains two types of data—a six-digit integer and a four-digit number with two decimal places—is described. The name of the entire table is EMPLOYEE-NUMBER-RATE-TABLE. EMPLOYEE-NUMBER-RATE-TABLE may be used in the PROCEDURE DIVISION to address all of the subordinate data items (50 bytes of data—five occurrences of six bytes plus five occurrences of four bytes). Each subordinate data item is

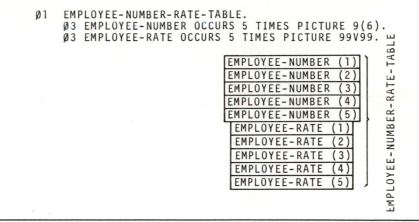

```
Ø1  EMPLOYEE-NUMBER-RATE-TABLE.
    Ø3 EMPLOYEE-NUMBER OCCURS 5 TIMES PICTURE 9(6).
    Ø3 EMPLOYEE-RATE OCCURS 5 TIMES PICTURE 99V99.
```

Figure 13.3 Two One-Dimensional Tables with Separate Occurrences

```
Ø1 EMPLOYEE-NUMBER-RATE-TABLE.
   Ø3 NUMBER-RATE-PAIRS OCCURS 5 TIMES.
      Ø5 EMPLOYEE-NUMBER PICTURE 9(6).
      Ø5 EMPLOYEE-RATE PICTURE 99V99.
```

EMPLOYEE-NUMBER (1)	EMPLOYEE-RATE (1)	NUMBER-RATE-PAIRS (1)
EMPLOYEE-NUMBER (2)	EMPLOYEE-RATE (2)	NUMBER-RATE-PAIRS (2)
EMPLOYEE-NUMBER (3)	EMPLOYEE-RATE (3)	NUMBER-RATE-PAIRS (3)
EMPLOYEE-NUMBER (4)	EMPLOYEE-RATE (4)	NUMBER-RATE-PAIRS (4)
EMPLOYEE-NUMBER (5)	EMPLOYEE-RATE (5)	NUMBER-RATE-PAIRS (5)

EMPLOYEE-NUMBER-RATE-TABLE

Figure 13.4 Two Single-Dimension Tables with Interleaved Occurrences

associated with an OCCURS clause. Since each OCCURS clause is independent of the other, the table is one-dimensional—only one subscript is necessary
when addressing either EMPLOYEE-NUMBER or EMPLOYEE- RATE. Each of
the elementary data items (EMPLOYEE-NUMBER and EMPLOYEE-RATE)
OCCURS five times. It is not necessary that both EMPLOYEE-NUMBER and
EMPLOYEE-RATE occur the same number of times. The important point is
that since each OCCURS clause is independent of the other, the data are internally structured such that all occurrences of EMPLOYEE-NUMBER are *followed* by all occurrences of EMPLOYEE-RATE.

Figure 13.4 provides an additional method of describing single-dimension
tables. (This form of table description is sometimes called a pseudo-two-
dimension table.) EMPLOYEE-NUMBER-RATE-TABLE still represents all of
the data subordinate to it (50 bytes); however, in this example, a group item
(NUMBER-RATE-PAIRS) has been coded with an OCCURS clause. Any item
subordinate to NUMBER-RATE-PAIRS will occur five times. Thus, there are
five occurrences of EMPLOYEE-NUMBER and EMPLOYEE-RATE (as in the
second example). In this case, however, the occurrences of the data items alternate. The first occurrence of EMPLOYEE-NUMBER is logically followed by
the first occurrence of EMPLOYEE-RATE; the second occurrence of
EMPLOYEE-NUMBER is followed by the second occurrence of EMPLOYEE-
RATE, and so forth. EMPLOYEE-NUMBER and EMPLOYEE-RATE must still

be referenced by a single subscript when addressed in the PROCEDURE DIVI-SION. A single occurrence of EMPLOYEE-NUMBER addresses six bytes, and EMPLOYEE-RATE addresses four bytes. Since a single occurrence of NUMBER-RATE-PAIRS addresses one occurrence of EMPLOYEE-NUMBER *and* EMPLOYEE-RATE, NUMBER-RATE-PAIRS must be accompanied by one subscript (within the range from 1 to 5) when referenced in the PRO-CEDURE DIVISION.

Multi-Dimension Tables

When a data-name associated with an OCCURS clause is subordinate to another OCCURS clause, the portion of the table described by the data-name is considered two-dimensional. That is, the data-name associated with one OCCURS clause that is subordinate to another may be logically thought of as having rows and columns—the data-name represents a matrix. In this representation, the integer value associated with the first OCCURS clause (from top to bottom) provides the number of rows of the table. The integer value associated with the second (subordinate) OCCURS provides the number of columns of the table. When a data item is described as being two-dimensional, two subscripts should be used to reference a single value from the table. As with single-dimension tables, the subscripts may be integer values or data-names that describe integer fields. Both subscript values should be enclosed in one set of parentheses and separated by a comma.

Figure 13.5 provides an example of a record description representing a two-dimension table. The record-name TRANSPORTATION-CHARGES may be used to address the entire table (360 bytes—ten rows by six columns by individual six-digit fields). As before, the table name may be referenced in the

```
01  TRANSPORTATION-CHARGES.
    05  WAREHOUSE-LOCATION OCCURS 10 TIMES.
        10  REC-PT          OCCURS 6 TIMES.
            15  CHARGE        PIC  9(4)V99.
```

WAREHOUSE-LOCATION (1)	CHARGE (1, 1) REC-PT (1, 1)	CHARGE (1, 2) REC-PT (1, 2)	CHARGE (1, 3) REC-PT (1, 3)	CHARGE (1, 4) REC-PT (1, 4)	CHARGE (1, 5) REC-PT (1, 5)	CHARGE (1, 6) REC-PT (1, 6)
WAREHOUSE-LOCATION (2)	CHARGE (2, 1) REC-PT (2, 1)	CHARGE (2, 2) REC-PT (2, 2)	CHARGE (2, 3) REC-PT (2, 3)	CHARGE (2, 4) REC-PT (2, 4)	CHARGE (2, 5) REC-PT (2, 5)	CHARGE (2, 6) REC-PT (2, 6)
WAREHOUSE-LOCATION (3)	CHARGE (3, 1) REC-PT (3, 1)	CHARGE (3, 2) REC-PT (3, 2)	CHARGE (3, 3) REC-PT (3, 3)	CHARGE (3, 4) REC-PT (3, 4)	CHARGE (3, 5) REC-PT (3, 5)	CHARGE (3, 6) REC-PT (3, 6)
WAREHOUSE-LOCATION (4)	CHARGE (4, 1) REC-PT (4, 1)	CHARGE (4, 2) REC-PT (4, 2)	CHARGE (4, 3) REC-PT (4, 3)	CHARGE (4, 4) REC-PT (4, 4)	CHARGE (4, 5) REC-PT (4, 5)	CHARGE (4, 6) REC-PT (4, 6)
WAREHOUSE-LOCATION (5)	CHARGE (5, 1) REC-PT (5, 1)	CHARGE (5, 2) REC-PT (5, 2)	CHARGE (5, 3) REC-PT (5, 3)	CHARGE (5, 4) REC-PT (5, 4)	CHARGE (5, 5) REC-PT (5, 5)	CHARGE (5, 6) REC-PT (5, 6)
WAREHOUSE-LOCATION (6)	CHARGE (6, 1) REC-PT (6, 1)	CHARGE (6, 2) REC-PT (6, 2)	CHARGE (6, 3) REC-PT (6, 3)	CHARGE (6, 4) REC-PT (6, 4)	CHARGE (6, 5) REC-PT (6, 5)	CHARGE (6, 6) REC-PT (6, 6)
WAREHOUSE-LOCATION (7)	CHARGE (7, 1) REC-PT (7, 1)	CHARGE (7, 2) REC-PT (7, 2)	CHARGE (7, 3) REC-PT (7, 3)	CHARGE (7, 4) REC-PT (7, 4)	CHARGE (7, 5) REC-PT (7, 5)	CHARGE (7, 6) REC-PT (7, 6)
WAREHOUSE-LOCATION (8)	CHARGE (8, 1) REC-PT (8, 1)	CHARGE (8, 2) REC-PT (8, 2)	CHARGE (8, 3) REC-PT (8, 3)	CHARGE (8, 4) REC-PT (8, 4)	CHARGE (8, 5) REC-PT (8, 5)	CHARGE (8, 6) REC-PT (8, 6)
WAREHOUSE-LOCATION (9)	CHARGE (9, 1) REC-PT (9, 1)	CHARGE (9, 2) REC-PT (9, 2)	CHARGE (9, 3) REC-PT (9, 3)	CHARGE (9, 4) REC-PT (9, 4)	CHARGE (9, 5) REC-PT (9, 5)	CHARGE (9, 6) REC-PT (9, 6)
WAREHOUSE-LOCATION (10)	CHARGE (10, 1) REC-PT (10, 1)	CHARGE (10, 2) REC-PT (10, 2)	CHARGE (10, 3) REC-PT (10, 3)	CHARGE (10, 4) REC-PT (10, 4)	CHARGE (10, 5) REC-PT (10, 5)	CHARGE (10, 6) REC-PT (10, 6)

TRANSPORTATION-CHARGES

Figure 13.5 A Two-Dimension Table

PROCEDURE DIVISION, but should *not* be written with a subscript. The first OCCURS clause is associated with WAREHOUSE-LOCATION. WARE-HOUSE-LOCATION is a group-name even though it is jointly a single-dimension table. Thus, WAREHOUSE-LOCATION may be referenced in the PROCEDURE DIVISION and should be written with one subscript. The next data item in the description is REC-PT (receiving point), which is at the 10 level and is, therefore, subordinate to WAREHOUSE-LOCATION. REC-PT OCCURS six times. For each occurrence of WAREHOUSE-LOCATION, there are six data items known as REC-PT. WAREHOUSE-LOCATION OCCURS 10 times, giving 60 data items in the entire table known as REC-PT. Each of these can be uniquely referenced by a particular subscript. Each cell of the TRANSPORTATION-CHARGES table may be referenced either by the group-name REC-PT and a particular row-column pair (an alphanumeric field) or by the data-name CHARGES and a particular row-column pair (a numeric-nonedited field).

Figure 13.6 illustrates a table composed of a mixture of tables. EMPLOYEE-RATE-AND-HOURS-TABLE, a record-name that describes all of the subordinate data (125 bytes), should not be written with a subscript in the PROCEDURE DIVISION. RATES-AND-HOURS, a group-name, is written with an OCCURS clause. RATES-AND-HOURS must be accompanied by one subscript when written in the PROCEDURE DIVISION; each occurrence addresses 25 bytes of internal memory. RATE is subordinate to the OCCURS clause associated with RATES-AND-HOURS. RATE occurs five times and must be written with one subscript in the PROCEDURE DIVISION; each occurrence addresses 4 bytes of memory. HOURS is subordinate to RATES-AND-HOURS and is written with an OCCURS clause, creating a two-dimensional table. HOURS is structured so that it logically appears to have five rows (from the OCCURS 5 TIMES associated with RATES-AND-HOURS) and seven columns (from the OCCURS 7 TIMES associated with HOURS), giving 35 distinct areas that can be referenced within HOURS. When HOURS is used in the PROCEDURE DIVISION, it must be written with two subscripts, with the first ranging from 1 to 5 and the second, from 1 to 7. In the logical representation of the computer's memory, the first occurrence of RATE is followed by the first row of HOURS. The "row" as a group is represented by a single occurrence of RATE-AND-HOURS.

```
Ø1  EMPLOYEE-RATE-AND-HOURS-TABLE.
    Ø3 RATE-AND-HOURS   OCCURS 5 TIMES.
       Ø5 RATE PICTURE 99V99.
       Ø5 HOURS OCCURS 7 TIMES PICTURE 99V9.
```

RATE (1)	HOURS (1,1)	HOURS (1,2)	HOURS (1,3)	HOURS (1,4)	HOURS (1,5)	HOURS (1,6)	HOURS (1,7)
RATE (2)	HOURS (2,1)	HOURS (2,2)	HOURS (2,3)	HOURS (2,4)	HOURS (2,5)	HOURS (2,6)	HOURS (2,7)
RATE (3)	HOURS (3,1)	HOURS (3,2)	HOURS (3,3)	HOURS (3,4)	HOURS (3,5)	HOURS (3,6)	HOURS (3,7)
RATE (4)	HOURS (4,1)	HOURS (4,2)	HOURS (4,3)	HOURS (4,4)	HOURS (4,5)	HOURS (4,6)	HOURS (4,7)
RATE (5)	HOURS (5,1)	HOURS (5,2)	HOURS (5,3)	HOURS (5,4)	HOURS (5,5)	HOURS (5,6)	HOURS (5,7)

```
RATE-AND-HOURS (5)
RATE-AND-HOURS (4)              EMPLOYEE-RATE-AND-HOURS-TABLE
RATE-AND-HOURS (3)
RATE-AND-HOURS (2)
RATE-AND-HOURS (1)
```

Figure 13.6 Mixture of One- and Two-Dimension Tables

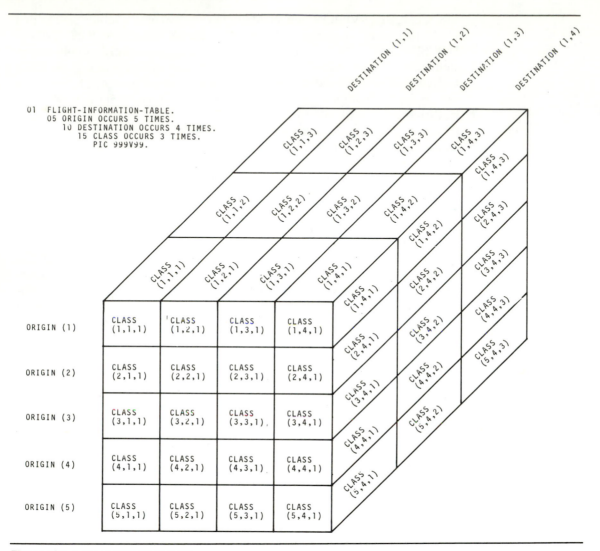

Figure 13.7 A Three-Dimension Table

When a data item associated with an OCCURS clause is subordinate to another OCCURS clause, which is itself subordinate to an OCCURS clause, the portion of the table addressed by the data item is considered three-dimensional. Logically a three-dimension table may be thought of as "cubic," with data defined in rows (length), columns (width), and ranks (depth). To address data at the lowest level of this table requires three subscripts. The first references rows; the second, columns; and the third, ranks. As before, these subscripts should be enclosed in parentheses and separated by commas.

Figure 13.7 illustrates a three-dimension table. In this example, FLIGHT-INFORMATION-TABLE references the entire table of 60 cells (360 bytes) and should not be subscripted when referred to in the PROCEDURE DIVISION. ORIGIN should be accompanied by one subscript. Each occurrence of

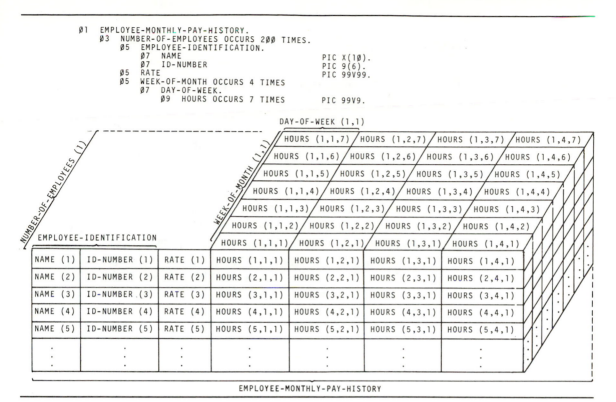

```
Ø1   EMPLOYEE-MONTHLY-PAY-HISTORY.
  Ø3   NUMBER-OF-EMPLOYEES OCCURS 2ØØ TIMES.
    Ø5   EMPLOYEE-IDENTIFICATION.
         Ø7   NAME                        PIC X(1Ø).
         Ø7   ID-NUMBER                   PIC 9(6).
    Ø5   RATE                             PIC 99V99.
    Ø5   WEEK-OF-MONTH OCCURS 4 TIMES
         Ø7   DAY-OF-WEEK.
              Ø9   HOURS OCCURS 7 TIMES   PIC 99V9.
```

Figure 13.8 A Three-Dimension Table with Appended One-Dimension Table

ORIGIN references 12 cells of the table. If ORIGIN(1) appeared in the PROCEDURE DIVISION, a reference would be made to all cells within the table having 1 as the first subscript value. DESTINATION provides for the four columns of the table since it OCCURS four times and is subordinate to ORIGIN. When referenced in the PROCEDURE DIVISION, DESTINATION should be accompanied by two subscripts. Each reference to DESTINATION in the PROCEDURE DIVISION addresses three cells of the table. For example, if DESTINATION (1, 1) appeared in the PROCEDURE DIVISION, CLASS (1, 1, 1), CLASS (1, 1, 2), and CLASS (1, 1, 3) would be referenced. Finally, the elementary data item CLASS appears in the record description. Since CLASS appears with an OCCURS clause and is subordinate to both DESTINATION and ORIGIN, CLASS represents the third level of the table. All references to CLASS in the PROCEDURE DIVISION address a single cell of the table and should appear with three subscripts.

The final example, presented in Figure 13.8, provides a description of a three-dimension table associated with one-dimension tables. Suppose a company wanted to store 200 employee payroll records in one table. This information might be stored for an entire month, with an area reserved for each day of the month. In the description of this table, EMPLOYEE-MONTHLY-PAY-HISTORY is a record-name which addresses all 6,200 addressable cells of the table (20,800 bytes). NUMBER-OF-EMPLOYEES is associated with an OCCURS clause that provides for 200 employees (subordinate items). Each oc-

$$\text{data-name-1} \quad \left[\left\{\begin{matrix}\underline{OF}\\\underline{IN}\end{matrix}\right\} \quad \text{data-name-2} \quad \left[\left\{\begin{matrix}\underline{OF}\\\underline{IN}\end{matrix}\right\} \text{data-name-3}\right]\right] \quad \ldots$$

$$(\text{subscript-1}[, \text{ subscript-2}[, \text{ subscript-3}]])$$

Figure 13.9 Format Requirements for Qualifying and Subscripting a Data Item

currence of NUMBER-OF-EMPLOYEES would logically reference one "layer" of the table. That is, the first occurrence of NUMBER-OF-EMPLOYEES would reference the first occurrence of NAME, ID-NUMBER, and RATE and HOURS from (1, 1, 1) to (1, 4, 7) (the top layer). Thus, each occurrence of NUMBER-OF-EMPLOYEES references 104 bytes of data. EMPLOYEE-IDEN-TIFICATION, which is subordinate to NUMBER-OF-EMPLOYEES, it OCCURS 200 times. Each occurrence of EMPLOYEE-IDENTIFICATION provides a single occurrence of NAME and ID-NUMBER. NAME and ID-NUMBER are subordinate to NUMBER-OF-EMPLOYEES and each OCCURS 200 times within the group-name EMPLOYEE-IDENTIFICATION. RATE, which is directly subordinate to NUMBER-OF-EMPLOYEES, OCCURS 200 times.

The next item that appears in the table is WEEK-OF-MONTH, which has an OCCURS clause that provides for four items for each occurrence of WEEK-OF-MONTH or any subordinate items. However, since WEEK-OF-MONTH is subordinate to NUMBER-OF-EMPLOYEES, it describes a two-dimension data item that represents 800 items (200 rows and 4 columns). Each occurrence of WEEK-OF-MONTH should be accompanied by two subscripts when referenced in the PROCEDURE DIVISION, and it would reference 12 bytes of internal memory. For example, WEEK-OF-MONTH (1, 1) would address HOURS (1, 1, 1) through HOURS (1, 1, 7). DAY-OF-WEEK, a group-name subordinate to WEEK-OF-MONTH, would address the same data as WEEK-OF- MONTH. Thus, DAY-OF-WEEK (1, 1) is in every respect equivalent to WEEK-OF-MONTH (1, 1). The final entry in the table is HOURS. HOURS is an elementary data item associated with an OCCURS clause. This OCCURS clause is subordinate to both previous OCCURS clauses, making HOURS a representation of a three-dimension table. Therefore, HOURS is represented by 200 rows, 4 columns, and 7 ranks, providing 5,600 separately addressable data items called HOURS. In the PROCEDURE DIVISION, a single occurrence of HOURS addresses 3 bytes of data, and HOURS should be written with three subscripts.

If the data-name to be addressed in the PROCEDURE DIVISION is not a unique identifier, the data item must be qualified. Figure 13.9 shows how to qualify a data item that is (or is part of) a table. The first identifier (data-name-1) represents the subscript data item, and data-name-2 is a qualifier of data-name-1. For example, if HOURS in Figure 13.8 were not unique, it might be qualified as HOURS OF EMPLOYEE-MONTHLY-PAY-HISTORY (I, J, K), where I, J, and K are subscript identifiers.

Sales Summary Report

Figure 13.10 illustrates how COBOL programs might utilize tables. In this illustration, it is assumed that a number of sales records exist, with the possibility of several records for each inventory item. The records represent dates of sale during a 12-month period. There might be either multiple records with the same item number but with different month-of-sale values or multiple records with the same item number and the same month-of-sale value, or there might be both. The objective of the procedure is to collect all the data for a single item (with summation if more than one sale occurred during a given month) and produce a "by-month" sales summary.

Now examine the code of Figure 13.10. Two data tables have been developed—an ITEM-TABLE (lines 460–490) and a SALES-BY-MONTH-TABLE (lines 500–530). The ITEM-TABLE is used to retain the values of ITEM-NUMBER and ITEM-DESCRIPTION as they are read from the SALES-FILE. Since we anticipate duplicate values for ITEM-NUMBER and ITEM-DESCRIPTION (multiple records for the same item representing different sales), we wish to retain only one "copy" of this data. The procedure can handle a *maximum* of 30 different items.

The SALES-BY-MONTH-TABLE is two-dimensional with 30 rows, corresponding to the 30 anticipated items, by 12 columns, corresponding to 12 months of a year. The application assumes that the value of the MONTH-OF-SALE (line 280) corresponds to one of the columns. We may access all 12 months of sales data by using ITEMS-SOLD (along with a single subscript); however, the elementary-item field is addressable only by MONTHLY-SALES (which must be recorded with two subscripts in the PROCEDURE DIVISION.

One other table, MONTHLY-SALES-OUT (a single-dimension table in lines 700 and 710), is used to prepare data for printed output.

In the PROCEDURE DIVISION, the process begins with an initialization sequence. In this sequence, both data tables are initialized. In line 840 the ITEM-TABLE is initialized to spaces, and in line 850 the SALES-BY-MONTH-TABLE is initialized to zeros. The initialization of the SALES-BY-MONTH-TABLE to zeros permits us to *add* AMOUNT-OF-SALES to any applicable cell of the table without further initialization. In addition, any cell of MONTHLY-SALES that is not addressed will remain zero. (If it were not for this initialization procedure, MONTHLY-SALES could have simply been added to the bottom of the ITEM-TABLE definition to create a two-dimension table.) In the SALES- SUMMATION module (3000), the procedure determines when a new item (ITEM-NUMBER) is encountered. When this occurs, ITEM-COUNT is incremented, marking the location of the most recent item. (Until a new item is encountered, ITEM-COUNT will not be altered.) At the same time the current ITEM-NUMBER and ITEM-DESCRIPTION are moved into the indicated positions of ITEM-TABLE at the ITEM-COUNT location. The next step is to add the current AMOUNT-OF-SALES for the record involved to MONTHLY-SALES. (The location is specified by ITEM-COUNT *and* MONTH-OF-SALE. Thus, one subscript is generated internally and the other is generated as a result of an input operation.)

The final procedure is to print all the collected data. Because we have counted the number of items placed in ITEM-TABLE (and MONTHLY-SALES), all that is necessary is to dump data in the tables from 1 to ITEM-COUNT. The PERFORM statement at lines 770 and 780 loads the data from the ITEM-TABLE into the output line, and the procedure continues by loading individual MONTHLY-SALES entries into the appropriate output slot. This process is similar to extracting data from the ITEM-TABLE except that the number of months in a year is known.

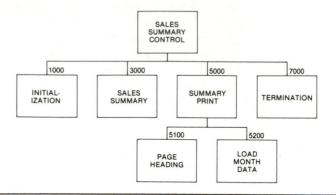

Figure 13.10 Sales Summary Report (Subscripted Tables) (Hierarchy Chart)

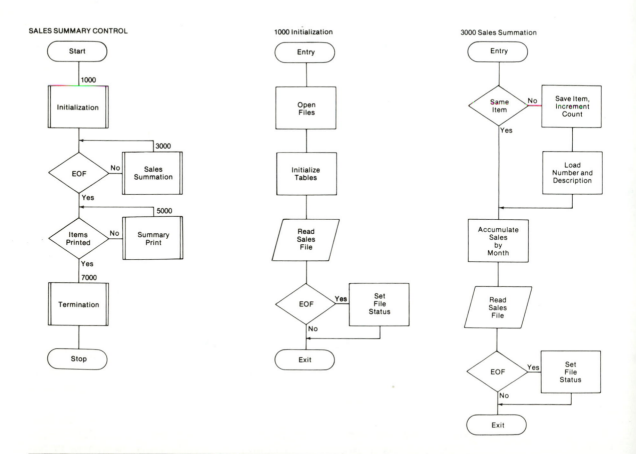

Figure 13.10 Sales Summary Report (Subscripted Tables) (Module Flowcharts) *Continued*

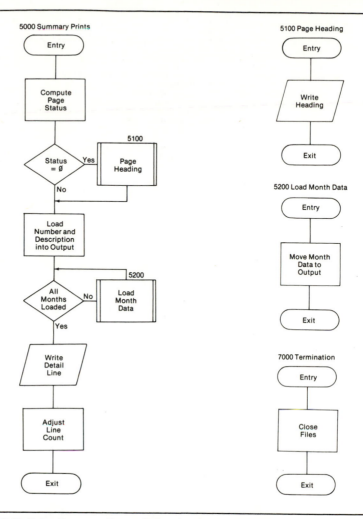

Figure 13.10 Sales Summary Report (Subscripted Tables) (Module Flowcharts) *Continued*

```
|     4     8     1     1     2     2     2     3     3     4     4     5     5     6     6     7     7     8|
|           2     6     0     4     8     2     6     0     4     8     2     6     0     4     8     2     6     0|
|000010 IDENTIFICATION DIVISION.                                                    FIG13.10|
|000020 PROGRAM-ID. SALES-SUMMARY.                                                  FIG13.10|
|000030 AUTHOR. J. WAYNE SPENCE.                                                    FIG13.10|
|000040 DATE-WRITTEN. JAN. 1, 1981.                                                 FIG13.10|
|000050 DATE-COMPILED. JAN. 1, 1981.                                                FIG13.10|
|000060*     PROCEDURE TO ACCUMULATE SALES OF ITEMS BY MONTH.                       FIG13.10|
|000070*     PROCEDURE USES A ONE DIMENSIONAL TABLE TO STORE THE                    FIG13.10|
|000080*     ITEM NUMBER AND NAME AND A TWO DIMENSIONAL TABLE TO                    FIG13.10|
|000090*     RECORD THE MONTHLY SALES OF EACH ITEM.                                 FIG13.10|
|000100 ENVIRONMENT DIVISION.                                                       FIG13.10|
|000110 CONFIGURATION SECTION.                                                      FIG13.10|
|000120 SOURCE-COMPUTER. IBM-370.                                                   FIG13.10|
|000130 OBJECT-COMPUTER. IBM-370.                                                   FIG13.10|
|000140 SPECIAL-NAMES.  C01 IS TOP-OF-PAGE.                                         FIG13.10|
|000150 INPUT-OUTPUT SECTION.                                                       FIG13.10|
|000160 FILE-CONTROL.                                                               FIG13.10|
|000170     SELECT SALES-FILE ASSIGN TO UT-S-SYSIN.                                 FIG13.10|
|000180     SELECT REPORT-FILE ASSIGN TO UT-S-SYSPRINT.                             FIG13.10|
```

Figure 13.10 Sales Summary Report (Subscripted Tables) *Continued*

```
|             1   1   2   2   2 . 3   3   4   4   4   5   5   6   6   6   7   7   8|
|     4       8   2   6   0   4   8   2   6   0   4   8   2   6   0   4   8   2   6   0|
------------------------------------------------------------------------------------
|000190 DATA DIVISION.                                                      FIG13.10|
|000200 FILE SECTION.                                                       FIG13.10|
|000210 FD  SALES-FILE                                                      FIG13.10|
|000220        LABEL RECORDS ARE OMITTED.                                   FIG13.10|
|000230 01  SALES-REC.                                                      FIG13.10|
|000240     05  ITEM-NUMBER              PIC 9(05).                         FIG13.10|
|000250     05  ITEM-DESCRIPTION         PIC X(30).                         FIG13.10|
|000260     05  FILLER                   PIC X(01).                         FIG13.10|
|000270     05  DATE-OF-SALE.                                               FIG13.10|
|000280         10  MONTH-OF-SALE        PIC 9(02).                         FIG13.10|
|000290         10  DAY-OF-SALE          PIC 9(02).                         FIG13.10|
|000300         10  YEAR-OF-SALE         PIC 9(02).                         FIG13.10|
|000310     05  FILLER                   PIC X(02).                         FIG13.10|
|000320     05  AMOUNT-OF-SALE           PIC S9(3)V99.                      FIG13.10|
|000330     05  FILLER                   PIC X(31).                         FIG13.10|
|000340 FD  REPORT-FILE                                                     FIG13.10|
|000350        LABEL RECORDS ARE STANDARD.                                  FIG13.10|
|000360 01  REPORT-LINE              PIC X(133).                            FIG13.10|
|000370 WORKING-STORAGE SECTION.                                            FIG13.10|
|000380 01  WORKING-VARIABLES.                                              FIG13.10|
|000390     05  FILE-STATUS              PIC X(10).                         FIG13.10|
|000400     05  ITEM                     PIC 9(02) VALUE ZERO.              FIG13.10|
|000410     05  MONTH                    PIC 9(02) VALUE ZERO.              FIG13.10|
|000420     05  ITEM-COUNT               PIC 9(02) VALUE ZERO.              FIG13.10|
|000430     05  LINE-COUNT               PIC 9(02) VALUE ZERO.              FIG13.10|
|000440     05  PAGE-STATUS              PIC V999.                          FIG13.10|
|000450     05  LAST-ITEM                PIC 9(05) VALUE ZERO.              FIG13.10|
|000460 01  ITEM-TABLE.                                                     FIG13.10|
|000470     05  ITEM-ENTRY OCCURS 30 TIMES.                                 FIG13.10|
|000480         10  ITEM-NUMBER-T      PIC 9(5).                           FIG13.10|
|000490         10  ITEM-DESCRIPTION-T PIC X(30).                           FIG13.10|
|000500 01  SALES-BY-MONTH-TABLE.                                           FIG13.10|
|000510     05  ITEMS-SOLD OCCURS 30 TIMES.                                 FIG13.10|
|000520         10  MONTHLY-SALES OCCURS 12 TIMES                           FIG13.10|
|000530                                 PIC S9(4)V99.                       FIG13.10|
|000540 01  PAGE-HEADING.                                                   FIG13.10|
|000550     05  FILLER                   PIC X(55) VALUE SPACES.            FIG13.10|
|000560     05  FILLER                   PIC X(22) VALUE                    FIG13.10|
|000570         *SALES SUMMARY BY MONTH*..                                  FIG13.10|
|000580 01  COLUMN-HEADING.                                                 FIG13.10|
|000590     05  FILLER                   PIC X(38) VALUE                    FIG13.10|
|000600         *  ITEM DESCRIPTION*.                                       FIG13.10|
|000610     05  FILLER                   PIC X(92) VALUE                    FIG13.10|
|000620     *JAN.   FEB.   MAR.   APR.   MAY    JUNE    JULY    AUG.FIG13.10|
|000630-    *  SEP.   OCT.   NOV.   DEC.*.                                   FIG13.10|
|000640 01  DETAIL-LINE.                                                    FIG13.10|
|000650     05  FILLER                   PIC X(01) VALUE SPACES.            FIG13.10|
|000660     05  ITEM-NUMBER-OUT          PIC 99B999.                        FIG13.10|
|000670     05  FILLER                   PIC X(01) VALUE SPACES.            FIG13.10|
|000680     05  ITEM-DESCRIPTION-OUT     PIC X(25).                         FIG13.10|
|000690     05  FILLER                   PIC X(01) VALUE SPACES.            FIG13.10|
|000700     05  MONTHLY-SALES-OUT OCCURS 12 TIMES                           FIG13.10|
|000710                                 PIC ZZZZZ.99.                       FIG13.10|
|000720 PROCEDURE DIVISION.                                                 FIG13.10|
|000730 SALES-SUMMARY-CONTROL.                                              FIG13.10|
|000740     PERFORM 1000-INITIALIZATION.                                    FIG13.10|
|000750     PERFORM 3000-SALES-SUMMATION                                    FIG13.10|
|000760        UNTIL FILE-STATUS = *DONE*.                                  FIG13.10|
|000770     PERFORM 5000-SUMMARY-PRINT                                      FIG13.10|
|000780        VARYING ITEM FROM 1 BY 1 UNTIL ITEM > ITEM-COUNT.            FIG13.10|
|000790     PERFORM 7000-TERMINATION.                                       FIG13.10|
|000800     STOP RUN.                                                       FIG13.10|
|000810 1000-INITIALIZATION.                                                FIG13.10|
|000820     OPEN INPUT SALES-FILE                                           FIG13.10|
|000830          OUTPUT REPORT-FILE.                                        FIG13.10|
|000840     MOVE SPACES TO ITEM-TABLE.                                      FIG13.10|
|000850     MOVE ZEROS TO SALES-BY-MONTH-TABLE.                             FIG13.10|
|000860     READ SALES-FILE                                                 FIG13.10|
|000870        AT END MOVE *DONE* TO FILE-STATUS.                           FIG13.10|
|000880 3000-SALES-SUMMATION.                                               FIG13.10|
|000890     IF ITEM-NUMBER NOT = LAST-ITEM                                  FIG13.10|
|000900        MOVE ITEM-NUMBER TO LAST-ITEM                                FIG13.10|
|000910        ADD 1 TO ITEM-COUNT                                          FIG13.10|
|000920        MOVE ITEM-NUMBER TO ITEM-NUMBER-T (ITEM-COUNT)               FIG13.10|
|000930        MOVE ITEM-DESCRIPTION TO ITEM-DESCRIPTION-T (ITEM-COUNT).FIG13.10|
|000940     ADD AMOUNT-OF-SALE TO                                           FIG13.10|
|000950        MONTHLY-SALES (ITEM-COUNT, MONTH-OF-SALE).                   FIG13.10|
|000960     READ SALES-FILE                                                 FIG13.10|
|000970        AT END MOVE *DONE* TO FILE-STATUS.                           FIG13.10|
```

Figure 13.10 Sales Summary Report (Subscripted Tables) *Continued*

```
         1   1   2   2   2   3   3   4   4   4   5   5   6   6   6   7   7   8
     4   8   2   6   0   4   8   2   6   0   4   8   2   6   0   4   8   2   6   0
-------------------------------------------------------------------------------
|000980 5000-SUMMARY-PRINT.                                              FIG13.10|
|000990     DIVIDE LINE-COUNT BY 25 GIVING PAGE-STATUS.                  FIG13.10|
|001000     IF PAGE-STATUS = 0                                           FIG13.10|
|001010         PERFORM 5100-PAGE-HEADING.                               FIG13.10|
|001020     MOVE ITEM-NUMBER-T (ITEM) TO ITEM-NUMBER-OUT.                FIG13.10|
|001030     MOVE ITEM-DESCRIPTION-T (ITEM) TO ITEM-DESCRIPTION-OUT.      FIG13.10|
|001040     PERFORM 5200-LOAD-MONTH-DATA                                 FIG13.10|
|001050         VARYING MONTH FROM 1 BY 1 UNTIL MONTH > 12.              FIG13.10|
|001060     WRITE REPORT-LINE FROM DETAIL-LINE AFTER ADVANCING 2 LINES.  FIG13.10|
|001070     ADD 2 TO LINE-COUNT.                                         FIG13.10|
|001080 5100-PAGE-HEADING.                                               FIG13.10|
|001090     WRITE REPORT-LINE FROM PAGE-HEADING                          FIG13.10|
|001100         AFTER ADVANCING TOP-OF-PAGE.                             FIG13.10|
|001110     WRITE REPORT-LINE FROM COLUMN-HEADING                        FIG13.10|
|001120         AFTER ADVANCING 2 LINES.                                 FIG13.10|
|001130 5200-LOAD-MONTH-DATA.                                            FIG13.10|
|001140     MOVE MONTHLY-SALES (ITEM, MONTH) TO                         FIG13.10|
|001150         MONTHLY-SALES-OUT (MONTH).                               FIG13.10|
|001160 7000-TERMINATION.                                                FIG13.10|
|001170     CLOSE SALES-FILE                                             FIG13.10|
|001180         REPORT-FILE.                                             FIG13.10|
```

Figure 13.10 Sales Summary Report (Subscripted Tables) *Continued*

```
|RECORD|1234567890123456789012345678901234567890123456789012345678901234567890| FIGURE NUMBER |
|   1|11232BALL POINT PEN                  011281  00198                |FIG13.10|
|   2|11232BALL POINT PEN                  090181  00198                |FIG13.10|
|   3|11232BALL POINT PEN                  090181  31522                |FIG13.10|
|   4|11232BALL POINT PEN                  090181  00198                |FIG13.10|
|   5|11232BALL POINT PEN                  090181  00198                |FIG13.10|
|   6|11232BALL POINT PEN                  090181  06170                |FIG13.10|
|   7|11232BALL POINT PEN                  021581  00225                |FIG13.10|
|   8|11232BALL POINT PEN                  022281  00035                |FIG13.10|
|   9|11232BALL POINT PEN                  022581  03300                |FIG13.10|
|  10|11232BALL POINT PEN                  030581  00210                |FIG13.10|
|  11|11232BALL POINT PEN                  031581  05115                |FIG13.10|
|  12|11232BALL POINT PEN                  090181  00198                |FIG13.10|
|  13|11232BALL POINT PEN                  053081  00550                |FIG13.10|
|  14|11232BALL POINT PEN                  060681  02235                |FIG13.10|
|  15|11232BALL POINT PEN                  042881  01422                |FIG13.10|
|  16|11232BALL POINT PEN                  012281  05765                |FIG13.10|
|  17|11232BALL POINT PEN                  121281  00098                |FIG13.10|
|  18|11232BALL POINT PEN                  070781  00555                |FIG13.10|
|  19|11232BALL POINT PEN                  111281  00450                |FIG13.10|
|  20|11232BALL POINT PEN                  051581  00995                |FIG13.10|
|  21|11232BALL POINT PEN                  101681  06100                |FIG13.10|
|  22|11232BALL POINT PEN                  111181  04599                |FIG13.10|
|  23|11232BALL POINT PEN                  010181  00155                |FIG13.10|
|  24|11232BALL POINT PEN                  081581  00699                |FIG13.10|
|  25|11232BALL POINT PEN                  040481  01555                |FIG13.10|
|  26|11232BALL POINT PEN                  062381  29914                |FIG13.10|
|  27|11232BALL POINT PEN                  092881  00814                |FIG13.10|
|  28|11232BALL POINT PEN                  090181  00335                |FIG13.10|
|  29|11232BALL POINT PEN                  030381  04125                |FIG13.10|
|  30|11232BALL POINT PEN                  082281  39900                |FIG13.10|
|  31|11232BALL POINT PEN                  060681  50000                |FIG13.10|
|  32|11232BALL POINT PEN                  041881  00444                |FIG13.10|
|  33|11232BALL POINT PEN                  022281  00245                |FIG13.10|
|  34|11232BALL POINT PEN                  011281  00516                |FIG13.10|
|  35|11232BALL POINT PEN                  081281  00198                |FIG13.10|
|  36|11232BALL POINT PEN                  101181  31935                |FIG13.10|
|  37|11232BALL POINT PEN                  053081  00485                |FIG13.10|
|  38|11232BALL POINT PEN                  061781  08840                |FIG13.10|
|  39|11232BALL POINT PEN                  112081  00198                |FIG13.10|
|  40|11232BALL POINT PEN                  122081  04400                |FIG13.10|
|  41|11232BALL POINT PEN                  090181  00198                |FIG13.10|
|  42|11232BALL POINT PEN                  090181  00198                |FIG13.10|
|  43|11232BALL POINT PEN                  050181  06170                |FIG13.10|
|  44|11232BALL POINT PEN                  090181  08820                |FIG13.10|
|  45|41127TYPING PAPER (BOND)             071381  01295                |FIG13.10|
|  46|41127TYPING PAPER (BOND)             041381  41480                |FIG13.10|
|  47|41127TYPING PAPER (BOND)             042281  81599                |FIG13.10|
```

Figure 13.10 Sales Summary Report (Subscripted Tables) (Data) *Continued*

```
--------------------------------------------------------------------------------
       |        1         2         3         4         5         6         7        8| FIGURE |
RECORD|12345678901234567890123456789012345678901234567890123456789012345678901234567890| NUMBER |
--------------------------------------------------------------------------------
        48|41127TYPING PAPER (BOND)              022081 02250                    |FIG13.10|
        49|41127TYPING PAPER (BOND)              122081 12200                    |FIG13.10|
        50|41127TYPING PAPER (BOND)              020181 01999                    |FIG13.10|
        51|41127TYPING PAPER (BOND)              053081 05650                    |FIG13.10|
        52|41127TYPING PAPER (BOND)              011681 09299                    |FIG13.10|
        53|55237COPY MACHINE                     032281 35990                    |FIG13.10|
        54|55237COPY MACHINE                     031581 71980                    |FIG13.10|
        55|55237COPY MACHINE                     011581 35990                    |FIG13.10|
        56|55237COPY MACHINE                     040181 71980                    |FIG13.10|
--------------------------------------------------------------------------------
```

Figure 13.10 Sales Summary Report (Subscripted Tables) (Data) *Continued*

SALES SUMMARY BY MONTH

ITEM DESCRIPTION	JAN.	FEB.	MAR.	APR.	MAY	JUNE	JULY	AUG.	SEP.	OCT.	NOV.	DEC.
11 232 BALL POINT PEN	66.34	38.05	94.50	34.21	82.00	909.89	5.55	407.97	488.49	380.35	52.47	44.98
41 127 TYPING PAPER (BOND)	92.99	42.49	.00	1230.79	56.50	.00	12.95	.00	.00	.00	.00	122.00
55 237 COPY MACHINE	359.90	.00	1079.70	719.80	.00	.00	.00	.00	.00	.00	.00	.00

Figure 13.10 Sales Summary Report (Subscripted Tables) (Output) *Continued*

Character Processing with Tables

Although tables are frequently used to process numeric data, tables may also be used to perform operations know as *character processing*. This simply means that tables are used to manipulate individual characters (or groups of characters) rather than what we normally think of as a field. In the example in Figure 13.11 the program accepts a numeric field (representing a dollar value

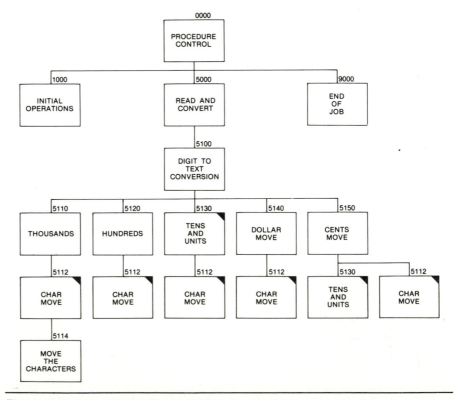

Figure 13.11 A Text Process Program (Hierarchy Chart)

such as the amount of a check) and translates the digits of the field into the words that represent those digits. The problem requires the decomposition of the number into single-digit components and the translation of the digits (and their respective locations in the field) into the text that represents those digits. The textual data is stored in a table through a MOVE statement (redefinitions are discussed in Chapter 19) and "looked-up" each time the digit corresponding to the text is found. The program does this by examining each individual character of a field to determine the presence of blanks, which represents the end of the text for a particular numeric value.

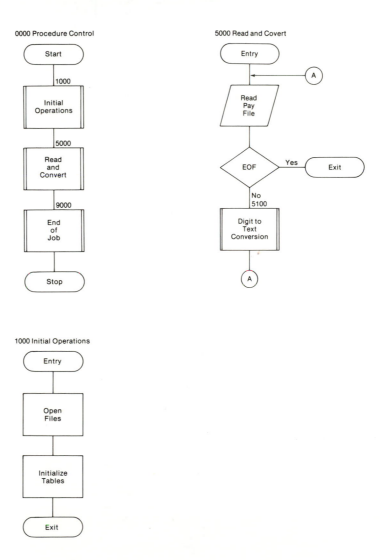

Figure 13.11 A Text Processing Program (Module Flowcharts) *Continued*

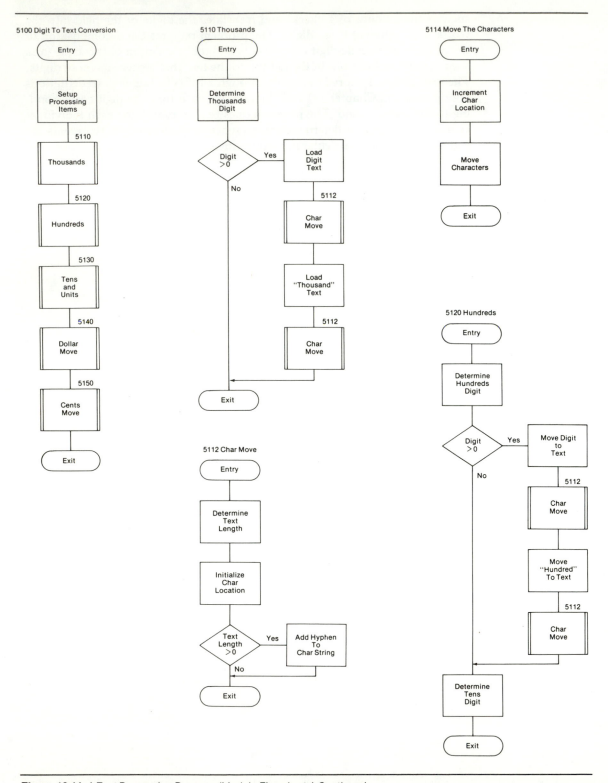

Figure 13.11 A Text Processing Program (Module Flowcharts) *Continued*

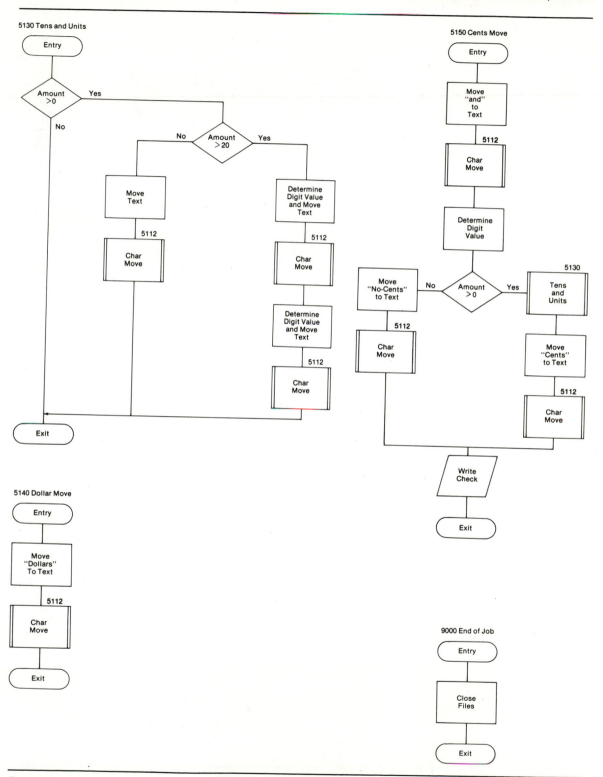

Figure 13.11 A Text Processing Program (Module Flowcharts) *Continued*

```
------------------------------------------------------------------------
|           1   1   2   2   2   3   3   4   4   4   5   5   6   6   6   7   7   8|
|   4   8   2   6   0   4   8   2   6   0   4   8   2   6   0   4   8   2   6   0|
------------------------------------------------------------------------
|000010 IDENTIFICATION DIVISION.                                      FIG13.11|
|000020 PROGRAM-ID. CHECK-WRITER.                                     FIG13.11|
|000030 AUTHOR. DON E. WILLIAMS.                                      FIG13.11|
|000040*    THIS PROGRAM PERFORM A NUMBER TO TEXT CONVERSION          FIG13.11|
|000050*    ON "AMOUNTS" AS MIGHT APPEAR ON A CHECK PRODUCED BY A     FIG13.11|
|000060*    COMPUTER PROGRAM.  NOTE THAT TABLES ARE USED IN THE       FIG13.11|
|000070*    PROCEDURE DIVISION WHICH HAVE VALUES ASSIGNED TO THEM     FIG13.11|
|000080*    THROUGH A MOVE STATEMENT IN THE PROCEDURE DIVISION.       FIG13.11|
|000090 ENVIRONMENT DIVISION.                                         FIG13.11|
|000100 CONFIGURATION SECTION.                                        FIG13.11|
|000110 SOURCE-COMPUTER. HONEYWELL.                                   FIG13.11|
|000120 OBJECT-COMPUTER. HONEYWELL.                                   FIG13.11|
|000130 INPUT-OUTPUT SECTION.                                         FIG13.11|
|000140 FILE-CONTROL.                                                 FIG13.11|
|000150     SELECT PAY-FILE ASSIGN TO UT-S-INFILE.                    FIG13.11|
|000160     SELECT CHECK-FILE ASSIGN TO UT-S-SYSPRINT.                FIG13.11|
|000170*              .RETNIRP OT NGISSA ELIF-KCEHC TCELES            FIG13.11|
|000180*              .REDAER-DRAC OT NGISSA ELIF-YAP TCELES          FIG13.11|
|000190 DATA DIVISION.                                                FIG13.11|
|000200 FILE SECTION.                                                 FIG13.11|
|000210 FD  PAY-FILE LABEL RECORDS ARE OMITTED.                       FIG13.11|
|000220 01  PAY-RECORD.                                               FIG13.11|
|000230     02 AMOUNT-OF-CHECK           PIC 9(04)V9(02).             FIG13.11|
|000240     02 FILLER                    PIC X(74).                   FIG13.11|
|000250 FD  CHECK-FILE LABEL RECORDS ARE OMITTED.                     FIG13.11|
|000260 01  CHECK                        PIC X(133).                  FIG13.11|
|000270 WORKING-STORAGE SECTION.                                      FIG13.11|
|000280 01  WORKING-VARIABLES.                                        FIG13.11|
|000290     05  WHOLE-AMOUNT             PIC 9(04) VALUE ZERO.        FIG13.11|
|000300     05  DIGIT-VALUE              PIC 9(04) VALUE ZERO.        FIG13.11|
|000310     05  CHAR-LOCATION            PIC 9(01) VALUE ZERO.        FIG13.11|
|000320     05  CHARACTER-LOCATION       PIC 9(02) VALUE ZERO.        FIG13.11|
|000330 01  DOLLARS-AND-CENTS.                                        FIG13.11|
|000340     02 DOLLARS                   PIC X(07) VALUE 'DOLLARS'.   FIG13.11|
|000350     02 CENTS                     PIC X(05) VALUE 'CENTS'.     FIG13.11|
|000360     02 NO-CENTS                  PIC X(08) VALUE 'NO-CENTS'.  FIG13.11|
|000370     02 AND-CENTS                 PIC X(03) VALUE 'AND'.       FIG13.11|
|000380 01  NAME-AMOUNT.                                              FIG13.11|
|000390     02 CHARS OCCURS 75 TIMES PIC X.                           FIG13.11|
|000400 01  WORKING-LINE.                                             FIG13.11|
|000410     02 CHRS OCCURS 9 TIMES PIC X.                             FIG13.11|
|000420 01  LIST-OF-UNITS.                                            FIG13.11|
|000430     02 FILLER                    PIC X(09) VALUE 'ONE'.       FIG13.11|
|000440     02 FILLER                    PIC X(09) VALUE 'TWO'.       FIG13.11|
|000450     02 FILLER                    PIC X(09) VALUE 'THREE'.     FIG13.11|
|000460     02 FILLER                    PIC X(09) VALUE 'FOUR'.      FIG13.11|
|000470     02 FILLER                    PIC X(09) VALUE 'FIVE'.      FIG13.11|
|000480     02 FILLER                    PIC X(09) VALUE 'SIX'.       FIG13.11|
|000490     02 FILLER                    PIC X(09) VALUE 'SEVEN'.     FIG13.11|
|000500     02 FILLER                    PIC X(09) VALUE 'EIGHT'.     FIG13.11|
|000510     02 FILLER                    PIC X(09) VALUE 'NINE'.      FIG13.11|
|000520     02 FILLER                    PIC X(09) VALUE 'TEN'.       FIG13.11|
|000530     02 FILLER                    PIC X(09) VALUE 'ELEVEN'.    FIG13.11|
|000540     02 FILLER                    PIC X(09) VALUE 'TWELVE'.    FIG13.11|
|000550     02 FILLER                    PIC X(09) VALUE 'THIRTEEN'.  FIG13.11|
|000560     02 FILLER                    PIC X(09) VALUE 'FOURTEEN'.  FIG13.11|
|000570     02 FILLER                    PIC X(09) VALUE 'FIFTEEN'.   FIG13.11|
|000580     02 FILLER                    PIC X(09) VALUE 'SIXTEEN'.   FIG13.11|
|000590     02 FILLER                    PIC X(09) VALUE 'SEVENTEEN'. FIG13.11|
|000600     02 FILLER                    PIC X(09) VALUE 'EIGHTEEN'.  FIG13.11|
|000610     02 FILLER                    PIC X(09) VALUE 'NINETEEN'.  FIG13.11|
|000620     02 FILLER                    PIC X(09) VALUE 'TWENTY'.    FIG13.11|
|000630     02 FILLER                    PIC X(09) VALUE 'THIRTY'.    FIG13.11|
|000640     02 FILLER                    PIC X(09) VALUE 'FORTY'.     FIG13.11|
|000650     02 FILLER                    PIC X(09) VALUE 'FIFTY'.     FIG13.11|
|000660     02 FILLER                    PIC X(09) VALUE 'SIXTY'.     FIG13.11|
|000670     02 FILLER                    PIC X(09) VALUE 'SEVENTY'.   FIG13.11|
|000680     02 FILLER                    PIC X(09) VALUE 'EIGHTY'.    FIG13.11|
|000690     02 FILLER                    PIC X(09) VALUE 'NINETY'.    FIG13.11|
|000700     02 FILLER                    PIC X(09) VALUE 'HUNDRED'.   FIG13.11|
|000710     02 FILLER                    PIC X(09) VALUE 'THOUSAND'.  FIG13.11|
|000720 01  DIGIT-TABLE.                                              FIG13.11|
|000730     02 DIGITS OCCURS 29 TIMES PIC X(9).                      FIG13.11|
|000740 01  AMOUNT-LINE.                                              FIG13.11|
|000750     02 FILLER                    PIC X(01).                   FIG13.11|
|000760     02 AMT-OF-CHECK              PIC 9(04).9(02).             FIG13.11|
|000770     02 FILLER                    PIC X(03) VALUE SPACES.      FIG13.11|
|000780     02 WRITTEN-AMOUNT            PIC X(75).                   FIG13.11|
```

Figure 13.11 A Text Processing Program *Continued*

```
|            1   1   2   2   2   3   3   4   4   4   5   5   6   6   6   7   7   8|
|  4   8     2   6   0   4   8   2   6   0   4   8   2   6   0   4   8   2   6   0|
-------------------------------------------------------------------------------
|000790 PROCEDURE DIVISION.                                           FIG13.11|
|000800 PROCEDURE-CONTROL SECTION.                                    FIG13.11|
|000810 0000-PROCEDURE-CONTROL.                                       FIG13.11|
|000820     PERFORM 1000-INITIAL-OPERATIONS.                          FIG13.11|
|000830     PERFORM 5000-READ-AND-CONVERT.                            FIG13.11|
|000840     PERFORM 9000-END-OF-JOB.                                  FIG13.11|
|000850     STOP RUN.                                                 FIG13.11|
|000860 1000-INITIAL-OPERATIONS SECTION.                              FIG13.11|
|000870 1001-INITIAL-OPERATIONS.                                      FIG13.11|
|000880     OPEN INPUT PAY-FILE, OUTPUT CHECK-FILE.                   FIG13.11|
|000890     MOVE LIST-OF-UNITS TO DIGIT-TABLE.                        FIG13.11|
|000900 1999-EXIT.                                                    FIG13.11|
|000910     EXIT.                                                     FIG13.11|
|000920 5000-READ-AND-CONVERT SECTION.                                FIG13.11|
|000930 5001-READ-AND-CONVERT.                                        FIG13.11|
|000940     READ PAY-FILE AT END                                      FIG13.11|
|000950         GO TO 5109-EXIT.                                      FIG13.11|
|000960     PERFORM 5100-DIGIT-TO-TEXT-CONVERSION.                    FIG13.11|
|000970     GO TO 5001-READ-AND-CONVERT.                              FIG13.11|
|000980 5109-EXIT.                                                    FIG13.11|
|000990     EXIT.                                                     FIG13.11|
|001000 5100-DIGIT-TO-TEXT-CONVERSION SECTION.                        FIG13.11|
|001010 5101-DIGIT-TO-TEXT.                                           FIG13.11|
|001020     MOVE 0 TO CHARACTER-LOCATION.                             FIG13.11|
|001030     MOVE SPACES TO NAME-AMOUNT, WORKING-LINE.                 FIG13.11|
|001040     MOVE AMOUNT-OF-CHECK TO WHOLE-AMOUNT.                     FIG13.11|
|001050     PERFORM 5110-THOUSANDS.                                   FIG13.11|
|001060     PERFORM 5120-HUNDREDS.                                    FIG13.11|
|001070     PERFORM 5130-TENS-AND-UNITS.                              FIG13.11|
|001080     PERFORM 5140-DOLLAR-MOVE.                                 FIG13.11|
|001090     PERFORM 5150-CENTS-MOVE.                                  FIG13.11|
|001100     GO TO 5999-END-CONVERSION.                                FIG13.11|
|001110 5110-THOUSANDS.                                               FIG13.11|
|001120     DIVIDE WHOLE-AMOUNT BY 1000 GIVING DIGIT-VALUE.           FIG13.11|
|001130     IF DIGIT-VALUE > 0                                        FIG13.11|
|001140         MOVE DIGITS (DIGIT-VALUE) TO WORKING-LINE;            FIG13.11|
|001150         PERFORM 5112-CHAR-MOVE;                               FIG13.11|
|001160         MOVE DIGITS (29) TO WORKING-LINE;                     FIG13.11|
|001170         PERFORM 5112-CHAR-MOVE.                               FIG13.11|
|001180 5112-CHAR-MOVE.                                               FIG13.11|
|001190*                                                              FIG13.11|
|001200********************************************************************** FIG13.11|
|001210*      THE EXAMINE STATEMENT BELOW IS DISCUSSED IN          *  FIG13.11|
|001220*      CHAPTER 21.                                          *  FIG13.11|
|001230*      THE VARIABLE "TALLY" WILL CONTAIN THE NUMBER OF      *  FIG13.11|
|001240*      CHARACTERS IN A WORD AS A RESULT OF THIS OPERATION.  *  FIG13.11|
|001250*      THE SAME OPERATION COULD BE ACHIEVED THROUGH THE USE *  FIG13.11|
|001260*      OF AN IF STATEMENT WITHIN A PERFORM VARYING, HOWEVER. *  FIG13.11|
|001270********************************************************************** FIG13.11|
|001280*                                                              FIG13.11|
|001290     EXAMINE WORKING-LINE TALLYING UNTIL FIRST SPACE.          FIG13.11|
|001300     MOVE 0 TO CHAR-LOCATION.                                  FIG13.11|
|001310     PERFORM 5114-MOVE-THE-CHARACTERS TALLY TIMES.             FIG13.11|
|001320     IF TALLY > 0                                              FIG13.11|
|001330         ADD 1 TO CHARACTER-LOCATION;                          FIG13.11|
|001340         MOVE "-" TO CHARS (CHARACTER-LOCATION).               FIG13.11|
|001350 5114-MOVE-THE-CHARACTERS.                                     FIG13.11|
|001360     ADD 1 TO CHAR-LOCATION, CHARACTER-LOCATION.               FIG13.11|
|001370     MOVE CHRS (CHAR-LOCATION) TO CHARS (CHARACTER-LOCATION).  FIG13.11|
|001380 5120-HUNDREDS.                                                FIG13.11|
|001390     COMPUTE WHOLE-AMOUNT = WHOLE-AMOUNT - DIGIT-VALUE * 1000. FIG13.11|
|001400     DIVIDE WHOLE-AMOUNT BY 100 GIVING DIGIT-VALUE.            FIG13.11|
|001410     IF DIGIT-VALUE > 0                                        FIG13.11|
|001420         MOVE DIGITS (DIGIT-VALUE) TO WORKING-LINE;            FIG13.11|
|001430         PERFORM 5112-CHAR-MOVE;                               FIG13.11|
|001440         MOVE DIGITS (28) TO WORKING-LINE;                     FIG13.11|
|001450         PERFORM 5112-CHAR-MOVE.                               FIG13.11|
|001460     COMPUTE WHOLE-AMOUNT = WHOLE-AMOUNT - DIGIT-VALUE * 100.  FIG13.11|
|001470 5130-TENS-AND-UNITS.                                          FIG13.11|
|001480     IF WHOLE-AMOUNT > 0                                       FIG13.11|
|001490       IF WHOLE-AMOUNT > 20                                    FIG13.11|
|001500         DIVIDE WHOLE-AMOUNT BY 10 GIVING DIGIT-VALUE;         FIG13.11|
|001510         ADD 18 TO DIGIT-VALUE;                                FIG13.11|
|001520         MOVE DIGITS (DIGIT-VALUE) TO WORKING-LINE;            FIG13.11|
|001530         PERFORM 5112-CHAR-MOVE; SUBTRACT 18 FROM DIGIT-VALUE;FIG13.11|
|001540         COMPUTE WHOLE-AMOUNT = WHOLE-AMOUNT -                 FIG13.11|
|001550             DIGIT-VALUE * 10;                                 FIG13.11|
|001560         IF WHOLE-AMOUNT = 0                                   FIG13.11|
```

Figure 13.11 A Text Processing Program *Continued*

```
-------------------------------------------------------------------------------
|         1  1  2  2  2  3  3  4  4  4  5  5  6  6  6  7  7  8|
|   4   8 2  6  0  4  8  2  6  0  4  8  2  6  0  4  8  2  6  0|
-------------------------------------------------------------------------------
|001570                       NEXT SENTENCE                        FIG13.11|
|001580              ELSE                                          FIG13.11|
|001590                   MOVE DIGITS (WHOLE-AMOUNT) TO WORKING-LINE;  FIG13.11|
|001600                   PERFORM 5112-CHAR-MOVE                   FIG13.11|
|001610            ELSE                                            FIG13.11|
|001620                MOVE DIGITS (WHOLE-AMOUNT) TO WORKING-LINE;  FIG13.11|
|001630                PERFORM 5112-CHAR-MOVE.                     FIG13.11|
|001640 5140-DOLLAR-MOVE.                                          FIG13.11|
|001650      MOVE DOLLARS TO WORKING-LINE.                         FIG13.11|
|001660      PERFORM 5112-CHAR-MOVE.                               FIG13.11|
|001670 5150-CENTS-MOVE.                                           FIG13.11|
|001680      MOVE AND-CENTS TO WORKING-LINE.                       FIG13.11|
|001690      PERFORM 5112-CHAR-MOVE.                               FIG13.11|
|001700      MOVE AMOUNT-OF-CHECK TO DIGIT-VALUE.                  FIG13.11|
|001710      COMPUTE WHOLE-AMOUNT = (AMOUNT-OF-CHECK - DIGIT-VALUE) FIG13.11|
|001720           * 100.                                           FIG13.11|
|001730      IF WHOLE-AMOUNT > 0                                   FIG13.11|
|001740          PERFORM 5130-TENS-AND-UNITS;                      FIG13.11|
|001750          MOVE CENTS TO WORKING-LINE;                       FIG13.11|
|001760          PERFORM 5112-CHAR-MOVE                            FIG13.11|
|001770      ELSE                                                  FIG13.11|
|001780          MOVE NO-CENTS TO WORKING-LINE;                    FIG13.11|
|001790          PERFORM 5112-CHAR-MOVE.                           FIG13.11|
|001800      MOVE NAME-AMOUNT TO WRITTEN-AMOUNT.                   FIG13.11|
|001810      MOVE AMOUNT-OF-CHECK TO AMT-OF-CHECK.                 FIG13.11|
|001820      WRITE CHECK FROM AMOUNT-LINE AFTER 1 LINES.           FIG13.11|
|001830 5999-END-CONVERSION.                                       FIG13.11|
|001840      EXIT.                                                 FIG13.11|
|001850 9000-END-OF-JOB SECTION.                                   FIG13.11|
|001860 9001-END-OF-JOB.                                           FIG13.11|
|001870      CLOSE PAY-FILE, CHECK-FILE.                           FIG13.11|
|001880 9999-EXIT.                                                 FIG13.11|
|001890      EXIT.                                                 FIG13.11|
-------------------------------------------------------------------------------
```

Figure 13.11 A Text Processing Program *Continued*

```
-------------------------------------------------------------------------------
|       |         1         2         3         4         5         6         7         8| FIGURE  |
|RECORD|12345678901234567890123456789012345678901234567890123456789012345678901234567890| NUMBER |
-------------------------------------------------------------------------------
|    1|500102                                                                           |FIG13.11|
|    2|002000                                                                           |FIG13.11|
|    3|069999                                                                           |FIG13.11|
|    4|021388                                                                           |FIG13.11|
|    5|005052                                                                           |FIG13.11|
|    6|953700                                                                           |FIG13.11|
|    7|046610                                                                           |FIG13.11|
|    8|002009                                                                           |FIG13.11|
|    9|000350                                                                           |FIG13.11|
|   10|032475                                                                           |FIG13.11|
|   11|300000                                                                           |FIG13.11|
|   12|765000                                                                           |FIG13.11|
|   13|465300                                                                           |FIG13.11|
|   14|022222                                                                           |FIG13.11|
-------------------------------------------------------------------------------
```

Figure 13.11 A Text Processing Program (Data) *Continued*

```
5001.02    FIVE-THOUSAND-ONE-DOLLARS-AND-TWO-CENTS-
0020.00    TWENTY-DOLLARS-AND-NO-CENTS-
0899.99    EIGHT-HUNDRED-NINETY-NINE-DOLLARS-AND-NINETY-NINE-CENTS-
0213.88    TWO-HUNDRED-THIRTEEN-DOLLARS-AND-EIGHTY-EIGHT-CENTS-
0050.52    FIFTY-DOLLARS-AND-FIFTY-TWO-CENTS-
9537.00    NINE-THOUSAND-FIVE-HUNDRED-THIRTY-SEVEN-DOLLARS-AND-NO-CENTS-
0466.10    FOUR-HUNDRED-SIXTY-SIX-DOLLARS-AND-TEN-CENTS-
0020.09    TWENTY-DOLLARS-AND-NINE-CENTS-
0003.50    THREE-DOLLARS-AND-FIFTY-CENTS-
0324.75    THREE-HUNDRED-TWENTY-FOUR-DOLLARS-AND-SEVENTY-FIVE-CENTS-
3000.00    THREE-THOUSAND-DOLLARS-AND-NO-CENTS-
7650.00    SEVEN-THOUSAND-SIX-HUNDRED-FIFTY-DOLLARS-AND-NO-CENTS-
4653.00    FOUR-THOUSAND-SIX-HUNDRED-FIFTY-THREE-DOLLARS-AND-NO-CENTS-
0222.22    TWO-HUNDRED-TWENTY-TWO-DOLLARS-AND-TWENTY-TWO-CENTS-
```

Figure 13.11 A Text Processing Program (Output) *Continued*

```
Format 2*


    OCCURS integer-1 TO integer-2 TIMES DEPENDING ON data-name-1
```
*Format, as written, is incomplete. Complete format provided in Chapter 14.

Figure 13.12 Format of the OCCURS/DEPENDING ON Clause

Variable-Length Tables

The second form of the OCCURS clause (Figure 13.12) permits the description of a *variable-length* table. A table is variable in length when its size may be changed during the execution of the program. This does *not* mean that COBOL can dynamically describe internal memory. A variable length table is considered to be static; for purposes of determining the amount of internal memory used, it is allocated the maximum number of occurrences.

In the Format 2 OCCURS clause, two integer values are specified. Integer-1 represents the minimum number of occurrences to be associated with a particular data-name. Integer-1 must be a non-negative integer value. Integer-2 provides for the maximum number of occurrences possible in the table. Integer-2 must be a positive integer value greater than integer-1. The DEPENDING ON clause is also used with the Format 2 OCCURS clause. Data-name-1, which follows the reserved words DEPENDING ON, specifies the actual number of usable occurrences within the range of integer-1 to integer-2. The table does not expand or contract with the positive integer value placed in data-name-1; the data-name indicates the logical size of the table. The table "appears" to contain data-name-1 occurrences, and only data-name-1 occurrences may be addressed with any reliability; however, the physical dimension of the table is specified by integer-2.

Data-name-1, as indicated above, must contain a positive integer value within the range of integer-1 to integer-2. The description of data-name-1 must not be subordinate to or associated with an OCCURS clause, except as presented in the DEPENDING ON option. Data-name-1 may appear in the same record description as a table that is described with the OCCURS DEPENDING ON clause but only before the variable portion of the table. If it is necessary, data-name-1 may be qualified in the same manner as other data names.

Summary

COBOL supports tables to a maximum of three dimensions. Tables are useful in solving problems that require the internal storage of massive quantities of data. In some cases these data may be homogeneous. In other cases, the data are simply interrelated.

In COBOL, tables are created through the use of one or more OCCURS clauses. When a single OCCURS clause appears in a record description, the data item (and all subordinate data items) is classified as a single-dimension table (a vector or list). When referenced in the PROCEDURE DIVISION, this data item (and subordinate data items) must be accompanied by a single subscript indicating the occurrence position to be addressed.

A two-dimension table is created when one OCCURS clause of a record description is subordinate to another OCCURS clause. This data matrix requires both row and column subscripts when addressed at the lowest level. Finally, three-dimension tables, a data "cube," are created when a record contains three OCCURS clauses. However, each OCCURS clause must be coded so that no two are on the same level (recorded with the same level number). Each reference to an elementary-item of a three-dimension table requires row, column, and rank subscripts. Tables may be coded so that they appear to be variable in size (variable-length tables).

Notes on Programming Style

Internal tables, though useful, are not a "cure-all" nor should they be used in all circumstances where your first impression leads you to believe they are warranted. When using tables, look out for the following situations:

1. subscript values outside the bounds of the table,
2. attempting to read into a table when the table is larger than the logical record,
3. storing more detail in a table than the problem warrants, and
4. assuming the table size you have decided upon is relative to the problem.

One frequent problem for beginning programmers is inattention to the value of subscripts. Suppose, for example, you have defined a table to contain ten elements. The only valid values for a subscript that references this table are 1, 2, 3, 4, 5, 6, 7, 8, 9, and 10. Because most compilers do not protect you from providing a subscript value that is less than 1 or greater than 10, your program could address data that immediately precedes or follows the actual table definition.

COBOL is designed to deal with logical records (at least as far as the FD description is concerned). When reading data that is a table, it is frequently necessary to read only a portion of the table from the external source and then load that portion into an internal (WORKING-STORAGE) table definition. By repeating this operation, the entire table will ultimately be reconstructed internally.

When designing a program to solve a particular problem that may require tables, we frequently rush into the solution without a thorough understanding of the requirements. If you are reading data that is to be stored in a table, ask yourself at least two questions. First, do you need all the fields presented in the record? Sometimes the answer is yes, and you may *also* find that additional fields are required. Second, do you need the detail of every record? Again, sometimes the answer is yes; however, at least you will have studied the problem requirements and are not just blindly following a solution to the problem.

Beginning programmers also frequently make assumptions about the size of a table that are too narrow. When program development begins, ask yourself "What is the biggest this table could ever be?" You should know the maximum size for each table involved in the problem. Creating tables to their maximum dimension generalizes your solution to handle problems other than those in the original problem statement. After all, you do not want to redesign a program just because you were not farsighted enough to realize that the next time the program was used there were to be a few more items stored in a table.

When generalizing the maximum table size, you should not assume that the table will always be full. If it is possible that the number of items may vary, *count them!*

Questions

Below fill in the blank(s) with the appropriate word, words, or phrases.

1. In COBOL, when it is necessary to store large amounts of data internally, _____ are often used.

2. In COBOL, a table is created through the use of a(n) _____ clause.

3. When the OCCURS clause is used in a record, it may appear anywhere from level _____ to level _____ .

4. COBOL supports tables to a maximum of _____ (number) dimensions.

5. A data item that is associated with only one OCCURS clause is referred to as a(n) _____ .

6. When a data item is written with an OCCURS clause, references to that data item in the PROCEDURE DIVISION must be accompanied by a(n) _____ .

7. An occurrence position within a table is specified through a(n) _____ .

8. When a data item OCCURS 20 TIMES, the valid occurrence positions within the table range from _____ (number) to _____ (number).

9. To create a two-dimension table (a table with rows and columns), a record must contain an OCCURS clause that is subordinate to a(n) _____ .

10. In a two-dimension table, the first OCCURS clause specifies the number of _____ (rows/columns) of the table, and the second clause indicates the number of _____ (rows/columns).

11. A two-dimension table may also be called a(n) _____ .

12. When a reference is made to a two-dimension table in the PROCEDURE DIVISION, _____ (number) subscripts must be used.

13. To construct a three-dimension table in COBOL, an OCCURS clause must be subordinate to an OCCURS clause which is subordinate to a(n) _____ .

14. The first subscript used to reference a three-dimension table represents the _____ (row, column, rank) position, the second, the _____ position, and the third, the _____ position.

15. In a variable-length table, the logically addressable positions (occurrences) of the table are specified by a(n) _____ .

16. In a variable-length table, the maximum physical size of the table is specified by _____ .

Answer the following questions by circling either "T" for True or "F" for False.

T F 17. An OCCURS clause may be associated with an independent-elementary-item.

T F 18. The OCCURS clause may be written only at the elementary-item level.

T F 19. In the format of the OCCURS clause that provides for the description of static tables, an identifier may be used to indicate the number of occurrences of the table.

T F 20. If an OCCURS clause is used at the group level, all items subordinate to that group are tables.

T F 21. A data item that is subordinate to another data item written with an OCCURS clause must be subscripted when referenced in the PROCEDURE DIVISION.

T F 22. A data item used as a subscript may not be used for any other purpose in the PROCEDURE DIVISION.

T F 23. When a table element is referenced with a subscript, the subscript must be enclosed in parentheses.

T F 24. Only a data-name may be used as a subscript.

T F 25. All records that contain two OCCURS clauses represent a two-dimension table.

T F 26. When referencing a two-dimension table in the PROCEDURE DIVISION, the first subscript is a row reference.

T F 27. In COBOL, a record could contain combinations of one- and two-dimension tables.

T F 28. In a two-dimension table, the second OCCURS clause must be followed by a subordinate elementary-item.

T F 29. In a two-dimension table, the second OCCURS clause is not permitted to have a subordinate elementary-item.

T F 30. Only three OCCURS clauses are permitted within a single record in COBOL.

T F 31. Variable-length tables in COBOL dynamically allocate memory.

Exercises

1. Complete a table with the indicated heading for each record description below. Each data-name in the record should be included in the table.

TABLE

Data-Name	Number of Rows	Columns	Ranks	Size of a Single Item	Number of Items In Description	Total Bytes In Description
a) Ø1 LIST-OF-CONTRIBUTORS.						
Ø2 CONTRIBUTOR OCCURS 20 TIMES				PIC X(20).		
b) Ø1 SALESMAN-TABLE.						
Ø2 SALESMAN-NAME OCCURS 50 TIMES.						
Ø3 NAME				PIC X(30).		
Ø3 ID-NUMBER				PIC 9(5).		
Ø3 PHONE				PIC 9(7).		
c) Ø1 COLLEGE-COURSES.						
Ø2 DEPARTMENT OCCURS 30 TIMES				PIC XXX.		
Ø2 COURSE-NUMBER OCCURS 90 TIMES				PIC 999.		
d) Ø1 LEDGER-TABLE.						
Ø2 ASSETS OCCURS 30 TIMES.						
Ø3 ASSET-NO				PIC 9(5).		
Ø3 ASSET-DESC				PIC X(25).		
Ø3 ASSET-BALANCE				PIC S9(5)V99.		
Ø2 LIABILITY OCCURS 10 TIMES.						
Ø3 LIAB-NO				PIC 9(5).		
Ø3 LIAB-DESC				PIC X(25).		
Ø3 LIAB-BALANCE				PIC S9(5)V99.		
e) Ø1 INTEREST-RATE-TABLE.						
Ø2 INTEREST-RATE OCCURS 10 TIMES.						
Ø3 YEARS-INVESTED OCCURS 20 TIMES.						
Ø4 INTEREST				PIC 9(5)V9(5).		

TABLE

Data-Name	Number of Rows	Columns	Ranks	Size of a Single Item	Number of Items In Description	Total Bytes In Description

f)   Ø1   STUDENT-INFORMATION-TABLE.

    Ø2   STUDENT OCCURS 400 TIMES.

        Ø3   NAME   PIC X(20).

        Ø3   ID-NUMBER   PIC 9(9).

        Ø3   CLASS   PIC XX

        Ø3   COURSE OCCURS 50 TIMES.

            Ø4   DEPT   PIC XXX.

            Ø4   COURSE-NO   PIC 999.

            Ø4   GRADE   PIC X.

g)   Ø1   DEMOGRAPHIC-DATA.

    Ø2   INCOME OCCURS 20 TIMES.

        Ø3   AGE OCCURS 40 TIMES.

            Ø4   SEX OCCURS 2 TIMES   PIC X

            Ø4   MARITAL-STATUS OCCURS 2 TIMES.   PIC X.

2. Below are a number of COBOL table descriptions. Sketch the logical appearance of each table, and indicate what portion of the table is addressed by each name.

    a)   Ø1   TABLE-1.

        Ø2   LEVEL-1 OCCURS 10 TIMES   PIC 9(5).

    b)   Ø1   TABLE-2.

        Ø2   LEVEL-1 OCCURS 3 TIMES.

            Ø3   LEVEL-1A   PIC 99.

            Ø3   LEVEL-1B   PIC X(4).

    c)   Ø1   TABLE-3.

        Ø2   LEVEL-1A OCCURS 5 TIMES   PIC 9(5).

        Ø2   LEVEL-1B OCCURS 7 TIMES   PIC 9V99.

    d)   Ø1   TABLE-4.

        Ø2   LEVEL-1 OCCURS 4 TIMES.

            Ø3   LEVEL-2 OCCURS 6 TIMES   PIC XX.

```
e)  Ø1  TABLE-5.

        Ø2  LEVEL-1 OCCURS 2 TIMES.

            Ø3  LEVEL-2 OCCURS 3 TIMES.

                Ø4  LEVEL-2A                      PIC 9(4).

                Ø4  LEVEL-2B                      PIC XX.


f)  Ø1  TABLE-6.

        Ø2  LEVEL-1 OCCURS 5 TIMES.

            Ø3  LEVEL-2 OCCURS 3 TIMES.

                Ø4  LEVEL-3 OCCURS 4 TIMES        PIC 9(5).


g)  Ø1  TABLE-7.

        Ø2  LEVEL-1 OCCURS 2 TIMES.

            Ø3  LEVEL-1A                          PIC XX

            Ø3  LEVEL-1B                          PIC 9.

            Ø3  LEVEL-2 OCCURS 4 TIMES.

                Ø4  LEVEL-2A                      PIC X.

                Ø4  LEVEL-2B                      PIC 999.
```

Problems

1. A series of records have been developed by the Personnel Department in preparation of the production of a company telephone book. The records contain the employees' names (last name first) and telephone numbers (see the multiple-card layout form).

   The report (see the print chart) is to conform to a standard similar to that produced by telephone utility companies. That is, each page consists of two columns. Each column is composed of individuals' names and telephone numbers. (Since our company is geographically dispersed, the area code is to be included in the telephone number.) To assist the telephone book user, any time the first letter of an employee's name changes, a blank area should appear in the column. For example, when the employee name "BACON, ALLEN D." is printed, his name should be preceded by a blank area (assuming of course that he is the first employee in the Bs.) In addition, for quick-referencing purposes, the first and last employee names on the page are to be printed at the bottom of each page. The location of the quick-reference line should be in the same place on every page.

   For purposes of this procedure, you may assume the data has been ordered by employee name.

MULTIPLE-CARD LAYOUT FORM

Company Learning COBOL, Inc.

Application Company Telephone Book _ _ _ _ by J. Wayne Spence _ _ _ _ _ _ _ _ Date 01/01/81 Job No. PROB 13.1 Sheet No. 1

Employee Name	Telephone			
	Area Code	Exchange	Number	
9 9 9 9 9 9 9 9 9 9 9 9 9 9 9 9 9 9 9 9	9 9 9	9 9	9 9 9 9	9 9 9 9 9 9 9 9 9 9 9 9 9 9 9 9 9 9 9 9 9 9 9 9 9 9 9 9 9 9 9 9 9 9 9 9 9 9 9 9 9 9 9 9 9 9 9 9 9 9

150/10/8 PRINT CHART   PROG. ID. Problem 13.1   PAGE 1
(SPACING: 150 POSITIONS AT 10 CHARACTERS PER INCH, 8 LINES PER VERTICAL INCH)   DATE 01/01/81
PROGRAM TITLE TELEPHONE BOOK
PROGRAMMER OR DOCUMENTALIST: J. Wayne Spence
CHART TITLE COMPANY TELEPHONE BOOK

```
              COMPANY TELEPHONE BOOK                    PAGE ZZ9

NAME                    PHONE NUMBER    NAME           PHONE NUMBER
X- - - - - - - - - - - -X   (XXX) XXX-XXXX    X- - - - - - - - - - -X   (XXX) XXX-XXXX
X- - - - - - - - - - - -X   (XXX) XXX-XXXX    X- - - - - - - - - - -X   (XXX) XXX-XXXX
X- - - - - - - - - - - -X   (XXX) XXX-XXXX                           (XXX) XXX-XXXX
X- - - - - - - - - - - -X   (XXX) XXX-XXXX    X- - - - - - - - - - -X   (XXX) XXX-XXXX
X- - - - - - - - - - - -X   (XXX) XXX-XXXX    X- - - - - - - - - - -X   (XXX) XXX-XXXX
Y- - - - - - - - - - - -X   (XXX) XXX-XXXX    X- - - - - - - - - - -X   (XXX) XXX-XXXX

                                        Change
                                        of First
                                        Letter
                                        in Last
                                        Name


X- - - - - - - - - - - -X   (XXX) XXX-XXXX    X- - - - - - - - - - -X   (XXX) XXX-XXXX

              X- - - - - - - - - - -X TO X- - - - - - - - - - -X
```

2. An instructor has just given a true-false and multiple-choice exam to his class, and he wishes to have a program developed that will grade the exam. In addition, the instructor wishes to use the same grading program for future exams and other classes. All questions will be equally weighted; however, each exam given (to separate classes) will not necessarily have the same number of questions. There will be a maximum of 50 questions on an exam and the maximum class size is 100 students. Furthermore, your procedure should be able to grade multiple classes in one execution.

We have devised the record formats presented in the multiple-card layout form to accomplish this task. Two record types will be used—the exam key record and student response records. The exam key record will be constructed such that the first three characters of the record will contain the word "KEY" followed by the exam identification and the correct responses to individual questions 1 through n. The correct responses to each question will occupy one record column each. A blank column in the key record means that the question is not to be graded (or did not appear on the exam). Student response records follow a similar format except that the first portion of the record contains the student identification number and the student's name.

Your procedure should determine (see the print chart):

1. the exam grade (score) for each student taking an exam;
2. the number of incorrect responses to each exam question;
3. the breakdown of student grades into As, Bs, Cs, Ds, and Fs;
4. the highest and lowest exam grade plus the grade range; and
5. the overall class average.

MULTIPLE-CARD LAYOUT FORM

Company Learning COBOL, INC.

Application Exam Grading   by J. Wayne Spence   Date 01/01/81   Job No. PROB 13.2   Sheet No. 1

Key Record

| KEY | Exam Identification | 1 2 3 | Correct Response to Question • • • 50 |

Student Response Record

| Student | | Student Response to Question |
| Identification Number | Name | 1 2 3 • • • 50 |

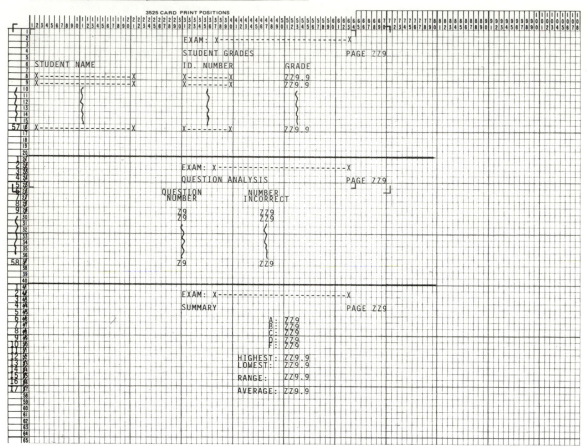

3. Expense records have been provided to us for all departments within the company. Each expense record contains three fields (see the multiple-card layout form):

   1. the department number of the department incurring an expense,
   2. the date on which the expense was paid (in a month-day-year format), and
   3. the amount of the expenditure.

   Corporate management wishes to see a summary of all expenditures of the company in two forms—by department and by the month in which the expense was incurred. As a consequence, the report designs shown on the print chart have been devised. Note that all department numbers (e.g., 100, 200, etc.) have been translated into the department name according to the following schedule:

Department Number(s)	Department Name
100-199	Accounting
200-239	Marketing-Sales
240-299	Marketing-Advertising & Research
300-399	Data Processing
600-699	Financial Controls & Budgets
700-799	Shipping & Receiving
800-819	Manufacturing-Fabrication
820-899	Manufacturing-Assembly & Packaging

You are to provide the name of the department in the departmental summary. Furthermore, you are to provide the name of the month (e.g., January, February, etc.) for the month number in the monthly summary.

MULTIPLE-CARD LAYOUT FORM

Company Learning COBOL, INC.

Application Expense Summary   by J. Wayne Spence   Date 01/01/81   Job No PROB 13.3   Sheet No. 1

Dept. Number	Date of Expense	Expense Amount	
999	99999	9999999999	999999999999999999999999999999999999999999999999999999999999

150/10/8 PRINT CHART   PROG. ID. Problem 13.3   PAGE 1
(SPACING: 150 POSITIONS AT 10 CHARACTERS PER INCH, 8 LINES PER VERTICAL INCH)   DATE 01/01/81
PROGRAM TITLE EXPENSE SUMMARY
PROGRAMMER OR DOCUMENTALIST: J. WAYNE SPENCE
CHART TITLE DEPARTMENTAL AND MONTHLY EXPENSE SUMMARY

3525 CARD PRINT POSITIONS

```
                    DEPARTMENTAL EXPENSE SUMMARY

                    DEPARTMENT              AMOUNT
                    ACCOUNTING        ZZZ,ZZZ,ZZZ.99
               MARKETING--SALES       ZZZ,ZZZ,ZZZ.99
    MARKETING--ADVERTISING & RESEARCH ZZZ,ZZZ,ZZZ.99
                          {                  {
MANUFACTURING--ASSEMBLY & PACKAGING   ZZZ,ZZZ,ZZZ.99
                                      --------------
               TOTAL EXPENSES         ZZZ,ZZZ,ZZZ.99


                    MONTHLY EXPENSE SUMMARY

                    MONTH               AMOUNT
                    JANUARY           ZZZ,ZZZ,ZZZ.99
                    FEBRUARY          ZZZ,ZZZ,ZZZ.99
                    MARCH             ZZZ,ZZZ,ZZZ.99
                      {                  {
                    DECEMBER          ZZZ,ZZZ,ZZZ.99
               TOTAL EXPENSES         ZZZ,ZZZ,ZZZ.99
```

14 Table Handling with Indexes

Data in a table can be handled more efficiently when the table is indexed rather than subscripted. Indexes (locations within a table) are determined by the number of bytes (displacement) from the beginning of the table. That is, an index value is based on the size of each of the items in the table. Thus, if the first item is to be addressed, the displacement (distance from the beginning of the table) would be zero bytes. If only one item is present in the table and each occurrence of the item is five bytes in length, the location of the second item in the table would be five bytes from the beginning of the table, the third item would be ten bytes from the beginning, and so forth.

When a table is subscripted, rather than indexed, the location of an item is determined in much the same way; however, the computer must first determine the occurrence number and then determine the location of the item on the basis of the number of bytes from the beginning of the table, which requires extra processing.

The process of creating an indexed table is similar to creating a subscripted table. An indexed table also uses an OCCURS clause; but, it requires other clauses, as indicated in Figure 14.1.

The clause that distinguishes an indexed table from a subscripted table is the INDEXED BY clause, which causes the creation of an index-name that is used only in conjunction with the particular level of the table to which it is attached. So, the index-name may be used to reference only *that* level of *that* table. The INDEXED BY clause automatically defines the index-name as a full-word binary integer field, eliminating the need for any other reference to the index-name in the DATA DIVISION. The index-name is automatically "synchronized" (adjusted to an appropriate internal boundary), which assists in speeding table processing. (With a subscripted table, the subscripts are user defined and could be DISPLAY data items, which the computer must translate into binary digits and adjust to the appropriate internal boundary before processing.)

An indexed table allows the addressing of a table item through both *direct* and *relative indexing*. With a subscripted table, a table item can be referenced

```
FORMAT 1:

    OCCURS integer TIMES

        ⎡ ⎧ASCENDING ⎫                                              ⎤
        ⎢ ⎨          ⎬ KEY IS data-name-1  [data-name-2] ...       ⎥ ...
        ⎣ ⎩DESCENDING⎭                                              ⎦

        [INDEXED BY index-name-1  [index-name-2]  ...]

- - - - - - - - - - - - - - - - - - - - - - - - - - - - - - - - - - - - - - -

FORMAT 2:

    OCCURS integer-1 TO integer-2 TIMES [DEPENDING ON data-name-3]

        ⎡ ⎧ASCENDING ⎫                                              ⎤
        ⎢ ⎨          ⎬ KEY IS data-name-1  [data-name-2] ...       ⎥ ...
        ⎣ ⎩DESCENDING⎭                                              ⎦

        [INDEXED BY index-name-1  [index-name-2]  ...]
```

Figure 14.1 Formats of the OCCURS Clause for Indexed Tables

only through direct addressing; i.e., the only valid reference (subscript) is an integer constant or a data item containing an integer value. An indexed table has that capability plus relative indexing.

Relative indexing means to address a table position with an index-name plus or minus an integer constant. For example, if TABLE-ITEM is the data-name used to reference a one-dimension table that is indexed by IND, the table could be addressed as TABLE-ITEM (1), TABLE-ITEM (IND), TABLE-ITEM (IND+2) or TABLE-ITEM (IND−5). (The first pair of notations represents direct indexing; the second pair, relative indexing.)

The PERFORM Statement

Though processing with indexed tables is more efficient, there are a number of restrictions on the modification of index-name values in the PROCEDURE DIVISION. When subscripts are used in conjunction with table processing, the programmer can use a wide range of statements to provide subscript values, such as the READ, ADD, SUBTRACT, MULTIPLY, DIVIDE, COMPUTE, MOVE, and PERFORM statements. Of these, only the PERFORM statement is permitted to modify the value associated with an index-name. The PER-FORM/VARYING statement, often used in conjunction with the processing of subscripted tables, may also be used to process indexed tables. As mentioned in Chapter 12, the PERFORM/VARYING statement may be used to modify the value of either an identifier or an index-name. Thus, if the statement

```
PERFORM PARA-A VARYING LCTN FROM 1 BY 1 UNTIL I = 100
```

appeared in a program, without examining the DATA DIVISION the programmer would be unable to determine whether LCTN represented a subscript or an index-name.

The SET Statement

Because index-name values are treated as byte displacements rather than as occurrence numbers, the MOVE, ADD, and SUBTRACT statements often used to create or modify the value of a subscript are not permitted to modify an index-name value. As a substitute, COBOL permits the SET statement to modify an index-name value in much the same way a MOVE, ADD, or SUBTRACT statement would modify a subscript.

The SET statement, shown in Figure 14.2, can be coded in two forms. The first format of the SET statement is a substitute for the MOVE statement; however, the order of the sending field and the receiving field(s) is the reverse of the MOVE statement. In other words, index-name-1 (or identifier-1) and index-name-2 (identifier-2) are *receiving* fields—their values are modified as a result of the execution of the SET statement. Index-name-3 (identifier-3 or literal-1) is the sending field. The index-names are implicitly described as integer fields. If identifiers are present, they must be described in the DATA DIVISION as integer fields, and literal-l (if used) must be a positive integer. If index-name-3 is used as the sending field, no conversion is made (from occurrence position to byte displacement) when it is placed in the receiving field. That is, index-name-3 contains the byte displacement for the data item with which it is associated before the SET statement is executed, and that value (byte displacement) is placed in the receiving field.

If the receiving field is an identifier, the identifier should be described in the DATA DIVISION with a USAGE IS INDEX clause. When the USAGE IS INDEX clause is associated with a data item in the DATA DIVISION, the data item is automatically defined as a full-word, binary integer storage position—no PICTURE clause is needed. This data item (generally called an *index-data-name*) is often used in conjunction with the processing of indexed tables. For example, when it is necessary to *save* the value associated with a particular index-name, the value might be placed in an index-data-name—a field with the same characteristics. However, an index-data-name is in no way directly connected with any table. Thus, an index-data-name could be used as a "generalized" storage position (the receiving field in the SET statement). In that case, when the sending field of a SET statement is an index-name, the value in index-

```
Format 1:

      ┌index-name-1┐ ┌index-name-2┐          ┌index-name-3┐
SET   │            │ │            │  ...  TO  │identifier-3│
      └identifier-1┘ └identifier-2┘          │literal-1   │
                                              └            ┘

- - - - - - - - - - - - - - - - - - - - - - - - - - - - - - - - - -

Format 2:

                                       ┌UP   BY┐  ┌identifier-4┐
SET index-name-4 [index-name-5] ...    │       │  │            │
                                       └DOWN BY┘  └literal-2   ┘
```

Figure 14.2 Formats of the SET Statement

name-3 (the sending field) is placed in index-data-name (the receiving field), i.e., the byte displacement transfers directly.

When identifier-3 is used as the sending field, the transmitted value depends on the description of the identifier. If identifier-3 is not an index-data-name, the value in identifier-3 is converted to the byte displacement for that occurrence number of the table indexed by index-name-1 (or index-name-2); only index-names may appear as receiving fields. If identifier-3 is an index-data-name, the value in the sending field is placed in the receiving field(s) without conversion. The receiving fields can be either index-names or index-data-names.

When literal-1 is used, the receiving field must be an index-name. The value from the sending field is converted into the byte displacement for itself and associated with the table indexed by index-name-1 (or index-name-2).

Figure 14.3 shows results of different options of the SET statement. All entries in the DATA DIVISION appear in the WORKING-STORAGE SECTION. The first entry shows the creation of an index-data-name. Notice that IND-X is accompanied by a USAGE IS INDEX clause. NON-IND is a normal data-name. Following WORKING-RECORD, two tables are described. In the first description, the table is represented by ten occurrences of TABLE-1. When a reference is made to TABLE-1 in the PROCEDURE DIVISION, it should be made through the use of IND-1, the index-name. Each occurrence of TABLE-1 consists of a five-digit number (five bytes). In the internal description of the table, which is provided below the DATA DIVISION entries, each occurrence number is associated with a byte displacement, which is used to reference each of the individual occurrence positions directly. So, a reference to occurrence-1 would be for a byte displacement of zero for a length of 5 bytes. If the second occurrence is addressed, the index value would be 5, for five bytes displacement from the beginning of the table.

The description of SECOND-TABLE is similar to FIRST-TABLE in that a one-dimension indexed table is created. There are six occurrences of TABLE-2, and each occurrence is 4 bytes long, for a total length of 24 bytes. The index-name could represent 0, 4, 8, 12, 16, or 20 bytes displacement from the beginning of the table.

In the SET statements that follow the internal organization of TABLE-1 and TABLE-2, remember that the index-names are directly associated with the tables with which they are coded. That is, TABLE-1 is indexed by IND-1, and TABLE-2 is indexed by IND-2. Thus, the determination of the index value is dependent on the characteristics of their respective tables. The first SET statement indicates that IND-1 and IND-2 are to be set to 1—the first occurrence positions of their respective tables. In each table, occurrence-1 begins at byte displacement 0. The second SET statement indicates that occurrence-5 is to be the value of IND-1 and IND-2. For TABLE-1, that is byte displacement 20, and for TABLE-2, byte displacement 16.

The third SET statement indicates that IND-1 is to be set to the third occurrence position. This would be byte displacement 10. The next SET statement places the value in IND-1 (10) into IND-2 and IND-X. Thus, IND-2 and IND-X will contain 10. However, notice that a byte displacement of 10 for TABLE-2 would begin in the middle of occurrence-3.

The next series of statements causes 6 to be moved to NON-IND and the value of NON-IND to be used to SET IND-1 and IND-2. The value of NON-IND is converted before being placed into IND-1 and IND-2 to give these two index-names values that address the 6th occurrence of their respective tables. The next SET statement uses an index-data-name (IND-X) to set the value of an index-name (IND-1). Because the value of IND-X already represents a byte displacement value (not an occurrence number), no conversion takes place

```
DATA DIVISION.

WORKING-STORAGE SECTION.
Ø1   WORKING-RECORD.
     Ø5 IND-X    USAGE IS INDEX.
     Ø5 NON-IND PIC 99.
Ø1   FIRST-TABLE.
     Ø2 TABLE-1 OCCURS 1Ø TIMES
               INDEXED BY IND-1
               PIC 9(5).
Ø1   SECOND-TABLE.
     Ø2 TABLE-2 OCCURS 6 TIMES
               INDEXED BY IND-2
               PIC X(4).
```

TABLE-1

1	2	3	4	5	6	7	8	9	10	Occurrence Number

0   5   10   15   20   25   30   35   40   45   50 Byte Displacement

TABLE-2

1	2	3	4	5	6	Occurrence Number

0   4   8   12   16   20   24 Byte Displacement

	Values of		
PROCEDURE DIVISION.	IND-1	IND-2	IND-X
SET IND-1, IND-2 TO 1.	0	0	–
SET IND-1, IND-2 TO 5.	20	16	–
SET IND-1 TO 3.	10	16	–
SET IND-2, IND-X TO IND-1.	10	10	10
MOVE 6 TO NON-IND. SET IND-1, IND-2 TO NON-IND.	25	20	10
SET IND-1 TO IND-X	10	20	10
SET IND-2 TO 3.	10	8	10

Figure 14.3 Examples of the SET Statement (Relative to Table Size)

with this process. Thus, IND-1 would have a value of 10 after the execution of SET IND-1 TO IND-X. The final example of the SET statement illustrates the use of a literal to set the value of an index-name. When IND-2 is set to occurrence-3, the value 3 is translated to byte displacement 8.

The second format of the SET statement is a substitute for the ADD and SUBTRACT statements, and is similar to their simple forms. (See Figure 14.2.) Index-name-4 (and index-name-5) must contain a value prior to execution. The programmer then has the option to either increment (UP BY) or decrement (DOWN BY) the index-name value. Identifier-4 (literal-2) is the amount by which the index-name value is to be modified. This amount is an occurrence number that is converted to a byte displacement amount before the index-name value is modified.

When this SET statement is executed, the index-name value is modified, allowing a programmer to "step through" a table by a specified displacement value. For example, if the statement

```
SET IND-1 UP BY 1
```

is placed in a program, each time the statement is executed, IND-1 is incremented by the number of bytes representing one occurrence. If the statement

```
SET IND-2 DOWN BY 3
```

is placed in a program, each time the statement is executed, IND-2 is reduced by the number of bytes representing three occurrences. Before the first execution of these statements, IND-1 and IND-2 must have values. Thereafter, the statements modify the index-name values when executed. If the literals 1 and 3 in the above examples were identifiers, a variable-stepping process would be possible.

The SEARCH Statement

With an indexed table, COBOL also permits use of the SEARCH statement. The SEARCH allows the programmer to "look through" items in a table for an occurrence that meets certain conditions.

The SEARCH statement causes the COBOL compiler to generate the code necessary to conduct a *linear* (or sequential) SEARCH of a table. The table is examined one occurrence at a time beginning with the last index-name setting, until a specified condition is encountered or the end of the table is reached. Figure 14.4 shows the format of the SEARCH statement. Identifier-1 must be a data-name representing an indexed table. The identifier itself cannot be subordinate to an OCCURS clause, but rather should be directly associated with the first OCCURS clause (using an INDEXED BY clause) in the record description. For example, suppose the following description of an indexed table is presented in the DATA DIVISION.

```
01   TABLE-NAME.
     02   TABLE-OCCURRENCES OCCURS
               25 TIMES INDEXED BY NUM.
          03   ITEM-A      PIC 9(5).
          03   ITEM-B      PIC XXX.
```

The only data-name in this description which could be used as identifier-1 is TABLE-OCCURRENCES. TABLE-OCCURRENCES would normally be written with an index (position) reference, but in the SEARCH statement only the data-name should be used.

```
SEARCH identifier-1   [VARYING  {index-name-1
                                 identifier-2}  [AT END imperative-statement-1]

    WHEN condition-1   {imperative-statement-2
                        NEXT SENTENCE}

[   WHEN condition-2   {imperative-statement-3
                        NEXT SENTENCE}]...
```

Figure 14.4 Format of the SEARCH Statement

The next clause that may appear in the SEARCH statement is the VARYING clause, which automatically modifies an index-name or an identifier. This index-name or identifier should *not* be the index-name associated with the table being searched. For example, the SEARCH statement will increment the index-name NUM associated with TABLE-NAME regardless of the presence or absence of the VARYING clause. The intent of the VARYING clause is to modify the index-name value of another table (or perhaps the subscript, though identifier-2, of another table). If an index-name is specified in the VARYING clause, the value of the index-name will be the same value as the index-name associated with the table being searched. That is, since index-name NUM is being modified by the SEARCH statement (in terms of byte displacement values), the value of index-name-1 would be modified by the same amount. (NUM and index-name-1 would have the same value only if set to the same value prior to the execution of the SEARCH statement.) If the VARYING clause is written with identifier-2, identifier-2 will be incremented by 1 every time the index-name of the table is incremented by one occurrence. (If identifier-2 is an index-data-name, the increment will be in byte displacement values rather than increments of 1.)

Another optional clause provided with the SEARCH statement is the AT END clause. This clause allows the programmer to specify the operations to take place if the end of the table is reached without any of the WHEN conditions being satisfied. The imperative statement is executed after the last occurrence of the table has been reached and no item in the table satisfies any of the specified conditions. If the AT END clause has not been specified (or the imperative statement does not perform an unconditional branch) when the end of the table is reached, the SEARCH statement is terminated, and execution continues with the statement immediately following the SEARCH statement.

It is important to note that the SEARCH statement will proceed through the table until the last occurrence is reached. This is true even if the table is not completely filled with data. When searching a partially filled (static) table, the programmer should provide for the termination of the SEARCH through one of the WHEN clauses. Otherwise, the programmer is forced to make the table a variable-length table (through the DEPENDING ON clause) or run the risk of encountering a position in the table that does not contain data.

Following the optional VARYING and AT END clauses, the programmer must specify one or more WHEN clauses. Each WHEN clause is written with a condition and an action to be taken (imperative statement or NEXT SEN-TENCE) when the condition is true. The WHEN clauses are roughly equivalent to an IF statement with only a true branch. (The false branch would be the next WHEN clause or the end of the SEARCH statement.) Thus, the reserved word IF is replaced with the reserved word WHEN, and the clause takes on the form of a conditional statement. The condition may be a relational test, a sign test, a class test, or a condition-name test. Furthermore, the logical operators NOT, AND, and OR may be used in each condition to create compound tests.

Each of the WHEN clauses is tested, in the order in which it appears, for each increment of the index associated with the table being searched. If none of the conditions is true, the index is incremented to the next occurrence position, and the tests are repeated. The process continues until the end of the table is reached or one of the conditions is found to be true. In either case the SEARCH statement is terminated. If the imperative statement does not cause an unconditional branch when the imperative statement is executed, the SEARCH statement is terminated, and execution continues with the statement immediately following the SEARCH statement.

Two additional issues should be mentioned. First, prior to the execution of the SEARCH statement, the index-name associated with the table must be initialized. Under most circumstances, the programmer desires to search the entire table rather than a portion of the table. In this case, prior to the initial execution of the SEARCH statement the index-name should be set to the first occurrence position. Otherwise, the operation begins with the last index setting for the table and continues a linear search from that point. If the index setting is for the last occurrence position in the table, the SEARCH will terminate immediately after examining the WHEN clause(s).

Second, only one index-name is modified by the SEARCH statement—the index-name associated with the lowest level of the table. Thus, if it is desirable to search a multi-dimension table, the SEARCH statement will increment only the last index of the table. The programmer must increment other index-names associated with the table and re-execute the SEARCH statement.

Figure 14.5 illustrates the searching of a table. In the first example, EMPLOYEE-TABLE describes a one-dimension table indexed by NUM. The desired process is to search the entire table (assuming it contains 100 entries) and locate the entries for employees who have worked more than 40 hours during the week. In the PROCEDURE DIVISION, NUM is SET to 1. Thus the search begins with the first occurrence of EMPLOYEE-TABLE. At the first occurrence position, NUMBER-OF-HOURS is checked to determine whether or not it exceeds 40. If it does not, NUM is incremented by 1 until the condition is true or the end of the table is reached. When the condition is true, the name of the employee and his location in the table are displayed. Execution of the true phrase normally would cause the termination of the SEARCH statement, but in this example the index is SET up by 1, and the SEARCH statement is restarted. Thus, the search begins again, immediately after the last NUMBER-OF-HOURS that was greater than 40. Thus, these statements search the entire table even if the condition is true one or more times. The operation is terminated only when the end of the table is reached and the perform indicator is set to "complete."

```
Example 1:

    DATA DIVISION.
                .
                .


    WORKING-STORAGE SECTION.
    Ø1   WORKING-RECORD.
       .  Ø5 NO-OF-EMPLOYEES          PIC 999 VALUE ZERO.
          Ø5 SEARCH-PROCESS           PIC X(1Ø).
    Ø1   EMPLOYEE-TABLE.
         Ø2 EMPLOYEE OCCURS 100 TIMES INDEXED BY NUM.
            Ø3 ID-NUMBER              PIC 9(6).
            Ø3 EMPLOYEE-NAME          PIC X(2Ø).
            Ø3 RATE-PER-HOUR          PIC 99V99.
            Ø3 NUMBER-OF-HOURS        PIC 99V9.
                     .
                     .

    PROCEDURE DIVISION.
                .
                .

        SET NUM TO 1.
        PERFORM SEARCH-ENTIRE-TABLE UNTIL SEARCH-PROCESS = 'COMPLETE'.
        PERFORM NEXT-PROCESS.
        STOP RUN.
    SEARCH-ENTIRE-TABLE.
        SEARCH EMPLOYEE        VARYING NO-OF-EMPLOYEES
            AT END MOVE 'COMPLETE' TO SEARCH-PROCESS.
            WHEN NUMBER-OF-HOURS (NUM) GREATER THAN 4Ø
                DISPLAY 'IN TABLE POSITION', NO-OF-EMPLOYEE, ' ',
                    EMPLOYEE (NUM), 'WORKED MORE THAN 4Ø HOURS';
                SET NUM UP BY 1.
    NEXT-PROCESS.
                .
                .
                .
```

```
Example 2:

    DATA DIVISION.
                .

    WORKING-STORAGE SECTION.
    Ø1   RATE-TABLE.
         Ø2 ORIGINS OCCURS 3Ø TIMES INDEXED BY ROWS.
            Ø3 DESTINATIONS OCCURS 5Ø TIMES INDEXED BY COLS.
               Ø4 RATE             PIC 9999V99.
                   .
                   .

    PROCEDURE DIVISION.
                .

        PERFORM TABLE-SEARCH VARYING ROWS FROM 1 BY 1 UNTIL ROWS GREATER THAN 4Ø.
        PERFORM NEXT-PROCESS.
        STOP RUN.
    TABLE-SEARCH.
        SET COLS TO 1.
        SEARCH ORGINS
            WHEN RATE (ROWS, COLS) IS ZERO OR NEGATIVE
                DISPLAY RATE (ROWS, COLS).
    NEXT-PROCESS.
                .
                .
```

Figure 14.5 Illustrations of the SEARCH Statement

```
SEARCH ALL identifier-1 [AT END imperative-statement-1]

    WHEN condition-1  ⎧imperative-statement-2⎫
                      ⎨                       ⎬
                      ⎩NEXT SENTENCE          ⎭
```

Figure 14.6 Format of the SEARCH ALL Statement

In the second example, RATE-TABLE describes a two-dimension table. The procedure checks the occurrence positions of the table to determine whether or not any occurrence in a particular column contains a RATE that is not positive. The table is organized such that the index-name ROWS addresses rows of the table. As previously mentioned, the SEARCH statement only modifies the lowest level of the table—i.e., that part of the table indexed by COLS. Thus, in the PROCEDURE DIVISION, a PERFORM statement is used to modify ROWS. In the TABLE-SEARCH paragraph, COLS is set to 1, indicating that each column of the table should be searched beginning with the first occurrence. The SEARCH statement begins searching the first column (since ROWS initially has a value of 1) until the first nonpositive RATE is found or until the end of the column has been encountered. When the SEARCH statement is terminated by the WHEN condition, the amount of RATE is displayed. There may be other nonpositive values below the location of the first, but they are not displayed.

When the end of the TABLE-SEARCH paragraph is encountered, the PERFORM statement increments ROWS by 1. This will cause a search of the second (third, fourth, etc.) column of the table. The operation is halted when the PERFORM has incremented ROWS past 30. NEXT-PROCESS is then performed.

The second form of the SEARCH statement, shown in Figure 14.6, is referred to as the SEARCH ALL statement. A SEARCH ALL may be conducted only for indexed tables that are *keyed*. The discussion of the ASCENDING/DESCENDING KEY clause, shown in Figure 14.1, has been delayed because the clause is necessary only when a SEARCH ALL statement is to be used. To refresh your memory, this clause (associated with the OCCURS clause) is written as:

```
⎡⎧ASCENDING ⎫                                                    ⎤
⎢⎨          ⎬      KEY IS data-name-2     [data-name-3] ...      ⎥  ...
⎣⎩DESCENDING⎭                                                    ⎦
```

The clause is used to direct the operation of the SEARCH ALL statement. That is, when the SEARCH ALL statement is executed, the data items in the table should be sequenced on (sorted by) data-name-2 (data-name-3, etc.).

When ASCENDING is specified, the data in the table should be arranged by the programmer in ascending order (from the smallest value to the largest value) by the data name(s) listed in the key(s) before the SEARCH ALL is executed. DESCENDING is an indication of ordering of data values from largest to smallest. (Note that the data does not have to be in the specified order when initially placed in the table. However, before the execution of the SEARCH ALL statement, the data should be organized in the indicated sequence.)

When the ASCENDING/DESCENDING KEY clause is specified, the keys (data-name-2, etc.) are listed in decreasing order of significance, i.e., data-name-2 is a major key, with data-name-3, etc. representing minor keys. There may be a maximum of 12 keys listed, but they must not exceed 256 bytes. The KEY data-name(s) must be subordinate to the table being searched but must not be written with an OCCURS clause or be subordinate to a level of a table other than that being searched.

The SEARCH ALL statement conducts a *binary* search of table items based on the keys described in the table. For larger tables, binary searching is more efficient than linear searching. Figure 14.7 illustrates this point. As demonstrated by the illustration, the first value examined is at the middle of the table. When the search for key 691 is being performed, a comparison of 691 and the value in the middle of the table (644) results in sought item being a larger value. By the process of elimination, the top half of the table is "disregarded" from the search—the solution, if it exists, cannot be in the top half of the table (since the table is ordered). Of the remaining items, the middle item is examined (position 12 of table). In this case, 691 is smaller than the table value (827). Again, by the process of elimination, the solution cannot be from position 12 to the end of the table. The key at the midpoint of the remaining items is inspected. The search is terminated with the location of item 691. As indicated in the illustration, a conclusion of the search is reached after three comparisons. The same operation done by a linear search would have required ten comparisons—a comparison of each key form position 1 to position 10 of the table.

Comparisons				
Binary Search for 691	Binary Search for 459	Table Position	Ascending Key	Contents of Record
		1	295	
		2	321	
		3	442	
	2nd —	4	454	
	4th —	5	515	
	3rd —	6	542	
		7	631	
1st ——	1st —	8	644	
		9	677	
3rd ———		10	691	
		11	827	
2nd ———		12	859	
		13	921	
		14	945	
		15	986	

Figure 14.7 Demonstration of a Binary Search

The second column of the table is a representation of what happens when a sought item does not exist in the table. The same process (dividing the remaining positions in half with every inspection) is followed. However, after the fourth inspection, all possible positions in the table have been exhausted without finding the item. Consequently, the search is terminated without a solution. For the illustrated table, four comparisons (the maximum) were required, whereas a linear search would take a minimum of five comparisons. (A SEARCH would inspect all fifteen key values of the table before reaching the conclusion that 459 did not exist because the data does not necessarily have to be in ascending (or descending) order for the SEARCH statement.)

In the SEARCH ALL statement, identifier-1 is the name of a table that is indexed and keyed. As with the SEARCH statement the identifier should be a data-name associated with the first OCCURS clause in the table description. The optional AT END clause operates in the same manner for the SEARCH ALL as it did for the SEARCH statement; however, the AT END is not invoked upon encountering the end of the table. Rather, the imperative statement is executed when the search has reached a *logical* conclusion without finding a match on a keyed item. (The "end" could be at any position in the table.)

The SEARCH ALL statement *does not* contain the VARYING clause, and only *one* WHEN clause is permitted. Furthermore, the condition is allowed to test only for equality, using the relational operators IS = or IS EQUAL TO. In addition, a compound condition is allowed only with the use of the logical operator AND. The imperative statement may take the same form as with the SEARCH statement. Termination of the SEARCH ALL statement is caused by the same conditions as for the SEARCH statement—by executing the WHEN clause imperative statement or the AT END imperative statement. When the AT END is omitted or the imperative statement connected to the WHEN clause does not perform an unconditional branch, the statement immediately following the SEARCH ALL statement will be executed.

Sales Summary Report with Indexed Tables

In Chapter 13, the Sales Summary Report procedure (Figure 13.10) was illustrated using subscripted tables. This procedure is repeated in Figure 14.8 using indexed tables. Although the two procedures produce the same result, a few differences are worth noting. First, a module called ZERO ITEM (3200) has been added to initialize the MONTHLY-SALES items of the table because the ITEM-TABLE in Figure 14.8 includes MONTHLY-SALES. In Figure 13.10 MONTHLY-SALES was recorded as a separate table. In Figure 13.10, all cells of the MONTHLY-SALES table were initialized by a MOVE statement in the INITIALIZATION module. In Figure 14.8, each "row" of the MONTHLY-SALES table is initialized as needed. Thus, only a part of the MONTHLY-SALES table includes legitimate numeric data—that part which is needed for processing purposes (see lines 890–900 and 970–980).

Of more direct concern is the definition of the ITEM-TABLE (lines 450–500). Notice that the clause INDEXED BY ITEM appears in conjunction with the first OCCURS clause at line 460. This transforms ITEM-TABLE from a subscripted table to an indexed table. Also, note that the data-name ITEM (the index-name) does not appear in the WORKING-VARIABLES record (as it did when it was used as a subscript in Figure 13.10). Next, note the INDEXED BY MONTH clause which appears at line 490. This clause completes the indexing operation. (Also notice that MONTH does not appear in WORKING-VARIABLES.) By virtue of these changes, only the index-names ITEM and MONTH may be used to address the ITEM-TABLE. ITEM is used to address ITEM-NUMBER-T and ITEM-DESCRIPTION-T in the PROCEDURE DIVISION. Both ITEM and MONTH are used to address MONTHLY-SALES. These are the *only* data-names permitted to serve in an addressing capacity in conjunction with the ITEM-TABLE.

In the PROCEDURE DIVISION, ITEM is modified through a SET statement at line 880. After this SET statement is executed, the value associated with ITEM will be the same as the value of ITEM-COUNT. (ITEM will not be the same *value*, but when ITEM-COUNT is 1, ITEM will point to the first occurrence position of ITEM-TABLE. When ITEM-COUNT is 2, ITEM will address the second occurrence position, and so on.) The index-name MONTH receives a value by virtue of a SET statement at line 930. Thus, the value associated with MONTH is generated from MONTH-OF-SALE.

Other manipulations of ITEM and MONTH occur during the SUMMARY-PRINT phase of the procedure. The PERFORM statement at line 740 generates values for ITEM such that ITEM will address the first, second, third, etc., occurrence positions of ITEM-TABLE. The values for MONTH are produced through the PERFORM statement at line 1050. Thus, MONTH addresses the first through the twelfth positions of MONTHLY-SALES at a specified position of ITEM.

Finally, note the SET statement at line 1150. Since the values associated with MONTH are not 1 through 12, but rather are the byte displacements represented by the first through the twelfth occurrence positions of MONTHLY-SALES, the statement will not accurately address the MONTHLY-SALES-OUT table (line 670); MONTH has to be converted first. To do this, an identifier (MONTH-NO) is SET to the value of an index-name (MONTH). MONTH-NO contains the values 1 through 12 (as a subscript value). This means that indexed and subscripted tables may be used in the *same* program.

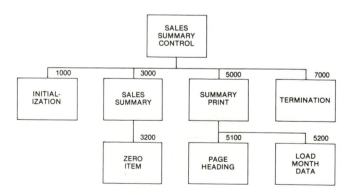

Figure 14.8 A Sales Summary Report (Indexed Tables) (Hierarchy Chart)

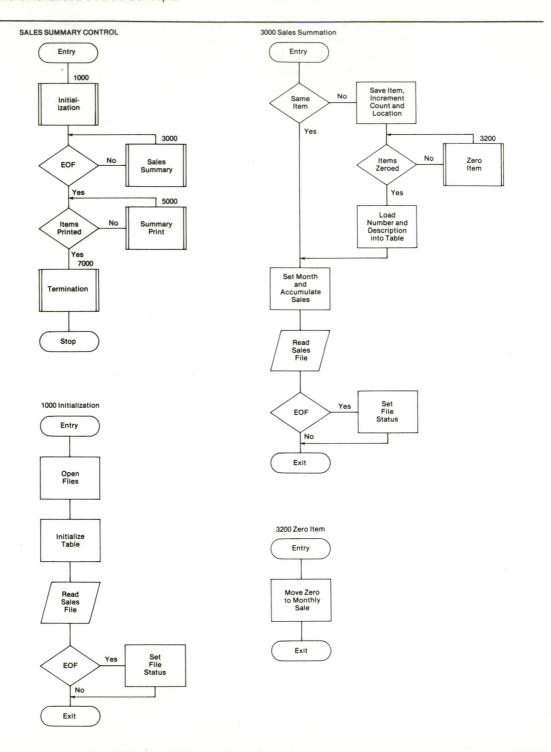

Figure 14.8 A Sales Summary Report (Indexed Tables) (Module Flowcharts) *Continued*

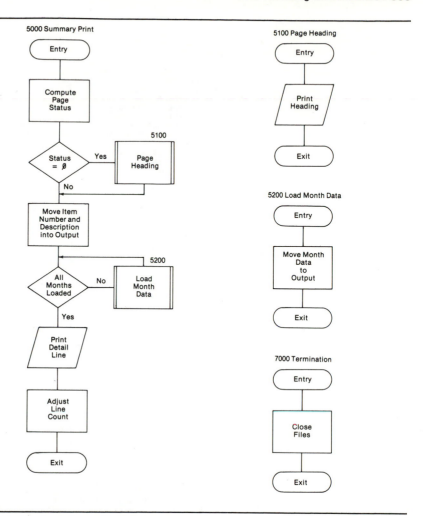

Figure 14.8 A Sales Summary Report (Indexed Tables) (Module Flowcharts) *Continued*

```
|         1   1   2   2   2   3   3   4   4   4   5   5   6   6   6   7   7   8|
|   4   8   2   6   0   4   8   2   6   0   4   8   2   6   0   4   8   2   6   0|
------------------------------------------------------------------------------
|000010 IDENTIFICATION DIVISION.                                    FIG 14.8|
|000020 PROGRAM-ID. SALES-SUMMARY-INDEXED.                          FIG 14.8|
|000030 AUTHOR. J. WAYNE SPENCE.                                    FIG 14.8|
|000040 DATE-WRITTEN. JAN. 1, 1981.                                 FIG 14.8|
|000050 DATE-COMPILED. JAN. 1, 1981.                                FIG 14.8|
|000060*     PROCEDURE TO ACCUMULATE SALES OF ITEMS BY MONTH.       FIG 14.8|
|000070*     PROCEDURE USES A ONE DIMENSIONAL TABLE TO STORE THE    FIG 14.8|
|000080*     ITEM NUMBER AND NAME AND A TWO DIMENSIONAL TABLE TO    FIG 14.8|
|000090*     RECORD THE MONTHLY SALES OF EACH ITEM.                 FIG 14.8|
|000100 ENVIRONMENT DIVISION.                                       FIG 14.8|
|000110 CONFIGURATION SECTION.                                      FIG 14.8|
|000120 SOURCE-COMPUTER. IBM-370.                                   FIG 14.8|
|000130 OBJECT-COMPUTER. IBM-370.                                   FIG 14.8|
|000140 SPECIAL-NAMES.  C01 IS TOP-OF-PAGE.                         FIG 14.8|
|000150 INPUT-OUTPUT SECTION.                                       FIG 14.8|
```

Figure 14.8 A Sales Summary Report (Indexed Tables) *Continued*

```
---------------------------------------------------------------------
|         1   1   2   2   2   3   3   4   4   4   5   5   6   6   6   7   7   8|
|   4   8   2   6   0   4   8   2   6   0   4   8   2   6   0   4   8   2   6   0|
---------------------------------------------------------------------
|000160 FILE-CONTROL.                                              FIG 14.8|
|000170     SELECT SALES-FILE ASSIGN TO UT-S-SYSIN.               FIG 14.8|
|000180     SELECT REPORT-FILE ASSIGN TO UT-S-SYSPRINT.           FIG 14.8|
|000190 DATA DIVISION.                                            FIG 14.8|
|000200 FILE SECTION.                                             FIG 14.8|
|000210 FD  SALES-FILE                                            FIG 14.8|
|000220         LABEL RECORDS ARE OMITTED.                        FIG 14.8|
|000230 01  SALES-REC.                                            FIG 14.8|
|000240     05  ITEM-NUMBER            PIC 9(05).                 FIG 14.8|
|000250     05  ITEM-DESCRIPTION       PIC X(30).                 FIG 14.8|
|000260     05  FILLER                 PIC X(01).                 FIG 14.8|
|000270     05  DATE-OF-SALE.                                     FIG 14.8|
|000280         10  MONTH-OF-SALE       PIC 9(02).                FIG 14.8|
|000290         10  DAY-OF-SALE         PIC 9(02).                FIG 14.8|
|000300         10  YEAR-OF-SALE        PIC 9(02).                FIG 14.8|
|000310     05  FILLER                 PIC X(02).                 FIG 14.8|
|000320     05  AMOUNT-OF-SALE         PIC S9(3)V99.              FIG 14.8|
|000330     05  FILLER                 PIC X(31).                 FIG 14.8|
|000340 FD  REPORT-FILE                                           FIG 14.8|
|000350         LABEL RECORDS ARE STANDARD.                       FIG 14.8|
|000360 01  REPORT-LINE                PIC X(133).                FIG 14.8|
|000370 WORKING-STORAGE SECTION.                                  FIG 14.8|
|000380 01  WORKING-VARIABLES.                                    FIG 14.8|
|000390     05  FILE-STATUS            PIC X(10).                 FIG 14.8|
|000400     05  MONTH-NO               PIC 9(02) VALUE ZERO.      FIG 14.8|
|000410     05  ITEM-COUNT             PIC 9(02) VALUE ZERO.      FIG 14.8|
|000420     05  LINE-COUNT             PIC 9(02) VALUE ZERO.      FIG 14.8|
|000430     05  PAGE-STATUS            PIC V999.                  FIG 14.8|
|000440     05  LAST-ITEM              PIC 9(05) VALUE ZERO.      FIG 14.8|
|000450 01  ITEM-TABLE.                                           FIG 14.8|
|000460     05  ITEM-ENTRY OCCURS 30 TIMES INDEXED BY ITEM.       FIG 14.8|
|000470         10  ITEM-NUMBER-T       PIC 9(5).                 FIG 14.8|
|000480         10  ITEM-DESCRIPTION-T  PIC X(30).                FIG 14.8|
|000490         10  MONTHLY-SALES OCCURS 12 TIMES INDEXED BY MONTH FIG 14.8|
|000500                                 PIC S9(4)V99.             FIG 14.8|
|000510 01  PAGE-HEADING.                                         FIG 14.8|
|000520     05  FILLER                 PIC X(55) VALUE SPACES.    FIG 14.8|
|000530     05  FILLER                 PIC X(22) VALUE            FIG 14.8|
|000540         'SALES SUMMARY BY MONTH'.                         FIG 14.8|
|000550 01  COLUMN-HEADING.                                       FIG 14.8|
|000560     05  FILLER                 PIC X(38) VALUE            FIG 14.8|
|000570         '  ITEM DESCRIPTION'.                             FIG 14.8|
|000580     05  FILLER                 PIC X(92) VALUE            FIG 14.8|
|000590         'JAN.    FEB.    MAR.    APR.    MAY    JUNE    JULY    AUG.FIG 14.8|
|000600-        '  SEP.   OCT.   NOV.   DEC.'.                    FIG 14.8|
|000610 01  DETAIL-LINE.                                          FIG 14.8|
|000620     05  FILLER                 PIC X(01) VALUE SPACES.    FIG 14.8|
|000630     05  ITEM-NUMBER-OUT        PIC 99B999.                FIG 14.8|
|000640     05  FILLER                 PIC X(01) VALUE SPACES.    FIG 14.8|
|000650     05  ITEM-DESCRIPTION-OUT   PIC X(25).                 FIG 14.8|
|000660     05  FILLER                 PIC X(01) VALUE SPACES.    FIG 14.8|
|000670     05  MONTHLY-SALES-OUT OCCURS 12 TIMES                 FIG 14.8|
|000680                                 PIC ZZZZZ.99.             FIG 14.8|
|000690 PROCEDURE DIVISION.                                       FIG 14.8|
|000700 SALES-SUMMARY-CONTROL.                                    FIG 14.8|
|000710     PERFORM 1000-INITIALIZATION.                          FIG 14.8|
|000720     PERFORM 3000-SALES-SUMMATION                          FIG 14.8|
|000730         UNTIL FILE-STATUS = 'DONE'.                       FIG 14.8|
|000740     PERFORM 5000-SUMMARY-PRINT                            FIG 14.8|
|000750         VARYING ITEM FROM 1 BY 1 UNTIL ITEM > ITEM-COUNT. FIG 14.8|
|000760     PERFORM 7000-TERMINATION.                             FIG 14.8|
|000770     STOP RUN.                                             FIG 14.8|
|000780 1000-INITIALIZATION.                                      FIG 14.8|
|000790     OPEN INPUT SALES-FILE                                 FIG 14.8|
|000800         OUTPUT REPORT-FILE.                               FIG 14.8|
|000810     MOVE SPACES TO ITEM-TABLE.                            FIG 14.8|
|000820     READ SALES-FILE                                       FIG 14.8|
|000830         AT END MOVE 'DONE' TO FILE-STATUS.                FIG 14.8|
|000840 3000-SALES-SUMMATION.                                     FIG 14.8|
|000850     IF ITEM-NUMBER NOT = LAST-ITEM                        FIG 14.8|
|000860         MOVE ITEM-NUMBER TO LAST-ITEM                     FIG 14.8|
|000870         ADD 1 TO ITEM-COUNT                               FIG 14.8|
|000880         SET ITEM TO ITEM-COUNT                            FIG 14.8|
|000890         PERFORM 3200-ZERO-ITEM                            FIG 14.8|
|000900             VARYING MONTH FROM 1 BY 1 UNTIL MONTH > 12    FIG 14.8|
|000910         MOVE ITEM-NUMBER TO ITEM-NUMBER-T (ITEM)          FIG 14.8|
|000920         MOVE ITEM-DESCRIPTION TO ITEM-DESCRIPTION-T (ITEM). FIG 14.8|
|000930     SET MONTH TO MONTH-OF-SALE.                           FIG 14.8|
|000940     ADD AMOUNT-OF-SALE TO MONTHLY-SALES (ITEM, MONTH).    FIG 14.8|
|000950     READ SALES-FILE                                       FIG 14.8|
```

Figure 14.8 A Sales Summary Report (Indexed Tables) *Continued*

```
|        1 1 2 2 2 3 3 4 4 4 5 5 6 6 6 7 7 8|
|  4   8 2 6 0 4 8 2 6 0 4 8 2 6 0 4 8 2 6 0|
|000960          AT END MOVE 'DONE' TO FILE-STATUS.                   FIG 14.8|
|000970 3200-ZERO-ITEM.                                               FIG 14.8|
|000980     MOVE ZERO TO MONTHLY-SALES (ITEM, MONTH).                 FIG 14.8|
|000990 5000-SUMMARY-PRINT.                                           FIG 14.8|
|001000     DIVIDE LINE-COUNT BY 25 GIVING PAGE-STATUS.               FIG 14.8|
|001010     IF PAGE-STATUS = 0                                        FIG 14.8|
|001020         PERFORM 5100-PAGE-HEADING.                            FIG 14.8|
|001030     MOVE ITEM-NUMBER-T (ITEM) TO ITEM-NUMBER-OUT.             FIG 14.8|
|001040     MOVE ITEM-DESCRIPTION-T (ITEM) TO ITEM-DESCRIPTION-OUT.   FIG 14.8|
|001050     PERFORM 5200-LOAD-MONTH-DATA                              FIG 14.8|
|001060         VARYING MONTH FROM 1 BY 1 UNTIL MONTH > 12.           FIG 14.8|
|001070     WRITE REPORT-LINE FROM DETAIL-LINE AFTER ADVANCING 2 LINES. FIG 14.8|
|001080     ADD 2 TO LINE-COUNT.                                      FIG 14.8|
|001090 5100-PAGE-HEADING.                                            FIG 14.8|
|001100     WRITE REPORT-LINE FROM PAGE-HEADING                       FIG 14.8|
|001110         AFTER ADVANCING TOP-OF-PAGE.                          FIG 14.8|
|001120     WRITE REPORT-LINE FROM COLUMN-HEADING                     FIG 14.8|
|001130         AFTER ADVANCING 2 LINES.                              FIG 14.8|
|001140 5200-LOAD-MONTH-DATA.                                         FIG 14.8|
|001150     SET MONTH-NO TO MONTH.                                    FIG 14.8|
|001160     MOVE MONTHLY-SALES (ITEM, MONTH) TO                       FIG 14.8|
|001170         MONTHLY-SALES-OUT (MONTH-NO).                         FIG 14.8|
|001180 7000-TERMINATION.                                             FIG 14.8|
|001190     CLOSE SALES-FILE                                          FIG 14.8|
|001200           REPORT-FILE.                                        FIG 14.8|
```

Figure 14.8 A Sales Summary Report (Indexed Tables) *Continued*

The Sales Analysis Program with SEARCH Statements

The Sales Analysis procedure illustrated in Figure 14.9 also uses indexed tables. Although the Sales Summary Report procedure and the Sales Analysis procedure are similar in design, the number, type, and use of tables are different. The first table used in the Sales Analysis procedure is defined in lines 580–670. It is defined as an indexed table by the INDEXED BY clause at line 590. The purpose of the SALESMAN-DATA-TABLE is similar to that of the ITEM-TABLE from the previous example—to retain and accumulate data.

The second table in Figure 14.9 is the STATE-CODE-TABLE (lines 840–890), which is used for internal purposes only. That is, when it becomes necessary to translate a district number from a numeric value to its corresponding state name, the STATE-CODE-TABLE will be employed. Notice, however, that the table definition not only indicates the table is indexed (INDEXED BY STATE), but that it is (or is capable of being) keyed (ASCENDING KEY IS STATE-CODE). In the PROCEDURE DIVISION the STATE-CODE-TABLE is loaded with the values in CODE-STATE-LIST (line 1270). The CODE-STATE-LIST contains a two-digit number (01 through 50, non-consecutive) in the first two bytes of each value, thus when these values are placed in the STATE-CODE-TABLE, the two-digit numbers are loaded into STATE-CODE (line 880), and the state names fall into STATE-NAME (line 890). As a result, the STATE-CODE values are ascending.

In the PROCEDURE DIVISION, several new variations of the use of indexes and indexed tables are presented. First, the index-names STATE and LCTN are initialized (to the first occurrence position) by a SET statement in line 1280. In the ZERO-TABLE module (lines 1330–1350) all elements of MAN-ID and DIST-NUM in the SALESMAN-DATA-TABLE are set to zero. The index LCTN is modified through the PERFORM statement in line 1290. The FIND-ENTRY module (lines 1470–1560) represents the first use of a SEARCH statement, which is to determine whether or not a particular salesman's record has been previously placed in the table. (A salesman is identified through the MAN-ID and DIST-NUM fields.) Unlike the Sales Summary Report procedure

(Figure 14.8), the Sales Analysis procedure does not assume any particular order for the data in the SALES-FILE. When the SEARCH statement is invoked (via the PERFORM statement at line 1440), LCTN is set to the first occurrence position (to make sure the complete table is searched if necessary). When a table entry containing zeros is found (before finding the sought salesman identification), it is assumed that the salesman's record is not present in the table. Thus, information contained in the salesmen's record is *added* to the table. The movement of SAVE-REORGANIZE-RECORD to SALESMAN-ENTRY places data in all fields of the SALESMAN-DATA-TABLE at the LCTN position. If, however, a match is found between the identifying fields in the SALES-RECORD and IDENTITY (a table group) in the SALESMAN-DATA-TABLE, the AMOUNT-OF-SALE is simply added to the existing value of AMOUNT in the table.

After all data has been loaded into the SALESMAN-DATA-TABLE, the data in the table are sorted. In this particular procedure, an *internal* sorting operation is performed. The sorting procedure selected (and illustrated in the SORT-FOR-REPORT and COMPARISON modules (lines 1570–1680) is generally known as the "bubble" or "triangular-method" sort. The procedure compares the IDENTITY field for two *adjacent* occurrence positions; if the value associated with IDENTITY of the first item is the larger of the two, the data are interchanged or swapped. (See lines 1640–1680.) This movement of data involves the first use of relative addressing—the use of LCTN+1 as an address reference. The procedure continues through all positions of the SALESMAN-DATA-TABLE comparing adjacent items and swapping oc-

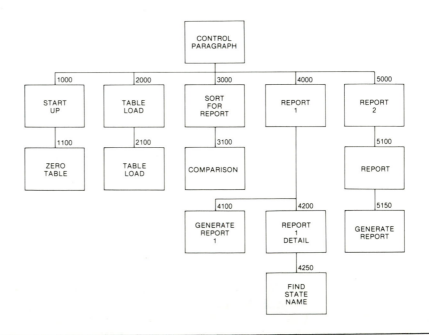

Figure 14.9 Sales Analysis (SEARCH Statements) (Hierarchy Chart)

currence positions as necessary. This is called "raising the bubble," even though the value is actually sinking like a rock. After one pass through the data, the data-name SORT-INDICATOR is tested, if no items have been swapped, the data has been ordered, and the sort is complete. If, however, even one pair of items has been swapped, the procedure is repeated.

The final use of an indexed table in the procedure is in conjunction with the SEARCH ALL statement in the FIND-STATE-NAME module. The SEARCH ALL statement "looks for" a match between the STATE-CODE value in the STATE-CODE-TABLE and the DISTRICT-NUMBER (which was loaded into the SAVE-REORGANIZE-RECORD from DIST-NUM of the SALESMAN-DATA-TABLE). Once a match is found, the STATE-NAME in the corresponding table position is retained to be placed in the output record for printing.

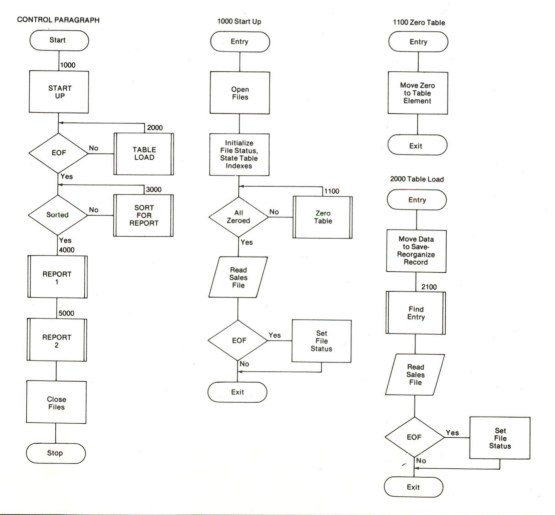

Figure 14.9 Sales Analysis (SEARCH Statements) (Module Flowcharts) *Continued*

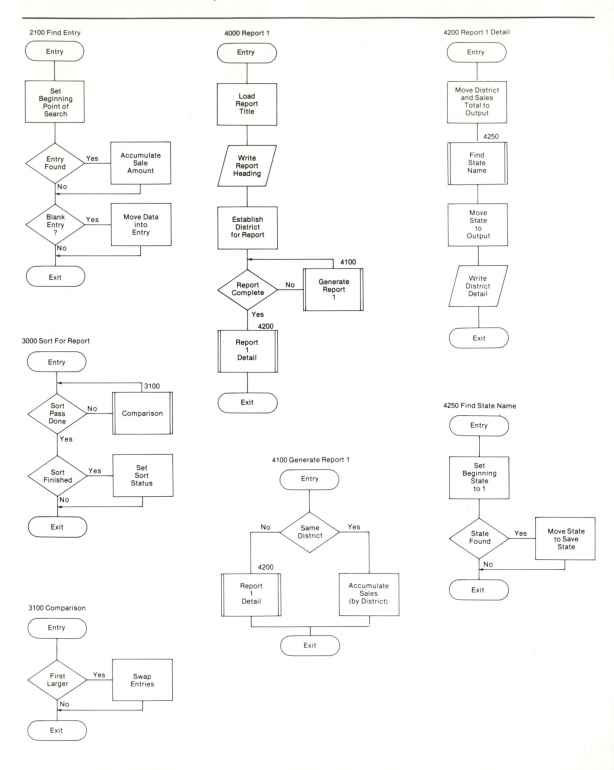

Figure 14.9 Sales Analysis (SEARCH Statements) (Module Flowcharts) *Continued*

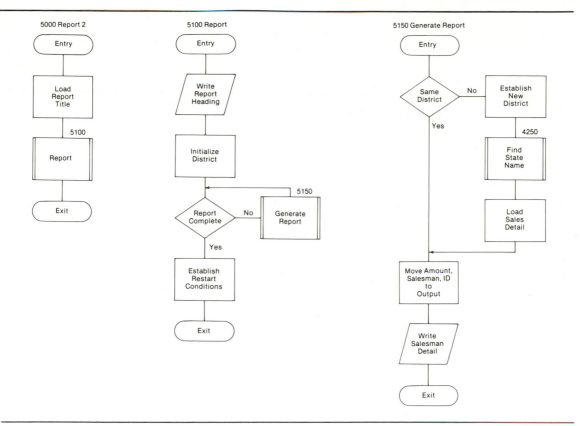

Figure 14.9 Sales Analysis (SEARCH Statements) (Module Flowcharts) *Continued*

```
|          1   1   2   2   2   3   3   4   4   4   5   5   6   6   6   7   7   8|
|   4   8   2   6   0   4   8   2   6   0   4   8   2   6   0   4   8   2   6   0|
----------------------------------------------------------------------------------
|000010 IDENTIFICATION DIVISION.                                      FIG 14.9|
|000020 PROGRAM-ID. SALES-ANALYSIS.                                   FIG 14.9|
|000030 AUTHOR. J. WAYNE SPENCE.                                      FIG 14.9|
|000040 DATE-WRITTEN. JANUARY 1, 1981.                                FIG 14.9|
|000050 DATE-COMPILED. JANUARY 1, 1981.                               FIG 14.9|
|000060*    THIS PROGRAM ILLUSTRATES THE USE OF INDEXED               FIG 14.9|
|000070*    TABLES.  IT DEFINES THE TABLES AND, IN SOME INSTANCES,    FIG 14.9|
|000080*    PROVIDES THE INITIAL VALUES TO BE PLACED IN THE TABLE.    FIG 14.9|
|000090*    IN THE PROCEDURE DIVISION, THE INDEXED TABLES ARE PROCESSED FIG 14.9|
|000100*    AND A "BUBBLE" SORT IS APPLIED TO REARRANGE THE DATA      FIG 14.9|
|000110*    INTERNALLY.  IN CONJUNCTION WITH THE TABLES, SET;         FIG 14.9|
|000120*    SEARCH; SEARCH ALL; AND INDEX-NAMES                       FIG 14.9|
|000130*    ARE USED.                                                 FIG 14.9|
|000140 ENVIRONMENT DIVISION.                                         FIG 14.9|
|000150 CONFIGURATION SECTION.                                        FIG 14.9|
|000160 SOURCE-COMPUTER. CDC-CYBER-72.                                FIG 14.9|
|000170 OBJECT-COMPUTER. CDC-CYBER-72.                                FIG 14.9|
|000180 SPECIAL-NAMES.  C01 IS PAGE-TOP.                              FIG 14.9|
|000190 INPUT-OUTPUT SECTION.                                         FIG 14.9|
|000200 FILE-CONTROL.                                                 FIG 14.9|
|000210     SELECT SALES-FILE ASSIGN TO UT-S-SYSIN.                   FIG 14.9|
|000220     SELECT REPORT-FILE ASSIGN TO UT-S-SYSPRINT.               FIG 14.9|
|000230 DATA DIVISION.                                                FIG 14.9|
|000240 FILE SECTION.                                                 FIG 14.9|
|000250 FD  SALES-FILE LABEL RECORDS ARE OMITTED.                     FIG 14.9|
|000260 01  SALES-RECORD.                                             FIG 14.9|
|000270     03 NAME.                                                  FIG 14.9|
|000280        05 LAST-NAME          PIC X(20).                       FIG 14.9|
```

Figure 14.9 Sales Analysis (SEARCH Statements) *Continued*

```
|------------------------------------------------------------------------
|         1   1   2   2   2   3   3   4   4   4   5   5   6   6   6   7   7   8|
|  4   8   2   6   0   4   8   2   6   0   4   8   2   6   0   4   8   2   6   0|
|------------------------------------------------------------------------
|000290            05  FIRST-NAME             PIC X(20).                FIG 14.9|
|000300            05  MIDDLE-INITIAL         PIC X(01).                FIG 14.9|
|000310        03  FILLER                     PIC X(08).                FIG 14.9|
|000320        03  ID-INFORMATION.                                      FIG 14.9|
|000330            05  SALESMAN-ID            PIC 9(05).                FIG 14.9|
|000340            05  FILLER                 PIC X(05).                FIG 14.9|
|000350            05  DISTRICT-NUMBER        PIC 9(02).                FIG 14.9|
|000360        03  FILLER                     PIC X(08).                FIG 14.9|
|000370        03  AMOUNT-OF-SALE             PIC 9(05)V9(02).          FIG 14.9|
|000380        03  FILLER                     PIC X(04).                FIG 14.9|
|000390 FD  REPORT-FILE LABEL RECORDS ARE OMITTED.                      FIG 14.9|
|000400 01  OUTPUT-LINE                       PIC X(133).               FIG 14.9|
|000410 WORKING-STORAGE SECTION.                                        FIG 14.9|
|000420 01  WORKING-VARIABLES.                                          FIG 14.9|
|000430        05  FILE-STATUS                PIC X(15).                FIG 14.9|
|000440        05  SORT-INDICATOR             PIC X(15).                FIG 14.9|
|000450        05  DISTRICT-TOTAL             PIC 9(07)V9(02).          FIG 14.9|
|000460        05  ITEMS-TO-BE-SORTED         PIC 9(03) VALUE ZERO.     FIG 14.9|
|000470        05  SAVE-STATE-NAME            PIC X(12).                FIG 14.9|
|000480        05  SALESMAN-COUNT             PIC 9(03) VALUE ZERO.     FIG 14.9|
|000490 01  SAVE-REORGANIZE-RECORD.                                     FIG 14.9|
|000500        03  ID-INFORMATION.                                      FIG 14.9|
|000510            05  DISTRICT-NUMBER        PIC 9(02).                FIG 14.9|
|000520            05  SALESMAN-ID            PIC 9(05).                FIG 14.9|
|000530        03  AMOUNT-OF-SALE             PIC 9(06)V9(02).          FIG 14.9|
|000540        03  NAME.                                                FIG 14.9|
|000550            05  LAST-NAME              PIC X(20).                FIG 14.9|
|000560            05  FIRST-NAME             PIC X(20).                FIG 14.9|
|000570            05  MIDDLE-INITIAL         PIC X(01).                FIG 14.9|
|000580 01  SALESMAN-DATA-TABLE.                                        FIG 14.9|
|000590     03  SALESMAN-ENTRY OCCURS 100 TIMES INDEXED BY LCTN.        FIG 14.9|
|000600            05  IDENTITY.                                        FIG 14.9|
|000610                07  DIST-NUM           PIC 9(02).                FIG 14.9|
|000620                07  MAN-ID             PIC 9(05).                FIG 14.9|
|000630            05  AMOUNT                 PIC 9(06)V9(02).          FIG 14.9|
|000640            05  SALESMAN-NAME.                                   FIG 14.9|
|000650                07  L-N                PIC X(20).                FIG 14.9|
|000660                07  F-N                PIC X(20).                FIG 14.9|
|000670                07  M-I                PIC X(01).                FIG 14.9|
|000680 01  CODE-STATE-LIST.                                            FIG 14.9|
|000690        02  FILLER                     PIC X(14) VALUE '01ALABAMA'.    FIG 14.9|
|000700        02  FILLER                     PIC X(14) VALUE '04ARKANSAS'.   FIG 14.9|
|000710        02  FILLER                     PIC X(14) VALUE '09FLORIDA'.    FIG 14.9|
|000720        02  FILLER                     PIC X(14) VALUE '10GEORGIA'.    FIG 14.9|
|000730        02  FILLER                     PIC X(14) VALUE '15IOWA'.       FIG 14.9|
|000740        02  FILLER                     PIC X(14) VALUE '25MISSOURI'.   FIG 14.9|
|000750        02  FILLER                     PIC X(14) VALUE '30NEW JERSEY'. FIG 14.9|
|000760        02  FILLER                     PIC X(14) VALUE '34NORTH DAKOTA'.FIG 14.9|
|000770        02  FILLER                     PIC X(14) VALUE '35OHIO'.       FIG 14.9|
|000780        02  FILLER                     PIC X(14) VALUE '36OKLAHOMA'.   FIG 14.9|
|000790        02  FILLER                     PIC X(14) VALUE '42TENNESSEE'.  FIG 14.9|
|000800        02  FILLER                     PIC X(14) VALUE '43TEXAS'.      FIG 14.9|
|000810        02  FILLER                     PIC X(14) VALUE '46VIRGINIA'.   FIG 14.9|
|000820        02  FILLER                     PIC X(14) VALUE '49WISCONSIN'.  FIG 14.9|
|000830        02  FILLER                     PIC X(14) VALUE '50WYOMING'.    FIG 14.9|
|000840 01  STATE-CODE-TABLE.                                           FIG 14.9|
|000850     02  STATE-CODE-ENTRIES OCCURS 15 TIMES                      FIG 14.9|
|000860          ASCENDING KEY IS STATE-CODE                            FIG 14.9|
|000870          INDEXED BY STATE.                                      FIG 14.9|
|000880            03  STATE-CODE             PIC 9(02).                FIG 14.9|
|000890            03  STATE-NAME             PIC X(12).                FIG 14.9|
|000900 01  REPORT-HEADING.                                             FIG 14.9|
|000910        02  FILLER                     PIC X(40) VALUE SPACES.   FIG 14.9|
|000920        02  FILLER                     PIC X(23) VALUE           FIG 14.9|
|000930   'SALESMAN WEEKLY REPORT '.                                    FIG 14.9|
|000940        02  TITLE                      PIC X(40).                FIG 14.9|
|000950 01  DISTRICT-DETAIL.                                            FIG 14.9|
|000960        02  FILLER                     PIC X(38) VALUE SPACES.   FIG 14.9|
|000970        02  DISTRICT-NUMBER-OUT        PIC Z9(01).               FIG 14.9|
|000980        02  FILLER                     PIC X(05) VALUE SPACES.   FIG 14.9|
|000990        02  STATE-NAME-OUT             PIC X(12).                FIG 14.9|
|001000        02  FILLER                     PIC X(05) VALUE SPACES.   FIG 14.9|
|001010        02  DIST-TOTAL                 PIC $$,$$$,$$$.99.        FIG 14.9|
|001020 01  SALESMAN-DETAIL.                                            FIG 14.9|
|001030        02  FILLER                     PIC X(21) VALUE SPACES.   FIG 14.9|
|001040        02  SALESMAN-NAME-OUT          PIC X(41).                FIG 14.9|
|001050        02  FILLER                     PIC X(05) VALUE SPACES.   FIG 14.9|
|001060        02  SALESMAN-NUMBER-OUT        PIC ZZZZZ9.               FIG 14.9|
|001070        02  FILLER                     PIC X(05) VALUE SPACES.   FIG 14.9|
```

Figure 14.9 Sales Analysis (SEARCH Statements) *Continued*

```
|         1   1   2   2   2   3   3   4   4   4   5   5   6   6   6   7   7   8|
|   4   8  2   6   0   4   8   2   6   0   4   8   2   6   0   4   8   2   6   0|
-----------------------------------------------------------------------------
|001080       02 DISTRICT-NUMBER-OUT        PIC Z9(01).                   FIG 14.9|
|001090       02 FILLER                     PIC X(05) VALUE SPACES.       FIG 14.9|
|001100       02 STATE-NAME-OUT             PIC X(12).                    FIG 14.9|
|001110       02 FILLER                     PIC X(05) VALUE SPACES.       FIG 14.9|
|001120       02 AMOUNT-OUT                 PIC $$$$,$$$.99.              FIG 14.9|
|001130 PROCEDURE DIVISION.                                              FIG 14.9|
|001140 CONTROL-PARAGRAPH.                                               FIG 14.9|
|001150       PERFORM 1000-START-UP.                                     FIG 14.9|
|001160       PERFORM 2000-TABLE-LOAD UNTIL FILE-STATUS = 'FILE COMPLETE'. FIG 14.9|
|001170       PERFORM 3000-SORT-FOR-REPORT                              FIG 14.9|
|001180            UNTIL SORT-INDICATOR = 'SORT COMPLETE'.               FIG 14.9|
|001190       PERFORM 4000-REPORT-1.                                     FIG 14.9|
|001200       PERFORM 5000-REPORT-2.                                     FIG 14.9|
|001210       CLOSE SALES-FILE, REPORT-FILE.                             FIG 14.9|
|001220       STOP RUN.                                                  FIG 14.9|
|001230 1000-START-UP.                                                   FIG 14.9|
|001240       OPEN INPUT SALES-FILE OUTPUT REPORT-FILE.                  FIG 14.9|
|001250       MOVE 'READING FILE' TO FILE-STATUS.                        FIG 14.9|
|001260       MOVE SPACES TO OUTPUT-LINE.                                FIG 14.9|
|001270       MOVE CODE-STATE-LIST TO STATE-CODE-TABLE.                  FIG 14.9|
|001280       SET STATE, LCTN TO 1.                                      FIG 14.9|
|001290       PERFORM 1100-ZERO-TABLE VARYING LCTN FROM 1 BY 1           FIG 14.9|
|001300            UNTIL LCTN > 100.                                     FIG 14.9|
|001310       READ SALES-FILE AT END                                     FIG 14.9|
|001320            MOVE 'FILE COMPLETE' TO FILE-STATUS.                  FIG 14.9|
|001330 1100-ZERO-TABLE.                                                 FIG 14.9|
|001340       MOVE 0 TO MAN-ID (LCTN), DIST-NUM (LCTN) AMOUNT            FIG 14.9|
|001350       (LCTN).                                                    FIG 14.9|
|001360 2000-TABLE-LOAD.                                                 FIG 14.9|
|001370       MOVE NAME OF SALES-RECORD TO NAME OF SAVE-REORGANIZE-RECORD. FIG 14.9|
|001380       MOVE SALESMAN-ID OF SALES-RECORD TO SALESMAN-ID           FIG 14.9|
|001390            OF SAVE-REORGANIZE-RECORD.                            FIG 14.9|
|001400       MOVE DISTRICT-NUMBER OF SALES-RECORD TO DISTRICT-NUMBER    FIG 14.9|
|001410            OF SAVE-REORGANIZE-RECORD.                            FIG 14.9|
|001420       MOVE AMOUNT-OF-SALE OF SALES-RECORD TO AMOUNT-OF-SALE      FIG 14.9|
|001430            OF SAVE-REORGANIZE-RECORD.                            FIG 14.9|
|001440       PERFORM 2100-FIND-ENTRY.                                   FIG 14.9|
|001450       READ SALES-FILE AT END                                     FIG 14.9|
|001460            MOVE 'FILE COMPLETE' TO FILE-STATUS.                  FIG 14.9|
|001470 2100-FIND-ENTRY.                                                 FIG 14.9|
|001480       SET LCTN TO 1.                                             FIG 14.9|
|001490       SEARCH SALESMAN-ENTRY                                      FIG 14.9|
|001500            WHEN MAN-ID (LCTN) = 0 AND DIST-NUM (LCTN) = 0        FIG 14.9|
|001510                MOVE SAVE-REORGANIZE-RECORD TO SALESMAN-ENTRY (LCTN) FIG 14.9|
|001520                ADD 1 TO SALESMAN-COUNT, ITEMS-TO-BE-SORTED       FIG 14.9|
|001530            WHEN IDENTITY (LCTN) = ID-INFORMATION OF             FIG 14.9|
|001540            SAVE-REORGANIZE-RECORD                                FIG 14.9|
|001550                ADD AMOUNT-OF-SALE OF SAVE-REORGANIZE-RECORD TO    FIG 14.9|
|001560                AMOUNT (LCTN).                                    FIG 14.9|
|001570 3000-SORT-FOR-REPORT.                                            FIG 14.9|
|001580       MOVE 'SORT COMPLETE' TO SORT-INDICATOR.                    FIG 14.9|
|001590       PERFORM 3100-COMPARISON VARYING LCTN FROM 1 BY 1           FIG 14.9|
|001600            UNTIL LCTN IS EQUAL TO ITEMS-TO-BE-SORTED.            FIG 14.9|
|001610       IF SORT-INDICATOR NOT EQUAL TO 'SORT COMPLETE'             FIG 14.9|
|001620                SUBTRACT 1 FROM ITEMS-TO-BE-SORTED.               FIG 14.9|
|001630 3100-COMPARISON.                                                 FIG 14.9|
|001640       IF IDENTITY (LCTN) IS GREATER THAN IDENTITY (LCTN + 1)     FIG 14.9|
|001650            MOVE SALESMAN-ENTRY (LCTN) TO SAVE-REORGANIZE-RECORD  FIG 14.9|
|001660            MOVE SALESMAN-ENTRY (LCTN + 1) TO SALESMAN-ENTRY (LCTN) FIG 14.9|
|001670            MOVE SAVE-REORGANIZE-RECORD TO SALESMAN-ENTRY (LCTN + 1) FIG 14.9|
|001680            MOVE 'ITEM SWITCHED' TO SORT-INDICATOR.               FIG 14.9|
|001690 4000-REPORT-1.                                                   FIG 14.9|
|001700       MOVE 'BY DISTRICT' TO TITLE.                               FIG 14.9|
|001710       SET LCTN TO 1.                                             FIG 14.9|
|001720       WRITE OUTPUT-LINE FROM REPORT-HEADING AFTER PAGE-TOP.      FIG 14.9|
|001730       MOVE AMOUNT (LCTN) TO DISTRICT-TOTAL.                      FIG 14.9|
|001740       MOVE DIST-NUM (LCTN) TO DISTRICT-NUMBER OF                 FIG 14.9|
|001750            SAVE-REORGANIZE-RECORD.                               FIG 14.9|
|001760       PERFORM 4100-GENERATE-REPORT-1 VARYING LCTN FROM 2 BY 1    FIG 14.9|
|001770            UNTIL LCTN IS GREATER THAN SALESMAN-COUNT.            FIG 14.9|
|001780       PERFORM 4200-REPORT-1-DETAIL.                             FIG 14.9|
|001790 4100-GENERATE-REPORT-1.                                          FIG 14.9|
|001800       IF DIST-NUM (LCTN) IS NOT EQUAL TO DISTRICT-NUMBER OF      FIG 14.9|
|001810            SAVE-REORGANIZE-RECORD PERFORM 4200-REPORT-1-DETAIL   FIG 14.9|
|001820            ELSE                                                  FIG 14.9|
|001830                ADD AMOUNT (LCTN) TO DISTRICT-TOTAL.              FIG 14.9|
|001840 4200-REPORT-1-DETAIL.                                            FIG 14.9|
|001850       MOVE DISTRICT-NUMBER OF SAVE-REORGANIZE-RECORD             FIG 14.9|
|001860            TO DISTRICT-NUMBER-OUT OF DISTRICT-DETAIL.            FIG 14.9|
```

Figure 14.9 Sales Analysis (SEARCH Statements) *Continued*

```
|        1   1   2   2   2   3   3   4   4   4   5   5   6   6   6   7   7   8|
|   4   8 2   6   0   4   8   2   6   0   4   8   2   6   0   4   8   2   6   0|
------------------------------------------------------------------------------
|001870      MOVE DISTRICT-TOTAL TO DIST-TOTAL.                      FIG 14.9|
|001880      PERFORM 4250-FIND-STATE-NAME.                           FIG 14.9|
|001890      MOVE SAVE-STATE-NAME TO STATE-NAME-OUT OF DISTRICT-DETAIL. FIG 14.9|
|001900      WRITE OUTPUT-LINE FROM DISTRICT-DETAIL AFTER 2 LINES.   FIG 14.9|
|001910      MOVE DIST-NUM (LCTN) TO DISTRICT-NUMBER OF             FIG 14.9|
|001920          SAVE-REORGANIZE-RECORD.                            FIG 14.9|
|001930      MOVE AMOUNT (LCTN) TO DISTRICT-TOTAL.                  FIG 14.9|
|001940 4250-FIND-STATE-NAME.                                       FIG 14.9|
|001950      SET STATE TO 1.                                        FIG 14.9|
|001960      SEARCH ALL STATE-CODE-ENTRIES WHEN STATE-CODE (STATE) IS  FIG 14.9|
|001970          EQUAL TO DISTRICT-NUMBER OF SAVE-REORGANIZE-RECORD FIG 14.9|
|001980          MOVE STATE-NAME (STATE) TO SAVE-STATE-NAME.        FIG 14.9|
|001990 5000-REPORT-2.                                              FIG 14.9|
|002000      MOVE 'BY SALESMAN NUMBER WITHIN DISTRICT' TO TITLE.    FIG 14.9|
|002010      PERFORM 5100-REPORT.                                   FIG 14.9|
|002020 5100-REPORT.                                                FIG 14.9|
|002030      WRITE OUTPUT-LINE FROM REPORT-HEADING AFTER PAGE-TOP.  FIG 14.9|
|002040      MOVE 0 TO DISTRICT-NUMBER OF SAVE-REORGANIZE-RECORD.   FIG 14.9|
|002050      PERFORM 5150-GENERATE-REPORT VARYING LCTN FROM 1 BY 1  FIG 14.9|
|002060          UNTIL LCTN IS GREATER THAN SALESMAN-COUNT.         FIG 14.9|
|002070      MOVE SALESMAN-COUNT TO ITEMS-TO-BE-SORTED.             FIG 14.9|
|002080      MOVE 'RESTART' TO SORT-INDICATOR.                      FIG 14.9|
|002090 5150-GENERATE-REPORT.                                       FIG 14.9|
|002100      IF DIST-NUM (LCTN) IS NOT EQUAL TO DISTRICT-NUMBER OF  FIG 14.9|
|002110        SAVE-REORGANIZE-RECORD                               FIG 14.9|
|002120          MOVE DIST-NUM (LCTN) TO                            FIG 14.9|
|002130              DISTRICT-NUMBER OF SAVE-REORGANIZE-RECORD;     FIG 14.9|
|002140          PERFORM 4250-FIND-STATE-NAME;                      FIG 14.9|
|002150          MOVE SAVE-STATE-NAME TO STATE-NAME-OUT OF          FIG 14.9|
|002160              SALESMAN-DETAIL;                               FIG 14.9|
|002170          MOVE DIST-NUM (LCTN) TO DISTRICT-NUMBER-OUT OF     FIG 14.9|
|002180              SALESMAN-DETAIL.                               FIG 14.9|
|002190      MOVE SALESMAN-NAME (LCTN) TO SALESMAN-NAME-OUT OF      FIG 14.9|
|002200          SALESMAN-DETAIL.                                   FIG 14.9|
|002210      MOVE AMOUNT (LCTN) TO AMOUNT-OUT.                      FIG 14.9|
|002220      MOVE MAN-ID (LCTN) TO SALESMAN-NUMBER-OUT OF           FIG 14.9|
|002230          SALESMAN-DETAIL.                                   FIG 14.9|
|002240      WRITE OUTPUT-LINE FROM SALESMAN-DETAIL AFTER 2 LINES.  FIG 14.9|
```

Figure 14.9 Sales Analysis (SEARCH Statements) *Continued*

```
|      |        1         2         3         4         5         6         7        8| FIGURE |
|RECORD|1234567890123456789012345678901234567890123456789012345678901234567890| NUMBER |
------------------------------------------------------------------------------------------
|    1 |ANDERSON          HEATHER          D       14250     43      0001995  |FIG 14.9|
|    2 |MILLER            HERMAN           T       20200     10      0002999  |FIG 14.9|
|    3 |JOHNSON           SUSAN            A       54220     25      0001500  |FIG 14.9|
|    4 |BAKER             WILLARD          V       12770     50      0004966  |FIG 14.9|
|    5 |BRUCE             FAYETTE          S       55500     49      0002245  |FIG 14.9|
|    6 |GRIFFIN           AMY              D       78980     30      0007599  |FIG 14.9|
|    7 |TUDDLE            JACKIE           F       69632     36      0008565  |FIG 14.9|
|    8 |GRIFFIN           AMY              D       78980     30      0002552  |FIG 14.9|
|    9 |MILLER            HERMAN           T       20200     10      0035050  |FIG 14.9|
|   10 |MARTIN            DIANE            C       33358     42      0014995  |FIG 14.9|
|   11 |MARTIN            DIANE            C       33358     42      0004554  |FIG 14.9|
|   12 |MARTIN            DIANE            C       33358     42      0002543  |FIG 14.9|
|   13 |SCHWARTZ          MONICA           B       64632     46      0000995  |FIG 14.9|
|   14 |JOHNSON           SUSAN            A       54220     25      0002988  |FIG 14.9|
|   15 |GRIFFIN           AMY              D       78980     30      0004875  |FIG 14.9|
|   16 |FELLMAN           ROBERT           R       99604     42      0000774  |FIG 14.9|
|   17 |ANDERSON          HEATHER          D       14250     43      0002550  |FIG 14.9|
|   18 |BAKER             WILLARD          V       12770     50      0009595  |FIG 14.9|
|   19 |WHITMAN           CLAUDETTE        E       10100     34      0001995  |FIG 14.9|
|   20 |BRADFORD          MICHAEL          D       45002     04      0003525  |FIG 14.9|
|   21 |KLINE             TRACEY           L       42130     01      0003449  |FIG 14.9|
|   22 |GRIFFIN           AMY              D       78980     30      0002995  |FIG 14.9|
|   23 |MAYES             DAVID            M       22250     15      0019595  |FIG 14.9|
|   24 |MARTIN            DIANE            C       33358     42      0001435  |FIG 14.9|
|   25 |MARTIN            DIANE            C       33358     42      0000950  |FIG 14.9|
|   26 |TUDDLE            JACKIE           F       69632     36      0000299  |FIG 14.9|
|   27 |TUDDLE            JACKIE           F       69632     36      0025621  |FIG 14.9|
```

Figure 14.9 Sales Analysis (SEARCH Statements) (Data) *Continued*

```
-------------------------------------------------------------------------------------------
|     |            1         2         3         4         5         6         7        8| FIGURE  |
|RECORD|12345678901234567890123456789012345678901234567890123456789012345678901234567890| NUMBER  |
-------------------------------------------------------------------------------------------
|    28|SCHWARTZ            MONICA            B      64632     46        0002995        |FIG 14.9|
|    29|SMITH              MARY              A      33320     35        0001525        |FIG 14.9|
|    30|SMITH              MARY              A      33320     35        0025000        |FIG 14.9|
|    31|MILLER             HERMAN            T      20200     10        0012500        |FIG 14.9|
|    32|SCHWARTZ            MONICA            B      64632     46        0006423        |FIG 14.9|
|    33|KLINE              TRACEY            L      42130     01        0002286        |FIG 14.9|
|    34|GRIFFIN             AMY               D      78980     30        0025350        |FIG 14.9|
|    35|JOHNSON             SUSAN             A      54220     25        0000999        |FIG 14.9|
|    36|BAKER               WILLARD           V      12770     50        0025099        |FIG 14.9|
|    37|MAYES              DAVID             M      22250     15        0002195        |FIG 14.9|
|    38|DOUGLAS             RICHARD           J      25600     09        0001139        |FIG 14.9|
|    39|WHITMAN             CLAUDETTE         E      10100     34        0052796        |FIG 14.9|
|    40|MAYES              DAVID             M      22250     15        0000965        |FIG 14.9|
|    41|TUDDLE              JACKIE            F      69632     36        0007329        |FIG 14.9|
|    42|MAYES              DAVID             M      22250     15        0000559        |FIG 14.9|
|    43|BRADFORD            MICHAEL           D      45002     04        0002589        |FIG 14.9|
|    44|BRADFORD            MICHAEL           D      45002     04        0001775        |FIG 14.9|
|    45|BRADFORD            MICHAEL           D      45002     04        0019995        |FIG 14.9|
|    46|KLINE              TRACEY            L      42130     01        0009995        |FIG 14.9|
|    47|FELLMAN             ROBERT            R      99604     42        0001875        |FIG 14.9|
|    48|FELLMAN             ROBERT            R      99604     42        0039999        |FIG 14.9|
|    49|BRADFORD            MICHAEL           D      45002     04        0001295        |FIG 14.9|
|    50|KLINE              TRACEY            L      42130     01        0008990        |FIG 14.9|
|    51|MAYES              DAVID             M      22250     15        0003529        |FIG 14.9|
|    52|TUDDLE              JACKIE            F      69632     36        0001995        |FIG 14.9|
|    53|SMITH              MARY              A      33320     35        0005489        |FIG 14.9|
|    54|BRUCE              FAYETTE           S      55500     49        0006969        |FIG 14.9|
|    55|JOHNSON             SUSAN             A      54220     25        0003000        |FIG 14.9|
|    56|DOUGLAS             RICHARD           J      25600     09        0059995        |FIG 14.9|
|    57|JOHNSON             SUSAN             A      54220     25        0004995        |FIG 14.9|
|    58|GRIFFIN             AMY               D      78980     30        0000599        |FIG 14.9|
|    59|KLINE              TRACEY            L      42130     01        0007642        |FIG 14.9|
|    60|GRIFFIN             AMY               D      78980     30        0001987        |FIG 14.9|
|    61|MAYES              DAVID             M      22250     15        00035288       |FIG 14.9|
```

Figure 14.9 Sales Analysis (SEARCH Statements) (Data) *Continued*

```
                    SALESMAN WEEKLY REPORT BY DISTRICT

            1      ALABAMA            $323.62

            4      ARKANSAS           $291.79

            9      FLORIDA            $611.34

           10      GEORGIA            $505.49

           15      IOWA               $303.71

           25      MISSOURI           $134.82

           30      NEW JERSEY         $459.57

           34      NORTH DAKOTA       $547.91

           35      OHIO               $320.14

           36      OKLAHOMA           $438.09

           42      TENNESSEE          $671.25

           43      TEXAS               $45.45

           46      VIRGINIA           $104.13

           49      WISCONSIN           $92.14

           50      WYOMING            $396.60
```

Figure 14.9 Sales Analysis (SEARCH Statements) (Output) *Continued*

```
             SALESMAN WEEKLY REPORT BY SALESMAN NUMBER WITHIN DISTRICT

    KLINE           TRACEY        L      42130      1      ALABAMA            $323.62

    BRADFORD        MICHAEL       D      45002      4      ARKANSAS           $291.79

    DOUGLAS         RICHARD       J      25600      9      FLORIDA            $611.34

    MILLER          HERMAN        T      20200     10      GEORGIA            $505.49

    MAYES           DAVID         M      22250     15      IOWA               $303.71

    JOHNSON         SUSAN         A      54220     25      MISSOURI           $134.82

    GRIFFIN         AMY           D      78980     30      NEW JERSEY         $459.57

    WHITMAN         CLAUDETTE     E      10100     34      NORTH DAKOTA       $547.91

    SMITH           MARY          A      33320     35      OHIO               $320.14

    TUDDLE          JACKIE        F      69632     36      OKLAHOMA           $438.09

    MARTIN          DIANE         C      33358     42      TENNESSEE          $244.77

    FELLMAN         ROBERT        R      99604     42      TENNESSEE          $426.48

    ANDERSON        HEATHER       D      14250     43      TEXAS               $45.45

    SCHWARTZ        MONICA        B      64632     46      VIRGINIA           $104.13

    BRUCE           FAYETTE       S      55500     49      WISCONSIN           $92.14

    BAKER           WILLARD       V      12770     50      WYOMING            $396.60
```

Figure 14.9 Sales Analysis (SEARCH Statements) (Output) *Continued*

The Sales Analysis Program with a Variable-Length Table

The program presented in Figure 14.10 is, for the most part, a duplication of the program in Figure 14.9, except that the SALESMAN-DATA-TABLE in Figure 14.10 is a variable-length table by virtue of the DEPENDING ON SALESMAN-COUNT clause in line 600. By using a variable-length table, two changes may be made in the program. First, it is not necessary to initialize the table to any known set of values—the ZERO TABLE module does not appear in the new program. Secondly, the SEARCH for corresponding salesman identification entries does not have to test to determine whether the end of the table has been encountered (see lines 1450–1540). Instead, the SEARCH statement simply *adds* a new item to the bottom of the existing table when no match on IDENTITY is found.

```
|            1   1   2   2   2   3   3   4   4   4   5   5   6   6   6   7   7   8|
|     4   8   2   6   0   4   8   2   6   0   4   8   2   6   0   4   8   2   6   0|
|-------------------------------------------------------------------------------
|000010 IDENTIFICATION DIVISION.                                      FIG14.10|
|000020 PROGRAM-ID. SALES-ANALYSIS.                                   FIG14.10|
|000030 AUTHOR. J. WAYNE SPENCE.                                      FIG14.10|
|000040 DATE-WRITTEN. JANUARY 1, 1981.                                FIG14.10|
|000050 DATE-COMPILED. JANUARY 1, 1981.                               FIG14.10|
|000060*    THIS PROGRAM ILLUSTRATES THE USE OF INDEXED               FIG14.10|
|000070*    TABLES.  IT DEFINES THE TABLES AND, IN SOME INSTANCES,    FIG14.10|
|000080*    PROVIDES THE INITIAL VALUES TO BE PLACED IN THE TABLE.    FIG14.10|
|000090*    IN THE PROCEDURE DIVISION, THE INDEXED TABLES ARE PROCESSED FIG14.10|
|000100*    AND A "BUBBLE" SORT IS APPLIED TO REARRANGE THE DATA      FIG14.10|
|000110*    INTERNALLY.  IN CONJUNCTION WITH THE TABLES, SET;         FIG14.10|
|000120*    SEARCH; SEARCH ALL; AND INDEX-NAMES                       FIG14.10|
|000130*    ARE USED.                                                 FIG14.10|
|000140 ENVIRONMENT DIVISION.                                         FIG14.10|
|000150 CONFIGURATION SECTION.                                        FIG14.10|
|000160 SOURCE-COMPUTER. CDC-CYBER-72.                                FIG14.10|
|000170 OBJECT-COMPUTER. CDC-CYBER-72.                                FIG14.10|
|000180 SPECIAL-NAMES.  C01 IS PAGE-TOP.                              FIG14.10|
```

Figure 14.10 Sales Analysis (Variable-Length Table)

```
|          1    1    2    2    2    3    3    4    4    4    5    5    6    6    6    7    7    8|
|    4    8    2    6    0    4    8    2    6    0    4    8    2    6    0    4    8    2    6    0|
--------------------------------------------------------------------------------------------------
|000190 INPUT-OUTPUT SECTION.                                        FIG14.10|
|000200 FILE-CONTROL.                                                FIG14.10|
|000210     SELECT SALES-FILE ASSIGN TO UT-S-SYSIN.                  FIG14.10|
|000220     SELECT REPORT-FILE ASSIGN TO UT-S-SYSPRINT.              FIG14.10|
|000230 DATA DIVISION.                                               FIG14.10|
|000240 FILE SECTION.                                                FIG14.10|
|000250 FD  SALES-FILE LABEL RECORDS ARE OMITTED.                    FIG14.10|
|000260 01  SALES-RECORD.                                            FIG14.10|
|000270     03 NAME.                                                 FIG14.10|
|000280         05 LAST-NAME          PIC X(20).                     FIG14.10|
|000290         05 FIRST-NAME         PIC X(20).                     FIG14.10|
|000300         05 MIDDLE-INITIAL     PIC X(01).                     FIG14.10|
|000310     03 FILLER                 PIC X(08).                     FIG14.10|
|000320     03 ID-INFORMATION.                                       FIG14.10|
|000330         05 SALESMAN-ID        PIC 9(05).                     FIG14.10|
|000340         05 FILLER             PIC X(05).                     FIG14.10|
|000350         05 DISTRICT-NUMBER    PIC 9(02).                     FIG14.10|
|000360     03 FILLER                 PIC X(08).                     FIG14.10|
|000370     03 AMOUNT-OF-SALE         PIC 9(05)V9(02).               FIG14.10|
|000380     03 FILLER                 PIC X(04).                     FIG14.10|
|000390 FD  REPORT-FILE LABEL RECORDS ARE OMITTED.                   FIG14.10|
|000400 01  OUTPUT-LINE               PIC X(133).                    FIG14.10|
|000410 WORKING-STORAGE SECTION.                                     FIG14.10|
|000420 01  WORKING-VARIABLES.                                       FIG14.10|
|000430     05  FILE-STATUS           PIC X(15).                     FIG14.10|
|000440     05  SORT-INDICATOR        PIC X(15).                     FIG14.10|
|000450     05  DISTRICT-TOTAL        PIC 9(07)V9(02).               FIG14.10|
|000460     05  ITEMS-TO-BE-SORTED    PIC 9(03) VALUE ZERO.          FIG14.10|
|000470     05  SAVE-STATE-NAME       PIC X(12).                     FIG14.10|
|000480     05  SALESMAN-COUNT        PIC 9(03) VALUE ZERO.          FIG14.10|
|000490 01  SAVE-REORGANIZE-RECORD.                                  FIG14.10|
|000500     03 ID-INFORMATION.                                       FIG14.10|
|000510         05 DISTRICT-NUMBER    PIC 9(02).                     FIG14.10|
|000520         05 SALESMAN-ID        PIC 9(05).                     FIG14.10|
|000530     03 AMOUNT-OF-SALE         PIC 9(06)V9(02).               FIG14.10|
|000540     03 NAME.                                                 FIG14.10|
|000550         05 LAST-NAME          PIC X(20).                     FIG14.10|
|000560         05 FIRST-NAME         PIC X(20).                     FIG14.10|
|000570         05 MIDDLE-INITIAL     PIC X(01).                     FIG14.10|
|000580 01  SALESMAN-DATA-TABLE.                                     FIG14.10|
|000590     03 SALESMAN-ENTRY OCCURS 0 TO 100 TIMES                  FIG14.10|
|000600            DEPENDING ON SALESMAN-COUNT                       FIG14.10|
|000610            INDEXED BY LCTN.                                  FIG14.10|
|000620         05 IDENTITY.                                         FIG14.10|
|000630             07 DIST-NUM       PIC 9(02).                     FIG14.10|
|000640             07 MAN-ID         PIC 9(05).                     FIG14.10|
|000650         05 AMOUNT             PIC 9(06)V9(02).               FIG14.10|
|000660         05 SALESMAN-NAME.                                    FIG14.10|
|000670             07 L-N            PIC X(20).                     FIG14.10|
|000680             07 F-N            PIC X(20).                     FIG14.10|
|000690             07 M-I            PIC X(01).                     FIG14.10|
|000700 01  CODE-STATE-LIST.                                         FIG14.10|
|000710     02 FILLER                 PIC X(14) VALUE '01ALABAMA'.   FIG14.10|
|000720     02 FILLER                 PIC X(14) VALUE '04ARKANSAS'.  FIG14.10|
|000730     02 FILLER                 PIC X(14) VALUE '09FLORIDA'.   FIG14.10|
|000740     02 FILLER                 PIC X(14) VALUE '10GEORGIA'.   FIG14.10|
|000750     02 FILLER                 PIC X(14) VALUE '15IOWA'.      FIG14.10|
|000760     02 FILLER                 PIC X(14) VALUE '25MISSOURI'.  FIG14.10|
|000770     02 FILLER                 PIC X(14) VALUE '30NEW JERSEY'.   FIG14.10|
|000780     02 FILLER                 PIC X(14) VALUE '34NORTH DAKOTA'.FIG14.10|
|000790     02 FILLER                 PIC X(14) VALUE '35OHIO'.      FIG14.10|
|000800     02 FILLER                 PIC X(14) VALUE '36OKLAHOMA'.  FIG14.10|
|000810     02 FILLER                 PIC X(14) VALUE '42TENNESSEE'. FIG14.10|
|000820     02 FILLER                 PIC X(14) VALUE '43TEXAS'.     FIG14.10|
|000830     02 FILLER                 PIC X(14) VALUE '46VIRGINIA'.  FIG14.10|
|000840     02 FILLER                 PIC X(14) VALUE '49WISCONSIN'. FIG14.10|
|000850     02 FILLER                 PIC X(14) VALUE '50WYOMING'.   FIG14.10|
|000860 01  STATE-CODE-TABLE.                                        FIG14.10|
|000870     02 STATE-CODE-ENTRIES OCCURS 15 TIMES                    FIG14.10|
|000880            ASCENDING KEY IS STATE-CODE                       FIG14.10|
|000890            INDEXED BY STATE.                                 FIG14.10|
|000900         03 STATE-CODE         PIC 9(02).                     FIG14.10|
|000910         03 STATE-NAME         PIC X(12).                     FIG14.10|
|000920 01  REPORT-HEADING.                                          FIG14.10|
|000930     02 FILLER                 PIC X(40) VALUE SPACES.        FIG14.10|
|000940     02 FILLER                 PIC X(23) VALUE                FIG14.10|
|000950     'SALESMAN WEEKLY REPORT '.                               FIG14.10|
|000960     02 TITLE                  PIC X(40).                     FIG14.10|
|000970 01  DISTRICT-DETAIL.                                         FIG14.10|
```

Figure 14.10 Sales Analysis (Variable-Length Table) *Continued*

```
|        1 1   2   2   2   3   3   4   4   4   5   5   6   6   6   7   7   8|
|   4    8 2   6   0   4   8   2   6   0   4   8   2   6   0   4   8   2   6   0|
-----------------------------------------------------------------------------
|000980      02 FILLER                    PIC X(38) VALUE SPACES.          FIG14.10|
|000990      02 DISTRICT-NUMBER-OUT        PIC Z9.                          FIG14.10|
|001000      02 FILLER                    PIC X(05) VALUE SPACES.          FIG14.10|
|001010      02 STATE-NAME-OUT            PIC X(12).                       FIG14.10|
|001020      02 FILLER                    PIC X(05) VALUE SPACES.          FIG14.10|
|001030      02 DIST-TOTAL                PIC $$,$$$,$$$.99.               FIG14.10|
|001040 01 SALESMAN-DETAIL.                                                FIG14.10|
|001050      02 FILLER                    PIC X(21) VALUE SPACES.          FIG14.10|
|001060      02 SALESMAN-NAME-OUT          PIC X(41).                       FIG14.10|
|001070      02 FILLER                    PIC X(05) VALUE SPACES.          FIG14.10|
|001080      02 SALESMAN-NUMBER-OUT        PIC ZZZZZ9.                      FIG14.10|
|001090      02 FILLER                    PIC X(05) VALUE SPACES.          FIG14.10|
|001100      02 DISTRICT-NUMBER-OUT        PIC Z9(01).                      FIG14.10|
|001110      02 FILLER                    PIC X(05) VALUE SPACES.          FIG14.10|
|001120      02 STATE-NAME-OUT            PIC X(12).                       FIG14.10|
|001130      02 FILLER                    PIC X(05) VALUE SPACES.          FIG14.10|
|001140      02 AMOUNT-OUT                PIC $$$$,$$$.9(02).              FIG14.10|
|001150 PROCEDURE DIVISION.                                                FIG14.10|
|001160 CONTROL-PARAGRAPH.                                                 FIG14.10|
|001170      PERFORM 1000-START-UP.                                        FIG14.10|
|001180      PERFORM 2000-TABLE-LOAD UNTIL FILE-STATUS = 'FILE COMPLETE'.  FIG14.10|
|001190      PERFORM 3000-SORT-FOR-REPORT                                  FIG14.10|
|001200          UNTIL SORT-INDICATOR = 'SORT COMPLETE'.                   FIG14.10|
|001210      PERFORM 4000-REPORT-1.                                        FIG14.10|
|001220      PERFORM 5000-REPORT-2.                                        FIG14.10|
|001230      CLOSE SALES-FILE, REPORT-FILE.                                FIG14.10|
|001240      STOP RUN.                                                     FIG14.10|
|001250 1000-START-UP.                                                     FIG14.10|
|001260      OPEN INPUT SALES-FILE OUTPUT REPORT-FILE.                     FIG14.10|
|001270      MOVE 'READING FILE' TO FILE-STATUS.                           FIG14.10|
|001280      MOVE SPACES TO OUTPUT-LINE.                                   FIG14.10|
|001290      MOVE CODE-STATE-LIST TO STATE-CODE-TABLE.                     FIG14.10|
|001300      SET STATE, LCTN TO 1.                                         FIG14.10|
|001310      READ SALES-FILE AT END                                       FIG14.10|
|001320          MOVE 'FILE COMPLETE' TO FILE-STATUS.                      FIG14.10|
|001330 2000-TABLE-LOAD.                                                   FIG14.10|
|001340      MOVE NAME OF SALES-RECORD TO NAME OF SAVE-REORGANIZE-RECORD.  FIG14.10|
|001350      MOVE SALESMAN-ID OF SALES-RECORD TO SALESMAN-ID              FIG14.10|
|001360          OF SAVE-REORGANIZE-RECORD.                                FIG14.10|
|001370      MOVE DISTRICT-NUMBER OF SALES-RECORD TO DISTRICT-NUMBER      FIG14.10|
|001380          OF SAVE-REORGANIZE-RECORD.                                FIG14.10|
|001390      MOVE AMOUNT-OF-SALE OF SALES-RECORD TO AMOUNT-OF-SALE        FIG14.10|
|001400          OF SAVE-REORGANIZE-RECORD.                                FIG14.10|
|001410      PERFORM 2100-FIND-ENTRY.                                      FIG14.10|
|001420      READ SALES-FILE AT END                                       FIG14.10|
|001430          MOVE 'FILE COMPLETE' TO FILE-STATUS.                      FIG14.10|
|001440 2100-FIND-ENTRY.                                                   FIG14.10|
|001450      SET LCTN TO 1.                                                FIG14.10|
|001460      SEARCH SALESMAN-ENTRY                                         FIG14.10|
|001470          AT END                                                    FIG14.10|
|001480              ADD 1 TO SALESMAN-COUNT, ITEMS-TO-BE-SORTED;         FIG14.10|
|001490              SET LCTN TO SALESMAN-COUNT;                           FIG14.10|
|001500              MOVE SAVE-REORGANIZE-RECORD TO SALESMAN-ENTRY (LCTN) FIG14.10|
|001510          WHEN IDENTITY (LCTN) = ID-INFORMATION OF                 FIG14.10|
|001520              SAVE-REORGANIZE-RECORD                                FIG14.10|
|001530              ADD AMOUNT-OF-SALE OF SAVE-REORGANIZE-RECORD TO      FIG14.10|
|001540                  AMOUNT (LCTN).                                    FIG14.10|
|001550 3000-SORT-FOR-REPORT.                                              FIG14.10|
|001560      MOVE 'SORT COMPLETE' TO SORT-INDICATOR.                       FIG14.10|
|001570      PERFORM 3100-COMPARISON VARYING LCTN FROM 1 BY 1             FIG14.10|
|001580          UNTIL LCTN IS EQUAL TO ITEMS-TO-BE-SORTED.                FIG14.10|
|001590      IF SORT-INDICATOR NOT EQUAL TO 'SORT COMPLETE'                FIG14.10|
|001600          SUBTRACT 1 FROM ITEMS-TO-BE-SORTED.                       FIG14.10|
|001610 3100-COMPARISON.                                                   FIG14.10|
|001620      IF IDENTITY (LCTN) IS GREATER THAN IDENTITY (LCTN + 1)       FIG14.10|
|001630          MOVE SALESMAN-ENTRY (LCTN) TO SAVE-REORGANIZE-RECORD     FIG14.10|
|001640          MOVE SALESMAN-ENTRY (LCTN + 1) TO SALESMAN-ENTRY (LCTN)  FIG14.10|
|001650          MOVE SAVE-REORGANIZE-RECORD TO SALESMAN-ENTRY (LCTN + 1) FIG14.10|
|001660          MOVE 'ITEM SWITCHED' TO SORT-INDICATOR.                   FIG14.10|
|001670 4000-REPORT-1.                                                     FIG14.10|
|001680      MOVE 'BY DISTRICT' TO TITLE.                                  FIG14.10|
|001690      SET LCTN TO 1.                                                FIG14.10|
|001700      WRITE OUTPUT-LINE FROM REPORT-HEADING AFTER PAGE-TOP.        FIG14.10|
|001710      MOVE AMOUNT (LCTN) TO DISTRICT-TOTAL.                         FIG14.10|
|001720      MOVE DIST-NUM (LCTN) TO DISTRICT-NUMBER OF                    FIG14.10|
|001730          SAVE-REORGANIZE-RECORD.                                   FIG14.10|
|001740      PERFORM 4100-GENERATE-REPORT-1 VARYING LCTN FROM 2 BY 1      FIG14.10|
|001750          UNTIL LCTN IS GREATER THAN SALESMAN-COUNT.                FIG14.10|
|001760      PERFORM 4200-REPORT-1-DETAIL.                                 FIG14.10|
```

Figure 14.10 Sales Analysis (Variable-Length Table) *Continued*

```
|             1   1   2   2   2   3   3   4   4   4   5   5   6   6   6   7   7   8|
|    4   8    2   6   0   4   8   2   6   0   4   8   2   6   0   4   8   2   6   0|
---------------------------------------------------------------------------------
|001770 4100-GENERATE-REPORT-1.                                          FIG14.10|
|001780     IF DIST-NUM (LCTN) IS NOT EQUAL TO DISTRICT-NUMBER OF        FIG14.10|
|001790        SAVE-REORGANIZE-RECORD PERFORM 4200-REPORT-1-DETAIL       FIG14.10|
|001800        ELSE                                                      FIG14.10|
|001810             ADD AMOUNT (LCTN) TO DISTRICT-TOTAL.                 FIG14.10|
|001820 4200-REPORT-1-DETAIL.                                            FIG14.10|
|001830     MOVE DISTRICT-NUMBER OF SAVE-REORGANIZE-RECORD               FIG14.10|
|001840        TO DISTRICT-NUMBER-OUT OF DISTRICT-DETAIL.                FIG14.10|
|001850     MOVE DISTRICT-TOTAL TO DIST-TOTAL.                           FIG14.10|
|001860     PERFORM 4250-FIND-STATE-NAME.                                FIG14.10|
|001870     MOVE SAVE-STATE-NAME TO STATE-NAME-OUT OF DISTRICT-DETAIL.   FIG14.10|
|001880     WRITE OUTPUT-LINE FROM DISTRICT-DETAIL AFTER 2 LINES.        FIG14.10|
|001890     MOVE DIST-NUM (LCTN) TO DISTRICT-NUMBER OF                   FIG14.10|
|001900        SAVE-REORGANIZE-RECORD.                                   FIG14.10|
|001910     MOVE AMOUNT (LCTN) TO DISTRICT-TOTAL.                        FIG14.10|
|001920 4250-FIND-STATE-NAME.                                            FIG14.10|
|001930     SET STATE TO 1.                                              FIG14.10|
|001940     SEARCH ALL STATE-CODE-ENTRIES WHEN STATE-CODE (STATE) IS     FIG14.10|
|001950        EQUAL TO DISTRICT-NUMBER OF SAVE-REORGANIZE-RECORD        FIG14.10|
|001960        MOVE STATE-NAME (STATE) TO SAVE-STATE-NAME.               FIG14.10|
|001970 5000-REPORT-2.                                                   FIG14.10|
|001980     MOVE 'BY SALESMAN NUMBER WITHIN DISTRICT' TO TITLE.          FIG14.10|
|001990     PERFORM 5100-REPORT.                                         FIG14.10|
|002000 5100-REPORT.                                                     FIG14.10|
|002010     WRITE OUTPUT-LINE FROM REPORT-HEADING AFTER PAGE-TOP.        FIG14.10|
|002020     MOVE 0 TO DISTRICT-NUMBER OF SAVE-REORGANIZE-RECORD.         FIG14.10|
|002030     PERFORM 5150-GENERATE-REPORT VARYING LCTN FROM 1 BY 1        FIG14.10|
|002040        UNTIL LCTN IS GREATER THAN SALESMAN-COUNT.                FIG14.10|
|002050     MOVE SALESMAN-COUNT TO ITEMS-TO-BE-SORTED.                   FIG14.10|
|002060     MOVE 'RESTART' TO SORT-INDICATOR.                            FIG14.10|
|002070 5150-GENERATE-REPORT.                                            FIG14.10|
|002080     IF DIST-NUM (LCTN) IS NOT EQUAL TO DISTRICT-NUMBER OF        FIG14.10|
|002090        SAVE-REORGANIZE-RECORD                                    FIG14.10|
|002100        MOVE DIST-NUM (LCTN) TO                                   FIG14.10|
|002110           DISTRICT-NUMBER OF SAVE-REORGANIZE-RECORD;             FIG14.10|
|002120        PERFORM 4250-FIND-STATE-NAME;                             FIG14.10|
|002130        MOVE SAVE-STATE-NAME TO STATE-NAME-OUT OF                 FIG14.10|
|002140           SALESMAN-DETAIL;                                       FIG14.10|
|002150     MOVE DIST-NUM (LCTN) TO DISTRICT-NUMBER-OUT OF               FIG14.10|
|002160        SALESMAN-DETAIL.                                          FIG14.10|
|002170     MOVE SALESMAN-NAME (LCTN) TO SALESMAN-NAME-OUT OF            FIG14.10|
|002180        SALESMAN-DETAIL.                                          FIG14.10|
|002190     MOVE AMOUNT (LCTN) TO AMOUNT-OUT.                            FIG14.10|
|002200     MOVE MAN-ID (LCTN) TO SALESMAN-NUMBER-OUT OF                 FIG14.10|
|002210        SALESMAN-DETAIL.                                          FIG14.10|
|002220     WRITE OUTPUT-LINE FROM SALESMAN-DETAIL AFTER 2 LINES.        FIG14.10|
```

Figure 14.10 Sales Analysis (Variable-Length Table) *Continued*

Summary

Although there is little difference in outward appearance between subscripted and indexed tables, the internal means of addressing a particular table position is considerably different. Subscripts are occurrence positions which must be translated into an internal memory address, whereas indexes are references to a byte displacement value from the beginning of the table—much more nearly the value used to address an internal memory position.

Indexed tables are created through the combination of the OCCURS and IN-DEXED BY clauses; however, an index is a different type of storage position than a subscript, and therefore, only a selected set of statements is permitted to modify the value of an index. As with a subscripted table, a PERFORM statement is permitted to modify an index. Where MOVE, ADD, and SUBTRACT statements may be used to alter the value of a subscript, a SET statement may be used to alter an index. Two forms of the SEARCH statement are also capable of altering the value of an index.

The SEARCH statement provides the programmer with the means of "automatically" conducting a linear search through an indexed table. In addition, the SEARCH ALL statement may be employed to conduct a binary search operation.

Notes on Programming Style
Although we have been discussing indexed tables, their treatment in a program is governed by the same set of general rules laid out in the programming style notes in Chapter 13. Although most systems scrutinize the value associated with an index more closely than the value of a subscript, it is still possible to address erroneous data. Of course, the other concerns relating to tables should be examined for indexed tables—reading directly into a table, storing more detail than is necessary, and determining a rationale for the size of tables.

Questions

Below fill in the blank(s) with the appropriate word, words, or phrases.

1. In determining a table reference position, subscripted tables internally utilize _____ while indexed tables utilize _____ .

2. A displacement value for an indexed table is measured in_____and represents _____ .

3. The clause that distinguishes an indexed from a subscripted table is the _____ clause.

4. Unlike a subscript, a(n) _____ is directly associated with a given level of a given table.

5. A subscripted table must use direct (subscript) addressing, whereas indexed tables are permitted to use both direct and _____ addressing.

6. If ITEM was the name of an indexed table (vector), the reference ITEM (LCTN) is an example of _____ addressing, while ITEM (LCTN + 4) is an example of _____ addressing.

7. The only statements permitted to create or modify an index-name are _____ , _____ , and _____ .

8. An index-data-name may be created only through the use of a(n) _____ clause.

9. The identifier referred to in a simple SET statement is generally a(n) _____ .

10. Though the MOVE statement is similar to the simple SET statement, the _____ statement, used in conjunction with indexed tables, is similar to both the ADD and SUBTRACT statements.

11. In the SET UP/DOWN BY statement, the value to be added to/subtracted from an index-name must be a(n) _____ or a(n) _____ .

12. The SEARCH statement may be used only in conjunction with a(n) _____ (subscripted/indexed) table.

13. The SEARCH statement performs a(n) _____ searching process through a table, while a SEARCH ALL statement performs a _____ searching operation.

14. The identifier that specifies the table to be examined through a SEARCH statement is that identifier in a table description which _____ .

15. The VARYING option of the SEARCH statement is used to modify _____ .

16. The AT END option of the SEARCH statement is executed when _____ .

17. A SEARCH statement is terminated when _____ or when _____ .

18. A SEARCH ALL statement may be used on an indexed table only if the table description includes a(n) _____ clause.

19. In an ASCENDING/DESCENDING KEY clause, the keys are listed in _____ (increasing/decreasing) order of importance.

20. Before a SEARCH ALL statement is executed on a table, the table must be _____ .

21. The conditions associated with the WHEN phrase of the SEARCH statement may be _____ (condition type(s)), while only a _____ (condition type) may be stated in the SEARCH ALL WHEN phrase.

Answer the following questions by circling either "T" for True or "F" for False.

T F 22. Indexed tables are more efficient than subscripted tables.

T F 23. An index-name, which appears in an INDEXED BY clause, requires no further reference in the DATA DIVSION.

T F 24. Both subscripted and indexed tables may be addressed by both direct and relative means.

T F 25. The statements that might be used to create or modify a subscript may also create or modify an index-name.

T F 26. An index-name is the same thing as an index-data-name.

T F 27. An index-name never requires a PICTURE clause.

T F 28. An index-data-name never requires a PICTURE clause.

T F 29. An index-data-name, like an index-name, is directly associated with a particular indexed table.

T F 30. When an index-name is the receiving field of a SET statement, the value in the sending field is always converted to byte displacement mode prior to being placed in the index-name.

T F 31. When an index-data-name is the receiving field of a SET statement and the sending field is an index-name, conversion never takes place.

T F 32. When the sending field in a SET statement is a literal, the value is always converted before being placed in the receiving field.

T F 33. In the simple SET statement, the receiving field must contain a value prior to the execution of the statement.

T F 34. In the SET UP/DOWN BY statement, the receiving field must contain a value prior to the execution of the statement.

T F 35. In a SET UP/DOWN BY statement, the value to be added to/subtracted from the index-name is always converted to byte displacement mode prior to the incrementing/decrementing process.

T F 36. The ASCENDING/DESCENDING KEY clause must be used in the description of an indexed table to permit the use of the SEARCH statement in the PROCEDURE DIVISION.

T F 37. The VARYING option of the SEARCH statement is used to vary the index-name of the table being searched.

T F 38. The VARYING option may be used on either the SEARCH or SEARCH ALL statement.

T F 39. The AT END phrase may be used in both the SEARCH and SEARCH ALL statements.

T F 40. When an indexed table is accompanied by an ASCENDING/DESCENDING KEY clause, data must be placed in the table in the order specified by the key clause.

T F 41. Only one key may be specified in an ASCENDING/DESCENDING KEY clause.

Exercises

1. Below are a series of indexed tables. Diagram each table, and jointly indicate occurrence positions and beginning byte displacements of each cell of the tables.

```
a)   Ø1   CODE-TO-RATE-CONVERSION.

     Ø2   RATE OCCURS 8 TIMES

          INDEXED BY CODE              PIC 99V99.


b)   Ø1   FEDERAL-TAX-TABLE.

     Ø2   TAX-BRACKET OCCURS 7 TIMES

          INDEXED BY INCOME.

          Ø3   LOWER-LIMIT             PIC 9(5)V99.

          Ø3   UPPER-LIMIT             PIC 9(5)V99.

          Ø3   BASE-TAX                PIC 9(4)V99.

          Ø3   PERCENT-TAX             PIC V99.


c)   Ø1   RATE-PREMIUM-CONVERSION.

     Ø2   PAY-SCALE OCCURS 5 TIMES

          INDEXED BY PAY-CODE.

          Ø3   SHIFT OCCURS 3 TIMES

               INDEXED BY SHIFT-CODE.

               Ø4   ADJUSTMENT         PIC 9V999.
```

2. Given the DATA DIVISION entries below, determine the actual value of the index-name or identifier in each SET statement.

```
WORKING-STORAGE SECTION.

Ø1   WORKING-RECORD.

     Ø5   IND-ALT             USAGE IS INDEX.

     Ø5   LCTN                PIC 999.

Ø1   DATA-TABLE.

     Ø2   DATA-ITEM OCCURS 15 TIMES

          INDEXED BY IND-1

          PIC 999.

Ø1   ITEM-TABLE.

     Ø2   ITEM OCCURS 7 TIMES

          INDEXED BY IND-2

          PIC 9(5).
```

a) SET IND-1 TO 3.   <u>Result</u>.

b) SET IND-2 TO 5.

c) MOVE 5 TO LCTN.

SET IND-1 TO LCTN.

d) SET IND-1 TO 2.

SET IND-ALT TO IND-1.

SET IND-2 TO IND-ALT.

e) SET IND-2 TO 4.

SET IND-ALT TO IND-2.

SET IND-2 TO IND-ALT.

3. In each of the following situations, write the SEARCH statement (and supporting code) necessary to fulfill the searching situation. Assume the presence of the indicated table below, as appropriate.

```
Ø1   INVENTORY-TABLE.

    Ø2   INVENTORY-ITEM OCCURS 300 TIMES

    INDEXED BY ITEM.

        Ø3   ITEM-NUMBER              PIC 9(5).

        Ø3   VENDOR-CODE              PIC XXX.

        Ø3   UNITS-ON-HAND            PIC 9(5).

        Ø3   PRICE                    PIC 9(5)V99.

        Ø3   COST                     PIC 9(5)V99.

        Ø3   MINIMUM-LEVEL            PIC 999.


Ø1   VENDOR-TABLE.

    Ø2   VENDOR-SUPPLIER OCCURS 30 TIMES

    INDEXED BY VEND.

        Ø3   VENDOR-NUMBER            PIC 9(7).

        Ø3   VEND-CODE                PIC XXX.

        Ø3   VENDOR-NAME              PIC X(30).

        Ø3   TERMS                    PIC 9(4).
```

a. Find the inventory item that carries the number "14728," and print all the values in the table for that item. If it is not found in the table, print an error message.
b. Find and print *all* inventory item numbers where the minimum level is greater than or equal to the units on hand.
c. Find the vendor code "RXT" and print the vendor's name. If that particular vendor is not in the table, add it to the end of the table, move "NEW VENDOR" to the vendor's name, assign the vendor number of the previous last vendor + 1 as the new vendor number, and put zeros in the numeric fields. All unused positions in the vendor table show blank in the vendor code.

d. Find *all* inventory items with a vendor code of "SRV" and print the vendor code, item number, and units on hand.

e. Print *all* items in the inventory table where the investment is greater than $10,000 (e.g., units on hand times the price per unit is greater than $10,000).

f. Print all records in the inventory table vendor code and print the name of each vendor along with the inventory item information.

4. In the following situations write the code necessary to conduct a binary search as indicated. Use the table definitions in Exercise 3, and modify them accordingly. You may assume the data is ordered in the table in any order you wish, so long as you state the assumed order. You may also assume you know the number of positions in the table that actually contain data. (This value, if used, may be assumed in a data-name called ACTIVE.)

a. Find the inventory item number "04782" and print the vendor code for that record. If not found, write an error message.

b. Verify that each vendor code that appears in the inventory table coexists in the vendor table. If the code does not exist, write an error message, otherwise do nothing.

c. Determine whether or not the vendor number "147" is associated with vendor code "RCB" in the vendor table.

Problems

1. A list of purchase-order records have been prepared representing the purchase of individual line items of inventory. Each record (see the multiple-card layout form) contains the inventory item number purchased, the vendor code (see below), the date of purchase (MMDDYY), the purchased quantity, and the total dollar cost to purchase the items. You are to produce a breakdown of these purchase-order records by a) the vendor—such that we may determine the total dollar cost of all items purchased from a single vendor and b) an exceptions list containing all individual inventory items to be purchased provided the dollar cost of purchasing the item is $10,000 or more. (See the print chart.)

When the vendor summary is produced, the vendor code should be accompanied by the vendor's name. The permitted (legal acceptable) vendor codes and names are as follows:

Vendor Code	Vendor Name
AMC	Apex Manufacturing Company
ASM	Adams and Sons Manufacturing
BBB	Biltmore Breaker Boxes
CH	Clinton-Hall
ECE	East Coast Electrical Supply
LLF	Lincoln Lighting and Fixtures
NL	Northern Lights
RTC	Reynolds Terminal Connectors
SWI	South Wire Incorporated
WGE	West Gate Electric Company

These names are to be stored in a table (internally, without any data being read) and utilized when the vendor summary is printed.

MULTIPLE-CARD LAYOUT FORM

Company LEARNING COBOL, INC.

Application Vendor Summary   by J. Wayne Spence   Date 01/01/81   Job No. PROB 14.1   Sheet No. 1

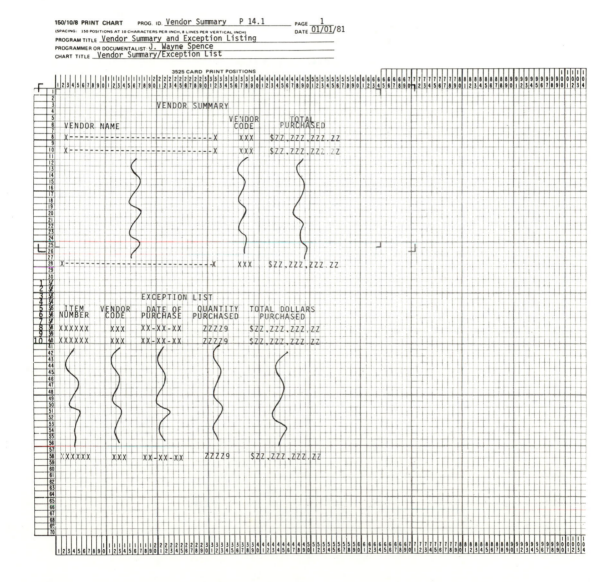

2. You are provided with a set of historical sales records for different products. The historical sales records are composed of a product number, a product name, a date of sale (MMYY), and the sales volume in units for the month (see multiple-card layout form). You will receive the past 12 monthly records (not necessarily a calendar year) in no particular order, as a group. You are to graph the sales performance of each product in the form demonstrated on the print chart.

Note: Since several products are to be displayed in this manner, you should consider (1) scaling the data over the range of sales specified in the monthly records (since there are limited printing positons that may be used to reflect magnitude), (2) the possibility that the origin does not represent zero units sold (thus providing greater dispersion of values on the graph), (3) the monthly sequence (e.g., July to June) may not be the same for all products (e.g., January to December). The month numbers are to be translated into month names.

MULTIPLE-CARD LAYOUT FORM

Company LEARNING COBOL, INC.
Application SALES PERFORMANCE   by J. Wayne Spence   Date 01/01/81   Job No. PROB 14.2   Sheet No. 1

3. You are to create a limited Bill Of Materials Processing (BOMP) system. A bill of materials is simply a list of all the materials (and their quantities) necessary to create a particular product. For example, if you were going to produce (manufacture) a single lawnmower, you would need:

Item	Quantity
Mower deck	1
Engine	1
Wheels	4
Mower blade	1
Wheel nut	4
Cotter pin	4
Medium washer	8
Heavy duty bolt	3
Blade safety nut	1
Heavy duty washer	2
Handle assembly	2
Handle grip	2
Throttle assembly	1

Presuming this is a complete list of materials necessary to build one basic lawnmower, it should be a simple task to determine the number of parts necessary to build 500 lawnmowers. As a result, we may easily determine if we have enough parts on hand to build that number of lawnmowers.

Now assume that we also make two different versions of the lawnmower—a basic model and a self-propelled unit. We would not necessarily have a completely different list of materials to make both products. Perhaps the only difference between the two models is a different mower deck type, a wheel driving assembly, and a mechanism to engage the wheel driving assembly. Of course, we could add garden tillers and other related home and garden implements. Soon we would find that certain materials appear in more than one product (e.g., an engine), but not necessarily in the same numbers (e.g., the garden tiller has only two wheels) or perhaps not at all (e.g., the garden tiller blades are hardly interchangeable with lawnmower blades). However, it is possible to determine what materials are necessary to produce 500 basic lawnmowers, 125 self-propelled lawnmowers, and 30 garden tillers.

Now, suppose that we manufacture 20 different product lines and each line will require no more than 10 different materials (i.e., product 1 may require 10 materials, and product 2 may require 10 materials—some of which may be the same as used in product 1). Now examine the multiple-card layout form. To perform the BOMP activities, four record types will be used. The first record type will contain a product number and the product name. After all product number-name records, a blank record will be inserted (as a delimiter). These records are to be read and stored for future reference. The second type of record contains material names and numbers. These names and numbers are also to be stored in a table for later use. These records will also be followed by a blank record. The third record type will contain single product number, a single material number and the quantity of the material needed to produce one unit of the product. In other words, several type-3 records (in no particular order) will be necessary to construct a complete bill of materials for an individual product. Of course the same would be true to complete the bill of materials of all other products involved. After all the product number-material number-quantity records, a blank record will appear. Finally, the fourth record type will contain a product number and the quantity to be produced.

Processing requirements call for the determination of the number of units of each material necessary to produce the indicated quantity of the product (see the multiple-card layout form) and a summary list indicating the materials and the amounts which should be on hand to meet the indicated production levels.

MULTIPLE-CARD LAYOUT FORM

Company LEARNING COBOL, INC.

Application BOMP by J. Wayne Spence Date 01/01/81 Job No. PROB 14.3 Sheet No. 1

150/10/8 PRINT CHART PROG. ID. Problem 14.3 PAGE 1
(SPACING: 150 POSITIONS AT 10 CHARACTERS PER INCH, 8 LINES PER VERTICAL INCH) DATE 01/01/81
PROGRAM TITLE BILL OF MATERIALS PROCESSING
PROGRAMMER OR DOCUMENTALIST: J. Wayne Spence
CHART TITLE BOMP/MATERIALS LIST

part **3 Fundamental File
Processing Concepts**

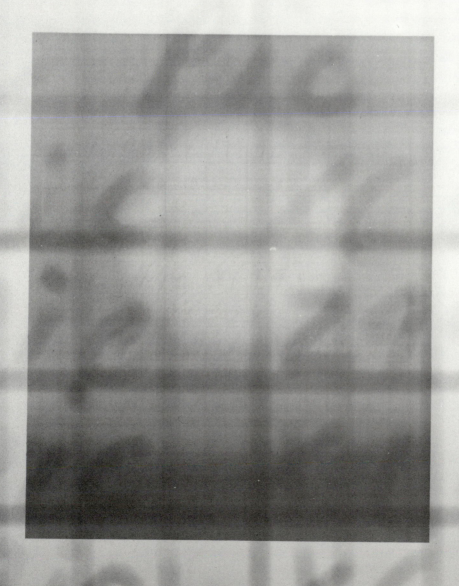

15 The SORT Statement

In some commercial installations, as much as 60 to 80 percent of the computer's time is spent sorting data. *Sorting* simply means the arrangement of data into a specified sequence. Many problems require data to be in a particular sequence. With others, the process is greatly simplified (or more efficient) if data are in a known sequence. As a consequence, sorting is often a necessary first step toward solving a problem.

The Sorting Process

The only problem presented thus far in the text which rearranged (sorted) data was the Sales Analysis problem in Chapter 14, in which an *internal* sort was coded into the program. Unfortunately, all internal sorts suffer the same difficulty—all the data to be sorted must be placed into the computer's memory. The problem presented in Figure 14.9 could accommodate up to 100 individual salesman entries in a table, but what would happen if we were required to sort 1,000 records, or 10,000 records, or 100,000 records? The internal sort would require sufficient internal memory to retain all this data (in addition to which, the sorting time might be prohibitive).

The procedure provided through the SORT statement is an *external* sort. This procedure requires only enough computer memory to store the actual program code and a segment of the data to be sorted; most of the data are temporarily stored on an external medium (e.g., magnetic tape or disk) until it is needed. The procedure is known as a *sort-merge* procedure. That is, a limited amount of data is sorted internally and then stored on an external medium. This "sorting and writing" process is repeated until all the data has been accepted. Then, the groups of sorted data are *merged*.

Consider for a moment a deck of regular playing cards. Suppose you wished to order all the playing cards into a specified sequence. Because it is more difficult with all 52 cards, you divide the deck into four equal stacks each containing 13 cards. You then proceed to order the playing cards in each stack into the appropriate order. After the four stacks have been ordered, you start merging the stacks. You examine stacks 1 and 2. After looking at the first card in each stack, you decide which is higher and you place this card in a new

```
SORT sort-file-name ON {ASCENDING / DESCENDING} KEY identifier-1 [identifier-2] . . .

[ON {ASCENDING / DESCENDING} KEY identifier-m [identifier-n] . . .] . . .

    {USING file-name-1
     INPUT PROCEDURE IS    section-name-1 [THRU    section-name-2]}

    {GIVING file-name-2
     OUTPUT PROCEDURE IS    section-name-3 [THRU    section-name-4]}
```

Figure 15.1 The SORT Statement

stack. You then compare the two cards that now appear on the top of each stack, and you select the higher card, adding it to the new stack. The process continues until you have "merged" the two smaller stacks into one stack containing 26 cards. You then repeat the process for stacks 3 and 4 to build another stack of 26 cards in the appropriate order. Finally, you perform the merging process on the two stacks of 26 cards, building a single stack of 52 cards. The result is an ordered deck of playing cards. The procedure performed by the SORT statement is very similar. The biggest difference is that rather than laying stacks of playing cards on a table, the SORT statement records these groups of ordered data on a magnetic medium for later recall.

The form of the SORT statement is presented in Figure 15.1. The statement has four distinct phases—the identification of the sort file, the specification of sort keys, a description of the input process, and an indication of the output process. Each of these phases will be discussed in turn.

The SORT File   The statement begins with the required reserved word SORT, followed by a "sort-file-name." All previous descriptions of files in COBOL have simply identified a "file-name." As is the case with other files, the sort-file-name must appear in a SELECT clause in the FILE-CONTROL paragraph of the ENVIRONMENT DIVISION. The sort-file must be assigned (via an ASSIGN clause) to a device consistent with the use of magnetic media. Because ASSIGN clause requirements are different from installation to installation, check with your computer center to determine the specific requirements for a sort file.

All files used in a COBOL program must be described in the FILE SECTION of the DATA DIVISION. The sort-file is no exception; however, the sort-file is described with an SD entry instead of an FD entry. Figure 15.2 illustrates a "typical" file and a sort-file. Note that both an INVOICE-FILE and an INVOICE-SORT-FILE are selected in the FILE-CONTROL paragraph. An FD description is presented in the FILE SECTION for the INVOICE-FILE. Following the description of the INVOICE-FILE, the SD for the INVOICE-SORT-FILE is provided.

```
ENVIRONMENT DIVISION.
CONFIGURATION SECTION.
SOURCE-COMPUTER.  IBM-37Ø.
OBJECT-COMPUTER.  IBM-37Ø.
INPUT-OUTPUT SECTION.
FILE-CONTROL.
     SELECT INVOICE-FILE ASSIGN TO UT-S-SYSIN.
     SELECT INVOICE-SORT-FILE ASSIGN TO UT-S-SORTWKØ1,
                                        SORTWKØ2,
                                        SORTWKØ3.
DATA DIVISION.
FILE SECTION.
FD  INVOICE-FILE
        LABEL RECORDS ARE OMITTED.
Ø1  INVOICE-RECORD.
    Ø5 INVOICE-NUMBER            PIC 9(Ø5).
    Ø5 CUSTOMER-NUMBER           PIC X(1Ø).
    Ø5 DATE-OF-PURCHASE.
       1Ø MONTH-PUR             PIC 9(Ø2).
       1Ø DAY-PUR               PIC 9(Ø2).
       1Ø YEAR-PUR              PIC 9(Ø2).
    Ø5 PURCHASE-AMOUNT           PIC 9(Ø5)V99.
    Ø5 DISCOUNT-AMOUNT           PIC 9(Ø3)V99.
    Ø5 TAX-AMOUNT                PIC 9(Ø3)V99.
    Ø5 FILLER                   PIC X(42).
SD  INVOICE-SORT-FILE.
Ø1  INVOICE-RECORD-SORT.
    Ø5 INVOICE-NUMBER-SORT       PIC 9(Ø5).
    Ø5 CUSTOMER-NUMBER-SORT      PIC X(1Ø).
    Ø5 DATE-OF-PURCHASE-SORT.
       1Ø MONTH-PUR-SORT        PIC 9(Ø2).
       1Ø DAY-PUR-SORT          PIC 9(Ø2).
       1Ø YEAR-PUR-SORT         PIC 9(Ø2).
    Ø5 PURCHASE-AMOUNT-SORT      PIC 9(Ø5)V99.
    Ø5 DISCOUNT-AMOUNT-SORT      PIC 9(Ø3)V99.
    Ø5 TAX-AMOUNT-SORT           PIC 9(Ø3)V99.
```

Figure 15.2 An Illustration of a Sort File SD

The Specification of Sort Keys

Immediately following the identification of the sort-file in Figure 15.1, the SORT statement specifies the keys on which the data are to be sorted. Keys are specified as either ASCENDING (from lowest to highest value) or DESCENDING (from highest to lowest value) according to the collating sequence of the computer you are using, EBCDIC or ASCII. These collating sequences are repeated in Table 15.1. To illustrate the importance of the collating sequence, assume that you wished to sort a customer address field in ASCENDING order. If you were using an EBCDIC machine (e.g., IBM) you would expect P.O. Box addresses to appear before street addresses— street addresses begin with digits. In other words, letters have a lower value on the EBCDIC collating sequence than do digits. Conversely, if you performed the same sort on an ASCII machine (e.g., Honeywell), you would expect the street addresses to appear before P.O. Box addresses—digits are lower in value in the ASCII collating sequence than are letters.

The ordering of sort keys is also important. In Figure 15.1, notice that several identifiers (identifier-1, identifier-2, etc.) may be listed after the words ASCENDING or DESCENDING. The identifiers are listed in the order of their

TABLE 15.1 The COBOL Character Sets
(in Collating Sequence Order from Lowest Value to Highest Value)

EBCDIC		ASCII	
	space		space
.	period or decimal point	''	quote symbol
<	less than symbol	$	currency symbol
(	left parenthesis	'	apostrophe
+	plus symbol	(	left parenthesis
$	currency symbol	(	right parenthesis
*	asterisk	*	asterisk
)	right parenthesis	+	plus symbol
;	semicolon	,	comma
−	hyphen or minus symbol	−	hyphen or minus symbol
/	slash	.	period or decimal point
,	comma	/	slash
>	greater than symbol	0 – 9	numeric characters (digits)
'	apostrophe	;	semicolon
=	equal symbol	<	less than symbol
''	quote symbol	=	equal symbol
A – Z	alphabetic characters (letters)	>	greater than symbol
0 – 9	numeric characters (digits)	A – Z	alphabetic characters (letters)

importance. Identifier-1 is the *major* sort key. Only when values of identifier-1 are equal will identifier-2 have any effect on the sequence of sorted data. When more than one sort record has the same value for identifier-1, they will be ordered by identifier-2. Figure 15.3 illustrates. In part A, a single key (INVOICE-NUMBER-SORT) is specified in an ASCENDING order. Compare the order of the data before and after the sorting operation. The data has been ordered on an ascending sequence based on INVOICE-NUMBER-SORT. In part B, multiple ASCENDING keys are specified—CUSTOMER-NUMBER-SORT, YEAR-PUR-SORT, MONTH-PUR-SORT, and DAY-PUR-SORT. Again, compare the sequence of the data before and after the sorting operation. The CUSTOMER-NUMBER-SORT has been ordered in an ascending sequence, however, the last two records contain the same customer number. Thus, during the sorting process, the values of YEAR-PUR-SORT were compared (80 versus 81). If more than one record had contained the same year, then the sorting procedure would have compared the values of MONTH-PUR-SORT to determine the appropriate sequence. If more than one record contained the same customer number, year, and month, DAY-PUR-SORT would have been examined.

In part C, a DESCENDING key of PURCHASE-AMOUNT-SORT has been specified, and the purchase amount field has been ordered from *largest to smallest* value. In part D, both the ASCENDING and DESCENDING phrases are specified in the same sorting operation. Examining the results of this process indicates that the data have been ordered by year and month (ASCENDING). In the final two records of the result, the year and month values are the same. Thus, the invoice number of these two items are compared and the larger of the two values is recorded first (since the key sequence for INVOICE-NUMBER-SORT is DESCENDING).

A)...ASCENDING KEY INVOICE-NUMBER-SORT...

Data BEFORE Sorting

INVOICE NUMBER SORT	CUSTOMER NUMBER SORT	DATE OF PURCHASE SORT			PURCHASE AMOUNT SORT	DISCOUNT AMOUNT SORT	TAX AMOUNT SORT
		MONTH PUR SORT	DAY PUR SORT	YEAR PUR SORT			
44193	113R397ƀƀƀ	Ø4	15	81	ØØØ24∧65	ØØØ∧24	ØØ1∧33
31962	227A5Ø3ƀƀƀ	Ø4	22	81	ØØ221∧33	ØØ2∧21	Ø11∧Ø7
631ØØ	Ø89U846ƀƀƀ	Ø3	1Ø	81	Ø335Ø∧ØØ	Ø33∧5Ø	167∧5Ø
Ø1862	227A5Ø3ƀƀƀ	12	15	8Ø	ØØ792∧15	ØØ7∧92	Ø39∧61

Data AFTER Sorting

INVOICE NUMBER SORT	CUSTOMER NUMBER SORT	DATE OF PURCHASE SORT			PURCHASE AMOUNT SORT	DISCOUNT AMOUNT SORT	TAX AMOUNT SORT
		MONTH PUR SORT	DAY PUR SORT	YEAR PUR SORT			
Ø1862	227A5Ø3ƀƀƀ	12	15	8Ø	ØØ792∧15	ØØ7∧92	Ø39∧61
31962	227A5Ø3ƀƀƀ	Ø4	22	81	ØØ221∧33	ØØ2∧21	Ø11∧Ø7
44193	113R397ƀƀƀ	Ø4	15	81	ØØØ24∧65	ØØØ∧24	ØØ1∧33
631ØØ	Ø89U846ƀƀƀ	Ø3	1Ø	81	Ø335Ø∧ØØ	Ø33∧5Ø	167∧5Ø

B)...ASCENDING KEY CUSTOMER-NUMBER-SORT, YEAR-PUR-SORT
MONTH-PUR-SORT, DAY-PUR-SORT ...

Data BEFORE Sorting

INVOICE NUMBER SORT	CUSTOMER NUMBER SORT	DATE OF PURCHASE SORT			PURCHASE AMOUNT SORT	DISCOUNT AMOUNT SORT	TAX AMOUNT SORT
		MONTH PUR SORT	DAY PUR SORT	YEAR PUR SORT			
44193	113R397ƀƀƀ	Ø4	15	81	ØØØ24∧65	ØØØ∧24	ØØ1∧33
31962	227A5Ø3ƀƀƀ	Ø4	22	81	ØØ221∧33	ØØ2∧21	Ø11∧Ø7
631ØØ	Ø89U846ƀƀƀ	Ø3	1Ø	81	Ø335Ø∧ØØ	Ø33∧5Ø	167∧5Ø
Ø1862	227A5Ø3ƀƀƀ	12	15	8Ø	ØØ792∧15	ØØ7∧92	Ø39∧61

Data AFTER Sorting

INVOICE NUMBER SORT	CUSTOMER NUMBER SORT	DATE OF PURCHASE SORT			PURCHASE AMOUNT SORT	DISCOUNT AMOUNT SORT	TAX AMOUNT SORT
		MONTH PUR SORT	DAY PUR SORT	YEAR PUR SORT			
631ØØ	Ø89U846ƀƀƀ	Ø3	1Ø	81	Ø335Ø∧ØØ	Ø33∧5Ø	167∧5Ø
44193	113R397ƀƀƀ	Ø4	15	81	ØØØ24∧65	ØØØ∧24	ØØ1∧33
Ø1862	227A5Ø3ƀƀƀ	12	15	8Ø	ØØ792∧15	ØØ7∧92	Ø39∧61
31962	227A5Ø3ƀƀƀ	Ø4	22	81	ØØ221∧33	ØØ2∧21	Ø11∧Ø7

C)...DESCENDING KEY PURCHASE-AMOUNT-SORT...

Data BEFORE Sorting

INVOICE NUMBER SORT	CUSTOMER NUMBER SORT	DATE OF PURCHASE SORT			PURCHASE AMOUNT SORT	DISCOUNT AMOUNT SORT	TAX AMOUNT SORT
		MONTH PUR SORT	DAY PUR SORT	YEAR PUR SORT			
44193	113R397ƀƀƀ	Ø4	15	81	ØØØ24∧65	ØØØ∧24	ØØ1∧33
31962	227A5Ø3ƀƀƀ	Ø4	22	81	ØØ221∧33	ØØ2∧21	Ø11∧Ø7
631ØØ	Ø89U846ƀƀƀ	Ø3	1Ø	81	Ø335Ø∧ØØ	Ø33∧5Ø	167∧5Ø
Ø1862	227A5Ø3ƀƀƀ	12	15	8Ø	ØØ792∧15	ØØ7∧15	Ø39∧61

Figure 15.3 Illustrations of the ASCENDING/DESCENDING KEY Clause

Data AFTER Sorting

INVOICE NUMBER SORT	CUSTOMER NUMBER SORT	DATE OF PURCHASE SORT			PURCHASE AMOUNT SORT	DISCOUNT AMOUNT SORT	TAX AMOUNT SORT
		MONTH PUR SORT	DAY PUR SORT	YEAR PUR SORT			
63100	089U846ØØØ	Ø3	1Ø	81	Ø335Ø∧ØØ	Ø33∧5Ø	167∧5Ø
Ø1862	227A5Ø3ØØØ	12	15	8Ø	ØØ792∧15	ØØ7∧92	Ø39∧61
31962	227A5Ø3ØØØ	Ø4	22	81	ØØ221∧33	ØØ2∧21	Ø11∧Ø7
44193	113R397ØØØ	Ø4	15	81	ØØØ24∧65	ØØØ∧24	ØØ1∧33

D)...ASCENDING KEY YEAR-PUR-SORT, MONTH-PUR-SORT
  DESCENDING KEY INVOICE-NUMBER-SORT...

Data BEFORE Sorting

INVOICE NUMBER SORT	CUSTOMER NUMBER SORT	DATE OF PURCHASE SORT			PURCHASE AMOUNT SORT	DISCOUNT AMOUNT SORT	TAX AMOUNT SORT
		MONTH PUR SORT	DAY PUR SORT	YEAR PUR SORT			
44193	113R397ØØØ	Ø4	15	81	ØØØ24∧65	ØØØ∧24	ØØ1∧33
31962	227A5Ø3ØØØ	Ø4	22	81	ØØ221∧33	ØØ2∧21	Ø11∧Ø7
63100	089U846ØØØ	Ø3	1Ø	81	Ø335Ø∧5Ø	Ø33∧5Ø	167∧5Ø
Ø1862	227A5Ø3ØØØ	12	15	8Ø	ØØ792∧15	ØØ7∧92	Ø39∧61

Data AFTER Sorting

INVOICE NUMBER SORT	CUSTOMER NUMBER SORT	DATE OF PURCHASE SORT			PURCHASE AMOUNT SORT	DISCOUNT AMOUNT SORT	TAX AMOUNT SORT
		MONTH PUR SORT	DAY PUR SORT	YEAR PUR SORT			
Ø1862	227A5Ø3ØØØ	12	15	8Ø	ØØ792∧15	ØØ7∧92	Ø39∧61
63100	089U846ØØØ	Ø3	1Ø	81	Ø335Ø∧ØØ	Ø33∧5Ø	167∧5Ø
44193	113R397ØØØ	Ø4	15	81	ØØØ24∧65	ØØØ∧24	ØØ1∧33
31962	227A5Ø3ØØØ	Ø4	22	81	ØØ221∧33	ØØ2∧21	Ø11∧Ø7

Figure 15.3 Illustrations of the ASCENDING/DESCENDING KEY Clause *Continued*

All sort key fields *must* be recorded in the sort-record description, i.e., they must be subordinate to an SD. The number and maximum length of all keys combined may be restricted. For example, IBM compilers permit a maximum of 12 keys; the total length of which may not exceed 256 bytes. If multiple record descriptions are provided with the SD, the key must be the same displacement from the beginning of the record in all descriptions. And, the programmer is not limited with regard to the type of data definition used in conjunction with a sort key. Sort keys may be either numeric or alphanumeric. In addition, the sort key could be a group-name or an elementary-item described as numeric-edited, binary, packed decimal, alphabetic, and so forth. (Binary and packed-decimal data types are described in Chapter 20.)

The Input Process

Figure 15.1 shows that the programmer has a choice of two phrases designed to accommodate the input of data into the sorting process— USING and INPUT PROCEDURE. The programmer selects one of these two options depending on the requirements of the problems. The first option, USING file-name-1, indicates that data is to be extracted from file-name-1 and transmitted to the sorting process. That is, the SORT statement with the USING phrase causes file-name-1 to be OPENed in the INPUT mode, data from file-name-1 to be

```
ENVIRONMENT DIVISION.
CONFIGURATION SECTION.
SOURCE-COMPUTER.  IBM.
OBJECT-COMPUTER.  IBM.
INPUT-OUTPUT SECTION.
FILE-CONTROL.
     SELECT INVOICE-FILE ASSIGN TO UT-S-SYSIN.
     SELECT INVOICE-SORT-FILE ASSIGN TO UT-S-SORTWKØ1
                                  UT-S-SORTWKØ2,
                                  UT-S-SORTWKØ3.
          .
          .
          .

DATA DIVISION.
FILE SECTION.
FD  INVOICE-FILE
    LABEL RECORDS ARE OMITTED.
Ø1  INVOICE-RECORD              PIC X(8Ø).
SD  INVOICE-SORT-FILE.
Ø1  INVOICE-SORT-RECORD.
    Ø5 INVOICE-NUMBER-SORT      PIC 9(Ø5).
    Ø5 CUSTOMER-NUMBER-SORT     PIC X(1Ø).
    Ø5 DATE-OF-PURCHASE-SORT.
       1Ø   MONTH-PUR-SORT      PIC 9(Ø2).
       1Ø   DAY-PUR-SORT        PIC 9(Ø2).
       1Ø   YEAR-PUR-SORT       PIC 9(Ø2).
    Ø5 PURCHASE-AMOUNT-SORT     PIC 9(Ø5)V99.
    Ø5 DISCOUNT-AMOUNT-SORT     PIC 9(Ø3)V99.
    Ø5 TAX-AMOUNT-SORT          PIC 9(Ø3)V99.
    Ø5 FILLER                   PIC X(42).
          .
          .
          .

PROCEDURE DIVISION.
SORT-CONTROL SECTION.
     SORT INVOICE-SORT-FILE
          ASCENDING KEY PURCHASE-AMOUNT-SORT
          USING INVOICE-FILE . . .
          .
          .
          .
```

Figure 15.4 An Illustration of the USING Phrase

READ into memory, the content of the input record to be MOVEd to the sort-record description, the sort-record to be written to the sort-file and, when all records from file-name-1 have been processed, file-name-1 is CLOSEd. For the USING phrase to be employed, file-name-1 must exist, it must be standard sequential file, and the length of the input record must be the same as the sort record.

Figure 15.4 illustrates the USING phrase. Notice that the record description in Figure 15.4 is a general record description—PIC X(80). The programmer will not be using the fields of the input file in the PROCEDURE DIVISION. Rather, the field-names in the sort record will be used after the sorting has been completed. Also, notice that the record lengths of INVOICE-RECORD and INVOICE-SORT-RECORD are exactly the same. Finally, note that it is not necessary that the first field of the sort be used as the sort key.

```
RELEASE sort-record-name [FROM identifier]
```

Figure 15.5 The RELEASE Statement

The second alternative available to the programmer for input processing is the INPUT PROCEDURE. As indicated in Figure 15.1, the identification of the INPUT PROCEDURE is specified by a SECTION name (or perhaps a range of sections as is permitted with the PERFORM statements). With this option, it is the programmer's responsibility to provide all the COBOL code necessary to accept input data and send data to the sort procedure. There are a number of situations when the USING phrase cannot be used and the INPUT PROCEDURE is required. If the input file is not a sequential file, the USING phrase cannot be used. If the programmer wishes to lengthen the sort-record by adding more fields or shorten the record by eliminating fields that are not needed in the output phase, the INPUT PROCEDURE must be used. The same is true if the programmer wishes to eliminate some records from being sorted or if data must be joined from two or more files in the sort-file. Likewise, if the programmer wished to select particular records or edit the records before sorting, an INPUT PROCEDURE must be used. Of course there are other reasons for using INPUT PROCEDURE, but those identified above provide sufficient cause for *not* employing the USING phrase.

Since the programmer is responsible for providing code to satisfy the input phase of the sort when the INPUT PROCEDURE is used, the programmer must OPEN the input file, READ the records from the file, MOVE the data to the sort-record description, write the sort-record to the sort-file, and CLOSE the input file. However, since the sort-file is a special file (notice that opening and closing the sort-file has *not* been mentioned), the programmer is not permitted to use a WRITE statement to transmit data to the sort-file. Instead, the programmer uses a RELEASE statement, as illustrated in Figure 15.5. The function (and appearance) of the RELEASE statement is highly similar to the WRITE statement. In fact, if the ADVANCING clause were to be dropped from the WRITE statement and the word *WRITE* were replaced with the word *RELEASE*, the two would be identical. Thus, the statement causes data in the sort-file (under the sort-record description) to be transmitted to the sorting process. If an INPUT PROCEDURE is used, the SECTION(s) identifying the COBOL code *must* contain a RELEASE statement—otherwise no data is transmitted to the sorting process.

Figure 15.6 illustrates one possible use of the INPUT PROCEDURE. Note the change in PICTURE descriptions of INVOICE-NUMBER and PURCHASE-AMOUNT of INVOICE-RECORD from that in previous illustrations. The procedure is to check the invoice number to insure it is numeric and to verify that the purchase amount is positive. In addition, notice that the record lengths of INVOICE-RECORD and INVOICE-SORT-RECORD are not the same. Only those fields necessary for the output process have been included in the sort-record description. In the PROCEDURE DIVISION, the SORT statement identifies the INPUT PROCEDURE as 300-CHECK-INVOICES—a SECTION. Upon entering 300-CHECK-INVOICES, a series of procedures are per-

```
ENVIRONMENT DIVISION.
CONFIGURATION SECTION.
SOURCE-COMPUTER.  IBM.
OBJECT-COMPUTER.  IBM.
INPUT-OUTPUT SECTION.
FILE-CONTROL.
    SELECT INVOICE-FILE ASSIGN TO UT-S-SYSIN.
    SELECT INVOICE-SORT-FILE ASSIGN TO UT-S-SORTWKØ1,
                                       UT-S-SORTWKØ2,
                                       UT-S-SORTWKØ3.

        .
        .
        .

DATA DIVISION.
FILE SECTION.
FD  INVOICE-FILE
    LABEL RECORDS ARE OMITTED.
Ø1  INVOICE-RECORD.
    Ø5 INVOICE-NUMBER           PIC X(Ø5).
    Ø5 CUSTOMER-NUMBER          PIC X(1Ø).
    Ø5 DATE-OF-PURCHASE         PIC 9(Ø6).
    Ø5 PURCHASE-AMOUNT          PIC S9(Ø5)V99.
    Ø5 DISCOUNT-AMOUNT          PIC 9(Ø3)V99.
    Ø5 TAX-AMOUNT               PIC 9(Ø3)V99.
    Ø5 FILLER                   PIC X(43).
SD  INVOICE-SORT-FILE.
Ø1  INVOICE-SORT-RECORD.
    Ø5 INVOICE-NUMBER-SORT      PIC 9(Ø5).
    Ø5 DATE-OF-PURCHASE-SORT    PIC 9(Ø6).
    Ø5 PURCHASE-AMOUNT-SORT     PIC 9(Ø5)V99.

        .
        .
        .

WORKING-STORAGE SECTION.
Ø1  WORKING-VARIABLES.
    Ø5 SORT-STATUS              PIC X(1Ø).

        .
        .
        .

PROCEDURE DIVISION.
SORT-CONTROL SECTION.
    SORT INVOICE-SORT-FILE
        ASCENDING KEY INVOICE-NUMBER-SORT.
        INPUT PROCEDURE 300-CHECK-INVOICES . . .

        .
        .
        .

300-CHECK-INVOICES SECTION.
    PERFORM 320-INITIALIZE-INPUT.
    PERFORM 340-EDIT-INVOICES.
    PERFORM 360-TERMINATE-INPUT.
320-INITIALIZE-INPUT SECTION.
    OPEN INPUT INVOICE-FILE.
340-EDIT-INVOICES SECTION.
    READ INVOICE-FILE
        AT END GO TO 349-EXIT.
    MOVE 'RELEASE' TO SORT-STATUS.
```

Figure 15.6 An Illustration of the INPUT PROCEDURE

```
        IF INVOICE-NUMBER NOT NUMERIC
            MOVE 'NO RELEASE' TO SORT-STATUS.
        IF PURCHASE-AMOUNT NOT POSITIVE
            MOVE 'NO RELEASE' TO SORT-STATUS.
        IF SORT-STATUS = 'RELEASE'
            MOVE INVOICE-NUMBER TO INVOICE-NUMBER-SORT
            MOVE DATE-OF-PURCHASE TO DATE-OF-PURCHASE-SORT
            MOVE PURCHASE-AMOUNT TO PURCHASE-AMOUNT-SORT
            RELEASE INVOICE-SORT-RECORD.
        GO TO 340-EDIT-INVOICES.
    349-EXIT.
        EXIT.
    360-TERMINATE-INPUT SECTION.
        CLOSE INVOICE-FILE.

                    .
                    .
                    .
```

Figure 15.6 An Illustration of the INPUT PROCEDURE *Continued*

formed; however, notice that each of the procedures PERFORMed are also SECTIONs. Thus, when 300-CHECK-INVOICES is finished, another SECTION is encountered—causing a return to the output phase of the SORT statement. As the procedure continues, the input file is opened (320-INITIALIZE-INPUT SECTION) and an iterative process begins (340-EDIT-INVOICES SECTION), which verifies the accuracy of the input data. If the input data is correct, within the guidelines previously established, the desired data are moved to the sort-record, and the sort-record is RELEASEd to the sort process. This procedure continues until an end-of-file is encountered on the INVOICE-FILE—which causes an unconditional branch to 349-EXIT—terminating the 340-EDIT-INVOICES SECTION. Finally, 360-TERMINATE-INPUT is executed. After the termination sequence has been completed, the INPUT PROCEDURE is finished, causing a return to the SORT statement.

The Output Process

Like the input phase, the output phase of the SORT statement provides two options—GIVING and OUTPUT PROCEDURE. These options mirror the options provided in the input phase. The GIVING phrase allows the programmer to create an output file from the sorted data. Like the USING phrase, with the GIVING phrase, the output file must be a standard sequential file, and the record lengths of the sort-file and the output file must be the same. The GIVING phrase creates file-name-2.

The OUTPUT PROCEDURE allows the programmer to access individual records as they are returned from the sort-file. Again, since the programmer is to provide the code to accomplish the output task, the procedure must OPEN the output file, read records from the sort-file, MOVE data from the sort record to the output record, WRITE the output record and, after all data has been read from the sort-file, CLOSE the output file. However, since the sort-file is a specialized file, the programmer is not permitted to READ the sort-file. Figure 15.7 illustrates the RETURN statement, which provides the programmer with the tool by which records may be retrieved from the sort-file. The only difference between the READ statement for a sequential file and the RETURN statement is that the word *READ* has been replaced with the word *RETURN*.

```
RETURN sort-file-name [INTO identifier]
    AT END imperative-statement
```

Figure 15.7 The RETURN Statement

The Inventory Sort Problem

Figure 15.8 illustrates the use of a SORT statement in the context of a complete program. This procedure utilizes a SORT statement with INPUT PROCEDURE and OUTPUT PROCEDURE options (see lines 890–920). The record descriptions in the FILE SECTION are all of different lengths. In the PROCEDURE DIVISION, the INPUT PROCEDURE is a section; the remaining parts of the INPUT PROCEDURE are coded at the paragraph level. To terminate the INPUT PROCEDURE, it is necessary to execute an unconditional branch to the end of the SECTION (190-INPUT-TERMINATION). The processing sequence involves an examination of each input record to determine whether or not the quantity ON-HAND is below the MIN-STOCK-LEVEL. If insufficient stock is ON-HAND, the record is transmitted to the sort process via 165-MOVE-AND-RELEASE.

After the INPUT PROCEDURE has been completed, the OUTPUT PROCEDURE proceeds to print a report based on the sorted data. Thus, records are RETURNed from the sort-file at lines 1290 and 1440. Note the similarity between the OUTPUT PROCEDURE of this problem and that in problems which did not use the SORT statement. If the RETURN statements were replaced by READ statements, the OUTPUT PROCEDURE could be a standalone program. After the OUTPUT PROCEDURE is terminated (by the unconditional branch to 290-OUTPUT-TERMINATION), control passes back to the sort statement, the sorting process is completed, and the STOP RUN statement is encountered.

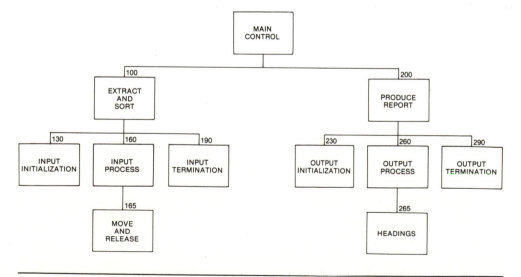

Figure 15.8 Inventory Sort (Hierarchy Chart)

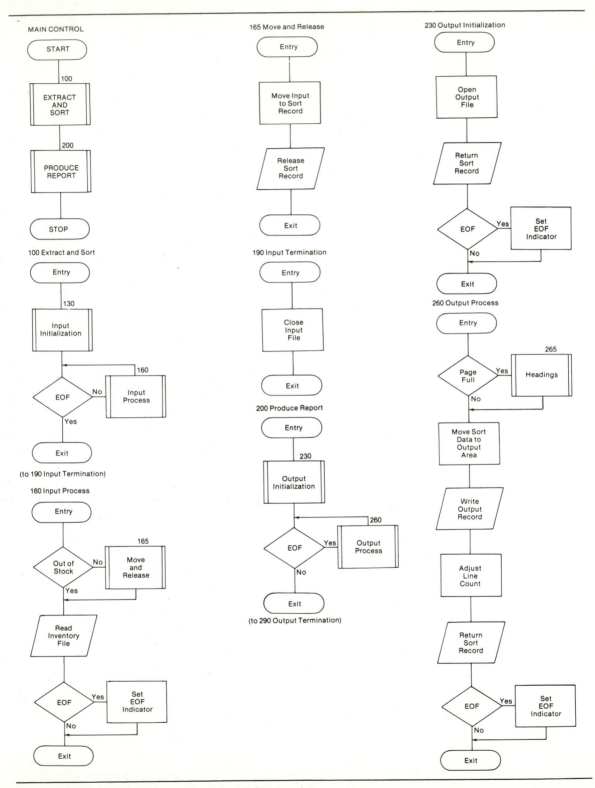

Figure 15.8 Inventory Sort (Module Flowcharts) *Continued*

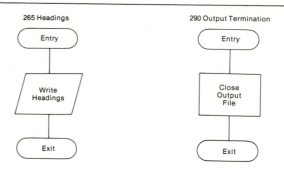

265 Headings

290 Output Termination

Figure 15.8 Inventory Sort (Module Flowcharts) *Continued*

```
|           1   1   2   2   2   3   3   4   4   4   5   5   6   6   6   7   7   8|
|   4   8   2   6   0   4   8   2   6   0   4   8   2   6   0   4   8   2   6   0|
|000010 IDENTIFICATION DIVISION.                                    FIG 15.8|
|000020 PROGRAM-ID.  INVENTORY-SORT.                                FIG 15.8|
|000030 AUTHOR.  DAWN LLOYD.                                        FIG 15.8|
|000040 DATE-WRITTEN.  JAN. 1, 1981.                                FIG 15.8|
|000050 DATE-COMPILED. JAN. 1, 1981.                                FIG 15.8|
|000060 ENVIRONMENT DIVISION.                                       FIG 15.8|
|000070 CONFIGURATION SECTION.                                      FIG 15.8|
|000080 SOURCE-COMPUTER.  IBM-370.                                  FIG 15.8|
|000090 OBJECT-COMPUTER.  IBM-370.                                  FIG 15.8|
|000100 SPECIAL-NAMES.                                              FIG 15.8|
|000110     C01 IS PAGE-TOP.                                        FIG 15.8|
|000120 INPUT-OUTPUT SECTION.                                       FIG 15.8|
|000130 FILE-CONTROL.                                               FIG 15.8|
|000140     SELECT INVENTORY-FILE ASSIGN TO UT-S-SYSIN.             FIG 15.8|
|000150     SELECT OUTPUT-FILE ASSIGN TO UT-S-SYSPRINT.             FIG 15.8|
|000160     SELECT SORT-FILE ASSIGN TO UT-S-SORTWK01.               FIG 15.8|
|000170 DATA DIVISION.                                              FIG 15.8|
|000180 FILE SECTION.                                               FIG 15.8|
|000190 FD  INVENTORY-FILE                                          FIG 15.8|
|000200     LABEL RECORDS ARE OMITTED.                              FIG 15.8|
|000210 01  INVENTORY-REC.                                          FIG 15.8|
|000220     05  ITEM               PIC X(06).                       FIG 15.8|
|000230     05  DESCRIPTION        PIC X(30).                       FIG 15.8|
|000240     05  VENDOR             PIC X(03).                       FIG 15.8|
|000250     05  ON-HAND            PIC X(05).                       FIG 15.8|
|000260     05  MIN-STOCK-LEVEL    PIC X(05).                       FIG 15.8|
|000270     05  UNIT-COST          PIC 9(05)V99.                    FIG 15.8|
|000280     05  UNIT-PRICE         PIC 9(05)V99.                    FIG 15.8|
|000290     05  YTD-SALES          PIC X(12).                       FIG 15.8|
|000300     05  FILLER             PIC X(05).                       FIG 15.8|
|000310 SD  SORT-FILE                                               FIG 15.8|
|000320     LABEL RECORDS ARE STANDARD.                             FIG 15.8|
|000330 01  SORT-REC.                                               FIG 15.8|
|000340     05  ITEM-SORT          PIC X(06).                       FIG 15.8|
|000350     05  DESCRIPTION-SORT   PIC X(30).                       FIG 15.8|
|000360     05  VENDOR-SORT        PIC X(03).                       FIG 15.8|
|000370     05  ON-HAND-SORT       PIC X(05).                       FIG 15.8|
|000380     05  MIN-STOCK-SORT     PIC X(05).                       FIG 15.8|
|000390     05  UNIT-COST-SORT     PIC 9(05)V99.                    FIG 15.8|
|000400     05  YTD-SALES-SORT     PIC 9(12).                       FIG 15.8|
|000410 FD  OUTPUT-FILE                                             FIG 15.8|
|000420     LABEL RECORDS ARE OMITTED                               FIG 15.8|
|000430     RECORD CONTAINS 133 CHARACTERS.                         FIG 15.8|
|000440 01  OUTPUT-REC         PIC X(133).                          FIG 15.8|
|000450 WORKING-STORAGE SECTION.                                    FIG 15.8|
|000460 01  WORKING-VARIABLES.                                      FIG 15.8|
|000470     05  END-OF-FILE        PIC X(03)  VALUE 'NO '.          FIG 15.8|
|000480     05  LINE-CNTR          PIC 9(02)  VALUE ZERO.           FIG 15.8|
|000490 01  HEADING1.                                               FIG 15.8|
|000500     05  FILLER             PIC X(55)  VALUE SPACES.         FIG 15.8|
|000510     05  FILLER             PIC X(20)  VALUE                 FIG 15.8|
|000520     'LEARNING COBOL, INC.'.                                 FIG 15.8|
|000530     05  FILLER             PIC X(58)  VALUE SPACES.         FIG 15.8|
|000540 01  HEADING2.                                               FIG 15.8|
|000550     05  FILLER             PIC X(08)  VALUE SPACES.         FIG 15.8|
|000560     05  FILLER             PIC X(04)  VALUE 'ITEM'.         FIG 15.8|
```

Figure 15.8 Inventory Sort *Continued*

```
------------------------------------------------------------------------------
|         1   1   2   2   2   3   3   4   4   4   5   5   6   6   6   7   7   8|
|   4   8 2   6   0   4   8   2   6   0   4   8   2   6   0   4   8   2   6   0|
------------------------------------------------------------------------------
|000570        05  FILLER                   PIC X(16)   VALUE SPACES.        FIG 15.8|
|000580        05  FILLER                   PIC X(11)   VALUE 'DESCRIPTION'. FIG 15.8|
|000590        05  FILLER                   PIC X(19)   VALUE SPACES.        FIG 15.8|
|000600        05  FILLER                   PIC X(06)   VALUE 'VENDOR'.      FIG 15.8|
|000610        05  FILLER                   PIC X(05)   VALUE SPACES.        FIG 15.8|
|000620        05  FILLER                   PIC X(07)   VALUE 'ON HAND'.     FIG 15.8|
|000630        05  FILLER                   PIC X(06)   VALUE SPACES.        FIG 15.8|
|000640        05  FILLER                   PIC X(07)   VALUE 'MINIMUM'.     FIG 15.8|
|000650        05  FILLER                   PIC X(08)   VALUE SPACES.        FIG 15.8|
|000660        05  FILLER                   PIC X(04)   VALUE 'COST'.        FIG 15.8|
|000670        05  FILLER                   PIC X(11)   VALUE SPACES.        FIG 15.8|
|000680        05  FILLER                   PIC X(09)   VALUE 'YTD SALES'.   FIG 15.8|
|000690        05  FILLER                   FIC X(12)   VALUE SPACES.        FIG 15.8|
|000700 01  REPORT-LINE.                                                     FIG 15.8|
|000710        05  FILLER                   PIC X(08)   VALUE SPACES.        FIG 15.8|
|000720        05  ITEM-OUT                 PIC X(06)   VALUE SPACES.        FIG 15.8|
|000730        05  FILLER                   PIC X(08)   VALUE SPACES.        FIG 15.8|
|000740        05  DESCRIPTION-OUT          PIC X(30)   VALUE SPACES.        FIG 15.8|
|000750        05  FILLER                   PIC X(08)   VALUE SPACES.        FIG 15.8|
|000760        05  VENDOR-OUT               PIC X(03)   VALUE SPACES.        FIG 15.8|
|000770        05  FILLER                   PIC X(05)   VALUE SPACES.        FIG 15.8|
|000780        05  ON-HAND-OUT              PIC Z(04)9  VALUE ZERO.          FIG 15.8|
|000790        05  FILLER                   PIC X(08)   VALUE SPACES.        FIG 15.8|
|000800        05  MINIMUM-OUT              PIC Z(04)9  VALUE ZERO.          FIG 15.8|
|000810        05  FILLER                   PIC X(07)   VALUE SPACES.        FIG 15.8|
|000820        05  UNIT-COST-OUT            PIC $$,$$$.99  VALUE ZERO.       FIG 15.8|
|000830        05  FILLER                   FIC X(04)   VALUE SPACES.        FIG 15.8|
|000840        05  YTD-SALES-OUT            PIC Z(11)9  VALUE ZERO.          FIG 15.8|
|000850        05  FILLER                   PIC X(15)   VALUE SPACES.        FIG 15.8|
|000860 PROCEDURE DIVISION.                                                  FIG 15.8|
|000870 MAIN-CONTROL.                                                        FIG 15.8|
|000880        MOVE 50000 TO SORT-CORE-SIZE.                                 FIG 15.8|
|000890        SORT SORT-FILE                                                FIG 15.8|
|000900            ASCENDING KEY VENDOR-SORT, ITEM-SORT                      FIG 15.8|
|000910            INPUT PROCEDURE 100-EXTRACT-AND-SORT                      FIG 15.8|
|000920            OUTPUT PROCEDURE 200-PRODUCE-REPORT.                      FIG 15.8|
|000930        STOP RUN.                                                     FIG 15.8|
|000940 100-EXTRACT-AND-SORT SECTION.                                        FIG 15.8|
|000950        PERFORM 130-INPUT-INITIALIZATION.                            FIG 15.8|
|000960        PERFORM 160-INPUT-PROCESS                                     FIG 15.8|
|000970            UNTIL END-OF-FILE = 'YES'.                                FIG 15.8|
|000980        GO TO 190-INPUT-TERMINATION.                                  FIG 15.8|
|000990 130-INPUT-INITIALIZATION.                                            FIG 15.8|
|001000        OPEN INPUT INVENTORY-FILE.                                    FIG 15.8|
|001010        READ INVENTORY-FILE                                           FIG 15.8|
|001020            AT END MOVE 'YES' TO END-OF-FILE.                         FIG 15.8|
|001030 160-INPUT-PROCESS.                                                   FIG 15.8|
|001040        IF ON-HAND < MIN-STOCK-LEVEL                                  FIG 15.8|
|001050            PERFORM 165-MOVE-AND-RELEASE.                             FIG 15.8|
|001060        READ INVENTORY-FILE                                           FIG 15.8|
|001070            AT END MOVE 'YES' TO END-OF-FILE.                         FIG 15.8|
|001080 165-MOVE-AND-RELEASE.                                                FIG 15.8|
|001090        MOVE ITEM TO ITEM-SORT.                                       FIG 15.8|
|001100        MOVE DESCRIPTION TO DESCRIPTION-SORT.                         FIG 15.8|
|001110        MOVE VENDOR TO VENDOR-SORT.                                   FIG 15.8|
|001120        MOVE ON-HAND TO ON-HAND-SORT.                                 FIG 15.8|
|001130        MOVE MIN-STOCK-LEVEL TO MIN-STOCK-SORT.                       FIG 15.8|
|001140        MOVE UNIT-COST TO UNIT-COST-SORT.                             FIG 15.8|
|001150        MOVE YTD-SALES TO YTD-SALES-SORT.                             FIG 15.8|
|001160        RELEASE SORT-REC.                                             FIG 15.8|
|001170 190-INPUT-TERMINATION.                                               FIG 15.8|
|001180        CLOSE INVENTORY-FILE.                                         FIG 15.8|
|001190 200-PRODUCE-REPORT SECTION.                                          FIG 15.8|
|001200        PERFORM 230-OUTPUT-INITIALIZATION.                           FIG 15.8|
|001210        PERFORM 260-OUTPUT-PROCESS                                    FIG 15.8|
|001220            UNTIL END-OF-FILE = 'YES'.                                FIG 15.8|
|001230        GO TO 290-OUTPUT-TERMINATION.                                 FIG 15.8|
|001240 230-OUTPUT-INITIALIZATION.                                           FIG 15.8|
|001250        OPEN OUTPUT OUTPUT-FILE.                                      FIG 15.8|
|001260        MOVE 'NO ' TO END-OF-FILE.                                    FIG 15.8|
|001270        MOVE 45 TO LINE-CNTR.                                         FIG 15.8|
|001280        RETURN SORT-FILE                                              FIG 15.8|
|001290            AT END MOVE 'YES' TO END-OF-FILE.                         FIG 15.8|
|001300 260-OUTPUT-PROCESS.                                                  FIG 15.8|
|001310        IF LINE-CNTR > 40                                             FIG 15.8|
|001320            PERFORM 265-HEADINGS.                                     FIG 15.8|
|001330        MOVE ITEM-SORT TO ITEM-OUT.                                   FIG 15.8|
|001340        MOVE DESCRIPTION-SORT TO DESCRIPTION-OUT.                     FIG 15.8|
|001350        MOVE VENDOR-SORT TO VENDOR-OUT.                               FIG 15.8|
```

Figure 15.8 Inventory Sort *Continued*

```
|                 1   1   2   2   2   3   3   4   4   4   5   5   6   6   6   7   7   8|
|    4       8    2   6   0   4   8   2   6   0   4   8   2   6   0   4   8   2   6   0|
-------------------------------------------------------------------------------------
|001360        MOVE ON-HAND-SORT TO ON-HAND-OUT.                                FIG 15.8|
|001370        MOVE MIN-STOCK-SORT TO MINIMUM-OUT.                              FIG 15.8|
|001380        MOVE UNIT-COST-SORT TO UNIT-COST-OUT.                            FIG 15.8|
|001390        MOVE YTD-SALES-SORT TO YTD-SALES-OUT.                            FIG 15.8|
|001400        WRITE OUTPUT-REC FROM REPORT-LINE                                FIG 15.8|
|001410            AFTER ADVANCING 2 LINES.                                     FIG 15.8|
|001420        ADD 2 TO LINE-CNTR.                                              FIG 15.8|
|001430        RETURN SORT-FILE                                                 FIG 15.8|
|001440            AT END MOVE 'YES' TO END-OF-FILE.                            FIG 15.8|
|001450    265-HEADINGS.                                                        FIG 15.8|
|001460        MOVE 0 TO LINE-CNTR.                                             FIG 15.8|
|001470        WRITE OUTPUT-REC FROM HEADING1                                   FIG 15.8|
|001480            AFTER ADVANCING PAGE-TOP.                                    FIG 15.8|
|001490        WRITE OUTPUT-REC FROM HEADING2                                   FIG 15.8|
|001500            AFTER ADVANCING 3 LINES.                                     FIG 15.8|
|001510    290-OUTPUT-TERMINATION.                                              FIG 15.8|
|001520        CLOSE OUTPUT-FILE.                                               FIG 15.8|
```

Figure 15.8 Inventory Sort *Continued*

```
|       |        1         2         3         4         5         6         7        8| FIGURE  |
|RECORD |1234567890123456789012345678901234567890123456789012345678901234567890| NUMBER  |
|     1 |ALBUM JESUS CHRIST SUPERSTAR       555000510005000009900002500000000000250 |FIG 15.8|
|     2 |8TRACKTHE PRETENDER - JACKSON BROWNE111000910008000004990000250000000000400 |FIG 15.8|
|     3 |8TRACKNIGHTWATCH - KENNY LOGGINS   111000418110000054900008990000000000545 |FIG 15.8|
|     4 |ALBUM RUNNING ON EMPTYJACKSON BROWNE222000810010000004990000899000000000490 |FIG 15.8|
|     5 |8TRACKHOME TO MYSELF - MANCHESTER  555000720007500004290000899000000000375 |FIG 15.8|
|     6 |CASSETTHE DREAM WEAVER - GARY WRIGHT222000820007500003990000699000000000370 |FIG 15.8|
|     7 |CASSETLONDON TOWN - WINGS          222000690005000003490000659000000000240 |FIG 15.8|
|     8 |8TRACKVENUS AND MARS - WINGS       777000290002500003990000799000000000120 |FIG 15.8|
|     9 |ALBUM ICE WATER - LEO KOTTKE       444000880009000004490000799000000000440 |FIG 15.8|
|    10 |ALBUM CAT STEVENS GREATEST HITS    333000620005000004250000789000000000240 |FIG 15.8|
|    11 |ALBUM FINALE-LOGGINS AND MESSINA   333000710008500004990000899000000000420 |FIG 15.8|
|    12 |CASSETRUMOURS - FLEETWOOD MAC      333000420006000004290000729000000000285 |FIG 15.8|
|    13 |CASSETLACE AND WHISKEY -ALICE COOPER333000770008000003990000699000000000390 |FIG 15.8|
|    14 |8TRACKEAGLES THEIR GREATEST HITS   111009200100000052900009790000000000495 |FIG 15.8|
|    15 |8TRACKBARRY MANILOW LIVE           444000410003500005990001129000000000175 |FIG 15.8|
|    16 |ALBUM THE BEACH BOYS ENDLESS SUMMER444000520005500006590000997000000000260 |FIG 15.8|
|    17 |8TRACKI'M IN YOU - PETER FRAMPTON  111000940009500004290000979000000000455 |FIG 15.8|
|    18 |CASSETGREENHOUSE - LEO KOTTKE      222000400005500004290000799000000000265 |FIG 15.8|
|    19 |8TRACKTUPELO HONEY - VAN MORRISON  222000750007000005290000999000000000340 |FIG 15.8|
|    20 |ALBUM LINDA RONSTADT GREATEST HITS 222000600006500005290000699000000000320 |FIG 15.8|
|    21 |ALBUM WINGS OVER AMERICA-MCCARTNEY 111000220002500004950000699000000000103 |FIG 15.8|
|    22 |8TRACKTHICK AS A BRICK - TULL      111002750020000005900000899000000000550 |FIG 15.8|
|    23 |8TRACKTHE BEST OF JETHRO TULL - TULL222001490015000004990000829000000000428 |FIG 15.8|
|    24 |8TRACKSWEET BABY JAMES-JAMES TAYLOR555001200010000005290000899000000000520 |FIG 15.8|
|    25 |CASSETMUD SLIDE SLIM - JAMES TAYLOR444000950010000004990000729000000000515 |FIG 15.8|
|    26 |8TRACKJT - JAMES TAYLOR            777000750015000005990000999000000000685 |FIG 15.8|
|    27 |ALBUM GORILLA - JAMES TAYLOR       333009200100000059900008990000000000497 |FIG 15.8|
|    28 |ALBUM TEASER AND THE FIRECAT-STEVENS222002900050000003990000899000000000235 |FIG 15.8|
|    29 |CASSETNIGHT MOVES - BOB SEGER      111001500012500003990000699000000000520 |FIG 15.8|
|    30 |CASSETI'LL PLAY FOR YOU-SEALS&CROFTS222000870008000004190000688000000000325 |FIG 15.8|
|    31 |CASSETSEALS AND CROFTS GREATEST HITS333000590007500003990000699000000000310 |FIG 15.8|
|    32 |8TRACKSILK DEGREES - BOZ SCAGGS    555001020014500005490000999000000000650 |FIG 15.8|
|    33 |8TRACKWILL O' THE WISP-LEON RUSSELL777000790007500004990000949000000000300 |FIG 15.8|
|    34 |ALBUM A NIGHT AT THE OPERA - QUEEN 444000910010000004880000695000000000515 |FIG 15.8|
|    35 |ALBUM DANCE - PURE PRAIRIE LEAGUE  111001270015000005500000850000000000690 |FIG 15.8|
|    36 |ALBUM BLUE SKY NIGHT THUNDER-MURPHEY111000890011000005990000899000000000550 |FIG 15.8|
|    37 |8TRACKCOURT AND SPARK -JONI MITCHELL222001050015500005490000997000000000580 |FIG 15.8|
|    38 |8TRACKON STAGE - LOGGINS & MESSINA 222000720007077776990001249000000000330 |FIG 15.8|
|    39 |CASSETNATIVE SONS-LOGGINS & MESSINA444001200012500004290000729000000000400 |FIG 15.8|
|    40 |CASSETCELEBRATE ME HOME - LOGGINS  777000920010000004520000749000000000500 |FIG 15.8|
|    41 |ALBUM MUSIC - CAROLE KING          555000620007500005490000895000000000325 |FIG 15.8|
|    42 |ALBUM ALL THINGS MUST PASS -HARRISON222000590005000005500000899000000000260 |FIG 15.8|
|    43 |8TRACKTHE BEST OF THE GUESS WHO    111000720007000004490000999000000000320 |FIG 15.8|
|    44 |8TRACKCAPTURED ANGEL-DAN FOGELBERG 222000640007500005290000998000000000375 |FIG 15.8|
|    45 |ALBUM HARD RAIN - BOB DYLAN        444000610006000005990000899000000000305 |FIG 15.8|
|    46 |ALBUM SLOWHAND - ERIC CLAPTON      555001030010000004750000799000000000515 |FIG 15.8|
|    47 |ALBUM AMERICA'S GREATEST HITS      555000980010000004890000799000000000520 |FIG 15.8|
|    48 |8TRACK52ND STREET - BILLY JOEL     444001440015000005420000998000000000750 |FIG 15.8|
|    49 |CASSETMOTHER LODE-LOGGINS & MESSINA222001200012500005190000699000000000700 |FIG 15.8|
|    50 |CASSETBACK HOME AGAIN - JOHN DENVER777001150010000004990000698000000000520 |FIG 15.8|
|    51 |8TRACKTHE STRANGER - BILLY JOEL    777001010012500005290000998000000000535 |FIG 15.8|
|    52 |ALBUM CITY TO CITY-JERRY RAFFERTY  444000900007500004500000899000000000400 |FIG 15.8|
```

Figure 15.8 Inventory Sort (Data) *Continued*

LEARNING COBOL, INC.

ITEM	DESCRIPTION	VENDOR	ON HAND	MINIMUM	COST	YTD SALES
ALBUM	BLUE SKY NIGHT THUNDER-MURPHEY	111	89	110	$5.99	550
ALBUM	DANCE - PURE PRAIRIE LEAGUE	111	127	150	$5.50	690
ALBUM	WINGS OVER AMERICA-MCCARTNEY	111	22	25	$4.95	103
8TRACK	I'M IN YOU - PETER FRAMPTON	111	94	95	$4.29	455
8TRACK	EAGLES THEIR GREATEST HITS	111	92	100	$5.29	495
8TRACK	NIGHTWATCH - KENNY LOGGINS	111	4	18110	$5.49	545
ALBUM	RUNNING ON EMPTYJACKSON BROWNE	222	81	100	$4.99	490
ALBUM	LINDA RONSTADT GREATEST HITS	222	60	65	$5.29	320
ALBUM	TEASER AND THE FIRECAT-STEVENS	222	29	50	$5.99	235
CASSET	MOTHER LODE-LOGGINS & MESSINA	222	112	125	$5.19	700
CASSET	GREENHOUSE - LEO KOTTKE	222	40	55	$4.29	265
8TRACK	THE BEST OF JETHRO TULL - TULL	222	149	150	$4.99	428
8TRACK	COURT AND SPARK -JONI MITCHELL	222	105	155	$5.49	580
8TRACK	CAPTURED ANGEL-DAN FOGELBERG	222	64	75	$5.29	375
ALBUM	GORILLA - JAMES TAYLOR	333	92	100	$5.99	497
ALBUM	FINALE-LOGGINS AND MESSINA	333	71	85	$4.99	420
CASSET	LACE AND WHISKEY -ALICE COOPER	333	77	80	$3.99	390
CASSET	RUMOURS - FLEETWOOD MAC	333	42	60	$4.29	285
CASSET	SEALS AND CROFTS GREATEST HITS	333	59	75	$3.99	310
ALBUM	A NIGHT AT THE OPERA - QUEEN	444	91	100	$4.88	515
ALBUM	THE BEACH BOYS ENDLESS SUMMER	444	52	55	$6.59	260

LEARNING COBOL, INC.

ITEM	DESCRIPTION	VENDOR	ON HAND	MINIMUM	COST	YTD SALES
ALBUM	ICE WATER - LEO KOTTKE	444	88	90	$4.49	440
CASSET	MUD SLIDE SLIM - JAMES TAYLOR	444	95	100	$4.99	515
CASSET	NATIVE SONS-LOGGINS & MESSINA	444	120	125	$4.29	400
8TRACK	52ND STREET - BILLY JOEL	444	144	150	$5.42	750
ALBUM	AMERICA'S GREATEST HITS	555	98	100	$4.89	520
ALBUM	MUSIC - CAROLE KING	555	62	75	$5.49	325
8TRACK	SILK DEGREES - BOZ SCAGGS	555	102	145	$5.49	650
8TRACK	HOME TO MYSELF - MANCHESTER	555	72	75	$4.29	375
CASSET	CELEBRATE ME HOME - LOGGINS	777	92	100	$4.52	500
8TRACK	THE STRANGER - BILLY JOEL	777	101	125	$5.29	535
8TRACK	JT - JAMES TAYLOR	777	75	150	$5.99	685

Figure 15.8 Inventory Sort (Output) *Continued*

General Limitations

Although not previously noted, there are a few general limitations on using the SORT statement. First, COBOL does not permit two SORT statements to be active *at the same time*; however, multiple SORT statements can still appear in the same program. Second, although COBOL will permit procedures in an OUTPUT PROCEDURE to be accessed (possibly by a PERFORM statement) from the INPUT PROCEDURE, a RETURN statement must not be encountered while in the OUTPUT PROCEDURE. If in the OUTPUT PROCEDURE, procedure-names in the INPUT PROCEDURE are invoked, a RELEASE statement must not be encountered. Third, magnetic media, i.e., magnetic tape or disk, must be available on the system to permit the use of the SORT statement. Recall that sort-work files are necessary. Finally, the SORT statement requires at least some limited amount of internal memory in which to order sets of records. Some COBOL compilers (e.g., IBM) provide a special register called SORT-CORE-SIZE to provide the programmer with the option of indicating the amount of memory to be allocated to the internal sorting process. Figure 15.8 illustrates the use of this special register in line 880. The MOVE statement causes 50,000 bytes of internal memory to be set aside for the internal sorting process. Thus, a rather significant number of records could be ordered in memory before being transmitted to a tape or disk work file.

Summary

In this chapter, the SORT statement has been described. The sorting process performed by the SORT statement may be viewed as being a "sort-merge" process with four distinct phases:

1. identification of the sort-file,
2. specification of sort keys and sequence for sorting,
3. a reference to the input phase, and
4. a reference to the output phase.

The statement permits multiple sort keys, which may be specified in ASCENDING or DESCENDING sequences. The programmer has a choice of a USING or an INPUT PROCEDURE phrase for the input phase and a GIVING or an OUTPUT PROCEDURE phrase for the output phase.

Notes on Programming Style

The SORT statement is a powerful statement that can manipulate large data files into a desired sequence. Although the programmer may have any combination of phrases in the input and output phases of the process, one would not typically choose a USING/GIVING set. Although COBOL places no restrictions on the combination of these phrases, the USING/GIVING combination is typically not an effective use of either machine or programmer time. A USING/GIVING set causes a sequential file to be read and sorted and the results written to an output sequential file. Fortunately, sort *utilities* are typically available at most installations. These utilities perform exactly the same process and typically require very little code. For example, a complete COBOL program could be replaced by four or five records.

Questions

Below fill in the blank(s) with the appropriate word, words or phrases.

1. The overall function of the SORT statement is to _____ .

2. When the programmer supplies the code to order data within a program (e.g., a bubble sort), the procedure is known as a(n) _____ sort, while the SORT statement is generally known as a(n) _____ sort.

3. The SORT statement is capable of ordering large data sets because only groups of data are sequenced internally in what is referred to as the _____ phase, then those groups are joined during a process known as the _____ phase.

4. The reserved words in a SORT statement that indicate the direction of ordering data are _____ and _____ .

5. The record length of the sort-record and the input record must be the same when _____ is used for the input phase.

6. If the INPUT PROCEDURE is specified, a(n) _____ statement must appear in the procedure.

7. If an INPUT PROCEDURE is specified, code in the PROCEDURE DIVISION that identifies the input process must be coded at the _____ level.

8. When a GIVING phrase is specified, the input file must be organized as a(n) _____ file type.

9. The output phase of a SORT statement is specified by the _____ and _____ phrases.

10. Each OUTPUT PROCEDURE must contain at least one _____ statement.

Answer the following questions by circling either "T" for True or "F" for False.

T F 11. A sort-file-name must appear in a SELECT clause.

T F 12. In the DATA DIVISION, a sort-file is described with an FD entry.

T F 13. Record descriptions for records in the sort-file are essentially the same as records in a typical file.

T F 14. It is possible for a sort-record description to be shorter than the record description of an input file to be sorted.

T F 15. It is possible for a sort-record description to be longer than the record description of an input file to be sorted.

T F 16. It is possible to sort records from two files into the same sort-file.

T F 17. If the GIVING phrase is specified in the SORT statement, the same sort statement may also use the INPUT PROCEDURE phrase.

T F 18. Sort keys must be numeric.

T F 19. Only one sort key may be specified for a single SORT statement.

T F 20. The SORT statement is only capable of sorting data from largest to smallest value.

T F 21. Both ascending and descending keys may be specified in one SORT statement.

T F 22. If an INPUT PROCEDURE is specified for the input phase, an OUTPUT PROCEDURE must be specified for the output phase.

T F 23. If an input file contains 100 records, it is always necessary to sort all 100 records.

T F 24. Two SORT statements could appear in the same program.

T F 25. The SORT statements always requires both an input and output phase.

Exercises

1. Below are a series of situations in which a SORT statement is used. Given the FILE SECTION entries below, identify all possible errors related to the correct usage of the SORT statements.

```
FILE SECTION.
FD  INPUT-FILE
    LABEL RECORDS OMITTED.
Ø1  INPUT-RECORD.
    Ø5  IN-FIELD-1        PIC X(1Ø).
    Ø5  IN-FIELD-2        PIC 9(Ø3).
    Ø5  IN-GROUP-1.
        1Ø  IN-FIELD-3    PIC 99V99.
        1Ø  IN-FIELD-4    PIC X(Ø5).
FD  OUTPUT-FILE LABEL RECORDS OMITTED.
Ø1  OUTPUT-RECORD        PIC X(9Ø).
SD  SORT-FILE.
Ø1  SORT-RECORD.
    Ø2  SORT-FIELD-1      PIC X(Ø5).
    Ø2  SORT-GROUP-1.
        Ø4  SORT-FIELD-2  PIC X(1Ø).
        Ø4  SORT-FIELD-3  PIC 9(Ø7).

a)  SORT SORT-FILE
        ASCENDING KEY SORT-FIELD-1
        USING INPUT-FILE
        OUTPUT PROCEDURE 2ØØ-REPORT.
            .
            .
            .
2ØØ-REPORT SECTION

b)  SORT SORT-FILE
        ASCENDING KEY IN-FIELD-1
        DESCENDING KEY IN-FIELD-4
        USING INPUT-FILE
        GIVING OUTPUT-FILE.

c)  SORT INPUT-FILE
        ASCENDING KEY SORT-GROUP-1
        INPUT PROCEDURE 1ØØ-TEST.
            .
            .
            .
1ØØ-TEST.

d)  SORT SORT-FILE
        DESCENDING SORT-RECORD
        INPUT INPUT-FILE
        OUTPUT PROCEDURE 5ØØ-DUMP-REC.
            .
            .
            .
5ØØ-DUMP-REC SECTION.

e)  SORT SORT-FILE
        ON DESCENDING SORT-FIELD-2
        INPUT PROCEDURE 2ØØ-SUM-VALUES
        GIVING OUTPUT-FILE.
            .
            .
            .
```

```
2ØØ-SUM-VALUES SECTION.

f)  SORT SORT-FILE.
        DECENDING KEY IS SORT-FIELD-1.
        INPUT PROCEDURE 2ØØ-FIRST.
        OUTPUT PROCEDURE 3ØØ-LAST.
            .
            .
            .
2ØØ-FIRST SECTION.
            .
            .
            .
        RETURN SORT-FILE
            AT END GO TO 3ØØ-LAST.
            .
            .
            .
3ØØ-LAST SECTION.
            .
            .
            .
        RELEASE SORT-FILE.
            .
            .
            .
        SORT SORT-FILE DESCENDING TEST-1
            USING INPUT-FILE GIVING
            OUTPUT-FILE.
```

2. Below is a set of data which is to be sorted. For each part below, indicate the sequence in which the data would appear after it was sorted with the specified key phrases.

DATA BEFORE SORTING

CHECK NUMBER	PAYEE NAME	CHECK AMOUNT	CHECK DATE	CHECK YEAR	VOUCHER NUMBER	CLEARED BY	CONTROL NUMBER
1129	JOHN PHILLIPS	033ᴧ45	04-15	81	395	RLS	44193
1039	MARK ANDERSON	062ᴧ15	04-02	81	287	BBR	83642
1427	JAMES HARRIS	731ᴧ44	05-05	81	528	JWS	83953
1319	MARK ANDERSON	005ᴧ95	04-19	81	407	JWS	41294
1220	JOHN JONES	062ᴧ88	04-20	81	401	RLS	79830
0921	MARK ANDERSON	314ᴧ14	03-26	81	263	BBR	97541
1006	ANDREW SMITH	842ᴧ15	03-30	81	270	DCD	06272

```
a) . . . ASCENDING CHECK-NUMBER . . .

b) . . . ASCENDING PAYEE-NAME, CHECK-NUMBER . . .

c) . . . DESCENDING CHECK-AMOUNT . . .

d) . . . DESCENDING CLEARED-BY
         ASCENDING CHECK-AMOUNT . . .

e) . . . DESCENDING CONTROL-NUMBER . . .

f) . . . ASCENDING CHECK-YEAR, CHECK-DATE, CHECK-NUMBER . . .

g) . . . ASCENDING PAYEE-NAME
         DESCENDING VOUCHER-NUMBER . . .

h) . . . ASCENDING CLEARED-BY
         DESCENDING PAYEE-NAME
         ASCENDING CHECK-YEAR, CHECK-DATE . . .
```

Problems

1. To update the customer file without processing errors or undue overhead in the updating procedure, we have been asked to edit invoice records to insure that they are legitimate (or at least reasonable). The invoice records contain a number of fields, each of which is subject to one or more errors. The fields, listed with possible errors, are specified below:

Field	Possible Error
Invoice Number	Duplicated
	Missing, i.e., nonconsecutive
	Non-numeric
Customer Number	Blank (Other checks would be made if we were to access the Customer File)
Date of Invoice	Month Error (not within the legitimate range of month values)
	Day Error (not within the legitimate range of day values)
	Year Error (not the same year as other invoice records)
Amount of Invoice	Non-numeric

Field	Possible Error
Amount of Tax	Non-numeric Tax not 0, 4, 5 , or 6 % of invoice amount
Amount of Discount	Discount not 0, 5,10, or 15 % of invoice amount Non-numeric
Amount of Cost	Non-numeric Cost greater than invoice amount

Many of these checks may (and should) be made before the data is ordered (for purposes of checking for duplicate/missing invoices). However, only invoices which indicate non-numeric invoice numbers are to be excluded from the sorting procedure.

The report format presented in the print chart should be used for this procedure.

MULTIPLE-CARD LAYOUT FORM

Company LEARNING COBOL, INC.

Application INVOICE EDITING   by J. Wayne Spence   Date 01/01/81   Job No. PROB 15.1   Sheet No. 1

150/10/8 PRINT CHART   PROG. ID. PROBLEM 15.1   PAGE 1   DATE 1/1/81
(SPACING: 150 POSITIONS AT 10 CHARACTERS PER INCH, 8 LINES PER VERTICAL INCH)
PROGRAM TITLE   INVOICE EDITING
PROGRAMMER OR DOCUMENTALIST J. Wayne Spence
CHART TITLE   INVOICE EDITING LIST

2. The inventory control manager is interested in developing a profit profile for all items in inventory. The profit profile is to be produced by outlet number. Within each outlet, inventory records are to be listed by vendor code. Finally, within each vendor group, items are to be listed by item number.

The report (illustrated in the printer spacing chart) is to be printed such that it adheres to the following guidelines:

a. All pages should be numbered at the right margin on both the top and bottom of each page.
b. Each outlet is to begin on a new page, and the outlet number should appear both in the heading and at the lower left margin of each page.
c. A heading should appear each time the vendor group changes and should be preceded and followed by two blank lines.
d. Group subtotals should be produced for each vendor group, as indicated.
e. Subtotals should be printed for each outlet.
f. Grand totals should be printed for each company.

Note: Gross profit is calculated as year-to-date sales less year-to-date cost.

MULTIPLE-CARD LAYOUT FORM

Company LEARNING COBOL, INC.

Application PROFIT PROFILE   by J. Wayne Spence   Date 01/01/81   Job No. PROB 15.2 & 3 Sheet No. 1

(Record Continued--Bytes 81-160)

(Record Continued--Bytes 161-171)

150/10/8 **PRINT CHART** PROG. ID. Problem 15.2 PAGE 1
(SPACING: 150 POSITIONS AT 10 CHARACTERS PER INCH, 8 LINES PER VERTICAL INCH) DATE 1/1/81
PROGRAM TITLE PROFIT PROFILE
PROGRAMMER OR DOCUMENTALIST J. Wayne Spence
CHART TITLE PROFIT PROFILE REPORT

```
                                           PROFIT PROFILE REPORT                                    PAGE ZZ9
OUTLET GROUP: 99999
        VENDOR GROUP: XXX
ITEM
NUMBER   ITEM DESCRIPTION              YTD SALES        YTD COST        YTD PROFIT
XXXXX    XXXXXXXXXXXXXXXXXXXXXXXXXXXX  Z,ZZZ,ZZZ,ZZZ.99 Z,ZZZ,ZZZ,ZZZ.99 Z,ZZZ,ZZZ,ZZZ.99
XXXXX    XXXXXXXXXXXXXXXXXXXXXXXXXXXX  Z,ZZZ,ZZZ,ZZZ.99 Z,ZZZ,ZZZ,ZZZ.99 Z,ZZZ,ZZZ,ZZZ.99
  {          {                              {                {                {
XXXXX    XXXXXXXXXXXXXXXXXXXXXXXXXXXX  Z,ZZZ,ZZZ,ZZZ.99 Z,ZZZ,ZZZ,ZZZ.99 Z,ZZZ,ZZZ,ZZZ.99

        VENDOR GROUP XXX TOTAL PROFIT                                     ZZZ,ZZZ,ZZZ,ZZZ.99
        VENDOR GROUP: XXX
ITEM
NUMBER   ITEM DESCRIPTION              YTD SALES        YTD COST        YTD PROFIT
XXXXX    XXXXXXXXXXXXXXXXXXXXXXXXXXXX  Z,ZZZ,ZZZ,ZZZ.99 Z,ZZZ,ZZZ,ZZZ.99 Z,ZZZ,ZZZ,ZZZ.99
  {          {                              {                {                {
XXXXX    XXXXXXXXXXXXXXXXXXXXXXXXXXXX  Z,ZZZ,ZZZ,ZZZ.99 Z,ZZZ,ZZZ,ZZZ.99 Z,ZZZ,ZZZ,ZZZ.99
        VENDOR GROUP XXX TOTAL PROFIT                                     ZZZ,ZZZ,ZZZ,ZZZ.99
OUTLET GROUP 99999 TOTAL PROFIT                                        ZZZ,ZZZ,ZZZ,ZZZ.99

OUTLET GROUP: 99999                                                                                PAGE ZZ9

─────────────────────────────────────────────────────────────────────────────────────────────────────

                                           PROFIT PROFILE REPORT                                    PAGE ZZ9
OUTLET GROUP: 99999
        VENDOR GROUP: XXX
ITEM
NUMBER   ITEM DESCRIPTION              YTD SALES        YTD COST        YTD PROFIT
XXXXX    XXXXXXXXXXXXXXXXXXXXXXXXXXXX  Z,ZZZ,ZZZ,ZZZ.99 Z,ZZZ,ZZZ,ZZZ.99 Z,ZZZ,ZZZ,ZZZ.99
  {          {                              {                {                {
        VENDOR GROUP XXX TOTAL PROFIT                                     ZZZ,ZZZ,ZZZ,ZZZ.99
OUTLET GROUP 99999 TOTAL PROFIT                                        ZZZ,ZZZ,ZZZ,ZZZ.99
***** COMPANY TOTAL *****                                           ZZZ,ZZZ,ZZZ,ZZZ.99
```

3. The inventory control manager wishes to receive an analysis of inventory movement. The particular analysis requested is referred to as "A-B-C Analysis." The inventory data to be used is in the same format as illustrated for problem #2.

A-B-C Analysis is an examination of the inventory on the basis of the level of investment in each inventory item. The level of investment is based on the total cost of units on hand. (That is, the on-hand quantity multiplied by cost per unit.) The A-B-C breakdown should be as follows:

Class A—The top 10% of the inventory items based on the level of investment.
Class B—The next 20% of the inventory items.
Class C—The remaining 70% of the inventory items.

For each inventory item, the reorder report should contain the item number, vendor, description, reorder point, amount on hand, cost, level of investment, cumulative level of investment for all items (including the current item) within the class, and cumulative level of investment of all items without regard to class.

Each class should be clearly labeled on the printout (i.e., A, B, or C) with page breaks between classes. Pages should be numbered and have appropriate headings. Each column should have appropriate column headings. If the level of investment for two or more items is equivalent, the items of equivalent value should be listed in vendor-code order. If the level of investment of two or more items is equivalent for the same vendor, the items should be listed in item-number order.

150/10/8 PRINT CHART   PROG. ID. PROBLEM 15.3   PAGE 1
(SPACING: 150 POSITIONS AT 10 CHARACTERS PER INCH, 8 LINES PER VERTICAL INCH)   DATE 1/1/81
PROGRAM TITLE ABC ANALYSIS
PROGRAMMER OR DOCUMENTALIST: J. Wayne Spence
CHART TITLE ABC ANALYSIS REPORT

```
              ABC INVENTORY ANALYSIS REPORT
                    CLASS A (TOP 10%)                                    PAGE ZZ9

ITEM                        VENDOR  MINIMUM   AMOUNT              LEVEL OF          CUMULATIVE
                            CODE    STOCK     ON        PER       INVESTMENT        INVESTMENT
NUMBER  ITEM DESCRIPTION            LEVEL     HAND      UNIT
XXXXX   XXXXXXXXXXXXXXXXXXXXXXXXXXXXXX  XXX  ZZZ,ZZ9  ZZZ,ZZ9  $ZZZ,ZZZ.99  $Z,ZZZ,ZZZ,ZZZ,ZZZ.99  $Z,ZZZ,ZZZ,ZZZ,ZZZ.99
XXXXX   XXXXXXXXXXXXXXXXXXXXXXXXXXXXXX  XXX  ZZZ,ZZ9  ZZZ,ZZ9  $ZZZ,ZZZ.99  $Z,ZZZ,ZZZ,ZZZ,ZZZ.99  $Z,ZZZ,ZZZ,ZZZ,ZZZ.99




XXXXX   XXXXXXXXXXXXXXXXXXXXXXXXXXXXXX  XXX  ZZZ,ZZ9  ZZZ,ZZ9  $ZZZ,ZZZ.99  $Z,ZZZ,ZZZ,ZZZ,ZZZ.99  $Z,ZZZ,ZZZ,ZZZ,ZZZ.99
```

16 Sequential File Processing

Although most of this text has been devoted to processing files based on a card-oriented input medium and a print-oriented output medium, most computer installations also use other media for the retention and manipulation of data. Among the most common media types are magnetic tape and magnetic disk. Magnetic media provide a number of very important advantages over punched cards and printed paper.

The first advantage is that magnetic media are reusable. Data may be erased, and new data may be recorded, making data modification possible. It is not possible to modify data on punched cards. Once holes have been punched into cards the medium is expended.

Second, once data has been written to a magnetic medium, it can also be read. Thus, a mass amount of data may be stored for future reference. Of course, data on punched cards may be reread, but first the programmer must reload the cards into a card reader.

Third, records on a magnetic medium are as long (or as short) as necessary to record the needed data. To retain 35 characters (bytes) of data, the record need only be 35 bytes long. To retain 300 bytes of data, the record may be 300 bytes long. Both the punched cards and printed media are fixed-length media. Punched cards are 80 columns long, whether or not all 80 columns contain data. Printed lines are typically 133 columns, whether or not all 133 columns contain printing.

Fourth, data stored on magnetic media may be read from or written to much more rapidly than reading data from punched cards or writing data to a printer.

Fifth, data stored on magnetic media is much more compact than data stored in either a printed or punched-card form. A typical magnetic tape could contain 48 million characters or more, and a magnetic disk could contain 200 million characters or more. To record 48 million characters on punched cards would require approximately 300 *boxes* (2,000 cards per box) or approximately 5,500 printed pages.

Finally, the magnetic media allow more flexibility in dealing with both *logical* and *physical* records. A logical record is application-oriented, i.e., the record the programmer views when writing a program. In COBOL, a logical record is coded for each FD in the FILE SECTION. A physical record is composed of one or more logical records. A physical record is read or written by a device (e.g., card reader, tape drive, or disk drive). Physical records are placed in the input buffers for a file or are written from output buffers (see Chapter 4). The programmer may decide the number of logical records in a physical record for magnetic media. To a card reader, a physical record is one card, and to a line printer, a physical record is one print line.

Why is the distinction between logical and physical records important? There are two reasons—space conservation and speed. As shown in Figure 16.1, magnetic media require that a space (called an *inter-record gap*—IRG) to be present between each physical record. On a magnetic tape, this space is typically expressed in inches and may require one-half to three-quarters of an inch of tape. On a magnetic disk, this space is typically expressed in bytes of recording surface and may require as much as 150 bytes of recording surface. Note that the recording of data in sequential form on tape requires the data to be spread down the length of the tape, while on disk, the data is recorded in concentric rings called *tracks*.

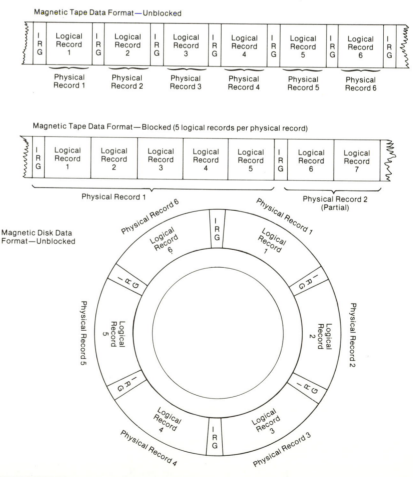

Figure 16.1 Physical Versus Logical Records

When data is recorded on a magnetic medium in an unblocked (one logical record per physical record) form, an inter-record gap is placed between each record. Suppose we were recording data on a magnetic tape with a recording density of 1,600 bytes per inch (BPI), logical record lengths of 200 bytes, and an inter-record gap of one-half inch. To record 1,000 records would require 625 inches (approximately 52 feet) of tape (200/1600×1000 + .5×1000 = 625). In this case the data occupies one-eighth inch per record, and the gap is one-half inch—more of the tape is gap than data. If, however, a *blocking factor* of 5 (5 logical records per physical record) is used, the amount of tape used falls to 225 inches (approximately 19 feet)! That is, 200 physical records times 1000/1600 inches per physical record plus one-half inch per block. This not only amounts to a substantial savings of media but also results in improved input-output performance for the data file.

How does input-output performance improve? The answer is simple. When we request data from the file (e.g., by a READ statement), two blocks are retrieved—10 logical records are placed in the two input buffers. As a result, our program will only have to communicate to the device once for every 10 logical READs in the procedure. When the CPU has to "converse" with a device, an *input-output interrupt* is generated by the operating system, which, in effect, causes the CPU to *wait* for the device to either transmit data to the CPU or the CPU to transmit data to the device. This is often called an *I-O wait state*. Thus, our program only has to "slow down" to device speed every ten READs in our program rather than every two. Therefore, the more logical records we can transmit to the CPU at one time, the fewer the wait states and the faster a procedure can peform I-O operations.

The procedure would be the same for magnetic disk. The major difference between tape and disk in handling sequential files is that tape is read and writ-

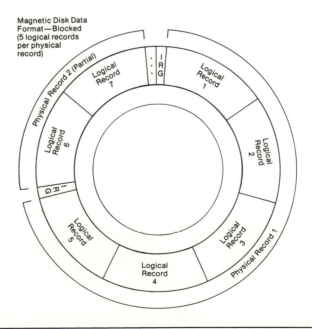

Figure 16.1 Physical Versus Logical Records *Continued*

ten serially down the length of the tape. The same process on a magnetic disk drive might require repositioning read-write heads to jump from track to track.

ENVIRONMENT DIVISION Considerations

To utilize magnetic tape and disk files in COBOL may require a few alterations in the ENVIRONMENT DIVISION. The basic format of the FILE-CONTROL paragraph (see Chapter 4) is repeated in Figure 16.2 to refresh your memory. The ASSIGN clause is the only change necessary to process sequential tape and disk files. The ASSIGN clause must reflect a system-name that designates your choice of a tape or disk file. It is possible to have multiple tape and disk files within one program. Figure 16.3 illustrates. In this figure, four files are assigned in the form necessary for an IBM system using the OS operating system. Notice that the file-names are similar to those appearing in previous

```
          .
          .
          .
[INPUT-OUTPUT SECTION.
 FILE-CONTROL.
        SELECT file-name
        ASSIGN TO system-name

  ┌                                              ┐
  │                 ⎧NO     ⎫              ⎡AREA ⎤│
  │  RESERVE        ⎨       ⎬ ALTERNATE    ⎢     ⎥│
  │                 ⎩integer⎭              ⎣AREAS⎦│
  └                                              ┘

        [ACCESS MODE IS SEQUENTIAL*]
        [PROCESSING MODE IS SEQUENTIAL]. . . .]
```
*The paragraph, as shown, is incomplete.

Figure 16.2 The Format of the INPUT-OUTPUT SECTION

```
          .
          .
          .
ENVIRONMENT DIVISION.
CONFIGURATION SECTION.
SOURCE-COMPUTER.   IBM-37Ø.
OBJECT-COMPUTER.   IBM-37Ø.
SPECIAL-NAMES.   CØ1 IS TOP-OF-PAGE.
INPUT-OUTPUT SECTION.
FILE-CONTROL.
        SELECT INVOICE-FILE ASSIGN TO UT-S-OLDMAST.
        SELECT NEW-INVOICE-FILE ASSIGN TO UT-S-NEWMAST.
        SELECT REPORT-FILE ASSIGN TO UT-S-SYSPRINT.
        SELECT SALES-FILE ASSIGN TO UT-S-TRANS.
          .
          .
          .
```

Figure 16.3 Data File ASSIGNments

programs; however, the assignment sequence is somewhat different. All file assignments are still prefixed by "UT-S" (utility—sequential), but a new series of programmer-selected names (OLDMAST, NEWMAST, and TRANS) have been supplied to complete the system-name. These programmer selected names are referred to as *ddnames* and are used to interface the program to JCL statements that provide additional information about the file. (Additional JCL is frequently necessary when using tape and/or disk files.)

Because we may now be faced with several input files and several output files, a new type of flowchart, the *system flowchart*, is often necessary to describe the types, number, and usage of different files. It provides a logical flow pattern for data entering and exiting a procedure. To specify media types and relations to a procedure, a new series of symbols is necessary, as shown in Figure 16.4. Each symbol shown in this figure identifies a particular type of medium (or procedure) and its possible uses in a system flowchart.

Figure 16.5 illustrates the relationship of the system flowchart to a procedure, using the file assignments in Figure 16.3. The system flowchart assumes that the INVOICE-FILE and the SALES-FILE are input files to the procedure and NEW-INVOICE-FILE and REPORT-FILE are produced as output files.

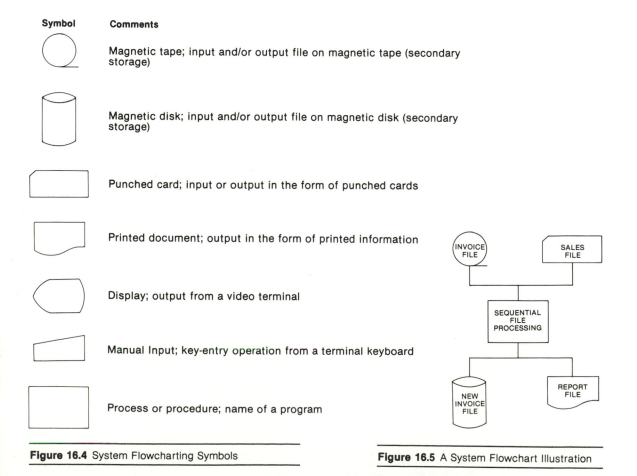

Symbol	Comments
	Magnetic tape; input and/or output file on magnetic tape (secondary storage)
	Magnetic disk; input and/or output file on magnetic disk (secondary storage)
	Punched card; input or output in the form of punched cards
	Printed document; output in the form of printed information
	Display; output from a video terminal
	Manual Input; key-entry operation from a terminal keyboard
	Process or procedure; name of a program

Figure 16.4 System Flowcharting Symbols

Figure 16.5 A System Flowchart Illustration

DATA DIVISION Considerations

As in previous programs, it is necessary to describe each file SELECTed with an FD in the FILE SECTION of the DATA DIVISION. For a sequential file FD a number of new clauses are needed (see Figure 16.6). The first new clause is the BLOCK CONTAINS clause, which indicates the blocking factor for records recorded on a magnetic medium. (A punched-card file and a printer file must be unblocked.) Integer-2 must be a nonnegative integer number. It specifies either the number of characters in a physical record (block) or the number of logical records in a physical record. For example, if the clause was written as:

BLOCK CONTAINS 500 CHARACTERS

COBOL would assume that the physical record was 500 bytes in length. The (logical) record description for this file should be a multiple of 500 (e.g., five 100-byte records). If the clause was written as:

BLOCK CONTAINS 5 RECORDS

COBOL would assume the physical record length to be five times the (logical) record length. (Note that IBM COBOL permits integer-2 to be zero—indicating that the blocking factor is to be defaulted to that specified in the JCL.) If integer-1 is specified, integer-1 must be a positive integer number that represents the minimum length of a physical record. Then, integer-2 becomes the maximum record length (and must be greater in value than integer-1). This option permits the specification of variable-length blocks in COBOL, i.e., all physical records do not necessarily have to be the same length. If the BLOCK CONTAINS clause is omitted, the file is unblocked.

The RECORD CONTAINS clause may be used to specify the logical record length. As in the BLOCK CONTAINS clause, integer-2 represents the maximum length of a (logical) record. COBOL checks the length specified against the cumulative total of the PICTURE clauses to determine whether or not the record description total length has been accurately stated. The LABEL RECORDS clause has been previously discussed; however, Figure 16.6 shows that a file may either possess no label (OMITTED) or a STANDARD label. Data files recorded on magnetic media generally are recorded with STANDARD, system-generated labels.

Finally, the DATA RECORDS clause allows the programmer to identify the record-names (data-name-1, data-name-2, etc.) that are written in conjunction with each file description. The DATA RECORDS clause is treated as a comment.

```
DATA DIVISION.
[FILE SECTION.
 FD  file-name

    [BLOCK CONTAINS [integer-1 TO]  integer-2  {CHARACTERS}
                                               {RECORDS   }]

    [RECORD CONTAINS [integer-1 TO]  integer-2 CHARACTERS]

    LABEL {RECORD IS  }  {OMITTED }
          {RECORDS ARE}  {STANDARD}

    [DATA {RECORD IS  } data-name-1 [data-name-2] . . .]  .]
          {RECORDS ARE}
```

Figure 16.6 Sequential File FDs

Figure 16.7 illustrates the relationship of files to the description of the files in the FILE SECTION. The INVOICE-FILE is a standard sequential (tape) file, thus the LABEL RECORDS clause is set to STANDARD. The logical record for this file is 100 bytes, and 50 logical records compose each physical record. The NEW-INVOICE-FILE is also standard sequential—perhaps a disk file and has 100-byte logical records. The BLOCK CONTAINS clause indicates, however, that the physical record length is 5,000 bytes (50 times 100). The REPORT-FILE is a print-oriented file; thus, the LABEL RECORDS ARE OMITTED, the record length is 133 bytes, and the file is unblocked (no BLOCK CONTAINS clause). In addition, the DATA RECORDS clause indicates that the record-names PRINT-LINE and MESSAGE-LINE are to appear in conjunction with the FD. Finally, the FD for SALES-FILE is provided. SALES-FILE is assumed to be a punched-card file. LABEL RECORDS ARE OMITTED and the logical record length is 80 bytes. However, in the FILE-CONTROL paragraph, 16 buffers (15 ALTERNATE AREAS) are indicated, providing the capability to read 16 cards at a time.

```
                    .
                    .
                    .
        FILE-CONTROL.
            SELECT INVOICE-FILE
                ASSIGN TO UT-S-OLDMAST.
            SELECT NEW-INVOICE-FILE.
                ASSIGN TO UT-S-NEWMAST.
            SELECT REPORT-FILE
                ASSIGN TO UT-S-SYSPRINT.
            SELECT SALES-FILE
                ASSIGN TO UT-S-SYSIN
                RESERVE 15 ALTERNATE AREAS.
        DATA DIVISION.
        FILE SECTION.
        FD  INVOICE-FILE
                LABEL RECORDS ARE STANDARD
                BLOCK CONTAINS 5Ø RECORDS
                RECORD CONTAINS 1ØØ CHARACTERS.
        Ø1  INVOICE-RECORD              PIC X(1ØØ).
        FD  NEW-INVOICE-FILE
                LABEL RECORDS ARE STANDARD
                BLOCK CONTAINS 5ØØØ CHARACTERS
                RECORD CONTAINS 1ØØ CHARACTERS.
        Ø1  NEW-INVOICE-RECORD.
            Ø5  INVOICE-NUMBER          PIC 9(Ø6).
            Ø5  CUSTOMER-NUMBER         PIC X(1Ø).
            Ø5  FILLER                  PIC X(Ø6).
            Ø5  PURCHASE-AMOUNT         PIC S9(Ø6)V99.
            Ø5  FILLER                  PIC X(67).
        FD  REPORT-FILE
                LABEL RECORDS ARE OMITTED
                RECORD CONTAINS 133 CHARACTERS
                DATA RECORDS ARE PRINT-LINE, MESSAGE-LINE.
        Ø1  PRINT-LINE                  PIC X(133).
        Ø1  MESSAGE-LINE.
            Ø5  FILLER                  PIC X(83).
            Ø5  MESSAGE-OUT             PIC X(5Ø).
        FD  SALES-FILE
                LABEL RECORDS ARE OMITTED
                RECORD CONTAINS 8Ø CHARACTERS.
        Ø1  SALES-RECORD                PIC X(8Ø).
```

Figure 16.7 Illustrations of Sequential File FDs

**Processing
Sequential
Files—New
Statement
Options**
Figure 16.8 provides a new look at the OPEN statement. New options are pro-
vided in this statement because of the media involved. Note that an INPUT file
may be opened REVERSED. That is, a standard sequential file may be opened
such that it is positioned at the end of the file and may be read *backwards!*
This option applies primarily to magnetic tape, allowing the programmer to
read (or reread) a file without rewinding it. The NO REWIND option of the
OPEN statement is treated as a comment. And, a new option is added to the
OPEN statement. A file may be opened in an INPUT, OUTPUT, or *I-O*
mode. That is, both reading and writing activity may take place in conjunction
with a file in one processing sequence. However, to be opened in an I-O mode,
the file must previously exist and the file must be on a mass storage device
(e.g., magnetic disk).

```
OPEN  [INPUT    file-name   ⌈REVERSED        ⌉      . . .]
                            ⌊WITH NO REWIND⌋

      [OUTPUT   file-name   [WITH NO REWIND]    . . .]

      [I-O   file-name   . . .]
```

Figure 16.8 Sequential File OPEN Statement

As with the OPEN statement, the CLOSE statement has new options when
used in conjunction with standard sequential files (see Figure 16.9). Both the
REEL and NO REWIND options apply to sequential files on magnetic tape.
The optional reserved word REEL may be used for documentation purposes to
make explicit the use of a magnetic tape. The NO REWIND option, if present,
forces the operating system to leave the magnetic tape at the end-of-file when it
is CLOSEd. In the absence of the NO REWIND option, the file is rewound
(repositioned for magnetic disk) to the beginning of the file. The LOCK option
specifies that after the file has been rewound further operations on the file are
to be inhibited for the remainder of the program. Without this option, the file
could be reopened and processed again. The LOCK option can be used with
tape or disk. Finally, the UNIT reserved word may be used to identify a mass
storage medium type and, like the REEL option, it is treated as a comment.

```
CLOSE file-name   ⌈REEL⌉     [WITH   ⎧NO REWIND⎫  ]
                  ⌊UNIT⌋             ⎩LOCK     ⎭
      [file-name  ⌈REEL⌉     [WITH   ⎧NO REWIND⎫  ]]. . .
                  ⌊UNIT⌋             ⎩LOCK     ⎭
```

Figure 16.9 Sequential File CLOSE Statement

The WRITE statement is also modified (Figure 16.10) when creating a standard sequential file. The BEFORE/AFTER ADVANCING option, previously
presented in conjunction with output to a printer, has been dropped. That is,
top-of-form, single-space, etc., have no meaning to a magnetic tape or disk.

(In addition, it should be mentioned that the READ statement, previously described in conjunction with punched card input files, is not altered when dealing with standard sequential files.)

```
WRITE record-name  [FROM identifier]
```

Figure 16.10 Sequential File WRITE Statement

Building a Sequential File

To be considered a standard sequential file, the file must have one record sequentially following another. For file processing purposes, however, many files are ordered on the basis of a particular field to permit efficient manipulation of the file. For example, compare the file sequences provided in Figure 16.11. Both illustrations represent sequential files; however, the second file would be somewhat easier to manipulate—customer number 400 is preceded by customer number 380 and followed by 405. On the other hand, suppose we are "looking" for a record not in the file, say a record identified by customer number 305. To determine that this record does not exist in the first file, we

File 1:   Unordered

	FIELD
CUSTOMER NUMBER	REMAINDER OF RECORD
320	--
405	--
180	--
310	--
400	--
570	--
260	--
380	--
605	--
410	--

File 2:   Ordered by Customer Number

	FIELD
CUSTOMER NUMBER	REMAINDER OF RECORD
180	--
260	--
310	--
320	--
380	--
400	--
405	--
410	--
570	--
605	--

Figure 16.11 Unordered Versus Ordered Sequential Files

would have to read the entire file. When processing the second file, since it is sequenced on the customer number field, encountering customer number 310 (without having previously encountered 305) would mean that customer number 305 is not present in the file. Thus, standard sequential files are frequently ordered on some identifying field to simplify file processing requirements.

Now turn to Figure 16.12. This program is responsible for building a standard sequential CUSTOMER file. For this type of file customer numbers should be unique. The procedure specifies that the CUSTOMER-IN file is presumed to be an unordered file. Thus, the PROCEDURE DIVISION begins with a SORT statement (with a USING phrase—see Chapter 15). When the OUTPUT PROCEDURE begins, the data has been ordered, and any duplicate CUSTOMER-NUMBERs will be adjacent to each other (CUSTOMER-NUMBER-SORT is the sort key). As records are returned from the CUSTOMER-SORT file (lines 1020 and 1120), they are checked to determine whether or not they are the same as that of the previous record (line 1070). If the customer number is a duplicate, the duplication is noted on the EXCEPTION-REPORT, and the record is omitted from the output file. If the customer number is not a duplicate, the customer record (from the sort file) is placed in the newly created output file (CUSTOMER-OUT) with the WRITE statement in line 1300. Thus, a new file has been created (sequenced on the customer number field) and retained for further processing.

One final note about building sequential files: the building process is typically required only *once*. That is, after the data has been examined for correctness, and the sequence has been established, all further processing works from this sequence.

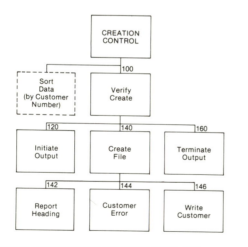

Figure 16.12 Building a Sequential File (Hierarchy Chart)

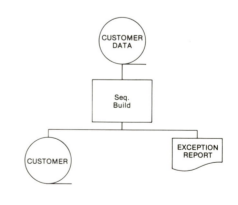

Figure 16.12 Building a Sequential File (System Flowchart) *Continued*

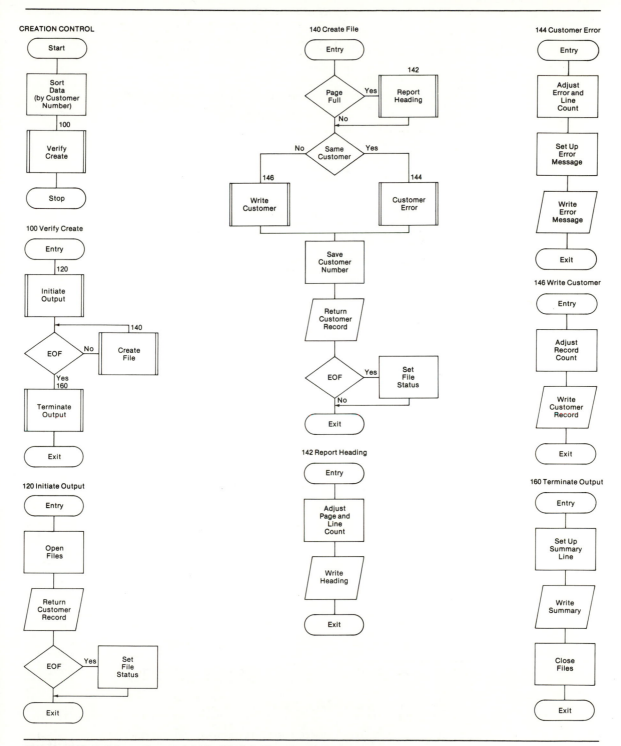

Figure 16.12 Building a Sequential File (Module Flowcharts) *Continued*

```
|         1   1   2   2   2   3   3   4   4   5   5   6   6   6   7   7   8|
|   4   8   2   6   0   4   8   2   6   0   4   8   2   6   0   4   8   2   6   0|
--------------------------------------------------------------------------------
|000010 IDENTIFICATION DIVISION.                                        FIG16.12|
|000020 PROGRAM-ID. SEQ-BUILD.                                          FIG16.12|
|000030 AUTHOR. J. WAYNE SPENCE.                                        FIG16.12|
|000040 DATE-WRITTEN. JAN 1, 1981.                                      FIG16.12|
|000050 DATE-COMPILED. JAN 1, 1981.                                     FIG16.12|
|000060*    THE PURPOSE OF THIS PROCEDURE IS TO PRODUCE A SEQUENTIAL    FIG16.12|
|000070*    DATA FILE BASED ON CUSTOMER RECORDS.  THE FILE IS TO BE     FIG16.12|
|000080*    ORDERED ON THE CUSTOMER NUMBER FIELD.                       FIG16.12|
|000090 ENVIRONMENT DIVISION.                                           FIG16.12|
|000100 CONFIGURATION SECTION.                                          FIG16.12|
|000110 SOURCE-COMPUTER. IBM-370.                                       FIG16.12|
|000120 OBJECT-COMPUTER. IBM-370.                                       FIG16.12|
|000130 SPECIAL-NAMES.                                                  FIG16.12|
|000140     C01 IS TOP-OF-PAGE.                                         FIG16.12|
|000150 INPUT-OUTPUT SECTION.                                           FIG16.12|
|000160 FILE-CONTROL.                                                   FIG16.12|
|000170     SELECT CUSTOMER-IN ASSIGN TO UT-S-CUSTIN.                   FIG16.12|
|000180     SELECT CUSTOMER-OUT ASSIGN TO UT-S-CUSTOUT.                 FIG16.12|
|000190     SELECT CUSTOMER-SORT ASSIGN TO UT-S-SORTWK01.               FIG16.12|
|000200     SELECT EXCEPTION-REPORT ASSIGN TO UT-S-SYSPRINT.            FIG16.12|
|000210 DATA DIVISION.                                                  FIG16.12|
|000220 FILE SECTION.                                                   FIG16.12|
|000230 FD  CUSTOMER-IN                                                 FIG16.12|
|000240     LABEL RECORDS ARE STANDARD                                  FIG16.12|
|000250     RECORD CONTAINS 124 CHARACTERS                             FIG16.12|
|000260     BLOCK CONTAINS 0 RECORDS.                                   FIG16.12|
|000270 01  CUSTOMER-REC-IN            PIC X(124).                      FIG16.12|
|000280 FD  CUSTOMER-OUT                                                FIG16.12|
|000290     LABEL RECORDS ARE STANDARD                                  FIG16.12|
|000300     RECORD CONTAINS 124 CHARACTERS                             FIG16.12|
|000310     BLOCK CONTAINS 0 RECORDS.                                   FIG16.12|
|000320 01  CUSTOMER-REC-OUT.                                           FIG16.12|
|000330     05  CUSTOMER-NUMBER-OUT    PIC X(10).                       FIG16.12|
|000340     05  CUSTOMER-NAME-OUT      PIC X(30).                       FIG16.12|
|000350     05  CUSTOMER-ADDRESS-OUT   PIC X(30).                       FIG16.12|
|000360     05  CUSTOMER-CITY-OUT      PIC X(20).                       FIG16.12|
|000370     05  CUSTOMER-STATE-OUT     PIC X(02).                       FIG16.12|
|000380     05  CUSTOMER-ZIP-OUT       PIC X(10).                       FIG16.12|
|000390     05  OUTSTANDING-BALANCE-OUT PIC S9(9)V99.                   FIG16.12|
|000400     05  CREDIT-LIMIT-OUT       PIC S9(9)V99.                    FIG16.12|
|000410 SD  CUSTOMER-SORT.                                              FIG16.12|
|000420 01  CUSTOMER-REC-SORT.                                          FIG16.12|
|000430     05  CUSTOMER-NUMBER-SORT   PIC X(10).                       FIG16.12|
|000440     05  FILLER                 PIC X(114).                      FIG16.12|
|000450 FD  EXCEPTION-REPORT                                            FIG16.12|
|000460     LABEL RECORDS ARE OMITTED.                                  FIG16.12|
|000470 01  REPORT-LINE                PIC X(133).                      FIG16.12|
|000480 WORKING-STORAGE SECTION.                                        FIG16.12|
|000490 01  PROGRAM-CONTROL-VARIABLES.                                  FIG16.12|
|000500     05  FILE-STATUS            PIC X(04) VALUE SPACES.          FIG16.12|
|000510     05  LAST-CUSTOMER-NUMBER   PIC X(10) VALUE SPACES.          FIG16.12|
|000520     05  LINE-NUMBER            PIC 9(02) VALUE 99.              FIG16.12|
|000530     05  PAGE-NUMBER            PIC 9(02) VALUE ZERO.            FIG16.12|
|000540     05  ERROR-COUNT            PIC 9(04) VALUE ZERO.            FIG16.12|
|000550     05  CUSTOMER-COUNT         PIC 9(04) VALUE ZERO.            FIG16.12|
|000560 01  HEADING-1.                                                  FIG16.12|
|000570     05  FILLER                 PIC X(32) VALUE SPACES.          FIG16.12|
|000580     05  FILLER                 PIC X(16) VALUE                  FIG16.12|
|000590     'EXCEPTION REPORT'.                                         FIG16.12|
|000600     05  FILLER                 PIC X(25) VALUE SPACES.          FIG16.12|
|000610     05  FILLER                 PIC X(05) VALUE 'PAGE'.          FIG16.12|
|000620     05  PAGE-OUT               PIC Z9.                          FIG16.12|
|000630 01  HEADING-2.                                                  FIG16.12|
|000640     05  FILLER                 PIC X(20) VALUE                  FIG16.12|
|000650     ' CUSTOMER NUMBER'.                                         FIG16.12|
|000660     05  FILLER                 PIC X(20) VALUE                  FIG16.12|
|000670     'COMMENTS'.                                                 FIG16.12|
|000680 01  HEADING-3.                                                  FIG16.12|
|000690     05  FILLER                 PIC X(01) VALUE SPACES.          FIG16.12|
|000700     05  FILLER                 PIC X(80) VALUE ALL '-'.         FIG16.12|
|000710 01  ERROR-LINE.                                                 FIG16.12|
|000720     05  FILLER                 PIC X(02) VALUE SPACES.          FIG16.12|
|000730     05  CUSTOMER-NUMBER-ERROR  PIC X(10).                       FIG16.12|
|000740     05  FILLER                 PIC X(08) VALUE SPACES.          FIG16.12|
|000750     05  FILLER                 PIC X(50) VALUE                  FIG16.12|
|000760     'CUSTOMER NUMBER DUPLICATE ENCOUNTERED--ELIMINATED'.        FIG16.12|
|000770 01  SUMMARY-LINE.                                               FIG16.12|
|000780     05  FILLER                 PIC X(01) VALUE SPACES.          FIG16.12|
|000790     05  CUSTOMER-COUNT-OUT     PIC +,**9.                       FIG16.12|
```

Figure 16.12 Building a Sequential File *Continued*

```
|      1 1 2 2 2 3 3 4 4 4 5 5 6 6 6 7 7 8|
|  4 8 2 6 0 4 8 2 6 0 4 8 2 6 0 4 8 2 6 0|
-----------------------------------------------------------------------------
|000800     05  FILLER                  PIC X(27) VALUE              FIG16.12|
|000810       ' CUSTOMER RECORDS WRITTEN--'.                         FIG16.12|
|000820     05  ERROR-COUNT-OUT          PIC *,**9.                  FIG16.12|
|000830     05  FILLER                  PIC X(25) VALUE              FIG16.12|
|000840       ' DUPLICATES ENCOUNTERED'.                             FIG16.12|
|000850 PROCEDURE DIVISION.                                          FIG16.12|
|000860 CREATION-CONTROL SECTION.                                    FIG16.12|
|000870     SORT CUSTOMER-SORT                                       FIG16.12|
|000880         ASCENDING KEY CUSTOMER-NUMBER-SORT                   FIG16.12|
|000890         USING CUSTOMER-IN                                    FIG16.12|
|000900         OUTPUT PROCEDURE 100-VERIFY-CREATE.                  FIG16.12|
|000910     STOP RUN.                                                FIG16.12|
|000920 100-VERIFY-CREATE SECTION.                                   FIG16.12|
|000930 100-VERIFY-CREATE-CONTROL.                                   FIG16.12|
|000940     PERFORM 120-INITIATE-OUTPUT.                             FIG16.12|
|000950     PERFORM 140-CREATE-FILE                                  FIG16.12|
|000960         UNTIL FILE-STATUS = 'DONE'.                          FIG16.12|
|000970     PERFORM 160-TERMINATE-OUTPUT.                            FIG16.12|
|000980     GO TO 199-EXIT.                                          FIG16.12|
|000990 120-INITIATE-OUTPUT.                                         FIG16.12|
|001000     OPEN OUTPUT CUSTOMER-OUT                                 FIG16.12|
|001010         EXCEPTION-REPORT.                                    FIG16.12|
|001020     RETURN CUSTOMER-SORT INTO CUSTOMER-REC-OUT               FIG16.12|
|001030         AT END MOVE 'DONE' TO FILE-STATUS.                   FIG16.12|
|001040 140-CREATE-FILE.                                             FIG16.12|
|001050     IF LINE-NUMBER IS GREATER THAN 40                        FIG16.12|
|001060         PERFORM 142-REPORT-HEADING.                          FIG16.12|
|001070     IF CUSTOMER-NUMBER-SORT = LAST-CUSTOMER-NUMBER           FIG16.12|
|001080         PERFORM 144-CUSTOMER-ERROR                           FIG16.12|
|001090     ELSE                                                     FIG16.12|
|001100         PERFORM 146-WRITE-CUSTOMER.                          FIG16.12|
|001110     MOVE CUSTOMER-NUMBER-SORT TO LAST-CUSTOMER-NUMBER.       FIG16.12|
|001120     RETURN CUSTOMER-SORT INTO CUSTOMER-REC-OUT               FIG16.12|
|001130         AT END MOVE 'DONE' TO FILE-STATUS.                   FIG16.12|
|001140 142-REPORT-HEADING.                                          FIG16.12|
|001150     ADD 1 TO PAGE-NUMBER.                                    FIG16.12|
|001160     MOVE PAGE-NUMBER TO PAGE-OUT.                            FIG16.12|
|001170     WRITE REPORT-LINE FROM HEADING-1 AFTER ADVANCING TOP-OF-PAGE.FIG16.12|
|001180     WRITE REPORT-LINE FROM HEADING-2 AFTER ADVANCING 3 LINES.FIG16.12|
|001190     WRITE REPORT-LINE FROM HEADING-3 AFTER ADVANCING 1 LINES.FIG16.12|
|001200     MOVE SPACES TO REPORT-LINE.                              FIG16.12|
|001210     WRITE REPORT-LINE AFTER ADVANCING 1 LINES.               FIG16.12|
|001220     MOVE 0 TO LINE-NUMBER.                                   FIG16.12|
|001230 144-CUSTOMER-ERROR.                                          FIG16.12|
|001240     ADD 1 TO ERROR-COUNT.                                    FIG16.12|
|001250     MOVE CUSTOMER-NUMBER-OUT TO CUSTOMER-NUMBER-ERROR.       FIG16.12|
|001260     WRITE REPORT-LINE FROM ERROR-LINE AFTER ADVANCING 1 LINES.FIG16.12|
|001270     ADD 1 TO LINE-NUMBER.                                    FIG16.12|
|001280 146-WRITE-CUSTOMER.                                          FIG16.12|
|001290     ADD 1 TO CUSTOMER-COUNT.                                 FIG16.12|
|001300     WRITE CUSTOMER-REC-OUT.                                  FIG16.12|
|001310 160-TERMINATE-OUTPUT.                                        FIG16.12|
|001320     MOVE ERROR-COUNT TO ERROR-COUNT-OUT.                     FIG16.12|
|001330     MOVE CUSTOMER-COUNT TO CUSTOMER-COUNT-OUT.               FIG16.12|
|001340     WRITE REPORT-LINE FROM SUMMARY-LINE AFTER ADVANCING 2 LINES.FIG16.12|
|001350     CLOSE EXCEPTION-REPORT                                   FIG16.12|
|001360         CUSTOMER-OUT.                                        FIG16.12|
|001370 199-EXIT.                                                    FIG16.12|
|001380     EXIT.                                                    FIG16.12|
```

Figure 16.12 Building a Sequential File *Continued*

```
         1         2         3         4         5         6         7         8         9         1         1         1
123456789012345678901234567890123456789012345678901234567890123456789012345678901234567890123456798012345678901234

4412X47390MARSHALL SILVERMAN         2219 WEST 7TH STREET          CLEVELAND        OH30119   0000000000000000500000
3199127X33JAMES THOMPKINS            44339 SOUTH WACKER DRIVE      CHICAGO          IL60606   0000002291800000500000
1141944103EDWIN WILLIAMS             2139 SOUTH COLGATE STREET     PERRYTON         TX79070   0000033193300035000000
6213937661JASON MADISON              8831 CEDAR DRIVE N.W.         NORWICH          CN00218   0000041452300003000000
5270215827CHARLES EVEREST            8821 OCEAN PARKWAY            MIAMI            FL51332   0000000000000000000000
3333333333JULIA HARRISTON            6132 MILL ROAD AVENUE         SHREVEPORT       LA63341   0000035134300005000000
3498966451JACOB R. SULLIVAN          6134 MALIBU DRIVE             LOS ANGELES      CA96512   0000000000000004400000
1RX14219-3JOHN P. VILLIMAN           8887 PEACH TREE LANE          DALLAS           TX75002   0000003143000050000000
6427633-94MARK U. LEMON              P. O. BOX 51244               NEW YORK         NY03158   0000000000000000005000
773194221BHELEN B. OVERSTREET        3153 YELLOW BRICK ROAD        YELLOW STONE PARK MT41229  0000012842000000000000
9X0-334RDSANTHONY P. JONES           EXECUTIVE OFFICE BUILDING     WASHINGTON       DC00000   0000000000000000000000
3333333333RAYMOND J. TAYLOR          912 DUSTY ROAD                PLAINS           GA39100   0000052353600010000000
```

Figure 16.12 Building a Sequential File (Data—CUSTOMER-IN) *Continued*

```
            1  1  2  2  2  3  3  4  4  4  5  5  6  6  6  7  7  8  8  8  9  9  1  1  1  1  1  1  1
            1  1  2  2  2  3  3  4  4  4  5  5  6  6  6  7  7  8  8  8  9  9  0  0  0  1  1  2  2
   4  8  2  6  0  4  8  2  6  0  4  8  2  6  0  4  8  2  6  0  4  8  2  6  0  4  8  2  6  0  4
----------------------------------------------------------------------------------------------------
1RX14219-3JOHN P. VILLIMAN          8887 PEACH TREE LANE        DALLAS            TX75002    00000003143000005000000
1141944103EDWIN WILLIAMS            2139 SOUTH COLGATE STREET   PERRYTON          TX79070    00000033193300035000000
3199127X33JAMES THOMPKINS           44339 SOUTH WACKER DRIVE    CHICAGO           IL60606    00000022918000005000000
3333333333JULIA HARRISTON           6132 MILL ROAD AVENUE       SHREVEPORT        LA63341    00000351343000050000000
3498966451JACOB R. SULLIVAN         6134 MALIBU DRIVE           LOS ANGELES       CA96512    00000000000000004400000
4412X47390MARSHALL SILVERMAN        2219 WEST 7TH STREET        CLEVELAND         OH30119    00000000000000000500000
5270215827CHARLES EVEREST           8821 OCEAN PARKWAY          MIAMI             FL51332    00000000000000000500000
6213937661JASON MADISON             8831 CEDAR DRIVE N.W.       NORWICH           CN00218    00000414523000030000000
6427633-94MARK U. LEMON             P. O. BOX 51244             NEW YORK          NY03158    00000000000000000005000
773194221BHELEN B. OVERSTREET       3153 YELLOW BRICK ROAD      YELLOW STONE PARK MT41229    00000012842000000000000
9X0-334RDSANTHONY P. JONES          EXECUTIVE OFFICE BUILDING   WASHINGTON        DC00000    00000000000000000000000
```

Figure 16.12 Building a Sequential File (Data—CUSTOMER-OUT) *Continued*

```
                                              EXCEPTION REPORT                              PAGE   1


         CUSTOMER NUMBER       COMMENTS
         ----------------------------------------------------------------------------------

           3333333333          CUSTOMER NUMBER DUPLICATE ENCOUNTERED--ELIMINATED

         ***11 CUSTOMER RECORDS WRITTEN--****1 DUPLICATES ENCOUNTERED
```

Figure 16.12 Building a Sequential File (Output) *Continued*

Updating a Sequential File

Unlike the building process, file updating is typically a repetitive process. That is, periodically a file may be modified to reflect more current information. For example, the customer file may be updated by altering the customer's address, modifying the credit limit, or incrementing (decrementing) the outstanding balance to reflect sales (and payments). To be able to update a record in a file properly, it is necessary for both the record to be updated and the update itself (for a particular record) to be processed at the same time. Figure 16.13 illustrates the logic of this process. Note that the CUSTOMER FILE (sometimes referred to as a *MASTER* file) and the SALES FILE (sometimes referred to as a *TRANSACTION* file) are both sequenced on the customer number. Further notice that for a particular customer number in the CUSTOMER FILE there may be no corresponding record in the SALES FILE. In other cases, however, one or more records in the SALES FILE could have a corresponding customer number. Finally, there may be customer numbers in the SALES FILE that do not exist in the CUSTOMER FILE—a probable error.

How do we determine what to do with each customer record in the CUSTOMER FILE and when to do it? To simplify the update logic, the programmer only has to be concerned with three basic relationships between the customer number of the CUSTOMER FILE and the customer number of the SALES FILE, as illustrated in Figure 16.14. Of course, we anticipate finding situations in which the customer number from the two files are equal (e.g., 260, 320, and 410 appear in both files). However, there may be circumstances under which a customer record is not updated (e.g., customer numbers 180, 310, 380, 400, 405, 570, and 605 of the CUSTOMER FILE). Finally, there may be customer numbers in the transaction file that do not have corresponding numbers in the CUSTOMER FILE (e.g., 350 in the SALES FILE).

Now examine Figure 16.14. First, we read one record from each file, i.e., 180 from the CUSTOMER FILE and 260 from the SALES FILE. Since 180 is less than 260, we write customer record 180 to a new file and read the next customer record—260—from the CUSTOMER FILE. Now, the two customer numbers match, the affected fields are modified, and the next record from the SALES FILE is read—320. The customer number from the CUSTOMER FILE is again less than that from the SALES FILE (260 is less than 320). The *changed* customer record is written to a new file and the next customer record from the CUSTOMER FILE (310) is read. The customer number from the CUSTOMER

CUSTOMER FILE (Master File)

CUSTOMER NUMBER	REMAINDER OF RECORD
180	---
260	---
310	---
320	---
380	---
400	---
405	---
410	---
570	---
605	---

SALES FILE (Transaction File)

CUSTOMER NUMBER	CONTENT OF UPDATE
260	--------------------------------------
320	--------------------------------------
320	--------------------------------------
350	--------------------------------------
410	--------------------------------------
410	--------------------------------------
410	--------------------------------------
410	--------------------------------------

Figure 16.13 Master Files and Transaction Files

UPDATE LOGIC

(Modification of fields in existing records in an old master file based on data found in a transaction file)

Key Relationship	Procedure
Master = Transaction	Change the indicated field(s), as appropriate, in the old master-file record, and read a new transaction record. (Procedure will accommodate one or more transactions per master record.)
Master < Transaction	Write a new record into the new master file from the old master file, and read another record from the old master file. (Create a new, updated record in the new master file or copy a nonupdated record from the old master file to the new master file.)
Master > Transaction	Error—no old master record contains the key specified in the transaction record. Write an error message and read a new transaction record.

Figure 16.14 Sequential File Update Logic (No duplicate master-file keys assumed)

FILE is still less than that from the SALES FILE. The customer record is written (copied), as was done with 180, and the next record (320) is read from the CUSTOMER FILE. The customer numbers are again equal, the affected field in the customer record is changed, and the next SALES RECORD (320) is read. The customer numbers are still equal, so another change is made to the customer record, and another record (350) is read from the SALES FILE. The customer number from the CUSTOMER FILE is now less than the customer number from the SALES FILE (320 is less than 350), the changed customer record is written to the new CUSTOMER FILE, and a new customer record (380) is read from the old CUSTOMER FILE. The current value of the customer number from the CUSTOMER FILE is *greater than* that from the SALES FILE (350)—a condition which can exist only if 350 is not present in the CUSTOMER FILE. Therefore, we declare 350 to be an error—if it had existed in the CUSTOMER file we would have read it prior to 380. An error message is written, and a new record (410) is read from the SALES FILE. After this, records 380, 400, and 405 will be copied to the new CUSTOMER FILE; CUSTOMER FILE record will be updated four times; and CUSTOMER FILE records 410, 570, and 605 will be written to the new CUSTOMER FILE. Thus, a complete file update has been performed.

The program presented in Figure 16.15 performs such an update. One problem not addressed with Figures 16.13 and 16.14 was the end-of-file process for the two files. By examining the PERFORM statement in lines 1030 through 1050, one can establish the condition under which 1400-UPDATE-FILE is terminated—both the CUSTOMER-NUMBER and CUSTOMER-NUMBER-SORT (associated with the sorted sales records) are HIGH-VALUES. It is unlikely that a customer number would be HIGH-VALUES (the highest value in the computer's collating sequence); thus, this value is generated by some other means. Now, turn to the procedures responsible for getting input data from the sort file (the RETURN statement in line 1540) and the customer file (the READ statement in line 1660). Note that the end-of-file condition for each statement causes HIGH-VALUES to be moved to their respective key fields. Thus, if we were to encounter the end of the sort file first, CUSTOMER-NUMBER would be *less than* CUSTOMER-NUMBER-SORT, forcing the remainder of the records in the CUSTOMER file to be copied to the new

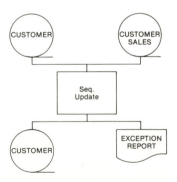

Figure 16.15 Updating a Sequential File (System Flowchart)

CUSTOMER-OUT file. On the other hand, if the end of the CUSTOMER file is encountered first, HIGH-VALUES is moved to CUSTOMER-NUMBER. From this point forward, the CUSTOMER-NUMBER would be *greater than* CUSTOMER-NUMBER-SORT—all remaining sales records would be identified as an error. Thus, no exceptional processing is required to handle end-of-file processing.

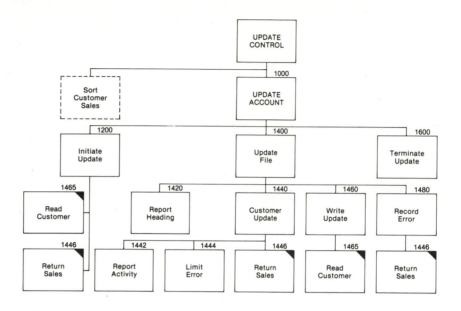

Figure 16.15 Updating a Sequential File (Hierarchy Chart) *Continued*

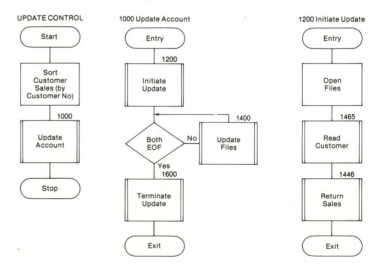

Figure 16.15 Updating a Sequential File (Module Flowcharts) *Continued*

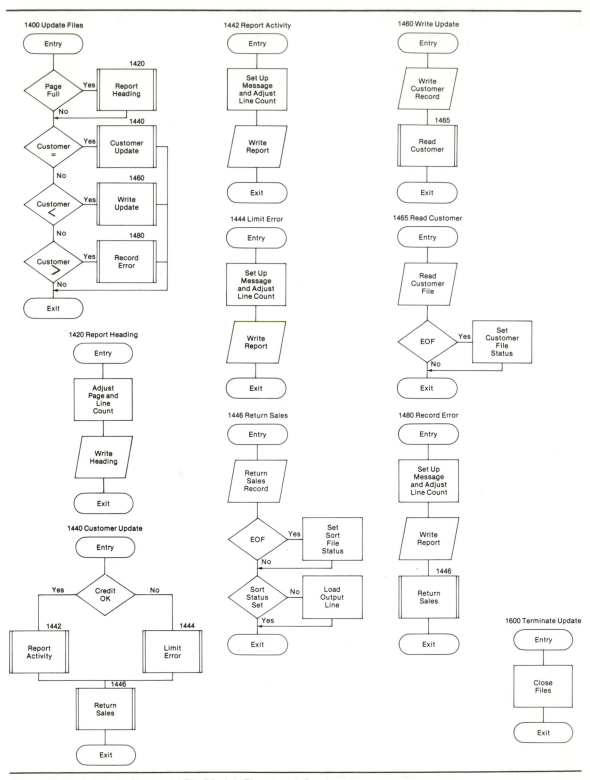

Figure 16.15 Updating a Sequential File (Module Flowcharts) *Continued*

```
|          1  1  2  2  2  3  3  4  4  5  5  6  6  6  7  7  8|
|   4   8  2  6  0  4  8  2  6  0  4  8  2  6  0  4  8  2  6  0|
------------------------------------------------------------------
|000010 IDENTIFICATION DIVISION.                                    FIG16.15|
|000020 PROGRAM-ID. SEQ-UPDATE.                                     FIG16.15|
|000030 AUTHOR. J. WAYNE SPENCE.                                    FIG16.15|
|000040 DATE-WRITTEN. JAN 1, 1981.                                  FIG16.15|
|000050 DATE-COMPILED. JAN 1, 1981.                                 FIG16.15|
|000060*     THE PURPOSE OF THIS PROCEDURE IS TO UPDATE AN EXISTING FIG16.15|
|000070*     SEQUENTIAL (CUSTOMER) FILE ON THE BASIS OF INFORMATION FIG16.15|
|000080*     CONTAINED IN A SALES FILE.  MULTIPLE UPDATES PER CUSTOMER FIG16.15|
|000090*     RECORD ARE PERMITTED AND CUSTOMER UPDATES (SALES RECORDS) FIG16.15|
|000100*     WITHOUT A CORRESPONDING CUSTOMER RECORD ARE IDENTIFIED. FIG16.15|
|000110 ENVIRONMENT DIVISION.                                       FIG16.15|
|000120 CONFIGURATION SECTION.                                      FIG16.15|
|000130 SOURCE-COMPUTER. IBM-370.                                   FIG16.15|
|000140 OBJECT-COMPUTER. IBM-370.                                   FIG16.15|
|000150 SPECIAL-NAMES.                                              FIG16.15|
|000160     C01 IS TOP-OF-PAGE.                                     FIG16.15|
|000170 INPUT-OUTPUT SECTION.                                       FIG16.15|
|000180 FILE-CONTROL.                                               FIG16.15|
|000190     SELECT CUSTOMER-SALES ASSIGN TO UT-S-SALES.             FIG16.15|
|000200     SELECT CUSTOMER ASSIGN TO UT-S-CUST.                    FIG16.15|
|000210     SELECT CUSTOMER-OUT ASSIGN TO UT-S-CUSTOUT.             FIG16.15|
|000220     SELECT SALES-SORT ASSIGN TO UT-S-SORTWK01.              FIG16.15|
|000230     SELECT EXCEPTION-REPORT ASSIGN TO UT-S-SYSPRINT.        FIG16.15|
|000240 DATA DIVISION.                                              FIG16.15|
|000250 FILE SECTION.                                               FIG16.15|
|000260 FD  CUSTOMER-SALES                                          FIG16.15|
|000270     LABEL RECORDS ARE STANDARD                              FIG16.15|
|000280     RECORD CONTAINS 80 CHARACTERS                           FIG16.15|
|000290     BLOCK CONTAINS 0 RECORDS.                               FIG16.15|
|000300 01  CUSTOMER-SALES-REC        PIC X(80).                    FIG16.15|
|000310 FD  CUSTOMER                                                FIG16.15|
|000320     LABEL RECORDS ARE STANDARD                              FIG16.15|
|000330     RECORD CONTAINS 124 CHARACTERS                          FIG16.15|
|000340     BLOCK CONTAINS 0 RECORDS.                               FIG16.15|
|000350 01  CUSTOMER-REC              PIC X(124).                   FIG16.15|
|000360 FD  CUSTOMER-OUT                                            FIG16.15|
|000370     LABEL RECORDS ARE STANDARD                              FIG16.15|
|000380     RECORD CONTAINS 124 CHARACTERS                          FIG16.15|
|000390     BLOCK CONTAINS 0 RECORDS.                               FIG16.15|
|000400 01  CUSTOMER-REC-OUT.                                       FIG16.15|
|000410     05  CUSTOMER-NUMBER       PIC X(10).                    FIG16.15|
|000420     05  CUSTOMER-NAME         PIC X(30).                    FIG16.15|
|000430     05  CUSTOMER-ADDRESS      PIC X(30).                    FIG16.15|
|000440     05  CUSTOMER-CITY         PIC X(20).                    FIG16.15|
|000450     05  CUSTOMER-STATE        PIC X(02).                    FIG16.15|
|000460     05  CUSTOMER-ZIP          PIC X(10).                    FIG16.15|
|000470     05  OUTSTANDING-BALANCE   PIC S9(9)V99.                 FIG16.15|
|000480     05  CREDIT-LIMIT          PIC S9(9)V99.                 FIG16.15|
|000490 SD  SALES-SORT.                                             FIG16.15|
|000500 01  SALES-REC-SORT.                                         FIG16.15|
|000510     05  CUSTOMER-NUMBER-SORT  PIC X(10).                    FIG16.15|
|000520     05  DATE-OF-PURCHASE.                                   FIG16.15|
|000530         10  PUR-MONTH         PIC XX.                       FIG16.15|
|000540         10  PUR-DAY           PIC XX.                       FIG16.15|
|000550         10  PUR-YEAR          PIC XX.                       FIG16.15|
|000560     05  ITEM-PURCHASED        PIC X(10).                    FIG16.15|
|000570     05  PURCHASE-AMOUNT       PIC S9(9)V99.                 FIG16.15|
|000580     05  FILLER                PIC X(43).                    FIG16.13|
|000590 FD  EXCEPTION-REPORT                                        FIG16.15|
|000600     LABEL RECORDS ARE OMITTED.                              FIG16.15|
|000610 01  REPORT-LINE               PIC X(80).                    FIG16.15|
|000620 WORKING-STORAGE SECTION.                                    FIG16.15|
|000630 01  PROGRAM-CONTROL-VARIABLES.                              FIG16.15|
|000640     05  LINE-NUMBER           PIC 9(02) VALUE 99.           FIG16.15|
|000650     05  PAGE-NUMBER           PIC 9(02) VALUE ZERO.         FIG16.15|
|000660 01  HEADING-1.                                              FIG16.15|
|000670     05  FILLER                PIC X(32) VALUE SPACES.       FIG16.15|
|000680     05  FILLER                PIC X(16) VALUE               FIG16.15|
|000690         'EXCEPTION REPORT'.                                 FIG16.15|
|000700     05  FILLER                PIC X(25) VALUE SPACES.       FIG16.15|
|000710     05  FILLER                PIC X(05) VALUE 'PAGE'.       FIG16.15|
|000720     05  PAGE-OUT              PIC Z9.                       FIG16.15|
|000730 01  HEADING-2.                                              FIG16.15|
|000740     05  FILLER                PIC X(20) VALUE               FIG16.15|
|000750         ' CUSTOMER NUMBER'.                                 FIG16.15|
|000760     05  FILLER                PIC X(50) VALUE               FIG16.15|
|000770         ' DATE    PURCHASE AMOUNT     COMMENTS'.            FIG16.15|
|000780 01  HEADING-3.                                              FIG16.15|
|000790     05  FILLER                PIC X(01) VALUE SPACES.       FIG16.15|
```

Figure 16.15 Updating a Sequential File *Continued*

```
|-----------------------------------------------------------------------|
|        1   1   2   2   2   3   3   4   4   4   5   5   6   6   6   7   7   8|
|  4   8   2   6   0   4   8   2   6   0   4   8   2   6   0   4   8   2   6   0|
|-----------------------------------------------------------------------|
|000800     05  FILLER                  PIC X(80) VALUE ALL '-'.      FIG16.15|
|000810 01  ERROR-LINE.                                              FIG16.15|
|000820     05  FILLER                  PIC X(02) VALUE SPACES.       FIG16.15|
|000830     05  CUSTOMER-NUMBER-OUT      PIC X(10).                   FIG16.15|
|000840     05  FILLER                  PIC X(08) VALUE SPACES.       FIG16.15|
|000850     05  MONTH-OUT               PIC X(02).                   FIG16.15|
|000860     05  FILLER                  PIC X(01) VALUE '/'.         FIG16.15|
|000870     05  DAY-OUT                 PIC X(02).                   FIG16.15|
|000880     05  FILLER                  PIC X(01) VALUE '/'.         FIG16.15|
|000890     05  YEAR-OUT                PIC X(02).                   FIG16.15|
|000900     05  FILLER                  PIC X(05) VALUE SPACES.       FIG16.15|
|000910     05  AMOUNT-OUT              PIC ZZZ,ZZZ,ZZZ.ZZ.          FIG16.15|
|000920     05  FILLER                  PIC X(05) VALUE SPACES.       FIG16.15|
|000930     05  MESSAGE-OUT             PIC X(50) VALUE SPACES.       FIG16.15|
|000940 PROCEDURE DIVISION.                                          FIG16.15|
|000950 UPDATE-CONTROL SECTION.                                      FIG16.15|
|000960     SORT SALES-SORT                                          FIG16.15|
|000970         ASCENDING KEY CUSTOMER-NUMBER-SORT                   FIG16.15|
|000980         USING CUSTOMER-SALES                                 FIG16.15|
|000990         OUTPUT PROCEDURE 1000-UPDATE-ACCOUNT.                FIG16.15|
|001000     STOP RUN.                                               FIG16.15|
|001010 1000-UPDATE-ACCOUNT SECTION.                                 FIG16.15|
|001020 1000-UPDATE-ACCOUNT-CONTROL.                                 FIG16.15|
|001030     PERFORM 1200-INITIATE-UPDATE.                            FIG16.15|
|001040     PERFORM 1400-UPDATE-FILE                                 FIG16.15|
|001050         UNTIL CUSTOMER-NUMBER = HIGH-VALUES                  FIG16.15|
|001060             AND CUSTOMER-NUMBER-SORT = HIGH-VALUES.          FIG16.15|
|001070     PERFORM 1600-TERMINATE-UPDATE.                           FIG16.15|
|001080 1099-EXIT.                                                   FIG16.15|
|001090     EXIT.                                                    FIG16.15|
|001100 1200-INITIATE-UPDATE SECTION.                                FIG16.15|
|001110     OPEN INPUT CUSTOMER                                      FIG16.15|
|001120         OUTPUT EXCEPTION-REPORT                              FIG16.15|
|001130             CUSTOMER-OUT.                                    FIG16.15|
|001140     PERFORM 1465-READ-CUSTOMER.                              FIG16.15|
|001150     PERFORM 1446-RETURN-SALES.                               FIG16.15|
|001160 1299-EXIT.                                                   FIG16.15|
|001170     EXIT.                                                    FIG16.15|
|001180 1400-UPDATE-FILE SECTION.                                    FIG16.15|
|001190     IF LINE-NUMBER IS GREATER THAN 40                        FIG16.15|
|001200         PERFORM 1420-REPORT-HEADING.                         FIG16.15|
|001210     IF CUSTOMER-NUMBER = CUSTOMER-NUMBER-SORT                FIG16.15|
|001220         PERFORM 1440-CUSTOMER-UPDATE                         FIG16.15|
|001230         GO TO 1499-EXIT.                                     FIG16.15|
|001240     IF CUSTOMER-NUMBER < CUSTOMER-NUMBER-SORT                FIG16.15|
|001250         PERFORM 1460-WRITE-UPDATE                            FIG16.15|
|001260         GO TO 1499-EXIT.                                     FIG16.15|
|001270     IF CUSTOMER-NUMBER > CUSTOMER-NUMBER-SORT                FIG16.15|
|001280         PERFORM 1480-RECORD-ERROR                            FIG16.15|
|001290         GO TO 1499-EXIT.                                     FIG16.15|
|001300 1420-REPORT-HEADING.                                         FIG16.15|
|001310     ADD 1 TO PAGE-NUMBER.                                    FIG16.15|
|001320     MOVE PAGE-NUMBER TO PAGE-OUT.                            FIG16.15|
|001330     MOVE 0 TO LINE-NUMBER.                                   FIG16.15|
|001340     WRITE REPORT-LINE FROM HEADING-1 AFTER ADVANCING TOP-OF-PAGE.FIG16.15|
|001350     WRITE REPORT-LINE FROM HEADING-2 AFTER ADVANCING 2 LINES. FIG16.15|
|001360     WRITE REPORT-LINE FROM HEADING-3 AFTER ADVANCING 1 LINES. FIG16.15|
|001370     MOVE SPACES TO REPORT-LINE.                              FIG16.15|
|001380     WRITE REPORT-LINE AFTER ADVANCING 1 LINES.               FIG16.15|
|001390 1440-CUSTOMER-UPDATE.                                        FIG16.15|
|001400     IF OUTSTANDING-BALANCE + PURCHASE-AMOUNT > CREDIT-LIMIT  FIG16.15|
|001410         PERFORM 1444-LIMIT-ERROR                             FIG16.15|
|001420     ELSE                                                     FIG16.15|
|001430         ADD PURCHASE-AMOUNT TO OUTSTANDING-BALANCE           FIG16.15|
|001440         PERFORM 1442-REPORT-ACTIVITY.                        FIG16.15|
|001450     PERFORM 1446-RETURN-SALES.                               FIG16.15|
|001460 1442-REPORT-ACTIVITY.                                        FIG16.15|
|001470     MOVE 'CUSTOMER RECORD UPDATED' TO MESSAGE-OUT.           FIG16.15|
|001480     WRITE REPORT-LINE FROM ERROR-LINE AFTER ADVANCING 1 LINES. FIG16.15|
|001490     ADD 1 TO LINE-NUMBER.                                    FIG16.15|
|001500 1444-LIMIT-ERROR.                                            FIG16.15|
|001510     MOVE 'CREDIT LIMIT EXCEEDED' TO MESSAGE-OUT.             FIG16.15|
|001520     WRITE REPORT-LINE FROM ERROR-LINE AFTER ADVANCING 1 LINES. FIG16.15|
|001530     ADD 1 TO LINE-NUMBER.                                    FIG16.15|
|001540 1446-RETURN-SALES.                                           FIG16.15|
|001550     RETURN SALES-SORT                                        FIG16.15|
```

Figure 16.15 Updating a Sequential File *Continued*

```
|        1   1   2   2   2   3   3   4   4   4   5   5   6   6   6   7   7   8|
|  4   8  2   6   0   4   8   2   6   0   4   8   2   6   0   4   8   2   6   0|
-----------------------------------------------------------------------------
|001560            AT END MOVE HIGH-VALUES TO CUSTOMER-NUMBER-SORT.    FIG16.15|
|001570        IF CUSTOMER-NUMBER-SORT NOT = HIGH-VALUES              FIG16.15|
|001580            MOVE CUSTOMER-NUMBER-SORT TO CUSTOMER-NUMBER-OUT    FIG16.15|
|001590            MOVE PUR-MONTH TO MONTH-OUT                         FIG16.15|
|001600            MOVE PUR-DAY TO DAY-OUT                             FIG16.15|
|001610            MOVE PUR-YEAR TO YEAR-OUT                           FIG16.15|
|001620            MOVE PURCHASE-AMOUNT TO AMOUNT-OUT.                 FIG16.15|
|001630    1460-WRITE-UPDATE.                                          FIG16.15|
|001640        WRITE CUSTOMER-REC-OUT.                                 FIG16.15|
|001650        PERFORM 1465-READ-CUSTOMER.                             FIG16.15|
|001660    1465-READ-CUSTOMER.                                         FIG16.15|
|001670        READ CUSTOMER INTO CUSTOMER-REC-OUT                     FIG16.15|
|001680            AT END MOVE HIGH-VALUES TO CUSTOMER-NUMBER.         FIG16.15|
|001690    1480-RECORD-ERROR.                                          FIG16.15|
|001700        MOVE ALL '-' TO REPORT-LINE.                            FIG16.15|
|001710        WRITE REPORT-LINE AFTER ADVANCING 2 LINES.              FIG16.15|
|001720        MOVE 'CUSTOMER RECORD NOT FOUND' TO MESSAGE-OUT.        FIG16.15|
|001730        WRITE REPORT-LINE FROM ERROR-LINE AFTER ADVANCING 1 LINES. FIG16.15|
|001740        MOVE ALL '-' TO REPORT-LINE.                            FIG16.15|
|001750        WRITE REPORT-LINE AFTER ADVANCING 1 LINES.              FIG16.15|
|001760        MOVE SPACES TO REPORT-LINE.                             FIG16.15|
|001770        WRITE REPORT-LINE AFTER ADVANCING 1 LINES.              FIG16.15|
|001780        ADD 5 TO LINE-NUMBER.                                   FIG16.15|
|001790        PERFORM 1446-RETURN-SALES.                             FIG16.15|
|001800    1499-EXIT.                                                  FIG16.15|
|001810        EXIT.                                                   FIG16.15|
|001820    1600-TERMINATE-UPDATE SECTION.                              FIG16.15|
|001830        CLOSE CUSTOMER,                                         FIG16.15|
|001840              EXCEPTION-REPORT                                  FIG16.15|
|001850              CUSTOMER-OUT.                                     FIG16.15|
```

Figure 16.15 Updating a Sequential File *Continued*

```
-----------------------------------------------------------------------------------------------------------
|        |         1         2         3         4         5         6         7         8| FIGURE  |
|RECORD|1234567890123456789012345678901234567890123456789012345678901234567890123456789012345678901234567890| NUMBER |

|    1|333333333305818144129400000044125                                                       |FIG16.15|
|    2|9X0-334RDS05158129-4331900000041232                                                     |FIG16.15|
|    3|114194410305148841933700000712911                                                       |FIG16.15|
|    4|333333333305148100005122529                                                             |FIG16.15|
|    5|41255927930501818888888888805122951 47                                                  |FIG16.15|
|    6|4412X473900501814 5-RTS00000056902                                                      |FIG16.15|
|    7|333333333306098 1BXR-3329400022212219                                                   |FIG16.15|
|    8|527021582705058100000112697                                                             |FIG16.15|
|    9|551229414805158100000004123                                                             |FIG16.15|
|   10|349896645105178199-457-33100000476110                                                   |FIG16.15|
|   11|4412X4739005228155144290220000000003312                                                 |FIG16.15|
|   12|114194410305258100000012000                                                             |FIG16.15|
```

Figure 16.15 Updating a Sequential File (Data—SALES-FILE) *Continued*

```
        1         2         3         4         5         6         7         8         9         1         1         1
                                                                                                  0         1         2
12345678901234567890123456789012345678901234567890123456789012345678901234567890123456789012345678901234567890123456789012345678901234
---------------------------------------------------------------------------------------------------------------------------------------
1RX14219-3JOHN P. VILLIMAN        8887 PEACH TREE LANE        DALLAS           TX75002    00000003143000000500000
1141944103EDWIN WILLIAMS          2139 SOUTH COLGATE STREET   PERRYTON         TX79070    00000392970000350000 0
3199127X33JAMES THOMPKINS         44339 SOUTH WACKER DRIVE    CHICAGO          IL60606    00000022918000000500000
3333333333JULIA HARRISTON         6132 MILL ROAD AVENUE       SHREVEPORT       LA63341    0000190500J00005000000
3498966451JACOB R. SULLIVAN       6134 MALIBU DRIVE           LOS ANGELES      CA96512    0000047611 00004400000
4412X47390MARSHALL SILVERMAN      2219 WEST 7TH STREET        CLEVELAND        0H30119    0000006021M00000500000
5270215827CHARLES EVEREST         8821 OCEAN PARKWAY          MIAMI            FL51332    0000011269P00000500000
6213937661JASON MADISON           8831 CEDAR DRIVE N.W.       NORWICH          CN00218    00000414523000030000 00
6427633-94MARK U. LEMON           P. O. BOX 51244             NEW YORK         NY03158    00000000000000000005000
773194221BHELEN B. OVERSTREET     3153 YELLOW BRICK ROAD      YELLOW STONE PARK MT41229   00000012842000000000000
9X0-334RDSANTHONY P. JONES        EXECUTIVE OFFICE BUILDING   WASHINGTON       DC00000    00000000000000000000000
```

Figure 16.15 Updating a Sequential File (Data—CUSTOMER-OUT) *Continued*

```
                                EXCEPTION REPORT                           PAGE   1

        CUSTOMER NUMBER      DATE       PURCHASE AMOUNT      COMMENTS
        ---------------------------------------------------------------------------------

           1141944103      05/25/81            120.00       CUSTOMER RECORD UPDATED
           1141944103      05/14/88          7,129.11       CUSTOMER RECORD UPDATED
           3333333333      05/14/81         51,225.29       CREDIT LIMIT EXCEEDED
           3333333333      05/81/81            441.25       CUSTOMER RECORD UPDATED
           3333333333      06/09/81         22,122.19       CUSTOMER RECORD UPDATED
           3498966451      05/17/81          4,761.10       CUSTOMER RECORD UPDATED
        ---------------------------------------------------------------------------------

           4125592793      05/01/81       5,122,951.47      CUSTOMER RECORD NOT FOUND
        ---------------------------------------------------------------------------------

           4412X47390      05/01/81            569.02       CUSTOMER RECORD UPDATED
           4412X47390      05/22/81             33.12       CUSTOMER RECORD UPDATED
           5270215827      05/05/81          1,126.97       CUSTOMER RECORD UPDATED
        ---------------------------------------------------------------------------------

           5512294148      05/15/81             41.23       CUSTOMER RECORD NOT FOUND
        ---------------------------------------------------------------------------------

           9X0-334RDS      05/15/81            412.32       CREDIT LIMIT EXCEEDED
        ---------------------------------------------------------------------------------
```

Figure 16.15 Updating a Sequential File (Output) *Continued*

Adding to a Sequential File

Unfortunately, files like the CUSTOMER file do not usually remain static—they are subject to changes in addition to the update process described in the previous section. For example, suppose a new customer (or series of new customers) is to be added to the file. Usually, the new customer records are interspersed with existing customer records.

As with the update process, three relationships are possible between a master CUSTOMER FILE and a transaction ADDITION FILE. These three relationships, along with probable responses, are shown in Figure 16.16. If a customer number from the CUSTOMER FILE is equal to a customer number from the ADDITION file, a duplicate record exists. If the customer number from the CUSTOMER FILE is greater than that from the ADDITION FILE, the

---

ADDITION LOGIC

(Addition of new records to an old master file based on records in a transaction file)

Key Relationship	Procedure
Master = Transaction	DUPLICATE RECORD: If no duplicates are to be allowed in the master file, write an error message indicating the attempt to add a duplicate, and read another record from the transaction file. If duplicates are to be allowed and the old master record is to appear first in the new master file, write the old record to the new master file, and read another record from the old master file. If duplicates are to be allowed and the transaction record is to appear first in the new master file, write the transaction record to the new master file, and read another transaction.
Master > Transaction	Write the transaction record to the new master file, and read another transaction record.
Master < Transaction	Write the old record to the new master file, and read another record from the old master file.

Figure 16.16 Sequential File Addition Logic

location of the record to be added has been found and the ADDITION FILE record is written. If the customer number from the CUSTOMER FILE is less than that from the ADDITION FILE, the existing customer record must be copied before proceeding by writing it to the new master file.

The program illustrated in Figure 16.17 performs the addition process. As explained in Figure 16.16, each of the three possible relationships between keys is provided in 1400-ADD-RECORDS SECTION (lines 970–1080). The end-of-file process is handled exactly the same as explained in Figure 16.15.

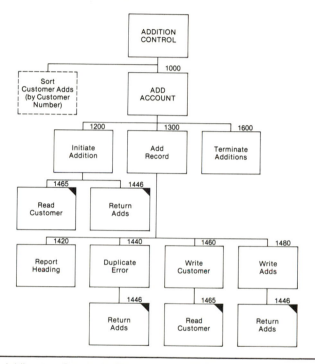

Figure 16.17 Adding to a Sequential File (Hierarchy Chart)

Figure 16.17 Adding to a Sequential File (System Flowchart) *Continued*

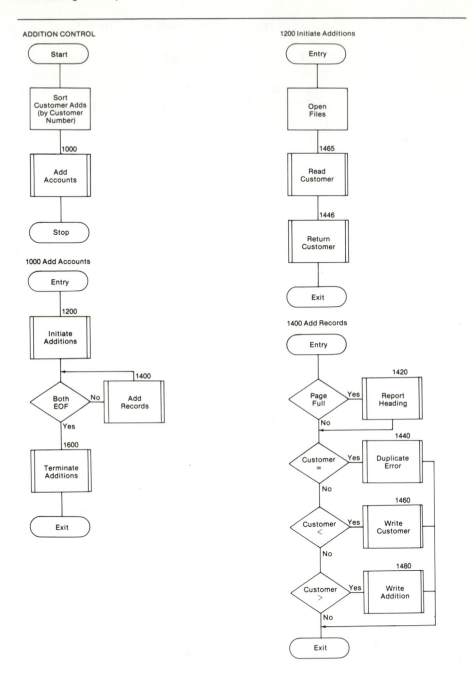

Figure 16.17 Adding to a Sequential File (Module Flowcharts) *Continued*

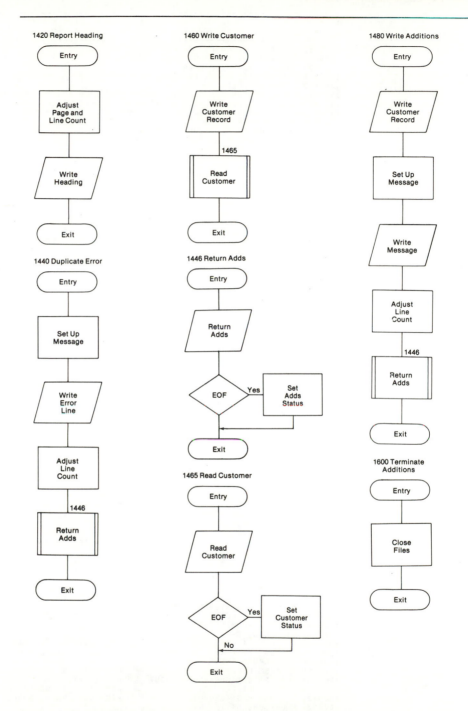

Figure 16.17 Adding to a Sequential File (Module Flowcharts) *Continued*

```
------------------------------------------------------------------------
|              1   1   2   2   3   3   4   4   4   5   5   6   6   6   7   7   8|
|      4   8   2   6   0   4   8   2   6   0   4   8   2   6   0   4   8   2   6   0|
------------------------------------------------------------------------
|000010 IDENTIFICATION DIVISION.                                        FIG16.17|
|000020 PROGRAM-ID. SEQ-ADDITION.                                       FIG16.17|
|000030 AUTHOR. J. WAYNE SPENCE.                                        FIG16.17|
|000040 DATE-WRITTEN. JAN 1, 1981.                                      FIG16.17|
|000050 DATE-COMPILED. JAN 1, 1981.                                     FIG16.17|
|000060*     THE PURPOSE OF THIS PROCEDURE IS TO ADD RECORDS (NEW CUSTOMEFIG16.17|
|000070*     TO AN EXISTING SEQUENTIAL (CUSTOMER) FILE.  THE PROCEDURE  FIG16.17|
|000080*     PROHIBITS DUPLICATE CUSTOMER RECORDS WITH THE SAME CUSTOMER FIG16.17|
|000090*     NUMBER.                                                    FIG16.17|
|000100 ENVIRONMENT DIVISION.                                           FIG16.17|
|000110 CONFIGURATION SECTION.                                          FIG16.17|
|000120 SOURCE-COMPUTER. IBM-370.                                       FIG16.17|
|000130 OBJECT-COMPUTER. IBM-370.                                       FIG16.17|
|000140 SPECIAL-NAMES.                                                  FIG16.17|
|000150     C01 IS TOP-OF-PAGE.                                         FIG16.17|
|000160 INPUT-OUTPUT SECTION.                                           FIG16.17|
|000170 FILE-CONTROL.                                                   FIG16.17|
|000180     SELECT CUSTOMER-ADDS ASSIGN TO UT-S-ADDS.                   FIG16.17|
|000190     SELECT CUSTOMER ASSIGN TO UT-S-CUST.                        FIG16.17|
|000200     SELECT CUSTOMER-OUT ASSIGN TO UT-S-CUSTOUT.                 FIG16.17|
|000210     SELECT ADDS-SORT ASSIGN TO UT-S-SORTWK01.                   FIG16.17|
|000220     SELECT EXCEPTION-REPORT ASSIGN TO UT-S-SYSPRINT.            FIG16.17|
|000230 DATA DIVISION.                                                  FIG16.17|
|000240 FILE SECTION.                                                   FIG16.17|
|000250 FD  CUSTOMER-ADDS                                               FIG16.17|
|000260     LABEL RECORDS ARE STANDARD                                  FIG16.17|
|000270     RECORD CONTAINS 124 CHARACTERS                             FIG16.17|
|000280     BLOCK CONTAINS 0 RECORDS.                                   FIG16.17|
|000290 01  CUSTOMER-ADDS-REC          PIC X(124).                      FIG16.17|
|000300 FD  CUSTOMER                                                    FIG16.17|
|000310     LABEL RECORDS ARE STANDARD                                  FIG16.17|
|000320     RECORD CONTAINS 124 CHARACTERS                             FIG16.17|
|000330     BLOCK CONTAINS 0 RECORDS.                                   FIG16.17|
|000340 01  CUSTOMER-REC.                                               FIG16.17|
|000350     05  CUSTOMER-NUMBER        PIC X(10).                       FIG16.17|
|000360     05  FILLER                 PIC X(114).                      FIG16.17|
|000370 FD  CUSTOMER-OUT                                                FIG16.17|
|000380     LABEL RECORDS ARE STANDARD                                  FIG16.17|
|000390     RECORD CONTAINS 124 CHARACTERS                             FIG16.17|
|000400     BLOCK CONTAINS 0 RECORDS.                                   FIG16.17|
|000410 01  CUSTOMER-REC-OUT           PIC X(124).                      FIG16.17|
|000420 SD  ADDS-SORT.                                                  FIG16.17|
|000430 01  ADDS-REC-SORT.                                              FIG16.17|
|000440     05  CUSTOMER-NUMBER-SORT   PIC X(10).                       FIG16.17|
|000450     05  FILLER                 PIC X(114).                      FIG16.17|
|000460 FD  EXCEPTION-REPORT                                            FIG16.17|
|000470     LABEL RECORDS ARE OMITTED.                                  FIG16.17|
|000480 01  REPORT-LINE                PIC X(80).                       FIG16.17|
|000490 WORKING-STORAGE SECTION.                                        FIG16.17|
|000500 01  PROGRAM-CONTROL-VARIABLES.                                  FIG16.17|
|000510     05  LINE-NUMBER            PIC 9(02) VALUE 99.              FIG16.17|
|000520     05  PAGE-NUMBER            PIC 9(02) VALUE ZERO.            FIG16.17|
|000530 01  HEADING-1.                                                  FIG16.17|
|000540     05  FILLER                 PIC X(32) VALUE SPACES.          FIG16.17|
|000550     05  FILLER                 PIC X(16) VALUE                  FIG16.17|
|000560     'EXCEPTION REPORT'.                                         FIG16.17|
|000570     05  FILLER                 PIC X(25) VALUE SPACES.          FIG16.17|
|000580     05  FILLER                 PIC X(05) VALUE 'PAGE'.          FIG16.17|
|000590     05  PAGE-OUT               PIC 29.                          FIG16.17|
|000600 01  HEADING-2.                                                  FIG16.17|
|000610     05  FILLER                 PIC X(20) VALUE                  FIG16.17|
|000620     ' CUSTOMER NUMBER'.                                         FIG16.17|
|000630     05  FILLER                 PIC X(50) VALUE                  FIG16.17|
|000640     'COMMENTS'.                                                 FIG16.17|
|000650 01  HEADING-3.                                                  FIG16.17|
|000660     05  FILLER                 PIC X(01) VALUE SPACES.          FIG16.17|
|000670     05  FILLER                 PIC X(80) VALUE ALL '-'.         FIG16.17|
|000680 01  ERROR-LINE.                                                 FIG16.17|
|000690     05  FILLER                 PIC X(02) VALUE SPACES.          FIG16.17|
|000700     05  CUSTOMER-NUMBER-OUT    PIC X(10).                       FIG16.17|
|000710     05  FILLER                 PIC X(08) VALUE SPACES.          FIG16.17|
|000720     05  MESSAGE-OUT            PIC X(50) VALUE SPACES.          FIG16.17|
|000730 PROCEDURE DIVISION.                                             FIG16.17|
|000740 ADDITION-CONTROL SECTION.                                       FIG16.17|
|000750     SORT ADDS-SORT                                              FIG16.17|
|000760         ASCENDING KEY CUSTOMER-NUMBER-SORT                      FIG16.17|
|000770         USING CUSTOMER-ADDS                                     FIG16.17|
```

Figure 16.17 Adding to a Sequential File *Continued*

```
|            1  1     2     2     2     3     3     4     4     4     5     5     6     6     6     7     7     8|
|    4     8  2  6     0     4     8     2     6     0     4     8     2     6     0     4     8     2     6     0|
----------------------------------------------------------------------------------------------------------------
|000780          OUTPUT PROCEDURE 1000-UPDATE-ACCOUNT.                                                  FIG16.17|
|000790       STOP RUN.                                                                                 FIG16.17|
|000800  1000-UPDATE-ACCOUNT SECTION.                                                                   FIG16.17|
|000810  1000-UPDATE-ACCOUNT-CONTROL.                                                                   FIG16.17|
|000820       PERFQRM 1200-INITIATE-ADDITION.                                                           FIG16.17|
|000830       PERFORM 1400-ADD-RECORDS                                                                  FIG16.17|
|000840          UNTIL CUSTOMER-NUMBER = HIGH-VALUES                                                     FIG16.17|
|000850             AND CUSTOMER-NUMBER-SORT = HIGH-VALUES.                                              FIG16.17|
|000860       PERFORM 1600-TERMINATE-ADDITION.                                                          FIG16.17|
|000870  1099-EXIT.                                                                                     FIG16.17|
|000880       EXIT.                                                                                     FIG16.17|
|000890  1200-INITIATE-ADDITION SECTION.                                                                FIG16.17|
|000900       OPEN INPUT CUSTOMER                                                                       FIG16.17|
|000910            OUTPUT EXCEPTION-REPORT                                                               FIG16.17|
|000920                   CUSTOMER-OUT.                                                                  FIG16.17|
|000930       PERFORM 1465-READ-CUSTOMER.                                                                FIG16.17|
|000940       PERFORM 1446-RETURN-ADDS.                                                                  FIG16.17|
|000950  1299-EXIT.                                                                                     FIG16.17|
|000960       EXIT.                                                                                     FIG16.17|
|000970  1400-ADD-RECORDS SECTION.                                                                      FIG16.17|
|000980       IF LINE-NUMBER IS GREATER THAN 40                                                         FIG16.17|
|000990          PERFORM 1420-REPORT-HEADING.                                                           FIG16.17|
|001000       IF CUSTOMER-NUMBER = CUSTOMER-NUMBER-SORT                                                 FIG16.17|
|001010          PERFORM 1440-DUPLICATE-ERROR                                                           FIG16.17|
|001020          GO TO 1499-EXIT.                                                                       FIG16.17|
|001030       IF CUSTOMER-NUMBER < CUSTOMER-NUMBER-SORT                                                 FIG16.17|
|001040          PERFORM 1460-WRITE-CUSTOMER                                                            FIG16.17|
|001050          GO TO 1499-EXIT.                                                                       FIG16.17|
|001060       IF CUSTOMER-NUMBER > CUSTOMER-NUMBER-SORT                                                 FIG16.17|
|001070          PERFORM 1480-WRITE-ADDITION                                                            FIG16.17|
|001080          GO TO 1499-EXIT.                                                                       FIG16.17|
|001090  1420-REPORT-HEADING.                                                                           FIG16.17|
|001100       ADD 1 TO PAGE-NUMBER.                                                                     FIG16.17|
|001110       MOVE PAGE-NUMBER TO PAGE-OUT.                                                             FIG16.17|
|001120       MOVE 0 TO LINE-NUMBER.                                                                    FIG16.17|
|001130       WRITE REPORT-LINE FROM HEADING-1 AFTER ADVANCING TOP-OF-PAGE.FIG16.17|
|001140       WRITE REPORT-LINE FROM HEADING-2 AFTER ADVANCING 2 LINES.    FIG16.17|
|001150       WRITE REPORT-LINE FROM HEADING-3 AFTER ADVANCING 1 LINES.    FIG16.17|
|001160       MOVE SPACES TO REPORT-LINE.                                                               FIG16.17|
|001170       WRITE REPORT-LINE AFTER ADVANCING 1 LINES.                                                FIG16.17|
|001180  1440-DUPLICATE-ERROR.                                                                          FIG16.17|
|001190       MOVE CUSTOMER-NUMBER-SORT TO CUSTOMER-NUMBER-OUT.                                         FIG16.17|
|001200       MOVE 'ATTEMPT TO ADD A DUPLICATE RECORD' TO MESSAGE-OUT.                                  FIG16.17|
|001210       WRITE REPORT-LINE FROM ERROR-LINE AFTER 2.                                                FIG16.17|
|001220       ADD 2 TO LINE-NUMBER.                                                                     FIG16.17|
|001230       PERFORM 1446-RETURN-ADDS.                                                                 FIG16.17|
|001240  1446-RETURN-ADDS.                                                                              FIG16.17|
|001250       RETURN ADDS-SORT                                                                          FIG16.17|
|001260          AT END MOVE HIGH-VALUES TO CUSTOMER-NUMBER-SORT.                                       FIG16.17|
|001270  1460-WRITE-CUSTOMER.                                                                           FIG16.17|
|001280       WRITE CUSTOMER-REC-OUT FROM CUSTOMER-REC.                                                 FIG16.17|
|001290       PERFORM 1465-READ-CUSTOMER.                                                               FIG16.17|
|001300  1465-READ-CUSTOMER.                                                                            FIG16.17|
|001310       READ CUSTOMER                                                                             FIG16.17|
|001320          AT END MOVE HIGH-VALUES TO CUSTOMER-NUMBER.                                            FIG16.17|
|001330  1480-WRITE-ADDITION.                                                                           FIG16.17|
|001340       WRITE CUSTOMER-REC-OUT FROM ADDS-REC-SORT.                                                FIG16.17|
|001350       MOVE CUSTOMER-NUMBER-SORT TO CUSTOMER-NUMBER-OUT.                                         FIG16.17|
|001360       MOVE 'CUSTOMER RECORD ADDED' TO MESSAGE-OUT.                                              FIG16.17|
|001370       WRITE REPORT-LINE FROM ERROR-LINE AFTER ADVANCING 2 LINES.                                FIG16.17|
|001380       ADD 2 TO LINE-NUMBER.                                                                     FIG16.17|
|001390       PERFORM 1446-RETURN-ADDS.                                                                 FIG16.17|
|001400  1499-EXIT.                                                                                     FIG16.17|
|001410       EXIT.                                                                                     FIG16.17|
|001420  1600-TERMINATE-ADDITION SECTION.                                                               FIG16.17|
|001430       CLOSE CUSTOMER,                                                                           FIG16.17|
|001440             EXCEPTION-REPORT                                                                    FIG16.17|
|001450             CUSTOMER-OUT.                                                                       FIG16.17|
```

Figure 16.17 Adding to a Sequential File *Continued*

```
         1         2         3         4         5         6         7         8         9         1         1         1
         1234567890123456789012345678901234567890123456789012345678901234567890123456789012345678901234567890123456789012345678901234
-------------------------------------------------------------------------------------------------------------------------------------
X14339-278ROGER P. EVANS             1422 N. W. CLASSEN BLVD.    OKLAHOMA CITY   OK65124    00000000000000000300000
2199428878STEWART A. ALEXANDER       5112 HAMILTON PARKWAY       MINNEAPOLIS     MN21132    00000622390000001000000
3333333333GEORGE P. MARTIN           LAS VEGAS HILTON            LAS VEGAS       NV81222    99999999999000000000000
5122314151MARK R. WHITE              55123 WAR MEMORIAL DRIVE    CLEVELAND       OH41229    00000041233000000050000
```

Figure 16.17 Adding to a Sequential File (Data—CUSTOMER-ADDS) *Continued*

```
       1         2         3         4         5         6         7         8         9         1         1         1
                                                                                                     0         1         2
1234567890123456789012345678901234567890123456789012345678901234567890123456789012345678901234567890123456789012345678901234
1RX14219-3JOHN P. VILLIMAN           8887 PEACH TREE LANE        DALLAS            TX75002   00000003143000000500000
1141944103EDWIN WILLIAMS            2139 SOUTH COLGATE STREET   PERRYTON          TX79070   00000331933000035000000
3199127X33JAMES THOMPKINS           44339 SOUTH WACKER DRIVE    CHICAGO           IL60606   00000022918000000500000
3333333333JULIA HARRISTON           6132 MILL ROAD AVENUE       SHREVEPORT        LA63341   00000351343000005000000
3498966451JACOB R. SULLIVAN         6134 MALIBU DRIVE           LOS ANGELES       CA96512   00000000000000000440000
4412X47390MARSHALL SILVERMAN        2219 WEST 7TH STREET        CLEVELAND         OH30119   00000000000000000500000
5270215827CHARLES EVEREST           8821 OCEAN PARKWAY          MIAMI             FL51332   00000000000000000500000
6213937661JASON MADISON             8831 CEDAR DRIVE N.W.       NORWICH           CN00218   00000414523000030000000
6427633-94MARK U. LEMON             P. O. BOX 51244             NEW YORK          NY03158   00000000000000000005000
773194221BHELEN B. OVERSTREET       3153 YELLOW BRICK ROAD      YELLOW STONE PARK MT41229   00000012842000000000000
9X0-334RDSANTHONY P. JONES          EXECUTIVE OFFICE BUILDING   WASHINGTON        DC00000   00000000000000000000000
```

Figure 16.17 Adding to a Sequential File (Data—CUSTOMER-OUT) *Continued*

```
                                            EXCEPTION REPORT                              PAGE  1

        CUSTOMER NUMBER       COMMENTS
        ---------------------------------------------------------------------------------

          X14339-278          CUSTOMER RECORD ADDED

          2199428878          CUSTOMER RECORD ADDED

          3333333333          ATTEMPT TO ADD A DUPLICATE RECORD

          5122314151          CUSTOMER RECORD ADDED
```

Figure 16.17 Adding to a Sequential File (Output) *Continued*

Deleting from a Sequential File

Often, we will also have to delete existing records. For example, customers may go out of business, choose not to do business with us, or move away. In any case, if we continually add to a file without periodically eliminating unneeded records, our file would grow until it became unmanageable. Figure 16.18 illustrates the deletion process based, again, on the three primary relationships between keys. If the customer number from the CUSTOMER FILE is

---

DELETION LOGIC

(Delete an existing record from the master file
based on the key of a transaction file record)

Key Relationship	Procedure
Master = Transaction	If duplicates *do not* exist in the master file, read a new transaction record *and* another record from the old master file.
	If duplicates *do* exist in the master file and all records with a specified key are to be deleted, read the next record from the old master file and indicate the transaction has been employed.
Master > Transaction	If duplicates do not exist in the master file, write an error (the transaction key value was not found), and read another transaction record.
	If duplicates exist and were to be deleted from the master file, check to determine whether or not the transaction key has been employed. If the transaction key was not used, execute the same sequence perform the operations as defined for files without duplicates. If the transaction key has been used, read the next transaction record.
Master < Transaction	Write the old master record to the new master file and read the next record from the old master file.

Figure 16.18 Sequential File Deletion Logic

equal to the customer number of the DELETE FILE, we have located the record to be deleted. Deletion is accomplished by *not writing* the record to the new CUSTOMER FILE. Since both records, in effect have been dealt with, it is necessary to read a record from both the old CUSTOMER FILE *and* the DELETE FILE. If the customer number of the CUSTOMER FILE is greater than that of the DELETE FILE, it is not in the CUSTOMER FILE. Then, an error message is to be written and a new record from the DELETE FILE is to be read. If the customer number of the CUSTOMER FILE is less than that of the DELETE FILE, the customer record is copied to the new CUSTOMER FILE, and another record from the old CUSTOMER FILE is read.

The process described above causes the *physical deletion* of a record; however, it might be desired to suspend or *logically delete* a record. In that case, the deletion process is the same as the update process. The update would cause an alteration of an existing field (the customer name field might be replaced with the word *DELETE*). Thus, the record would still be in the file. A much more likely circumstance is that a special field representing record status would be added to the record description during the initial development of the customer records system. Thus, the customer record might be 125 bytes or more. The extra space would be used to record the status of individual customers. However, since the record would still be present in the file, it would be read along with other records. Therefore, the programmer's code would have to be modified to reflect that deleted records should be read and bypassed, if found.

Sequential File Processing with Magnetic Disk

All of the processes previously described may be performed either on magnetic tape or disk. However, we have additional latitude with magnetic disk. Recall from the first part of this chapter that a mass storage device (e.g., magnetic disk) can be OPENed in an *I-O* mode. That is, records may be read or written in one procedure (without virtue of multiple open and close statements). This additional capability only impacts the update (and perhaps logical deletion) process. File building, adding new records, and physically deleting records remains the same.

When a disk file is opened I-O, it is assumed that updates will be placed in the existing master file, i.e., records will be read from the master file, changed, and rewritten. Most systems require a special statement to perform this rewriting (or *overwriting*) process. The REWRITE statement, as illustrated in Figure 16.19, performs this function. (Check your compiler to determine which statement causes the rewriting function.) The function of the REWRITE statement, like the WRITE statement, is to cause data to be written to a device. (In the case of a REWRITE statement, the device is magnetic disk or other mass storage medium.) However, while the WRITE statement directs the *next* record to be written to a file, the REWRITE statement for a file causes the *last*

```
REWRITE record-name  [FROM identifier]
```

Figure 16.19 The REWRITE Statement (for Sequential Files)

record READ to be overwritten. Consequently, during the update process, it would no longer be necessary to write a record if it were not changed, eliminating the "copying" operation. Therefore, the logic of the update process would require that a status field be updated each time a record is changed. Then, when the master file key is less than the transaction file key, it would be necessary to determine whether or not the status field showed a change for the existing record. If not, the next master record is read. If the status field indicated a change, the existing record would be rewritten, the status field would be changed for the new record, and the next master record would be read. All other operations would remain the same.

Summary

In this chapter, the COBOL statements and the logic necessary to perform sequential file processing on magnetic tape or disk have been illustrated. Modifications to the OPEN, CLOSE, and WRITE statements may become useful to accomplish certain tasks related to sequential file processing. Furthermore, the characteristics of the ENVIRONMENT and DATA DIVISIONs may be slightly altered to handle data more efficiently. An example of the more efficient manipulation of data from sequential files is the use of the BLOCK CONTAINS clause to record multiple logical records per physical record. Finally, the logic and procedure necessary to build, update, add records, and delete records in a sequential file were presented.

Notes on Programming Style

The structure presented in this chapter can be improved upon in a couple of ways. For example, the end-of-file processing illustrated in the programs in this chapter could be handled more efficiently by a specialized routine to copy records, identify errors, or add records. Specialized routines would be more efficient because a decision on the relationship of keys would not have to be established.

A second modification of the procedures illustrated might be a change to the paragraph level for the decision-making (key comparison) process. It would be possible to have a single paragraph perform the same function that a SECTION performed and eliminate the GO TO statements causing an unconditional branch to the exit. One word of caution is necessary. If you choose to use a "fall through" procedure (checking the next decision in the key relationship sequence regardless of whether or not a previous decision was true), the equality relationship should be the first test. Otherwise, it is possible to have both the master key and the transaction key assigned HIGH-VALUES, and therefore the test would presume a valid relationship for illegal data—an error!

Questions

Below, fill in the blank(s) with the appropriate word, words, or phrases.

1. Data which are recorded on _____ can be erased.

2. Relative to punched card and printed output devices, data is transmitted at a _____ rate than when compared to the transmission rate of magnetic media.

3. In terms of storage space, data stored on magnetic media requires _____ than the equivalent data stored on punched cards.

4. One _____ record may contain one or more _____ records.

5. Relative to the length of a physical record, one buffer is (longer than, the same size as, shorter than) _____ a buffer.

6. Two reasons for blocking a data file are _____ and _____ .

7. An unblocked file means _____ (number) logical record per physical record.

8. On a magnetic medium, a(n) _____ separates two physical records.

9. Data stored on magnetic disk is recorded around concentric rings called _____ .

10. An input-output interrupt is generated each time the CPU interfaces with a(n) _____ .

11. A diagram that illustrates the types of devices (or media) to be interfaced to a procedure (program) is called a(n) _____ .

12. The _____ clause of the DATA DIVISION is used to control the number of logical records per physical record; the _____ clause of the ENVIRONMENT DIVSION is used to control the number of buffers per file.

13. A disk file can be opened in the _____ , _____ , or _____ mode.

14. Before a file can be read, it must first be opened in the _____ mode and written.

15. If a magnetic media file is closed, without the use of any special options, the file is _____ .

16. Under the strictest definition of a sequential file, the records in the file must be _____ related to each other.

17. For processing purposes, a sequential file is generally _____ before file manipulation begins.

18. The statement that causes records to be placed in a file is the _____ statement.

19. A process known as _____ results in the modification or change in the existing records of a sequential file.

20. The three relationships that should be tested between a master key and a transaction key to determine the appropriate process are _____, _____, and _____.

21. The process of incorporating new records into an existing file is often referred to as _____ .

22. The process of eliminating existing records from a file that are no longer needed is referred to as _____ .

23. A _____ statement is capable of overwriting existing data in a magnetic disk file.

Answer the following questions by circling either "T" for True or "F" for False.

T	F	24. A punched card record is 80 bytes long even if only 50 columns are used.
T	F	25. A logical record on magnetic tape must be less than 500 bytes in length.
T	F	26. A block can contain more than one physical record.
T	F	27. A block can contain more than one logical record.
T	F	28. Physical records on magnetic disk are separated by an area called an inter-record gap.
T	F	29. A buffer may contain one or more physical records.
T	F	30. Data may be transmitted to the CPU from magnetic tape faster than the CPU is capable of handling it.
T	F	31. A logical record is the same as a physical record.
T	F	32. Magnetic tape is a more compact medium than punched cards.
T	F	33. The ACCESS MODE clause is required in the ENVIRONMENT DIVISION for sequential files.
T	F	34. More than two files may be ASSIGNed in one program.
T	F	35. A program flowchart and a system flowchart serve the same purpose.
T	F	36. The number of logical records per physical record is controlled by the REVERSE clause.
T	F	37. The number of logical records per physical record is controlled by the RECORD CONTAINS clause.
T	F	38. The DATA RECORDS clause is required when two or more record descriptions are recorded for a single file.
T	F	39. The LABEL RECORDS clause is required for sequential files.
T	F	40. When a file is LOCKed on the CLOSE statement, it means the file may not be used again in the same program.
T	F	41. A WRITE statement that transmits data to a magnetic disk file would normally have a BEFORE/AFTER ADVANCING clause.
T	F	42. A file may be opened in an I-O mode before it has been created.
T	F	43. The READ statement used to get data from a sequential tape file uses the same format as the READ statement used to get data from a punched card file.
T	F	44. To update a file means to change some characteristic of an existing record or series of records.
T	F	45. A file which is referred to as a MASTER file is the same as a TRANSACTION file.
T	F	46. To be processed correctly for an update process, the master file must be ordered on an ascending basis.
T	F	47. If, during the addition process, the master key and the transaction key are the same value, it means that a duplicate record is about to be added to the master file.
T	F	48. A record is physically deleted from a sequential file by not writing it to the new file.
T	F	49. Logically deleted records are the same as physically deleted records.
T	F	50. Record addition for a magnetic tape file is fundamentally different from the addition process for a magnetic disk file.

Problems

1. We are requested to develop a system capable of processing inventory records. The system is to be limited to four procedures:

   a. building an inventory file from data,
   b. adding to an existing inventory file,
   c. updating an inventory file from sales records, and
   d. producing an inventory reorder report.

   The relationships among these processes is presented in the System Flowchart for inventory processing.

   ### Part A. Building an Inventory File

   The system flowchart indicates that an inventory file (for processing purposes) is to be developed. An inventory data file is to be provided as input to the process. (See the multiple-card layout form of an inventory record. The same record format will be used for all procedures, except that the record is to be expanded to 200 bytes—a FILLER at the end of the record— to accommodate future applications using the inventory file.) The procedure is to order the data by item number, vendor, and outlet. Individual item numbers, vendors, and outlets will not necessarily be unique; however, if coupled together an item number-vendor-outlet set should be unique. If a particular item number-vendor-outlet set is not unique, it is a duplicate record and only the first such record should be placed in the inventory file. The creation report should reflect all duplicates. Only the item number, vendor, and outlet number need appear on the report. In addition, the number of records placed in the file should appear on the report. Use your judgment in the design of the report from the standpoint of headings, page numbers, etc.

   ### Part B. Adding to the Inventory File

   The second procedure illustrated in the system flowchart is to perform an addition operation. The records in the Addition file are in the same format as those in the inventory data file. The process should cause new records to be placed in the inventory file in their appropriate position (relative to item number-vendor-outlet number keys). The data file is not ordered on any particular basis. The Addition Report is to reflect any attempt to add a duplicate record to the file. Like the Creation Report, it is only necessary to identify the duplicate records by item number, vendor and outlet number fields. Duplicate records should not be added to the file.

   ### Part C. Updating the Inventory File

   The third procedure is to perform an update operation on the basis of data found in the Sales file. (See the record format of a sales record. The data in this file is not ordered in any particular way.) Multiple updates for a single inventory record are possible as well as no update for a particular inventory record.

   The update procedure should accommodate the following operations (if matching item number-vendor-outlet number keys are found in both the inventory and sales files):

   a. *Provided the on-hand amount of the inventory record is not less than the quantity sold*, subtract the quantity sold from the amount on hand.
   b. Record the date of (last) sale from the sales file to the date of last sale in the inventory file. The date should be changed only if it is a more current date.

c. Add the quantity sold to the year-to-date and month-to-date sales in units field.
d. Adjust the year-to-date and month-to-date sales in dollars fields. The amount of adjustment is the quantity sold multiplied by the price per unit.
e. Adjust the year-to-date and month-to-date cost in dollars fields. The amount of the adjustment is the quantity sold multiplied by the cost per unit.

If the quantity sold is greater than the on-hand amount, *no update is to be performed.* That is, all fields of the record should be exactly the same both before and after processing the sales record.

Examine the report layout to determine the requirements of this procedure from the standpoint of printed output.

Part D. Producing a Reorder Report

The final procedure in the system is to produce a report indicating those inventory items for which the on-hand amount is either equal to or less than the minimum stock level (reorder point). The data printed on this report should be ordered by vendor, item number, and outlet. Each vendor should begin on a separate page. See the multiple-card layout form for additional details of the Reorder Report.

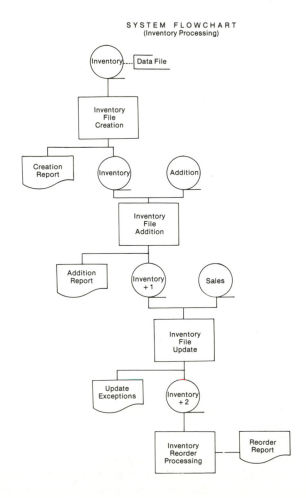

SYSTEM FLOWCHART
(Inventory Processing)

MULTIPLE-CARD LAYOUT FORM

Company LEARNING COBOL, INC.

Application INVENTORY PROCESSING   by J. Wayne Spence   Date 01/01/81   Job No. PROB 16.1   Sheet No. 1

Inventory Record

ITEM NUMBER	VENDOR CODE	ITEM DESCRIPTION	PRODUCT GROUP	OUTLET NUMBER	UNITS ON HAND	MINIMUM STOCK LEVEL	PRICE PER UNIT	COST PER UNIT	MEASURE.	
9 9 9 9 9 9	9 9 9	9 9 9 9 9 9 9 9 9 9 9 9 9 9 9 9 9 9 9 9 9 9 9 9 9 9 9 9 9 9 9	9 9 9	9 9 9	9 9 9 9 9	9 9 9 9 9	9 9 9 9 9 9 9	9 9 9 9 9 9 9	9 9 9	9
1 2 3 4 5 6	7 8 9	10 11 12 13 14 15 16 17 18 19 20 21 22 23 24 25 26 27 28 29 30 31 32 33 34 35 36 37 38 39	40 41 42 43 44	45 46 47 48 49	50 51 52 53 54 55	56 57 58 59 60 61	62 63 64 65 66 67 68 69	70 71 72 73 74 75 76 77	78 79 80	

(Inventory Record Continued--Bytes 81 - 160)

DATE LAST PURCHASE	DATE LAST RECEIVED	PURCHASE QUANTITY	DATE LAST SOLD	YTD SALES (UNITS)	YTD SALES (DOLLARS)	YTD COST (DOLLARS)	MTD SALES (UNITS)	MTD SALES (DOLLARS)
9 9 9 9 9	9 9 9 9 9 9	9 9 9 9 9 9	9 9 9 9 9 9	9 9 9 9 9 9 9 9 9	9 9 9 9 9 9 9 9 9 9 9	9 9 9 9 9 9 9 9 9 9 9	9 9 9 9 9 9 9 9 9	9 9 9 9 9 9 9 9 9 9 9 9 9
1 2 3 4 5	6 7 8 9 10 11	12 13 14 15 16 17	18 19 20 21 22 23	24 25 26 27 28 29 30 31 32 33	34 35 36 37 38 39 40 41 42 43 44 45	46 47 48 49 50 51 52 53 54 55 56	57 58 59 60 61 62 63 64 65 66 67	68 69 70 71 72 73 74 75 76 77 78 79 80

(Inventory Record Continued--Bytes 161 - 171)

MTD COST (DOLLARS)	
9 9 9 9 9 9 9 9 9 9 9	9 9 9 9 9 9 9 9 9 9 9 9 9 9 9 9 9 9 9 9 9 9 9 9 9 9 9 9 9 9 9 9 9 9 9 9 9 9 9 9 9 9 9 9 9 9 9 9 9 9 9 9 9 9 9 9 9 9 9 9 9 9 9 9 9 9 9 9 9
1 2 3 4 5 6 7 8 9 10 11	12 13 14 15 16 17 18 19 20 21 22 23 24 25 26 27 28 29 30 31 32 33 34 35 36 37 38 39 40 41 42 43 44 45 46 47 48 49 50 51 52 53 54 55 56 57 58 59 60 61 62 63 64 65 66 67 68 69 70 71 72 73 74 75 76 77 78 80

MULTIPLE-CARD LAYOUT FORM

Company LEARNING COBOL, INC.

Application INVENTORY PROCESSING   by J. Wayne Spence   Date 01/01/81   Job No. PROB 16.1   Sheet No. 1

Sales Record

CUSTOMER NUMBER	SALESMAN CODE	ITEM NUMBER	VENDOR CODE	OUTLET NUMBER	QUANTITY SOLD	DATE OF SALE	
9 9 9 9 9 9	9 9 9	9 9 9 9 9 9	9 9 9	9 9 9	9 9 9 9 9 9	9 9 9 9 9 9	9 9 9 9 9 9 9 9 9 9 9 9 9 9 9 9 9 9 9 9 9 9 9 9 9 9 9 9 9 9 9 9 9 9 9 9 9 9 9 9 9 9 9 9 9
1 2 3 4 5 6	7 8 9	10 11 12 13 14 15	16 17 18	19 20 21 22 23	24 25 26 27 28 29	30 31 32 33 34 35	36 37 38 39 40 41 42 43 44 45 46 47 48 49 50 51 52 53 54 55 56 57 58 59 60 61 62 63 64 65 66 67 68 69 70 71 72 73 74 75 76 77 78 79 80

	9 9 9 9 9 9 9 9 9 9 9 9 9 9 9 9 9 9 9 9 9 9 9 9 9 9 9 9 9 9 9 9 9 9 9 9 9 9 9 9 9 9 9 9 9 9 9 9 9 9 9 9 9 9 9 9 9 9 9 9 9 9 9 9 9 9 9 9 9 9 9 9 9 9 9 9 9 9 9 9
	1 2 3 4 5 6 7 8 9 10 11 12 13 14 15 16 17 18 19 20 21 22 23 24 25 26 27 28 29 30 31 32 33 34 35 36 37 38 39 40 41 42 43 44 45 46 47 48 49 50 51 52 53 54 55 56 57 58 59 60 61 62 63 64 65 66 67 68 69 70 71 72 73 74 75 76 77 78 79 80

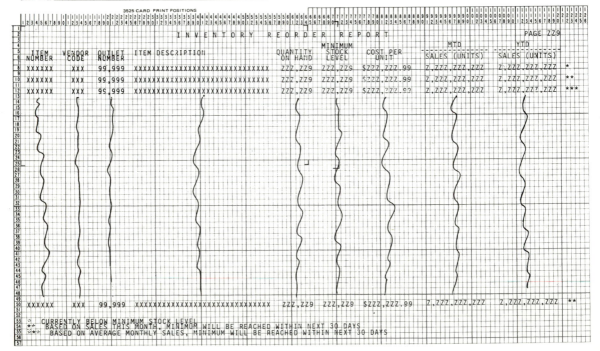

2. You are to create a system including all the properties illustrated in the attached System Flowchart for Customer Processing. This processing consists of four parts:

Part A: Building the Customer File

The record layout of the data in this file is shown in the multiple-card layout form. The data should be ordered by customer number to create the Customer File. The format of the Customer File should be the same as shown in the multiple-card layout form. The Creation Report should be generated in customer number order. The report should identify duplicate customer numbers, and duplicates should be eliminated from the file. In addition, any customer record for which the past due balance is greater than zero should be printed on the report, along with the values of the outstanding balance. (The outstanding balance is the sum of 30-day, 60-day, and 90-day balances.)

Part B: Add Records to the Customer File

The Addition file contains records in the same format as the Customer File. The records in the Addition file should be added in the appropriate location in the Customer File with respect to the customer number field. The Addition file is in no particular order. The Addition Report should identify all attempts to add a duplicate record. When all additions have attempted, the Addition Report should indicate the number of records which were in the original Customer File, the number of records added to the new Customer File, the number of duplicate records rejected, and the total number of records in the new Customer File.

Part C: Update the Customer File

The customer file is to be updated using a series of sales records. The graphic record layout of records which are in the sales file is given in problem #1. The fields in the customer record to be updated are in current balance and date of last purchase. The QUANTITY SOLD field of the sales record is to be interpreted as a dollars and cents field representing the amount of purchase. This value is to be added to the current-balance field. The date-of-last-purchase field in the customer record is to be replaced by the date-of-purchase field in the sales record (provided the sales record contains the more current date). The Update Report is to identify each customer record updated, the number of updates for the individual record and the total new sales posted to the customer record (current balance field).

Part D: Customer Accounts Receivable Processing

After the other processes have been completed, an Accounts Receivable Report is to be produced (see the print chart) by the total value of receivables. A customer record is to appear on the Accounts Receivable Report only if the customer has an outstanding balance.

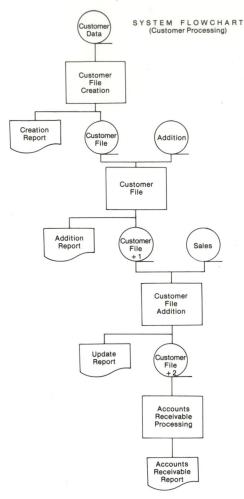

SYSTEM FLOWCHART
(Customer Processing)

MULTIPLE-CARD LAYOUT FORM

Company	LEARNING COBOL, INC.

Application CUSTOMER PROCESS   by J. Wayne Spence   Date 01/01/81   Job No. PROB 16.2   Sheet No. 1

Customer Record

CUSTOMER NUMBER	LAST NAME	FIRST NAME	MIDDLE NAME	STREET ADDRESS/P O BOX
999999	999999999999999	999999999999999	99999999999999	9999999999999999999999999999999
1 2 3 4 5 6	7 8 9 10 11 12 13 14 15 16 17 18 19 20 21	22 23 24 25 26 27 28 29 30 31 32 33 34 35 36	37 38 39 40 41 42 43 44 45 46 47 48 49 50 51	52 53 54 55 56 57 58 59 60 61 62 63 64 65 66 67 68 69 70 71 72 73 74 75 76 77 78 79 80

(Customer Record Continued--Bytes 81 - 160)

CITY	STATE	ZIP CODE	CURRENT BALANCE	30-DAY BALANCE	60-DAY BALANCE	90-DAY BALANCE	DATE LAST STMT
9999999999999999999999	99	9999999999	999999999	99999999	99999999	99999999	9999999
1 2 3 4 5 6 7 8 9 10 11 12 13 14 15 16 17 18 19 20 21	22 23	24 25 26 27 28 29 30 31 32 33	34 35 36 37 38 39 40 41 42 43	44 45 46 47 48 49 50 51 52 53	54 55 56 57 58 59 60 61 62 63	64 65 66 67 68 69 70 71 72 73	74 75 76 77 78 79 80

(Customer Record Continued--Bytes 161 - 171)

DATE LAST PAYMENT	DATE LAST PURCHASE	
99999	99999	9999999999999999999999999999999999999999999999999999999999999999999999
1 2 3 4 5	6 7 8 9 10 11	12 13 14 15 16 17 18 19 20 21 22 23 24 25 26 27 28 29 30 31 32 33 34 35 36 37 38 39 40 41 42 43 44 45 46 47 48 49 50 51 52 53 54 55 56 57 58 59 60 61 62 63 64 65 66 67 68 69 70 71 72 73 74 75 76 77 78 79 80

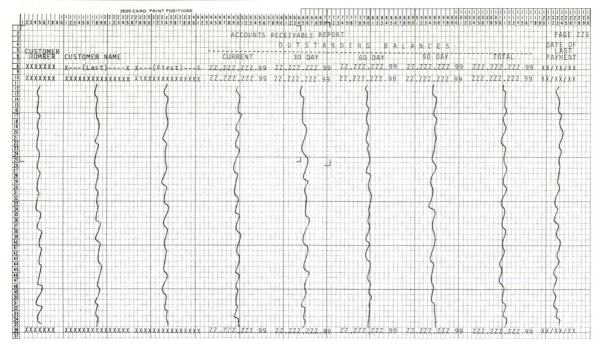

3. We are requested by the inventory control manager to perform processing of purchase order records for inventory records. The processing requirements are in four parts.

Part A: Building an Inventory File

We are to build an inventory file using inventory data. Use the record layout and processing requirements of Part A in problem #1.

Part B: Process Purchase Orders

We are to update the inventory records to reflect the receipt of purchased inventory items. That is, we have ordered from our vendors to replenish quantities on hand. The records in the purchase-order file are in no particular order. When we find a matching inventory item (by item number, vendor, and outlet number), we are to perform the following update sequence:

a. add the quantity in the purchase-order record to the on-hand field of the inventory record.
b. replace the date last purchased of the inventory record with the date of purchase of the purchase-order record (provided the purchase-order date is more current than the existing date of last purchase).

The Purchase-Order Report is to reflect the update activity. That is, the Purchase-Order Report should indicate all inventory records updated, the change in the on-hand amount, and any purchase orders for which an inventory record cannot be located. Finally, the report should indicate whether or not the inventory record still falls into the reorder category (minimum stock level greater than on-hand quantity) after all updates have been completed.

Part C: Inventory Record Addition/Deletion

The Add/Delete File is an unordered file containing records to be either added to or deleted from the inventory file. The format of the records in the Add/Delete File is the same as the inventory record. Records to be added will have data in all fields. Records to be deleted will have data only in the item number, vendor, and outlet fields—all other fields will be blank. The Add/Delete Report should reflect the consequence of each add/delete record. Do not add duplicate records. It is possible that a record to be deleted may not exist.

Part D: Inventory Reorder Processing

Complete Part D as specified for problem #1.

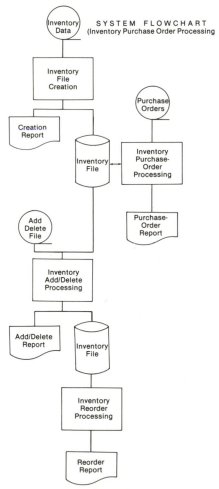

SYSTEM FLOWCHART
(Inventory Purchase Order Processing

MULTIPLE-CARD LAYOUT FORM

Company LEARNING COBOL, INC.

Application PURCHASE ORDER PROCESS   by J. Wayne Spence   Date 01/01/81   Job No. PROB 16.3   Sheet No. 1

Purchase Order Record

VENDOR CODE	ITEM NUMBER	OUTLET NUMBER	QUANTITY PURCHASED	DATE OF PURCHASE		
9 9 9	9 9 9 9 9 9	9 9 9 9 9	9 9 9 9 9 9	9 9 9 9 9 9	9 9 9 9 9 9 9 9 9 9 9 9 9 9 9 9 9 9 9 9 9 9 9 9 9 9 9 9 9 9 9 9 9 9 9 9 9 9 9 9 9 9 9 9 9 9 9 9 9 9 9 9 9 9	

17 Indexed File Processing

An indexed (or keyed) data file allows each record in the file to be uniquely addressed. In a sequential file the programmer's only access option is to get the next sequential record. This accessing procedure *may* be used with an indexed or keyed file, but the programmer may also supply an index or key to allow retrieval of specific records. That is, records in an indexed file may be retrieved at random, without consideration to the present location in the file.

Figure 17.1 shows how an indexed file may be accessed randomly. Of course, random access is not truly random, but rather it is based on a value provided from a transaction file. Thus, when it is necessary to move from one area of the file to another, all that is necessary is to provide the appropriate key value and the operating system takes care of the file positioning.

Although most systems provide some type of indexed or keyed file, the implementation of the file type varies from one manufacturer to another. The basis for this chapter is the indexed sequential access method (ISAM), as implemented by IBM.

ENVIRONMENT DIVISION Considerations

Although the INPUT-OUTPUT SECTION of the ENVIRONMENT DIVISION (see Figure 17.2) is similar to that presented in Chapter 16, three clauses are either new or modified. The first is the ACCESS MODE clause, which had previously specified only SEQUENTIAL access. Since sequential access is assumed if the clause is absent from the FILE-CONTROL paragraph, all previous files were sequential. Indexed sequential files may be accessed in either SEQUENTIAL or RANDOM mode, however.

The second change in the INPUT-OUTPUT SECTION is the addition of the RECORD KEY clause. The RECORD KEY clause must always be present in the file definition of an indexed sequential file (whether the access is sequential or random). Identifier-1 must be a field in the indexed sequential file record. The limitations on identifier-1 are that its total length must not exceed 256 bytes and, if record delete codes are to be used or the file is unblocked, identifier-1 must not start in the first byte of the indexed-sequential-file record description. (Delete codes are discussed more fully in the DATA DIVISION considerations.)

INDEXED FILE (MASTER): File keyed on CUSTOMER NUMBER

RECORD NUMBER	CUSTOMER NUMBER	REMAINDER OF RECORD
1.	180	--
2.	210	--
3.	250	--
4.	300	--
5.	305	--
6.	310	--
7.	370	--
8.	400	--
9.	420	--
10.	500	--
11.	670	--

TRANSACTION FILE: Sequential File Type

CUSTOMER NUMBER	REMAINDER OF RECORD	COMMENTS
305	-----------------------------------	Jump to record 5
500	-----------------------------------	Jump from record 5 to record 10
210	-----------------------------------	Jump from record 10 to record 2
400	-----------------------------------	Jump from record 2 to record 8
305	-----------------------------------	Jump from record 8 to record 5
300	-----------------------------------	Jump from record 5 to record 4
670	-----------------------------------	Jump from record 4 to record 11
210	-----------------------------------	Jump from record 11 to record 2

Figure 17.1 An Illustration of Random Access

```
ENVIRONMENT DIVISION.

        .
        .
        .

[INPUT-OUTPUT SECTION.
 FILE-CONTROL.
      SELECT file-name
      ASSIGN TO system-name

     [RESERVE {NO     } . ALTERNATE  [AREA ]]
             {integer}              [AREAS]

     [ACCESS MODE IS {SEQUENTIAL}  ]
                     {RANDOM    }
     [PROCESSING MODE IS SEQUENTIAL ]
     [RECORD KEY IS identifier-1]
     [NOMINAL KEY IS identifier-2].  . . .]
```

Figure 17.2 INPUT-OUTPUT SECTION for IBM Indexed-Sequential-File Organization

The final change in the INPUT-OUTPUT SECTION is the addition of the NOMINAL KEY clause (an IBM extension). The NOMINAL KEY clause is only necessary when records are to be accessed in a RANDOM mode. Identifier-2 must be defined in the WORKING-STORAGE SECTION, it must be a fixed displacement from the beginning of a record (it must not be subsequent to an OCCURS/DEPENDING ON), it may not exceed 256 bytes in length, and the definition of the item should be consistent with the definition of the RECORD KEY identifier. That is, since the identifier specified as the NOMINAL KEY will be used to "find" records in the indexed sequential file, it must match the value of the RECORD KEY identifier exactly. Thus, if the RECORD KEY identifier was described in the indexed sequential record as a PICTURE 9(Ø5) and the NOMINAL KEY identifier's description in WORKING-STORAGE was PICTURE X(1Ø), the values in these two identifiers would never be the same. (THE WORKING-STORAGE item is longer, and at a minimum, would contain blanks if loaded with the same value as was placed in the RECORD KEY identifier.

The file described as an indexed sequential file *must be recorded on a mass storage device* (e.g., magnetic disk). The file type is no longer purely sequential—requiring a change to the IBM system-name. Thus, the prefix of "DA-I" before a ddname indicates that the file will be placed on a direct access (DA) device and the file type is indexed (I). Indexed sequential files must be recorded on magnetic disk in *cylinders*. A cylinder is the same track number on all recording surfaces (platters) of a disk pack. While this requirement does not necessarily have any direct impact on COBOL code, JCL modifications will be necessary. (Consult your installation guide for information concerning the allocation requirements for indexed sequential files.)

Figure 17.3 illustrates the appearance of the ENVIRONMENT DIVISION in a program using an indexed sequential file. Note from the illustration that CUSTOMER-FILE is ASSIGNed to the system-name DA-I-MASTER, which specifically indicates that an indexed sequential file is being used. Next, the ACCESS MODE clause is specified, indicating RANDOM access. The RECORD KEY clause, always required for an indexed sequential file, indicates that the field which identifies individual records is called CUSTOMER-NUMBER. The NOMINAL KEY clause (required when the ACCESS MODE is RANDOM), identifies the data-name LOCATE-CUSTOMER as the field to be used when it is necessary to locate a particular indexed sequential record. (Note: When the access to an indexed sequential file is sequential, neither the ACCESS MODE nor the NOMINAL KEY clause is required.)

```
ENVIRONMENT DIVISION.
CONFIGURATION SECTION.
SOURCE-COMPUTER. IBM.
OBJECT-COMPUTER. IBM.
INPUT-OUTPUT SECTION.
FILE-CONTROL
     SELECT CUSTOMER-FILE
         ASSIGN TO DA-I-MASTER
         ACCESS MODE IS RANDOM
         RECORD KEY IS CUSTOMER-NUMBER
         NOMINAL KEY IS LOCATE-CUSTOMER.
```

Figure 17.3 An Illustration of the ENVIRONMENT DIVISION for an Indexed Sequential File

**DATA
DIVISION
Considerations**

The options for using the LABEL RECORDS, BLOCK CONTAINS, RECORD CONTAINS, and DATA RECORDS clauses are the same for indexed sequential files as they are for sequential files. There may be differences in the record description of the same file between standard sequential files and indexed sequential files, however. The identifier specified as the RECORD KEY in the FILE-CONTROL paragraph of the ENVIRONMENT DIVISION must appear in the indexed sequential file record and may be located in other than the first bytes of the record. The RECORD KEY could be a group-item or an elementary-item; however, the *contents* of the field *must be unique* among all the records in the file. Records with duplicate RECORD KEY values are not permitted in an indexed sequential file.

The second possible modification of the indexed-sequential-file record deals with the possible deletion of records in the file. The first byte (character) position of an indexed-sequential-file record is a special byte. If this position in the record contains HIGH-VALUES, the record is assumed to be a deleted record. It will be treated as though it had been physically deleted (e.g., READ statements will bypass the record), even though the record may still be physically present in the file. If the first byte contains any other value, the record is assumed to be a valid record for processing purposes.

**PROCEDURE
DIVISION
Considerations**

All the processing described in Chapter 16 related to updating, adding, and deleting records on a magnetic disk medium apply equally to an indexed sequential file. So long as a RECORD KEY has been assigned for a file, an indexed sequential file may be READ in exactly the same manner as used for a standard sequential file. But, because the file is a "keyed" file and may be addressed in either SEQUENTIAL or RANDOM mode, some statements may be slightly modified.

The READ statement, shown in Figure 17.4, is given an INVALID KEY phrase in the same area occupied by the AT END phrase. If the ACCESS MODE is SEQUENTIAL, the programmer must supply the RECORD KEY in the FILE-CONTROL paragraph for the indexed sequential file, and the READ statement will employ the AT END phrase. The AT END imperative statement is executed when the end of file is encountered. If the programmer has selected ACCESS MODE IS RANDOM, both the RECORD KEY and NOMINAL KEY must be supplied in the FILE-CONTROL paragraph, the NOMINAL KEY must be loaded with a value equal to that of the RECORD KEY of the record to be located and read, and the READ statement must employ the INVALID KEY phrase. The INVALID KEY imperative statement is executed in the event that (a) the specified NOMINAL KEY value cannot be located in the file, (b) an attempt is made to read past the end-of-file, or (c) a device error occurs. In other words, if the specified record is *not found* for whatever reason, the imperative statement is executed.

The WRITE statement, Figure 17.5, is also modified to include an INVALID KEY phrase. For indexed sequential files, the WRITE statement is used to build a file or to add records to an existing file—it is not always necessary to create a new file when it is necessary to add records. The INVALID KEY imperative statement is executed in the event that (a) an attempt is made to place a record

```
READ file-name RECORD [INTO identifier]

 ⎰AT END  imperative-statement        ⎱
 ⎱INVALID KEY imperative-statement⎰
```

Figure 17.4 Indexed Sequential File READ Statement

```
WRITE record-name [FROM identifier]

[INVALID KEY imperative-statement]
```

Figure 17.5 Indexed Sequential File WRITE Statement

```
REWRITE record-name [FROM identifier

[INVALID KEY imperative-statement]
```

Figure 17.6 Indexed Sequential File REWRITE Statement

with a *duplicate* RECORD KEY value in the file (either during the building or adding process), (b) file space has been exhausted, or (c) a device error occurs. During the file building process, the ACCESS MODE should be SEQUENTIAL, and a RECORD KEY clause must appear in the FILE-CONTROL paragraph. If records are to be added to a file, the ACCESS MODE could be either SEQUENTIAL or RANDOM. The RECORD KEY and NOMINAL KEY clause should be provided, and the NOMINAL KEY should be loaded with the RECORD KEY value of the record to be added. Thus, if the value of the NOMINAL KEY is found in the file, the INVALID KEY (for a duplicate RECORD KEY) is executed.

For purposes of updating an indexed sequential file, the REWRITE statement, Figure 17.6, is used. Like the REWRITE statement for updating sequential files on mass storage devices (as illustrated in Chapter 16), the REWRITE statement for an indexed sequential file causes an existing record to be over written—replacing old data with new data. Like the sequential REWRITE operation, the rewritten data are placed in the same location as the data last READ by the procedure. Thus, a READ statement should always precede a REWRITE statement in the PROCEDURE DIVISION; however, a REWRITE should *not* follow a READ statement that has encountered the end-of-file. The INVALID KEY clause is included for consistency and is never executed for a REWRITE on an indexed sequential file— the READ activity would encounter an INVALID KEY prior to the execution of the REWRITE statement!

Format 1:

```
START file-name

    [INVALID KEY imperative-statement]
```

Format 2:

```
START file-name

    USING KEY identifier-1 {EQUAL TO}    identifier-2
                           {  =   }

    [INVALID KEY imperative-statement]
```

Figure 17.7 The START Statement

The START statement, illustrated in Figure 17.7, is the only new statement type included for use with indexed sequential files. The START statement is used when the programmer wishes to process an indexed sequential file in a sequential manner (i.e., ACCESS MODE is SEQUENTIAL) but wishes to initiate the process at a record location other than the first (next) record in the file. In other words, the START statement permits the programmer to "jump ahead" in the file to the position of the *next* record to be processed. The START statement, if used, must be executed prior to the execution of a READ statement.

In the Format 1 version of the START statement, the value placed in the NOMINAL KEY field is used to locate the (next) record. Therefore, the NOMINAL KEY clause is required when this format is used, and the NOMINAL KEY identifier must contain the value of the record to be located prior to the execution of the START statement. The INVALID KEY imperative statement is executed in the event the specified NOMINAL KEY value cannot be located in the file.

When the Format 2 version of the START statement is used, the NOMINAL KEY clause is not *required*. Identifier-1 must be the RECORD KEY identifier. Identifier-2 is referred to as a *generic key*. That is, identifier-2 is defined in the DATA DIVISION but is in no way associated with any key clause in the FILE-CONTROL paragraph of the ENVIRONMENT DIVISION. Identifier-2 may be less than or equal to the length of the RECORD KEY identifier and should not be a part of the indexed-sequential-file record. Upon execution of the Format 2 START statement, the system searches for the first RECORD KEY value that matches the value of the generic key. Thus, if the definition of the generic key is shorter than the RECORD KEY identifier, this START statement may be used to find the first record in an indexed sequential file that begins with the generic key "prefix." That is, if the generic key is three characters long and the RECORD KEY identifier is eight characters long (and perhaps contains a series of values prefixed with the same first three characters) the START statement will locate the first occurrence of this "prefix" in the indexed sequential file.

Building an Indexed Sequential File

The building or development of an indexed sequential file follows many of the characteristics of building a standard sequential file. As illustrated in the System Flowchart of Figure 17.8, a sequential file (perhaps on magnetic tape) is processed into an output file (which must be on a mass storage device) in an indexed sequential form. The same basic procedure illustrated in Chapter 16 is provided in the procedure of Figure 17.8. First, turn to the definition of the file in the ENVIRONMENT DIVISION. Note that the CUSTOMER-OUT file is assigned to a direct access (DA) device, and the RECORD KEY is CUSTO-MER-NUMBER-OUT. The ACCESS MODE is specifically identified as SE-QUENTIAL, although sequential access would be assumed in the absence of the clause. Next, examine the record description of the indexed sequential file (lines 330–420). As indicated by the RECORD CONTAINS clause, the output record contains 125 characters (as opposed to the 124-byte input record). Note that the first field of the output record is DELETE-BYTE—a one-byte field to be used to delete records, if necessary. The next field of the output record is CUSTOMER-NUMBER-OUT—the RECORD KEY field.

Turning to the PROCEDURE DIVISION, notice that the input file is to be sorted on the CUSTOMER-SORT field. To create an indexed sequential file, the data placed in the RECORD KEY field (CUSTOMER-NUMBER-OUT) must be ordered on an *ascending* basis. In the OUTPUT PROCEDURE, during the process initialization phase, the output file (CUSTOMER-OUT) is opened in an OUTPUT mode. Thus, in this procedure, only output data will be accepted by the file. As the process progresses, data is RETURNed to the CUSTOMER-SORT file in preparation for writing the first record. Notice that both this RETURN statement and the second RETURN statement in line 1190 place the data from the sort file into RECORD-CONTENTS (line 600). Further examination of the DATA DIVISION in the area of RECORDS-CONTENTS shows that the field is preceded by a one-byte field, which will contain a space. This one-byte field, will ultimately be placed in the DELETE-BYTE position of the CUSTOMER-OUT record. In 140-CREATE-FILE (a repetitive procedure), the status variable OUTPUT-STATUS is loaded with a value of "RECORD-ED"—in anticipation of writing a record to the indexed sequential file. The CUSTOMER-OUT-REC is then loaded with the data of INPUT-OUTPUT-RECORD (at which time the RECORD KEY receives its value). An attempt is then made to WRITE the new record. If the WRITE operation works, a record is placed in the indexed sequential file. If, however, it does not, the INVALID KEY phrase is executed—loading OUTPUT-STATUS with "DUPLICATE" (the assumed reason for the execution of the imperative statement). Shortly thereafter, the next record is RETURNed, and the process is repeated until an end-of-file has been encountered for CUSTOMER-SORT. When the output file (CUSTOMER-OUT) is closed in line 1400, the creation process has been completed.

As with sequential files, the building process only occurs once. However, unlike a sequential file, an indexed sequential file is often copied or rebuilt periodically to restructure the file and eliminate records that contain a HIGH-VALUE delete-byte value.

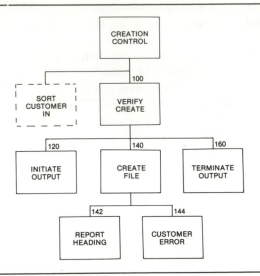

Figure 17.8 Building an Indexed Sequential File (Hierarchy Chart)

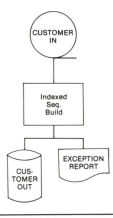

Figure 17.8 Building an Indexed Sequential File (System Flowchart)

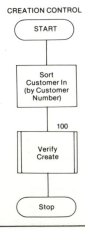

Figure 17.8 Building an Indexed Sequential File (Module Flowchart) *Continued*

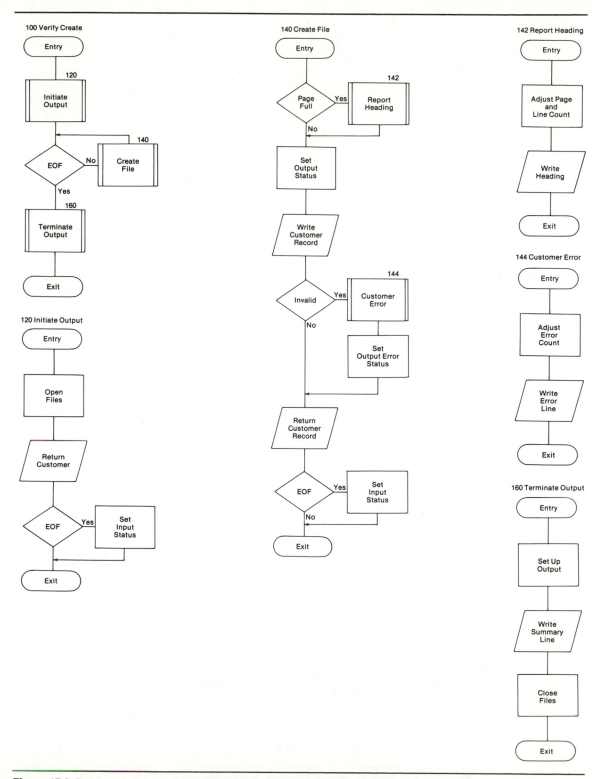

Figure 17.8 Building an Indexed Sequential File (Module Flowcharts) *Continued*

```
|-----------------------------------------------------------------------------|
|        1   1   2   2   2   3   3   4   4   4   5   5   6   6   6   6   7   7  8|
|   4    8   2   6   0   4   8   2   6   0   4   8   2   6   0   4   8   2   6  0|
|-----------------------------------------------------------------------------|
|000010 IDENTIFICATION DIVISION.                                      FIG 17.8|
|000020 PROGRAM-ID. INDEXED-SEQ-BUILD.                                FIG 17.8|
|000030 AUTHOR. J. WAYNE SPENCE.                                      FIG 17.8|
|000040 DATE-WRITTEN. JAN 1, 1981.                                    FIG 17.8|
|000050 DATE-COMPILED. JAN 1, 1981.                                   FIG 17.8|
|000060*    THE PURPOSE OF THIS PROCEDURE IS TO PRODUCE AN INDEXED    FIG 17.8|
|000070*    SEQUENTIAL DATA FILE BASED ON CUSTOMER RECORDS.. THE FILE FIG 17.8|
|000080*    IS TO BE KEYED ON THE CUSTOMER NUMBER FIELD.              FIG 17.8|
|000090 ENVIRONMENT DIVISION.                                         FIG 17.8|
|000100 CONFIGURATION SECTION.                                        FIG 17.8|
|000110 SOURCE-COMPUTER. IBM-370.                                     FIG 17.8|
|000120 OBJECT-COMPUTER. IBM-370.                                     FIG 17.8|
|000130 SPECIAL-NAMES.                                                FIG 17.8|
|000140     C01 IS TOP-OF-PAGE.                                       FIG 17.8|
|000150 INPUT-OUTPUT SECTION.                                         FIG 17.8|
|000160 FILE-CONTROL.                                                 FIG 17.8|
|000170     SELECT CUSTOMER-IN ASSIGN TO UT-S-CUSTIN.                 FIG 17.8|
|000180     SELECT CUSTOMER-OUT ASSIGN TO DA-I-CUSTOUT.               FIG 17.8|
|000190        RECORD KEY IS CUSTOMER-NUMBER-OUT                      FIG 17.8|
|000200        ACCESS IS SEQUENTIAL.                                  FIG 17.8|
|000210     SELECT CUSTOMER-SORT ASSIGN TO UT-S-SORTWK01.             FIG 17.8|
|000220     SELECT EXCEPTION-REPORT ASSIGN TO UT-S-SYSPRINT.          FIG 17.8|
|000230 DATA DIVISION.                                                FIG 17.8|
|000240 FILE SECTION.                                                 FIG 17.8|
|000250 FD  CUSTOMER-IN                                               FIG 17.8|
|000260     LABEL RECORDS ARE STANDARD                                FIG 17.8|
|000270     RECORD CONTAINS 124 CHARACTERS                            FIG 17.8|
|000280     BLOCK CONTAINS 0 RECORDS.                                 FIG 17.8|
|000290 01  CUSTOMER-REC-IN          PIC X(124).                      FIG 17.8|
|000300 FD  CUSTOMER-OUT                                              FIG 17.8|
|000310     LABEL RECORDS ARE STANDARD                                FIG 17.8|
|000320     RECORD CONTAINS 125 CHARACTERS.                           FIG 17.8|
|000330 01  CUSTOMER-REC-OUT.                                         FIG 17.8|
|000340     05  DELETE-BYTE          PIC X(01).                       FIG 17.8|
|000350     05  CUSTOMER-NUMBER-OUT  PIC X(10).                       FIG 17.8|
|000360     05  CUSTOMER-NAME-OUT    PIC X(30).                       FIG 17.8|
|000370     05  CUSTOMER-ADDRESS-OUT PIC X(30).                       FIG 17.8|
|000380     05  CUSTOMER-CITY-OUT    PIC X(20).                       FIG 17.8|
|000390     05  CUSTOMER-STATE-OUT   PIC X(02).                       FIG 17.8|
|000400     05  CUSTOMER-ZIP-OUT     PIC X(10).                       FIG 17.8|
|000410     05  OUTSTANDING-BALANCE-OUT PIC S9(9)V99.                 FIG 17.8|
|000420     05  CREDIT-LIMIT-OUT     PIC S9(9)V99.                    FIG 17.8|
|000430 SD  CUSTOMER-SORT.                                            FIG 17.8|
|000440 01  CUSTOMER-REC-SORT.                                        FIG 17.8|
|000450     05  CUSTOMER-NUMBER-SORT PIC X(10).                       FIG 17.8|
|000460     05  FILLER               PIC X(114).                      FIG 17.8|
|000470 FD  EXCEPTION-REPORT                                          FIG 17.8|
|000480     LABEL RECORDS ARE OMITTED.                                FIG 17.8|
|000490 01  REPORT-LINE              PIC X(133).                      FIG 17.8|
|000500 WORKING-STORAGE SECTION.                                      FIG 17.8|
|000510 01  PROGRAM-CONTROL-VARIABLES.                                FIG 17.8|
|000520     05  FILE-STATUS          PIC X(04) VALUE SPACES.          FIG 17.8|
|000530     05  OUTPUT-STATUS        PIC X(10) VALUE SPACES.          FIG 17.8|
|000540     05  LINE-NUMBER          PIC 9(02) VALUE 99.              FIG 17.8|
|000550     05  PAGE-NUMBER          PIC 9(02) VALUE ZERO.            FIG 17.8|
|000560     05  ERROR-COUNT          PIC 9(04) VALUE ZERO.            FIG 17.8|
|000570     05  CUSTOMER-COUNT       PIC 9(04) VALUE ZERO.            FIG 17.8|
|000580     05  INPUT-OUTPUT-RECORD.                                  FIG 17.8|
|000590         10  FILLER           PIC X(01) VALUE SPACES.          FIG 17.8|
|000600         10  RECORD-CONTENTS  PIC X(124).                      FIG 17.8|
|000610 01  HEADING-1.                                                FIG 17.8|
|000620     05  FILLER               PIC X(32) VALUE SPACES.          FIG 17.8|
|000630     05  FILLER               PIC X(16) VALUE                  FIG 17.8|
|000640     'EXCEPTION REPORT'.                                       FIG 17.8|
|000650     05  FILLER               PIC X(25) VALUE SPACES.          FIG 17.8|
|000660     05  FILLER               PIC X(05) VALUE 'PAGE'.          FIG 17.8|
|000670     05  PAGE-OUT             PIC Z9.                          FIG 17.8|
|000680 01  HEADING-2.                                                FIG 17.8|
|000690     05  FILLER               PIC X(20) VALUE                  FIG 17.8|
|000700     ' CUSTOMER NUMBER'.                                       FIG 17.8|
|000710     05  FILLER               PIC X(20) VALUE                  FIG 17.8|
|000720     'COMMENTS'.                                               FIG 17.8|
|000730 01  HEADING-3.                                                FIG 17.8|
|000740     05  FILLER               PIC X(01) VALUE SPACES.          FIG 17.8|
|000750     05  FILLER               PIC X(80) VALUE ALL '-'.         FIG 17.8|
|000760 01  ERROR-LINE.                                               FIG 17.8|
|000770     05  FILLER               PIC X(02) VALUE SPACES.          FIG 17.8|
|000780     05  CUSTOMER-NUMBER-ERROR PIC X(10).                      FIG 17.8|
|000790     05  FILLER               PIC X(08) VALUE SPACES.          FIG 17.8|
```

Figure 17.8 Building an Indexed Sequential File *Continued*

```
|        1  1  2  2  3  3  4  4  4  5  6  6  6  7  7  8|
|  4  8  2  6  0  4  8  2  6  0  4  8  2  6  0  4  8  2  6  0|
---------------------------------------------------------------
|000800      05  FILLER                PIC X(50) VALUE        FIG 17.8|
|000810          *CUSTOMER NUMBER DUPLICATE ENCOUNTERED--ELIMINATED*.  FIG 17.8|
|000820 01  SUMMARY-LINE.                                    FIG 17.8|
|000830      05  FILLER                PIC X(01) VALUE SPACES.  FIG 17.8|
|000840      05  CUSTOMER-COUNT-OUT    PIC *,**9.             FIG 17.8|
|000850      05  FILLER                PIC X(27) VALUE        FIG 17.8|
|000860          * CUSTOMER RECORDS WRITTEN--*.              FIG 17.8|
|000870      05  ERROR-COUNT-OUT       PIC *,**9.             FIG 17.8|
|000880      05  FILLER                PIC X(25) VALUE        FIG 17.8|
|000890          * DUPLICATES ENCOUNTERED*.                  FIG 17.8|
|000900 PROCEDURE DIVISION.                                  FIG 17.8|
|000910 CREATION-CONTROL SECTION.                            FIG 17.8|
|000920      MOVE 45000 TO SORT-CORE-SIZE.                   FIG 17.8|
|000930      SORT CUSTOMER-SORT                              FIG 17.8|
|000940          ASCENDING KEY CUSTOMER-NUMBER-SORT          FIG 17.8|
|000950          USING CUSTOMER-IN                           FIG 17.8|
|000960          OUTPUT PROCEDURE 100-VERIFY-CREATE.         FIG 17.8|
|000970      STOP RUN.                                       FIG 17.8|
|000980 100-VERIFY-CREATE SECTION.                           FIG 17.8|
|000990 100-VERIFY-CREATE-CONTROL.                           FIG 17.8|
|001000      PERFORM 120-INITIATE-OUTPUT.                    FIG 17.8|
|001010      PERFORM 140-CREATE-FILE                         FIG 17.8|
|001020          UNTIL FILE-STATUS = *DONE*.                 FIG 17.8|
|001030      PERFORM 160-TERMINATE-OUTPUT.                   FIG 17.8|
|001040      GO TO 199-EXIT.                                 FIG 17.8|
|001050 120-INITIATE-OUTPUT.                                 FIG 17.8|
|001060      OPEN OUTPUT CUSTOMER-OUT                        FIG 17.8|
|001070              EXCEPTION-REPORT.                       FIG 17.8|
|001080      RETURN CUSTOMER-SORT INTO RECORD-CONTENTS       FIG 17.8|
|001090          AT END MOVE *DONE* TO FILE-STATUS.          FIG 17.8|
|001100 140-CREATE-FILE.                                     FIG 17.8|
|001110      IF LINE-NUMBER IS GREATER THAN 40               FIG 17.8|
|001120          PERFORM 142-REPORT-HEADING.                 FIG 17.8|
|001130      MOVE *RECORDED* TO OUTPUT-STATUS.               FIG 17.8|
|001140      WRITE CUSTOMER-REC-OUT FROM INPUT-OUTPUT-RECORD  FIG 17.8|
|001150          INVALID KEY PERFORM 144-CUSTOMER-ERROR      FIG 17.8|
|001160              MOVE *DUPLICATE* TO OUTPUT-STATUS.      FIG 17.8|
|001170      IF OUTPUT-STATUS = *RECORDED*                   FIG 17.8|
|001180          ADD 1 TO CUSTOMER-COUNT.                    FIG 17.8|
|001190      RETURN CUSTOMER-SORT INTO RECORD-CONTENTS       FIG 17.8|
|001200          AT END MOVE *DONE* TO FILE-STATUS.          FIG 17.8|
|001210 142-REPORT-HEADING.                                  FIG 17.8|
|001220      ADD 1 TO PAGE-NUMBER.                           FIG 17.8|
|001230      MOVE PAGE-NUMBER TO PAGE-OUT.                   FIG 17.8|
|001240      WRITE REPORT-LINE FROM HEADING-1 AFTER ADVANCING TOP-OF-PAGE.FIG 17.8|
|001250      WRITE REPORT-LINE FROM HEADING-2 AFTER ADVANCING 3 LINES.  FIG 17.8|
|001260      WRITE REPORT-LINE FROM HEADING-3 AFTER ADVANCING 1 LINES.  FIG 17.8|
|001270      MOVE SPACES TO REPORT-LINE.                     FIG 17.8|
|001280      WRITE REPORT-LINE AFTER ADVANCING 1 LINES.      FIG 17.8|
|001290      MOVE 0 TO LINE-NUMBER.                          FIG 17.8|
|001300 144-CUSTOMER-ERROR.                                  FIG 17.8|
|001310      ADD 1 TO ERROR-COUNT.                           FIG 17.8|
|001320      MOVE CUSTOMER-NUMBER-OUT TO CUSTOMER-NUMBER-ERROR.  FIG 17.8|
|001330      WRITE REPORT-LINE FROM ERROR-LINE AFTER ADVANCING 1 LINES.  FIG 17.8|
|001340      ADD 1 TO LINE-NUMBER.                           FIG 17.8|
|001350 160-TERMINATE-OUTPUT.                                FIG 17.8|
|001360      MOVE ERROR-COUNT TO ERROR-COUNT-OUT.            FIG 17.8|
|001370      MOVE CUSTOMER-COUNT TO CUSTOMER-COUNT-OUT.      FIG 17.8|
|001380      WRITE REPORT-LINE FROM SUMMARY-LINE AFTER ADVANCING 2 LINES. FIG 17.8|
|001390      CLOSE EXCEPTION-REPORT                          FIG 17.8|
|001400              CUSTOMER-OUT.                           FIG 17.8|
|001410 199-EXIT.                                            FIG 17.8|
|001420      EXIT.                                           FIG 17.8|
```

Figure 17.8 Building an Indexed Sequential File *Continued*

```
        1         2         3         4         5         6         7         8         9         1         1         1
                                                                                                  0         1         2
1234567890123456789012345678901234567890123456789012345678901234567890123456789012345678901234567980123456789012345678901234
---------------------------------------------------------------------------------------------------------------------------
4412X47390MARSHALL SILVERMAN      2219 WEST 7TH STREET        CLEVELAND        OH30119  0000000000000000500000
3199127X33JAMES THOMPKINS         44339 SOUTH WACKER DRIVE    CHICAGO          IL60606  0000002291800000500000
1141944103EDWIN WILLIAMS          2139 SOUTH COLGATE STREET   PERRYTON         TX79070  0000033193300035000000
6213937661JASON MADISON           8831 CEDAR DRIVE N.W.       NORWICH          CN00218  0000041452300000300000
5270215827CHARLES EVEREST         8821 OCEAN PARKWAY          MIAMI            FL51332  0000000000000000500000
3333333333JULIA HARRISTON         6132 MILL ROAD AVENUE       SHREVEPORT       LA63341  0000035134300005000000
3498966451JACOB R. SULLIVAN       6134 MALIBU DRIVE           LOS ANGELES      CA96512  0000000000000004400000
1RX14219-3JOHN P. VILLIMAN        8887 PEACH TREE LANE        DALLAS           TX75002  0000000314300000500000
6427633-94MARK U. LEMON           P. O. BOX 51244             NEW YORK         NY03158  0000000000000000005000
773194221BHELEN B. OVERSTREET     3153 YELLOW BRICK ROAD      YELLOW STONE PARK MT41229  0000001284200000000000
9X0-334RDSANTHONY P. JONES        EXECUTIVE OFFICE BUILDING   WASHINGTON       DC00000  0000000000000000000000
3333333333RAYMOND J. TAYLOR       912 DUSTY ROAD              PLAINS           GA39100  0000052353600010000000
```

Figure 17.8 Building an Indexed Sequential File (Data—CUSTOMER-IN) *Continued*

```
      RECORD 00001
1RX14219-3JOHN P. VILLIMAN            8887 PEACH TREE LANE         DALLAS            TX75002    00000003143000005
00000
      RECORD 00002
1141944103EDWIN WILLIAMS             2139 SOUTH COLGATE STREET    PERRYTON          TX79070    00000331933000350
00000
      RECORD 00003
3199127X33JAMES THOMPKINS            44339 SOUTH WACKER DRIVE     CHICAGO           IL60606    00000022918000005
00000
      RECORD 00004
3333333333JULIA HARRISTON            6132 MILL ROAD AVENUE        SHREVEPORT        LA63341    00000351343000050
00000
      RECORD 00005
3498966451JACOB R. SULLIVAN          6134 MALIBU DRIVE            LOS ANGELES       CA96512    00000000000000044
00000
      RECORD 00006
4412X47390MARSHALL SILVERMAN         2219 WEST 7TH STREET         CLEVELAND         OH30119    00000000000000005
00000
      RECORD 00007
5270215P27CHARLES EVEREST            8821 OCEAN PARKWAY           MIAMI             FL51332    00000000000000005
00000
      RECORD 00008
6213937661JASON MADISON              8831 CEDAR DRIVE N.W.        NORWICH           CN00218    00000414523000030
00000
      RECORD 00009
6427633-94MARK U. LEMON              P. O. BOX 51244              NEW YORK          NY03158    00000000000000000
05000
      RECORD 00010
7731942210HELEN B. OVERSTREET        3153 YELLOW BRICK ROAD       YELLOW STONE PARK MT41229    00000012842000000
00000
      RECORD 00011
9X0-334RDSANTHONY P. JONES           EXECUTIVE OFFICE BUILDING    WASHINGTON        DC00000    00000000000000000
00000
***END OF OUTPUT
```

Figure 17.8 Building an Indexed Sequential File (Data—CUSTOMER-OUT) *Continued*

```
                                       EXCEPTION REPORT                          PAGE   1


        CUSTOMER NUMBER      COMMENTS
        --------------------------------------------------------------------------------

          3333333333         CUSTOMER NUMBER DUPLICATE ENCOUNTERED--ELIMINATED

        ***11 CUSTOMER RECORDS WRITTEN--****1 DUPLICATES ENCOUNTERED
```

Figure 17.8 Building an Indexed Sequential File (Output) *Continued*

Updating an Indexed Sequential File

Although the building process for sequential and indexed sequential files is similar, the updating process may be considerably different. Recall from the sequential file update process in Chapter 16 that it was necessary to establish a greater than, equal to, or less than relationship between the CUSTOMER (master) file and the SALES (transaction) file. Unless a mass storage device was employed for the master file, a new file had to be created that contained the updated data. In addition, the transaction file had to be ordered in the same sequence as the master file.

If the programmer selects the random mode (ACCESS MODE IS RANDOM) to update an indexed sequential file, none of these conditions are required specifically. Turn to Figure 17.9—a random update of the CUSTOMER file. In the System Flowchart, the CUSTOMER file is used both for input and output purposes, as indicated by the two-way arrow. In the ENVIRONMENT DIVISION, the specification of the file indicates that again the CUSTOMER file is assigned to a mass storage device (DA), and CUSTOMER-NUMBER is the RECORD KEY. In addition, a NOMINAL KEY variable of CUSTOMER-NUMBER-FIND (defined in line 600) and ACCESS MODE IS RANDOM are provided.

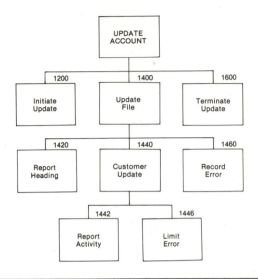

Figure 17.9 Updating an Indexed Sequential File (Hierarchy Chart)

The PROCEDURE DIVISION is initiated (without a SORT statement), and in the 1400-INITIATE-UPDATE SECTION, the CUSTOMER file is opened in an I-O mode—both reading and writing operations are permitted. During the actual updating procedure (lines 1070–1240), a record is READ from the CUSTOMER-SALES file, the NOMINAL KEY value is established via the MOVE statement in line 1110, an INPUT-STATUS indicator is set (presuming a record will be successfully read), and an attempt is made to READ the record to be updated. If the indicated record is successfully read, i.e., the value placed in the NOMINAL KEY variable matches one of the RECORD KEY values, the 1440-CUSTOMER-UPDATE procedure is invoked. Otherwise, the INPUT-STATUS indicator is set to "NOT FOUND" by the INVALID KEY phrase of the READ statement (the NOMINAL KEY and any RECORD KEY value did not match exactly), and an error routine (1460-RECORD-ERROR) is invoked.

During the update sequence (lines 1340–1500), if the transaction contains a legitimate change (the credit limit is not exceeded), the OUTSTANDING-BALANCE field is modified, and the record is rewritten to the indexed sequential file (line 1420). Otherwise, a limit error is printed (1444-LIMIT-ERROR). Notice that if the record is not modified—if a limit error is encountered—the record from the indexed sequential file does not have to be rewritten. Since nothing in the record was modified, rewriting the record would be pointless—the file contains the data currently in memory. Finally, notice that the update sequence from the transaction file is in no particular order. Examine either the output in the EXCEPTION-RECORD or the data in the CUSTOMER-SALES file. Notice that only the contents of the record in the CUSTOMER file have been modified—the sequence of the records in the indexed sequential file has not been affected.

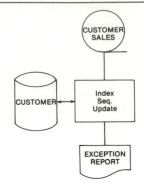

Figure 17.9 Updating an Indexed Sequential File (System Flowchart) *Continued*

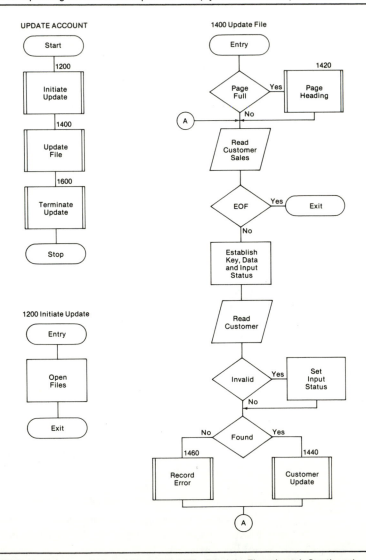

Figure 17.9 Updating an Indexed Sequential File (Module Flowcharts) *Continued*

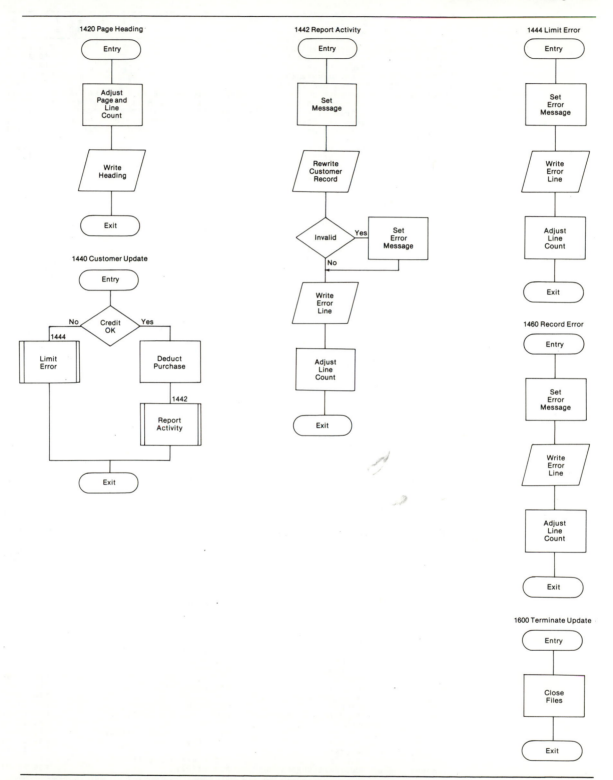

Figure 17.9 Updating an Indexed Sequential File (Module Flowcharts) *Continued*

```
|                1  1   2   2   2   3   3   4   4   4   5   5   6   6   6   7   7   8|
|   4    8       2  6   0   4   8   2   6   0   4   8   2   6   0   4   8   2   6   0|
-------------------------------------------------------------------------------------
|000010 IDENTIFICATION DIVISION.                                          FIG 17.9|
|000020 PROGRAM-ID. INDEX-SEQ-UPDATE.                                     FIG 17.9|
|000030 AUTHOR. J. WAYNE SPENCE.                                          FIG 17.9|
|000040 DATE-WRITTEN. JAN 1, 1981.                                        FIG 17.9|
|000050 DATE-COMPILED. JAN 1, 1981.                                       FIG 17.9|
|000060*     THE PURPOSE OF THIS PROCEDURE IS TO UPDATE AN EXISTING       FIG 17.9|
|000070*     INDEXED SEQUENTIAL FILE (CUSTOMER) ON THE BASIS OF INFORMATIFIG 17.9|
|000080*     CONTAINED IN A SALES FILE.  MULTIPLE UPDATES PER CUSTOMER    FIG 17.9|
|000090*     RECORDS ARE PERMITTED (IN RANDOM ORDER) AND CUSTOMER UPDATESFIG 17.9|
|000100*     (SALES RECORDS) WITHOUT A CORRESPONDING CUSTOMER RECORD ARE  FIG 17.9|
|000110*     IDENTIFIED.                                                  FIG 17.9|
|000120 ENVIRONMENT DIVISION.                                             FIG 17.9|
|000130 CONFIGURATION SECTION.                                            FIG 17.9|
|000140 SOURCE-COMPUTER. IBM-370.                                         FIG 17.9|
|000150 OBJECT-COMPUTER. IBM-370.                                         FIG 17.9|
|000160 SPECIAL-NAMES.                                                    FIG 17.9|
|000170     C01 IS TOP-OF-PAGE.                                           FIG 17.9|
|000180 INPUT-OUTPUT SECTION.                                             FIG 17.9|
|000190 FILE-CONTROL.                                                     FIG 17.9|
|000200     SELECT CUSTOMER-SALES ASSIGN TO UT-S-SALES.                   FIG 17.9|
|000210     SELECT CUSTOMER ASSIGN TO DA-I-CUST                           FIG 17.9|
|000220         RECORD KEY IS CUSTOMER-NUMBER                             FIG 17.9|
|000230         NOMINAL KEY IS CUSTOMER-NUMBER-FIND                       FIG 17.9|
|000240         ACCESS IS RANDOM.                                         FIG 17.9|
|000250     SELECT EXCEPTION-REPORT ASSIGN TO UT-S-SYSPRINT.              FIG 17.9|
|000260 DATA DIVISION.                                                    FIG 17.9|
|000270 FILE SECTION.                                                     FIG 17.9|
|000280 FD  CUSTOMER-SALES                                                FIG 17.9|
|000290     LABEL RECORDS ARE STANDARD                                    FIG 17.9|
|000300     RECORD CONTAINS 80 CHARACTERS                                 FIG 17.9|
|000310     BLOCK CONTAINS 0 RECORDS.                                     FIG 17.9|
|000320 01  SALES-REC.                                                    FIG 17.9|
|000330     05  CUSTOMER-NUMBER-SALES   PIC X(10).                        FIG 17.9|
|000340     05  DATE-OF-PURCHASE.                                         FIG 17.9|
|000350         10  PUR-MONTH           PIC XX.                           FIG 17.9|
|000360         10  PUR-DAY             PIC XX.                           FIG 17.9|
|000370         10  PUR-YEAR            PIC XX.                           FIG 17.9|
|000380     05  ITEM-PURCHASED          PIC X(10).                        FIG 17.9|
|000390     05  PURCHASE-AMOUNT         PIC S9(9)V99.                     FIG 17.9|
|000400 05  FILLER  PIC X(43).                                            FIG 17.9|
|000410 FD  CUSTOMER                                                      FIG 17.9|
|000420     LABEL RECORDS ARE STANDARD                                    FIG 17.9|
|000430     RECORD CONTAINS 125 CHARACTERS.                               FIG 17.9|
|000440 01  CUSTOMER-REC.                                                 FIG 17.9|
|000450     05  DELETE-BYTE             PIC X(01).                        FIG 17.9|
|000460     05  CUSTOMER-NUMBER         PIC X(10).                        FIG 17.9|
|000470     05  CUSTOMER-NAME           PIC X(30).                        FIG 17.9|
|000480     05  CUSTOMER-ADDRESS        PIC X(30).                        FIG 17.9|
|000490     05  CUSTOMER-CITY           PIC X(20).                        FIG 17.9|
|000500     05  CUSTOMER-STATE          PIC X(02).                        FIG 17.9|
|000510     05  CUSTOMER-ZIP            PIC X(10).                        FIG 17.9|
|000520     05  OUTSTANDING-BALANCE     PIC S9(9)V99.                     FIG 17.9|
|000530     05  CREDIT-LIMIT            PIC S9(9)V99.                     FIG 17.9|
|000540 FD  EXCEPTION-REPORT                                              FIG 17.9|
|000550     LABEL RECORDS ARE OMITTED.                                    FIG 17.9|
|000560 01  REPORT-LINE                 PIC X(80).                        FIG 17.9|
|000570 WORKING-STORAGE SECTION.                                          FIG 17.9|
|000580 01  PROGRAM-CONTROL-VARIABLES.                                    FIG 17.9|
|000590     05  INPUT-STATUS            PIC X(10) VALUE SPACES.           FIG 17.9|
|000600     05  CUSTOMER-NUMBER-FIND    PIC X(10).                        FIG 17.9|
|000610     05  LINE-NUMBER             PIC 9(02) VALUE 99.               FIG 17.9|
|000620     05  PAGE-NUMBER             PIC 9(02) VALUE ZERO.             FIG 17.9|
|000630 01  HEADING-1.                                                    FIG 17.9|
|000640     05  FILLER                  PIC X(32) VALUE SPACES.           FIG 17.9|
|000650     05  FILLER                  PIC X(16) VALUE                   FIG 17.9|
|000660     'EXCEPTION REPORT'.                                           FIG 17.9|
|000670     05  FILLER                  PIC X(25) VALUE SPACES.           FIG 17.9|
|000680     05  FILLER                  PIC X(05) VALUE 'PAGE'.           FIG 17.9|
|000690     05  PAGE-OUT                PIC Z9.                           FIG 17.9|
|000700 01  HEADING-2.                                                    FIG 17.9|
|000710     05  FILLER                  PIC X(20) VALUE                   FIG 17.9|
|000720     ' CUSTOMER NUMBER'.                                           FIG 17.9|
|000730     05  FILLER                  PIC X(50) VALUE                   FIG 17.9|
|000740     ' DATE      PURCHASE AMOUNT      COMMENTS'.                   FIG 17.9|
|000750 01  HEADING-3.                                                    FIG 17.9|
|000760     05  FILLER                  PIC X(01) VALUE SPACES.           FIG 17.9|
|000770     05  FILLER                  PIC X(80) VALUE ALL '-'.          FIG 17.9|
|000780 01  ERROR-LINE.                                                   FIG 17.9|
|000790     05  FILLER                  PIC X(02) VALUE SPACES.           FIG 17.9|
|000800     05  CUSTOMER-NUMBER-OUT     PIC X(10).                        FIG 17.9|
```

Figure 17.9 Updating an Indexed Sequential File *Continued*

```
|    1   1   2   2   2   3   3   4   4   4   5   5   6   6   6   7   7   8|
| 4  8   2   6   0   4   8   2   6   0   4   8   2   6   0   4   8   2   6   0|
---------------------------------------------------------------------------
|000810     05  FILLER                    PIC X(08) VALUE SPACES.      FIG 17.9|
|000820     05  MONTH-OUT                 PIC X(02).                   FIG 17.9|
|000830     05  FILLER                    PIC X(01) VALUE '/'.         FIG 17.9|
|000840     05  DAY-OUT                   PIC X(02).                   FIG 17.9|
|000850     05  FILLER                    PIC X(01) VALUE '/'.         FIG 17.9|
|000860     05  YEAR-OUT                  PIC X(02).                   FIG 17.9|
|000870     05  FILLER                    PIC X(05) VALUE SPACES.      FIG 17.9|
|000880     05  AMOUNT-OUT                PIC ZZZ,ZZZ,ZZZ.ZZ.          FIG 17.9|
|000890     05  FILLER                    PIC X(05) VALUE SPACES.      FIG 17.9|
|000900     05  MESSAGE-OUT               PIC X(50) VALUE SPACES.      FIG 17.9|
|000910 PROCEDURE DIVISION.                                           FIG 17.9|
|000920 1000-UPDATE-ACCOUNT SECTION.                                  FIG 17.9|
|000930 1000-UPDATE-ACCOUNT-CONTROL.                                  FIG 17.9|
|000940     PERFORM 1200-INITIATE-UPDATE.                             FIG 17.9|
|000950     PERFORM 1400-UPDATE-FILE.                                 FIG 17.9|
|000960     PERFORM 1600-TERMINATE-UPDATE.                            FIG 17.9|
|000970     STOP RUN.                                                 FIG 17.9|
|000980 1099-EXIT.                                                    FIG 17.9|
|000990     EXIT.                                                     FIG 17.9|
|001000 1200-INITIATE-UPDATE SECTION.                                 FIG 17.9|
|001010     OPEN I-O CUSTOMER                                         FIG 17.9|
|001020         INPUT CUSTOMER-SALES                                  FIG 17.9|
|001030         OUTPUT EXCEPTION-REPORT.                              FIG 17.9|
|001040 1299-EXIT.                                                    FIG 17.9|
|001050     EXIT.                                                     FIG 17.9|
|001060 1400-UPDATE-FILE SECTION.                                     FIG 17.9|
|001070     IF LINE-NUMBER IS GREATER THAN 40                         FIG 17.9|
|001080         PERFORM 1420-REPORT-HEADING.                          FIG 17.9|
|001090     READ CUSTOMER-SALES                                       FIG 17.9|
|001100         AT END GO TO 1499-EXIT.                               FIG 17.9|
|001110     MOVE CUSTOMER-NUMBER-SALES TO CUSTOMER-NUMBER-OUT         FIG 17.9|
|001120                                   CUSTOMER-NUMBER-FIND.       FIG 17.9|
|001130     MOVE PUR-MONTH TO MONTH-OUT.                              FIG 17.9|
|001140     MOVE PUR-DAY TO DAY-OUT.                                  FIG 17.9|
|001150     MOVE PUR-YEAR TO YEAR-OUT.                                FIG 17.9|
|001160     MOVE PURCHASE-AMOUNT TO AMOUNT-OUT.                       FIG 17.9|
|001170     MOVE 'FOUND' TO INPUT-STATUS.                             FIG 17.9|
|001180     READ CUSTOMER                                             FIG 17.9|
|001190         INVALID KEY MOVE 'NOT FOUND' TO INPUT-STATUS.         FIG 17.9|
|001200     IF INPUT-STATUS = 'FOUND'                                 FIG 17.9|
|001210         PERFORM 1440-CUSTOMER-UPDATE                          FIG 17.9|
|001220     ELSE                                                      FIG 17.9|
|001230         PERFORM 1460-RECORD-ERROR.                            FIG 17.9|
|001240     GO TO 1400-UPDATE-FILE.                                   FIG 17.9|
|001250 1420-REPORT-HEADING.                                          FIG 17.9|
|001260     ADD 1 TO PAGE-NUMBER.                                     FIG 17.9|
|001270     MOVE PAGE-NUMBER TO PAGE-OUT.                             FIG 17.9|
|001280     MOVE 0 TO LINE-NUMBER.                                    FIG 17.9|
|001290     WRITE REPORT-LINE FROM HEADING-1 AFTER ADVANCING TOP-OF-PAGE.FIG 17.9|
|001300     WRITE REPORT-LINE FROM HEADING-2 AFTER ADVANCING 2 LINES. FIG 17.9|
|001310     WRITE REPORT-LINE FROM HEADING-3 AFTER ADVANCING 1 LINES. FIG 17.9|
|001320     MOVE SPACES TO REPORT-LINE.                               FIG 17.9|
|001330     WRITE REPORT-LINE AFTER ADVANCING 1 LINES.                FIG 17.9|
|001340 1440-CUSTOMER-UPDATE.                                         FIG 17.9|
|001350     IF OUTSTANDING-BALANCE + PURCHASE-AMOUNT > CREDIT-LIMIT   FIG 17.9|
|001360         PERFORM 1444-LIMIT-ERROR                              FIG 17.9|
|001370     ELSE                                                      FIG 17.9|
|001380         ADD PURCHASE-AMOUNT TO OUTSTANDING-BALANCE            FIG 17.9|
|001390         PERFORM 1442-REPORT-ACTIVITY.                         FIG 17.9|
|001400 1442-REPORT-ACTIVITY.                                         FIG 17.9|
|001410     MOVE 'CUSTOMER RECORD UPDATED' TO MESSAGE-OUT.            FIG 17.9|
|001420     REWRITE CUSTOMER-REC                                      FIG 17.9|
|001430         INVALID KEY MOVE 'ERROR--RECORD NOT UPDATED' TO       FIG 17.9|
|001440                     MESSAGE-OUT.                              FIG 17.9|
|001450     WRITE REPORT-LINE FROM ERROR-LINE AFTER ADVANCING 1 LINES.FIG 17.9|
|001460     ADD 1 TO LINE-NUMBER.                                     FIG 17.9|
|001470 1444-LIMIT-ERROR.                                             FIG 17.9|
|001480     MOVE 'CREDIT LIMIT EXCEEDED' TO MESSAGE-OUT.              FIG 17.9|
|001490     WRITE REPORT-LINE FROM ERROR-LINE AFTER ADVANCING 1 LINES.FIG 17.9|
|001500     ADD 1 TO LINE-NUMBER.                                     FIG 17.9|
|001510 1460-RECORD-ERROR.                                            FIG 17.9|
|001520     MOVE ALL '-' TO REPORT-LINE.                              FIG 17.9|
|001530     WRITE REPORT-LINE AFTER ADVANCING 2 LINES.                FIG 17.9|
|001540     MOVE 'CUSTOMER RECORD NOT FOUND' TO MESSAGE-OUT.          FIG 17.9|
|001550     WRITE REPORT-LINE FROM ERROR-LINE AFTER ADVANCING 1 LINES.FIG 17.9|
|001560     MOVE ALL '-' TO REPORT-LINE.                              FIG 17.9|
|001570     WRITE REPORT-LINE AFTER ADVANCING 1 LINES.                FIG 17.9|
|001580     MOVE SPACES TO REPORT-LINE.                               FIG 17.9|
|001590     WRITE REPORT-LINE AFTER ADVANCING 1 LINES.                FIG 17.9|
|001600     ADD 5 TO LINE-NUMBER.                                     FIG 17.9|
```

Figure 17.9 Updating an Indexed Sequential File *Continued*

```
|     1   1   2   2   2   3   3   4   4   4   5   5   6   6   6   7   7   8|
|   4   8   2   6   0   4   8   2   6   0   4   8   2   6   0   4   8   2   6   0|
-------------------------------------------------------------------------------
|001610 1499-EXIT.                                                  FIG 17.9|
|001620     EXIT.                                                   FIG 17.9|
|001630 1600-TERMINATE-UPDATE SECTION.                              FIG 17.9|
|001640     CLOSE CUSTOMER,                                         FIG 17.9|
|001650             CUSTOMER-SALES                                  FIG 17.9|
|001660             EXCEPTION-REPORT.                               FIG 17.9|
```

Figure 17.9 Updating an Indexed Sequential File

```
|       |       1         2         3         4         5         6         7         8| FIGURE |
|RECORD|12345678901234567890123456789012345678901234567890123456789012345678901234567890| NUMBER |
|    1 |333333333305818144129400000044125                                               |FIG 17.9|
|    2 |9X0-334RDS05158129-43319  00000041232                                           |FIG 17.9|
|    3 |114194410305148841933700000712911                                               |FIG 17.9|
|    4 |333333333051481          00005122529                                            |FIG 17.9|
|    5 |412559279305018181888888888800512295147                                         |FIG 17.9|
|    6 |4412X4739005018145-RTS    00000056902                                           |FIG 17.9|
|    7 |3333333333060981BXR-33294 00002212219                                           |FIG 17.9|
|    8 |527021582705058100000112697                                                     |FIG 17.9|
|    9 |5512294148051581          00000004123                                           |FIG 17.9|
|   10 |349896645105178199-457-33100000476110                                           |FIG 17.9|
|   11 |4412X4739005228155144290220000000003312                                         |FIG 17.9|
|   12 |114194410305258100000012000                                                     |FIG 17.9|
```

Figure 17.9 Updating an Indexed Sequential File (Sales Data) *Continued*

```
     RECORD 00001
1RX14219-3JOHN P. VILLIMAN        8887 PEACH TREE LANE       DALLAS          TX75002    00000003143000005
00000
     RECORD 00002
1141944103EDWIN WILLIAMS          2139 SOUTH COLGATE STREET   PERRYTON        TX79070    0000105684D000350
00000
     RECORD 00003
3199127X33JAMES THOMPKINS         44339 SOUTH WACKER DRIVE    CHICAGO         IL60606    00000022918000005
00000
     RECORD 00004
3333333333JULIA HARRISTON         6132 MILL ROAD AVENUE       SHREVEPORT      LA63341    0000260768G000050
00000
     RECORD 00005
3498966451JACOB R. SULLIVAN       6134 MALIBU DRIVE           LOS ANGELES     CA96512    0000047611 000044
00000
     RECORD 00006
4412X47390MARSHALL SILVERMAN      2219 WEST 7TH STREET        CLEVELAND       OH30119    0000006021D000005
00000
     RECORD 00007
5270215827CHARLES EVEREST         8821 OCEAN PARKWAY          MIAMI           FL51332    00000112696000005
00000
     RECORD 00008
6213937661JASON MADISON           8831 CEDAR DRIVE N.W.       NORWICH         CN00218    00000414523000030
00000
     RECORD 00009
6427633-94MARK U. LEMON           P. O. BOX 51244             NEW YORK        NY03158    00000000000000000
05000
     RECORD 00010
773194221BHELEN B. OVERSTREET     3153 YELLOW BRICK ROAD      YELLOW STONE PARK  MT41229 00000012842000000
00000
     RECORD 00011
9X0-334RDSANTHONY P. JONES        EXECUTIVE OFFICE BUILDING   WASHINGTON      DC00000    00000000000000000
00000
***END OF OUTPUT
```

Figure 17.9 Updating an Indexed Sequential File (CUSTOMER—After Update) *Continued*

Adding to an Indexed Sequential File

Recall from Chapter 16 that the addition process for a sequential file requires that a new file be created. In the System Flowchart in Figure 17.10, note that only one CUSTOMER file is required to perform additions for an indexed sequential file. Whether a standard sequential file is recorded on magnetic tape or a mass storage medium, it must be rewritten to add records to any position of the file except at its end. In the indexed sequential file illustrated in Figure 17.10, records are added at the beginning of the file and interspersed with existing records of the file.

```
                                    EXCEPTION REPORT                          PAGE   1
      CUSTOMER NUMBER        DATE       PURCHASE AMOUNT      COMMENTS
      ------------------------------------------------------------------------------------

         3333333333        05/81/81              441.25      CUSTOMER RECORD UPDATED
         9X0-334RDS        05/15/81              412.32      CREDIT LIMIT EXCEEDED
         1141944103        05/14/88            7,129.11      CUSTOMER RECORD UPDATED
         3333333333        05/14/81           51,225.29      CREDIT LIMIT EXCEEDED
      ------------------------------------------------------------------------------------

         4125592793        05/01/81        5,122,951.47      CUSTOMER RECORD NOT FOUND
      ------------------------------------------------------------------------------------

         4412X47390        05/01/81              569.02      CUSTOMER RECORD UPDATED
         3333333333        06/09/81           22,122.19      CUSTOMER RECORD UPDATED
         5270215827        05/05/81            1,126.97      CUSTOMER RECORD UPDATED
      ------------------------------------------------------------------------------------

         5512294148        05/15/81               41.23      CUSTOMER RECORD NOT FOUND
      ------------------------------------------------------------------------------------

         3498966451        05/17/81            4,761.10      CUSTOMER RECORD UPDATED
         4412X47390        05/22/81               33.12      CUSTOMER RECORD UPDATED
         1141944103        05/25/81              120.00      CUSTOMER RECORD UPDATED
```

Figure 17.9 Updating an Indexed Sequential File (Output) *Continued*

In the ENVIRONMENT DIVISION, the RANDOM access mode has been selected, thus both the RECORD KEY and the NOMINAL KEY are required. In the PROCEDURE DIVISION, the CUSTOMER file is opened in an I-O mode. In the repetitive procedure of the 1400-ADD-RECORDS SECTION, a record is read from the CUSTOMER-ADDS file, and the NOMINAL KEY variable is initialized with the MOVE statement at line 910.

The process varies somewhat from the update process at this point. Instead of setting a status variable and *reading* a record from the indexed sequential file, the process sets the status variable and *writes* a (new) record to the indexed sequential file. Provided the WRITE operation is successful, an output routine in invoked to print a message reflecting the addition of the record. However, if an INVALID KEY is caused by the WRITE operation, the attempt to place the new record in the file causes a duplication of an existing RECORD KEY—the record is not placed in the file and a message indicating the situation is printed. (Of course, if a large number of records have been added to the file, the "DUPLICATE" message might be in error. Existing file space *could* have been exhausted.)

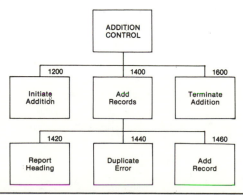

Figure 17.10 Adding to an Indexed Sequential File (Hierarchy Chart)

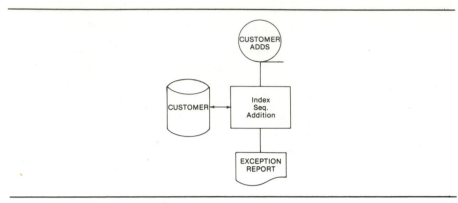

Figure 17.10 Adding to an Indexed Sequential File (System Flowchart) *Continued*

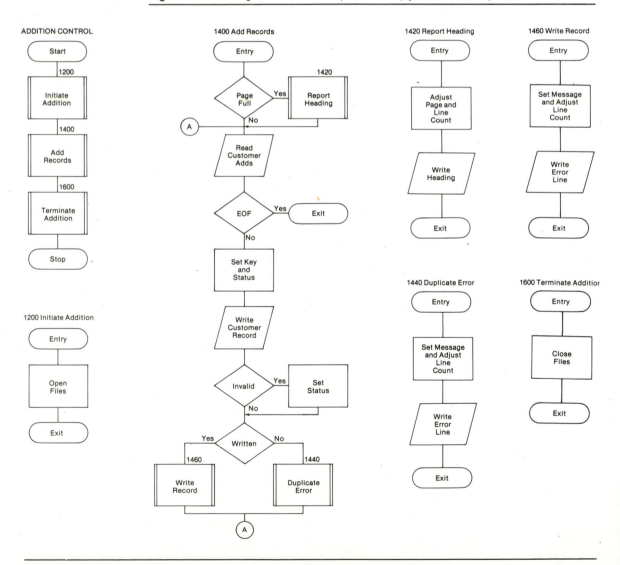

Figure 17.10 Adding to an Indexed Sequential File (Module Flowcharts) *Continued*

```
|          1   1   2   2   3   3   4   4   4   5   5   6   6   6   7   7   8|
|  4   8   2   6   0   4   8   2   6   0   4   8   2   6   0   4   8   2   6   0|
--------------------------------------------------------------------------------
|000010 IDENTIFICATION DIVISION.                                      FIG17.10|
|000020 PROGRAM-ID. INDEX-SEQ-ADDITION.                               FIG17.10|
|000030 AUTHOR. J. WAYNE SPENCE.                                      FIG17.10|
|000040 DATE-WRITTEN. JAN 1, 1981.                                    FIG17.10|
|000050 DATE-COMPILED. JAN 1, 1981.                                   FIG17.10|
|000060*     THE PURPOSE OF THIS PROCEDURE IS TO ADD RECORDS (NEW CUSTOMEFIG17.10|
|000070*     TO AN EXISTING INDEXED SEQUENTIAL (CUSTOMER) FILE.  THE PROCFIG17.10|
|000080*     PROHIBITS DUPLICATE CUSTOMER RECORDS WITH THE SAME CUSTOMER FIG17.10|
|000090*     NUMBER.                                                  FIG17.10|
|000100 ENVIRONMENT DIVISION.                                         FIG17.10|
|000110 CONFIGURATION SECTION.                                        FIG17.10|
|000120 SOURCE-COMPUTER. IBM-370.                                     FIG17.10|
|000130 OBJECT-COMPUTER. IBM-370.                                     FIG17.10|
|000140 SPECIAL-NAMES.                                                FIG17.10|
|000150     C01 IS TOP-OF-PAGE.                                       FIG17.10|
|000160 INPUT-OUTPUT SECTION.                                         FIG17.10|
|000170 FILE-CONTROL.                                                 FIG17.10|
|000180     SELECT CUSTOMER-ADDS ASSIGN TO UT-S-ADDS.                 FIG17.10|
|000190     SELECT CUSTOMER ASSIGN TO DA-I-CUST                       FIG17.10|
|000200         RECORD KEY IS CUSTOMER-NUMBER                         FIG17.10|
|000210         NOMINAL KEY IS CUSTOMER-NUMBER-FIND                   FIG17.10|
|000220         ACCESS IS RANDOM.                                     FIG17.10|
|000230     SELECT EXCEPTION-REPORT ASSIGN TO UT-S-SYSPRINT.          FIG17.10|
|000240 DATA DIVISION.                                                FIG17.10|
|000250 FILE SECTION.                                                 FIG17.10|
|000260 FD  CUSTOMER-ADDS                                             FIG17.10|
|000270     LABEL RECORDS ARE STANDARD                                FIG17.10|
|000280     RECORD CONTAINS 124 CHARACTERS                            FIG17.10|
|000290     BLOCK CONTAINS 0 RECORDS.                                 FIG17.10|
|000300 01  CUSTOMER-REC-ADDS.                                        FIG17.10|
|000310     05  CUSTOMER-NUMBER-ADDS    PIC X(10).                    FIG17.10|
|000320     05  FILLER                  PIC X(114).                   FIG17.10|
|000330 FD  CUSTOMER                                                  FIG17.10|
|000340     LABEL RECORDS ARE STANDARD                                FIG17.10|
|000350     RECORD CONTAINS 125 CHARACTERS.                           FIG17.10|
|000360 01  CUSTOMER-REC.                                             FIG17.10|
|000370     05  DELETE-CODE             PIC X(01).                    FIG17.10|
|000380     05  CUSTOMER-NUMBER         PIC X(10).                    FIG17.10|
|000390     05  FILLER                  PIC X(114).                   FIG17.10|
|000400 FD  EXCEPTION-REPORT                                          FIG17.10|
|000410     LABEL RECORDS ARE OMITTED.                                FIG17.10|
|000420 01  REPORT-LINE                 PIC X(80).                    FIG17.10|
|000430 WORKING-STORAGE SECTION.                                      FIG17.10|
|000440 01  PROGRAM-CONTROL-VARIABLES.                                FIG17.10|
|000450     05  OUTPUT-STATUS           PIC X(15).                    FIG17.10|
|000460     05  CUSTOMER-NUMBER-FIND    PIC X(10).                    FIG17.10|
|000470     05  LINE-NUMBER             PIC 9(02) VALUE 99.           FIG17.10|
|000480     05  PAGE-NUMBER             PIC 9(02) VALUE ZERO.         FIG17.10|
|000490     05  INPUT-OUTPUT-RECORD.                                  FIG17.10|
|000500         10  FIRST-BYTE          PIC X(01) VALUE SPACES.       FIG17.10|
|000510         10  RECORD-CONTENTS     PIC X(124).                   FIG17.10|
|000520 01  HEADING-1.                                                FIG17.10|
|000530     05  FILLER                  PIC X(32) VALUE SPACES.       FIG17.10|
|000540     05  FILLER                  PIC X(16) VALUE               FIG17.10|
|000550     'EXCEPTION REPORT'.                                       FIG17.10|
|000560     05  FILLER                  PIC X(25) VALUE SPACES.       FIG17.10|
|000570     05  FILLER                  PIC X(05) VALUE 'PAGE'.       FIG17.10|
|000580     05  PAGE-OUT                PIC Z9.                       FIG17.10|
|000590 01  HEADING-2.                                                FIG17.10|
|000600     05  FILLER                  PIC X(20) VALUE               FIG17.10|
|000610     ' CUSTOMER NUMBER'.                                       FIG17.10|
|000620     05  FILLER                  PIC X(50) VALUE               FIG17.10|
|000630     'COMMENTS'.                                               FIG17.10|
|000640 01  HEADING-3.                                                FIG17.10|
|000650     05  FILLER                  PIC X(01) VALUE SPACES.       FIG17.10|
|000660     05  FILLER                  PIC X(80) VALUE ALL '-'.      FIG17.10|
|000670 01  ERROR-LINE.                                               FIG17.10|
|000680     05  FILLER                  PIC X(02) VALUE SPACES.       FIG17.10|
|000690     05  CUSTOMER-NUMBER-OUT     PIC X(10).                    FIG17.10|
|000700     05  FILLER                  PIC X(08) VALUE SPACES.       FIG17.10|
|000710     05  MESSAGE-OUT             PIC X(50) VALUE SPACES.       FIG17.10|
|000720 PROCEDURE DIVISION.                                           FIG17.10|
|000730 1000-ADDITION-CONTROL SECTION.                                FIG17.10|
|000740     PERFORM 1200-INITIATE-ADDITION.                           FIG17.10|
|000750     PERFORM 1400-ADD-RECORDS.                                 FIG17.10|
|000760     PERFORM 1600-TERMINATE-ADDITION.                          FIG17.10|
|000770     STOP RUN.                                                 FIG17.10|
|000780 1099-EXIT.                                                    FIG17.10|
|000790     EXIT.                                                     FIG17.10|
```

Figure 17.10 Adding to an Indexed Sequential File *Continued*

```
|               1   1   2   .2   2   3   4   4   4   5   5   6   6   6   7   7   8|
|    4      8   2   6   0    4   8   2   4   8   2   6   0   4   8   2   6   0   4   8   2   6   0|
-------------------------------------------------------------------------------------------------
|000800 1200-INITIATE-ADDITION SECTION.                                          FIG17.10|
|000810     OPEN I-O CUSTOMER                                                    FIG17.10|
|000820          INPUT CUSTOMER-ADDS                                             FIG17.10|
|000830          OUTPUT EXCEPTION-REPORT.                                        FIG17.10|
|000840 1299-EXIT.                                                               FIG17.10|
|000850     EXIT.                                                                FIG17.10|
|000860 1400-ADD-RECORDS SECTION.                                                FIG17.10|
|000870     IF LINE-NUMBER IS GREATER THAN 40                                    FIG17.10|
|000880         PERFORM 1420-REPORT-HEADING.                                     FIG17.10|
|000890     READ CUSTOMER-ADDS INTO RECORD-CONTENTS                              FIG17.10|
|000900         AT END GO TO 1499-EXIT.                                          FIG17.10|
|000910     MOVE CUSTOMER-NUMBER-ADDS TO CUSTOMER-NUMBER-OUT                      FIG17.10|
|000920                                CUSTOMER-NUMBER-FIND.                      FIG17.10|
|000930     MOVE *NO DUPLICATE* TO OUTPUT-STATUS.                                FIG17.10|
|000940     WRITE CUSTOMER-REC FROM INPUT-OUTPUT-RECORD                          FIG17.10|
|000950         INVALID KEY MOVE *DUPLICATE* TO OUTPUT-STATUS.                    FIG17.10|
|000960     IF OUTPUT-STATUS = *DUPLICATE*                                       FIG17.10|
|000970         PERFORM 1440-DUPLICATE-ERROR                                     FIG17.10|
|000980     ELSE                                                                 FIG17.10|
|000990         PERFORM 1460-WRITE-RECORD.                                       FIG17.10|
|001000     GO TO 1400-ADD-RECORDS.                                              FIG17.10|
|001010 1420-REPORT-HEADING.                                                     FIG17.10|
|001020     ADD 1 TO PAGE-NUMBER.                                                FIG17.10|
|001030     MOVE PAGE-NUMBER TO PAGE-OUT.                                        FIG17.10|
|001040     MOVE 0 TO LINE-NUMBER.                                               FIG17.10|
|001050     WRITE REPORT-LINE FROM HEADING-1 AFTER ADVANCING TOP-OF-PAGE.FIG17.10|
|001060     WRITE REPORT-LINE FROM HEADING-2 AFTER ADVANCING 2 LINES.             FIG17.10|
|001070     WRITE REPORT-LINE FROM HEADING-3 AFTER ADVANCING 1 LINES.             FIG17.10|
|001080     MOVE SPACES TO REPORT-LINE.                                          FIG17.10|
|001090     WRITE REPORT-LINE AFTER ADVANCING 1 LINES.                           FIG17.10|
|001100 1440-DUPLICATE-ERROR.                                                    FIG17.10|
|001110     MOVE *ATTEMPT TO ADD A DUPLICATE RECORD* TO MESSAGE-OUT.             FIG17.10|
|001120     WRITE REPORT-LINE FROM ERROR-LINE AFTER 2.                           FIG17.10|
|001130     ADD 2 TO LINE-NUMBER.                                                FIG17.10|
|001140 1460-WRITE-RECORD.                                                       FIG17.10|
|001150     MOVE *RECORD ADDED* TO MESSAGE-OUT.                                  FIG17.10|
|001160     WRITE REPORT-LINE FROM ERROR-LINE AFTER 2.                           FIG17.10|
|001170     ADD 2 TO LINE-NUMBER.                                                FIG17.10|
|001180 1499-EXIT.                                                               FIG17.10|
|001190     EXIT.                                                                FIG17.10|
|001200 1600-TERMINATE-ADDITION SECTION.                                         FIG17.10|
|001210     CLOSE CUSTOMER,                                                      FIG17.10|
|001220          EXCEPTION-REPORT                                                FIG17.10|
|001230          CUSTOMER-ADDS.                                                  FIG17.10|
```

Figure 17.10 Adding to an Indexed Sequential File *Continued*

```
        1         2         3         4         5         6         7         8         9         1         1 .       1
12345678901234567890123456789012345678901234567890123456789012345678901234567890123456789012345670123456789012345678901234
----------------------------------------------------------------------------------------------------------------------------
X14339-278ROGER P. EVANS          1422 N. W. CLASSEN BLVD.    OKLAHOMA CITY   OK65124   00000000000000000300000
2199428878STEWART A. ALEXANDER    5112 HAMILTON PARKWAY        MINNEAPOLIS     MN21132   00000622390000001000000
3333333333GEORGE P. MARTIN        LAS VEGAS HILTON             LAS VEGAS       NV81222   99999999999900000000000
5122314151MARK R. WHITE           55123 WAR MEMORIAL DRIVE     CLEVELAND       OH41229   00000041233000000050000
----------------------------------------------------------------------------------------------------------------------------
```

Figure 17.10 Adding to an Indexed Sequential File (Data—ADDS) *Continued*

```
      RECORD 00001
    X14339-278ROGER P. EVANS         1422 N. W. CLASSEN BLVD.     OKLAHOMA CITY   OK65124   00000000000000003
00000
      RECORD 00002
    1RX14219-3JOHN P. VILLIMAN        8887 PEACH TREE LANE         DALLAS          TX75002   00000003143000005
00000
      RECORD 00003
    1141944103EDWIN WILLIAMS          2139 SOUTH COLGATE STREET    PERRYTON        TX79070   0000105684D000350
00000
      RECORD 00004
    2199428878STEWART A. ALEXANDER    5112 HAMILTON PARKWAY        MINNEAPOLIS     MN21132   00000622390000010
00000
      RECORD 00005
    3199127X33JAMES THOMPKINS         44339 SOUTH WACKER DRIVE     CHICAGO         IL60606   00000022918000005
00000
      RECORD 00006
    3333333333JULIA HARRISTON         6132 MILL ROAD AVENUE        SHREVEPORT      LA63341   0000260768G000050
00000
```

Figure 17.10 Adding to an Indexed Sequential File (CUSTOMER—After Additions) *Continued*

```
        RECORD 00007
  3498966451JACOB R. SULLIVAN        6134 MALIBU DRIVE           LOS ANGELES       CA96512    0000047611 000044
00000
        RECORD 00008
  4412X47390MARSHALL SILVERMAN       2219 WEST 7TH STREET        CLEVELAND         OH30119    0000006021D000005
00000
        RECORD 00009
  5122314151MARK R. WHITE            55123 WAR MEMORIAL DRIVE    CLEVELAND         OH41229    0000004123300000
50000
        RECORD 00010
  5270215827CHARLES EVEREST          8821 OCEAN PARKWAY          MIAMI             FL51332    000001126960000005
00000
        RECORD 00011
  6213937661JASON MADISON            8831 CEDAR DRIVE N.W.       NORWICH           CN00218    000004145230000030
00000
        RECORD 00012
  6427633-94MARK U. LEMON            P. O. BOX 51244             NEW YORK          NY03158    000000000000000000
05000
        RECORD 00013
  7731942218HELEN B. OVERSTREET      3153 YELLOW BRICK ROAD      YELLOW STONE PARK MT41229    00000012842000000
00000
        RECORD 00014
  9X0-334RDSANTHONY P. JONES         EXECUTIVE OFFICE BUILDING   WASHINGTON        DC00000    000000000000000000
00000
***END OF OUTPUT
```

Figure 17.10 Adding to an Indexed Sequential File (CUSTOMER—After Additions) *Continued*

```
                                         EXCEPTION REPORT                        PAGE   1

        CUSTOMER NUMBER    COMMENTS
        --------------------------------------------------------------------------------

          X14339-278       RECORD ADDED

          2199428878       RECORD ADDED

          3333333333       ATTEMPT TO ADD A DUPLICATE RECORD

          5122314151       RECORD ADDED
```

Figure 17.10 Adding to an Indexed Sequential File (Output) *Continued*

Summary

In this chapter, the process of building, updating, and adding records to an indexed sequential file has been illustrated. Files of this type may be read or written either sequentially or randomly. Records may be updated, added, or deleted without rewriting the file. If the records in the file are to be updated randomly, only those records affected by the update would be accessed. Other records in the file would not be either read or written. Records may be added to the file at the beginning or at the end of the file, or interspersed throughout, provided sufficient space for the records remains in the file. Records may be logically deleted (such that they are transparent to the programmer) by simply loading HIGH-VALUES in the first byte of the record. Sequential file processing may be improved through the use of a specific or generic key in the START statement—permitting sequential access and processing of an indexed sequential file at other than the first (next) serial record.

Notes on Programming Style

While it might seem that no one in their right mind would select a sequential file organization for a master file over an indexed sequential file, there are a number of excellent reasons for using other file types. First, indexed sequential files require more media space than does a sequential file. RECORD KEYs occupy additional space in the indexed sequential file. "Deleted" records may also occupy needed space. Other disadvantages are the manner in which records are added to the file and the retention and manipulation of indexes (also stored in the file). As you progress in your career in data processing, you will become aware of other choices which should provide a more complete picture of data access arrangements in today's commercial environment.

Questions

Below, answer each question by supplying the appropriate word, words, or phrase.

1. Another term that indicates a file is indexed is that it is _____ .

2. An indexed file may be accessed either _____ or _____ .

3. For an indexed sequential file the _____ KEY clause is always required.

4. An index sequential file must be recorded on a _____ medium.

5. When an indexed sequential file is to be accessed in a RANDOM mode, the _____ clause is required.

6. An indexed sequential file that is READ sequentially should use a(n) _____ clause prior to the imperative statement.

7. An indexed sequential file that is READ randomly should use a(n) _____ clause prior to the imperative statement.

8. The identifier used as the RECORD KEY must appear in the _____ record description.

9. The identifier used as the NOMINAL KEY must appear as a field in the _____ SECTION.

10. A(n) _____ statement is used to build or add records to an indexed sequential file, while a(n) _____ statement is used to update the file.

11. The space on a magnetic disk must be allocated by _____ for an indexed sequential file.

12. If records are to be deleted from an indexed sequential file using the delete byte, the value _____ must be moved to the _____ byte of the record description.

13. When an indexed sequential file is built, the values in the RECORD KEY variable must be _____ and must be arranged in an _____ order.

14. The most likely reason for the execution of an imperative statement of a READ statement using the INVALID KEY phrase is that _____ .

15. The most likely reason for the execution of an imperative statement of the WRITE statement is that _____ .

16. If an indexed sequential file is to be read sequentially, the first record accessed may be other than the first physical record if the _____ statement is employed.

17. The only condition under which an item may be addressed using a value other than an exact match of the RECORD KEY in an operation designed to locate existing records is when a(n) _____ key is used in a(n) _____ statement.

For the questions below, answer by circling "T" for True and "F" for False.

T F 18. Records may be added to an indexed sequential file with a REWRITE statement.

T F 19. The identifier specified as a RECORD KEY must appear in the record description of the indexed sequential file.

T F 20. For an indexed sequential file, the RECORD KEY must be specified only under certain conditions.

T F 21. The description of a RECORD KEY must be numeric.

T F 22. The description of the RECORD KEY must be the same as the NOMINAL KEY identifier.

T F 23. An indexed sequential file must not be blocked.

T F 24. An indexed sequential file must be recorded on a direct access type of storage device.

T F 25. Media space on a magnetic disk for an indexed sequential file may be specified in either tracks or cylinders.

T F 26. The description of the NOMINAL KEY variable, depending on the application, may appear in the FILE SECTION.

T F 27. An INVALID KEY imperative statement for an indexed-sequential-file reading operation may be caused by the location of a duplicate record in the file.

T F 28. A REWRITE statement should always be logically preceded by a READ statement.

T F 29. A NOMINAL KEY clause must be supplied whenever a START statement is used.

T F 30. A generic key for the START statement may have a description that is shorter than the RECORD KEY description.

T F 31. It is always necessary that prior to the actual update of an indexed sequential file, the transaction records must be ordered in the same sequence as the indexed sequential file.

Problems

1. Complete problem #1 of Chapter 16. Alter the file type of the inventory file to indexed sequential. Alter the requirements of the Update Exceptions report so that updated records are printed after each record from the Sales file has been processed. In other words, do not reorder the Sales file to conform to the order of the Inventory file. Finally, some reorganization of the inventory record may be required to create a single "field" which represents the key for the record.

2. Complete problem #2 of Chapter 16. Alter the file type of the customer file to indexed sequential. Order the Sales file data such that all updates for a single customer record may be handled at one time.

3. Complete problem #3 of Chapter 16. Alter the file type of the inventory file to indexed sequential. The purchase orders are to be handled in the sequence they appear in the Purchase- Order file. Some reorganization of the inventory record may be required to create a single "field" that represents the key for the record. In addition, the length of the record may be altered to accommodate record deletions.

part **4** **Special Usage COBOL Concepts**

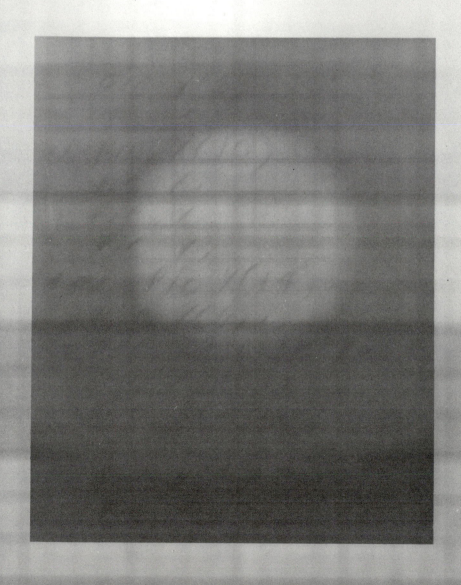

18 More GO TO Statements

In Chapter 6, a simple unconditional GO TO statement was presented for the purpose of illustrating the looping process—a series of statements that are repeated due to the action of the GO TO statement. Another form of the GO TO statement is available in the.COBOL language—the GO TO/DEPENDING ON. This statement is useful under very limited sets of circumstances; however, under those circumstances, programming using the GO TO/DEPENDING ON statement is greatly simplified.

The GO TO/ DEPENDING ON Statement

The GO TO/DEPENDING ON statement, illustrated in Figure 18.1, provides the capability of branching on the basis of the value of a particular data item. From a single point in a program, one of several paths may be taken depending on the value contained by the identifier in Figure 18.1. The identifier must be defined in the DATA DIVISION as being a numeric-elementary data item and must contain an integer value. The PICTURE string for this data item must be four digits or less.

Upon execution of the GO TO/DEPENDING ON statement, the value of the identifier is examined. If the value of the identifier is 1, a branch to procedure-name-1 is executed. If the value of the identifier is 2, a branch to procedure-name-2 is executed, and so forth. If the value of the identifier is either less than 1 or greater than the maximum number of the procedure-names provided in the statement, the GO TO/DEPENDING ON statement is ignored. In this case, the program execution continues with the next statement.

Figure 18.2 demonstrates the use of the GO TO/DEPENDING ON statement. In Chapters 8 and 11, a program for translating a numeric average of three student exam scores into its letter grade equivalent was presented. The

```
GO TO procedure-name-1 [procedure-name-2] . . .DEPENDING ON identifier
```

Figure 18.1 Format of the GO TO/DEPENDING ON Statement

process was accomplished in a number of different ways using various forms of the IF statement. In the program presented in Figure 18.2, the same process is accomplished through the use of a GO TO/DEPENDING ON statement. However, since exam averages do not generally begin with the value 1 (with increments of 1), it is necessary to "scale" the averages so that a grade of 59.4 or less receives a value of 1 (or less); 59.5 to 69.4 is scaled to a value of 2; 69.5 to 79.4, a value of 3; and so forth. The only changes necessary in the procedure from that shown in Figure 10.8 are the DETERMINE GRADE module and paragraph of the program.

A COMPUTE statement in the program provides a value for data-name BRANCH and is responsible for the scaling of the average scores. Note that 40 is subtracted from the AVERAGE. By doing this, most averages will then fall into a 60 to 0 range. (Subtracting 40 will also cause some averages to become negative but if the value of the identifier (BRANCH) is less than one, the GO TO/DEPENDING ON statement is ignored—causing execution of the next sequential statement. In the program any average that would result in a negative number after having 40 subtracted from it would normally receive the letter grade F. Notice that if the GO TO/DEPENDING ON statement is ignored, the next statement moves F to LETTER-GRADE.) However, subtracting 40 from 59.5 and then dividing the result by 10 would cause the value of BRANCH to be 1 (because BRANCH is an integer field). Thus, .5 is added to the result of the subtraction, causing any fraction of .5 or more to be "rounded up" after the division takes place. As a result, averages between 49.5 and 59.4 would be recoded to 1; 59.5 to 69.4 would cause BRANCH to receive a value of 2; 69.5 to 79.4, the value 3; 79.5 to 89.4, the value 4; and 89.5 to 99.4 would result in BRANCH receiving the value 5. One minor problem is that values over 99.4 will be recoded to 6; however, this value also represents an average which should receive the letter grade A; thus, the extra GRADE-A paragraph name. Without this extra paragraph name, anyone having an average score between 99.5 and 100 would receive the letter grade F—a major program error.

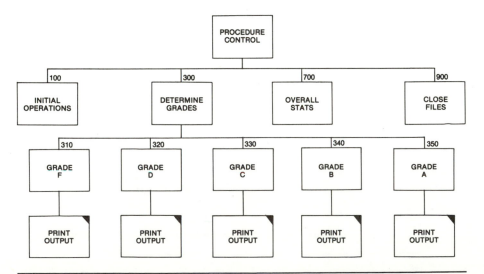

Figure 18.2 An Illustration of the GO TO/DEPENDING ON Statement (Hierarchy Chart)

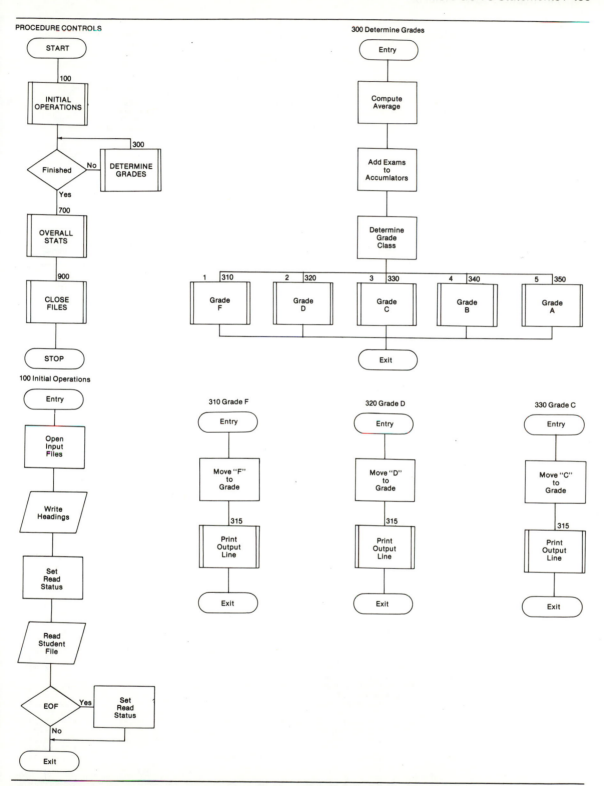

Figure 18.2 An Illustration of the GO TO/DEPENDING ON Statement (Module Flowcharts) *Continued*

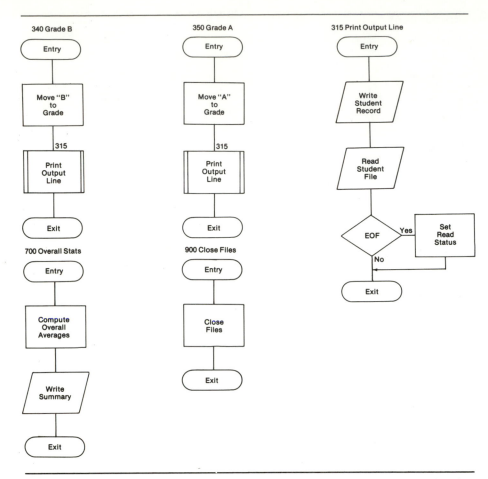

Figure 18.2 An Illustration of the GO TO/DEPENDING ON Statement (Module Flowcharts) *Continued*

```
|          1   1   2   2   2   3   3   4   4   4   5   5   6   6   6   7   7   8|
|    4   8  2   6   0   4   8   2   6   0   4   8   2   6   0   4   8   2   6   0|
------------------------------------------------------------------------------
|000010 IDENTIFICATION DIVISION.                                      FIG 18.2|
|000020 PROGRAM-ID. GRADES-ANALYSIS.                                  FIG 18.2|
|000030 AUTHOR. J. WAYNE SPENCE.                                      FIG 18.2|
|000040 DATE-WRITTEN.  JAN 1, 1981.                                   FIG 18.2|
|000050 DATE-COMPILED. JAN 1, 1981.                                   FIG 18.2|
|000060*    THIS PROGRAM ILLUSTRATES THE USE OF                       FIG 18.2|
|000070*    THE GO TO/DEPENDING ON STATEMENT.                         FIG 18.2|
|000080*    IN ADDITION, ARITHMETIC STATEMENTS; ACCUMULATORS;         FIG 18.2|
|000090*    EXAM-COUNTERS; EDITED OUTPUT AND VALUE CLAUSES ARE USED.  FIG 18.2|
|000100 ENVIRONMENT DIVISION.                                         FIG 18.2|
|000110 CONFIGURATION SECTION.                                        FIG 18.2|
|000120 SOURCE-COMPUTER. IBM-370-158.                                 FIG 18.2|
|000130 OBJECT-COMPUTER. IBM-370-158.                                 FIG 18.2|
|000140 SPECIAL-NAMES.  C01 IS HEAD-OF-PAGE.                          FIG 18.2|
|000150 INPUT-OUTPUT SECTION.                                         FIG 18.2|
|000160 FILE-CONTROL.                                                 FIG 18.2|
|000170     SELECT STUDENT-FILE ASSIGN TO UT-S-SYSIN.                 FIG 18.2|
|000180     SELECT GRADE-REPORT ASSIGN TO UT-S-SYSPRINT.              FIG 18.2|
|000190 DATA DIVISION.                                                FIG 18.2|
|000200 FILE SECTION.                                                 FIG 18.2|
|000210 FD  STUDENT-FILE LABEL RECORDS ARE OMITTED.                   FIG 18.2|
```

Figure 18.2 An Illustration of the GO TO/DEPENDING ON Statement *Continued*

```
|                 1  1  2  2  2  3  3  4  4  4  5  5  6  6  6  7  7  8|
|    4     8      2  4  8  2  6  0  4  8  2  6  0  4  8  2  6  0  4  8  2  6  0|
|000220 01   CARD-REC.                                              FIG 18.2|
|000230      03 NAME-STUDENT          PIC X(20).                    FIG 18.2|
|000240      03 FILLER                PIC X(10).                    FIG 18.2|
|000250      03 GRADES.                                             FIG 18.2|
|000260         05 EXAM-1             PIC 9(03).                    FIG 18.2|
|000270         05 EXAM-2             PIC 9(03).                    FIG 18.2|
|000280         05 EXAM-3             PIC 9(03).                    FIG 18.2|
|000290      03 FILLER                PIC X(41).                    FIG 18.2|
|000300 FD   GRADE-REPORT LABEL RECORDS ARE OMITTED.               FIG 18.2|
|000310 01   PRINT-LINE               PIC X(133).                   FIG 18.2|
|000320 WORKING-STORAGE SECTION.                                    FIG 18.2|
|000330 01   WORKING-VARIABLES.                                     FIG 18.2|
|000340      05   EXAM-COUNTER        PIC 9(03) VALUE ZERO.         FIG 18.2|
|000350      05   EXAM-1-TOTAL        PIC 9(05) VALUE ZERO.         FIG 18.2|
|000360      05   EXAM-2-TOTAL        PIC 9(05) VALUE ZERO.         FIG 18.2|
|000370      05   EXAM-3-TOTAL        PIC 9(05) VALUE ZERO.         FIG 18.2|
|000380      05   GRAND-TOTAL         PIC 9(06) VALUE ZERO.         FIG 18.2|
|000390      05   AVERAGE             PIC 9(03)V9(01).              FIG 18.2|
|000400      05   ALL-STUDENTS        PIC X(08).                    FIG 18.2|
|000410      05   BRANCH              PIC 9(01).                    FIG 18.2|
|000420 01   TITLE-LINE.                                            FIG 18.2|
|000430      02 FILLER                PIC X(55) VALUE SPACES.       FIG 18.2|
|000440      02 FILLER                PIC X(22) VALUE               FIG 18.2|
|000450      'STUDENT GRADE AVERAGES'.                              FIG 18.2|
|000460      02 FILLER                PIC X(56) VALUE SPACES.       FIG 18.2|
|000470 01   REPORT-COL-HEADINGS.                                   FIG 18.2|
|000480      02 FILLER                PIC X(41) VALUE SPACES.       FIG 18.2|
|000490      02 FILLER                PIC X(12) VALUE               FIG 18.2|
|000500      'STUDENT NAME'.                                        FIG 18.2|
|000510      02 FILLER                PIC X(10) VALUE SPACES.       FIG 18.2|
|000520      02 FILLER                PIC X(07) VALUE 'AVERAGE'.    FIG 18.2|
|000530      02 FILLER                PIC X(10) VALUE SPACES.       FIG 18.2|
|000540      02 FILLER                PIC X(12) VALUE 'LETTER GRADE'.FIG 18.2|
|000550 01   ASTER-ROW.                                             FIG 18.2|
|000560      02 FILLER                PIC X(41) VALUE SPACES.       FIG 18.2|
|000570      02 FILLER                PIC X(51) VALUE ALL '*'.      FIG 18.2|
|000580 01   STUDENT-REC.                                           FIG 18.2|
|000590      02 FILLER                PIC X(41) VALUE SPACES.       FIG 18.2|
|000600      02 STUDENT-NAME          PIC X(20).                    FIG 18.2|
|000610      02 FILLER                PIC X(03) VALUE SPACES.       FIG 18.2|
|000620      02 AVERAGE-GRADE         PIC ZZ9.9.                    FIG 18.2|
|000630      02 FILLER                PIC X(16) VALUE SPACES.       FIG 18.2|
|000640      02 LETTER-GRADE          PIC X(01).                    FIG 18.2|
|000650 01   STATISTICS.                                            FIG 18.2|
|000660      02 FILLER                PIC X(27) VALUE SPACES.       FIG 18.2|
|000670      02 FILLER                PIC X(24) VALUE               FIG 18.2|
|000680      'SUMMARY CLASS STATISTICS'.                            FIG 18.2|
|000690      02 FILLER                PIC X(05) VALUE SPACES.       FIG 18.2|
|000700      02 EXAM-1-AVERAGE        PIC ZZ9.9.                    FIG 18.2|
|000710      02 FILLER                PIC X(05) VALUE SPACES.       FIG 18.2|
|000720      02 EXAM-2-AVERAGE        PIC ZZ9.9.                    FIG 18.2|
|000730      02 FILLEP                PIC X(05) VALUE SPACES.       FIG 18.2|
|000740      02 EXAM-3-AVERAGE        PIC ZZ9.9.                    FIG 18.2|
|000750      02 FILLER                PIC X(05) VALUE SPACES.       FIG 18.2|
|000760      02 OVERALL-AVERAGE       PIC ZZ9.9.                    FIG 18.2|
|000770 PROCEDURE DIVISION.                                         FIG 18.2|
|000780 PROCEDURE-CONTROL SECTION.                                  FIG 18.2|
|000790      PERFORM 100-INITIAL-OPERATIONS.                        FIG 18.2|
|000800      PERFORM 300-DETERMINE-GRADES                           FIG 18.2|
|000810         UNTIL ALL-STUDENTS = 'FINISHED'.                    FIG 18.2|
|000820      PERFORM 700-OVERALL-STATS.                             FIG 18.2|
|000830      PERFORM 900-CLOSE-FILES.                               FIG 18.2|
|000840      STOP RUN.                                              FIG 18.2|
|000850 100-INITIAL-OPERATIONS SECTION.                             FIG 18.2|
|000860      OPEN INPUT STUDENT-FILE, OUTPUT GRADE-REPORT.          FIG 18.2|
|000870      WRITE PRINT-LINE FROM TITLE-LINE AFTER HEAD-OF-PAGE.   FIG 18.2|
|000880      WRITE PRINT-LINE FROM REPORT-COL-HEADINGS AFTER 1 LINES. FIG 18.2|
|000890      WRITE PRINT-LINE FROM ASTER-ROW AFTER 1 LINES.         FIG 18.2|
|000900      MOVE 'READING' TO ALL-STUDENTS.                        FIG 18.2|
|000910      READ STUDENT-FILE AT END MOVE 'FINISHED' TO ALL-STUDENTS. FIG 18.2|
|000920 300-DETERMINE-GRADES SECTION.                               FIG 18.2|
|000930      COMPUTE AVERAGE ROUNDED = (EXAM-1 + EXAM-2 + EXAM-3) / 3. FIG 18.2|
|000940      ADD EXAM-1 TO EXAM-1-TOTAL, GRAND-TOTAL.               FIG 18.2|
|000950      ADD EXAM-2 TO EXAM-2-TOTAL, GRAND-TOTAL.               FIG 18.2|
|000960      ADD EXAM-3 TO EXAM-3-TOTAL, GRAND-TOTAL.               FIG 18.2|
|000970      ADD 1 TO EXAM-COUNTER.                                 FIG 18.2|
|000980      COMPUTE BRANCH = (AVERAGE - 40) / 10 + .5.             FIG 18.2|
|000990      GO TO 310-GRADE-F, 320-GRADE-D, 330-GRADE-C,          FIG 18.2|
|001000         340-GRADE-B, 350-GRADE-A,                           FIG 18.2|
```

Figure 18.2 An Illustration of the GO TO/DEPENDING ON Statement *Continued*

```
|                 1   1   2   2   2   3   3   4   4   4   5   5   6   6   6   7   7   8|
|    4   8        2   6   0   4   8   2   6   0   4   8   2   6   0   4   8   2   6   0|
---------------------------------------------------------------------------------------
|001010          DEPENDING ON BRANCH.                                       FIG 18.2|
|001020 310-GRADE-F.                                                        FIG 18.2|
|001030     MOVE 'F' TO LETTER-GRADE.                                       FIG 18.2|
|001040     PERFORM 315-PRINT-OUTPUT-LINE.                                  FIG 18.2|
|001050     GO TO 399-EXIT.                                                 FIG 18.2|
|001060 320-GRADE-D.                                                        FIG 18.2|
|001070     MOVE 'D' TO LETTER-GRADE.                                       FIG 18.2|
|001080     PERFORM 315-PRINT-OUTPUT-LINE.                                  FIG 18.2|
|001090     GO TO 399-EXIT.                                                 FIG 18.2|
|001100 330-GRADE-C.                                                        FIG 18.2|
|001110     MOVE 'C' TO LETTER-GRADE.                                       FIG 18.2|
|001120     PERFORM 315-PRINT-OUTPUT-LINE.                                  FIG 18.2|
|001130     GO TO 399-EXIT.                                                 FIG 18.2|
|001140 340-GRADE-B.                                                        FIG 18.2|
|001150     MOVE 'B' TO LETTER-GRADE.                                       FIG 18.2|
|001160     PERFORM 315-PRINT-OUTPUT-LINE.                                  FIG 18.2|
|001170     GO TO 399-EXIT.                                                 FIG 18.2|
|001180 350-GRADE-A.                                                        FIG 18.2|
|001190     MOVE 'A' TO LETTER-GRADE.                                       FIG 18.2|
|001200 315-PRINT-OUTPUT-LINE.                                              FIG 18.2|
|001210     MOVE NAME-STUDENT TO STUDENT-NAME.                              FIG 18.2|
|001220     MOVE AVERAGE TO AVERAGE-GRADE.                                  FIG 18.2|
|001230     WRITE PRINT-LINE FROM STUDENT-REC AFTER 2 LINES.                FIG 18.2|
|001240     READ STUDENT-FILE AT END MOVE 'FINISHED' TO ALL-STUDENTS.       FIG 18.2|
|001250 399-EXIT.                                                           FIG 18.2|
|001260     EXIT.                                                           FIG 18.2|
|001270 700-OVERALL-STATS SECTION.                                          FIG 18.2|
|001280     WRITE PRINT-LINE FROM ASTER-ROW AFTER 2 LINES.                  FIG 18.2|
|001290     DIVIDE EXAM-1-TOTAL BY EXAM-COUNTER GIVING EXAM-1-AVERAGE       FIG 18.2|
|001300          ROUNDED.                                                   FIG 18.2|
|001310     DIVIDE EXAM-2-TOTAL BY EXAM-COUNTER GIVING EXAM-2-AVERAGE       FIG 18.2|
|001320          ROUNDED.                                                   FIG 18.2|
|001330     DIVIDE EXAM-3-TOTAL BY EXAM-COUNTER GIVING EXAM-3-AVERAGE       FIG 18.2|
|001340          ROUNDED.                                                   FIG 18.2|
|001350     COMPUTE OVERALL-AVERAGE ROUNDED = GRAND-TOTAL /                 FIG 18.2|
|001360          (EXAM-COUNTER * 3).                                        FIG 18.2|
|001370     WRITE PRINT-LINE AFTER ADVANCING 2 LINES.                       FIG 18.2|
|001380     WRITE PRINT-LINE FROM STATISTICS AFTER 2 LINES.                 FIG 18.2|
|001390 900-CLOSE-FILES SECTION.                                            FIG 18.2|
|001400     CLOSE STUDENT-FILE, GRADE-REPORT.                               FIG 18.2|
```

Figure 18.2 An Illustration of the GO TO/DEPENDING ON Statement *Continued*

```
|        |          1         2         3         4         5         6         7         8| FIGURE  |
|RECORD  |1234567890123456789012345678901234567890123456789012345678901234567890| NUMBER  |
|    1|ADAMS, FOREST            053051051                                         |FIG 18.2|
|    2|BALLES, WILLIAM          070075072                                         |FIG 18.2|
|    3|BOND, GEORGE             090096090                                         |FIG 18.2|
|    4|BROADUS, CATHY           086080081                                         |FIG 18.2|
|    5|CESARIO, WINNIE          068051058                                         |FIG 18.2|
|    6|CLEMENT, DEBORA          094093085                                         |FIG 18.2|
|    7|DECKER, LAWRENCE         044045050                                         |FIG 18.2|
|    8|EDMISTON, GARY           079071074                                         |FIG 18.2|
|    9|ELLIOTT, JOSE            081080084                                         |FIG 18.2|
|   10|FORD, JAMES              086084061                                         |FIG 18.2|
|   11|GAPINSKI, MAUREEN        054057051                                         |FIG 18.2|
|   12|HAFFEY, ERNEST           093090094                                         |FIG 18.2|
|   13|HEALTON, TIM             084095098                                         |FIG 18.2|
|   14|HILL, ROBERT             077070071                                         |FIG 18.2|
|   15|HOOSON, KIM              076075076                                         |FIG 18.2|
|   16|KASKADDEN, NANCY         081086080                                         |FIG 18.2|
|   17|KEYES, ANDY              063054080                                         |FIG 18.2|
|   18|KLAVON, KEVIN            084088085                                         |FIG 18.2|
|   19|KOS, JANIE               100099099                                         |FIG 18.2|
|   20|LORENZ, LINDA            082087081                                         |FIG 18.2|
|   21|MEYER, ROBERT            099092095                                         |FIG 18.2|
|   22|MILLER, MARK             071069068                                         |FIG 18.2|
|   23|MYERS, AUDREY            072075070                                         |FIG 18.2|
|   24|ROEHL, MARTY             081093095                                         |FIG 18.2|
|   25|SENGER, MARVIN           053053055                                         |FIG 18.2|
```

Figure 18.2 An Illustration of the GO TO/DEPENDING ON Statement (Data) *Continued*

```
|-------------------------------------------------------------------------------------
| |       1         2         3         4         5         6         7        8| FIGURE |
|RECORD|1234567890123456789012345678901234567890123456789012345678901234567890| NUMBER |
|   26|SHOGREN, MARCUS            091094089                                     |FIG 18.2|
|   27|SMITH, DENNIS             025072028                                      |FIG 18.2|
|   28|SWANSON, JEFF             100100100                                      |FIG 18.2|
|   29|TIDWELL, JANE             065066067                                      |FIG 18.2|
```

Figure 18.2 An Illustration of the GO TO/DEPENDING ON Statement (Data) *Continued*

```
                          STUDENT GRADE AVERAGES
              STUDENT NAME           AVERAGE        LETTER GRADE
              *******************************************************

              ADAMS, FOREST           51.7              F

              BALLES, WILLIAM         72.3              C

              BOND, GEORGE            92.0              A

              BROADUS, CATHY          92.3              B

              CESARIO, WINNIE         59.0              D

              CLEMENT, DEBORA         90.7              A

              DECKER, LAWRENCE        46.3              F

              EDMISTON, GARY          74.7              C

              ELLIOTT, JOSE           81.7              B

              FORD, JAMES             77.0              B

              GAPINSKI, MAUREEN       54.0              F

              HAFFEY, ERNEST          92.3              A

              HEALTON, TIM            92.3              A

              HILL, ROBERT            72.7              C

              HODSON, KIM             75.7              B

              KASKADDEN, NANCY        82.3              B

              KEYES, ANDY             65.7              C

              KLAVON, KEVIN           85.7              A

              KOS, JANIE              99.3              F

              LORENZ, LINDA           83.3              B

              MEYER, ROBERT           95.3              F

              MILLER, MARK            69.3              C

              MYERS, AUDREY           72.3              C

              ROEHL, MARTY            89.7              A

              SENGER, MARVIN          53.7              F

              SHOGREN, MARCUS         91.3              A

              SMITH, DENNIS           41.7              F

              SWANSON, JEFF           100.0             F

              TIDWELL, JANE           66.0              C

              *******************************************************

              *******************************************************

      SUMMARY CLASS STATISTICS     75.9      77.3      75.4      76.2
```

Figure 18.2 An Illustration of the GO TO/DEPENDING ON Statement (Output) *Continued*

Summary   In this chapter, an additional form of the GO TO statement has been presented. The GO TO/DEPENDING ON statement is capable of executing an unconditional branch to a procedure name by "selecting" a particular procedure-name from a list of procedures. This selection is used on a correspondence between the value of an identifier associated with the GO TO/DEPENDING ON statement and the location (first, second, third, etc.) of a procedure in the list of procedures.

Notes on Programming Style   The case structure is probably best approximated in COBOL through the use of the GO TO/DEPENDING ON statement. However, do not get yourself trapped when designing code to use this statement. You will frequently find it necessary to use the SECTION level in the PROCEDURE DIVISION. Otherwise, you will have to cancel a PERFORM statement that is probably controlling the overall procedure. You will be calling for help from your favorite deity if that happens.

Questions

Fill in the following blank(s) with the appropriate word, words, or phrase.

1. In total, there are _____ (number) formats of the GO TO statement.

2. The types of GO TO statements provided in COBOL include the _____ and _____ statements.

3. The simple GO TO statement provides for a single, unconditional branch; the GO TO/DEPENDING ON statement provides for _____ .

Answer the following questions by circling "T" for True or "F" for False.

T   F   4. The identifier associated with the GO TO/DEPENDING ON statement must be defined as an integer field.

T   F   5. The identifier associated with the GO TO/DEPENDING ON statement could contain zero.

T   F   6. If the identifier associated with a GO TO/DEPENDING ON statement contained a negative value, the GO TO/DEPENDING ON statement is executed.

19 Multiple Record Descriptions, Redefinitions, and Renaming of Data Items

Some problems require that the definitions of records, groups of items, or elementary-items describe the same space in the computer's memory. Two benefits are derived from this technique. First, by describing two or more data items (records, groups, or elementary-items) to occupy the same place, the computer's internal memory is conserved. Second, alternate descriptions (with varied field sizes and characteristics) for the same area of the computer's memory are provided.

Multiple Record Descriptions

Under some circumstances, the input data for a program has varied formats (i.e., all of the input records have different field designations or sizes and characteristics). If it were not possible to have multiple record descriptions for these records, it would be difficult to input and interpret their meanings. Multiple record descriptions can be placed in the FILE SECTION to be associated with one file or FD. If a problem requires the input (or output) of two or more records with differing characteristics and if the programmer codes these records in one FD record, the program can accommodate those variations.

As an illustration of this process, assume a program must handle three different types of records from the same file (see Figure 19.1). If the programmer incorporates multiple record descriptions in the file description for this file, all of these records can be read into the computer's memory. The record descriptions for these three records are also shown in Figure 19.1. Note that each of the descriptions begins with the level number Ø1—the COBOL notation for records—and that the fields and their characteristics are different from one record to another. Also, some fields in the same columns of the respective records use different labels (data-names). When data is needed in the PROCEDURE DIVISION, the programmer must determine which of the record descriptions contains the correct interpretation of the record last read. This is often done by placing a code field in one of the columns of the record. In the example, the programmer could use the code in column 80 of each record to determine which record description to use in the PROCEDURE DIVISION. (If the code is 1, the first record description should be used; if the code is 2, the second record description should be used; and so forth.)

MULTIPLE-CARD LAYOUT FORM

Company   ABC MANUFACTURING COMPANY

Application   INVENTORY RECORD DESCRIPTIONS   by   J. WAYNE SPENCE   Date 1/1/78   Job No. ABC-123   Sheet No. 1

RECORD 1

ITEM NUMBER	ITEM DESCRIPTION	ON HAND	MIN. ORDER LEVEL	UNIT INFORMATION CUMULATIVE ANNUAL DISBURSEMENT	ACQUISITION	AVERAGE PRICE	LAST SUPPLIER	DATE OF LAST DISBURSEMENT D M Y	ACQUISITION D M Y	CARD TYPE

RECORD 2

ITEM NUMBER	QUANTITY RECEIVED	DATE RECEIVED D M Y	PRICE PER UNIT	SUPPLIER NAME	STREET ADDRESS	CITY	STATE	ZIP CODE	ID. CODE	CARD TYPE

RECORD 3

ITEM NUMBER	QUANTITY DISBURSED	DATE DISBURSED D M Y	AGENCY DISBURSED TO= NAME	STREET ADDRESS	CITY	STATE	ZIP CODE	CARD TYPE

Figure 19.1 Multiple Record Layouts

The COBOL compiler assumes that the three record descriptions in the FILE SECTION of Figure 19.2 describe the same space in the computer's memory. The compiler makes no such assumption about records described in the WORKING-STORAGE SECTION. Therefore, these three record descriptions occupy 80 characters of computer memory if located in the FILE SECTION but 240 characters of memory, if in the WORKING-STORAGE SECTION.

The records illustrated in Figure 19.1 are different in many respects, including different field names (e.g., ITEM DESCRIPTION in record 1 versus QUANTITY DISBURSED in record 2) and different field characteristics (e.g., ITEM DESCRIPTION of record 1 is an alphanumeric field; QUANTITY RECEIVED and QUANTITY DISBURSED of records 2 and 3 are numeric fields). Even though the records are different, they may be read into the same buffer. Recall from Chapters 3 and 5 that the FILE SECTION of the DATA DIVISION represents internal computer memory employed for input and output buffers. The program can accept any type of data in the input buffer. It is only when data are to be accessed in the PROCEDURE DIVISION that they must be referenced with an appropriate PICTURE string. That is, to *utilize* data in an input buffer, they must be matched with a data item description. Then, data can be read; otherwise, a fatal error may result.

After data have been read into an input buffer, the programmer must use the appropriate data-names to access the data. The approach used in Figure 19.2 is a code (CARD-TYPE), which indicates the difference between the formats. Thus, if the CARD-TYPE contained the value 1, the programmer could interpret this to mean that a MASTER-RECORD has entered the buffer. The value 2 could be used for RECEIPT-RECORD identification, and the value 3 could represent a DISBURSEMENT-RECORD. However, this is not the only means to distinguish among records. For example, to distinguish between a MASTER-RECORD and a RECEIPT-RECORD, the STATE field of the RECEIPT-RECORD could be examined to determine whether its contents was alphabetic. (If the statement IF STATE OF RECEIPT-RECORD IS ALPHABETIC was placed in the program, a false result would indicate that a MASTER-

```
DATA DIVISION.
FILE SECTION.
FD   INVENTORY-FILE LABEL RECORDS ARE OMITTED.
Ø1   MASTER-RECORD.
     Ø3 INVENTORY-NUMBER        PIC 9(6).
     Ø3 ITEM-DESCRIPTION        PIC X(21).
     Ø3 UNIT-INFORMATION.
        Ø5 ON-HAND              PIC 9(7).
        Ø5 MINIMUM-ORDER-LEVEL  PIC 9(4).
        Ø5 CUMULATIVE-ANNUAL.
           Ø7 DISBURSEMENTS     PIC 9(1Ø).
           Ø7 ACQUISITIONS      PIC 9(1Ø).
        Ø5 AVERAGE-PRICE        PIC 9(4)V99.
     Ø3 LAST-SUPPLIER           PIC 999.
     Ø3 DATE-OF-LAST.
        Ø5 DISBURSEMENT
           Ø7 DAY               PIC 99.
           Ø7 MONTH             PIC 99.
           Ø7 YEAR              PIC 99.
        Ø5 ACQUISITION.
           Ø7 DAY               PIC 99.
           Ø7 MONTH             PIC 99.
           Ø7 YEAR              PIC 99.
     Ø3 CARD-TYPE               PIC 9.
Ø1   RECEIPT-RECORD.
     Ø3 ITEM-NUMBER             PIC 9(6).
     Ø3 QUANTITY-RECEIVED       PIC 9(6).
     Ø3 DATE-RECEIVED.
        Ø5 DAY                  PIC 99.
        Ø5 MONTH                PIC 99.
        Ø5 YEAR                 PIC 99.
     Ø3 PRICE-PER-UNIT          PIC 9999V99.
     Ø3 SUPPLIER.
        Ø5 NAME                 PIC X(2Ø).
        Ø5 STREET               PIC X(15).
        Ø5 CITY                 PIC X(9).
        Ø5 STATE                PIC XX.
        Ø5 ZIP CODE             PIC 9(5).
     Ø3 ID-CODE                 PIC 9999.
     Ø3 CARD-CODE               PIC 9.
Ø1   DISBURSEMENT-RECORD.
     Ø3 ITEM-NUMBER             PIC 9(6).
     Ø3 QUANTITY-DISBURSED      PIC 9(6).
     Ø3 DATE-DISBURSED.
        Ø5 DAY                  PIC 99.
        Ø5 MONTH                PIC 99.
        Ø5 YEAR                 PIC 99.
     Ø3 AGENCY-DISBURSED-TO.
        Ø5 NAME                 PIC X(2Ø).
        Ø5 STREET-ADDRESS       PIC X(2Ø).
        Ø5 CITY                 PIC X(1Ø).
        Ø5 STATE                PIC XX.
        Ø5 ZIP-CODE             PIC 9(5).
     Ø3 FILLER                  PIC XXXX.
     Ø3 CARD-TYPE               PIC 9.
```

Figure 19.2 Multiple Record Descriptions in the FILE SECTION

RECORD was in the input buffer—assuming the DATE-OF-LAST-DISBURSEMENT was recorded as a number.) To distinguish between a RECEIPT-RECORD and a DISBURSEMENT-RECORD, the ID-CODE of RECEIPT-RECORD could be examined to determine whether its contents was a number (the appropriate contents for an ID-CODE) or spaces (the normal contents of FILLER). Thus, the programmer does not have to rely totally on the foresight of those responsible for designing input records.

The REDEFINES Clause

In some cases, the records to be read by a program have highly similar characteristics. For example, the input-record descriptions presented in Figure 19.1 include an ITEM-NUMBER in the first six columns of each record. Each of the records presents a CARD-TYPE code in column 80.

By using the REDEFINES clause in the description of records, any fields that are present in one or more records (or groups) do not have to be recoded. Only the different portions of the records (in size or characteristics) need be coded by the programmer. In addition, one WORKING-STORAGE SECTION record description may be *overlaid* on another by using the REDEFINES clause in *either* the FILE SECTION or the WORKING-STORAGE SECTION. Thus, by placing one record (or a portion of a record) in the same internal computer memory location as another, space in the WORKING-STORAGE SECTION may be conserved. The format of the REDEFINES clause is presented in Figure 19.3.

Data-name-1, as specified in Figure 19.3, must not be the name of a record in the FILE SECTION. As seen in the discussion of multiple records in the FILE SECTION, a redefinition of these records at level-Ø1 is redundant—the records are already implicitly redefined. Data-name-1 also must not be a level-66 or 88 data item. Level-66 is used with the RENAMES clause, which is discussed later in this chapter. Level-88 is used with condition-names as described in Chapter 11. Both data-name-1 and data-name-2 may represent a table (a data item which is accompanied by an OCCURS clause—see Chapter 13). Neither data-name-1 nor data-name-2 may be a variable-length table. Data-name-2 may not be written with or subordinate to an OCCURS clause, but it may have an OCCURS clause with one of *its* subordinate items.

The level number associated with the REDEFINES clause is the key to understanding the redefinition process. Data-name-2 must appear in a description of data prior to the redefinition itself. The level number associated with data-name-2 must be the same level number as the redefinition. For example, if data-name-2 is coded at level-Ø3 the redefinition must be at level-Ø3. If data-name-2 is an elementary data item, the redefinition must immediately follow the data-name-2 entry. If data-name-2 is a group (or record), the redefinition must follow data-name-2 at the programmer's first opportunity to enter a level number equivalent to that of data-name-2. For example, if data-name-2 is coded at level-Ø2 redefinition must begin before the next level-2 which would normally appear in the record description.

The redefinition is terminated by the occurrence of a level that is higher than or equal to that of the redefinition. If the redefinition begins with level-Ø4 the redefinition is terminated with the next occurrence of level-Ø1, Ø2, Ø3, or Ø4. The redefinition should be exactly the same length as the original definition of the data being redefined. That is, if the original description of the data (in or subordinate to data-name-2) is 3Ø characters or digits, the redefinition should also represent 3Ø characters or digits. If multiple redefinitions of the same data

```
level-number data-name-1 REDEFINES data-name-2
```

Figure 19.3 Format of the REDEFINES Clause

fields are necessary, each redefinition should use the name (data-name-2) of the original data description. (Some compilers—e.g., IBM—permit a redefinition *of* a redefinition.) It is also possible to have a redefinition *within* a redefinition. That is, COBOL allows the programmer to redefine a portion of a record description which is associated with a REDEFINES clause.

Figure 19.4 shows how the REDEFINES clause is used. This illustration provides an alternative to the FILE SECTION entries in Figure 19.2, using the same description of data presented in Figure 19.1. However, this description is somewhat shorter and does not require PROCEDURE DIVISION qualification of the data-names ITEM-NUMBER and CARD-TYPE.

```
DATA DIVISION
FILE SECTION
FD   INVENTORY-FILE LABEL RECORDS ARE OMITTED.
Ø1   INVENTORY-RECORDS.
     Ø3 ITEM-NUMBER                        PIC 9(6).
     Ø3 BODY-OF-RECORD.
         Ø5 ITEM-DESCRIPTION               PIC X(21).
         Ø5 UNIT-INFORMATION.
             Ø7 ON-HAND                    PIC 9(7).
             Ø7 MIN-ORDER-LEVEL            PIC 9999.
             Ø7 CUMULATIVE-ANNUAL.
                 Ø9 DISBURSEMENTS          PIC 9(1Ø).
                 Ø9 ACQUISITIONS           PIC 9(1Ø).
             Ø7 AVERAGE-PRICE              PIC 9999V99.
         Ø5 LAST-SUPPLIER                  PIC 999.
         Ø5 DATE-OF-LAST.
             Ø7 DISBURSEMENT.
                 Ø9 DAY                    PIC 99.
                 Ø9 MONTH                  PIC 99.
                 Ø9 YEAR                   PIC 99.
             Ø7 ACQUISITION.
                 Ø9 DAY                    PIC 99.
                 Ø9 MONTH                  PIC 99.
                 Ø9 YEAR                   PIC 99.
     Ø3 RECEIPT-DISBURSEMENT-RECORD REDEFINES BODY-OF-RECORD.
         Ø5 QUANTITY-RECEIVED-DISBURSED  PIC 9(6).
         Ø5 DATE-RECEIVED-DISBURSED.
             Ø7 DAY                        PIC 99.
             Ø7 MONTH                      PIC 99.
             Ø7 YEAR                       PIC 99.
         Ø5 RECEIPT-INFORMATION.
             Ø7 PRICE-PER-UNIT             PIC 9999V99.
             Ø7 SUPPLIER.
                 Ø9 NAME                   PIC X(2Ø).
                 Ø9 ADDRESS               PIC X(15).
                 Ø9 CITY                   PIC X(9).
                 Ø9 STATE                  PIC XX.
                 Ø9 ZIP-CODE               PIC 9(5).
                 Ø9 ID-CODE                PIC 9999.
         Ø5 DISBURSEMENT-INFORMATION REDEFINES RECEIPT-INFORMATION.
             Ø7 NAME                       PIC X(2Ø).
             Ø7 ADDRESS                    PIC X(2Ø).
             Ø7 CITY                       PIC X(1Ø).
             Ø7 STATE                      PIC XX.
             Ø7 ZIP-CODE                   PIC 9(5).
             Ø7 FILLER                     PIC XXXX
     Ø3 CARD-TYPE                          PIC 9.
```

Figure 19.4 An Illustration of the REDEFINES Clause

Redefinition of Tables

It is often useful to have a table constructed in the computer's memory that is provided with data prior to program execution. That is, during the creation of the table, the table is "loaded" with data. This may be done with the REDEFINES clause. Recall that the REDEFINES clause may be used with OC-CURS clauses to provide alternate descriptions of the same area of the computer's memory. The programmer should also remember that a VALUE clause cannot be written with or subordinate to an OCCURS clause, except as might be used with condition-names. Thus, unless the programmer plans to MOVE data into a table during the execution of the PROCEDURE DIVISION, the only alternative to loading a table with data values prior to program execution is to utilize the REDEFINES clause.

Figure 19.5 provides an example of how the REDEFINES clause is used to provide initial values for table items. (It is assumed that the code of Figure 19.5 is in the WORKING-STORAGE SECTION, since the VALUE clause is being employed.) Notice that it is first necessary to construct a "dummy" record containing the data values to be placed in the table. DATA-RECORD is such a record. The sole purpose of DATA-RECORD is to provide values to be placed in certain positions with TABLE-OF-MONTHS. VALUE clauses may be used with the FILLER items of DATA-RECORD, but they could not be used with any item associated with TABLE-OF-MONTHS. The programmer must be

```
Ø1    DATA-RECORD.
      Ø2 FILLER PIC X(11) VALUE 'Ø1JANUARY'.
      Ø2 FILLER PIC X(11) VALUE 'Ø2FEBRUARY'.
      Ø2 FILLER PIC X(11) VALUE 'Ø3MARCH'.
      Ø2 FILLER PIC X(11) VALUE 'Ø4APRIL'.
      Ø2 FILLER PIC X(11) VALUE 'Ø5MAY'.
      Ø2 FILLER PIC X(11) VALUE 'Ø6JUNE'.
      Ø2 FILLER PIC X(11) VALUE 'Ø7JULY'.
      Ø2 FILLER PIC X(11) VALUE 'Ø8AUGUST'.
      Ø2 FILLER PIC X(11) VALUE 'Ø9SEPTEMBER'.
      Ø2 FILLER PIC X(11) VALUE '1ØOCTOBER'.
      Ø2 FILLER PIC X(11) VALUE '11NOVEMBER'.
      Ø2 FILLER PIC X(11) VALUE '12DECEMBER'.

Ø1    TABLE-OF-MONTHS REDEFINES DATA-RECORD.
      Ø2 MONTH-NAME-NUMBER OCCURS 12 TIMES.
         Ø3 MONTH-NUMBER PIC 99.
         Ø3 MONTH-NAME   PIC X(9).
```

TABLE-OF-MONTHS

```
MONTH-NUMBER (1)    | Ø1 | JANUARY   |   MONTH-NAME (1)
MONTH-NUMBER (2)    | Ø2 | FEBRUARY  |   MONTH-NAME (2)
MONTH-NUMBER (3)    | Ø3 | MARCH     |   MONTH-NAME (3)
MONTH-NUMBER (4)    | Ø4 | APRIL     |   MONTH-NAME (4)
MONTH-NUMBER (5)    | Ø5 | MAY       |   MONTH-NAME (5)
MONTH-NUMBER (6)    | Ø6 | JUNE      |   MONTH-NAME (6)
MONTH-NUMBER (7)    | Ø7 | JULY      |   MONTH-NAME (7)
MONTH-NUMBER (8)    | Ø8 | AUGUST    |   MONTH-NAME (8)
MONTH-NUMBER (9)    | Ø9 | SEPTEMBER |   MONTH-NAME (9)
MONTH-NUMBER (1Ø)   | 1Ø | OCTOBER   |   MONTH-NAME (1Ø)
MONTH-NUMBER (11)   | 11 | NOVEMBER  |   MONTH-NAME (11)
MONTH-NUMBER (12)   | 12 | DECEMBER  |   MONTH-NAME (12)
```

Figure 19.5 An Example of Table Initialization

careful when providing data values to be placed in a table. The description of the data must be consistent with the description of the table. In Figure 19.5, MONTH-NUMBER and MONTH-NAME (each of which OCCURS 12 times) alternate in the computer's memory. (The alternating process was described in Chapter 13.) Thus, the description of the data values to be placed in the table must alternate.

Figure 19.6 illustrates the same type of data arrangement as in Figure 19.5; however, in this illustration, the table is described in such a way that all occurrences of MONTH-NUMBER appear before the first occurrence of MONTH-NAME. Thus, the data placed into DATA-RECORD must be organized so that all values for MONTH-NUMBER are provided before the value to be placed in the first occurrence of MONTH-NAME.

The RENAMES Clause

The final clause to be discussed in this chapter is the RENAMES clause. This clause allows the programmer to change the names of data items or groups or create totally new groupings of data items. The RENAMES clause is different from the REDEFINES clause in a number of respects. As the format of the RENAMES clause in Figure 19.7 indicates it is always accompanied by a level-66 number. This level number should be coded in Area A of a COBOL

```
Ø1    DATA-RECORD.
      Ø2 FILLER PIC X(24) VALUE 'Ø1Ø2Ø3Ø4Ø5Ø6Ø7Ø8Ø9101112'.
      Ø2 FILLER PIC X(1Ø8)  VALUE 'JANUARY   FEBRUARY MARCH      APRIL
      '   MAY       JUNE     JULY      AUGUST   SEPTEMBEROCTOBER   NO
      'VEMBER DECEMBER'.
Ø1    MONTH-NAME-NUMBER-TABLE REDEFINES DATA-RECORD.
      Ø2 MONTH-NUMBER OCCURS 12 TIMES PIC 99.
      Ø2 MONTH-NAME   OCCURS 12 TIMES PIC X(9).
```

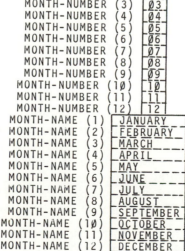

Figure 19.6 A Second Illustration of Table Initialization

entry. The RENAMES clause should appear immediately *after* a record description—not within the record description, as with the REDEFINES clause. In addition, the REDEFINES clause may be accompanied by a PICTURE clause or have subordinate data items that modify the original characteristics of the same data area. The RENAMES clause may not be written with a PICTURE clause, i.e., the RENAMES clause may only be used to provide an alternate name for data already described. In addition, there may be no data items subordinate to a RENAMES clause. Thus, the RENAMES clause cannot change the characteristics of a data area. Finally, the RENAMES clause cannot be used to provide alternate data-names for other items accompanied by level numbers Ø1, 66, 77, or 88.

In Figure 19.7, data-name-1 represents a new data-name which acts as an alternate to data-name-2 (which should appear in the preceding record). That is, in the PROCEDURE DIVISION, data-name-1 and data-name-2 may be used interchangeably—both represent the same data. If data-name-2 is an elementary data item, data-name-1 is assumed to be an elementary data item with the same characteristics. If data-name-2 is a group item, data-name-1 is also considered to be a group item. The only difference between data-name-1 and data-name-2 is that data-name-1 may not be used in the qualification of a data-name that is subordinate to data-name-2.

When both data-name-2 and data-name-3 are used, data-name-1 is considered to be a group item. Data-name-2 and data-name-3 should not be the same name. Data-name-3 should physically follow data-name-2 in the record description, but data-name-3 should not be subordinate to data-name-2. When the RENAMES is complete, data-name-1 is considered to be a group item which includes all data items between data-name-2 and data-name-3 (and if data-name-3 is a group name, data-name-1 includes all data items subordinate to data-name-3). Data-name-2 and data-name-3 may be either elementary data items or group names.

The RENAMES clause may be used in the description of the inventory records presented in Figures 19.2 and 19.4. Figure 19.8 presents a demonstration of the use of multiple records, REDEFINES clauses, and RENAMES clauses. This illustration provides a description of the MASTER-RECORD and a RECEIPT-DISBURSEMENT-RECORD, which is used jointly by both receipts and disbursements. Note that in the RECEIPT-DISBURSEMENT-RECORD the redefinition is slightly different from the redefinition in Figure 19.4. Only the portions of the receipt and disbursement records that are different are included in the redefined area. Thus, STATE and ZIP-CODE, being in the same columns in both records, are *not* redefined. Immediately following the RECEIPT-DISBURSEMENT-RECORD are a series of RENAMES clauses. The first RENAMES clause is used to provide an alternate name for QUANTITY-RECEIVED. In the PROCEDURE DIVISION, columns 7 through 12 of the input record could be represented by either QUANTITY-RECEIVED or QUANTITY-DISBURSED (i.e., they are both numeric elementary data

```
66 data-name-1 RENAMES data-name-2 [THRU data-name-3]
```

Figure 19.7 Format of the RENAMES Clause

items). The second RENAMES clause is used to provide an alternate name for DATE-RECEIVED—a group name. Thus, DATE-DISBURSED could be used in the PROCEDURE DIVISION as a group representation for DAY, MONTH, and YEAR.

The third RENAMES clause is used to regroup data items which were separated during the redefinition process. In the receipt record, the PRICE-PER-UNIT, NAME, ADDRESS, CITY, STATE, ZIP-CODE, and ID-CODE are placed in a group called SUPPLIER-INFORMATION. (Note that with the RENAMES clause, PRICE-PER-UNIT could be replaced by SUPPLIER-

```
DATA DIVISION
FILE SECTION
FD  INVENTORY-FILE LABEL RECORDS ARE OMITTED.
Ø1  MASTER-RECORD.
    Ø3 INVENTORY-NUMBER        PIC 9(6).
    Ø3 ITEM-DESCRIPTION        PIC X(21).
    Ø3 UNIT-INFORMATION.
        Ø5 ON-HAND             PIC 9(7).
        Ø5 MIN-ORDER-LEVEL     PIC 9(1Ø).
        Ø5 CUMULATIVE-ANNUAL.
            Ø7 DISBURSEMENTS   PIC 9(1Ø).
            Ø7 ACQUISITIONS    PIC 9(1Ø).
        Ø5 AVERAGE-PRICE       PIC 9999V99.
        Ø5 DATE-OF-LAST.
            Ø7 DISBURSEMENT.
                Ø9 DAY         PIC 99.
                Ø9 MONTH       PIC 99.
                Ø9 YEAR        PIC 99.
            Ø7 ACQUISITION.
                Ø9 DAY         PIC 99.
                Ø9 MONTH       PIC 99.
                Ø9 YEAR        PIC 99.
    Ø3 CARD-TYPE               PIC 9.
Ø1  RECEIPT-DISBURSEMENT-RECORD
    Ø3 ITEM-NUMBER             PIC 9(6)
    Ø3 QUANTITY-RECEIVED       PIC 9(6)
    Ø3 DATE-RECEIVED.
        Ø5 DAY                 PIC 99.
        Ø5 MONTH               PIC 99.
        Ø5 YEAR                PIC 99.
    Ø3 RECEIPT-DISBURSEMENT-INFORMATION.
        Ø5 SUPPLIER-SPECIFIC-INFORMATION.
            Ø7 PRICE-PER-UNIT  PIC 9999V99.
            Ø7 SUPPLIER.
                Ø9 NAME        PIC X(2Ø).
                Ø9 ADDRESS     PIC X(15).
                Ø9 CITY        PIC X(9).
        Ø5 DISBURSE-SPECIFIC-INFORMATION REDEFINES SUPPLIER-SPECIFIC-INFORMATION.
            Ø7 NAME            PIC X(2Ø).
            Ø7 ADDRESS         PIC X(2Ø).
            Ø7 CITY            PIC X(1Ø).
        Ø5 STATE               PIC XX.
        Ø5 ZIP-CODE            PIC 9(5).
    Ø3 ID-CODE                 PIC 9999.
    Ø3 CARD-TYPE               PIC 9.
66  QUANTITY-DISBURSED RENAMES QUANTITY-RECEIVED.
66  DATE-DISBURSED RENAMES DATE-RECEIVED.
66  SUPPLIER-INFORMATION RENAMES PRICE-PER-UNIT THRU ID-CODE.
66  AGENCY-DISBURSED-TO RENAMES PRICE-PER-UNIT THRU ZIP-CODE.
```

Figure 19.8 An Illustration of Multiple Record Descriptions, REDEFINES Clauses, and RENAMES Clauses

SPECIFIC-INFORMATION or RECEIPT-DISBURSEMENT-INFORMATION with the same result.) The last RENAMES clause presented in the illustration is used to regroup items that would normally be associated with a disbursement. Thus, NAME, ADDRESS, CITY (all of which are part of a redefinition), STATE, and ZIP-CODE are grouped together to form a group known as AGENCY-DISBURSED-TO. (Note that PRICE-PER-UNIT could be replaced with either DISBURSE-SPECIFIC-INFORMATION, NAME OF DISBURSE-SPECIFIC-INFORMATION, or either of the two identifiers mentioned with the previous renaming process with the same result.)

Figure 19.9 provides multiple records used in the context of a program. (The completed program appears in Chapter 10.) The purpose of the program is to compute a summary of the information that would be produced on a customer bill by an electric utility company. The input to the program consists of four types of records. The first record is a previous history card containing the customer account number, electricity usage meter reading from the past month, and any customer account balance carried forward from the previous month's bill. The second card is an account payment record. It contains the customer's account number and an amount of payment. The third card format is the electricity usage during the current month. Each of the records contains a code number in column 80 to allow the programmer to distinguish between the records. (Note that redefinitions are used in this program. However, these redefinitions could be replaced by RENAMES clauses since all meter readings and amounts appear in the same input record columns.) The last record to be used by this program is a record containing the current date. (Note that some compilers have special registers that allow the transmission of the current date to the programmer's work area. For example, a programmer using an IBM computer may reference the special register CURRENT-DATE to receive the date entered into the computer at the beginning of the day's operation.)

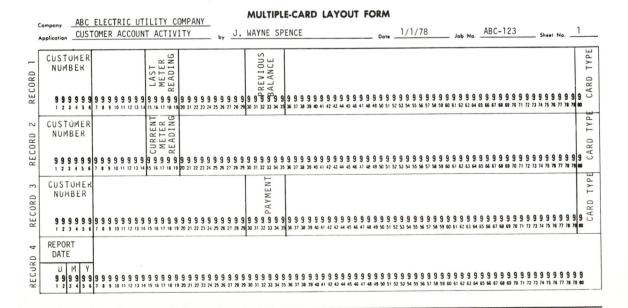

Figure 19.9 A Program Illustration (Record Layouts)

Figure 19.10 provides three separate examples of how the records presented in Figure 19.9 might be incorporated into such a program. Example 1 demonstrates the use of multiple record descriptions. Example 2 uses a single record description into which redefinitions have been introduced. Example 3 uses a single record description, redefinitions, and renaming of data items.

```
Example 1:   Multiple Record Descriptions

     FD  INFO-CARDS LABEL RECORDS ARE OMITTED.
     Ø1  HISTORY-RECORD.
         Ø3 CUSTOMER-NUMBER          PIC 9(6).
         Ø3 FILLER                   PIC X(8).
         Ø3 LAST-METER-READING       PIC 9(5).
         Ø3 FILLER                   PIC X(10).
         Ø3 PREVIOUS-BALANCE         PIC 9999V99.
         Ø3 FILLER                   PIC X(44).
         Ø3 CARD-TYPE                PIC 9.
            88 HISTORY               VALUE 1.
     Ø1  PAYMENT-RECORD.
         Ø3 FILLER                   PIC X(29).
         Ø3 PAYMENT                  PIC 9999V99.
         Ø3 FILLER                   PIC X(44).
         Ø3 CARD-TYPE                PIC 9.
            88 ACCOUNT-PAYMENT       VALUE 2.
     Ø1  METER-READING-RECORD.
         Ø3 FILLER                   PIC X(14).
         Ø3 CURRENT-METER-READING    PIC 9(5).
         Ø3 FILLER                   PIC X(60).
         Ø3 CARD-TYPE                PIC 9.
            88 CURRENT-INFO          VALUE 3.
     Ø1  DATE-CARD.
         Ø2 REPORT-DAY               PIC 99.
         Ø2 REPORT-MONTH             PIC 99.
         Ø2 REPORT-YEAR              PIC 99.
         Ø2 FILLER                   PIC X(74).

Example 2:   REDEFINES Clause

     FD  INFO-CARDS LABEL RECORDS ARE OMITTED.
     Ø1  CARD-LAYOUTS.
         Ø3 CUSTOMER-NUMBER          PIC 9(6).
         Ø3 DATE-CARD REDEFINES CUSTOMER-NUMBER.
            Ø5 REPORT-DAY            PIC 99.
            Ø5 REPORT-MONTH          PIC 99.
            Ø5 REPORT-YEAR           PIC 99.
         Ø3 FILLER                   PIC X(8).
         Ø3 HISTORY-INFORMATION.
            Ø5 LAST-METER-READING    PIC 9(5)
            Ø5 FILLER                PIC X(10).
            Ø5 PREVIOUS-BALANCE      PIC 9999V99.
         Ø3 PAYMENT-INFORMATION REDEFINES HISTORY-INFORMATION.
            Ø5 FILLER                PIC X(15).
            Ø5 PAYMENT               PIC 9999V99.
         Ø3 CURRENT-INFORMATION REDEFINES HISTORY-INFORMATION.
            Ø5 CURRENT-METER-READING PIC 9(5).
            Ø5 FILLER                PIC X(16).
         Ø3 FILLER                   PIC X(44).
         Ø3 CARD-TYPE                PIC 9.
            88 HISTORY               VALUE 1.
            88 ACCOUNT-PAYMENT       VALUE 2.
            88 CURRENT-INFO          VALUE 3.
```

Figure 19.10 Program Illustrations of Multiple Record Descriptions, REDEFINES Clauses, and RENAMES Clauses

```
Example 3:   RENAMES Clause
    FD  INFO-CARDS LABEL RECORDS ARE OMITTED.
    Ø1  CARD-LAYOUTS.
        Ø3 CUSTOMER-NUMBER              PIC 9(6).
        Ø3 DATE-CARD REDEFINES CUSTOMER-NUMBER.
            Ø5 REPORT-DAY               PIC 99.
            Ø5 REPORT-MONTH             PIC 99.
            Ø5 REPORT-YEAR              PIC 99.
        Ø3 FILLER                       PIC X(8).
        Ø3 LAST-METER-READING           PIC 9(5).
        Ø3 FILLER                       PIC X(1Ø).
        Ø3 PREVIOUS-BALANCE             PIC 999V99.
        Ø3 FILLER                       PIC X(44).
        Ø3 CARD-TYPE                    PIC 9.
            88 HISTORY                  VALUE 1.
            88 ACCOUNT-PAYMENT          VALUE 2.
            88 CURRENT-INFO             VALUE 3.
    66  CURRENT-METER-READING RENAMES LAST-METER-READING.
    66  PAYMENT RENAMES PREVIOUS-BALANCE.
```

Figure 19.10 Program Illustrations of Multiple Record Descriptions, REDEFINES Clauses, and RENAMES Clauses *Continued*

Figure 19.11 illustrates the use of redefinitions to "load" a table with initial values. The code shown in Example 1 was originally presented in Chapter 14. In that problem, it was necessary to MOVE CODE-STATE-LIST TO STATE-CODE-TABLE in the PROCEDURE DIVISION. If the code in Example 1 were used as a replacement (with STATE-CODE-TABLE REDEFINES CODE-STATE-LIST included), the MOVE statement could be eliminated. In the second example, the program code comes from a problem (CHECK-WRITER) in Chapter 13. Again, a redefinition is used to initialize DIGIT-TABLE so that it contains the various words necessary to perform the digit-to-text conversion.

Summary   This chapter has compared three interrelated facets of the DATA DIVISION—multiple record descriptions on the FILE SECTION, the REDEFINES clause, and the RENAMES clause. Each of these alternatives in the DATA DIVISION has an impact on the ease of coding the PROCEDURE DIVISION and the amount of internal memory used. In the FILE SECTION, multiple record descriptions can be provided in one FD. When several types of input records are anticipated from a single file, the programmer has only to write the record descriptions for each anticipated record type. Data does not have to match the field types recorded in the input-record description when a record is read. However, the programmer is responsible for insuring the data matches the field description when the data-name is referenced.

The REDEFINES clause is *not* limited only to the FILE SECTION. It may also be used in the WORKING-STORAGE SECTION. Furthermore, redefinitions may be used at the record, group, or elementary-item level. While the length of a redefinition must generally be the same as the original data description, field characters may be changed.

Example 1:

```
01   CODE-STATE-LIST.
     02 FILLER                        PIC X(14) VALUE '01ALABAMA'.
     02 FILLER                        PIC X(14) VALUE '04ARKANSAS'.
     02 FILLER                        PIC X(14) VALUE '09FLORIDA'.
     02 FILLER                        PIC X(14) VALUE '10GEORGIA'.
     02 FILLER                        PIC X(14) VALUE '15IOWA'.
     02 FILLER                        PIC X(14) VALUE '25MISSOURI'.
     02 FILLER                        PIC X(14) VALUE '30NEW JERSEY'.
     02 FILLER                        PIC X(14) VALUE '34NORTH DAKOTA'.
     02 FILLER                        PIC X(14) VALUE '35OHIO'.
     02 FILLER                        PIC X(14) VALUE '36OKLAHOMA'.
     02 FILLER                        PIC X(14) VALUE '42TENNESSEE'.
     02 FILLER                        PIC X(14) VALUE '43TEXAS'.
     02 FILLER                        PIC X(14) VALUE '46VIRGINIA'.
     02 FILLER                        PIC X(14) VALUE '49WISCONSIN'.
     02 FILLER                        PIC X(14) VALUE '50WYOMING'.
01   STATE-CODE-TABLE REDEFINES CODE-STATE-LIST.
     02 STATE-CODE-ENTRIES OCCURS 15 TIMES
        ASCENDING KEY IS STATE-CODE
        INDEXED BY STATE.
        03 STATE-CODE                 PIC 99.
        03 STATE-NAME                 PIC X(12).
```

Example 2:

```
01   LIST-OF-UNITS.
     02 FILLER                        PIC X(9) VALUE 'ONE'.
     02 FILLER                        PIC X(9) VALUE 'TWO'.
     02 FILLER                        PIC X(9) VALUE 'THREE'.
     02 FILLER                        PIC X(9) VALUE 'FOUR'.
     02 FILLER                        PIC X(9) VALUE 'FIVE'.
     02 FILLER                        PIC X(9) VALUE 'SIX'.
     02 FILLER                        PIC X(9) VALUE 'SEVEN'.
     02 FILLER                        PIC X(9) VALUE 'EIGHT'.
     02 FILLER                        PIC X(9) VALUE 'NINE'.
     02 FILLER                        PIC X(9) VALUE 'TEN'.
     02 FILLER                        PIC X(9) VALUE 'ELEVEN'.
     02 FILLER                        PIC X(9) VALUE 'TWELVE'.
     02 FILLER                        PIC X(9) VALUE 'THIRTEEN'.
     02 FILLER                        PIC X(9) VALUE 'FOURTEEN'.
     02 FILLER                        PIC X(9) VALUE 'FIFTEEN'.
     02 FILLER                        PIC X(9) VALUE 'SIXTEEN'.
     02 FILLER                        PIC X(9) VALUE 'SEVENTEEN'.
     02 FILLER                        PIC X(9) VALUE 'EIGHTEEN'.
     02 FILLER                        PIC X(9) VALUE 'NINETEEN'.
     02 FILLER                        PIC X(9) VALUE 'TWENTY'.
     02 FILLER                        PIC X(9) VALUE 'THIRTY'.
     02 FILLER                        PIC X(9) VALUE 'FORTY'.
     02 FILLER                        PIC X(9) VALUE 'FIFTY'.
     02 FILLER                        PIC X(9) VALUE 'SIXTY'.
     02 FILLER                        PIC X(9) VALUE 'SEVENTY'.
     02 FILLER                        PIC X(9) VALUE 'EIGHTY'.
     02 FILLER                        PIC X(9) VALUE 'NINETY'.
     02 FILLER                        PIC X(9) VALUE 'HUNDRED'.
     02 FILLER                        PIC X(9) VALUE 'THOUSAND'.
01   DIGIT-TABLE REDEFINES LIST-OF-UNITS.
     02 DIGITS OCCURS 29 TIMES PIC X(9).
```

Figure 19.11 Table Initialization through Redefinition

Finally, the RENAMES clause may appear in both the FILE and WORKING-STORAGE SECTIONs. The purpose of the RENAMES clause is to provide alternate names for identifiers. In addition, the clause may be used to form alternate groupings of data items.

Notes on Programming Style

Most of the commercial programming standards of which this author is aware suggest a reduction in the use (if not the total elimination) of the RENAMES clause. The rationale behind this position is that the data item should have been named properly to begin with or data should be explicitly moved to the data item. Thus, by avoiding the use of the RENAMES clause, the programmer should never get confused about how a particular data item received its value.

Current opinions regarding the use of the REDEFINES clause range from "its the best thing to come along since sliced bread" to "don't let me catch you using that again." There are several positive arguments for the use of the REDEFINES clause including the concise presentation of a wide variety of data representations for a single area of memory. Most of these representations, however could be separately coded and the data moved into them. Your best bet is to check the coding standards in your shop before using the REDEFINES clause.

Questions

Below, fill in the blank(s) with the appropriate word, words, or phrases.

1. The advantages of having two or more data-names address the same memory locations are _____ and _____ .

2. If four 80-byte record descriptions are provided under one FD in the FILE SECTION, the minimum amount of internal memory used would be _____ bytes.

3. The REDEFINES clause may be used at the _____ or _____ level in the FILE SECTION.

4. The REDEFINES clause may be used at the _____ , _____ , or _____ level in the WORKING-STORAGE SECTION.

5. Both the original description of data and its redefinition must be coded at the _____ level number.

6. If a programmer wishes to redefine an elementary-item, the redefinition must _____ .

7. The redefinition of a group item is assumed to be terminated when _____ .

8. If a data area of 10 bytes is to be redefined, the redefinition should be _____ (number) bytes in length.

9. When multiple redefinition of the same area is required, each subsequent redefinition should reference (as data-name-2) _____ .

10. Level-66 is always associated with the _____ clause.

11. Level-66 items used in conjunction with a particular record must be located _____ the record.

12. The purpose of the RENAMES clause is to _____ or _____ .

13. When the THRU option of the RENAMES clause is used, the newly created data item is assumed to represent a _____ level item.

Answer the following questions by circling either "T" for True or "F" for False.

T F 14. It is possible for two data-names to address the same positions in the computer's memory.

T F 15. Only one record description is permitted within one FD in the FILE SECTION.

T F 16. It is possible to have an internal memory address with two different characteristics (e.g., accessed as a number in one case and as an alphanumeric field in the second).

T F 17. Regardless of the number of records associated with a single FD, no more space is consumed than for a single record description.

T F 18. Each record description in the WORKING-STORAGE SECTION, unless redefined, utilizes additional memory.

T F 19. The REDEFINES clause may be used in both the FILE SECTION and WORKING-STORAGE SECTION.

T F 20. Records can be REDEFINED in the FILE SECTION.

T F 21. Records can be REDEFINED in the WORKING-STORAGE SECTION.

T F 22. A REDEFINES clause can be used to place two table descriptions in the same location in the computer's memory.

T F 23. A redefinition may be longer (in bytes) than the original description of the data.

T F 24. A redefinition can always be redefined by additional code.

T F 25. A redefinition can include a redefinition.

T F 26. A redefinition can physically precede the description of the data to be redefined in the program code.

T F 27. It is possible to alter an elementary-item's PICTURE description with a REDEFINES clause.

T F 28. It is possible to alter an elementary-item's PICTURE description with a RENAMES clause.

T F 29. An elementary-item may be subordinate to a level-66.

T F 30. A level-66 item may rename an elementary-item.

T F 31. A level-66 item may rename a group item.

T F 32. The new name created through a RENAMES clause may be qualified.

T F 33. It is possible to create a totally new grouping of data (a grouping not indicated in the prior record description) with the RENAMES clause.

20 Non-Character-Oriented Data Storage

Up to this point in the text, the discussion of data storage has revolved around a type of data representation called DISPLAY. When PICTURE clauses were presented in the DATA DIVISION (Chapter 5), each elementary-item was assumed to have a USAGE IS DISPLAY clause attached. The DISPLAY usage is a representation of data in a "character" form. Each 9, A, or Z in a PICTURE clause requires one character position (or byte) of computer memory. DISPLAY usage is required when the input medium is punched cards and the output medium is printed paper. However, within the computer's memory (or on non-unit record media) it is possible to store numeric data in a more compact form than one digit per byte.

A *byte* is generally the smallest unit of the computer's memory which can be directly addressed as a data-storage position in COBOL. A byte is normally six or eight bits. A *bit* is the smallest unit of storage in the computer's memory. ("Bit" is an acronym for *binary digit*. A *binary digit* is a digit value of either Ø or 1 in the binary numbering system.) The internal storage capacity of most computers is specified by the number of bytes or "words" which the computer can store at one time. The size of each *word* of storage is often stated in terms of the number of bits or bytes it contains. For example, one type of computer may be characterized as a 60-bit word machine (e.g., CDC), while others may be classified as a 32-bit word or 4-byte word machine (e.g., IBM), while still another machine may be based on a 16-bit word (e.g., PDP-11). For the sake of simplicity the examples in this chapter are based on a 32-bit word computer (using four 8-bit bytes). The coding scheme used by an IBM computer—EBCDIC—will be used when necessary. (Remember, the other coding scheme is ASCII.) If you want more information about the internal architecture of the computer you are using, consult with the computer personnel at your installation.

As previously indicated, there are alternative ways in which numeric data may be described. (Numeric data, in this context, means a nonedited numeric field associated with an elementary data item.) The types of internal representation provided by all computers (with the use of a COBOL compiler) are DISPLAY (also called external decimal or character data) and COMPUTA-

```
[USAGE IS]  { DISPLAY
              COMPUTATIONAL
              COMP
              COMPUTATIONAL-1*
              COMP-1*
              COMPUTATIONAL-2*
              COMP-2*
              COMPUTATIONAL-3*
              COMP-3* }
```

*Permitted by some COBOL compilers, but not by ANS COBOL standards.

Figure 20.1 Format of the USAGE Clause

DATA VALUE PLACED IN THE FIELD	PICTURE CLAUSE DESCRIBED WITH A USAGE IS DISPLAY	INTERNAL REPRESENTATION*
27	99	F:2 | F:7
− 27	99	F:2 | F:7
− 27	S99	F:2 | D:7
12473	S9(5)	F:1 | F:2 | F:4 | F:7 | F:3
− 6418	S9(5)	F:Ø | F:6 | F:4 | F:1 | D:8
+ 1738	S9(4)	F:1 | F:7 | F:3 | C:8

*Internal representation based on a machine using a 32-bit word, 8-bit byte and and EBCDIC coding scheme. Each box represents one byte.

Figure 20.2 Illustrations of Numeric Data Stored with a DISPLAY Usage

TIONAL (also called binary data.) In addition, many computers offer data representations in COMPUTATIONAL-1 (known as "short" floating-point data), COMPUTATIONAL-2 ("long" floating-point data), and COMPUTATIONAL-3 (packed-decimal). Most of the internal data representations used in COBOL are DISPLAY, COMPUTATIONAL, or COMPUTATIONAL-3.

The format of the USAGE clause is provided in Figure 20.1. The clause is optional; when the USAGE clause is omitted, USAGE IS DISPLAY is assumed. (Any other USAGE for a non-numeric or edited-numeric field will result in an error.)

DISPLAY Data Items

When an elementary data item is coded with a USAGE IS DISPLAY clause or without a USAGE clause, the data described by the item is recorded in external decimal (or character form). Figure 20.2 presents a number of examples of data storage where the USAGE IS DISPLAY clause accompanies a PICTURE clause. For every 9 that appears in a numeric PICTURE clause, one byte of internal storage is allocated. For example, the first illustration of Figure 20.2 assumes that the elementary data item is described with a PICTURE 99 USAGE IS DISPLAY entry. The stored result (internal representation) requires two bytes of internal memory. Each byte of the field is composed of high-order and low-order half-bytes (four-bits each in the example). For an unsigned field, each of the high-order half-bytes contains the hexadecimal number F. The low-order half-bytes contain the digit value placed in the field. Thus, the value 27, when placed in a data field described by PICTURE 99 USAGE IS DISPLAY entry, is recorded internally as F2F7.

The other illustrations in Figure 20.2 follow a similar pattern except some of the data values and PICTURE clauses result in signed data being stored. The sign for a DISPLAY data item is recorded in the high-order half-byte of the last full byte of the field. The sign position contains the hexadecimal value F if the number is unsigned (as in the first example), the value C if the number is positive, and D if the number is negative. However, remember that both the data and the PICTURE clause must be combined for a sign to be stored. That is, if the data contains a sign, but the PICTURE clause does not permit a sign, the resulting data value will be unsigned. In addition, if the PICTURE clause permits a sign, but the data value is unsigned the stored value is unsigned.

Binary Data Items

The second form of the USAGE clause is for a COMPUTATIONAL data item. The reserved word COMPUTATIONAL (or its abbreviation COMP) indicates that a numeric data item is to be stored in a binary form. Storing data in binary form has two basic advantages. First, data stored in binary can be manipulated faster by a computer than data stored in DISPLAY form. The reason for this is that DISPLAY data must be translated into its binary equivalent before an arithmetic manipulation may be made, and once the manipulation is complete, data being stored in a DISPLAY field must be converted from binary to "character" form. Second, data stored in binary form may require less internal storage than the same data stored in a DISPLAY form.

Although COMPUTATIONAL usage is permitted under ANS COBOL, the COMPUTATIONAL data item is described differently by the programmer depending on the computer. Some COBOL compilers (e.g., IBM) require that COMPUTATIONAL data items be accompanied by a PICTURE clause. With this type of compiler, a PICTURE clause of a single digit (9) to four digits (9999) will require a half-word (2 bytes) of internal memory. A PICTURE clause that contains five digits (9(5)) to nine digits (9(9)) uses a full word of computer memory. PICTURE clauses containing 10 digits (9(10)) to 18 digits (9(18)) require two words of internal storage. A COMPUTATIONAL data item may contain an operational sign and an implied decimal point. (Any unsigned COMPUTATIONAL field is assumed to contain only positive values.) Other computers (e.g., Honeywell) do not permit PICTURE clauses in conjuction with a COMPUTATIONAL data item. In this situation, the COBOL compiler assumes the data field to be one full word in size; it can contain up to a nine-digit, signed, integer number.

Figure 20.3 illustrates the internal representation of data stored in a COMPUTATIONAL field. Each of the elementary-items in this example must be accompanied by a USAGE IS COMPUTATIONAL or a USAGE IS COMP clause. The sign in a COMPUTATIONAL data item is stored in the high-order (leftmost) *bit* in the field. For a positive number the sign bit is zero. For a negative number the sign bit is one. Also notice that negative numbers are stored in *"two's complement" form* so that the first bit of the field is the binary digit 1.

DATA VALUE PLACED IN THE FIELD	PICTURE CLAUSE DESCRIBED WITH A USAGE IS COMPUTATIONAL	INTERNAL REPRESENTATION*			
27	99 COMPUTATIONAL	0000:0000	0001:1011		
− 27	S9(4) COMP	1111:1111	1110:0010		
+ 5729	S9(4) COMP	0001:0110	0110:0001		
− 7982	S9(4) COMPUTATIONAL	1110:0000	1101:0001		
462985	S9(9) COMPUTATIONAL	0000:0000 0000:0111	0001:0000 1000:1001		

*Internal representation based on a computer using a 32-bit word, 8-bit byte, and a COBOL compiler permitting the use of a PICTURE clause with a COMPUTATIONAL data item. Each box represents one byte.

Figure 20.3 Illustrations of Numeric Data Stored with a COMPUTATIONAL Usage

For those compilers that *do not* permit a PICTURE clause to be associated with a COMPUTATIONAL data item, the amount of internal memory used for a field is a full word. For a computer using a 32-bit word, the amount of storage would be the same as for the last example in Figure 20.3. Thus, if any of the first four data values presented in Figure 20.3 were to be stored in a computer that did not permit a PICTURE clause, the COMPUTATIONAL field would be twice as large as the internal representation in the examples. If any of the examples had contained an implied decimal point, there would be no equivalent storage in a COMPUTATIONAL field.

Packed-Decimal Data Items

Another type of data storage often available with COBOL compilers is COMPUTATIONAL-3. A COMPUTATIONAL-3 data item is often referred to as a *packed-decimal* data item. In other words, the data is internally stored in a form similar to DISPLAY. However, in DISPLAY almost half of the data storage area is wasted. In a DISPLAY field, most of the high-order half-bytes (sometimes called zone-bits) are filled with a character code for a number (a hexadecimal F). While these characters codes are useful in the recording of alphabetic and special characters, they serve no useful purpose in a numeric field. Thus, in a COMPUTATIONAL-3 data field each of the unnecessary character codes (zone codes) is eliminated—leaving only the digits and a code for the sign of the data.

Figure 20.4 illustrates data stored in a COMPUTATIONAL-3 field. Notice from the examples that each field is recorded in terms of full bytes (i.e., half-byte addressing in COBOL is not permitted). One character (zone) code is retained (the zone code for the sign of the number); however, this code is placed in the low-order half-byte of each field. (As with DISPLAY data fields, the hexadecimal digit F represents an unsigned data value, C represents a positive value, and D indicates a negative value.) Comparing the amount of internal memory required for a packed-decimal field to that which is required when the data is in DISPLAY form, about one-half of the internal storage is used. (The amount of internal storage used would be exactly half the number of digits in the PICTURE clause if it were not necessary to store the sign of the data value.)

DATA VALUE PLACED IN THE FIELD	PICTURE CLAUSE DESCRIBED WITH A USAGE IS COMPUTATIONAL-3	INTERNAL REPRESENTATION*
27	99 COMPUTATIONAL-3	Ø:2 | 7:F
− 684	S999 COMPUTATIONAL-3	6:8 | 4:D
+ 6295	S9(4) COMP-3	Ø:6 | 2:9 | 5:C
− 93874	9(5) COMP-3	9:3 | 8:7 | 4:F

*Internal representation based on a computer using a 32-bit word, 8-bit byte, and an EBCDIC coding scheme. Each box represents one byte.

Figure 20.4 Illustrations of Numeric Data Stored with a COMPUTATIONAL-3 Usage

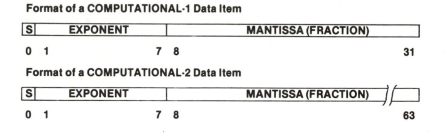

Format of a COMPUTATIONAL-1 Data Item

S	EXPONENT	MANTISSA (FRACTION)

0   1   7   8   31

Format of a COMPUTATIONAL-2 Data Item

S	EXPONENT	MANTISSA (FRACTION)

0   1   7   8   63

Figure 20.5 Internal Formats of COMPUTATIONAL-1 and COMPUTATIONAL-2 Data Items

Floating-Point Data Items

The final two types of data storage are called COMPUTATIONAL-1 (COMP-1) and COMPUTATIONAL-2 (COMP-2). These two internal representations of data are not part of ANS COBOL and are available with a limited number of compilers. Both COMPUTATIONAL-1 and COMPUTATIONAL-2 are often referred to as internal floating-point data storage. The term *floating-point* is frequently used in conjunction with data stored within the computer's memory in exponential form. Neither a COMPUTATIONAL-1 nor a COMPUTATIONAL-2 data description is written with a PICTURE clause. When USAGE IS COMPUTATIONAL-1 is declared for an elementary-item, one full word of computer memory is allocated to the field. When USAGE IS COMPUTATIONAL-2 is specified, two full words of internal storage are used. For this reason, and because of the resulting capability to store more significant digits, COMPUTATIONAL-1 is referred to as *short* floating-point; COMPUTATIONAL-2 is called *long* floating-point. The format of a data item stored in COMPUTATIONAL-1 or COMPUTATIONAL-2 is presented in Figure 20.5.

With both COMPUTATIONAL-1 and COMPUTATIONAL-2 the internal formats of the data represented are basically the same. Bit Ø of either a 32-bit word or a 64-bit double word contains the sign of the data value. The next seven bits (bits 1 through 7) are used to store the *exponent* of the data value (i.e., the exponent represents the power of ten to be multiplied by the *mantissa* or fraction). The function of the exponent is to move the location of the as-

```
[BLANK WHEN ZERO]
```

Figure 20.6 Format of the BLANK WHEN ZERO Clause

Figure 20.7 Format of the JUSTIFIED Clause

sumed decimal point in the data value either to the left or to the right a specified number of positions, depending on the positive or negative value stored in bits 1 through 7. The mantissa or fraction (bits 8 through 31 for COMPUTATIONAL-1 and bits 8 through 63 for COMPUTATIONAL-2) is a decimal fraction containing the significant digits of the data value itself. (COMPUTATIONAL-1 provides sufficient space for a value that can be represented by approximately seven significant decimal digits; COMPUTATIONAL-2 permits a value equivalent to approximately 16 significant digits.) Thus, these field types provide the capability to store a number of extremely large or extremely small magnitude. Values which can be stored in COMPUTATIONAL-1 and COMPUTATIONAL-2 fields range from a minimum magnitude of $\pm 5.4 \times 10^{-79}$ to a maximum magnitude of $\pm 7.2 \times 10^{75}$.

Other Clauses Related to the Descriptions of Data

Four other clauses are permitted in the DATA DIVISION of an ANS COBOL program. Each of these clauses permits a specialized treatment of the data itself in the location of that data within the computer's memory. These clauses are BLANK WHEN ZERO, JUSTIFIED, SIGN, and SYNCHRONIZED.

The BLANK WHEN ZERO clause (Figure 20.6) may be used in conjunction with a numeric (DISPLAY) or a numeric-edited field. When the clause accompanies a numeric field, the field is treated as a numeric-edited field. The purpose of the BLANK WHEN ZERO clause is to cause the entire numeric field to be replaced with spaces when the value placed in the field is zero. This action is taken regardless of the PICTURE characters used to describe the numeric field. The clause may not be used in conjunction with a level-66 or 88 data items.

The JUSTIFIED clause (Figure 20.7) is used to alter the normal alignment of data placed in an alphabetic or alphanumeric field. Normally, when data is placed in an alphabetic or alphanumeric field, the data is left-justified (i.e., the data begins at the leftmost position within the field and is either truncated or blank-filled to the right as necessary). The JUSTIFIED (JUST) clause reverses the normal alignment so that the data is right-justified. The clause causes the last character of the data to be placed in the rightmost position of the field. If the field is larger than the data, blanks will be inserted to the left until the field is filled. If the field is smaller than the length of the data being supplied, characters are truncated from the left until the data exactly fill the field. The JUSTIFIED clause may be specified only for an elementary data item, and it may not be used in conjunction with a level-66 or 88 data item.

The SIGN clause, presented in Figure 20.8, is used to modify the location of the operational sign of a numeric field. When the clause is used, it may only be used in conjunction with a numeric (DISPLAY) data item (although if coded at the group level, it pertains to all subordinate numeric fields). As noted in Figure 20.2, when numeric data is placed in a DISPLAY data item, the sign of the number is placed in the high-order half-byte of the *last* byte of the field—the normal location of the operational sign. The location of the sign would not be changed if the clause SIGN IS TRAILING was added to the description of the data item. However, if the clause SIGN IS LEADING was specified, the sign of the number would be in the high-order half-byte of the *first* byte of the field. In either case, the operational sign character (S) does not cause any additional space to be added to the field.

When the phrase SEPARATE CHARACTER is added to the SIGN clause, an additional byte is added to the field. If the reserved word TRAILING is used, the extra bytes is added to the end of the field and the sign is placed in this byte. If LEADING is specified, the extra byte is added before the first byte which would normally be in the field, and the sign is placed in this byte. Thus, the sign is placed in a SEPARATE CHARACTER position. When the SEPARATE CHARACTER phrase is employed, the data *must* contain an operational sign. The character "+" should be used for a positive operational sign, and the character "−" should be used for a negative operational sign. Since the compiler expects one of these two characters to be present, the absence of one of these characters will cause a fatal error, and the program will be terminated. When the data item is used in the PROCEDURE DIVISION, any conversion of the sign necessary for manipulation, computation, or comparsion automatically takes place prior to the operation.

The format of the SYNCHRONIZED clause is presented in Figure 20.9. The clause causes the COBOL compiler to generate extra instructions for a data alignment appropriate to the particular type of data item being described.

Figure 20.8 Format of the SIGN Clause

Figure 20.9 Format of the SYNCHRONIZED Clause

Data alignment internally shifts a data field so that it is located on the proper boundaries within the computer's memory. This improves overall operating efficiency when the data is being used for arithmetic manipulation. By aligning fields properly within the computer's memory, the amount of time required to locate data, process it and if necessary, return it to the field is reduced. This shifting of data items within internal memory often uses additional memory.

The key reserved word in the clause is SYNCHRONIZED, or its abbreviation SYNC. The clause may appear only in conjunction with an elementary data item. Following the reserved word SYNCHRONIZED, the programmer may specify the reserved words LEFT or RIGHT; however, under most circumstances LEFT and RIGHT are treated as comments. As was the case with noncharacter data storage presented earlier in this chapter, the function or the SYNCHRONIZED clause varies with particular COBOL compilers. For example, Honeywell COBOL compilers automatically "synchronize" COMPUTATIONAL (as well as COMPUTATIONAL-1, COMPUTATIONAL-2, and COMPUTATIONAL-3) data items. Then, the SYCHRONIZED clause is treated as a comment. Other compilers do not automatically synchronize or align the data on the natural internal boundaries of the computer's memory. For an IBM COBOL program (as well as others) it may be necessary to use the SYNCHRONIZED clause to indicate to the COBOL compiler that proper data alignment is desired.

Figure 20.10 illustrates the action taken by a COBOL compiler to align data on an appropriate internal boundary. In this illustration, the same record is coded without SYNCHRONIZED clauses and with SYNCHRONIZED clauses. In the first record description, the data are placed in one byte after another without regard for the natural internal boundaries used by the computer. The only natural boundary sought by the compiler in placing the record into the computer's memory is a double-word boundary. In this example (assumed to be for an IBM computer), each record is aligned on a double-word boundary, and the bytes described by the record are allocated beginning with this boundary.

In the second record description, a boundary alignment is sought for each of the elementary data items coded with a SYNCHRONIZED clause. For data described (either implicitly or explicitly) as DISPLAY, the SYNCHRONIZED clause is ignored. For COMPUTATIONAL data items the alignment depends on the size of the field. If a COMPUTATIONAL data item contains from one to four digits it requires one half-word (2 bytes) of computer storage. These data are aligned on a half-word internal boundary. For COMPUTATIONAL data items of five to eighteen digits, the alignment is on a full-word boundary (not necessarily a double word). COMPUTATIONAL-1 data items are placed on a full-word boundary, and COMPUTATIONAL-2 data items are aligned on a double-word boundary. If a data field does not fall on the proper internal boundary by default, extra bytes (often called "slack bytes") are added to the field so that the data are placed on the appropriate boundary. Notice from the second record description and its internal mapping that extra bytes have been inserted between some data items so that proper alignment is maintained.

SYNCHRONIZED data items also require careful handling. Since data items can be redefined (with a REDEFINES clause) the original data description may be SYNCHRONIZED without the redefinition being SYNCHRONIZED. This

```
Ø1   DATA-RECORD-1.                         Ø1   DATA-RECORD-2.
     Ø3   FIELD-1   PIC X(6).                    Ø3   FIELD-1   PIC X(6).
     Ø3   FIELD-2   PIC 9(5)V99 COMP.            Ø3   FIELD-2   PIC 9(5)V99 COMP SYNC.
     Ø3   FIELD-3   PIC 9.                       Ø3   FIELD-3   PIC 9.
     Ø3   FIELD-4   PIC S99V99 COMP.             Ø3   FIELD-4   PIC S99V99 COMP SYNC.
     Ø3   FIELD-5   PIC X(1Ø).                   Ø3   FIELD-5   PIC X(1Ø).
     Ø3   FIELD-6   PIC S9(12)V99 COMP.          Ø3   FIELD-6   PIC S9(12)V99 COMP SYNC.
     Ø3   FIELD-7   PIC X.                        Ø3   FIELD-7   PIC X.
     Ø3   FIELD-8   PIC S9(6)V99 COMP.           Ø3   FIELD-8   PIC S9(6)V99 COMP SYNC.
     Ø3   FIELD-9   PIC X(14).                   Ø3   FIELD-9   PIC X(14).
     Ø3   FIELD-1Ø PIC S9(7) COMP.               Ø3   FIELD-1Ø PIC S9(7) COMP SYNC.
     Ø3   FIELD-11 PIC 9(4) COMP.                Ø3   FIELD-11 PIC 9(4) COMP SYNC.
```

Internal Mappings of Records*

DATA-RECORD-1

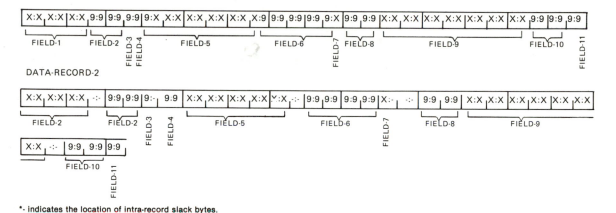

DATA-RECORD-2

*- indicates the location of intra-record slack bytes.

Figure 20.10 Illustrations of Internal Mappings of Record Descriptions

is only important for the redefinition because the numeric data items in the redefined area do not necessarily fall on the same natural boundaries as the original data items. Furthermore, since extra bytes may be used in the internal alignment of the original data items, the original record may be longer than the PICTURE strings of the elementary-items indicate. If the redefinition contains SYNCHRONIZED clauses and the original data description does not contain SYNCHRONIZED clauses, it is the programmer's responsibility to align the original data items such that the SYNCHRONIZED redefined items fall on the appropriate boundries.

Non-Character-Oriented Data, Tables, and the SYNCHRONIZED Clause

Although the majority of this text has assumed data to be in character form, it is possible to describe elementary-items (or groups of items) more efficiently as binary or packed-decimal numeric fields as already noted. This is extremely important in the description of data items that are included in tables. With very little effort on the part of the programmer, mass areas of storage may be allocated through the OCCURS clause. This mass of data area may be somewhat reduced in size and processed more efficiently if the programmer carefully studies the organization of the table, the characteristics of the data items in the table, and the expected amount of use of each of the data items.

Figure 20.11 illustrates this point. The first table is described using character-oriented (DISPLAY) data fields. The second table provides the same capability to store numeric data values, but the numeric data items have all been declared to be COMPUTATIONAL (except for the alphanumeric field—FIELD-3). (Note that the COMPUTATIONAL data items are presumed to allow PICTURE clauses.) The third table is a representation of each numeric

```
a)   Ø1   TABLE-RECORD.
          Ø2   TABLE-ITEMS OCCURS 1ØØ TIMES.
               Ø3   FIELD-1          PIC 9(Ø1).
               Ø3   FIELD-2          PIC 9(Ø6).
               Ø3   FIELD-3          PIC X(2Ø).
               Ø3   FIELD-4          PIC 9(Ø9).
               Ø3   FIELD-5          PIC 9(Ø2).
               Ø3   FIELD-6          PIC 9(12).
               Ø3   FIELD-7          PIC 9(Ø3)V99.
               Ø3   FIELD-8          PIC 9(Ø3).

     Length per Occurrence--58 bytes
     Total Length of Table--5,800 bytes

b)   Ø1   TABLE-RECORD.
          Ø2   TABLE-ITEMS OCCURS 1ØØ TIMES.
               Ø3   FIELD-1          PIC 9(Ø1) COMP.
               Ø3   FIELD-2          PIC 9(Ø6) COMP.
               Ø3   FIELD-3          PIC X(2Ø).
               Ø3   FIELD-4          PIC 9(Ø9) COMP.
               Ø3   FIELD-5          PIC 9(Ø2) COMP.
               Ø3   FIELD-6          PIC 9(12) COMP.
               Ø3   FIELD-7          PIC 9(Ø3)V99 COMP.
               Ø3   FIELD-8          PIC 9(Ø3) COMP.

     Length per Occurrence--46 bytes
     Total Length of Table--4,600 bytes

c)   Ø1   TABLE-RECORD.
          Ø2   TABLE-ITEMS OCCURS 1ØØ TIMES.
               Ø3   FIELD-1          PIC 9(Ø1) COMP-3.
               Ø3   FIELD-2          PIC 9(Ø6) COMP-3.
               Ø3   FIELD-3          PIC X(2Ø).
               Ø3   FIELD-4          PIC 9(Ø9) COMP-3.
               Ø3   FIELD-5          PIC 9(Ø2) COMP-3.
               Ø3   FIELD-6          PIC 9(12) COMP-3.
               Ø3   FIELD-7          PIC 9(Ø3)V99 COMP-3.
               Ø3   FIELD-8          PIC 9(Ø3) COMP-3.

     Length per Occurrence--47 bytes
     Total Length of Table--4,700 bytes

d)   Ø1   TABLE-RECORD.
          Ø2   TABLE-ITEMS OCCURS 1ØØ TIMES.
               Ø3   FIELD-1          PIC 9(Ø1). (or COMP-3)
               Ø3   FIELD-2          PIC 9(Ø6) COMP. (or COMP-3)
               Ø3   FIELD-3          PIC X(2Ø).
               Ø3   FIELD-4          PIC 9(Ø9) COMP.
               Ø3   FIELD-5          PIC 9(Ø2) COMP. (or COMP-3)
               Ø3   FIELD-6          PIC 9(12) COMP-3.
               Ø3   FIELD-7          PIC 9(Ø3)V99 COMP-3.
               Ø3   FIELD-8          PIC 9(Ø3) COMP. (or COMP-3)

     Length per Occurrence--43 bytes
     Total Length of Table--4,300 bytes
```

Figure 20.11 Illustrations of Table Descriptions with Various Usages

data item if coded with a COMPUTATIONAL-3 usage. Again, the table requires less space (COMPUTATION-3 is *not* always shorter than COMPUTATIONAL.) The final alternative is a table coded with the type of USAGE which would result in the least amount of space being used for each data item. When the number of bytes is totaled, the fourth record description takes the most advantage of the internal memory of the computer.

Suppose that for efficiency an entire record is classified as COMPUTATIONAL. To make table processing more efficient, each of the COMPUTATIONAL items should also be SYNCHRONIZED. The record might then be described as presented in Figure 20.12. The synchronization of the COMPUTATIONAL items results in slack bytes being inserted, as indicated in the memory layout that appears below the record. Each occurrence of the data items occupies 50 bytes, although only 46 bytes of data are described. In the physical layout, slack bytes (sometimes referred to as *intra-occurrence* slack bytes) have been added so that the COMPUTATIONAL data fall on the appropriate internal boundaries. In addition, 2 bytes are not used at the end of each occurrence in the table. These extra bytes (called *inter-occurrence* slack bytes) are added so that each occurrence of the table requires 52 bytes, and the entire table will use 5,200 bytes of internal memory.

Now compare this record description to the record description in Figure 20.13. If the programmer has the latitude to arrange the table, he or she might reorganize the data items in the table to conserve internal memory, while maintaining processing efficiency. The tables created in Figures 20.12 and 20.13 both describe the same amount of data. However, a single occurrence of the table in Figure 20.13 requires only 46 bytes for data and 2 bytes for inter-occurrence slack bytes. The new table uses 48 bytes per occurrence. The table requires 4,800 bytes in total. This amounts to a savings of 800 bytes in the description of this rather small table.

```
01    TABLE-RECORD.
      02 TABLE-ITEMS OCCUR 100 TIMES.
         03 FIELD-1 PIC 9 COMP SYNC.
         03 FIELD-2 PIC 9(6) COMP SYNC.
         03 FIELD-3 PIC X(20).
         03 FIELD-4 PIC 9(9) COMP SYNC.
         03 FIELD-5 PIC 99 COMP SYNC.
         03 FIELD-6 PIC 9(12) COMP SYNC.
         03 FIELD-7 PIC 999V99 COMP SYNC.
         03 FIELD-8 PIC 999 COMP SYNC.
```

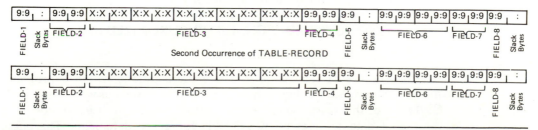

Figure 20.12 An Illustration of COMPUTATIONAL and SYNCHRONIZED Table Items (Slack Bytes Added)

```
Ø1    TABLE-RECORD.
      Ø2 TABLE-ITEMS OCCURS 1ØØ TIMES.
         Ø3 FIELD-1 PIC 9 COMP SYNC.
         Ø3 FIELD-5 PIC 99 COMP SYNC.
         Ø3 FIELD-2 PIC 9(6) COMP SYNC.
         Ø3 FIELD-3 PIC X(2Ø).
         Ø3 FIELD-4 PIC 9(9) COMP SYNC.
         Ø3 FIELD-6 PIC 9(12) COMP SYNC.
         Ø3 FIELD-7 PIC 999V99 COMP SYNC.
         Ø3 FIELD-8 PIC 999.
```

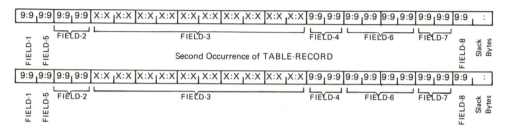

Figure 20.13 An Illustration of COMPUTATIONAL and SYCHRONIZED Table Items (Slack Bytes Eliminated)

Summary

In this chapter, various means of describing numeric data have been discussed. Normally, numeric data is described in DISPLAY mode; however, the USAGE clause may be added to the description of non-edited-numeric data items to achieve alternate forms of internal data storage. Although data must be described in DISPLAY mode (character form) for input-output operations involving card readers and line printers, other forms of data representation may be used for internally accessed data items and for data recorded on disk and tape media.

Besides DISPLAY data items, data may be represented in COMPUTATIONAL (binary), COMPUTATIONAL-1 (short floating-point), COMPUTATIONAL-2 (long floating-point), and COMPUTATIONAL-3 (packed-decimal) formats. Each of these data types has its own impact on the computer's ability to manipulate numeric values quickly and on the amount of internal memory used.

Table 20.1 presents the completed table of allowable movements of data for COBOL that provides for the USAGE clauses discussed in this chapter. In addition, other clauses may be added to the description of data items to either enhance the programmer's capability to manipulate data values or to improve the computer's access to data values in memory. They are the BLANK WHEN ZERO, JUSTIFIED, SIGN, and SYNCHRONIZED clauses.

Notes on Programming Style

The use of noncharacter data representations within a program seems to follow a similar line to many of the other special usage items described in Part 4 of this text. Almost every shop would like to use the most efficient form of data representation available for every data item. The question again arises—"What will the negative impact be if we employ this type of code?" Unfortunately, many companies have been forced to use DISPLAY representation exclusively because of the lack of sophistication of many of their entry-level programmers. This lack of familiarity with noncharacter representations,

Table 20.1 The Complete Table of Allowable Moves in COBOL

Sending Field	Receiving Field								
	Group	Alphabetic	Alphanumeric	Alphanumeric-edited	Numeric (DISPLAY)	Numeric-edited	Binary (COMP)	Floating-point (COMP-1/COMP-2)	Packed-decimal (COMP-3)
Group	Y	Y	Y	Y[1]	Y[1]	Y[1]	Y[1]	Y[1]	Y[1]
Alphabetic (A)	Y	Y	Y	Y	N	N	N	N	N
Alphanumeric (X)	Y	Y	Y	Y	Y[4]	Y[4]	Y[4]	Y[4]	Y[4]
Alphanumeric-edited	Y	Y	Y	Y	N	N	N	N	N
Numeric (DISPLAY) (9)	Y[1]	N	Y[2]	Y[2]	Y	Y	Y	Y	Y
Numeric-edited	Y	N	Y	Y	N	N	N	N	N
Binary (COMP)	Y[1]	N	Y[2]	Y[2]	Y	Y	Y	Y	Y
Floating-point (COMP-1/COMP-2)	Y[1]	N	N	N	Y	Y	Y	Y	Y
Packed-decimal (COMP-3)	Y[1]	N	Y[2]	Y[2]	Y	Y	Y	Y	Y
Figurative Constants ZEROS	Y	N	Y	Y	Y[3]	Y[3]	Y[3]	Y[3]	Y[3]
SPACES	Y	Y	Y	Y	N	N	N	N	N
HIGH-VALUE LOW-VALUE QUOTE	Y	N	Y	Y	N	N	N	N	N
ALL literal	Y	Y	Y	Y	Y[5]	Y[5]	Y[5]	N	Y[5]
Numeric literal	Y[1]	N	Y[2]	Y[2]	Y	Y	Y	Y	Y
Nonnumeric literal	Y	Y	Y	Y	Y[5]	Y[5]	Y[5]	N	Y[5]

LEGEND: Y = yes; N = no
1. move treated like an alphanumeric to alphanumeric move—no data conversion is made
2. decimal point must be to the right of the least significant digit treated as a numeric move
3. treated as a numeric move
4. alphanumeric field treated as an integer numeric (DISPLAY) field
5. literal treated as an integer numeric (DISPLAY) field and may contain only numeric characters

coupled with a slight advantage in program debugging (you can see the numeric representations when displayed), have caused many companies to stay away from noncharacter data. Thus, "human efficiency" seems to be winning out over "program efficiency" or "space efficiency."

Questions

Below fill in the blank(s) with the appropriate word, words, or phrases.

1. When a USAGE clause is not specified for a data item, the assumed usage is _____.

2. In a DISPLAY mode, each 9 in a PICTURE string requires one _____ of internal memory.

3. When data is being read from a punched-card device, all data fields must be described in _____ mode.

4. The smallest unit of memory generally addressable in COBOL is the _____ .

5. Bit is an acronym for _____ _____ .

6. A byte is a combination of _____ .

7. Most computer internal memory capacity is stated in terms of _____ or _____ .

8. The two most frequently used internal coding schemes are _____ and _____ .

9. Another term which means the same as DISPLAY-mode data is _____ .

10. Data that are stored in COMPUTATIONAL-mode are stored in _____ form.

11. Data that are stored in COMPUTATIONAL-3 mode are stored in _____ form.

12. The sign of numeric DISPLAY data is recorded in the _____ .

13. For an unsigned, numeric DISPLAY data value, the high-order half-byte for each digit position contains the hexadecimal digit _____ .

14. The two advantages that COMPUTATIONAL data has over DISPLAY data are that COMPUTATIONAL data _____ and _____ .

15. The sign of a COMPUTATIONAL data item is stored in the _____ .

16. Provided a PICTURE clause is permitted in conjunction with a COMPUTATIONAL data item, the PICTURE characters which may be used to describe the field include _____ , _____ , and _____ .

17. The sign bit of positive COMPUTATIONAL data contains a binary value of _____ .

18. Negative binary data is stored in _____ form.

19. Packed-decimal data may be described by using the USAGE IS _____ clause.

20. Another term for "high-order" bits is _____ bits.

21. In a packed-decimal format, each byte of computer memory may contain up to _____ (number) digits.

22. Where data is described as being in COMP-3 mode, the sign is recorded in the _____ .

23. Both COMP-1 and COMP-2 provide for internal data representation in _____ form.

24. COMP-1 requires _____ of memory, and COMP-2 requires _____ .

25. The sign bit of a COMP-1 field is in the same location and has the same representation as data stored in the _____ mode.

26. The BLANK WHEN ZERO clause may be used only in conjuction with fields declared to be in _____ mode.

27. When the JUSTIFIED RIGHT clause is attached to an alphanumeric field description, data placed in the field is _____ -justified.

28. When the SIGN IS TRAILING clause is added to the description of a data item, the sign is located in the _____ .

29. When the SEPARATE CHARACTER phrase is added to the SIGN clause, the length of the data field is _____ .

30. The SYNCHRONIZED clause is used to insure _____ of numeric data.

31. To achieve the proper internal alignment, SYNCHRONIZED fields often cause _____ to be added to the internal definition of the data, if necessary.

32. If SYNCHRONIZED clauses are used in conjunction with a table, _____ and _____ may be generated to achieve proper internal boundary alignment.

Answer the following questions by circling either "T" for True or "F" for False.

T F 33. The internal architecture of all computers is the same.
T F 34. Only numeric data may be described in non-DISPLAY form.
T F 35. The only forms in which data may be stored in COBOL are external-decimal, binary, and packed-decimal.
T F 36. It is possible to mix data types (e.g., DISPLAY and COMP) in one program.
T F 37. Regardless of the type of computer used, DISPLAY data items always require a PICTURE clause.
T F 38. Regardless of the type of computer used, COMPUTATIONAL data items always require a PICTURE clause.
T F 39. Regardless of the type of computer used, COMPUTATIONAL data items are always integers (whole numbers).
T F 40. Data stored in COMP-1 mode is recorded in an exponential format.
T F 41. COMP-1 and COMP-2 fields require PICTURE clauses with their descriptions.
T F 42. It is possible to store a fractional value in a COMP-1 field.
T F 43. A new type of PICTURE string character is available when data is stored in COMP-3 form.

T F 44. HIGH-VALUES may be moved to a COMPUTATIONAL field.

T F 45. The BLANK WHEN ZERO clause, when properly used, causes a field to contain blanks regardless of the PICTURE description when the data value of zero is placed in the field.

T F 46. Normally, data in an alphanumeric field is left-justified.

T F 47. The SIGN clause may be used only in conjuction with numeric data fields in the COMP mode.

T F 48. When the SIGN IS SEPARATE clause is used, the data description (PICTURE string) must include the operational sign character.

T F 49. When the SIGN IS SEPARATE clause is used, the data must contain a sign.

T F 50. Data which is SYNCHRONIZED may be manipulated by the computer more quickly than nonsynchronized data.

T F 51. Data which is SYNCHRONIZED requires less internal memory than nonsynchronized data.

21 Character-Oriented Data Processing

The STRING and UNSTRING statements are useful to manipulate character strings. The STRING statement's function is *concatenation*—to take data values in two or more fields and place these values together in a single field. The UNSTRING statement performs a *parsing* operating—taking data in one field and separating it into two or more fields. The STRING and UNSTRING statements were added to ANS COBOL in 1974. For this reason, unless your installation is using a current ANS COBOL compiler, these statements may not be available. Other statement types, including INSPECT, EXAMINE, and TRANSFORM, are also available for field examination and manipulation. These statements, however, are not uniformly available in COBOL compilers.

The STRING Statement

The format of the STRING statement is provided in Figure 21.1. In this statement, identifier-1 (literal-1), identifier-2 (literal-2), identifier-4 (literal-4), identifier-5 (literal-5) represents sending fields. Each of these identifiers must be implicitly or explicitly described with the USAGE IS DISPLAY clause. None of these identifiers may use the character P in a PICTURE string. Identifier-7 must be a nonedited-alphanumeric elementary data item. All literals must be non-numeric literals or figurative constants other than ALL.

The effect of the STRING statement is to copy one character at a time (from left to right) from the sending field into the receiving field (from left to right). This process is completed for identifier-1 before the examination and transmission of any characters from subsequent fields.

Two optional clauses may be used with the STRING statement. The POINTER clause may be used to indicate a count of the number of characters placed in the receiving field. That is, each character placed in the receiving field will cause identifier-8 to be incremented by one. Identifier-8 must be described as a nonedited-numeric integer data item. It should be capable of storing a value equal to the maximum number of characters in the receiving field (identifier-7) plus one digit. The programmer is responsible for initializing identifier-8 prior to each execution of the STRING statement. The initial value of the identifier must be a positive integer. The programmer may also use this identifier in other statements of his program.

```
STRING   {identifier-1}  [identifier-2]  . . .DELIMITED BY {identifier-3}
         {literal-1   }  [literal-2   ]                   {literal-3   }
                                                          {SIZE        }

         [{identifier-4}  [identifier-5]  . . .DELIMITED BY {identifier-6}]. . .
         [{literal-4   }  [literal-5   ]                    {literal-6   }]
                                                            {SIZE        }

         INTO identifier-7 [WITH POINTER identifier-8]

         [ON OVERFLOW imperative-statement]
```

Figure 21.1 Format of the STRING Statement

The OVERFLOW clause allows the programmer to specify execution of the imperative statement when an attempt is made to place more characters in a receiving field than it is capable of holding. Any receiving field that appears after the identifier causing the overflow will not have its value altered.

Figure 21.2 presents several examples of the STRING statement. Ordinarily, data would not be placed in the sending fields by MOVE statements immediately preceding the STRING statement. However, suppose that ALPHA-1, ALPHA-2, and ALPHA-3 (in the first two examples) are 15-character alphanumeric fields. In the first example, the blank after the character C of ALPHA-1 is eliminated in the receiving field due to the DELIMITED BY clause. The data is placed in ALPHA-3, left-justified, and blank filled. In the second example, the character E of ALPHA-2 is not transmitted to ALPHA-3. Also notice that a literal may be used as a sending field.

The third example is used to demonstrate a way of compressing data values which represent name fields to produce a field which is more normal in appearance for an individual's name. That is, each of the sending fields, except MIDDLE-INITIAL, might be 10 or more characters in length. Thus, the STRING statement is used to "squeeze" unnecessary blanks from the data fields as characters are placed in a receiving field.

The last two examples demonstrate the use of the optional clauses. With the fourth example, the POINTER clause is used to count the number of characters placed in the receiving field. The example assumes that ZIP is described as a five-digit integer field. Notice that CHAR-COUNT is initialized to 1 prior to the execution of the statement. If the value of CHAR-COUNT was not changed prior to the execution of the statement, CHAR-COUNT would be incremented from the last value it contained.

The last example employs the OVERFLOW clause. Assuming the field size for STREET-ADDRESS is 20 characters, an overflow would exist for this statement and the value in STREET-NUMBER, STREET-NAME and ST-AVE-ETC would be displayed. Note that data would be placed in the receiving field, even though an overflow condition exists.

In Chapter 13 a program was presented which accepted a dollar amount as input and translated the digits into the text representing those digits. The text-

```
Example 1:
        MOVE 'ABC' TO ALPHA-1.
        MOVE 'DEF' TO ALPHA-2.
        STRING ALPHA-1, ALPHA-2 DELIMITED BY SPACE INTO ALPHA-3.
                (ALPHA-3 = ABCDEF)
```

```
Example 2:
        MOVE 'ABCDEFGHIJ' TO ALPHA-1.
        MOVE "NOPE" TO ALPHA-2.
        STRING ALPHA-1, 'KLM' DELIMITED BY SIZE
                ALPHA-2 DELIMITED BY 'E' INTO ALPHA-3.
                (ALPHA-3 = ABCDEFGHIJKLMNOP)
```

```
Example 3:
        MOVE 'JEFFERSON' TO LAST-NAME.
        MOVE 'ANDREW' TO FIRST-NAME.
        MOVE 'R' TO MIDDLE-INITIAL.
        STRING FIRST-NAME DELIMITED BY SPACE
                ' ', MIDDLE-INITIAL, '. ' DELIMITED BY SIZE
                LAST-NAME DELIMITED BY SPACE INTO NAME-FIELD.
                (NAME-FIELD = ANDREW R. JEFFERSON)
```

```
Example 4:
        MOVE 1 TO CHAR-COUNT.
        MOVE 'CHICAGO' TO CITY.
        MOVE 'ILLINOIS' TO STATE.
        MOVE 60606 TO ZIP.
        STRING CITY DELIMITED BY SPACE ', ' DELIMITED BY SIZE
                STATE DELIMITED BY SPACE ' ', ZIP DELIMITED BY SIZE
                INTO ADDRESS WITH POINTER CHAR-COUNT.
                (ADDRESS = CHICAGO, ILLINOIS 60606)
                (CHAR-COUNT = 23)
```

```
Example 5:
        MOVE '12345' TO STREET-NUMBER.
        MOVE 'MOCKINGBIRD' TO STREET-NAME.
        MOVE 'BOULEVARD' TO ST-AVE-ETC.
        STRING STREET-NUMBER DELIMITED BY SPACE ' ' DELIMITED BY SIZE
                STREET-NAME DELIMITED BY SPACE ' ' DELIMITED BY SIZE
                ST-AVE-ETC DELIMITED BY SPACE INTO STREET-ADDRESS
                ON OVERFLOW DISPLAY STREET-NUMBER, STREET-NAME, ST-AVE-ETC.
                (STREET-ADDRESS = 12345 MOCKINGBIRD BO)
```

Figure 21.2 Examples of the STRING Statement

processing program is repeated in Figure 21.3. However, in this illustration, the STRING statement is used to concatenate the words that represent the digits. The STRING statement greatly simplifies the program.

The UNSTRING Statement

The UNSTRING statement is the logical complement of the STRING statement. It separates data from one field into several fields.

The format of the UNSTRING statement is shown in Figure 21.4. In this statement identifier-1 is the sending field and identifier-4 (identifier-7, etc.) is the receiving field. Identifier-1 must be described as an alphanumeric field. Identifier-4 (identifier-7, etc.) must be described as a nonedited-numeric field that does not contain the PICTURE character P and is implicitly or explicitly described as a DISPLAY field.

When the UNSTRING statement is executed, the sending field is examined, one-character-at-a-time from left to right. The characters are placed in the first receiving field until the character specified in the DELIMITED BY clause is encountered. Identifier-2 (identifiter-3, etc.) of the DELIMITED BY clause must be an alphanumeric data item. Literal-1 (literal-2, etc.) must be a non-numeric literal or a figurative constant other than ALL. Thus, when this character is encountered in the sending field, the movement of characters from the sending field to the first receiving field is terminated. If a second (third, etc.) receiving field is specified, movement of data continues, as before, with the character immediately following the character that caused the termination of the previous movement of data.

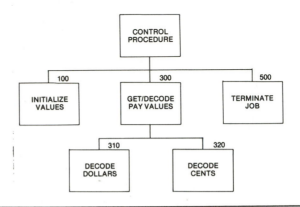

Figure 21.3 A Text-Processing Program (Hierarchy Chart)

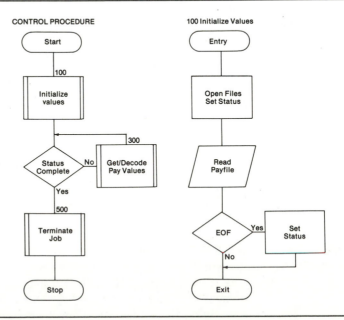

Figure 21.3 A Text-Processing Program (Module Flowchart) *Continued*

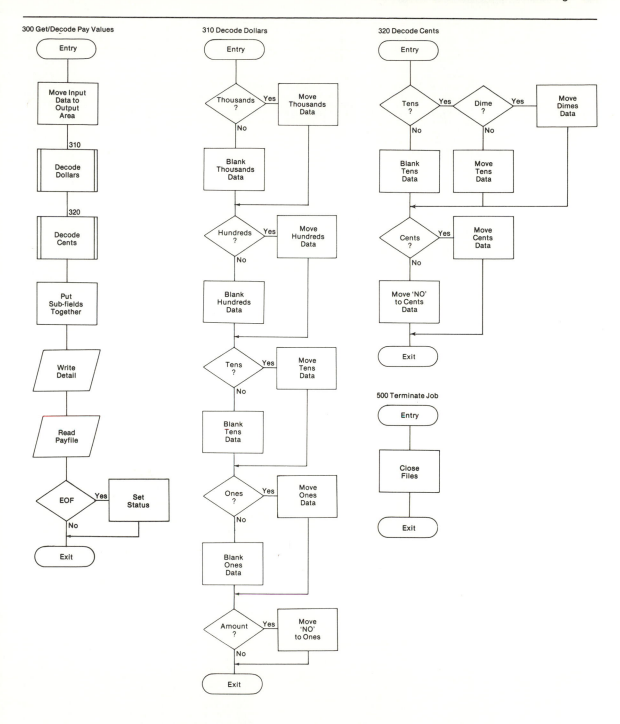

Figure 21.3 A Text-Processing Program (Module Flowchart) *Continued*

```
|                1    1    2    2    2    3    3    4    4    4    5    5    6    6    6    7    7    8|
|    4    8       2    6    0    4    8    2    6    0    4    8    2    6    0    4    8    2    6    0|
--------------------------------------------------------------------------------------------------------
|000010 IDENTIFICATION DIVISION.                                                      FIG 21.3|
|000020 PROGRAM-ID. CHECK-WRITER.                                                     FIG 21.3|
|000030 AUTHOR. DON E. WILLIAMS.                                                      FIG 21.3|
|000040*    THIS PROGRAM PERFORMS A NUMBER TO TEXT CONVERSION                         FIG 21.3|
|000050*    ON "AMOUNTS" AS MIGHT APPEAR ON A CHECK PRODUCED BY A                     FIG 21.3|
|000060*    COMPUTER PROGRAM.  NOTE THAT TABLES ARE USED IN THE                       FIG 21.3|
|000070*    PROCEDURE DIVISION WHICH HAVE VALUES ASSIGNED TO THEM                     FIG 21.3|
|000080*    IN THE DATA DIVISION THROUGH A REDEFINITION.                              FIG 21.3|
|000090*    THE AMOUNT TO TEXT CONVERSION IS DONE BY THE STRING                       FIG 21.3|
|000100*    STATEMENT.                                                                FIG 21.3|
|000110 ENVIRONMENT DIVISION.                                                         FIG 21.3|
|000120 CONFIGURATION SECTION.                                                        FIG 21.3|
|000130 SOURCE-COMPUTER. IBM-370.                                                     FIG 21.3|
|000140 OBJECT-COMPUTER. IBM-370.                                                     FIG 21.3|
|000150 INPUT-OUTPUT SECTION.                                                         FIG 21.3|
|000160 FILE-CONTROL.                                                                 FIG 21.3|
|000170     SELECT PAY-FILE ASSIGN TO UT-S-SYSIN.                                     FIG 21.3|
|000180     SELECT CHECK-FILE ASSIGN TO UT-S-SYSPRINT.                                FIG 21.3|
|000190 DATA DIVISION.                                                                FIG 21.3|
|000200 FILE SECTION.                                                                 FIG 21.3|
|000210 FD  PAY-FILE LABEL RECORDS ARE OMITTED.                                       FIG 21.3|
|000220 01  PAY-RECORD.                                                               FIG 21.3|
|000230     02 AMOUNT-OF-CHECK           PIC 9(04)V9(02).                             FIG 21.3|
|000240     02 AMOUNT REDEFINES AMOUNT-OF-CHECK.                                      FIG 21.3|
|000250        03 DIGITS OCCURS 6 TIMES PIC 9(01).                                    FIG 21.3|
|000260     02 FILLER                    PIC X(74).                                   FIG 21.3|
|000270 FD  CHECK-FILE LABEL RECORDS ARE OMITTED.                                     FIG 21.3|
|000280 01  CHECK                        PIC X(133).                                  FIG 21.3|
|000290 WORKING-STORAGE SECTION.                                                      FIG 21.3|
|000300 01  WORKING-VARIABLES.                                                        FIG 21.3|
|000310     05  FILE-STATUS        PIC X(15).                                         FIG 21.3|
|000320     05  THOUSANDS          PIC X(10).                                         FIG 21.3|
|000330     05  HUNDREDS           PIC X(10).                                         FIG 21.3|
|000340     05  TENS               PIC X(10).                                         FIG 21.3|
|000350     05  ONES               PIC X(10).                                         FIG 21.3|
|000360     05  TENS-OF-CENTS      PIC X(10).                                         FIG 21.3|
|000370     05  SINGLE-CENTS       PIC X(10).                                         FIG 21.3|
|000380     05  THOU               PIC X(10).                                         FIG 21.3|
|000390     05  HUND               PIC X(10).                                         FIG 21.3|
|000400     05  BODY               PIC 9(02).                                         FIG 21.3|
|000410 01  DOLLARS-AND-CENTS.                                                        FIG 21.3|
|000420     02 DOLLARS-AND         PIC X(12) VALUE                                    FIG 21.3|
|000430     'DOLLARS-AND-'.                                                           FIG 21.3|
|000440     02 CENTS               PIC X(05) VALUE 'CENTS'.                           FIG 21.3|
|000450 01  LIST-OF-UNITS.                                                            FIG 21.3|
|000460     02 FILLER              PIC X(10) VALUE 'ONE-'.                            FIG 21.3|
|000470     02 FILLER              PIC X(10) VALUE 'TWO-'.                            FIG 21.3|
|000480     02 FILLER              PIC X(10) VALUE 'THREE-'.                          FIG 21.3|
|000490     02 FILLER              PIC X(10) VALUE 'FOUR-'.                           FIG 21.3|
|000500     02 FILLER              PIC X(10) VALUE 'FIVE-'.                           FIG 21.3|
|000510     02 FILLER              PIC X(10) VALUE 'SIX-'.                            FIG 21.3|
|000520     02 FILLER              PIC X(10) VALUE 'SEVEN-'.                          FIG 21.3|
|000530     02 FILLER              PIC X(10) VALUE 'EIGHT-'.                          FIG 21.3|
|000540     02 FILLER              PIC X(10) VALUE 'NINE-'.                           FIG 21.3|
|000550     02 FILLER              PIC X(10) VALUE 'TEN-'.                            FIG 21.3|
|000560     02 FILLER              PIC X(10) VALUE 'ELEVEN-'.                         FIG 21.3|
|000570     02 FILLER              PIC X(10) VALUE 'TWELVE-'.                         FIG 21.3|
|000580     02 FILLER              PIC X(10) VALUE 'THRITEEN-'.                       FIG 21.3|
|000590     02 FILLER              PIC X(10) VALUE 'FOURTEEN-'.                       FIG 21.3|
|000600     02 FILLER              PIC X(10) VALUE 'FIFTEEN-'.                        FIG 21.3|
|000610     02 FILLER              PIC X(10) VALUE 'SIXTEEN-'.                        FIG 21.3|
|000620     02 FILLER              PIC X(10) VALUE 'SEVENTEEN-'.                      FIG 21.3|
|000630     02 FILLER              PIC X(10) VALUE 'EIGHTEEN-'.                        FIG 21.3|
|000640     02 FILLER              PIC X(10) VALUE 'NINETEEN-'.                       FIG 21.3|
|000650     02 FILLER              PIC X(10) VALUE 'TWENTY-'.                         FIG 21.3|
|000660     02 FILLER              PIC X(10) VALUE 'THIRTY-'.                         FIG 21.3|
|000670     02 FILLER              PIC X(10) VALUE 'FORTY-'.                          FIG 21.3|
|000680     02 FILLER              PIC X(10) VALUE 'FIFTY-'.                          FIG 21.3|
|000690     02 FILLER              PIC X(10) VALUE 'SIXTY-'.                          FIG 21.3|
|000700     02 FILLER              PIC X(10) VALUE 'SEVENTY-'.                        FIG 21.3|
|000710     02 FILLER              PIC X(10) VALUE 'EIGHTY-'.                         FIG 21.3|
|000720     02 FILLER              PIC X(10) VALUE 'NINETY-'.                         FIG 21.3|
|000730     02 FILLER              PIC X(10) VALUE 'HUNDRED-'.                        FIG 21.3|
|000740     02 FILLER              PIC X(10) VALUE 'THOUSAND-'.                       FIG 21.3|
|000750 01  DIGIT-TABLE REDEFINES LIST-OF-UNITS.                                      FIG 21.3|
|000760     02 LETTER OCCURS 29 TIMES PIC X(10).                                      FIG 21.3|
```

Figure 21.3 A Text-Processing Program *Continued*

```
|          1 1 2 2 2 3 3 4 4 5 5 6 6 6 7 7 8|
|  4   8   2 6 0 4 8 2 6 0 4 8 2 6 0 4 8 2 6 0|
------------------------------------------------
|000770 01  AMOUNT-LINE.                                    FIG 21.3|
|000780    02  FILLER                PIC X(01).             FIG 21.3|
|000790    02  AMT-OF-CHECK          PIC 9(04).9(02).       FIG 21.3|
|000800    02  FILLER                PIC X(03) VALUE SPACES. FIG 21.3|
|000810    02  WRITTEN-AMOUNT        PIC X(72).             FIG 21.3|
|000820 PROCEDURE DIVISION.                                 FIG 21.3|
|000830 CONTROL-PROCEDURE.                                  FIG 21.3|
|000840    PERFORM 100-INITIALIZE-VALUES.                   FIG 21.3|
|000850    PERFORM 300-GET-DECODE-PAY-VALUES UNTIL          FIG 21.3|
|000860       FILE-STATUS = 'FILE COMPLETE'.                FIG 21.3|
|000870    PERFORM 500-TERMINATE-JOB.                       FIG 21.3|
|000860    STOP RUN.                                        FIG 21.3|
|000890 100-INITIALIZE-VALUES.                              FIG 21.3|
|000900    OPEN INPUT PAY-FILE, OUTPUT CHECK-FILE.          FIG 21.3|
|000910    MOVE 'START FILE' TO FILE-STATUS.                FIG 21.3|
|000920    READ PAY-FILE                                    FIG 21.3|
|000930       AT END MOVE 'FILE COMPLETE' TO FILE-STATUS.   FIG 21.3|
|000940 300-GET-DECODE-PAY-VALUES.                          FIG 21.3|
|000950    MOVE AMOUNT-OF-CHECK TO AMT-OF-CHECK.            FIG 21.3|
|000960    MOVE SPACES TO WRITTEN-AMOUNT.                   FIG 21.3|
|000970    PERFORM 310-DECODE-DOLLARS.                      FIG 21.3|
|000980    PERFORM 320-DECODE-CENTS.                        FIG 21.3|
|000990    STRING THOUSANDS, THOU, HUNDREDS, HUND, TENS, ONES, FIG 21.3|
|001000       DOLLARS-AND, TENS-OF-CENTS, SINGLE-CENTS, CENTS FIG 21.3|
|001010       DELIMITED BY SPACE INTO WRITTEN-AMOUNT.       FIG 21.3|
|001020    WRITE CHECK FROM AMOUNT-LINE AFTER ADVANCING 1 LINES. FIG 21.3|
|001030    READ PAY-FILE                                    FIG 21.3|
|001040       AT END MOVE 'FILE COMPLETE' TO FILE-STATUS.   FIG 21.3|
|001050 310-DECODE-DOLLARS.                                 FIG 21.3|
|001060    IF DIGITS (1) > 0                                FIG 21.3|
|001070       MOVE DIGITS (1) TO BODY                       FIG 21.3|
|001080       MOVE LETTER (BODY) TO THOUSANDS               FIG 21.3|
|001090       MOVE LETTER (29) TO THOU                      FIG 21.3|
|001100    ELSE                                             FIG 21.3|
|001110       MOVE SPACES TO THOUSANDS, THOU.               FIG 21.3|
|001120    IF DIGITS (2) > 0                                FIG 21.3|
|001130       MOVE DIGITS (2) TO BODY                       FIG 21.3|
|001140       MOVE LETTER (BODY) TO HUNDREDS                FIG 21.3|
|001150       MOVE LETTER (28) TO HUND                      FIG 21.3|
|001160    ELSE                                             FIG 21.3|
|001170       MOVE SPACES TO HUNDREDS, HUND.                FIG 21.3|
|001180    MOVE SPACES TO TENS.                             FIG 21.3|
|001190    IF DIGITS (3) = 1                                FIG 21.3!
|001200       ADD 10, DIGITS (4) GIVING BODY                FIG 21.3|
|001210       MOVE LETTER (BODY) TO TENS                    FIG 21.3|
|001220       MOVE SPACES TO ONES.                          FIG 21.3|
|001230    IF DIGITS (3) > 1                                FIG 21.3|
|001240       ADD 18, DIGITS (3) GIVING BODY                FIG 21.3|
|001250       MOVE LETTER (BODY) TO TENS.                   FIG 21.3|
|001260    IF DIGITS (4) > 0 AND DIGITS (3) NOT = 1         FIG 21.3|
|001270       MOVE DIGITS (4) TO BODY                       FIG 21.3|
|001280       MOVE LETTER (BODY) TO ONES                    FIG 21.3|
|001290    ELSE                                             FIG 21.3|
|001300       MOVE SPACES TO ONES.                          FIG 21.3|
|001310    IF AMOUNT-OF-CHECK < 1                           FIG 21.3|
|001320       MOVE 'NO-' TO ONES.                           FIG 21.3|
|001330 320-DECODE-CENTS.                                   FIG 21.3|
|001340    MOVE SPACES TO TENS-OF-CENTS.                    FIG 21.3|
|001350    IF DIGITS (5) = 1                                FIG 21.3|
|001360       ADD 10, DIGITS (6) GIVING BODY                FIG 21.3|
|001370       MOVE LETTER (BODY) TO TENS-OF-CENTS           FIG 21.3|
|001380       MOVE SPACES TO SINGLE-CENTS.                  FIG 21.3|
|001390    IF DIGITS (5) > 1                                FIG 21.3|
|001400       ADD 18, DIGITS (5) GIVING BODY                FIG 21.3|
|001410       MOVE LETTER (BODY) TO TENS-OF-CENTS.          FIG 21.3|
|001420    IF DIGITS (6) > 0 AND DIGITS (5) NOT = 1         FIG 21.3|
|001430       MOVE DIGITS (6) TO BODY                       FIG 21.3|
|001440       MOVE LETTER (BODY) TO SINGLE-CENTS.           FIG 21.3|
|001450    MOVE SPACES TO SINGLE-CENTS.                     FIG 21.3|
|001460    IF DIGITS (6) > 0 AND DIGITS (5) NOT = 1         FIG 21.3|
|001470       MOVE DIGITS (6) TO BODY                       FIG 21.3|
|001480       MOVE LETTER (BODY) TO SINGLE-CENTS.           FIG 21.3|
|001490    IF DIGITS (5) = 0 AND DIGITS (6) = 0             FIG 21.3|
|001500       MOVE 'NO-' TO SINGLE-CENTS.                   FIG 21.3|
|001510 500-TERMINATE-JOB.                                  FIG 21.3|
|001520    CLOSE PAY-FILE, CHECK-FILE.                      FIG 21.3|
```

Figure 21.3 A Text-Processing Program *Continued*

```
-------------------------------------------------------------------------------------------
|      |          1         2         3         4         5         6         7        8| FIGURE |
|RECORD|12345678901234567890123456789012345678901234567890123456789012345678901234567890| NUMBER |
-------------------------------------------------------------------------------------------
|    1|000575                                                                          |FIG 21.3|
|    2|023568                                                                          |FIG 21.3|
|    3|008512                                                                          |FIG 21.3|
|    4|064599                                                                          |FIG 21.3|
|    5|165307                                                                          |FIG 21.3|
|    6|990130                                                                          |FIG 21.3|
|    7|100000                                                                          |FIG 21.3|
|    8|659709                                                                          |FIG 21.3|
|    9|001080                                                                          |FIG 21.3|
|   10|603009                                                                          |FIG 21.3|
|   11|004600                                                                          |FIG 21.3|
|   12|400005                                                                          |FIG 21.3|
```

Figure 21.3 A Text-Processing Progam (Data) *Continued*

```
0005.75    FIVE-DOLLARS-AND-SEVENTY-FIVE-CENTS
0235.68    TWO-HUNDRED-THIRTY-FIVE-DOLLARS-AND-SIXTY-EIGHT-CENTS
0085.12    EIGHTY-FIVE-DOLLARS-AND-TWELVE-CENTS
0645.99    SIX-HUNDRED-FOURTY-FIVE-DOLLARS-AND-NINETY-NINE-CENTS
1653.07    ONE-THOUSAND-SIX-HUNDRED-FIFTY-THREE-DOLLARS-AND-SEVEN-CENTS
9901.30    NINE-THOUSAND-NINE-HUNDRED-ONE-DOLLARS-AND-THIRTY-CENTS
1000.00    ONE-THOUSAND-DOLLARS-AND-NO-CENTS
6597.09    SIX-THOUSAND-FIVE-HUNDRED-NINETY-SEVEN-DOLLARS-AND-NINE-CENTS
0010.80    TEN-DOLLARS-AND-EIGHTY-CENTS
6030.09    SIX-THOUSAND-THIRTY-DOLLARS-AND-NINE-CENTS
0046.00    FOURTY-SIX-DOLLARS-AND-NO-CENTS
4000.05    FOUR-THOUSAND-DOLLARS-AND-FIVE-CENTS
```

Figure 21.3 A Text-Processing Program (Output) *Continued*

```
UNSTRING identifier-1

   ┌                   ┌identifier-2┐          ┌identifier-3┐   ┐
   │ DELIMITED BY [ALL] │            │ OR [ALL] │            │...│
   └                   └literal-1   ┘          └literal-2   ┘   ┘

      INTO identifier-4 [DELIMITER IN identifier-5][COUNT IN identifier-6]

          [identifier-7 [DELIMITER IN identifier-8][COUNT IN identifier-9]]...

   [WITH POINTER identifier-10] [TALLYING IN identifier-11]

   [ON OVERFLOW imperative-statement]
```

Figure 21.4 Format of the UNSTRING Statement

When the DELIMITED BY clause is specified, the DELIMITER IN and the COUNT IN clause may be listed for the receiving field(s). Unless the DELIMITER IN clause is specified, the character that caused the termination of the movement of data from the sending field will be lost. Since the DELIMITED BY clause could cause the termination of character movement on the basis of several characters, the DELIMITER IN clause may be used to retain the delimiter for further reference. The location of the delimiter character will be identifier-5 (identifier-7, etc.). This identifier must be a nonedited-alphanumeric field.

The COUNT IN clause may be used to count the number of characters placed in a receiving field. This count does not include an increment for the delimiter character. Identifier-6 (identifier-9, etc.) must be a nonedited-numeric field without the PICTURE character P. These identifiers will be initialized to zero and incremented by one for each character moved into the receiving field. If two successive delimiting characters are encountered, the count will remain zero for that receiving field.

Three optional clauses accompany the UNSTRING statement—the POINTER clause, the TALLYING clause, and the OVERFLOW clause. As with the STRING statement, the POINTER clause is used to keep track of the character being examined in the sending field of the UNSTRING statement. Identifier-10 must be a nonedited-numeric elementary-item which cannot contain the character P in the PICTURE string. The UNSTRING statement increments the identifier by one for each character examined; the programmer is responsible for initializing the identifier to some positive value prior to each execution of the statement. The TALLYING option follows the same basic form as the POINTER clause. That is, the characteristics of identifier-11 are the same as those for identifier-10; however, identifier-11 contains a count of the number of receiving fields which have received data from the sending field.

An OVERFLOW condition is caused by either of two situations: (1) when the POINTER identifier contains a value less than 1, or (2) when all receiving fields have received data and characters remain unexamined in identifier-1. When either of these conditions occurs, the UNSTRING statement is terminated, and the OVERFLOW imperative statement is executed.

Now look at Figure 21.5. This illustration provides several examples of the use of UNSTRING statements. The first example illustrates how to extract the "prefix" from a character string. Data is placed in FEDERAL-ID-GROUP until a hyphen is encountered (e.g., to extract hyphens from a social security number). In the second example, a portion of the sending field (the first six characters) is to be bypassed such that the parsing operation begins at the seventh character of the field. The third example illustrates more the of the full potential of the UNSTRING statement. In this example, data from one field is divided into several receiving fields, when each delimiter is retained for data reference. The fourth example is similar to the third example, but the delimiters are not retained.

The final example demonstrates how other PROCEDURE DIVISION statements are used in such a way that the UNSTRING statement is executed until all the data from the sending field has been examined. The UNSTRING statement must avoid beginning at the first character position of the sending field each time the statement is executed, thus the POINTER clause is employed. The data that is parsed with each execution of the UNSTRING statement is placed in a table along with its length.

```
Example 1:
    MOVE '75-1234567' TO FEDERAL-ID-NUMBER.
    UNSTRING FEDERAL-ID-NUMBER DELIMITED BY '—'
        INTO FEDERAL-ID-GROUP.
    (FEDERAL-ID-GROUP = 75)
```

Figure 21.5 Examples of the UNSTRING Statement

Example 2:

```
MOVE 7 TO JUMP-PAST-AREA-CODE.
MOVE '(214) 382-8671' TO PHONE-NUMBER.
UNSTRING PHONE-NUMBER DELIMITED BY '-'
    INTO EXCHANGE
    WITH POINTER JUMP-PAST-AREA-CODE.
(EXCHANGE = 382)
```

Example 3:

```
MOVE '$5,277.Ø8' TO DOLLAR-CHARACTERS.
UNSTRING DOLLAR-CHARACTERS
    DELIMITED BY '$' INTO LEADING-BLANKS
        DELIMITER IN DOLLAR-SIGN
    DELIMITED BY ',' INTO THOUSANDS
        DELIMITER IN COMMA-CHARACTER
    DELIMITED BY '.' HUNDREDS-TENS-ONES
        DELIMITER IN DECIMAL-POINT
    DELIMTED BY SPACE INTO CENTS.
(LEADING-BLANKS = NO DATA
DOLLAR-SIGN = $
THOUSANDS = 5
COMMA-CHARACTER = ,
HUNDREDS-TENS-ONES = 277
DECIMAL-POINT = .
CENTS = Ø8)
```

Example 4:

```
MOVE 'JULY 4, 1947' TO DATE-OF-BIRTH.
UNSTRING DATE-OF-BIRTH
    DELIMITED BY SPACE INTO DOB-MONTH
    DELIMITED BY ',' INTO DOB-DAY
    DELIMITED BY '9' OR '8' INTO UNNEEDED-DATA
    DELIMITED BY SPACE INTO DOB-YEAR.

(DOB-MONTH = JULY
DOB-DAY = 4
UNNEEDED-DATA = 19
DOB-YEAR = 47
DELIMITERS NOT SAVED)
```

Figure 21.5 Examples of the UNSTRING Statement *Continued*

```
Example 5:
    MOVE 0 TO WORD-COUNT.
    MOVE 1 TO BEGIN-AT.
    MOVE 'THE QUICK BROWN FOX JUMPED
        OVER THE LAZY DOG.' TO TEXT-STRING
    PERFORM PARSE-TEXT VARYING 1 FROM
        1 BY 1 UNTIL INDICATOR = 'STOP'.
            .
            .
            .
PARSE-TEXT
    MOVE 0 TO WORD-LENGTH (I).
    UNSTRING TEXT-STRING
        DELIMITED BY SPACE INTO TEXT-WORD (I)
        DELIMITER IN SPACE-BETWEEN
        COUNT IN WORD-LENGTH (I)
        WITH POINTER BEGIN-AT
        TALLYING IN WORD-COUNT
        ON OVERFLOW MOVE 'STOP' TO INDICATOR.
    ADD 1, WORD-LENGTH (1) TO BEGIN-AT.
```

```
(TEXT-WORD (1) - THE      ; WORD-LENGTH (1) = 3
         "    (2) = QUICK          "    (2) = 5
         "    (3) = BROWN          "    (3) = 5
         "    (4) = FOX            "    (4) = 3
         "    (5) = JUMPED         "    (5) = 6
         "    (6) = OVER           "    (6) = 4
         "    (7) = THE            "    (7) = 3
         "    (8) = LAZY           "    (8) = 4
         "    (9) = DOG            "    (9) = 3
WORD-COUNT = 9)
```

Figure 21.5 Examples of the UNSTRING Statement *Continued*

Key Word in Context

The process known as "key word in context" scans a specified text for one or more occurrences of a specified word or phrase. The process is illustrated in Figure 21.6. The problem can be divided into three distinct phases (1) reading the text to be searched (the READ-TEXT procedure—3200), (2) writing the text which has been read (the WRITE-TEXT procedure—3400), and (3) the searching for one or more key words or phrases (the PROCESS-KEY-WORDS procedure—3600).

The procedure, as designed, utilizes an UNSTRING statement within the key word searching segment. After the text has been read and a key word is available, the identifier BODY is searched. BODY contains all of the text. The delimiter sought in the searching sequence is the key word. To ensure that only the key word (without trailing blanks) is sought, the key word is placed in KEY-WORD-TABLE. To determine whether or not a key word was found, the DELIMITER IN phrase is used. When WORD-CHECK has the question mark symbol after searching, a key word *has not* been found. The STRING-LENGTH identifier is used to determine the number of characters that precede the key word, and the BEGIN-POINT identifier establishes where searching is to begin. (If BEGIN-POINT were not used, searching would always begin at the beginning of the string—the first character—and the same key word would repetitively be found.) To determine the number of times the key word is found, the TALLYING phrase is used to increment WORDS-FOUND each time the UNSTRING activity is attempted.

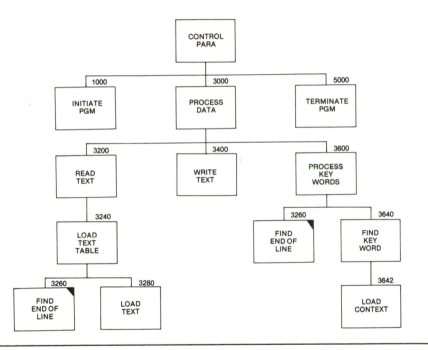

Figure 21.6 Key Word in Context (Hierarchy Chart)

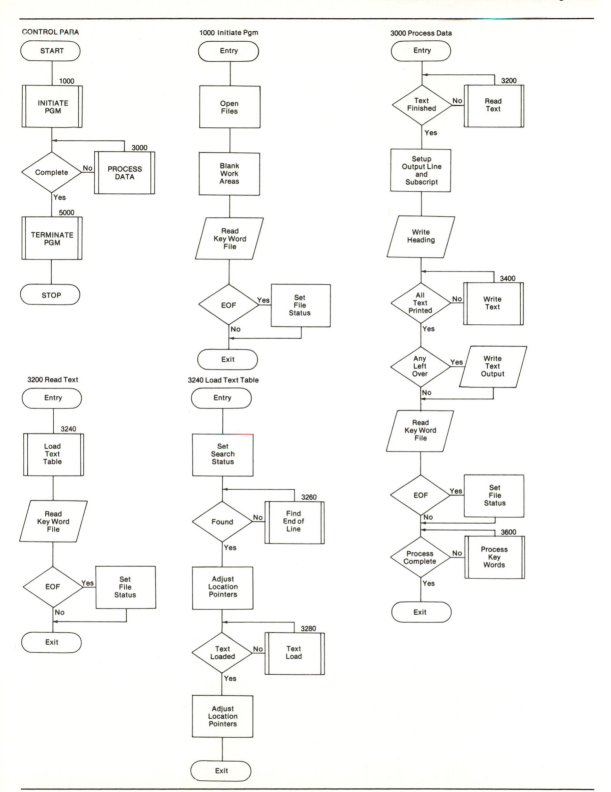

Figure 21.6 Key Word in Context (Module Flowcharts) *Continued*

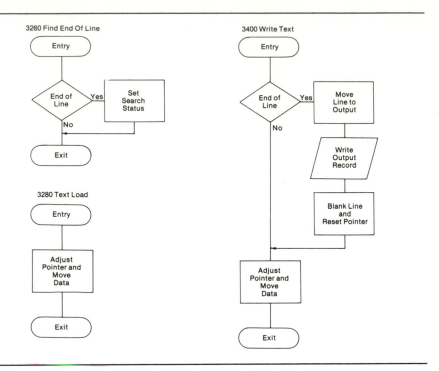

Figure 21.6 Key Word in Context (Module Flowcharts) *Continued*

```
---------------------------------------------------------------------------
|          1   1   2   2   2   3   3   4   4   4   5   5   6   6   6   7   7   8|
|  4   8   2   6   0   4   8   2   6   0   4   8   2   6   0   4   8   2   6   0|
---------------------------------------------------------------------------
|000010 IDENTIFICATION DIVISION.                                       FIG 21.6|
|000020 PROGRAM-ID. KWIC.                                              FIG 21.6|
|000030 DATE-WRITTEN. JANUARY 1, 1981.                                 FIG 21.6|
|000040 DATE-COMPILED. JANUAPY 1, 1981.                                FIG 21.6|
|000050 ENVIRONMENT DIVISION.                                          FIG 21.6|
|000060 CONFIGURATION SECTION.                                         FIG 21.6|
|000070 SOURCE-COMPUTER.  IBM-3033.                                    FIG 21.6|
|000080 OBJECT-COMPUTER.  IBM-3033.                                    FIG 21.6|
|000090 SPECIAL-NAMES. C01 IS TOP-OF-PAGE.                             FIG 21.6|
|000100 INPUT-OUTPUT SECTION.                                          FIG 21.6|
|000110 FILE-CONTROL.                                                  FIG 21.6|
|000120     SELECT KEY-WORD-FILE ASSIGN TO UT-S-SYSIN.                 FIG 21.6|
|000130     SELECT OUTPUT-FILE ASSIGN TO UT-S-SYSPRINT.                FIG 21.6|
|000140 DATA DIVISION.                                                 FIG 21.6|
|000150 FILE SECTION.                                                  FIG 21.6|
|000160 FD  KEY-WORD-FILE LABEL RECORDS ARE OMITTED.                   FIG 21.6|
|000170 01  TEXT-RECORD.                                               FIG 21.6|
|000180     02 INPUT-CHAR OCCURS 80 TIMES PIC X(01).                   FIG 21.6|
|000190 01  KEY-WORD-RECORD.                                           FIG 21.6|
|000200     02 KEY-WORD              PIC X(80).                        FIG 21.6|
|000210 FD  OUTPUT-FILE LABEL RECORDS ARE OMITTED.                     FIG 21.6|
|000220 01  OUTPUT-RECORD.                                             FIG 21.6|
|000230     02 FILLER                PIC X(01).                        FIG 21.6|
|000240     02 OUTPUT-LINE           PIC X(132).                       FIG 21.6|
|000250 WORKING-STORAGE SECTION.                                       FIG 21.6|
|000260 01  WORKING-STATUS-VARIABLES.                                  FIG 21.6|
|000270     02 FILE-STATUS           PIC X(10).                        FIG 21.6|
|000280     02 SEARCH-STATUS         PIC X(10).                        FIG 21.6|
|000290     02 BEGIN-LOAD            PIC S9(04) VALUE 1.               FIG 21.6|
|000300     02 END-LOAD              PIC 9(04) VALUE 0.                FIG 21.6|
```

Figure 21.6 Key Word in Context *Continued*

```
|                 1  1  2  2  2  3  3  4  4  4  5  5  6  6  6  7  7  8|
|    4     8      2  6  0  4  8  2  6  0  4  8  2  6  0  4  8  2  6  0|
------------------------------------------------------------------------
|000310     02 LCTN                    PIC 9(04).                FIG 21.6|
|000320     02 ORIG                    PIC 9(04).                FIG 21.6|
|000330     02 WORDS-FOUND             PIC 9(02).                FIG 21.6|
|000340     02 WORD-CHECK              PIC X(01).                FIG 21.6|
|000350     02 BEGIN-POINT             PIC 9(04).                FIG 21.6|
|000360     02 STRING-LENGTH           PIC 9(04).                FIG 21.6|
|000370     02 WORD-LENGTH             PIC 9(02).                FIG 21.6|
|000380 01  BODY.                                               FIG 21.6|
|000390     02 TEXT-CHARACTER OCCURS 2500 TIMES PIC X(01).      FIG 21.6|
|000400 01  TEXT-OUTPUT.                                        FIG 21.6|
|000410     02 OUTPUT-CHARACTER OCCURS 2500 TIMES PIC X(01).    FIG 21.6|
|000420 01  KEY-WORD-TABLE.                                     FIG 21.6|
|000430     05 KEY-WORD-CHAR OCCURS 1 TO 80 TIMES              FIG 21.6|
|000440        DEPENDING ON WORD-LENGTH PIC X(01).             FIG 21.6|
|000450 01  KEY-WORD-LINE.                                      FIG 21.6|
|000460     02 FILLER                  PIC X(01) VALUE SPACES.  FIG 21.6|
|000470     02 FILLER                  PIC X(22) VALUE          FIG 21.6|
|000480     *SEARCH FOR KEY WORD:*.                             FIG 21.6|
|000490     02 KEY-WORD-OUT            PIC X(80).               FIG 21.6|
|000500 01  COUNT-LINE.                                         FIG 21.6|
|000510     02 FILLER                  PIC X(01) VALUE SPACES.  FIG 21.6|
|000520     02 FILLER                  PIC X(28) VALUE          FIG 21.6|
|000530     *NUMBER OF KEY WORDS FOUND:*.                       FIG 21.6|
|000540     02 WORD-COUNT              PIC Z9.                  FIG 21.6|
|000550 PROCEDURE DIVISION.                                     FIG 21.6|
|000560 CONTROL-PARA.                                           FIG 21.6|
|000570     PERFORM 1000-INITIATE-PGM.                          FIG 21.6|
|000580     PERFORM 3000-PROCESS-DATA                           FIG 21.6|
|000590        UNTIL FILE-STATUS = *COMPLETE*.                  FIG 21.6|
|000600     PERFORM 5000-TERMINATE-PGM.                         FIG 21.6|
|000610     STOP RUN.                                           FIG 21.6|
|000620 1000-INITIATE-PGM.                                      FIG 21.6|
|000630     OPEN INPUT KEY-WORD-FILE, OUTPUT OUTPUT-FILE.       FIG 21.6|
|000640     MOVE SPACES TO BODY, TEXT-OUTPUT, OUTPUT-RECORD.    FIG 21.6|
|000650     READ KEY-WORD-FILE                                  FIG 21.6|
|000660        AT END MOVE *COMPLETE* TO FILE-STATUS;           FIG 21.6|
|000670            MOVE ALL *+* TO TEXT-RECORD.                 FIG 21.6|
|000680 3000-PROCESS-DATA.                                      FIG 21.6|
|000690     PERFORM 3200-READ-TEXT                              FIG 21.6|
|000700        UNTIL TEXT-RECORD = ALL *+*.                     FIG 21.6|
|000710     MOVE 0 TO ORIG.                                     FIG 21.6|
|000720     MOVE *TEXT AS READ:* TO OUTPUT-LINE.                FIG 21.6|
|000730     WRITE OUTPUT-RECORD AFTER ADVANCING TOP-OF-PAGE.    FIG 21.6|
|000740     MOVE SPACES TO OUTPUT-LINE.                         FIG 21.6|
|000750     WRITE OUTPUT-RECORD AFTER ADVANCING 2 LINES.        FIG 21.6|
|000760     PERFORM 3400-WRITE-TEXT                             FIG 21.6|
|000770        VARYING LCTN FROM 1 BY 1 UNTIL LCTN > BEGIN-LOAD.FIG 21.6|
|000780     IF TEXT-OUTPUT NOT = SPACES                         FIG 21.6|
|000790        MOVE TEXT-OUTPUT TO OUTPUT-LINE                  FIG 21.6|
|000800        WRITE OUTPUT-RECORD AFTER 1 LINES.               FIG 21.6|
|000810     READ KEY-WORD-FILE                                  FIG 21.6|
|000820        AT END MOVE *COMPLETE* TO FILE-STATUS.           FIG 21.6|
|000830     PERFORM 3600-PROCESS-KEY-WORDS                      FIG 21.6|
|000840        UNTIL TEXT-RECORD = ALL *+* OR FILE-STATUS = *COMPLETE*. FIG 21.6|
|000850 3200-READ-TEXT.                                         FIG 21.6|
|000860     PERFORM 3240-LOAD-TEXT-TABLE.                       FIG 21.6|
|000870     READ KEY-WORD-FILE                                  FIG 21.6|
|000880        AT END MOVE *COMPLETE* TO FILE-STATUS;           FIG 21.6|
|000890            MOVE ALL *+* TO TEXT-RECORD.                 FIG 21.6|
|000900 3240-LOAD-TEXT-TABLE.                                   FIG 21.6|
|000910     MOVE *LOOKING* TO SEARCH-STATUS.                    FIG 21.6|
|000920     PERFORM 3260-FIND-END-OF-LINE                       FIG 21.6|
|000930        VARYING LCTN FROM 80 BY -1 UNTIL LCTN < 1        FIG 21.6|
|000940        OR SEARCH-STATUS = *FOUND*.                      FIG 21.6|
|000950     ADD LCTN, 1 TO END-LOAD.                            FIG 21.6|
|000960     MOVE 0 TO ORIG.                                     FIG 21.6|
|000970     PERFORM 3280-TEXT-LOAD                              FIG 21.6|
|000980        VARYING LCTN FROM BEGIN-LOAD BY 1 UNTIL LCTN > END-LOAD FIG 21.6|
|000990        OR 2500.                                         FIG 21.6|
|001000     ADD 1 TO END-LOAD.                                  FIG 21.6|
|001010     ADD END-LOAD 1 GIVING BEGIN-LOAD.                   FIG 21.6|
|001020 3260-FIND-END-OF-LINE.                                  FIG 21.6|
|001030     IF INPUT-CHAR (LCTN) NOT = SPACE                    FIG 21.6|
|001040        MOVE *FOUND* TO SEARCH-STATUS.                   FIG 21.6|
|001050 3280-TEXT-LOAD.                                         FIG 21.6|
|001060     ADD 1 TO ORIG.                                      FIG 21.6|
|001070     MOVE INPUT-CHAR (ORIG) TO TEXT-CHARACTER (LCTN).    FIG 21.6|
|001080 3400-WRITE-TEXT.                                        FIG 21.6|
|001090     IF ORIG > 80 AND TEXT-CHARACTER (LCTN) = SPACE      FIG 21.6|
|001100        MOVE TEXT-OUTPUT TO OUTPUT-LINE                  FIG 21.6|
```

Figure 21.6 Key Word in Context *Continued*

```
|                1   1   2   2   2   3   3   4   4   4   5   5   6   6   6   6   7   7   8|
|    4       8   2   6   0   4   8   2   6   0   4   8   2   6   0   4   8   2   6   0|
|001110          WRITE OUTPUT-RECORD AFTER 1 LINES                           FIG 21.6|
|001120          MOVE SPACES TO TEXT-OUTPUT                                   FIG 21.6|
|001130          MOVE 0 TO ORIG.                                             FIG 21.6|
|001140      ADD 1 TO ORIG.                                                  FIG 21.6|
|001150      MOVE TEXT-CHARACTER (LCTN) TO OUTPUT-CHARACTER (ORIG).          FIG 21.6|
|001160 3600-PROCESS-KEY-WORDS.                                              FIG 21.6|
|001170      MOVE 1 TO BEGIN-POINT.                                          FIG 21.6|
|001180      MOVE 0 TO STRING-LENGTH, WORDS-FOUND.                           FIG 21.6|
|001190      MOVE *SEARCH* TO SEARCH-STATUS.                                 FIG 21.6|
|001200      PERFORM 3260-FIND-END-OF-LINE                                   FIG 21.6|
|001210          VARYING LCTN FROM 80 BY -1 UNTIL                            FIG 21.6|
|001220              SEARCH-STATUS = *FOUND* OR LCTN < 1.                     FIG 21.6|
|001230      ADD LCTN, 1 GIVING WORD-LENGTH.                                 FIG 21.6|
|001240      MOVE KEY-WORD TO KEY-WORD-TABLE, KEY-WORD-OUT.                  FIG 21.6|
|001250      WRITE OUTPUT-RECORD FROM KEY-WORD-LINE                          FIG 21.6|
|001260          AFTER ADVANCING TOP-OF-PAGE.                                FIG 21.6|
|001270      MOVE SPACES TO OUTPUT-LINE.                                     FIG 21.6|
|001280      WPITE OUTPUT-RECORD AFTER ADVANCING 2 LINES.                    FIG 21.6|
|001290      PERFORM 3640-FIND-KEY-WORD                                      FIG 21.6|
|001300          UNTIL BEGIN-POINT > 2500.                                   FIG 21.6|
|001310      SUBTRACT 1 FROM WORDS-FOUND GIVING WORD-COUNT.                  FIG 21.6|
|001320      WRITE OUTPUT-RECORD FROM COUNT-LINE AFTER 4 LINES.             FIG 21.6|
|001330      READ KEY-WORD-FILE                                              FIG 21.6|
|001340          AT END MOVE *COMPLETE* TO FILE-STATUS.                      FIG 21.6|
|001350 3640-FIND-KEY-WORD.                                                  FIG 21.6|
|001360      MOVE *?* TO WORD-CHECK.                                         FIG 21.6|
|001370      UNSTRING BODY                                                   FIG 21.6|
|001380          DELIMITED BY KEY-WORD-TABLE                                 FIG 21.6|
|001390          INTO TEXT-OUTPUT                                            FIG 21.6|
|001400          DELIMITER IN WORD-CHECK                                     FIG 21.6|
|001410          COUNT IN STRING-LENGTH                                      FIG 21.6|
|001420          WITH POINTER BEGIN-POINT                                    FIG 21.6|
|001430          TALLYING IN WORDS-FOUND.                                    FIG 21.6|
|001440      MOVE 0 TO ORIG.                                                 FIG 21.6|
|001450      MOVE SPACES TO TEXT-RECORD, TEXT-OUTPUT                         FIG 21.6|
|001460      SUBTRACT 40 FROM BEGIN-POINT GIVING BEGIN-LOAD.                 FIG 21.6|
|001470      ADD BEGIN-LOAD, 82, WORD-LENGTH GIVING END-LOAD.               FIG 21.6|
|001480      PERFORM 3642-LOAD-CONTEXT                                       FIG 21.6|
|001490          VARYING LCTN FROM BEGIN-LOAD BY 1                           FIG 21.6|
|001500          UNTIL LCTN > END-LOAD OR 2500.                              FIG 21.6|
|001510      MOVE TEXT-OUTPUT TO OUTPUT-LINE.                                FIG 21.6|
|001520      IF WORD-CHECK NOT = *?*                                         FIG 21.6|
|001530          WRITE OUTPUT-RECORD AFTER ADVANCING 2 LINES.                FIG 21.6|
|001540      ADD WORD-LENGTH TO BEGIN-POINT.                                 FIG 21.6|
|001550 3642-LOAD-CONTEXT.                                                   FIG 21.6|
|001560      ADD 1 TO ORIG.                                                  FIG 21.6|
|001570      IF LCTN > 0                                                     FIG 21.6|
|001580          MOVE TEXT-CHARACTER (LCTN) TO OUTPUT-CHARACTER (ORIG)       FIG 21.6|
|001590      ELSE                                                            FIG 21.6|
|001600          MOVE SPACE TO OUTPUT-CHARACTER (ORIG).                      FIG 21.6|
|001610 5000-TERMINATE-PGM.                                                  FIG 21.6|
|001620      CLOSE KEY-WORD-FILE, OUTPUT-FILE.                               FIG 21.6|
```

Figure 21.6 Key Word in Context *Continued*

```
|       |          1         2         3         4         5         6         7        8| FIGURE |
|RECORD|1234567890123456789012345678901234567890123456789012345678901234567890| NUMBER |

|    1|*ANY ORGANIZATION INTERESTED IN REPRODUCING THE COBOL REPORT AND SPECIFICATIONS |FIG 21.6|
|    2|IN WHOLE OR IN PART, USING IDEAS TAKEN FROM THIS REPORT AS A BASIS FOR AN        |FIG 21.6|
|    3|INSTRUCTION MANUAL OR FOR ANY OTHER PURPOSE IS FREE TO DO SO.  HOWEVER, ALL      |FIG 21.6|
|    4|SUCH ORGANIZATIONS ARE REQUESTED TO REPRODUCE THIS SECTION AS PART OF THE        |FIG 21.6|
|    5|INTRODUCTION TO THE DOCUMENT.   THOSE USING A SHORT PASSAGE, AS IN A BOOK REVIEW,|FIG 21.6|
|    6|ARE REQUESTED TO MENTION *COBOL* IN ACKNOWLEDGEMENT OF THE SOURCE, BUT NEED NOT  |FIG 21.6|
|    7|QUOTE THIS ENTIRE SECTION.  COBOL IS AN INDUSTRY LANGUAGE AND IS NOT THE         |FIG 21.6|
|    8|PROPERTY OF ANY COMPANY OR GROUP OF COMPANIES, OR OF ANY ORGANIZATION OR GROUP   |FIG 21.6|
|    9|OF ORGANIZATIONS.  NO WARRANTY, EXPRESSED OR IMPLIED, IS MADE BY ANY CONTRIBUTOR|FIG 21.6|
|   10|OR BY THE COBOL COMMITTEE AS TO THE ACCURACY AND FUNCTIONING OF THE PROGRAMMING  |FIG 21.6|
|   11|SYSTEM AND LANGUAGE.  MOREOVER, NO RESPONSIBILITY IS ASSUMED BY ANY CONTRIBUTOR, |FIG 21.6|
|   12|OR BY THE COMMITTEE, IN CONNECTION THEREWITH.  PROCEDURES HAVE BEEN ESTABLISHED  |FIG 21.6|
|   13|FOR THE MAINTENANCE OF COBOL.  INQUIRIES CONCERNING THE PROCEDURES FOR PROPOSED  |FIG 21.6|
|   14|CHANGES SHOULD BE DIRECTED TO THE EXECUTIVE COMMITTEE OF THE CONFERENCE ON DATA  |FIG 21.6|
|   15|SYSTEM LANGUAGES.                                                               |FIG 21.6|
|   16|***************************************************************************************|FIG 21.6|
|   17|COBOL                                                                           |FIG 21.6|
|   18|REPORT                                                                          |FIG 21.6|
|   19|PROCEDURES                                                                      |FIG 21.6|
|   20|COMMITTEE                                                                       |FIG 21.6|
|   21|LANGUAGE                                                                        |FIG 21.6|
```

Figure 21.6 Key Word in Context (Data) *Continued*

TEXT AS READ:

"ANY ORGANIZATION INTERESTED IN REPRODUCING THE COBOL REPORT AND SPECIFICATIONS IN
WHOLE OR IN PART, USING IDEAS TAKEN FROM THIS REPORT AS A BASIS FOR AN INSTRUCTION
MANUAL OR FOR ANY OTHER PURPOSE IS FREE TO DO SO. HOWEVER, ALL SUCH ORGANIZATIONS
ARE REQUESTED TO REPRODUCE THIS SECTION AS PART OF THE INTRODUCTION TO THE DOCUMENT.
 THOSE USING A SHORT PASSAGE, AS IN A BOOK REVIEW, ARE REQUESTED TO MENTION "COBOL"
IN ACKNOWLEDGEMENT OF THE SOURCE, BUT NEED NOT QUOTE THIS ENTIRE SECTION. COBOL
IS AN INDUSTRY LANGUAGE AND IS NOT THE PROPERTY OF ANY COMPANY OR GROUP OF COMPANIES,
OR OF ANY ORGANIZATION OR GROUP OF ORGANIZATIONS. NO WARRANTY, EXPRESSED OR IMPLIED,
IS MADE BY ANY CONTRIBUTOR OR BY THE COBOL COMMITTEE AS TO THE ACCURACY AND FUNCTIONING
OF THE PROGRAMMING SYSTEM AND LANGUAGE. MOREOVER, NO RESPONSIBILITY IS ASSUMED BY
ANY CONTRIBUTOR, OR BY THE COMMITTEE, IN CONNECTION THEREWITH. PROCEDURES HAVE BEEN
ESTABLISHED FOR THE MAINTENANCE OF COBOL. INQUIRIES CONCERNING THE PROCEDURES FOR
PROPOSED CHANGES SHOULD BE DIRECTED TO THE EXECUTIVE COMMITTEE OF THE CONFERENCE
ON DATA SYSTEM LANGUAGES.

SEARCH FOR KEY WORD: COBOL

TION INTERESTED IN REPRODUCING THE COBOL REPORT AND SPECIFICATIONS IN WHOLE OR IN PART,

 REVIEW, ARE REQUESTED TO MENTION "COBOL" IN ACKNOWLEDGEMENT OF THE SOURCE, BUT NEED NOT

ED NOT QUOTE THIS ENTIRE SECTION. COBOL IS AN INDUSTRY LANGUAGE AND IS NOT THE PROPERTY

 MADE BY ANY CONTRIBUTOR OR BY THE COBOL COMMITTEE AS TO THE ACCURACY AND FUNCTIONING OF

ESTABLISHED FOR THE MAINTENANCE OF COBOL. INQUIRIES CONCERNING THE PROCEDURES FOR PROPO

NUMBER OF KEY WORDS FOUND: 5

SEARCH FOR KEY WORD: REPORT

TERESTED IN REPRODUCING THE COBOL REPORT AND SPECIFICATIONS IN WHOLE OR IN PART, USING ID

PART, USING IDEAS TAKEN FROM THIS REPORT AS A BASIS FOR AN INSTRUCTION MANUAL OR FOR ANY

NUMBER OF KEY WORDS FOUND: 2

SEARCH FOR KEY WORD: PROCEDURES

EE, IN CONNECTION THEREWITH. PROCEDURES HAVE BEEN ESTABLISHED FOR THE MAINTENANCE OF COBOL.

OL. INQUIRIES CONCERNING THE PROCEDURES FOR PROPOSED CHANGES SHOULD BE DIRECTED TO THE EXECU

NUMBER OF KEY WORDS FOUND: 2

SEARCH FOR KEY WORD: COMMITTEE

NY CONTRIBUTOR OR BY THE COBOL COMMITTEE AS TO THE ACCURACY AND FUNCTIONING OF THE PROGRAMMI

 BY ANY CONTRIBUTOR, OR BY THE COMMITTEE, IN CONNECTION THEREWITH. PROCEDURES HAVE BEEN EST

D BE DIRECTED TO THE EXECUTIVE COMMITTEE OF THE CONFERENCE ON DATA SYSTEM LANGUAGES.

NUMBER OF KEY WORDS FOUND: 3

Figure 21.6 Key Word in Context (Output) *Continued*

```
SEARCH FOR KEY WORD:  LANGUAGE

SECTION.  COBOL IS AN INDUSTRY LANGUAGE AND IS NOT THE PROPERTY OF ANY COMPANY OR GROUP OF

G OF THE PROGRAMMING SYSTEM AND LANGUAGE.  MOREOVER, NO RESPONSIBILITY IS ASSUMED BY ANY CO

F THE CONFERENCE ON DATA SYSTEM LANGUAGES.

NUMBER OF KEY WORDS FOUND:   3
```

Figure 21.6 Key Word in Context (Output) *Continued*

The INSPECT Statement

The INSPECT statement allows the programmer to scrutinize the contents of a data item with the possible aim of counting the number of occurrences of specific characters, replacing occurrences of certain characters with other characters, or both. The purpose of the INSPECT statement is to interrogate the contents of a data field.

The formats of the INSPECT statement, shown in Figure 21.7, are among the most complex in the COBOL language because of the number of options available to the programmer. The three forms of the INSPECT statement are INSPECT TALLYING, INSPECT REPLACING, and INSPECT TALLYING/REPLACING. The function of the TALLYING option is to count the occurrences of specific types of characters in a data item (identifier-1). Identifier-1 in all three options of the INSPECT statement must be either an elementary-item or a group-name that appears in DISPLAY (USAGE IS DISPLAY) form. Identifier-2 (of formats 1 and 2) contains a count of the number of characters for which the tally is to be taken. The identifier must be defined as a numeric elementary-item. Identifier-2 is not initialized by the INSPECT statement; it is the programmer's responsibility to provide the initial value for identifier-2. All remaining identifiers (and literals) in the INSPECT statement (format 1) must be single-character fields (or single-character non-numeric literals or figurative constants except ALL). The identifiers must be elementary data items.

The format 1 INSPECT statement permits the programmer to select between two types of tallying operations. The first option provides for the tallying of either ALL or LEADING occurrences of the character indicated by identifier-3 (literal-1). Using the reserved word ALL, all of the characters within the specified portion of identifier-1 are counted. When LEADING is indicated, only the leading characters within the specified portion of identifier-1 are tallied. (If either ALL or LEADING is specified, identifier-3 or literal-1 must be specified.) When using the second option by selecting the reserved word CHARACTERS in this position, *any* character that falls within the specified portion of identifier-1 is counted. The count is performed by examining the characters contained in identifier-1 one at a time. If the specified character is located, the counter (identifier-2) is incremented by one.

The final option of the format 1 INSPECT statement allows the programmer to indicate the character position within identifier-1 at which the inspection is to begin. For example, the programmer may specify that scanning of identifier-1 is to end BEFORE the first occurrence of identifier-4 (literal-2). If the BEFORE/AFTER option is omitted, the entire field is examined for the character indicated in the ALL/LEADING or CHARACTERS option.

```
Format 1:

    INSPECT identifier-1 TALLYING

        {identifier-2 FOR  { {ALL      }  {identifier-3} }
                             {LEADING  }  {literal-1   }
                             {CHARACTERS}

        [{BEFORE}  INITIAL  {identifier-4}]} ...  } ...
         {AFTER }           {literal-2   }
```

```
Format 2:

    INSPECT identifier-1 REPLACING

    {  CHARACTERS BY {identifier-6} [{BEFORE}  INITIAL  {identifier-7}]
                     {literal-4   }  {AFTER }           {literal-5   }

           {ALL     } {identifier-5}  BY  {identifier-6}
           {LEADING } {literal-3   }      {literal-4   }
           {FIRST   }

        [{BEFORE}  INITIAL  {identifier-7}] } ...  } ...
         {AFTER }           {literal-5   }
```

```
Format 3:

    INSPECT identifier-1 TALLYING

        {identifier-2 FOR  { {ALL       }  {identifier-3} }
                             {LEADING   }  {literal-1   }
                             {CHARACTERS}

        [{BEFORE}  INITIAL  {identifier-4}]} ...  } ...
         {AFTER }           {literal-2   }

    REPLACING

    {  CHARACTERS BY {identifier-6} [{BEFORE}  INITIAL  {identifier-4}]
                     {literal-4   }  {AFTER }           {literal-2   }

         { {ALL     } {identifier-5}  BY  {identifier-6} }
         { {LEADING } {literal-3   }      {literal-4   } }
         { {FIRST   }

        [{BEFORE}  INITIAL  {identifier-7}]} }  ... } ...
         {AFTER }           {literal-5   }
```

Figure 21.7 Formats of the INSPECT Statement

Format 2 of the INSPECT statement is the REPLACING option. Its primary function is to locate specific characters in identifier-1 and replace them with characters indicated by one of the options. With the CHARACTERS BY option, the INSPECT statement will replace any character that appears in identifier-1 (within the specified range) with identifier-6 (literal-4). As with the TALLYING option of the INSPECT statement all identifiers (except identifier-1) must be single-character elementary data items. Literals must be single-character non-numeric literal or figurative constants (except ALL). The REPLACING option is also similar to the TALLYING option in that the programmer can specify a beginning or ending point for scanning by indicating the BEFORE or AFTER option. An alternative to the CHARACTERS BY option allows the programmer to select a specific character for replacement using the reserved word ALL, LEADING, or FIRST. As with the TALLYING option, the reserved word ALL causes the replacement of all of the identifier-5 (literal-3) character *BY* identifier-6 (literal-4) characters. The reserved word LEADING has the same connotation as in the TALLYING option, that the specified characters are replaced and not counted. The optional BEFORE/AFTER phrase, used to indicate beginning or ending points of the scanning operations, is also available with this form of the REPLACING option.

The final format of the INSPECT statement is simply a combination of formats 1 and 2. Format 3 permits a programmer to both count and replace specific characters in identifier-1. The rules that apply to the identifiers specified in formats 1 and 2 also apply to the format 3 INSPECT statement. It is possible to count characters of one type while replacing other characters.

Examples of the three versions of the INSPECT statement are presented in Figure 21.8. The INSPECT statement is especially useful because it allows the programmer to interrogate data fields that might cause an error. Recall from

INSPECT Statement Illustration	Contents of TEST-FIELD*		Result in CHAR-COUNT**
	Before	After	
INSPECT TEST-FIELD TALLYING CHAR-COUNT FOR ALL SPACES.	P.ƀ0.ƀBOXƀ	P.ƀ0.ƀBOXƀ	3
INSPECT TEST-FIELD TALLYING CHAR-COUNT FOR LEADING ZEROS.	001403700	001403700	2
INSPECT TEST-FIELD TALLYING CHAR-COUNT FOR ALL 'X' AFTER SPACE.	AXBXƀNXXDX	AXBXƀNXXDX	3
INSPECT TEST-FIELD TALLYING CHAR-COUNT FOR LEADING SPACES BEFORE 'X'	1ƀ3ƀ3ƀXƀ4ƀ	1ƀ3ƀ3ƀXƀ4ƀ	1
INSPECT TEST-FIELD TALLYING CHAR-COUNT FOR CHARACTERS.	P.ƀ0.ƀBOXƀ	P.ƀ0.ƀBOXƀ	7
INSPECT TEST-FIELD REPLACING CHARACTERS BY ZERO.	1ƀ3ƀ3ƀXƀ4ƀ	1ƀ3ƀ3ƀ0ƀ4ƀ	-
INSPECT TEST-FIELD REPLACING CHARACTERS BY 'X' AFTER SPACE.	P.ƀ0.ƀBOXƀ	P.ƀXXƀXXXƀ	-
INSPECT TEST-FIELD REPLACING ALL SPACES BY ZERO.	ƀƀ14037ƀƀ	001403700	-
INSPECT TEST-FIELD REPLACING LEADING 'A' BY 'B'.	AAAABBBAA	BBBBBBBAA	-
INSPECT TEST-FIELD REPLACING FIRST '1' BY 'X'.	ƀ5Aƀ115	ƀ5AƀX15	-
INSPECT TEST-FIELD REPLACING ALL SPACES BY '0' AFTER 'X'.	Pƀ0ƀBOXƀ5ƀ	Pƀ0ƀBOX050	-
INSPECT TEST-FIELD TALLYING CHAR-COUNT FOR ALL SPACES REPLACING CHARACTERS BY ZERO.	ƀƀ14037 0ƀƀ	ƀƀ000000ƀƀ	4
INSPECT TEST-FIELD TALLYING CHAR-COUNT FOR LEADING ZEROS REPLACING LEADING ZEROS BY SPACES.	000120340	ƀƀƀ120340	3
INSPECT TEST-FIELD TALLYING CHAR-COUNT FOR CHARACTERS REPLACING ALL 'A' BY 'B' LEADING SPACES BY ZERO AFTER 'B'.	ƀƀAABBAAƀ	ƀƀBBBBBB0	6

* The character ƀ indicates the location of blanks in the TEST-FIELD data item contents.
**CHAR-COUNT is assumed to be initialized to zero before the execution of each INSPECT Statement.

Figure 21.8 Examples of the INSPECT Statement

Chapter 10 that a numeric data item is not permitted to contain blanks. If the processing of this data item had included an arithmetic manipulation, the program would have encountered a fatal error resulting in an abnormal termination. However, if the programmer suspects that one or more of the numeric data fields may contain blanks, he can resolve the problem by inspecting those fields and replacing all occurrences of blanks with zeros. Figure 21.9 illustrates the procedure for STUDENT-ID. When the STUDENT-ID for BEN FRANKLIN is encountered, the INSPECT statement will encounter blanks and will convert blanks to zeros.

```
|           1    1    2    2    3    3    4    4    5    5    6    6    6    7    7    8|
|     4     8    2    6    0    4    8    2    6    0    4    8    2    6    0    4    8    2    6    0|
---------------------------------------------------------------------------------
|000010 IDENTIFICATION DIVISION.                                    FIG 21.9|
|000020 PROGRAM-ID.  EXAMPLE-INSPECT.                               FIG 21.9|
|000030 AUTHOR. CARI DIANE SPENCE.                                  FIG 21.9|
|000040 DATE-WRITTEN. JANUARY 1, 1981.                              FIG 21.9|
|000050 DATE-COMPILED. JANUARY 1, 1981.                             FIG 21.9|
|000060*    THIS PROGRAM DEMONSTRATES THE USE OF AN INSPECT         FIG 21.9|
|000070*    STATEMENT TO MODIFY INCORRECTLY CODED NUMERIC DATA.     FIG 21.9|
|000080 ENVIRONMENT DIVISION.                                       FIG 21.9|
|000090 CONFIGURATION SECTION.                                      FIG 21.9|
|000100 SOURCE-COMPUTER. IBM-370-145.                               FIG 21.9|
|000110 OBJECT-COMPUTER. IBM-370-145.                               FIG 21.9|
|000120 SPECIAL-NAMES.  C01 IS TOP-OF-NEXT-PAGE.                    FIG 21.9|
|000130 INPUT-OUTPUT SECTION.                                       FIG 21.9|
|000140 FILE-CONTROL.                                               FIG 21.9|
|000150     SELECT STUDENT-FILE ASSIGN TO UR-S-SYSIN.               FIG 21.9|
|000160     SELECT PRINTOUT ASSIGN TO UR-S-SYSPRINT.                FIG 21.9|
|000170 DATA DIVISION.                                              FIG 21.9|
|000180 FILE SECTION.                                               FIG 21.9|
|000190 FD  STUDENT-FILE LABEL RECORDS ARE OMITTED.                 FIG 21.9|
|000200 01  STUDENT-REC.                                            FIG 21.9|
|000210     05 STUDENT-IDENTIFICATION.                              FIG 21.9|
|000220        10 LAST-NAME           PIC X(10).                    FIG 21.9|
|000230        10 FIRST-NAME          PIC X(10).                    FIG 21.9|
|000240        10 MIDDLE-INITIAL      PIC X(01).                    FIG 21.9|
|000250        10 STUDENT-ID          PIC 9(09).                    FIG 21.9|
|000260     05 FILLER                 PIC X(05).                    FIG 21.9|
|000270     05 ENROLLMENT-INFO.                                     FIG 21.9|
|000280        10 CLASSIFICATION      PIC X(02).                    FIG 21.9|
|000290        10 TOTAL-HOURS         PIC 9(03).                    FIG 21.9|
|000300        10 HOURS-THIS-SEM      PIC 9(02).                    FIG 21.9|
|000310        10 MAJOR               PIC X(03).                    FIG 21.9|
|000320     05  FILLER                PIC X(35).                    FIG 21.9|
|000330 FD  PRINTOUT LABEL RECORDS ARE OMITTED.                     FIG 21.9|
|000340 01  PRINT-LINE                PIC X(133).                   FIG 21.9|
|000350 WORKING-STORAGE SECTION.                                    FIG 21.9|
|000360 01  WORKING-VARIABLES.                                      FIG 21.9|
|000370     05  INDICATOR             PIC X(16).                    FIG 21.9|
|000380 01  OUTPUT-REC.                                             FIG 21.9|
|000390        08 FILLER              PIC X(03) VALUE ' '.          FIG 21.9|
|000400        08 1ST-NAME            PIC X(11).                    FIG 21.9|
|000410        08 M-I                 PIC X(01).                    FIG 21.9|
|000420        08 FILLER              PIC X(02) VALUE '.'.          FIG 21.9|
|000430        08 SUR-NAME            PIC X(10).                    FIG 21.9|
|000440        08 FILLER              PIC X(04) VALUE ' '.          FIG 21.9|
|000450        08 ID-NUM              PIC 9(09).                    FIG 21.9|
|000460        08 FILLER              PIC X(05) VALUE '  '.         FIG 21.9|
|000470        08 CLASS               PIC X(02).                    FIG 21.9|
|000480        08 FILLER              PIC X(06) VALUE '   '.        FIG 21.9|
|000490        08 MAJ                 PIC X(03).                    FIG 21.9|
|000500        08 FILLER              PIC X(08) VALUE '  '.         FIG 21.9|
|000510        08 CURRENT-HOURS       PIC 9(02).                    FIG 21.9|
|000520        08 FILLER              PIC X(08) VALUE '   '.        FIG 21.9|
|000530        08 TOT-HOURS           PIC 9(03).                    FIG 21.9|
|000540        08 FILLER              PIC X(03) VALUE ' '.          FIG 21.9|
|000550 PROCEDURE DIVISION.                                         FIG 21.9|
|000560 CONTROL-PROCEDURE.                                          FIG 21.9|
|000570     PERFORM 100-INITIALIZATION.                             FIG 21.9|
|000580     PERFORM 300-READ-RECORDS-PRINT-DETAILS                  FIG 21.9|
|000590        UNTIL INDICATOR = 'PROCESS COMPLETE'.                FIG 21.9|
|000600     PERFORM 500-TERMINATION.                                FIG 21.9|
|000610     STOP RUN.                                               FIG 21.9|
```

Figure 21.9 An Illustration of the INSPECT Statement

```
|         1   1   2   2   2   3   3   4   4   4   5   5   6   6   6   7   7   8|
|    4   8   2   6   0   4   8   2   6   0   4   8   2   6   0   4   8   2   6   0|
-------------------------------------------------------------------------------
|000620 100-INITIALIZATION.                                           FIG 21.9|
|000630     MOVE "PROCESS START" TO INDICATOR.                        FIG 21.9|
|000640     OPEN INPUT STUDENT-FILE, OUTPUT PRINTOUT.                 FIG 21.9|
|000650     READ STUDENT-FILE                                         FIG 21.9|
|000660         AT END MOVE "PROCESS COMPLETE" TO INDICATOR.          FIG 21.9|
|000670 300-READ-RECORDS-PRINT-DETAILS.                               FIG 21.9|
|000680     INSPECT STUDENT-ID REPLACING ALL " " BY "0".             FIG 21.9|
|000690     MOVE STUDENT-ID TO ID-NUM.                                FIG 21.9|
|000700     MOVE LAST-NAME TO SUR-NAME.                               FIG 21.9|
|000710     MOVE FIRST-NAME TO 1ST-NAME.                              FIG 21.9|
|000720     MOVE MIDDLE-INITIAL TO M-I.                               FIG 21.9|
|000730     MOVE CLASSIFICATION TO CLASS.                             FIG 21.9|
|000740     MOVE TOTAL-HOURS TO TOT-HOURS.                            FIG 21.9|
|000750     MOVE HOURS-THIS-SEM TO CURRENT-HOURS.                     FIG 21.9|
|000760     MOVE MAJOR TO MAJ.                                        FIG 21.9|
|000770     WRITE PRINT-LINE FROM OUTPUT-REC AFTER 2 LINES.           FIG 21.9|
|000780     READ STUDENT-FILE                                         FIG 21.9|
|000790         AT END MOVE "PROCESS COMPLETE" TO INDICATOR.          FIG 21.9|
|000800 500-TERMINATION.                                              FIG 21.9|
|000810     CLOSE STUDENT-FILE, PRINTOUT.                             FIG 21.9|
```

Figure 21.9 An Illustration of the INSPECT Statement *Continued*

```
|       |         1         2         3         4         5         6         7        8| FIGURE |
|RECORD |1234567890123456789012345678901234567890123456789012345678901234567890| NUMBER |
-----------------------------------------------------------------------------------------------
|    1|ADAMS     JOHN      Q343564321     GR21900CSC                              |FIG 21.9|
|    2|BROWN     JOHN      A555667777     FR03515MKT                              |FIG 21.9|
|    3|CULVER    MATT      N456789012     JR09408MGT                              |FIG 21.9|
|    4|DORSETT   ANTHONY   R353492761     SR13816ECO                              |FIG 21.9|
|    5|ELDRIDGE  DAVID     Q376495268     SO04712FIN                              |FIG 21.9|
|    6|FRANKLIN  BEN       V         2    GR18912GBU                              |FIG 21.9|
|    7|GERBER    KENNETH   A537903251     SO02816MGT                              |FIG 21.9|
|    8|HAMILTON  MARK      C486762389     JR09618CSC                              |FIG 21.9|
|    9|ISSACS    MATT      H474653790     SR12018ECO                              |FIG 21.9|
|   10|JENNINGS  HAROLD    Q502326955     FR01818MGT                              |FIG 21.9|
|   11|KENNIMER  FLOYD     R476329092     JR06012MKT                              |FIG 21.9|
|   12|LINCOLN   STEVEN    0442648942     SO04515MKT                              |FIG 21.9|
|   13|MARCUS    JEFF      V546677219     SR09918CSC                              |FIG 21.9|
```

Figure 21.9 An Illustration of the INSPECT Statement (Data) *Continued*

```
*  JOHN        Q.  ADAMS       *  343564321   *  GR  *  CSC  *    00   *  219  *

*  JOHN        A.  BROWN       *  555667777   *  FR  *  MKT  *    15   *  035  *

*  MATT        N.  CULVER      *  456789012   *  JR  *  MGT  *    08   *  094  *

*  ANTHONY     R.  DORSETT     *  353492761   *  SR  *  ECO  *    16   *  138  *

*  DAVID       Q.  ELDRIDGE    *  376495268   *  SO  *  FIN  *    12   *  047  *

*  BEN         V.  FRANKLIN    *  000000002   *  GR  *  GBU  *    12   *  189  *

*  KENNETH     A.  GERBER      *  537903251   *  SO  *  MGT  *    16   *  028  *

*  MARK        C.  HAMILTON    *  486762389   *  JR  *  CSC  *    18   *  096  *

*  MATT        H.  ISSACS      *  474653790   *  SR  *  ECO  *    18   *  120  *

*  HAROLD      Q.  JENNINGS    *  502326955   *  FR  *  MGT  *    18   *  018  *

*  FLOYD       R.  KENNIMER    *  476329092   *  JR  *  MKT  *    12   *  060  *

*  STEVEN      O.  LINCOLN     *  442648942   *  SO  *  MKT  *    15   *  045  *

*  JEFF        V.  MARCUS      *  546677219   *  SR  *  CSC  *    18   *  099  *
```

Figure 21.9 An Illustration of the INSPECT Statement (Output) *Continued*

The EXAMINE and TRANSFORM Statements

Some computer manufacturers do not include the INSPECT statement in their ANS COBOL compilers. Those compilers that do not contain the INSPECT statement often support the EXAMINE or the TRANSFORM statement. IBM COBOL compilers do not contain the INSPECT statement, but they do contain both the EXAMINE and the TRANSFORM statements. (A few compilers that do contain the INSPECT statement also permit the use of the EXAMINE statement.)

Both statements are intended as a substitute for the INSPECT statement. The EXAMINE statement, shown in Figure 21.10, has two formats. The first format is similar to the format 3 INSPECT statement—it is capable of both TALLYING and REPLACING characters that appear in an identifier. As with the INSPECT statement, the identifier that appears immediately after the reserved word EXAMINE must be described as a DISPLAY elementary-item or group. No other identifiers appear in the formats of the EXAMINE statement. The first format of the statement can count the occurrences of the specified character (literal-1). Compilers which support the EXAMINE statement provide a *special register* called TALLY. TALLY is implicitly defined by the compiler as being a numeric data item which may contain up to a five-digit integer number. When the TALLYING form of the EXAMINE statement is used, the value of TALLY is automatically set to zero before each execution of the statement. The character count contained in TALLY may then be used as an internal data-name in other COBOL statements.

The EXAMINE statement is also similar to the INSPECT statement in that it permits an inspection of a data field as dictated by the reserved words ALL and LEADING. And, a procedure for scanning the data field is provided with the reserved words UNTIL FIRST. As with the INSPECT statement, when ALL is specified, every occurrence of literal-1 is counted (in TALLY) and replaced with the character specified by literal-2. (Both literal-1 and literal-2 must be single-character non-numeric literals or a figurative constant, except ALL.) When LEADING is chosen, the leading characters are indicated as an uninterrupted string of the literal-1 character, beginning with the leftmost character in the field. That is, the first non-literal-1 character found in the data field ter-

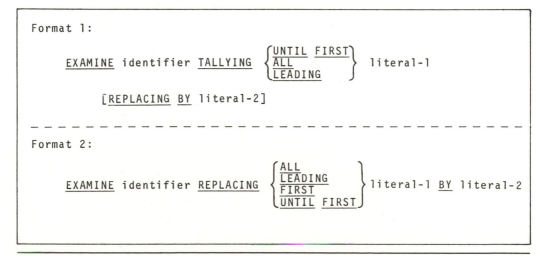

Figure 21.10 Formats of the EXAMINE Statement (Non-ANS Standard)

minates the EXAMINE statement. With UNTIL FIRST, the character string to be inspected by the EXAMINE statement is that string of characters (from left to right) which is terminated by the first occurrence of the literal-1 character.

Format 2 of the EXAMINE statement is similar to the format 2 INSPECT statement. The purpose of this form is to locate the occurrence(s) of literal-1 and replace it (them) with the literal-2 character. Like format 1 of the EXAMINE statement, format 2 utilizes the reserved words ALL, LEADING, and UNTIL FIRST to control the character scanning operation. These words have the same meaning in format 2 as they have in format 1. However, like format 2 of the INSPECT statement, format 2 of the EXAMINE statement also permits the use of the reserved word FIRST. The use of FIRST allows only a single replacement of literal-1 *BY* literal-2. That is, only the first occurrence of literal-1 in the identifier is replaced by literal-2.

Another non-ANS statement, the TRANSFORM statement, performs some of the same functions as the INSPECT statement. The format of the TRANSFORM statement is presented in Figure 21.11. As with the identifier being INSPECTed or EXAMINEd, identifier-3 of the TRANSFORM statement must be an elementary data item or a group-name that is described in DISPLAY form. The essence of the TRANSFORM statement is like that of the INSPECT REPLACING or the EXAMINE REPLACING. The character(s) represented by figurative-constant-1, non-numeric-literal-1, or identifier-1 are replaced by the character(s) represented by figurative-constant-2, non-numeric-literal-2, or identifier-2. There is a major difference in the description of identifier-1 (literal-1) and identifier-2 (literal-2), however. These identifiers (and literals) may be composed of one *or more* characters. The identifier must still be described as an elementary data item in DISPLAY form.

When identifier-1 (or literal-1) is used, identifier-2 (or literal-2) must be the same length as identifier-1 (or literal-1) or a single character. Figurative constants in either position are treated as a single character. In this case, every occurrence of the first item in the characters of identifier-3 is replaced by the second item. If the first item is longer than one character and the second item is a single character, any character that appears in both identifier-3 and the first item is replaced by the second item (character). When the first item and second item are both longer than one character, both items (regardless of their type) must be the same length. During the inspection of identifier-3, any occurrence of the first character of the first item is replaced by the first character of the second item; the second character in the first item is replaced by the second

```
TRANSFORM identifier-3 CHARACTERS FROM  ⎧figurative-constant-1⎫
                                        ⎨non-numeric-literal-1⎬
                                        ⎩identifier-1         ⎭

     ⎧figurative-constant-2⎫
  TO ⎨non-numeric-literal-2⎬
     ⎩identifier-2         ⎭
```

Figure 21.11 Format of the TRANSFORM Statement (Non-ANS Standard)

character of the second item; and so forth. Thus, the replacement of characters is performed character by character (or character *for* character) for the first item and the second item.

Figure 21.12 illustrates both the EXAMINE statement and the TRANS-FORM statement. Many of the examples presented in the illustration are similar to those included in Figure 21.10 (Examples of the INSPECT Statement).

Finally, Figure 21.13 illustrates the use of an EXAMINE statement. Recall that in Figure 21.9 an INSPECT statement was used to scan the characters in STUDENT-ID and replace any occurrence of a blank with a zero. Line 670 of Figure 21.13 performs the same conversion process, except an EXAMINE statement has been substituted for the INSPECT statement.

EXAMINE and TRANSFORM Statement Illustrations	Contents of TEST-FIELD*		Results in TALLY**
	Before	After	
EXAMINE TEST-FIELD TALLYING ALL SPACES.	P.ƀ0.ƀBOXƀ	P.ƀ0.ƀBOXƀ	3
EXAMINE TEST-FIELD TALLYING LEADING ZEROS.	001403700	001403700	2
EXAMINE TEST-FIELD TALLYING ALL 'X'.	AXBXƀNXXDX	AXBXƀNXXDX	5
EXAMINE TEST-FIELD TALLYING UNTIL FIRST 'X'.	P.ƀ0.ƀBOXƀ	P.ƀ0.ƀBOXƀ	8
EXAMINE TEST-FIELD REPLACING ALL SPACES BY ZERO. or TRANSFORM TEST-FIELD FROM SPACES TO ZERO.	ƀƀ14037ƀƀ	001403700	-
EXAMINE TEST-FIELD REPLACING LEADING 'A' BY 'B'.	AAAABBBAA	BBBBBBBAA	-
EXAMINE TEST-FIELD REPLACING FIRST '1' BY 'X'.	ƀ5Aƀ115	ƀ5AƀX15	-
EXAMINE TEST-FIELD REPLACING UNTIL FIRST 'X' BY 'Ø'.	P.ƀ0.ƀBOXƀ	00000000Xƀ	-
EXAMINE TEST-FIELD TALLYING ALL SPACES REPLACING BY ZERO.	ƀƀ140370ƀƀ	0014037000	4
EXAMINE TEST-FIELD TALLYING LEADING ZEROS REPLACING BY SPACES.	000120340	ƀƀƀ120340	3
TRANSFORM TEST-FIELD FROM 'X' TO 'Ø'.	AXBXƀNXXDX	A0B0ƀN00D0	-
TRANSFORM TEST-FIELD FROM 'ABC' TO '123'.	AABACADABA	112131D121	-
TRANSFORM TEST-FIELD FROM 'ABC' TO 'BCD'.	AABACADABA	DDDDDDDDDD	-
TRANSFORM TEST-FIELD FROM 'Ø123456789' TO SPACE.	ƀƀ140370ƀƀ	ƀƀƀƀƀƀƀƀƀ	-

* The character ƀ indicates the location of blanks in the contents of TEST-FIELD.
**TALLY is automatically initialized to zero before the execution of each EXAMINE statement.

Figure 21.12 Examples of the EXAMINE and TRANSFORM Statements

```
|            1   1   2   2   2   3   3   4   4   4   5   5   6   6   6   7   7   8|
|   4    8   2   6   0   4   8   2   6   0   4   8   2   6   0   4   8   2   6   0|
--------------------------------------------------------------------------------
|000010 IDENTIFICATION DIVISION.                                    FIG21.13|
|000020 PROGRAM-ID.  EXAMPLE-EXAMINE.                               FIG21.13|
|000030 AUTHOR. MARTHA WORKMAN.                                     FIG21.13|
|000040 DATE-WRITTEN. JANUARY 1, 1981.                              FIG21.13|
|000050 DATE-COMPILED. JANUARY 1, 1981.                             FIG21.13|
|000060*    THIS PROGRAM DEMONSTRATES THE USE OF AN EXAMINE         FIG21.13|
|000070*    STATEMENT TO MODIFY INCORRECTLY CODED NUMERIC DATA.     FIG21.13|
|000080 ENVIRONMENT DIVISION.                                       FIG21.13|
|000090 CONFIGURATION SECTION.                                      FIG21.13|
|000100 SOURCE-COMPUTER. IBM-370-145.                               FIG21.13|
|000110 OBJECT-COMPUTER. IBM-370-145.                               FIG21.13|
|000120 SPECIAL-NAMES.  C01 IS TOP-OF-NEXT-PAGE.                    FIG21.13|
|000130 INPUT-OUTPUT SECTION.                                       FIG21.13|
|000140 FILE-CONTROL.                                               FIG21.13|
|000150     SELECT STUDENT-FILE ASSIGN TO UR-S-SYSIN.              FIG21.13|
|000160     SELECT PRINTOUT ASSIGN TO UR-S-SYSPRINT.               FIG21.13|
|000170 DATA DIVISION.                                              FIG21.13|
|000180 FILE SECTION.                                               FIG21.13|
|000190 FD   STUDENT-FILE LABEL RECORDS ARE OMITTED.               FIG21.13|
|000200 01   STUDENT-REC.                                           FIG21.13|
|000210     05 STUDENT-IDENTIFICATION.                              FIG21.13|
|000220        10 LAST-NAME           PIC X(10).                   FIG21.13|
|000230        10 FIRST-NAME          PIC X(10).                   FIG21.13|
|000240        10 MIDDLE-INITIAL      PIC X(01).                   FIG21.13|
|000250        10 STUDENT-ID          PIC X(09).                   FIG21.13|
|000260     05 FILLER                 PIC X(05).                   FIG21.13|
|000270     05 ENROLLMENT-INFO.                                     FIG21.13|
|000280        10 CLASSIFICATION      PIC X(02).                   FIG21.13|
|000290        10 TOTAL-HOURS         PIC 9(03).                   FIG21.13|
|000300        10 HOURS-THIS-SEM      PIC 9(02).                   FIG21.13|
|000310        10 MAJOR               PIC X(03).                   FIG21.13|
|000320     05   FILLER               PIC X(35).                   FIG21.13|
|000330 FD   PRINTOUT LABEL RECORDS ARE OMITTED.                   FIG21.13|
|000340 01   PRINT-LINE               PIC X(133).                  FIG21.13|
|000350 WORKING-STORAGE SECTION.                                    FIG21.13|
|000360 01   WORKING-VARIABLES.                                     FIG21.13|
|000370     05 INDICATOR              PIC X(16).                   FIG21.13|
|000380 01   OUTPUT-REC.                                            FIG21.13|
|000390        08 FILLER              PIC X(03) VALUE ' *'.        FIG21.13|
|000400        08 1ST-NAME            PIC X(11).                   FIG21.13|
|000410        08 M-I                 PIC X(01).                   FIG21.13|
|000420        08 FILLER              PIC X(02) VALUE '.'.         FIG21.13|
|000430        08 SUR-NAME            PIC X(10).                   FIG21.13|
|000440        08 FILLER              PIC X(04) VALUE ' *'.        FIG21.13|
|000450        08 ID-NUM              PIC 9(09).                   FIG21.13|
|000460        08 FILLER              PIC X(05) VALUE '  *'.       FIG21.13|
|000470        08 CLASS               PIC X(02).                   FIG21.13|
|000480        08 FILLER              PIC X(06) VALUE '   *'.      FIG21.13|
|000490        08 MAJ                 PIC X(03).                   FIG21.13|
|000500        08 FILLER              PIC X(08) VALUE ' *'.        FIG21.13|
|000510        08 CURRENT-HOURS       PIC 9(02).                   FIG21.13|
|000520        08 FILLER              PIC X(08) VALUE '    *'.     FIG21.13|
|000530        08 TOT-HOURS           PIC 9(03).                   FIG21.13|
|000540        08 FILLER              PIC X(03) VALUE ' *'.        FIG21.13|
|000550 PROCEDURE DIVISION.                                         FIG21.13|
|000560 CONTROL-PROCEDURE.                                          FIG21.13|
|000570     PERFORM 100-INITIALIZATION.                            FIG21.13|
|000580     PERFORM 300-READ-RECORD-PRINT-DETAIL                   FIG21.13|
|000590         UNTIL INDICATOR = 'PROCESS COMPLETE'.              FIG21.13|
|000600     PERFORM 500-TERMINATION.                               FIG21.13|
|000610     STOP RUN.                                              FIG21.13|
|000620 100-INITIALIZATION.                                         FIG21.13|
|000630     MOVE 'PROCESS START' TO INDICATOR.                     FIG21.13|
|000640     OPEN INPUT STUDENT-FILE, OUTPUT PRINTOUT.              FIG21.13|
|000650     READ STUDENT-FILE                                      FIG21.13|
|000660         AT END MOVE 'PROCESS COMPLETE' TO INDICATOR.       FIG21.13|
|000670 300-READ-RECORD-PRINT-DETAIL.                               FIG21.13|
|000680     EXAMINE STUDENT-ID REPLACING ALL ' ' BY '0'.          FIG21.13|
|000690     MOVE STUDENT-ID TO ID-NUM.                             FIG21.13|
|000700     MOVE LAST-NAME TO SUR-NAME.                            FIG21.13|
|000710     MOVE FIRST-NAME TO 1ST-NAME.                           FIG21.13|
|000720     MOVE MIDDLE-INITIAL TO M-I.                            FIG21.13|
|000730     MOVE CLASSIFICATION TO CLASS.                          FIG21.13|
|000740     MOVE TOTAL-HOURS TO TOT-HOURS.                         FIG21.13|
|000750     MOVE HOURS-THIS-SEM TO CURRENT-HOURS.                  FIG21.13|
|000760     MOVE MAJOR TO MAJ.                                     FIG21.13|
|000770     WRITE PRINT-LINE FROM OUTPUT-REC AFTER 2 LINES.        FIG21.13|
|000780     READ STUDENT-FILE                                      FIG21.13|
|000790         AT END MOVE 'PROCESS COMPLETE' TO INDICATOR.       FIG21.13|
|000800 500-TERMINATION.                                            FIG21.13|
|000810     CLOSE STUDENT-FILE, PRINTOUT.                          FIG21.13|
```

Figure 21.13 An Illustration of the EXAMINE Statement

*	JOHN	Q. ADAMS	*	343564321	*	GR	*	CSC	*	00	*	219	*
*	JOHN	A. BROWN	*	555667777	*	FP	*	MKT	*	15	*	035	*
*	MATT	N. CULVER	*	456789012	*	JR	*	MGT	*	08	*	094	*
*	ANTHONY	R. DORSETT	*	353492761	*	SR	*	ECO	*	16	*	138	*
*	DAVID	Q. ELDRIDGE	*	376495268	*	SO	*	FIN	*	12	*	047	*
*	BEN	V. FRANKLIN	*	000000002	*	GR	*	GRU	*	12	*	189	*
*	KENNETH	A. GERBER	*	537903251	*	SO	*	MGT	*	16	*	028	*
*	MARK	C. HAMILTON	*	486762389	*	JR	*	CSC	*	18	*	096	*
*	MATT	H. ISSACS	*	474653790	*	SR	*	ECO	*	18	*	120	*
*	HAROLD	Q. JENNINGS	*	502326955	*	FR	*	MGT	*	18	*	018	*
*	FLOYD	R. KENNIMER	*	476329092	*	JR	*	MKT	*	12	*	060	*
*	STEVEN	O. LINCOLN	*	442648942	*	SO	*	MKT	*	15	*	045	*
*	JEFF	V. MARCUS	*	546677219	*	SR	*	CSC	*	18	*	099	*

Figure 21.13 An Illustration of the EXAMINE Statement (Output) *Continued*

Summary

This chapter has presented statements specifically designed to manipulate character data. The STRING statement may be used to copy data from two or more fields into one receiving field. With the use of optional clauses, the STRING statement may count the characters placed in the receiving field and indicate the procedure to be executed in the event that the data to be strung together overflows the receiving field.

The UNSTRING statement, on the other hand, allows the programmer to extract data from one field and have the result placed in multiple receiving fields. In addition, the UNSTRING statement provides options that allow the programmer to count the number of characters moved to each receiving field, initializing UNSTRING operations in a location other than the first character of the sending field, count the number of receiving fields, and indicate the procedure to be executed in the event that all receiving fields did not receive data as a consequence of the unstringing operation.

The INSPECT, EXAMINE and TRANSFORM statements serve a slightly different function in that they are capable of manipulating existing data in a single field. In addition, the INSPECT and EXAMINE statements are also capable of performing a counting function.

Notes on Programming Style

The STRING and UNSTRING statements have been left to last in this text because these statements represent the direction in which COBOL is moving. That is, the STRING and UNSTRING statements were not included in the ANS COBOL standard instruction set until 1974. These statements obviously have very specialized uses, as will be the case when other statements or type representations are added to the language in the future.

Future programming may require better communication with the user. An operator sitting at a CRT terminal may request certain operations to be performed in the form of a sentence or phrase, and it will be the program's task to determine from the sentence or phrase what is being requested. Furthermore, responses to the operator may be more textual than they are today. Thus, it may be the program's responsibility to *construct* meaningful sentences or phrases to respond to user requests. Both of these functions would obviously be much easier to handle with the availability of statements like STRING and UNSTRING. The next version of COBOL will likely include more string-oriented operations than the current versions.

One word of caution about the EXAMINE and TRANSFORM statements. Since these are not ANS standard COBOL statements, the possibility exists that the manufacturers that support these statements may choose to withdraw that support at any time. Therefore, many installations choose not to use these statements to avoid incompatibility with future compilers, and so that switching to other computers is more easily accomplished.

Questions

Below fill in the blank(s) with the appropriate word, words, or phrases.

1. The STRING and the UNSTRING statement are used in the manipulation of _____ .

2. The STRING statement provides the programmer with the function of _____ .

3. The UNSTRING statement provides the programmer with the function of _____ .

4. The STRING statement causes data to be copied from the sending field into the receiving field until the situation or value specified in the _____ phrase is encountered.

5. In a STRING operation, the programmer is provided the capability of counting the number of characters moved through the _____ option.

6. When the operation of the STRING statement attempts to place more characters in the receiving field than it is capable of retaining, the _____ option is invoked, if present.

7. The movement of data from the sending field to the first receiving field in the UNSTRING statement is terminated by _____ .

8. Statement types which may be used to manipulate the contents of existing fields include _____ , _____ , and _____ .

9. If one wished to count the number of occurrences of a particular character in a field, one might use the _____ or _____ statement.

Answer the following questions by circling either "T" for True or "F" for False.

T F 10. Concatenation means to place two or more items together.

T F 11. Parsing means to segment one item into two or more items.

T F 12. The receiving field of a STRING statement must be an alphanumeric field.

T F 13. The identifier used in the POINTER option of the STRING statement is automatically initialized by the execution of the STRING statement.

T F 14. In the STRING statement no more than one receiving field may be employed.

T F 15. In the UNSTRING statement no more than one receiving field may be employed.
T F 16. Data must be described in DISPLAY form to be used in either the STRING or UNSTRING statement.
T F 17. In the STRING statement, no more than one sending field may be employed.
T F 18. In the UNSTRING statement, no more than one sending field may be employed.
T F 19. In the STRING statement, one sending field may be employed.
T F 20. In the UNSTRING statement, one receiving field may be employed.

Appendixes

A List of Reserved Words

ACCEPT
ACCESS
+ ACTIVE
* ACTUAL
ADD
* ADDRESS
ADVANCING
AFTER
ALL
ALPHABETIC
ALPHANUMERIC
ALPHANUMERIC-EDITED
ALTER
ALTERNATE
+ AN
AND
+ ANY
* APPLY
ARE
AREA
AREAS
ASCENDING
@ ASCII
+ ASM
ASSIGN
AT
AUTHOR

BASIS
BEFORE
* BEGINNING
@ BINARY
BLANK
BLOCK
BOTTOM
BY

CALL
CANCEL
* CARD-PUNCH
* CARD-READER
# CBL
CD
CF
+ CFH
CH
* CHANGED
@ CHANNEL
CHARACTER
CHARACTERS
CLOCK-UNITS
CLOSE
COBOL
CODE
CODE-SET
COLLATING
COLUMN
COM-REG
COMMA
* COMMON-STORAGE
COMMUNICATION
COMP
* COMP-1
* COMP-2
* COMP-3
* COMP-4
+ COMPACT
COMPUTATIONAL
* COMPUTATIONAL-1
* COMPUTATIONAL-2
* COMPUTATIONAL-3
* COMPUTATIONAL-4
COMPUTE

CONFIGURATION
* CONSOLE
# CONSTANT
CONTAINS
CONTROL
CONTROLS
COPY
* CORE-INDEX
CORR
CORRESPONDING
COUNT
+ CREATION-DATE
# CSP
CURRENCY
CURRENT-DATE
+ CYCLES
# CYL-INDEX
# CYL-OVERFLOW
# CØ1
# CØ2

DATA
DATE
DATE-COMPILED
DATE-WRITTEN
+ DATE-TIME
DAY
DAY-OF-WEEK
DE
DEBUG-CONTENTS
DEBUG-ITEM
DEBUG-LINE
DEBUG-NAME
DEBUG-SUB-1
DEBUG-SUB-2
DEBUG-SUB-3

* Adopted by multiple manufacturers
@ Digital Equipment Corporation
# IBM (VS, OS, DOS)
& Honeywell/Xerox
+ Univac

DEBUGGING
DECIMAL-POINT
DECLARATIVES
@ DEFERRED
DELETE
DELIMITED
DELIMITER
@ DENSITY
DEPENDING
* DEPTH
DESCENDING
DESTINATION
DETAIL
+ DIRECT
DISABLE
* DISP
DISPLAY
DISPLAY-ST
* DISPLAY-n
DIVISION
DOWN
DUPLICATES
DYNAMIC

@ EBCDIC
EGI
# EJECT
ELSE
EMI
ENABLE
END
END-OF-PAGE
* ENDING
ENTER
* ENTRY
ENVIRONMENT
+ EOF
EOP
EQUAL
* EQUALS
ERROR
ESI
* ETI
+ EVEN
EVERY
* EXAMINE
* EXCEEDS
EXCEPTION
* EXHIBIT
+ EXREF
EXIT
EXTEND
EXTENDED-SEARCH

FD
FILE
+ FILE-ACCESS
FILE-CONTROL
+ FILE-ID
* FILE-LIMIT
* FILE-LIMITS
+ FILE-QUALIFIER
FILLER
FINAL
FIRST
FOOTING
FOR
+ FORMnn
+ FORM-REQUEST
FOR
* FORTRAN
@ FORTRAN IV
+ FREE
FROM

GENERATE
GIVING
GO
* GOBACK
GREATER
GROUP

HEADING
HIGH-VALUE
HIGH-VALUES
* HOLD

I-O
I-O CONTROL
* ID
IDENTIFICATION
IF
IN
+ INACTIVE
& INCLUDE
INDEX
INDEX-n
INDEXED
INDICATE
INITIAL
INITIALIZE
INITIATE
+ INLINE
INPUT
INPUT-OUTPUT
INSERT
INSPECT

INSTALLATION
+ INTER-LOCK
+ INTERNAL
INTO
INVALID
IS

JUST
JUSTIFIED

KEY
* KEYS

LABEL
LABEL-RETURN
LAST
LEADING
LEAVE
LEFT
LENGTH
LESS
LIBRARY
LIMIT
LIMITS
LINAGE
LINAGE-COUNTER
LINE
LINE-COUNTER
@ LINE-PRINTER
LINES
LINKAGE
+ LION
+ LOCATION
LOCK
LOW-VALUE
LOW-VALUES
* LOWER-BOUND
* LOWER-BOUNDS

@ MACRO
@ MAP 4
@ MAP 5
@ MAP 6
@ MAP 7
@ MAP 8
+ MASS-STORAGE
# MASTER-INDEX
+ MCFLAG
MEMORY
MERGE
MESSAGE
MODE
MODULES

* Adopted by multiple manufacturers
@ Digital Equipment Corporation
# IBM (VS, OS, DOS)
& Honeywell/Xerox
+ Univac

+	MONITOR	+	POINTS		RESET
#	MORE-LABELS		POSITION		RETURN
	MOVE	#	POSITIONING	#	RETURN-CODE
	MULTIPLE		POSITIVE		REVERSED
	MULTIPLY	#	PREPARED		REWIND
		*	PRINTER		REWRITE
*	NAMED		PRINTING		RF
	NATIVE	@	PRINT-CONTROL		RH
	NEGATIVE	#	PRINT-SWITCH		RIGHT
	NEXT	#	PRIORITY		ROUNDED
	NO		PROCEDURE		RUN
#	NOMINAL		PROCEDURES		
	NOT		PROCEED	#	SA
*	NOTE		PROCESS		SAME
#	NSTD-REELS	*	PROCESSING		SD
	NUMBER		PROGRAM		SEARCH
	NUMERIC		PROGRAM-ID		SECTION
#	NUMERIC-EDITED	+	PROTECT		SECURITY
		+	PURGE-DATE	*	SEEK
	OBJECT-COMPUTER				SEGMENT
#	OBJECT-PROGRAM		QUEUE		SEGMENT-LIMIT
	OCCURS		QUOTE		SELECT
@	ODD		QUOTES	#	SELECTED
	OF				SEND
	OFF		RANDOM		SENTENCE
	OH	#	RANGE		SEPARATE
	OMITTED		READ		SEQUENCE
	ON	@	READ-AHEAD		SEQUENTIAL
	OPEN	*	READY	#	SERVICE
	OPTIONAL		RECEIVE		SET
	OR		RECORD	+	SET-ID
	ORGANIZATION	#	RECORD-OVERFLOW		SIGN
*	OTHERWISE	*	RECORDING		SIZE
	OUTPUT		RECORDS	#	SKIP 1
#	OV		REDEFINES	#	SKIP 2
	OVERFLOW		REEL	#	SKIP 3
			REFERENCES		SORT
	PAGE		RELATIVE	#	SORT-CORE-SIZE
	PAGE-COUNTER		RELEASE	#	SORT-FILE-SIZE
@	PAPER-TAPE-PUNCH	#	RELOAD		SORT-MERGE
@	PAPER-TAPE-READER		REMAINDER	#	SORT-MESSAGE
@	PARITY	*	REMARKS	#	SORT-MODE-SIZE
#	PASSWORD		REMOVAL	#	SORT-OPTION
	PERFORM		RENAMES	#	SORT-RETURN
	PF	&	RENAMING		SOURCE
	PH	#	REORG-CRITERIA		SOURCE-COMPUTER
	PIC		REPLACING		SPACE
	PICTURE		REPORT		SPACES
+	PLACE		REPORTING		SPECIAL-NAMES
+	PLACES		REPORTS		STANDARD
	PLUS	#	REREAD		STANDARD-1
+	POINT		RERUN		START
	POINTER		RESERVE		STATUS

* Adopted by multiple manufacturers
@ Digital Equipment Corporation
# IBM (VS, OS, DOS)
& Honeywell/Xerox
+ Univac

STOP
STRING
SUB-QUEUE-1
SUB-QUEUE-2
SUB-QUEUE-3
SUBTRACT
SUM
\# SUPERVISOR
SUPPRESS
\# SUSPEND
* SWITCH
SYMBOLIC
SYNC
SYNCHRONIZED
\# SYSIN
\# SYSIPT
\# SYSLST
\# SYSOUT
\# SYSPLH
\# SYSPUNCH
\# SØ1
\# SØ2

TABLE
* TALLY
TALLYING
TAPE
TERMINAL
TERMINATE
TEXT
THAN

\# THEN
THROUGH
THRU
TIME
\# TIME-OF-DAY
TIMES
TO
@ TODAY
TOP
\# TOTALED
\# TOTALING
* TRACE
\# TRACK
\# TRACK-AREA
\# TRACK-LIMIT
\# TRACKS
TRAILING
* TRANSFORM
TYPE

\# UNEQUAL
UNIT
+ UNISERVO
+ UNISERVOS
+ UNLOCK
UNSTRING
UNTIL
UP
* UPPER-BOUND
* UPPER-BOUNDS
UPON

\# UPSI Ø
\# UPSI 1
\# UPSI 2
\# UPSI 3
\# UPSI 4
\# UPSI 5
\# UPSI 6
\# UPSI 7
USAGE
USE
@ USER-NUMBER
USING

VALUE
VALUES
VARYING

WHEN
\# WHEN-COMPILED
WITH
+ WORD
WORDS
WORKING-STORAGE
WRITE
@ WRITE-BEHIND
* WRITE-ONLY
\# WRITE-VERIFY

ZERO
ZEROES
ZEROS

*   Adopted by multiple manufacturers
@ Digital Equipment Corporation
\#   IBM (VS, OS, DOS)
&   Honeywell/Xerox
+   Univac

B General Forms of COBOL Statements

The following are the general formats for all COBOL Statements used in this text

REFERENCE   **GENERAL FORMAT FOR IDENTIFICATION DIVISION**

Chapter 3

```
IDENTIFICATION DIVISION.

PROGRAM-ID. program-name.

[AUTHOR. [comment-entry] ...]

[INSTALLATION. [comment-entry] ...]

[DATE-WRITTEN. [comment-entry] ...]

[DATE-COMPILED. [comment-entry] ...]

[SECURITY. [comment-entry] ...]
```

GENERAL FORMAT FOR ENVIRONMENT DIVISION

Chapter 4

```
ENVIRONMENT DIVISION.

CONFIGURATION SECTION.
```

Appendix E

```
SOURCE-COMPUTER. computer-name [WITH DEBUGGING MODE]

OBJECT-COMPUTER. computer-name

[SPECIAL-NAMES. system-name IS mnemonic-name.]

[INPUT-OUTPUT SECTION.

FILE-CONTROL.

[SELECT [OPTIONAL] file-name

ASSIGN TO implementor-name-1 [, implementor-name-2] ...
```

Chapter 16

```
[; RESERVE {NO / integer-1} ALTERNATE [AREA / AREAS]]

[; ORGANIZATION IS SEQUENTIAL]

[; ACCESS MODE IS SEQUENTIAL]
```

REFERENCE

Chapter 17

$$\left[\text{\underline{SELECT}} \text{ file-name}\right.$$

$$\text{\underline{ASSIGN}} \text{ TO implementor-name-1 } [, \text{ implementor-name-2}] \quad \dots$$

$$\left[; \text{ \underline{RESERVE}} \begin{Bmatrix} \underline{NO} \\ \text{integer-1} \end{Bmatrix} \text{ ALTERNATE } \begin{bmatrix} \text{AREA} \\ \text{AREAS} \end{bmatrix}\right]$$

$$; \text{ \underline{ORGANIZATION}} \text{ IS \underline{INDEXED}}$$

$$\left[; \text{ \underline{ACCESS}} \text{ MODE IS } \begin{Bmatrix} \underline{\text{SEQUENTIAL}} \\ \underline{\text{RANDOM}} \end{Bmatrix}\right]$$

$$; \text{ \underline{RECORD}} \text{ KEY IS data-name-1}$$

$$\left[, \text{ \underline{NOMINAL}} \text{ KEY IS data-name-2}\right]$$

GENERAL FORMAT FOR DATA DIVISION

Chapter 5

$$\text{\underline{DATA}} \text{ \underline{DIVISION}.}$$

$$[\text{\underline{FILE}} \text{ \underline{SECTION}.}$$

$$[\text{\underline{FD}} \text{ file-name}$$

Chapter 16

$$\left[; \text{ \underline{BLOCK}} \text{ CONTAINS } [\text{integer-1 \underline{TO}}] \text{ integer-2 } \begin{Bmatrix} \text{\underline{RECORDS}} \\ \text{\underline{CHARACTERS}} \end{Bmatrix}\right]$$

$$[; \text{ \underline{RECORD}} \text{ CONTAINS } [\text{integer-3 \underline{TO}}] \text{ integer-4 CHARACTERS}]$$

$$; \text{ \underline{LABEL}} \begin{Bmatrix} \underline{\text{RECORD}} \text{ IS} \\ \underline{\text{RECORDS}} \text{ ARE} \end{Bmatrix} \begin{Bmatrix} \underline{\text{STANDARD}} \\ \underline{\text{OMITTED}} \end{Bmatrix}$$

$$\left[; \text{ \underline{DATA}} \begin{Bmatrix} \underline{\text{RECORD}} \text{ IS} \\ \underline{\text{RECORDS}} \text{ ARE} \end{Bmatrix} \text{ data-name-3 } [, \text{ data-name-4}] \quad \dots\right]$$

$$[\text{record-description-entry}] \quad \dots] \quad \dots$$

Chapter 15

$$[\text{\underline{SD}} \text{ file-name}$$

$$[; \text{ \underline{RECORD}} \text{ CONTAINS } [\text{integer-1 \underline{TO}}] \text{ integer-2 CHARACTERS}]$$

$$\left[; \text{ \underline{DATA}} \begin{Bmatrix} \underline{\text{RECORD}} \text{ IS} \\ \underline{\text{RECORDS}} \text{ ARE} \end{Bmatrix} \text{ data-name-1 } [, \text{ data-name-2}] \quad \dots \right].$$

$$\begin{Bmatrix} \text{record-description-entry} \end{Bmatrix} \quad \dots \quad] \quad \dots]$$

$$[\text{\underline{WORKING-STORAGE}} \text{ \underline{SECTION}.}$$

$$\begin{bmatrix} \text{77-level-description-entry} \\ \text{record-description-entry} \end{bmatrix} \dots]$$

REFERENCE   **GENERAL FORMAT FOR DATA DESCRIPTION ENTRY**

FORMAT 1:

Chapter 5

```
level-number   {data-name-1}
               {FILLER     }
```

Chapter 19

```
[; REDEFINES data-name-2]
```

Chapters 5, 9, 20

```
[; {PICTURE}  IS character-string]
   {PIC    }
```

Chapter 20

```
[; [USAGE IS] {COMPUTATIONAL}]
              {COMP         }
              {DISPLAY      }
              {INDEX        }
```

Chapter 20

```
[; [SIGN IS] {LEADING }  [SEPARATE CHARACTER]]
             {TRAILING}
```

Chapters 13, 14

```
[; OCCURS {integer-1 TO integer-2 TIMES DEPENDING ON data-name-3}
          {integer-2 TIMES                                      }
```

Chapter 14

```
   [{ASCENDING }  KEY IS data-name-4  [, data-name-5]...]...
    {DESCENDING}
```

Chapter 14

```
   [INDEXED BY index-name-1  [, index-name-2]  ...]]
```

Chapter 20

```
[; {SYNCHRONIZED}  [LEFT ]]
   {SYNC        }  [RIGHT]
```

Chapter 20

```
[; {JUSTIFIED}  RIGHT]
   {JUST     }
```

Chapter 20

```
[; BLANK WHEN ZERO]
```

Chapter 5

```
[; VALUE IS literal]
```

FORMAT 2:

Chapter 19

```
66  data-name-1; RENAMES data-name-2 [{THROUGH}  data-name-3]
                                      {THRU   }
```

FORMAT 3:

Chapter 11

```
88 condition-name; {VALUE  IS } literal-1[{THROUGH}  literal-2]
                   {VALUES ARE}           {THRU   }

   [, literal-3 [{THROUGH}  literal-4]]  ...    .
                 {THRU   }
```

REFERENCE

GENERAL FORMAT FOR PROCEDURE DIVISION

Chapters 6, 7   <u>PROCEDURE DIVISION</u>.

Appendix E   [<u>DECLARATIVES</u>.

     $\left\{ \text{section-name } \underline{\text{SECTION}}. \quad \text{declarative-sentence}. \right.$

     [paragraph-name.   [sentence] ...] ... $\left.\right\}$ ...

     <u>END</u> <u>DECLARATIVES</u>.]

     $\left\{ \text{section-name } \underline{\text{SECTION}} \right.$

     [paragraph-name.   [sentence] ...] ... $\left.\right\}$ ...

GENERAL FORMAT FOR VERBS

Chapter 10

$\underline{\text{ADD}} \left\{ \begin{matrix} \text{identifier-1} \\ \text{literal-1} \end{matrix} \right\} \left[\begin{matrix} , \text{ identifier-2} \\ , \text{ literal-2} \end{matrix} \right] ... \underline{\text{TO}} \text{ identifier-m } [\underline{\text{ROUNDED}}]$

     [,identifier-n [<u>ROUNDED</u>]] ...

     [; ON <u>SIZE-ERROR</u> imperative-statement]

Chapter 10

$\underline{\text{ADD}} \left\{ \begin{matrix} \text{identifier-1} \\ \text{literal-1} \end{matrix} \right\} , \left\{ \begin{matrix} \text{identifier-2} \\ \text{literal-2} \end{matrix} \right\} \left[\begin{matrix} , \text{ identifier-3} \\ , \text{ literal-3} \end{matrix} \right] ...$

     <u>GIVING</u> identifier-m   [<u>ROUNDED</u>]   [, identifier-n [<u>ROUNDED</u>]] ...

     [; ON <u>SIZE ERROR</u> imperative-statement]

Chapters 6, 16

$\underline{\text{CLOSE}} \text{ file-name-1} \left[\begin{matrix} \left\{ \begin{matrix} \underline{\text{REEL}} \\ \underline{\text{UNIT}} \end{matrix} \right\} \left[\begin{matrix} \text{WITH NO REWIND} \\ \text{FOR } \underline{\text{REMOVAL}} \end{matrix} \right] \\ \text{WITH} \left\{ \begin{matrix} \underline{\text{NO REWIND}} \\ \underline{\text{LOCK}} \end{matrix} \right\} \end{matrix} \right]$

$\left[, \text{ file-name-2} \left[\begin{matrix} \left\{ \begin{matrix} \underline{\text{REEL}} \\ \underline{\text{UNIT}} \end{matrix} \right\} \left[\begin{matrix} \text{WITH NO REWIND} \\ \text{FOR } \underline{\text{REMOVAL}} \end{matrix} \right] \\ \text{WITH} \left\{ \begin{matrix} \underline{\text{NO REWIND}} \\ \underline{\text{LOCK}} \end{matrix} \right\} \end{matrix} \right] \right] ...$

Chapters 6, 16

<u>CLOSE</u> file-name-1 [WITH <u>LOCK</u>] [, file-name-2 [WITH <u>LOCK</u>]] ...

Chapter 10

<u>COMPUTE</u> identifier-1[<u>ROUNDED</u>] [, identifier-2 [<u>ROUNDED</u>]] ...

     = arithmetic-expression [; ON <u>SIZE ERROR</u> imperative-statement]

Appendix E

$\underline{\text{DISPLAY}} \left\{ \begin{matrix} \text{identifier-1} \\ \text{literal-1} \end{matrix} \right\} \left[\begin{matrix} , \text{identifier-2} \\ , \text{literal-2} \end{matrix} \right] ... [\underline{\text{UPON}} \text{ mnemonic-name}]$

Chapter 10

$\underline{\text{DIVIDE}} \left\{ \begin{matrix} \text{identifier-1} \\ \text{literal-1} \end{matrix} \right\} \underline{\text{INTO}} \text{ identifier-2 } [\underline{\text{ROUNDED}}]$

     [, identifier-3   [<u>ROUNDED</u>]]   ...

     [; ON <u>SIZE ERROR</u> imperative-statement]

REFERENCE

Chapter 10   DIVIDE $\left\{\begin{matrix} \text{identifier-1} \\ \text{literal-1} \end{matrix}\right\}$ INTO $\left\{\begin{matrix} \text{identifier-2} \\ \text{literal-2} \end{matrix}\right\}$

GIVING identifier-3 [ROUNDED]

[, identifier-4 [ROUNDED]] ...

[; ON SIZE ERROR imperative-statement]

Chapter 10   DIVIDE $\left\{\begin{matrix} \text{identifier-1} \\ \text{literal-1} \end{matrix}\right\}$ BY $\left\{\begin{matrix} \text{identifier-2} \\ \text{literal-2} \end{matrix}\right\}$

GIVING identifier-3 [ROUNDED]

[, identifier-4 [ROUNDED]] ...

[; ON SIZE ERROR imperative-statement]

Chapter 10   DIVIDE $\left\{\begin{matrix} \text{identifier-1} \\ \text{literal-1} \end{matrix}\right\}$ INTO $\left\{\begin{matrix} \text{identifier-2} \\ \text{literal-2} \end{matrix}\right\}$

GIVING identifier-3 [ROUNDED]

REMAINDER identifier-4 [; ON SIZE ERROR imperative-statement]

Chapter 10   DIVIDE $\left\{\begin{matrix} \text{identifier-1} \\ \text{literal-1} \end{matrix}\right\}$ BY $\left\{\begin{matrix} \text{identifier-2} \\ \text{literal-2} \end{matrix}\right\}$

GIVING identifier-3 [ROUNDED]

REMAINDER identifier-4 [; ON SIZE ERROR imperative-statement]

Chapter 8   EXIT.

Chapter 6   GO TO procedure-name.

Chapter 18   GO TO procedure-name-1 [, procedure-name-2] ...
, procedure-name-n

DEPENDING ON identifier

Chapters 8, 11   IF condition; $\left\{\begin{matrix} \text{statement-1} \\ \text{NEXT SENTENCE} \end{matrix}\right\}$ $\left\{\begin{matrix} \text{; ELSE statement-2} \\ \text{; ELSE NEXT SENTENCE} \end{matrix}\right\}$

Chapter 21   INSPECT identifier-1 TALLYING

$\left\{, \text{identifier-2 } \underline{FOR} \left\{, \left\{\begin{matrix} \underline{ALL} \\ \underline{LEADING} \\ \underline{CHARACTERS} \end{matrix}\right\} \left\{\begin{matrix} \text{identifier-3} \\ \text{literal-1} \end{matrix}\right\} \right.\right.$

$\left.\left.\left[\left\{\begin{matrix} \underline{BEFORE} \\ \underline{AFTER} \end{matrix}\right\} \text{ INITIAL } \left\{\begin{matrix} \text{identifier-4} \\ \text{literal-2} \end{matrix}\right\}\right]\right\} \cdots \right\} \cdots$

REFERENCE

Chapter 21

```
INSPECT identifier-1 REPLACING
```

$$
\left\{
\begin{array}{l}
\text{CHARACTERS } \underline{\text{BY}} \left\{ \begin{array}{l} \text{identifier-6} \\ \text{literal-4} \end{array} \right\} \left[\left\{ \begin{array}{l} \underline{\text{BEFORE}} \\ \underline{\text{AFTER}} \end{array} \right\} \text{INITIAL} \left\{ \begin{array}{l} \text{identifier-7} \\ \text{literal-5} \end{array} \right\} \right] \\[4mm]
\left\{ , \left\{ \begin{array}{l} \underline{\text{ALL}} \\ \underline{\text{LEADING}} \\ \underline{\text{FIRST}} \end{array} \right\} \left\{ , \left\{ \begin{array}{l} \text{identifier-5} \\ \text{literal-3} \end{array} \right\} \underline{\text{BY}} \left\{ \begin{array}{l} \text{identifier-6} \\ \text{literal-4} \end{array} \right\} \right. \right. \\[4mm]
\left. \left. \left[\left\{ \begin{array}{l} \underline{\text{BEFORE}} \\ \underline{\text{AFTER}} \end{array} \right\} \text{INITIAL} \left\{ \begin{array}{l} \text{identifier-7} \\ \text{literal-5} \end{array} \right\} \right] \right\} \dots \right\} \dots
\end{array}
\right\}
$$

Chapter 21

```
INSPECT identifier-1 TALLYING
```

$$
\left\{ , \text{identifier-2 } \underline{\text{FOR}} \left\{ , \left\{ \begin{array}{l} \underline{\text{ALL}} \\ \underline{\text{LEADING}} \\ \underline{\text{CHARACTERS}} \end{array} \right\} \left\{ \begin{array}{l} \text{identifier-3} \\ \text{literal-1} \end{array} \right\} \right. \right.
$$

$$
\left. \left. \left[\left\{ \begin{array}{l} \underline{\text{BEFORE}} \\ \underline{\text{AFTER}} \end{array} \right\} \text{INITIAL} \left\{ \begin{array}{l} \text{identifier-4} \\ \text{literal-2} \end{array} \right\} \right] \right\} \dots \right\} \dots
$$

```
REPLACING
```

$$
\left\{
\begin{array}{l}
\text{CHARACTERS } \underline{\text{BY}} \left\{ \begin{array}{l} \text{identifier-6} \\ \text{literal-4} \end{array} \right\} \left[\left\{ \begin{array}{l} \underline{\text{BEFORE}} \\ \underline{\text{AFTER}} \end{array} \right\} \text{INITIAL} \left\{ \begin{array}{l} \text{identifier-7} \\ \text{literal-5} \end{array} \right\} \right] \\[4mm]
\left\{ , \left\{ \begin{array}{l} \underline{\text{ALL}} \\ \underline{\text{LEADING}} \\ \underline{\text{FIRST}} \end{array} \right\} \left\{ , \left\{ \begin{array}{l} \text{identifier-5} \\ \text{literal-3} \end{array} \right\} \underline{\text{BY}} \left\{ \begin{array}{l} \text{identifier-6} \\ \text{literal-4} \end{array} \right\} \right. \right. \\[4mm]
\left. \left. \left[\left\{ \begin{array}{l} \underline{\text{BEFORE}} \\ \underline{\text{AFTER}} \end{array} \right\} \text{INITIAL} \left\{ \begin{array}{l} \text{identifier-7} \\ \text{literal-5} \end{array} \right\} \right] \right\} \dots \right\} \dots
\end{array}
\right\}
$$

Chapters 6, 9, 20

$$
\underline{\text{MOVE}} \left\{ \begin{array}{l} \text{identifier-1} \\ \text{literal} \end{array} \right\} \text{TO identifier-2 [, identifier-3]} \dots
$$

Chapter 10

$$
\underline{\text{MULTIPLY}} \left\{ \begin{array}{l} \text{identifier-1} \\ \text{literal-1} \end{array} \right\} \underline{\text{BY}} \text{ identifier-2 } [\underline{\text{ROUNDED}}]
$$

$$
[, \text{identifier-3 } [\underline{\text{ROUNDED}}]] \dots
$$

$$
[; \text{ON } \underline{\text{SIZE}} \ \underline{\text{ERROR}} \text{ imperative-statement}]
$$

Chapter 10

$$
\underline{\text{MULTIPLY}} \left\{ \begin{array}{l} \text{identifier-1} \\ \text{literal-1} \end{array} \right\} \underline{\text{BY}} \left\{ \begin{array}{l} \text{identifier-2} \\ \text{literal-2} \end{array} \right\}
$$

$$
\underline{\text{GIVING}} \text{ identifier-3 } [\underline{\text{ROUNDED}}]
$$

REFERENCE

$$\left[, \text{ identifier-4 } [\underline{ROUNDED}]\right] \ldots$$

$$[; \text{ ON } \underline{SIZE} \text{ } \underline{ERROR} \text{ imperative-statement}]$$

Chapters 16, 17

$$\underline{OPEN} \left\{ \begin{array}{l} \underline{INPUT} \text{ file-name-1 } \left[\frac{\underline{REVERSED}}{\underline{WITH} \text{ } \underline{NO} \text{ } \underline{REWIND}}\right][, \text{ file-name-2} \\ \left[\frac{\underline{REVERSED}}{\underline{WITH} \text{ } \underline{NO} \text{ } \underline{REWIND}}\right]\right] \ldots \\ \underline{OUTPUT} \text{ file-name-3 } [\underline{WITH} \text{ } \underline{NO} \text{ } \underline{REWIND}][, \text{ file-name-4} \\ [\underline{WITH} \text{ } \underline{NO} \text{ } \underline{REWIND}]] \ldots \ldots \\ \underline{I-O} \text{ file-name-5 } [, \text{ file-name-6}] \ldots \end{array} \right.$$

Chapters 6, 16, 17

$$\underline{OPEN} \left\{ \begin{array}{l} \underline{INPUT} \text{ file-name-1 } [, \text{ file-name-2}] \ldots \\ \underline{OUTPUT} \text{ file-name-3 } [, \text{ file-name-4}] \ldots \\ \underline{I-O} \text{ file-name-5 } [, \text{ file-name-6}] \ldots \end{array} \right\} \ldots$$

Chapter 8

$$\underline{PERFORM} \text{ procedure-name-1 } \left[\left\{\frac{\underline{THROUGH}}{\underline{THRU}}\right\} \text{ procedure-name-2}\right]$$

Chapter 12

$$\underline{PERFORM} \text{ procedure-name-1 } \left[\left\{\frac{\underline{THROUGH}}{\underline{THRU}}\right\} \text{ procedure-name-2}\right]$$

$$\left\{\begin{array}{l} \text{identifier-1} \\ \text{integer-1} \end{array}\right\} \text{ } \underline{TIMES}$$

Chapter 8

$$\underline{PERFORM} \text{ procedure-name-1 } \left[\left\{\frac{\underline{THROUGH}}{\underline{THRU}}\right\} \text{ procedure-name-2}\right]$$

$$\underline{UNTIL} \text{ condition-1}$$

Chapter 12

$$\underline{PERFORM} \text{ procedure-name-1 } \left[\left\{\frac{\underline{THROUGH}}{\underline{THRU}}\right\} \text{ procedure-name-2}\right]$$

$$\underline{VARYING} \left\{\begin{array}{l} \text{identifier-2} \\ \text{index-name-1} \end{array}\right\} \text{ } \underline{FROM} \left\{\begin{array}{l} \text{identifier-3} \\ \text{index-name-4} \\ \text{literal-1} \end{array}\right\}$$

$$\underline{BY} \left\{\begin{array}{l} \text{identifier-4} \\ \text{literal-3} \end{array}\right\} \text{ } \underline{UNTIL} \text{ condition-1}$$

$$\left[\underline{AFTER} \left\{\begin{array}{l} \text{identifier-5} \\ \text{index-name-3} \end{array}\right\} \text{ } \underline{FROM} \left\{\begin{array}{l} \text{identifier-6} \\ \text{index-name-4} \\ \text{literal-3} \end{array}\right\}\right.$$

$$\underline{BY} \left\{\begin{array}{l} \text{identifier-7} \\ \text{literal-4} \end{array}\right\} \text{ } \underline{UNTIL} \text{ condition-2}$$

$$\left[\underline{AFTER} \left\{\begin{array}{l} \text{identifier-8} \\ \text{index-name-5} \end{array}\right\} \text{ } \underline{FROM} \left\{\begin{array}{l} \text{identifier-9} \\ \text{index-name-6} \\ \text{literal-5} \end{array}\right\}\right.$$

$$\left.\left.\underline{BY} \left\{\begin{array}{l} \text{identifier-10} \\ \text{literal-6} \end{array}\right\} \text{ } \underline{UNTIL} \text{ condition-3}\right]\right]$$

Chapters 6, 16, 17

$$\underline{READ} \text{ file-name RECORD } [\underline{INTO} \text{ identifier}]$$

$$[; \text{ AT } \underline{END} \text{ imperative-statement}]$$

REFERENCE

Chapter 17

```
READ file-name RECORD [INTO identifier]
        [; INVALID KEY imperative-statement]
```

Chapter 15

```
RELEASE record-name [FROM identifier]
```

Chapter 15

```
RETURN file-name RECORD [INTO identifier]  ;
        AT END imperative-statement
```

Chapter 16

```
REWRITE record-name [FROM identifier]
```

Chapter 17

```
REWRITE record-name [FROM identifier]
        [; INVALID KEY imperative-statement]
```

Chapter 14

$$\text{SEARCH identifier-1} \left[\underline{\text{VARYING}} \left\{ \begin{array}{l} \text{identifier-2} \\ \text{index-name-1} \end{array} \right\} \right]$$

$$[; \text{ AT } \underline{\text{END}} \text{ imperative-statement-1}]$$

$$; \underline{\text{WHEN}} \text{ condition-1} \left\{ \begin{array}{l} \text{imperative-statement-2} \\ \underline{\text{NEXT}} \ \underline{\text{SENTENCE}} \end{array} \right\}$$

$$\left[; \underline{\text{WHEN}} \text{ condition-2} \left\{ \begin{array}{l} \text{imperative-stetement-3} \\ \underline{\text{NEXT}} \ \underline{\text{SENTENCE}} \end{array} \right\} \right] \ \ldots$$

Chapter 14

$$\text{SEARCH } \underline{\text{ALL}} \text{ identifier-1} \quad [; \text{ AT } \underline{\text{END}} \text{ imperative-statement-1}]$$

$$; \underline{\text{WHEN}} \left[\left\{ \begin{array}{l} \text{data-name-1} \left\{ \begin{array}{l} \text{IS } \underline{\text{EQUAL}} \ \underline{\text{TO}} \\ \text{IS } = \end{array} \right\} \left\{ \begin{array}{l} \text{identifier-3} \\ \text{literal-1} \\ \text{arithmetic-expression-1} \end{array} \right\} \\ \text{condition-name-1} \end{array} \right. \right]$$

$$\left[\underline{\text{AND}} \left\{ \begin{array}{l} \text{data-name-2} \left\{ \begin{array}{l} \text{IS } \underline{\text{EQUAL}} \ \underline{\text{TO}} \\ \text{IS } = \end{array} \right\} \left\{ \begin{array}{l} \text{identifier-4} \\ \text{literal-2} \\ \text{arithmetic-expression-2} \end{array} \right\} \\ \text{condition-name-2} \end{array} \right. \right] \ldots$$

$$\left\{ \begin{array}{l} \text{imperative-statement-2} \\ \underline{\text{NEXT}} \ \underline{\text{SENTENCE}} \end{array} \right\}$$

Chapter 14

$$\underline{\text{SET}} \left\{ \begin{array}{ll} \text{identifier-1} & [, \text{ identifier-2}] \ \ldots \\ \text{index-name-1} & [, \text{ index-name-2}] \ \ldots \end{array} \right\} \quad \underline{\text{TO}} \left\{ \begin{array}{l} \text{identifier-3} \\ \text{index-name-3} \\ \text{integer-1} \end{array} \right\}$$

Chapter 14

$$\underline{\text{SET}} \text{ index-name-4 } [, \text{ index-name-5}] \ \ldots \left\{ \begin{array}{l} \underline{\text{UP}} \ \underline{\text{BY}} \\ \underline{\text{DOWN}} \ \underline{\text{BY}} \end{array} \right\} \left\{ \begin{array}{l} \text{identifier-4} \\ \text{integer-2} \end{array} \right\}$$

Chapter 15

$$\underline{\text{SORT}} \text{ file-name-1 ON} \left\{ \begin{array}{l} \underline{\text{ASCENDING}} \\ \underline{\text{DESCENDING}} \end{array} \right\}$$

$$\text{KEY data-name-1 } [, \text{ data-name-2}] \ \ldots$$

$$\left[\text{ON} \left\{ \begin{array}{l} \underline{\text{ASCENDING}} \\ \underline{\text{DESCENDING}} \end{array} \right\} \text{ KEY data-name-3 } [, \text{ data-name-4}] \ \ldots \right] \ \ldots$$

$$\left\{ \begin{array}{l} \underline{\text{INPUT}} \ \underline{\text{PROCEDURE}} \text{ IS section-name-1} \left[\begin{array}{l} \underline{\text{THROUGH}} \\ \underline{\text{THRU}} \end{array} \right] \text{ section-name-2} \\ \underline{\text{USING}} \text{ file-name-2 } [, \text{ file-name-3}] \ \ldots \end{array} \right.$$

$$\left. \begin{array}{l} \underline{\text{OUTPUT}} \ \underline{\text{PROCEDURE}} \text{ IS section-name-3} \left[\left\{ \begin{array}{l} \underline{\text{THROUGH}} \\ \underline{\text{THRU}} \end{array} \right\} \text{ section-name-4} \right] \\ \underline{\text{GIVING}} \text{ file-name-4} \end{array} \right\}$$

REFERENCE

Chapter 17

$$\text{START file-name} \left[\underline{\text{KEY}} \begin{Bmatrix} \text{IS } \underline{\text{EQUAL}} \text{ TO} \\ \text{IS } \underline{=} \\ \text{IS } \underline{\text{GREATER}} \text{ THAN} \\ \text{IS } \underline{>} \\ \text{IS } \underline{\text{NOT LESS}} \text{ THAN} \\ \text{IS } \underline{\text{NOT}}< \end{Bmatrix} \text{data-name} \right]$$

[; <u>INVALID</u> KEY imperative-statement]

Chapter 6

$$\underline{\text{STOP}} \begin{Bmatrix} \underline{\text{RUN}} \\ \text{literal} \end{Bmatrix}$$

Chapter 21

$$\underline{\text{STRING}} \begin{Bmatrix} \text{identifier-1} \\ \text{literal-1} \end{Bmatrix} \left[\begin{matrix} , \text{ identifier-2} \\ , \text{ literal-2} \end{matrix} \right] \ \dots$$

$$\underline{\text{DELIMITED}} \text{ BY } \begin{Bmatrix} \text{identifier-3} \\ \text{literal-3} \\ \underline{\text{SIZE}} \end{Bmatrix}$$

$$\left[, \begin{Bmatrix} \text{identifier-4} \\ \text{literal-4} \end{Bmatrix} \left[\begin{matrix} , \text{ identifier-5} \\ , \text{ literal-5} \end{matrix} \right] \ \dots \right.$$

$$\left. \underline{\text{DELIMITED}} \text{ BY } \begin{Bmatrix} \text{identifier-6} \\ \text{literal-6} \\ \underline{\text{SIZE}} \end{Bmatrix} \right] \ \dots$$

<u>INTO</u> identifier-7 [WITH <u>POINTER</u> identifier-8]

[; ON <u>OVERFLOW</u> imperative-statement]

Chapter 10

$$\underline{\text{SUBTRACT}} \begin{Bmatrix} \text{identifier-1} \\ \text{literal-1} \end{Bmatrix} \left[\begin{matrix} , \text{ identifier-2} \\ , \text{ literal-2} \end{matrix} \right] \ \dots$$

<u>FROM</u> identifier-m [<u>ROUNDED</u>]

$$\left[, \text{ identifier-n } [\underline{\text{ROUNDED}}] \right] \ \dots$$

[; ON <u>SIZE</u> <u>ERROR</u> imperative-statement]

Chapter 10

$$\underline{\text{SUBTRACT}} \begin{Bmatrix} \text{identifier-1} \\ \text{literal-1} \end{Bmatrix} \left[\begin{matrix} , \text{ identifier-2} \\ , \text{ literal-2} \end{matrix} \right] \ \dots$$

$$\underline{\text{FROM}} \begin{Bmatrix} \text{identifier-m} \\ \text{literal-m} \end{Bmatrix}$$

<u>GIVING</u> identifier-n [<u>ROUNDED</u>]

$$\left[, \text{ identifier-o } [\underline{\text{ROUNDED}}] \right] \ \dots$$

[; ON <u>SIZE</u> <u>ERROR</u> imperative-statement]

Chapter 21

<u>UNSTRING</u> identifier-1

$$\left[\underline{\text{DELIMITED}} \text{ BY } [\underline{\text{ALL}}] \begin{Bmatrix} \text{identifier-2} \\ \text{literal-1} \end{Bmatrix} \right.$$

$$\left. \left[, \underline{\text{OR}} \ [\underline{\text{ALL}}] \begin{Bmatrix} \text{identifier-3} \\ \text{literal-2} \end{Bmatrix} \right] \ \dots \right]$$

<u>INTO</u> identifier-4 [, <u>DELIMITER</u> IN identifier-5]

[, <u>COUNT</u> IN identifier-6]

REFERENCE

```
              [, identifier-7  [, DELIMITER IN identifier-8]

              [, COUNT IN identifier-9]] ...

       [WITH POINTER identifier-10]  [TALLYING IN identifier-11]

       [; ON OVERFLOW imperative-statement]
```

Appendix E
```
                                        ⎧[ALL REFERENCES OF] identifier-1⎫
       USE FOR DEBUGGING ON             ⎨file-name-1                     ⎬
                                        ⎪procedure-name-1                ⎪
                                        ⎩ALL PROCEDURES                  ⎭

           ⎡  ⎧[ALL REFERENCES OF] identifier-2⎫⎤
           ⎢  ⎨file-name-2                     ⎬⎥ ...  .
           ⎢, ⎪procedure-name-2                ⎪⎥
           ⎣  ⎩ALL PROCEDURES                  ⎭⎦
```

Chapters 6, 16
```
       WRITE record-name  [FROM identifier-1]

           ⎡                      ⎧identifier-2⎫ ⎡LINE ⎤⎤
           ⎢⎧BEFORE⎫              ⎨integer     ⎬ ⎣LINES⎦⎥
           ⎢⎨AFTER ⎬  ADVANCING   ⎩            ⎭        ⎥
           ⎢⎩      ⎭              ⎧mnemonic-name⎫       ⎥
           ⎣                      ⎩PAGE         ⎭       ⎦

           ⎡      ⎧END-OF-PAGE⎫                     ⎤
           ⎢; AT  ⎨EOP        ⎬  imperative-statement⎥
           ⎣      ⎩           ⎭                     ⎦
```

Chapter 17
```
       WRITE record-name  [FROM identifier]
              [; INVALID KEY imperative-statement]
```

GENERAL FORMAT FOR CONDITIONS

Chapter 8
```
       RELATION CONDITION:

       ⎧identifier-1           ⎫  ⎡IS [NOT] GREATER THAN⎤
       ⎨literal-1              ⎬  ⎢IS [NOT] LESS THAN   ⎥
       ⎪arithmetic-expression-1⎪  ⎢IS [NOT] EQUAL TO    ⎥
       ⎩index-name-1          ⎭  ⎢IS [NOT] >           ⎥
       ⎧identifier-2           ⎫  ⎢IS [NOT] <           ⎥
       ⎨literal-2              ⎬  ⎣IS [NOT] =           ⎦
       ⎪arithmetic-expression-2⎪
       ⎩index-name-2          ⎭
```

Chapter 11
```
       CLASS CONDITION:

       identifier IS [NOT] ⎧NUMERIC   ⎫
                          ⎩ALPHABETIC⎭
```

REFERENCE

Chapter 11   SIGN CONDITION:

arithmetic-expression is [NOT] $\begin{Bmatrix} \text{POSITIVE} \\ \text{NEGATIVE} \\ \text{ZERO} \end{Bmatrix}$

Chapter 11   CONDITION-NAME CONDITION:

condition-name

Chapter 8   NEGATED SIMPLE CONDITION:

NOT simple-condition

Chapter 8   COMBINED CONDITION:

condition $\begin{Bmatrix} \begin{Bmatrix} \text{AND} \\ \text{OR} \end{Bmatrix} & \text{condition} \end{Bmatrix}$ ...

Chapter 8   ABBREVIATED COMBINED RELATION CONDITION:

relation-condition $\begin{Bmatrix} \begin{Bmatrix} \text{AND} \\ \text{OR} \end{Bmatrix} & \text{[NOT][relational-operator]} & \text{object} \end{Bmatrix}$ ...

MISCELLANEOUS FORMATS

Chapter 13   SUBSCRIPTING:

$\begin{Bmatrix} \text{data-name} \\ \text{condition-name} \end{Bmatrix}$ (subscript-1 [, subscript-2 [, subscript-3]])

Chapter 14   INDEXING:

$\begin{Bmatrix} \text{data-name} \\ \text{condition-name} \end{Bmatrix}$ ($\begin{Bmatrix} \text{index-name-1 } [\{\pm\} \text{ literal-2}] \\ \text{literal-1} \end{Bmatrix}$

$\left[, \begin{Bmatrix} \text{index-name-2 } [\{\pm\} \text{ literal-4}] \\ \text{literal-3} \end{Bmatrix} \right.$

$\left. \left[, \begin{Bmatrix} \text{index-name-3 } [\{\pm\} \text{ literal-6}] \\ \text{literal-5} \end{Bmatrix} \right] \right]$)

Chapter 13   IDENTIFIER: FORMAT 2

data-name-1 $\left[\begin{Bmatrix} \text{OF} \\ \text{IN} \end{Bmatrix} \text{data-name-2} \right]$ ...   [(subscript-1

[, subscript-2   [, subscript-3]])]

REFERENCE

Chapter 14

$$\underline{IDENTIFIER: FORMAT\ 2}$$

$$\text{data-name-1} \left[\left\{\frac{OF}{IN}\right\} \text{ data-name-2}\right] \dots$$

$$\left[\left(\left\{ \begin{matrix} \text{index-name-1 } [\{\pm\} \text{ literal-2}] \\ \text{literal-1} \end{matrix} \right. \right.\right.$$

$$\left[, \left\{ \begin{matrix} \text{index-name-2 } [\{\pm\} \text{ literal-4}] \\ \text{literal-3} \end{matrix} \right. \right.$$

$$\left. \left[, \left\{ \begin{matrix} \text{index-name-3 } [\{\pm\} \text{ literal-6}] \\ \text{literal-5} \end{matrix} \right\} \right] \right] \left. \right) \right]$$

C Table of Allowable Data Movements

Sending Field	Receiving Field								
	Group	Alphabetic	Alphanumeric	Alphanumeric-edited	Numeric (DISPLAY)	Numeric-edited	Binary (COMP)	Floating-point (COMP-1/COMP-2)	Packed-decimal (COMP-3)
Group	Y	Y	Y	Y[1]	Y[1]	Y[1]	Y[1]	Y[1]	Y[1]
Alphabetic (A)	Y	Y	Y	Y	N	N	N	N	N
Alphanumeric (X)	Y	Y	Y	Y	Y[4]	Y[4]	Y[4]	Y[4]	Y[4]
Alphanumeric-edited	Y	Y	Y	Y	N	N	N	N	N
Numeric (DISPLAY) (9)	Y[1]	N	Y[2]	Y[2]	Y	Y	Y	Y	Y
Numeric-edited	Y	N	Y	Y	N	N	N	N	N
Binary (COMP)	Y[1]	N	Y[2]	Y[2]	Y	Y	Y	Y	Y
Floating-point (COMP-1/COMP-2)	Y[1]	N	N	N	Y	Y	Y	Y	Y
Packed-decimal (COMP-3)	Y[1]	N	Y[2]	Y[2]	Y	Y	Y	Y	Y
Figurative Constants ZEROS	Y	N	Y	Y	Y[3]	Y[3]	Y[3]	Y[3]	Y[3]
SPACES	Y	Y	Y	Y	N	N	N	N	N
HIGH-VALUE LOW-VALUE QUOTE	Y	N	Y	Y	N	N	N	N	N
ALL literal	Y	Y	Y	Y	Y[5]	Y[5]	Y[5]	N	Y[5]
Numeric literal	Y[1]	N	Y[2]	Y[2]	Y	Y	Y	Y	Y
Nonnumeric literal	Y	Y	Y	Y	Y[5]	Y[5]	Y[5]	N	Y[5]

LEGEND: Y = yes; N = no
1. move treated like an alphanumeric to alphanumeric move—no data conversion is made
2. decimal point must be to the right of the least significant digit treated as a numeric move
3. treated as a numeric move
4. alphanumeric field treated as an integer numeric (DISPLAY) field
5. literal treated as an integer numeric (DISPLAY) field and may contain only numeric characters

D Answers to Selected Questions and Exercises

Chapter 1 Answers to Questions

1. COmmon Business-Oriented Language
3. commercial/business-oriented
5. Committee On Data System Languages
7. U.S. Government (Defense Department); universities (educators); computer manufacturers; computer users
9. American National Standards Institute
11. COBOL
13. disciplined
15. central processing unit (CPU), tape and/or disk units
17. software
19. operating system
21. object
23. application
25. Job Control Language (JCL)
27. data
29. a. not a highly mathematical language
    b. wordy-lengthy
    c. not the easiest language to learn
    d. not the best language for structured design

Chapter 2 Answers to Questions

1. DIVISION
3. SECTIONs: paragraphs
5. IDENTIFICATION; PROCEDURE
7. PROCEDURE
9. identify the resources (computers and devices) needed by the program
11. DATA
13. PROCEDURE
15. hyphen; seven
17. A
19. numeric; alphabetic; special characters
21. period
23. reserved words; programmer-supplied-names
25. DATA
27. constants
29. 120
31. reserved
33. F—IDENTIFICATION DIVISION does not

35. F—statement
37. F—only in the PROCEDURE DIVISION
39. F—only when reserved words, data-names, or constants are broken
41. T
43. T
45. F—but this is desirable from a coding standpoint
47. F—period
49. F—e.g., procedure-names
51. T
53. F—they are reserved words
55. F—not with a decimal point

Answers to Exercises

1. a. legal
3. b. illegal—$ is a special character
   c. legal
   d. legal for a procedure-name only
   e. legal
   f. illegal—must be a continuous character string (use hyphens)
   g. illegal—exceeds 30 characters
   h. illegal—decimal point/period is an illegal character
   i. illegal—a reserved word
   j. legal

Chapter 3   Answers to Questions

1. IDENTIFICATION
3. SECTION
5. A
7. DATE-COMPILED
9. period
11. F—the specified order must be maintained
13. F—the PROGRAM-ID paragraph must be first
15. T
17. T—and a space must follow the period
19. F—these entries must fall wholly within columns 12 through 72

Answers to Exercises

1. a. period after division heading
   b. PROGRAM-ID omitted
   c. period after author's name is missing
   d. DATE-COMPILED precedes DATE-WRITTEN
   e. DATE-COMPILED must be hyphenated
   f. DATE-WRITTEN is misspelled
   g. a period must immediately follow SECURITY paragraph name
   h. "PART II . . ." should begin in Area B—columns 12 through 72
3. IDENTIFICATION DIVISION.
   PROGRAM-ID. DFCM214.

Chapter 4   Answers to Questions

1. the resources necessary to execute the program
3. SOURCE-COMPUTER; OBJECT-COMPUTER
5. top of form—the top of the printer page
7. INPUT-OUTPUT
9. ASSIGN
11. BUFFER
13. one (1)

15. F—the ENVIRONMENT DIVISION is system sensitive
17. T
19. F—the entries may be used to interface special system functions to a COBOL program
21. F
23. F—not necessarily
25. T

Answers to Exercises

1. a. ENVIRONMENT is misspelled
   b. CONFIGURATION SECTION is not hyphenated
   c. OBJECT-COMPUTER is hyphenated
   d. SPECIAL-NAMES not "TERMS"
   e. CØ1 should be a continuous string
   f. period should appear after NEXT-PAGE
   g. INPUT-OUTPUT should be followed by the reserved word SECTION
   h. FILE-CONTROL paragraph is missing
   i. period after MY-INPUT-FILE should be omitted
   j. SELECT MY-PRINT-FILE should begin in Area B
   k. ALTERNATIVE should be ALTERNATE

Chapter 5   Answers to Questions

1. FILE; WORKING-STORAGE
3. WORKING-STORAGE
5. eighty (80)
7. groups; elementary-items
9. Ø1
11. PICTURE (PIC)
13. alphabetic; alphanumeric; numeric
15. Sign character (S); first (leftmost); minus sign overpunched; last (rightmost)
17. replication factor in parentheses
19. eighty (80); 160
21. T
23. T
25. T
27. F—level numbers are Ø1 through 49
29. T
31. T—unless multiple lines are necessary (two cannot appear on the same line)
33. T—this is also true for record-names
35. F—it may not be the rightmost character
37. T—it must be described as an alphanumeric field
39. T
41. T—level-77 data items must immediately follow the WORKING-STORAGE SECTION heading
43. F—SPACE(S) is an illegal value for a numeric data item
45. T

Answers to Exercises

1.   Record Description

Data-Name	Group or Elementary-Item	Length	Columns or Positions
INVOICE-RECORD	Group	75	1–75
DESCRIPTIVE-INFORMATION	Group	70	1–70
INVOICE-NUMBER	Elementary-Item	5	1–5
CUSTOMER-NUMBER	Group	9	6–14

Data-Name	Group or Elementary-Item	Length	Columns or Positions
CUSTOMER-GROUP	Elementary-Item	2	6–7
CUSTOMER-SUFFIX	Elementary-Item	7	8–14
ITEM-INFORMATION	Group	56	15–70
ITEM-NUMBER	Elementary-Item	10	15–24
ITEM-DESCRIPTION	Elementary-Item	30	25–54
QUANTITY-PURCHASED	Elementary-Item	5	55–59
PRICE-PER-UNIT	Elementary-Item	5	60–64
COST-PER-UNIT	Elementary-Item	5	65–69
UNIT-MEASUREMENT	Elementary-Item	1	70
FILLER	Elementary-Item	5	71–75

```
3.  a)  Ø1  NAME-ADDRESS-LABEL
            Ø2 CONTACT-NAME      PIC X(2Ø).
            Ø2 BUSINESS-NAME     PIC X(19).
            Ø2 STREET-ADDRESS    PIC X(2Ø).
            Ø2 CITY              PIC A(14).
            Ø2 STATE             PIC XX.
            Ø2 ZIP-CODE          PIC X(5).

    b)  Ø1  INVENTORY-RECORD.
            Ø2 IDENTIFICATION-INFORMATION.
                Ø3 ITEM-NUMBER        PIC 9(9).
                Ø3 ITEM-DESCRIPTION   PIC X(3Ø).
            Ø2 CURRENT-INFORMATION.
                Ø3 PRICE-GROUP        PIC 9(5).
                Ø3 UNIT-PRICE         PIC 9(4)V99.
                Ø3 UNIT-COST          PIC 9(4)V99.
                Ø3 ON-HAND            PIC 9(6).
            Ø2 STATISTICAL-INFORMATION.
                Ø3 MTD-SALES          PIC 9(8).
                Ø3 YTD-SALES          PIC 9(8).
            Ø2 FILLER             PIC XX.

    c)  Ø1  STUDENT-GRADE-RECORD.
            Ø2 STUDENT-NAME       PIC X(2Ø).
            Ø2 STUDENT-ID-NUMBER  PIC 9(9).
            Ø2 EXAM-GRADES.
                Ø3 EXAM-1         PIC 999V9.
                Ø3 EXAM-2         PIC 999V9.
                Ø3 EXAM-3         PIC 999V9.
                Ø3 EXAM-4         PIC 999V9.
            Ø2 COURSE-DATE.
                Ø3 PREFIX         PIC XXXX.
                Ø3 NUMBER         PIC 9999.
                Ø3 COURSE-TITLE   PIC X(27).

5.  WORKING-STORAGE SECTION.
    Ø1  HEADING-1.
        Ø2 FILLER                  PIC X(23) VALUE SPACES.
        Ø2 FILLER                  PIC X(22) VALUE 'INVENTORY USAGE REPORT'.
    Ø1  HEADING-2.
        Ø2 FILLER                  PIC X(24) VALUE SPACES.
        Ø2 FILLER                  PIC X(12) VALUE 'REPORT DATE'.
        Ø2 MONTH                   PIC 99.
        Ø2 FILLER                  PIC X VALUE '/'.
        Ø2 DAY                     PIC 99.
        Ø2 FILLER                  PIC X VALUE '/'.
        Ø2 YEAR                    PIC 99.
        Ø2 FILLER                  PIC X(15) VALUE SPACES.
        Ø2 PAGE-NO                 PIC 99.
    Ø1  HEADING-3.
        Ø2 FILLER                  PIC X(14) VALUE ' ITEM'.
        Ø2 FILLER                  PIC X(22) VALUE 'ITEM'.
```

```
        Ø2 FILLER                    PIC X(14) VALUE 'UNITS ON'.
        Ø2 FILLER                    PIC X(8)  VALUE 'MONTH TO'.
    Ø1  HEADING-4.
        Ø2 FILLER                    PIC X VALUE SPACES.
        Ø2 FILLER                    PIC X(59) VALUE
        'NUMBER      DESCRIPTION              HAND      DATE USAGE'.
    Ø1  HEADING-5.
        Ø2 FILLER                    PIC X(6Ø) VALUE ALL '*'.
```

Chapter 6   Answers to Questions

1. sentence; statement
3. DATA; PROCEDURE; PROCEDURE
5. SELECT; FD
7. CLOSE
9. PHYSICAL
11. SENTENCE
13. one (1)
15. FROM
17. integer; identifier; mnemonic-name
19. SPECIAL-NAMES; ENVIRONMENT
21. sending
23. right; left
25. the repetitive execution of statements without the means to terminate the operation
27. STOP RUN; logical
29. F—READ a file, WRITE a record
31. T—resulting in no advance of the printer page
33. F—groups are treated as alphanumeric regardless of their subordinate definition
35. F—it is always required
37. T
39. T—the entire procedure could be composed of paragraphs
41. F—files must be opened before they can be used
43. F—as many as the programmer desires
45. F—one or the other but not both
47. F—once the file has been closed, all input-output activity must cease until the file has been reopened
49. F—they are independent of each other with respect to order
51. T—depending on the number of buffers assigned through the RESERVE clause (normally two) in the ENVIRONMENT DIVISION
53. T—with the use of the INTO option
55. F—types may be different

1.   Answers to Exercises

Data-Name	Value from First Read	Value from Second Read
POLICY-NUMBER	AX-14293-4	R42219-CØØ
CLIENT-NUMBER	ØØ5Ø2148	1Ø852102
POLICY-ANNIVERSARY-DATE*	Ø415	Ø831
ANNIVERSARY-MONTH	Ø4	Ø8
ANNIVERSARY-DAY	15	31
POLICY-EXPIRATION-DATE*	Ø22682	1Ø2881
EXPIRATION-MONTH	Ø2	1Ø
EXPIRATION-DAY	26	28
EXPIRATION-YEAR	82	81
PREMIUM-AMOUNT	ØØ723ˆ88	Ø1911ˆ76
COMMISSION-AMOUNT	Ø86ˆ90	116ˆ62
SALESMAN-CODE	JWS	DEW
STATE-CODE	TX	IL

*Group-names—the record-name references all the data

Chapter 7 Answers to Questions

1. analysis
3. bugs
5. flowchart
7. arrowheads
9. functionally
11. a. simple sequence
    b. if-then-else
    c. do-while
13. a. larger, more complex problems may be approached on the basis of smaller, less complex subproblems
    b. time required to develop a program is reduced
    c. errors may be located and eliminated more quickly
    d. the program may be developed in sections
    e. standardization is promoted
15. tree; stair step
17. indicator
19. control module
21. case
23. F—normally repetitive debugging operations follow the first attempted execution of a program
25. F—one block may be used to represent a series of similar operations (e.g., a series of MOVEs)
27. T
29. F—only when an error exit is desired should a module have multiple exit points
31. T
33. T

Chapter 8 Answers to Questions

1. PROCEDURE
3. relational
5. class
7. AND; OR
9. OR
11. paragraph; SECTION
13. the end of the procedure has been encountered
15. the end of the procedure has been encountered; the PERFORM/UNTIL condition is true
17. T
19. T
21. T
23. T
25. F
27. F—the subject may be implied
29. F—logical operators may never be implied
31. T
33. F—the procedure may be either above or below the PERFORM
35. F—a range of procedures may be executed with the THRU option
37. F—either paragraphs or SECTIONs
39. F—individual PERFORM statements are independent of each other
41. T
43. F—all condition types are permitted

Answers to Exercises

1. a. correct; True: MOVE 'OVERTIME WORKED' TO MESSAGE
             False: MOVE 'NO OVERTIME' TO MESSAGE

    b. correct; True: NEXT SENTENCE

             False: MOVE Ø TO DEDUCTION-AMOUNT

    c. incorrect; relations should be NOT EQUAL *TO*

    d. correct; True: PERFORM EIC-LOOKUP

             False: none stated

    e. incorrect; GO TO NEXT-OPERATION can never be executed because it is preceded by another GO TO statement

    f. incorrect; no true statement has been provided—NEXT SENTENCE should be supplied

3. a. A-PART

    B-PART

  b. 1ST-PARA

    2ND-PARA

    1ST-PARA   } will continue to be executed infinitely

  c. PARA-A

    PARA-B

    PARA-C

    PARA-B

  d. PART-1

    PART-2

    PART-1—fall through

    PART-2

    PART-2—fall through

    PART-3—fall through

  e. DO-1ST

    DO-2ND

    DO-3RD

    DO-2ND

    DO-LAST

    DO-2ND

    DO-2ND—fall through

    DO-3RD—fall through

    DO-2ND

    DO-LAST

    DO-2ND

    DO-LAST—fall through

    DO-2ND

Chapter 9   Answers to Questions

1. Fixed insertion
3. Minus (−) insertion
5. floating
7. Ø and B
9. * and Z
11. F—e.g., +, −, and $ are both fixed- and floating-insertion characters
13. F—it may also appear on the right side of the PICTURE clause
15. F—., ,, Ø, B, CR, and DB are only fixed-insertion characters
17. T
19. F—combinations may be used (e.g., $999,999.99-)
21. F—only one character per PICTURE string may be either a floating or replacement character
23. T
25. T—e.g., in the PICTURE string $$$,$$$.$$ a $ will replace the comma when the value placed in the field is less than 1,000
27. T—e.g., as illustrated in the answer to question #25
29. F
31. T—e.g., ZZZ,ZZZ when the value in the field is less than 1,000, the comma is replaced with a blank

Answers to Exercises

		Length
1.	Result*	
	a. 69,274	6
	b. Ø3,192.88	9
	c. − ØØ24.76	8
	d. − 627.ØØ	7
	e. + 27	3
	f. 677.44ØØ	8
	g. $7,621.88Ø −	11
	h. Ø$4,562.89	10
	i. ØØØ$.Ø1	7
	j. $855.97	7
	k. − Ø$9,884.6Ø	11
	l. ØØØØØØØ	7
	m. + $**462.88	10
	n. 12Ø86ØØØ	8
	o. HELPØØME	8

Chapter 10 Answers to Questions

1. ADD; SUBTRACT; MULTIPLY; DIVIDE; COMPUTE
3. ADD or COMPUTE
5. data items; numeric literals
7. ON SIZE ERROR
9. one (1); two (2)
11. data items
13. GIVING
15. division by zero
17. dividend
19. numeric data items, numeric literals, operators (+ , − , *, /, **); parentheses
21. T
23. T—e.g., ADD 1 TO A, B.
25. F—only identifiers may appear as receiving fields
27. T
29. F—i.e., ADD A, B GIVING C—the GIVING form of the statement does not contain the reserved word TO
31. F—the receiving field (data-name following GIVING) does not have to contain a value prior to the execution of the statement.
33. T
35. F—only in a simple SUBTRACT statement
37. F—although generally desirable, neither form of the SUBTRACT statement requires an operational sign (S) on the receiving field
39. T
41. F—BY is permitted only in the GIVING form of the DIVIDE statement
43. T
45. T—since it only acts as a receiving field
47. T—this sequence can only be altered by the use of parentheses

Answers to Exercises

1. a. FIELD-2 = 89
   b. FIELD-2 = 36 (both overflow and underflow occurs)
   c. FIELD-4 = Ø274.62
   d. FIELD-3 = 129.5Ø
   e. FIELD-4 = Ø134.7Ø (rounding occurs)

*represents the location of the blank character

    f. FIELD-2 = 72

    g. FIELD-2 = 49

    h. FIELD-2 = 13 (a positive value since FIELD-2 does not contain an operational sign)

    i. FIELD-1 = 48 (rounding occurs)

    j. FIELD-3 = Ø (ON SIZE ERROR option executed since the result will cause an overflow of the receiving field)

3. a. NUM-3 = 15ØØ

    b. NUM-2 = Ø25 (a positive value)

    c. NUM-4 = 11.1Ø

    d. NUM-1 = ØØ (overflow occurs)

    e. NUM-2 = 125

    f. NUM-5 = $1,5ØØ.ØØ

    g. NUM-3 = 27 (no operational sign; thus the value is positive, and the fractional part of the result is truncated)

    h. NUM-2 = ØØ1 (.999 is rounded to 1)

    i. NUM-5 = ØØØ$27.75 (no sign option, thus the negative sign is dropped)

    j. NUM-3 = Ø25Ø (ON SIZE ERROR option is not invoked by the dropping of the sign)

5. a. VAL-1 = ØØ5Ø.ØØ

    b. VAL-2 = 5Ø.ØØ

    c. VAL-3 = ØØ17.5Ø

    d. VAL-2 = 25.ØØ

    e. VAL-4 = Ø.5ØØ

    f. VAL-5 = Ø625.ØØ

    g. VAL-1 = Ø16

    h. VAL-3 = − ØØ6Ø.ØØ

Chapter 11   Answers to Questions

1. numeric
3. NUMERIC; ALPHABETIC
5. ascending
7. F—not by themselves, but may be used when in an arithmetic expression
9. F—only an identifier may be tested in the condition
11. T
13. F—for example, testing a field for contents of a nonnumeric literal may be performed in a relational test

Answers to Exercises

1. a. correct; sign; true:

    MOVE 'DIVISION ERROR—PROCEDURE ABORTED' TO OUTPUT-LINE
    WRITE OUTPUT-LINE AFTER ADVANCING 1 LINES
    STOP RUN

    b. correct; class; true: PERFORM DEPENDENT-DEDUCTIONS
                           false: NEXT SENTENCE (redundant)

    c. incorrect; a numeric literal may not be tested by itself in a sign test

    d. correct; class; true: MOVE 'W-2 FILED' TO EMPLOYEE-STATUS
                           false: MOVE 'NO W-2' TO EMPLOYEE-STATUS

3. Relational Tests:

```
MOVE SPACES TO BASE, OVERTIME.        IF PAY-CODE = '0'
IF PAY-CODE = 'S'                          MOVE 'SALARY' TO BASE
    MOVE 'SALARY' TO BASE                  MOVE 'YES' TO OVERTIME.
    MOVE 'NO' TO OVERTIME.
```

```
IF PAY-CODE = 'X'                        MOVE 'ERROR' TO BASE, OVERTIME.
    MOVE 'HOURLY' TO BASE                IF PAY-CODE = 'S' OR 'O'
    MOVE 'NO' TO OVERTIME.                   MOVE 'SALARY' TO BASE.
IF PAY-CODE = 'H'                        IF PAY-CODE = 'X' OR 'H'
    MOVE 'HOURLY' TO BASE                    MOVE 'HOURLY' TO BASE.
    MOVE 'YES' TO OVERTIME.              IF PAY-CODE = 'S' OR 'X'
IF BASE = SPACES OR OVERTIME = SPACES        MOVE 'NO' TO OVERTIME.
    MOVE 'ERROR' TO BASE, OVERTIME.     IF PAY-CODE = 'O' OR 'H'
                                             MOVE 'YES' TO OVERTIME.


Condition-name Test:
    Ø5 PAY-CODE                     PIC X.
        88 SALARIED-EXEMPT          VALUE 'S'.
        88 SALARIED-NON-EXEMPT      VALUE 'O'.
        88 HOURLY-EXEMPT            VALUE 'X'.
        88 HOURLY-NON-EXEMPT        VALUE 'H'.


    MOVE 'ERROR' TO BASE, OVERTIME.
    IF SALARIED-EXEMPT OR SALARIED-NON-EXEMPT
        MOVE 'SALARY' TO BASE.
    IF HOURLY-EXEMPT OR HOURLY-NON-EXEMPT
        MOVE 'HOURLY' TO BASE.
    IF SALARIED-EXEMPT OR HOURLY-EXEMPT
        MOVE 'NO' TO OVERTIME.
    IF SALARIED-NON-EXEMPT OR HOURLY-NON-EXEMPT
        MOVE 'YES' TO OVERTIME.
```

Chapter 12   Answers to Questions

1. four (4)
3. numeric identifier or numeric literal
5. three (3)
7. EXIT
9. T
11. F—altering the identifier has no impact on the number of times the procedure is repeated
13. F—it may contain a negative value, but the procedure will not be executed
15. F—the increment may be negative
17. F—it may be any of the condition types, including compound conditions
19. F—one condition must be stated with the VARYING phrase and one condition must be specified for each AFTER option used
21. T
23. T
25. F—syntax requirements dictate the location of these reserved words
27. T—the EXIT statement must be the only statement in the paragraph.

Answers to Exercises

1. a.	PARA-1		PARA-3	d.	PARA-1
	PARA-2		PARA-3		PARA-3
	PARA-2		PARA-1		PARA-2
	PARA-2		PARA-2		PARA-2
	PARA-2		PARA-3		PARA-2
	PARA-2		PARA-3		PARA-2
b.	PARA-1	c.	PARA-1	e.	PARA-1
	PARA-2		PARA-1		PARA-2 (fall through)
	PARA-3		PARA-1		PARA-1
	PARA-3		PARA-1		PARA-3 (fall through)
	PARA-1		PARA-2		PARA-4
	PARA-2		PARA-2		PARA-4
					PARA-4

Chapter 13   Answers to Questions

1. tables
3. Ø2; 49
5. single-dimension table (list, vector)
7. subscript
9. OCCURS clause
11. matrix
13. OCCURS clause
15. identifier
17. F—tables may be defined only within record descriptions
19. F—the identifier is used only for variable-length tables
21. T
23. T
25. F—only if one OCCURS clause is subordinate to another OCCURS clause
27. T
29. F—the subordinate description may be used to describe one, two, or more interrelated tables.

1. Answers to Exercises

Data-name	Number of			Length of a Single Item	# of Items In Descrip.	Total Bytes In Descrip.
	Rows	Cols	Ranks			
1. a. LIST-OF-CONTRIBUTORS	-	-	-	400	1	400
CONTRIBUTOR	20	-	-	20	20	400
b. SALESMAN—TABLE	-	-	-	2010	1	2010
SALESMAN-NAME	50	-	-	42	50	2010
NAME	50	-	-	30	50	1500
ID-NUMBER	50	-	-	5	50	250
PHONE	50	-	-	7	50	350
c. COLLEGE-COURSE	-	-	-	360	1	360
DEPARTMENT	30	-	-	3	30	90
COURSE-NUMBER	90	-	-	3	90	270
d. LEDGER-TABLE	-	-	-	1480	1	1480
ASSETS	30	-	-	37	30	1110
ASSET-NO	30	-	-	5	30	150
ASSET-DESC	30	-	-	25	30	750
ASSET-BALANCE	30	-	-	7	30	210
LIABILITY	10	-	-	37	10	370
LIAB-NO	10	-	-	5	10	50
LIAB-DESC	10	-	-	25	10	250
LIAB-BALANCE	10	-	-	7	10	70
e. INTEREST-RATE-TABLE	-	-	-	2000	1	2000
INTEREST-RATE	10	-	-	200	10	2000
YEARS-INVESTED	10	20	-	10	200	2000
INTEREST	10	20	-	10	200	2000
f. STUDENT-INFORMATION-TABLE	-	-	-	26400	1	26400
STUDENT	400	-	-	31	400	12400
NAME	400	-	-	20	400	8000
ID-NUMBER	400	-	-	9	400	3600
CLASS	400	-	-	2	400	800
COURSE	400	50	-	7	2000	14000
DEPT	400	50	-	3	2000	6000
COURSE-NO	400	50	-	3	2000	6000
GRADE	400	50	-	1	2000	2000

Data-name	Number of			Length of a Single Item	# of Items In Descrip.	Total Bytes In Descrip.
	Rows	Cols	Ranks			
g. DEMOGRAPHIC-DATA	-	-	-	3200	1	3200
INCOME	20	-	-	160	20	3200
AGE	20	40	-	4	800	3200
SEX	20	40	2	1	1600	1600
MARITAL-STATUS	20	40	2	1	1600	1600

Chapter 14   Answers to Questions

1. occurrence positions; byte displacement
3. INDEXED BY
5. relative
7. PERFORM; SET; SEARCH
9. index-name
11. numeric literal; identifier
13. linear; binary
15. the index-name of another table
17. the specified condition is found to be true; the logical end of the searching process has been encountered
19. decreasing
21. relational, sign, class, or condition-name conditions; relational condition
23. T—the identifier is implicitly defined as a full-word, binary, integer storage position
25. F—of the statements generally used to modify a subscript, only the PERFORM statement is permitted to modify an index
27. T—it is implicitly defined by its appearance in an INDEXED BY clause
29. F—an index-data-name is not directly related to a table—it may be used in conjunction with the processing of several tables
31. T—the actual byte displacement value is placed in the index-data-name
33. F—the receiving fields in the SET statement are treated similar to those used as the receiving fields of MOVE statements
35. T
37. F—it is used to vary the index of another, perhaps related, table
39. T—but the logic behind the execution of each is different
41. F—several keys, in decreasing order of importance, may be stated

Answers to Exercises

1. a.

CODE-TO-RATE-CONVERSION	Byte Displacement	
	Begins	Ends
RATE (1)	0	3
RATE (2)	4	7'
RATE (3)	8	11
RATE (4)	12	15
RATE (5)	16	19
RATE (6)	20	23
RATE (7)	24	27
RATE (8)	28	31

b.

FEDERAL-TAX-TABLE

TAX-BRACKET (1) (0–21)	LOWER-LIMIT (1) (0–6)	UPPER-LIMIT (1) (7–13)	BASE-TAX (1) (14–19)	PERCENT-TAX (1) (20–21)
TAX-BRACKET (2) (22–43)	LOWER-LIMIT (2) (22–28)	UPPER-LIMIT (2) (29–35)	BASE-TAX (2) (36–41)	PERCENT-TAX (2) (42–43)
TAX-BRACKET (3) (44–65)	LOWER-LIMIT (3) (44–50)	UPPER-LIMIT (3) (51–57)	BASE-TAX (3) (58–63)	PERCENT-TAX (3) (64–65)
TAX-BRACKET (4) (66–87)	LOWER-LIMIT (4) (66–72)	UPPER-LIMIT (4) (73–79)	BASE-TAX (4) (80–85)	PERCENT-TAX (4) (86–87)
TAX-BRACKET (5) (88–109)	LOWER-LIMIT (5) (88–94)	UPPER-LIMIT (5) (95–101)	BASE-TAX (5) (102–107)	PERCENT-TAX (5) (108–109)
TAX-BRACKET (6) (110–131)	LOWER-LIMIT (6) (110–116)	UPPER-LIMIT (6) (117–123)	BASE-TAX (6) (124–129)	PERCENT-TAX (6) (130–131)
TAX-BRACKET (7) (132–153)	LOWER-LIMIT (7) (132–138)	UPPER-LIMIT (7) (139–145)	BASE-TAX (7) (146–151)	PERCENT-TAX (7) (152–153)

c.

RATE-PREMIUM-CONVERSION

PAY-SCALE (1) (0–11)	SHIFT (1,1) ADJUSTMENT (1,1) (0–3)	SHIFT (1,2) ADJUSTMENT (1,2) (4–7)	SHIFT (1,3) ADJUSTMENT (1,3) (8–11)
PAY-SCALE (2) (12–23)	SHIFT (2,1) ADJUSTMENT (2,1) (12–15)	SHIFT (2,2) ADJUSTMENT (2,2) (16–19)	SHIFT (2,3) ADJUSTMENT (2,3) (20–23)
PAY-SCALE (3) (24–35)	SHIFT (3,1) ADJUSTMENT (3,1) (24–27)	SHIFT (3,2) ADJUSTMENT (3,2) (28–31)	SHIFT (3,3) ADJUSTMENT (3,3) (32–35)
PAY-SCALE (4) (36–47)	SHIFT (4,1) ADJUSTMENT (4,1) (36–39)	SHIFT (4,2) ADJUSTMENT (4,2) (40–43)	SHIFT (4,3) ADJUSTMENT (4,3) (44–47)
PAY-SCALE (5) (48–59)	SHIFT (5,1) ADJUSTMENT (5,1) (48–51)	SHIFT (5,2) ADJUSTMENT (5,2) (52–55)	SHIFT (5,3) ADJUSTMENT (5,3) (56–59)

3. d)
```
        SET ITEM TO 1.
        MOVE 'BEGIN' TO SEARCH-STATUS.
        PERFORM SEARCH-ITEMS
            UNTIL SEARCH-STATUS = 'COMPLETE'.
        STOP RUN.
     SEARCH-ITEMS.
        SEARCH INVENTORY-ITEMS
            AT END
                MOVE 'COMPLETE' TO SEARCH-STATUS
            WHEN VENDOR-CODE (ITEM) = 'SRV'
                DISPLAY 'ITEM ', ITEM-NUMBER (ITEM),
                        ' VENDOR ', VENDOR-CODE (ITEM),
                        ' UNITS ', UNITS-ON-HAND (ITEM).
```

e)
```
        SET ITEM TO 1.
        MOVE 'BEGIN' TO SEARCH-STATUS.
        PERFORM SEARCH-ITEMS
            UNTIL SEARCH-STATUS = 'COMPLETE'.
        STOP RUN.
```

```
    SEARCH-ITEMS.
        SEARCH INVENTORY-ITEMS
            AT END
                MOVE 'COMPLETE' TO SEARCH-STATUS
            WHEN
                PRICE (ITEM) * UNITS-ON-HAND (ITEM) GREATER THAN 10000
                DISPLAY ITEM-NUMBER (ITEM).

f)      PERFORM OUTPUT-INVENTORY
            VARYING ITEM FROM 1 BY 1 UNTIL ITEM GREATER THAN 300.
        STOP RUN.
    OUTPUT-INVENTORY.
        SET VEND TO 1.
        MOVE ITEM-NUMBER (ITEM) TO ITEM-OUT.
        MOVE VENDOR-CODE (ITEM) TO VENDOR-OUT.
        SEARCH VENDOR-SUPPLIER
            AT END MOVE 'NOT FOUND' TO VENDOR-NAME-OUT
            WHEN VENDOR-CODE (ITEM) = VEND-CODE (VEND)
                MOVE VENDOR-NAME (VEND) TO VENDOR-NAME-OUT.
        WRITE OUTPUT-LINE AFTER ADVANCING 1 LINES.

4.  a) 01 INVENTORY-TABLE.
        02 INVENTORY-ITEM
                OCCURS 0 TO 300 TIMES DEPENDING ON ACTIVE
                ASCENDING KEY IS ITEM-NUMBER
                INDEXED BY ITEM.
                    .
                    .
                    .
    (assume ITEM has previously been set to some legitimate value)
        SEARCH ALL INVENTORY-ITEM
            AT END DISPLAY ' ITEM NOT FOUND'
            WHEN ITEM-NUMBER (ITEM) = 4782
                DISPLAY 'ITEM ', ITEM-NUMBER (ITEM),
                        ' VENDOR ', VENDOR-CODE (ITEM).
```

Chapter 15   Answers to Questions

1. to order data into a specified sequence
3. sort; merge
5. USING
7. SECTION
9. GIVING; OUTPUT PROCEDURE
11. T
13. T
15. T—provided the USING phrase is not employed
17. F—only one of the two phrases may be employed
19. F—multiple keys may be specified (up to a maximum of 12)
21. T
23. F—the desired records may be selected for RELEASE in the INPUT PROCEDURE
25. T

Answers to Exercises

1. a. correct; provided 200-REPORT contains a RETURN statement
   b. incorrect; record length of OUTPUT-FILE is longer than the SORT-FILE
      incorrect; IN-FIELD-1 and IN-FIELD-2 are not in the SORT-RECORD description
   c. incorrect; no output phrase is specified
      incorrect; 100-TEST is a paragraph name
      incorrect; INPUT-FILE is not a sort-file-name
   d. incorrect; required reserved word PROCEDURE omitted from input phrase
   e. incorrect; OUTPUT-FILE not the same length as SORT-FILE

f. incorrect; DESCENDING misspelled
incorrect; RETURN statement must not appear in an INPUT PROCEDURE
incorrect; RELEASE statement must not appear in an OUTPUT PROCEDURE
incorrect; SORT statement must not appear in an OUTPUT PROCEDURE
incorrect; TEST-1 not defined as a sort key
incorrect; OUTPUT-FILE not the same length as SORT-FILE
incorrect; GO TO 300-LAST causes execution of an OUTPUT PROCEDURE without a return to the SORT statement

Chapter 16 Answers to Questions

1. magnetic medium
3. less space
5. the same size as
7. one (1)
9. tracks
11. system flowchart
13. INPUT, OUTPUT, I-O
15. rewound
17. sorted or ordered
19. updating
21. addition
23. REWRITE
25. F—the limitation is different from system to system, but none restrict the user to 500 bytes or less
27. T
29. F—a buffer is exactly one physical record in length
31. F—only when a file is unblocked; then they are the same in length but different in meaning
33. F—the access mode is assumed to be sequential if omitted
35. F—a system flowchart is global in nature, while a program flowchart concentrates solely on the procedure
37. F—it is controlled by the BLOCK CONTAINS clause
39. T—it is required for all files (except a SORT file)
41. F— a disk, for example, does not know what the top of page means
43. T
45. F—a master file is more permanent in nature and typically retains historical data
47. T—provided the procedure is capable of adding a duplicate
49. F—logically deleted records appear in the file; physically deleted records do not

Chapter 17 Answers to Questions

1. keyed
3. RECORD
5. NOMINAL KEY
7. INVALID KEY
9. WORKING-STORAGE
11. cylinders
13. unique; ascending
15. a duplicate RECORD KEY value already exists in the file
17. generic; START
19. T
21. F—the description could be alphanumeric, for example
23. F—it may be blocked at the programmers discretion
25. F—only cylinder allocation is permitted
27. F—duplicate records are only identified by WRITE statements
29. F—the second form of the START statement does not require the NOMINAL KEY clause
31. F—since the records may be accessed randomly, ordering the transaction records may be pointless

Chapter 18   Answers to Questions

1. two (2)
3. multiple branches from a single location
5. T

Chapter 19   Answers to Questions

1. memory usage is conserved; alternate (more descriptive) naming of data items is possible
3. WORKING-STORAGE SECTION; group (not record) level (or below)
5. same
7. a level number equivalent (or higher) to that at the beginning of the redefinition is encountered
9. the original definition of the data item
11. immediately after
13. group
15. F—as many as needed may appear in one FD, and they are assumed to be implicit redefinitions of each other
17. T—the length of the longest record if all are not the same length
19. T— but only at the group or elementary-item level in the FILE SECTION
21. T
23. F—most compilers require the redefinition to be the same length as the original description; none will permit the redefinition to be shorter
25. T—but it cannot redefine the entire redefinition
27. T—although if only an elementary-item is being redefined, it still must be the same length
29. F—66-levels do not have subordinate definition
31. T
33. T

Chapter 20   Answers to Questions

1. DISPLAY (zone decimal or external decimal)
3. DISPLAY
5. *binary digits*
7. bytes; words
9. zone decimal (external decimal)
11. packed decimal
13. F
15. first bit
17. zero (0)
19. COMPUTATIONAL-3 (COMP-3)
21. two (2)
23. floating point
25. COMPUTATIONAL-2 (COMP-2)
27. right
29. increased by one byte
31. slack bytes
33. F
35. F—COMP-1 and COMP-2 (short and long floating point) are permitted by some compilers
37. T
39. F—this is true only when a PICTURE clause is not permitted
41. F
43. F
45. F—may only be used in conjunction with DISPLAY fields
47. F—DISPLAY mode only

49. T
51. F—at least the same (and more if slack bytes must be inserted)

Chapter 21   Answers to Questions

1. character data
3. parsing
5. POINTER
7. DELIMITED BY
9. INSPECT, EXAMINE
11. T
13. F—the programmer must initialize the pointer variable
15. F
17. F
19. T

E Debugging COBOL Programs

Unfortunately, programmers are human and humans are not perfect. As a consequence, programs written by humans are prone to have *bugs*. The word "bug" is a data processing term meaning error. There are two broad categories of errors related to programming—*compilation errors* and *execution errors*.

Compilation errors are errors discovered by the compiler in an attempt to translate a source-language program (e.g., a COBOL program) into an object-language program. These errors are generally caused by a violation of the *syntax* (e.g., format or grammar) rules specified for a particular programming language, such as the incorrect spelling of a reserved word in COBOL. Such an error would cause a message to be printed by the compiler. These *diagnostics* assist the programmer in eliminating syntax errors.

Not all errors identified by the compiler will terminate a program before it begins execution. Most compilers generate at least two levels of error messages. The first category of compiler-detected errors is *fatal errors*. These terminate the program before execution begins. The second category is *warning errors*. The messages produced by a compiler in this category are intended to bring the programmer's attention to a potential problem. In most cases, warnings will not cause program termination. One additional note with regard to compilation errors—certain violations of syntax rules will cause the compiler to generate several error messages. In many cases, the compiler will provide alternative explanations for the cause of the error. Also, many compilers are prone to provide error messages because of a condition previously found in the program. For this reason, the programmer should concentrate initial corrections on the top portion of the program and proceed from top to bottom.

Execution errors are those errors detected by the computer while acting on the instructions within a program. In some cases, these errors are caused by the interaction of data with the program instructions. In other situations, these errors may be due to incorrect program logic. Both kinds may be difficult to trace because of the possibility that they are caused by interacting conditions or may occur at many locations within the program code. While both data errors and logic errors are frustrating, logic errors are generally more difficult to eliminate because of the varied conditions that may cause them and because the logical requirements of a program vary from one program to another. Thus, there may be no standard pattern for the elimination of logic errors. However, structured design (discussed in Chapter 7) is often helpful in the elimination of these errors.

Errors produced by the interaction of data with the program code are generally caused by a discrepancy between the description of the data item and the actual contents of the data item. Therefore, the problem could be that the description of the data item is inconsistent with the allowed use of that type of data item (e.g., using an edited-numeric data item in a position intended for a nonedited item) or the contents of the data item are not consistent with the PICTURE string (e.g., a numeric field that contains non-numeric data). Under these circumstances, the computer may produce a message like DATA EXCEPTION or ILLEGAL DECIMAL. These messages are designed to indicate to the programmer that one of the two above conditions exist. In most cases, the computer will not indicate *where* the problem arose. If the computer indicates the location (address) of the error, it is likely to be a location that has meaning to the computers, but not necessarily to the programmer. Thus, it is often left up to the programmer to employ his own devices to locate and correct the error.

All compilers can produce what is called a *core dump*. A core dump is a printed listing of the contents of the computer's primary storage unit, i.e., in most cases magnetic core memory. The only problem with analyzing a core dump is that the organization and content of the printout is different for computers manufactured by different companies (and in some cases, different within the same company). It is often difficult to read (or analyze) a core dump unless the programmer is familiar with the computer being used, its internal architecture (structure), and its assembly language.

To make debugging more manageable, most computer systems can provide more limited (and to the novice, more useful) information regarding the source of an error. This type of diagnostic assistance varies from computer to computer; however, generally available diagnostic aids such as a DATA DIVISION mapping, and a condensed listing of the verbs present in the PROCEDURE DIVISION (e.g., an IBM CQBOL CLIST) are often useful in debugging. The information contained in these diagnotics is not as detailed as a core dump, but they require only knowledge of the hexadecimal or octal numbering systems (depending on the computer) and how to subtract in these numbering systems. In most cases a simple subtraction will provide the address of the COBOL statement which caused the error. (The operation usually requires subtracting the address of the program load point—where the program was located in the computer's memory—from the address of the instruction causing the error.) This address is a computer storage address and it is necessary to translate this number to find the COBOL statement which caused the error. (A CLIST or PROCEDURE DIVISION mapping will often provide this type of information. For further details on the availability and use of computer generated diagnostics mentioned above, consult with your computer installation.)

The DISPLAY Statement

After locating the statement that produced the error, the cause of the error may not be apparent. Thus, other diagnostic aids may be necessary to further isolate the problem. One of these diagnostic aids is the DISPLAY statement, which is presented in Figure E.1. It is capable of producing textual types of information (non-numeric literals) and the contents of storage positions (identifiers). Both identifiers and literals (except the figurative constant ALL) or combinations of identifiers and literals may appear in the DISPLAY statement, which makes it useful in the detection of both data and logical errors.

By using a combination of identifiers (and possibly literals), the programmer can use the DISPLAY statement to print the contents of data items. These items (noted as identifiers in the format) may be elementary-items, groups, or records. If the data is in an unreadable form—not in DISPLAY form—it will be converted. (Non-DISPLAY descriptions of data items are presented in Chapter 20.)

The size of these items is sometimes limited. The product of the DISPLAY statement is produced on the system output device designated in the UPON clause. The UPON clause is optional and may provide a system-name known by the COBOL compiler or a mnemonic-name which was presented in the SPECIAL-NAMES paragraph of the ENVIRONMENT DIVISION. If the clause is omitted, the default system output device will be used. This device may be a line printer or the computer operator console. Before employing the DISPLAY statement check with your computer installation to determine which device is used by default.

Figure E.2 provides an illustration of how the DISPLAY statement might be used to locate a data value which is causing an error. Two DISPLAY statements appear in the PROCEDURE DIVISION. The first is used to advance one line before the second is executed. The extra DISPLAY statement is sometimes necessary to keep the displayed data from being "overwritten" by output produced by a WRITE statement. In the absence of the first DISPLAY statement in Figure E.2 the output produced by the second DISPLAY may be on the same line as (and some of the same printed columns as) a line produced by a WRITE statement. Thus, in the statement DISPLAY 'STUDENT ID. NUMBER', STUDENT-ID causes the printing of each value of STUDENT-ID as it appears on the input record along with a message prior to the execution of the WRITE statement.

```
DISPLAY   {literal-1    }  [literal-2    ]  ...  [UPON  {system-name    }  ]
          {identifier-1 }  [identifier-2 ]         {mnemonic-name }
```

Figure E.1 Format of the DISPLAY Statement

```
|         1   1   2   2   2   3   3   4   4   4   5   5   6   6   6   7   7   8|
|   4   8   2   6   0   4   8   2   6   0   4   8   2   6   0   4   8   2   6   0|
----------------------------------------------------------------------------
|000010 IDENTIFICATION DIVISION.                                    FIG  E.2|
|000020 PROGRAM-ID.  EXAMPLE-DISPLAY.                               FIG  E.2|
|000030 AUTHOR.  PATRICK THOMAS SPENCE.                             FIG  E.2|
|000040 DATE-WRITTEN. JANUARY 1, 1981.                             FIG  E.2|
|000050 DATE-COMPILED. JANUARY 1, 1981.                           FIG  E.2|
|000060*    THIS PROGRAM DEMONSTRATES THE USE OF DISPLAY STATEMENTS FIG  E.2|
|000070*    USED FOR THE PURPOSE OF DETERMINING THE CONTENTS OF     FIG  E.2|
|000080*     AN IDENTIFIER WHICH SEEMS TO BE PRODUCING A PROBLEM.   FIG  E.2|
|000090 ENVIRONMENT DIVISION.                                      FIG  E.2|
|000100 CONFIGURATION SECTION.                                     FIG  E.2|
|000110 SOURCE-COMPUTER. IBM-370-145.                              FIG  E.2|
|000120 OBJECT-COMPUTER. IBM-370-145.                              FIG  E.2|
|000130 SPECIAL-NAMES.  C01 IS TOP-OF-NEXT-PAGE.                   FIG  E.2|
|000140 INPUT-OUTPUT SECTION.                                      FIG  E.2|
|000150 FILE-CONTROL.                                              FIG  E.2|
|000160     SELECT STUDENT-FILE ASSIGN TO UR-S-SYSIN.              FIG  E.2|
```

Figure E.2 An Illustration of the DISPLAY Statement

```
|         1   1   2   2   2   3   3   4   4   4   5   5   6   6   6   7   7   8|
|   4    8  2   6   0   4   8   2   6   0   4   8   2   6   0   4   8   2   6   0|
-----------------------------------------------------------------------------------
|000170       SELECT PRINTOUT ASSIGN TO UR-S-SYSPRINT.                    FIG E.2|
|000180 DATA DIVISION.                                                    FIG E.2|
|000190 FILE SECTION.                                                     FIG E.2|
|000200 FD  STUDENT-FILE LABEL RECORDS ARE OMITTED.                       FIG E.2|
|000210 01  STUDENT-REC.                                                  FIG E.2|
|000220     05 STUDENT-IDENTIFICATION.                                    FIG E.2|
|000230        10 LAST-NAME            PIC X(10).                         FIG E.2|
|000240        10 FIRST-NAME           PIC X(10).                         FIG E.2|
|000250        10 MIDDLE-INITIAL       PIC X(01).                         FIG E.2|
|000260        10 STUDENT-ID           PIC 9(09).                         FIG E.2|
|000270     05 FILLER                  PIC X(05).                         FIG E.2|
|000280     05 ENROLLMENT-INFO.                                           FIG E.2|
|000290        10 CLASSIFICATION       PIC X(02).                         FIG E.2|
|000300        10 TOTAL-HOURS          PIC 9(03).                         FIG E.2|
|000310        10 HOURS-THIS-SEM       PIC 9(02).                         FIG E.2|
|000320        10 MAJOR                PIC X(03).                         FIG E.2|
|000330     05 FILLER                  PIC X(35).                         FIG E.2|
|000340 FD  PRINTOUT LABEL RECORDS ARE OMITTED.                           FIG E.2|
|000350 01  PRINT-LINE                 PIC X(133).                        FIG E.2|
|000360 WORKING-STORAGE SECTION.                                          FIG E.2|
|000370 01  WORKING-VARIABLES.                                            FIG E.2|
|000380     05  OUTPUT-REC.                                               FIG E.2|
|000390        08 FILLER               PIC X(03) VALUE ' *'.              FIG E.2|
|000400        08 1ST-NAME             PIC X(11).                         FIG E.2|
|000410        08 M-I                  PIC X(01).                         FIG E.2|
|000420        08 FILLER               PIC X(02) VALUE '.'.               FIG E.2|
|000430        08 SUR-NAME             PIC X(10).                         FIG E.2|
|000440        08 FILLER               PIC X(04) VALUE ' *'.              FIG E.2|
|000450        08 ID-NUM               PIC 9(09).                         FIG E.2|
|000460        08 FILLER               PIC X(05) VALUE '  *'.             FIG E.2|
|000470        08 CLASS                PIC X(02).                         FIG E.2|
|000480        08 FILLER               PIC X(06) VALUE '   *'.            FIG E.2|
|000490        08 MAJ                  PIC X(03).                         FIG E.2|
|000500        08 FILLER               PIC X(08) VALUE '   *'.            FIG E.2|
|000510        08 CURRENT-HOURS        PIC 9(02).                         FIG E.2|
|000520        08 FILLER               PIC X(08) VALUE '      *'.         FIG E.2|
|000530        08 TOT-HOURS            PIC 9(03).                         FIG E.2|
|000540        08 FILLER               PIC X(03) VALUE ' *'.              FIG E.2|
|000550 01  PROCESS-STATUS.                                               FIG E.2|
|000560     05  INDICATOR              PIC X(16) VALUE SPACES.            FIG E.2|
|000570 PROCEDURE DIVISION.                                               FIG E.2|
|000580 CONTROL-PROCEDURE.                                                FIG E.2|
|000590     PERFORM 100-INITIALIZATION.                                   FIG E.2|
|000600     PERFORM 300-READ-RECORDS-PRINT-DETAILS                        FIG E.2|
|000610         UNTIL INDICATOR = 'PROCESS COMPLETE'.                     FIG E.2|
|000620     PERFORM 500-TERMINATION.                                      FIG E.2|
|000630     STOP RUN.                                                     FIG E.2|
|000640 100-INITIALIZATION.                                               FIG E.2|
|000650     MOVE 'PROCESS START' TO INDICATOR.                            FIG E.2|
|000660     OPEN INPUT STUDENT-FILE, OUTPUT PRINTOUT.                     FIG E.2|
|000670     READ STUDENT-FILE                                             FIG E.2|
|000680         AT END MOVE 'PROCESS COMPLETE' TO INDICATOR.             FIG E.2|
|000690 300-READ-RECORDS-PRINT-DETAILS.                                   FIG E.2|
|000700     DISPLAY ' '.                                                  FIG E.2|
|000710     DISPLAY 'STUDENT ID. NUMBER ', STUDENT-ID.                    FIG E.2|
|000720     MOVE STUDENT-ID TO ID-NUM.                                    FIG E.2|
|000730     MOVE LAST-NAME TO SUR-NAME.                                   FIG E.2|
|000740     MOVE FIRST-NAME TO 1ST-NAME.                                  FIG E.2|
|000750     MOVE MIDDLE-INITIAL TO M-I.                                   FIG E.2|
|000760     MOVE CLASSIFICATION TO CLASS.                                 FIG E.2|
|000770     MOVE TOTAL-HOURS TO TOT-HOURS.                                FIG E.2|
|000780     MOVE HOURS-THIS-SEM TO CURRENT-HOURS.                         FIG E.2|
|000790     MOVE MAJOR TO MAJ.                                            FIG E.2|
|000800     WRITE PRINT-LINE FROM OUTPUT-REC AFTER 2 LINES.               FIG E.2|
|000810     READ STUDENT-FILE                                             FIG E.2|
|000820         AT END MOVE 'PROCESS COMPLETE' TO INDICATOR.             FIG E.2|
|000830 500-TERMINATION.                                                  FIG E.2|
|000840     CLOSE STUDENT-FILE, PRINTOUT.                                 FIG E.2|
```

Figure E.2 An Illustration of the DISPLAY Statement *Continued*

```
|    |        1         2         3         4         5         6         7         8| FIGURE  |
|RECORD|123456789012345678901234567890123456789012345678901234567890123456789012345678901234567890| NUMBER |
```

```
|    1|ADAMS      JOHN      Q3435643P1     GR21900CSC                                    |FIG  E.2|
|    2|BROWN      JOHN      A555667777     FR03515MKT                                    |FIG  E.2|
|    3|CULVER     MATT      N456789012     JR09408MGT                                    |FIG  E.2|
|    4|DORSETT    ANTHONY   R353492761     SR13816ECO                                    |FIG  E.2|
|    5|ELDRIDGE   DAVID     Q376495268     SO04712FIN                                    |FIG  E.2|
|    6|FRANKLIN   BEN       V000000002     GR18912GBU                                    |FIG  E.2|
|    7|GERBER     KENNETH   A537903251     SO02816MGT                                    |FIG  E.2|
|    8|HAMILTON   MARK      C486762389     JR09618CSC                                    |FIG  E.2|
|    9|ISSACS     MATT      H474653790     SR12018ECO                                    |FIG  E.2|
|   10|JENNINGS   HAROLD    G502326955     FR01818MGT                                    |FIG  E.2|
|   11|KENNIMER   FLOYD     R476329092     JR06012MKT                                    |FIG  E.2|
|   12|LINCOLN    STEVEN    0442648942     SO04515MKT                                    |FIG  E.2|
|   13|MARCUS     JEFF      V546677219     SR09918CSC                                    |FIG  E.2|
```

Figure E.2 An Illustration of the DISPLAY Statement (Data) *Continued*

a. **Displayed Results:**

```
STUDENT ID. NUMBER 343564321

STUDENT ID. NUMBER 555667777

STUDENT ID. NUMBER 456789012

STUDENT ID. NUMBER 353492761

STUDENT ID. NUMBER 376495268

STUDENT ID. NUMBER 000000002

STUDENT ID. NUMBER 537903251

STUDENT ID. NUMBER 486762389

STUDENT ID. NUMBER 474653790

STUDENT ID. NUMBER 502326955

STUDENT ID. NUMBER 476329092

STUDENT ID. NUMBER 442648942

STUDENT ID. NUMBER 546677219
```

b. **Printed (Written) Results:**

```
* JOHN      Q. ADAMS     * 343564321 * GR * CSC *   00   * 219 *

* JOHN      A. BROWN     * 555667777 * FR * MKT *   15   * 035 *

* MATT      N. CULVER    * 456789012 * JR * MGT *   08   * 094 *

* ANTHONY   R. DORSETT   * 353492761 * SR * ECO *   16   * 138 *

* DAVID     Q. ELDRIDGE  * 376495268 * SO * FIN *   12   * 047 *

* BEN       V. FRANKLIN  * 000000002 * GR * GBU *   12   * 189 *

* KENNETH   A. GERBER    * 537903251 * SO * MGT *   16   * 028 *

* MARK      C. HAMILTON  * 486762389 * JR * CSC *   18   * 096 *

* MATT      H. ISSACS    * 474653790 * SR * ECO *   18   * 120 *

* HAROLD    G. JENNINGS  * 502326955 * FR * MGT *   18   * 018 *

* FLOYD     R. KENNIMER  * 476329092 * JR * MKT *   12   * 060 *

* STEVEN    O. LINCOLN   * 442648942 * SO * MKT *   15   * 045 *

* JEFF      V. MARCUS    * 546677219 * SR * CSC *   18   * 099 *
```

Figure E.2 An Illustration of the DISPLAY Statement (Output) *Continued*

The DISPLAY statement can also be employed for the detection of logical error. DISPLAY statements could be placed in the suspect paragraphs to determine whether the correct logical sequence of paragraphs is being executed. Under many circumstances, the DISPLAY of data items is not necessary. Thus, specific messages (non-numeric literals) would be included in the DISPLAY statement so the programmer could determine whether the correct logical sequence is being properly executed. This procedure might be called a logical tracing of the execution of a program.

DISPLAY statements are very useful for debugging programs, but some programmers use them for other purposes (e.g., instead of WRITE statements in the production of output). The programmer should be cautioned against such practices. WRITE statements are more efficient (faster) in the production of output than DISPLAY statements. (WRITE statements utilize output buffers; DISPLAY statements do not.) Therefore, DISPLAY statements should be used sparingly, if at all, in the final version of a program.

The USE FOR DEBUGGING Statement

One ANS COBOL statement is specifically designed for the purpose of debugging programs. The USE FOR DEBUGGING statement, though not available on all computers (including IBM) is very useful as a diagnostic tool. To activate the procedure it is necessary to modify the SOURCE-COMPUTER paragraph of the ENVIRONMENT DIVISION by adding the phrase WITH DEBUGGING MODE after the SOURCE-COMPUTER computer-name. The error-checking process specified in the PROCEDURE is activated by this phrase, allowing a variety of diagnostic messages to be produced. (The words DEBUGGING and MODE are required; WITH is optional.) The format of the USE FOR DEBUGGING statement appears in Figure E.3.

A number of alternative USE FOR DEBUGGING statements can be used to debug a program. The programmer may produce his own diagnostics or procedures using *interrupts* based on (1) a particular data-name (identifier), (2) a particular file-name, (3) a particular procedure (paragraph or SECTION name), or (4) all procedures in the PROCEDURE DIVISION. On encountering any of the indentifiers, files, or procedures listed in the USE FOR DEBUGGING statement, the execution of the body of the PROCEDURE DIVISION is temporarily interrupted until the procedure accompanying the USE FOR DEBUGGING statement is executed. After the USE FOR DEBUGGING procedure is completed, execution of the body of the PROCEDURE DIVISION continues from the point where the interrupt occurred.

```
                           ┌[ALL REFERENCES OF] identifier-1┐
                           │file-name-1                     │
USE FOR DEBUGGING ON       ┤PROCEDURE procedure-name-1      ├
                           └ALL PROCEDURES                  ┘

                          ┌┌[ALL REFERENCES OF] identifier-2┐┐
                          ││file-name-2                     ││
                          ┤│PROCEDURE procedure-name-2      ││  . . .
                          └└ALL PROCEDURES                  ┘┘
```

Figure E.3 Format of the USE FOR DEBUGGING Statement

An identifier, file-name, or procedure-name that appears in one USE FOR DEBUGGING statement cannot appear in any other USE FOR DEBUGGING statement.

When identifier-1 (or identifier-2, etc.) is specified in the USE FOR DEBUGGING statement, *any* occurrence of that identifier in the PROCEDURE DIVISION will cause the programmer-supplied procedure associated with the USE FOR DEBUGGING statement to be executed. The identifier must not be a data item described in the REPORT SECTION of a program. However, the data item may be a table or a part of a table (a data item subordinate to an OCCURS clause—as discussed in Chapter 13). However, when a table name is used, the table name should appear in the USE FOR DEBUGGING statement without subscripts or indexes.

When file-name is specified, the programmer-supplied procedure is executed after the execution of any OPEN, CLOSE, or READ statement that does not cause the AT END imperative statement to be executed. If the procedure-name (a paragraph or SECTION name) is specified, the programmer-supplied procedure associated with the USE FOR DEBUGGING is executed upon encountering the procedure-name during the execution of the program. When ALL PROCEDURES is specified, the programmer-supplied procedure is executed for every paragraph or SECTION encountered during the execution of the program, except those paragraphs or SECTIONs which appear in DECLARATIVES.

Although it is not often necessary (or desirable) to execute portions of the programmer-supplied procedure associated with the USE FOR DEBUGGING statement from the normal code of a program, within a limited set of circumstances the programmer is allowed to access instructions which appear in DECLARATIVES. However, procedures connected with the USE FOR DEBUGGING statements cannot be executed directly from the normal code. Within DECLARATIVES, the procedure specified for one USE FOR DEBUGGING statement may be PERFORMed by the procedure associated with another USE FOR DEBUGGING statement. (The PERFORM statement is discussed in Chapter 8.) Other than this one exception, USE FOR DEBUGGING statements and their procedures cannot be connected to each other or to the remaining code of the program.

The USE FOR DEBUGGING statement and the accompanying procedure must be located in the PROCEDURE DIVISION immediately after a DECLARATIVES heading. (The DECLARATIVES section of a program is often used for special purpose operations including, but not limited to, the debugging for a program.) The location of the DECLARATIVES heading relative to other parts of a program is shown in Figure E.4.

```
----------------------------------------------------------------------------
|       1  1  2  2  2  3  3  4  4  4  5  5  6  6  6  7  7  8|
|  4  8  2  6  0  4  8  2  6  0  4  8  2  6  0  4  8  2  6  0|
----------------------------------------------------------------------------
|000010 IDENTIFICATION DIVISION.                                   FIG  E.4|
|000020 PROGRAM-ID.  EXAMPLE-DEBUG.                                FIG  E.4|
|000030 AUTHOR. MARK BRYAN.                                        FIG  E.4|
|000040 DATE-WRITTEN. JANUARY 1, 1981.                            FIG  E.4|
|000050 DATE-COMPILED. JANUARY 1, 1981.                            FIG  E.4|
|000060*    THIS PROGRAM ILLUSTRATES THE USE OF THE DEBUGGING      FIG  E.4|
|000070*    FACILITY AVAILABLE IN MOST ANS COBOL COMPILERS.        FIG  E.4|
|000080*    THE "USE FOR DEBUGGING" STATEMENT APPEARS IN THE       FIG  E.4|
|000090*    DECLARATIVES AND DEBUG-ITEM (A SPECIAL RECORD) IS      FIG  E.4|
|000100*    DISPLAYED.                                             FIG  E.4|
|000110 ENVIRONMENT DIVISION.                                      FIG  E.4|
|000120 CONFIGURATION SECTION.                                     FIG  E.4|
|000130 SOURCE-COMPUTER. XEROX-560 WITH DEBUGGING MODE.            FIG  E.4|
|000140 OBJECT-COMPUTER. XEROX-560.                                FIG  E.4|
```

Figure E.4 An Illustration of the USE FOR DEBUGGING Statement

```
|             1   1   2   2   3   3   4   4   4   5   5   6   6   6   7   7   8|
|    4   8    2   6   0   4   8   2   6   0   4   8   2   6   0   4   8   2   6   0|
-------------------------------------------------------------------------------
|000150 SPECIAL-NAMES.  *1* IS TOP-OF-NEXT-PAGE.                      FIG  E.4|
|000160 INPUT-OUTPUT SECTION.                                         FIG  E.4|
|000170 FILE-CONTROL.                                                 FIG  E.4|
|000180     SELECT STUDENT-FILE ASSIGN TO CARD-READER.               FIG  E.4|
|000190     SELECT PRINTOUT ASSIGN TO PRINTER.                       FIG  E.4|
|000200 DATA DIVISION.                                                FIG  E.4|
|000210 FILE SECTION.                                                 FIG  E.4|
|000220 FD  STUDENT-FILE LABEL RECORDS ARE OMITTED.                  FIG  E.4|
|000230 01  STUDENT-REC.                                              FIG  E.4|
|000240     05 STUDENT-IDENTIFICATION.                               FIG  E.4|
|000250        10 LAST-NAME           PIC X(10).                     FIG  E.4|
|000260        10 FIRST-NAME          PIC X(10).                     FIG  E.4|
|000270        10 MIDDLE-INITIAL      PIC X(01).                     FIG  E.4|
|000280        10 STUDENT-ID          PIC 9(09).                     FIG  E.4|
|000290     05 FILLER                 PIC X(05).                     FIG  E.4|
|000300     05 ENROLLMENT-INFO.                                      FIG  E.4|
|000310        10 CLASSIFICATION      PIC X(02).                     FIG  E.4|
|000320        10 TOTAL-HOURS         PIC 9(03).                     FIG  E.4|
|000330        10 HOURS-THIS-SEM      PIC 9(02).                     FIG  E.4|
|000340        10 MAJOR               PIC X(03).                     FIG  E.4|
|000350     05  FILLER                PIC X(35).                     FIG  E.4|
|000360 FD  PRINTOUT LABEL RECORDS ARE OMITTED.                      FIG  E.4|
|000370 01  PRINT-LINE                PIC X(133).                    FIG  E.4|
|000380 WORKING-STORAGE SECTION.                                     FIG  E.4|
|000390 01  WORKING-VARIABLES.                                       FIG  E.4|
|000400     05  INDICATOR            PIC X(16).                      FIG  E.4|
|000410 01  OUTPUT-REC.                                              FIG  E.4|
|000420        08 FILLER             PIC X(03) VALUE * *.            FIG  E.4|
|000430        08 1ST-NAME           PIC X(11).                      FIG  E.4|
|000440        08 M-I                PIC X(01).                      FIG  E.4|
|000450        08 FILLER             PIC X(02) VALUE *.*.            FIG  E.4|
|000460        08 SUR-NAME           PIC X(10).                      FIG  E.4|
|000470        08 FILLER             PIC X(04) VALUE * *.            FIG  E.4|
|000480        08 ID-NUM             PIC 9(09).                      FIG  E.4|
|000490        08 FILLER             PIC X(05) VALUE *  *.           FIG  E.4|
|000500        08 CLASS              PIC X(02).                      FIG  E.4|
|000510        08 FILLER             PIC X(06) VALUE *   *.          FIG  E.4|
|000520        08 MAJ                PIC X(03).                      FIG  E.4|
|000530        08 FILLER             PIC X(08) VALUE *  *.           FIG  E.4|
|000540        08 CURRENT-HOURS      PIC 9(02).                      FIG  E.4|
|000550        08 FILLER             PIC X(08) VALUE *    *.         FIG  E.4|
|000560        08 TOT-HOURS          PIC 9(03).                      FIG  E.4|
|000570        08 FILLER             PIC X(03) VALUE *  *.           FIG  E.4|
|000580 PROCEDURE DIVISION.                                          FIG  E.4|
|000590 DECLARATIVES.                                                FIG  E.4|
|000600 PGM-DEBUG SECTION.                                           FIG  E.4|
|000610     USE FOR DEBUGGING ON ALL REFERENCES OF STUDENT-ID.       FIG  E.4|
|000620 DISPLAY-PARA.                                                FIG  E.4|
|000630     DISPLAY * * UPON PRINTER.                                FIG  E.4|
|000640     DISPLAY DEBUG-ITEM UPON PRINTER.                         FIG  E.4|
|000650 END DECLARATIVES.                                            FIG  E.4|
|000660 PGM-CODE SECTION.                                            FIG  E.4|
|000670 CONTROL-PROCEDURE.                                           FIG  E.4|
|000680     PERFORM 100-INITIALIZATION.                              FIG  E.4|
|000690     PERFORM 300-READ-RECORDS-PRINT-DETAILS                   FIG  E.4|
|000700         UNTIL INDICATOR = *PROCESS COMPLETE*.                FIG  E.4|
|000710     PERFORM 500-TERMINATION.                                 FIG  E.4|
|000720     STOP RUN.                                                FIG  E.4|
|000730 100-INITIALIZATION.                                          FIG  E.4|
|000740     MOVE *PROCESS START* TO INDICATOR.                       FIG  E.4|
|000750     OPEN INPUT STUDENT-FILE, OUTPUT PRINTOUT.                FIG  E.4|
|000760     READ STUDENT-FILE                                        FIG  E.4|
|000770         AT END MOVE *PROCESS COMPLETE* TO INDICATOR.         FIG  E.4|
|000780 300-READ-RECORDS-PRINT-DETAILS.                              FIG  E.4|
|000790     MOVE STUDENT-ID TO ID-NUM.                               FIG  E.4|
|000800     MOVE LAST-NAME TO SUR-NAME.                              FIG  E.4|
|000810     MOVE FIRST-NAME TO 1ST-NAME.                             FIG  E.4|
|000820     MOVE MIDDLE-INITIAL TO M-I.                              FIG  E.4|
|000830     MOVE CLASSIFICATION TO CLASS.                            FIG  E.4|
|000840     MOVE TOTAL-HOURS TO TOT-HOURS.                           FIG  E.4|
|000850     MOVE HOURS-THIS-SEM TO CURRENT-HOURS.                    FIG  E.4|
|000860     MOVE MAJOR TO MAJ.                                       FIG  E.4|
|000870     WRITE PRINT-LINE FROM OUTPUT-REC AFTER 2 LINES.          FIG  E.4|
|000880     READ STUDENT-FILE                                        FIG  E.4|
|000890         AT END MOVE *PROCESS COMPLETE* TO INDICATOR.         FIG  E.4|
|000900 500-TERMINATION.                                             FIG  E.4|
|000910     CLOSE STUDENT-FILE, PRINTOUT.                            FIG  E.4|
```

Figure E.4 An Illustration of the USE FOR DEBUGGING Statement *Continued*

```
000078 STUDENT-ID                                            343564321

* JOHN       Q. ADAMS      *  343564321  *  GR  *  CSC  *      00     *  219  *
000078 STUDENT-ID                                            555667777

* JOHN       A. BROWN      *  555667777  *  FR  *  MKT  *      15     *  035  *
000078 STUDENT-ID                                            456789012

* MATT       N. CULVER     *  456789012  *  JR  *  MGT  *      08     *  094  *
000078 STUDENT-ID                                            353492761

* ANTHONY    R. DORSETT    *  353492761  *  SR  *  ECO  *      16     *  138  *
000078 STUDENT-ID                                            376495268

* DAVID      Q. ELDRIDGE   *  376495268  *  SO  *  FIN  *      12     *  047  *
000078 STUDENT-ID                                            000000002

* BEN        V. FRANKLIN   *  000000002  *  GR  *  GBU  *      12     *  189  *
000078 STUDENT-ID                                            537903251

* KENNETH    A. GERBER     *  537903251  *  SO  *  MGT  *      16     *  028  *
000078 STUDENT-ID                                            486762389

* MARK       C. HAMILTON   *  486762389  *  JR  *  CSC  *      18     *  096  *
000078 STUDENT-ID                                            474653790

* MATT       H. ISSACS     *  474653790  *  SR  *  ECO  *      18     *  120  *
000078 STUDENT-ID                                            502326955

* HAROLD     Q. JENNINGS   *  502326955  *  FR  *  MGT  *      18     *  018  *
000078 STUDENT-ID                                            476329092

* FLOYD      R. KENNIMER   *  476329092  *  JR  *  MKT  *      12     *  060  *
000078 STUDENT-ID                                            442648942

* STEVEN     O. LINCOLN    *  442648942  *  SO  *  MKT  *      15     *  045  *
000078 STUDENT-ID                                            546677219

* JEFF       V. MARCUS     *  546677219  *  SR  *  CSC  *      18     *  099  *
```

Figure E.4 An Illustration of the USE FOR DEBUGGING Statement and DECLARATIVES (Output) *Continued*

The USE FOR DEBUGGING statement and its accompanying procedure must appear within a SECTION. In the program PGM-DEBUG SECTION is a programmer-supplied SECTION name. The USE FOR DEBUGGING statement should immediately follow this SECTION name. The procedure that accompanies the USE FOR DEBUGGING statement must appear in a paragraph immediately following the USE FOR DEBUGGING statement. In the example program, DISPLAY-PARA indicates the procedure to be executed when the USE FOR DEBUGGING statement is invoked. DISPLAY statements are used in the example, but any set of COBOL statements (except another USE FOR DEBUGGING statement) may appear in this paragraph. The code is not limited to a single paragraph. The procedure associated with a particular USE FOR DEBUGGING is terminated with the appearance of another SECTION name in the DECLARATIVES or the END DECLARATIVES heading. In the example, END DECLARATIVES terminates the procedure. Thus, if multiple USE FOR DEBUGGING statements were required within a program, each such set of statements would be placed within a SECTION, isolating it within that SECTION from other USE FOR DEBUGGING statements or other commands.

The DECLARATIVES section of a program is terminated by the END DECLARATIVES marker. Under usual conditions, the program should not begin with the DECLARATIVES portion of a program. Execution of the program should begin with the first executable statement following the END DECLARATIVES marker. In the example program, the first executable statement is the PERFORM statement in the CONTROL-PROCEDURE paragraph.

However, most systems require a SECTION name to follow the END DECLARATIVES. Therefore, the PGM-CODE SECTION was added to the program to satisfy this requirement. (This makes the paragraph name CONTROL-PROCEDURE unnecessary in some systems, but it is retained as a reference point.)

As the program in Figure E.4 is executed, the program checks for an occurrence of the data item STUDENT-ID. (The statement USE FOR DEBUGGING ON ALL REFERENCES OF STUDENT-ID causes this action.) When STUDENT-ID is found during program execution, the statements in DISPLAY-PARA (two DISPLAY statements) are executed. The first DISPLAY statement is used to avoid overwriting of the message to be produced by the second DISPLAY statement. The second statement reads DISPLAY DEBUG-ITEM UPON PRINTER. Upon examining the entire program, the programmer will notice that there is no description of DEBUG-ITEM in the DATA DIVISION. When the USE FOR DEBUGGING statement appears in a program, the COBOL compiler automatically inserts the description of DEBUG-ITEM. Thus, DEBUG-ITEM is a special record. Its description is as follows:

```
Ø1    DEBUG-ITEM.
      Ø2    DEBUG-LINE          PICTURE X(6).
      Ø2    FILLER              PICTURE X VALUE IS SPACES.
      Ø2    DEBUG-NAME          PICTURE X(3Ø).
      Ø2    FILLER              PICTURE X VALUE IS SPACES.
      Ø2    DEBUG-SUB-1         PICTURE 9999.
      Ø2    FILLER              PICTURE X VALUE IS SPACES.
      Ø2    DEBUG-SUB-2         PICTURE 9999.
      Ø2    FILLER              PICTURE X VALUE IS SPACES.
      Ø2    DEBUG-SUB-3         PICTURE 9999.
      Ø2    FILLER              PICTURE X VALUE IS SPACES.
      Ø2    DEBUG-CONTENTS      PICTURE X(n).
```

DEBUG-ITEM is an implicit record description which does not appear in the program code. Each of the elementary-items in this record description is often referred to as a *special* COBOL *register*. Depending on the particular option specified in the USE FOR DEBUGGING statement, the appropriate information will be placed in these special registers. Table E.1 presents a summary of the types of information to be placed in these special registers.

Descriptions of DEBUG-LINE, DEBUG-NAME, and DEBUG-CONTENTS are presented in Table E.1, but DEBUG-SUB-1, DEBUG-SUB-2, and DEBUG-SUB-3 are not mentioned. These special registers contain information only when the identifier indicated in the USE FOR DEBUGGING statement is a table. (Tables are discussed in Chapters 13 and 14.) The content of these special registers is the subscript (or index) value of the identifier (table). If an identifier is not used in the statement or the identifier is not a table (or part of a table), these special registers contain spaces.

Figure E.5 further illustrates the USE FOR DEBUGGING statement. This program is similar to the program presented in Figure E.4; however, here the USE FOR DEBUGGING statement references the procedure-name READ-RECORDS-AND-PRINT-DETAILS. In all other respects the programs are the same. In the output produced by the execution of this program, the first DISPLAY of DEBUG-ITEM produces the program line number that invoked the procedure (the PERFORM statement at line 69), the procedure-name executed (READ-DATA-AND-PRINT-DETAILS), and the condition under which the procedure was reached (FALL THROUGH from the PERFORM statement). Thereafter, the procedure-name is displayed as a result of the re-execution of the paragraph caused by the PERFORM statement.

Table E.1 The Contents of DEBUG-ITEM on the Execution of a USE FOR DEBUGGING Statement

Field	USE FOR DEBUGGING ON			
			procedure-name-1 when	
	identifier-1	file-name-1	encountered by branching	encountered sequentially
DEBUG-LINE	Identifies the source statement containing identifier-1 (The statement line number.)	Identifies the source statement referencing file-name-1	Identifies the source statement that caused the branch to take place.	Identifies the source statement immediately prior to the procedure-name
DEBUG-NAME	The data name of the identifier	File-name-1	Procedure-name-1	Procedure-name-1
DEBUG-CONTENTS	The data value contained in identifier-1 after the statement containing the identifier is executed	Spaces for OPEN and CLOSE statements; the contents of the input record for READ statements	Spaces (except when an ALTER statement has caused the branch. In this case, procedure-name-2 of the ALTER statement is produced.)	The nonnumeric literal FALL THROUGH

```
|        1  1  2  2  2  3  3  4  4  4  5  5  6  6  6  7  7  8|
|     4  8  2  6  0  4  8  2  6  0  4  8  2  6  0  4  8  2  6  0|
----------------------------------------------------------------
|000010 IDENTIFICATION DIVISION.                                    FIG E.5|
|000020 PROGRAM-ID.  EXAMPLE-DEBUG.                                 FIG E.5|
|000030 AUTHOR.  MARK BRYAN.                                        FIG E.5|
|000040 DATE-WRITTEN.  JANUARY 1, 1981.                             FIG E.5|
|000050 DATE-COMPILED.  JANUARY 1, 1981.                            FIG E.5|
|000060*    THIS PROGRAM ILLUSTRATES THE USE OF THE DEBUGGING       FIG E.5|
|000070*    FACILITY AVAILABLE IN MOST ANS COBOL COMPILERS.         FIG E.5|
|000080*    THE "USE FOR DEBUGGING" STATEMENT APPEARS IN THE        FIG E.5|
|000090*    DECLARATIVES AND DEBUG-ITEM (A SPECIAL RECORD) IS       FIG E.5|
|000100*    DISPLAYED.                                              FIG E.5|
|000110 ENVIRONMENT DIVISION.                                       FIG E.5|
|000120 CONFIGURATION SECTION.                                      FIG E.5|
|000130 SOURCE-COMPUTER.  XEROX-560 WITH DEBUGGING MODE.            FIG E.5|
|000140 OBJECT-COMPUTER.  XEROX-560.                                FIG E.5|
|000150 SPECIAL-NAMES.  "1" IS TOP-OF-NEXT-PAGE.                    FIG E.5|
|000160 INPUT-OUTPUT SECTION.                                       FIG E.5|
|000170 FILE-CONTROL.                                               FIG E.5|
|000180     SELECT STUDENT-FILE ASSIGN TO CARD-READER.             FIG E.5|
|000190     SELECT PRINTOUT ASSIGN TO PRINTER.                     FIG E.5|
|000200 DATA DIVISION.                                              FIG E.5|
|000210 FILE SECTION.                                               FIG E.5|
|000220 FD  STUDENT-FILE LABEL RECORDS ARE OMITTED.                FIG E.5|
|000230 01  STUDENT-REC.                                            FIG E.5|
|000240     05 STUDENT-IDENTIFICATION.                             FIG E.5|
|000250         10 LAST-NAME            PIC X(10).                 FIG E.5|
|000260         10 FIRST-NAME           PIC X(10).                 FIG E.5|
|000270         10 MIDDLE-INITIAL       PIC X(01).                 FIG E.5|
|000280         10 STUDENT-ID           PIC 9(09).                 FIG E.5|
|000290     05 FILLER                   PIC X(05).                 FIG E.5|
|000300     05 ENROLLMENT-INFO.                                    FIG E.5|
|000310         10 CLASSIFICATION       PIC X(02).                 FIG E.5|
|000320         10 TOTAL-HOURS          PIC 9(03).                 FIG E.5|
|000330         10 HOURS-THIS-SEM       PIC 9(02).                 FIG E.5|
|000340         10 MAJOR                PIC X(03).                 FIG E.5|
|000350 FD  PRINTOUT LABEL RECORDS ARE OMITTED.                    FIG E.5|
|000360 01  PRINT-LINE                  PIC X(133).                FIG E.5|
|000370 WORKING-STORAGE SECTION.                                   FIG E.5|
|000380 01  WORKING-VARIABLES.                                     FIG E.5|
|000390     05  INDICATOR               PIC X(16).                 FIG E.5|
```

Figure E.5 A Second Illustration of the USE FOR DEBUGGING Statement

```
|-----------------------------------------------------------------------------|
|        1   1   2   2   2   3   3   4   4   4   5   5   6   6   6   7   7   8| |
|  4   8   2   6   0   4   8   2   6   0   4   8   2   6   0   4   8   2   6   0| |
|000400 01   OUTPUT-REC.                                               FIG  E.5|
|000410         08  FILLER            PIC  X(03)  VALUE ' '.           FIG  E.5|
|000420         08  1ST-NAME          PIC  X(11).                      FIG  E.5|
|000430         08  M-I               PIC  X(01).                      FIG  E.5|
|000440         08  FILLER            PIC  X(02)  VALUE ' '.           FIG  E.5|
|000450         08  SUR-NAME          PIC  X(10).                      FIG  E.5|
|000460         08  FILLER            PIC  X(04)  VALUE ' '.           FIG  E.5|
|000470         08  ID-NUM            PIC  9(09).                      FIG  E.5|
|000480         08  FILLER            PIC  X(05)  VALUE '   '.         FIG  E.5|
|000490         08  CLASS             PIC  X(02).                      FIG  E.5|
|000500         08  FILLER            PIC  X(06)  VALUE '    '.        FIG  E.5|
|000510         08  MAJ               PIC  X(03).                      FIG  E.5|
|000520         08  FILLER            PIC  X(08)  VALUE '   '.         FIG  E.5|
|000530         08  CURRENT-HOURS     PIC  9(02).                      FIG  E.5|
|000540         08  FILLER            PIC  X(08)  VALUE '     '.       FIG  E.5|
|000550      05   FILLER              PIC  X(35).                      FIG  E.5|
|000560         08  TOT-HOURS         PIC  9(03).                      FIG  E.5|
|000570         08  FILLER            PIC  X(03)  VALUE ' '.           FIG  E.5|
|000580 PROCEDURE DIVISION.                                           FIG  E.5|
|000590 DECLARATIVES.                                                 FIG  E.5|
|000600 PGM-DEBUG SECTION.                                            FIG  E.5|
|000610      USE FOR DEBUGGING ON                                     FIG  E.5|
|000620          PROCEDURE READ-RECORDS-AND-PRINT-DETAILS.            FIG  E.5|
|000630 DISPLAY-PARA.                                                 FIG  E.5|
|000640      DISPLAY ' ' UPON PRINTER.                                FIG  E.5|
|000650      DISPLAY DEBUG-ITEM UPON PRINTER.                         FIG  E.5|
|000660 END DECLARATIVES.                                             FIG  E.5|
|000670 PGM-CODE SECTION.                                             FIG  E.5|
|000680 CONTROL-PROCEDURE.                                            FIG  E.5|
|000690      PERFORM 100-INITIALIZATION.                              FIG  E.5|
|000700      PERFORM 300-READ-RECORDS-PRINT-DETAILS                   FIG  E.5|
|000710          UNTIL INDICATOR = 'PROCESS COMPLETE'.                FIG  E.5|
|000720      PERFORM 500-TERMINATION.                                 FIG  E.5|
|000730      STOP RUN.                                                FIG  E.5|
|000740 100-INITIALIZATION.                                           FIG  E.5|
|000750      MOVE 'PROCESS START' TO INDICATOR.                       FIG  E.5|
|000760      OPEN INPUT STUDENT-FILE, OUTPUT PRINTOUT.                FIG  E.5|
|000770      READ STUDENT-FILE                                        FIG  E.5|
|000780          AT END MOVE 'PROCESS COMPLETE' TO INDICATOR.         FIG  E.5|
|000790 300-READ-RECORDS-PRINT-DETAILS.                               FIG  E.5|
|000800      MOVE STUDENT-ID TO ID-NUM.                               FIG  E.5|
|000810      MOVE LAST-NAME TO SUR-NAME.                              FIG  E.5|
|000820      MOVE FIRST-NAME TO 1ST-NAME.                             FIG  E.5|
|000830      MOVE MIDDLE-INITIAL TO M-I.                              FIG  E.5|
|000840      MOVE CLASSIFICATION TO CLASS.                            FIG  E.5|
|000850      MOVE TOTAL-HOURS TO TOT-HOURS.                           FIG  E.5|
|000860      MOVE HOURS-THIS-SEM TO CURRENT-HOURS.                    FIG  E.5|
|000870      MOVE MAJOR TO MAJ.                                       FIG  E.5|
|000880      WRITE PRINT-LINE FROM OUTPUT-REC AFTER 2 LINES.          FIG  E.5|
|000890      READ STUDENT-FILE                                        FIG  E.5|
|000900          AT END MOVE 'PROCESS COMPLETE' TO INDICATOR.         FIG  E.5|
|000910 500-TERMINATION.                                              FIG  E.5|
|000920      CLOSE STUDENT-FILE, PRINTOUT.                            FIG  E.5|
```

Figure E.5 A Second Illustration of the USE FOR DEBUGGING Statement *Continued*

The EXHIBIT Statement

Although the USE FOR DEBUGGING statement is an ANS COBOL statement, COBOL compilers produced by some computer manufacturers do not include the statement. However, the compilers that do not contain the USE FOR DEBUGGING statement often support other nonstandard statements that perform some of the same debugging functions. For example, IBM COBOL compilers support the EXHIBIT statement.

The format of the EXHIBIT statement, shown in Figure E.6, is similar to the DISPLAY statement. The function of the EXHIBIT statement is to produce on the system output device (usually a line printer) values associated with one or more identifiers. Unlike the DISPLAY statement, however, the EXHIBIT statement may produce other helpful information (and in some cases, it does not produce the information which is not essential).

```
000069  READ-RECORDS-AND-PRINT-DETAILS                          FALL THROUGH

* JOHN        Q. ADAMS     * 343564321  * GR * CSC *    00    * 219 *
              READ-RECORDS-AND-PRINT-DETAILS

* JOHN        A. BROWN     * 555667777  * FR * MKT *    15    * 035 *
              READ-RECORDS-AND-PRINT-DETAILS

* MATT        N. CULVER    * 456789012  * JR * MGT *    08    * 094 *
              READ-RECORDS-AND-PRINT-DETAILS

* ANTHONY     R. DORSETT   * 353492761  * SR * ECO *    16    * 138 *
              READ-RECORDS-AND-PRINT-DETAILS

* DAVID       Q. ELDRIDGE  * 376495268  * SO * FIN *    12    * 047 *
              READ-RECORDS-AND-PRINT-DETAILS

* BEN         V. FRANKLIN  * 000000002  * GR * GBU *    12    * 189 *
              READ-RECORDS-AND-PRINT-DETAILS

* KENNETH     A. GERBER    * 537903251  * SO * MGT *    16    * 028 *
              READ-RECORDS-AND-PRINT-DETAILS

* MARK        C. HAMILTON  * 486762389  * JR * CSC *    18    * 096 *
              READ-RECORDS-AND-PRINT-DETAILS

* MATT        H. ISSACS    * 474653790  * SR * ECO *    18    * 120 *
              READ-RECORDS-AND-PRINT-DETAILS

* HAROLD      Q. JENNINGS  * 502326955  * FR * MGT *    18    * 018 *
              READ-RECORDS-AND-PRINT-DETAILS

* FLOYD       R. KENNIMER  * 476329092  * JR * MKT *    12    * 060 *
              READ-RECORDS-AND-PRINT-DETAILS

* STEVEN      O. LINCOLN   * 442648942  * SO * MKT *    15    * 045 *
              READ-RECORDS-AND-PRINT-DETAILS

* JEFF        V. MARCUS    * 546677219  * SR * CSC *    18    * 099 *
```

Figure E.5 A Second Illustration of the USE FOR DEBUGGING Statement (Output)
Continued

The three reserved words that follow the word EXHIBIT are used to control the output produced by the statement. If the reserved word NAMED is specified in the EXHIBIT statement, both the data-name and the contents of the data-name are produced for each identifier shown in the statement. Thus, if the statement

```
EXHIBIT NAMED STUDENT-ID, LAST-NAME
```

were placed in a program, when the statement is executed the identifier-name (i.e., STUDENT-ID and LAST-NAME) would be written along with the current value stored in those storage positions. If the statement contains a non-numeric literal, the literal is displayed along with the data item names and values.

```
             ⎧ NAMED          ⎫ ⎧ identifier-1            ⎫ ⎡ identifier-2            ⎤
EXHIBIT      ⎨ CHANGED  NAMED ⎬ ⎨ non-numeric-literal-1   ⎬ ⎢ non-numeric-literal-2   ⎥ . . .
             ⎩ CHANGED        ⎭ ⎩                         ⎭ ⎣                         ⎦
```

Figure E.6 Format of the EXHIBIT Statement (Non-ANS Standard)

When the CHANGED NAMED option of the EXHIBIT statement is used, the identifiers and their values are displayed only if the values have been altered since the last execution of the EXHIBIT statement. The EXHIBIT automatically produces all values and data item names when initially encountered in the program, but thereafter the output of the statement depends on the values of the identifiers. If the value of an identifier changes, the value and name of the identifier is displayed; otherwise, no output is generated. Non-numeric literals are produced by this statement, if present, in the same manner as with the NAMED option.

The last option of the EXHIBIT statement includes the reserved word CHANGED. It is similar to the CHANGED NAMED option in that output is produced only if the value of an identifier has changed from one execution of the statement to the next encounter with the EXHIBIT statement. Unlike the CHANGED NAMED (or the NAMED) option, however, the identifier-name is *not* displayed with the value of the identifier with the CHANGED option. For this reason, the output produced by this form of the EXHIBIT statement is in a fixed columnar format. This allows the programmer to determine more easily which identifier value has been changed. With either the CHANGED NAMED or the CHANGED options, if no values are changed from one execution of the EXHIBIT statement to another, a blank will be produced on the output.

Figure E.7 illustrates the use of an EXHIBIT statement in a program. At line 690, an EXHIBIT is used to display the values of STUDENT-ID and MAJOR, along with the data-names themselves, when their data values change. In the output from this program, STUDENT-ID changes for every record, and the data-name and value are printed every time. However, an examination of MAJOR demonstrates one instance where the value of the data item did not change. Between the records for Floyd R. Kennimer and Steven O. Lincoln, a blank line is printed. An examination of the output indicates that both individuals are "MKT" students. As a consequence the value for MAJOR is not printed.

```
|              1   1   2   2   2   3   3   4   4   4   5   5   6   6   6   7   7   8|
|    4     8   2   6   0   4   8   2   6   0   4   8   2   6   0   4   8   2   6   0|
----------------------------------------------------------------------------------
|000010 IDENTIFICATION DIVISION.                                        FIG  E.7|
|000020 PROGRAM-ID.  EXHIBIT-STATEMENT.                                 FIG  E.7|
|000030 AUTHOR. CLARENE TROWBRIDGE.                                     FIG  E.7|
|000040 DATE-WRITTEN. JANUARY 1, 1981.                                  FIG  E.7|
|000050 DATE-COMPILED. JANUARY 1, 1981.                                 FIG  E.7|
|000060*    THIS PROGRAM ILLUSTRATES THE USE OF THE                     FIG  E.7|
|000070*    EXHIBIT STATEMENT TO TRACE THE VALUES PLACED IN             FIG  E.7|
|000080*    IDENTIFIERS.                                                FIG  E.7|
|000090 ENVIRONMENT DIVISION.                                           FIG  E.7|
|000100 CONFIGURATION SECTION.                                          FIG  E.7|
|000110 SOURCE-COMPUTER. IBM-370-145.                                   FIG  E.7|
|000120 OBJECT-COMPUTER. IBM-370-145.                                   FIG  E.7|
|000130 SPECIAL-NAMES.  C01 IS TOP-OF-NEXT-PAGE.                        FIG  E.7|
|000140 INPUT-OUTPUT SECTION.                                           FIG  E.7|
|000150 FILE-CONTROL.                                                   FIG  E.7|
```

Figure E.7 An Illustration of the EXHIBIT Statement

```
|               1   1   2   2   2   3   3   4   4   5   5   6   6   6   7   7   8|
|   4   8       2   6   0   4   8   2   6   0   4   8   2   6   0   4   8   2   6   0|
-------------------------------------------------------------------------------
|000160    SELECT STUDENT-FILE ASSIGN TO UR-S-SYSIN.              FIG E.7|
|000170    SELECT PRINTOUT ASSIGN TO UR-S-SYSPRINT.              FIG E.7|
|000180 DATA DIVISION.                                           FIG E.7|
|000190 FILE SECTION.                                            FIG E.7|
|000200 FD  STUDENT-FILE LABEL RECORDS ARE OMITTED.             FIG E.7|
|000210 01  STUDENT-REC.                                        FIG E.7|
|000220    05 STUDENT-IDENTIFICATION.                           FIG E.7|
|000230       10 LAST-NAME           PIC X(10).                 FIG E.7|
|000240       10 FIRST-NAME          PIC X(10).                 FIG E.7|
|000250       10 MIDDLE-INITIAL      PIC X(01).                 FIG E.7|
|000260       10 STUDENT-ID          PIC 9(09).                 FIG E.7|
|000270    05 FILLER                 PIC X(05).                 FIG E.7|
|000280    05 ENROLLMENT-INFO.                                  FIG E.7|
|000290       10 CLASSIFICATION      PIC X(02).                 FIG E.7|
|000300       10 TOTAL-HOURS         PIC 9(03).                 FIG E.7|
|000310       10 HOURS-THIS-SEM      PIC 9(02).                 FIG E.7|
|000320       10 MAJOR               PIC X(03).                 FIG E.7|
|000330    05 FILLER                 PIC X(35).                 FIG E.7|
|000340 FD  PRINTOUT LABEL RECORDS ARE OMITTED.                FIG E.7|
|000350 01  PRINT-LINE               PIC X(133).                FIG E.7|
|000360 WORKING-STORAGE SECTION.                                FIG E.7|
|000370 01  WORKING-VARIABLES.                                  FIG E.7|
|000380    05  INDICATOR             PIC X(16).                 FIG E.7|
|000390 01  OUTPUT-REC.                                         FIG E.7|
|000400       08 FILLER              PIC X(03) VALUE ' *'.      FIG E.7|
|000410       08 1ST-NAME            PIC X(11).                 FIG E.7|
|000420       08 M-I                 PIC X(01).                 FIG E.7|
|000430       08 FILLER              PIC X(02) VALUE '.'.       FIG E.7|
|000440       08 SUR-NAME            PIC X(10).                 FIG E.7|
|000450       08 FILLER              PIC X(04) VALUE ' *'.      FIG E.7|
|000460       08 ID-NUM              PIC 9(09).                 FIG E.7|
|000470       08 FILLER              PIC X(05) VALUE '  *'.     FIG E.7|
|000480       08 CLASS               PIC X(02).                 FIG E.7|
|000490       08 FILLER              PIC X(06) VALUE '   *'.    FIG E.7|
|000500       08 MAJ                 PIC X(03).                 FIG E.7|
|000510       08 FILLER              PIC X(08) VALUE '   *'.    FIG E.7|
|000520       08 CURRENT-HOURS       PIC 9(02).                 FIG E.7|
|000530       08 FILLER              PIC X(08) VALUE '     *'.  FIG E.7|
|000540       08 TOT-HOURS           PIC 9(03).                 FIG E.7|
|000550       08 FILLER              PIC X(03) VALUE '  *'.     FIG E.7|
|000560 PROCEDURE DIVISION.                                     FIG E.7|
|000570 CONTROL-PROCEDURE.                                      FIG E.7|
|000580    PERFORM 100-INITIALIZATION.                          FIG E.7|
|000590    PERFORM 300-READ-RECORDS-PRINT-DETAILS               FIG E.7|
|000600       UNTIL INDICATOR = 'PROCESS COMPLETE'.            FIG E.7|
|000610    PERFORM 500-TERMINATION.                             FIG E.7|
|000620    STOP RUN.                                            FIG E.7|
|000630 100-INITIALIZATION.                                     FIG E.7|
|000640    MOVE 'PROCESS START' TO INDICATOR.                  FIG E.7|
|000650    OPEN INPUT STUDENT-FILE, OUTPUT PRINTOUT.           FIG E.7|
|000660    READ STUDENT-FILE                                    FIG E.7|
|000670       AT END MOVE 'PROCESS COMPLETE' TO INDICATOR.     FIG E.7|
|000680 300-READ-RECORDS-PRINT-DETAILS.                         FIG E.7|
|000690    DISPLAY ' '.                                         FIG E.7|
|000700    EXHIBIT CHANGED NAMED STUDENT-ID, MAJOR.            FIG E.7|
|000710    MOVE STUDENT-ID TO ID-NUM.                           FIG E.7|
|000720    MOVE LAST-NAME TO SUR-NAME.                          FIG E.7|
|000730    MOVE FIRST-NAME TO 1ST-NAME.                         FIG E.7|
|000740    MOVE MIDDLE-INITIAL TO M-I.                          FIG E.7|
|000750    MOVE CLASSIFICATION TO CLASS.                        FIG E.7|
|000760    MOVE TOTAL-HOURS TO TOT-HOURS.                       FIG E.7|
|000770    MOVE HOURS-THIS-SEM TO CURRENT-HOURS.                FIG E.7|
|000780    MOVE MAJOR TO MAJ.                                   FIG E.7|
|000790    WRITE PRINT-LINE FROM OUTPUT-REC AFTER 2 LINES.     FIG E.7|
|000800    READ STUDENT-FILE                                    FIG E.7|
|000810       AT END MOVE 'PROCESS COMPLETE' TO INDICATOR.     FIG E.7|
|000820 500-TERMINATION.                                        FIG E.7|
|000830    CLOSE STUDENT-FILE, PRINTOUT.                        FIG E.7|
```

Figure E.7 An Illustration of the Exhibit Statement *Continued*

a. Exhibited Results:

```
STUDENT-ID = 343564321 MAJOR = CSC

STUDENT-ID = 555667777 MAJOR = MKT

STUDENT-ID = 456789012 MAJOR = MGT

STUDENT-ID = 353492761 MAJOR = ECO

STUDENT-ID = 376495268 MAJOR = FIN

STUDENT-ID = 000000002 MAJOR = GBU

STUDENT-ID = 537903251 MAJOR = MGT

STUDENT-ID = 486762389 MAJOR = CSC

STUDENT-ID = 474653790 MAJOR = ECO

STUDENT-ID = 502326955 MAJOR = MGT

STUDENT-ID = 476329092 MAJOR = MKT

STUDENT-ID = 442648942

STUDENT-ID = 546677219 MAJOR = CSC
```

b. Printed (Written) Results:

```
*  JOHN        Q.  ADAMS      *  343564321  *  GR  *  CSC  *  00  *  219  *

*  JOHN        A.  BROWN      *  555667777  *  FR  *  MKT  *  15  *  035  *

*  MATT        N.  CULVER     *  456789012  *  JR  *  MGT  *  08  *  094  *

*  ANTHONY     R.  DORSETT    *  353492761  *  SR  *  ECO  *  16  *  138  *

*  DAVID       Q.  ELDRIDGE   *  376495268  *  SO  *  FIN  *  12  *  047  *

*  BEN         V.  FRANKLIN   *  000000002  *  GR  *  GBU  *  12  *  189  *

*  KENNETH     A.  GERBER     *  537903251  *  SO  *  MGT  *  16  *  028  *

*  MARK        C.  HAMILTON   *  486762389  *  JR  *  CSC  *  18  *  096  *

*  MATT        H.  ISSACS     *  474653790  *  SR  *  ECO  *  18  *  120  *

*  HAROLD      G.  JENNINGS   *  502326955  *  FR  *  MGT  *  18  *  018  *

*  FLOYD       R.  KENNIMER   *  476329092  *  JR  *  MKT  *  12  *  060  *

*  STEVEN      O.  LINCOLN    *  442648942  *  SO  *  MKT  *  15  *  045  *

*  JEFF        V.  MARCUS     *  546677219  *  SR  *  CSC  *  18  *  099  *
```

Figure E.7 An Illustration of the EXHIBIT Statement (Output) *Continued*

The TRACE Statement

TRACE is another statement that is often included in COBOL compilers but is not a part of ANS COBOL. The TRACE statement allows the programmer to determine the logical flow of a program from one procedure to another during execution of the program. Each paragraph or SECTION name encountered while the TRACE is active will cause the paragraph or SECTION name (or line number in the program) to be produced on the system output device (e.g., line printer). The TRACE statement is accompanied by two additional reserved words—READY and RESET. To initiate a trace of the procedure-names encountered during execution of a program, the programmer enters READY TRACE. An example of the tracing of the procedure-names is presented in Figure E.8. Notice that on the output of the program, the paragraph names that were reached while the trace was active (caused by the READY TRACE statement) are printed at the left margin. Upon completing the CONTROL-PROCEDURE paragraph, the trace is deactivated by RESET TRACE. In the example, all of the paragraphs of the program (except the CONTROL-PRO-CEDURE paragraph) were subjected to the trace. However, if the program were longer and more complex, performing a trace from the beginning of the program to the end would not necessarily be desirable. The trace could be localized to concentrate on those areas of a program that are the likely source of the error. If several areas of the program are suspect, several sets of READY TRACE and RESET TRACE may be necessary to turn the trace "on" and "off." This approach is generally more useful and does not overburden the programmer with a mass of unneeded tracing.

```
---------------------------------------------------------------------------
|           1   1   2   2   2   3   3   4   4   4   5   5   6   6   6   7   7   8|
|   4   8   2   6   0   4   8   2   6   0   4   8   2   6   0   4   8   2   6   0|
---------------------------------------------------------------------------
|000010 15.8:   AN ILLUSTRATION OF THE READY AND RESET TRACE STATEMENTS     FIG  E.8|
|000020 IDENTIFICATION DIVISION.                                            FIG  E.8|
|000030 PROGRAM-ID. PROCEDURE-TRACE.                                        FIG  E.8|
|000040 AUTHOR. STACY BRYAN.                                                FIG  E.8|
|000050 DATE-WRITTEN. JANUARY 1, 1981.                                      FIG  E.8|
|000060 DATE-COMPILED. JANUARY 1, 1981.                                     FIG  E.8|
|000070*     PROGRAM ILLUSTRATES THE USE OF THE TRACE                       FIG  E.8|
|000080*     STATEMENT TO PROVIDE THE MEANS FOR FOLLOWING THE               FIG  E.8|
|000090*     EXECUTION SEQUENCE OF THE PROGRAM.                             FIG  E.8|
|000100 ENVIRONMENT DIVISION.                                               FIG  E.8|
|000110 CONFIGURATION SECTION.                                              FIG  E.8|
|000120 SOURCE-COMPUTER. CDC-6600.                                          FIG  E.8|
|000130 OBJECT-COMPUTER. CDC-6600.                                          FIG  E.8|
|000140 SPECIAL-NAMES.  C01 IS TOP-OF-NEXT-PAGE.                            FIG  E.8|
|000150 INPUT-OUTPUT SECTION.                                               FIG  E.8|
|000160 FILE-CONTROL.                                                       FIG  E.8|
|000170     SELECT STUDENT-FILE ASSIGN TO UT-S-SYSIN.                       FIG  E.8|
|000180     SELECT PRINTOUT ASSIGN TO UT-S-SYSPRINT.                        FIG  E.8|
|000190 DATA DIVISION.                                                      FIG  E.8|
|000200 FILE SECTION.                                                       FIG  E.8|
|000210 FD  STUDENT-FILE LABEL RECORDS ARE OMITTED.                         FIG  E.8|
|000220 01  STUDENT-REC.                                                    FIG  E.8|
|000230     05 STUDENT-IDENTIFICATION.                                      FIG  E.8|
|000240        10 LAST-NAME              PIC X(10).                         FIG  E.8|
|000250        10 FIRST-NAME             PIC X(10).                         FIG  E.8|
|000260        10 MIDDLE-INITIAL         PIC X(01).                         FIG  E.8|
|000270        10 STUDENT-ID             PIC 9(09).                         FIG  E.8|
|000280     05 FILLER                    PIC X(05).                         FIG  E.8|
|000290     05 ENROLLMENT-INFO.                                             FIG  E.8|
|000300        10 CLASSIFICATION         PIC X(02).                         FIG  E.8|
|000310        10 TOTAL-HOURS            PIC 9(03).                         FIG  E.8|
|000320        10 HOURS-THIS-SEM         PIC 9(02).                         FIG  E.8|
|000330        10 MAJOR                  PIC X(03).                         FIG  E.8|
|000340     05  FILLER                   PIC X(35).                         FIG  E.8|
|000350 FD  PRINTOUT LABEL RECORDS ARE OMITTED.                             FIG  E.8|
|000360 01  PRINT-LINE                   PIC X(133).                        FIG  E.8|
|000370 WORKING-STORAGE SECTION.                                            FIG  E.8|
|000380 01  WORKING-VARIABLES.                                              FIG  E.8|
|000390     05  INDICATOR                PIC X(16).                         FIG  E.8|
|000400 01  REPORT-HEADING.                                                 FIG  E.8|
|000410     03 FILLER                    PIC X(29) VALUE SPACES.            FIG  E.8|
|000420     03 FILLER                    PIC X(21) VALUE                    FIG  E.8|
|000430     *SEMESTER STUDENT LIST*.                                        FIG  E.8|
|000440 01  SEPARATOR-LINE.                                                 FIG  E.8|
|000450     03 FILLER                    PIC X(01) VALUE SPACES.            FIG  E.8|
|000460     03 FILLER                    PIC X(79)  VALUE ALL *.*.          FIG  E.8|
|000470 01  COLUMN-HEADING-1.                                               FIG  E.8|
|000480     02 FILLER                    PIC X(01) VALUE SPACES.            FIG  E.8|
|000490     02 FILLER                    PIC X(79) VALUE *.        STUDENT  FIG  E.8|
|000500-     *NAME       * STUDENT ID. * CLASS * MAJOR *  CURRENT   * TOTA  FIG  E.8|
|000510-     *L *.                                                          FIG  E.8|
|000520 01  COLUMN-HEADING-2.                                               FIG  E.8|
|000530     02 FILLER                    PIC X(28) VALUE * *.               FIG  E.8|
|000540     02 FILLER                    PIC X(14) VALUE *.  NUMBER*.       FIG  E.8|
|000550     02 FILLER                    PIC X(08) VALUE *.*.               FIG  E.8|
|000560     02 FILLER                    PIC X(08) VALUE *.*.               FIG  E.8|
|000570     02 FILLER                    PIC X(22) VALUE *. ENROLLMENT * H  FIG  E.8|
|000580-     *OURS *.                                                       FIG  E.8|
|000590 01  OUTPUT-REC.                                                     FIG  E.8|
|000600        08 FILLER                 PIC X(03) VALUE * *.               FIG  E.8|
|000610        08 1ST-NAME               PIC X(11).                         FIG  E.8|
```

Figure E.8 An Illustration of the READY and RESET TRACE Statements

```
|      1  1  2  2  2  3  3  4  4  4  5  5  6  6  6  7  7  8|
|   4  8  2  6  0  4  8  2  6  0  4  8  2  6  0  4  8  2  6  0|
------------------------------------------------------------------
|000620         08 M-I                 PIC X(01).              FIG E.8|
|000630         08 FILLER              PIC X(02) VALUE '.'.    FIG E.8|
|000640         08 SUR-NAME            PIC X(10).              FIG E.8|
|000650         08 FILLER              PIC X(04) VALUE ' *'.   FIG E.8|
|000660         08 ID-NUM              PIC 9(09).              FIG E.8|
|000670         08 FILLER              PIC X(05) VALUE '   *'. FIG E.8|
|000680         08 CLASS               PIC X(02).              FIG E.8|
|000690         08 FILLER              PIC X(06) VALUE '    *'.FIG E.8|
|000700         08 MAJ                 PIC X(03).              FIG E.8|
|000710         08 FILLER              PIC X(08) VALUE '   *'. FIG E.8|
|000720         08 CURRENT-HOURS       PIC 9(02).              FIG E.8|
|000730         08 FILLER              PIC X(08) VALUE '      *'.FIG E.8|
|000740         08 TOT-HOURS           PIC 9(03).              FIG E.8|
|000750         08 FILLER              PIC X(03) VALUE '  *'.  FIG E.8|
|000760 PROCEDURE DIVISION.                                    FIG E.8|
|000770 CONTROL-PROCEDURE.                                     FIG E.8|
|000780     READY TRACE.                                       FIG E.8|
|000790     PERFORM 100-INITIALIZATION.                        FIG E.8|
|000800     PERFORM 300-REPORT-HEADING.                        FIG E.8|
|000810     PERFORM 500-READ-RECORDS-PRINT-DETAILS             FIG E.8|
|000820         UNTIL INDICATOR = 'PROCESS COMPLETE'.          FIG E.8|
|000830     PERFORM 700-TERMINATION.                           FIG E.8|
|000840     RESET TRACE.                                       FIG E.8|
|000850     STOP RUN.                                          FIG E.8|
|000860 100-INITIALIZATION.                                    FIG E.8|
|000870     MOVE 'PROCESS START' TO INDICATOR.                 FIG E.8|
|000880     OPEN INPUT STUDENT-FILE, OUTPUT PRINTOUT.          FIG E.8|
|000890     READ STUDENT-FILE                                  FIG E.8|
|000900         AT END MOVE 'PROCESS COMPLETE' TO INDICATOR.   FIG E.8|
|000910 300-REPORT-HEADING.                                    FIG E.8|
|000920     WRITE PRINT-LINE FROM REPORT-HEADING AFTER         FIG E.8|
|000930         TOP-OF-NEXT-PAGE.                              FIG E.8|
|000940     WRITE PRINT-LINE FROM SEPARATOR-LINE AFTER 2 LINES.FIG E.8|
|000950     WRITE PRINT-LINE FROM COLUMN-HEADING-1 AFTER 1.    FIG E.8|
|000960     WRITE PRINT-LINE FROM COLUMN-HEADING-2 AFTER 1.    FIG E.8|
|000970     WRITE PRINT-LINE FROM SEPARATOR-LINE AFTER 1.      FIG E.8|
|000980 500-READ-RECORDS-PRINT-DETAILS.                        FIG E.8|
|000990     MOVE STUDENT-ID TO ID-NUM.                         FIG E.8|
|001000     MOVE LAST-NAME TO SUR-NAME.                        FIG E.8|
|001010     MOVE FIRST-NAME TO 1ST-NAME.                       FIG E.8|
|001020     MOVE MIDDLE-INITIAL TO M-I.                        FIG E.8|
|001030     MOVE CLASSIFICATION TO CLASS.                      FIG E.8|
|001040     MOVE TOTAL-HOURS TO TOT-HOURS.                     FIG E.8|
|001050     MOVE HOURS-THIS-SEM TO CURRENT-HOURS.              FIG E.8|
|001060     MOVE MAJOR TO MAJ.                                 FIG E.8|
|001070     WRITE PRINT-LINE FROM OUTPUT-REC AFTER 2 LINES.    FIG E.8|
|001080     READ STUDENT-FILE                                  FIG E.8|
|001090         AT END MOVE 'PROCESS COMPLETE' TO INDICATOR.   FIG E.8|
|001100     DISPLAY ' '.                                       FIG E.8|
|001110 700-TERMINATION.                                       FIG E.8|
|001120     CLOSE STUDENT-FILE, PRINTOUT.                      FIG E.8|
```

Figure E.8 An Illustration of the READY and RESET Statements *Continued*

a. Tracing Results:

```
85
90
97

97

97

97

97

97

97

97

97

97

97

97

110
```

b. Printed (Written) Results:

SEMESTER STUDENT LIST

	STUDENT NAME		STUDENT ID. NUMBER	CLASS	MAJOR	CURRENT ENROLLMENT	TOTAL HOURS
JOHN	Q.	ADAMS	343564321	GR	CSC	00	219
JOHN	A.	BROWN	555667777	FR	MKT	15	035
MATT	N.	CULVER	456789012	JR	MGT	08	094
ANTHONY	R.	DORSETT	353492761	SR	ECO	16	138
DAVID	Q.	ELDRIDGE	376495268	SO	FIN	12	047
BEN	V.	FRANKLIN	000000002	GR	GBU	12	189
KENNETH	A.	GERBER	537903251	SO	MGT	16	028
MARK	C.	HAMILTON	486762389	JR	CSC	18	096
MATT	H.	ISSACS	474653790	SR	ECO	18	120
HAROLD	Q.	JENNINGS	502326955	FR	MGT	18	018
FLOYD	R.	KENNIMER	476329092	JR	MKT	12	060
STEVEN	O.	LINCOLN	442648942	SO	MKT	15	045
JEFF	V.	MARCUS	546677219	SR	CSC	18	099

Figure E.8 An Illustration of the READY and RESET TRACE Statements (Output—Type 1) *Continued*

a. Tracing Results:

```
100-INITIALIZATION ,300-REPORT-HEADING ,500-READ-RECORDS-PRINT-DETAILS ,
500-READ-RECORDS-PRINT-DETAILS ,
500-READ-RECORDS-PRINT-DETAILS ,
500-READ-RECORDS-PRINT-DETAILS ,
500-READ-RECORDS-PRINT-DETAILS ,
500-READ-RECORDS-PRINT-DETAILS ,
500-READ-RECORDS-PRINT-DETAILS ,
500-READ-RECORDS-PRINT-DETAILS ,
500-READ-RECORDS-PRINT-DETAILS ,
500-READ-RECORDS-PRINT-DETAILS ,
500-READ-RECORDS-PRINT-DETAILS ,
500-READ-RECORDS-PRINT-DETAILS ,
500-READ-RECORDS-PRINT-DETAILS ,
700-TERMINATION ,
```

b. Printed (Written) Results:

SEMESTER STUDENT LIST

STUDENT NAME	STUDENT ID. NUMBER	CLASS	MAJOR	CURRENT ENROLLMENT	TOTAL HOURS
JOHN Q. ADAMS	343564321	GR	CSC	00	219
JOHN A. BROWN	555667777	FR	MKT	15	035
MATT N. CULVER	456789012	JR	MGT	08	094
ANTHONY R. DORSETT	353492761	SR	ECO	16	138
DAVID Q. ELDRIDGE	376495268	SO	FIN	12	047
BEN V. FRANKLIN	000000002	GR	GBU	12	189
KENNETH A. GERBER	537903251	SO	MGT	16	028
MARK C. HAMILTON	486762389	JR	CSC	18	096
MATT H. ISSACS	474653790	SR	ECO	18	120
HAROLD Q. JENNINGS	502326955	FR	MGT	18	018
FLOYD R. KENNIMER	476329092	JR	MKT	12	060
STEVEN O. LINCOLN	442648942	SO	MKT	15	045
JEFF V. MARCUS	546677219	SR	CSC	18	099

Figure E.8 An Illustration of the READY and RESET TRACE Statements (Output—Type 2) *Continued*

F COBOL '81—Suggestions for the New Standard

At press time, a number of alterations of COBOL were under consideration by the American National Standards Institute. This new standard, to be known as COBOL 81, has not yet been formally accepted. However, a number of changes seem destined to become a part of the future COBOL standard. This appendix provides a brief summary of the anticipated changes. For additional details concerning these changes, consult COBOL Information Bulletin Number 19, X3J4 COBOL Technical Committee, May 1980. This publication is available from the Computer Business Equipment Manufacturers Association by writing to:

X3 Secretariat
C.B.E.M.A.
1828 L Street NW (Suite 1200)
Washington, D.C. 20036

Characteristic of Change	Affected Chapters
1. Addition of the following reserved words: ALPHABET ALPHANUMERIC ALPHANUMERIC-EDITED ANY BIT BITS COMMIT COMMON CONNECT CONTENT CONTINUE CONVERSION CONVERTING CURRENT DAY-OF-WEEK DB-EXCEPTION DB-RECORD-NAME DB-SET-NAME DB-STATUS DEBUG-LENGTH DEBUG-NUMERIC-CONTENTS DEBUG-SIZE DEBUG-START DEBUG-SUB DEBUG-SUB-ITEM DEBUG-SUB-N DEBUG-SUB-NUM DISCONNECT DUPLICATE EMPTY END-ADD END-CALL END-COMPUTE END-DELETE END-DIVIDE END-EVALUATE END-IF END-MULTIPLY END-PERFORM END-READ END-RECEIVE END-RETURN END-REWRITE ERASE EVALUATE EXCLUSIVE EXTERNAL FALSE FIND FINISH FREE GET GLOBAL INITIALIZE KEEP LD LOCALLY MEMBER MODIFY NULL ORDER OTHER OWNER PADDING PRIOR PROTECTED PURGE READY REALM REALMS RECONNECT REFERENCE REFERENCE-MODIFIER REPLACE RETAINING RETRIEVAL ROLLBACK SETS STANDARD-2 STORE TENANT TEST THEN TRUE UPDATE USAGE-MODE WITHIN	2; A
2. Data-names not required to be unique (or uniquely qualified) if not referenced	2

581

Characteristic of Change	Affected Chapters
3. Punctuation characters of comma, semicolon, and space may be used interchangeably	2
4. Data-names and system-names may be the same	2
5. Addition of colon to the COBOL character set for purposes of reference modification	2; 21
6. Elimination of the AUTHOR, INSTALLATION, DATE-WRITTEN, and DATE-COMPILED paragraphs from the IDENTIFICATION DIVISION	3
7. Optional use of the ENVIRONMENT, DATA, and PROCEDURE DIVISIONs	4; 5; 6
8. Optional CONFIGURATION SECTION	4
9. SOURCE-COMPUTER and OBJECT-COMPUTER name optional	4
10. Reserved word IS optional (in SPECIAL-NAMES paragraph)	4
11. ALL literals cannot be associated with a numeric or numeric-edited data item	5
12. PICTURE string character A and the category ALPHABETIC assigned to a transitional category	5; 11
13. LABEL RECORDS clause optional (assumed to be standard if not present) and assigned to a transitional category	5; 16; 17
14. DATA RECORDS clause assigned to a transitional category	5; 16; 17
15. Level-77-data items assigned to a transitional category	5
16. Non-numeric literals to have an upper limit of 160 characters	5
17. Addition of the INITIALIZE statement to set specified data fields to predetermined values	6
18. Alternation of the READ statement to permit (a) the INTO to accept variable-length records, (b) execution of the READ after execution of the AT END phrase, and (c) addition of the optional reserved word NEXT for reading sequential files	6; 16; 17
19. Program nesting with the addition of reserved words INITIAL (specification of program initial state), COMMON (data references across programs), GLOBAL (to made data-names globally defined across programs), EXTERNAL (to reference another program within the same run unit, and END PROGRAM (to terminate a "contained" program).	6; 7
20. ADVANCING PAGE and END-OF-PAGE not permitted in the same WRITE statement for a print-oriented file	6
21. END-READ statement added to terminate imperative statement	6; 16; 17
22. Left-to-right evaluation of connected conditions within a hierarchical level (condition level—AND or OR)	8; 11

Characteristic of Change	Affected Chapters
23. END-IF statement added to terminate imperative statement	8; 11
24. THEN added as an optional reserved word following condition in IF statement	8; 11
25. In-line PERFORM statement to permit iteration without referencing a procedure-name	8; 12
26. END-PERFORM statement added to terminate PERFORM statements	8; 12
27. TEST BEFORE/AFTER added to permit both "do-while" and "do-until" structured logic	8; 12
28. Insertion characters of period or comma permitted to be the last character of a PICTURE string (followed by a period)	9
29. Addition of a "de-edit" feature to permit data to be retrieved (in a numeric sense) from numeric-edited fields	9
30. Figurative constant ZERO permitted in arithmetic expressions	10
31. Intermediate result of the evaluation of an arithmetic expression not limited to 18 digits	10
32. END-ADD, END-COMPUTE, END-DIVIDE, END-SUBTRACT, and END-MULTIPLY statements added to terminate imperative statement	10
33. Class test for ALPHABETIC characters to include lowercase characters as well as uppercase.	11
34. Permits an unlimited number of AFTER phrases in the PERFORM/VARYING statement	12
35. Subscripting (and dimensioning) up to 48 levels (currently only three levels are supported)	13; 14
36. Both indexes and subscript data-names may both be used to reference an individual occurrence of a multidimension table	13; 14
37. Relative subscripting (subscript + or − an integer) permitted	13
38. Minimum number of occurrences of a variable-length table may be zero	13; 14
39. Allows data moved to a variable-length table (OCCURS/DEPENDING ON) to be fully received up to the maximum table size, regardless of the current value of the identifier indicating table size	13; 14
40. END-RETURN added to terminate imperative statement	15
41. RETURN INTO allowed for variable-length records, and RETURN permitted to be executed after AT END phrase	15
42. SORT file description permitted to contain variable-length records	15

Characteristic of Change	Affected Chapters
43. Duplicate keys permitted in the sort-file and ordering will be maintained from input file	15
44. Multiple GIVING file-names permitted	15
45. A GIVING file may be indexed	15; 17
46. When magnetic tape is used, USING and GIVING files may be on the same physical reel	15
47. Variable-length records may be explicitly defined by using the RECORD clause	16; 17
48. The NO REWIND clause may not be used with the UNIT/REEL option of the CLOSE statement	16
49. The REVERSED phrase of the OPEN statement has been deleted	16
50. The I-O and EXTENDED options of the OPEN statement cause a file to be created if one does not exist	16; 17
51. The ACCESS MODE, RECORD KEY, ALTERNATE RECORD KEY, and FILE STATUS entries of the ENVIRONMENT DIVISION have been placed in a transitional category and added to the FD entry of the FILE SECTION	16; 17
52. The BLOCK clause has been placed in a transitional category	16; 17
53. A specified padding character may be requested to complete a partially filled block	16; 17
54. The OPTIONAL phrase of the SELECT clause may be used with both sequential and indexed files	16; 17
55. The EXTENDED option of the OPEN statement may be used in sequential and indexed files	16; 17
56. CORRESPONDING options of the MOVE, ADD, and SUBTRACT statements have been placed in a transitional category	6; 10
57. The ALTER statement is to be deleted	18
58. The GO TO/DEPENDING ON statement may provide only one procedure-name	18
59. The EVALUATE statement has been added to provide COBOL with a true "case" structure	18
60. An END-EVALUATE statement is added to terminate an imperative statement	18
61. The RENAMES clause has been placed in the transitional category	19
62. Qualification of a data-name may occur to 50 levels	19
63. The reserved word FILLER may be used as the subject of a REDEFINES clause	19

Characteristic of Change	Affected Chapters
64. A redefinition may be shorter than the original definition	19
65. A Boolean-type variable (value of zero or one) may be created for evaluation in Boolean expressions	20
66. SIGN clauses may be specified at multiple levels within the hierarchy of a record description	20
67. Index-data-names (USAGE IS INDEX) may be SYNCHRONIZED	20
68. The INSPECT statement with both TALLYING and REPLACING phrases has been placed in the transitional category	21
69. One or more characters may be placed in a string to be operated on by an INSPECT statement with the CONVERTING phrase	21
70. Multiple BEFORE/AFTER phrases may be used in conjunction with the INSPECT statement with the TALLYING or REPLACING options	21
71. Subscripting and indexing evaluation has been added to the capability of the STRING and UNSTRING statements	21
72. END-STRING and END-UNSTRING have been added to terminate the imperative statements	21
73. The WITH NO ADVANCING phrase has been added to the DISPLAY statement for interaction with line-oriented devices	E
74. The record description of DEBUG-ITEM has been altered	E

Index

access mode, 36, 40
ACCESS MODE clause, 425–27, 429
ADD statement, 189–91
addition of records, 406–12, 442–47
ADVANCING, 73
algorithm, 6
ALL literal, 24, 58–59, 172
ALPHABETIC, 230
alphabetic data (A), 50, 76
alphabetic edited data, 167–68
alphanumeric data (X), 50, 76
alphanumeric edited data, 167–68
analysis, 99
AND, 131–32, 328, 332
ANSI (ANS), 4, 74, 581
apostrophe ('), 23, 58
application software, 6
Area A, 16, 18, 32, 46, 58, 467
Area B, 16, 18, 32, 46
arithmetic expressions, 132, 195–97
arithmetic operators, 195
ASCII, 23, 50–51, 363, 477
assembler, 6, 562
ASSIGN clause, 37–38, 46, 69, 362, 388, 427
asterisk (*), 17–18
AUTHOR, 31

batch, 10
binary data, 479–80
binary digit, 477
binary search, 331–32
bit, 477, 479
BLANK WHEN ZERO clause, 482
BLOCK CONTAINS clause, 390–91, 428
blocking factor, 387, 390
bottom-up design, 122
branching operation, 67, 77, 128
buffer, 38–40, 72, 386, 387, 462–63

bugs, 100, 561
building of files, 393–98, 431–36
byte, 477, 478
byte displacement, 321, 324–26
bytes per inch (BPI), 387

card reader, 69–70, 71, 385, 386
carriage control, 36, 73, 74
case structure, 121–23, 460
Cathode Ray Tube (CRT), 10
CBEMA, 581
character data, 477, 478
character processing, 302, 493–519
character set, 18, 51
class test, 127, 139, 229, 230, 328
clause, 13
CLIST, 562
CLOSE statement, 37, 69, 70, 392
closed loop, 77
COBOL '81, 581–85
CODASYL, 3–4
coding form, 16–18
collating sequence, 51, 363, 364, 400
column headings, 79
columns, 292–94
comma (,), 19, 21, 292, 294
comment entries, 31–32, 35
comments, 16, 17–18
compilation errors, 561
compiler, compilation, 6, 8, 10, 31
COMPUTATIONAL, COMP, 478, 479–80
COMPUTATIONAL-1, COMP-1, 478, 481
COMPUTATIONAL-2, COMP-2, 478, 481
COMPUTATIONAL-3, COMP-3, 478, 480
COMPUTE statement, 189, 190, 195–97
computer system, 6
concatenation, 493
condition-names, 22, 127, 231–33, 464, 466

condition-name test, 127, 139, 229, 230–33, 328
CONFIGURATION SECTION, 14, 35–36
constants, 23
continuation, 16–17, 24–25
control break, 146, 149, 217
control variable, 15, 112
core dump, 562
critical event design, 122
CURRENT-DATE, 470
cylinders, 427

data, data file, 6, 9
data base management system, 5
DATA DIVISION, 13–14, 45–59
data editing, 167–72, 240–52
data errors, 561–62
data-names, 22, 67, 70
DATA RECORDS clause, 47, 54, 390–91, 428
data representations, 477–81
   binary, 479–80
   external decimal, 477–79
   long floating-point, 481
   packed decimal, 480
   short floating-point, 481
   zone decimal, 477–79
DATE-COMPILED, 31–32
DATE-WRITTEN, 31
ddnames, 389, 427
DEBUG-ITEM, 570
debugging, 27, 68, 99–100, 561–80
decimal point, 52, 167, 168, 479
   implied, 52, 479
   insertion, 167, 168
decision tree, 105–6
DECLARATIVES, 567–69
decomposition, 108, 124
default logic, 131
delete codes, 425, 428
deletion of records, 412–13, 428
diagnostics, 561
direct indexing, 321–22
DISPLAY statement, 36, 562–66
DISPLAY usage, 49, 477–79, 482–83
DIVIDE statement, 189, 190, 193–95
division, 13
do-until structure, 105, 107
do-while structure, 104–5, 107
double-word boundary, 484

EBCDIC, 23, 50–51, 363, 477
edited data, 167–72

editing symbols, 167–72
   +, 167–70
   −, 167–70
   $, 167–70
   ., 167–68
   ,, 167–68
   *, 171
   0, 167–68
   B, 167–68
   CR, 167–68
   DB, 167–68
   Z, 171
elementary-item-names, 22, 47–48
END DECLARATIVES, 569
end-of-file (EOF), 71
entry, 13
ENVIRONMENT DIVISION, 13–14, 35–42
EQUAL TO (=), 128, 430
errors, 561–62, 566
   compilation, 561
   data, 561–62
   execution, 561
   fatal, 561
   logical, 561–62, 566
   warnings, 561
evaluation of IF statement logic, 132
EXAMINE statement, 493, 515–17
execution, 9, 10
execution errors, 561
EXHIBIT statement, 572–76
EXIT statement, 142
exponential form, 481
exponentiation, 189, 195
external decimal, 477–79
external-name, 32, 36, 46

fall through, 117, 137, 141
fatal errors, 561
FD (File Description), 37, 46–47, 54–56, 68–73, 390–91, 461
figurative constants, 23–24, 58, 172
FILE-CONTROL, 37, 46, 54, 362
file-names, 22, 36, 37, 46, 54–56, 68–69, 71, 367, 388, 567
FILE SECTION, 45–56, 74, 362, 390–91, 461–62, 464
FILLER, 49, 56, 58–59, 74, 466
firmware, 7
fixed-insertion editing, 167–68
floating-insertion editing, 167, 169–70
floating-point, 481

flowcharting, 99–103, 389
full-word boundary, 484

generic key, 430
GO TO statement, 71, 77–78, 111, 128, 135–36, 453
  DEPENDING ON, 121–22, 453–60
GREATER THAN (>), 128
group-names, 22, 47–49, 76, 290, 293, 296

hard-copy, 10, 70
hardware, 6, 99
hexadecimal, 562
hierarchy chart, 115–16
high-order digits, 190, 191
HIGH-VALUE, HIGH-VALUES, 24, 172, 400–1, 428
Hollerith code, 51
host programming language, 4
hyphen (-), 17, 19, 21, 24

I-O wait state, 387
IDENTIFICATION DIVISION, 13, 31–33
IF statement 127–35, 229–52
  class test, 127, 139, 229, 230
  condition-name test, 127, 139, 230–33
  nesting, 107, 134–35, 230
  relational test, 127–31, 139
  sign test, 127, 139, 229–30
if-then-else structure, 104–7, 127
imperative statement, 71, 128, 229, 327, 332
implementation, 99
implied decimal point (V), 52, 479
implied relational operator, 133
implied subject (IF statement), 133, 230
independent elementary-item-names, 22, 58
index-data-names, 22, 323–25
index-names, 22, 263, 321–32, 567
index sequential access method (ISAM), 425–47
INDEXED BY clause, 321–32
indexed files, 425–47
  adding to, 442–47
  building of, 431–36
  deleting from, 428
  updating of, 436–42
indexed tables, 321–32
indicator variables, 112, 114–15
input data, 52
input-output buffers, 38–40, 72, 386, 387, 462–63
input-output interrupt, 387
INPUT-OUTPUT SECTION, 14, 37–42
INSPECT statement, 493, 510–13

INSTALLATION, 31
inter-occurrence slack bytes, 487
inter-record gap (IRG), 386–87
interactive, 10
internal-name, 36, 37
internal sort, 338
internal storage, 6
interpreter, 6
interrupt, 387, 566
intersection, 131
intra-occurrence slack bytes, 487

job, job stream, 7–9
job control language (JCL), 6–9, 389, 390, 427
job queue, 10
JUSTIFIED clause, 482–83

key word in context, 503
keyed file, 10, 425, 428
keyed table, 330

LABEL RECORDS clause, 46–47, 54–56, 390–91,
    428
left justify, 59, 76, 494
LESS THAN (<), 128
level numbers, 47–49, 464
  01, 48, 289, 461, 468
  02-48, 48–49, 289
  49, 48, 289
  66, 289, 464, 467–68
  77, 58, 289, 468
  88, 231–32, 289, 464, 468
line printer, 70, 167, 385, 386, 477
linear search, 326–30
literals, 23
loading, 9
logic tree, 106–7, 115
logical deletion, 413
logical errors, 561–62, 566
logical input-output, 39
logical operators, 131–32
logical records, 385–87, 390
long floating-point, 481
looping, 77, 107, 110, 453
low-order digits, 77, 191
LOW-VALUE, LOW-VALUES, 24, 172

machine language, 9
magnetic disk, 385, 386, 387, 388, 392, 413–14, 427
magnetic media, 385, 386, 390

magnetic tape, 385, 386, 388, 392
mantissa, 481–82
mass storage devices, 6, 413, 427, 429
master file, 398, 406, 436
matrix, 292
merging, 361
mnemonic-names, 22, 36, 73–74, 563
modification and maintenance, 100
modules, 104
modulo division, 194
MOVE statement, 76–77, 171–72, 541
MULTIPLY statement, 189, 192–93

NEGATIVE, 229
negative data, 50–52, 479, 480, 482
nested IF statements, 107, 134–35, 230
NOMINAL KEY clause, 426–29, 430
non-numeric literals, 23, 58–59, 172
NOT, 128, 132, 328
NUMERIC, 230
numeric data (9), 50–52
numeric edited data, 167–72
numeric literals, 23, 58, 172

OBJECT-COMPUTER, 35
object program, 6, 9, 31, 35, 561
occurrence number, 321
OCCURS clause, 289–98, 321–32, 466–67, 485–88
    ASCENDING/DESCENDING KEY, 330–32
    DEPENDING ON, 309, 327
    INDEXED BY, 321–22
octal, 562
on-line, 10
OPEN statement, 37, 68, 69, 71, 73, 392
operating system, 6, 8–9, 32, 85, 387, 388, 392
operational sign (S), 51–52, 192, 479, 483
OR, 131–32, 328
output data, 56

packed decimal, 480
page break, 217
page number, 17
paragraph-names, 13, 22, 67–68, 77, 135–36, 142,
    149–51, 261
parentheses, 132, 196, 289, 292, 294
parsing, 493
PERFORM statement, 112, 127, 135–39, 261
    TIMES, 261–63
    UNTIL, 127, 139–42
    VARYING, 261, 263–69, 322
period (.), 19, 21
Phillippakis, Andrew, 4
physical deletion, 413
physical input-output, 39
physical records, 385–87, 390
PICTURE (PIC), 47–52, 167–72, 477–81
pointer, 39
POSITIVE, 229
predefined process, 108

PROCEDURE DIVISION, 13, 15–16
procedure-names, 22–23, 67, 135–36, 261, 376, 567
PROCESSING MODE clause, 36, 40
program, 6
program development, 99–100
program flowcharting, 99–103
PROGRAM-ID, 31–32
program load point, 562
program-name, 32
programmer-supplied-name, 20–23, 32
punctuation, 19

QUOTE, QUOTES, 24, 172
quote character ("), 23, 58

random access, 425
ranks, 294
READ statement, 37, 70–72, 393
    INVALID KEY, 428–29, 430
read-write heads, 388
READY TRACE, 576
receiving fields, 76, 172, 190, 193, 195, 323–24,
    493–501
RECORD CONTAINS clause, 47, 54, 390, 428
record-names, 22, 47, 73–76, 290, 292, 391
RECORD KEY clause, 425–29
records, 385–87, 390
    logical, 385–87, 390
    physical, 385–87, 390
recursive decomposition, 124
REDEFINES clause, 464–67, 484
relational operators, 128, 132
relational test, 127–31, 139, 328
relative indexing, 321–22
RELEASE statement, 368, 376
REMAINDER, 194
RENAMES clause, 464, 467–72
replacement character editing, 167, 171–72
replication factor, 52
report headings, 79, 82–83
RESERVE clause, 38–40
reserved words, 20–21, 525–28
RESET TRACE, 576
RETURN statement, 370, 376
REWRITE statement, 413–14
    INVALID KEY, 429
ROUNDED, 190
rows, 292–94

scaling factor (P), 52
SD (Sort Description), 362, 366
SEARCH statement, 326–32
    SEARCH ALL, 330–32
    VARYING, 327
    WHEN, 327–28, 332
section-name, 13, 67, 77, 135–36, 150–52, 368
SECURITY, 31
SELECT clause, 37–38, 46, 54, 68–70
sending fields, 76, 172, 323, 324, 493–501

sentence, 13
sequence numbers, 16
sequence structure, 105
sequential files, 385–414
  addition to, 406–12
  building of, 393–98
  deletion from, 412–13
  updating of, 398–406
sequential search, 326–30
serial numbers, 17
service module, 117
SET statement, 323–26
short floating-point, 481
sign, 479, 480
  bit, 479
  negative, 479, 480, 482
  positive, 479, 480, 482
  unsigned, 479, 480
SIGN clause, 482, 483
sign test, 127, 139, 229–30, 328
SIZE ERROR, 190
slack bytes, 484, 487
  inter-occurrence, 487
  intra-occurrence, 487
software, 6, 99
SORT-CORE-SIZE, 377
sort-file-name, 22, 362
sort-merge, 361
sort-record-name, 22
SORT statement, 362–70, 394
  ASCENDING/DESCENDING KEY, 363–66
  GIVING, 370
  INPUT PROCEDURE, 366–70, 376
  OUTPUT PROCEDURE, 370, 376, 394
  RELEASE statement, 368, 376
  RETURN statement, 370–71, 376
  USING, 366–67, 394
sorting, 338, 361, 377
  bubble, 338
  external, 361
  internal, 338, 361
SOURCE-COMPUTER, 35, 566
source file, 10
source program, 6, 9, 31, 35, 561
SPACE, SPACES, 24, 58, 59, 172
SPECIAL-NAMES, 22, 35, 36, 73–74, 563
special registers, 377, 470, 515
  CURRENT-DATE, 470
  DEBUG-ITEM, 570
  SORT-CORE-SIZE, 377
  TALLY, 515
START statement, 430
statement, 13
stepwise refinement, 124
STOP statement, 78
subscripted tables, 289–92

table handling, 263, 289–96, 321–32, 485–88, 567
  indexed, 321–32
  multi-dimension, 292–96
  pseudo-two dimension, 291
  redefinition of, 466–67
  single dimension, 289–92
  subscripted, 289–96
  three dimension, 294–96
  two dimension, 292–93
table look-up, 303
TALLY, 515
testing, 99
text editor file, 10
text processing, 494–95
top-down design, 122
TRACE statement, 576–80
tracks, 386, 388
transaction file, 398, 406, 412, 436
TRANSFORM statement, 493, 515–17
truncation, 59, 76–77, 190
two's complement form, 479

unconditional branching, 128
union, 131
UNSTRING statement, 493, 495–503
updating of records, 398–406, 436–42
USAGE clause, 323, 324, 478
  COMPUTATIONAL, COMP, 478, 479–80, 484
  COMPUTATIONAL-1, COMP-1, 478, 481
  COMPUTATIONAL-2, COMP-2, 478, 481
  COMPUTATIONAL-3, COMP-3, 478, 480
  DISPLAY, 477–79, 482–83
  INDEX, 323, 324
USE FOR DEBUGGING statement, 566–72
utility module, 117

VALUE clause, 58–59, 231–32, 466
variable length blocks, 390
variable length tables, 309
vector, 289
Visual Table of Contents (VTOC), 115–16

warnings, 561
words, 19–20, 477
WORKING-STORAGE SECTION, 15, 45, 56–59, 71, 73, 74, 462, 464, 466
WRITE statement, 36, 72–76, 394, 413
  INVALID KEY, 428–29

ZERO, ZEROS, ZEROES, 23, 58, 172, 229
zone-bits, 480
zone decimal, 477–79